Stan Lee Presents:

ESSENTIAL THE AVENGERS VOL. 3

Collecting Avengers #47-68 & Annual #2

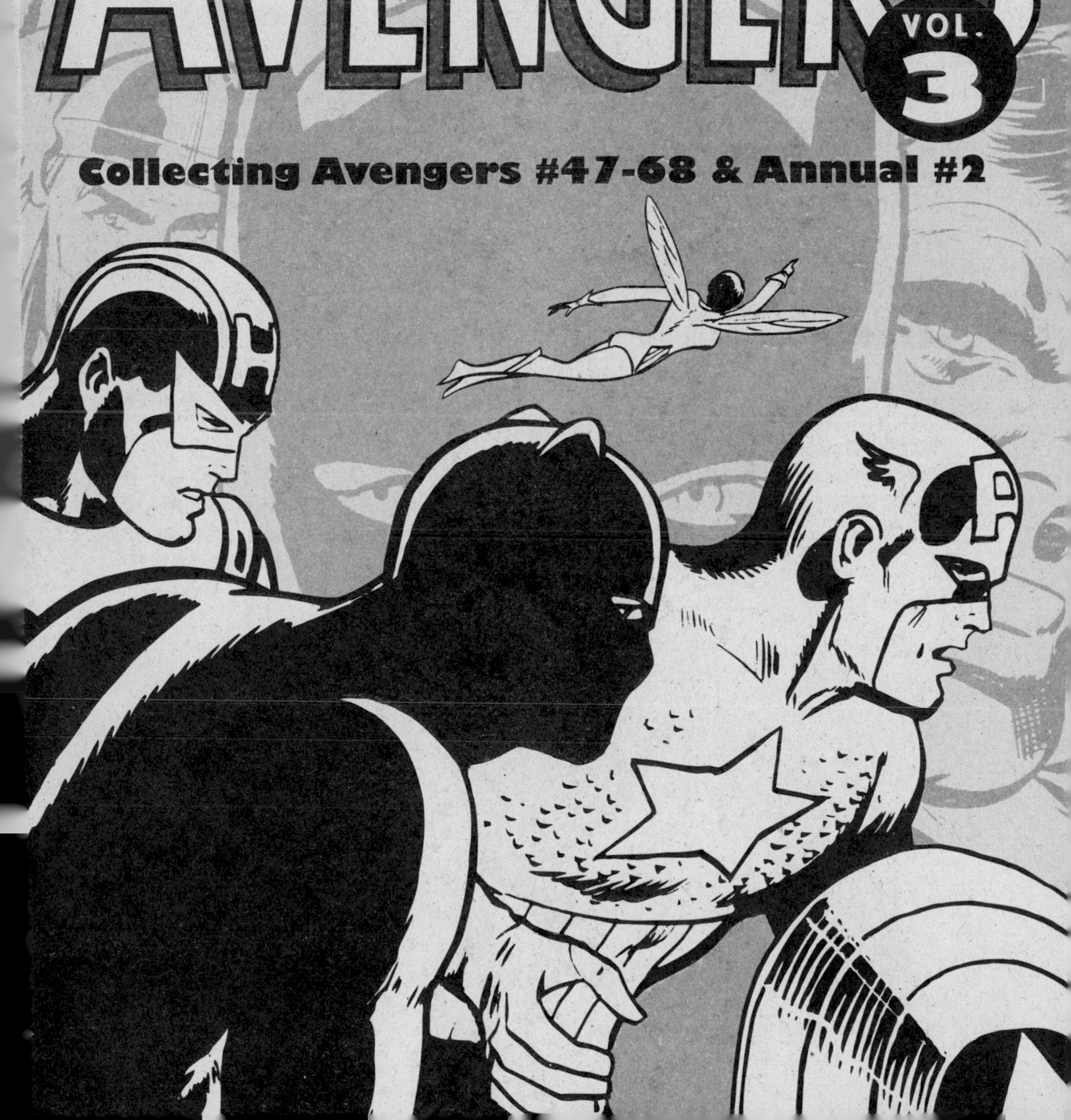

Stan Lee Presents:

ESSENTIAL THE AVENGERS VOL. 3

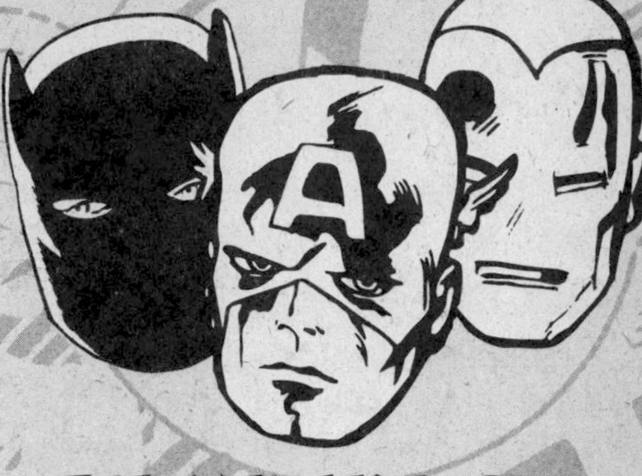

THE AVENGERS #47:
SCRIPT: ROY THOMAS
PENCILS: JOHN BUSCEMA
INKS: GEORGE TUSKA
LETTERS: L.P. GREGOR

THE AVENGERS #48:
SCRIPT: ROY THOMAS
ART: GEORGE TUSKA
LETTERS: ARTIE SIMEK

THE AVENGERS #49:
SCRIPT: ROY THOMAS
ART: JOHN BUSCEMA
LETTERS: ARTIE SIMEK

THE AVENGERS #50:
SCRIPT: ROY THOMAS
ART: JOHN BUSCEMA
LETTERS: SAM ROSEN

THE AVENGERS #51:
SCRIPT: ROY THOMAS
PENCILS: JOHN BUSCEMA
INKS: GEORGE TUSKA
LETTERS: SAM ROSEN

THE AVENGERS #52:
SCRIPT: ROY THOMAS
PENCILS: JOHN BUSCEMA
INKS: VINCE COLLETTA
LETTERS: SAM ROSEN

THE AVENGERS #53:
SCRIPT: ROY THOMAS
PENCILS: JOHN BUSCEMA
INKS: GEORGE TUSKA
LETTERS: SAM ROSEN

THE AVENGERS #54:
SCRIPT: ROY THOMAS
PENCILS: JOHN BUSCEMA
INKS: GEORGE TUSKA
LETTERS: SAM ROSEN

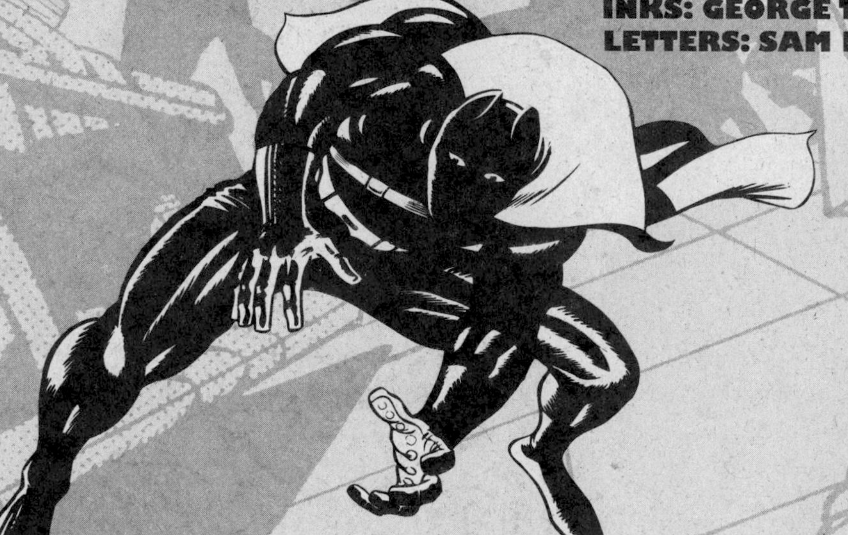

THE AVENGERS #55:
SCRIPT: ROY THOMAS
PENCILS: JOHN BUSCEMA
INKS: GEORGE KLEIN
LETTERS: SAM ROSEN

THE AVENGERS #56:
SCRIPT: ROY THOMAS
PENCILS: JOHN BUSCEMA
INKS: GEORGE KLEIN
LETTERS: SAM ROSEN

AVENGERS ANNUAL #2:
SCRIPT: ROY THOMAS
ARTISTS: DON HECK
& WERNER ROTH
INKS: VINCE COLLETTA
LETTERS: JOE ROSEN

THE AVENGERS #57:
SCRIPT: ROY THOMAS
PENCILS: JOHN BUSCEMA
INKS: GEORGE KLEIN
LETTERS: SAM ROSEN

THE AVENGERS #58:
SCRIPT: ROY THOMAS
PENCILS: JOHN BUSCEMA
INKS: GEORGE KLEIN
LETTERS: SAM ROSEN

THE AVENGERS #59:
SCRIPT: ROY THOMAS
PENCILS: JOHN BUSCEMA
INKS: GEORGE KLEIN
LETTERS: SAM ROSEN

THE AVENGERS #60:
SCRIPT: ROY THOMAS
PENCILS: JOHN BUSCEMA
INKS: MICKEY DEMEO
LETTERS: SAM ROSEN

THE AVENGERS #61:
SCRIPT: ROY THOMAS
PENCILS: JOHN BUSCEMA
INKS: GEORGE KLEIN
LETTERS: SAM ROSEN

THE AVENGERS #62:
SCRIPT: ROY THOMAS
PENCILS: JOHN BUSCEMA
INKS: GEORGE KLEIN
LETTERS: ARTIE SIMEK

THE AVENGERS #63:
SCRIPT: ROY THOMAS
PENCILS: GENE COLAN
INKS: GEORGE KLEIN
LETTERS: ARTIE SIMEK

THE AVENGERS #64
SCRIPT: ROY THOMAS
PENCILS: GENE COLAN
INKS: GEORGE KLEIN
LETTERS: SAM ROSEN

THE AVENGERS #65
SCRIPT: ROY THOMAS
PENCILS: GENE COLAN
INKS: SAM GRAINGER
LETTERS: SAM ROSEN

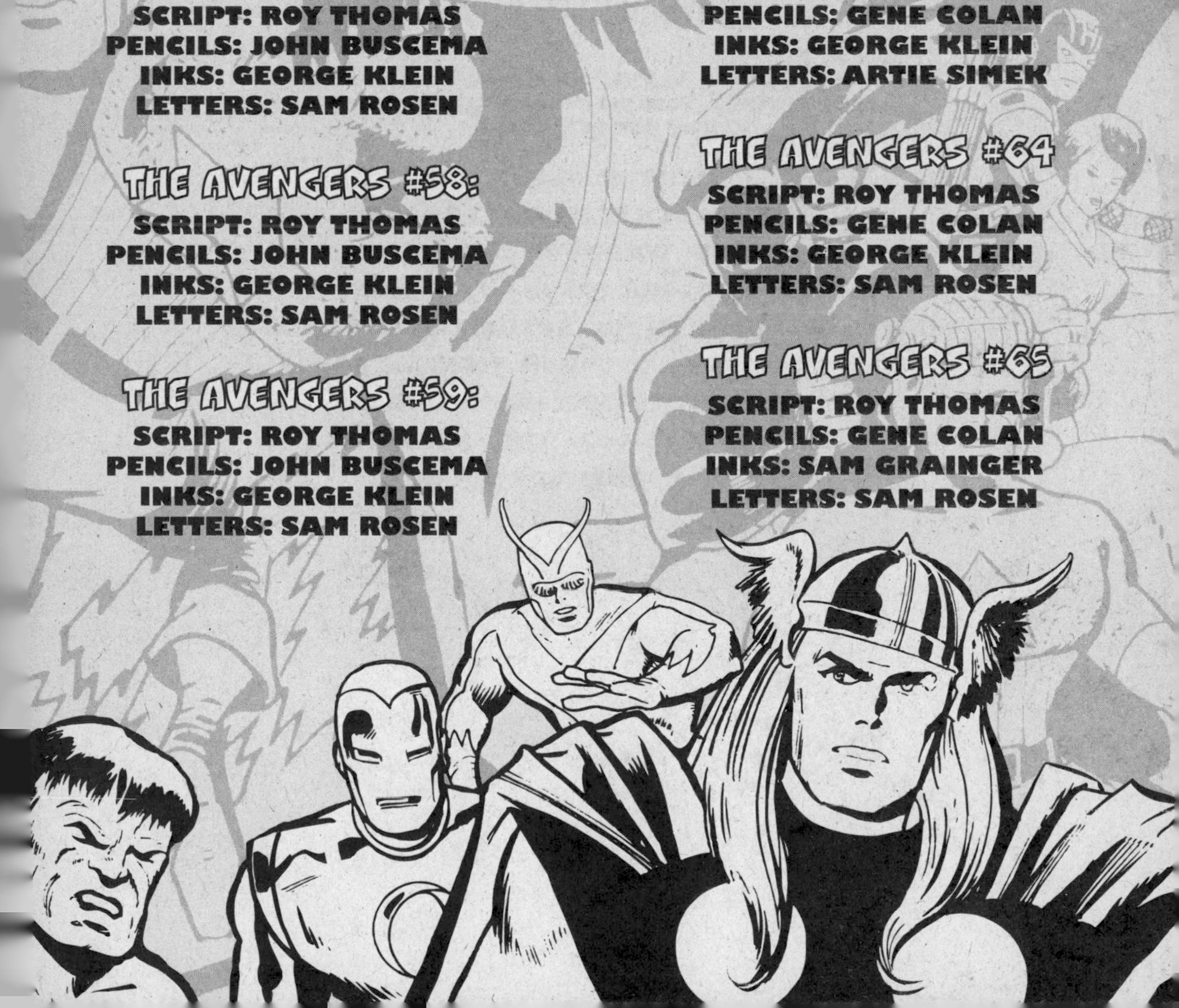

Stan Lee Presents:

ESSENTIAL
THE AVENGERS
VOL. 3

THE AVENGERS #66:
SCRIPT: ROY THOMAS
PENCILS: BARRY SMITH
INKS: SYD SHORES
LETTERS: ARTIE SIMEK

THE AVENGERS #67:
SCRIPT: ROY THOMAS
PENCILS: BARRY SMITH
INKS: GEORGE KLEIN
LETTERS: ARTIE SIMEK

THE AVENGERS #68:

SCRIPT: ROY THOMAS
PENCILS: SAL BUSCEMA
INKS: SAM GRAINGER
LETTERS: SAM ROSEN

SPECIAL THANKS:
Elizabeth Maya, Tom Brevoort, Doreen Mulryan,
and Jared Osborne

REPRINT CREDITS:

COVER PENCILS: STUART IMMONEN

COVER INKS: WADE VON GRAWBADGER

COVER COLORS: STEVE BUCCELLATO

COVER DESIGN: JOHN "JG" ROSHELL OF COMICRAFT

INTERIOR DESIGN & RETOUCH: MIKHAIL BORTNIK

ASSITANT EDITOR: MATTY RYAN

COLLECTION EDITOR: BEN ABERNATHY

EDITOR IN CHIEF: JOE QUESADA

Stan Lee Presents:

ESSENTIAL
THE AVENGERS
VOL. 3

ESSENTIAL AVENGERS® VOL. 3 Contains material originally published in magazine form as AVENGERS Vol. 1 #'s 47-68, AVENGERS ANNUAL # 2. Published by MARVEL COMICS, ...ill Jemas, President; Frank Fochetta, Senior Vice President, Publishing; Joe Quesada, Editor-in-Chief; Stan Lee, Chairman Emeritus. OFFICE OF PUBLICATION: 387 PARK AVENUE ...OUTH, NEW YORK, N.Y. 10016. Copyright © 1967, 1968 and 2001 Marvel Characters, Inc. All rights reserved. AVENGERS (including all prominent characters featured in this issue ...d the distinctive likenesses thereof) is a registered trademark of MARVEL CHARACTERS, INC. No part of this book may be printed or reproduced in any manner without the written ...ermission of the publiser Printed in the U.S.A. First Printing, March, 2001. ISBN: 0-7851-0741-X. GST #R127032852. MARVEL COMICS is a division of MARVEL ENTERPRISES, INC. ...eter Cuneo, Chief Executive Officer; Avi Arad, Chief Creative Officer.

9 8 7 6 5 4 3 2 1

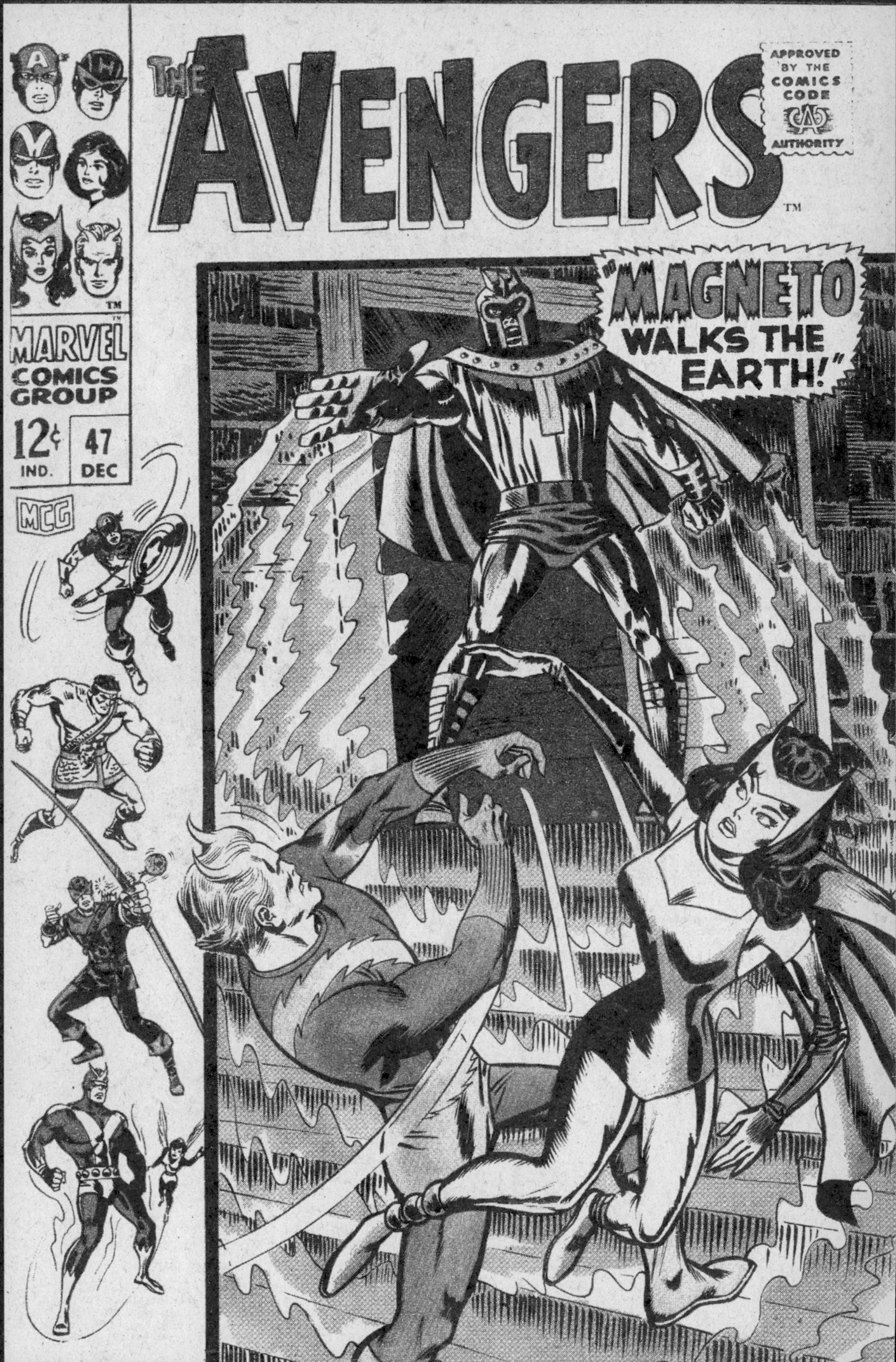
THE AVENGERS
APPROVED BY THE COMICS CODE AUTHORITY
MARVEL COMICS GROUP
12¢ IND.
47 DEC
MCG
"MAGNETO WALKS THE EARTH!"

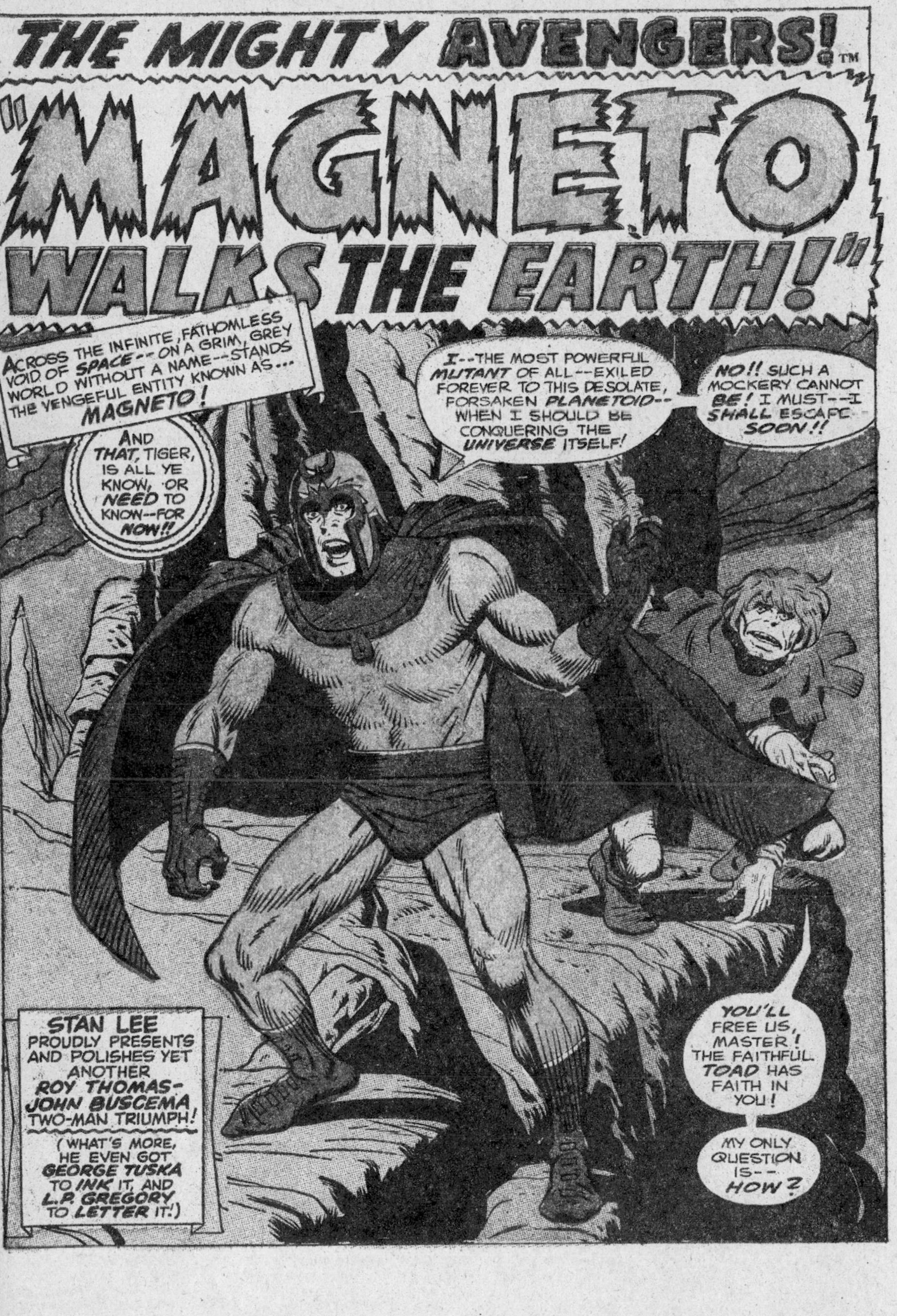
THE MIGHTY AVENGERS!™
"MAGNETO WALKS THE EARTH!"
ACROSS THE INFINITE, FATHOMLESS VOID OF SPACE-- ON A GRIM, GREY WORLD WITHOUT A NAME--STANDS THE VENGEFUL ENTITY KNOWN AS... MAGNETO!
AND THAT, TIGER, IS ALL YE KNOW, OR NEED TO KNOW--FOR NOW!!
I--THE MOST POWERFUL MUTANT OF ALL--EXILED FOREVER TO THIS DESOLATE, FORSAKEN PLANETOID-- WHEN I SHOULD BE CONQUERING THE UNIVERSE ITSELF!
NO!! SUCH A MOCKERY CANNOT BE! I MUST--I SHALL ESCAPE SOON!!
YOU'LL FREE US, MASTER! THE FAITHFUL TOAD HAS FAITH IN YOU!
MY ONLY QUESTION IS-- HOW?
STAN LEE PROUDLY PRESENTS AND POLISHES YET ANOTHER ROY THOMAS-JOHN BUSCEMA TWO-MAN TRIUMPH!
(WHAT'S MORE, HE EVEN GOT GEORGE TUSKA TO INK IT, AND L.P. GREGORY TO LETTER IT!)

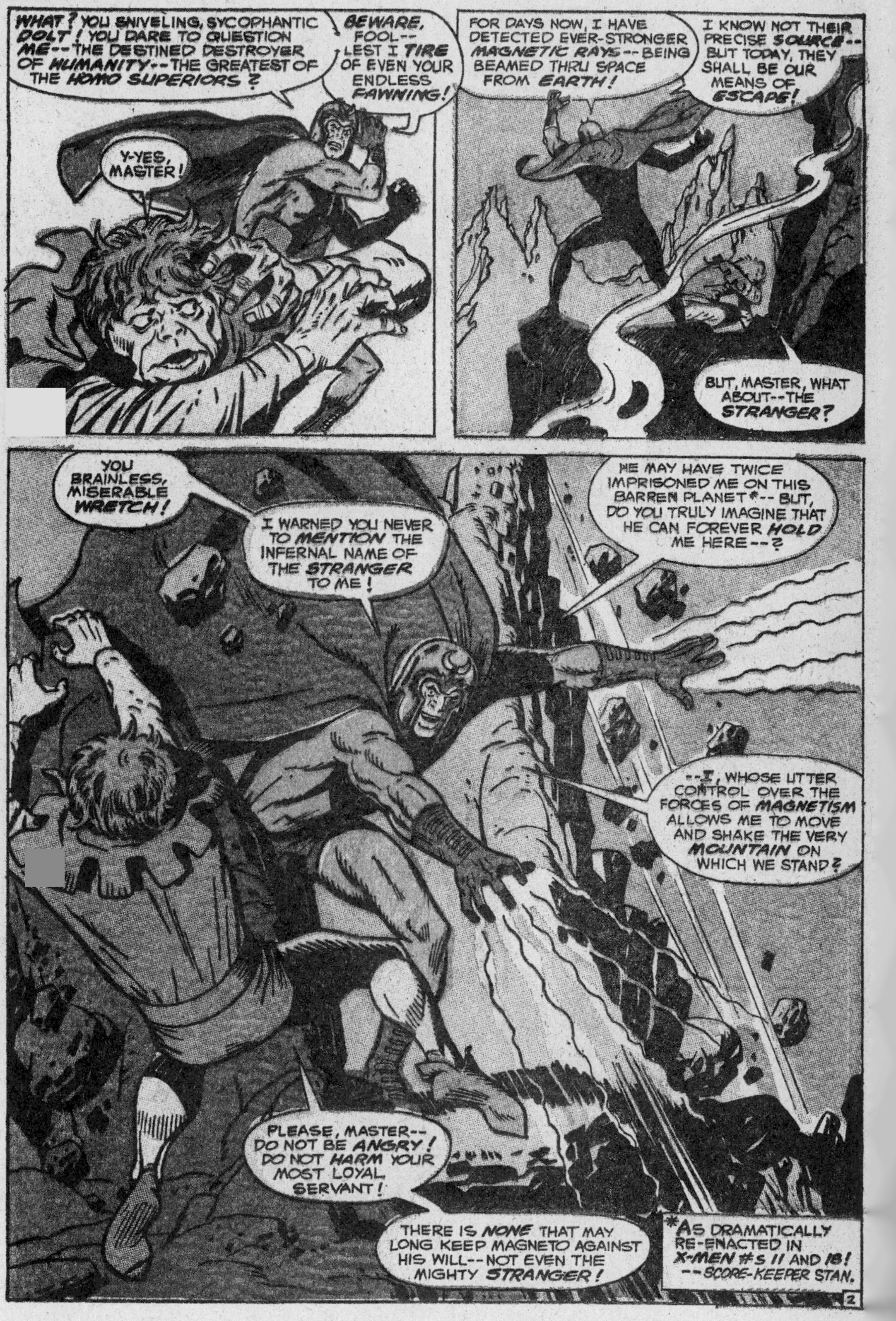
WHAT? YOU SNIVELING, SYCOPHANTIC DOLT! YOU DARE TO QUESTION ME--THE DESTINED DESTROYER OF HUMANITY--THE GREATEST OF THE HOMO SUPERIORS?
BEWARE, FOOL--LEST I TIRE OF EVEN YOUR ENDLESS FAWNING!
Y-YES, MASTER!
FOR DAYS NOW, I HAVE DETECTED EVER-STRONGER MAGNETIC RAYS--BEING BEAMED THRU SPACE FROM EARTH!
I KNOW NOT THEIR PRECISE SOURCE--BUT TODAY, THEY SHALL BE OUR MEANS OF ESCAPE!
BUT, MASTER, WHAT ABOUT--THE STRANGER?
YOU BRAINLESS, MISERABLE WRETCH!
I WARNED YOU NEVER TO MENTION THE INFERNAL NAME OF THE STRANGER TO ME!
HE MAY HAVE TWICE IMPRISONED ME ON THIS BARREN PLANET*--BUT, DO YOU TRULY IMAGINE THAT HE CAN FOREVER HOLD ME HERE--?
--I, WHOSE UTTER CONTROL OVER THE FORCES OF MAGNETISM ALLOWS ME TO MOVE AND SHAKE THE VERY MOUNTAIN ON WHICH WE STAND?
PLEASE, MASTER--DO NOT BE ANGRY! DO NOT HARM YOUR MOST LOYAL SERVANT!
THERE IS NONE THAT MAY LONG KEEP MAGNETO AGAINST HIS WILL--NOT EVEN THE MIGHTY STRANGER!
*AS DRAMATICALLY RE-ENACTED IN X-MEN #s 11 AND 18! --SCORE-KEEPER STAN.
2

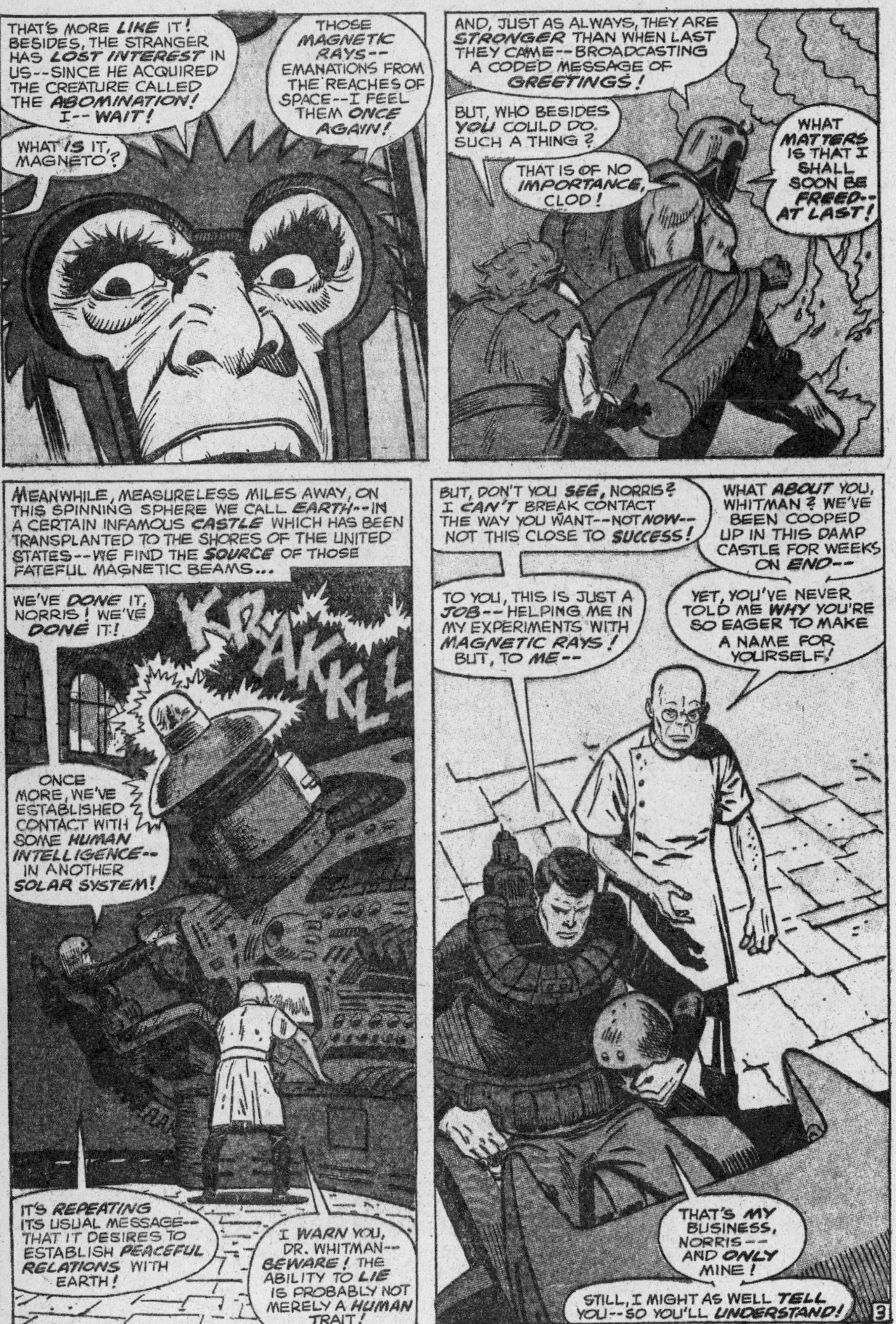

THAT'S MORE LIKE IT! BESIDES, THE STRANGER HAS LOST INTEREST IN US--SINCE HE ACQUIRED THE CREATURE CALLED THE ABOMINATION! I--WAIT!
WHAT IS IT, MAGNETO?
THOSE MAGNETIC RAYS--EMANATIONS FROM THE REACHES OF SPACE--I FEEL THEM ONCE AGAIN!
AND, JUST AS ALWAYS, THEY ARE STRONGER THAN WHEN LAST THEY CAME--BROADCASTING A CODED MESSAGE OF GREETINGS!
BUT, WHO BESIDES YOU COULD DO SUCH A THING?
THAT IS OF NO IMPORTANCE, CLOD!
WHAT MATTERS IS THAT I SHALL SOON BE FREED--AT LAST!
MEANWHILE, MEASURELESS MILES AWAY, ON THIS SPINNING SPHERE WE CALL EARTH--IN A CERTAIN INFAMOUS CASTLE WHICH HAS BEEN TRANSPLANTED TO THE SHORES OF THE UNITED STATES--WE FIND THE SOURCE OF THOSE FATEFUL MAGNETIC BEAMS...
WE'VE DONE IT, NORRIS! WE'VE DONE IT!
KRAKKLL
ONCE MORE, WE'VE ESTABLISHED CONTACT WITH SOME HUMAN INTELLIGENCE--IN ANOTHER SOLAR SYSTEM!
IT'S REPEATING ITS USUAL MESSAGE--THAT IT DESIRES TO ESTABLISH PEACEFUL RELATIONS WITH EARTH!
I WARN YOU, DR. WHITMAN--BEWARE! THE ABILITY TO LIE IS PROBABLY NOT MERELY A HUMAN TRAIT!
BUT, DON'T YOU SEE, NORRIS? I CAN'T BREAK CONTACT THE WAY YOU WANT--NOT NOW--NOT THIS CLOSE TO SUCCESS!
TO YOU, THIS IS JUST A JOB--HELPING ME IN MY EXPERIMENTS WITH MAGNETIC RAYS! BUT, TO ME--
WHAT ABOUT YOU, WHITMAN? WE'VE BEEN COOPED UP IN THIS DAMP CASTLE FOR WEEKS ON END--
YET, YOU'VE NEVER TOLD ME WHY YOU'RE SO EAGER TO MAKE A NAME FOR YOURSELF!
THAT'S MY BUSINESS, NORRIS--AND ONLY MINE!
STILL, I MIGHT AS WELL TELL YOU--SO YOU'LL UNDERSTAND!
3

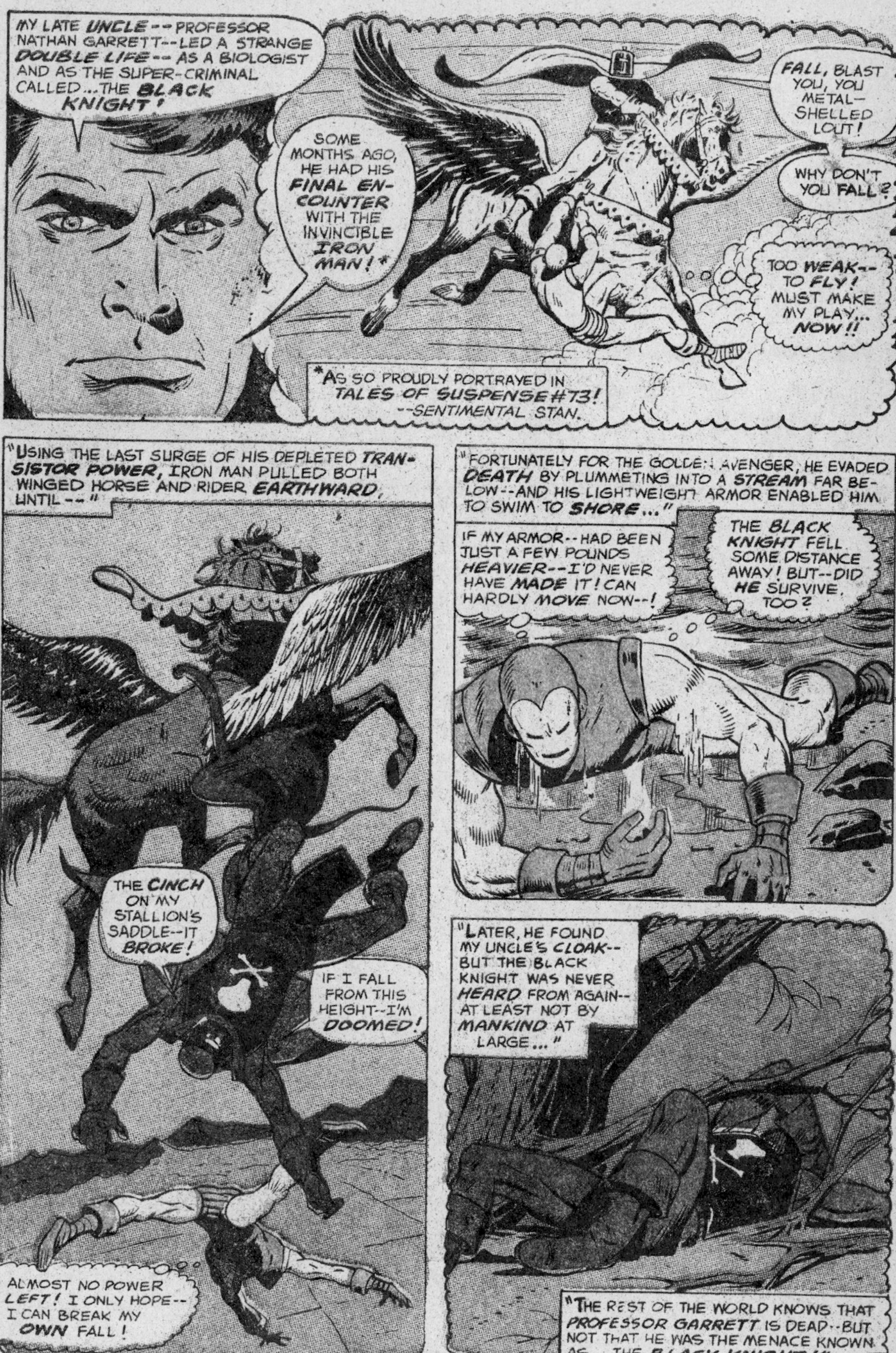
MY LATE UNCLE--PROFESSOR NATHAN GARRETT--LED A STRANGE DOUBLE LIFE--AS A BIOLOGIST AND AS THE SUPER-CRIMINAL CALLED...THE BLACK KNIGHT!
SOME MONTHS AGO, HE HAD HIS FINAL ENCOUNTER WITH THE INVINCIBLE IRON MAN!*
FALL, BLAST YOU, YOU METAL-SHELLED LOUT!
WHY DON'T YOU FALL?
TOO WEAK--TO FLY! MUST MAKE MY PLAY... NOW!!
*AS SO PROUDLY PORTRAYED IN TALES OF SUSPENSE #73! --SENTIMENTAL STAN.
"USING THE LAST SURGE OF HIS DEPLETED TRANSISTOR POWER, IRON MAN PULLED BOTH WINGED HORSE AND RIDER EARTHWARD, UNTIL--"
THE CINCH ON MY STALLION'S SADDLE--IT BROKE!
IF I FALL FROM THIS HEIGHT--I'M DOOMED!
ALMOST NO POWER LEFT! I ONLY HOPE--I CAN BREAK MY OWN FALL!
"FORTUNATELY FOR THE GOLDEN AVENGER, HE EVADED DEATH BY PLUMMETING INTO A STREAM FAR BELOW--AND HIS LIGHTWEIGHT ARMOR ENABLED HIM TO SWIM TO SHORE..."
IF MY ARMOR--HAD BEEN JUST A FEW POUNDS HEAVIER--I'D NEVER HAVE MADE IT! CAN HARDLY MOVE NOW--!
THE BLACK KNIGHT FELL SOME DISTANCE AWAY! BUT--DID HE SURVIVE, TOO?
"LATER, HE FOUND MY UNCLE'S CLOAK--BUT THE BLACK KNIGHT WAS NEVER HEARD FROM AGAIN--AT LEAST NOT BY MANKIND AT LARGE..."
"THE REST OF THE WORLD KNOWS THAT PROFESSOR GARRETT IS DEAD--BUT NOT THAT HE WAS THE MENACE KNOWN AS...THE BLACK KNIGHT!"
4

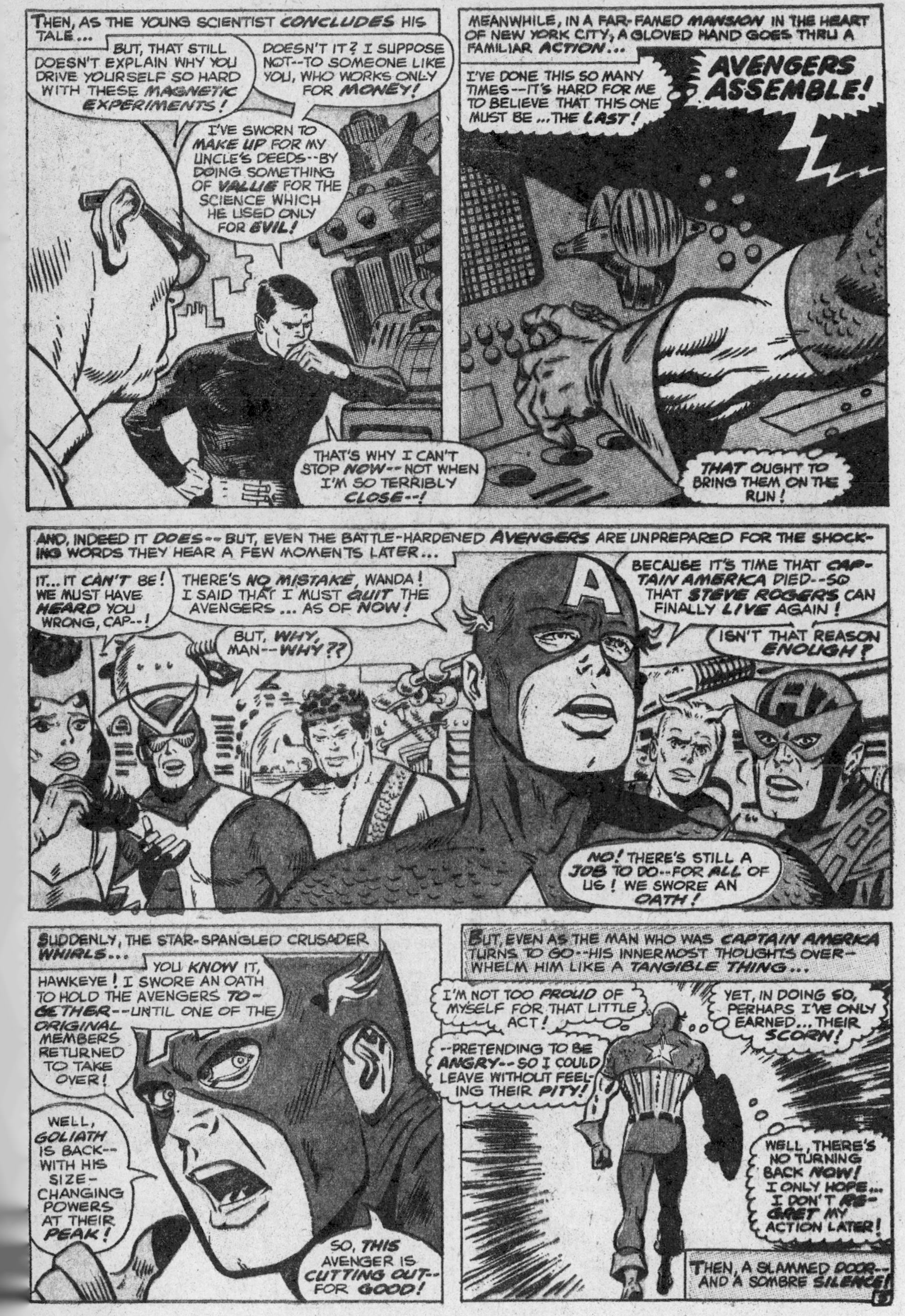
THEN, AS THE YOUNG SCIENTIST CONCLUDES HIS TALE...
BUT, THAT STILL DOESN'T EXPLAIN WHY YOU DRIVE YOURSELF SO HARD WITH THESE MAGNETIC EXPERIMENTS!
DOESN'T IT? I SUPPOSE NOT--TO SOMEONE LIKE YOU, WHO WORKS ONLY FOR MONEY!
I'VE SWORN TO MAKE UP FOR MY UNCLE'S DEEDS--BY DOING SOMETHING OF VALUE FOR THE SCIENCE WHICH HE USED ONLY FOR EVIL!
THAT'S WHY I CAN'T STOP NOW--NOT WHEN I'M SO TERRIBLY CLOSE--!
MEANWHILE, IN A FAR-FAMED MANSION IN THE HEART OF NEW YORK CITY, A GLOVED HAND GOES THRU A FAMILIAR ACTION...
I'VE DONE THIS SO MANY TIMES--IT'S HARD FOR ME TO BELIEVE THAT THIS ONE MUST BE ...THE LAST!
AVENGERS ASSEMBLE!
THAT OUGHT TO BRING THEM ON THE RUN!
AND, INDEED IT DOES--BUT, EVEN THE BATTLE-HARDENED AVENGERS ARE UNPREPARED FOR THE SHOCKING WORDS THEY HEAR A FEW MOMENTS LATER...
IT...IT CAN'T BE! WE MUST HAVE HEARD YOU WRONG, CAP--!
THERE'S NO MISTAKE, WANDA! I SAID THAT I MUST QUIT THE AVENGERS ... AS OF NOW!
BUT, WHY, MAN--WHY??
BECAUSE IT'S TIME THAT CAPTAIN AMERICA DIED--SO THAT STEVE ROGERS CAN FINALLY LIVE AGAIN!
ISN'T THAT REASON ENOUGH?
NO! THERE'S STILL A JOB TO DO--FOR ALL OF US! WE SWORE AN OATH!
SUDDENLY, THE STAR-SPANGLED CRUSADER WHIRLS...
YOU KNOW IT, HAWKEYE! I SWORE AN OATH TO HOLD THE AVENGERS TOGETHER--UNTIL ONE OF THE ORIGINAL MEMBERS RETURNED TO TAKE OVER!
WELL, GOLIATH IS BACK--WITH HIS SIZE-CHANGING POWERS AT THEIR PEAK!
SO, THIS AVENGER IS CUTTING OUT--FOR GOOD!
BUT, EVEN AS THE MAN WHO WAS CAPTAIN AMERICA TURNS TO GO--HIS INNERMOST THOUGHTS OVERWHELM HIM LIKE A TANGIBLE THING...
I'M NOT TOO PROUD OF MYSELF FOR THAT LITTLE ACT!
--PRETENDING TO BE ANGRY--SO I COULD LEAVE WITHOUT FEELING THEIR PITY!
YET, IN DOING SO, PERHAPS I'VE ONLY EARNED... THEIR SCORN!
WELL, THERE'S NO TURNING BACK NOW! I ONLY HOPE... I DON'T REGRET MY ACTION LATER!
THEN, A SLAMMED DOOR--AND A SOMBRE SILENCE!
5

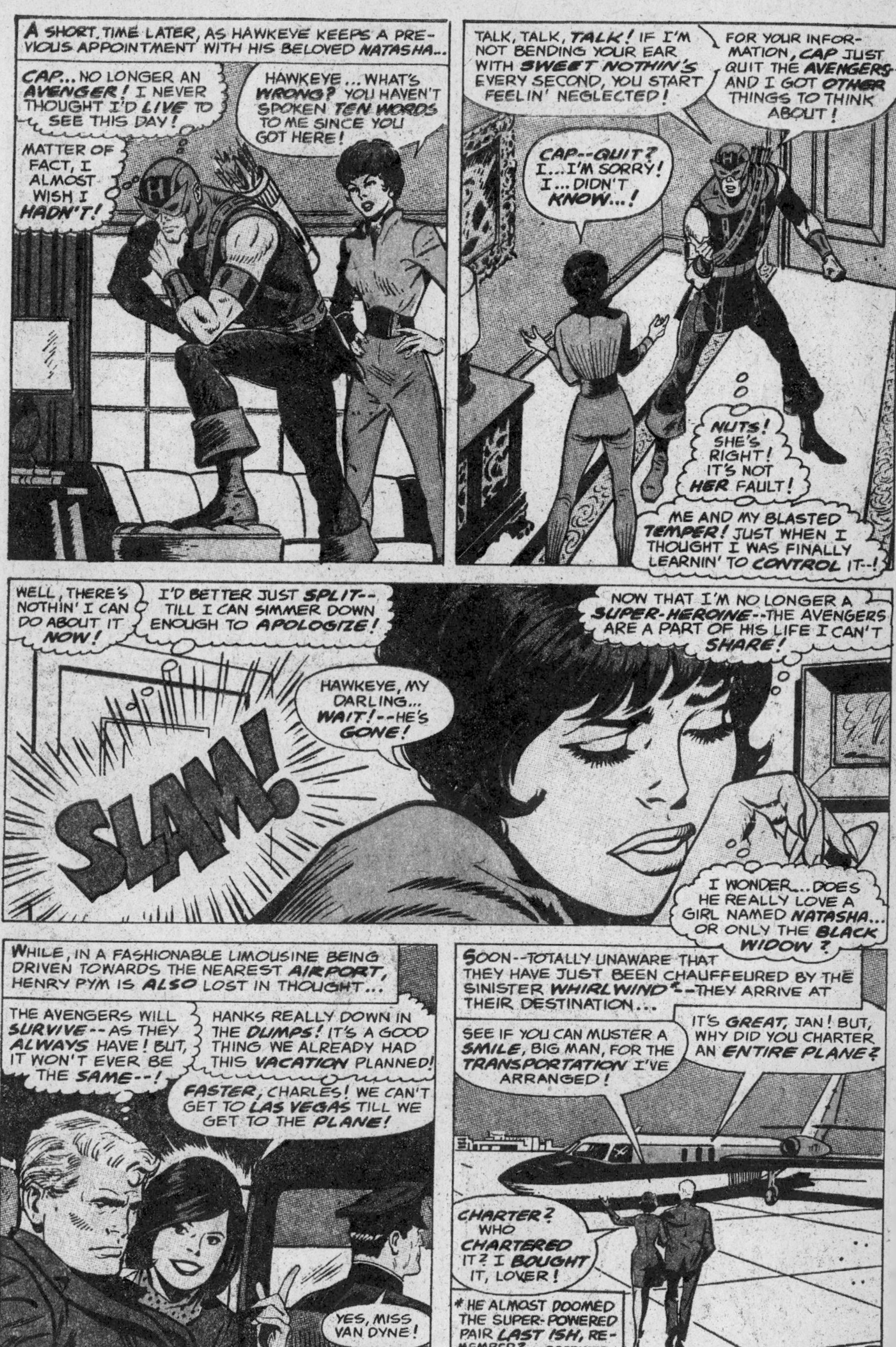
A SHORT TIME LATER, AS HAWKEYE KEEPS A PREVIOUS APPOINTMENT WITH HIS BELOVED NATASHA...
CAP... NO LONGER AN AVENGER! I NEVER THOUGHT I'D LIVE TO SEE THIS DAY!
MATTER OF FACT, I ALMOST WISH I HADN'T!
HAWKEYE ... WHAT'S WRONG? YOU HAVEN'T SPOKEN TEN WORDS TO ME SINCE YOU GOT HERE!
TALK, TALK, TALK! IF I'M NOT BENDING YOUR EAR WITH SWEET NOTHIN'S EVERY SECOND, YOU START FEELIN' NEGLECTED!
FOR YOUR INFORMATION, CAP JUST QUIT THE AVENGERS AND I GOT OTHER THINGS TO THINK ABOUT!
CAP--QUIT? I... I'M SORRY! I... DIDN'T KNOW...!
NUTS! SHE'S RIGHT! IT'S NOT HER FAULT!
ME AND MY BLASTED TEMPER! JUST WHEN I THOUGHT I WAS FINALLY LEARNIN' TO CONTROL IT--!
WELL, THERE'S NOTHIN' I CAN DO ABOUT IT NOW!
I'D BETTER JUST SPLIT-- TILL I CAN SIMMER DOWN ENOUGH TO APOLOGIZE!
SLAM!
HAWKEYE, MY DARLING... WAIT!--HE'S GONE!
NOW THAT I'M NO LONGER A SUPER-HEROINE--THE AVENGERS ARE A PART OF HIS LIFE I CAN'T SHARE!
I WONDER... DOES HE REALLY LOVE A GIRL NAMED NATASHA... OR ONLY THE BLACK WIDOW?
WHILE, IN A FASHIONABLE LIMOUSINE BEING DRIVEN TOWARDS THE NEAREST AIRPORT, HENRY PYM IS ALSO LOST IN THOUGHT...
THE AVENGERS WILL SURVIVE--AS THEY ALWAYS HAVE! BUT, IT WON'T EVER BE THE SAME--!
HANKS REALLY DOWN IN THE DUMPS! IT'S A GOOD THING WE ALREADY HAD THIS VACATION PLANNED!
FASTER, CHARLES! WE CAN'T GET TO LAS VEGAS TILL WE GET TO THE PLANE!
YES, MISS VAN DYNE!
SOON--TOTALLY UNAWARE THAT THEY HAVE JUST BEEN CHAUFFEURED BY THE SINISTER WHIRLWIND*--THEY ARRIVE AT THEIR DESTINATION...
SEE IF YOU CAN MUSTER A SMILE, BIG MAN, FOR THE TRANSPORTATION I'VE ARRANGED!
IT'S GREAT, JAN! BUT, WHY DID YOU CHARTER AN ENTIRE PLANE?
CHARTER? WHO CHARTERED IT? I BOUGHT IT, LOVER!
* HE ALMOST DOOMED THE SUPER-POWERED PAIR LAST ISH, REMEMBER? --FOOTNOTE--WEARY STAN.
6

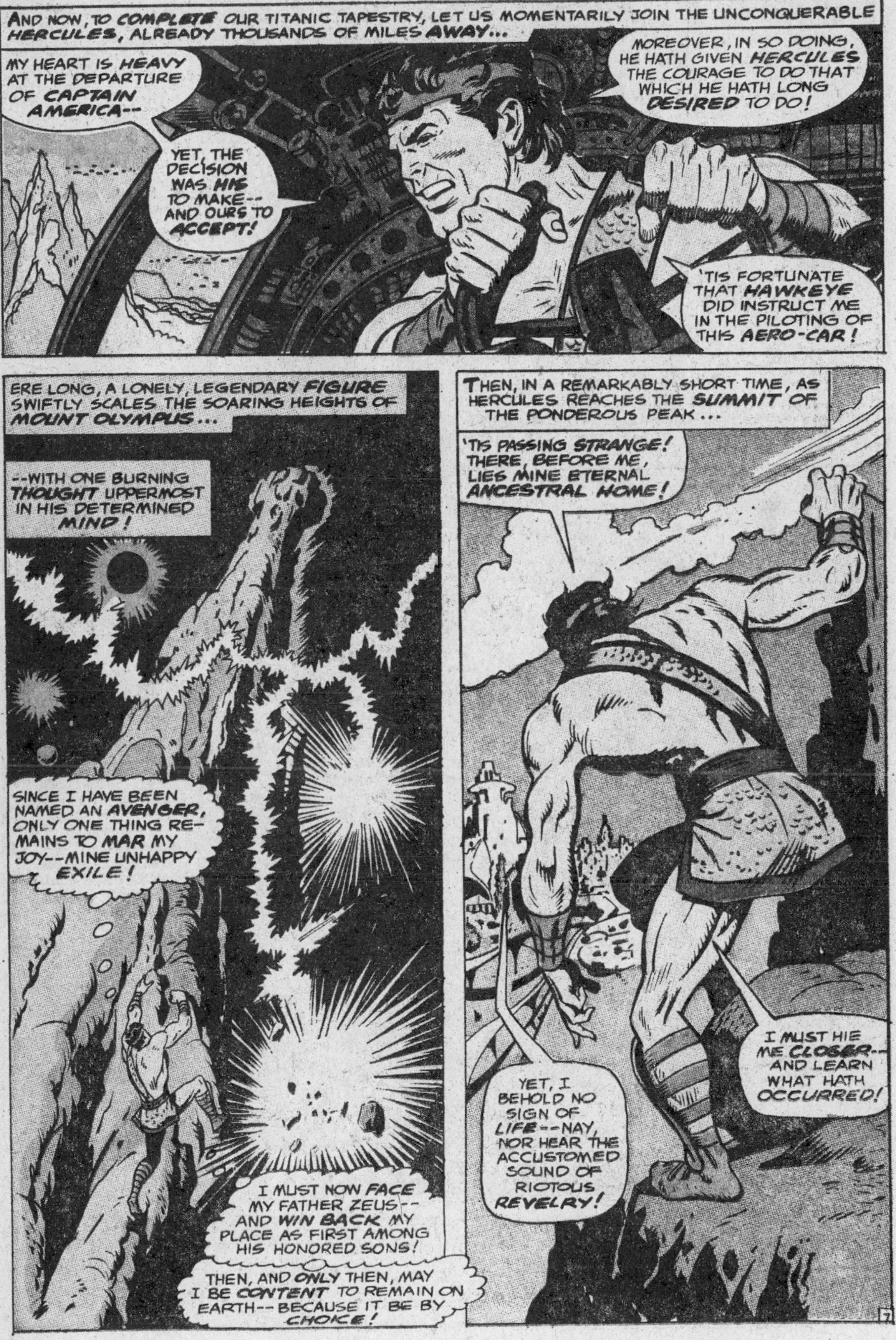

AND NOW, TO COMPLETE OUR TITANIC TAPESTRY, LET US MOMENTARILY JOIN THE UNCONQUERABLE HERCULES, ALREADY THOUSANDS OF MILES AWAY...
MY HEART IS HEAVY AT THE DEPARTURE OF CAPTAIN AMERICA--
YET, THE DECISION WAS HIS TO MAKE-- AND OURS TO ACCEPT!
MOREOVER, IN SO DOING, HE HATH GIVEN HERCULES THE COURAGE TO DO THAT WHICH HE HATH LONG DESIRED TO DO!
'TIS FORTUNATE THAT HAWKEYE DID INSTRUCT ME IN THE PILOTING OF THIS AERO-CAR!
ERE LONG, A LONELY, LEGENDARY FIGURE SWIFTLY SCALES THE SOARING HEIGHTS OF MOUNT OLYMPUS...
--WITH ONE BURNING THOUGHT UPPERMOST IN HIS DETERMINED MIND!
SINCE I HAVE BEEN NAMED AN AVENGER, ONLY ONE THING RE-MAINS TO MAR MY JOY--MINE UNHAPPY EXILE!
I MUST NOW FACE MY FATHER ZEUS-- AND WIN BACK MY PLACE AS FIRST AMONG HIS HONORED SONS!
THEN, AND ONLY THEN, MAY I BE CONTENT TO REMAIN ON EARTH-- BECAUSE IT BE BY CHOICE!
THEN, IN A REMARKABLY SHORT TIME, AS HERCULES REACHES THE SUMMIT OF THE PONDEROUS PEAK...
'TIS PASSING STRANGE! THERE, BEFORE ME, LIES MINE ETERNAL ANCESTRAL HOME!
I MUST HIE ME CLOSER-- AND LEARN WHAT HATH OCCURRED!
YET, I BEHOLD NO SIGN OF LIFE--NAY, NOR HEAR THE ACCUSTOMED SOUND OF RIOTOUS REVELRY!
7

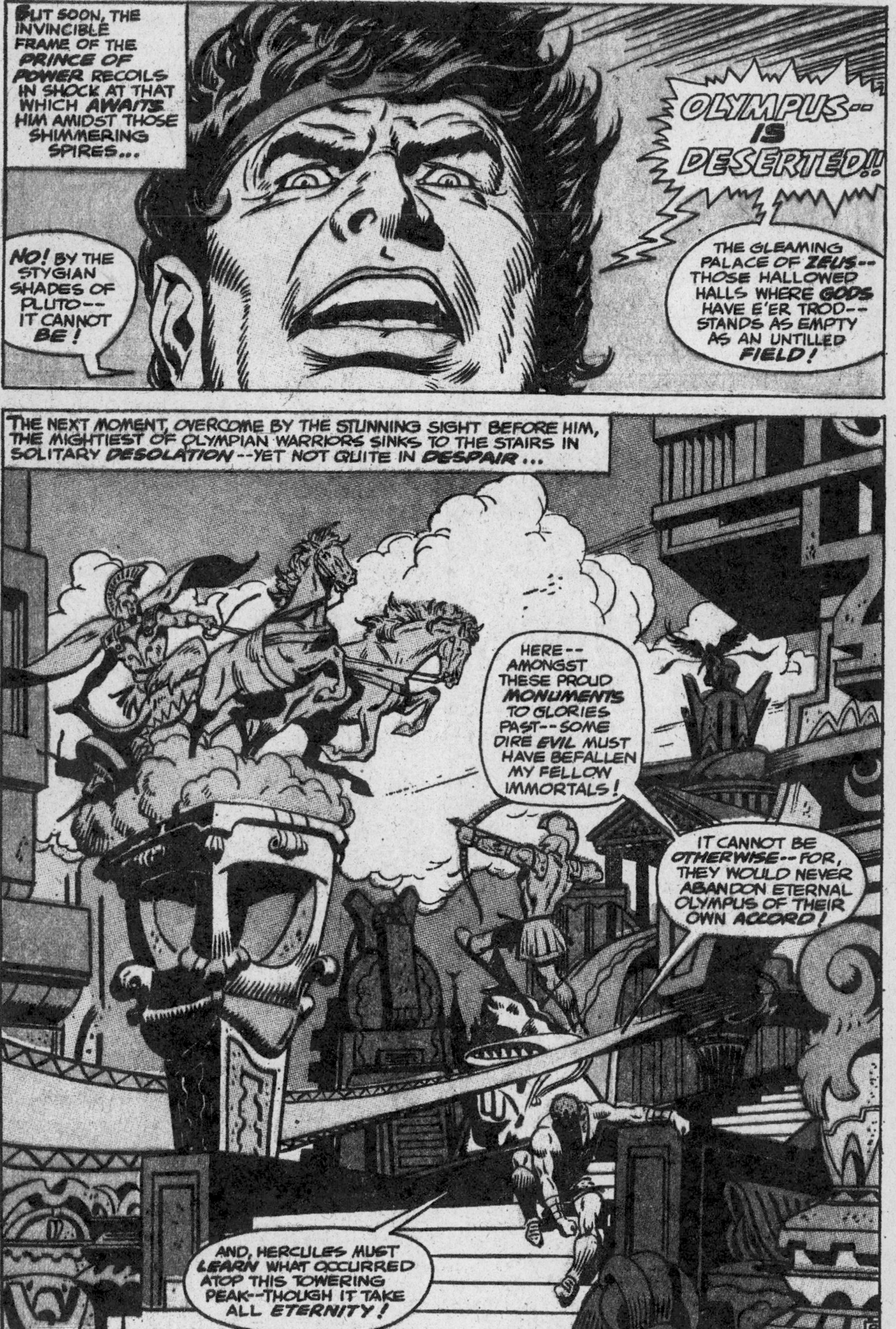

BUT SOON, THE INVINCIBLE FRAME OF THE PRINCE OF POWER RECOILS IN SHOCK AT THAT WHICH AWAITS HIM AMIDST THOSE SHIMMERING SPIRES...
OLYMPUS-- IS DESERTED!!
NO! BY THE STYGIAN SHADES OF PLUTO-- IT CANNOT BE!
THE GLEAMING PALACE OF ZEUS-- THOSE HALLOWED HALLS WHERE GODS HAVE E'ER TROD-- STANDS AS EMPTY AS AN UNTILLED FIELD!
THE NEXT MOMENT, OVERCOME BY THE STUNNING SIGHT BEFORE HIM, THE MIGHTIEST OF OLYMPIAN WARRIORS SINKS TO THE STAIRS IN SOLITARY DESOLATION --YET NOT QUITE IN DESPAIR...
HERE-- AMONGST THESE PROUD MONUMENTS TO GLORIES PAST--SOME DIRE EVIL MUST HAVE BEFALLEN MY FELLOW IMMORTALS!
IT CANNOT BE OTHERWISE--FOR, THEY WOULD NEVER ABANDON ETERNAL OLYMPUS OF THEIR OWN ACCORD!
AND, HERCULES MUST LEARN WHAT OCCURRED ATOP THIS TOWERING PEAK--THOUGH IT TAKE ALL ETERNITY!
8

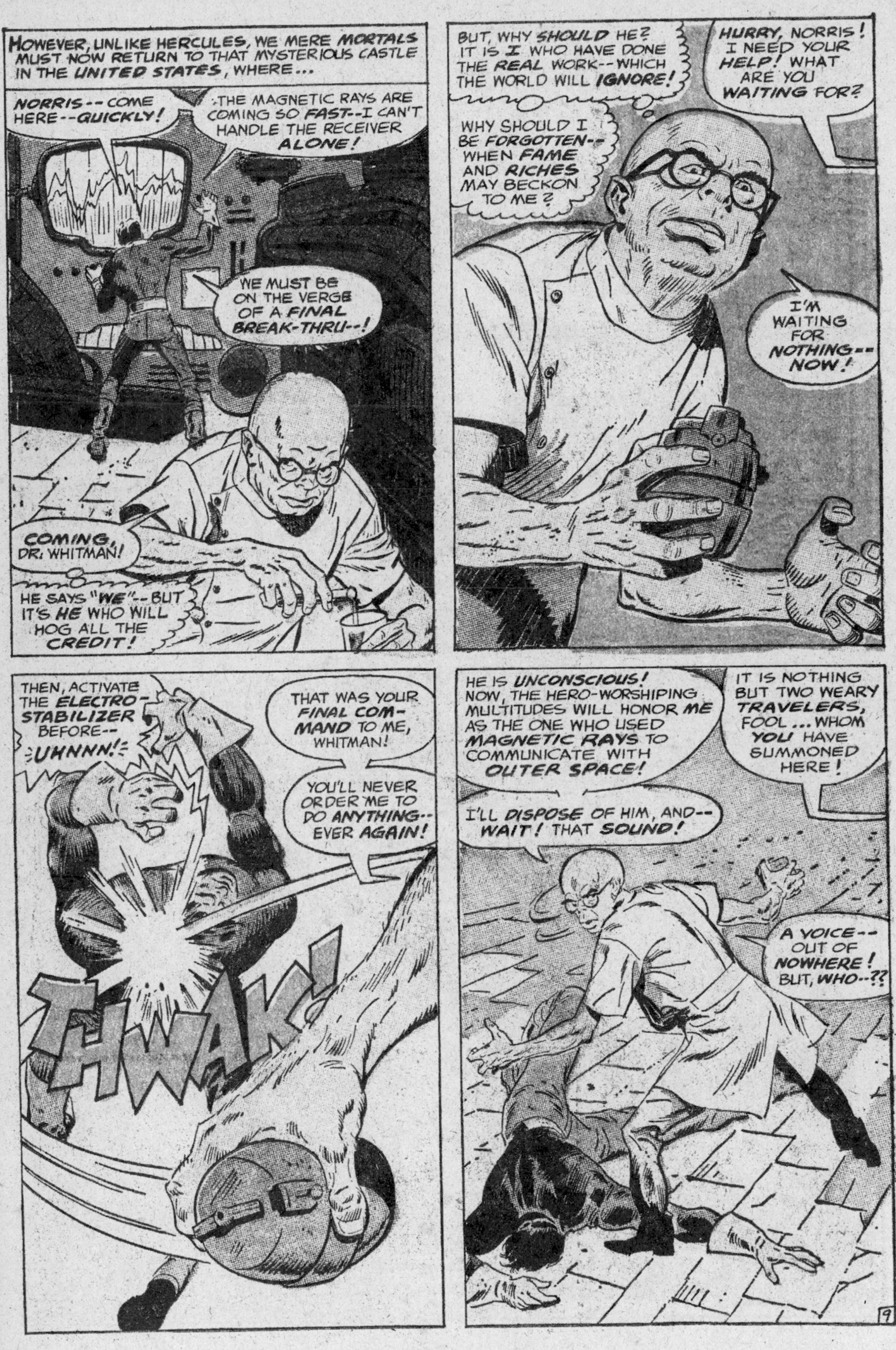

HOWEVER, UNLIKE HERCULES, WE MERE MORTALS MUST NOW RETURN TO THAT MYSTERIOUS CASTLE IN THE UNITED STATES, WHERE...
NORRIS--COME HERE--QUICKLY!
THE MAGNETIC RAYS ARE COMING SO FAST--I CAN'T HANDLE THE RECEIVER ALONE!
WE MUST BE ON THE VERGE OF A FINAL BREAK-THRU--!
COMING, DR. WHITMAN!
HE SAYS "WE"--BUT IT'S HE WHO WILL HOG ALL THE CREDIT!
BUT, WHY SHOULD HE? IT IS I WHO HAVE DONE THE REAL WORK--WHICH THE WORLD WILL IGNORE!
WHY SHOULD I BE FORGOTTEN--WHEN FAME AND RICHES MAY BECKON TO ME?
HURRY, NORRIS! I NEED YOUR HELP! WHAT ARE YOU WAITING FOR?
I'M WAITING FOR NOTHING--NOW!
THEN, ACTIVATE THE ELECTRO-STABILIZER BEFORE--
UHNNN!
THAT WAS YOUR FINAL COMMAND TO ME, WHITMAN!
YOU'LL NEVER ORDER ME TO DO ANYTHING--EVER AGAIN!
THWAK!
HE IS UNCONSCIOUS! NOW, THE HERO-WORSHIPING MULTITUDES WILL HONOR ME AS THE ONE WHO USED MAGNETIC RAYS TO COMMUNICATE WITH OUTER SPACE!
I'LL DISPOSE OF HIM, AND--WAIT! THAT SOUND!
IT IS NOTHING BUT TWO WEARY TRAVELERS, FOOL... WHOM YOU HAVE SUMMONED HERE!
A VOICE--OUT OF NOWHERE! BUT, WHO--??
9

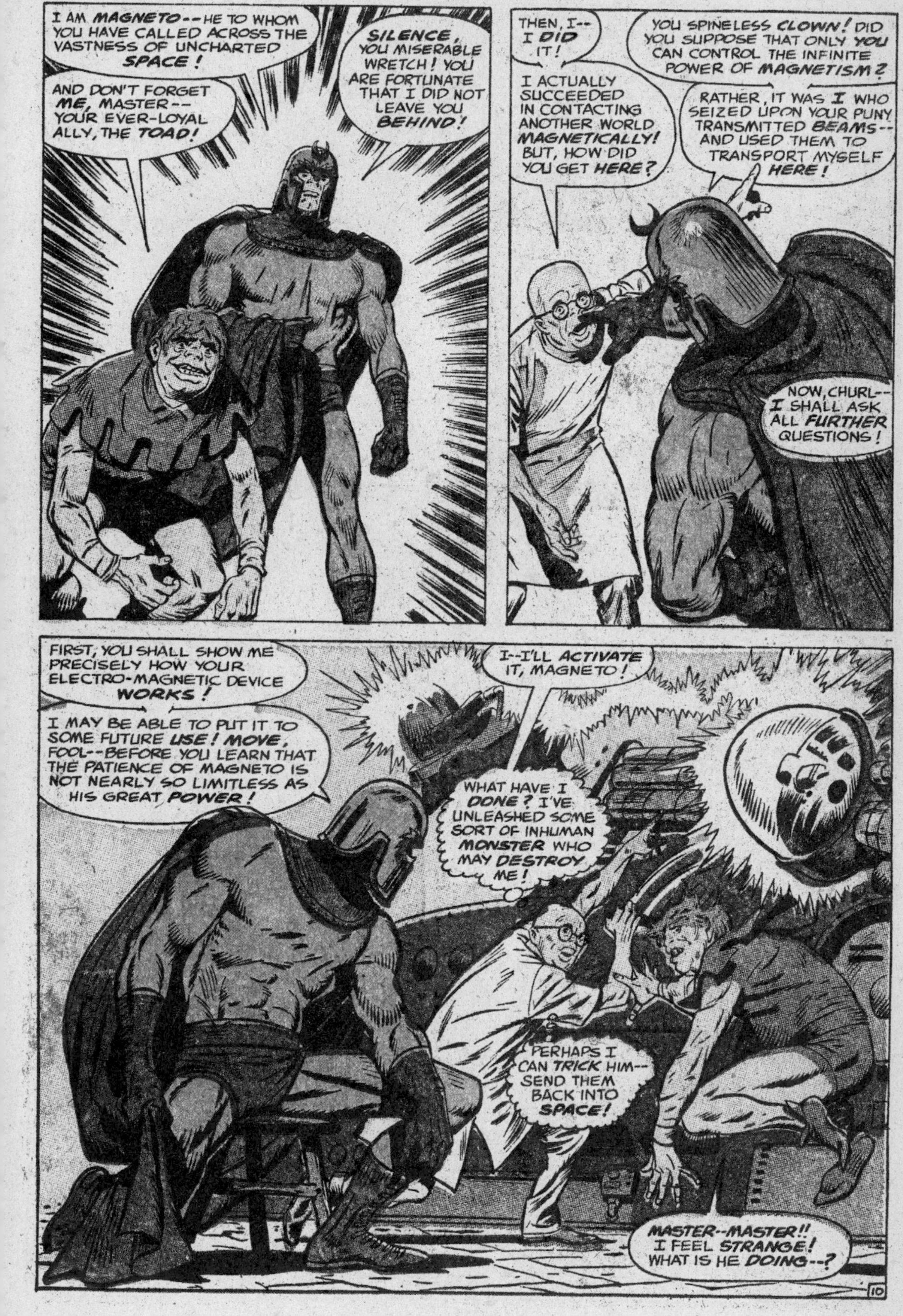
I AM MAGNETO--HE TO WHOM YOU HAVE CALLED ACROSS THE VASTNESS OF UNCHARTED SPACE!
AND DON'T FORGET ME, MASTER--YOUR EVER-LOYAL ALLY, THE TOAD!
SILENCE, YOU MISERABLE WRETCH! YOU ARE FORTUNATE THAT I DID NOT LEAVE YOU BEHIND!
THEN, I--I DID IT!
I ACTUALLY SUCCEEDED IN CONTACTING ANOTHER WORLD MAGNETICALLY! BUT, HOW DID YOU GET HERE?
YOU SPINELESS CLOWN! DID YOU SUPPOSE THAT ONLY YOU CAN CONTROL THE INFINITE POWER OF MAGNETISM?
RATHER, IT WAS I WHO SEIZED UPON YOUR PUNY TRANSMITTED BEAMS--AND USED THEM TO TRANSPORT MYSELF HERE!
NOW, CHURL--I SHALL ASK ALL FURTHER QUESTIONS!
FIRST, YOU SHALL SHOW ME PRECISELY HOW YOUR ELECTRO-MAGNETIC DEVICE WORKS!
I MAY BE ABLE TO PUT IT TO SOME FUTURE USE! MOVE, FOOL--BEFORE YOU LEARN THAT THE PATIENCE OF MAGNETO IS NOT NEARLY SO LIMITLESS AS HIS GREAT POWER!
I--I'LL ACTIVATE IT, MAGNETO!
WHAT HAVE I DONE? I'VE UNLEASHED SOME SORT OF INHUMAN MONSTER WHO MAY DESTROY ME!
PERHAPS I CAN TRICK HIM--SEND THEM BACK INTO SPACE!
MASTER--MASTER!! I FEEL STRANGE! WHAT IS HE DOING--?
10

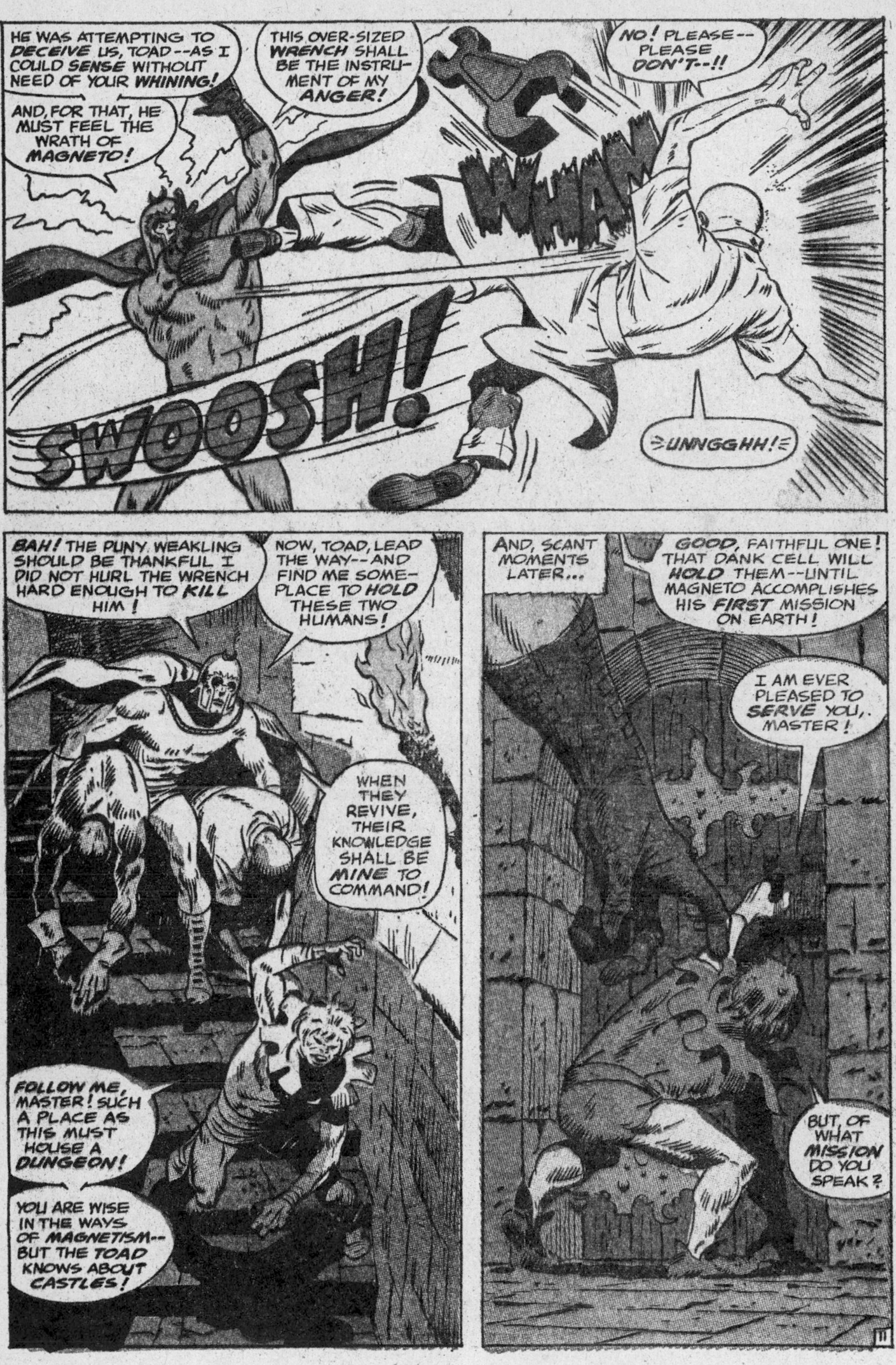
HE WAS ATTEMPTING TO DECEIVE US, TOAD--AS I COULD SENSE WITHOUT NEED OF YOUR WHINING!
AND, FOR THAT, HE MUST FEEL THE WRATH OF MAGNETO!
THIS OVER-SIZED WRENCH SHALL BE THE INSTRUMENT OF MY ANGER!
NO! PLEASE-- PLEASE DON'T--!!
WHAM
SWOOSH!
UNNGGHH!
BAH! THE PUNY WEAKLING SHOULD BE THANKFUL I DID NOT HURL THE WRENCH HARD ENOUGH TO KILL HIM!
NOW, TOAD, LEAD THE WAY--AND FIND ME SOME-PLACE TO HOLD THESE TWO HUMANS!
WHEN THEY REVIVE, THEIR KNOWLEDGE SHALL BE MINE TO COMMAND!
FOLLOW ME, MASTER! SUCH A PLACE AS THIS MUST HOUSE A DUNGEON!
YOU ARE WISE IN THE WAYS OF MAGNETISM-- BUT THE TOAD KNOWS ABOUT CASTLES!
AND, SCANT MOMENTS LATER...
GOOD, FAITHFUL ONE! THAT DANK CELL WILL HOLD THEM--UNTIL MAGNETO ACCOMPLISHES HIS FIRST MISSION ON EARTH!
I AM EVER PLEASED TO SERVE YOU, MASTER!
BUT, OF WHAT MISSION DO YOU SPEAK?
11

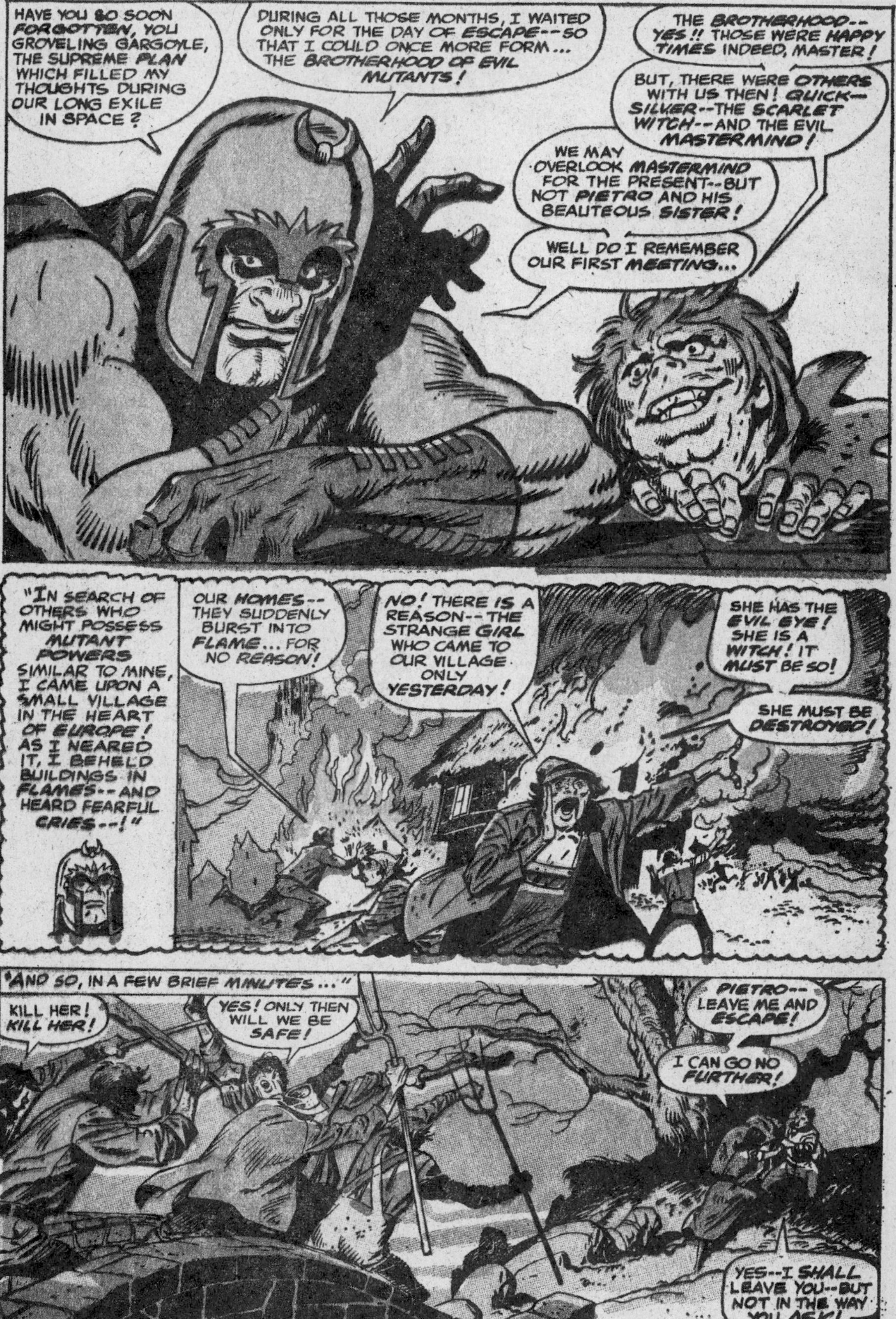
HAVE YOU SO SOON FORGOTTEN, YOU GROVELING GARGOYLE, THE SUPREME PLAN WHICH FILLED MY THOUGHTS DURING OUR LONG EXILE IN SPACE?
DURING ALL THOSE MONTHS, I WAITED ONLY FOR THE DAY OF ESCAPE--SO THAT I COULD ONCE MORE FORM... THE BROTHERHOOD OF EVIL MUTANTS!
THE BROTHERHOOD--YES!! THOSE WERE HAPPY TIMES INDEED, MASTER!
BUT, THERE WERE OTHERS WITH US THEN! QUICK-SILVER--THE SCARLET WITCH--AND THE EVIL MASTERMIND!
WE MAY OVERLOOK MASTERMIND FOR THE PRESENT--BUT NOT PIETRO AND HIS BEAUTEOUS SISTER!
WELL DO I REMEMBER OUR FIRST MEETING...
"IN SEARCH OF OTHERS WHO MIGHT POSSESS MUTANT POWERS SIMILAR TO MINE, I CAME UPON A SMALL VILLAGE IN THE HEART OF EUROPE! AS I NEARED IT, I BEHELD BUILDINGS IN FLAMES--AND HEARD FEARFUL CRIES--!"
OUR HOMES--THEY SUDDENLY BURST INTO FLAME... FOR NO REASON!
NO! THERE IS A REASON--THE STRANGE GIRL WHO CAME TO OUR VILLAGE ONLY YESTERDAY!
SHE HAS THE EVIL EYE! SHE IS A WITCH! IT MUST BE SO!
SHE MUST BE DESTROYED!
"AND SO, IN A FEW BRIEF MINUTES..."
KILL HER! KILL HER!
YES! ONLY THEN WILL WE BE SAFE!
PIETRO--LEAVE ME AND ESCAPE!
I CAN GO NO FURTHER!
YES--I SHALL LEAVE YOU--BUT NOT IN THE WAY YOU ASK!
12

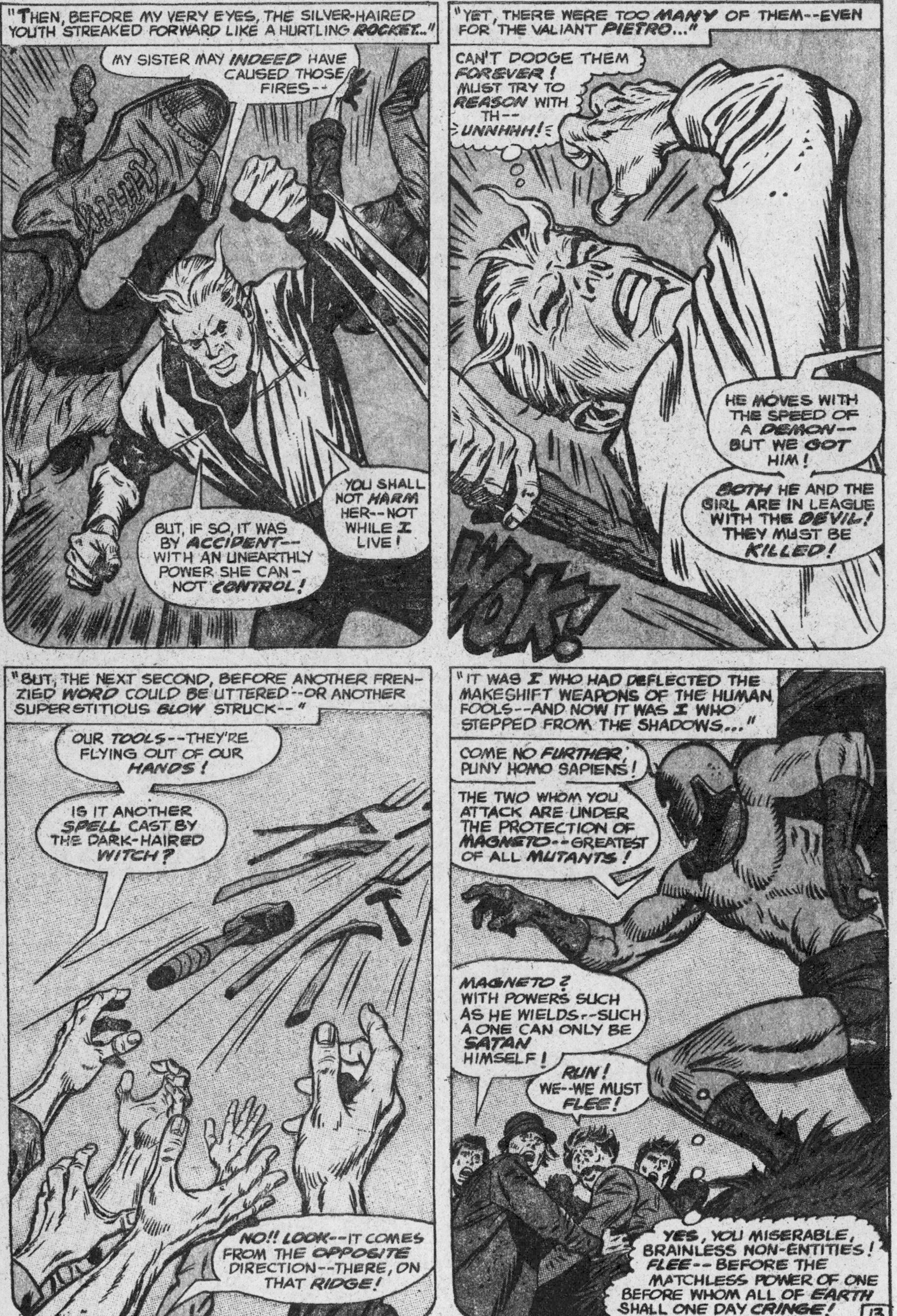
"THEN, BEFORE MY VERY EYES, THE SILVER-HAIRED YOUTH STREAKED FORWARD LIKE A HURTLING ROCKET..."
MY SISTER MAY INDEED HAVE CAUSED THOSE FIRES--
BUT, IF SO, IT WAS BY ACCIDENT--WITH AN UNEARTHLY POWER SHE CAN-NOT CONTROL!
YOU SHALL NOT HARM HER--NOT WHILE I LIVE!
"YET, THERE WERE TOO MANY OF THEM--EVEN FOR THE VALIANT PIETRO..."
CAN'T DODGE THEM FOREVER! MUST TRY TO REASON WITH TH-- UNNHHH!
HE MOVES WITH THE SPEED OF A DEMON--BUT WE GOT HIM!
BOTH HE AND THE GIRL ARE IN LEAGUE WITH THE DEVIL! THEY MUST BE KILLED!
WOK!
"BUT, THE NEXT SECOND, BEFORE ANOTHER FREN-ZIED WORD COULD BE UTTERED--OR ANOTHER SUPERSTITIOUS BLOW STRUCK--"
OUR TOOLS--THEY'RE FLYING OUT OF OUR HANDS!
IS IT ANOTHER SPELL CAST BY THE DARK-HAIRED WITCH?
NO!! LOOK--IT COMES FROM THE OPPOSITE DIRECTION--THERE, ON THAT RIDGE!
"IT WAS I WHO HAD DEFLECTED THE MAKESHIFT WEAPONS OF THE HUMAN FOOLS--AND NOW IT WAS I WHO STEPPED FROM THE SHADOWS..."
COME NO FURTHER, PUNY HOMO SAPIENS!
THE TWO WHOM YOU ATTACK ARE UNDER THE PROTECTION OF MAGNETO--GREATEST OF ALL MUTANTS!
MAGNETO? WITH POWERS SUCH AS HE WIELDS--SUCH A ONE CAN ONLY BE SATAN HIMSELF!
RUN! WE--WE MUST FLEE!
YES, YOU MISERABLE, BRAINLESS NON-ENTITIES! FLEE--BEFORE THE MATCHLESS POWER OF ONE BEFORE WHOM ALL OF EARTH SHALL ONE DAY CRINGE!
13

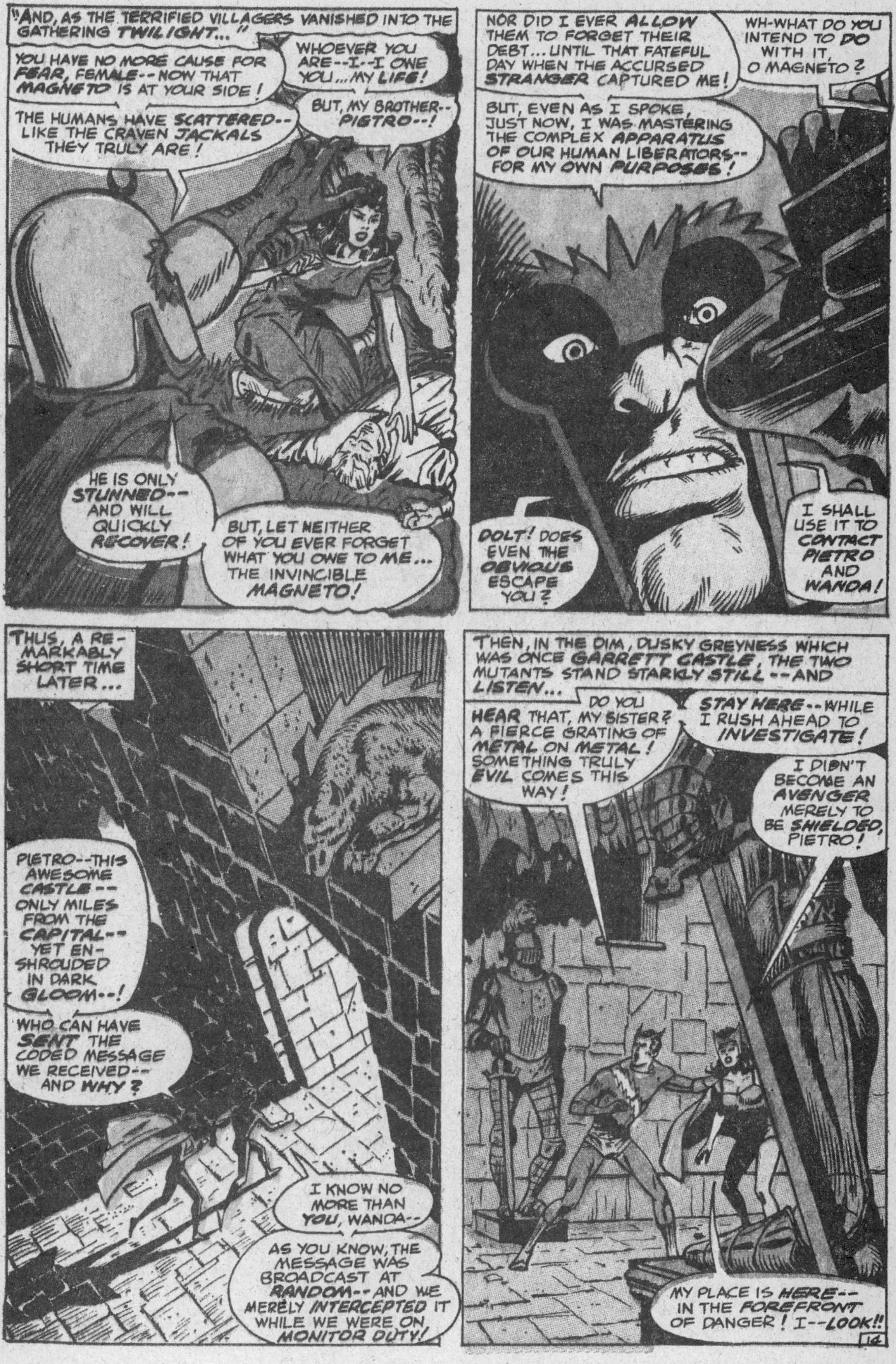
"AND, AS THE TERRIFIED VILLAGERS VANISHED INTO THE GATHERING TWILIGHT..."
YOU HAVE NO MORE CAUSE FOR FEAR, FEMALE--NOW THAT MAGNETO IS AT YOUR SIDE!
WHOEVER YOU ARE--I--I OWE YOU...MY LIFE!
BUT, MY BROTHER--PIETRO--!
THE HUMANS HAVE SCATTERED--LIKE THE CRAVEN JACKALS THEY TRULY ARE!
HE IS ONLY STUNNED--AND WILL QUICKLY RECOVER!
BUT, LET NEITHER OF YOU EVER FORGET WHAT YOU OWE TO ME... THE INVINCIBLE MAGNETO!
NOR DID I EVER ALLOW THEM TO FORGET THEIR DEBT...UNTIL THAT FATEFUL DAY WHEN THE ACCURSED STRANGER CAPTURED ME!
BUT, EVEN AS I SPOKE, JUST NOW, I WAS MASTERING THE COMPLEX APPARATUS OF OUR HUMAN LIBERATORS--FOR MY OWN PURPOSES!
WH-WHAT DO YOU INTEND TO DO WITH IT, O MAGNETO?
DOLT! DOES EVEN THE OBVIOUS ESCAPE YOU?
I SHALL USE IT TO CONTACT PIETRO AND WANDA!
THUS, A REMARKABLY SHORT TIME LATER...
PIETRO--THIS AWESOME CASTLE--ONLY MILES FROM THE CAPITAL--YET ENSHROUDED IN DARK GLOOM--!
WHO CAN HAVE SENT THE CODED MESSAGE WE RECEIVED--AND WHY?
I KNOW NO MORE THAN YOU, WANDA--
AS YOU KNOW, THE MESSAGE WAS BROADCAST AT RANDOM--AND WE MERELY INTERCEPTED IT WHILE WE WERE ON MONITOR DUTY!
THEN, IN THE DIM, DUSKY GREYNESS WHICH WAS ONCE GARRETT CASTLE, THE TWO MUTANTS STAND STARKLY STILL--AND LISTEN...
DO YOU HEAR THAT, MY SISTER? A FIERCE GRATING OF METAL ON METAL! SOMETHING TRULY EVIL COMES THIS WAY!
STAY HERE--WHILE I RUSH AHEAD TO INVESTIGATE!
I DIDN'T BECOME AN AVENGER MERELY TO BE SHIELDED, PIETRO!
MY PLACE IS HERE--IN THE FOREFRONT OF DANGER! I--LOOK!!
14

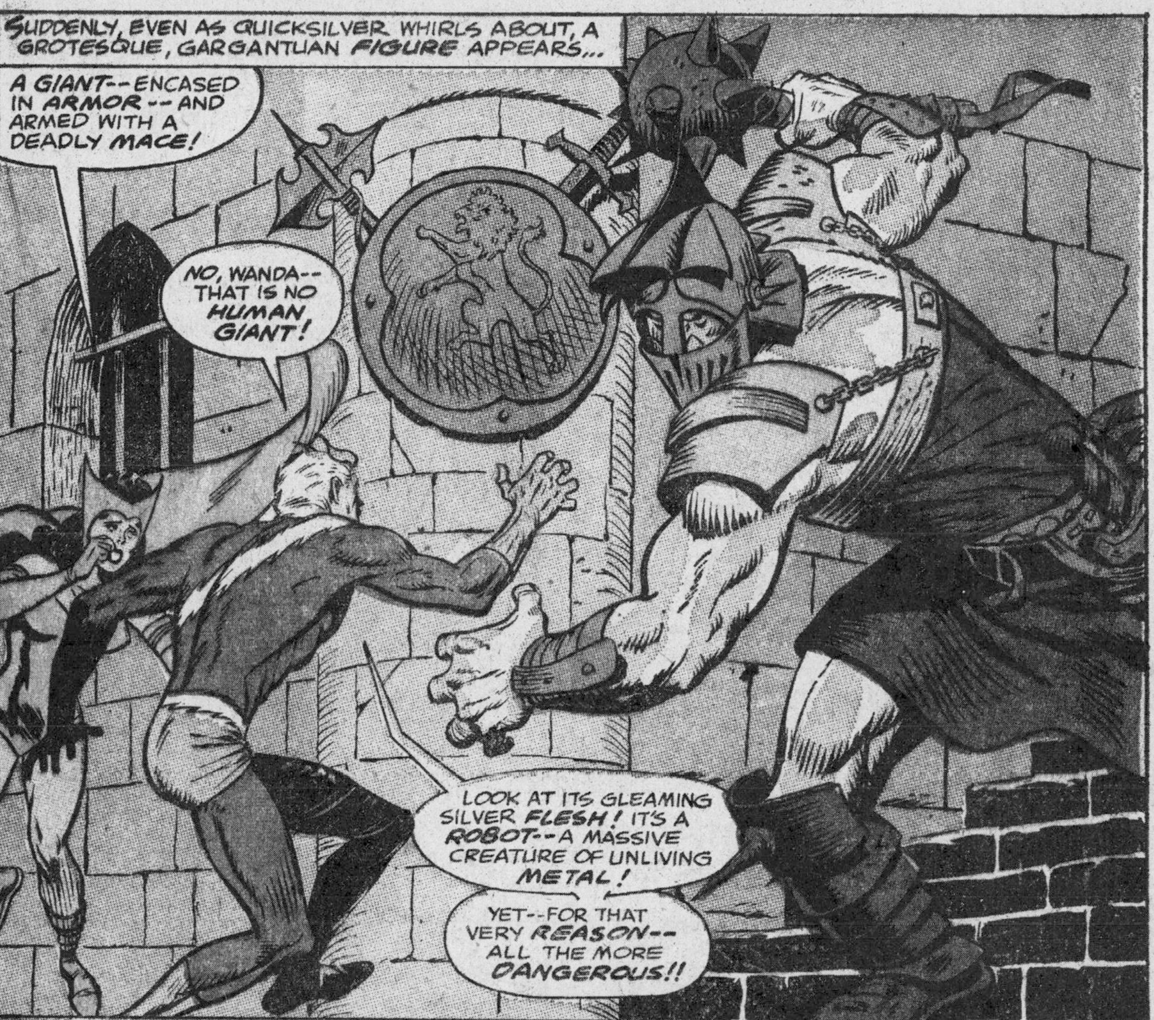
SUDDENLY, EVEN AS QUICKSILVER WHIRLS ABOUT, A GROTESQUE, GARGANTUAN FIGURE APPEARS...
A GIANT--ENCASED IN ARMOR--AND ARMED WITH A DEADLY MACE!
NO, WANDA--THAT IS NO HUMAN GIANT!
LOOK AT ITS GLEAMING SILVER FLESH! IT'S A ROBOT--A MASSIVE CREATURE OF UNLIVING METAL!
YET--FOR THAT VERY REASON--ALL THE MORE DANGEROUS!!

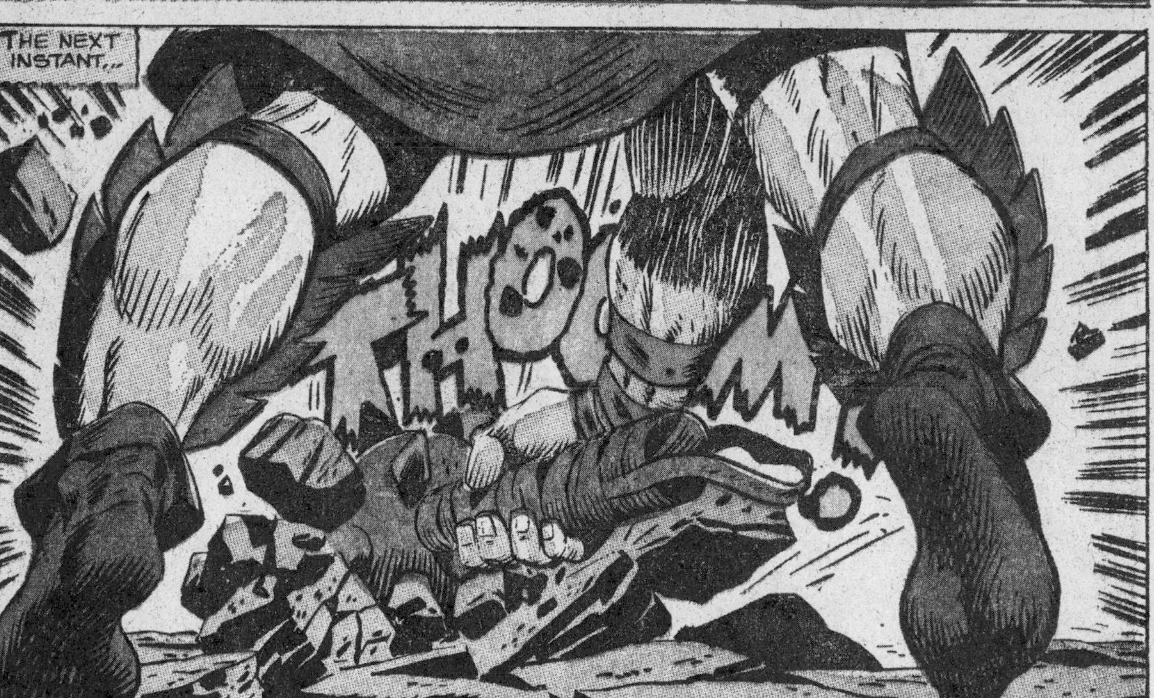
THE NEXT INSTANT...

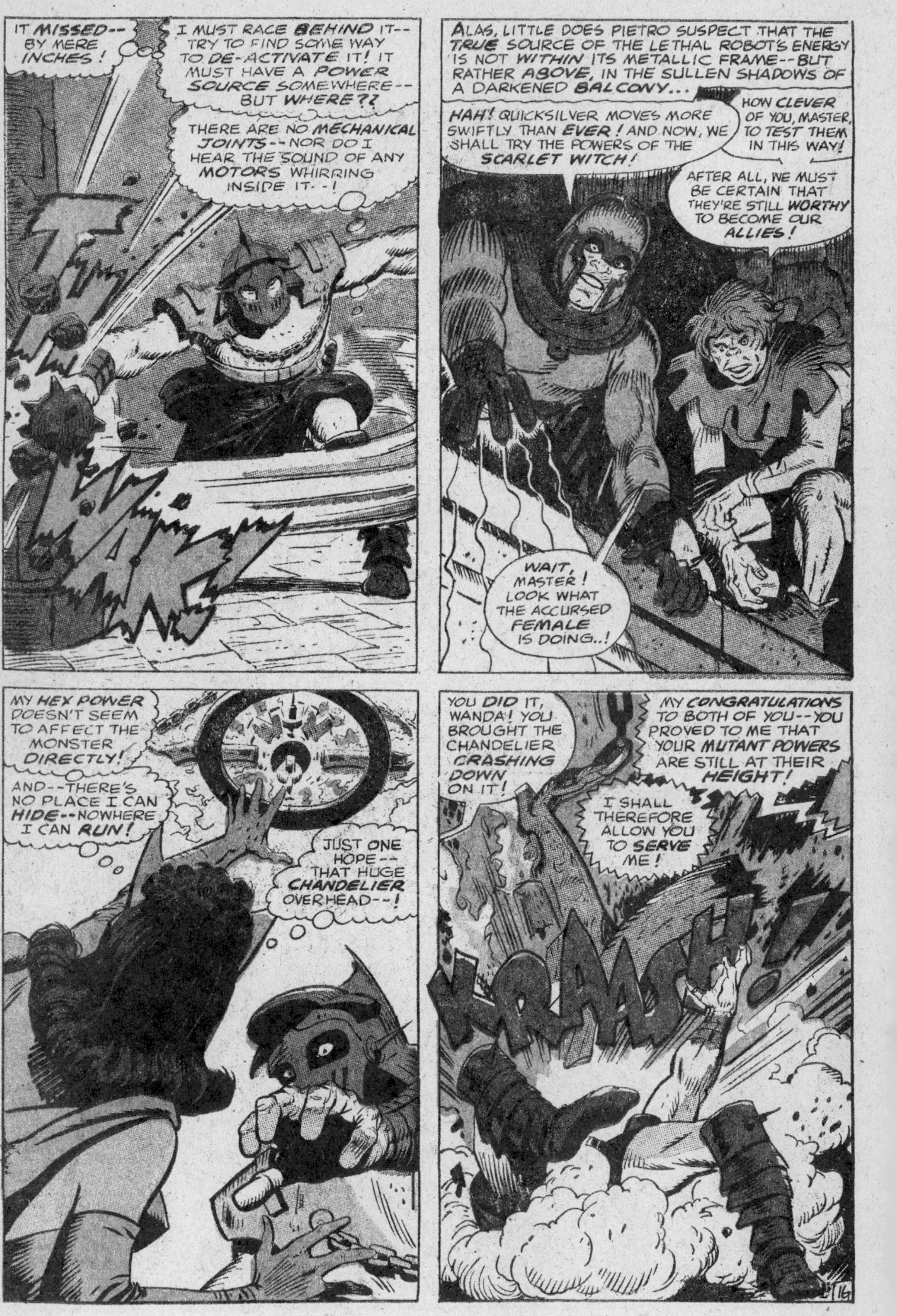
IT MISSED-- BY MERE INCHES!
I MUST RACE BEHIND IT-- TRY TO FIND SOME WAY TO DE-ACTIVATE IT! IT MUST HAVE A POWER SOURCE SOMEWHERE-- BUT WHERE??
THERE ARE NO MECHANICAL JOINTS--NOR DO I HEAR THE SOUND OF ANY MOTORS WHIRRING INSIDE IT--!
ALAS, LITTLE DOES PIETRO SUSPECT THAT THE TRUE SOURCE OF THE LETHAL ROBOT'S ENERGY IS NOT WITHIN ITS METALLIC FRAME--BUT RATHER ABOVE, IN THE SULLEN SHADOWS OF A DARKENED BALCONY...
HAH! QUICKSILVER MOVES MORE SWIFTLY THAN EVER! AND NOW, WE SHALL TRY THE POWERS OF THE SCARLET WITCH!
HOW CLEVER OF YOU, MASTER, TO TEST THEM IN THIS WAY!
AFTER ALL, WE MUST BE CERTAIN THAT THEY'RE STILL WORTHY TO BECOME OUR ALLIES!
WAIT, MASTER! LOOK WHAT THE ACCURSED FEMALE IS DOING..!
MY HEX POWER DOESN'T SEEM TO AFFECT THE MONSTER DIRECTLY!
AND--THERE'S NO PLACE I CAN HIDE--NOWHERE I CAN RUN!
JUST ONE HOPE-- THAT HUGE CHANDELIER OVERHEAD--!
YOU DID IT, WANDA! YOU BROUGHT THE CHANDELIER CRASHING DOWN ON IT!
MY CONGRATULATIONS TO BOTH OF YOU--YOU PROVED TO ME THAT YOUR MUTANT POWERS ARE STILL AT THEIR HEIGHT!
I SHALL THEREFORE ALLOW YOU TO SERVE ME!
KRAASSH!
16

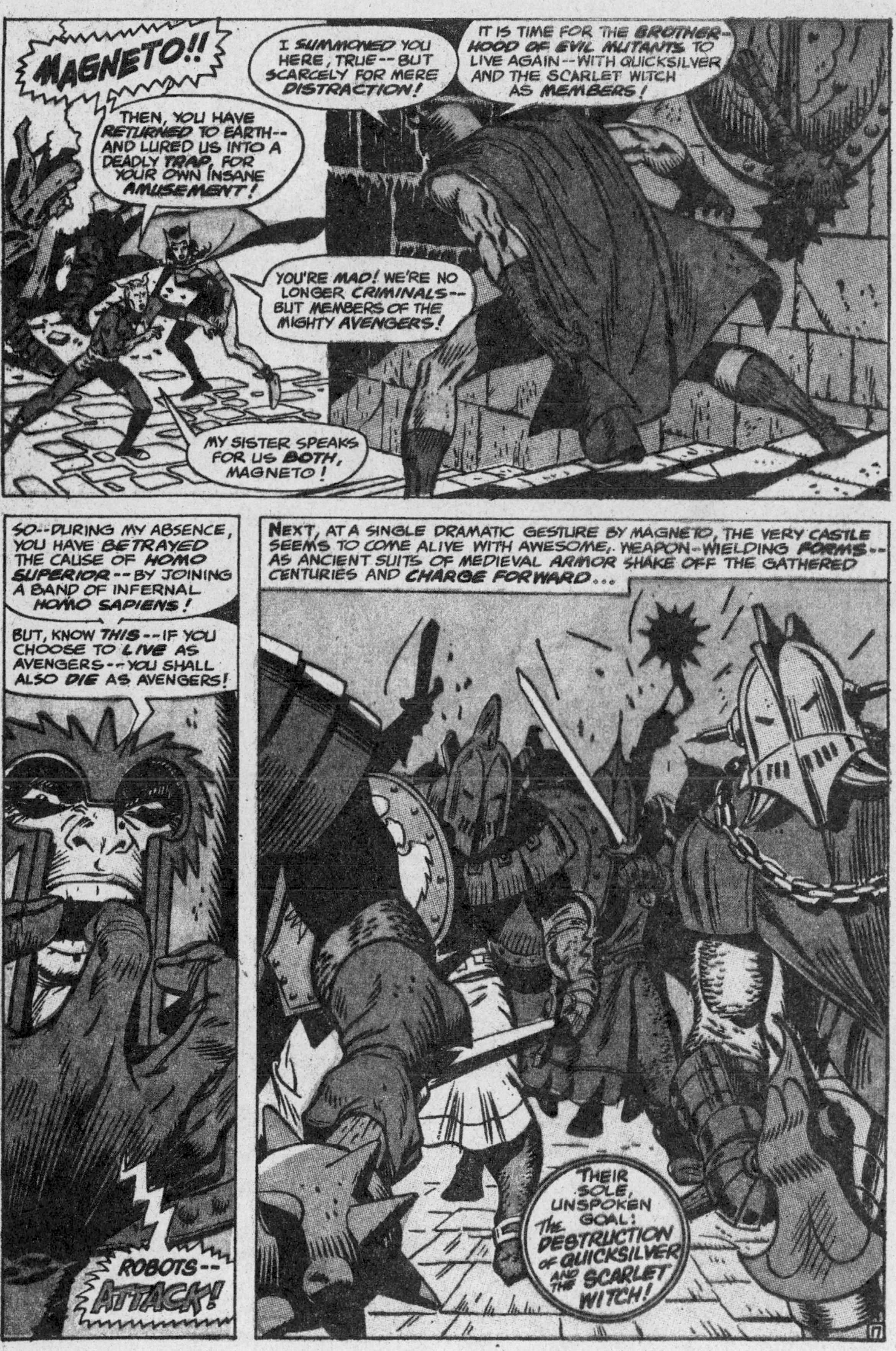

MAGNETO!!
THEN, YOU HAVE RETURNED TO EARTH-- AND LURED US INTO A DEADLY TRAP, FOR YOUR OWN INSANE AMUSEMENT!
I SUMMONED YOU HERE, TRUE--BUT SCARCELY FOR MERE DISTRACTION!
IT IS TIME FOR THE BROTHERHOOD OF EVIL MUTANTS TO LIVE AGAIN--WITH QUICKSILVER AND THE SCARLET WITCH AS MEMBERS!
YOU'RE MAD! WE'RE NO LONGER CRIMINALS-- BUT MEMBERS OF THE MIGHTY AVENGERS!
MY SISTER SPEAKS FOR US BOTH, MAGNETO!
SO--DURING MY ABSENCE, YOU HAVE BETRAYED THE CAUSE OF HOMO SUPERIOR--BY JOINING A BAND OF INFERNAL HOMO SAPIENS!
BUT, KNOW THIS--IF YOU CHOOSE TO LIVE AS AVENGERS--YOU SHALL ALSO DIE AS AVENGERS!
ROBOTS-- ATTACK!
NEXT, AT A SINGLE DRAMATIC GESTURE BY MAGNETO, THE VERY CASTLE SEEMS TO COME ALIVE WITH AWESOME, WEAPON-WIELDING FORMS-- AS ANCIENT SUITS OF MEDIEVAL ARMOR SHAKE OFF THE GATHERED CENTURIES AND CHARGE FORWARD...
THEIR SOLE, UNSPOKEN GOAL: THE DESTRUCTION OF QUICKSILVER AND THE SCARLET WITCH!
17

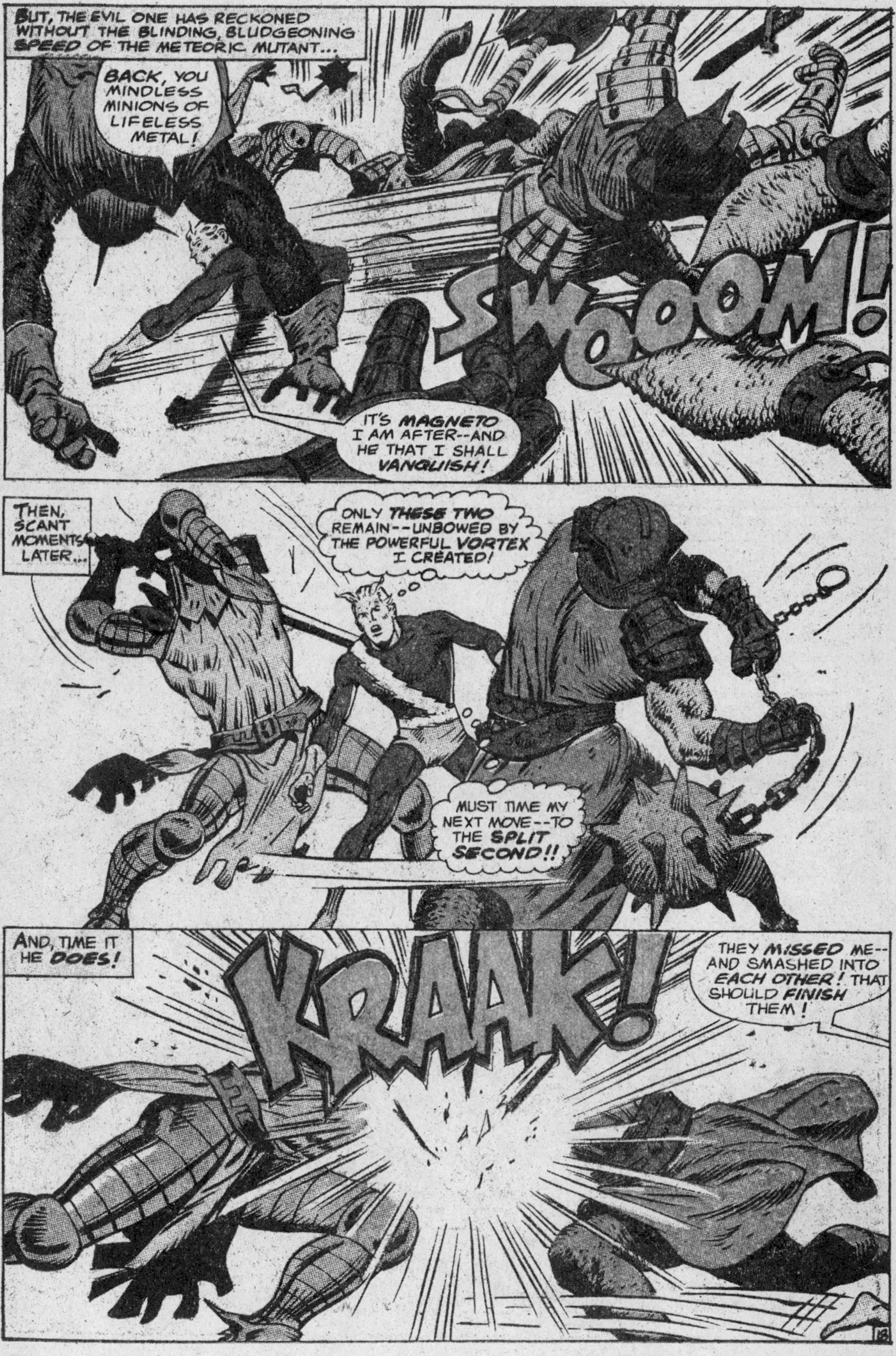

BUT, THE EVIL ONE HAS RECKONED WITHOUT THE BLINDING, BLUDGEONING SPEED OF THE METEORIC MUTANT...
BACK, YOU MINDLESS MINIONS OF LIFELESS METAL!
SWOOOM!
IT'S MAGNETO I AM AFTER--AND HE THAT I SHALL VANQUISH!
THEN, SCANT MOMENTS LATER...
ONLY THESE TWO REMAIN--UNBOWED BY THE POWERFUL VORTEX I CREATED!
MUST TIME MY NEXT MOVE--TO THE SPLIT SECOND!!
AND, TIME IT HE DOES!
KRAAK!
THEY MISSED ME--AND SMASHED INTO EACH OTHER! THAT SHOULD FINISH THEM!
18

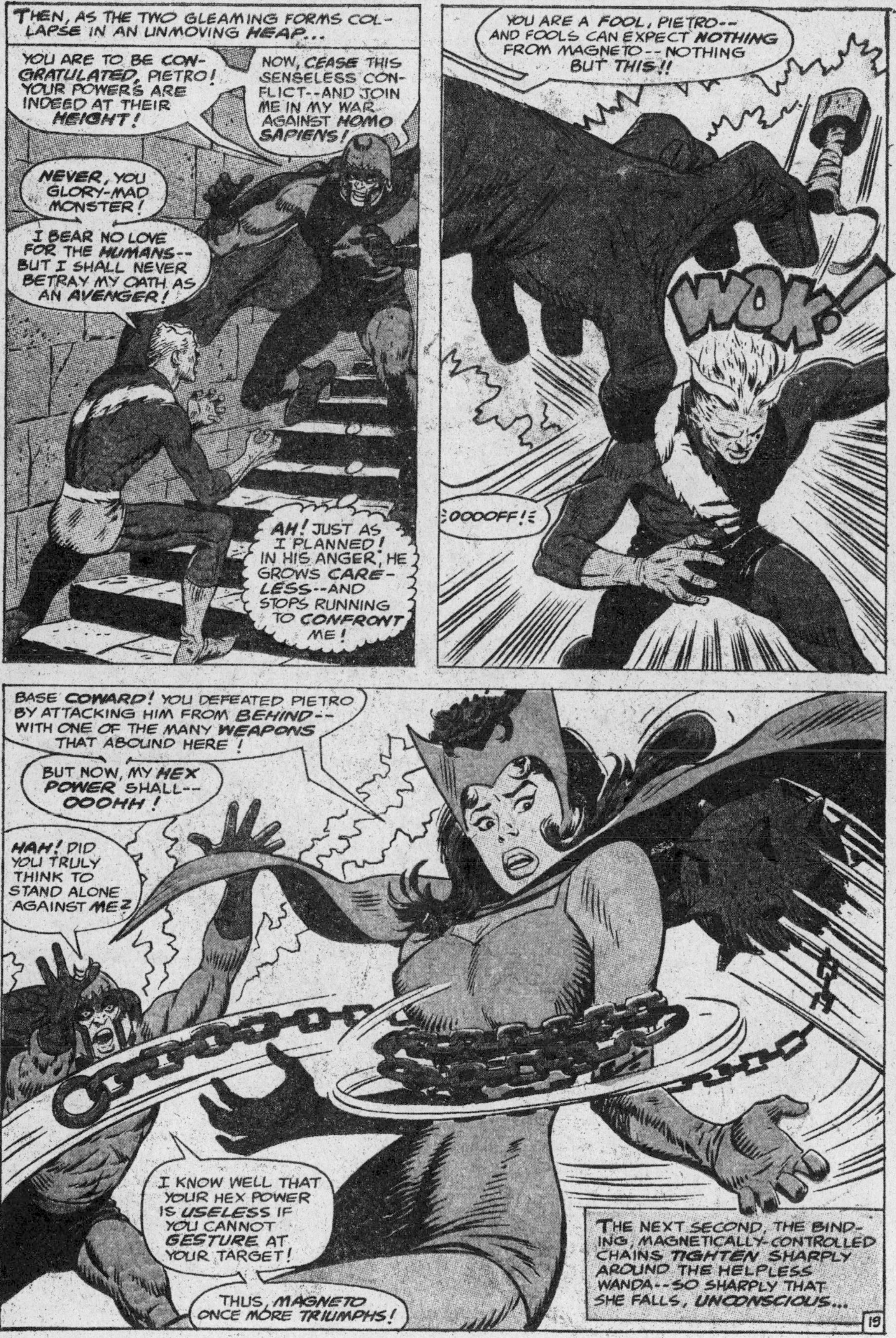

THEN, AS THE TWO GLEAMING FORMS COL-LAPSE IN AN UNMOVING HEAP...
YOU ARE TO BE CON-GRATULATED, PIETRO! YOUR POWERS ARE INDEED AT THEIR HEIGHT!
NOW, CEASE THIS SENSELESS CON-FLICT--AND JOIN ME IN MY WAR AGAINST HOMO SAPIENS!
NEVER, YOU GLORY-MAD MONSTER!
I BEAR NO LOVE FOR THE HUMANS-- BUT I SHALL NEVER BETRAY MY OATH AS AN AVENGER!
AH! JUST AS I PLANNED! IN HIS ANGER, HE GROWS CARE-LESS--AND STOPS RUNNING TO CONFRONT ME!
YOU ARE A FOOL, PIETRO-- AND FOOLS CAN EXPECT NOTHING FROM MAGNETO--NOTHING BUT THIS!!
WOK!
OOOOFF!
BASE COWARD! YOU DEFEATED PIETRO BY ATTACKING HIM FROM BEHIND-- WITH ONE OF THE MANY WEAPONS THAT ABOUND HERE!
BUT NOW, MY HEX POWER SHALL-- OOOHH!
HAH! DID YOU TRULY THINK TO STAND ALONE AGAINST ME?
I KNOW WELL THAT YOUR HEX POWER IS USELESS IF YOU CANNOT GESTURE AT YOUR TARGET!
THUS, MAGNETO ONCE MORE TRIUMPHS!
THE NEXT SECOND, THE BIND-ING, MAGNETICALLY-CONTROLLED CHAINS TIGHTEN SHARPLY AROUND THE HELPLESS WANDA--SO SHARPLY THAT SHE FALLS, UNCONSCIOUS...

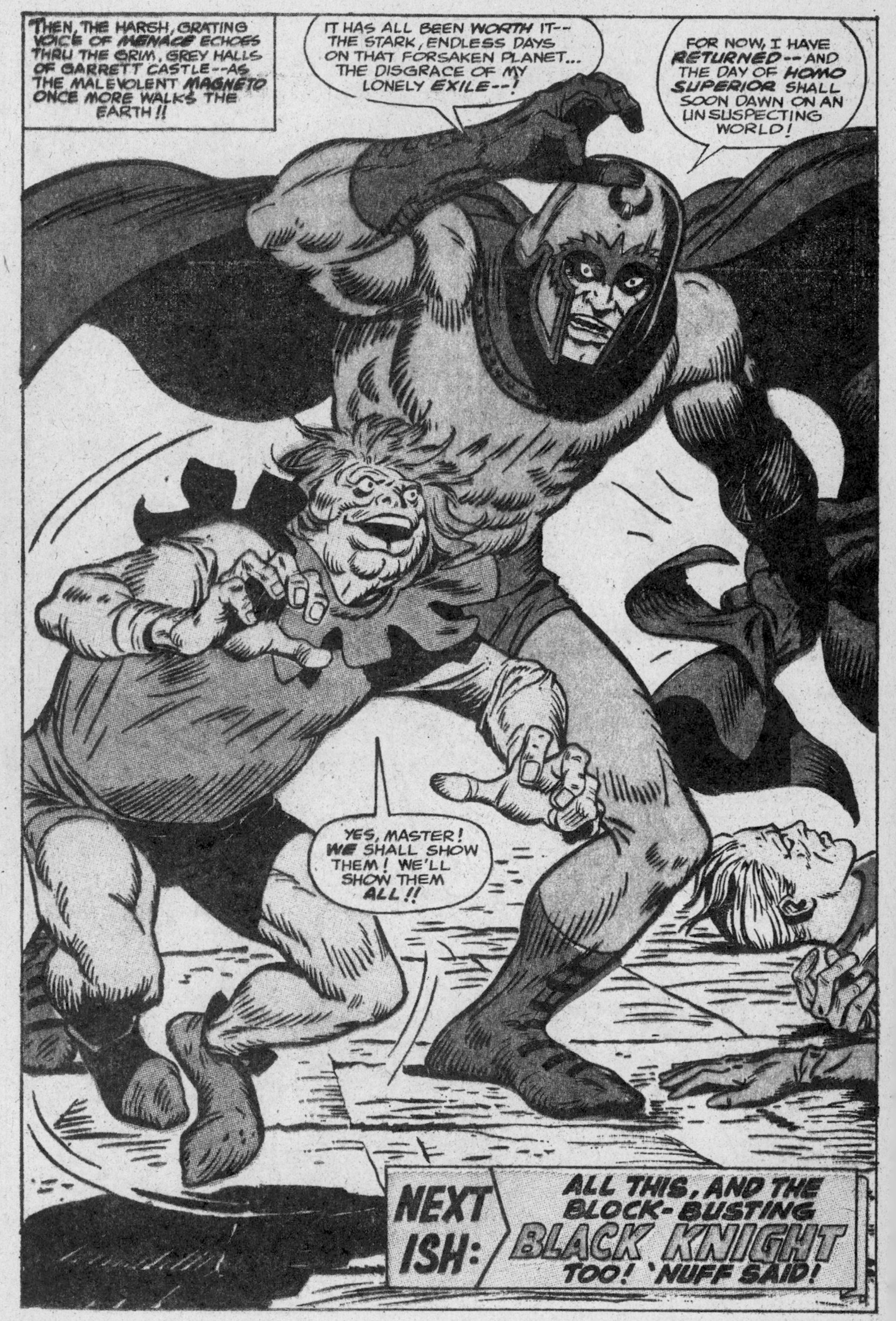
THEN, THE HARSH, GRATING VOICE OF MENACE ECHOES THRU THE GRIM, GREY HALLS OF GARRETT CASTLE--AS THE MALEVOLENT MAGNETO ONCE MORE WALKS THE EARTH!!
IT HAS ALL BEEN WORTH IT-- THE STARK, ENDLESS DAYS ON THAT FORSAKEN PLANET... THE DISGRACE OF MY LONELY EXILE--!
FOR NOW, I HAVE RETURNED-- AND THE DAY OF HOMO SUPERIOR SHALL SOON DAWN ON AN UNSUSPECTING WORLD!
YES, MASTER! WE SHALL SHOW THEM! WE'LL SHOW THEM ALL!!
NEXT ISH:
ALL THIS, AND THE BLOCK-BUSTING BLACK KNIGHT TOO! 'NUFF SAID!

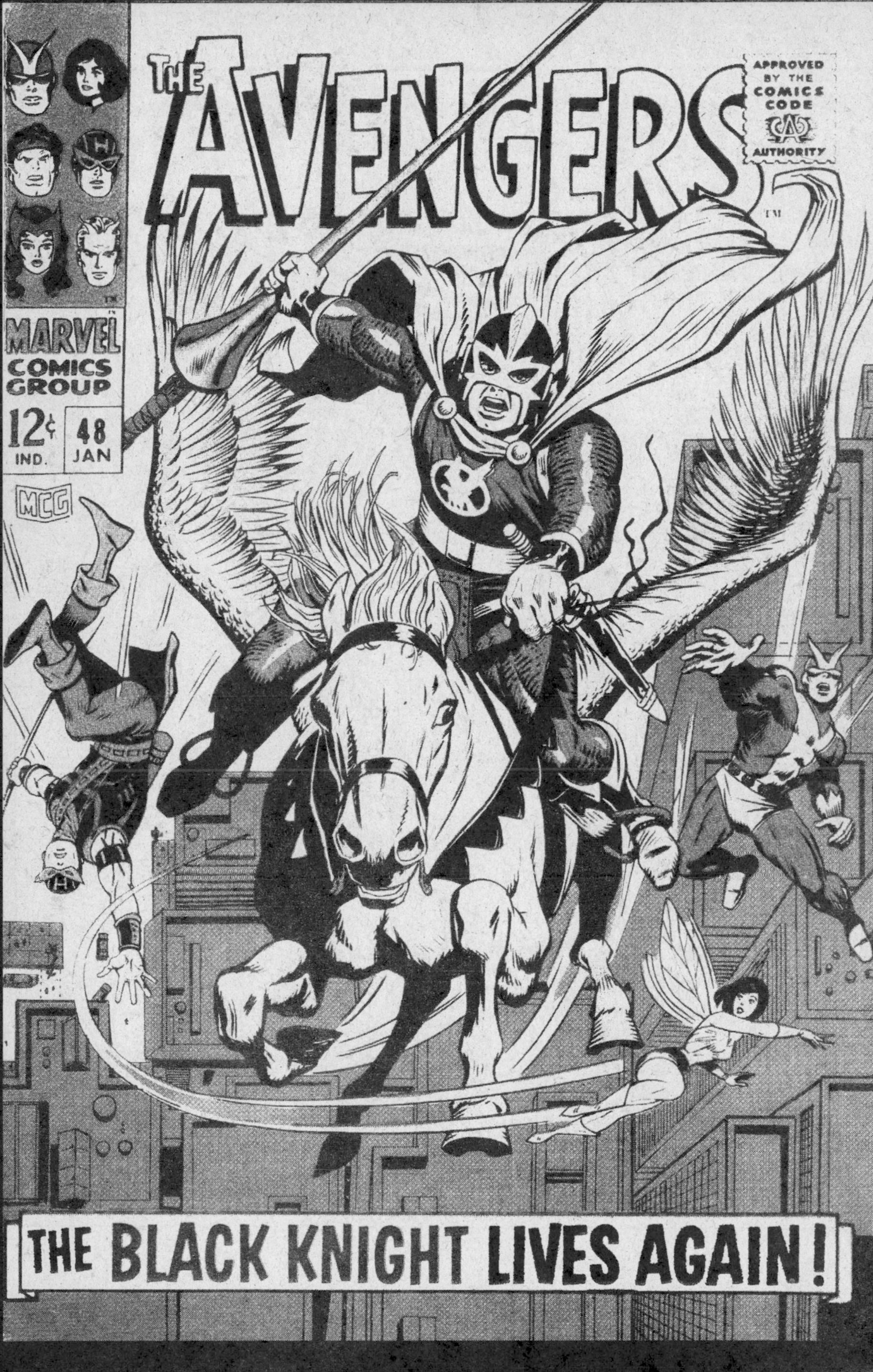
THE AVENGERS
APPROVED BY THE COMICS CODE AUTHORITY
MARVEL COMICS GROUP
12¢ IND.
48 JAN
MCG
THE BLACK KNIGHT LIVES AGAIN!

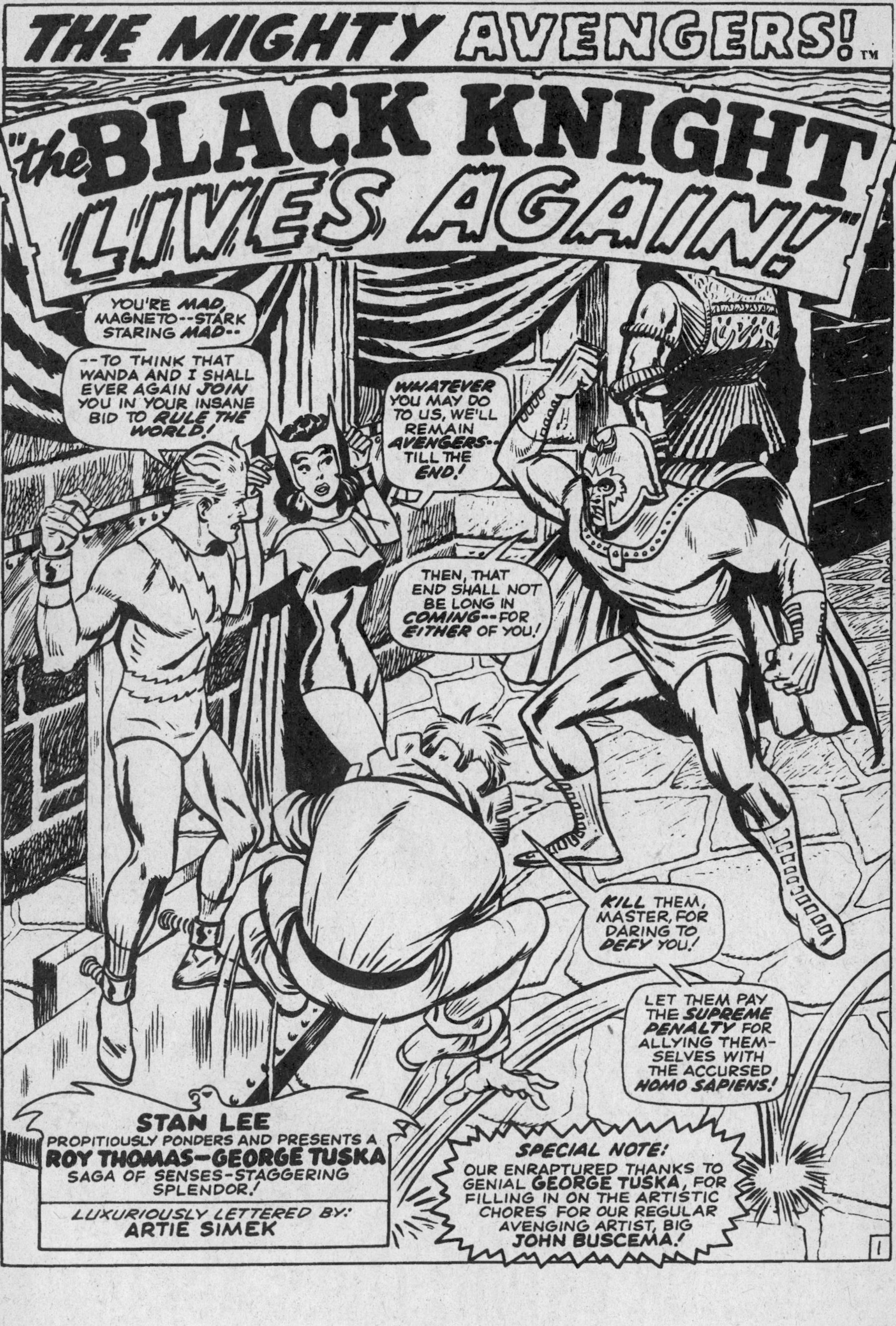
THE MIGHTY AVENGERS!™
"the BLACK KNIGHT LIVES AGAIN!"
YOU'RE MAD, MAGNETO--STARK STARING MAD--
--TO THINK THAT WANDA AND I SHALL EVER AGAIN JOIN YOU IN YOUR INSANE BID TO RULE THE WORLD!
WHATEVER YOU MAY DO TO US, WE'LL REMAIN AVENGERS-- TILL THE END!
THEN, THAT END SHALL NOT BE LONG IN COMING--FOR EITHER OF YOU!
KILL THEM, MASTER, FOR DARING TO DEFY YOU!
LET THEM PAY THE SUPREME PENALTY FOR ALLYING THEMSELVES WITH THE ACCURSED HOMO SAPIENS!
STAN LEE PROPITIOUSLY PONDERS AND PRESENTS A ROY THOMAS—GEORGE TUSKA SAGA OF SENSES-STAGGERING SPLENDOR!
LUXURIOUSLY LETTERED BY: ARTIE SIMEK
SPECIAL NOTE! OUR ENRAPTURED THANKS TO GENIAL GEORGE TUSKA, FOR FILLING IN ON THE ARTISTIC CHORES FOR OUR REGULAR AVENGING ARTIST, BIG JOHN BUSCEMA!
1

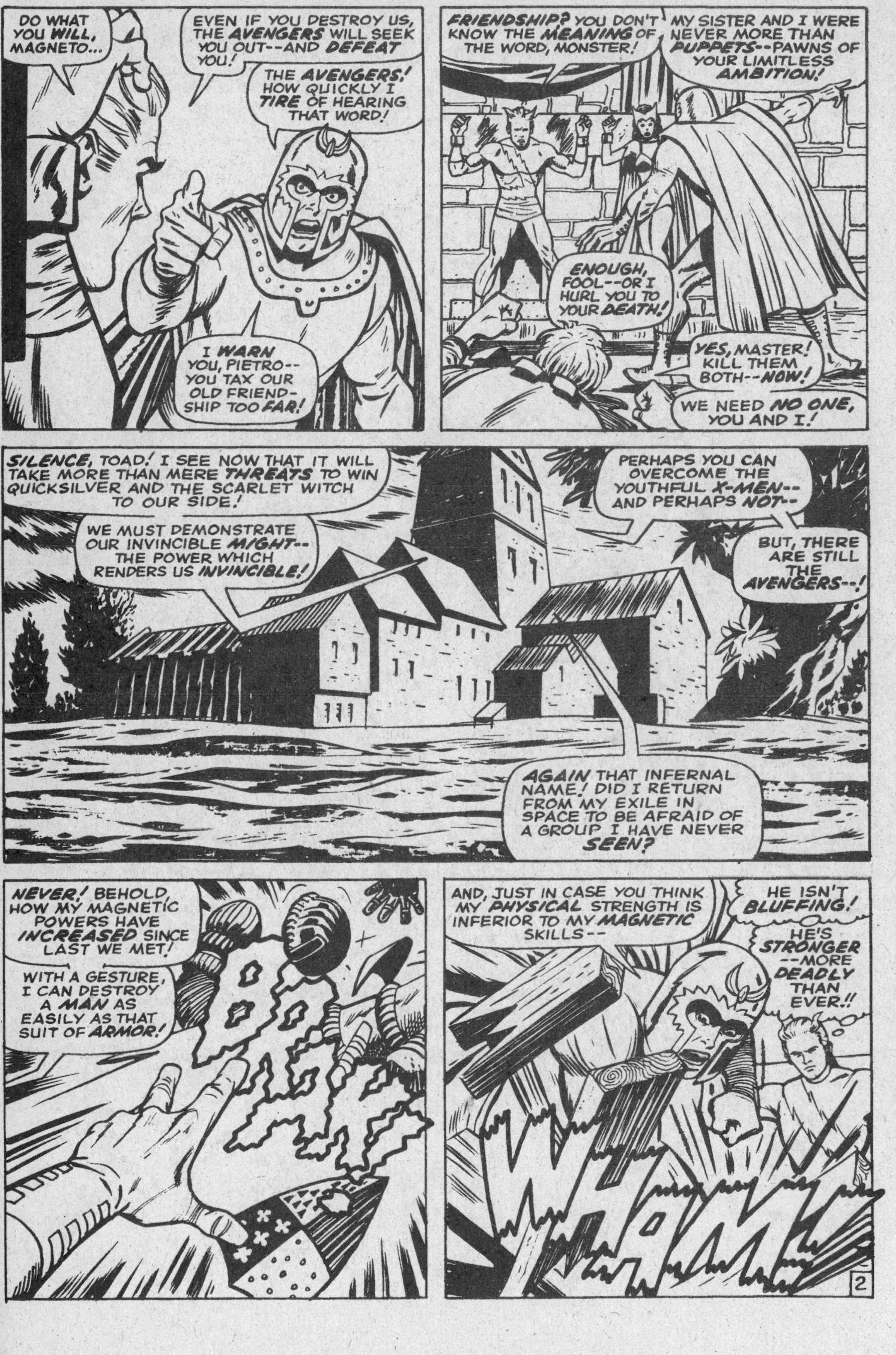
DO WHAT YOU WILL, MAGNETO...
EVEN IF YOU DESTROY US, THE AVENGERS WILL SEEK YOU OUT--AND DEFEAT YOU!
THE AVENGERS! HOW QUICKLY I TIRE OF HEARING THAT WORD!
I WARN YOU, PIETRO--YOU TAX OUR OLD FRIENDSHIP TOO FAR!
FRIENDSHIP? YOU DON'T KNOW THE MEANING OF THE WORD, MONSTER!
MY SISTER AND I WERE NEVER MORE THAN PUPPETS--PAWNS OF YOUR LIMITLESS AMBITION!
ENOUGH, FOOL--OR I HURL YOU TO YOUR DEATH!
YES, MASTER! KILL THEM BOTH--NOW!
WE NEED NO ONE, YOU AND I!
SILENCE, TOAD! I SEE NOW THAT IT WILL TAKE MORE THAN MERE THREATS TO WIN QUICKSILVER AND THE SCARLET WITCH TO OUR SIDE!
WE MUST DEMONSTRATE OUR INVINCIBLE MIGHT--THE POWER WHICH RENDERS US INVINCIBLE!
PERHAPS YOU CAN OVERCOME THE YOUTHFUL X-MEN--AND PERHAPS NOT--
BUT, THERE ARE STILL THE AVENGERS--!
AGAIN THAT INFERNAL NAME! DID I RETURN FROM MY EXILE IN SPACE TO BE AFRAID OF A GROUP I HAVE NEVER SEEN?
NEVER! BEHOLD HOW MY MAGNETIC POWERS HAVE INCREASED SINCE LAST WE MET!
WITH A GESTURE, I CAN DESTROY A MAN AS EASILY AS THAT SUIT OF ARMOR!
AND, JUST IN CASE YOU THINK MY PHYSICAL STRENGTH IS INFERIOR TO MY MAGNETIC SKILLS--
HE ISN'T BLUFFING!
HE'S STRONGER--MORE DEADLY THAN EVER!!
WHAM
2

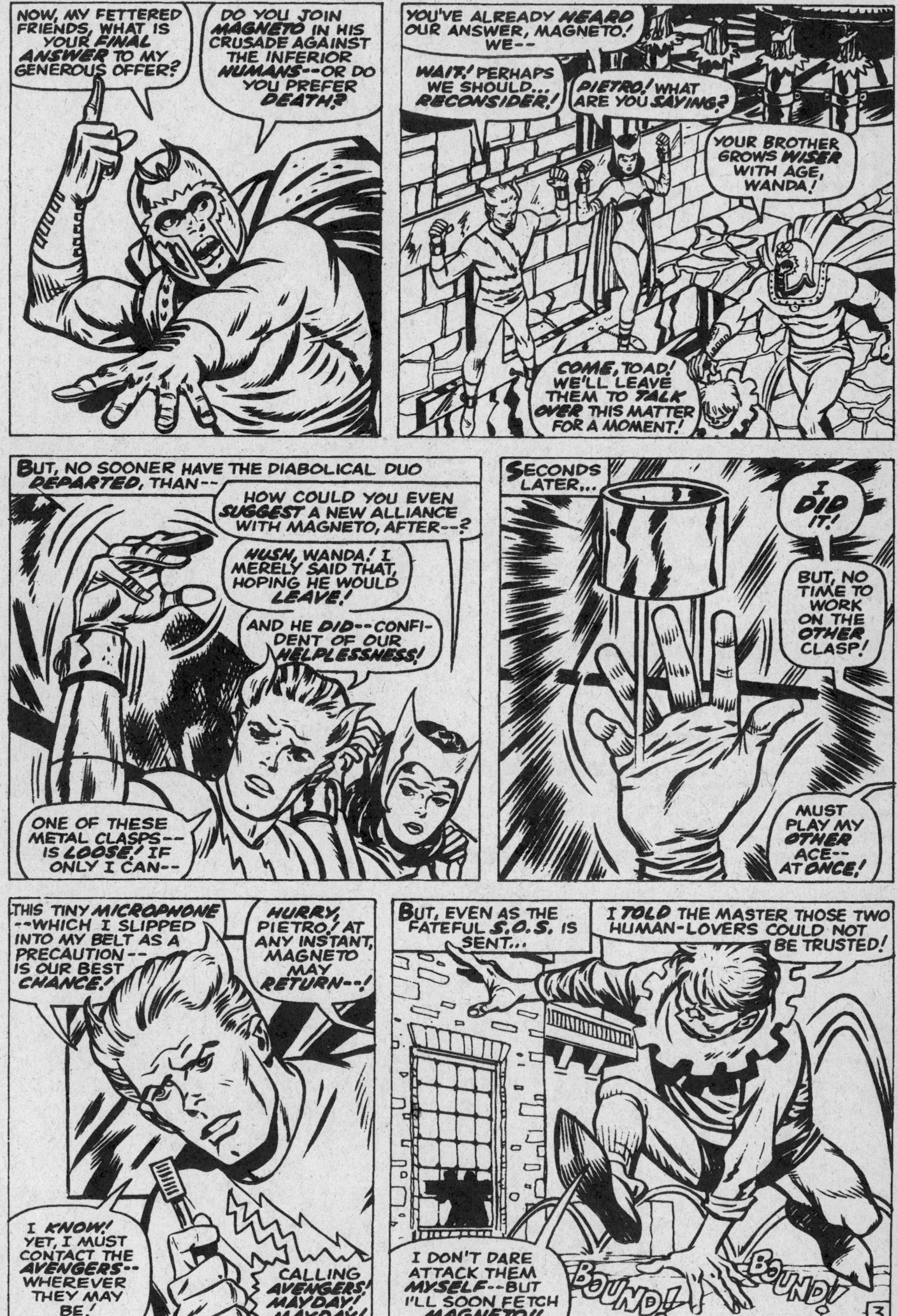
NOW, MY FETTERED FRIENDS, WHAT IS YOUR FINAL ANSWER TO MY GENEROUS OFFER?
DO YOU JOIN MAGNETO IN HIS CRUSADE AGAINST THE INFERIOR HUMANS--OR DO YOU PREFER DEATH?
YOU'VE ALREADY HEARD OUR ANSWER, MAGNETO! WE--
WAIT! PERHAPS WE SHOULD... RECONSIDER!
PIETRO! WHAT ARE YOU SAYING?
YOUR BROTHER GROWS WISER WITH AGE, WANDA!
COME, TOAD! WE'LL LEAVE THEM TO TALK OVER THIS MATTER FOR A MOMENT!
BUT, NO SOONER HAVE THE DIABOLICAL DUO DEPARTED, THAN--
HOW COULD YOU EVEN SUGGEST A NEW ALLIANCE WITH MAGNETO, AFTER--?
HUSH, WANDA! I MERELY SAID THAT, HOPING HE WOULD LEAVE!
AND HE DID--CONFIDENT OF OUR HELPLESSNESS!
ONE OF THESE METAL CLASPS--IS LOOSE! IF ONLY I CAN--
SECONDS LATER...
I DID IT!
BUT, NO TIME TO WORK ON THE OTHER CLASP!
MUST PLAY MY OTHER ACE--AT ONCE!
THIS TINY MICROPHONE--WHICH I SLIPPED INTO MY BELT AS A PRECAUTION--IS OUR BEST CHANCE!
HURRY, PIETRO! AT ANY INSTANT, MAGNETO MAY RETURN--!
I KNOW! YET, I MUST CONTACT THE AVENGERS--WHEREVER THEY MAY BE!
CALLING AVENGERS! MAYDAY! MAYDAY!
BUT, EVEN AS THE FATEFUL S.O.S. IS SENT...
I TOLD THE MASTER THOSE TWO HUMAN-LOVERS COULD NOT BE TRUSTED!
I DON'T DARE ATTACK THEM MYSELF--BUT I'LL SOON FETCH MAGNETO!!
BOUND!
BOUND!
3

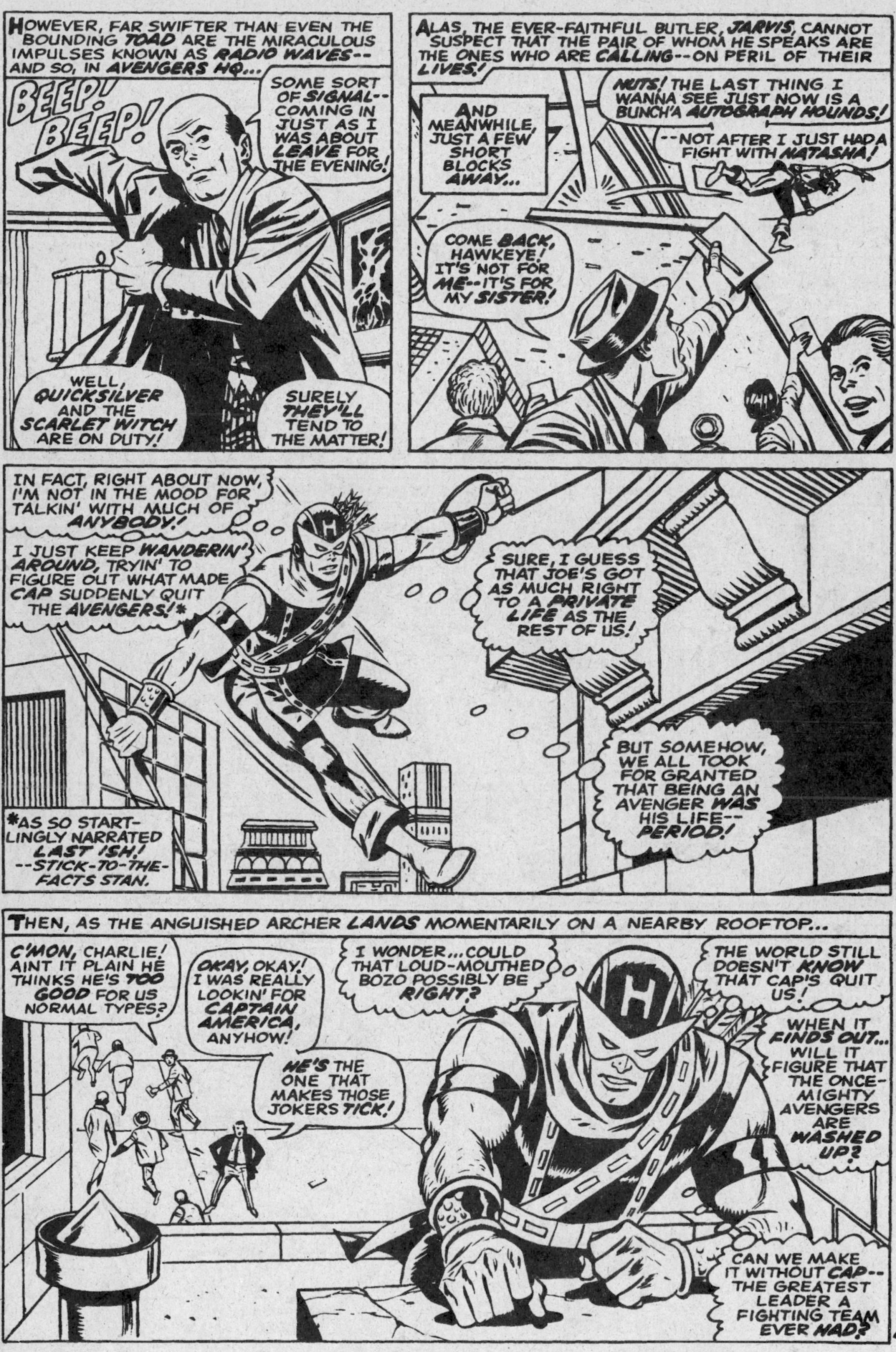
HOWEVER, FAR SWIFTER THAN EVEN THE BOUNDING TOAD ARE THE MIRACULOUS IMPULSES KNOWN AS RADIO WAVES-- AND SO, IN AVENGERS HQ...
BEEP! BEEP!
SOME SORT OF SIGNAL-- COMING IN JUST AS I WAS ABOUT LEAVE FOR THE EVENING!
WELL, QUICKSILVER AND THE SCARLET WITCH ARE ON DUTY!
SURELY THEY'LL TEND TO THE MATTER!
ALAS, THE EVER-FAITHFUL BUTLER, JARVIS, CANNOT SUSPECT THAT THE PAIR OF WHOM HE SPEAKS ARE THE ONES WHO ARE CALLING--ON PERIL OF THEIR LIVES!
AND MEANWHILE, JUST A FEW SHORT BLOCKS AWAY...
NUTS! THE LAST THING I WANNA SEE JUST NOW IS A BUNCH'A AUTOGRAPH HOUNDS!
--NOT AFTER I JUST HAD A FIGHT WITH NATASHA!
COME BACK, HAWKEYE! IT'S NOT FOR ME--IT'S FOR MY SISTER!
IN FACT, RIGHT ABOUT NOW, I'M NOT IN THE MOOD FOR TALKIN' WITH MUCH OF ANYBODY!
I JUST KEEP WANDERIN' AROUND, TRYIN' TO FIGURE OUT WHAT MADE CAP SUDDENLY QUIT THE AVENGERS!*
SURE, I GUESS THAT JOE'S GOT AS MUCH RIGHT TO A PRIVATE LIFE AS THE REST OF US!
BUT SOMEHOW, WE ALL TOOK FOR GRANTED THAT BEING AN AVENGER WAS HIS LIFE-- PERIOD!
*AS SO STARTLINGLY NARRATED LAST ISH! --STICK-TO-THE-FACTS STAN.
THEN, AS THE ANGUISHED ARCHER LANDS MOMENTARILY ON A NEARBY ROOFTOP...
C'MON, CHARLIE! AINT IT PLAIN HE THINKS HE'S TOO GOOD FOR US NORMAL TYPES?
OKAY, OKAY! I WAS REALLY LOOKIN' FOR CAPTAIN AMERICA, ANYHOW!
HE'S THE ONE THAT MAKES THOSE JOKERS TICK!
I WONDER... COULD THAT LOUD-MOUTHED BOZO POSSIBLY BE RIGHT?
THE WORLD STILL DOESN'T KNOW THAT CAP'S QUIT US!
WHEN IT FINDS OUT... WILL IT FIGURE THAT THE ONCE-MIGHTY AVENGERS ARE WASHED UP?
CAN WE MAKE IT WITHOUT CAP-- THE GREATEST LEADER A FIGHTING TEAM EVER HAD?
4

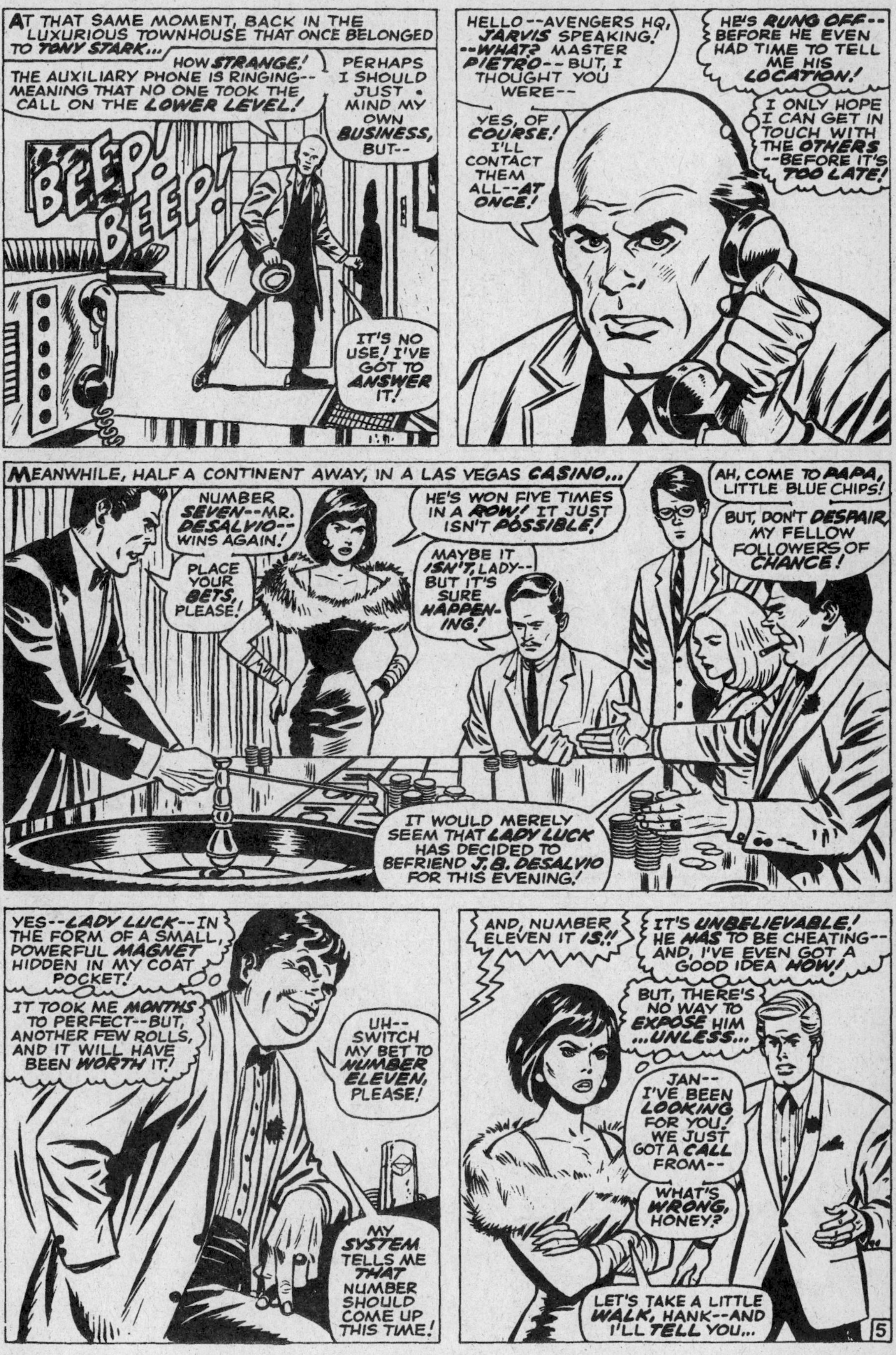
AT THAT SAME MOMENT, BACK IN THE LUXURIOUS TOWNHOUSE THAT ONCE BELONGED TO TONY STARK...
HOW STRANGE! THE AUXILIARY PHONE IS RINGING-- MEANING THAT NO ONE TOOK THE CALL ON THE LOWER LEVEL!
PERHAPS I SHOULD JUST MIND MY OWN BUSINESS, BUT--
BEEP! BEEP!
IT'S NO USE! I'VE GOT TO ANSWER IT!
HELLO--AVENGERS HQ, JARVIS SPEAKING! --WHAT? MASTER PIETRO--BUT, I THOUGHT YOU WERE--
YES, OF COURSE! I'LL CONTACT THEM ALL--AT ONCE!
HE'S RUNG OFF-- BEFORE HE EVEN HAD TIME TO TELL ME HIS LOCATION!
I ONLY HOPE I CAN GET IN TOUCH WITH THE OTHERS --BEFORE IT'S TOO LATE!
MEANWHILE, HALF A CONTINENT AWAY, IN A LAS VEGAS CASINO...
NUMBER SEVEN--MR. DESALVIO--WINS AGAIN!
PLACE YOUR BETS, PLEASE!
HE'S WON FIVE TIMES IN A ROW! IT JUST ISN'T POSSIBLE!
MAYBE IT ISN'T, LADY-- BUT IT'S SURE HAPPENING!
AH, COME TO PAPA, LITTLE BLUE CHIPS!
BUT, DON'T DESPAIR, MY FELLOW FOLLOWERS OF CHANCE!
IT WOULD MERELY SEEM THAT LADY LUCK HAS DECIDED TO BEFRIEND J.B. DESALVIO FOR THIS EVENING!
YES--LADY LUCK--IN THE FORM OF A SMALL, POWERFUL MAGNET HIDDEN IN MY COAT POCKET!
IT TOOK ME MONTHS TO PERFECT--BUT, ANOTHER FEW ROLLS, AND IT WILL HAVE BEEN WORTH IT!
UH-- SWITCH MY BET TO NUMBER ELEVEN, PLEASE!
MY SYSTEM TELLS ME THAT NUMBER SHOULD COME UP THIS TIME!
AND, NUMBER ELEVEN IT IS!!
IT'S UNBELIEVABLE! HE HAS TO BE CHEATING-- AND, I'VE EVEN GOT A GOOD IDEA HOW!
BUT, THERE'S NO WAY TO EXPOSE HIM ...UNLESS...
JAN-- I'VE BEEN LOOKING FOR YOU! WE JUST GOT A CALL FROM--
WHAT'S WRONG, HONEY?
LET'S TAKE A LITTLE WALK, HANK--AND I'LL TELL YOU...
5

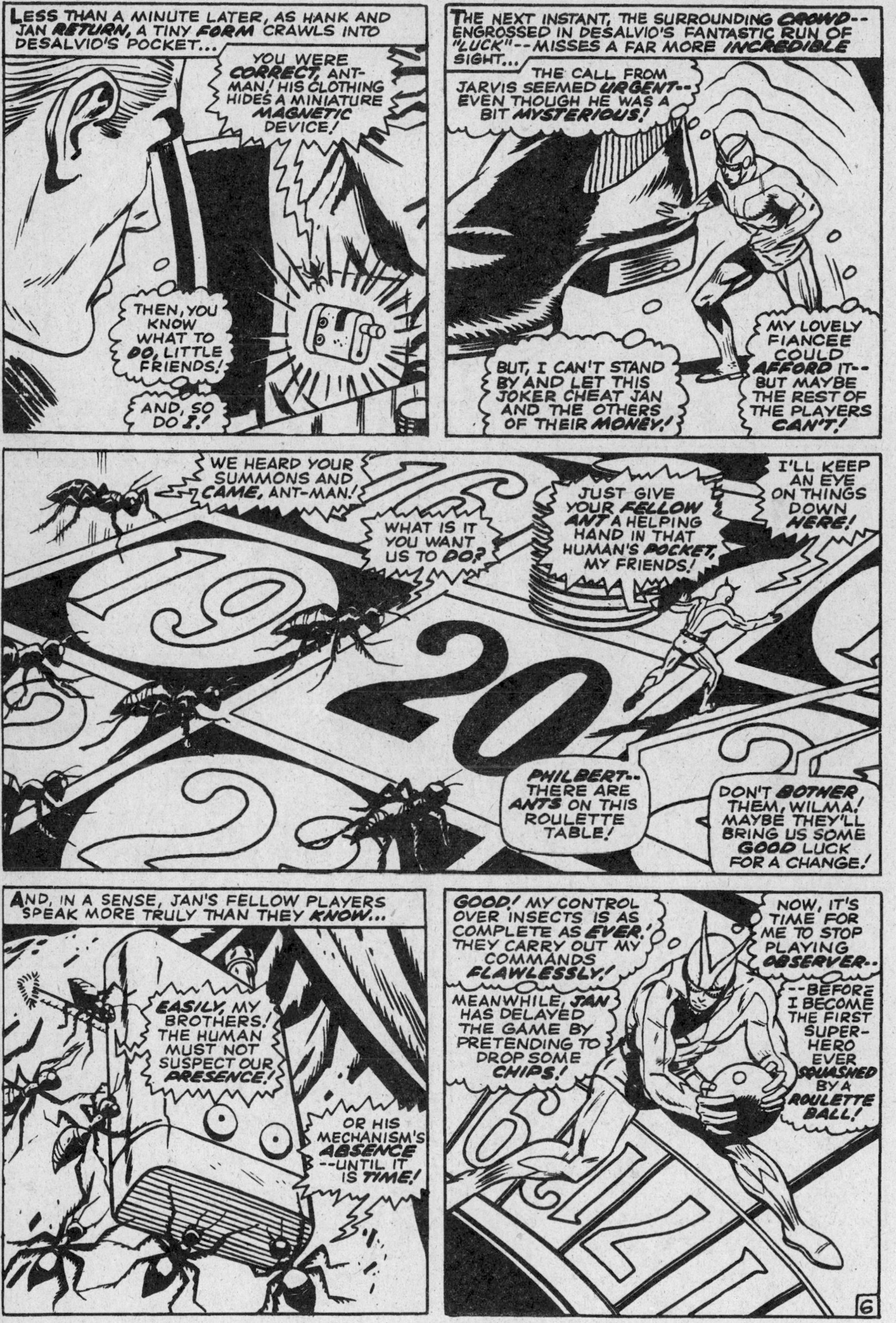
LESS THAN A MINUTE LATER, AS HANK AND JAN RETURN, A TINY FORM CRAWLS INTO DESALVIO'S POCKET...
YOU WERE CORRECT, ANT-MAN! HIS CLOTHING HIDES A MINIATURE MAGNETIC DEVICE!
THEN, YOU KNOW WHAT TO DO, LITTLE FRIENDS!
AND, SO DO I!
THE NEXT INSTANT, THE SURROUNDING CROWD--ENGROSSED IN DESALVIO'S FANTASTIC RUN OF "LUCK"--MISSES A FAR MORE INCREDIBLE SIGHT...
THE CALL FROM JARVIS SEEMED URGENT--EVEN THOUGH HE WAS A BIT MYSTERIOUS!
BUT, I CAN'T STAND BY AND LET THIS JOKER CHEAT JAN AND THE OTHERS OF THEIR MONEY!
MY LOVELY FIANCEE COULD AFFORD IT--BUT MAYBE THE REST OF THE PLAYERS CAN'T!
WE HEARD YOUR SUMMONS AND CAME, ANT-MAN!
WHAT IS IT YOU WANT US TO DO?
JUST GIVE YOUR FELLOW ANT A HELPING HAND IN THAT HUMAN'S POCKET, MY FRIENDS!
I'LL KEEP AN EYE ON THINGS DOWN HERE!
PHILBERT--THERE ARE ANTS ON THIS ROULETTE TABLE!
DON'T BOTHER THEM, WILMA! MAYBE THEY'LL BRING US SOME GOOD LUCK FOR A CHANGE!
AND, IN A SENSE, JAN'S FELLOW PLAYERS SPEAK MORE TRULY THAN THEY KNOW...
EASILY, MY BROTHERS! THE HUMAN MUST NOT SUSPECT OUR PRESENCE!
OR HIS MECHANISM'S ABSENCE--UNTIL IT IS TIME!
GOOD! MY CONTROL OVER INSECTS IS AS COMPLETE AS EVER! THEY CARRY OUT MY COMMANDS FLAWLESSLY!
MEANWHILE, JAN HAS DELAYED THE GAME BY PRETENDING TO DROP SOME CHIPS!
NOW, IT'S TIME FOR ME TO STOP PLAYING OBSERVER--
--BEFORE I BECOME THE FIRST SUPER-HERO EVER SQUASHED BY A ROULETTE BALL!
6

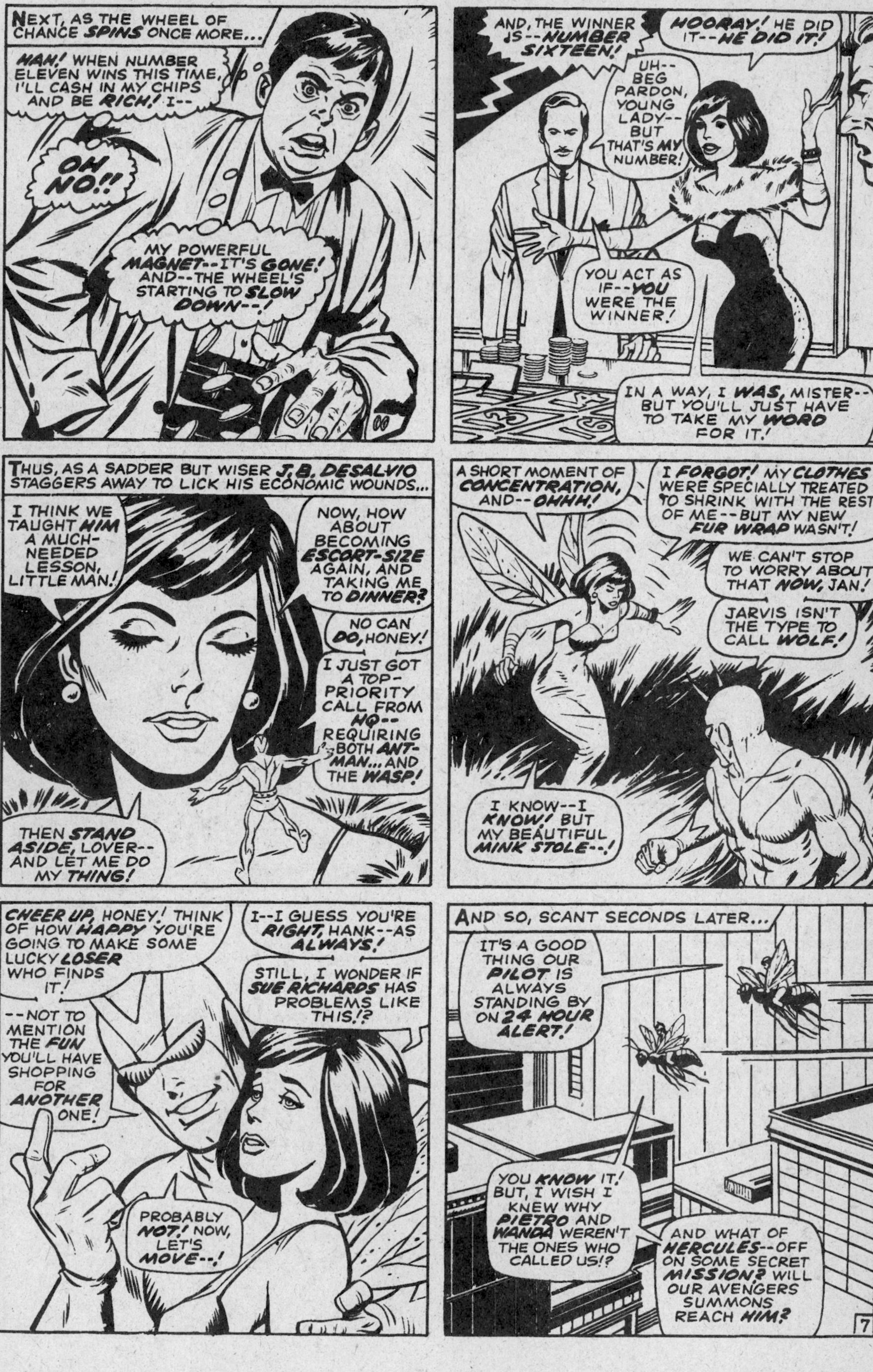
NEXT, AS THE WHEEL OF CHANCE SPINS ONCE MORE...
MAN! WHEN NUMBER ELEVEN WINS THIS TIME, I'LL CASH IN MY CHIPS AND BE RICH! I--
OH NO!!
MY POWERFUL MAGNET--IT'S GONE! AND--THE WHEEL'S STARTING TO SLOW DOWN--!
AND, THE WINNER IS--NUMBER SIXTEEN!
HOORAY! HE DID IT--HE DID IT!
UH--BEG PARDON, YOUNG LADY--BUT THAT'S MY NUMBER!
YOU ACT AS IF--YOU WERE THE WINNER!
IN A WAY, I WAS, MISTER--BUT YOU'LL JUST HAVE TO TAKE MY WORD FOR IT!
THUS, AS A SADDER BUT WISER J.B. DESALVIO STAGGERS AWAY TO LICK HIS ECONOMIC WOUNDS...
I THINK WE TAUGHT HIM A MUCH-NEEDED LESSON, LITTLE MAN!
NOW, HOW ABOUT BECOMING ESCORT-SIZE AGAIN, AND TAKING ME TO DINNER?
NO CAN DO, HONEY!
I JUST GOT A TOP-PRIORITY CALL FROM HQ--REQUIRING BOTH ANT-MAN... AND THE WASP!
THEN STAND ASIDE, LOVER--AND LET ME DO MY THING!
A SHORT MOMENT OF CONCENTRATION, AND--OHHH!
I FORGOT! MY CLOTHES WERE SPECIALLY TREATED TO SHRINK WITH THE REST OF ME--BUT MY NEW FUR WRAP WASN'T!
WE CAN'T STOP TO WORRY ABOUT THAT NOW, JAN!
JARVIS ISN'T THE TYPE TO CALL WOLF!
I KNOW--I KNOW! BUT MY BEAUTIFUL MINK STOLE--!
CHEER UP, HONEY! THINK OF HOW HAPPY YOU'RE GOING TO MAKE SOME LUCKY LOSER WHO FINDS IT!
--NOT TO MENTION THE FUN YOU'LL HAVE SHOPPING FOR ANOTHER ONE!
I--I GUESS YOU'RE RIGHT, HANK--AS ALWAYS!
STILL, I WONDER IF SUE RICHARDS HAS PROBLEMS LIKE THIS!?
PROBABLY NOT! NOW, LET'S MOVE--!
AND SO, SCANT SECONDS LATER...
IT'S A GOOD THING OUR PILOT IS ALWAYS STANDING BY ON 24 HOUR ALERT!
YOU KNOW IT! BUT, I WISH I KNEW WHY PIETRO AND WANDA WEREN'T THE ONES WHO CALLED US!?
AND WHAT OF HERCULES--OFF ON SOME SECRET MISSION? WILL OUR AVENGERS SUMMONS REACH HIM?
7

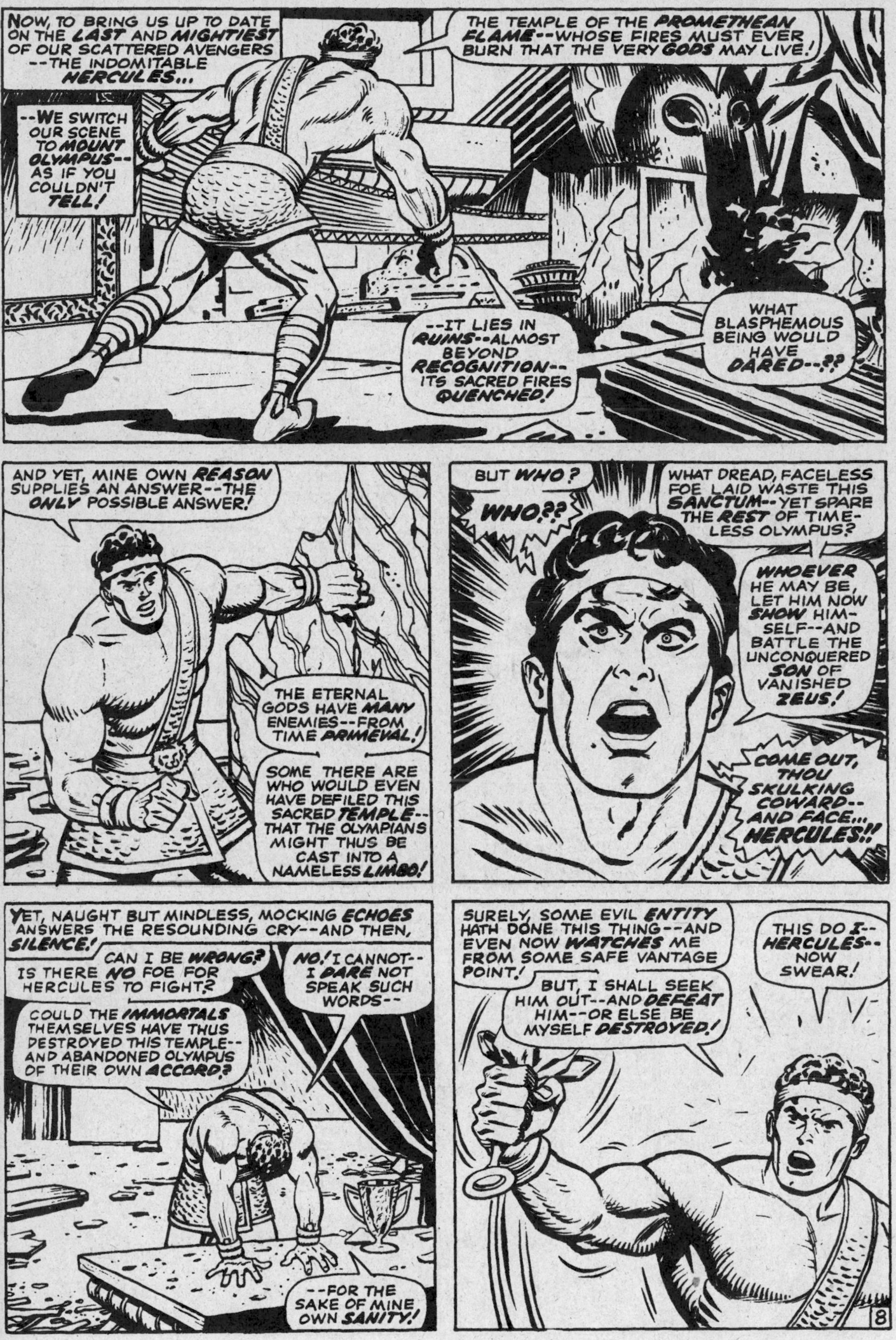

NOW, TO BRING US UP TO DATE ON THE LAST AND MIGHTIEST OF OUR SCATTERED AVENGERS --THE INDOMITABLE HERCULES...
--WE SWITCH OUR SCENE TO MOUNT OLYMPUS-- AS IF YOU COULDN'T TELL!
THE TEMPLE OF THE PROMETHEAN FLAME--WHOSE FIRES MUST EVER BURN THAT THE VERY GODS MAY LIVE!
--IT LIES IN RUINS--ALMOST BEYOND RECOGNITION--ITS SACRED FIRES QUENCHED!
WHAT BLASPHEMOUS BEING WOULD HAVE DARED--??
AND YET, MINE OWN REASON SUPPLIES AN ANSWER--THE ONLY POSSIBLE ANSWER!
THE ETERNAL GODS HAVE MANY ENEMIES--FROM TIME PRIMEVAL!
SOME THERE ARE WHO WOULD EVEN HAVE DEFILED THIS SACRED TEMPLE--THAT THE OLYMPIANS MIGHT THUS BE CAST INTO A NAMELESS LIMBO!
BUT WHO?
WHO??
WHAT DREAD, FACELESS FOE LAID WASTE THIS SANCTUM--YET SPARE THE REST OF TIME-LESS OLYMPUS?
WHOEVER HE MAY BE, LET HIM NOW SHOW HIM-SELF--AND BATTLE THE UNCONQUERED SON OF VANISHED ZEUS!
COME OUT, THOU SKULKING COWARD--AND FACE... HERCULES!!
YET, NAUGHT BUT MINDLESS, MOCKING ECHOES ANSWERS THE RESOUNDING CRY--AND THEN, SILENCE!
CAN I BE WRONG? IS THERE NO FOE FOR HERCULES TO FIGHT?
COULD THE IMMORTALS THEMSELVES HAVE THUS DESTROYED THIS TEMPLE--AND ABANDONED OLYMPUS OF THEIR OWN ACCORD?
NO! I CANNOT--I DARE NOT SPEAK SUCH WORDS--
--FOR THE SAKE OF MINE OWN SANITY!
SURELY, SOME EVIL ENTITY HATH DONE THIS THING--AND EVEN NOW WATCHES ME FROM SOME SAFE VANTAGE POINT!
BUT, I SHALL SEEK HIM OUT--AND DEFEAT HIM--OR ELSE BE MYSELF DESTROYED!
THIS DO I--HERCULES--NOW SWEAR!
8

BUT NOW, AS THE *PRINCE OF POWER* STALKS THE STREETS OF ETERNAL OLYMPUS, WE MUST RETURN TO *EARTH*, WHERE...

JARVIS SAYS HE GOT A SHORT MAYDAY CALL FROM *PIETRO AND WANDA*--WHICH WAS *RECORDED* AUTOMATICALLY ON TAPE!

SOMEONE MUST HAVE LURED THEM OFF *MONITOR DUTY* --AND *CAPTURED* THEM!

I WONDER...WHICH OF THE AVENGERS' MANY PAST FOES COULD IT HAVE *BEEN*?

MAYBE WE'LL SOON *KNOW*, HONEY!

ROLL THAT *TAPE*, HAWKEYE!

I DON'T SEEM TO RECALL CAP LEAVIN' *YOU* IN CHARGE WHEN HE QUIT US, MAN-MOUNTAIN!

LOOK, BOW-SLINGER--THIS IS HARDLY THE *TIME* FOR--

K-K!

OKAY, OKAY, I'M TURNIN' IT *ON* ALREADY!

DON'T GET YOUR *ANTENNAE* IN AN UPROAR!

THE NEXT SECOND, ANY FLARING ANIMOSITIES ARE SWIFTLY *FORGOTTEN*, AS...

CALLING AVENGERS--MAYDAY! MAYDAY! WANDA AND I HAVE BEEN CAPTURED BY *MAGNETO!* CONTACT *AVENGERS* WITHOUT DELAY--!

MAGNETO? BUT--HE'S THE GREATEST ENEMY OF THE *X-MEN!*

THEIR *MONOPOLY* ON HIM IS *OVER*, HAND-SOME!

WHEN HE CAPTURED *WANDA AND PIETRO*, HE TOOK ON THE *AVENGERS* AS WELL--AND YOU *KNOW* IT!

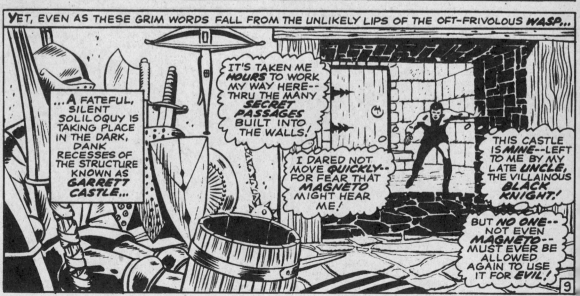

YET, EVEN AS THESE GRIM WORDS FALL FROM THE UNLIKELY LIPS OF THE OFT-FRIVOLOUS *WASP*...

...A FATEFUL, SILENT SOLILOQUY IS TAKING PLACE IN THE DARK, DANK RECESSES OF THE STRUCTURE KNOWN AS *GARRETT CASTLE*...

IT'S TAKEN ME *HOURS* TO WORK MY WAY HERE-- THRU THE MANY *SECRET PASSAGES* BUILT INTO THE WALLS!

I DARED NOT MOVE *QUICKLY*-- FOR FEAR THAT *MAGNETO* MIGHT HEAR ME!

THIS CASTLE IS *MINE*--LEFT TO ME BY MY *LATE UNCLE*, THE VILLAINOUS *BLACK KNIGHT!*

BUT *NO ONE*-- NOT EVEN *MAGNETO*-- MUST EVER BE ALLOWED AGAIN TO USE IT FOR *EVIL!*

9

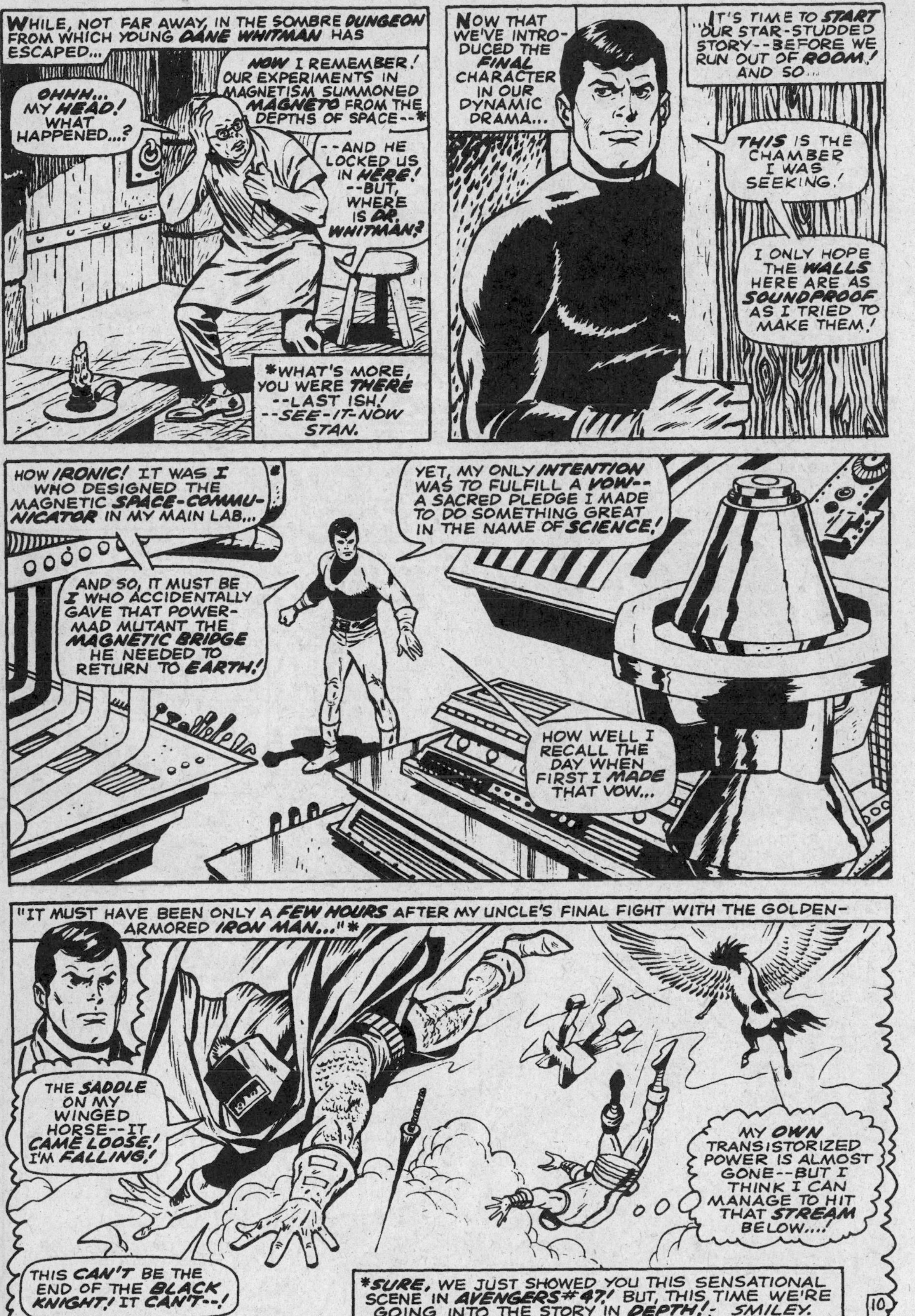
WHILE, NOT FAR AWAY, IN THE SOMBRE DUNGEON FROM WHICH YOUNG DANE WHITMAN HAS ESCAPED...
OHHH... MY HEAD! WHAT HAPPENED...?
NOW I REMEMBER! OUR EXPERIMENTS IN MAGNETISM SUMMONED MAGNETO FROM THE DEPTHS OF SPACE--*
--AND HE LOCKED US IN HERE! --BUT, WHERE IS DR. WHITMAN?
*WHAT'S MORE, YOU WERE THERE --LAST ISH! --SEE-IT-NOW STAN.
NOW THAT WE'VE INTRODUCED THE FINAL CHARACTER IN OUR DYNAMIC DRAMA...
...IT'S TIME TO START OUR STAR-STUDDED STORY--BEFORE WE RUN OUT OF ROOM! AND SO...
THIS IS THE CHAMBER I WAS SEEKING!
I ONLY HOPE THE WALLS HERE ARE AS SOUNDPROOF AS I TRIED TO MAKE THEM!
HOW IRONIC! IT WAS I WHO DESIGNED THE MAGNETIC SPACE-COMMUNICATOR IN MY MAIN LAB...
AND SO, IT MUST BE I WHO ACCIDENTALLY GAVE THAT POWER-MAD MUTANT THE MAGNETIC BRIDGE HE NEEDED TO RETURN TO EARTH!
YET, MY ONLY INTENTION WAS TO FULFILL A VOW--A SACRED PLEDGE I MADE TO DO SOMETHING GREAT IN THE NAME OF SCIENCE!
HOW WELL I RECALL THE DAY WHEN FIRST I MADE THAT VOW...
"IT MUST HAVE BEEN ONLY A FEW HOURS AFTER MY UNCLE'S FINAL FIGHT WITH THE GOLDEN-ARMORED IRON MAN..."*
THE SADDLE ON MY WINGED HORSE--IT CAME LOOSE! I'M FALLING!
MY OWN TRANSISTORIZED POWER IS ALMOST GONE--BUT I THINK I CAN MANAGE TO HIT THAT STREAM BELOW...!
THIS CAN'T BE THE END OF THE BLACK KNIGHT! IT CAN'T--!
*SURE, WE JUST SHOWED YOU THIS SENSATIONAL SCENE IN AVENGERS #47! BUT, THIS TIME WE'RE GOING INTO THE STORY IN DEPTH! - SMILEY.
10

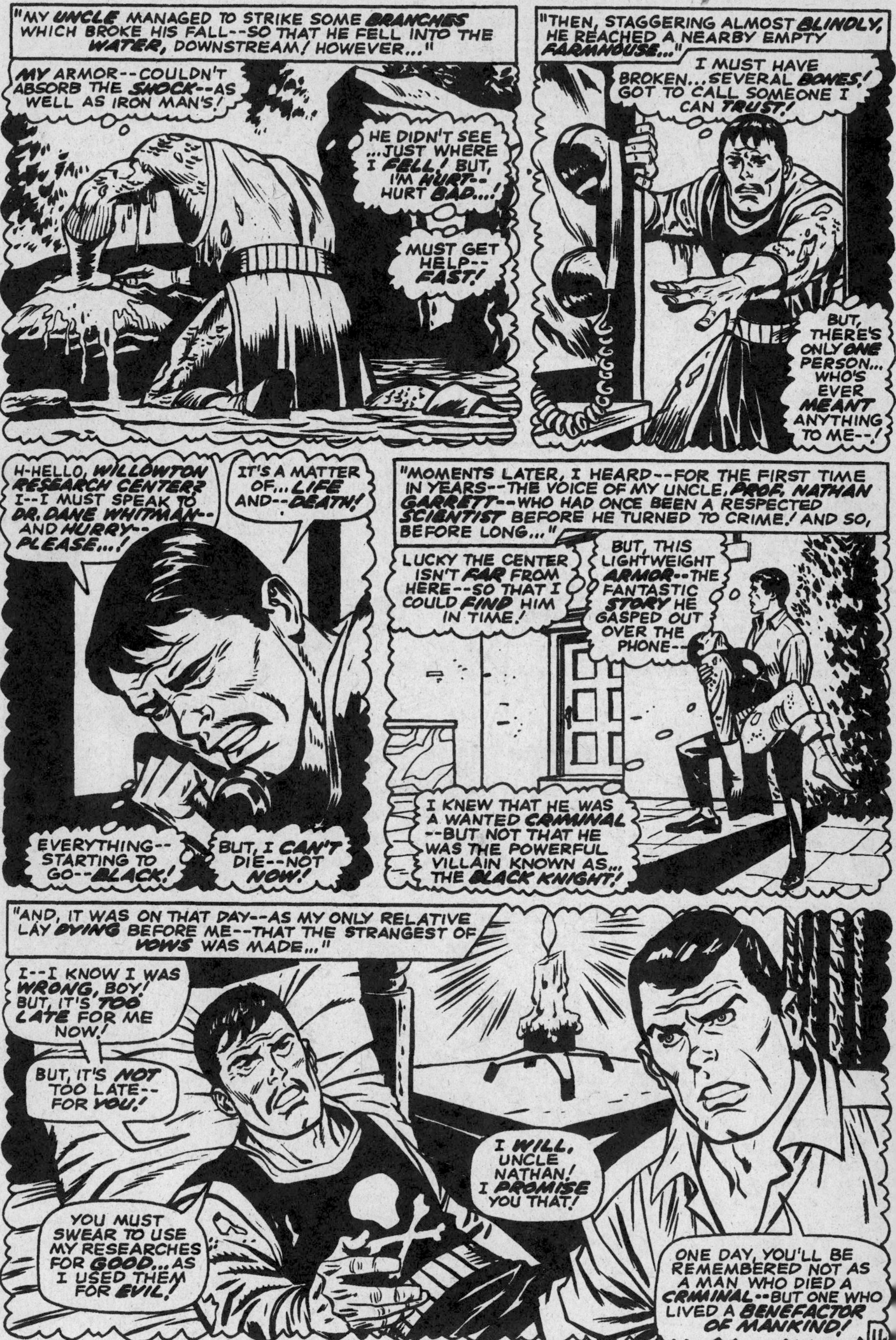

"MY UNCLE MANAGED TO STRIKE SOME BRANCHES WHICH BROKE HIS FALL--SO THAT HE FELL INTO THE WATER, DOWNSTREAM! HOWEVER..."
MY ARMOR--COULDN'T ABSORB THE SHOCK--AS WELL AS IRON MAN'S!
HE DIDN'T SEE ...JUST WHERE I FELL! BUT, I'M HURT-- HURT BAD...!
MUST GET HELP-- FAST!
"THEN, STAGGERING ALMOST BLINDLY, HE REACHED A NEARBY EMPTY FARMHOUSE..."
I MUST HAVE BROKEN...SEVERAL BONES! GOT TO CALL SOMEONE I CAN TRUST!
BUT, THERE'S ONLY ONE PERSON... WHO'S EVER MEANT ANYTHING TO ME--!
H-HELLO, WILLOWTON RESEARCH CENTER? I--I MUST SPEAK TO DR. DANE WHITMAN-- AND HURRY-- PLEASE...!
IT'S A MATTER OF... LIFE AND--DEATH!
EVERYTHING-- STARTING TO GO--BLACK!
BUT, I CAN'T DIE--NOT NOW!
"MOMENTS LATER, I HEARD--FOR THE FIRST TIME IN YEARS--THE VOICE OF MY UNCLE, PROF. NATHAN GARRETT--WHO HAD ONCE BEEN A RESPECTED SCIENTIST BEFORE HE TURNED TO CRIME! AND SO, BEFORE LONG..."
LUCKY THE CENTER ISN'T FAR FROM HERE--SO THAT I COULD FIND HIM IN TIME!
BUT, THIS LIGHTWEIGHT ARMOR--THE FANTASTIC STORY HE GASPED OUT OVER THE PHONE--
I KNEW THAT HE WAS A WANTED CRIMINAL --BUT NOT THAT HE WAS THE POWERFUL VILLAIN KNOWN AS... THE BLACK KNIGHT!
"AND, IT WAS ON THAT DAY--AS MY ONLY RELATIVE LAY DYING BEFORE ME--THAT THE STRANGEST OF VOWS WAS MADE..."
I--I KNOW I WAS WRONG, BOY! BUT, IT'S TOO LATE FOR ME NOW!
BUT, IT'S NOT TOO LATE-- FOR YOU!
I WILL, UNCLE NATHAN! I PROMISE YOU THAT!
YOU MUST SWEAR TO USE MY RESEARCHES FOR GOOD... AS I USED THEM FOR EVIL!
ONE DAY, YOU'LL BE REMEMBERED NOT AS A MAN WHO DIED A CRIMINAL--BUT ONE WHO LIVED A BENEFACTOR OF MANKIND!
11.

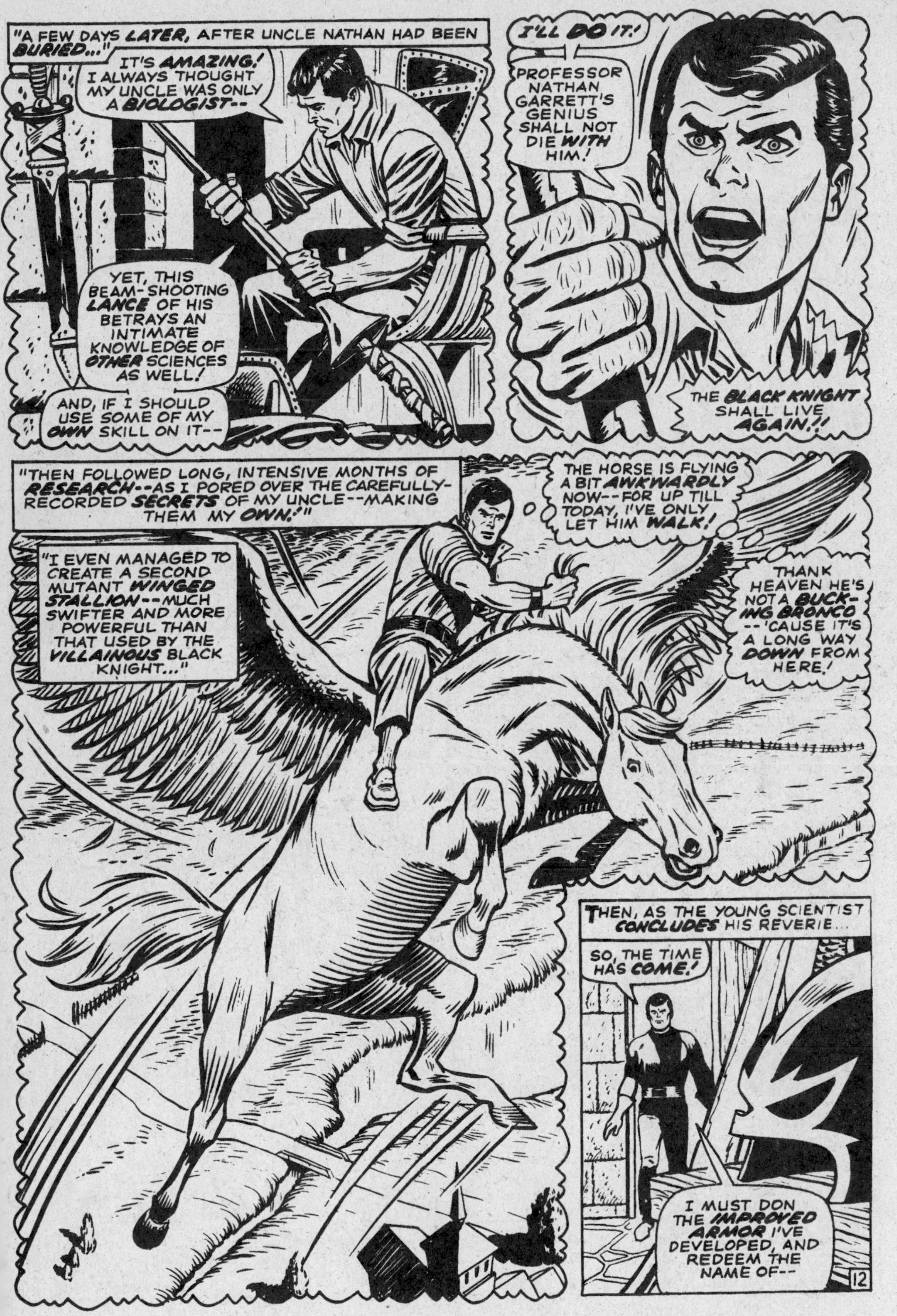
"A FEW DAYS LATER, AFTER UNCLE NATHAN HAD BEEN BURIED..."
IT'S AMAZING! I ALWAYS THOUGHT MY UNCLE WAS ONLY A BIOLOGIST--
YET, THIS BEAM-SHOOTING LANCE OF HIS BETRAYS AN INTIMATE KNOWLEDGE OF OTHER SCIENCES AS WELL!
AND, IF I SHOULD USE SOME OF MY OWN SKILL ON IT--
I'LL DO IT!
PROFESSOR NATHAN GARRETT'S GENIUS SHALL NOT DIE WITH HIM!
THE BLACK KNIGHT SHALL LIVE AGAIN!!
"THEN FOLLOWED LONG, INTENSIVE MONTHS OF RESEARCH--AS I PORED OVER THE CAREFULLY-RECORDED SECRETS OF MY UNCLE--MAKING THEM MY OWN!"
THE HORSE IS FLYING A BIT AWKWARDLY NOW--FOR UP TILL TODAY, I'VE ONLY LET HIM WALK!
"I EVEN MANAGED TO CREATE A SECOND MUTANT WINGED STALLION--MUCH SWIFTER AND MORE POWERFUL THAN THAT USED BY THE VILLAINOUS BLACK KNIGHT..."
THANK HEAVEN HE'S NOT A BUCKING BRONCO--'CAUSE IT'S A LONG WAY DOWN FROM HERE!
THEN, AS THE YOUNG SCIENTIST CONCLUDES HIS REVERIE...
SO, THE TIME HAS COME!
I MUST DON THE IMPROVED ARMOR I'VE DEVELOPED, AND REDEEM THE NAME OF--
12

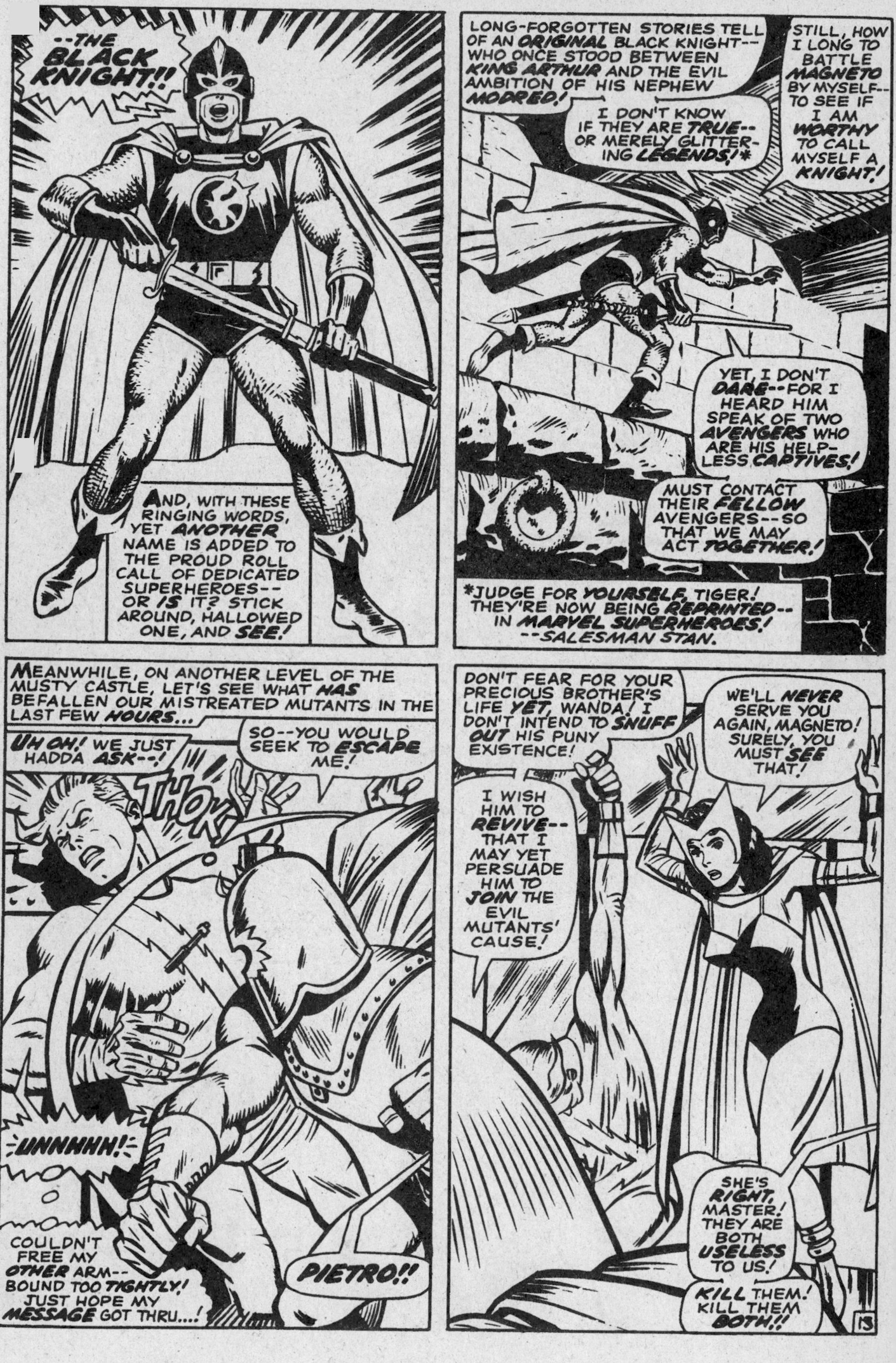

--THE BLACK KNIGHT!!
AND, WITH THESE RINGING WORDS, YET ANOTHER NAME IS ADDED TO THE PROUD ROLL CALL OF DEDICATED SUPERHEROES--OR IS IT? STICK AROUND, HALLOWED ONE, AND SEE!
LONG-FORGOTTEN STORIES TELL OF AN ORIGINAL BLACK KNIGHT--WHO ONCE STOOD BETWEEN KING ARTHUR AND THE EVIL AMBITION OF HIS NEPHEW MODRED!
I DON'T KNOW IF THEY ARE TRUE--OR MERELY GLITTERING LEGENDS!*
STILL, HOW I LONG TO BATTLE MAGNETO BY MYSELF--TO SEE IF I AM WORTHY TO CALL MYSELF A KNIGHT!
YET, I DON'T DARE--FOR I HEARD HIM SPEAK OF TWO AVENGERS WHO ARE HIS HELPLESS CAPTIVES!
MUST CONTACT THEIR FELLOW AVENGERS--SO THAT WE MAY ACT TOGETHER!
*JUDGE FOR YOURSELF, TIGER! THEY'RE NOW BEING REPRINTED--IN MARVEL SUPERHEROES! --SALESMAN STAN.
MEANWHILE, ON ANOTHER LEVEL OF THE MUSTY CASTLE, LET'S SEE WHAT HAS BEFALLEN OUR MISTREATED MUTANTS IN THE LAST FEW HOURS...
UH OH! WE JUST HADDA ASK--!
SO--YOU WOULD SEEK TO ESCAPE ME!
THOK
UNNNHH!
COULDN'T FREE MY OTHER ARM--BOUND TOO TIGHTLY! JUST HOPE MY MESSAGE GOT THRU...!
PIETRO!!
DON'T FEAR FOR YOUR PRECIOUS BROTHER'S LIFE YET, WANDA! I DON'T INTEND TO SNUFF OUT HIS PUNY EXISTENCE!
I WISH HIM TO REVIVE--THAT I MAY YET PERSUADE HIM TO JOIN THE EVIL MUTANTS' CAUSE!
WE'LL NEVER SERVE YOU AGAIN, MAGNETO! SURELY, YOU MUST SEE THAT!
SHE'S RIGHT, MASTER! THEY ARE BOTH USELESS TO US!
KILL THEM! KILL THEM BOTH!!
13

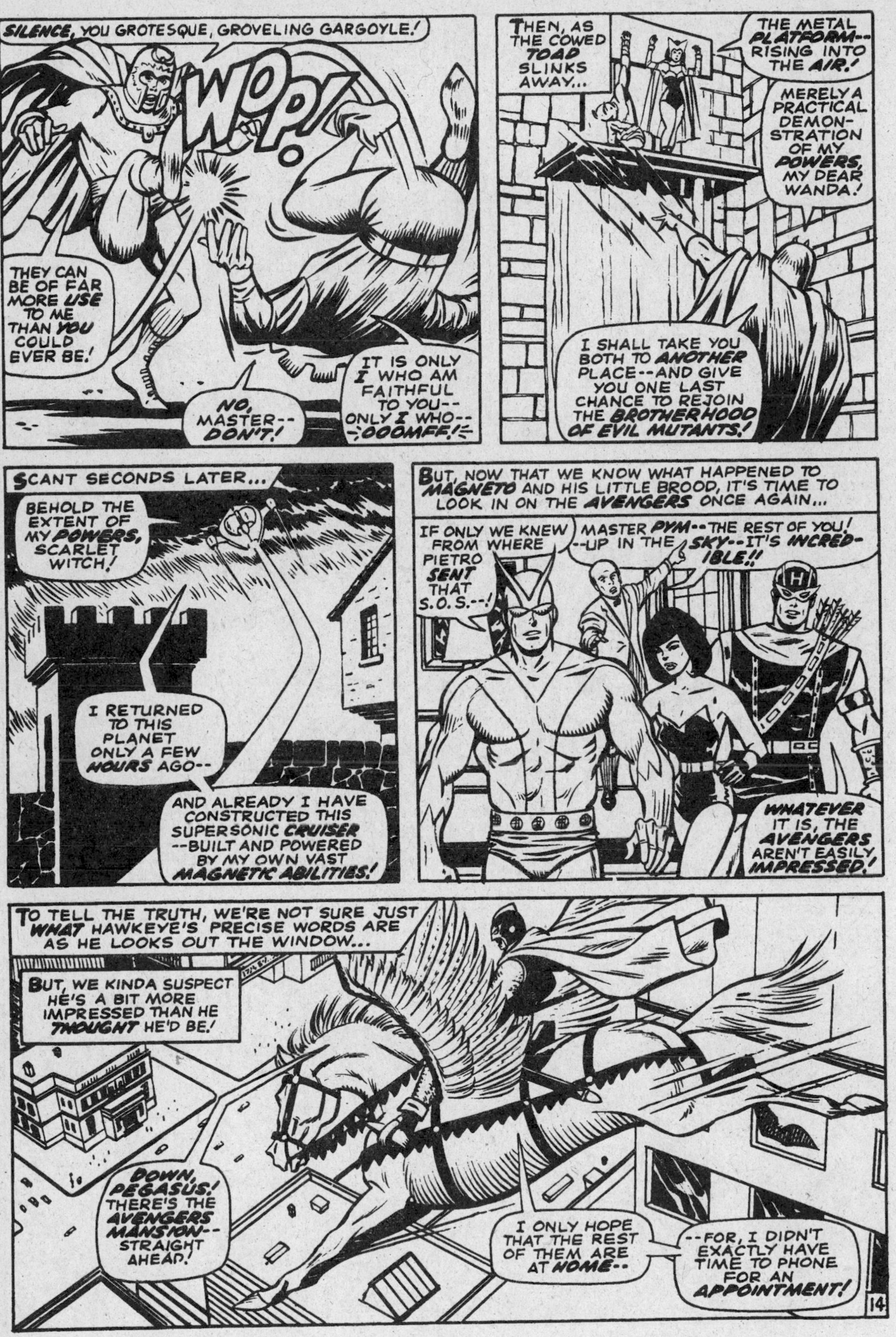
SILENCE, YOU GROTESQUE, GROVELING GARGOYLE!
WOP!
THEY CAN BE OF FAR MORE USE TO ME THAN YOU COULD EVER BE!
IT IS ONLY I WHO AM FAITHFUL TO YOU--ONLY I WHO--
OOOMFF!
NO, MASTER--DON'T!
THEN, AS THE COWED TOAD SLINKS AWAY...
THE METAL PLATFORM--RISING INTO THE AIR!
MERELY A PRACTICAL DEMONSTRATION OF MY POWERS, MY DEAR WANDA!
I SHALL TAKE YOU BOTH TO ANOTHER PLACE--AND GIVE YOU ONE LAST CHANCE TO REJOIN THE BROTHERHOOD OF EVIL MUTANTS!
SCANT SECONDS LATER...
BEHOLD THE EXTENT OF MY POWERS, SCARLET WITCH!
I RETURNED TO THIS PLANET ONLY A FEW HOURS AGO--
AND ALREADY I HAVE CONSTRUCTED THIS SUPERSONIC CRUISER --BUILT AND POWERED BY MY OWN VAST MAGNETIC ABILITIES!
BUT, NOW THAT WE KNOW WHAT HAPPENED TO MAGNETO AND HIS LITTLE BROOD, IT'S TIME TO LOOK IN ON THE AVENGERS ONCE AGAIN...
IF ONLY WE KNEW FROM WHERE PIETRO SENT THAT S.O.S.--!
MASTER PYM--THE REST OF YOU! --UP IN THE SKY--IT'S INCREDIBLE!!
WHATEVER IT IS, THE AVENGERS AREN'T EASILY IMPRESSED!
TO TELL THE TRUTH, WE'RE NOT SURE JUST WHAT HAWKEYE'S PRECISE WORDS ARE AS HE LOOKS OUT THE WINDOW...
BUT, WE KINDA SUSPECT HE'S A BIT MORE IMPRESSED THAN HE THOUGHT HE'D BE!
DOWN, PEGASUS! THERE'S THE AVENGERS MANSION--STRAIGHT AHEAD!
I ONLY HOPE THAT THE REST OF THEM ARE AT HOME--
--FOR, I DIDN'T EXACTLY HAVE TIME TO PHONE FOR AN APPOINTMENT!
14

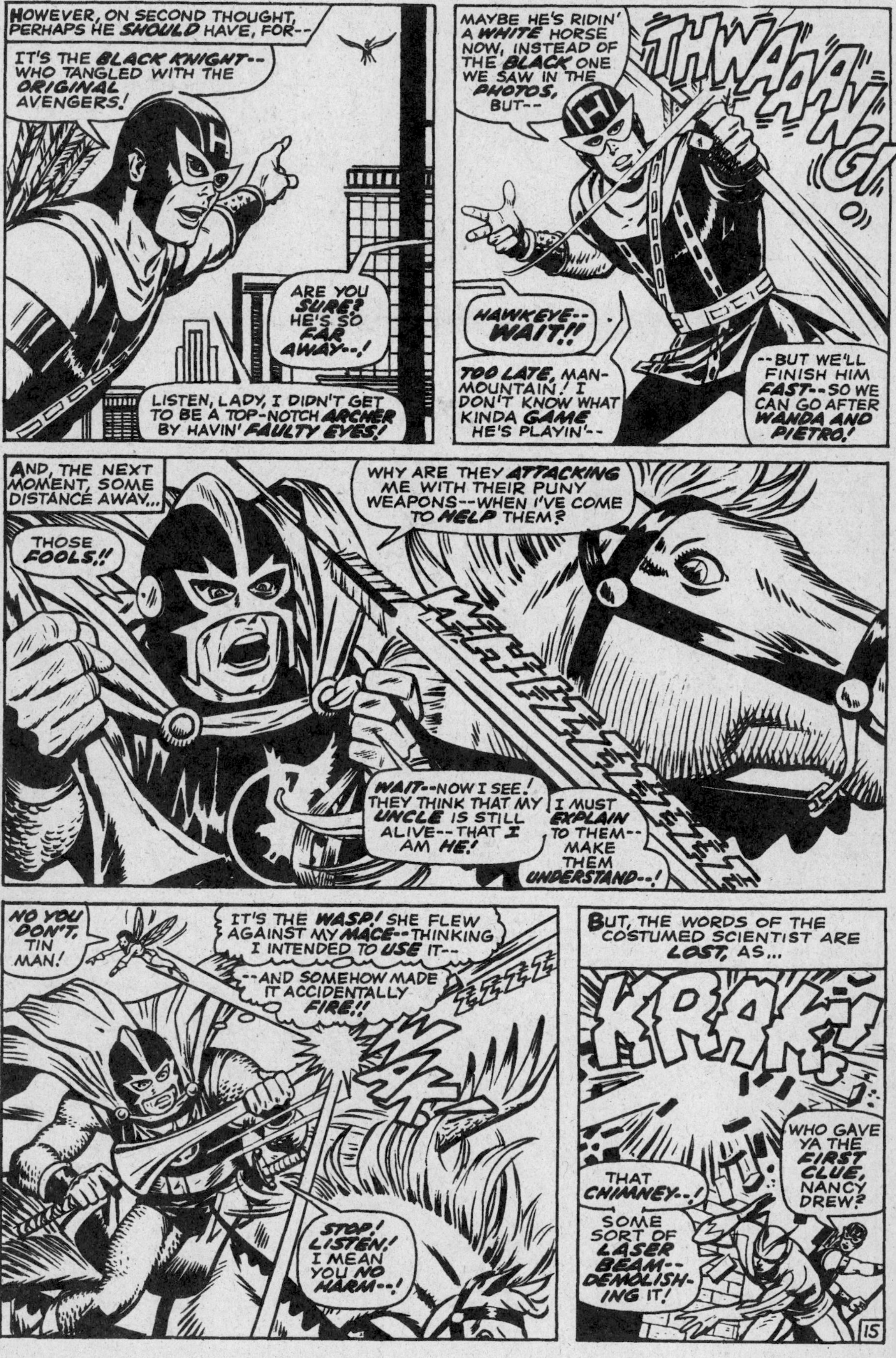
HOWEVER, ON SECOND THOUGHT, PERHAPS HE SHOULD HAVE, FOR--
IT'S THE BLACK KNIGHT-- WHO TANGLED WITH THE ORIGINAL AVENGERS!
ARE YOU SURE? HE'S SO FAR AWAY--!
LISTEN, LADY, I DIDN'T GET TO BE A TOP-NOTCH ARCHER BY HAVIN' FAULTY EYES!
MAYBE HE'S RIDIN' A WHITE HORSE NOW, INSTEAD OF THE BLACK ONE WE SAW IN THE PHOTOS, BUT--
THWAAANG!
HAWKEYE-- WAIT!!
TOO LATE, MAN-MOUNTAIN! I DON'T KNOW WHAT KINDA GAME HE'S PLAYIN'--
--BUT WE'LL FINISH HIM FAST--SO WE CAN GO AFTER WANDA AND PIETRO!
AND, THE NEXT MOMENT, SOME DISTANCE AWAY...
THOSE FOOLS!!
WHY ARE THEY ATTACKING ME WITH THEIR PUNY WEAPONS--WHEN I'VE COME TO HELP THEM?
WAIT--NOW I SEE! THEY THINK THAT MY UNCLE IS STILL ALIVE--THAT I AM HE!
I MUST EXPLAIN TO THEM-- MAKE THEM UNDERSTAND--!
NO YOU DON'T, TIN MAN!
IT'S THE WASP! SHE FLEW AGAINST MY MACE--THINKING I INTENDED TO USE IT--
--AND SOMEHOW MADE IT ACCIDENTALLY FIRE!!
STOP! LISTEN! I MEAN YOU NO HARM--!
BUT, THE WORDS OF THE COSTUMED SCIENTIST ARE LOST, AS...
KRAK!
WHO GAVE YA THE FIRST CLUE, NANCY DREW?
THAT CHIMNEY--!
SOME SORT OF LASER BEAM-- DEMOLISHING IT!
15

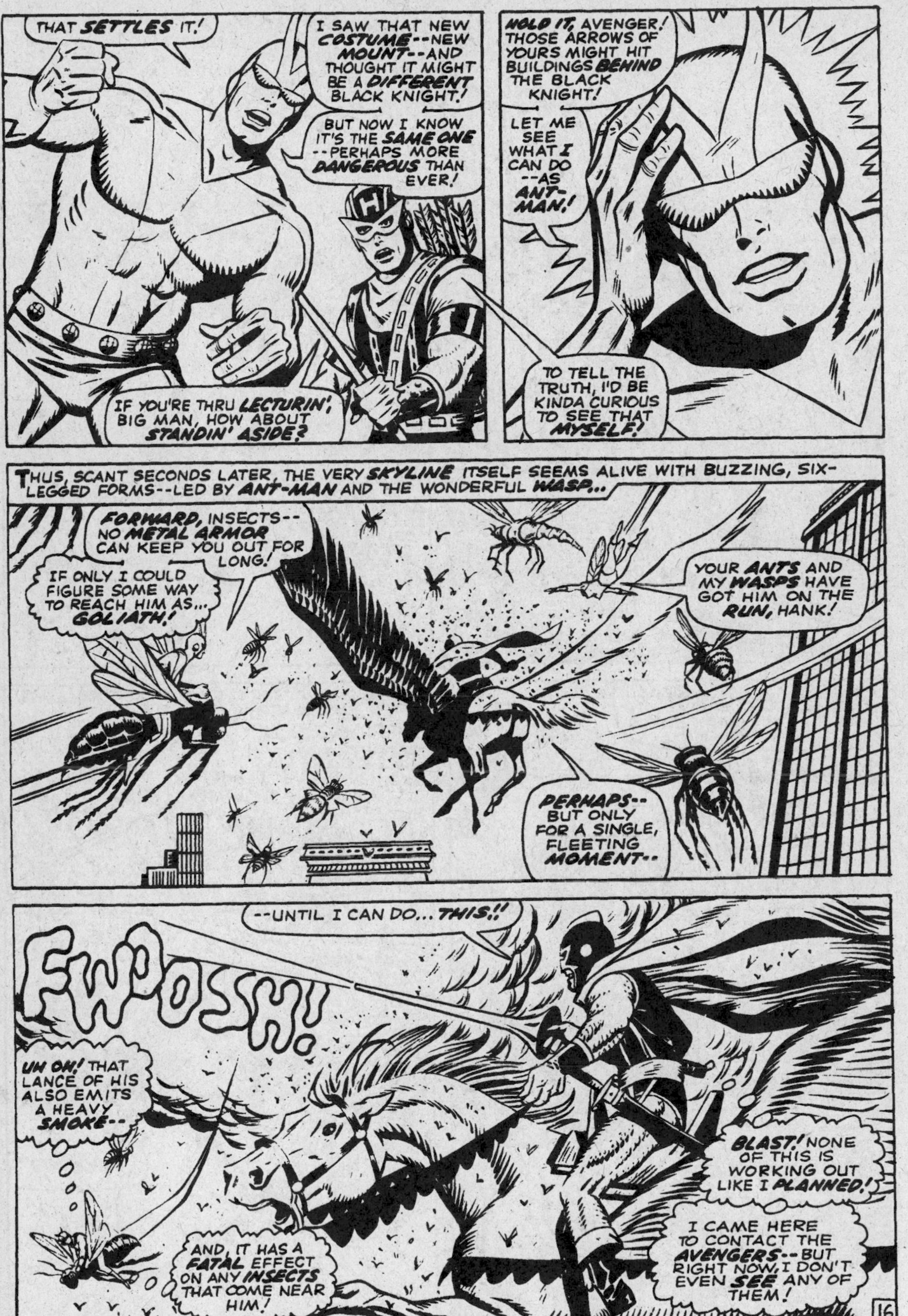

THAT SETTLES IT!
I SAW THAT NEW COSTUME--NEW MOUNT--AND THOUGHT IT MIGHT BE A DIFFERENT BLACK KNIGHT!
BUT NOW I KNOW IT'S THE SAME ONE --PERHAPS MORE DANGEROUS THAN EVER!
IF YOU'RE THRU LECTURIN', BIG MAN, HOW ABOUT STANDIN' ASIDE?
HOLD IT, AVENGER! THOSE ARROWS OF YOURS MIGHT HIT BUILDINGS BEHIND THE BLACK KNIGHT!
LET ME SEE WHAT I CAN DO --AS ANT-MAN!
TO TELL THE TRUTH, I'D BE KINDA CURIOUS TO SEE THAT MYSELF!
THUS, SCANT SECONDS LATER, THE VERY SKYLINE ITSELF SEEMS ALIVE WITH BUZZING, SIX-LEGGED FORMS--LED BY ANT-MAN AND THE WONDERFUL WASP...
FORWARD, INSECTS--NO METAL ARMOR CAN KEEP YOU OUT FOR LONG!
IF ONLY I COULD FIGURE SOME WAY TO REACH HIM AS... GOLIATH!
YOUR ANTS AND MY WASPS HAVE GOT HIM ON THE RUN, HANK!
PERHAPS--BUT ONLY FOR A SINGLE, FLEETING MOMENT--
--UNTIL I CAN DO... THIS!!
FWOOSH!
UH OH! THAT LANCE OF HIS ALSO EMITS A HEAVY SMOKE--
AND, IT HAS A FATAL EFFECT ON ANY INSECTS THAT COME NEAR HIM!
BLAST! NONE OF THIS IS WORKING OUT LIKE I PLANNED!
I CAME HERE TO CONTACT THE AVENGERS--BUT RIGHT NOW, I DON'T EVEN SEE ANY OF THEM!
16

PERHAPS DANE WHITMAN MAY BE *EXCUSED* FOR NOT SEEING THE MINUTE FORMS OF *HANK* AND *JAN* NEARBY! BUT, WHAT ABOUT *HAWKEYE*--?

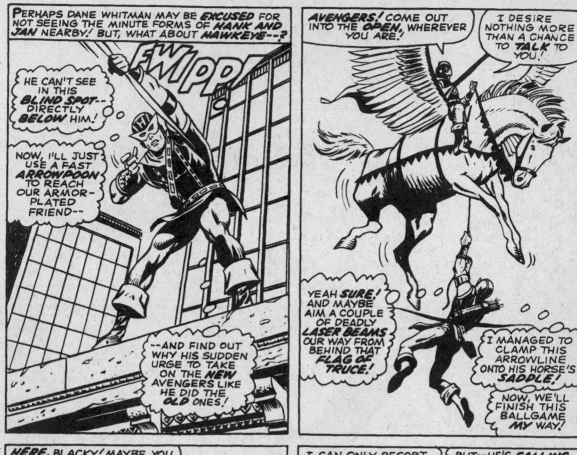

HE CAN'T SEE IN THIS *BLIND SPOT*-- DIRECTLY *BELOW* HIM!

NOW, I'LL JUST USE A FAST *ARROWPOON* TO REACH OUR ARMOR-PLATED FRIEND--

FWIPP

--AND FIND OUT WHY HIS SUDDEN URGE TO TAKE ON THE *NEW* AVENGERS LIKE HE DID THE *OLD* ONES!

AVENGERS! COME OUT INTO THE *OPEN,* WHEREVER YOU ARE!

I DESIRE NOTHING MORE THAN A CHANCE TO *TALK* TO YOU!

YEAH *SURE!* AND MAYBE AIM A COUPLE OF DEADLY *LASER BEAMS* OUR WAY FROM BEHIND THAT *FLAG OF TRUCE!*

I MANAGED TO CLAMP THIS *ARROWLINE* ONTO HIS HORSE'S *SADDLE!*

NOW, WE'LL FINISH THIS *BALLGAME MY* WAY!

HERE, BLACKY! MAYBE YOU MANAGED TO CLEAR ALL OF HANK'S LITTLE BABY *BUGS* OUTTA YOUR HAIR--

BUT, YOU'VE STILL GOT *BROTHER HAWKEYE* TO RECKON WITH!

-*UNNHHH!-- WAIT!* I-- I'VE COME ONLY TO--

IT'S *NO USE!* CAN'T *SPEAK*--! HE'S *LOOPED* HIS *BOW* AROUND ME TOO *TIGHTLY!*

I CAN ONLY RESORT TO --*VIOLENCE!*

THERE! CAUGHT HIM--A GLANCING BLOW WITH MY *LANCE!*

BUT--HE'S *FALLING* --MAYBE TO HIS *DEATH!* I DIDN'T *MEAN* TO--

WISSH

-*OOOOMFF!-*

17

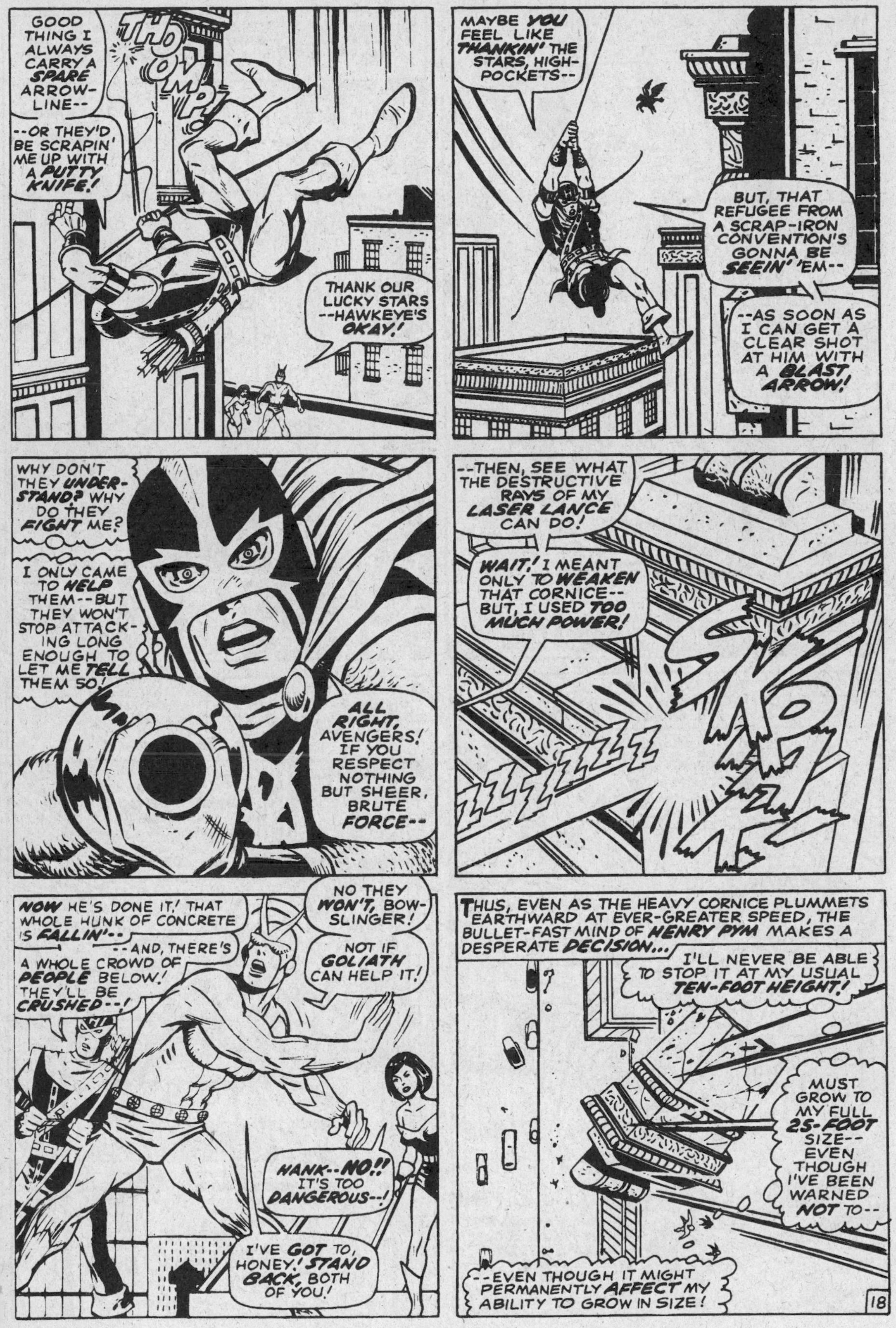

GOOD THING I ALWAYS CARRY A SPARE ARROW-LINE--
--OR THEY'D BE SCRAPIN' ME UP WITH A PUTTY KNIFE!
THOOMP!
THANK OUR LUCKY STARS --HAWKEYE'S OKAY!
MAYBE YOU FEEL LIKE THANKIN' THE STARS, HIGH-POCKETS--
BUT, THAT REFUGEE FROM A SCRAP-IRON CONVENTION'S GONNA BE SEEIN' 'EM--
--AS SOON AS I CAN GET A CLEAR SHOT AT HIM WITH A BLAST ARROW!
WHY DON'T THEY UNDERSTAND? WHY DO THEY FIGHT ME?
I ONLY CAME TO HELP THEM--BUT THEY WON'T STOP ATTACKING LONG ENOUGH TO LET ME TELL THEM SO!
ALL RIGHT, AVENGERS! IF YOU RESPECT NOTHING BUT SHEER, BRUTE FORCE--
--THEN, SEE WHAT THE DESTRUCTIVE RAYS OF MY LASER LANCE CAN DO!
WAIT! I MEANT ONLY TO WEAKEN THAT CORNICE--BUT, I USED TOO MUCH POWER!
SKOKK!
ZZZZZZZZ
NOW HE'S DONE IT! THAT WHOLE HUNK OF CONCRETE IS FALLIN'--
--AND, THERE'S A WHOLE CROWD OF PEOPLE BELOW! THEY'LL BE CRUSHED--!
NO THEY WON'T, BOW-SLINGER!
NOT IF GOLIATH CAN HELP IT!
HANK--NO!! IT'S TOO DANGEROUS--!
I'VE GOT TO, HONEY! STAND BACK, BOTH OF YOU!
THUS, EVEN AS THE HEAVY CORNICE PLUMMETS EARTHWARD AT EVER-GREATER SPEED, THE BULLET-FAST MIND OF HENRY PYM MAKES A DESPERATE DECISION...
I'LL NEVER BE ABLE TO STOP IT AT MY USUAL TEN-FOOT HEIGHT!
MUST GROW TO MY FULL 25-FOOT SIZE--EVEN THOUGH I'VE BEEN WARNED NOT TO--
--EVEN THOUGH IT MIGHT PERMANENTLY AFFECT MY ABILITY TO GROW IN SIZE!
18

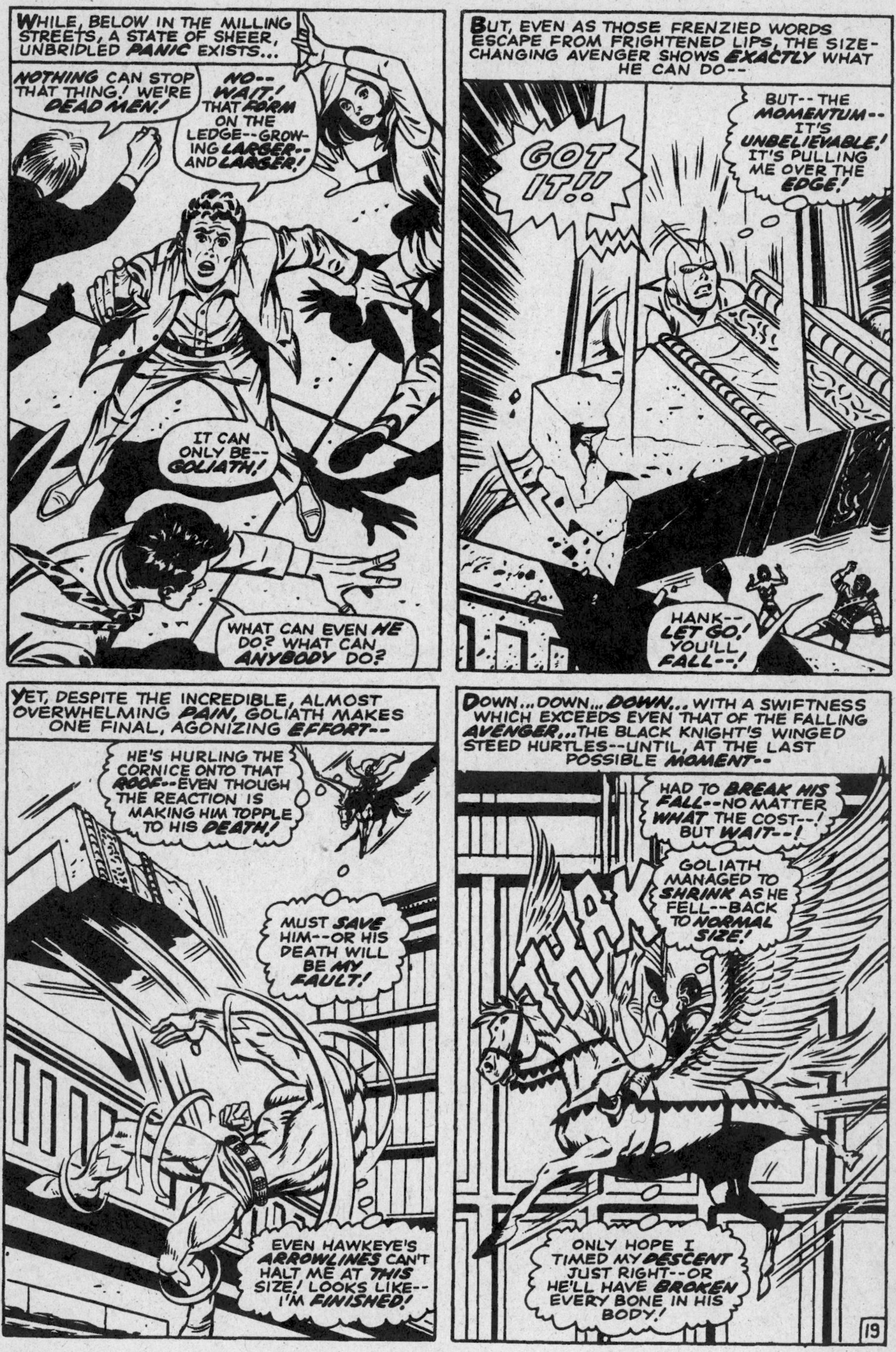
WHILE, BELOW IN THE MILLING STREETS, A STATE OF SHEER, UNBRIDLED PANIC EXISTS...
NOTHING CAN STOP THAT THING! WE'RE DEAD MEN!
NO-- WAIT! THAT FORM ON THE LEDGE--GROWING LARGER-- AND LARGER!
IT CAN ONLY BE-- GOLIATH!
WHAT CAN EVEN HE DO? WHAT CAN ANYBODY DO?
BUT, EVEN AS THOSE FRENZIED WORDS ESCAPE FROM FRIGHTENED LIPS, THE SIZE-CHANGING AVENGER SHOWS EXACTLY WHAT HE CAN DO--
GOT IT!!
BUT-- THE MOMENTUM-- IT'S UNBELIEVABLE! IT'S PULLING ME OVER THE EDGE!
HANK-- LET GO! YOU'LL FALL--!
YET, DESPITE THE INCREDIBLE, ALMOST OVERWHELMING PAIN, GOLIATH MAKES ONE FINAL, AGONIZING EFFORT--
HE'S HURLING THE CORNICE ONTO THAT ROOF--EVEN THOUGH THE REACTION IS MAKING HIM TOPPLE TO HIS DEATH!
MUST SAVE HIM--OR HIS DEATH WILL BE MY FAULT!
EVEN HAWKEYE'S ARROWLINES CAN'T HALT ME AT THIS SIZE! LOOKS LIKE-- I'M FINISHED!
DOWN...DOWN...DOWN... WITH A SWIFTNESS WHICH EXCEEDS EVEN THAT OF THE FALLING AVENGER...THE BLACK KNIGHT'S WINGED STEED HURTLES--UNTIL, AT THE LAST POSSIBLE MOMENT--
HAD TO BREAK HIS FALL--NO MATTER WHAT THE COST--! BUT WAIT--!
GOLIATH MANAGED TO SHRINK AS HE FELL--BACK TO NORMAL SIZE!
THAK
ONLY HOPE I TIMED MY DESCENT JUST RIGHT--OR HE'LL HAVE BROKEN EVERY BONE IN HIS BODY!
19

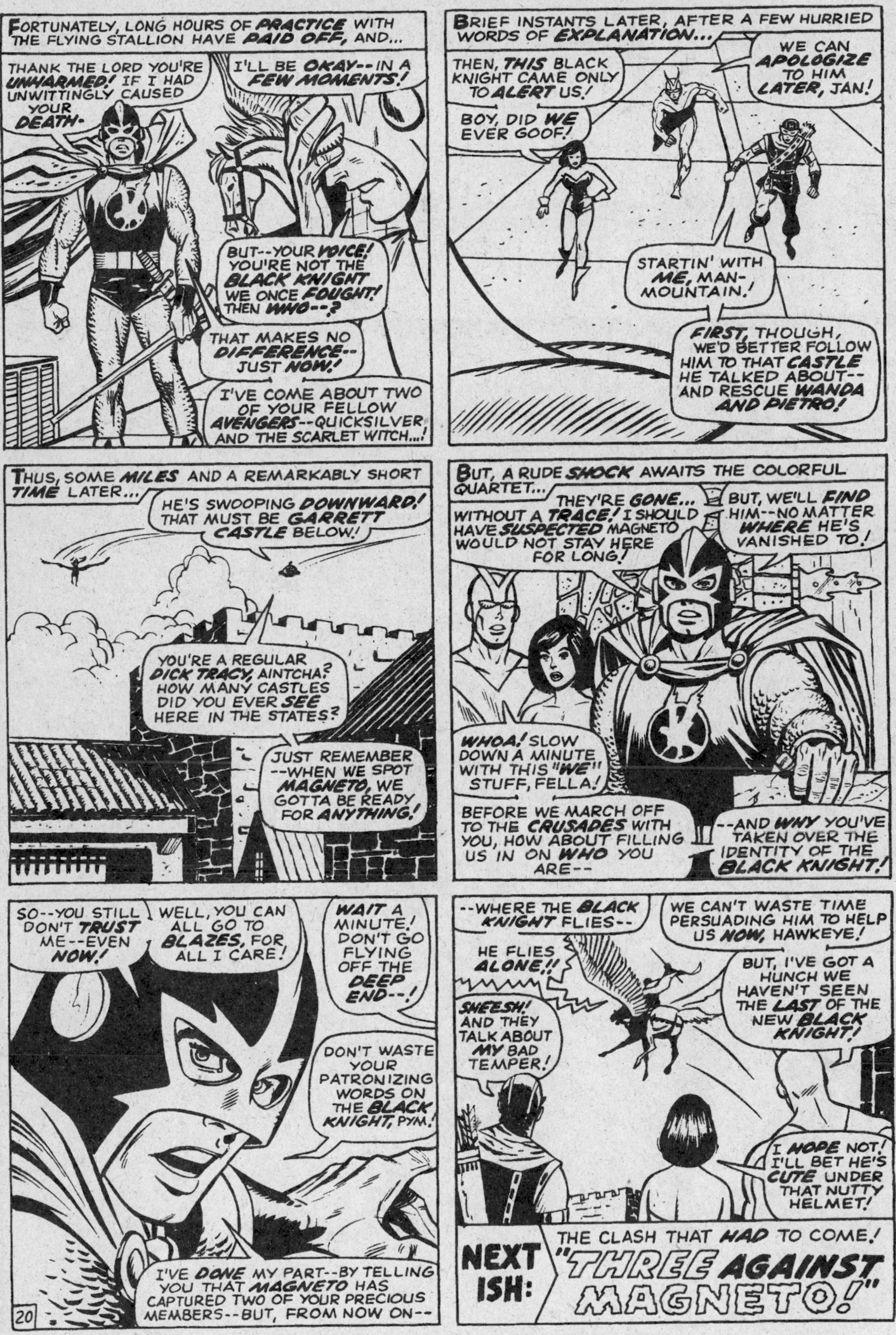
FORTUNATELY, LONG HOURS OF PRACTICE WITH THE FLYING STALLION HAVE PAID OFF, AND...
THANK THE LORD YOU'RE UNHARMED! IF I HAD UNWITTINGLY CAUSED YOUR DEATH-
I'LL BE OKAY--IN A FEW MOMENTS!
BUT--YOUR VOICE! YOU'RE NOT THE BLACK KNIGHT WE ONCE FOUGHT! THEN WHO--?
THAT MAKES NO DIFFERENCE--JUST NOW!
I'VE COME ABOUT TWO OF YOUR FELLOW AVENGERS--QUICKSILVER AND THE SCARLET WITCH...!
BRIEF INSTANTS LATER, AFTER A FEW HURRIED WORDS OF EXPLANATION...
THEN, THIS BLACK KNIGHT CAME ONLY TO ALERT US!
WE CAN APOLOGIZE TO HIM LATER, JAN!
BOY, DID WE EVER GOOF!
STARTIN' WITH ME, MAN-MOUNTAIN!
FIRST, THOUGH, WE'D BETTER FOLLOW HIM TO THAT CASTLE HE TALKED ABOUT--AND RESCUE WANDA AND PIETRO!
THUS, SOME MILES AND A REMARKABLY SHORT TIME LATER...
HE'S SWOOPING DOWNWARD! THAT MUST BE GARRETT CASTLE BELOW!
YOU'RE A REGULAR DICK TRACY, AINTCHA? HOW MANY CASTLES DID YOU EVER SEE HERE IN THE STATES?
JUST REMEMBER --WHEN WE SPOT MAGNETO, WE GOTTA BE READY FOR ANYTHING!
BUT, A RUDE SHOCK AWAITS THE COLORFUL QUARTET...
THEY'RE GONE... WITHOUT A TRACE! I SHOULD HAVE SUSPECTED MAGNETO WOULD NOT STAY HERE FOR LONG!
BUT, WE'LL FIND HIM--NO MATTER WHERE HE'S VANISHED TO!
WHOA! SLOW DOWN A MINUTE WITH THIS "WE" STUFF, FELLA!
BEFORE WE MARCH OFF TO THE CRUSADES WITH YOU, HOW ABOUT FILLING US IN ON WHO YOU ARE--
--AND WHY YOU'VE TAKEN OVER THE IDENTITY OF THE BLACK KNIGHT!
SO--YOU STILL DON'T TRUST ME--EVEN NOW!
WELL, YOU CAN ALL GO TO BLAZES, FOR ALL I CARE!
WAIT A MINUTE! DON'T GO FLYING OFF THE DEEP END--!
DON'T WASTE YOUR PATRONIZING WORDS ON THE BLACK KNIGHT, PYM!
I'VE DONE MY PART--BY TELLING YOU THAT MAGNETO HAS CAPTURED TWO OF YOUR PRECIOUS MEMBERS--BUT, FROM NOW ON--
20
--WHERE THE BLACK KNIGHT FLIES--
HE FLIES ALONE!!
WE CAN'T WASTE TIME PERSUADING HIM TO HELP US NOW, HAWKEYE!
BUT, I'VE GOT A HUNCH WE HAVEN'T SEEN THE LAST OF THE NEW BLACK KNIGHT!
SHEESH! AND THEY TALK ABOUT MY BAD TEMPER!
I HOPE NOT! I'LL BET HE'S CUTE UNDER THAT NUTTY HELMET!
NEXT ISH:
THE CLASH THAT HAD TO COME!
"THREE AGAINST MAGNETO!"

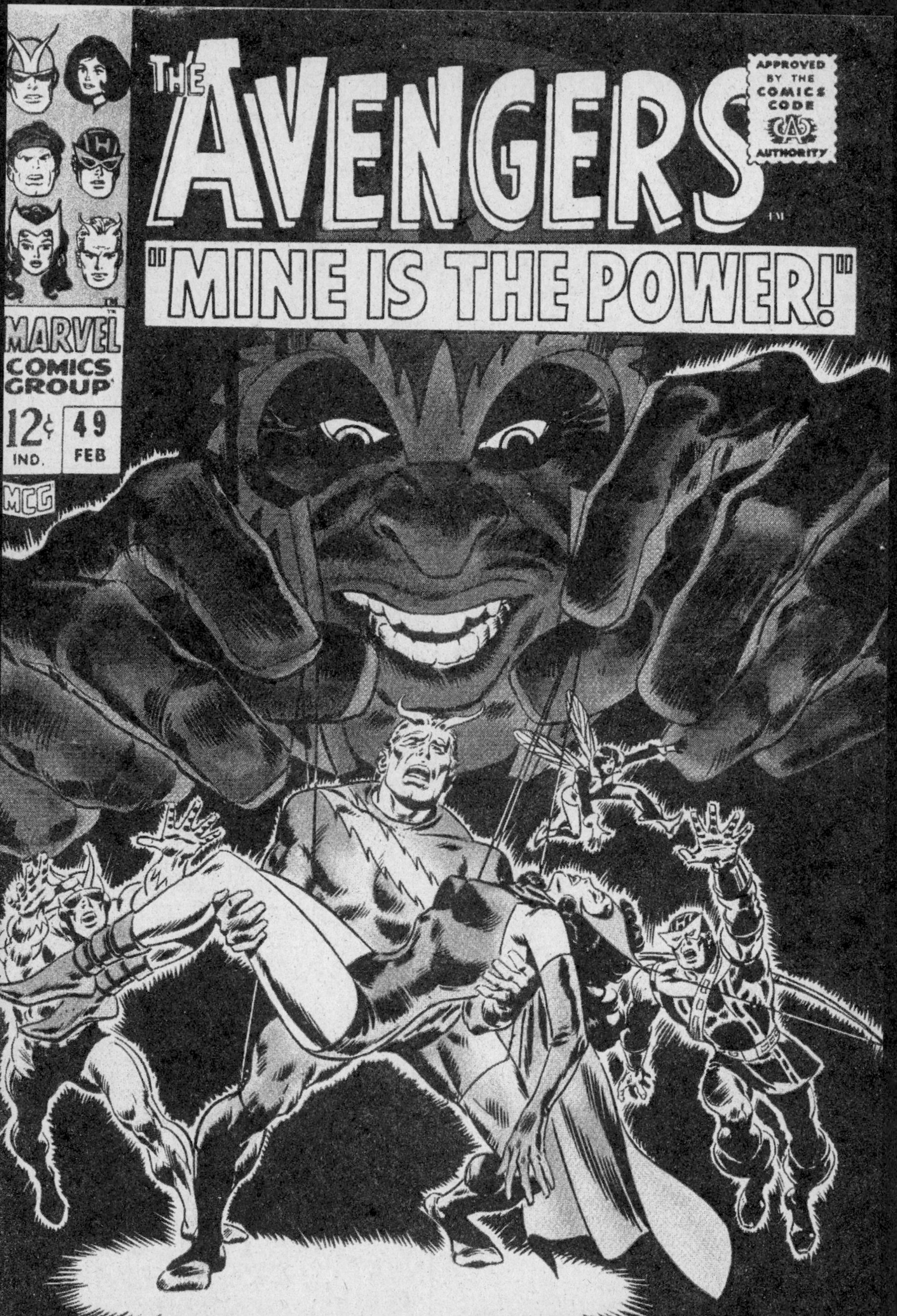
THE AVENGERS
"MINE IS THE POWER!"
APPROVED BY THE COMICS CODE AUTHORITY
MARVEL COMICS GROUP
12¢ IND.
49 FEB
MCG

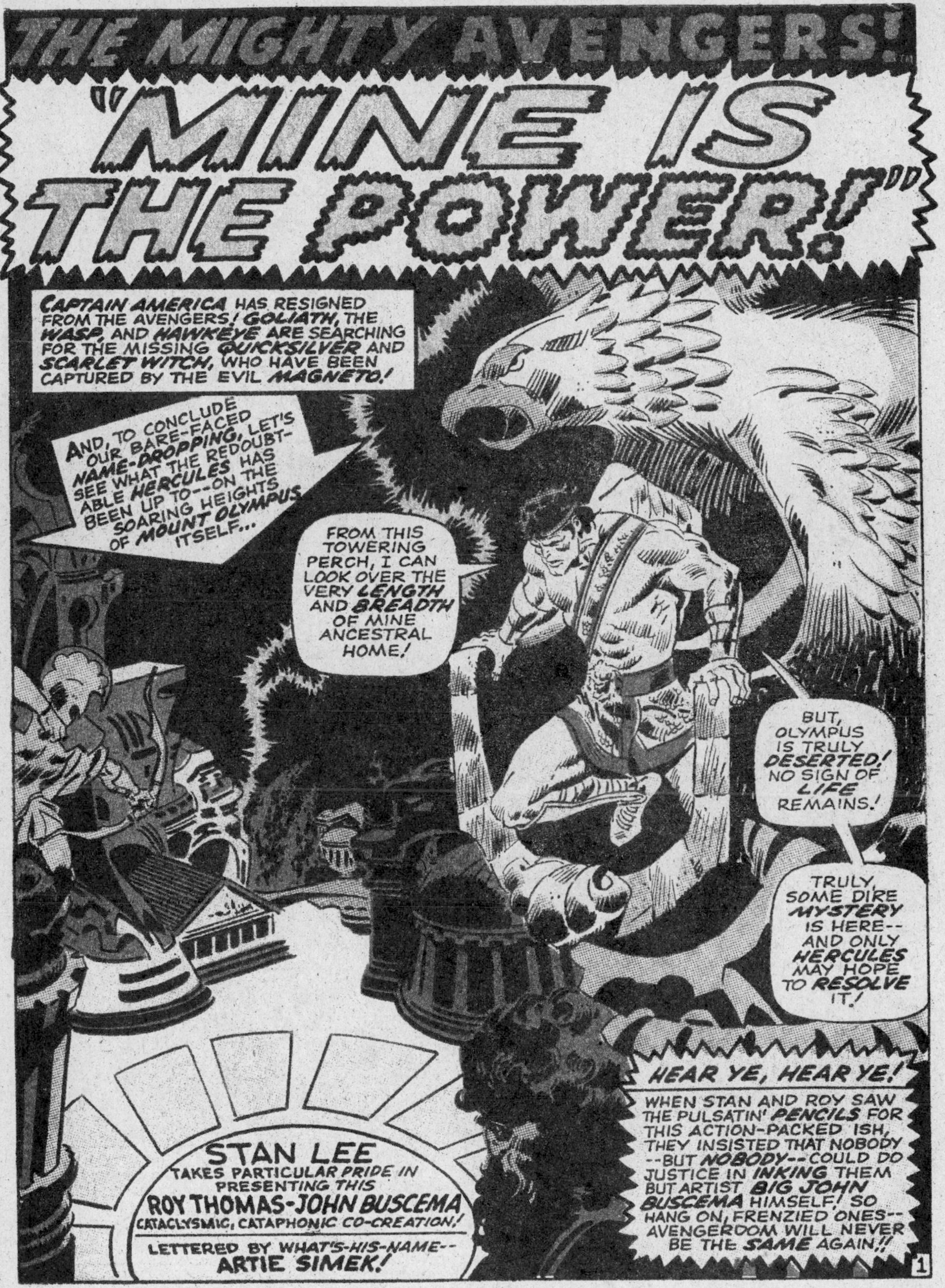
THE MIGHTY AVENGERS!
"MINE IS THE POWER!"
CAPTAIN AMERICA HAS RESIGNED FROM THE AVENGERS! GOLIATH, THE WASP, AND HAWKEYE ARE SEARCHING FOR THE MISSING QUICKSILVER AND SCARLET WITCH, WHO HAVE BEEN CAPTURED BY THE EVIL MAGNETO!
AND, TO CONCLUDE OUR BARE-FACED NAME-DROPPING, LET'S SEE WHAT THE REDOUBTABLE HERCULES HAS BEEN UP TO--ON THE SOARING HEIGHTS OF MOUNT OLYMPUS ITSELF...
FROM THIS TOWERING PERCH, I CAN LOOK OVER THE VERY LENGTH AND BREADTH OF MINE ANCESTRAL HOME!
BUT, OLYMPUS IS TRULY DESERTED! NO SIGN OF LIFE REMAINS!
TRULY, SOME DIRE MYSTERY IS HERE--AND ONLY HERCULES MAY HOPE TO RESOLVE IT!
STAN LEE TAKES PARTICULAR PRIDE IN PRESENTING THIS ROY THOMAS-JOHN BUSCEMA CATACLYSMIC, CATAPHONIC CO-CREATION!
LETTERED BY WHAT'S-HIS-NAME--ARTIE SIMEK!
HEAR YE, HEAR YE!
WHEN STAN AND ROY SAW THE PULSATIN' PENCILS FOR THIS ACTION-PACKED ISH, THEY INSISTED THAT NOBODY --BUT NOBODY--COULD DO JUSTICE IN INKING THEM BUT ARTIST BIG JOHN BUSCEMA HIMSELF! SO HANG ON, FRENZIED ONES--AVENGERDOM WILL NEVER BE THE SAME AGAIN!!
1

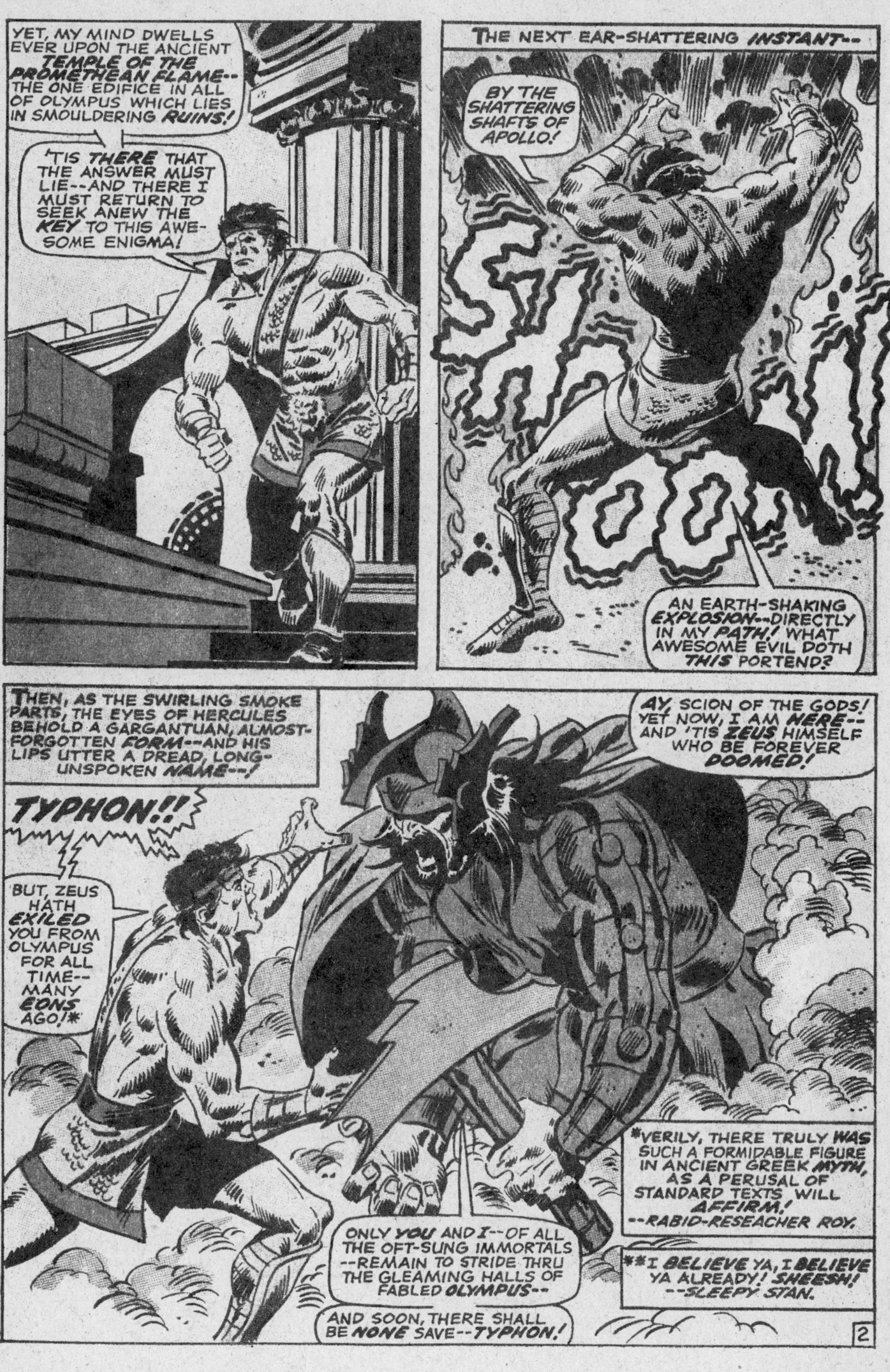

YET, MY MIND DWELLS EVER UPON THE ANCIENT TEMPLE OF THE PROMETHEAN FLAME-- THE ONE EDIFICE IN ALL OF OLYMPUS WHICH LIES IN SMOULDERING RUINS!
'TIS THERE THAT THE ANSWER MUST LIE--AND THERE I MUST RETURN TO SEEK ANEW THE KEY TO THIS AWESOME ENIGMA!
THE NEXT EAR-SHATTERING INSTANT--
BY THE SHATTERING SHAFTS OF APOLLO!
SHOOM
AN EARTH-SHAKING EXPLOSION--DIRECTLY IN MY PATH! WHAT AWESOME EVIL DOTH THIS PORTEND?
THEN, AS THE SWIRLING SMOKE PARTS, THE EYES OF HERCULES BEHOLD A GARGANTUAN, ALMOST-FORGOTTEN FORM--AND HIS LIPS UTTER A DREAD, LONG-UNSPOKEN NAME--!
TYPHON!!
BUT, ZEUS HATH EXILED YOU FROM OLYMPUS FOR ALL TIME-- MANY EONS AGO!*
AY, SCION OF THE GODS! YET NOW, I AM HERE-- AND 'TIS ZEUS HIMSELF WHO BE FOREVER DOOMED!
ONLY YOU AND I--OF ALL THE OFT-SUNG IMMORTALS --REMAIN TO STRIDE THRU THE GLEAMING HALLS OF FABLED OLYMPUS--
AND SOON, THERE SHALL BE NONE SAVE--TYPHON!
*VERILY, THERE TRULY WAS SUCH A FORMIDABLE FIGURE IN ANCIENT GREEK MYTH, AS A PERUSAL OF STANDARD TEXTS WILL AFFIRM! --RABID-RESEACHER ROY.
**I BELIEVE YA, I BELIEVE YA ALREADY! SHEESH! --SLEEPY STAN.
2

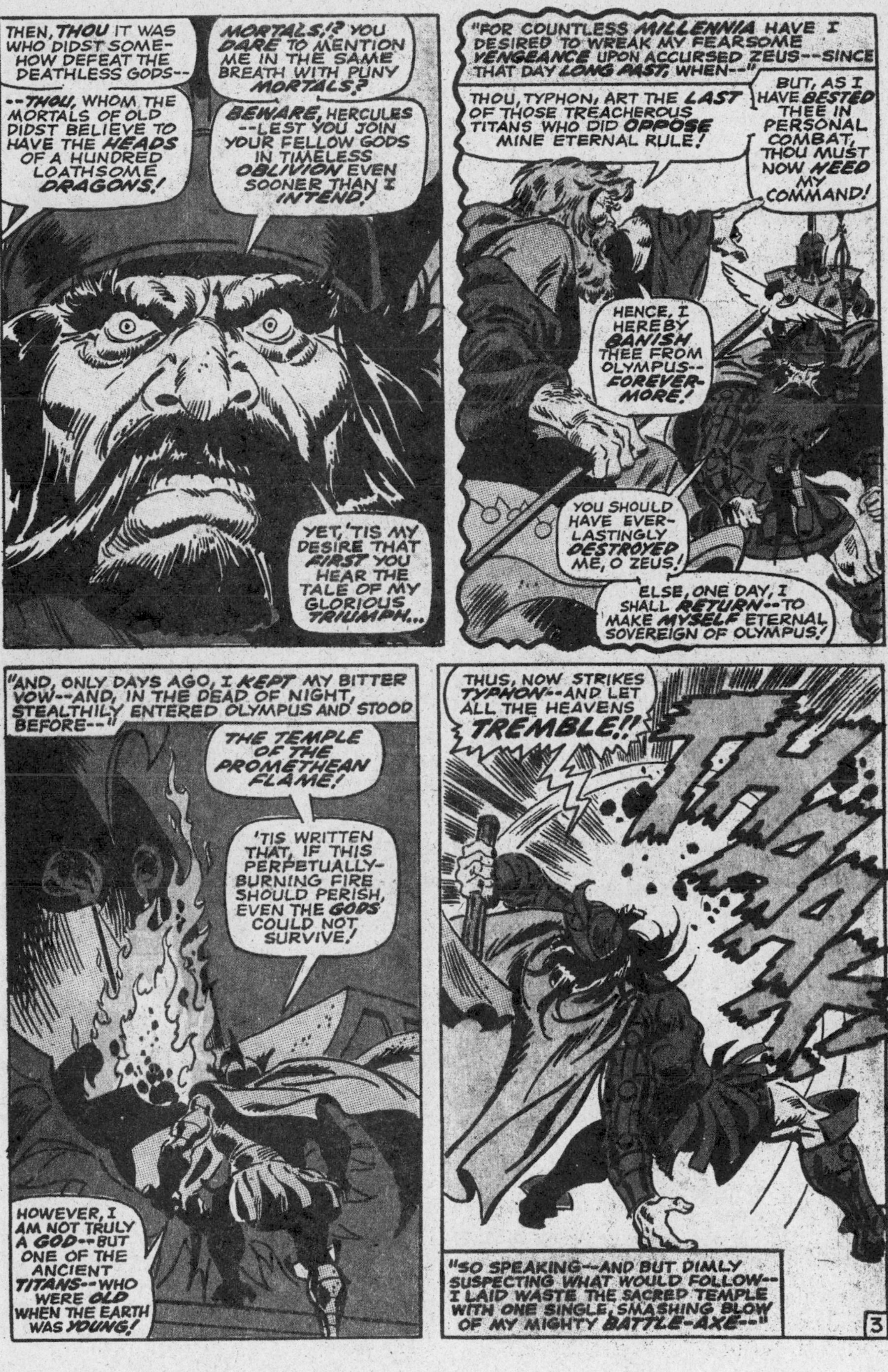

THEN, THOU IT WAS WHO DIDST SOMEHOW DEFEAT THE DEATHLESS GODS--
--THOU, WHOM THE MORTALS OF OLD DIDST BELIEVE TO HAVE THE HEADS OF A HUNDRED LOATHSOME DRAGONS!
MORTALS!? YOU DARE TO MENTION ME IN THE SAME BREATH WITH PUNY MORTALS?
BEWARE, HERCULES --LEST YOU JOIN YOUR FELLOW GODS IN TIMELESS OBLIVION EVEN SOONER THAN I INTEND!
YET, 'TIS MY DESIRE THAT FIRST YOU HEAR THE TALE OF MY GLORIOUS TRIUMPH...
"FOR COUNTLESS MILLENNIA HAVE I DESIRED TO WREAK MY FEARSOME VENGEANCE UPON ACCURSED ZEUS--SINCE THAT DAY LONG PAST, WHEN--"
THOU, TYPHON, ART THE LAST OF THOSE TREACHEROUS TITANS WHO DID OPPOSE MINE ETERNAL RULE!
BUT, AS I HAVE BESTED THEE IN PERSONAL COMBAT, THOU MUST NOW HEED MY COMMAND!
HENCE, I HEREBY BANISH THEE FROM OLYMPUS--FOREVERMORE!
YOU SHOULD HAVE EVERLASTINGLY DESTROYED ME, O ZEUS!
ELSE, ONE DAY, I SHALL RETURN--TO MAKE MYSELF ETERNAL SOVEREIGN OF OLYMPUS!
"AND, ONLY DAYS AGO, I KEPT MY BITTER VOW--AND, IN THE DEAD OF NIGHT, STEALTHILY ENTERED OLYMPUS AND STOOD BEFORE--"
THE TEMPLE OF THE PROMETHEAN FLAME!
'TIS WRITTEN THAT, IF THIS PERPETUALLY-BURNING FIRE SHOULD PERISH, EVEN THE GODS COULD NOT SURVIVE!
HOWEVER, I AM NOT TRULY A GOD--BUT ONE OF THE ANCIENT TITANS--WHO WERE OLD WHEN THE EARTH WAS YOUNG!
THUS, NOW STRIKES TYPHON--AND LET ALL THE HEAVENS TREMBLE!!
THAK
"SO SPEAKING--AND BUT DIMLY SUSPECTING WHAT WOULD FOLLOW--I LAID WASTE THE SACRED TEMPLE WITH ONE SINGLE, SMASHING BLOW OF MY MIGHTY BATTLE-AXE--"
3

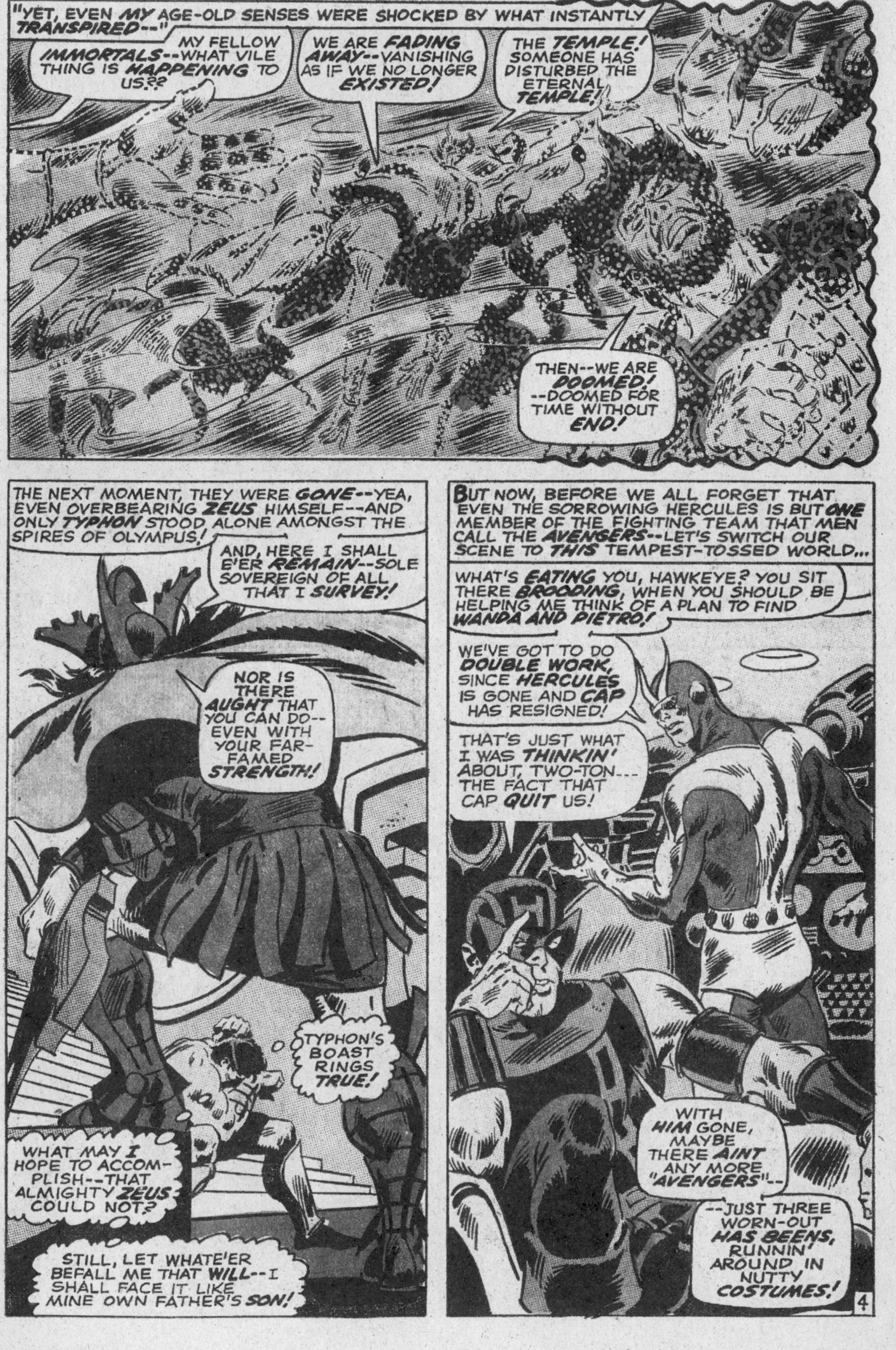

"YET, EVEN MY AGE-OLD SENSES WERE SHOCKED BY WHAT INSTANTLY TRANSPIRED--"
MY FELLOW IMMORTALS--WHAT VILE THING IS HAPPENING TO US?!?
WE ARE FADING AWAY--VANISHING AS IF WE NO LONGER EXISTED!
THE TEMPLE! SOMEONE HAS DISTURBED THE ETERNAL TEMPLE!
THEN--WE ARE DOOMED! --DOOMED FOR TIME WITHOUT END!
THE NEXT MOMENT, THEY WERE GONE--YEA, EVEN OVERBEARING ZEUS HIMSELF--AND ONLY TYPHON STOOD ALONE AMONGST THE SPIRES OF OLYMPUS!
AND, HERE I SHALL E'ER REMAIN--SOLE SOVEREIGN OF ALL THAT I SURVEY!
NOR IS THERE AUGHT THAT YOU CAN DO--EVEN WITH YOUR FAR-FAMED STRENGTH!
TYPHON'S BOAST RINGS TRUE!
WHAT MAY I HOPE TO ACCOMPLISH--THAT ALMIGHTY ZEUS COULD NOT?
STILL, LET WHATE'ER BEFALL ME THAT WILL--I SHALL FACE IT LIKE MINE OWN FATHER'S SON!
BUT NOW, BEFORE WE ALL FORGET THAT EVEN THE SORROWING HERCULES IS BUT ONE MEMBER OF THE FIGHTING TEAM THAT MEN CALL THE AVENGERS--LET'S SWITCH OUR SCENE TO THIS TEMPEST-TOSSED WORLD...
WHAT'S EATING YOU, HAWKEYE? YOU SIT THERE BROODING, WHEN YOU SHOULD BE HELPING ME THINK OF A PLAN TO FIND WANDA AND PIETRO!
WE'VE GOT TO DO DOUBLE WORK, SINCE HERCULES IS GONE AND CAP HAS RESIGNED!
THAT'S JUST WHAT I WAS THINKIN' ABOUT, TWO-TON--THE FACT THAT CAP QUIT US!
WITH HIM GONE, MAYBE THERE AINT ANY MORE "AVENGERS"--
--JUST THREE WORN-OUT HAS BEENS, RUNNIN' AROUND IN NUTTY COSTUMES!
4

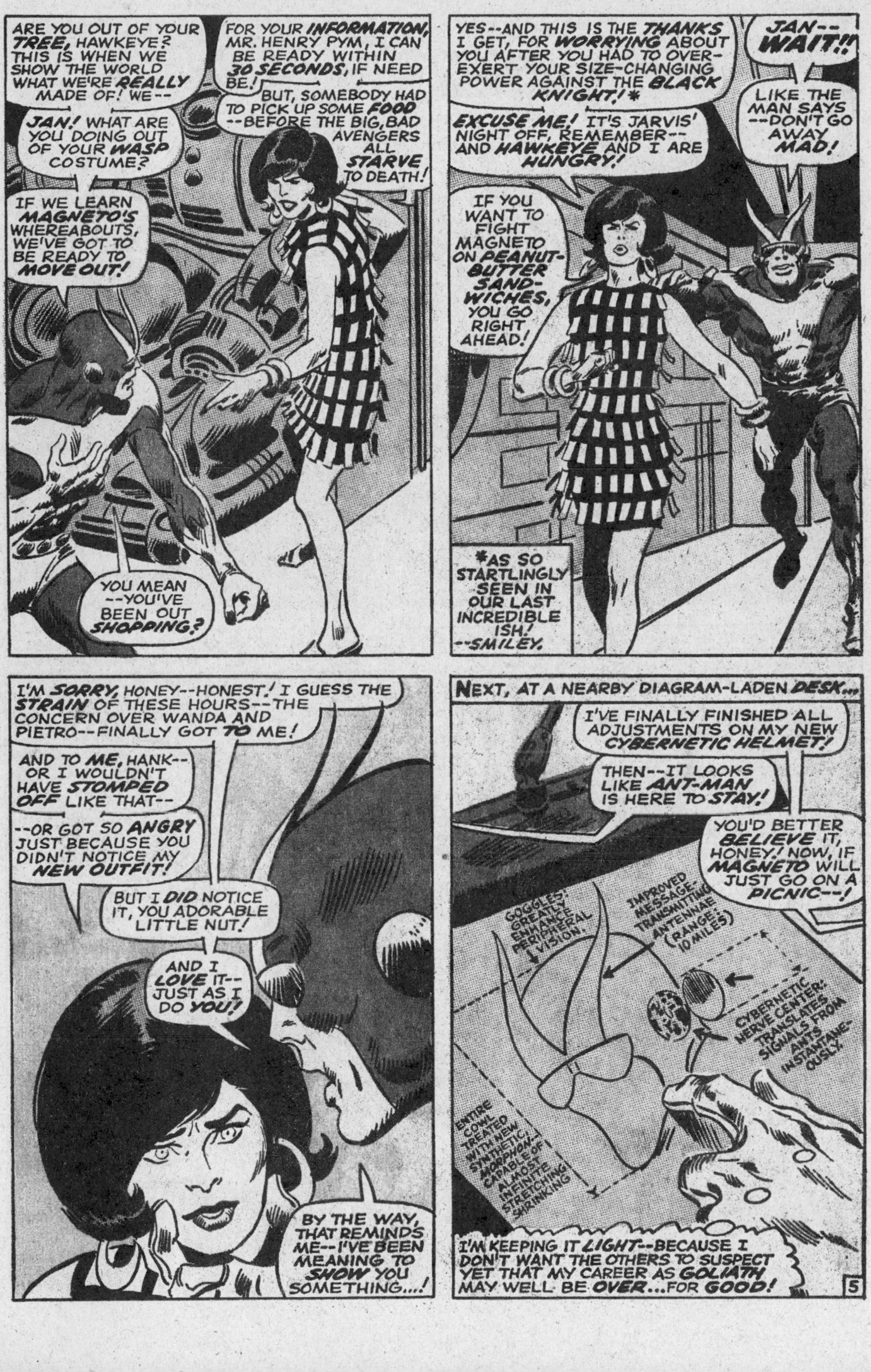
ARE YOU OUT OF YOUR TREE, HAWKEYE? THIS IS WHEN WE SHOW THE WORLD WHAT WE'RE REALLY MADE OF! WE--
FOR YOUR INFORMATION, MR. HENRY PYM, I CAN BE READY WITHIN 30 SECONDS, IF NEED BE!
BUT, SOMEBODY HAD TO PICK UP SOME FOOD --BEFORE THE BIG, BAD AVENGERS ALL STARVE TO DEATH!
JAN! WHAT ARE YOU DOING OUT OF YOUR WASP COSTUME?
IF WE LEARN MAGNETO'S WHEREABOUTS, WE'VE GOT TO BE READY TO MOVE OUT!
YOU MEAN --YOU'VE BEEN OUT SHOPPING?
YES--AND THIS IS THE THANKS I GET, FOR WORRYING ABOUT YOU AFTER YOU HAD TO OVER-EXERT YOUR SIZE-CHANGING POWER AGAINST THE BLACK KNIGHT! *
EXCUSE ME! IT'S JARVIS' NIGHT OFF, REMEMBER-- AND HAWKEYE AND I ARE HUNGRY!
IF YOU WANT TO FIGHT MAGNETO ON PEANUT-BUTTER SANDWICHES, YOU GO RIGHT AHEAD!
JAN-- WAIT!!
LIKE THE MAN SAYS --DON'T GO AWAY MAD!
*AS SO STARTLINGLY SEEN IN OUR LAST INCREDIBLE ISH! --SMILEY.
I'M SORRY, HONEY--HONEST! I GUESS THE STRAIN OF THESE HOURS--THE CONCERN OVER WANDA AND PIETRO--FINALLY GOT TO ME!
AND TO ME, HANK-- OR I WOULDN'T HAVE STOMPED OFF LIKE THAT--
--OR GOT SO ANGRY JUST BECAUSE YOU DIDN'T NOTICE MY NEW OUTFIT!
BUT I DID NOTICE IT, YOU ADORABLE LITTLE NUT!
AND I LOVE IT-- JUST AS I DO YOU!
BY THE WAY, THAT REMINDS ME--I'VE BEEN MEANING TO SHOW YOU SOMETHING...!
NEXT, AT A NEARBY DIAGRAM-LADEN DESK...
I'VE FINALLY FINISHED ALL ADJUSTMENTS ON MY NEW CYBERNETIC HELMET!
THEN--IT LOOKS LIKE ANT-MAN IS HERE TO STAY!
YOU'D BETTER BELIEVE IT, HONEY! NOW, IF MAGNETO WILL JUST GO ON A PICNIC--!
GOGGLES: GREATLY ENHANCE PERIPHERAL VISION.
IMPROVED MESSAGE-TRANSMITTING ANTENNAE (RANGE: 10 MILES)
CYBERNETIC NERVE CENTER: TRANSLATES SIGNALS FROM ANTS INSTANTANE-OUSLY.
ENTIRE COWL TREATED WITH NEW SYNTHETIC, MORPHON... CAPABLE OF ALMOST INFINITE STRETCHING! SHRINKING
I'M KEEPING IT LIGHT--BECAUSE I DON'T WANT THE OTHERS TO SUSPECT YET THAT MY CAREER AS GOLIATH MAY WELL BE OVER...FOR GOOD!
5

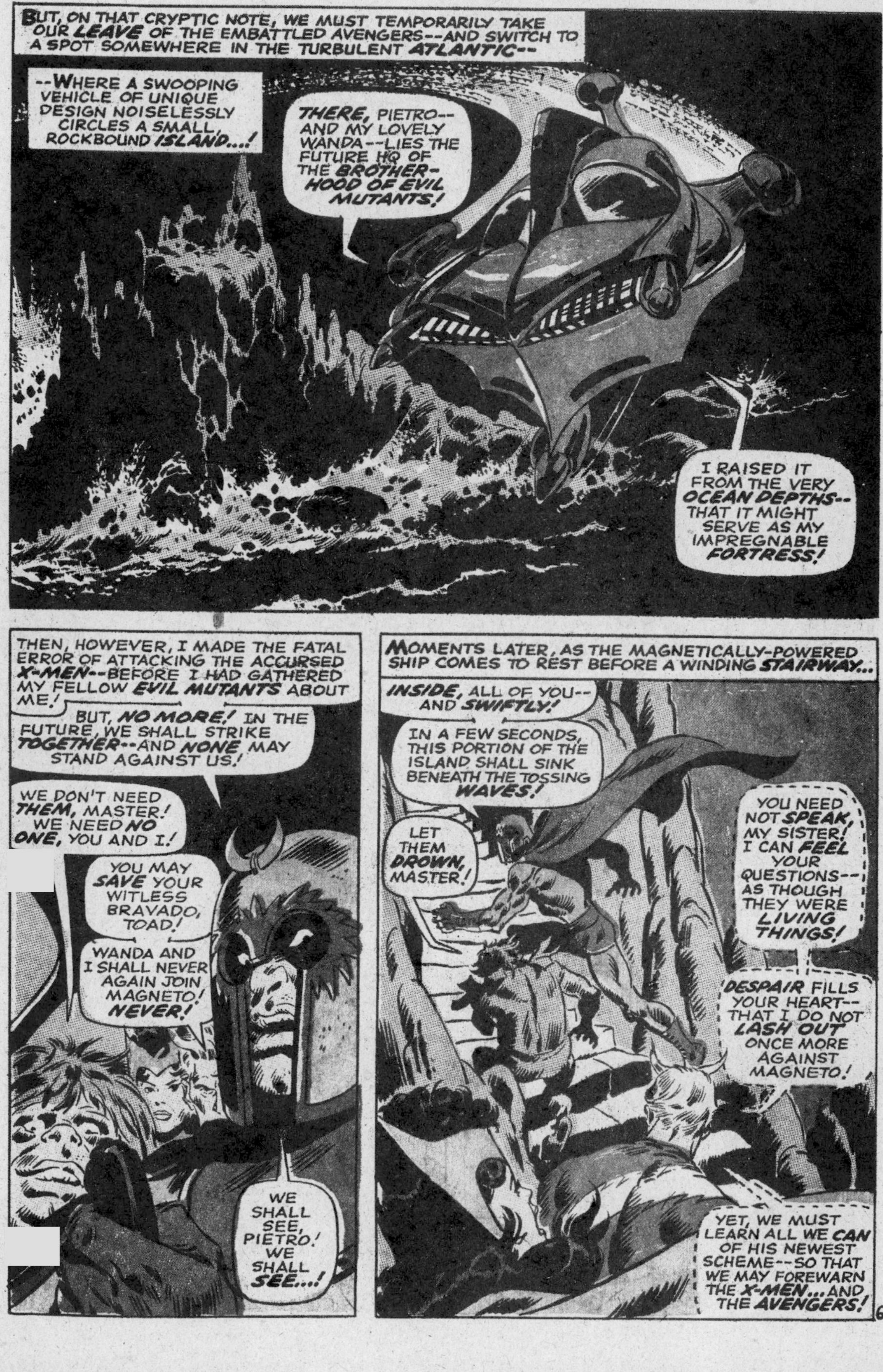
BUT, ON THAT CRYPTIC NOTE, WE MUST TEMPORARILY TAKE OUR LEAVE OF THE EMBATTLED AVENGERS--AND SWITCH TO A SPOT SOMEWHERE IN THE TURBULENT ATLANTIC--
--WHERE A SWOOPING VEHICLE OF UNIQUE DESIGN NOISELESSLY CIRCLES A SMALL, ROCKBOUND ISLAND...!
THERE, PIETRO--AND MY LOVELY WANDA--LIES THE FUTURE HQ OF THE BROTHER-HOOD OF EVIL MUTANTS!
I RAISED IT FROM THE VERY OCEAN DEPTHS--THAT IT MIGHT SERVE AS MY IMPREGNABLE FORTRESS!
THEN, HOWEVER, I MADE THE FATAL ERROR OF ATTACKING THE ACCURSED X-MEN--BEFORE I HAD GATHERED MY FELLOW EVIL MUTANTS ABOUT ME!
BUT, NO MORE! IN THE FUTURE, WE SHALL STRIKE TOGETHER--AND NONE MAY STAND AGAINST US!
WE DON'T NEED THEM, MASTER! WE NEED NO ONE, YOU AND I!
YOU MAY SAVE YOUR WITLESS BRAVADO, TOAD!
WANDA AND I SHALL NEVER AGAIN JOIN MAGNETO! NEVER!
WE SHALL SEE, PIETRO! WE SHALL SEE...!
MOMENTS LATER, AS THE MAGNETICALLY-POWERED SHIP COMES TO REST BEFORE A WINDING STAIRWAY...
INSIDE, ALL OF YOU--AND SWIFTLY!
IN A FEW SECONDS, THIS PORTION OF THE ISLAND SHALL SINK BENEATH THE TOSSING WAVES!
LET THEM DROWN, MASTER!
YOU NEED NOT SPEAK, MY SISTER! I CAN FEEL YOUR QUESTIONS--AS THOUGH THEY WERE LIVING THINGS!
DESPAIR FILLS YOUR HEART--THAT I DO NOT LASH OUT ONCE MORE AGAINST MAGNETO!
YET, WE MUST LEARN ALL WE CAN OF HIS NEWEST SCHEME--SO THAT WE MAY FOREWARN THE X-MEN...AND THE AVENGERS!
6.

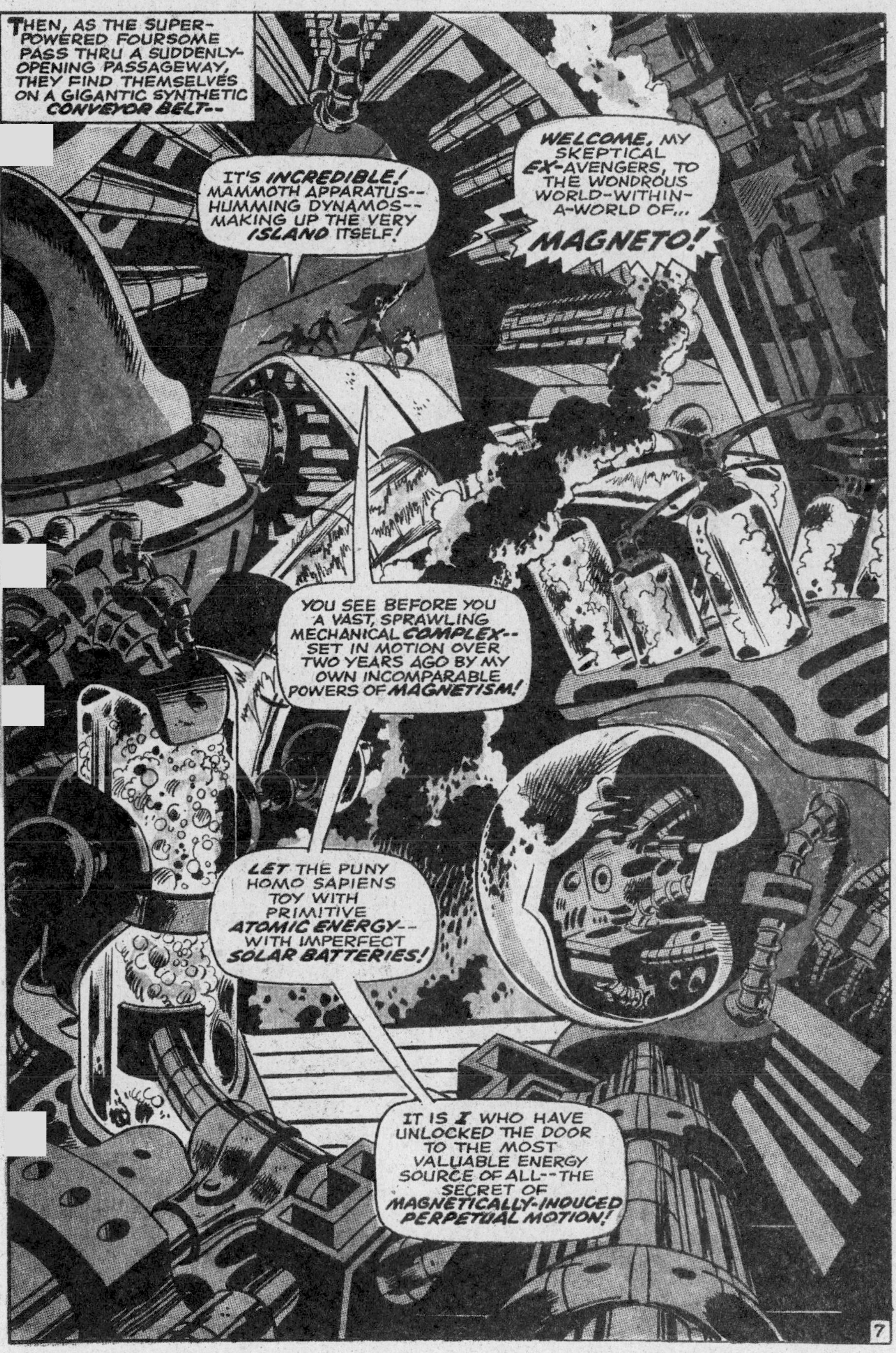

THEN, AS THE SUPER-POWERED FOURSOME PASS THRU A SUDDENLY-OPENING PASSAGEWAY, THEY FIND THEMSELVES ON A GIGANTIC SYNTHETIC CONVEYOR BELT--
IT'S INCREDIBLE! MAMMOTH APPARATUS--HUMMING DYNAMOS--MAKING UP THE VERY ISLAND ITSELF!
WELCOME, MY SKEPTICAL EX-AVENGERS, TO THE WONDROUS WORLD-WITHIN-A-WORLD OF... MAGNETO!
YOU SEE BEFORE YOU A VAST, SPRAWLING MECHANICAL COMPLEX--SET IN MOTION OVER TWO YEARS AGO BY MY OWN INCOMPARABLE POWERS OF MAGNETISM!
LET THE PUNY HOMO SAPIENS TOY WITH PRIMITIVE ATOMIC ENERGY--WITH IMPERFECT SOLAR BATTERIES!
IT IS I WHO HAVE UNLOCKED THE DOOR TO THE MOST VALUABLE ENERGY SOURCE OF ALL--THE SECRET OF MAGNETICALLY-INDUCED PERPETUAL MOTION!

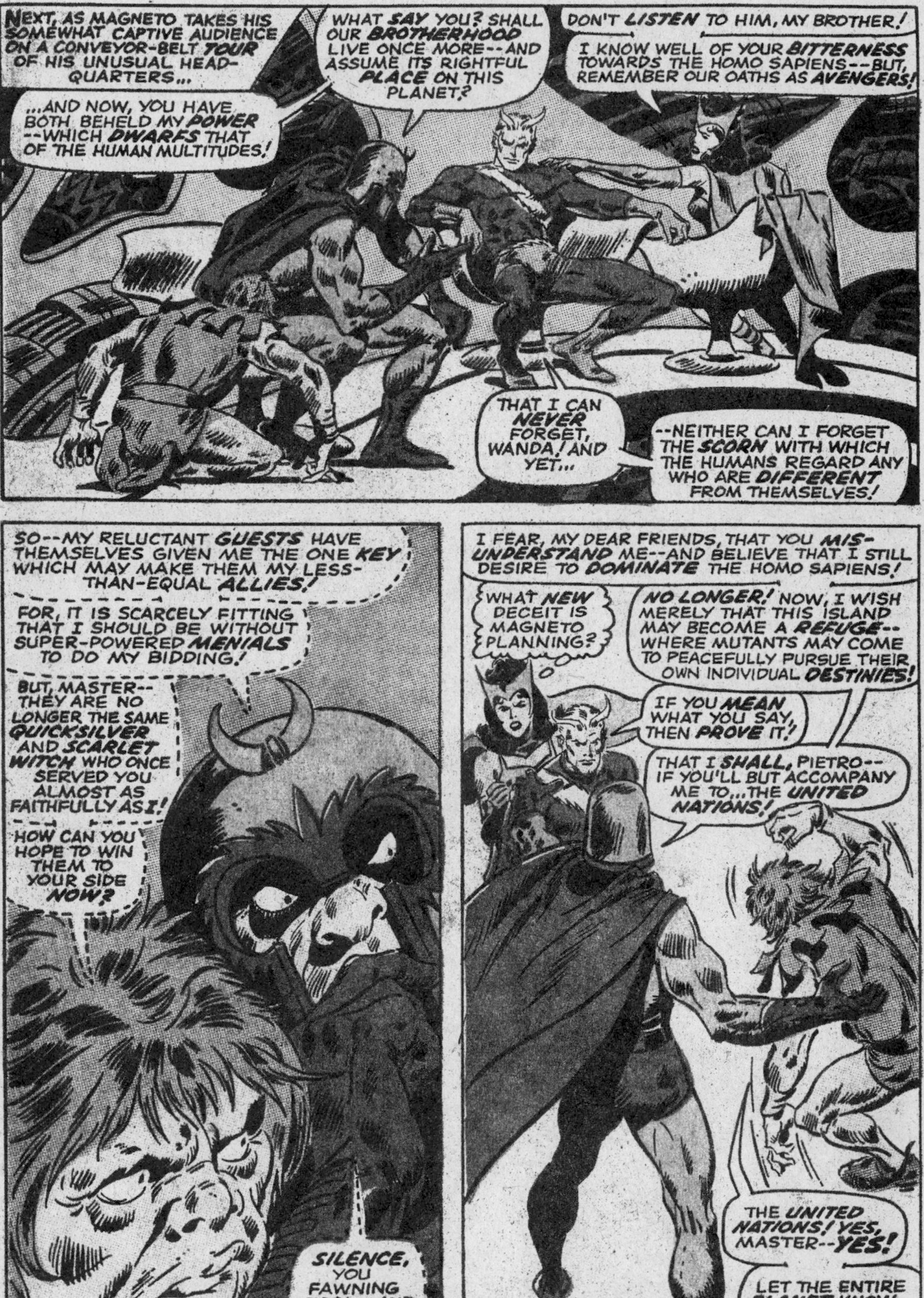
NEXT, AS MAGNETO TAKES HIS SOMEWHAT CAPTIVE AUDIENCE ON A CONVEYOR-BELT TOUR OF HIS UNUSUAL HEAD-QUARTERS...
...AND NOW, YOU HAVE BOTH BEHELD MY POWER --WHICH DWARFS THAT OF THE HUMAN MULTITUDES!
WHAT SAY YOU? SHALL OUR BROTHERHOOD LIVE ONCE MORE--AND ASSUME ITS RIGHTFUL PLACE ON THIS PLANET?
DON'T LISTEN TO HIM, MY BROTHER!
I KNOW WELL OF YOUR BITTERNESS TOWARDS THE HOMO SAPIENS--BUT, REMEMBER OUR OATHS AS AVENGERS!
THAT I CAN NEVER FORGET, WANDA! AND YET...
--NEITHER CAN I FORGET THE SCORN WITH WHICH THE HUMANS REGARD ANY WHO ARE DIFFERENT FROM THEMSELVES!
SO--MY RELUCTANT GUESTS HAVE THEMSELVES GIVEN ME THE ONE KEY WHICH MAY MAKE THEM MY LESS-THAN-EQUAL ALLIES!
FOR, IT IS SCARCELY FITTING THAT I SHOULD BE WITHOUT SUPER-POWERED MENIALS TO DO MY BIDDING!
BUT, MASTER--THEY ARE NO LONGER THE SAME QUICKSILVER AND SCARLET WITCH WHO ONCE SERVED YOU ALMOST AS FAITHFULLY AS I!
HOW CAN YOU HOPE TO WIN THEM TO YOUR SIDE NOW?
SILENCE, YOU FAWNING FOOL... AND OBSERVE!
I FEAR, MY DEAR FRIENDS, THAT YOU MIS-UNDERSTAND ME--AND BELIEVE THAT I STILL DESIRE TO DOMINATE THE HOMO SAPIENS!
WHAT NEW DECEIT IS MAGNETO PLANNING?
NO LONGER! NOW, I WISH MERELY THAT THIS ISLAND MAY BECOME A REFUGE--WHERE MUTANTS MAY COME TO PEACEFULLY PURSUE THEIR OWN INDIVIDUAL DESTINIES!
IF YOU MEAN WHAT YOU SAY, THEN PROVE IT!
THAT I SHALL, PIETRO--IF YOU'LL BUT ACCOMPANY ME TO... THE UNITED NATIONS!
THE UNITED NATIONS! YES, MASTER--YES!
LET THE ENTIRE PLANET KNOW THAT THE BROTHERHOOD OF EVIL MUTANTS IS BACK TO STAY!

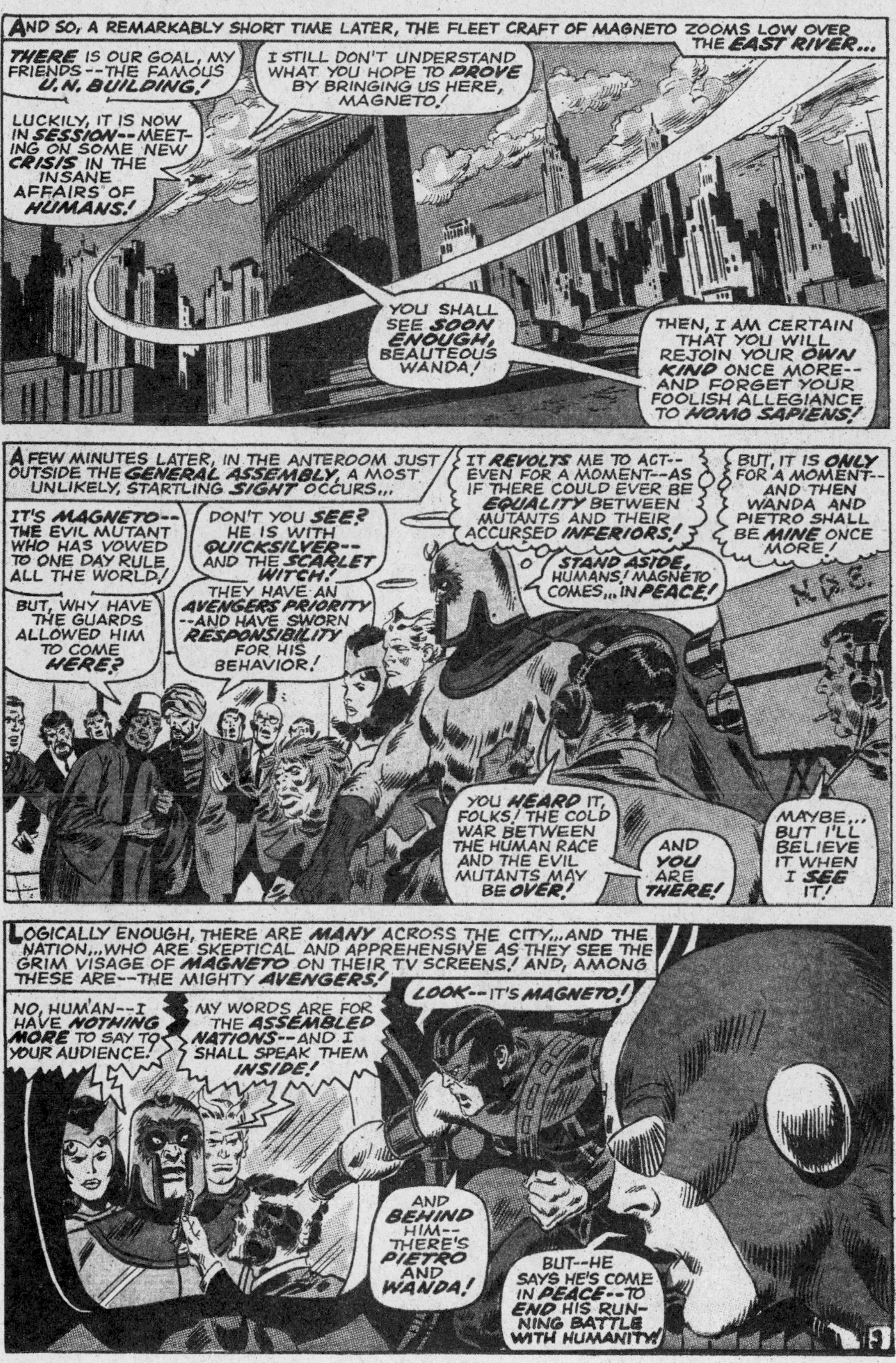
AND SO, A REMARKABLY SHORT TIME LATER, THE FLEET CRAFT OF MAGNETO ZOOMS LOW OVER THE EAST RIVER...
THERE IS OUR GOAL, MY FRIENDS--THE FAMOUS U.N. BUILDING!
LUCKILY, IT IS NOW IN SESSION--MEETING ON SOME NEW CRISIS IN THE INSANE AFFAIRS OF HUMANS!
I STILL DON'T UNDERSTAND WHAT YOU HOPE TO PROVE BY BRINGING US HERE, MAGNETO!
YOU SHALL SEE SOON ENOUGH, BEAUTEOUS WANDA!
THEN, I AM CERTAIN THAT YOU WILL REJOIN YOUR OWN KIND ONCE MORE--AND FORGET YOUR FOOLISH ALLEGIANCE TO HOMO SAPIENS!
A FEW MINUTES LATER, IN THE ANTEROOM JUST OUTSIDE THE GENERAL ASSEMBLY, A MOST UNLIKELY, STARTLING SIGHT OCCURS...
IT'S MAGNETO--THE EVIL MUTANT WHO HAS VOWED TO ONE DAY RULE ALL THE WORLD!
BUT, WHY HAVE THE GUARDS ALLOWED HIM TO COME HERE?
DON'T YOU SEE? HE IS WITH QUICKSILVER--AND THE SCARLET WITCH! THEY HAVE AN AVENGERS PRIORITY--AND HAVE SWORN RESPONSIBILITY FOR HIS BEHAVIOR!
IT REVOLTS ME TO ACT--EVEN FOR A MOMENT--AS IF THERE COULD EVER BE EQUALITY BETWEEN MUTANTS AND THEIR ACCURSED INFERIORS!
BUT, IT IS ONLY FOR A MOMENT--AND THEN WANDA AND PIETRO SHALL BE MINE ONCE MORE!
STAND ASIDE, HUMANS! MAGNETO COMES... IN PEACE!
N.B.C.
YOU HEARD IT, FOLKS! THE COLD WAR BETWEEN THE HUMAN RACE AND THE EVIL MUTANTS MAY BE OVER!
AND YOU ARE THERE!
MAYBE... BUT I'LL BELIEVE IT WHEN I SEE IT!
LOGICALLY ENOUGH, THERE ARE MANY ACROSS THE CITY... AND THE NATION... WHO ARE SKEPTICAL AND APPREHENSIVE AS THEY SEE THE GRIM VISAGE OF MAGNETO ON THEIR TV SCREENS! AND, AMONG THESE ARE--THE MIGHTY AVENGERS!
NO, HUMAN--I HAVE NOTHING MORE TO SAY TO YOUR AUDIENCE!
MY WORDS ARE FOR THE ASSEMBLED NATIONS--AND I SHALL SPEAK THEM INSIDE!
LOOK--IT'S MAGNETO!
AND BEHIND HIM--THERE'S PIETRO AND WANDA!
BUT--HE SAYS HE'S COME IN PEACE--TO END HIS RUNNING BATTLE WITH HUMANITY!

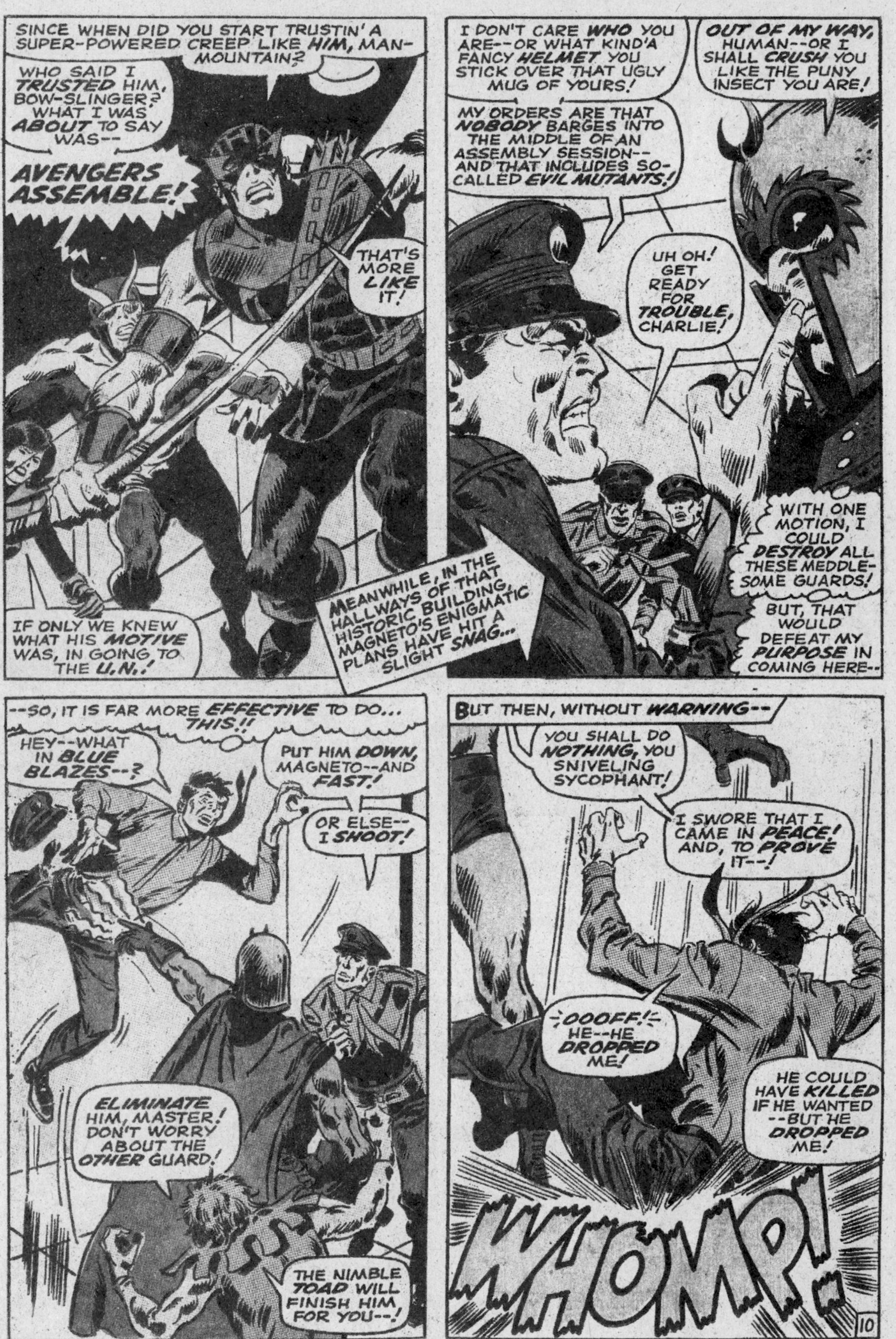

SINCE WHEN DID YOU START TRUSTIN' A SUPER-POWERED CREEP LIKE HIM, MAN-MOUNTAIN?
WHO SAID I TRUSTED HIM, BOW-SLINGER? WHAT I WAS ABOUT TO SAY WAS--
AVENGERS ASSEMBLE!
THAT'S MORE LIKE IT!
IF ONLY WE KNEW WHAT HIS MOTIVE WAS, IN GOING TO THE U.N.!
MEANWHILE, IN THE HALLWAYS OF THAT HISTORIC BUILDING, MAGNETO'S ENIGMATIC PLANS HAVE HIT A SLIGHT SNAG...
I DON'T CARE WHO YOU ARE--OR WHAT KIND'A FANCY HELMET YOU STICK OVER THAT UGLY MUG OF YOURS!
MY ORDERS ARE THAT NOBODY BARGES INTO THE MIDDLE OF AN ASSEMBLY SESSION--AND THAT INCLUDES SO-CALLED EVIL MUTANTS!
OUT OF MY WAY, HUMAN--OR I SHALL CRUSH YOU LIKE THE PUNY INSECT YOU ARE!
UH OH! GET READY FOR TROUBLE, CHARLIE!
WITH ONE MOTION, I COULD DESTROY ALL THESE MEDDLE-SOME GUARDS!
BUT, THAT WOULD DEFEAT MY PURPOSE IN COMING HERE--
--SO, IT IS FAR MORE EFFECTIVE TO DO... THIS!!
HEY--WHAT IN BLUE BLAZES--?
PUT HIM DOWN, MAGNETO--AND FAST!
OR ELSE--I SHOOT!
ELIMINATE HIM, MASTER! DON'T WORRY ABOUT THE OTHER GUARD!
THE NIMBLE TOAD WILL FINISH HIM FOR YOU--!
BUT THEN, WITHOUT WARNING--
YOU SHALL DO NOTHING, YOU SNIVELING SYCOPHANT!
I SWORE THAT I CAME IN PEACE! AND, TO PROVE IT--!
OOOFF! HE--HE DROPPED ME!
HE COULD HAVE KILLED IF HE WANTED--BUT HE DROPPED ME!
WHOMP!
10

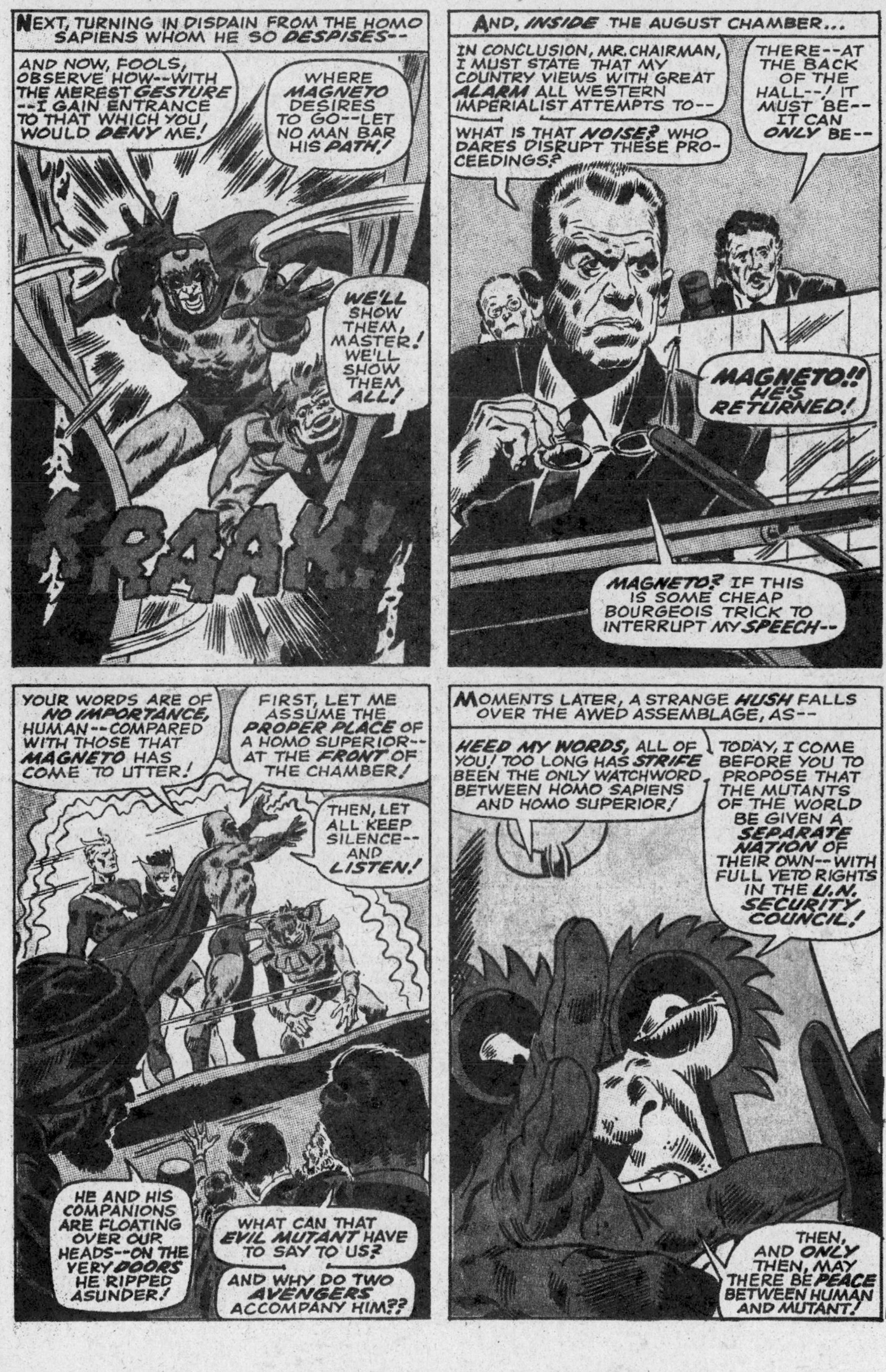

NEXT, TURNING IN DISDAIN FROM THE HOMO SAPIENS WHOM HE SO DESPISES--
AND NOW, FOOLS, OBSERVE HOW--WITH THE MEREST GESTURE--I GAIN ENTRANCE TO THAT WHICH YOU WOULD DENY ME!
WHERE MAGNETO DESIRES TO GO--LET NO MAN BAR HIS PATH!
WE'LL SHOW THEM, MASTER! WE'LL SHOW THEM ALL!
KRAAK!
AND, INSIDE THE AUGUST CHAMBER...
IN CONCLUSION, MR. CHAIRMAN, I MUST STATE THAT MY COUNTRY VIEWS WITH GREAT ALARM ALL WESTERN IMPERIALIST ATTEMPTS TO--
WHAT IS THAT NOISE? WHO DARES DISRUPT THESE PROCEEDINGS?
THERE--AT THE BACK OF THE HALL--! IT MUST BE--IT CAN ONLY BE--
MAGNETO!! HE'S RETURNED!
MAGNETO? IF THIS IS SOME CHEAP BOURGEOIS TRICK TO INTERRUPT MY SPEECH--
YOUR WORDS ARE OF NO IMPORTANCE, HUMAN--COMPARED WITH THOSE THAT MAGNETO HAS COME TO UTTER!
FIRST, LET ME ASSUME THE PROPER PLACE OF A HOMO SUPERIOR--AT THE FRONT OF THE CHAMBER!
THEN, LET ALL KEEP SILENCE--AND LISTEN!
HE AND HIS COMPANIONS ARE FLOATING OVER OUR HEADS--ON THE VERY DOORS HE RIPPED ASUNDER!
WHAT CAN THAT EVIL MUTANT HAVE TO SAY TO US?
AND WHY DO TWO AVENGERS ACCOMPANY HIM??
MOMENTS LATER, A STRANGE HUSH FALLS OVER THE AWED ASSEMBLAGE, AS--
HEED MY WORDS, ALL OF YOU! TOO LONG HAS STRIFE BEEN THE ONLY WATCHWORD BETWEEN HOMO SAPIENS AND HOMO SUPERIOR!
TODAY, I COME BEFORE YOU TO PROPOSE THAT THE MUTANTS OF THE WORLD BE GIVEN A SEPARATE NATION OF THEIR OWN--WITH FULL VETO RIGHTS IN THE U.N. SECURITY COUNCIL!
THEN, AND ONLY THEN, MAY THERE BE PEACE BETWEEN HUMAN AND MUTANT!
11.

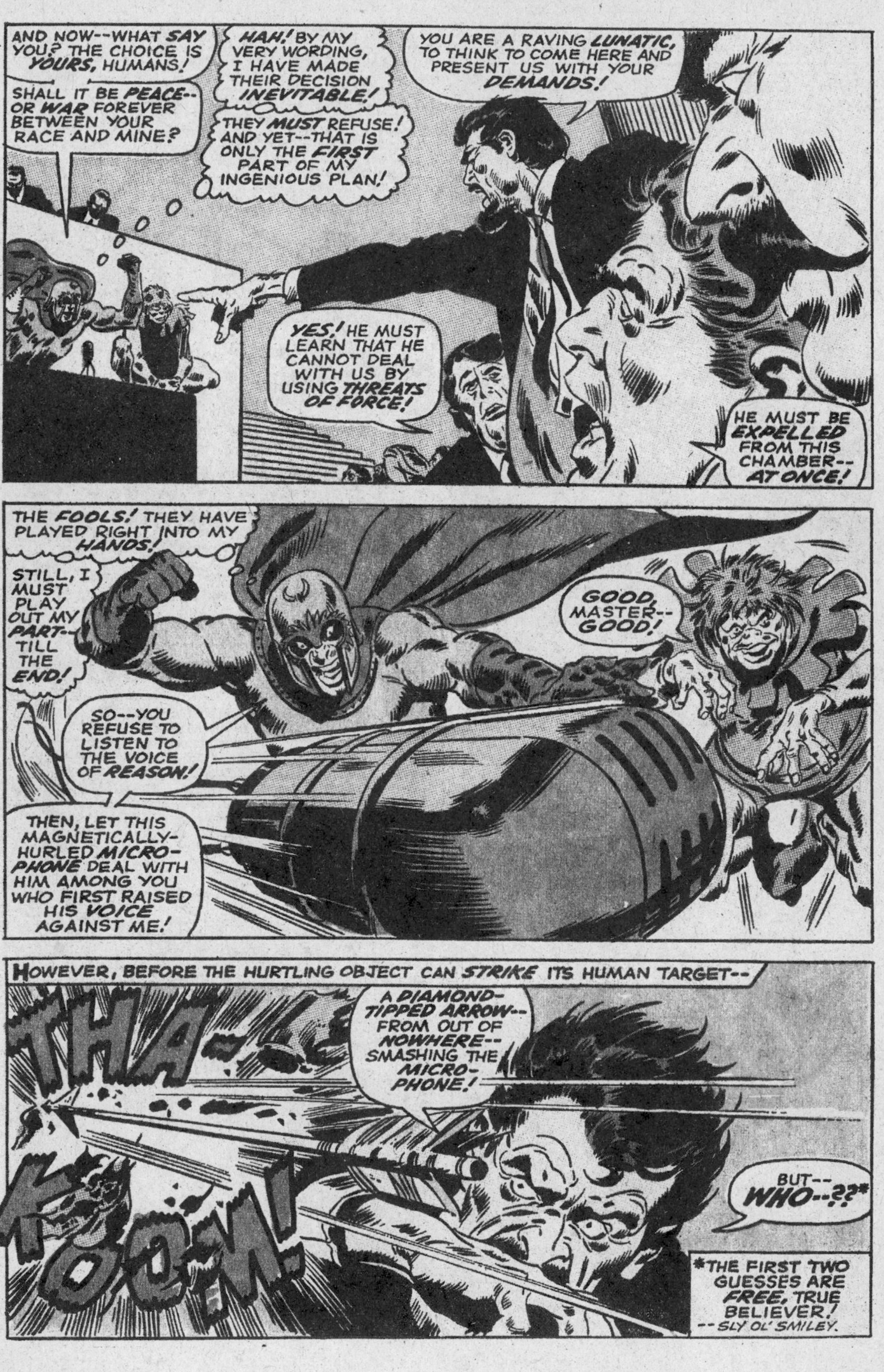

AND NOW--WHAT SAY YOU? THE CHOICE IS YOURS, HUMANS!
SHALL IT BE PEACE--OR WAR FOREVER BETWEEN YOUR RACE AND MINE?
HAH! BY MY VERY WORDING, I HAVE MADE THEIR DECISION INEVITABLE!
THEY MUST REFUSE! AND YET--THAT IS ONLY THE FIRST PART OF MY INGENIOUS PLAN!
YOU ARE A RAVING LUNATIC, TO THINK TO COME HERE AND PRESENT US WITH YOUR DEMANDS!
YES! HE MUST LEARN THAT HE CANNOT DEAL WITH US BY USING THREATS OF FORCE!
HE MUST BE EXPELLED FROM THIS CHAMBER--AT ONCE!
THE FOOLS! THEY HAVE PLAYED RIGHT INTO MY HANDS!
STILL, I MUST PLAY OUT MY PART--TILL THE END!
GOOD, MASTER--GOOD!
SO--YOU REFUSE TO LISTEN TO THE VOICE OF REASON!
THEN, LET THIS MAGNETICALLY-HURLED MICROPHONE DEAL WITH HIM AMONG YOU WHO FIRST RAISED HIS VOICE AGAINST ME!
HOWEVER, BEFORE THE HURTLING OBJECT CAN STRIKE ITS HUMAN TARGET--
THA-KOOM!
A DIAMOND-TIPPED ARROW--FROM OUT OF NOWHERE--SMASHING THE MICROPHONE!
BUT--WHO--??*
*THE FIRST TWO GUESSES ARE FREE, TRUE BELIEVER! --SLY OL' SMILEY.

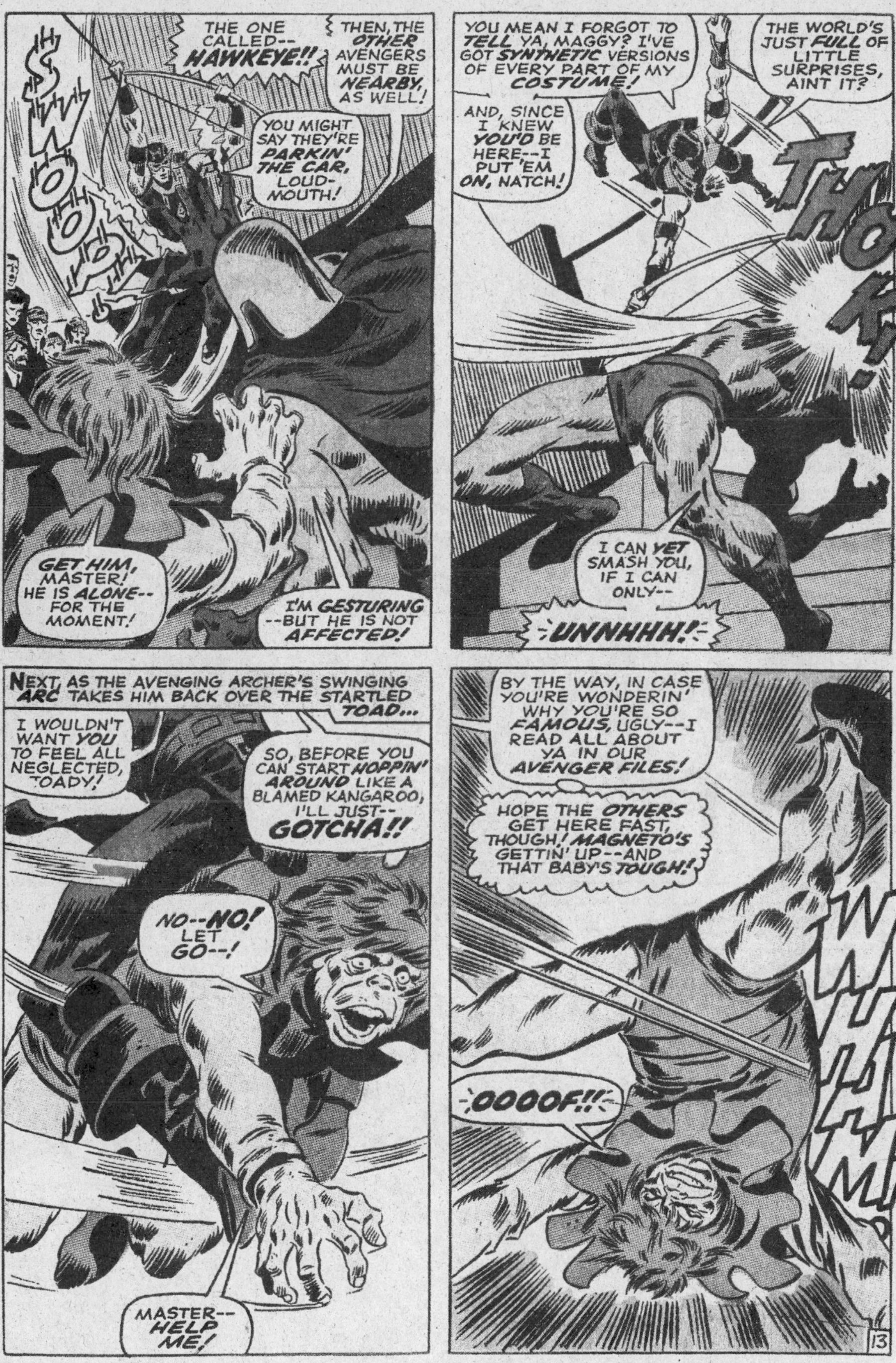
SWOOOSH
THE ONE CALLED-- HAWKEYE!!
THEN, THE OTHER AVENGERS MUST BE NEARBY, AS WELL!
YOU MIGHT SAY THEY'RE PARKIN' THE CAR, LOUD-MOUTH!
GET HIM, MASTER! HE IS ALONE-- FOR THE MOMENT!
I'M GESTURING --BUT HE IS NOT AFFECTED!
YOU MEAN I FORGOT TO TELL YA, MAGGY? I'VE GOT SYNTHETIC VERSIONS OF EVERY PART OF MY COSTUME!
AND, SINCE I KNEW YOU'D BE HERE--I PUT 'EM ON, NATCH!
THE WORLD'S JUST FULL OF LITTLE SURPRISES, AINT IT?
THOK!
I CAN YET SMASH YOU, IF I CAN ONLY--
UNNHHH!
NEXT, AS THE AVENGING ARCHER'S SWINGING ARC TAKES HIM BACK OVER THE STARTLED TOAD...
I WOULDN'T WANT YOU TO FEEL ALL NEGLECTED, TOADY!
SO, BEFORE YOU CAN START HOPPIN' AROUND LIKE A BLAMED KANGAROO, I'LL JUST-- GOTCHA!!
NO--NO! LET GO--!
MASTER-- HELP ME!
BY THE WAY, IN CASE YOU'RE WONDERIN' WHY YOU'RE SO FAMOUS, UGLY--I READ ALL ABOUT YA IN OUR AVENGER FILES!
HOPE THE OTHERS GET HERE FAST, THOUGH! MAGNETO'S GETTIN' UP--AND THAT BABY'S TOUGH!
WHHAM!
OOOOF!!
13

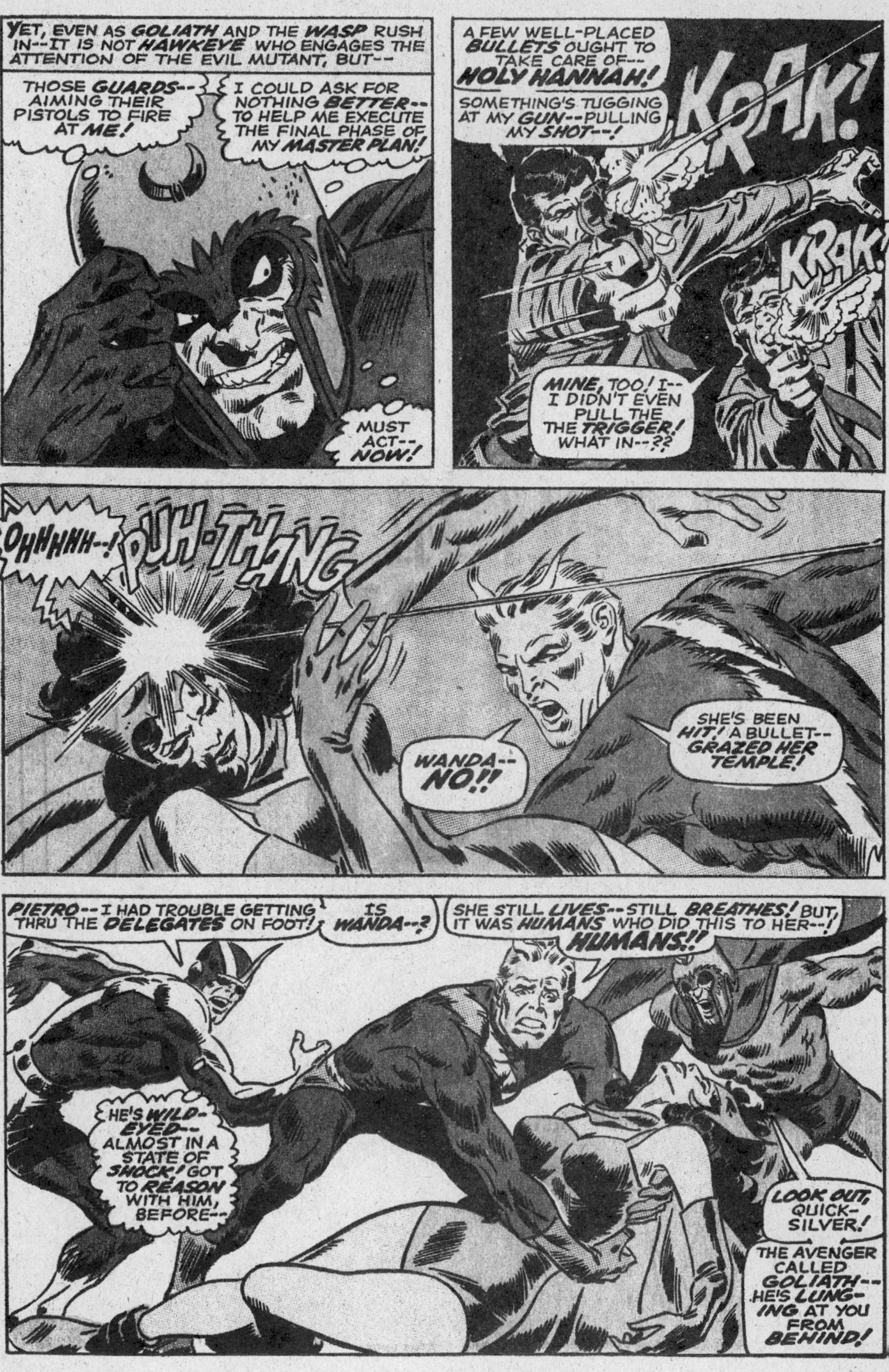
YET, EVEN AS GOLIATH AND THE WASP RUSH IN--IT IS NOT HAWKEYE WHO ENGAGES THE ATTENTION OF THE EVIL MUTANT, BUT--
THOSE GUARDS--AIMING THEIR PISTOLS TO FIRE AT ME!
I COULD ASK FOR NOTHING BETTER--TO HELP ME EXECUTE THE FINAL PHASE OF MY MASTER PLAN!
MUST ACT--NOW!
A FEW WELL-PLACED BULLETS OUGHT TO TAKE CARE OF--HOLY HANNAH!
SOMETHING'S TUGGING AT MY GUN--PULLING MY SHOT--!
KRAK!
KRAK!
MINE, TOO! I--I DIDN'T EVEN PULL THE THE TRIGGER! WHAT IN--??
OHHHHH--!
PUH-THANG
WANDA--NO!!
SHE'S BEEN HIT! A BULLET--GRAZED HER TEMPLE!
PIETRO--I HAD TROUBLE GETTING THRU THE DELEGATES ON FOOT!
IS WANDA--?
SHE STILL LIVES--STILL BREATHES! BUT, IT WAS HUMANS WHO DID THIS TO HER--! HUMANS!!
HE'S WILD-EYED--ALMOST IN A STATE OF SHOCK! GOT TO REASON WITH HIM, BEFORE--
LOOK OUT, QUICK-SILVER!
THE AVENGER CALLED GOLIATH--HE'S LUNGING AT YOU FROM BEHIND!

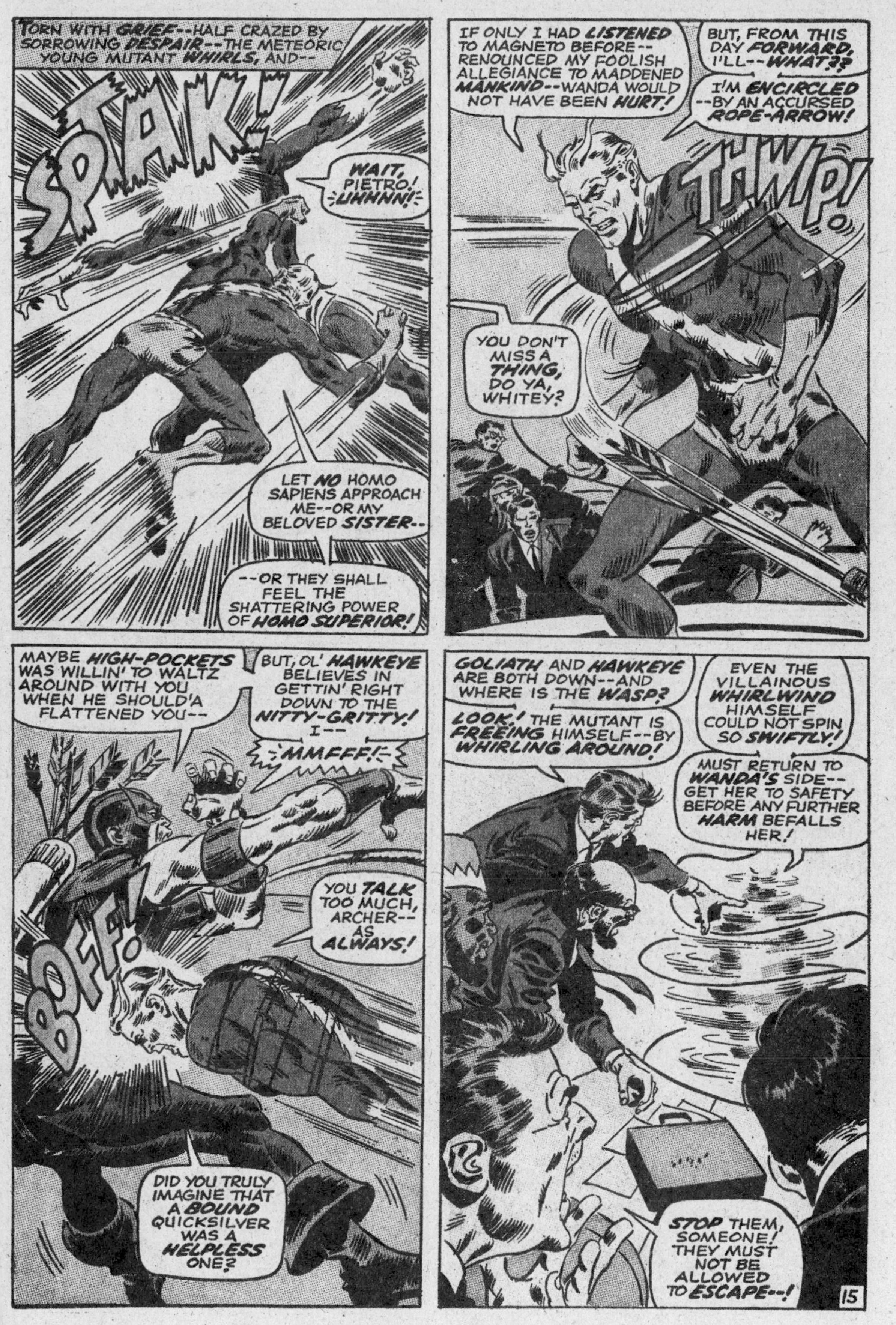
TORN WITH GRIEF--HALF CRAZED BY SORROWING DESPAIR--THE METEORIC YOUNG MUTANT WHIRLS, AND--
SPTAK!
WAIT, PIETRO! UHHNNN!
LET NO HOMO SAPIENS APPROACH ME--OR MY BELOVED SISTER--
--OR THEY SHALL FEEL THE SHATTERING POWER OF HOMO SUPERIOR!
IF ONLY I HAD LISTENED TO MAGNETO BEFORE--RENOUNCED MY FOOLISH ALLEGIANCE TO MADDENED MANKIND--WANDA WOULD NOT HAVE BEEN HURT!
BUT, FROM THIS DAY FORWARD, I'LL--WHAT??
I'M ENCIRCLED--BY AN ACCURSED ROPE-ARROW!
THWIP!
YOU DON'T MISS A THING, DO YA, WHITEY?
MAYBE HIGH-POCKETS WAS WILLIN' TO WALTZ AROUND WITH YOU WHEN HE SHOULD'A FLATTENED YOU--
BUT, OL' HAWKEYE BELIEVES IN GETTIN' RIGHT DOWN TO THE NITTY-GRITTY! I--
MMFFF!
YOU TALK TOO MUCH, ARCHER--AS ALWAYS!
BOFF!
DID YOU TRULY IMAGINE THAT A BOUND QUICKSILVER WAS A HELPLESS ONE?
GOLIATH AND HAWKEYE ARE BOTH DOWN--AND WHERE IS THE WASP?
LOOK! THE MUTANT IS FREEING HIMSELF--BY WHIRLING AROUND!
EVEN THE VILLAINOUS WHIRLWIND HIMSELF COULD NOT SPIN SO SWIFTLY!
MUST RETURN TO WANDA'S SIDE--GET HER TO SAFETY BEFORE ANY FURTHER HARM BEFALLS HER!
STOP THEM, SOMEONE! THEY MUST NOT BE ALLOWED TO ESCAPE--!
15

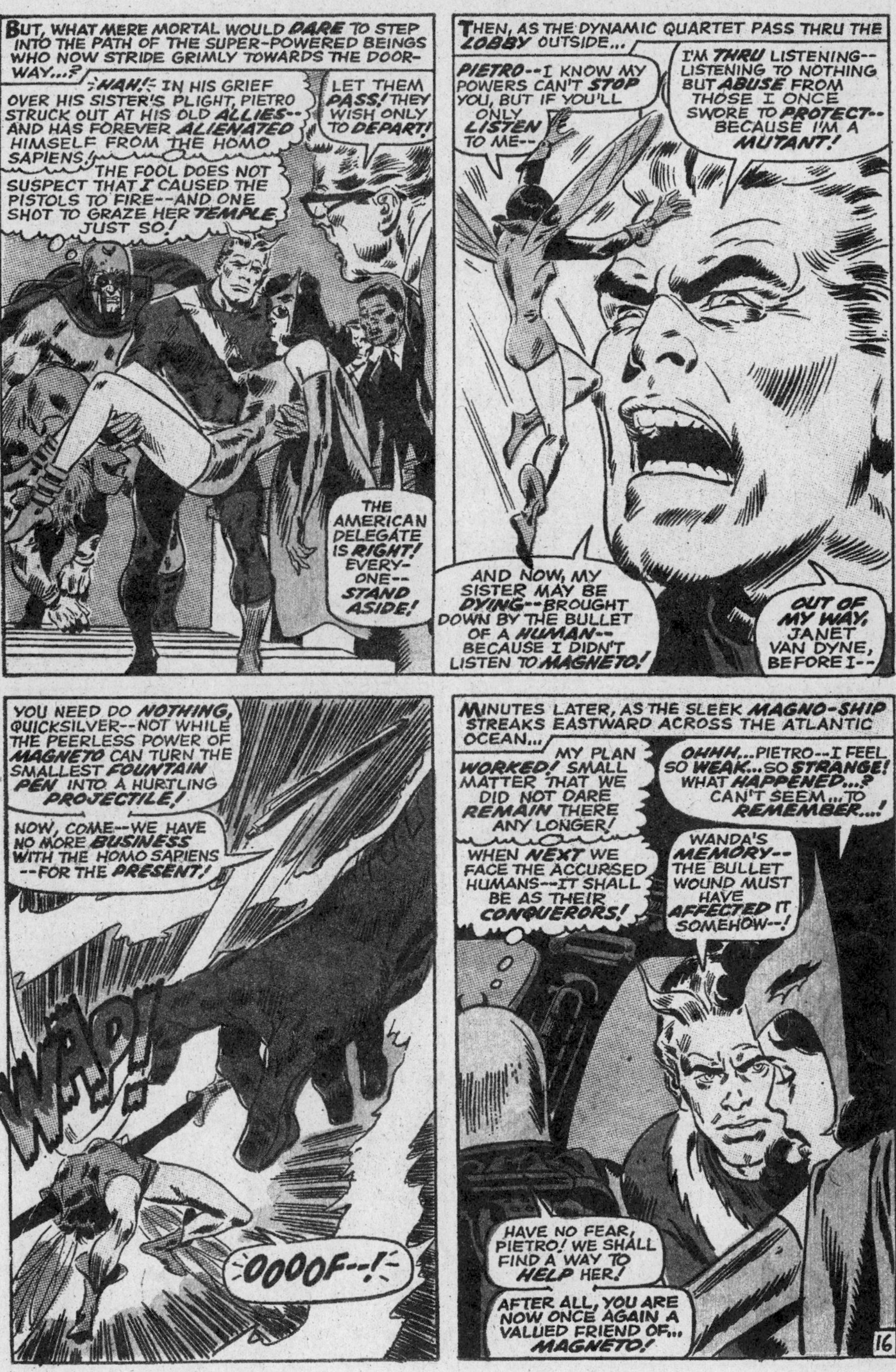
BUT, WHAT MERE MORTAL WOULD DARE TO STEP INTO THE PATH OF THE SUPER-POWERED BEINGS WHO NOW STRIDE GRIMLY TOWARDS THE DOOR-WAY...?
NAH! IN HIS GRIEF OVER HIS SISTER'S PLIGHT, PIETRO STRUCK OUT AT HIS OLD ALLIES--AND HAS FOREVER ALIENATED HIMSELF FROM THE HOMO SAPIENS!
THE FOOL DOES NOT SUSPECT THAT I CAUSED THE PISTOLS TO FIRE--AND ONE SHOT TO GRAZE HER TEMPLE JUST SO!
LET THEM PASS! THEY WISH ONLY TO DEPART!
THE AMERICAN DELEGATE IS RIGHT! EVERY-ONE--STAND ASIDE!
THEN, AS THE DYNAMIC QUARTET PASS THRU THE LOBBY OUTSIDE...
PIETRO--I KNOW MY POWERS CAN'T STOP YOU, BUT IF YOU'LL ONLY LISTEN TO ME--
I'M THRU LISTENING--LISTENING TO NOTHING BUT ABUSE FROM THOSE I ONCE SWORE TO PROTECT--BECAUSE I'M A MUTANT!
AND NOW, MY SISTER MAY BE DYING--BROUGHT DOWN BY THE BULLET OF A HUMAN--BECAUSE I DIDN'T LISTEN TO MAGNETO!
OUT OF MY WAY, JANET VAN DYNE, BEFORE I--
YOU NEED DO NOTHING, QUICKSILVER--NOT WHILE THE PEERLESS POWER OF MAGNETO CAN TURN THE SMALLEST FOUNTAIN PEN INTO A HURTLING PROJECTILE!
NOW, COME--WE HAVE NO MORE BUSINESS WITH THE HOMO SAPIENS--FOR THE PRESENT!
WAP!
OOOOF--!
MINUTES LATER, AS THE SLEEK MAGNO-SHIP STREAKS EASTWARD ACROSS THE ATLANTIC OCEAN...
MY PLAN WORKED! SMALL MATTER THAT WE DID NOT DARE REMAIN THERE ANY LONGER!
WHEN NEXT WE FACE THE ACCURSED HUMANS--IT SHALL BE AS THEIR CONQUERORS!
OHHH...PIETRO--I FEEL SO WEAK...SO STRANGE! WHAT HAPPENED...? CAN'T SEEM...TO REMEMBER...!
WANDA'S MEMORY--THE BULLET WOUND MUST HAVE AFFECTED IT SOMEHOW--!
HAVE NO FEAR, PIETRO! WE SHALL FIND A WAY TO HELP HER!
AFTER ALL, YOU ARE NOW ONCE AGAIN A VALUED FRIEND OF... MAGNETO!

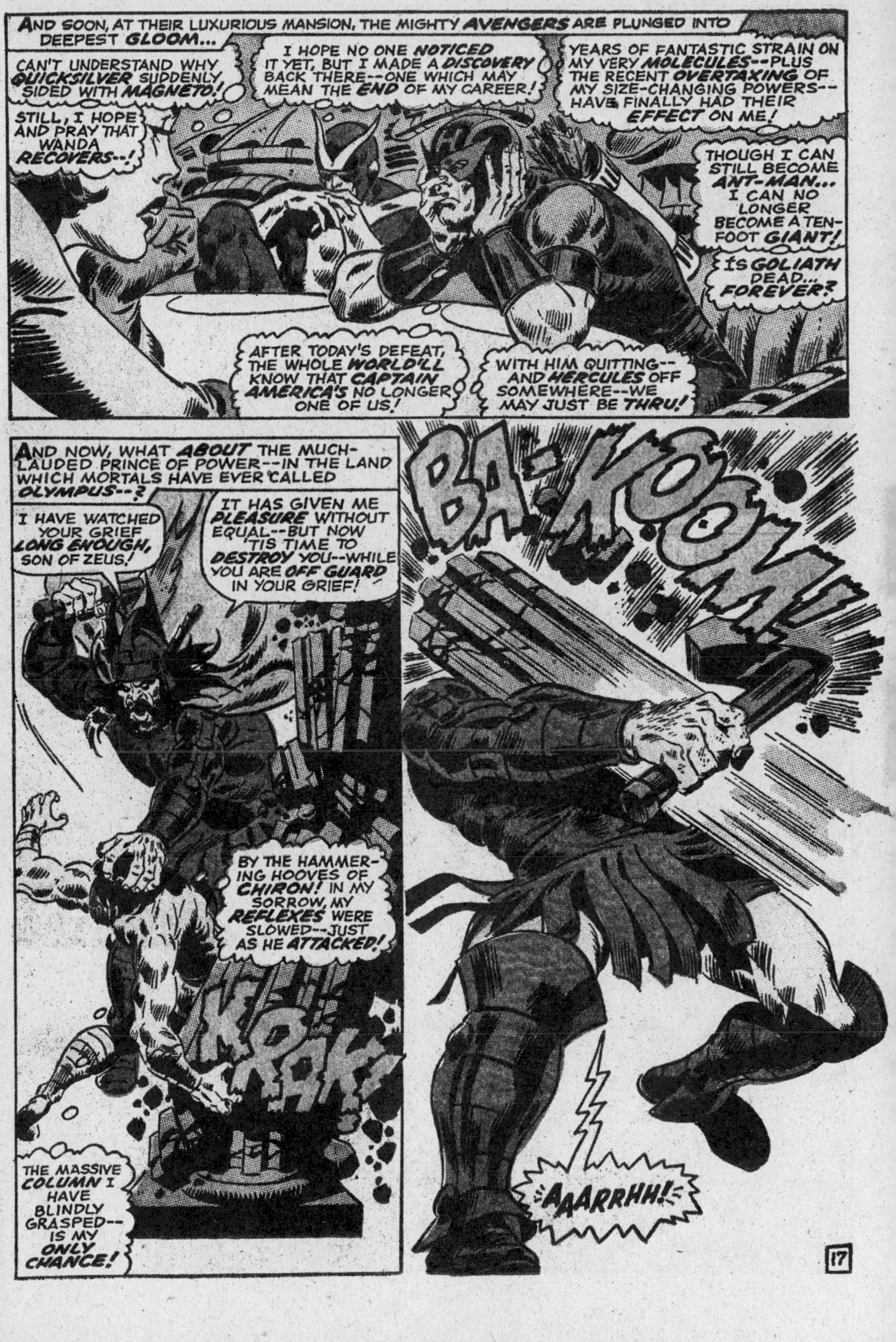
AND SOON, AT THEIR LUXURIOUS MANSION, THE MIGHTY AVENGERS ARE PLUNGED INTO DEEPEST GLOOM...
CAN'T UNDERSTAND WHY QUICKSILVER SUDDENLY SIDED WITH MAGNETO!
STILL, I HOPE AND PRAY THAT WANDA RECOVERS--!
I HOPE NO ONE NOTICED IT YET, BUT I MADE A DISCOVERY BACK THERE--ONE WHICH MAY MEAN THE END OF MY CAREER!
YEARS OF FANTASTIC STRAIN ON MY VERY MOLECULES--PLUS THE RECENT OVERTAXING OF MY SIZE-CHANGING POWERS--HAVE FINALLY HAD THEIR EFFECT ON ME!
THOUGH I CAN STILL BECOME ANT-MAN... I CAN NO LONGER BECOME A TEN-FOOT GIANT!
IS GOLIATH DEAD... FOREVER?
AFTER TODAY'S DEFEAT, THE WHOLE WORLD'LL KNOW THAT CAPTAIN AMERICA'S NO LONGER ONE OF US!
WITH HIM QUITTING--AND HERCULES OFF SOMEWHERE--WE MAY JUST BE THRU!
AND NOW, WHAT ABOUT THE MUCH-LAUDED PRINCE OF POWER--IN THE LAND WHICH MORTALS HAVE EVER CALLED OLYMPUS--?
I HAVE WATCHED YOUR GRIEF LONG ENOUGH, SON OF ZEUS!
IT HAS GIVEN ME PLEASURE WITHOUT EQUAL--BUT NOW 'TIS TIME TO DESTROY YOU--WHILE YOU ARE OFF GUARD IN YOUR GRIEF!
BA-KOOM!
BY THE HAMMERING HOOVES OF CHIRON! IN MY SORROW, MY REFLEXES WERE SLOWED--JUST AS HE ATTACKED!
KRAK!
THE MASSIVE COLUMN I HAVE BLINDLY GRASPED--IS MY ONLY CHANCE!
AAARRHH!

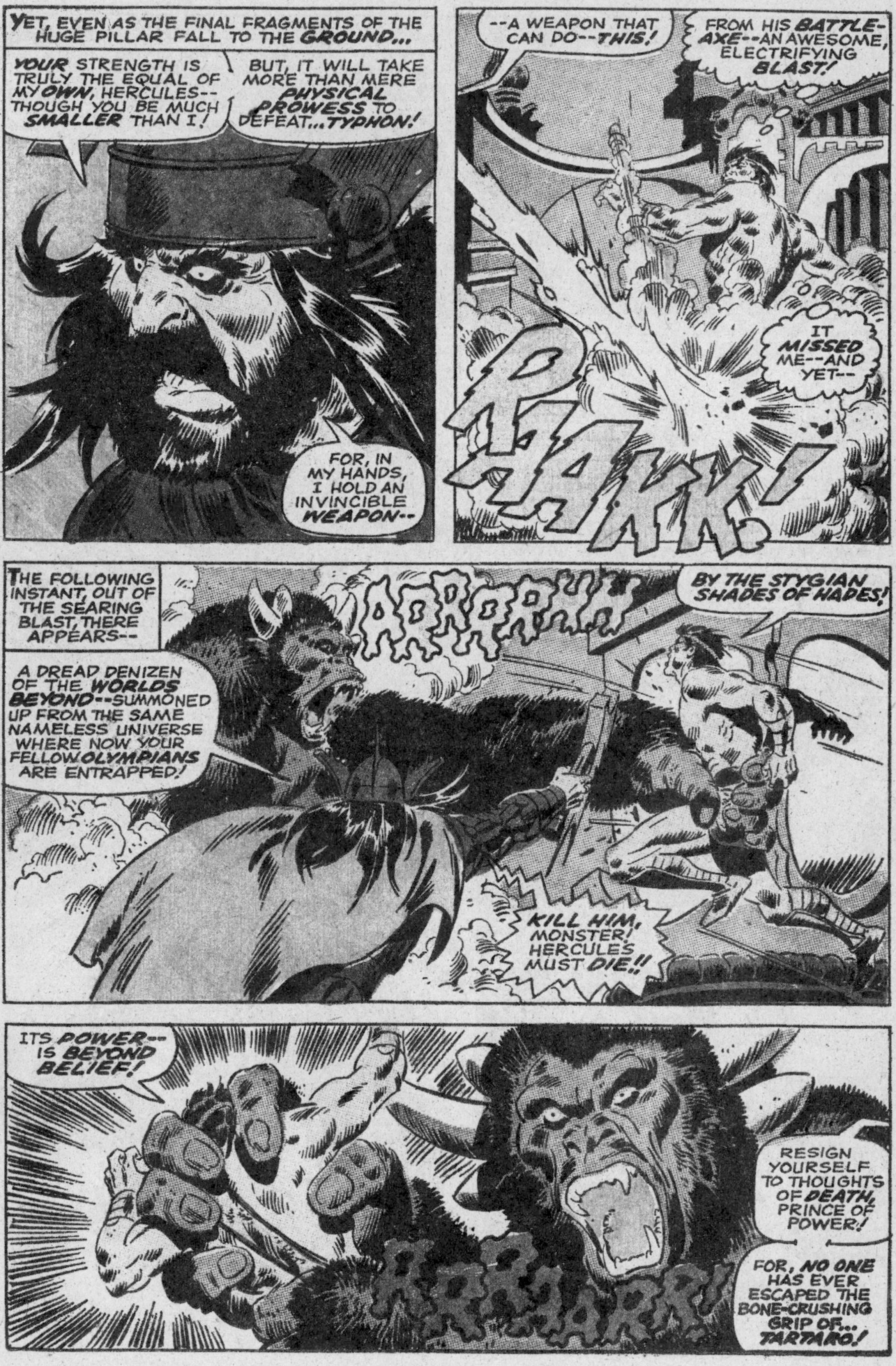
YET, EVEN AS THE FINAL FRAGMENTS OF THE HUGE PILLAR FALL TO THE GROUND...
YOUR STRENGTH IS TRULY THE EQUAL OF MY OWN, HERCULES-- THOUGH YOU BE MUCH SMALLER THAN I!
BUT, IT WILL TAKE MORE THAN MERE PHYSICAL PROWESS TO DEFEAT...TYPHON!
FOR, IN MY HANDS, I HOLD AN INVINCIBLE WEAPON--
--A WEAPON THAT CAN DO--THIS!
FROM HIS BATTLE-AXE--AN AWESOME, ELECTRIFYING BLAST!
IT MISSED ME--AND YET--
RAKK!
THE FOLLOWING INSTANT, OUT OF THE SEARING BLAST, THERE APPEARS--
ARRRRHH
BY THE STYGIAN SHADES OF HADES!
A DREAD DENIZEN OF THE WORLDS BEYOND--SUMMONED UP FROM THE SAME NAMELESS UNIVERSE WHERE NOW YOUR FELLOW OLYMPIANS ARE ENTRAPPED!
KILL HIM, MONSTER! HERCULES MUST DIE!!
ITS POWER--IS BEYOND BELIEF!
RESIGN YOURSELF TO THOUGHTS OF DEATH, PRINCE OF POWER!
FOR, NO ONE HAS EVER ESCAPED THE BONE-CRUSHING GRIP OF... TARTARO!
ARRHARR!

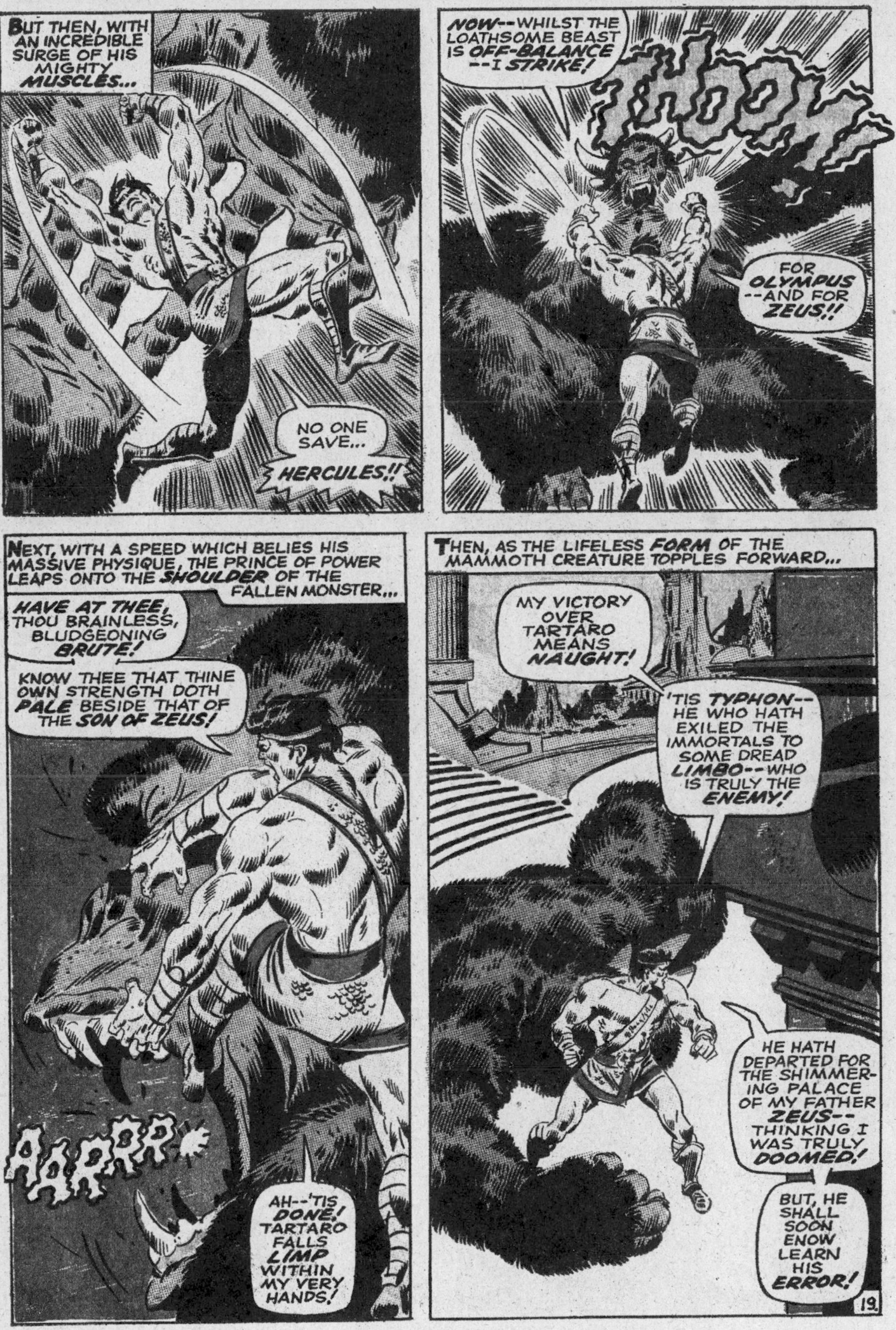
BUT THEN, WITH AN INCREDIBLE SURGE OF HIS MIGHTY MUSCLES...
NO ONE SAVE...
HERCULES!!
NOW--WHILST THE LOATHSOME BEAST IS OFF-BALANCE --I STRIKE!
THOOM
FOR OLYMPUS --AND FOR ZEUS!!
NEXT, WITH A SPEED WHICH BELIES HIS MASSIVE PHYSIQUE, THE PRINCE OF POWER LEAPS ONTO THE SHOULDER OF THE FALLEN MONSTER...
HAVE AT THEE, THOU BRAINLESS, BLUDGEONING BRUTE!
KNOW THEE THAT THINE OWN STRENGTH DOTH PALE BESIDE THAT OF THE SON OF ZEUS!
AARRRR
AH--'TIS DONE! TARTARO FALLS LIMP WITHIN MY VERY HANDS!
THEN, AS THE LIFELESS FORM OF THE MAMMOTH CREATURE TOPPLES FORWARD...
MY VICTORY OVER TARTARO MEANS NAUGHT!
'TIS TYPHON-- HE WHO HATH EXILED THE IMMORTALS TO SOME DREAD LIMBO--WHO IS TRULY THE ENEMY!
HE HATH DEPARTED FOR THE SHIMMERING PALACE OF MY FATHER ZEUS-- THINKING I WAS TRULY DOOMED!
BUT, HE SHALL SOON ENOW LEARN HIS ERROR!
19

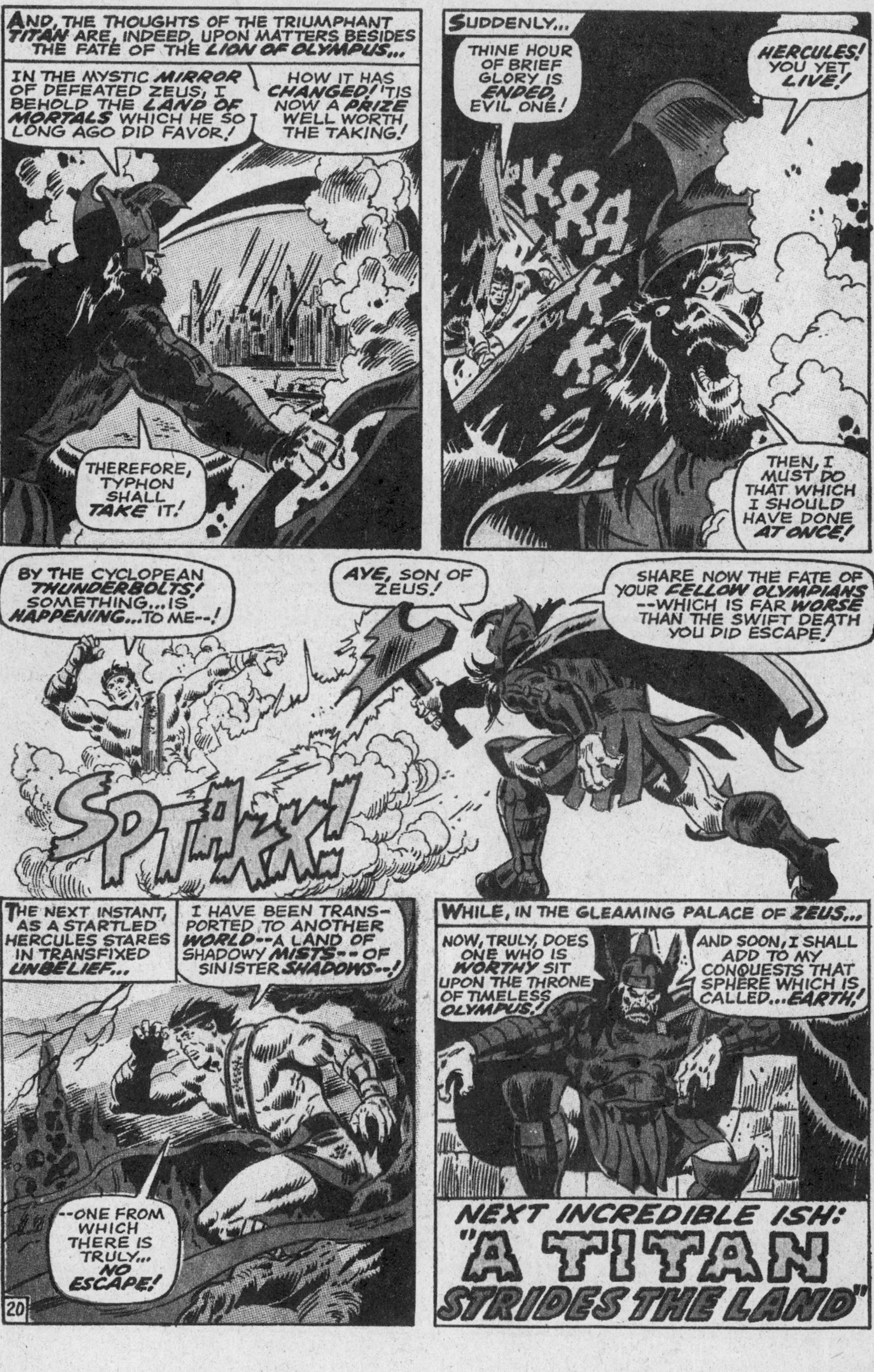
AND, THE THOUGHTS OF THE TRIUMPHANT TITAN ARE, INDEED, UPON MATTERS BESIDES THE FATE OF THE LION OF OLYMPUS...
IN THE MYSTIC MIRROR OF DEFEATED ZEUS, I BEHOLD THE LAND OF MORTALS WHICH HE SO LONG AGO DID FAVOR!
HOW IT HAS CHANGED! 'TIS NOW A PRIZE WELL WORTH THE TAKING!
THEREFORE, TYPHON SHALL TAKE IT!
SUDDENLY...
THINE HOUR OF BRIEF GLORY IS ENDED, EVIL ONE!
KRAKKK
HERCULES! YOU YET LIVE!
THEN, I MUST DO THAT WHICH I SHOULD HAVE DONE AT ONCE!
BY THE CYCLOPEAN THUNDERBOLTS! SOMETHING... IS HAPPENING... TO ME--!
AYE, SON OF ZEUS!
SHARE NOW THE FATE OF YOUR FELLOW OLYMPIANS --WHICH IS FAR WORSE THAN THE SWIFT DEATH YOU DID ESCAPE!
SPTAKK!
THE NEXT INSTANT, AS A STARTLED HERCULES STARES IN TRANSFIXED UNBELIEF...
I HAVE BEEN TRANSPORTED TO ANOTHER WORLD--A LAND OF SHADOWY MISTS--OF SINISTER SHADOWS--!
--ONE FROM WHICH THERE IS TRULY... NO ESCAPE!
20
WHILE, IN THE GLEAMING PALACE OF ZEUS...
NOW, TRULY, DOES ONE WHO IS WORTHY SIT UPON THE THRONE OF TIMELESS OLYMPUS!
AND SOON, I SHALL ADD TO MY CONQUESTS THAT SPHERE WHICH IS CALLED... EARTH!
NEXT INCREDIBLE ISH:
"A TITAN STRIDES THE LAND"

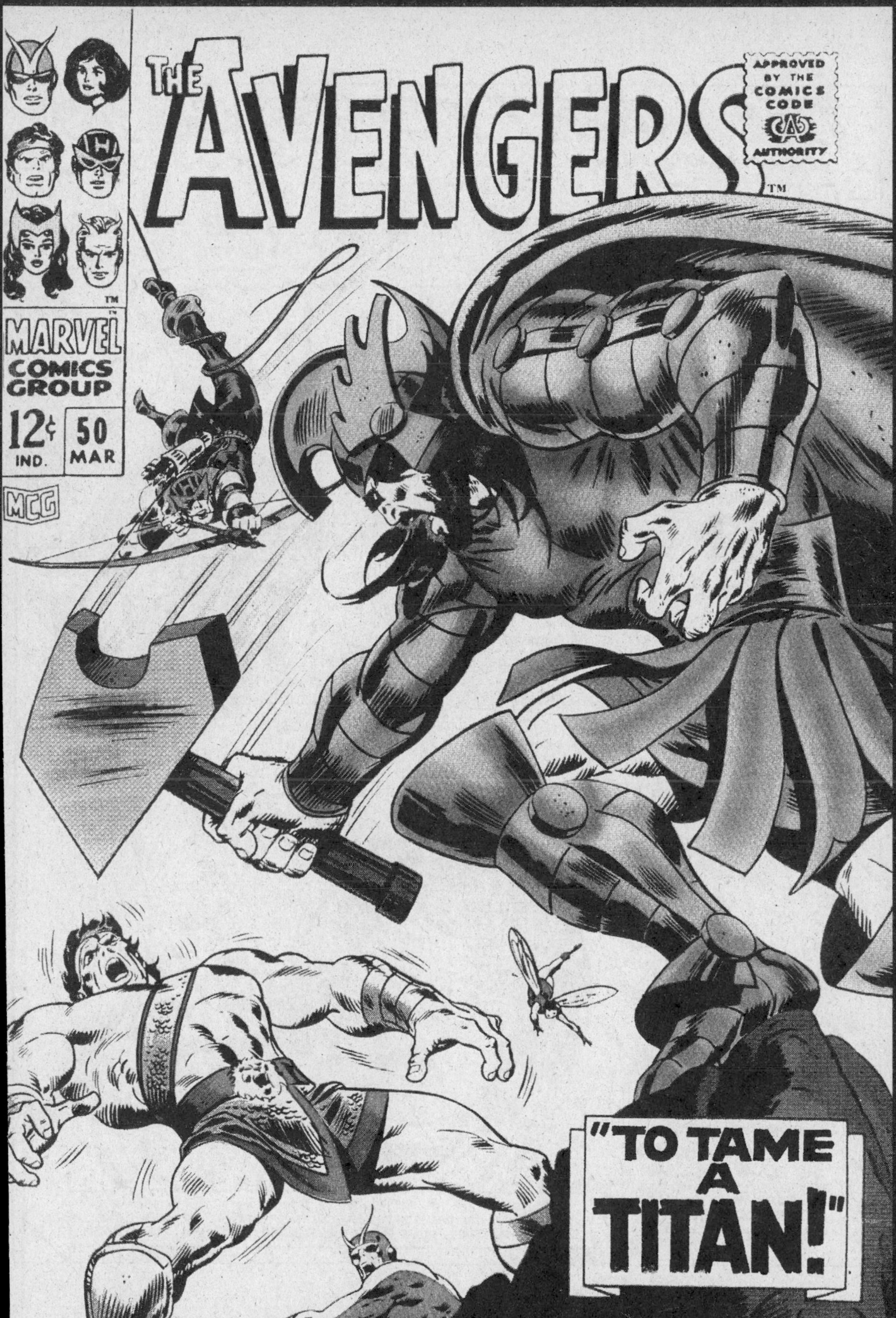
THE AVENGERS ™
APPROVED BY THE COMICS CODE CA AUTHORITY
MARVEL COMICS GROUP
12¢ IND.
50 MAR
MCG
"TO TAME A TITAN!"

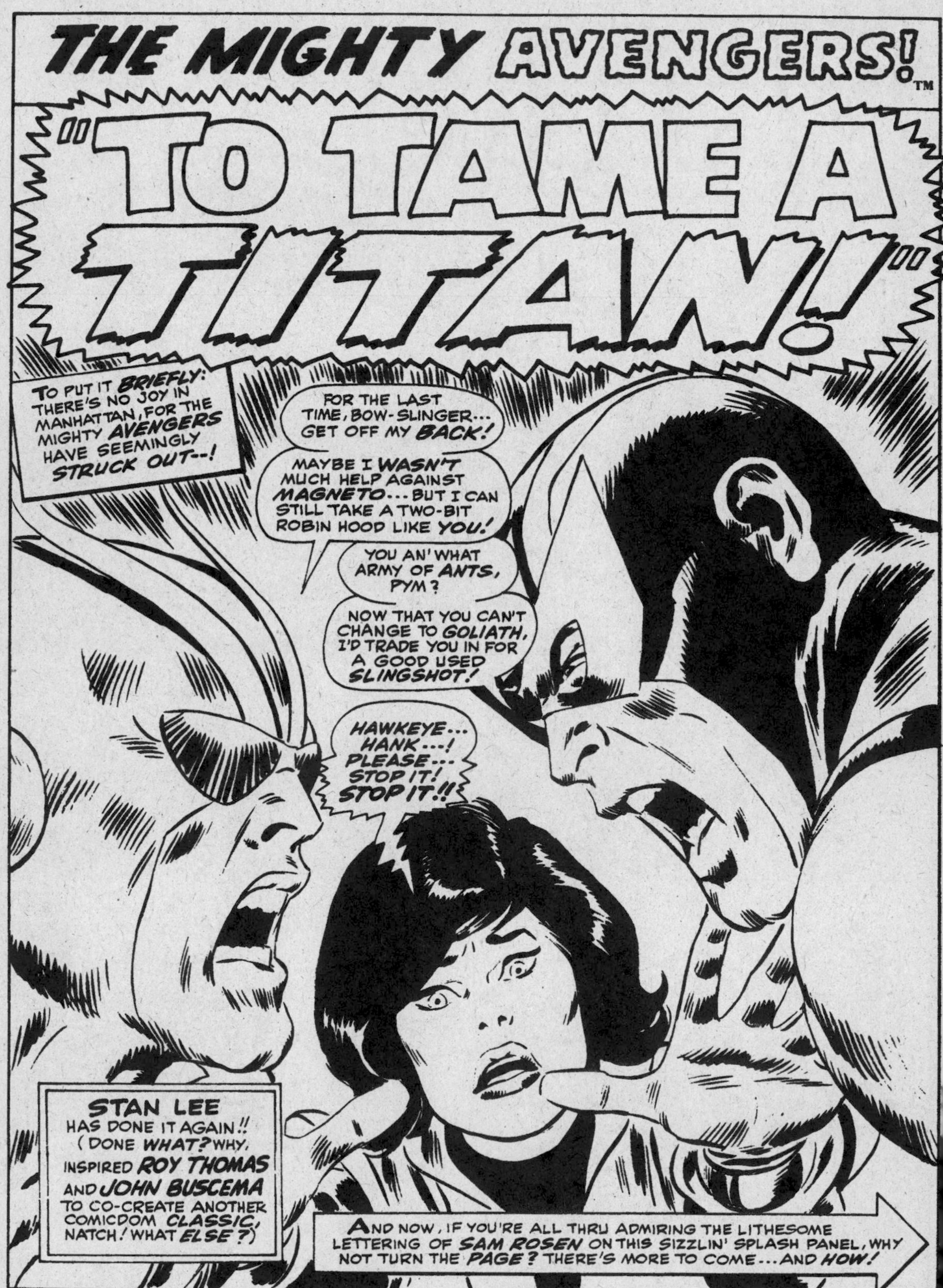
THE MIGHTY AVENGERS! TM
"TO TAME A TITAN!"
TO PUT IT BRIEFLY: THERE'S NO JOY IN MANHATTAN, FOR THE MIGHTY AVENGERS HAVE SEEMINGLY STRUCK OUT--!
FOR THE LAST TIME, BOW-SLINGER... GET OFF MY BACK!
MAYBE I WASN'T MUCH HELP AGAINST MAGNETO... BUT I CAN STILL TAKE A TWO-BIT ROBIN HOOD LIKE YOU!
YOU AN' WHAT ARMY OF ANTS, PYM?
NOW THAT YOU CAN'T CHANGE TO GOLIATH, I'D TRADE YOU IN FOR A GOOD USED SLINGSHOT!
HAWKEYE... HANK...! PLEASE... STOP IT! STOP IT!!
STAN LEE HAS DONE IT AGAIN!! (DONE WHAT? WHY, INSPIRED ROY THOMAS AND JOHN BUSCEMA TO CO-CREATE ANOTHER COMICDOM CLASSIC, NATCH! WHAT ELSE?)
AND NOW, IF YOU'RE ALL THRU ADMIRING THE LITHESOME LETTERING OF SAM ROSEN ON THIS SIZZLIN' SPLASH PANEL, WHY NOT TURN THE PAGE? THERE'S MORE TO COME... AND HOW!

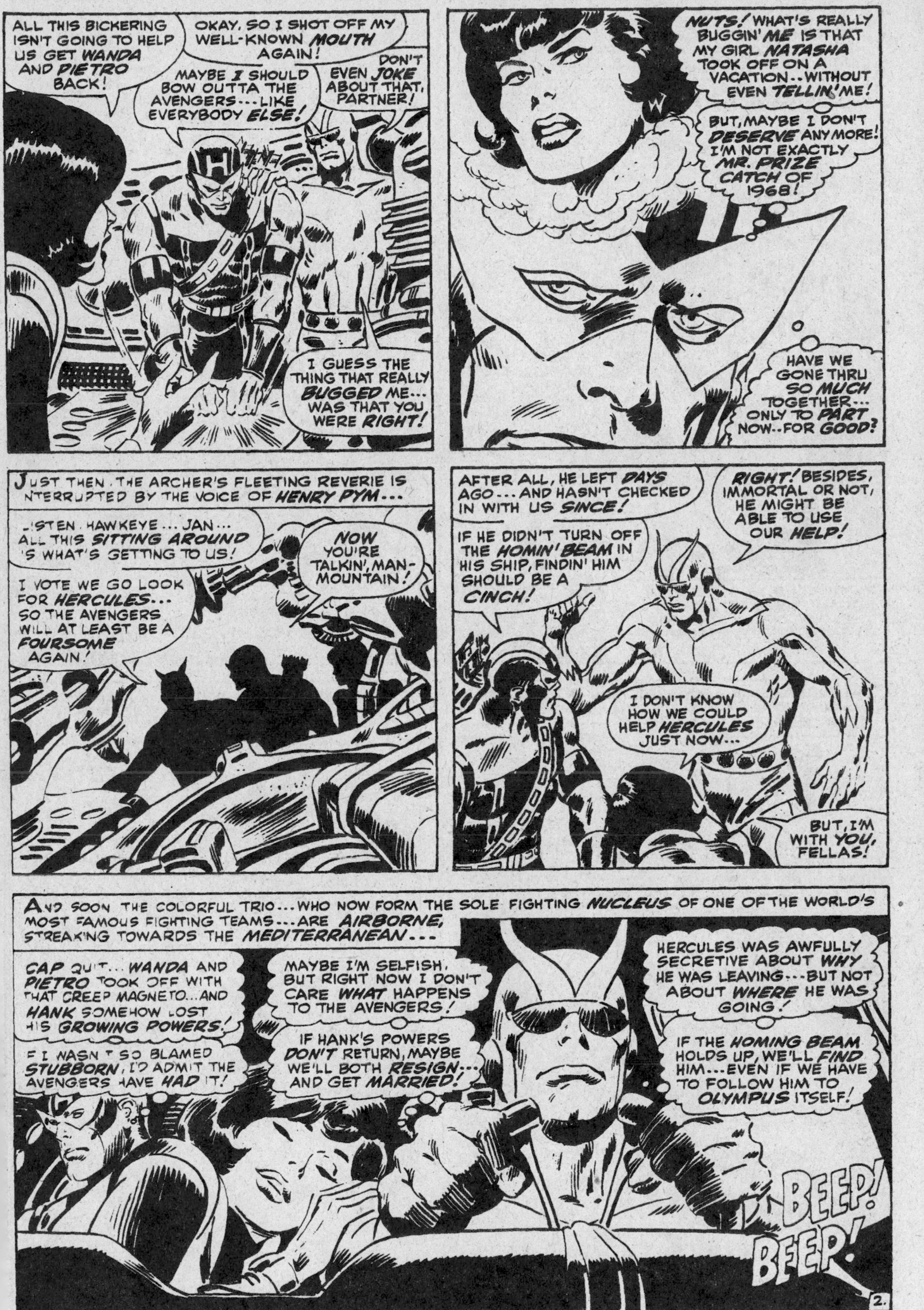

ALL THIS BICKERING ISN'T GOING TO HELP US GET WANDA AND PIETRO BACK!
OKAY, SO I SHOT OFF MY WELL-KNOWN MOUTH AGAIN!
MAYBE I SHOULD BOW OUTTA THE AVENGERS... LIKE EVERYBODY ELSE!
DON'T EVEN JOKE ABOUT THAT, PARTNER!
I GUESS THE THING THAT REALLY BUGGED ME... WAS THAT YOU WERE RIGHT!
NUTS! WHAT'S REALLY BUGGIN' ME IS THAT MY GIRL NATASHA TOOK OFF ON A VACATION -- WITHOUT EVEN TELLIN' ME!
BUT, MAYBE I DON'T DESERVE ANY MORE! I'M NOT EXACTLY MR. PRIZE CATCH OF 1968!
HAVE WE GONE THRU SO MUCH TOGETHER... ONLY TO PART NOW -- FOR GOOD?
JUST THEN, THE ARCHER'S FLEETING REVERIE IS INTERRUPTED BY THE VOICE OF HENRY PYM...
LISTEN, HAWKEYE... JAN... ALL THIS SITTING AROUND IS WHAT'S GETTING TO US!
NOW YOU'RE TALKIN', MAN-MOUNTAIN!
I VOTE WE GO LOOK FOR HERCULES... SO THE AVENGERS WILL AT LEAST BE A FOURSOME AGAIN!
AFTER ALL, HE LEFT DAYS AGO... AND HASN'T CHECKED IN WITH US SINCE!
RIGHT! BESIDES, IMMORTAL OR NOT, HE MIGHT BE ABLE TO USE OUR HELP!
IF HE DIDN'T TURN OFF THE HOMIN' BEAM IN HIS SHIP, FINDIN' HIM SHOULD BE A CINCH!
I DON'T KNOW HOW WE COULD HELP HERCULES JUST NOW...
BUT, I'M WITH YOU, FELLAS!
AND SOON THE COLORFUL TRIO... WHO NOW FORM THE SOLE FIGHTING NUCLEUS OF ONE OF THE WORLD'S MOST FAMOUS FIGHTING TEAMS... ARE AIRBORNE, STREAKING TOWARDS THE MEDITERRANEAN...
CAP QUIT... WANDA AND PIETRO TOOK OFF WITH THAT CREEP MAGNETO... AND HANK SOMEHOW LOST HIS GROWING POWERS!
IF I WASN'T SO BLAMED STUBBORN, I'D ADMIT THE AVENGERS HAVE HAD IT!
MAYBE I'M SELFISH, BUT RIGHT NOW I DON'T CARE WHAT HAPPENS TO THE AVENGERS!
IF HANK'S POWERS DON'T RETURN, MAYBE WE'LL BOTH RESIGN... AND GET MARRIED!
HERCULES WAS AWFULLY SECRETIVE ABOUT WHY HE WAS LEAVING... BUT NOT ABOUT WHERE HE WAS GOING!
IF THE HOMING BEAM HOLDS UP, WE'LL FIND HIM... EVEN IF WE HAVE TO FOLLOW HIM TO OLYMPUS ITSELF!
BEEP! BEEP!

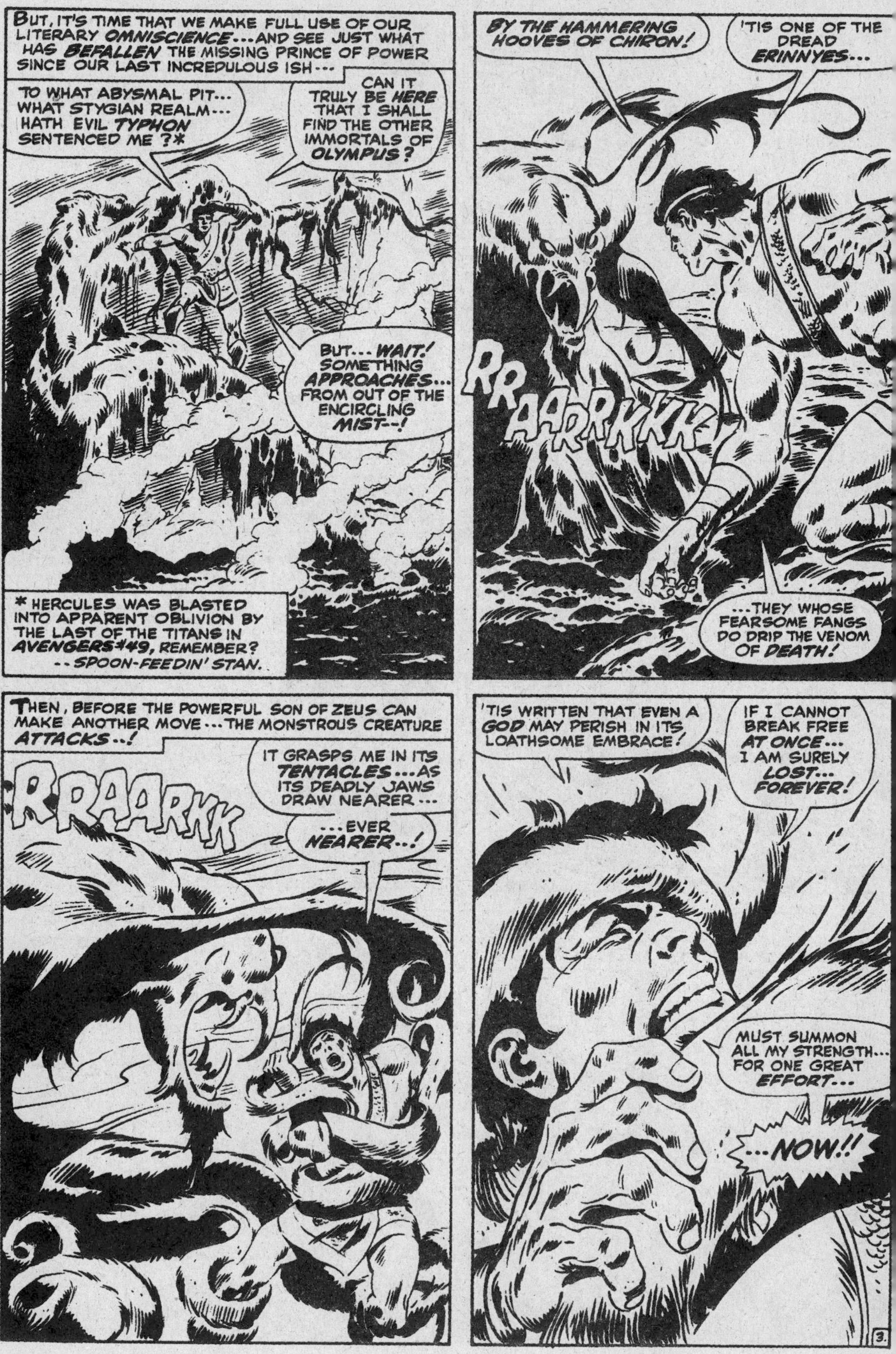

But, it's time that we make full use of our literary omniscience... and see just what has befallen the missing Prince of Power since our last incredulous ish...
To what abysmal pit... what Stygian realm... hath evil Typhon sentenced me?*
Can it truly be here that I shall find the other immortals of Olympus?
But... wait! Something approaches... from out of the encircling mist--!
* Hercules was blasted into apparent oblivion by the last of the Titans in Avengers #49, remember? --Spoon-feedin' Stan.
By the hammering hooves of Chiron!
'Tis one of the dread Erinnyes...
RRAARRKKK
...They whose fearsome fangs do drip the venom of death!
Then, before the powerful son of Zeus can make another move... the monstrous creature attacks..!
RRAARKKK
It grasps me in its tentacles... as its deadly jaws draw nearer...
...ever nearer..!
'Tis written that even a god may perish in its loathsome embrace!
If I cannot break free at once... I am surely lost... forever!
Must summon all my strength... for one great effort...
...Now!!
3.

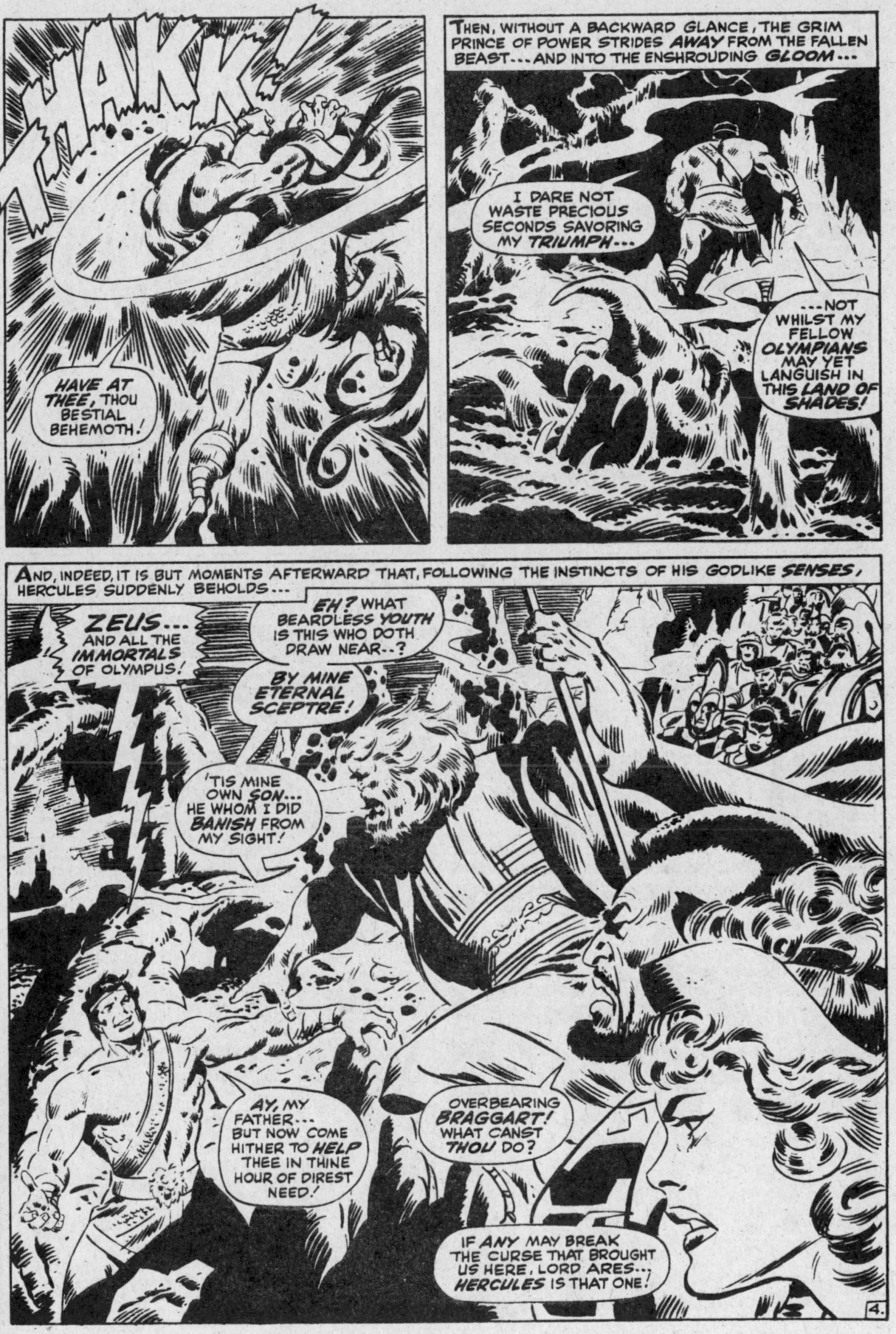
THAKK!
HAVE AT THEE, THOU BESTIAL BEHEMOTH!
THEN, WITHOUT A BACKWARD GLANCE, THE GRIM PRINCE OF POWER STRIDES AWAY FROM THE FALLEN BEAST... AND INTO THE ENSHROUDING GLOOM...
I DARE NOT WASTE PRECIOUS SECONDS SAVORING MY TRIUMPH...
...NOT WHILST MY FELLOW OLYMPIANS MAY YET LANGUISH IN THIS LAND OF SHADES!
AND, INDEED, IT IS BUT MOMENTS AFTERWARD THAT, FOLLOWING THE INSTINCTS OF HIS GODLIKE SENSES, HERCULES SUDDENLY BEHOLDS...
ZEUS... AND ALL THE IMMORTALS OF OLYMPUS!
EH? WHAT BEARDLESS YOUTH IS THIS WHO DOTH DRAW NEAR--?
BY MINE ETERNAL SCEPTRE!
'TIS MINE OWN SON... HE WHOM I DID BANISH FROM MY SIGHT!
AY, MY FATHER... BUT NOW COME HITHER TO HELP THEE IN THINE HOUR OF DIREST NEED!
OVERBEARING BRAGGART! WHAT CANST THOU DO?
IF ANY MAY BREAK THE CURSE THAT BROUGHT US HERE, LORD ARES... HERCULES IS THAT ONE!

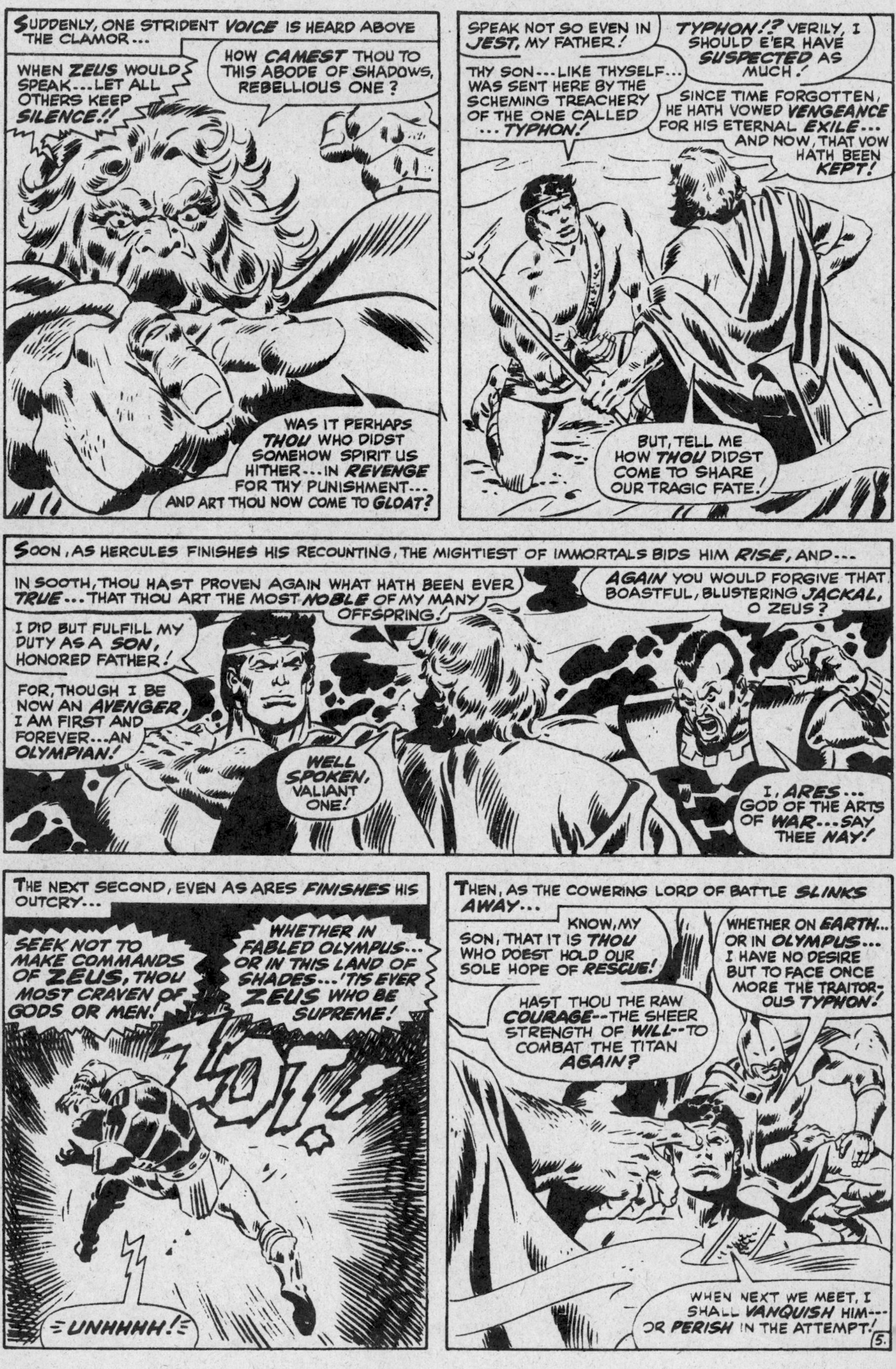
SUDDENLY, ONE STRIDENT VOICE IS HEARD ABOVE THE CLAMOR...
WHEN ZEUS WOULD SPEAK... LET ALL OTHERS KEEP SILENCE!!
HOW CAMEST THOU TO THIS ABODE OF SHADOWS, REBELLIOUS ONE?
WAS IT PERHAPS THOU WHO DIDST SOMEHOW SPIRIT US HITHER... IN REVENGE FOR THY PUNISHMENT... AND ART THOU NOW COME TO GLOAT?
SPEAK NOT SO EVEN IN JEST, MY FATHER!
THY SON... LIKE THYSELF... WAS SENT HERE BY THE SCHEMING TREACHERY OF THE ONE CALLED ...TYPHON!
TYPHON!? VERILY, I SHOULD E'ER HAVE SUSPECTED AS MUCH!
SINCE TIME FORGOTTEN, HE HATH VOWED VENGEANCE FOR HIS ETERNAL EXILE... AND NOW, THAT VOW HATH BEEN KEPT!
BUT, TELL ME HOW THOU DIDST COME TO SHARE OUR TRAGIC FATE!
SOON, AS HERCULES FINISHES HIS RECOUNTING, THE MIGHTIEST OF IMMORTALS BIDS HIM RISE, AND...
IN SOOTH, THOU HAST PROVEN AGAIN WHAT HATH BEEN EVER TRUE... THAT THOU ART THE MOST NOBLE OF MY MANY OFFSPRING!
I DID BUT FULFILL MY DUTY AS A SON, HONORED FATHER!
FOR, THOUGH I BE NOW AN AVENGER, I AM FIRST AND FOREVER... AN OLYMPIAN!
WELL SPOKEN, VALIANT ONE!
AGAIN YOU WOULD FORGIVE THAT BOASTFUL, BLUSTERING JACKAL, O ZEUS?
I, ARES... GOD OF THE ARTS OF WAR... SAY THEE NAY!
THE NEXT SECOND, EVEN AS ARES FINISHES HIS OUTCRY...
SEEK NOT TO MAKE COMMANDS OF ZEUS, THOU MOST CRAVEN OF GODS OR MEN!
WHETHER IN FABLED OLYMPUS... OR IN THIS LAND OF SHADES... 'TIS EVER ZEUS WHO BE SUPREME!
ZOT!
UNHHHH!
THEN, AS THE COWERING LORD OF BATTLE SLINKS AWAY...
KNOW, MY SON, THAT IT IS THOU WHO DOEST HOLD OUR SOLE HOPE OF RESCUE!
HAST THOU THE RAW COURAGE--THE SHEER STRENGTH OF WILL--TO COMBAT THE TITAN AGAIN?
WHETHER ON EARTH... OR IN OLYMPUS... I HAVE NO DESIRE BUT TO FACE ONCE MORE THE TRAITOROUS TYPHON!
WHEN NEXT WE MEET, I SHALL VANQUISH HIM--- OR PERISH IN THE ATTEMPT!
5.

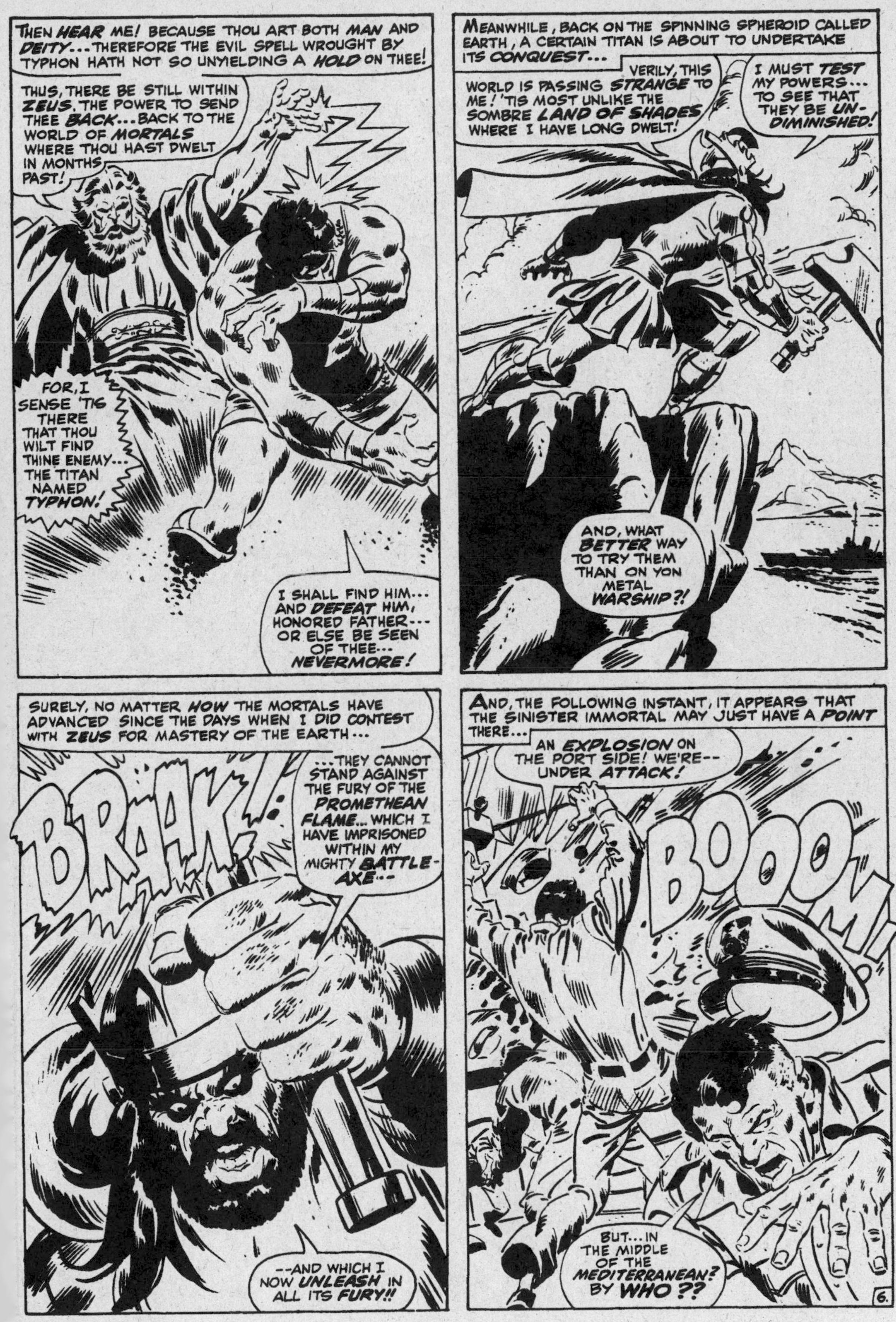
THEN HEAR ME! BECAUSE THOU ART BOTH MAN AND DEITY... THEREFORE THE EVIL SPELL WROUGHT BY TYPHON HATH NOT SO UNYIELDING A HOLD ON THEE!
THUS, THERE BE STILL WITHIN ZEUS, THE POWER TO SEND THEE BACK... BACK TO THE WORLD OF MORTALS WHERE THOU HAST DWELT IN MONTHS PAST!
FOR, I SENSE 'TIS THERE THAT THOU WILT FIND THINE ENEMY... THE TITAN NAMED TYPHON!
I SHALL FIND HIM... AND DEFEAT HIM, HONORED FATHER--- OR ELSE BE SEEN OF THEE--- NEVERMORE!
MEANWHILE, BACK ON THE SPINNING SPHEROID CALLED EARTH, A CERTAIN TITAN IS ABOUT TO UNDERTAKE ITS CONQUEST...
VERILY, THIS WORLD IS PASSING STRANGE TO ME! 'TIS MOST UNLIKE THE SOMBRE LAND OF SHADES WHERE I HAVE LONG DWELT!
I MUST TEST MY POWERS... TO SEE THAT THEY BE UN-DIMINISHED!
AND, WHAT BETTER WAY TO TRY THEM THAN ON YON METAL WARSHIP?!
SURELY, NO MATTER HOW THE MORTALS HAVE ADVANCED SINCE THE DAYS WHEN I DID CONTEST WITH ZEUS FOR MASTERY OF THE EARTH...
...THEY CANNOT STAND AGAINST THE FURY OF THE PROMETHEAN FLAME... WHICH I HAVE IMPRISONED WITHIN MY MIGHTY BATTLE-AXE--
BRAAK!
--AND WHICH I NOW UNLEASH IN ALL ITS FURY!!
AND, THE FOLLOWING INSTANT, IT APPEARS THAT THE SINISTER IMMORTAL MAY JUST HAVE A POINT THERE...
AN EXPLOSION ON THE PORT SIDE! WE'RE-- UNDER ATTACK!
BOOOM!
BUT... IN THE MIDDLE OF THE MEDITERRANEAN? BY WHO??
6.

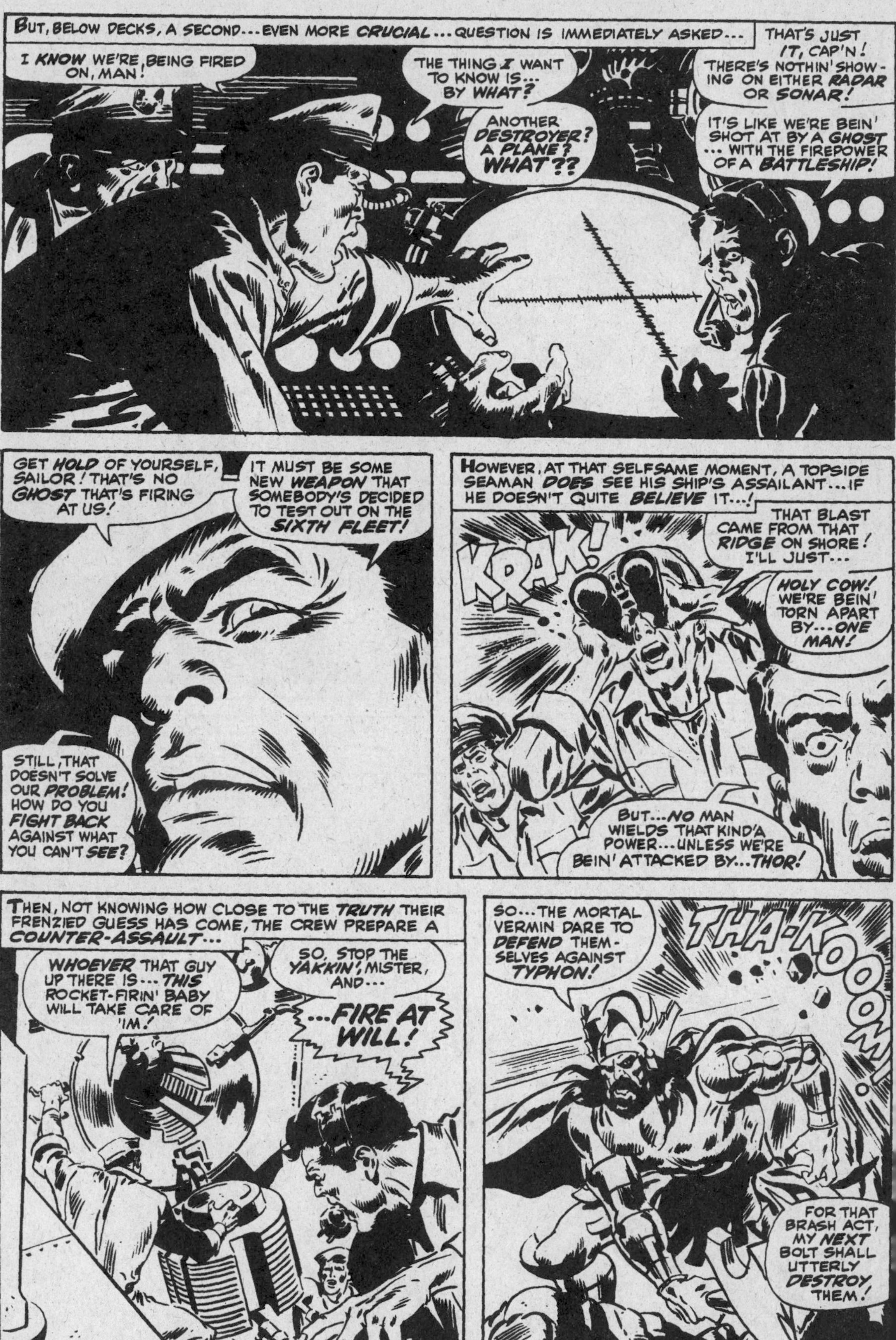

BUT, BELOW DECKS, A SECOND... EVEN MORE CRUCIAL... QUESTION IS IMMEDIATELY ASKED...
I KNOW WE'RE BEING FIRED ON, MAN!
THE THING I WANT TO KNOW IS... BY WHAT?
ANOTHER DESTROYER? A PLANE? WHAT??
THAT'S JUST IT, CAP'N! THERE'S NOTHIN' SHOWING ON EITHER RADAR OR SONAR!
IT'S LIKE WE'RE BEIN' SHOT AT BY A GHOST... WITH THE FIREPOWER OF A BATTLESHIP!
GET HOLD OF YOURSELF, SAILOR! THAT'S NO GHOST THAT'S FIRING AT US!
IT MUST BE SOME NEW WEAPON THAT SOMEBODY'S DECIDED TO TEST OUT ON THE SIXTH FLEET!
STILL, THAT DOESN'T SOLVE OUR PROBLEM! HOW DO YOU FIGHT BACK AGAINST WHAT YOU CAN'T SEE?
HOWEVER, AT THAT SELFSAME MOMENT, A TOPSIDE SEAMAN DOES SEE HIS SHIP'S ASSAILANT... IF HE DOESN'T QUITE BELIEVE IT...!
KRAK!
THAT BLAST CAME FROM THAT RIDGE ON SHORE! I'LL JUST...
HOLY COW! WE'RE BEIN' TORN APART BY... ONE MAN!
BUT... NO MAN WIELDS THAT KIND'A POWER... UNLESS WE'RE BEIN' ATTACKED BY... THOR!
THEN, NOT KNOWING HOW CLOSE TO THE TRUTH THEIR FRENZIED GUESS HAS COME, THE CREW PREPARE A COUNTER-ASSAULT...
WHOEVER THAT GUY UP THERE IS... THIS ROCKET-FIRIN' BABY WILL TAKE CARE OF 'IM!
SO, STOP THE YAKKIN', MISTER, AND...
...FIRE AT WILL!
SO... THE MORTAL VERMIN DARE TO DEFEND THEMSELVES AGAINST TYPHON!
THA-KOOOOM!
FOR THAT BRASH ACT, MY NEXT BOLT SHALL UTTERLY DESTROY THEM!
7.

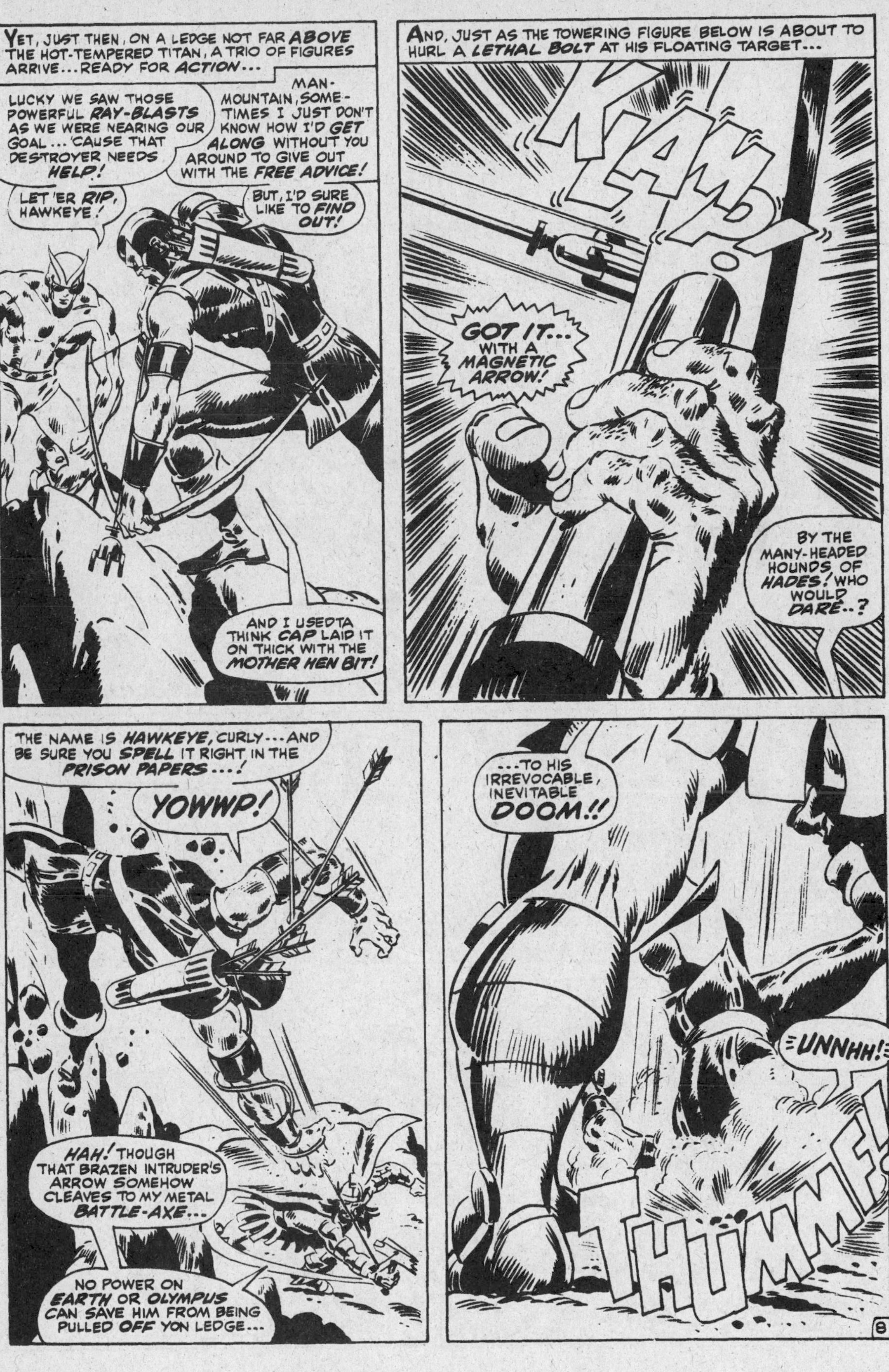
YET, JUST THEN, ON A LEDGE NOT FAR ABOVE THE HOT-TEMPERED TITAN, A TRIO OF FIGURES ARRIVE... READY FOR ACTION...
LUCKY WE SAW THOSE POWERFUL RAY-BLASTS AS WE WERE NEARING OUR GOAL... 'CAUSE THAT DESTROYER NEEDS HELP!
MAN-MOUNTAIN, SOMETIMES I JUST DON'T KNOW HOW I'D GET ALONG WITHOUT YOU AROUND TO GIVE OUT WITH THE FREE ADVICE!
LET 'ER RIP, HAWKEYE!
BUT, I'D SURE LIKE TO FIND OUT!
AND I USEDTA THINK CAP LAID IT ON THICK WITH THE MOTHER HEN BIT!
AND, JUST AS THE TOWERING FIGURE BELOW IS ABOUT TO HURL A LETHAL BOLT AT HIS FLOATING TARGET...
KLAMP!
GOT IT... WITH A MAGNETIC ARROW!
BY THE MANY-HEADED HOUNDS OF HADES! WHO WOULD DARE..?
THE NAME IS HAWKEYE, CURLY... AND BE SURE YOU SPELL IT RIGHT IN THE PRISON PAPERS...!
YOWWP!
HAH! THOUGH THAT BRAZEN INTRUDER'S ARROW SOMEHOW CLEAVES TO MY METAL BATTLE-AXE...
NO POWER ON EARTH OR OLYMPUS CAN SAVE HIM FROM BEING PULLED OFF YON LEDGE...
...TO HIS IRREVOCABLE, INEVITABLE DOOM!!
UNNHH!
THUMMF!
8

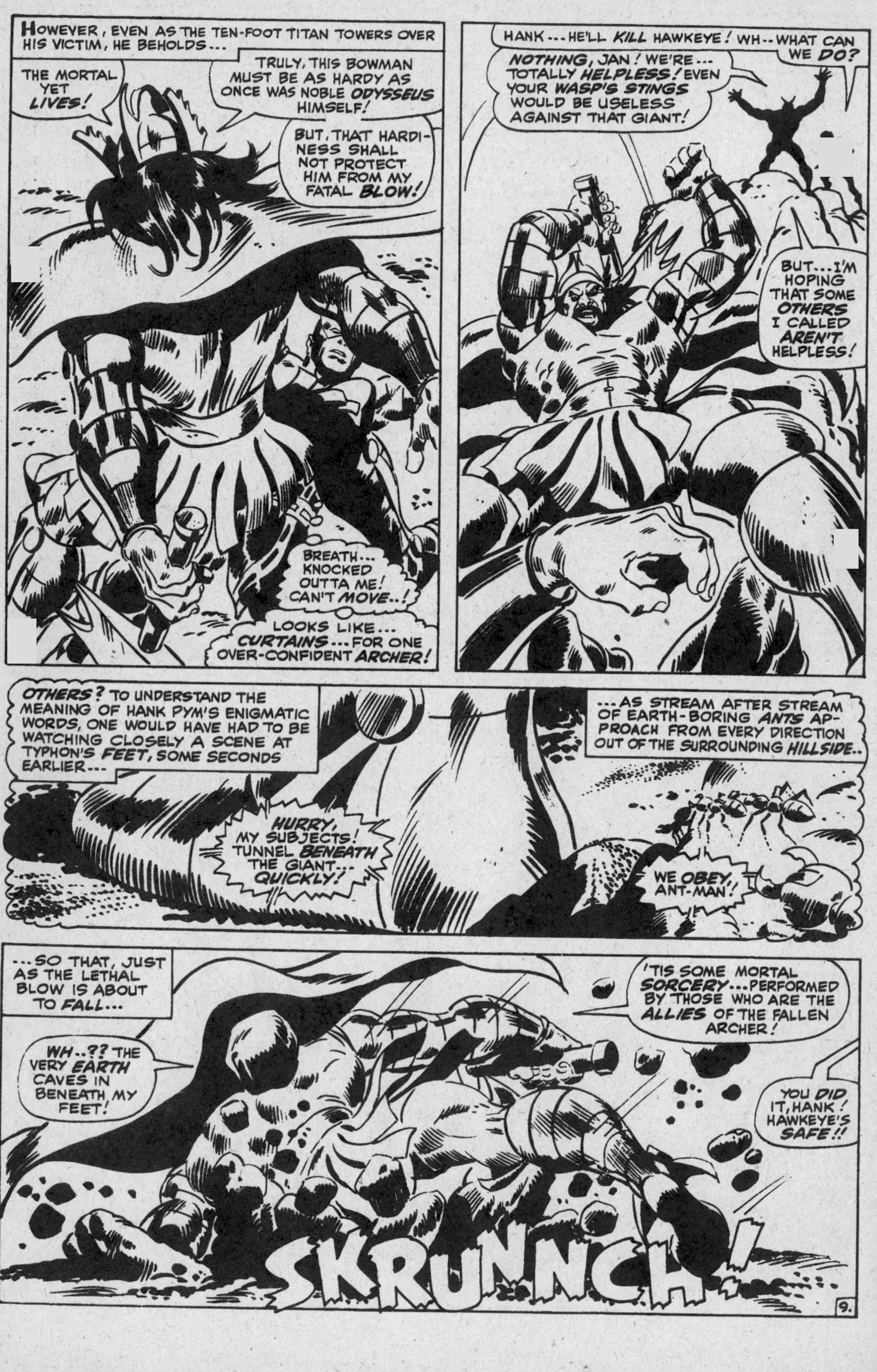

HOWEVER, EVEN AS THE TEN-FOOT TITAN TOWERS OVER HIS VICTIM, HE BEHOLDS...
THE MORTAL YET LIVES!
TRULY, THIS BOWMAN MUST BE AS HARDY AS ONCE WAS NOBLE ODYSSEUS HIMSELF!
BUT, THAT HARDINESS SHALL NOT PROTECT HIM FROM MY FATAL BLOW!
BREATH... KNOCKED OUTTA ME! CAN'T MOVE..!
LOOKS LIKE... CURTAINS... FOR ONE OVER-CONFIDENT ARCHER!
HANK... HE'LL KILL HAWKEYE! WH--WHAT CAN WE DO?
NOTHING, JAN! WE'RE... TOTALLY HELPLESS! EVEN YOUR WASP'S STINGS WOULD BE USELESS AGAINST THAT GIANT!
BUT... I'M HOPING THAT SOME OTHERS I CALLED AREN'T HELPLESS!
OTHERS? TO UNDERSTAND THE MEANING OF HANK PYM'S ENIGMATIC WORDS, ONE WOULD HAVE HAD TO BE WATCHING CLOSELY A SCENE AT TYPHON'S FEET, SOME SECONDS EARLIER...
...AS STREAM AFTER STREAM OF EARTH-BORING ANTS APPROACH FROM EVERY DIRECTION OUT OF THE SURROUNDING HILLSIDE..
HURRY, MY SUBJECTS! TUNNEL BENEATH THE GIANT... QUICKLY!
WE OBEY, ANT-MAN!
...SO THAT, JUST AS THE LETHAL BLOW IS ABOUT TO FALL...
'TIS SOME MORTAL SORCERY... PERFORMED BY THOSE WHO ARE THE ALLIES OF THE FALLEN ARCHER!
WH..?? THE VERY EARTH CAVES IN BENEATH MY FEET!
YOU DID IT, HANK! HAWKEYE'S SAFE!!
SKRUNNCH!

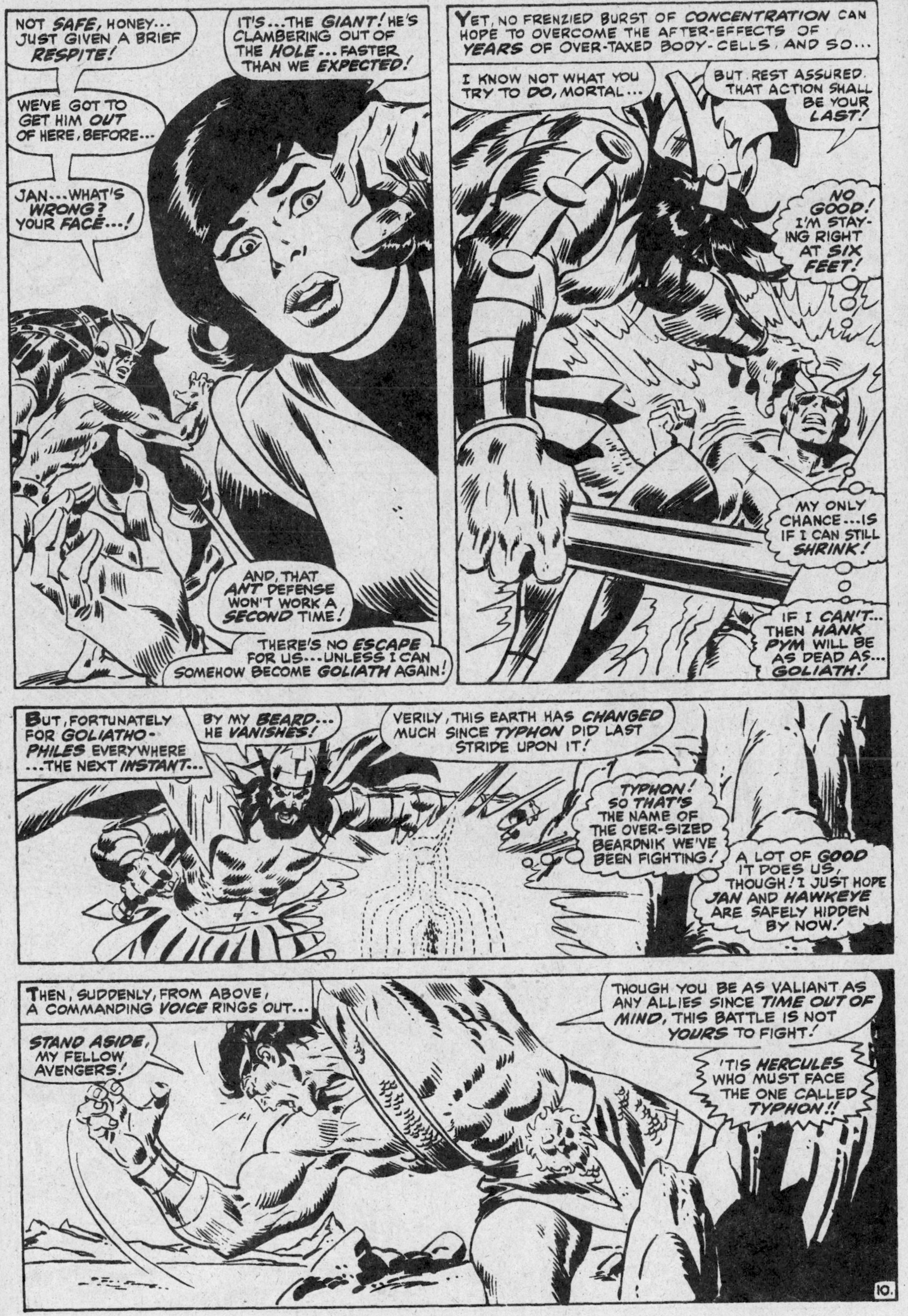
NOT SAFE, HONEY... JUST GIVEN A BRIEF RESPITE!
IT'S... THE GIANT! HE'S CLAMBERING OUT OF THE HOLE... FASTER THAN WE EXPECTED!
WE'VE GOT TO GET HIM OUT OF HERE, BEFORE...
JAN... WHAT'S WRONG? YOUR FACE...!
AND, THAT ANT DEFENSE WON'T WORK A SECOND TIME!
THERE'S NO ESCAPE FOR US... UNLESS I CAN SOMEHOW BECOME GOLIATH AGAIN!
YET, NO FRENZIED BURST OF CONCENTRATION CAN HOPE TO OVERCOME THE AFTER-EFFECTS OF YEARS OF OVER-TAXED BODY-CELLS, AND SO...
I KNOW NOT WHAT YOU TRY TO DO, MORTAL...
BUT REST ASSURED. THAT ACTION SHALL BE YOUR LAST!
NO GOOD! I'M STAYING RIGHT AT SIX FEET!
MY ONLY CHANCE... IS IF I CAN STILL SHRINK!
IF I CAN'T... THEN HANK PYM WILL BE AS DEAD AS... GOLIATH!
BUT, FORTUNATELY FOR GOLIATHO-PHILES EVERYWHERE ...THE NEXT INSTANT...
BY MY BEARD... HE VANISHES!
VERILY, THIS EARTH HAS CHANGED MUCH SINCE TYPHON DID LAST STRIDE UPON IT!
TYPHON! SO THAT'S THE NAME OF THE OVER-SIZED BEARDNIK WE'VE BEEN FIGHTING!
A LOT OF GOOD IT DOES US, THOUGH! I JUST HOPE JAN AND HAWKEYE ARE SAFELY HIDDEN BY NOW!
THEN, SUDDENLY, FROM ABOVE, A COMMANDING VOICE RINGS OUT...
STAND ASIDE, MY FELLOW AVENGERS!
THOUGH YOU BE AS VALIANT AS ANY ALLIES SINCE TIME OUT OF MIND, THIS BATTLE IS NOT YOURS TO FIGHT!
'TIS HERCULES WHO MUST FACE THE ONE CALLED TYPHON!!
10.

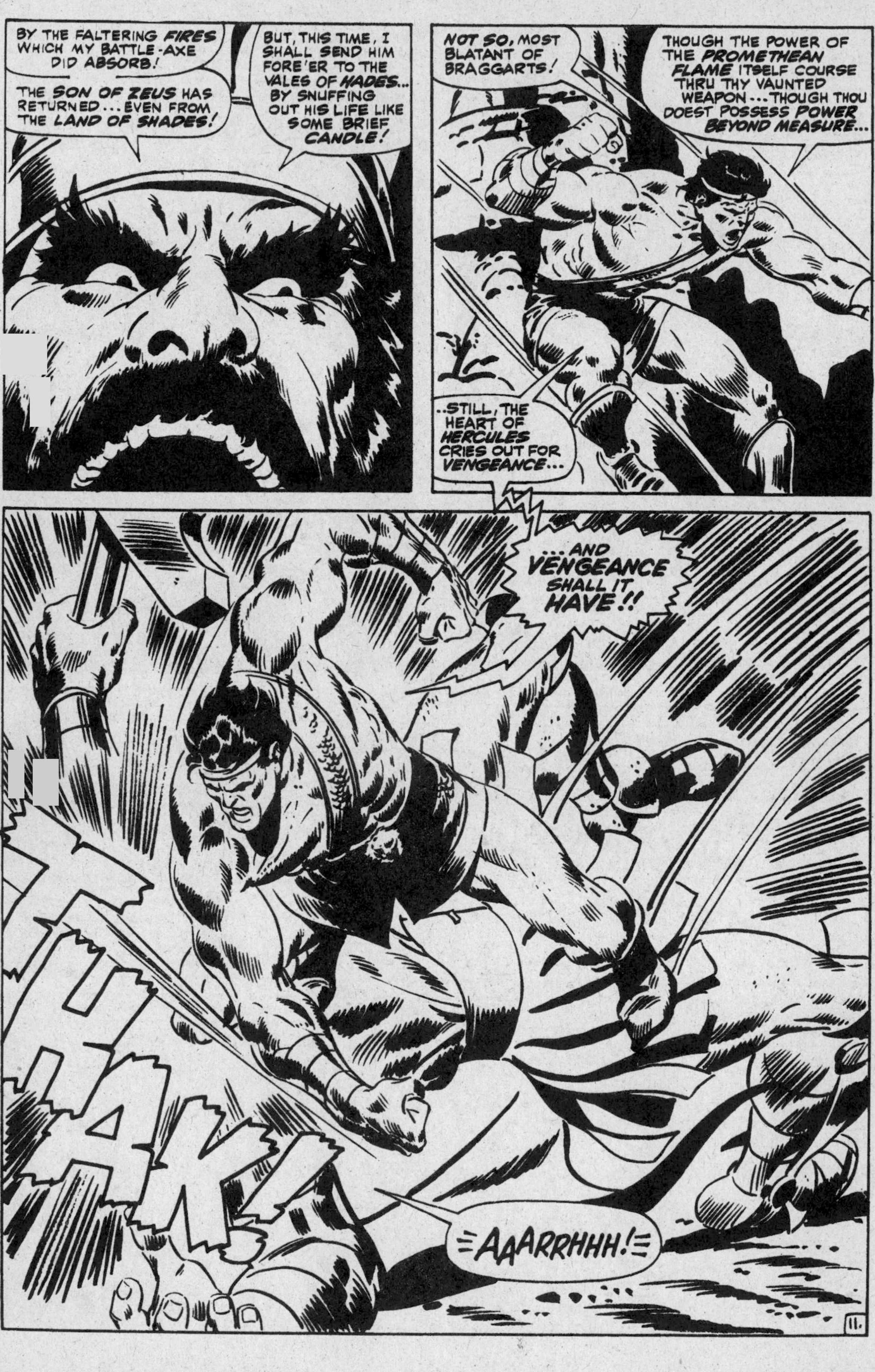

BY THE FALTERING FIRES WHICH MY BATTLE-AXE DID ABSORB!
THE SON OF ZEUS HAS RETURNED... EVEN FROM THE LAND OF SHADES!
BUT, THIS TIME, I SHALL SEND HIM FORE'ER TO THE VALES OF HADES... BY SNUFFING OUT HIS LIFE LIKE SOME BRIEF CANDLE!
NOT SO, MOST BLATANT OF BRAGGARTS!
THOUGH THE POWER OF THE PROMETHEAN FLAME ITSELF COURSE THRU THY VAUNTED WEAPON... THOUGH THOU DOEST POSSESS POWER BEYOND MEASURE...
..STILL, THE HEART OF HERCULES CRIES OUT FOR VENGEANCE...
...AND VENGEANCE SHALL IT HAVE!!
THAKK!
AAARRHHH!
11.

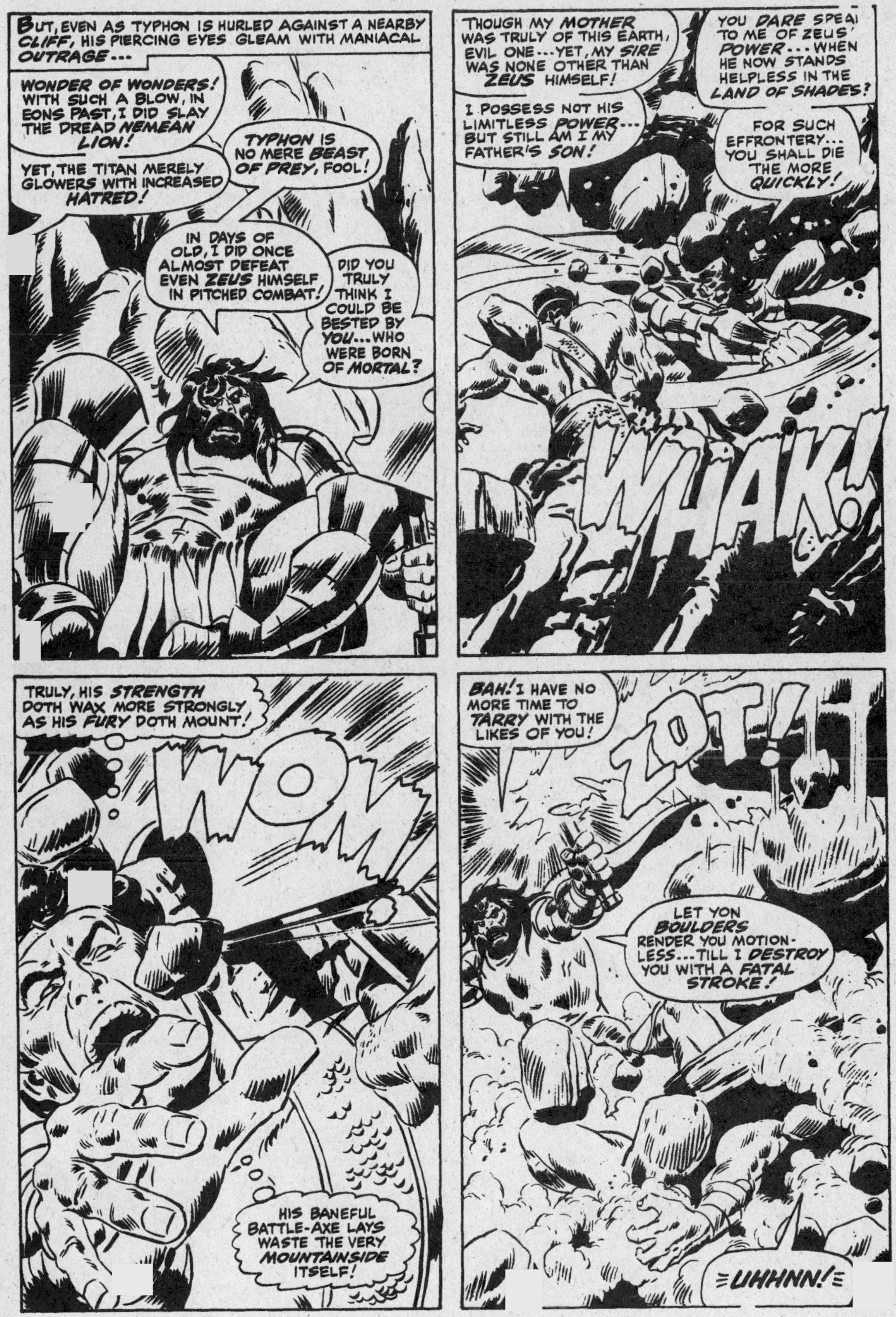
BUT, EVEN AS TYPHON IS HURLED AGAINST A NEARBY CLIFF, HIS PIERCING EYES GLEAM WITH MANIACAL OUTRAGE...
WONDER OF WONDERS! WITH SUCH A BLOW, IN EONS PAST, I DID SLAY THE DREAD NEMEAN LION!
YET, THE TITAN MERELY GLOWERS WITH INCREASED HATRED!
TYPHON IS NO MERE BEAST OF PREY, FOOL!
IN DAYS OF OLD, I DID ONCE ALMOST DEFEAT EVEN ZEUS HIMSELF IN PITCHED COMBAT!
DID YOU TRULY THINK I COULD BE BESTED BY YOU...WHO WERE BORN OF MORTAL?
THOUGH MY MOTHER WAS TRULY OF THIS EARTH, EVIL ONE...YET, MY SIRE WAS NONE OTHER THAN ZEUS HIMSELF!
I POSSESS NOT HIS LIMITLESS POWER... BUT STILL AM I MY FATHER'S SON!
YOU DARE SPEAK TO ME OF ZEUS' POWER...WHEN HE NOW STANDS HELPLESS IN THE LAND OF SHADES?
FOR SUCH EFFRONTERY... YOU SHALL DIE THE MORE QUICKLY!
WHAK!
TRULY, HIS STRENGTH DOTH WAX MORE STRONGLY AS HIS FURY DOTH MOUNT!
WOM
HIS BANEFUL BATTLE-AXE LAYS WASTE THE VERY MOUNTAINSIDE ITSELF!
BAH! I HAVE NO MORE TIME TO TARRY WITH THE LIKES OF YOU!
ZOT!
LET YON BOULDERS RENDER YOU MOTION-LESS...TILL I DESTROY YOU WITH A FATAL STROKE!
UHHNN!

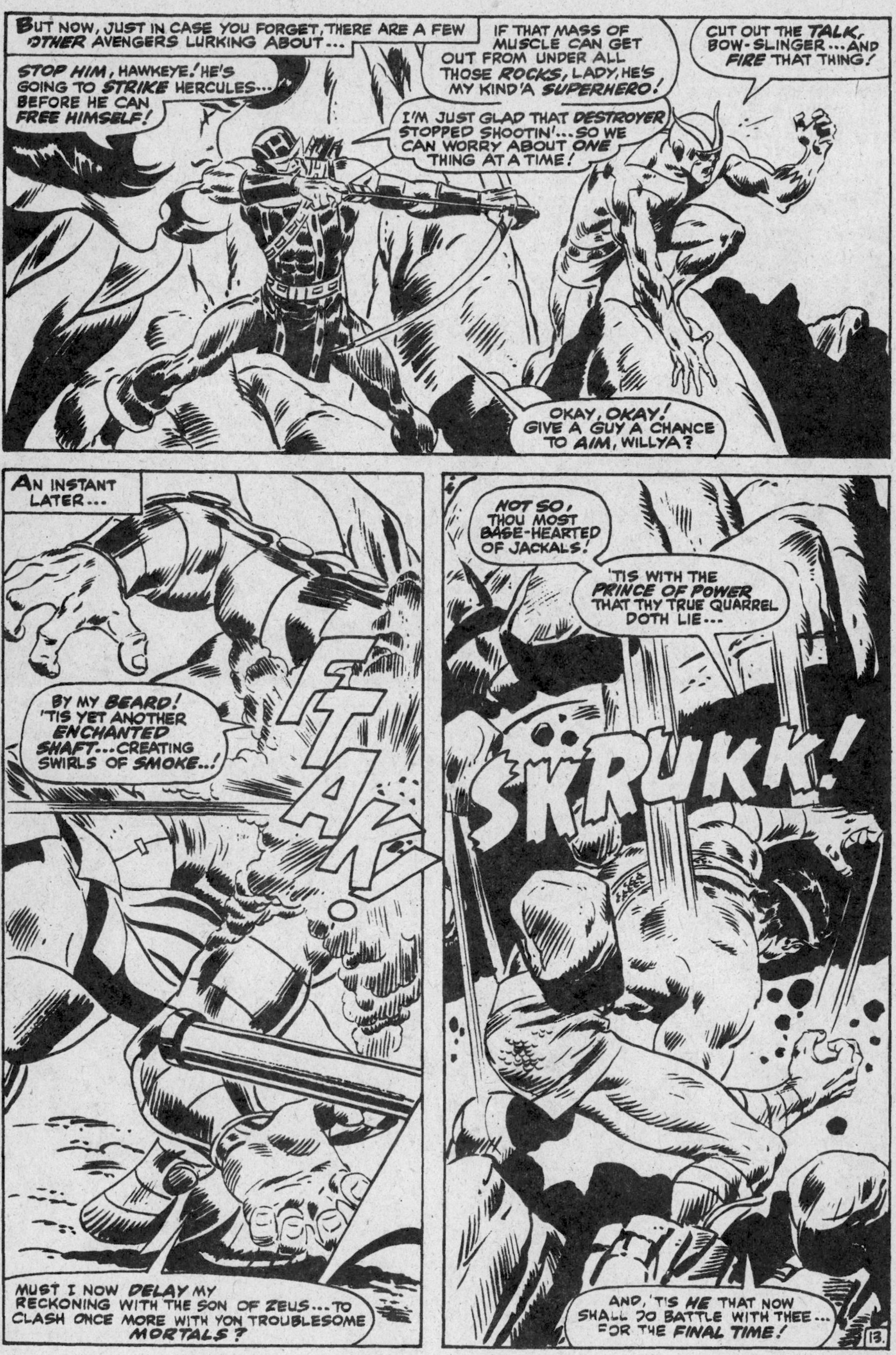

BUT NOW, JUST IN CASE YOU FORGET, THERE ARE A FEW OTHER AVENGERS LURKING ABOUT...
STOP HIM, HAWKEYE! HE'S GOING TO STRIKE HERCULES... BEFORE HE CAN FREE HIMSELF!
IF THAT MASS OF MUSCLE CAN GET OUT FROM UNDER ALL THOSE ROCKS, LADY, HE'S MY KIND'A SUPERHERO!
I'M JUST GLAD THAT DESTROYER STOPPED SHOOTIN'... SO WE CAN WORRY ABOUT ONE THING AT A TIME!
CUT OUT THE TALK, BOW-SLINGER... AND FIRE THAT THING!
OKAY, OKAY! GIVE A GUY A CHANCE TO AIM, WILLYA?
AN INSTANT LATER...
BY MY BEARD! 'TIS YET ANOTHER ENCHANTED SHAFT... CREATING SWIRLS OF SMOKE...!
FTAK!
MUST I NOW DELAY MY RECKONING WITH THE SON OF ZEUS... TO CLASH ONCE MORE WITH YON TROUBLESOME MORTALS?
NOT SO, THOU MOST BASE-HEARTED OF JACKALS!
'TIS WITH THE PRINCE OF POWER THAT THY TRUE QUARREL DOTH LIE...
SKRUKK!
AND, 'TIS HE THAT NOW SHALL DO BATTLE WITH THEE... FOR THE FINAL TIME!
13.

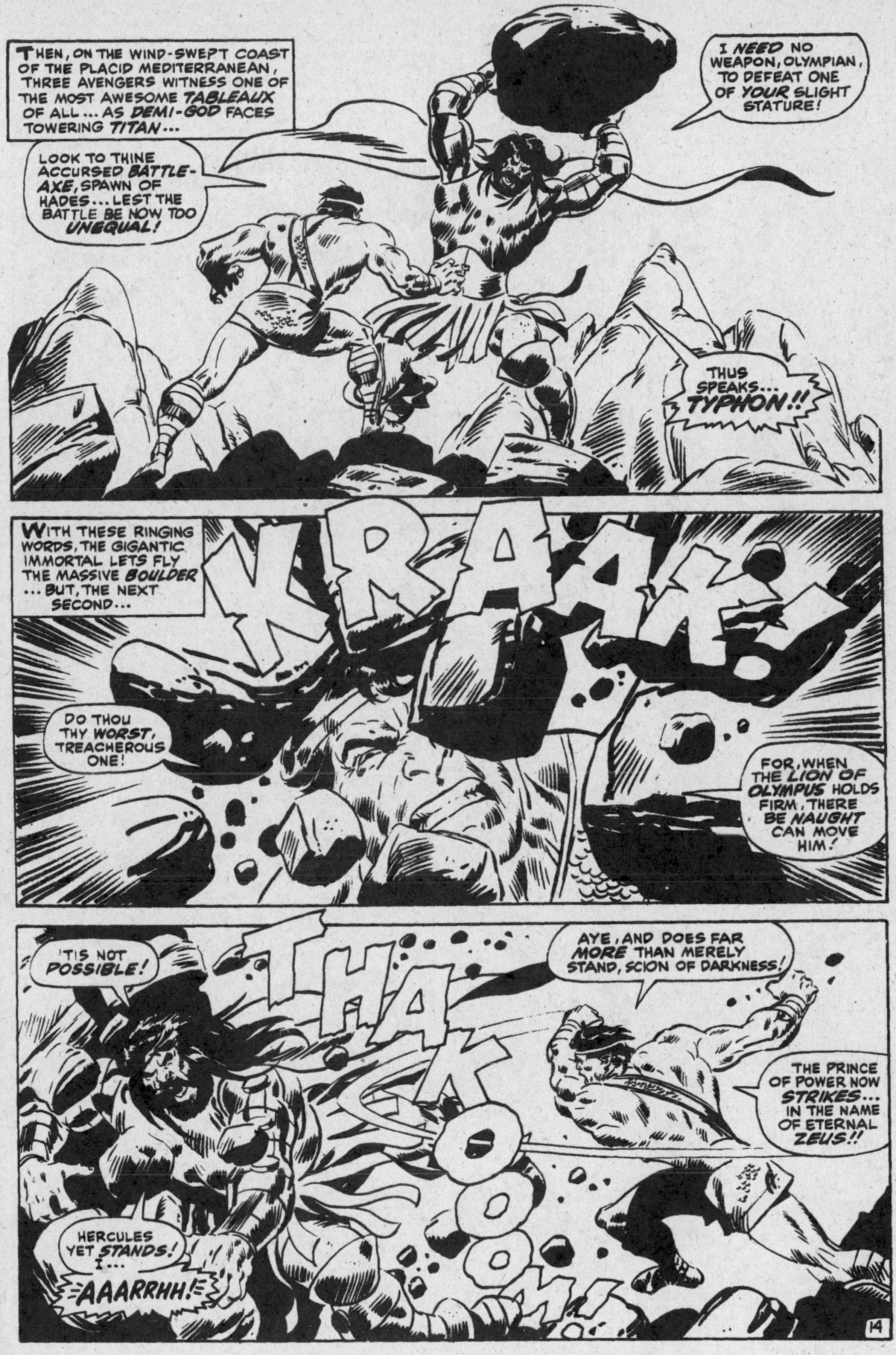
THEN, ON THE WIND-SWEPT COAST OF THE PLACID MEDITERRANEAN, THREE AVENGERS WITNESS ONE OF THE MOST AWESOME TABLEAUX OF ALL... AS DEMI-GOD FACES TOWERING TITAN...
I NEED NO WEAPON, OLYMPIAN, TO DEFEAT ONE OF YOUR SLIGHT STATURE!
LOOK TO THINE ACCURSED BATTLE-AXE, SPAWN OF HADES... LEST THE BATTLE BE NOW TOO UNEQUAL!
THUS SPEAKS... TYPHON!!
WITH THESE RINGING WORDS, THE GIGANTIC IMMORTAL LETS FLY THE MASSIVE BOULDER ... BUT, THE NEXT SECOND...
KRAAK!
DO THOU THY WORST, TREACHEROUS ONE!
FOR, WHEN THE LION OF OLYMPUS HOLDS FIRM, THERE BE NAUGHT CAN MOVE HIM!
'TIS NOT POSSIBLE!
THAK
AYE, AND DOES FAR MORE THAN MERELY STAND, SCION OF DARKNESS!
THE PRINCE OF POWER NOW STRIKES... IN THE NAME OF ETERNAL ZEUS!!
HERCULES YET STANDS! I...
AAARRHH!
OOOOM!
14

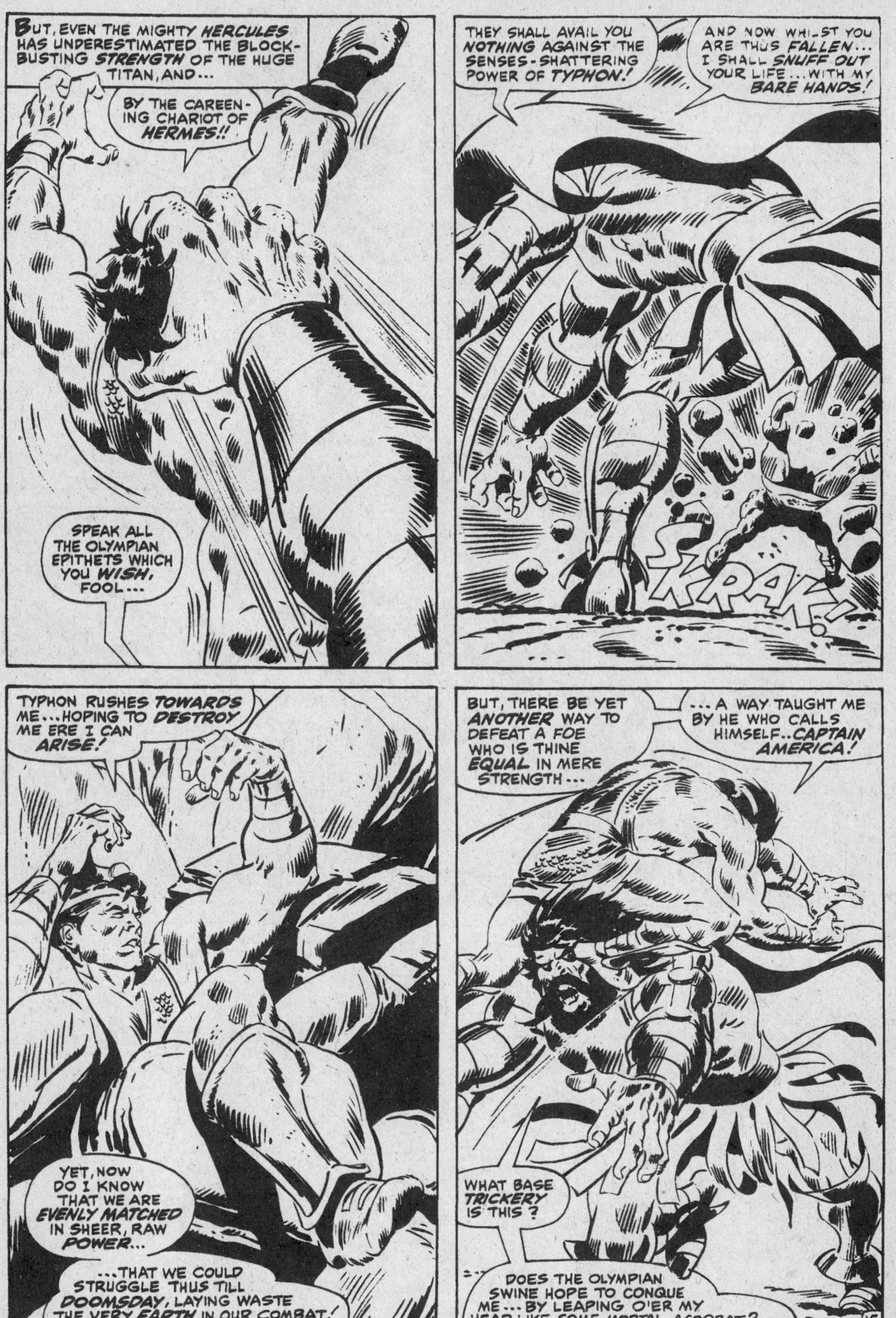
BUT, EVEN THE MIGHTY HERCULES HAS UNDERESTIMATED THE BLOCK-BUSTING STRENGTH OF THE HUGE TITAN, AND...
BY THE CAREENING CHARIOT OF HERMES!!
SPEAK ALL THE OLYMPIAN EPITHETS WHICH YOU WISH, FOOL...
THEY SHALL AVAIL YOU NOTHING AGAINST THE SENSES-SHATTERING POWER OF TYPHON!
AND NOW WHILST YOU ARE THUS FALLEN... I SHALL SNUFF OUT YOUR LIFE... WITH MY BARE HANDS!
SKRAK!
TYPHON RUSHES TOWARDS ME... HOPING TO DESTROY ME ERE I CAN ARISE!
YET, NOW DO I KNOW THAT WE ARE EVENLY MATCHED IN SHEER, RAW POWER...
...THAT WE COULD STRUGGLE THUS TILL DOOMSDAY, LAYING WASTE THE VERY EARTH IN OUR COMBAT!
BUT, THERE BE YET ANOTHER WAY TO DEFEAT A FOE WHO IS THINE EQUAL IN MERE STRENGTH...
...A WAY TAUGHT ME BY HE WHO CALLS HIMSELF..CAPTAIN AMERICA!
WHAT BASE TRICKERY IS THIS?
DOES THE OLYMPIAN SWINE HOPE TO CONQUE ME... BY LEAPING O'ER MY HEAD LIKE SOME MORTAL ACROBAT?
15.

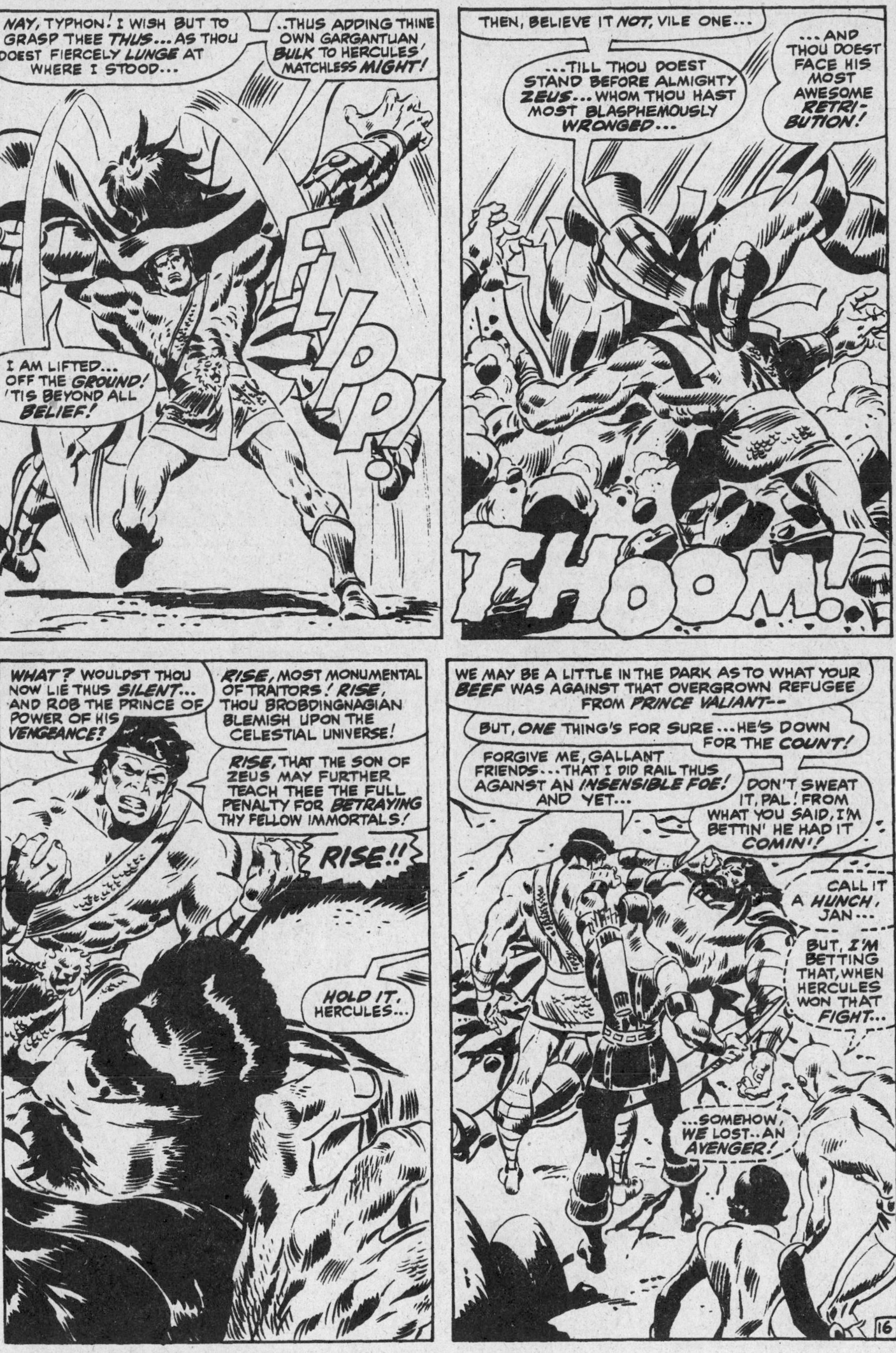
NAY, TYPHON! I WISH BUT TO GRASP THEE THUS... AS THOU DOEST FIERCELY LUNGE AT WHERE I STOOD...
..THUS ADDING THINE OWN GARGANTUAN BULK TO HERCULES' MATCHLESS MIGHT!
FLIPP!
I AM LIFTED... OFF THE GROUND! 'TIS BEYOND ALL BELIEF!
THEN, BELIEVE IT NOT, VILE ONE...
...TILL THOU DOEST STAND BEFORE ALMIGHTY ZEUS... WHOM THOU HAST MOST BLASPHEMOUSLY WRONGED...
...AND THOU DOEST FACE HIS MOST AWESOME RETRI-BUTION!
THOOM!
WHAT? WOULDST THOU NOW LIE THUS SILENT... AND ROB THE PRINCE OF POWER OF HIS VENGEANCE?
RISE, MOST MONUMENTAL OF TRAITORS! RISE, THOU BROBDINGNAGIAN BLEMISH UPON THE CELESTIAL UNIVERSE!
RISE, THAT THE SON OF ZEUS MAY FURTHER TEACH THEE THE FULL PENALTY FOR BETRAYING THY FELLOW IMMORTALS!
RISE!!
HOLD IT, HERCULES...
WE MAY BE A LITTLE IN THE DARK AS TO WHAT YOUR BEEF WAS AGAINST THAT OVERGROWN REFUGEE FROM PRINCE VALIANT--
BUT, ONE THING'S FOR SURE...HE'S DOWN FOR THE COUNT!
FORGIVE ME, GALLANT FRIENDS...THAT I DID RAIL THUS AGAINST AN INSENSIBLE FOE! AND YET...
DON'T SWEAT IT, PAL! FROM WHAT YOU SAID, I'M BETTIN' HE HAD IT COMIN'!
CALL IT A HUNCH, JAN...
BUT, I'M BETTING THAT, WHEN HERCULES WON THAT FIGHT...
...SOMEHOW, WE LOST..AN AVENGER!
16

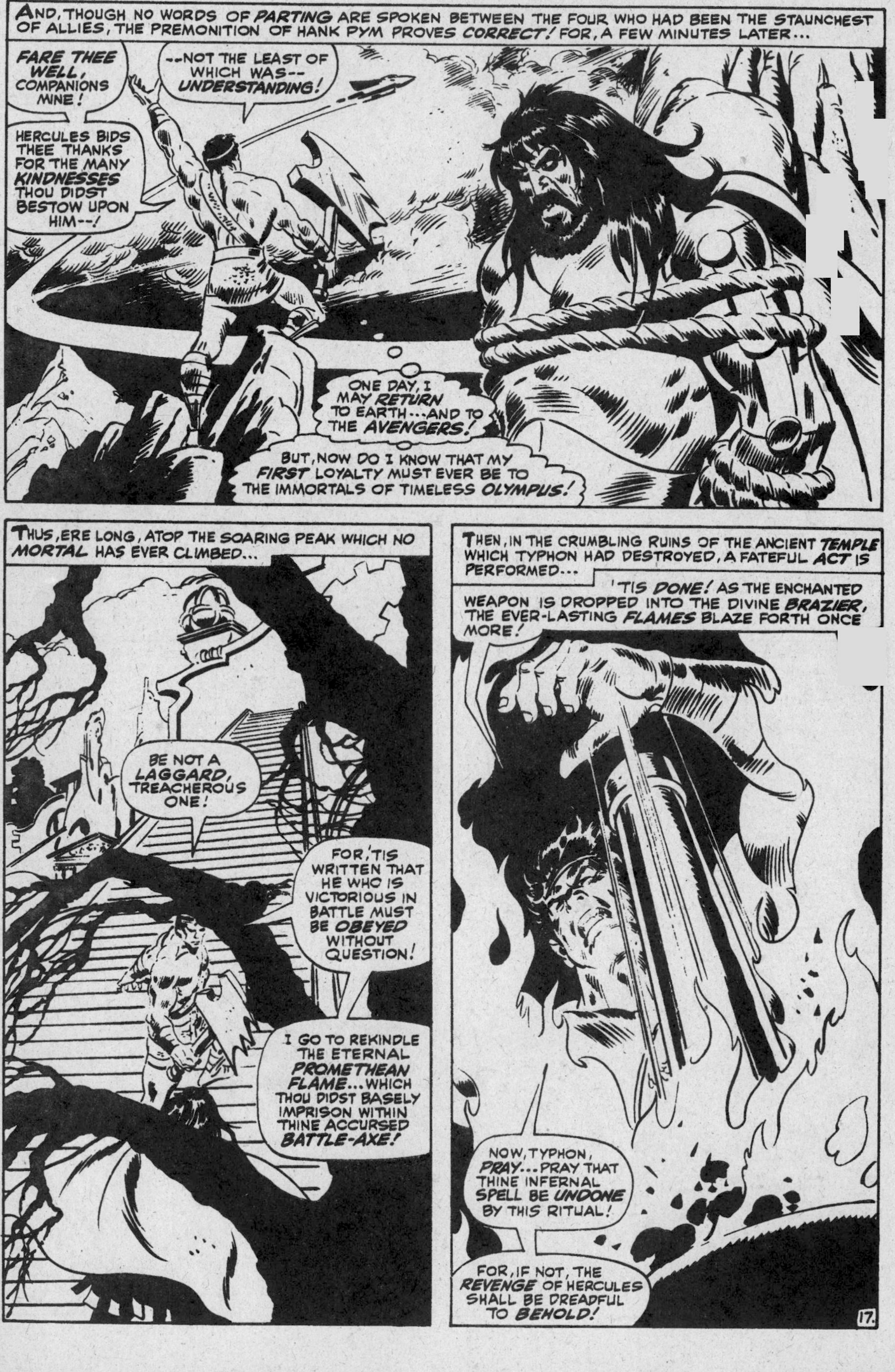
AND, THOUGH NO WORDS OF PARTING ARE SPOKEN BETWEEN THE FOUR WHO HAD BEEN THE STAUNCHEST OF ALLIES, THE PREMONITION OF HANK PYM PROVES CORRECT! FOR, A FEW MINUTES LATER...
FARE THEE WELL, COMPANIONS MINE!
HERCULES BIDS THEE THANKS FOR THE MANY KINDNESSES THOU DIDST BESTOW UPON HIM--!
--NOT THE LEAST OF WHICH WAS-- UNDERSTANDING!
ONE DAY, I MAY RETURN TO EARTH...AND TO THE AVENGERS!
BUT, NOW DO I KNOW THAT MY FIRST LOYALTY MUST EVER BE TO THE IMMORTALS OF TIMELESS OLYMPUS!
THUS, ERE LONG, ATOP THE SOARING PEAK WHICH NO MORTAL HAS EVER CLIMBED...
BE NOT A LAGGARD, TREACHEROUS ONE!
FOR, 'TIS WRITTEN THAT HE WHO IS VICTORIOUS IN BATTLE MUST BE OBEYED WITHOUT QUESTION!
I GO TO REKINDLE THE ETERNAL PROMETHEAN FLAME...WHICH THOU DIDST BASELY IMPRISON WITHIN THINE ACCURSED BATTLE-AXE!
THEN, IN THE CRUMBLING RUINS OF THE ANCIENT TEMPLE WHICH TYPHON HAD DESTROYED, A FATEFUL ACT IS PERFORMED...
'TIS DONE! AS THE ENCHANTED WEAPON IS DROPPED INTO THE DIVINE BRAZIER, THE EVER-LASTING FLAMES BLAZE FORTH ONCE MORE!
NOW, TYPHON, PRAY...PRAY THAT THINE INFERNAL SPELL BE UNDONE BY THIS RITUAL!
FOR, IF NOT, THE REVENGE OF HERCULES SHALL BE DREADFUL TO BEHOLD!
17.

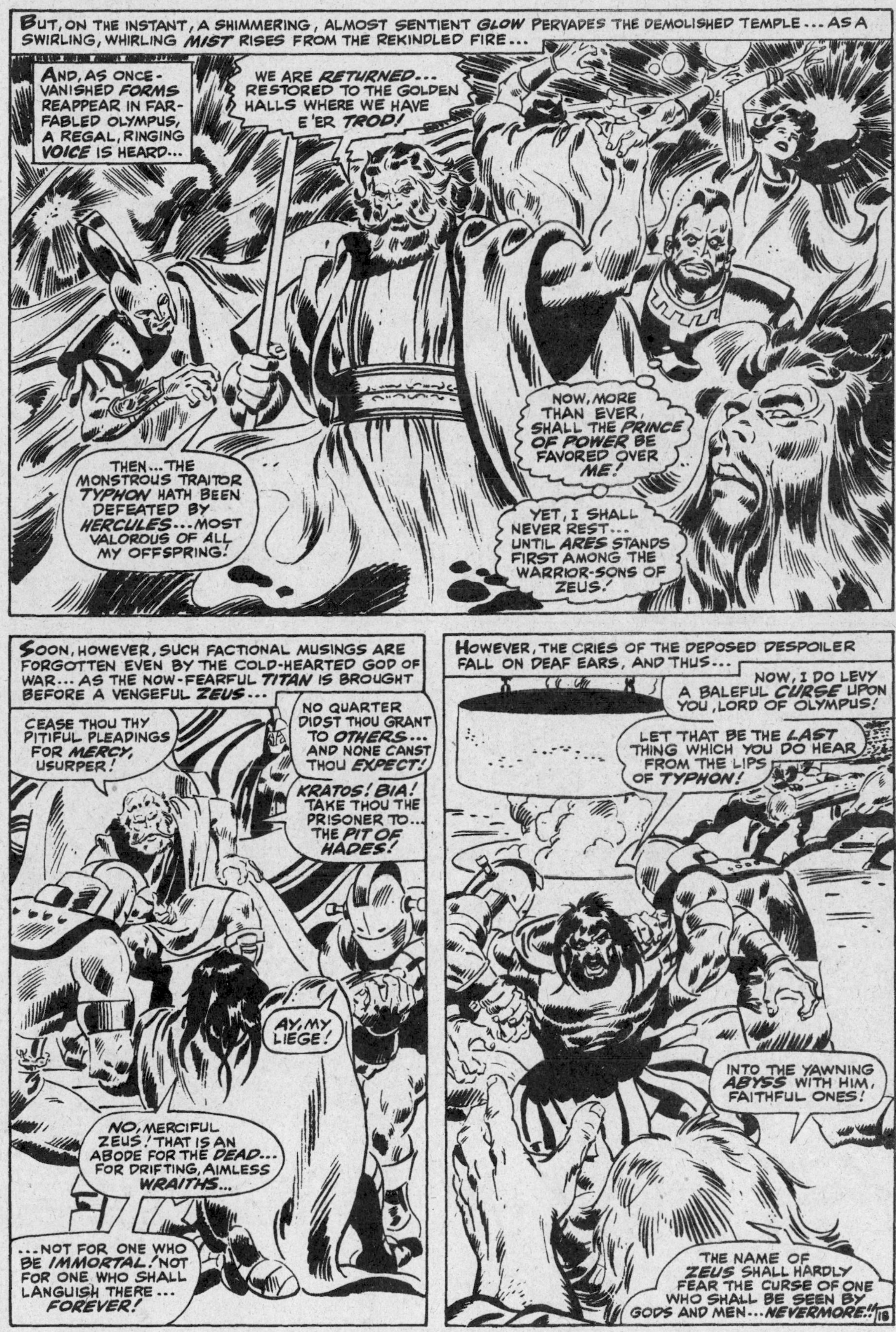

BUT, ON THE INSTANT, A SHIMMERING, ALMOST SENTIENT GLOW PERVADES THE DEMOLISHED TEMPLE... AS A SWIRLING, WHIRLING MIST RISES FROM THE REKINDLED FIRE...
AND, AS ONCE-VANISHED FORMS REAPPEAR IN FAR-FABLED OLYMPUS, A REGAL, RINGING VOICE IS HEARD...
WE ARE RETURNED... RESTORED TO THE GOLDEN HALLS WHERE WE HAVE E'ER TROD!
THEN... THE MONSTROUS TRAITOR TYPHON HATH BEEN DEFEATED BY HERCULES... MOST VALOROUS OF ALL MY OFFSPRING!
NOW, MORE THAN EVER, SHALL THE PRINCE OF POWER BE FAVORED OVER ME!
YET, I SHALL NEVER REST... UNTIL ARES STANDS FIRST AMONG THE WARRIOR-SONS OF ZEUS!
SOON, HOWEVER, SUCH FACTIONAL MUSINGS ARE FORGOTTEN EVEN BY THE COLD-HEARTED GOD OF WAR... AS THE NOW-FEARFUL TITAN IS BROUGHT BEFORE A VENGEFUL ZEUS...
CEASE THOU THY PITIFUL PLEADINGS FOR MERCY, USURPER!
NO QUARTER DIDST THOU GRANT TO OTHERS... AND NONE CANST THOU EXPECT!
KRATOS! BIA! TAKE THOU THE PRISONER TO... THE PIT OF HADES!
AY, MY LIEGE!
NO, MERCIFUL ZEUS! THAT IS AN ABODE FOR THE DEAD... FOR DRIFTING, AIMLESS WRAITHS...
...NOT FOR ONE WHO BE IMMORTAL! NOT FOR ONE WHO SHALL LANGUISH THERE... FOREVER!
HOWEVER, THE CRIES OF THE DEPOSED DESPOILER FALL ON DEAF EARS, AND THUS...
NOW, I DO LEVY A BALEFUL CURSE UPON YOU, LORD OF OLYMPUS!
LET THAT BE THE LAST THING WHICH YOU DO HEAR FROM THE LIPS OF TYPHON!
INTO THE YAWNING ABYSS WITH HIM, FAITHFUL ONES!
THE NAME OF ZEUS SHALL HARDLY FEAR THE CURSE OF ONE WHO SHALL BE SEEN BY GODS AND MEN... NEVERMORE!
18

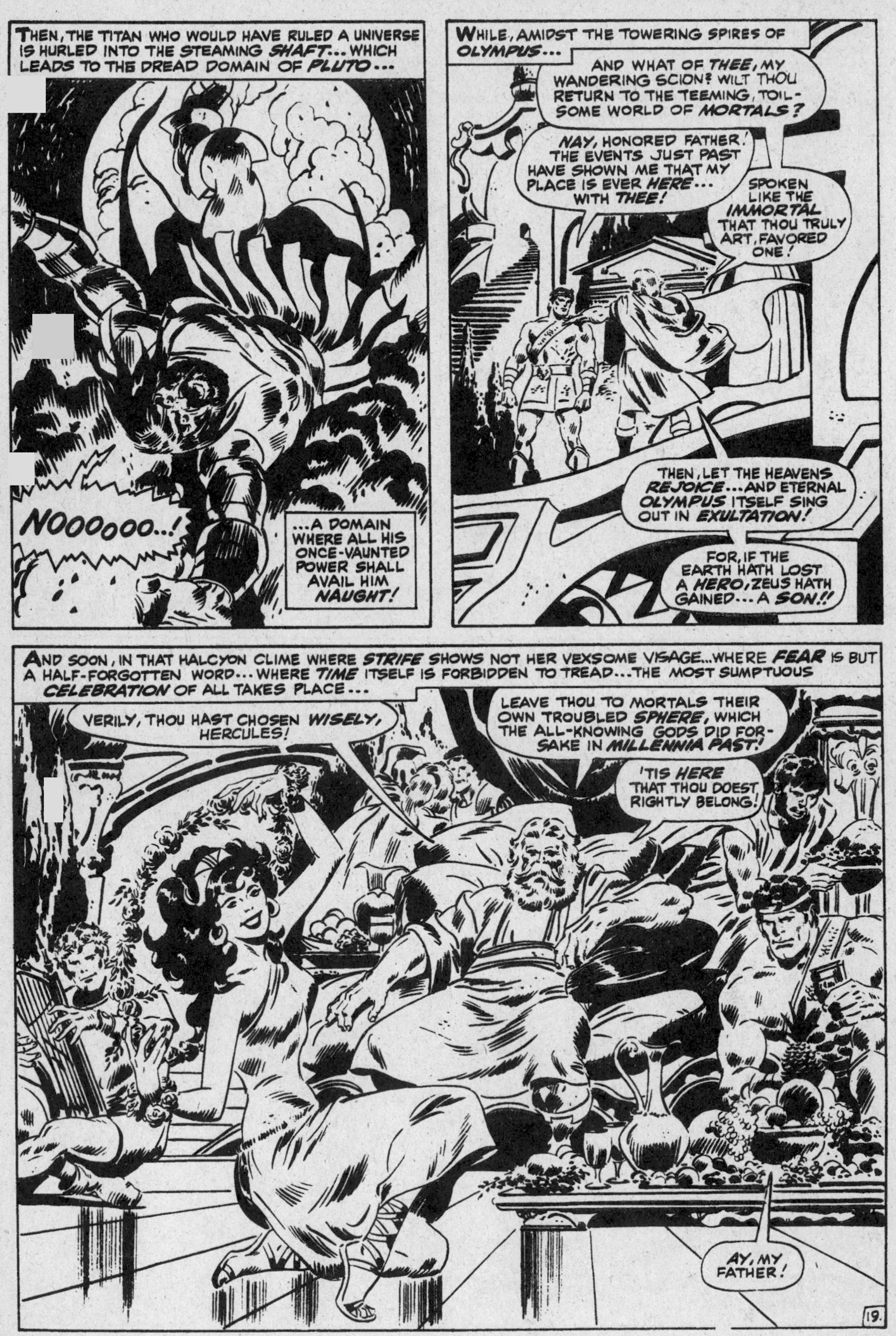
THEN, THE TITAN WHO WOULD HAVE RULED A UNIVERSE IS HURLED INTO THE STEAMING SHAFT... WHICH LEADS TO THE DREAD DOMAIN OF PLUTO...
NOOOOOO...!
...A DOMAIN WHERE ALL HIS ONCE-VAUNTED POWER SHALL AVAIL HIM NAUGHT!
WHILE, AMIDST THE TOWERING SPIRES OF OLYMPUS...
AND WHAT OF THEE, MY WANDERING SCION? WILT THOU RETURN TO THE TEEMING, TOIL-SOME WORLD OF MORTALS?
NAY, HONORED FATHER! THE EVENTS JUST PAST HAVE SHOWN ME THAT MY PLACE IS EVER HERE... WITH THEE!
SPOKEN LIKE THE IMMORTAL THAT THOU TRULY ART, FAVORED ONE!
THEN, LET THE HEAVENS REJOICE... AND ETERNAL OLYMPUS ITSELF SING OUT IN EXULTATION!
FOR, IF THE EARTH HATH LOST A HERO, ZEUS HATH GAINED... A SON!!
AND SOON, IN THAT HALCYON CLIME WHERE STRIFE SHOWS NOT HER VEXSOME VISAGE... WHERE FEAR IS BUT A HALF-FORGOTTEN WORD... WHERE TIME ITSELF IS FORBIDDEN TO TREAD... THE MOST SUMPTUOUS CELEBRATION OF ALL TAKES PLACE...
VERILY, THOU HAST CHOSEN WISELY, HERCULES!
LEAVE THOU TO MORTALS THEIR OWN TROUBLED SPHERE, WHICH THE ALL-KNOWING GODS DID FOR-SAKE IN MILLENNIA PAST!
'TIS HERE THAT THOU DOEST RIGHTLY BELONG!
AY, MY FATHER!

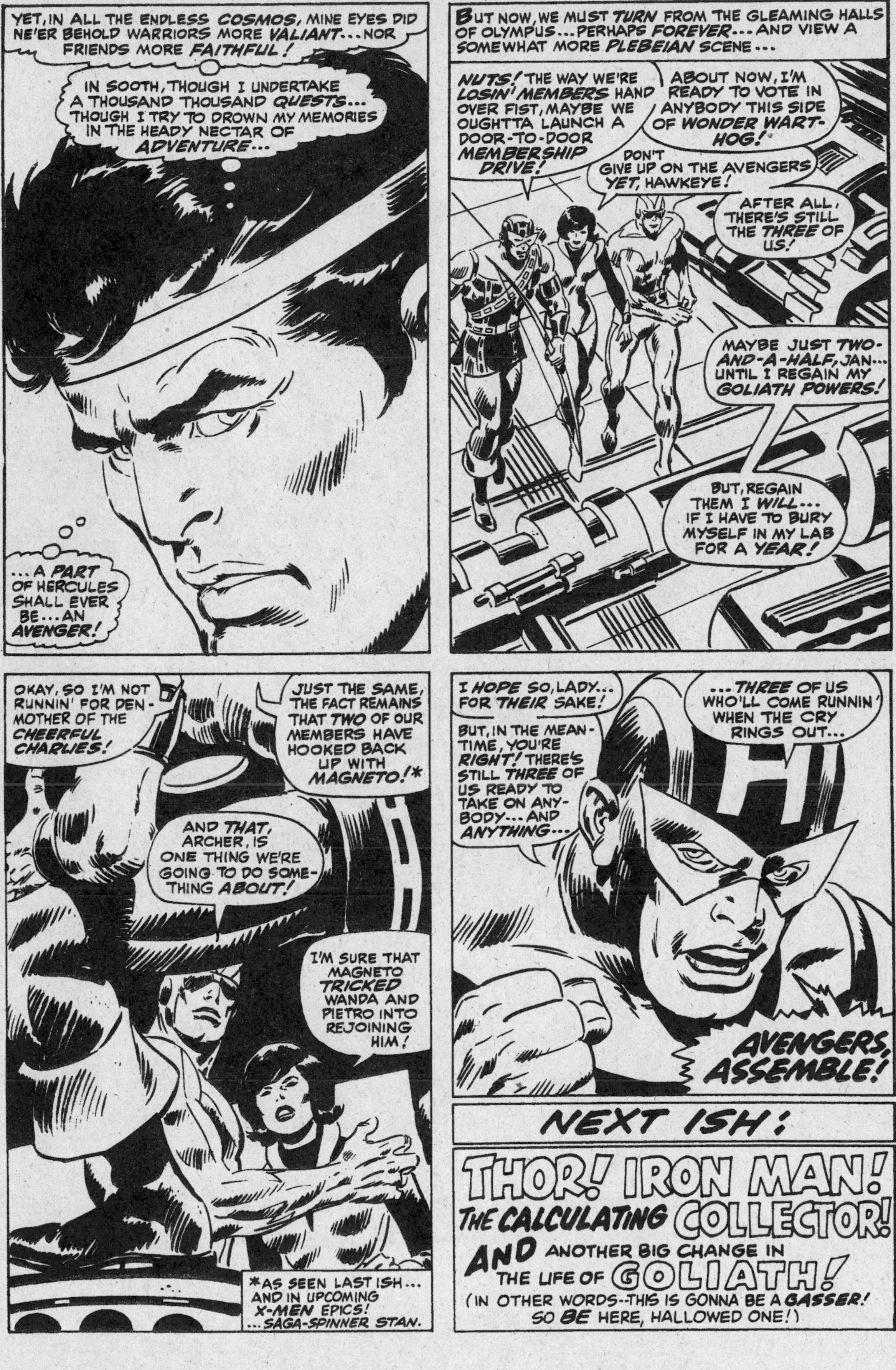
YET, IN ALL THE ENDLESS COSMOS, MINE EYES DID NE'ER BEHOLD WARRIORS MORE VALIANT... NOR FRIENDS MORE FAITHFUL!
IN SOOTH, THOUGH I UNDERTAKE A THOUSAND THOUSAND QUESTS... THOUGH I TRY TO DROWN MY MEMORIES IN THE HEADY NECTAR OF ADVENTURE...
...A PART OF HERCULES SHALL EVER BE... AN AVENGER!
BUT NOW, WE MUST TURN FROM THE GLEAMING HALLS OF OLYMPUS... PERHAPS FOREVER... AND VIEW A SOMEWHAT MORE PLEBEIAN SCENE...
NUTS! THE WAY WE'RE LOSIN' MEMBERS HAND OVER FIST, MAYBE WE OUGHTTA LAUNCH A DOOR-TO-DOOR MEMBERSHIP DRIVE!
ABOUT NOW, I'M READY TO VOTE IN ANYBODY THIS SIDE OF WONDER WART-HOG!
DON'T GIVE UP ON THE AVENGERS YET, HAWKEYE!
AFTER ALL, THERE'S STILL THE THREE OF US!
MAYBE JUST TWO-AND-A-HALF, JAN... UNTIL I REGAIN MY GOLIATH POWERS!
BUT, REGAIN THEM I WILL... IF I HAVE TO BURY MYSELF IN MY LAB FOR A YEAR!
OKAY, SO I'M NOT RUNNIN' FOR DEN-MOTHER OF THE CHEERFUL CHARLIES!
JUST THE SAME, THE FACT REMAINS THAT TWO OF OUR MEMBERS HAVE HOOKED BACK UP WITH MAGNETO!*
AND THAT, ARCHER, IS ONE THING WE'RE GOING TO DO SOMETHING ABOUT!
I'M SURE THAT MAGNETO TRICKED WANDA AND PIETRO INTO REJOINING HIM!
*AS SEEN LAST ISH... AND IN UPCOMING X-MEN EPICS! ...SAGA-SPINNER STAN.
I HOPE SO, LADY... FOR THEIR SAKE!
BUT, IN THE MEAN-TIME, YOU'RE RIGHT! THERE'S STILL THREE OF US READY TO TAKE ON ANY-BODY... AND ANYTHING...
...THREE OF US WHO'LL COME RUNNIN' WHEN THE CRY RINGS OUT...
AVENGERS, ASSEMBLE!
NEXT ISH:
THOR! IRON MAN! THE CALCULATING COLLECTOR! AND ANOTHER BIG CHANGE IN THE LIFE OF GOLIATH!
(IN OTHER WORDS--THIS IS GONNA BE A GASSER! SO BE HERE, HALLOWED ONE!)

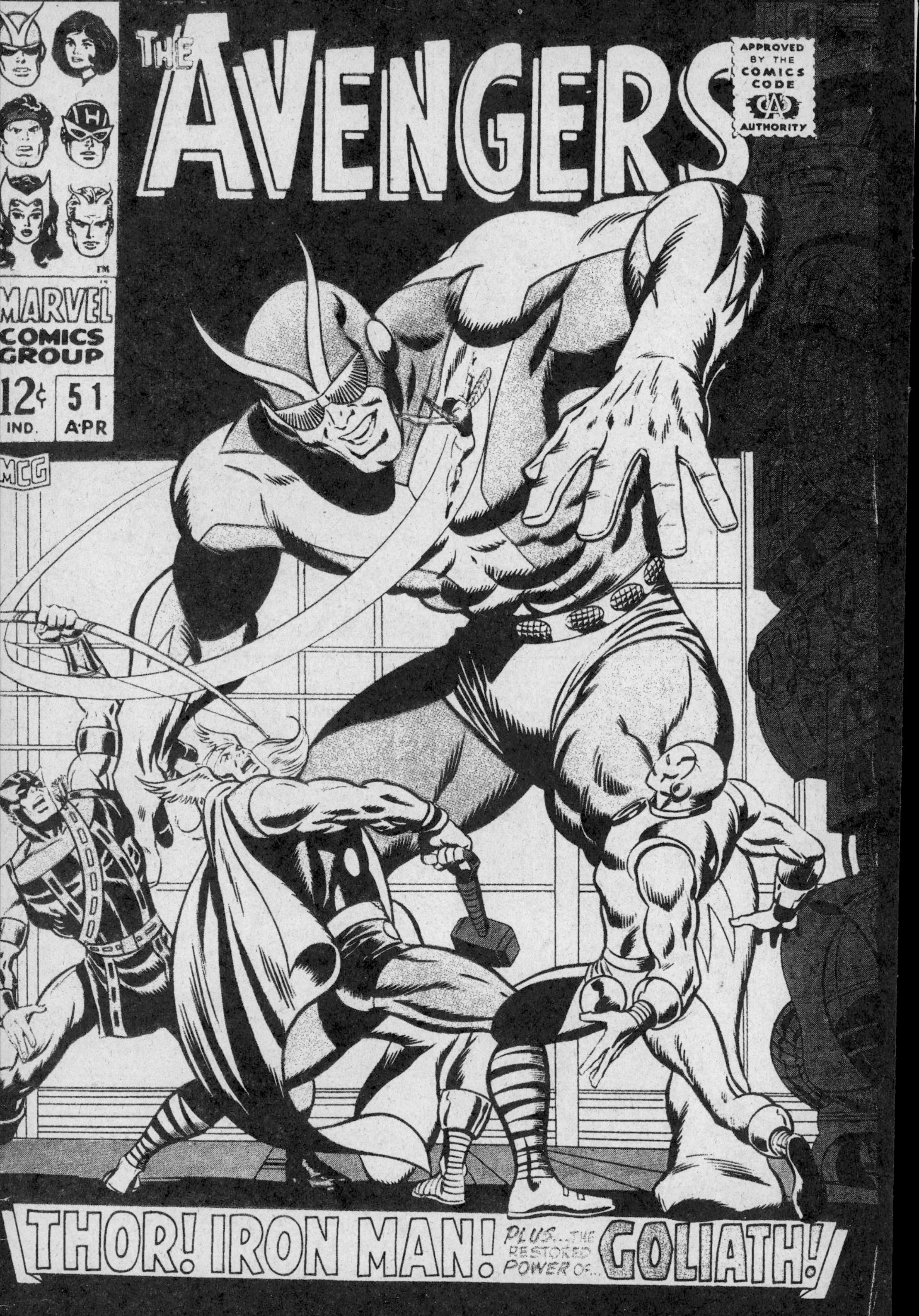

THE AVENGERS
APPROVED BY THE COMICS CODE CA AUTHORITY
TM
MARVEL COMICS GROUP
12¢ IND.
51 APR
MCG
THOR! IRON MAN! PLUS... THE RESTORED POWER OF... GOLIATH!

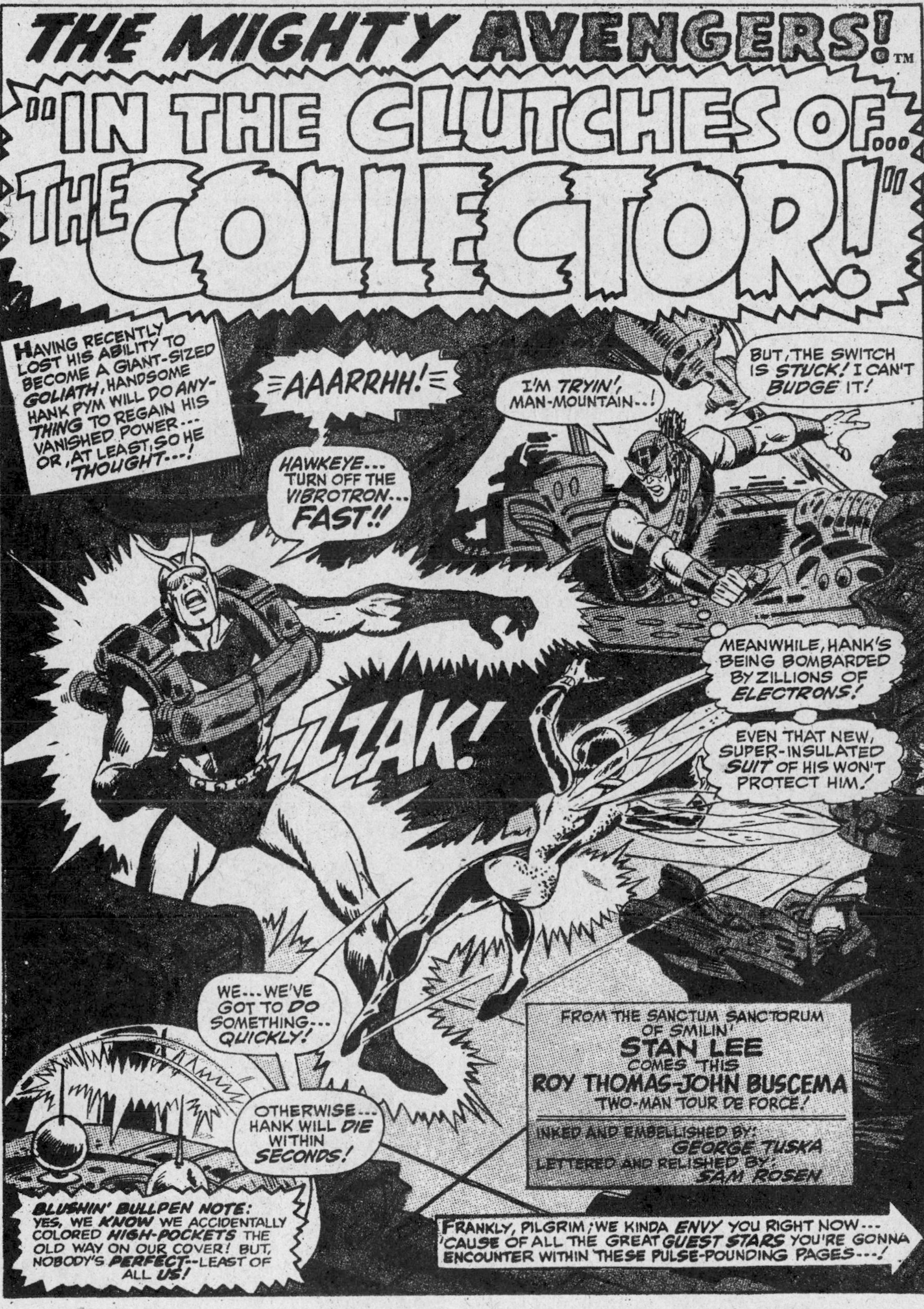
THE MIGHTY AVENGERS! TM
"IN THE CLUTCHES OF... THE COLLECTOR!"
HAVING RECENTLY LOST HIS ABILITY TO BECOME A GIANT-SIZED GOLIATH, HANDSOME HANK PYM WILL DO ANY-THING TO REGAIN HIS VANISHED POWER--- OR, AT LEAST, SO HE THOUGHT---!
AAARRHH!
I'M TRYIN', MAN-MOUNTAIN--!
BUT, THE SWITCH IS STUCK! I CAN'T BUDGE IT!
HAWKEYE... TURN OFF THE VIBROTRON... FAST!!
ZZAK!
MEANWHILE, HANK'S BEING BOMBARDED BY ZILLIONS OF ELECTRONS!
EVEN THAT NEW, SUPER-INSULATED SUIT OF HIS WON'T PROTECT HIM!
WE... WE'VE GOT TO DO SOMETHING... QUICKLY!
OTHERWISE... HANK WILL DIE WITHIN SECONDS!
FROM THE SANCTUM SANCTORUM OF SMILIN' STAN LEE COMES THIS ROY THOMAS-JOHN BUSCEMA TWO-MAN TOUR DE FORCE!
INKED AND EMBELLISHED BY: GEORGE TUSKA
LETTERED AND RELISHED BY: SAM ROSEN
BLUSHIN' BULLPEN NOTE: YES, WE KNOW WE ACCIDENTALLY COLORED HIGH-POCKETS THE OLD WAY ON OUR COVER! BUT, NOBODY'S PERFECT--LEAST OF ALL US!
FRANKLY, PILGRIM, WE KINDA ENVY YOU RIGHT NOW--- 'CAUSE OF ALL THE GREAT GUEST STARS YOU'RE GONNA ENCOUNTER WITHIN THESE PULSE-POUNDING PAGES---!

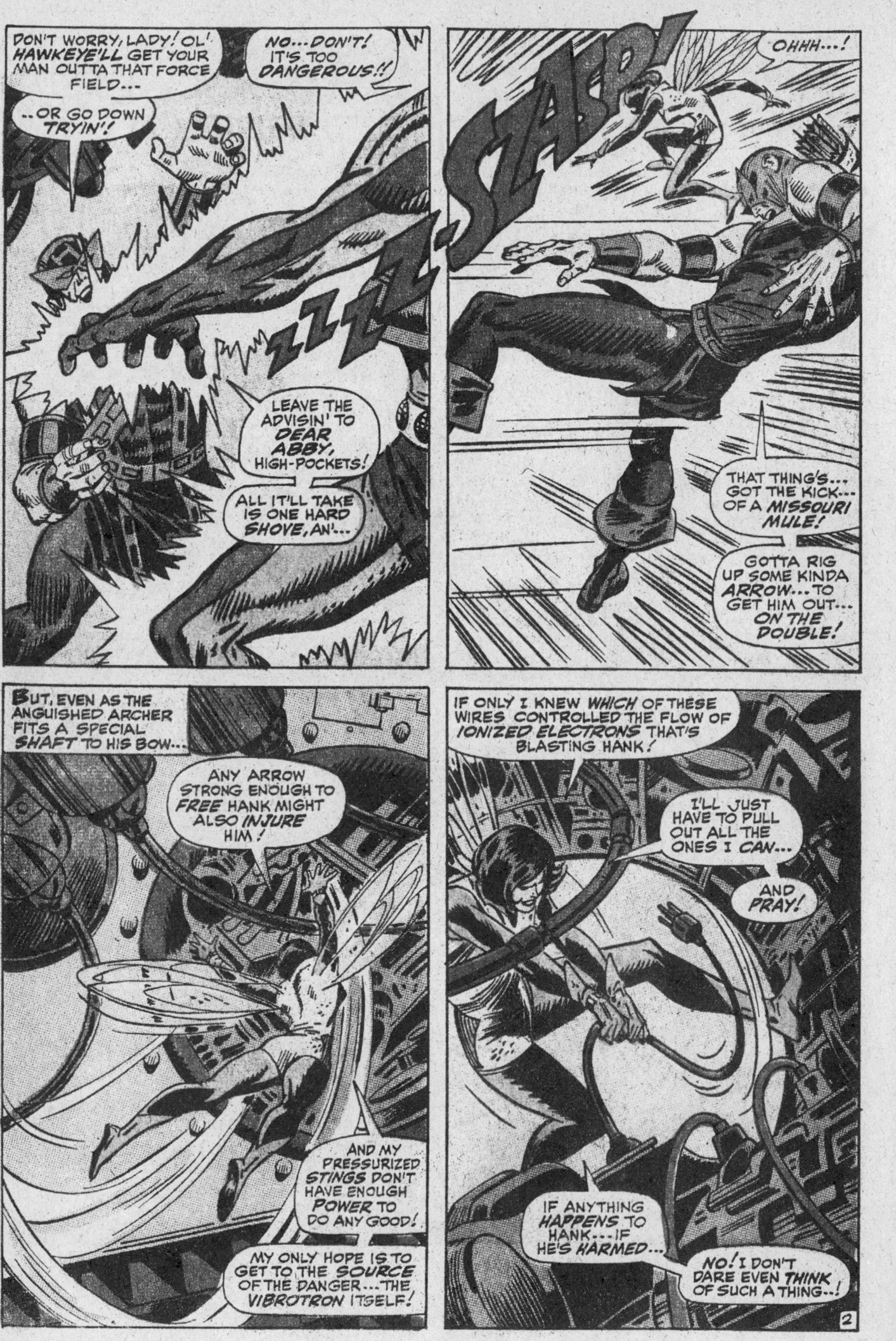
DON'T WORRY, LADY! OL' HAWKEYE'LL GET YOUR MAN OUTTA THAT FORCE FIELD...
NO...DON'T! IT'S TOO DANGEROUS!!
..OR GO DOWN TRYIN'!
ZZZZ-SZASP!
LEAVE THE ADVISIN' TO DEAR ABBY, HIGH-POCKETS!
ALL IT'LL TAKE IS ONE HARD SHOVE, AN'...
OHHH...!
THAT THING'S... GOT THE KICK... OF A MISSOURI MULE!
GOTTA RIG UP SOME KINDA ARROW... TO GET HIM OUT... ON THE DOUBLE!
BUT, EVEN AS THE ANGUISHED ARCHER FITS A SPECIAL SHAFT TO HIS BOW...
ANY ARROW STRONG ENOUGH TO FREE HANK MIGHT ALSO INJURE HIM!
AND MY PRESSURIZED STINGS DON'T HAVE ENOUGH POWER TO DO ANY GOOD!
MY ONLY HOPE IS TO GET TO THE SOURCE OF THE DANGER...THE VIBROTRON ITSELF!
IF ONLY I KNEW WHICH OF THESE WIRES CONTROLLED THE FLOW OF IONIZED ELECTRONS THAT'S BLASTING HANK!
I'LL JUST HAVE TO PULL OUT ALL THE ONES I CAN...
AND PRAY!
IF ANYTHING HAPPENS TO HANK...IF HE'S HARMED...
NO! I DON'T DARE EVEN THINK OF SUCH A THING...!
2

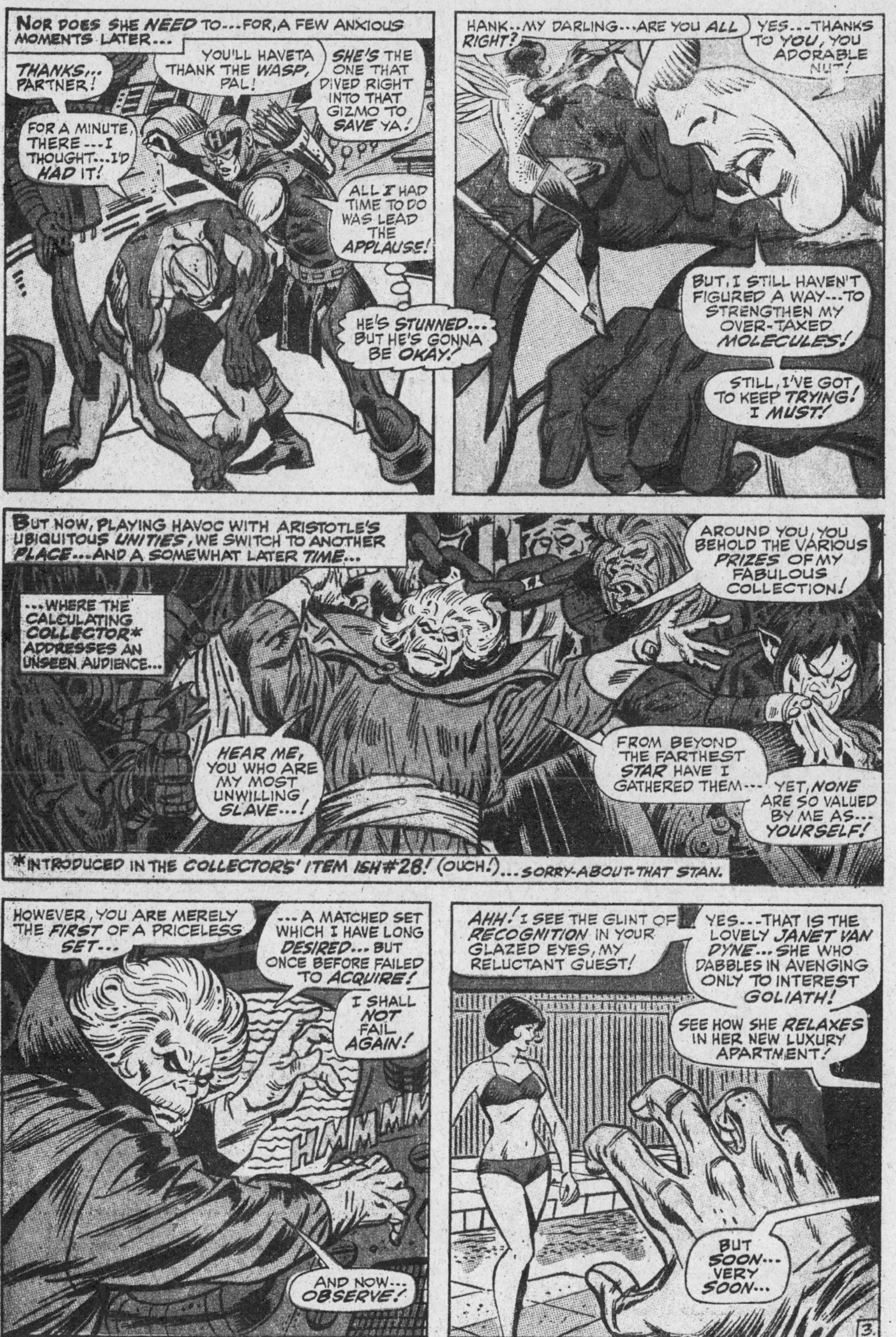
NOR DOES SHE NEED TO... FOR, A FEW ANXIOUS MOMENTS LATER...
THANKS... PARTNER!
YOU'LL HAVETA THANK THE WASP, PAL!
SHE'S THE ONE THAT DIVED RIGHT INTO THAT GIZMO TO SAVE YA!
FOR A MINUTE, THERE --- I THOUGHT... I'D HAD IT!
ALL I HAD TIME TO DO WAS LEAD THE APPLAUSE!
HE'S STUNNED... BUT HE'S GONNA BE OKAY!
HANK... MY DARLING... ARE YOU ALL RIGHT?
YES... THANKS TO YOU, YOU ADORABLE NUT!
BUT, I STILL HAVEN'T FIGURED A WAY --- TO STRENGTHEN MY OVER-TAXED MOLECULES!
STILL, I'VE GOT TO KEEP TRYING! I MUST!
BUT NOW, PLAYING HAVOC WITH ARISTOTLE'S UBIQUITOUS UNITIES, WE SWITCH TO ANOTHER PLACE... AND A SOMEWHAT LATER TIME...
...WHERE THE CALCULATING COLLECTOR* ADDRESSES AN UNSEEN AUDIENCE...
AROUND YOU, YOU BEHOLD THE VARIOUS PRIZES OF MY FABULOUS COLLECTION!
HEAR ME, YOU WHO ARE MY MOST UNWILLING SLAVE...!
FROM BEYOND THE FARTHEST STAR HAVE I GATHERED THEM---
YET, NONE ARE SO VALUED BY ME AS... YOURSELF!
*INTRODUCED IN THE COLLECTORS' ITEM ISH #28! (OUCH!)... SORRY-ABOUT-THAT STAN.
HOWEVER, YOU ARE MERELY THE FIRST OF A PRICELESS SET...
... A MATCHED SET WHICH I HAVE LONG DESIRED... BUT ONCE BEFORE FAILED TO ACQUIRE!
I SHALL NOT FAIL AGAIN!
HMMMM
AND NOW... OBSERVE!
AHH! I SEE THE GLINT OF RECOGNITION IN YOUR GLAZED EYES, MY RELUCTANT GUEST!
YES... THAT IS THE LOVELY JANET VAN DYNE... SHE WHO DABBLES IN AVENGING ONLY TO INTEREST GOLIATH!
SEE HOW SHE RELAXES IN HER NEW LUXURY APARTMENT!
BUT SOON... VERY SOON...
3.

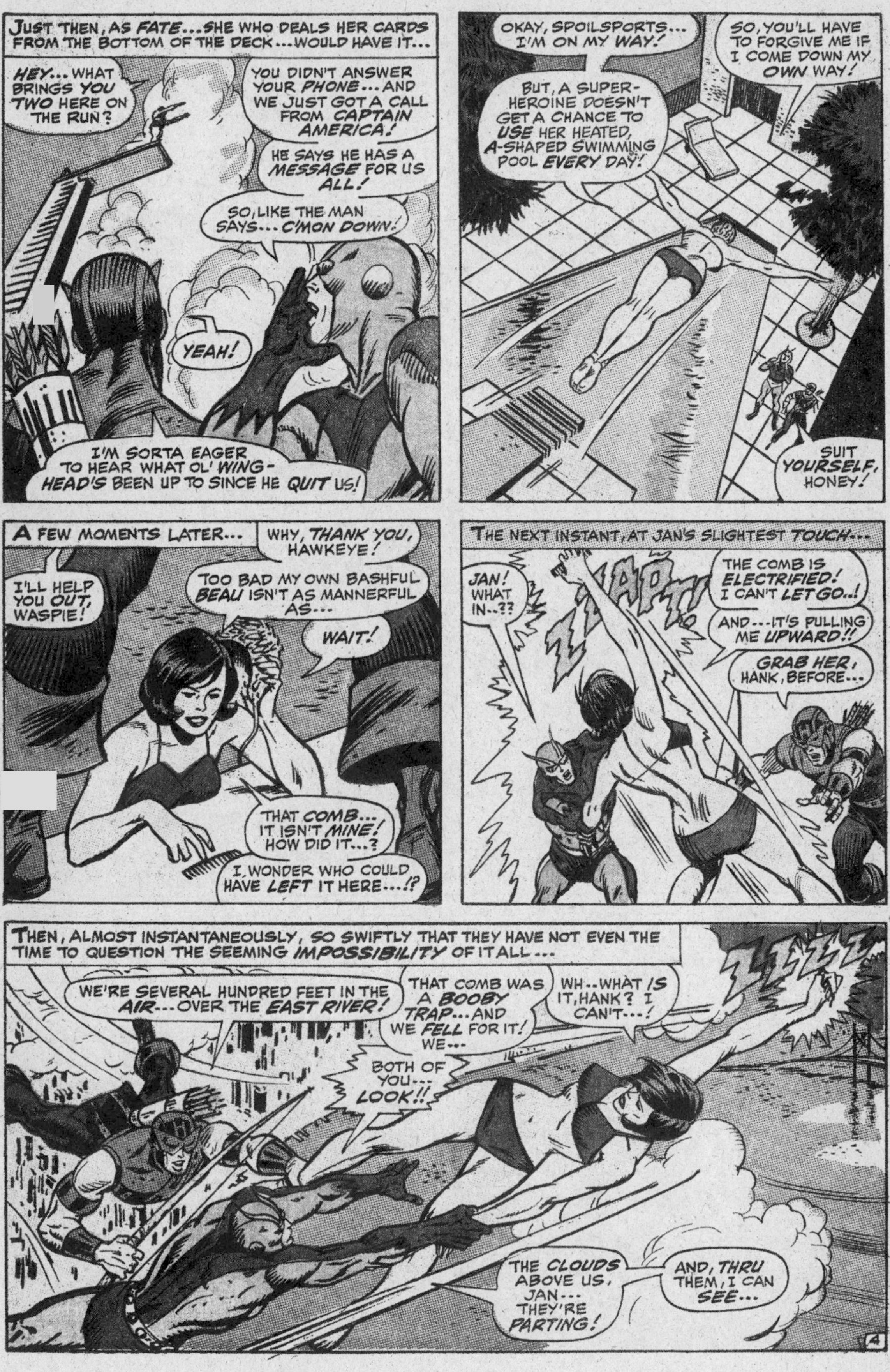
JUST THEN, AS FATE...SHE WHO DEALS HER CARDS FROM THE BOTTOM OF THE DECK...WOULD HAVE IT...
HEY... WHAT BRINGS YOU TWO HERE ON THE RUN?
YOU DIDN'T ANSWER YOUR PHONE... AND WE JUST GOT A CALL FROM CAPTAIN AMERICA!
HE SAYS HE HAS A MESSAGE FOR US ALL!
SO, LIKE THE MAN SAYS... C'MON DOWN!
YEAH!
I'M SORTA EAGER TO HEAR WHAT OL' WING-HEAD'S BEEN UP TO SINCE HE QUIT US!
OKAY, SPOILSPORTS... I'M ON MY WAY!
BUT, A SUPER-HEROINE DOESN'T GET A CHANCE TO USE HER HEATED, A-SHAPED SWIMMING POOL EVERY DAY!
SO, YOU'LL HAVE TO FORGIVE ME IF I COME DOWN MY OWN WAY!
SUIT YOURSELF, HONEY!
A FEW MOMENTS LATER...
I'LL HELP YOU OUT, WASPIE!
WHY, THANK YOU, HAWKEYE!
TOO BAD MY OWN BASHFUL BEAU ISN'T AS MANNERFUL AS---
WAIT!
THAT COMB... IT ISN'T MINE! HOW DID IT...?
I WONDER WHO COULD HAVE LEFT IT HERE...!?
THE NEXT INSTANT, AT JAN'S SLIGHTEST TOUCH...
JAN! WHAT IN..??
ZZAP!!
THE COMB IS ELECTRIFIED! I CAN'T LET GO..!
AND---IT'S PULLING ME UPWARD!!
GRAB HER, HANK, BEFORE...
THEN, ALMOST INSTANTANEOUSLY, SO SWIFTLY THAT THEY HAVE NOT EVEN THE TIME TO QUESTION THE SEEMING IMPOSSIBILITY OF IT ALL...
ZZZZ
WE'RE SEVERAL HUNDRED FEET IN THE AIR---OVER THE EAST RIVER!
THAT COMB WAS A BOOBY TRAP... AND WE FELL FOR IT! WE---
WH--WHAT IS IT, HANK? I CAN'T---!
BOTH OF YOU--- LOOK!!
THE CLOUDS ABOVE US, JAN--- THEY'RE PARTING!
AND, THRU THEM, I CAN SEE...
4

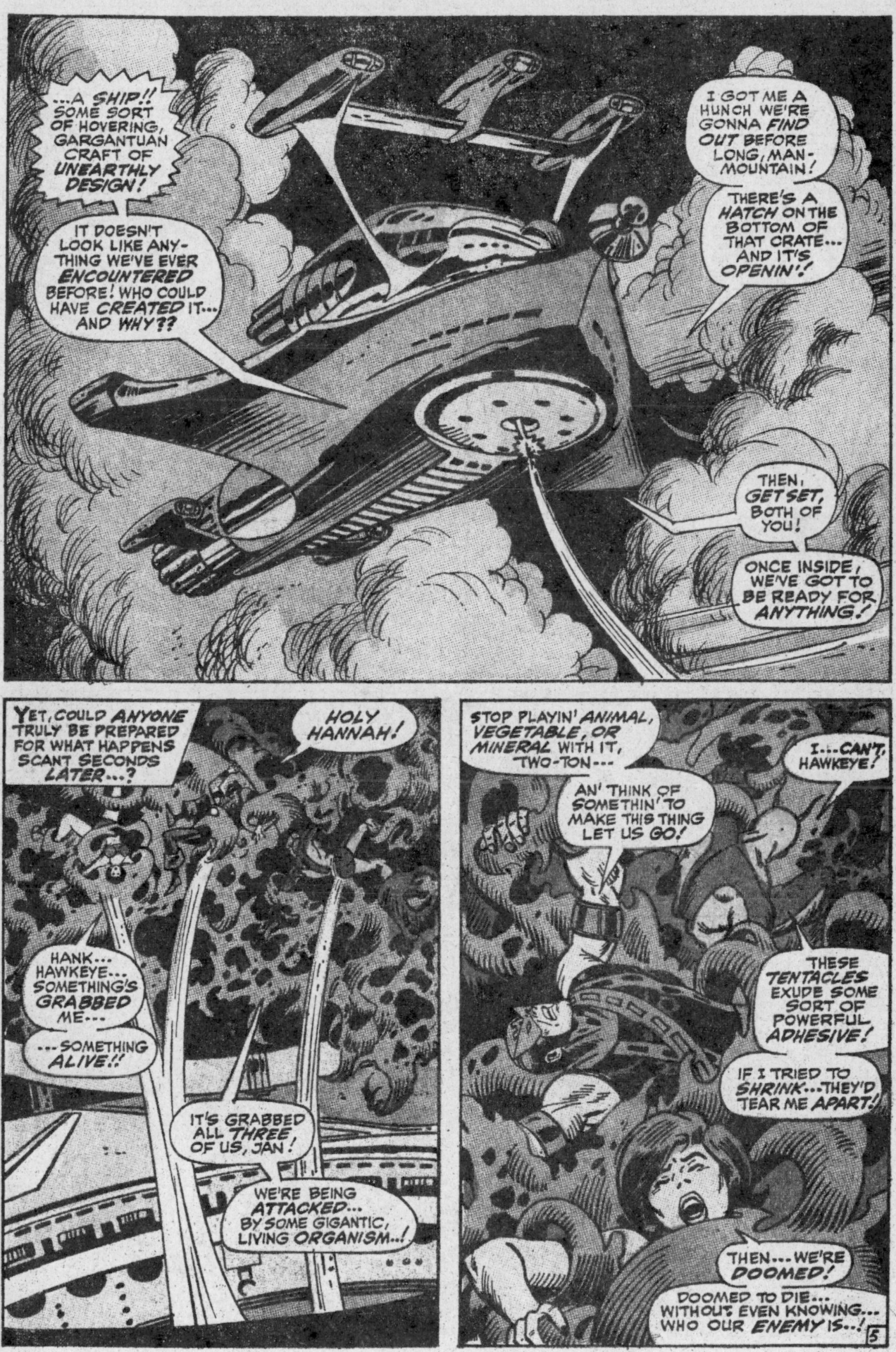
...A SHIP!! SOME SORT OF HOVERING, GARGANTUAN CRAFT OF UNEARTHLY DESIGN!
IT DOESN'T LOOK LIKE ANYTHING WE'VE EVER ENCOUNTERED BEFORE! WHO COULD HAVE CREATED IT... AND WHY??
I GOT ME A HUNCH WE'RE GONNA FIND OUT BEFORE LONG, MAN-MOUNTAIN!
THERE'S A HATCH ON THE BOTTOM OF THAT CRATE... AND IT'S OPENIN'!
THEN, GET SET, BOTH OF YOU!
ONCE INSIDE, WE'VE GOT TO BE READY FOR ANYTHING!
YET, COULD ANYONE TRULY BE PREPARED FOR WHAT HAPPENS SCANT SECONDS LATER...?
HOLY HANNAH!
HANK... HAWKEYE... SOMETHING'S GRABBED ME---
---SOMETHING ALIVE!!
IT'S GRABBED ALL THREE OF US, JAN!
WE'RE BEING ATTACKED... BY SOME GIGANTIC, LIVING ORGANISM...!
STOP PLAYIN' ANIMAL, VEGETABLE, OR MINERAL WITH IT, TWO-TON---
AN' THINK OF SOMETHIN' TO MAKE THIS THING LET US GO!
I...CAN'T, HAWKEYE!
THESE TENTACLES EXUDE SOME SORT OF POWERFUL ADHESIVE!
IF I TRIED TO SHRINK...THEY'D TEAR ME APART!
THEN... WE'RE DOOMED!
DOOMED TO DIE... WITHOUT EVEN KNOWING... WHO OUR ENEMY IS...!
5

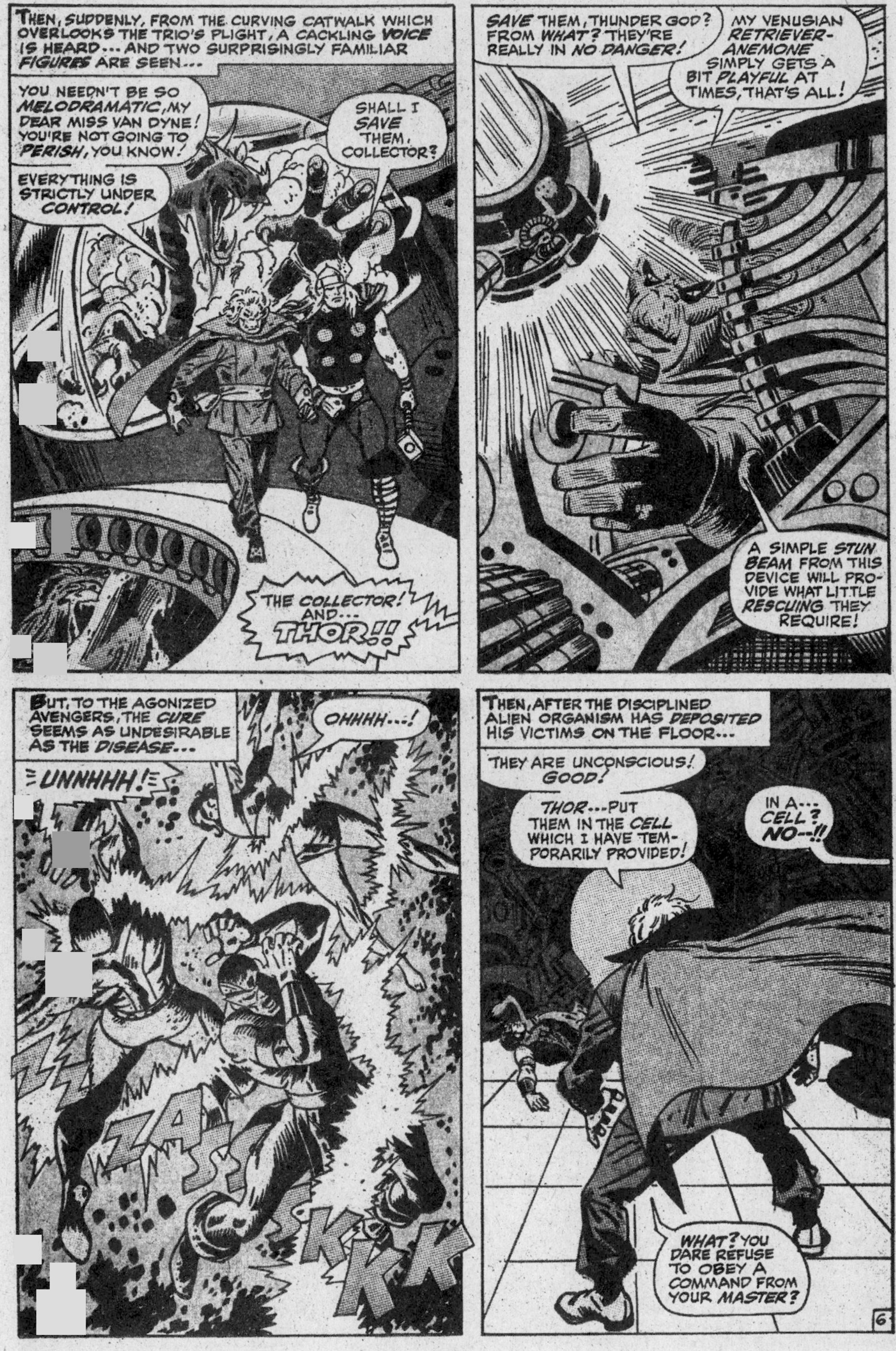
THEN, SUDDENLY, FROM THE CURVING CATWALK WHICH OVERLOOKS THE TRIO'S PLIGHT, A CACKLING VOICE IS HEARD... AND TWO SURPRISINGLY FAMILIAR FIGURES ARE SEEN...
YOU NEEDN'T BE SO MELODRAMATIC, MY DEAR MISS VAN DYNE! YOU'RE NOT GOING TO PERISH, YOU KNOW!
EVERYTHING IS STRICTLY UNDER CONTROL!
SHALL I SAVE THEM, COLLECTOR?
THE COLLECTOR! AND... THOR!!
SAVE THEM, THUNDER GOD? FROM WHAT? THEY'RE REALLY IN NO DANGER!
MY VENUSIAN RETRIEVER-ANEMONE SIMPLY GETS A BIT PLAYFUL AT TIMES, THAT'S ALL!
A SIMPLE STUN BEAM FROM THIS DEVICE WILL PROVIDE WHAT LITTLE RESCUING THEY REQUIRE!
BUT, TO THE AGONIZED AVENGERS, THE CURE SEEMS AS UNDESIRABLE AS THE DISEASE...
OHHHH...!
UNNHHH!
ZAS
SKKK
THEN, AFTER THE DISCIPLINED ALIEN ORGANISM HAS DEPOSITED HIS VICTIMS ON THE FLOOR...
THEY ARE UNCONSCIOUS! GOOD!
THOR...PUT THEM IN THE CELL WHICH I HAVE TEMPORARILY PROVIDED!
IN A... CELL? NO--!!
WHAT? YOU DARE REFUSE TO OBEY A COMMAND FROM YOUR MASTER?
6

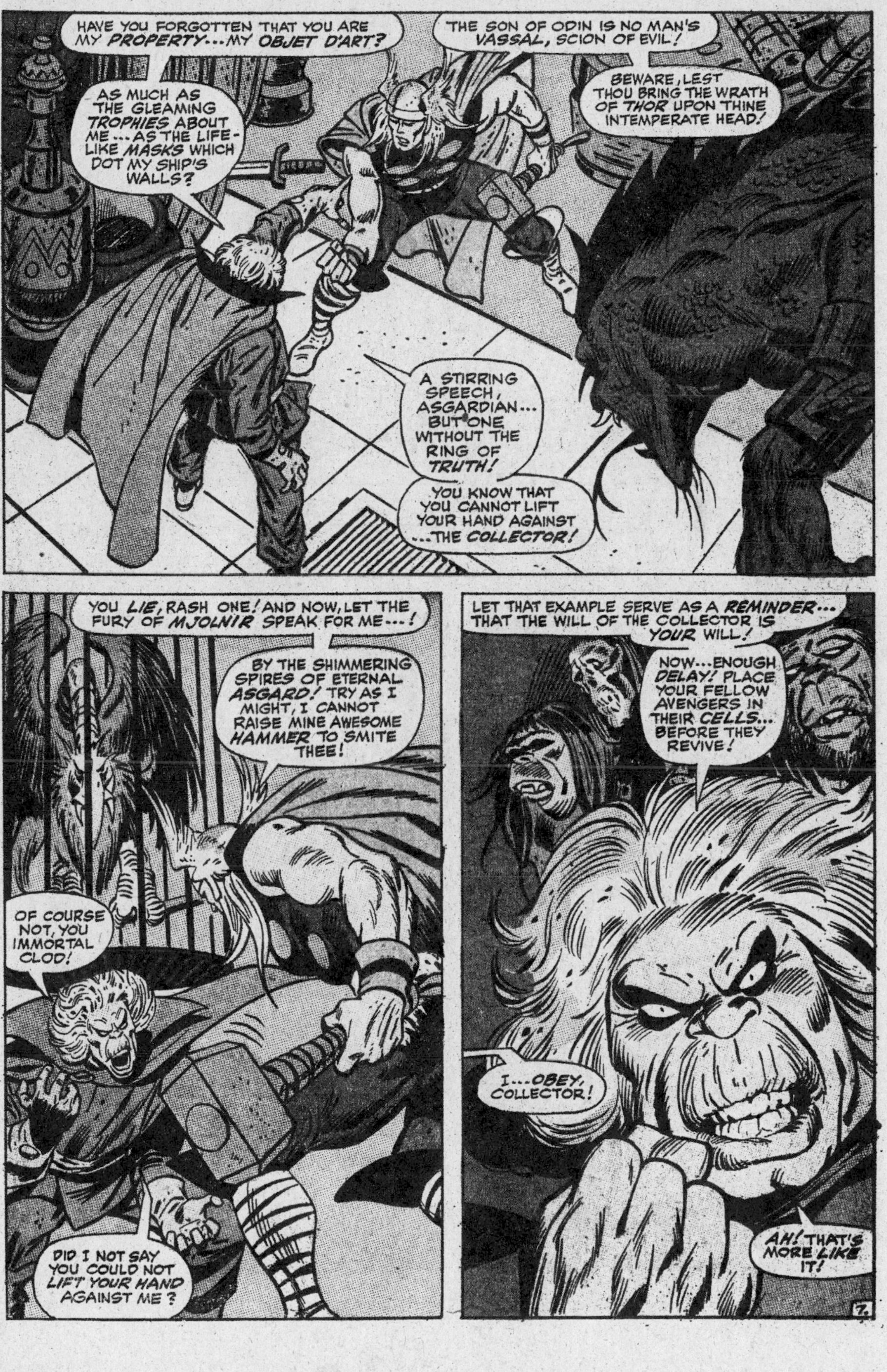
HAVE YOU FORGOTTEN THAT YOU ARE MY PROPERTY...MY OBJET D'ART?
AS MUCH AS THE GLEAMING TROPHIES ABOUT ME...AS THE LIFE-LIKE MASKS WHICH DOT MY SHIP'S WALLS?
THE SON OF ODIN IS NO MAN'S VASSAL, SCION OF EVIL!
BEWARE, LEST THOU BRING THE WRATH OF THOR UPON THINE INTEMPERATE HEAD!
A STIRRING SPEECH, ASGARDIAN... BUT ONE WITHOUT THE RING OF TRUTH!
YOU KNOW THAT YOU CANNOT LIFT YOUR HAND AGAINST ...THE COLLECTOR!
YOU LIE, RASH ONE! AND NOW, LET THE FURY OF MJOLNIR SPEAK FOR ME---!
BY THE SHIMMERING SPIRES OF ETERNAL ASGARD! TRY AS I MIGHT, I CANNOT RAISE MINE AWESOME HAMMER TO SMITE THEE!
OF COURSE NOT, YOU IMMORTAL CLOD!
DID I NOT SAY YOU COULD NOT LIFT YOUR HAND AGAINST ME?
LET THAT EXAMPLE SERVE AS A REMINDER... THAT THE WILL OF THE COLLECTOR IS YOUR WILL!
NOW...ENOUGH DELAY! PLACE YOUR FELLOW AVENGERS IN THEIR CELLS... BEFORE THEY REVIVE!
I...OBEY, COLLECTOR!
AH! THAT'S MORE LIKE IT!
7.

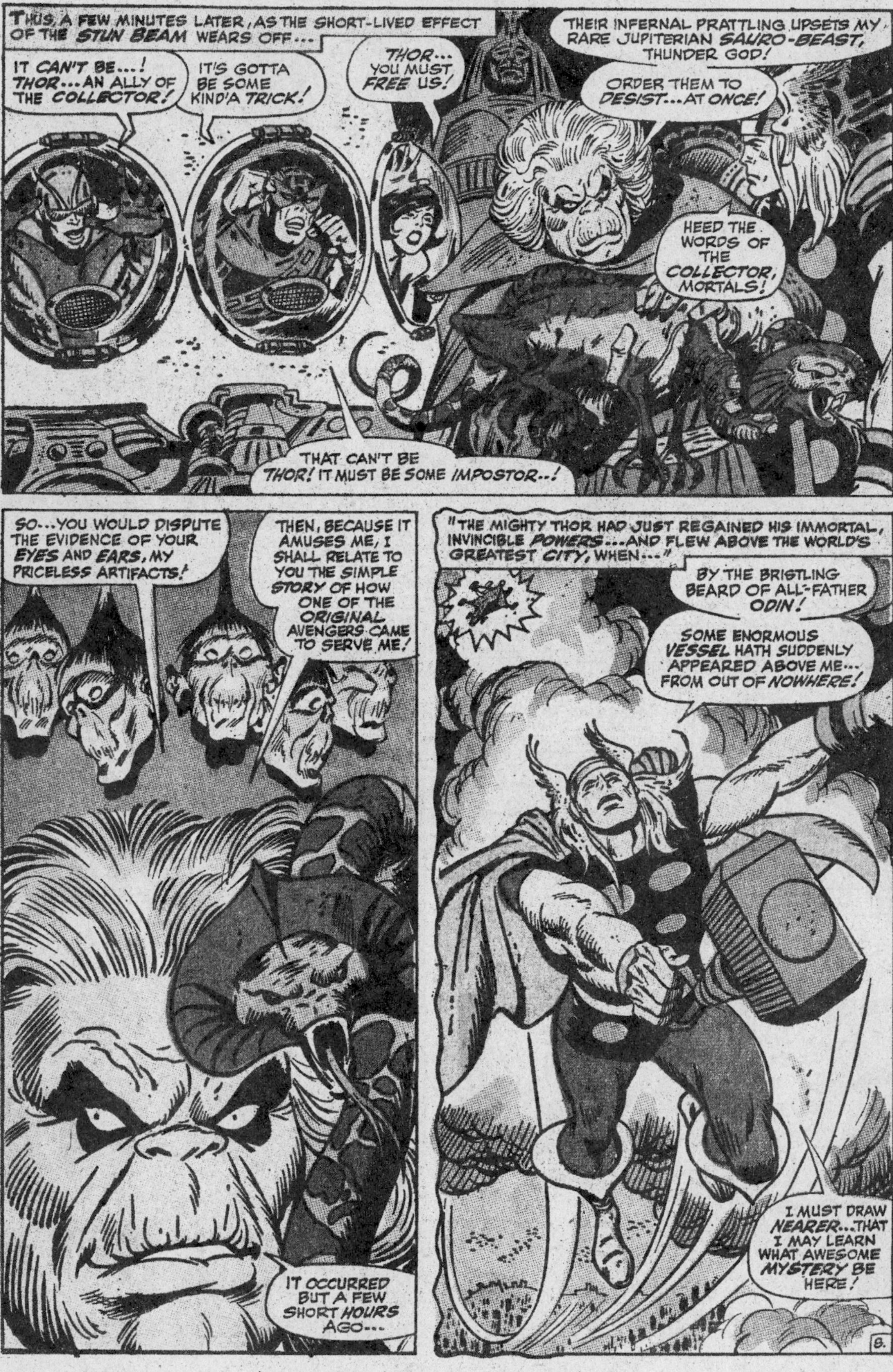

THUS, A FEW MINUTES LATER, AS THE SHORT-LIVED EFFECT OF THE STUN BEAM WEARS OFF...
IT CAN'T BE...! THOR...AN ALLY OF THE COLLECTOR!
IT'S GOTTA BE SOME KIND'A TRICK!
THOR... YOU MUST FREE US!
THEIR INFERNAL PRATTLING UPSETS MY RARE JUPITERIAN SAURO-BEAST, THUNDER GOD!
ORDER THEM TO DESIST...AT ONCE!
HEED THE WORDS OF THE COLLECTOR, MORTALS!
THAT CAN'T BE THOR! IT MUST BE SOME IMPOSTOR..!
SO...YOU WOULD DISPUTE THE EVIDENCE OF YOUR EYES AND EARS, MY PRICELESS ARTIFACTS!
THEN, BECAUSE IT AMUSES ME, I SHALL RELATE TO YOU THE SIMPLE STORY OF HOW ONE OF THE ORIGINAL AVENGERS CAME TO SERVE ME!
IT OCCURRED BUT A FEW SHORT HOURS AGO...
"THE MIGHTY THOR HAD JUST REGAINED HIS IMMORTAL, INVINCIBLE POWERS...AND FLEW ABOVE THE WORLD'S GREATEST CITY, WHEN..."
BY THE BRISTLING BEARD OF ALL-FATHER ODIN!
SOME ENORMOUS VESSEL HATH SUDDENLY APPEARED ABOVE ME... FROM OUT OF NOWHERE!
I MUST DRAW NEARER...THAT I MAY LEARN WHAT AWESOME MYSTERY BE HERE!
8.

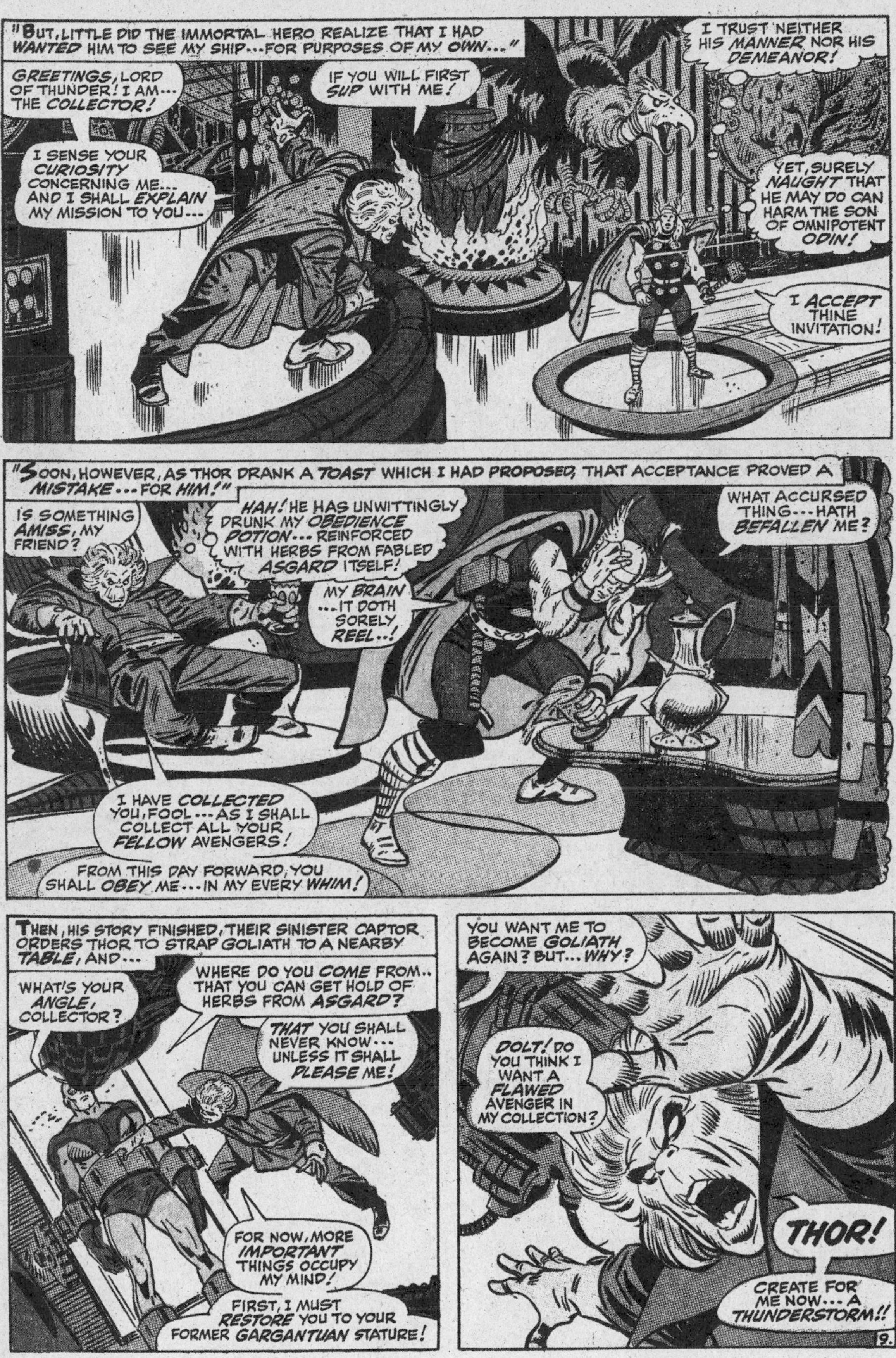

"BUT, LITTLE DID THE IMMORTAL HERO REALIZE THAT I HAD WANTED HIM TO SEE MY SHIP--- FOR PURPOSES OF MY OWN..."
GREETINGS, LORD OF THUNDER! I AM... THE COLLECTOR!
IF YOU WILL FIRST SUP WITH ME!
I TRUST NEITHER HIS MANNER NOR HIS DEMEANOR!
I SENSE YOUR CURIOSITY CONCERNING ME... AND I SHALL EXPLAIN MY MISSION TO YOU---
YET, SURELY NAUGHT THAT HE MAY DO CAN HARM THE SON OF OMNIPOTENT ODIN!
I ACCEPT THINE INVITATION!
"SOON, HOWEVER, AS THOR DRANK A TOAST WHICH I HAD PROPOSED, THAT ACCEPTANCE PROVED A MISTAKE--- FOR HIM!"
IS SOMETHING AMISS, MY FRIEND?
HAH! HE HAS UNWITTINGLY DRUNK MY OBEDIENCE POTION--- REINFORCED WITH HERBS FROM FABLED ASGARD ITSELF!
WHAT ACCURSED THING--- HATH BEFALLEN ME?
MY BRAIN ---IT DOTH SORELY REEL--!
I HAVE COLLECTED YOU, FOOL--- AS I SHALL COLLECT ALL YOUR FELLOW AVENGERS!
FROM THIS DAY FORWARD, YOU SHALL OBEY ME--- IN MY EVERY WHIM!
THEN, HIS STORY FINISHED, THEIR SINISTER CAPTOR ORDERS THOR TO STRAP GOLIATH TO A NEARBY TABLE, AND...
WHAT'S YOUR ANGLE, COLLECTOR?
WHERE DO YOU COME FROM.. THAT YOU CAN GET HOLD OF HERBS FROM ASGARD?
THAT YOU SHALL NEVER KNOW--- UNLESS IT SHALL PLEASE ME!
FOR NOW, MORE IMPORTANT THINGS OCCUPY MY MIND!
FIRST, I MUST RESTORE YOU TO YOUR FORMER GARGANTUAN STATURE!
YOU WANT ME TO BECOME GOLIATH AGAIN? BUT... WHY?
DOLT! DO YOU THINK I WANT A FLAWED AVENGER IN MY COLLECTION?
THOR!
CREATE FOR ME NOW... A THUNDERSTORM!!
9.

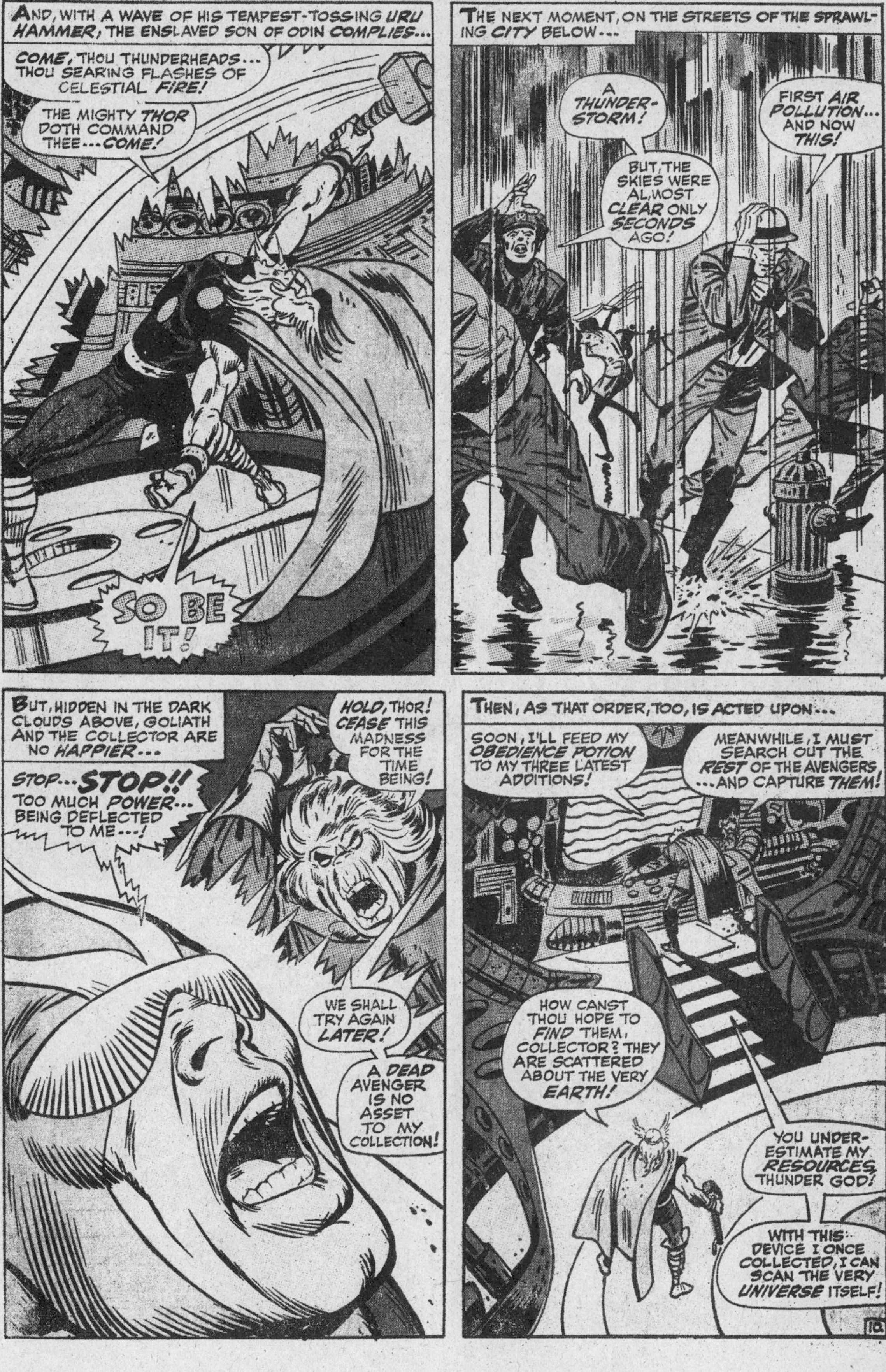

AND, WITH A WAVE OF HIS TEMPEST-TOSSING URU HAMMER, THE ENSLAVED SON OF ODIN COMPLIES...
COME, THOU THUNDERHEADS... THOU SEARING FLASHES OF CELESTIAL FIRE!
THE MIGHTY THOR DOTH COMMAND THEE---COME!
SO BE IT!
THE NEXT MOMENT, ON THE STREETS OF THE SPRAWLING CITY BELOW---
A THUNDER-STORM!
BUT, THE SKIES WERE ALMOST CLEAR ONLY SECONDS AGO!
FIRST AIR POLLUTION... AND NOW THIS!
BUT, HIDDEN IN THE DARK CLOUDS ABOVE, GOLIATH AND THE COLLECTOR ARE NO HAPPIER...
STOP...STOP!! TOO MUCH POWER... BEING DEFLECTED TO ME---!
HOLD, THOR! CEASE THIS MADNESS FOR THE TIME BEING!
WE SHALL TRY AGAIN LATER!
A DEAD AVENGER IS NO ASSET TO MY COLLECTION!
THEN, AS THAT ORDER, TOO, IS ACTED UPON...
SOON, I'LL FEED MY OBEDIENCE POTION TO MY THREE LATEST ADDITIONS!
MEANWHILE, I MUST SEARCH OUT THE REST OF THE AVENGERS ...AND CAPTURE THEM!
HOW CANST THOU HOPE TO FIND THEM, COLLECTOR? THEY ARE SCATTERED ABOUT THE VERY EARTH!
YOU UNDER-ESTIMATE MY RESOURCES, THUNDER GOD!
WITH THIS DEVICE I ONCE COLLECTED, I CAN SCAN THE VERY UNIVERSE ITSELF!
10

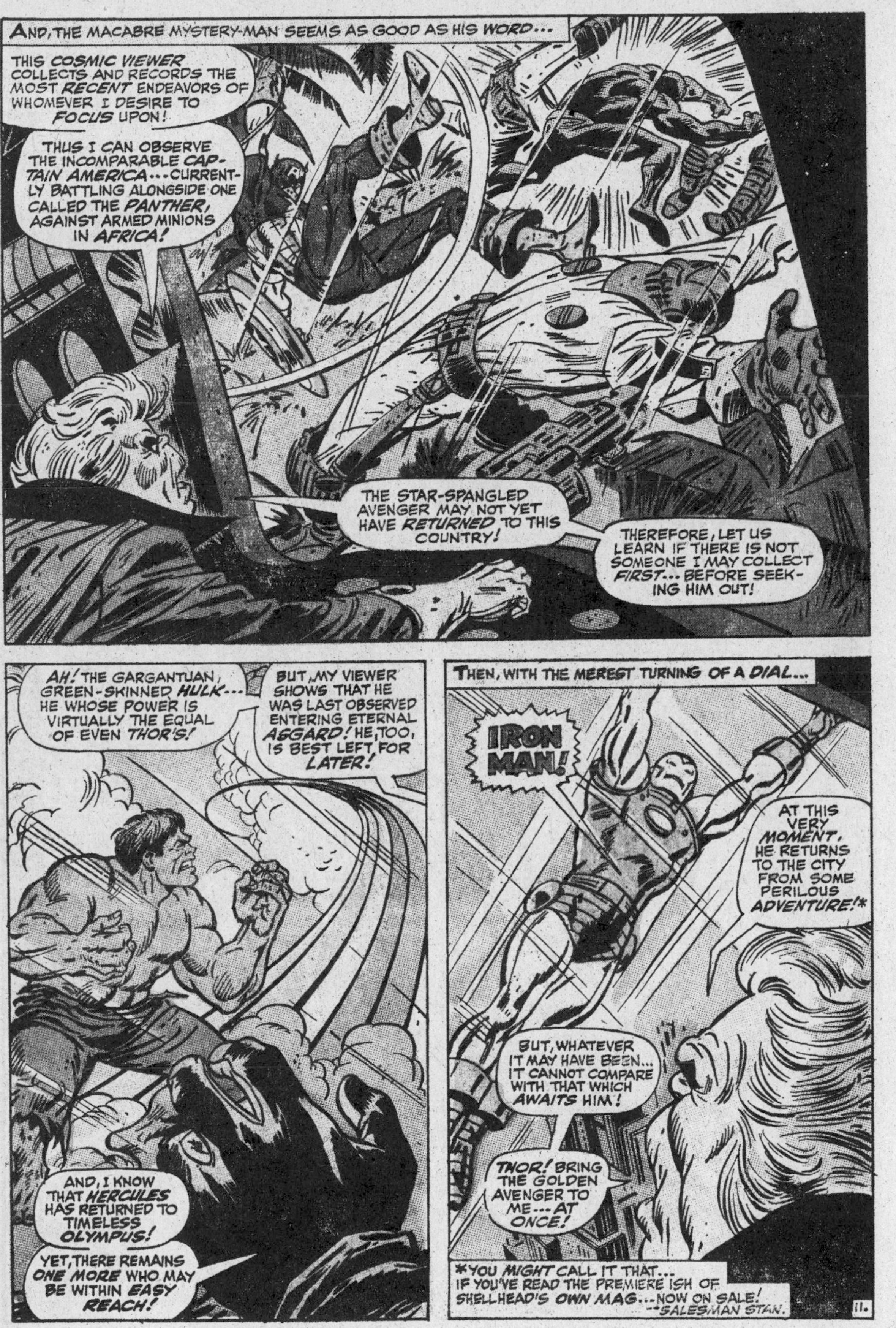
AND, THE MACABRE MYSTERY-MAN SEEMS AS GOOD AS HIS WORD...
THIS COSMIC VIEWER COLLECTS AND RECORDS THE MOST RECENT ENDEAVORS OF WHOMEVER I DESIRE TO FOCUS UPON!
THUS I CAN OBSERVE THE INCOMPARABLE CAPTAIN AMERICA... CURRENTLY BATTLING ALONGSIDE ONE CALLED THE PANTHER, AGAINST ARMED MINIONS IN AFRICA!
THE STAR-SPANGLED AVENGER MAY NOT YET HAVE RETURNED TO THIS COUNTRY!
THEREFORE, LET US LEARN IF THERE IS NOT SOMEONE I MAY COLLECT FIRST... BEFORE SEEKING HIM OUT!
AH! THE GARGANTUAN, GREEN-SKINNED HULK... HE WHOSE POWER IS VIRTUALLY THE EQUAL OF EVEN THOR'S!
BUT, MY VIEWER SHOWS THAT HE WAS LAST OBSERVED ENTERING ETERNAL ASGARD! HE, TOO, IS BEST LEFT FOR LATER!
AND, I KNOW THAT HERCULES HAS RETURNED TO TIMELESS OLYMPUS!
YET, THERE REMAINS ONE MORE WHO MAY BE WITHIN EASY REACH!
THEN, WITH THE MEREST TURNING OF A DIAL...
IRON MAN!
AT THIS VERY MOMENT, HE RETURNS TO THE CITY FROM SOME PERILOUS ADVENTURE!*
BUT, WHATEVER IT MAY HAVE BEEN... IT CANNOT COMPARE WITH THAT WHICH AWAITS HIM!
THOR! BRING THE GOLDEN AVENGER TO ME... AT ONCE!
*YOU MIGHT CALL IT THAT... IF YOU'VE READ THE PREMIERE ISH OF SHELLHEAD'S OWN MAG... NOW ON SALE! --SALESMAN STAN.
11.

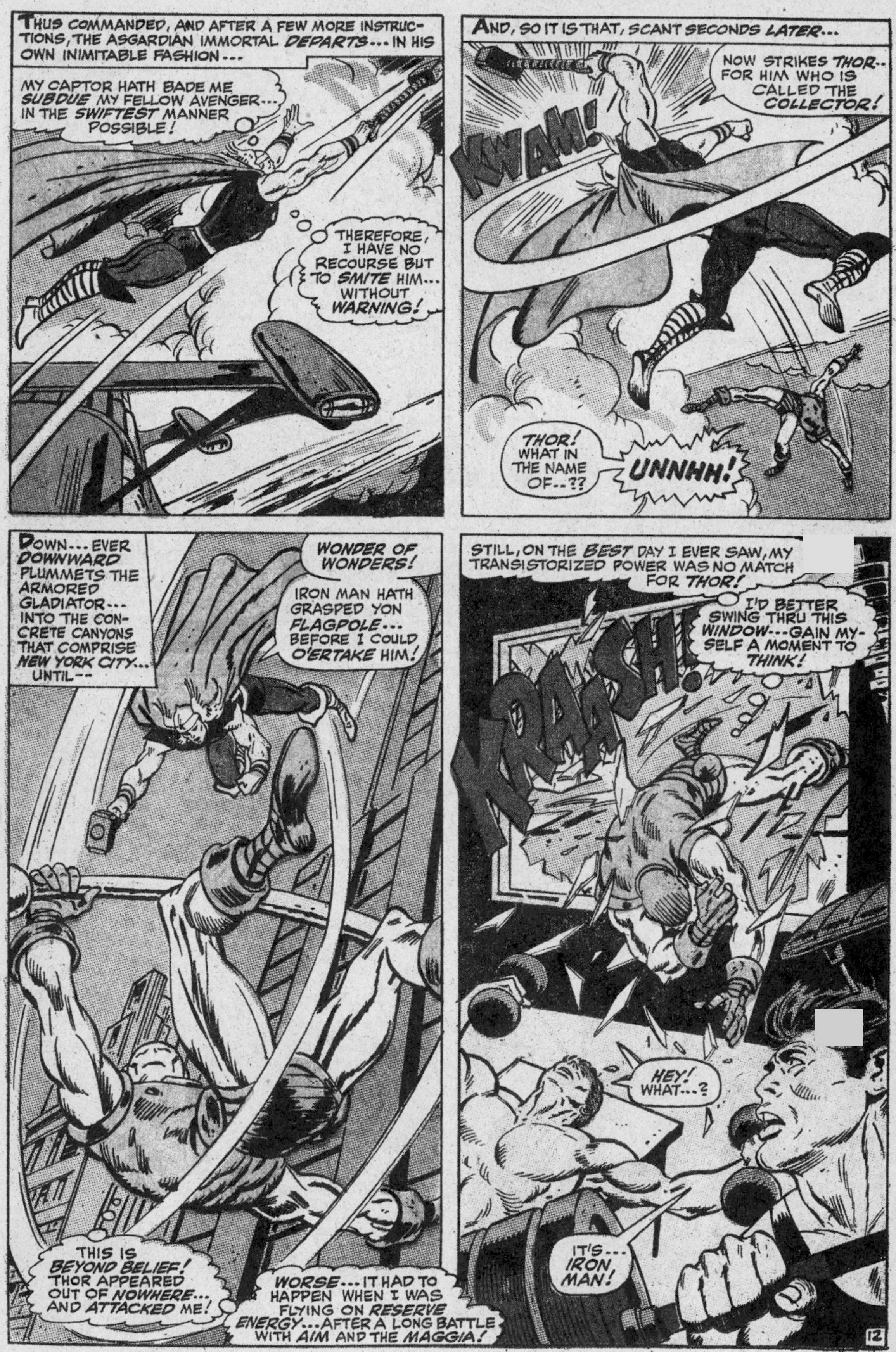
THUS COMMANDED, AND AFTER A FEW MORE INSTRUCTIONS, THE ASGARDIAN IMMORTAL DEPARTS... IN HIS OWN INIMITABLE FASHION...
MY CAPTOR HATH BADE ME SUBDUE MY FELLOW AVENGER... IN THE SWIFTEST MANNER POSSIBLE!
THEREFORE, I HAVE NO RECOURSE BUT TO SMITE HIM... WITHOUT WARNING!
AND, SO IT IS THAT, SCANT SECONDS LATER...
NOW STRIKES THOR-- FOR HIM WHO IS CALLED THE COLLECTOR!
KWAM!
THOR! WHAT IN THE NAME OF--??
UNNHH!
DOWN... EVER DOWNWARD PLUMMETS THE ARMORED GLADIATOR... INTO THE CONCRETE CANYONS THAT COMPRISE NEW YORK CITY... UNTIL--
WONDER OF WONDERS!
IRON MAN HATH GRASPED YON FLAGPOLE... BEFORE I COULD O'ERTAKE HIM!
THIS IS BEYOND BELIEF! THOR APPEARED OUT OF NOWHERE... AND ATTACKED ME!
WORSE... IT HAD TO HAPPEN WHEN I WAS FLYING ON RESERVE ENERGY... AFTER A LONG BATTLE WITH AIM AND THE MAGGIA!
STILL, ON THE BEST DAY I EVER SAW, MY TRANSISTORIZED POWER WAS NO MATCH FOR THOR!
I'D BETTER SWING THRU THIS WINDOW... GAIN MYSELF A MOMENT TO THINK!
KRAASH!
HEY! WHAT...?
IT'S... IRON MAN!

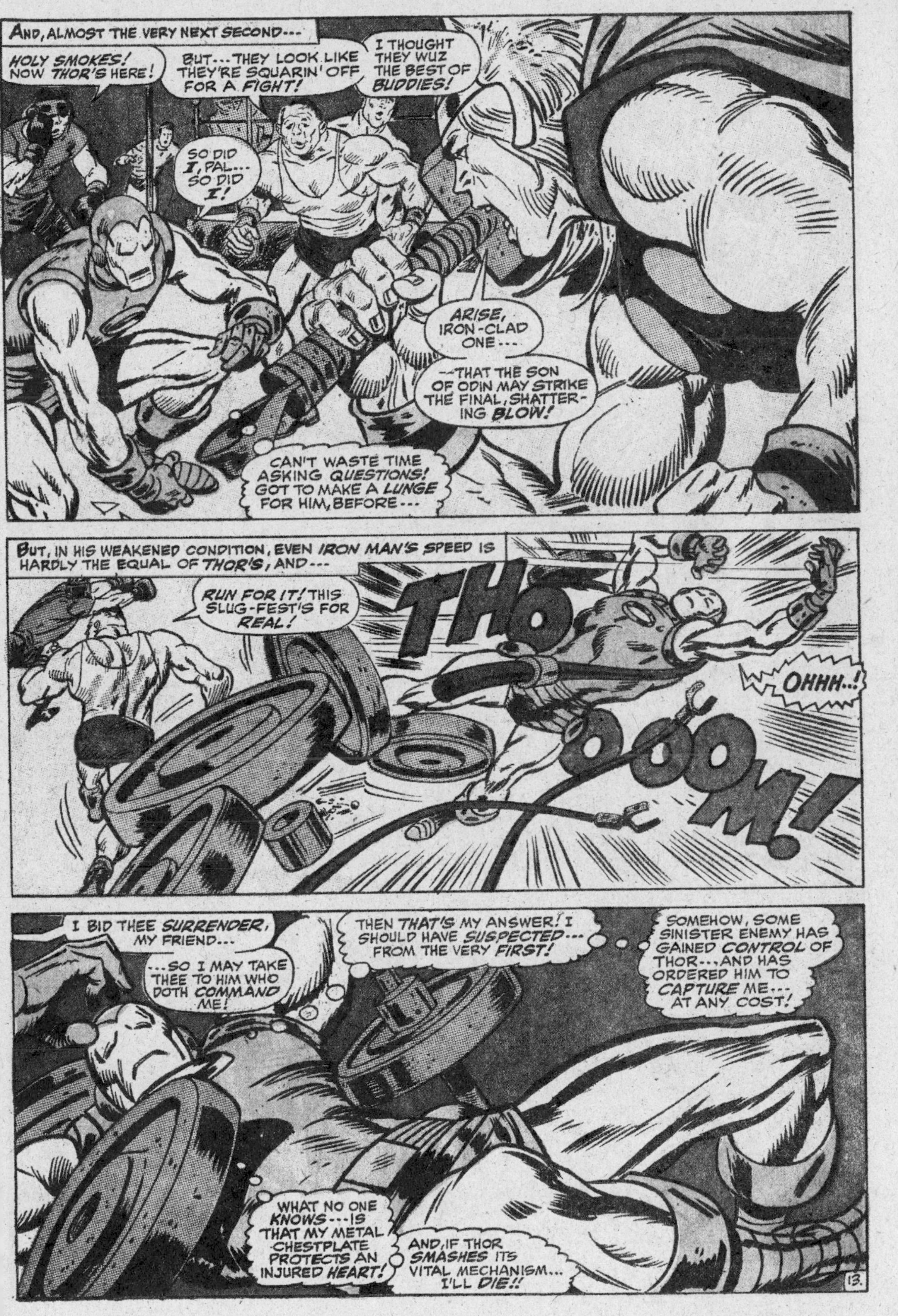

AND, ALMOST THE VERY NEXT SECOND---
HOLY SMOKES! NOW THOR'S HERE!
BUT--- THEY LOOK LIKE THEY'RE SQUARIN' OFF FOR A FIGHT!
I THOUGHT THEY WUZ THE BEST OF BUDDIES!
SO DID I, PAL... SO DID I!
ARISE, IRON-CLAD ONE---
--THAT THE SON OF ODIN MAY STRIKE THE FINAL, SHATTERING BLOW!
CAN'T WASTE TIME ASKING QUESTIONS! GOT TO MAKE A LUNGE FOR HIM, BEFORE---
BUT, IN HIS WEAKENED CONDITION, EVEN IRON MAN'S SPEED IS HARDLY THE EQUAL OF THOR'S, AND---
RUN FOR IT! THIS SLUG-FEST'S FOR REAL!
THOOOOM!
OHHH..!
I BID THEE SURRENDER, MY FRIEND---
...SO I MAY TAKE THEE TO HIM WHO DOTH COMMAND ME!
THEN THAT'S MY ANSWER! I SHOULD HAVE SUSPECTED--- FROM THE VERY FIRST!
SOMEHOW, SOME SINISTER ENEMY HAS GAINED CONTROL OF THOR---AND HAS ORDERED HIM TO CAPTURE ME--- AT ANY COST!
WHAT NO ONE KNOWS---IS THAT MY METAL CHESTPLATE PROTECTS AN INJURED HEART!
AND, IF THOR SMASHES ITS VITAL MECHANISM... I'LL DIE!!
13.

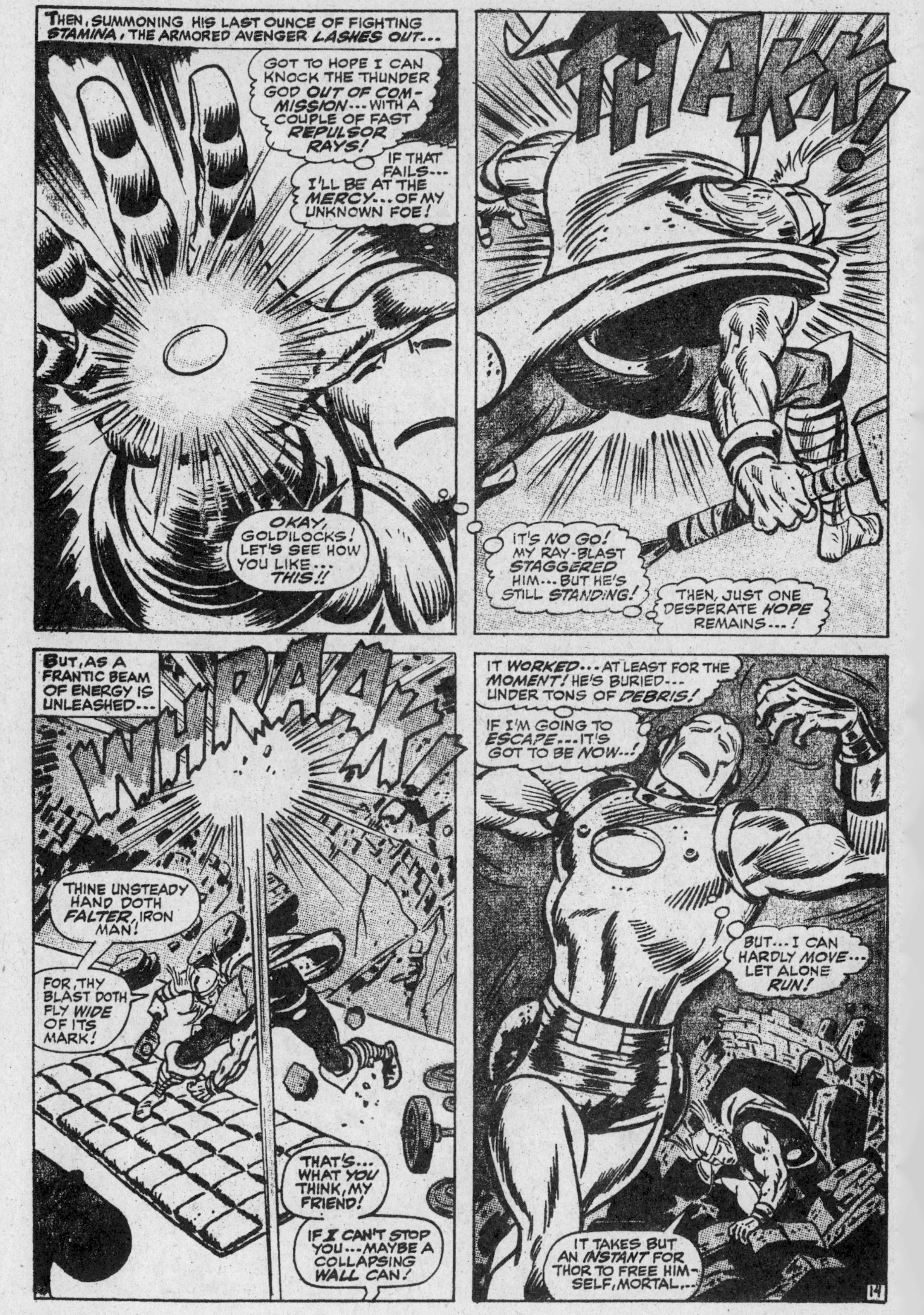
THEN, SUMMONING HIS LAST OUNCE OF FIGHTING STAMINA, THE ARMORED AVENGER LASHES OUT...
GOT TO HOPE I CAN KNOCK THE THUNDER GOD OUT OF COM-MISSION... WITH A COUPLE OF FAST REPULSOR RAYS!
IF THAT FAILS... I'LL BE AT THE MERCY... OF MY UNKNOWN FOE!
OKAY, GOLDILOCKS! LET'S SEE HOW YOU LIKE... THIS!!
THAKK!
IT'S NO GO! MY RAY-BLAST STAGGERED HIM... BUT HE'S STILL STANDING!
THEN, JUST ONE DESPERATE HOPE REMAINS...!
BUT, AS A FRANTIC BEAM OF ENERGY IS UNLEASHED...
WHRAAK!
THINE UNSTEADY HAND DOTH FALTER, IRON MAN!
FOR, THY BLAST DOTH FLY WIDE OF ITS MARK!
THAT'S... WHAT YOU THINK, MY FRIEND!
IF I CAN'T STOP YOU... MAYBE A COLLAPSING WALL CAN!
IT WORKED... AT LEAST FOR THE MOMENT! HE'S BURIED... UNDER TONS OF DEBRIS!
IF I'M GOING TO ESCAPE... IT'S GOT TO BE NOW...!
BUT... I CAN HARDLY MOVE... LET ALONE RUN!
IT TAKES BUT AN INSTANT FOR THOR TO FREE HIM-SELF, MORTAL...
14

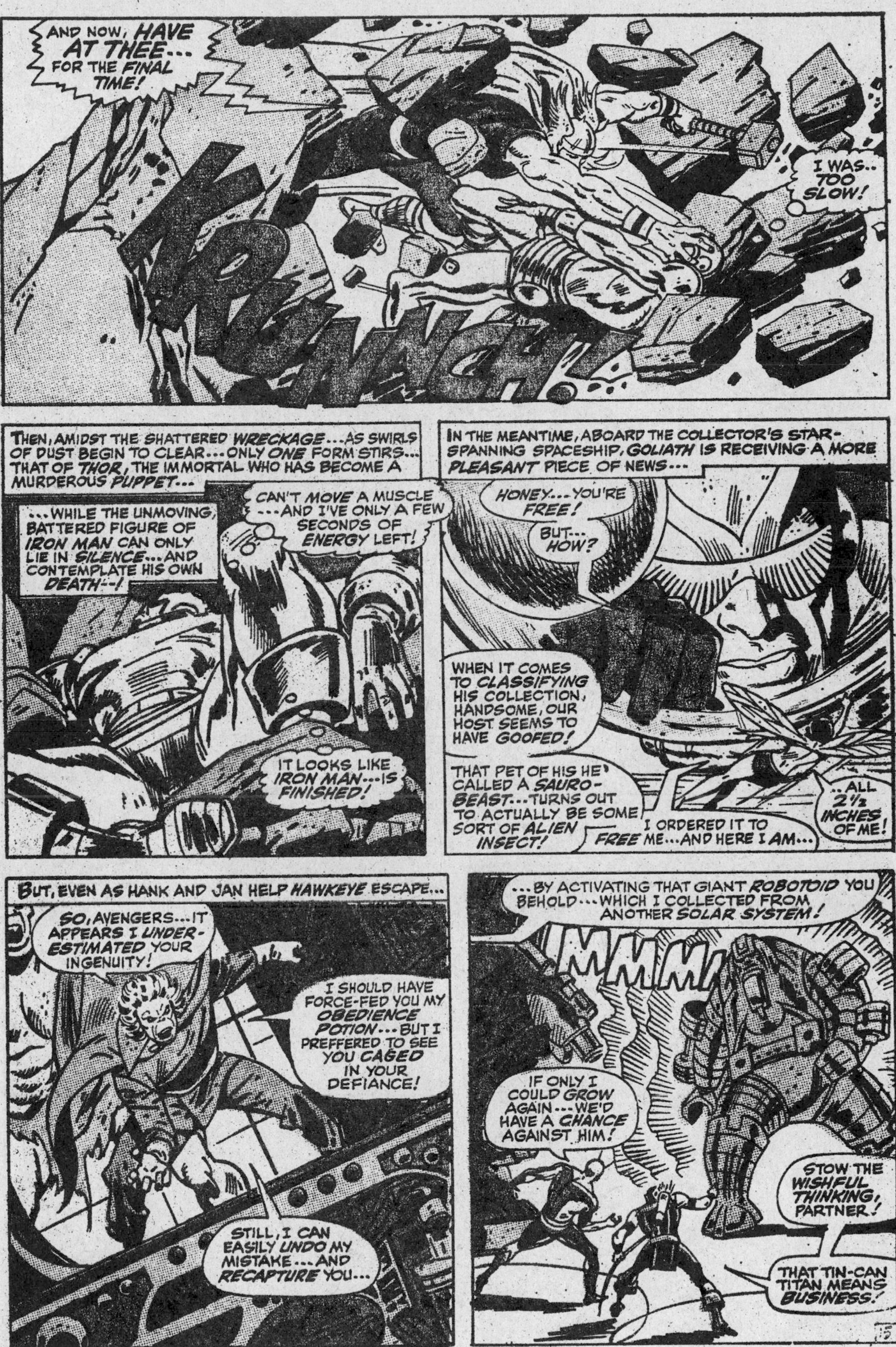
AND NOW, HAVE AT THEE... FOR THE FINAL TIME!
KRUNCH!
I WAS.. TOO SLOW!
THEN, AMIDST THE SHATTERED WRECKAGE... AS SWIRLS OF DUST BEGIN TO CLEAR... ONLY ONE FORM STIRS... THAT OF THOR, THE IMMORTAL WHO HAS BECOME A MURDEROUS PUPPET...
...WHILE THE UNMOVING, BATTERED FIGURE OF IRON MAN CAN ONLY LIE IN SILENCE... AND CONTEMPLATE HIS OWN DEATH--!
CAN'T MOVE A MUSCLE ---AND I'VE ONLY A FEW SECONDS OF ENERGY LEFT!
IT LOOKS LIKE IRON MAN---IS FINISHED!
IN THE MEANTIME, ABOARD THE COLLECTOR'S STAR-SPANNING SPACESHIP, GOLIATH IS RECEIVING A MORE PLEASANT PIECE OF NEWS...
HONEY... YOU'RE FREE!
BUT... HOW?
WHEN IT COMES TO CLASSIFYING HIS COLLECTION, HANDSOME, OUR HOST SEEMS TO HAVE GOOFED!
THAT PET OF HIS HE CALLED A SAURO-BEAST... TURNS OUT TO ACTUALLY BE SOME SORT OF ALIEN INSECT!
I ORDERED IT TO FREE ME... AND HERE I AM...
..ALL 2 1/2 INCHES OF ME!
BUT, EVEN AS HANK AND JAN HELP HAWKEYE ESCAPE...
SO, AVENGERS... IT APPEARS I UNDER-ESTIMATED YOUR INGENUITY!
I SHOULD HAVE FORCE-FED YOU MY OBEDIENCE POTION... BUT I PREFFERED TO SEE YOU CAGED IN YOUR DEFIANCE!
STILL, I CAN EASILY UNDO MY MISTAKE... AND RECAPTURE YOU...
...BY ACTIVATING THAT GIANT ROBOTOID YOU BEHOLD... WHICH I COLLECTED FROM ANOTHER SOLAR SYSTEM!
MMMM
IF ONLY I COULD GROW AGAIN... WE'D HAVE A CHANCE AGAINST HIM!
STOW THE WISHFUL THINKING, PARTNER!
THAT TIN-CAN TITAN MEANS BUSINESS!

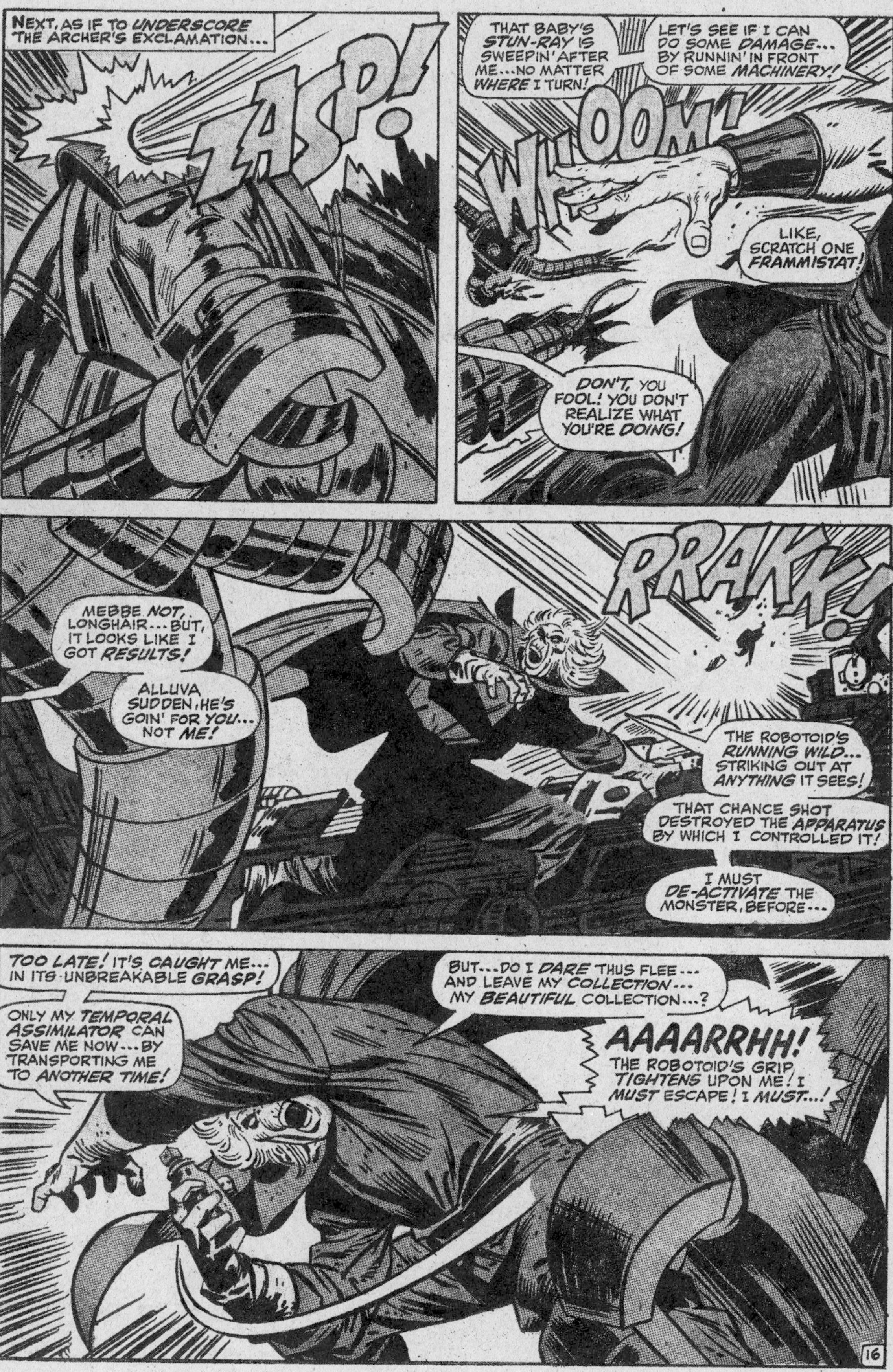
NEXT, AS IF TO UNDERSCORE THE ARCHER'S EXCLAMATION...
ZASP!
THAT BABY'S STUN-RAY IS SWEEPIN' AFTER ME...NO MATTER WHERE I TURN!
LET'S SEE IF I CAN DO SOME DAMAGE... BY RUNNIN' IN FRONT OF SOME MACHINERY!
WHOOOM!
LIKE, SCRATCH ONE FRAMMISTAT!
DON'T, YOU FOOL! YOU DON'T REALIZE WHAT YOU'RE DOING!
RRAKK!
MEBBE NOT, LONGHAIR... BUT, IT LOOKS LIKE I GOT RESULTS!
ALLUVA SUDDEN, HE'S GOIN' FOR YOU... NOT ME!
THE ROBOTOID'S RUNNING WILD... STRIKING OUT AT ANYTHING IT SEES!
THAT CHANCE SHOT DESTROYED THE APPARATUS BY WHICH I CONTROLLED IT!
I MUST DE-ACTIVATE THE MONSTER, BEFORE---
TOO LATE! IT'S CAUGHT ME... IN ITS UNBREAKABLE GRASP!
ONLY MY TEMPORAL ASSIMILATOR CAN SAVE ME NOW... BY TRANSPORTING ME TO ANOTHER TIME!
BUT... DO I DARE THUS FLEE--- AND LEAVE MY COLLECTION--- MY BEAUTIFUL COLLECTION...?
AAAARRHH!
THE ROBOTOID'S GRIP TIGHTENS UPON ME! I MUST ESCAPE! I MUST...!
16

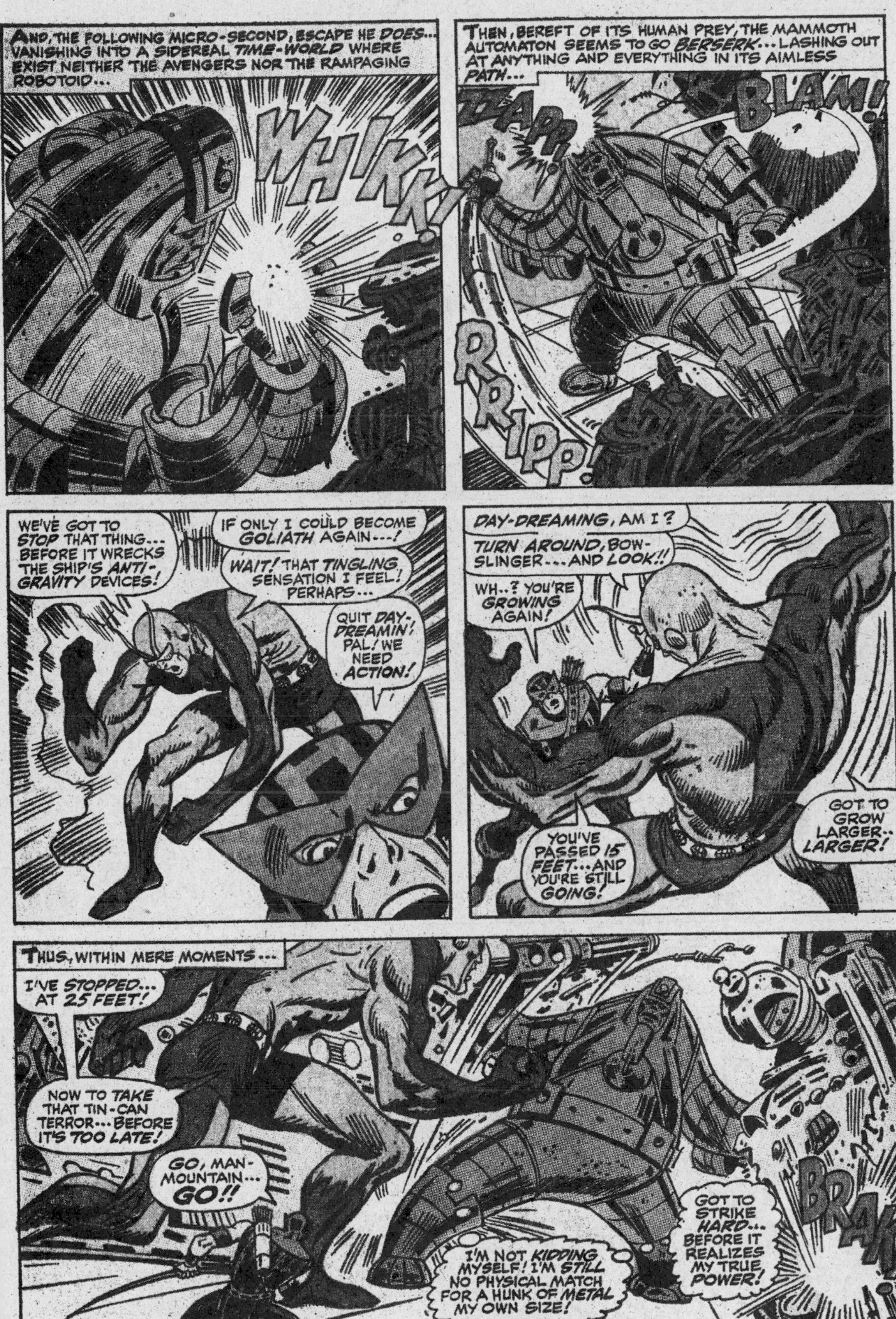
AND, THE FOLLOWING MICRO-SECOND, ESCAPE HE DOES... VANISHING INTO A SIDEREAL TIME-WORLD WHERE EXIST NEITHER THE AVENGERS NOR THE RAMPAGING ROBOTOID...
WHIKK!
THEN, BEREFT OF ITS HUMAN PREY, THE MAMMOTH AUTOMATON SEEMS TO GO BERSERK... LASHING OUT AT ANYTHING AND EVERYTHING IN ITS AIMLESS PATH...
ZZAPP!
BLAM!
RRIPP!
WE'VE GOT TO STOP THAT THING... BEFORE IT WRECKS THE SHIP'S ANTI-GRAVITY DEVICES!
IF ONLY I COULD BECOME GOLIATH AGAIN---!
WAIT! THAT TINGLING SENSATION I FEEL! PERHAPS...
QUIT DAY-DREAMIN', PAL! WE NEED ACTION!
DAY-DREAMING, AM I?
TURN AROUND, BOW-SLINGER---AND LOOK!!
WH..? YOU'RE GROWING AGAIN!
YOU'VE PASSED 15 FEET...AND YOU'RE STILL GOING!
GOT TO GROW LARGER.. LARGER!
THUS, WITHIN MERE MOMENTS...
I'VE STOPPED... AT 25 FEET!
NOW TO TAKE THAT TIN-CAN TERROR...BEFORE IT'S TOO LATE!
GO, MAN-MOUNTAIN... GO!!
I'M NOT KIDDING MYSELF! I'M STILL NO PHYSICAL MATCH FOR A HUNK OF METAL MY OWN SIZE!
GOT TO STRIKE HARD... BEFORE IT REALIZES MY TRUE POWER!
BRAKK!
17

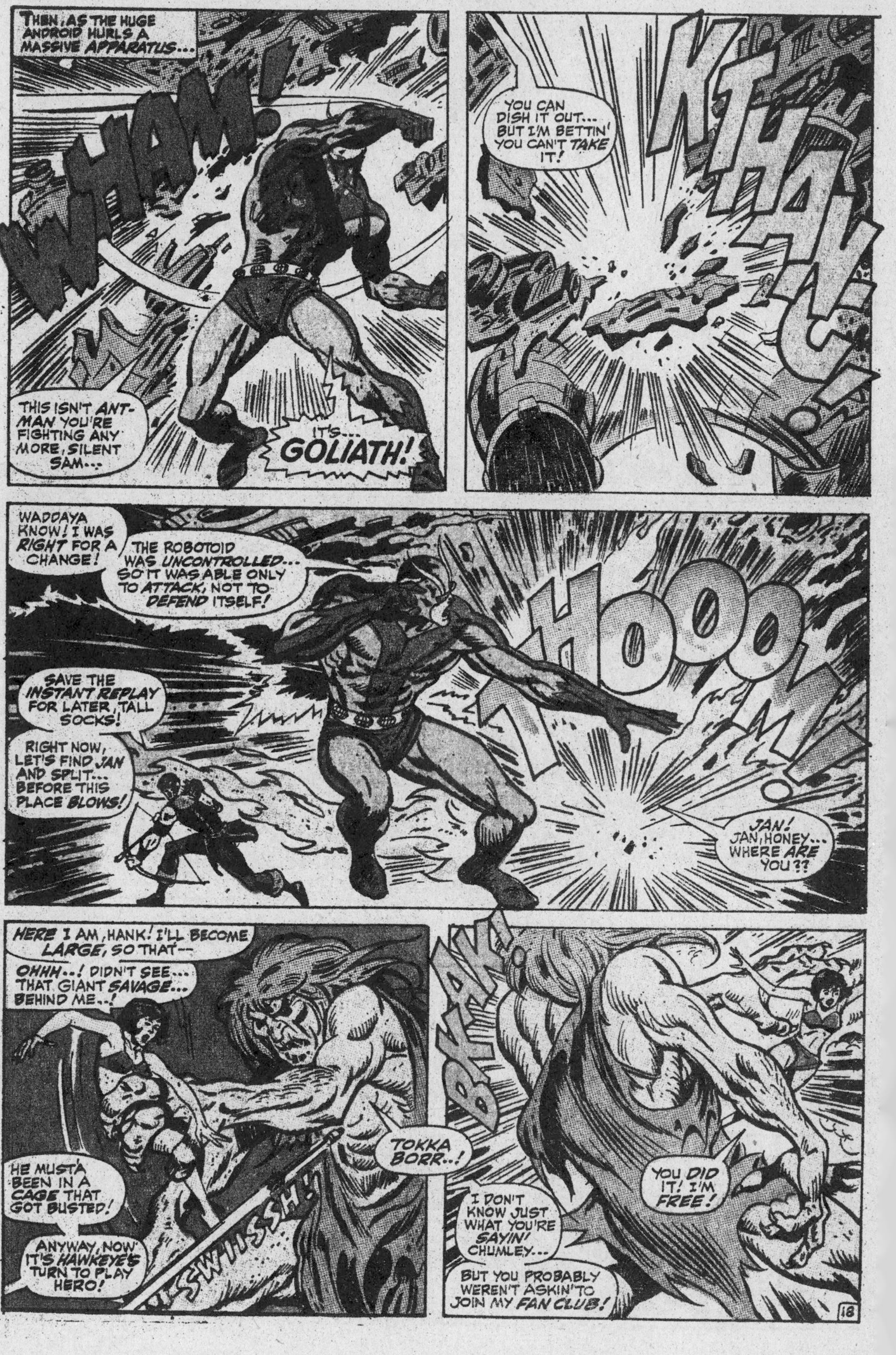
THEN, AS THE HUGE ANDROID HURLS A MASSIVE APPARATUS...
WHAM!
THIS ISN'T ANT-MAN YOU'RE FIGHTING ANY MORE, SILENT SAM...
IT'S... GOLIATH!
YOU CAN DISH IT OUT... BUT I'M BETTIN' YOU CAN'T TAKE IT!
KTHANC!
WADDAYA KNOW! I WAS RIGHT FOR A CHANGE!
THE ROBOTOID WAS UNCONTROLLED... SO IT WAS ABLE ONLY TO ATTACK, NOT TO DEFEND ITSELF!
THOOOM!
SAVE THE INSTANT REPLAY FOR LATER, TALL SOCKS!
RIGHT NOW, LET'S FIND JAN AND SPLIT... BEFORE THIS PLACE BLOWS!
JAN! JAN, HONEY... WHERE ARE YOU??
HERE I AM, HANK! I'LL BECOME LARGE, SO THAT--
OHHH..! DIDN'T SEE... THAT GIANT SAVAGE... BEHIND ME..!
TOKKA BORR..!
HE MUSTA BEEN IN A CAGE THAT GOT BUSTED!
ANYWAY, NOW IT'S HAWKEYE'S TURN TO PLAY HERO!
SWISSSH!
BAK!
YOU DID IT! I'M FREE!
I DON'T KNOW JUST WHAT YOU'RE SAYIN' CHUMLEY...
BUT YOU PROBABLY WEREN'T ASKIN' TO JOIN MY FAN CLUB!
18

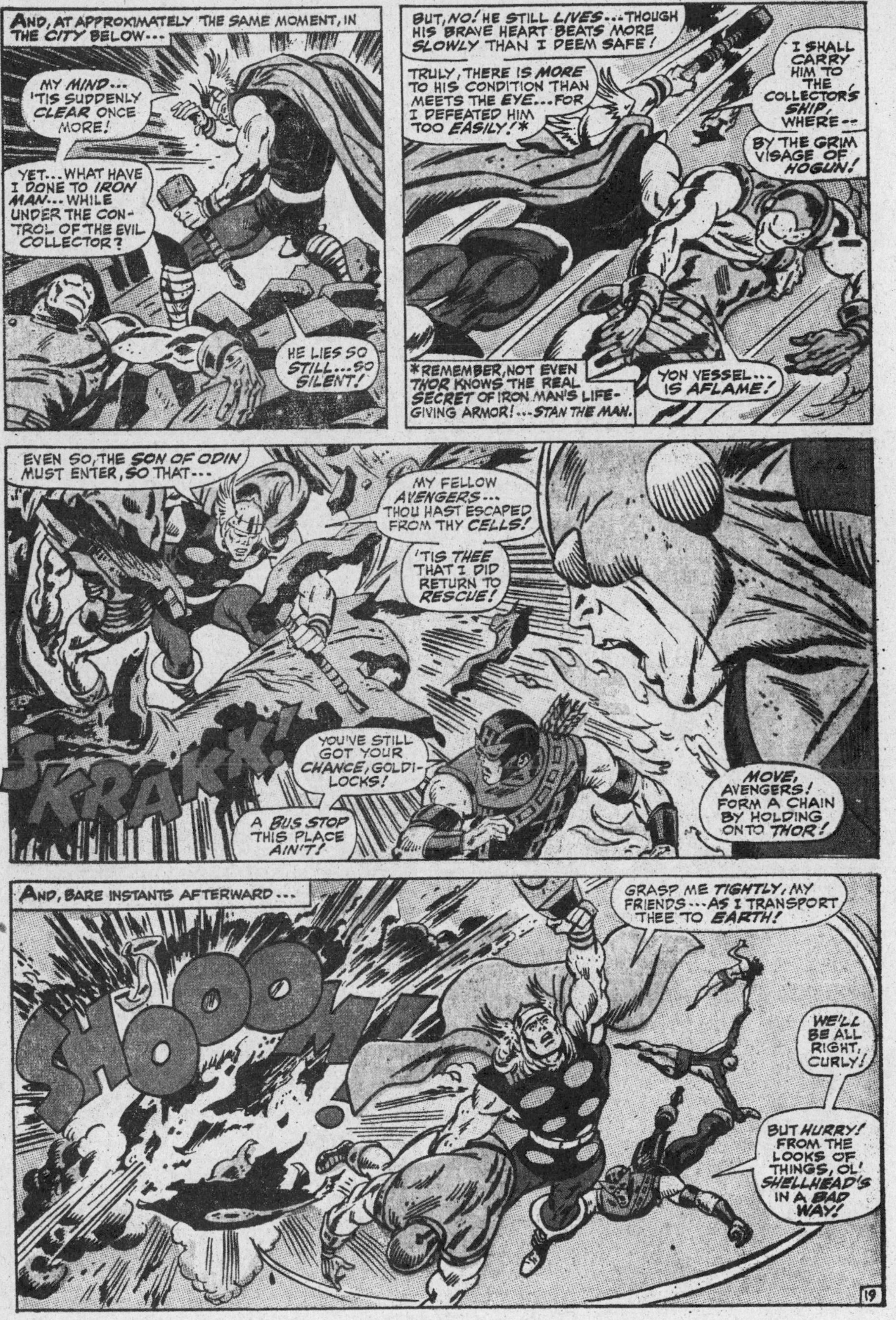
AND, AT APPROXIMATELY THE SAME MOMENT, IN THE CITY BELOW...
MY MIND... 'TIS SUDDENLY CLEAR ONCE MORE!
YET... WHAT HAVE I DONE TO IRON MAN... WHILE UNDER THE CONTROL OF THE EVIL COLLECTOR?
HE LIES SO STILL... SO SILENT!
BUT, NO! HE STILL LIVES... THOUGH HIS BRAVE HEART BEATS MORE SLOWLY THAN I DEEM SAFE!
TRULY, THERE IS MORE TO HIS CONDITION THAN MEETS THE EYE... FOR I DEFEATED HIM TOO EASILY!*
I SHALL CARRY HIM TO THE COLLECTOR'S SHIP, WHERE--
BY THE GRIM VISAGE OF HOGUN!
YON VESSEL... IS AFLAME!
*REMEMBER, NOT EVEN THOR KNOWS THE REAL SECRET OF IRON MAN'S LIFE-GIVING ARMOR! ...STAN THE MAN.
EVEN SO, THE SON OF ODIN MUST ENTER, SO THAT---
MY FELLOW AVENGERS... THOU HAST ESCAPED FROM THY CELLS!
'TIS THEE THAT I DID RETURN TO RESCUE!
SKRAKK!
YOU'VE STILL GOT YOUR CHANCE, GOLDILOCKS!
A BUS STOP THIS PLACE AIN'T!
MOVE, AVENGERS! FORM A CHAIN BY HOLDING ONTO THOR!
AND, BARE INSTANTS AFTERWARD...
GRASP ME TIGHTLY, MY FRIENDS---AS I TRANSPORT THEE TO EARTH!
SHOOOM!
WE'LL BE ALL RIGHT, CURLY!
BUT HURRY! FROM THE LOOKS OF THINGS, OL' SHELLHEAD'S IN A BAD WAY!

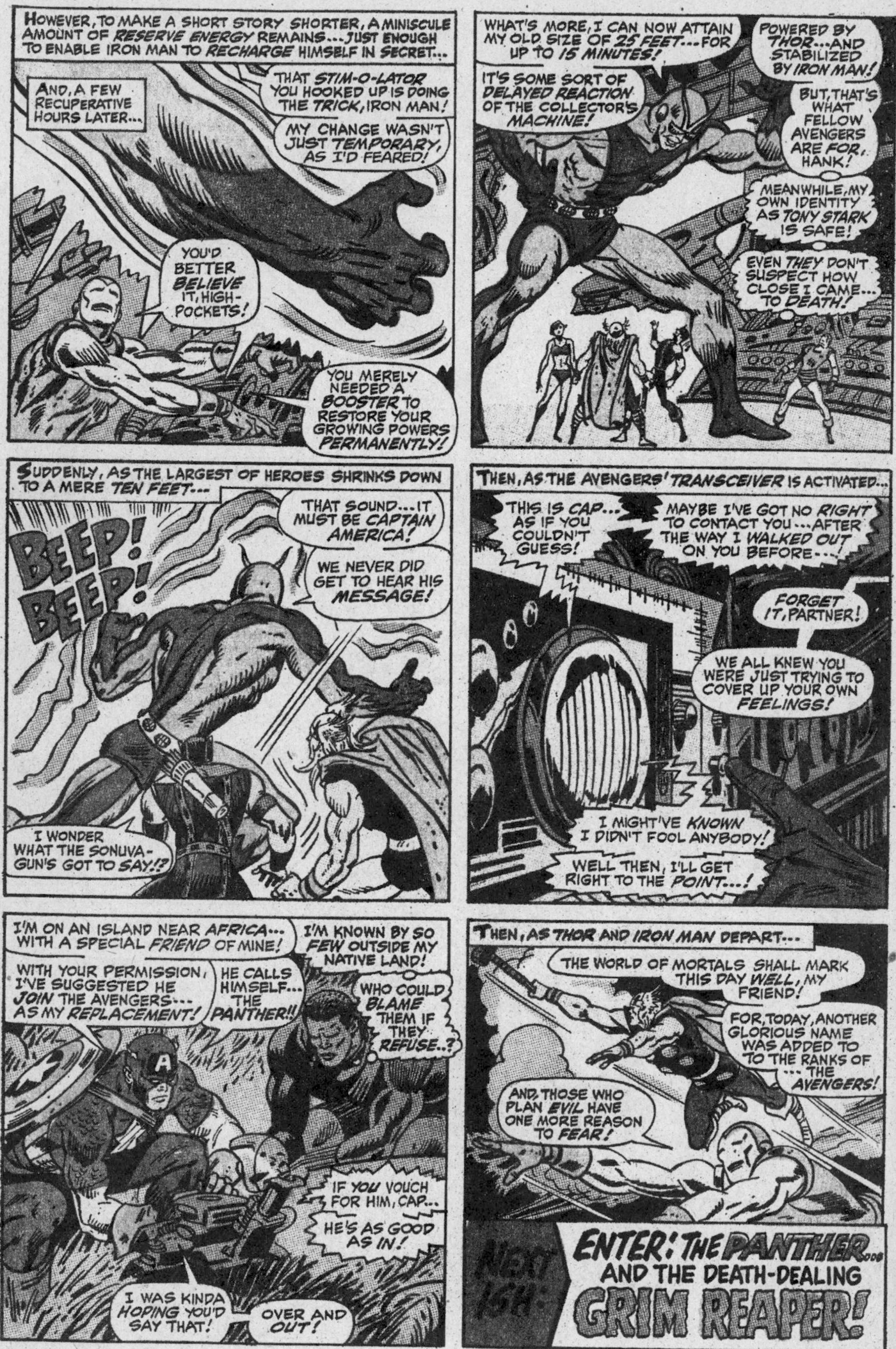
HOWEVER, TO MAKE A SHORT STORY SHORTER, A MINISCULE AMOUNT OF RESERVE ENERGY REMAINS... JUST ENOUGH TO ENABLE IRON MAN TO RECHARGE HIMSELF IN SECRET...
AND, A FEW RECUPERATIVE HOURS LATER...
THAT STIM-O-LATOR YOU HOOKED UP IS DOING THE TRICK, IRON MAN!
MY CHANGE WASN'T JUST TEMPORARY, AS I'D FEARED!
YOU'D BETTER BELIEVE IT, HIGH-POCKETS!
YOU MERELY NEEDED A BOOSTER TO RESTORE YOUR GROWING POWERS PERMANENTLY!
WHAT'S MORE, I CAN NOW ATTAIN MY OLD SIZE OF 25 FEET... FOR UP TO 15 MINUTES!
IT'S SOME SORT OF DELAYED REACTION OF THE COLLECTOR'S MACHINE!
POWERED BY THOR... AND STABILIZED BY IRON MAN!
BUT, THAT'S WHAT FELLOW AVENGERS ARE FOR, HANK!
MEANWHILE, MY OWN IDENTITY AS TONY STARK IS SAFE!
EVEN THEY DON'T SUSPECT HOW CLOSE I CAME... TO DEATH!
SUDDENLY, AS THE LARGEST OF HEROES SHRINKS DOWN TO A MERE TEN FEET...
BEEP! BEEP!
THAT SOUND... IT MUST BE CAPTAIN AMERICA!
WE NEVER DID GET TO HEAR HIS MESSAGE!
I WONDER WHAT THE SONUVA-GUN'S GOT TO SAY!?
THEN, AS THE AVENGERS' TRANSCEIVER IS ACTIVATED...
THIS IS CAP... AS IF YOU COULDN'T GUESS!
MAYBE I'VE GOT NO RIGHT TO CONTACT YOU... AFTER THE WAY I WALKED OUT ON YOU BEFORE...!
FORGET IT, PARTNER!
WE ALL KNEW YOU WERE JUST TRYING TO COVER UP YOUR OWN FEELINGS!
I MIGHT'VE KNOWN I DIDN'T FOOL ANYBODY!
WELL THEN, I'LL GET RIGHT TO THE POINT...!
I'M ON AN ISLAND NEAR AFRICA... WITH A SPECIAL FRIEND OF MINE!
I'M KNOWN BY SO FEW OUTSIDE MY NATIVE LAND!
WITH YOUR PERMISSION, I'VE SUGGESTED HE JOIN THE AVENGERS... AS MY REPLACEMENT!
HE CALLS HIMSELF... THE PANTHER!!
WHO COULD BLAME THEM IF THEY REFUSE..?
IF YOU VOUCH FOR HIM, CAP...
HE'S AS GOOD AS IN!
I WAS KINDA HOPING YOU'D SAY THAT!
OVER AND OUT!
THEN, AS THOR AND IRON MAN DEPART...
THE WORLD OF MORTALS SHALL MARK THIS DAY WELL, MY FRIEND!
FOR, TODAY, ANOTHER GLORIOUS NAME WAS ADDED TO TO THE RANKS OF ... THE AVENGERS!
AND, THOSE WHO PLAN EVIL HAVE ONE MORE REASON TO FEAR!
NEXT ISH:
ENTER: THE PANTHER... AND THE DEATH-DEALING GRIM REAPER!

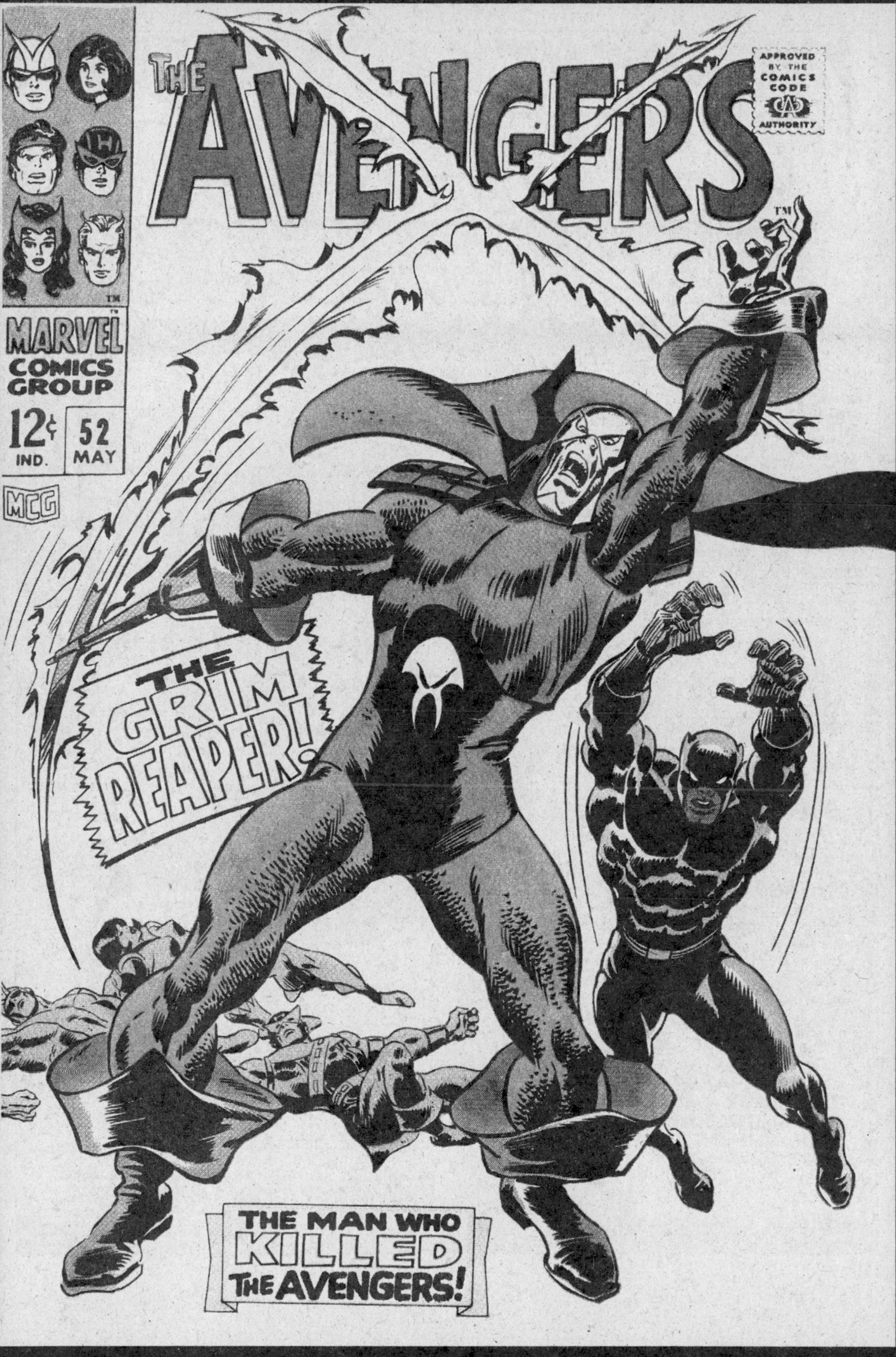
THE AVENGERS
APPROVED BY THE COMICS CODE AUTHORITY
MARVEL COMICS GROUP
12¢ IND.
52 MAY
MCG
THE GRIM REAPER!
THE MAN WHO KILLED THE AVENGERS!

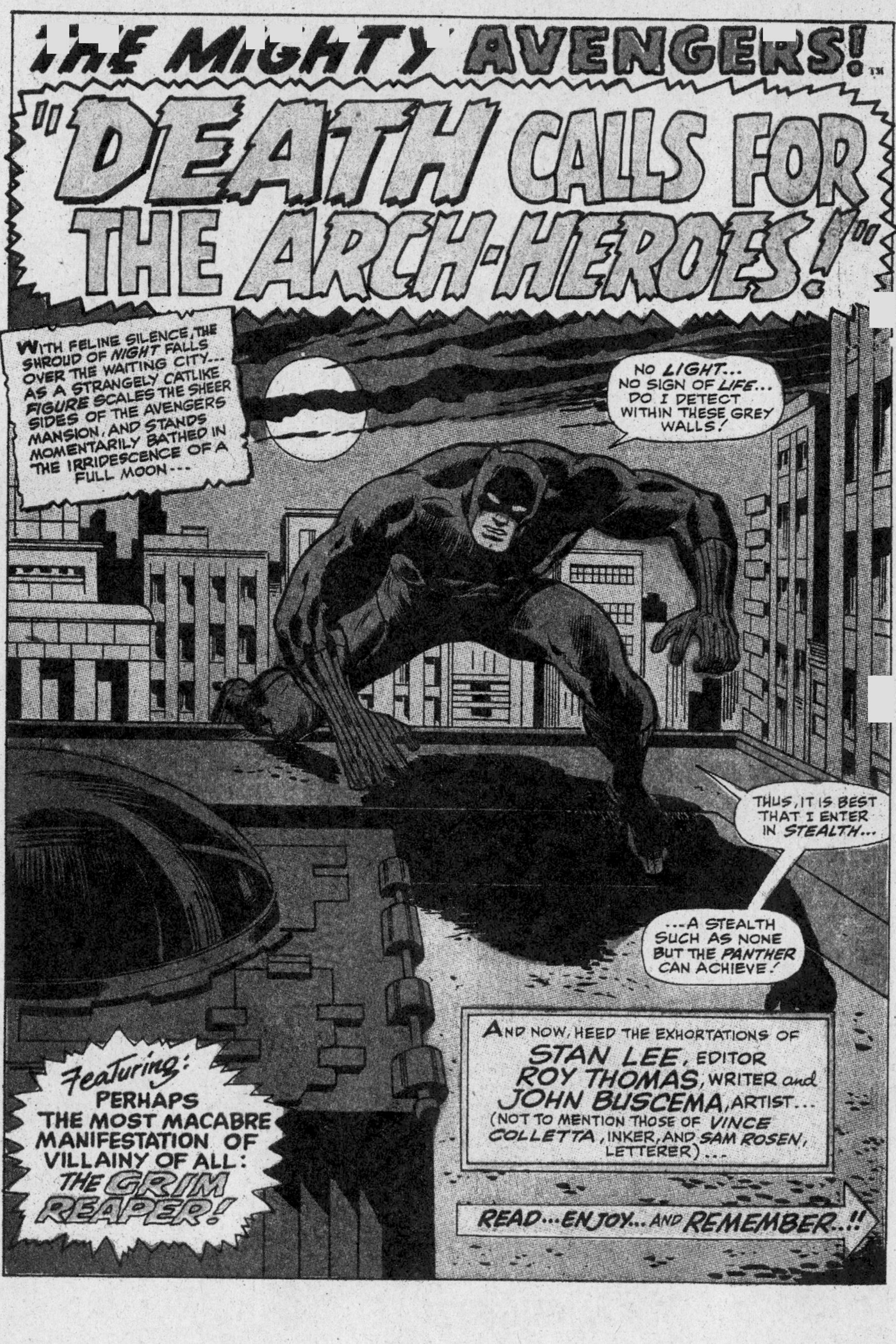
THE MIGHTY AVENGERS!
"DEATH CALLS FOR THE ARCH-HEROES!"
WITH FELINE SILENCE, THE SHROUD OF NIGHT FALLS OVER THE WAITING CITY--- AS A STRANGELY CATLIKE FIGURE SCALES THE SHEER SIDES OF THE AVENGERS MANSION, AND STANDS MOMENTARILY BATHED IN THE IRRIDESCENCE OF A FULL MOON---
NO LIGHT... NO SIGN OF LIFE... DO I DETECT WITHIN THESE GREY WALLS!
THUS, IT IS BEST THAT I ENTER IN STEALTH...
...A STEALTH SUCH AS NONE BUT THE PANTHER CAN ACHIEVE!
Featuring: PERHAPS THE MOST MACABRE MANIFESTATION OF VILLAINY OF ALL: THE GRIM REAPER!
AND NOW, HEED THE EXHORTATIONS OF STAN LEE, EDITOR ROY THOMAS, WRITER and JOHN BUSCEMA, ARTIST... (NOT TO MENTION THOSE OF VINCE COLLETTA, INKER, AND SAM ROSEN, LETTERER)...
READ...ENJOY...AND REMEMBER..!!

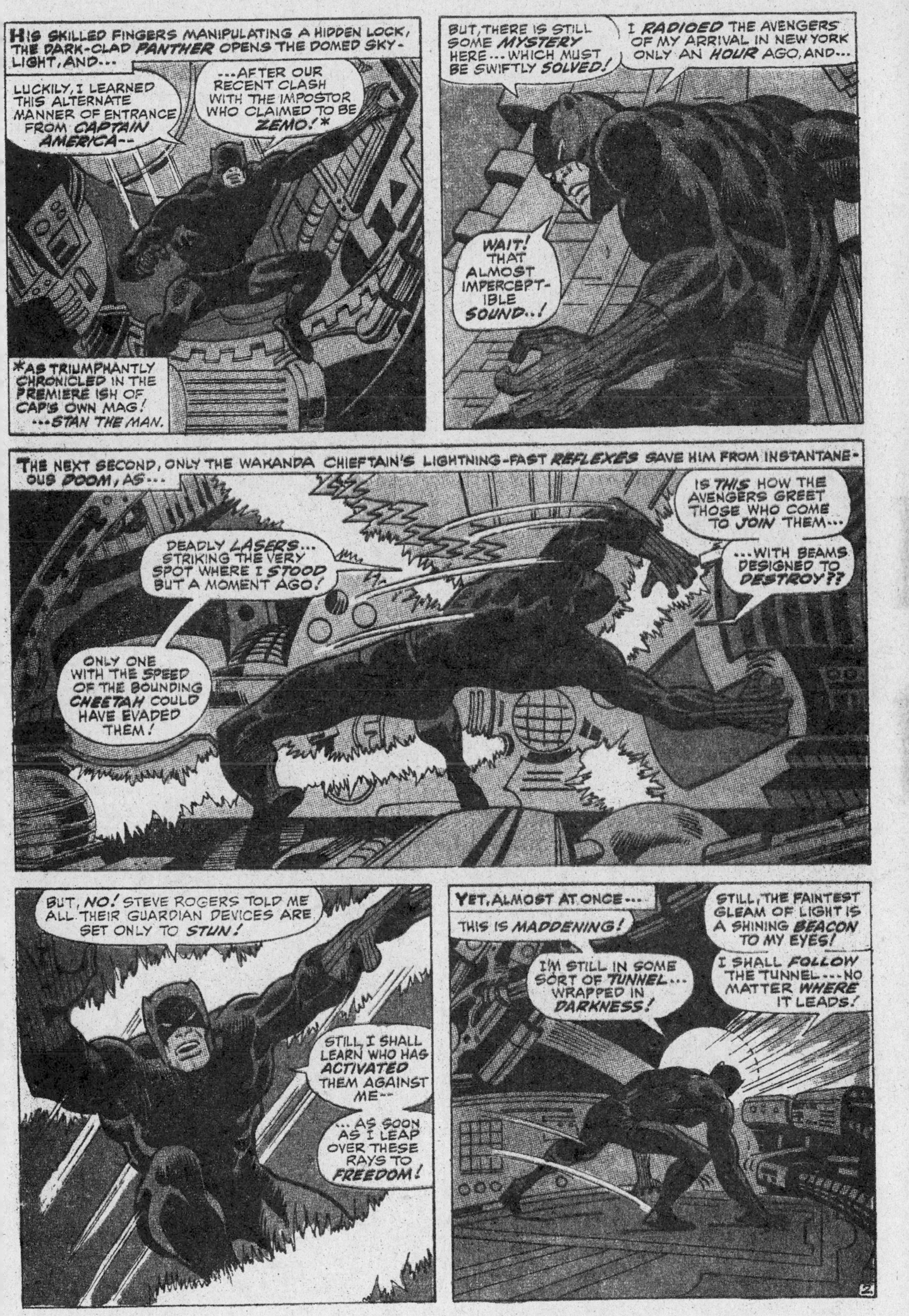
HIS SKILLED FINGERS MANIPULATING A HIDDEN LOCK, THE DARK-CLAD PANTHER OPENS THE DOMED SKY-LIGHT, AND...
LUCKILY, I LEARNED THIS ALTERNATE MANNER OF ENTRANCE FROM CAPTAIN AMERICA--
---AFTER OUR RECENT CLASH WITH THE IMPOSTOR WHO CLAIMED TO BE ZEMO!*
*AS TRIUMPHANTLY CHRONICLED IN THE PREMIERE ISH OF CAP'S OWN MAG! ---STAN THE MAN.
BUT, THERE IS STILL SOME MYSTERY HERE--- WHICH MUST BE SWIFTLY SOLVED!
I RADIOED THE AVENGERS OF MY ARRIVAL IN NEW YORK ONLY AN HOUR AGO, AND...
WAIT! THAT ALMOST IMPERCEPT-IBLE SOUND..!
THE NEXT SECOND, ONLY THE WAKANDA CHIEFTAIN'S LIGHTNING-FAST REFLEXES SAVE HIM FROM INSTANTANE-OUS DOOM, AS...
DEADLY LASERS... STRIKING THE VERY SPOT WHERE I STOOD BUT A MOMENT AGO!
ONLY ONE WITH THE SPEED OF THE BOUNDING CHEETAH COULD HAVE EVADED THEM!
IS THIS HOW THE AVENGERS GREET THOSE WHO COME TO JOIN THEM...
...WITH BEAMS DESIGNED TO DESTROY??
BUT, NO! STEVE ROGERS TOLD ME ALL THEIR GUARDIAN DEVICES ARE SET ONLY TO STUN!
STILL, I SHALL LEARN WHO HAS ACTIVATED THEM AGAINST ME--
...AS SOON AS I LEAP OVER THESE RAYS TO FREEDOM!
YET, ALMOST AT ONCE---
THIS IS MADDENING!
I'M STILL IN SOME SORT OF TUNNEL... WRAPPED IN DARKNESS!
STILL, THE FAINTEST GLEAM OF LIGHT IS A SHINING BEACON TO MY EYES!
I SHALL FOLLOW THE TUNNEL---NO MATTER WHERE IT LEADS!
2

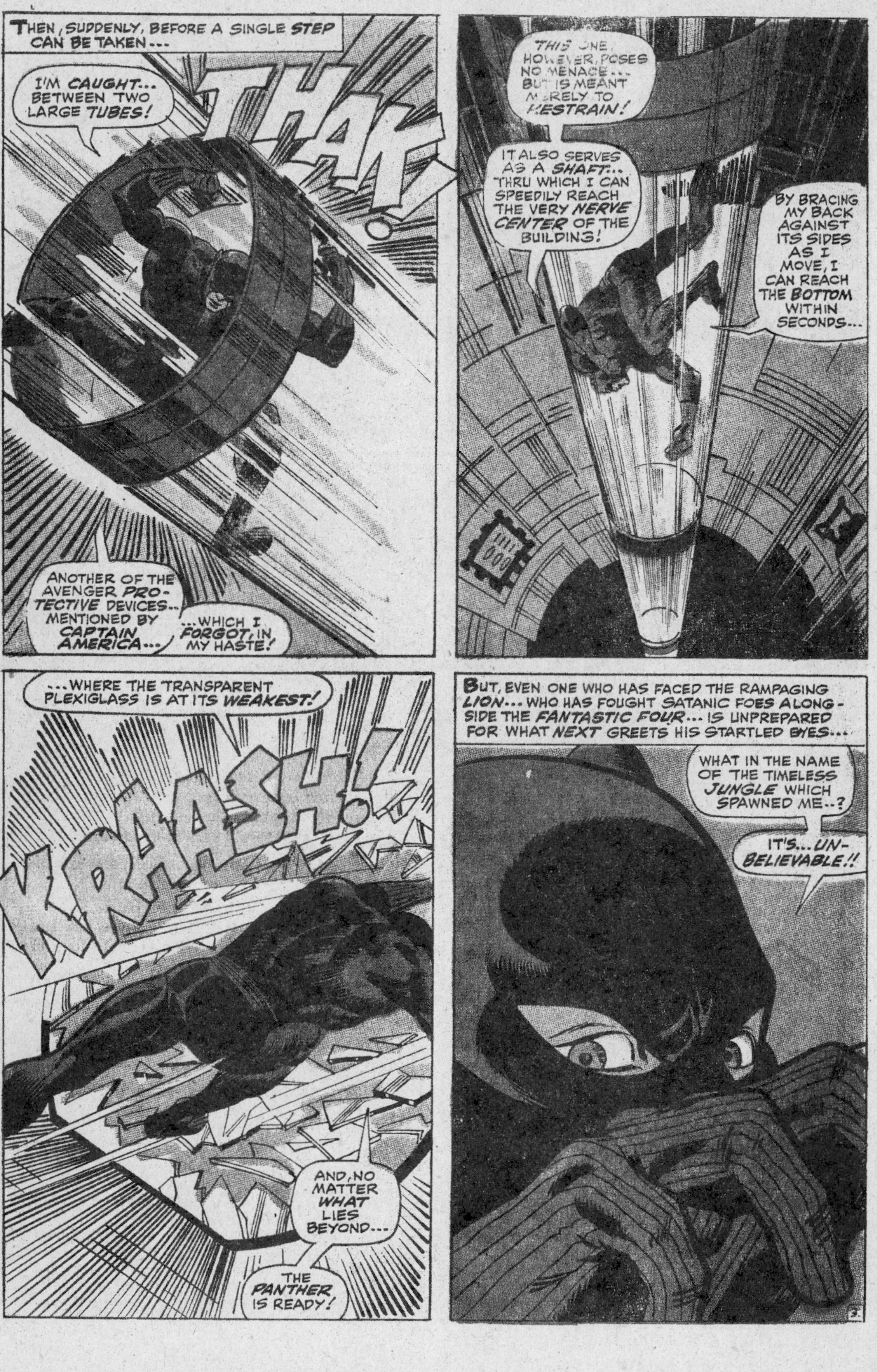
THEN, SUDDENLY, BEFORE A SINGLE STEP CAN BE TAKEN...
I'M CAUGHT... BETWEEN TWO LARGE TUBES!
THAK!
ANOTHER OF THE AVENGER PROTECTIVE DEVICES... MENTIONED BY CAPTAIN AMERICA...
...WHICH I FORGOT, IN MY HASTE!
THIS ONE, HOWEVER, POSES NO MENACE... BUT IS MEANT MERELY TO RESTRAIN!
IT ALSO SERVES AS A SHAFT... THRU WHICH I CAN SPEEDILY REACH THE VERY NERVE CENTER OF THE BUILDING!
BY BRACING MY BACK AGAINST ITS SIDES AS I MOVE, I CAN REACH THE BOTTOM WITHIN SECONDS...
...WHERE THE TRANSPARENT PLEXIGLASS IS AT ITS WEAKEST!
KRAASH!
AND, NO MATTER WHAT LIES BEYOND...
THE PANTHER IS READY!
BUT, EVEN ONE WHO HAS FACED THE RAMPAGING LION... WHO HAS FOUGHT SATANIC FOES ALONG-SIDE THE FANTASTIC FOUR... IS UNPREPARED FOR WHAT NEXT GREETS HIS STARTLED EYES...
WHAT IN THE NAME OF THE TIMELESS JUNGLE WHICH SPAWNED ME..?
IT'S...UN-BELIEVABLE!!

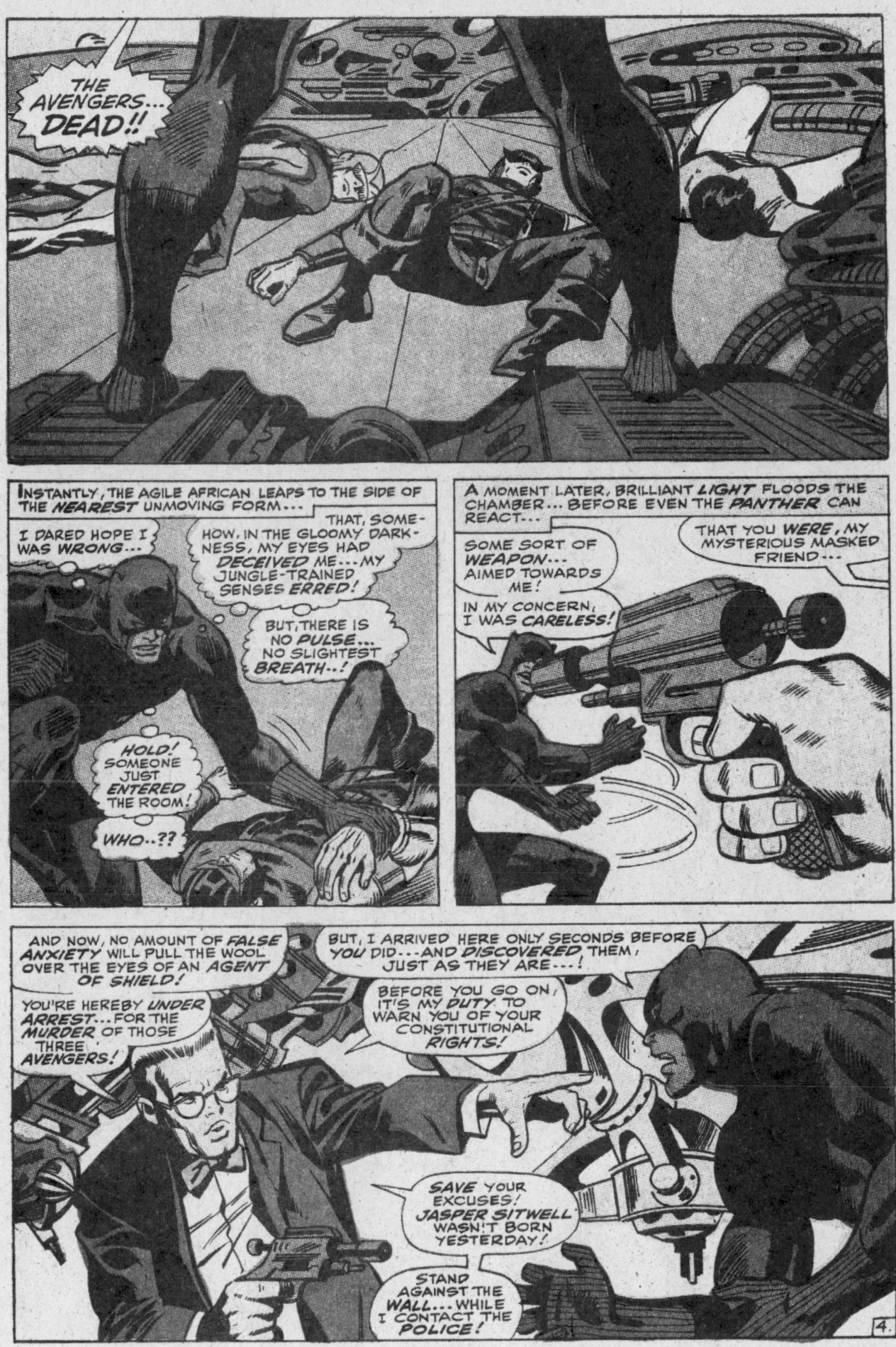

THE AVENGERS... DEAD!!
INSTANTLY, THE AGILE AFRICAN LEAPS TO THE SIDE OF THE NEAREST UNMOVING FORM...
I DARED HOPE I WAS WRONG...
THAT, SOMEHOW, IN THE GLOOMY DARKNESS, MY EYES HAD DECEIVED ME... MY JUNGLE-TRAINED SENSES ERRED!
BUT, THERE IS NO PULSE... NO SLIGHTEST BREATH..!
HOLD! SOMEONE JUST ENTERED THE ROOM!
WHO..??
A MOMENT LATER, BRILLIANT LIGHT FLOODS THE CHAMBER... BEFORE EVEN THE PANTHER CAN REACT...
SOME SORT OF WEAPON... AIMED TOWARDS ME!
IN MY CONCERN, I WAS CARELESS!
THAT YOU WERE, MY MYSTERIOUS MASKED FRIEND...
AND NOW, NO AMOUNT OF FALSE ANXIETY WILL PULL THE WOOL OVER THE EYES OF AN AGENT OF SHIELD!
YOU'RE HEREBY UNDER ARREST... FOR THE MURDER OF THOSE THREE AVENGERS!
BUT, I ARRIVED HERE ONLY SECONDS BEFORE YOU DID... AND DISCOVERED THEM, JUST AS THEY ARE...!
BEFORE YOU GO ON, IT'S MY DUTY TO WARN YOU OF YOUR CONSTITUTIONAL RIGHTS!
SAVE YOUR EXCUSES! JASPER SITWELL WASN'T BORN YESTERDAY!
STAND AGAINST THE WALL... WHILE I CONTACT THE POLICE!

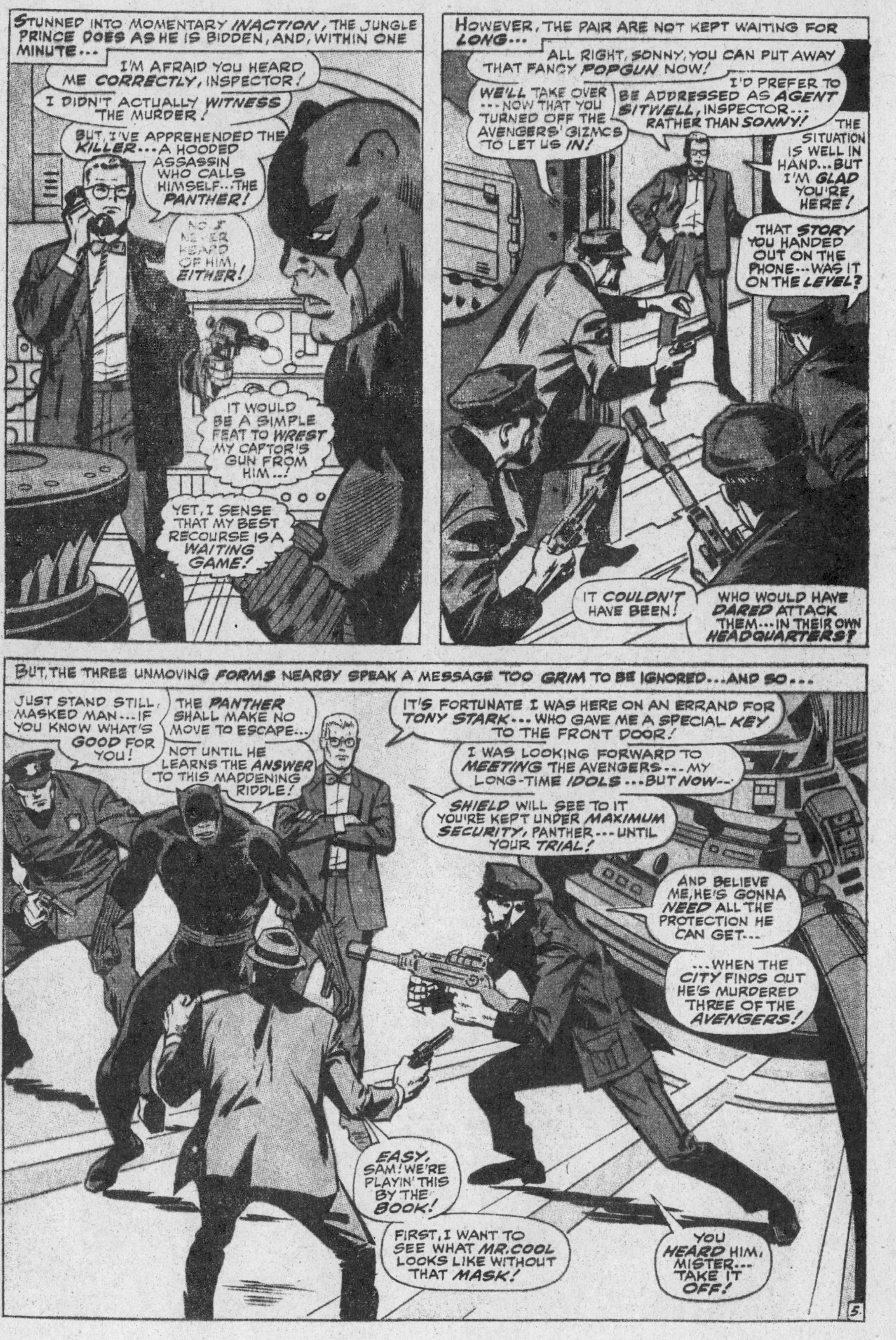

STUNNED INTO MOMENTARY INACTION, THE JUNGLE PRINCE DOES AS HE IS BIDDEN, AND, WITHIN ONE MINUTE...
I'M AFRAID YOU HEARD ME CORRECTLY, INSPECTOR!
I DIDN'T ACTUALLY WITNESS THE MURDER!
BUT, I'VE APPREHENDED THE KILLER... A HOODED ASSASSIN WHO CALLS HIMSELF... THE PANTHER!
NO, I NEVER HEARD OF HIM, EITHER!
IT WOULD BE A SIMPLE FEAT TO WREST MY CAPTOR'S GUN FROM HIM...!
YET, I SENSE THAT MY BEST RECOURSE IS A WAITING GAME!
HOWEVER, THE PAIR ARE NOT KEPT WAITING FOR LONG...
ALL RIGHT, SONNY, YOU CAN PUT AWAY THAT FANCY POPGUN NOW!
WE'LL TAKE OVER --- NOW THAT YOU TURNED OFF THE AVENGERS' GIZMOS TO LET US IN!
I'D PREFER TO BE ADDRESSED AS AGENT SITWELL, INSPECTOR... RATHER THAN SONNY!
THE SITUATION IS WELL IN HAND... BUT I'M GLAD YOU'RE HERE!
THAT STORY YOU HANDED OUT ON THE PHONE... WAS IT ON THE LEVEL?
IT COULDN'T HAVE BEEN!
WHO WOULD HAVE DARED ATTACK THEM... IN THEIR OWN HEADQUARTERS?
BUT, THE THREE UNMOVING FORMS NEARBY SPEAK A MESSAGE TOO GRIM TO BE IGNORED... AND SO...
JUST STAND STILL, MASKED MAN... IF YOU KNOW WHAT'S GOOD FOR YOU!
THE PANTHER SHALL MAKE NO MOVE TO ESCAPE...
NOT UNTIL HE LEARNS THE ANSWER TO THIS MADDENING RIDDLE!
IT'S FORTUNATE I WAS HERE ON AN ERRAND FOR TONY STARK... WHO GAVE ME A SPECIAL KEY TO THE FRONT DOOR!
I WAS LOOKING FORWARD TO MEETING THE AVENGERS... MY LONG-TIME IDOLS... BUT NOW--
SHIELD WILL SEE TO IT YOU'RE KEPT UNDER MAXIMUM SECURITY, PANTHER--- UNTIL YOUR TRIAL!
AND BELIEVE ME, HE'S GONNA NEED ALL THE PROTECTION HE CAN GET...
...WHEN THE CITY FINDS OUT HE'S MURDERED THREE OF THE AVENGERS!
EASY, SAM! WE'RE PLAYIN' THIS BY THE BOOK!
FIRST, I WANT TO SEE WHAT MR. COOL LOOKS LIKE WITHOUT THAT MASK!
YOU HEARD HIM, MISTER--- TAKE IT OFF!
5

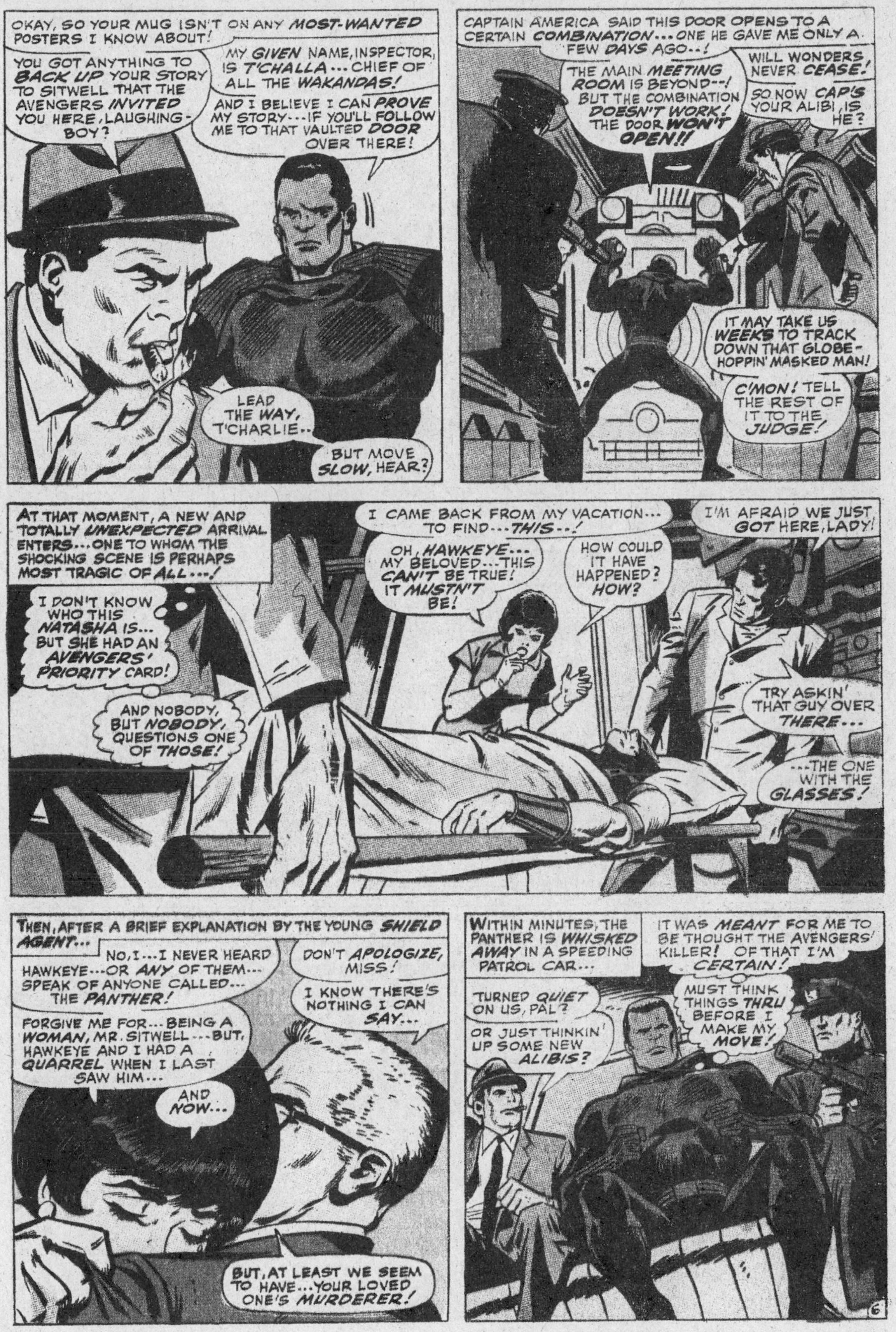
OKAY, SO YOUR MUG ISN'T ON ANY MOST-WANTED POSTERS I KNOW ABOUT!
YOU GOT ANYTHING TO BACK UP YOUR STORY TO SITWELL THAT THE AVENGERS INVITED YOU HERE, LAUGHING-BOY?
MY GIVEN NAME, INSPECTOR, IS T'CHALLA... CHIEF OF ALL THE WAKANDAS!
AND I BELIEVE I CAN PROVE MY STORY---IF YOU'LL FOLLOW ME TO THAT VAULTED DOOR OVER THERE!
LEAD THE WAY, T'CHARLIE...
BUT MOVE SLOW, HEAR?
CAPTAIN AMERICA SAID THIS DOOR OPENS TO A CERTAIN COMBINATION... ONE HE GAVE ME ONLY A FEW DAYS AGO--!
THE MAIN MEETING ROOM IS BEYOND--! BUT THE COMBINATION DOESN'T WORK! THE DOOR WON'T OPEN!!
WILL WONDERS NEVER CEASE!
SO NOW CAP'S YOUR ALIBI, IS HE?
IT MAY TAKE US WEEKS TO TRACK DOWN THAT GLOBE-HOPPIN' MASKED MAN!
C'MON! TELL THE REST OF IT TO THE JUDGE!
AT THAT MOMENT, A NEW AND TOTALLY UNEXPECTED ARRIVAL ENTERS... ONE TO WHOM THE SHOCKING SCENE IS PERHAPS MOST TRAGIC OF ALL...!
I DON'T KNOW WHO THIS NATASHA IS... BUT SHE HAD AN AVENGERS' PRIORITY CARD!
AND NOBODY, BUT NOBODY, QUESTIONS ONE OF THOSE!
I CAME BACK FROM MY VACATION... TO FIND... THIS--!
OH, HAWKEYE... MY BELOVED... THIS CAN'T BE TRUE! IT MUSTN'T BE!
HOW COULD IT HAVE HAPPENED? HOW?
I'M AFRAID WE JUST GOT HERE, LADY!
TRY ASKIN' THAT GUY OVER THERE...
...THE ONE WITH THE GLASSES!
THEN, AFTER A BRIEF EXPLANATION BY THE YOUNG SHIELD AGENT...
NO, I... I NEVER HEARD HAWKEYE... OR ANY OF THEM... SPEAK OF ANYONE CALLED... THE PANTHER!
FORGIVE ME FOR... BEING A WOMAN, MR. SITWELL... BUT, HAWKEYE AND I HAD A QUARREL WHEN I LAST SAW HIM...
AND NOW...
DON'T APOLOGIZE, MISS!
I KNOW THERE'S NOTHING I CAN SAY...
BUT, AT LEAST WE SEEM TO HAVE... YOUR LOVED ONE'S MURDERER!
WITHIN MINUTES, THE PANTHER IS WHISKED AWAY IN A SPEEDING PATROL CAR...
IT WAS MEANT FOR ME TO BE THOUGHT THE AVENGERS' KILLER! OF THAT I'M CERTAIN!
TURNED QUIET ON US, PAL?
OR JUST THINKIN' UP SOME NEW ALIBIS?
MUST THINK THINGS THRU BEFORE I MAKE MY MOVE!
6

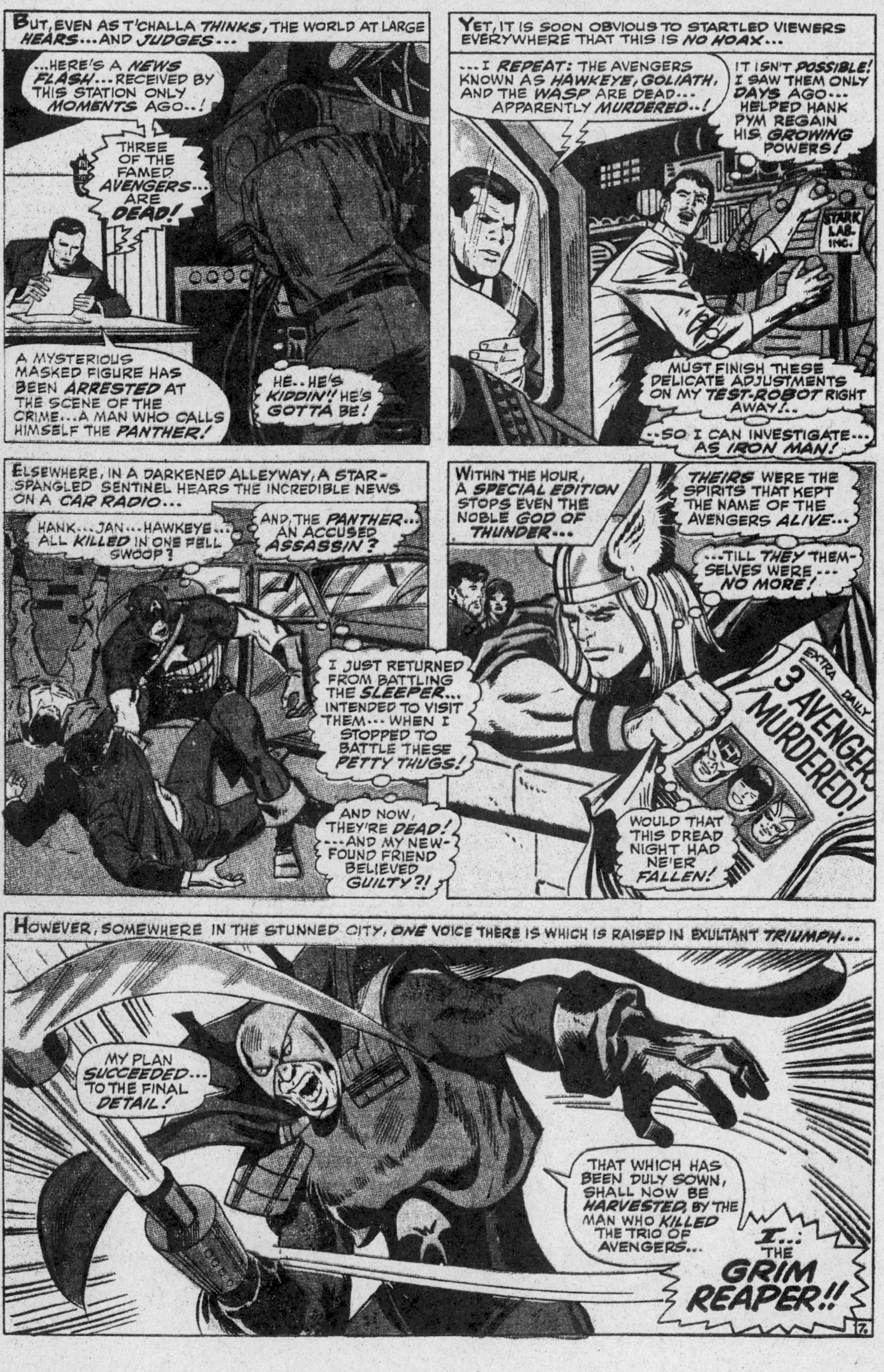

BUT, EVEN AS T'CHALLA THINKS, THE WORLD AT LARGE HEARS... AND JUDGES...
...HERE'S A NEWS FLASH... RECEIVED BY THIS STATION ONLY MOMENTS AGO..!
THREE OF THE FAMED AVENGERS... ARE DEAD!
A MYSTERIOUS MASKED FIGURE HAS BEEN ARRESTED AT THE SCENE OF THE CRIME... A MAN WHO CALLS HIMSELF THE PANTHER!
HE.. HE'S KIDDIN'! HE'S GOTTA BE!
YET, IT IS SOON OBVIOUS TO STARTLED VIEWERS EVERYWHERE THAT THIS IS NO HOAX...
...I REPEAT: THE AVENGERS KNOWN AS HAWKEYE, GOLIATH, AND THE WASP ARE DEAD... APPARENTLY MURDERED..!
IT ISN'T POSSIBLE! I SAW THEM ONLY DAYS AGO... HELPED HANK PYM REGAIN HIS GROWING POWERS!
STARK LAB. INC.
MUST FINISH THESE DELICATE ADJUSTMENTS ON MY TEST-ROBOT RIGHT AWAY!..
..SO I CAN INVESTIGATE... AS IRON MAN!
ELSEWHERE, IN A DARKENED ALLEYWAY, A STAR-SPANGLED SENTINEL HEARS THE INCREDIBLE NEWS ON A CAR RADIO...
HANK... JAN... HAWKEYE... ALL KILLED IN ONE FELL SWOOP?
AND THE PANTHER... AN ACCUSED ASSASSIN?
I JUST RETURNED FROM BATTLING THE SLEEPER... INTENDED TO VISIT THEM... WHEN I STOPPED TO BATTLE THESE PETTY THUGS!
AND NOW, THEY'RE DEAD! ...AND MY NEW-FOUND FRIEND BELIEVED GUILTY?!
WITHIN THE HOUR, A SPECIAL EDITION STOPS EVEN THE NOBLE GOD OF THUNDER...
THEIRS WERE THE SPIRITS THAT KEPT THE NAME OF THE AVENGERS ALIVE...
...TILL THEY THEMSELVES WERE... NO MORE!
EXTRA DAILY
3 AVENGERS MURDERED!
WOULD THAT THIS DREAD NIGHT HAD NE'ER FALLEN!
HOWEVER, SOMEWHERE IN THE STUNNED CITY, ONE VOICE THERE IS WHICH IS RAISED IN EXULTANT TRIUMPH...
MY PLAN SUCCEEDED... TO THE FINAL DETAIL!
THAT WHICH HAS BEEN DULY SOWN, SHALL NOW BE HARVESTED, BY THE MAN WHO KILLED THE TRIO OF AVENGERS...
I...: THE GRIM REAPER!!
7.

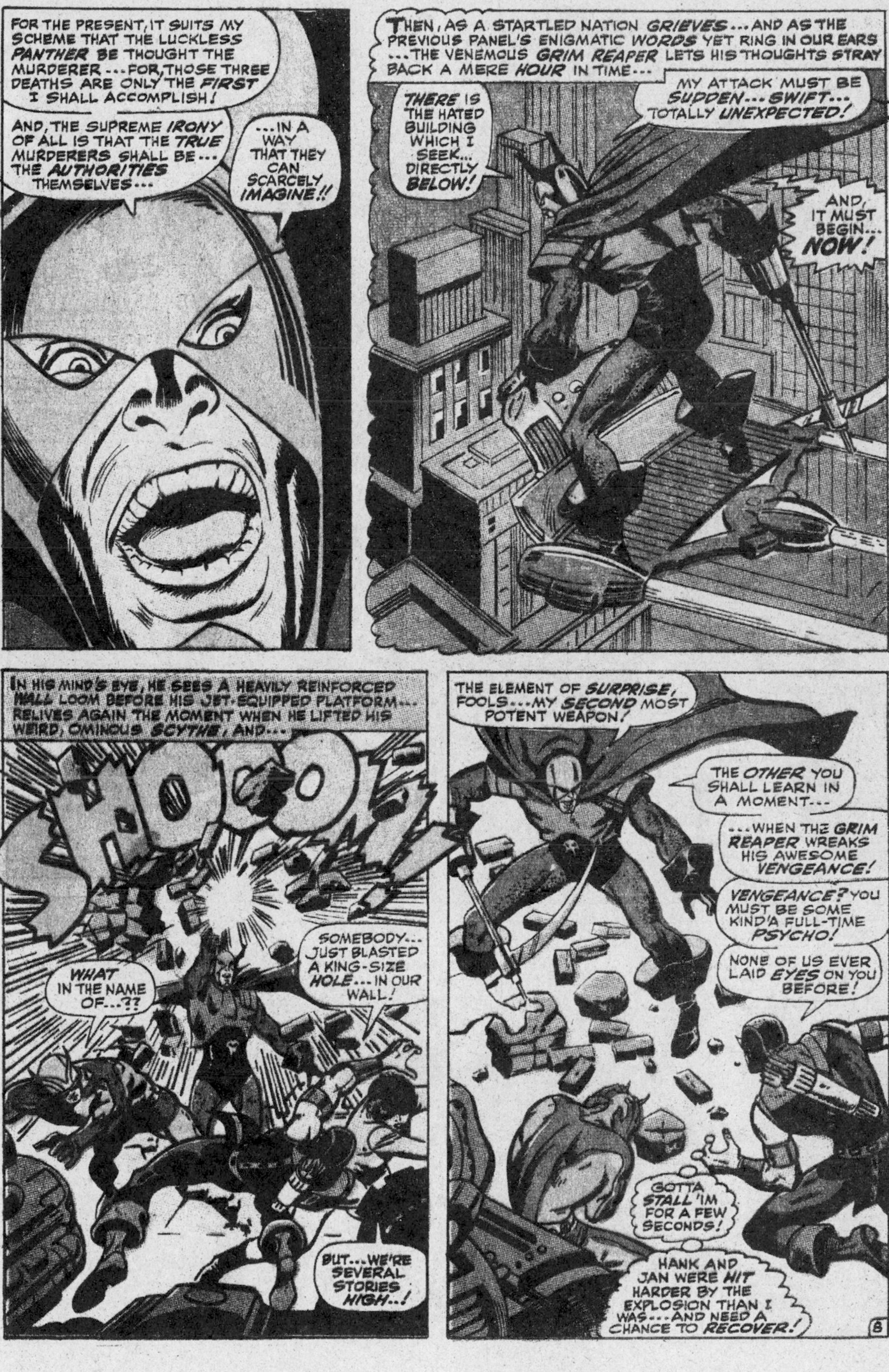

FOR THE PRESENT, IT SUITS MY SCHEME THAT THE LUCKLESS PANTHER BE THOUGHT THE MURDERER ... FOR, THOSE THREE DEATHS ARE ONLY THE FIRST I SHALL ACCOMPLISH!
AND, THE SUPREME IRONY OF ALL IS THAT THE TRUE MURDERERS SHALL BE... THE AUTHORITIES THEMSELVES...
...IN A WAY THAT THEY CAN SCARCELY IMAGINE!!
THEN, AS A STARTLED NATION GRIEVES... AND AS THE PREVIOUS PANEL'S ENIGMATIC WORDS YET RING IN OUR EARS ... THE VENEMOUS GRIM REAPER LETS HIS THOUGHTS STRAY BACK A MERE HOUR IN TIME...
THERE IS THE HATED BUILDING WHICH I SEEK... DIRECTLY BELOW!
MY ATTACK MUST BE SUDDEN... SWIFT... TOTALLY UNEXPECTED!
AND, IT MUST BEGIN... NOW!
IN HIS MIND'S EYE, HE SEES A HEAVILY REINFORCED WALL LOOM BEFORE HIS JET-EQUIPPED PLATFORM... RELIVES AGAIN THE MOMENT WHEN HE LIFTED HIS WEIRD, OMINOUS SCYTHE, AND...
SHOOOOM
WHAT IN THE NAME OF..??
SOMEBODY... JUST BLASTED A KING-SIZE HOLE... IN OUR WALL!
BUT... WE'RE SEVERAL STORIES HIGH...!
THE ELEMENT OF SURPRISE, FOOLS... MY SECOND MOST POTENT WEAPON!
THE OTHER YOU SHALL LEARN IN A MOMENT---
...WHEN THE GRIM REAPER WREAKS HIS AWESOME VENGEANCE!
VENGEANCE? YOU MUST BE SOME KIND'A FULL-TIME PSYCHO!
NONE OF US EVER LAID EYES ON YOU BEFORE!
GOTTA STALL 'IM FOR A FEW SECONDS!
HANK AND JAN WERE HIT HARDER BY THE EXPLOSION THAN I WAS... AND NEED A CHANCE TO RECOVER!
8

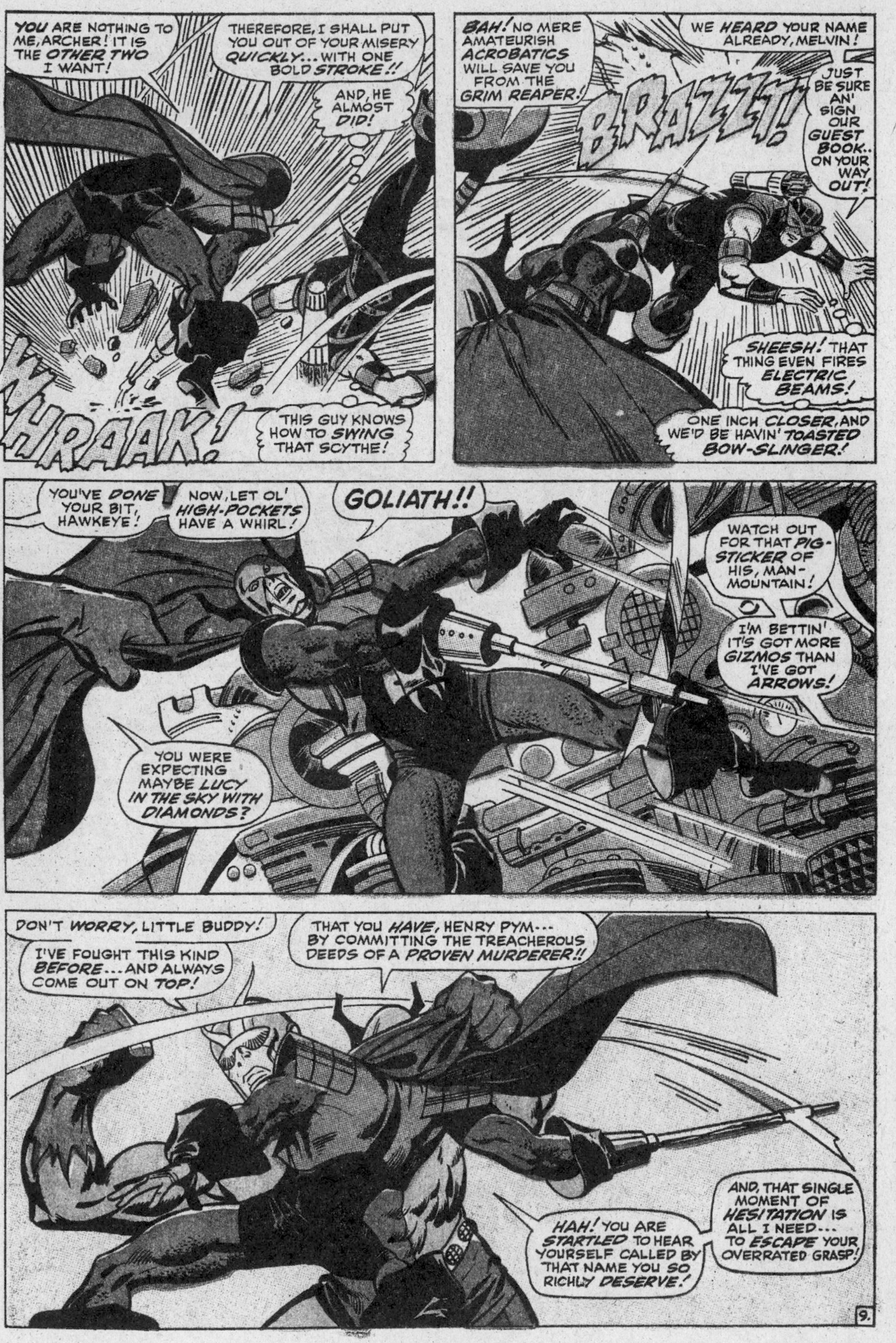

YOU ARE NOTHING TO ME, ARCHER! IT IS THE OTHER TWO I WANT!
THEREFORE, I SHALL PUT YOU OUT OF YOUR MISERY QUICKLY... WITH ONE BOLD STROKE!!
AND, HE ALMOST DID!
WHRAAK!
THIS GUY KNOWS HOW TO SWING THAT SCYTHE!
BAH! NO MERE AMATEURISH ACROBATICS WILL SAVE YOU FROM THE GRIM REAPER!
WE HEARD YOUR NAME ALREADY, MELVIN!
BRAZZT!
JUST BE SURE AN' SIGN OUR GUEST BOOK.. ON YOUR WAY OUT!
SHEESH! THAT THING EVEN FIRES ELECTRIC BEAMS!
ONE INCH CLOSER, AND WE'D BE HAVIN' TOASTED BOW-SLINGER!
YOU'VE DONE YOUR BIT, HAWKEYE!
NOW, LET OL' HIGH-POCKETS HAVE A WHIRL!
GOLIATH!!
WATCH OUT FOR THAT PIG-STICKER OF HIS, MAN-MOUNTAIN!
I'M BETTIN' IT'S GOT MORE GIZMOS THAN I'VE GOT ARROWS!
YOU WERE EXPECTING MAYBE LUCY IN THE SKY WITH DIAMONDS?
DON'T WORRY, LITTLE BUDDY!
I'VE FOUGHT THIS KIND BEFORE... AND ALWAYS COME OUT ON TOP!
THAT YOU HAVE, HENRY PYM--- BY COMMITTING THE TREACHEROUS DEEDS OF A PROVEN MURDERER!!
HAH! YOU ARE STARTLED TO HEAR YOURSELF CALLED BY THAT NAME YOU SO RICHLY DESERVE!
AND, THAT SINGLE MOMENT OF HESITATION IS ALL I NEED... TO ESCAPE YOUR OVERRATED GRASP!
9.

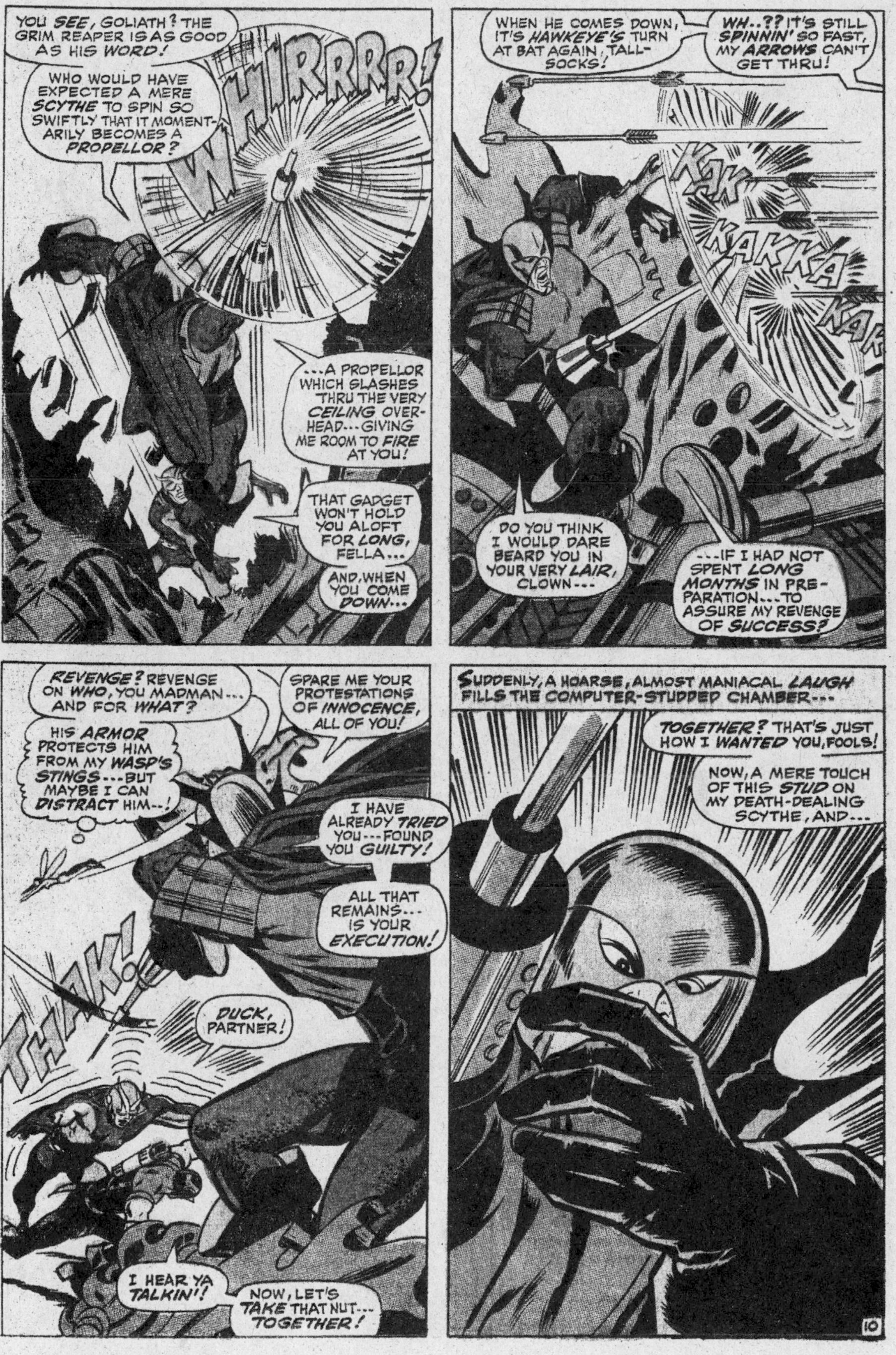
YOU SEE, GOLIATH? THE GRIM REAPER IS AS GOOD AS HIS WORD!
WHO WOULD HAVE EXPECTED A MERE SCYTHE TO SPIN SO SWIFTLY THAT IT MOMENTARILY BECOMES A PROPELLOR?
WHIRRRR!
...A PROPELLOR WHICH SLASHES THRU THE VERY CEILING OVERHEAD...GIVING ME ROOM TO FIRE AT YOU!
THAT GADGET WON'T HOLD YOU ALOFT FOR LONG, FELLA...
AND, WHEN YOU COME DOWN...
WHEN HE COMES DOWN, IT'S HAWKEYE'S TURN AT BAT AGAIN, TALL-SOCKS!
WH..?? IT'S STILL SPINNIN' SO FAST, MY ARROWS CAN'T GET THRU!
KAK
KAKKA
KAK
DO YOU THINK I WOULD DARE BEARD YOU IN YOUR VERY LAIR, CLOWN---
---IF I HAD NOT SPENT LONG MONTHS IN PREPARATION...TO ASSURE MY REVENGE OF SUCCESS?
REVENGE? REVENGE ON WHO, YOU MADMAN... AND FOR WHAT?
SPARE ME YOUR PROTESTATIONS OF INNOCENCE, ALL OF YOU!
HIS ARMOR PROTECTS HIM FROM MY WASP'S STINGS...BUT MAYBE I CAN DISTRACT HIM..!
I HAVE ALREADY TRIED YOU---FOUND YOU GUILTY!
ALL THAT REMAINS... IS YOUR EXECUTION!
THAK!
DUCK, PARTNER!
I HEAR YA TALKIN'!
NOW, LET'S TAKE THAT NUT--- TOGETHER!
SUDDENLY, A HOARSE, ALMOST MANIACAL LAUGH FILLS THE COMPUTER-STUDDED CHAMBER---
TOGETHER? THAT'S JUST HOW I WANTED YOU, FOOLS!
NOW, A MERE TOUCH OF THIS STUD ON MY DEATH-DEALING SCYTHE, AND...
10

...AND, BOTH THE MURDERER CALLED *GOLIATH*...AND HE WHO WOULD *PROTECT* HIM... ARE IRREVOCABLY *DOOMED!*

A WIDE-SPREAD ELECTRICAL CHARGE ...CATCHING US *BOTH!*

OUR ONLY CHANCE NOW...IS *JAN!*

BLACKING OUT...! CAN'T STAND...THE SEARING *PAIN!!*

ZZAT--KAZZAKKAK

BUT, THE LOVELY AVENGING *HEIRESS* IS NOT SPARED THE FATE OF HER CLOSEST COMRADES...

HANK AND HAWKEYE...DIDN'T KNOW I WAS *FLYING* JUST ABOVE THEM!

THAT CHARGE *OVERCAME*... MY MENTAL *SIZE- CONTROL!* I'M... GROWING *LARGER* AGAIN...!

ZZIKK

THEN, AS THE *LAST* OF THE TRIO SLUMPS INTO UN- CONSCIOUS- NESS...

YOU CANNOT *HEAR* ME...*ANY* OF YOU...

YET, I AM THE *ONE* FOE YOU HAD NO *CHANCE* AGAINST!

FOR, I AM THE EMBODIMENT OF *DEATH*... AND I STRUCK IN THE NAME OF JUST *VENGEANCE!*

"IF YOU COULD HEAR ME, I WOULD ASK YOU TO REMEMBER ONE CALLED... *WONDER MAN*...!*"

GET *HIM!* HE'S AN AGENT OF *ZEMO!*

*OUR ONCE-IN-A LIFETIME HERO-VILLAIN FROM ISH #9! ...SMILEY.

"YES, FOOLS... *WONDER MAN!* HE WHO BECAME VIRTUALLY AN *AVENGER*... IN ORDER TO *DESTROY* YOU FROM WITHIN---"

YOU *MISSED*, GIANT-MAN... BUT I SHALL *NOT!* THOUGH YOU *DWARF* ME, I'M AT LEAST YOUR *EQUAL* IN POWER!

11.

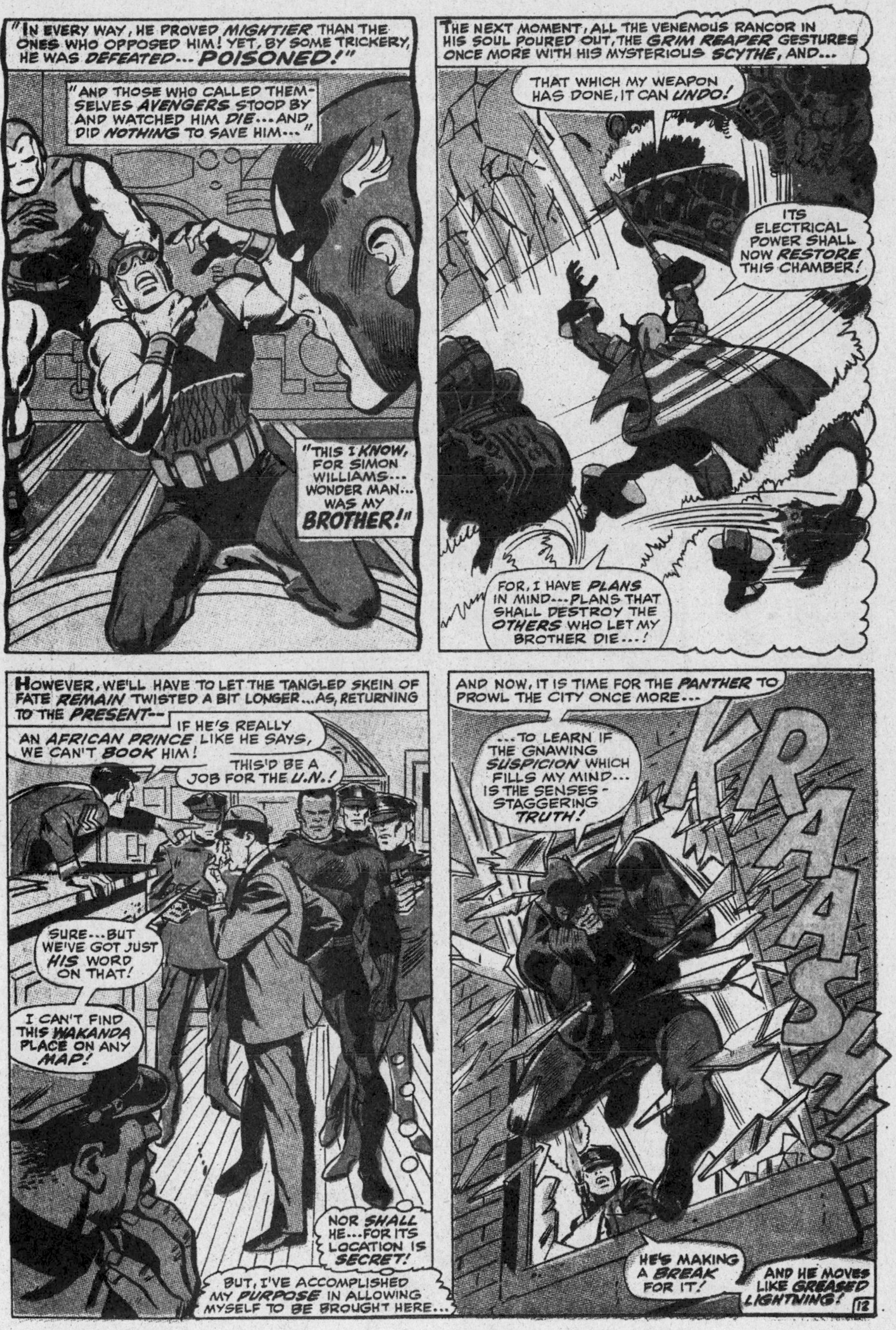
"IN EVERY WAY, HE PROVED MIGHTIER THAN THE ONES WHO OPPOSED HIM! YET, BY SOME TRICKERY, HE WAS DEFEATED... POISONED!"
"AND THOSE WHO CALLED THEMSELVES AVENGERS STOOD BY AND WATCHED HIM DIE... AND DID NOTHING TO SAVE HIM..."
"THIS I KNOW, FOR SIMON WILLIAMS... WONDER MAN... WAS MY BROTHER!"
THE NEXT MOMENT, ALL THE VENEMOUS RANCOR IN HIS SOUL POURED OUT, THE GRIM REAPER GESTURES ONCE MORE WITH HIS MYSTERIOUS SCYTHE, AND...
THAT WHICH MY WEAPON HAS DONE, IT CAN UNDO!
ITS ELECTRICAL POWER SHALL NOW RESTORE THIS CHAMBER!
FOR, I HAVE PLANS IN MIND... PLANS THAT SHALL DESTROY THE OTHERS WHO LET MY BROTHER DIE...!
HOWEVER, WE'LL HAVE TO LET THE TANGLED SKEIN OF FATE REMAIN TWISTED A BIT LONGER... AS, RETURNING TO THE PRESENT--
IF HE'S REALLY AN AFRICAN PRINCE LIKE HE SAYS, WE CAN'T BOOK HIM!
THIS'D BE A JOB FOR THE U.N.!
SURE... BUT WE'VE GOT JUST HIS WORD ON THAT!
I CAN'T FIND THIS WAKANDA PLACE ON ANY MAP!
NOR SHALL HE... FOR ITS LOCATION IS SECRET!
BUT, I'VE ACCOMPLISHED MY PURPOSE IN ALLOWING MYSELF TO BE BROUGHT HERE...
AND NOW, IT IS TIME FOR THE PANTHER TO PROWL THE CITY ONCE MORE...
...TO LEARN IF THE GNAWING SUSPICION WHICH FILLS MY MIND... IS THE SENSES-STAGGERING TRUTH!
K'RAASH
HE'S MAKING A BREAK FOR IT!
AND HE MOVES LIKE GREASED LIGHTNING!
12

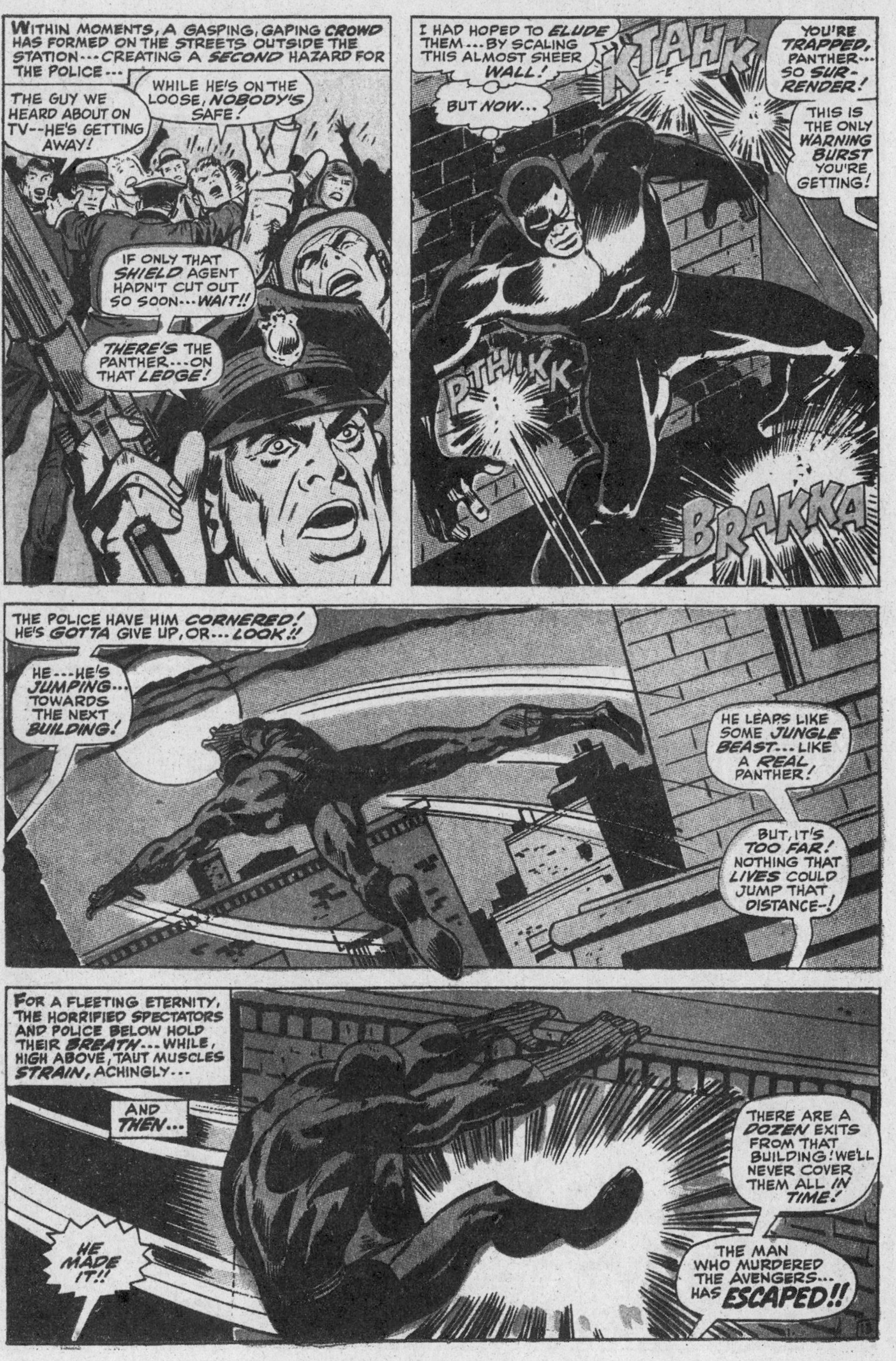
WITHIN MOMENTS, A GASPING, GAPING CROWD HAS FORMED ON THE STREETS OUTSIDE THE STATION --- CREATING A SECOND HAZARD FOR THE POLICE ---
THE GUY WE HEARD ABOUT ON TV--HE'S GETTING AWAY!
WHILE HE'S ON THE LOOSE, NOBODY'S SAFE!
IF ONLY THAT SHIELD AGENT HADN'T CUT OUT SO SOON --- WAIT!!
THERE'S THE PANTHER --- ON THAT LEDGE!
I HAD HOPED TO ELUDE THEM --- BY SCALING THIS ALMOST SHEER WALL!
BUT NOW...
KTAHK
YOU'RE TRAPPED, PANTHER --- SO SUR-RENDER!
THIS IS THE ONLY WARNING BURST YOU'RE GETTING!
PTHIKK
BRAKKA
THE POLICE HAVE HIM CORNERED! HE'S GOTTA GIVE UP, OR --- LOOK!!
HE --- HE'S JUMPING... TOWARDS THE NEXT BUILDING!
HE LEAPS LIKE SOME JUNGLE BEAST --- LIKE A REAL PANTHER!
BUT, IT'S TOO FAR! NOTHING THAT LIVES COULD JUMP THAT DISTANCE-!
FOR A FLEETING ETERNITY, THE HORRIFIED SPECTATORS AND POLICE BELOW HOLD THEIR BREATH --- WHILE, HIGH ABOVE, TAUT MUSCLES STRAIN, ACHINGLY ---
AND THEN ---
HE MADE IT!!
THERE ARE A DOZEN EXITS FROM THAT BUILDING! WE'LL NEVER COVER THEM ALL IN TIME!
THE MAN WHO MURDERED THE AVENGERS... HAS ESCAPED!!

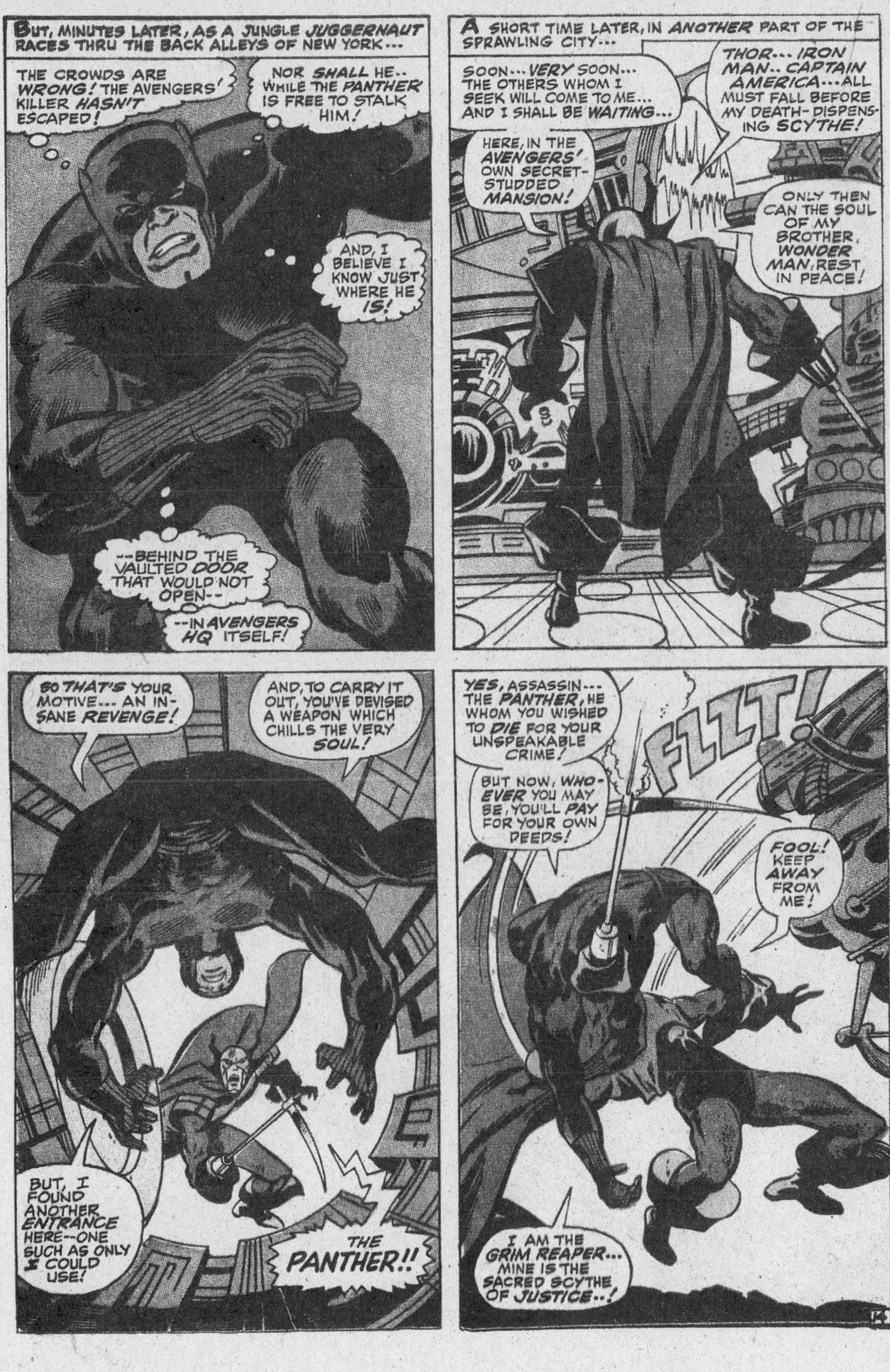

BUT, MINUTES LATER, AS A JUNGLE JUGGERNAUT RACES THRU THE BACK ALLEYS OF NEW YORK...
THE CROWDS ARE WRONG! THE AVENGERS' KILLER HASN'T ESCAPED!
NOR SHALL HE.. WHILE THE PANTHER IS FREE TO STALK HIM!
AND, I BELIEVE I KNOW JUST WHERE HE IS!
--BEHIND THE VAULTED DOOR THAT WOULD NOT OPEN--
--IN AVENGERS HQ ITSELF!
A SHORT TIME LATER, IN ANOTHER PART OF THE SPRAWLING CITY...
SOON... VERY SOON... THE OTHERS WHOM I SEEK WILL COME TO ME... AND I SHALL BE WAITING...
HERE, IN THE AVENGERS' OWN SECRET-STUDDED MANSION!
THOR... IRON MAN.. CAPTAIN AMERICA... ALL MUST FALL BEFORE MY DEATH-DISPENSING SCYTHE!
ONLY THEN CAN THE SOUL OF MY BROTHER, WONDER MAN, REST IN PEACE!
SO THAT'S YOUR MOTIVE... AN INSANE REVENGE!
AND, TO CARRY IT OUT, YOU'VE DEVISED A WEAPON WHICH CHILLS THE VERY SOUL!
BUT, I FOUND ANOTHER ENTRANCE HERE--ONE SUCH AS ONLY I COULD USE!
THE PANTHER!!
YES, ASSASSIN... THE PANTHER, HE WHOM YOU WISHED TO DIE FOR YOUR UNSPEAKABLE CRIME!
BUT NOW, WHOEVER YOU MAY BE, YOU'LL PAY FOR YOUR OWN DEEDS!
FZZT!
FOOL! KEEP AWAY FROM ME!
I AM THE GRIM REAPER... MINE IS THE SACRED SCYTHE OF JUSTICE..!
14

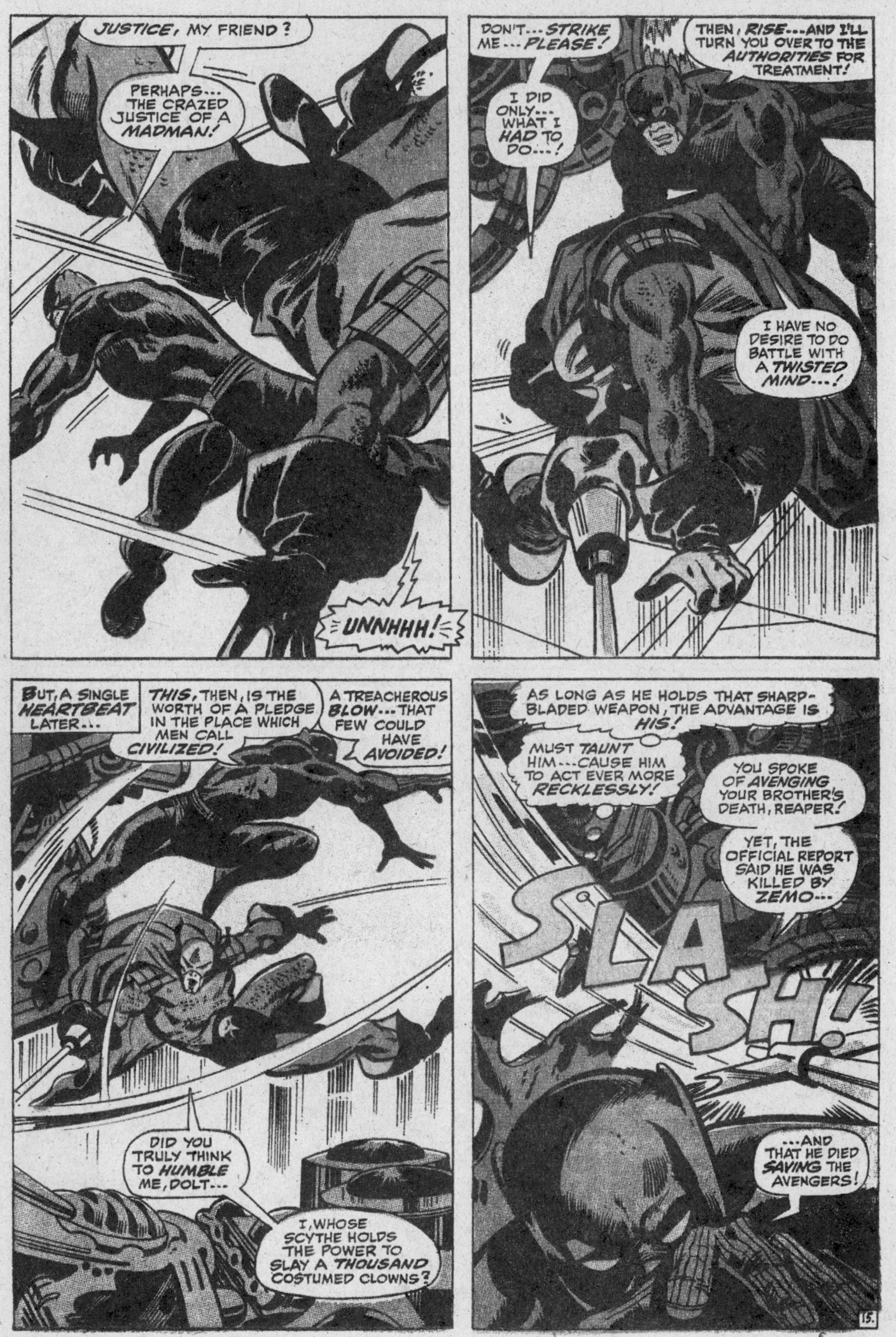
JUSTICE, MY FRIEND?
PERHAPS... THE CRAZED JUSTICE OF A MADMAN!
UNNHHH!
DON'T... STRIKE ME... PLEASE!
I DID ONLY... WHAT I HAD TO DO...!
THEN, RISE...AND I'LL TURN YOU OVER TO THE AUTHORITIES FOR TREATMENT!
I HAVE NO DESIRE TO DO BATTLE WITH A TWISTED MIND...!
BUT, A SINGLE HEARTBEAT LATER...
THIS, THEN, IS THE WORTH OF A PLEDGE IN THE PLACE WHICH MEN CALL CIVILIZED!
A TREACHEROUS BLOW...THAT FEW COULD HAVE AVOIDED!
DID YOU TRULY THINK TO HUMBLE ME, DOLT...
I, WHOSE SCYTHE HOLDS THE POWER TO SLAY A THOUSAND COSTUMED CLOWNS?
AS LONG AS HE HOLDS THAT SHARP-BLADED WEAPON, THE ADVANTAGE IS HIS!
MUST TAUNT HIM...CAUSE HIM TO ACT EVER MORE RECKLESSLY!
YOU SPOKE OF AVENGING YOUR BROTHER'S DEATH, REAPER!
YET, THE OFFICIAL REPORT SAID HE WAS KILLED BY ZEMO...
SLASH!
...AND THAT HE DIED SAVING THE AVENGERS!
15.

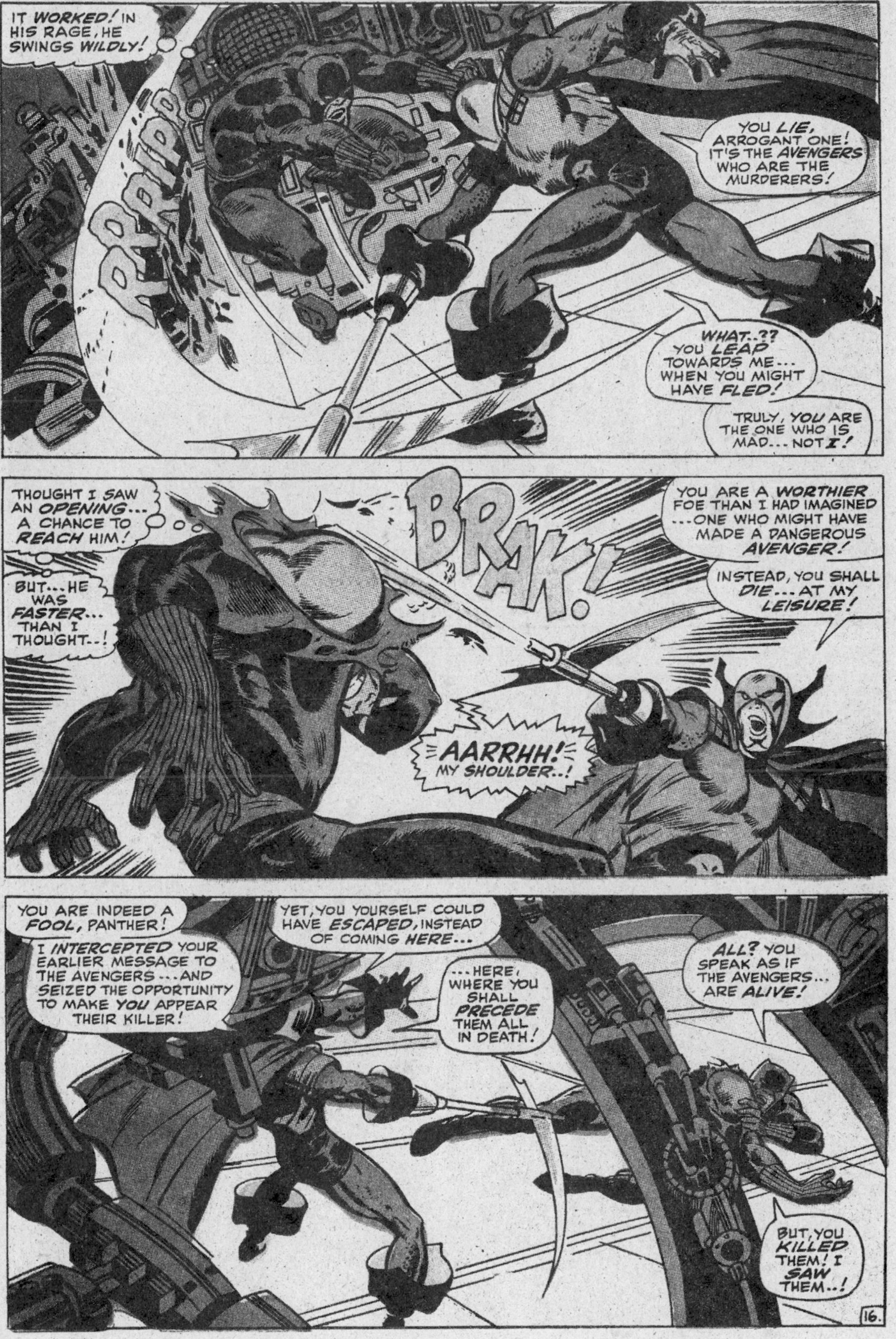
IT WORKED! IN HIS RAGE, HE SWINGS WILDLY!
RRRIPP
YOU LIE, ARROGANT ONE! IT'S THE AVENGERS WHO ARE THE MURDERERS!
WHAT..?? YOU LEAP TOWARDS ME... WHEN YOU MIGHT HAVE FLED!
TRULY, YOU ARE THE ONE WHO IS MAD... NOT I!
THOUGHT I SAW AN OPENING... A CHANCE TO REACH HIM!
BUT... HE WAS FASTER... THAN I THOUGHT--!
BRAK!
YOU ARE A WORTHIER FOE THAN I HAD IMAGINED ...ONE WHO MIGHT HAVE MADE A DANGEROUS AVENGER!
INSTEAD, YOU SHALL DIE... AT MY LEISURE!
AARRHH! MY SHOULDER..!
YOU ARE INDEED A FOOL, PANTHER!
I INTERCEPTED YOUR EARLIER MESSAGE TO THE AVENGERS ...AND SEIZED THE OPPORTUNITY TO MAKE YOU APPEAR THEIR KILLER!
YET, YOU YOURSELF COULD HAVE ESCAPED, INSTEAD OF COMING HERE...
...HERE, WHERE YOU SHALL PRECEDE THEM ALL IN DEATH!
ALL? YOU SPEAK AS IF THE AVENGERS... ARE ALIVE!
BUT, YOU KILLED THEM! I SAW THEM..!
16.

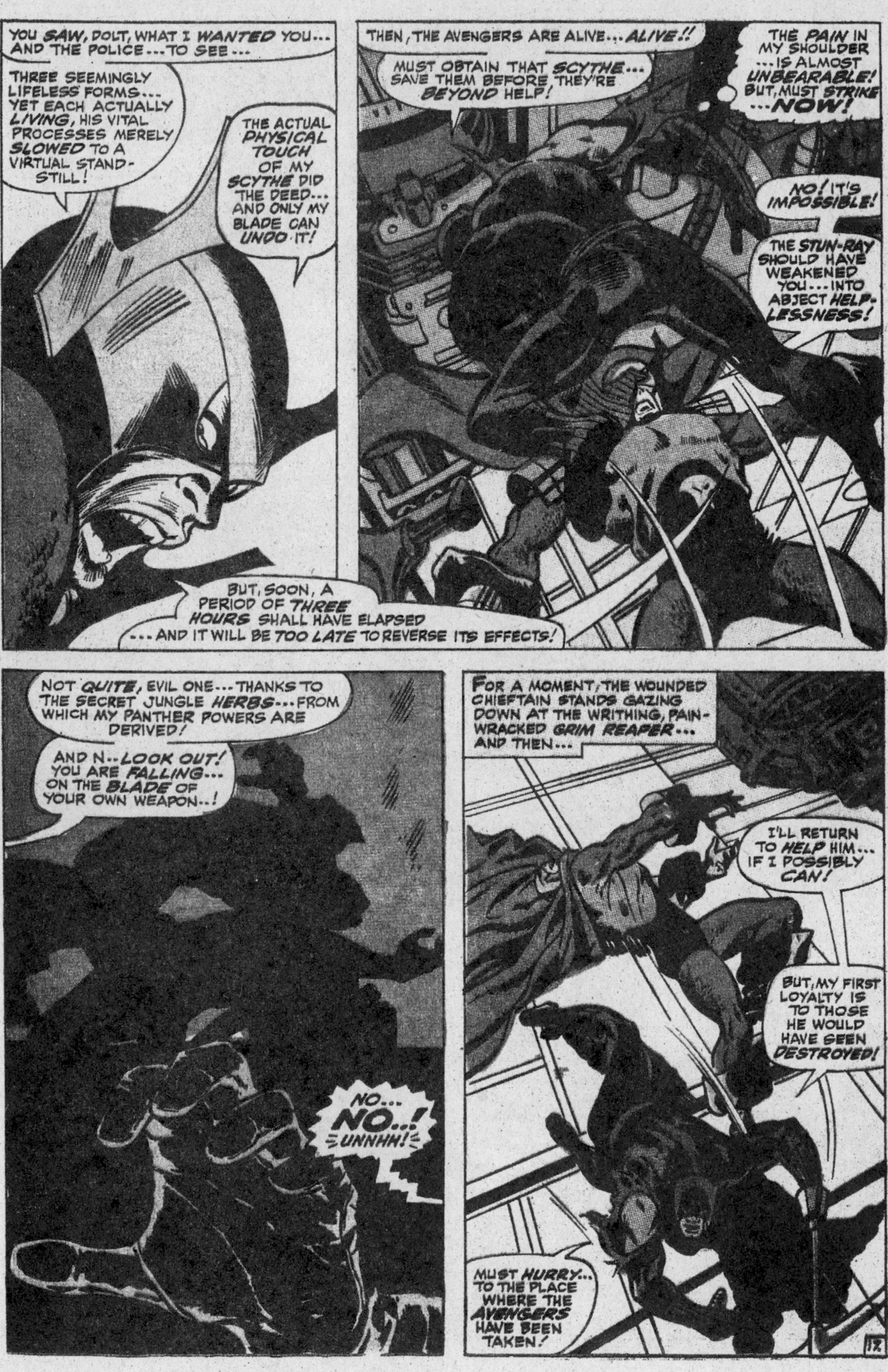
YOU SAW, DOLT, WHAT I WANTED YOU... AND THE POLICE... TO SEE...
THREE SEEMINGLY LIFELESS FORMS... YET EACH ACTUALLY LIVING, HIS VITAL PROCESSES MERELY SLOWED TO A VIRTUAL STAND-STILL!
THE ACTUAL PHYSICAL TOUCH OF MY SCYTHE DID THE DEED... AND ONLY MY BLADE CAN UNDO IT!
THEN, THE AVENGERS ARE ALIVE... ALIVE!!
MUST OBTAIN THAT SCYTHE... SAVE THEM BEFORE THEY'RE BEYOND HELP!
THE PAIN IN MY SHOULDER ...IS ALMOST UNBEARABLE! BUT, MUST STRIKE ...NOW!
NO! IT'S IMPOSSIBLE!
THE STUN-RAY SHOULD HAVE WEAKENED YOU... INTO ABJECT HELP-LESSNESS!
BUT, SOON, A PERIOD OF THREE HOURS SHALL HAVE ELAPSED ...AND IT WILL BE TOO LATE TO REVERSE ITS EFFECTS!
NOT QUITE, EVIL ONE... THANKS TO THE SECRET JUNGLE HERBS... FROM WHICH MY PANTHER POWERS ARE DERIVED!
AND N.. LOOK OUT! YOU ARE FALLING... ON THE BLADE OF YOUR OWN WEAPON..!
NO... NO..! UNNHH!
FOR A MOMENT, THE WOUNDED CHIEFTAIN STANDS GAZING DOWN AT THE WRITHING, PAIN-WRACKED GRIM REAPER... AND THEN...
I'LL RETURN TO HELP HIM... IF I POSSIBLY CAN!
BUT, MY FIRST LOYALTY IS TO THOSE HE WOULD HAVE SEEN DESTROYED!
MUST HURRY... TO THE PLACE WHERE THE AVENGERS HAVE BEEN TAKEN!
17

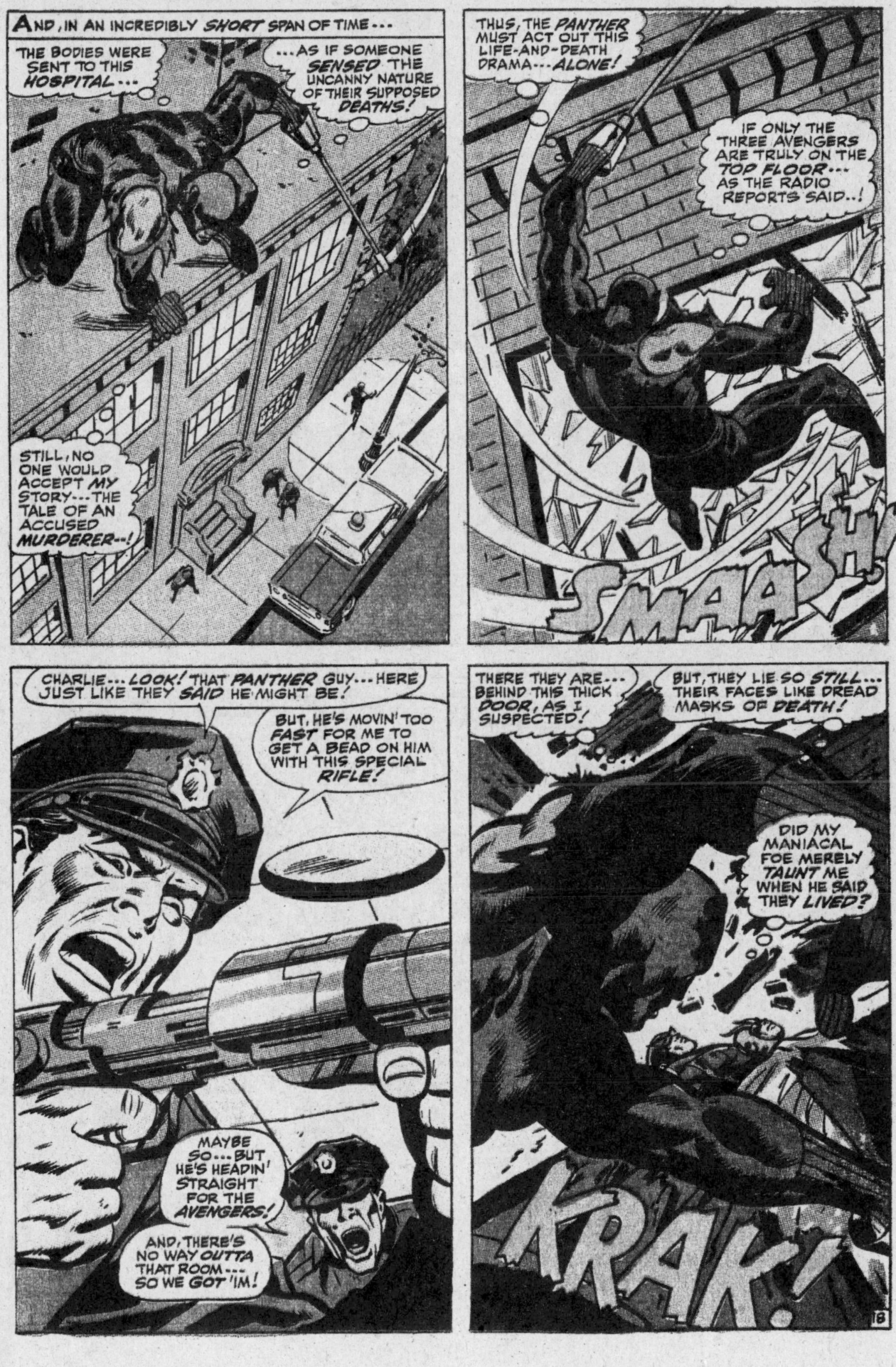
AND, IN AN INCREDIBLY SHORT SPAN OF TIME...
THE BODIES WERE SENT TO THIS HOSPITAL...
...AS IF SOMEONE SENSED THE UNCANNY NATURE OF THEIR SUPPOSED DEATHS!
STILL, NO ONE WOULD ACCEPT MY STORY---THE TALE OF AN ACCUSED MURDERER--!
THUS, THE PANTHER MUST ACT OUT THIS LIFE-AND-DEATH DRAMA---ALONE!
IF ONLY THE THREE AVENGERS ARE TRULY ON THE TOP FLOOR--- AS THE RADIO REPORTS SAID..!
SMAASH!
CHARLIE...LOOK! THAT PANTHER GUY...HERE JUST LIKE THEY SAID HE MIGHT BE!
BUT, HE'S MOVIN' TOO FAST FOR ME TO GET A BEAD ON HIM WITH THIS SPECIAL RIFLE!
MAYBE SO...BUT HE'S HEADIN' STRAIGHT FOR THE AVENGERS!
AND, THERE'S NO WAY OUTTA THAT ROOM--- SO WE GOT 'IM!
THERE THEY ARE--- BEHIND THIS THICK DOOR, AS I SUSPECTED!
BUT, THEY LIE SO STILL... THEIR FACES LIKE DREAD MASKS OF DEATH!
DID MY MANIACAL FOE MERELY TAUNT ME WHEN HE SAID THEY LIVED?
KRAK!
18

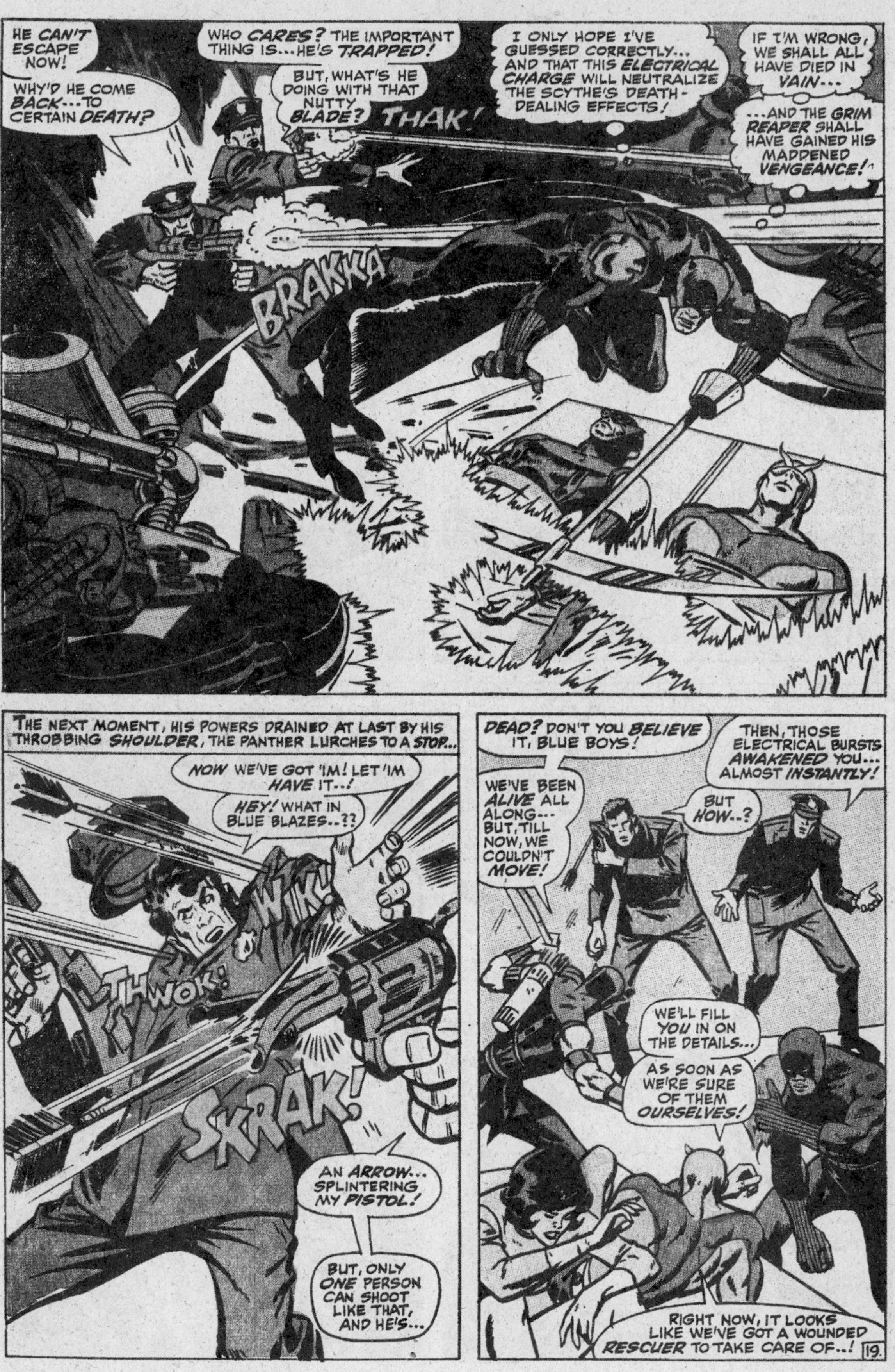
HE CAN'T ESCAPE NOW!
WHY'D HE COME BACK...TO CERTAIN DEATH?
WHO CARES? THE IMPORTANT THING IS...HE'S TRAPPED!
BUT, WHAT'S HE DOING WITH THAT NUTTY BLADE?
THAK!
I ONLY HOPE I'VE GUESSED CORRECTLY... AND THAT THIS ELECTRICAL CHARGE WILL NEUTRALIZE THE SCYTHE'S DEATH-DEALING EFFECTS!
IF I'M WRONG, WE SHALL ALL HAVE DIED IN VAIN...
...AND THE GRIM REAPER SHALL HAVE GAINED HIS MADDENED VENGEANCE!
BRAKKA
THE NEXT MOMENT, HIS POWERS DRAINED AT LAST BY HIS THROBBING SHOULDER, THE PANTHER LURCHES TO A STOP...
NOW WE'VE GOT 'IM! LET 'IM HAVE IT--!
HEY! WHAT IN BLUE BLAZES..??
WIK!
THWOK!
SKRAK!
AN ARROW... SPLINTERING MY PISTOL!
BUT, ONLY ONE PERSON CAN SHOOT LIKE THAT, AND HE'S...
DEAD? DON'T YOU BELIEVE IT, BLUE BOYS!
WE'VE BEEN ALIVE ALL ALONG... BUT, TILL NOW, WE COULDN'T MOVE!
THEN, THOSE ELECTRICAL BURSTS AWAKENED YOU... ALMOST INSTANTLY!
BUT HOW..?
WE'LL FILL YOU IN ON THE DETAILS...
AS SOON AS WE'RE SURE OF THEM OURSELVES!
RIGHT NOW, IT LOOKS LIKE WE'VE GOT A WOUNDED RESCUER TO TAKE CARE OF..!
19.

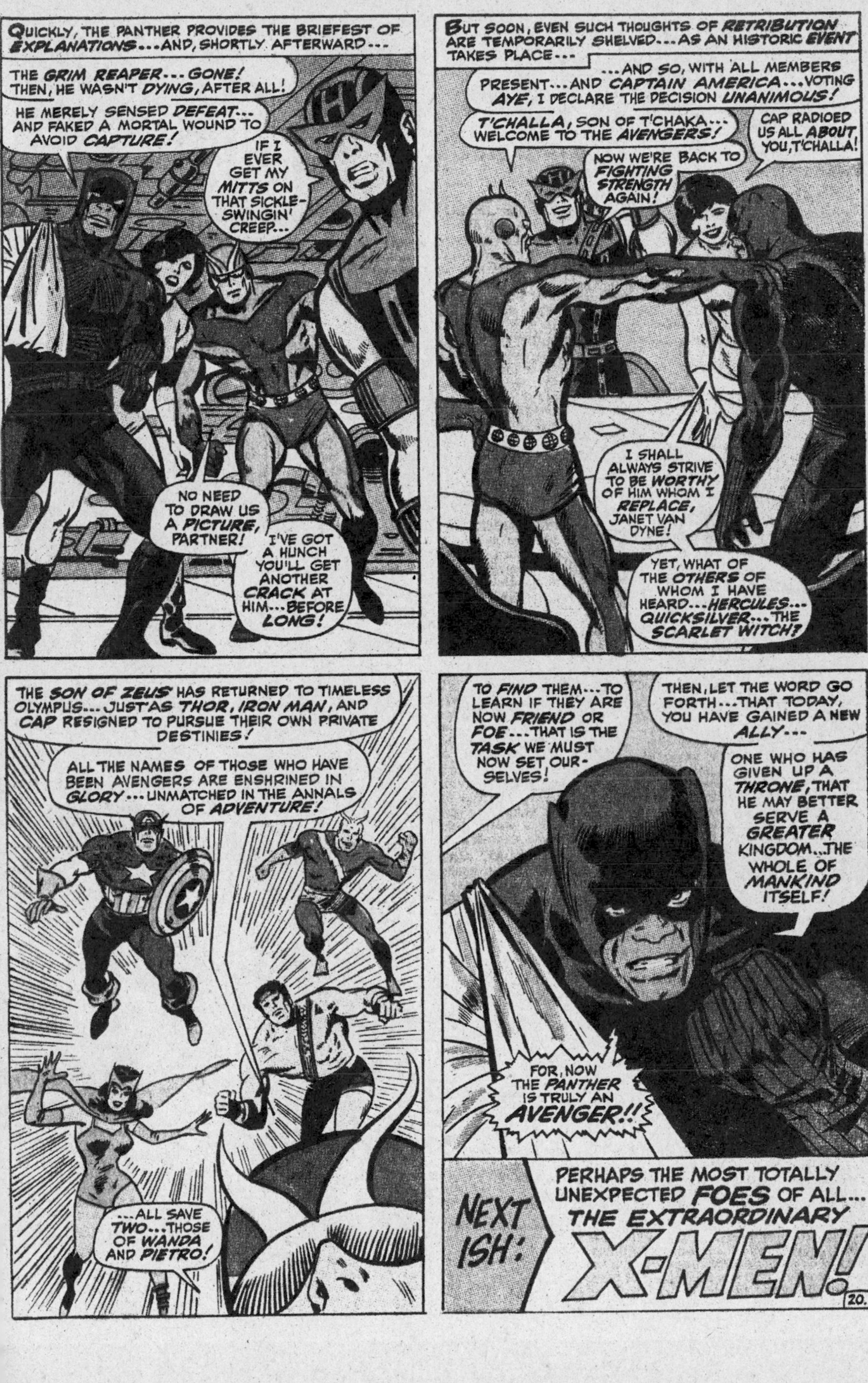

QUICKLY, THE PANTHER PROVIDES THE BRIEFEST OF EXPLANATIONS... AND, SHORTLY AFTERWARD...
THE GRIM REAPER... GONE! THEN, HE WASN'T DYING, AFTER ALL!
HE MERELY SENSED DEFEAT... AND FAKED A MORTAL WOUND TO AVOID CAPTURE!
IF I EVER GET MY MITTS ON THAT SICKLE-SWINGIN' CREEP...
NO NEED TO DRAW US A PICTURE, PARTNER!
I'VE GOT A HUNCH YOU'LL GET ANOTHER CRACK AT HIM... BEFORE LONG!
BUT SOON, EVEN SUCH THOUGHTS OF RETRIBUTION ARE TEMPORARILY SHELVED... AS AN HISTORIC EVENT TAKES PLACE...
...AND SO, WITH ALL MEMBERS PRESENT... AND CAPTAIN AMERICA... VOTING AYE, I DECLARE THE DECISION UNANIMOUS!
T'CHALLA, SON OF T'CHAKA... WELCOME TO THE AVENGERS!
CAP RADIOED US ALL ABOUT YOU, T'CHALLA!
NOW WE'RE BACK TO FIGHTING STRENGTH AGAIN!
I SHALL ALWAYS STRIVE TO BE WORTHY OF HIM WHOM I REPLACE, JANET VAN DYNE!
YET, WHAT OF THE OTHERS OF WHOM I HAVE HEARD... HERCULES... QUICKSILVER... THE SCARLET WITCH?
THE SON OF ZEUS HAS RETURNED TO TIMELESS OLYMPUS... JUST AS THOR, IRON MAN, AND CAP RESIGNED TO PURSUE THEIR OWN PRIVATE DESTINIES!
ALL THE NAMES OF THOSE WHO HAVE BEEN AVENGERS ARE ENSHRINED IN GLORY... UNMATCHED IN THE ANNALS OF ADVENTURE!
...ALL SAVE TWO... THOSE OF WANDA AND PIETRO!
TO FIND THEM... TO LEARN IF THEY ARE NOW FRIEND OR FOE... THAT IS THE TASK WE MUST NOW SET OUR-SELVES!
THEN, LET THE WORD GO FORTH... THAT TODAY, YOU HAVE GAINED A NEW ALLY...
ONE WHO HAS GIVEN UP A THRONE, THAT HE MAY BETTER SERVE A GREATER KINGDOM... THE WHOLE OF MANKIND ITSELF!
FOR, NOW THE PANTHER IS TRULY AN AVENGER!!
NEXT ISH: PERHAPS THE MOST TOTALLY UNEXPECTED FOES OF ALL... THE EXTRAORDINARY X-MEN!
20.

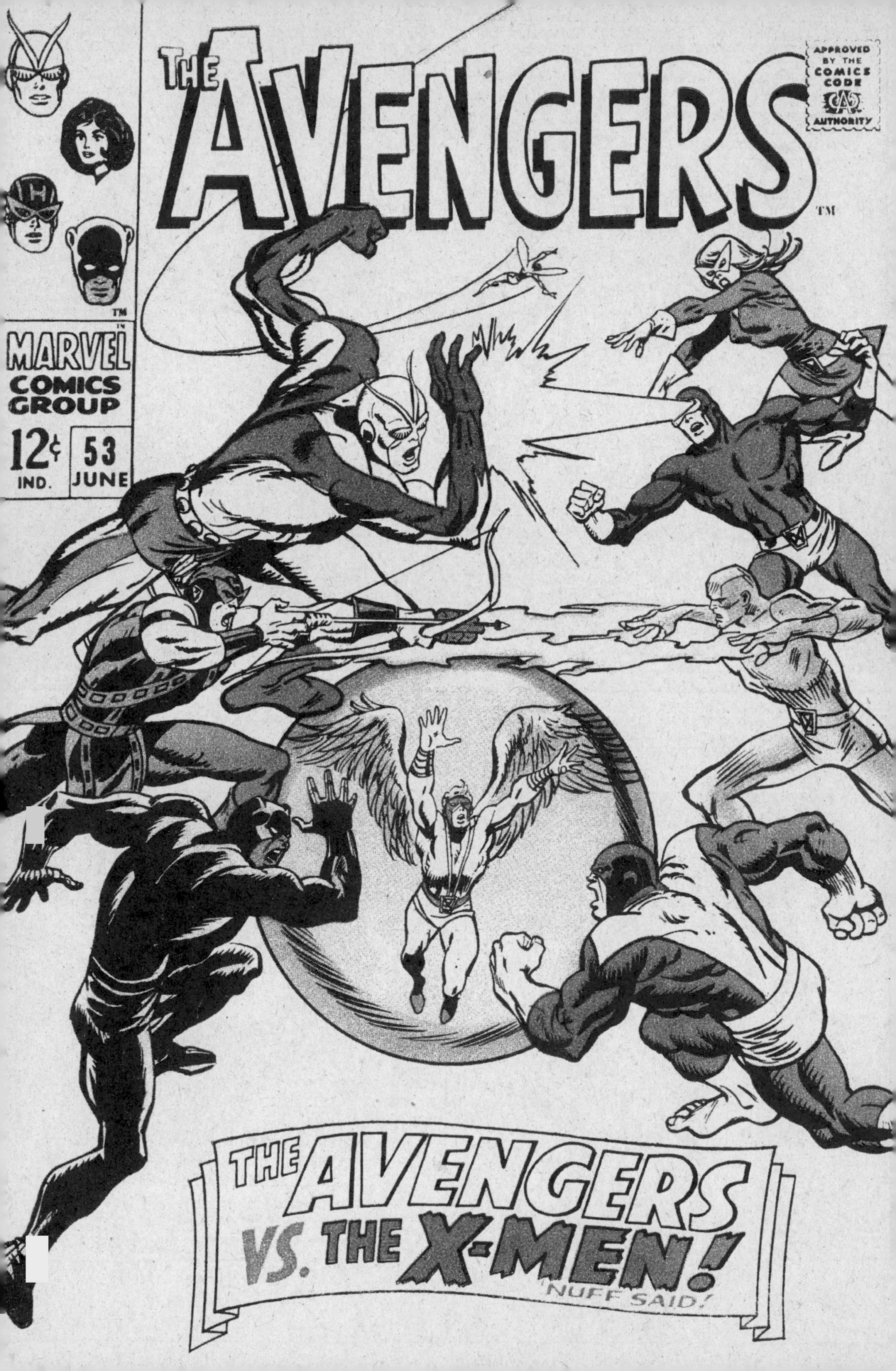

THE AVENGERS
APPROVED BY THE COMICS CODE CA AUTHORITY
MARVEL COMICS GROUP
12¢ IND.
53 JUNE
THE AVENGERS VS. THE X-MEN!
'NUFF SAID!

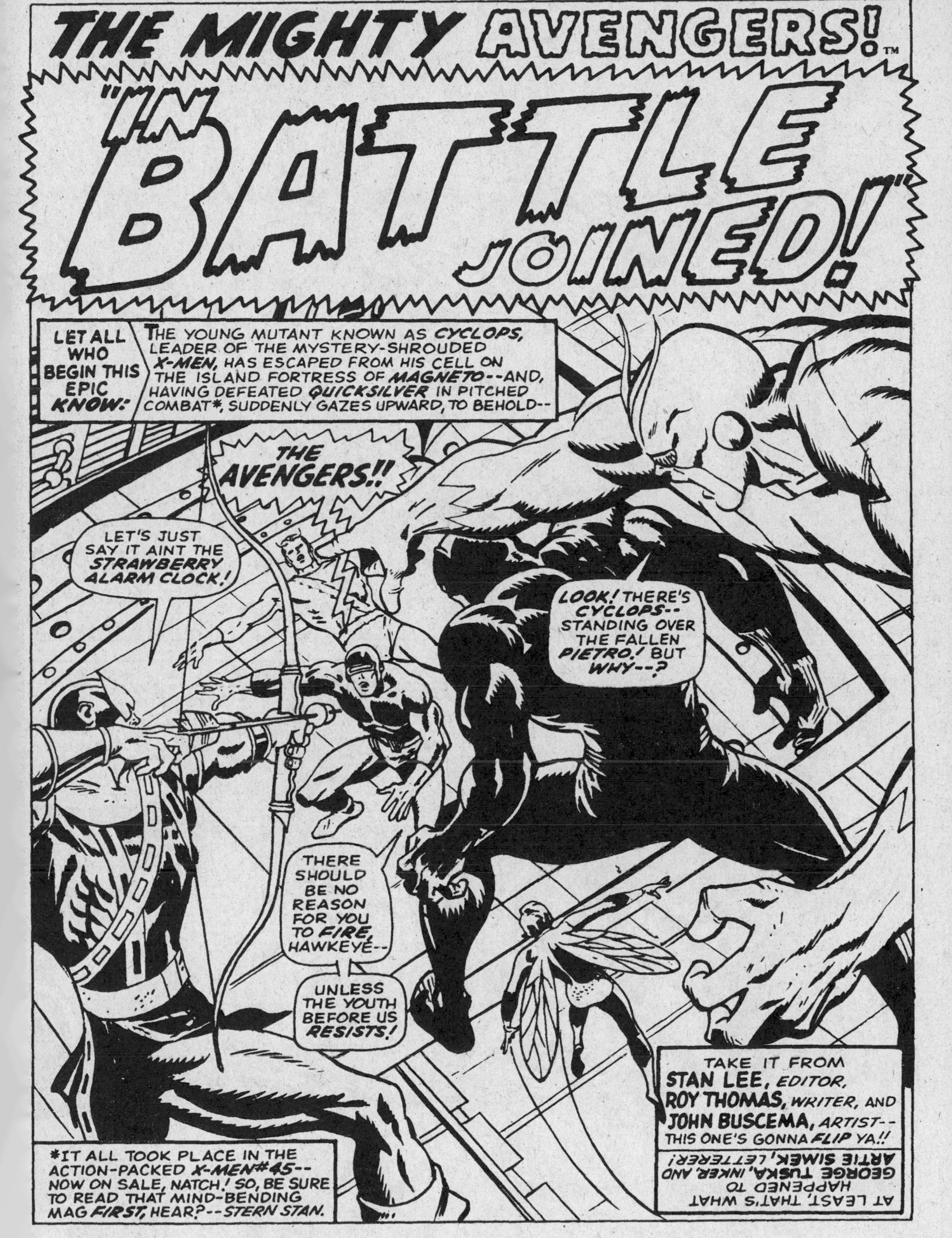

THE MIGHTY AVENGERS!™
"IN BATTLE JOINED!"
LET ALL WHO BEGIN THIS EPIC KNOW:
THE YOUNG MUTANT KNOWN AS CYCLOPS, LEADER OF THE MYSTERY-SHROUDED X-MEN, HAS ESCAPED FROM HIS CELL ON THE ISLAND FORTRESS OF MAGNETO--AND, HAVING DEFEATED QUICKSILVER IN PITCHED COMBAT*, SUDDENLY GAZES UPWARD, TO BEHOLD--
THE AVENGERS!!
LET'S JUST SAY IT AINT THE STRAWBERRY ALARM CLOCK!
LOOK! THERE'S CYCLOPS--STANDING OVER THE FALLEN PIETRO! BUT WHY--?
THERE SHOULD BE NO REASON FOR YOU TO FIRE, HAWKEYE--
UNLESS THE YOUTH BEFORE US RESISTS!
TAKE IT FROM STAN LEE, EDITOR, ROY THOMAS, WRITER, AND JOHN BUSCEMA, ARTIST--THIS ONE'S GONNA FLIP YA!!
AT LEAST, THAT'S WHAT HAPPENED TO GEORGE TUSKA, INKER, AND ARTIE SIMEK, LETTERER!
*IT ALL TOOK PLACE IN THE ACTION-PACKED X-MEN #45--NOW ON SALE, NATCH! SO, BE SURE TO READ THAT MIND-BENDING MAG FIRST, HEAR?--STERN STAN.

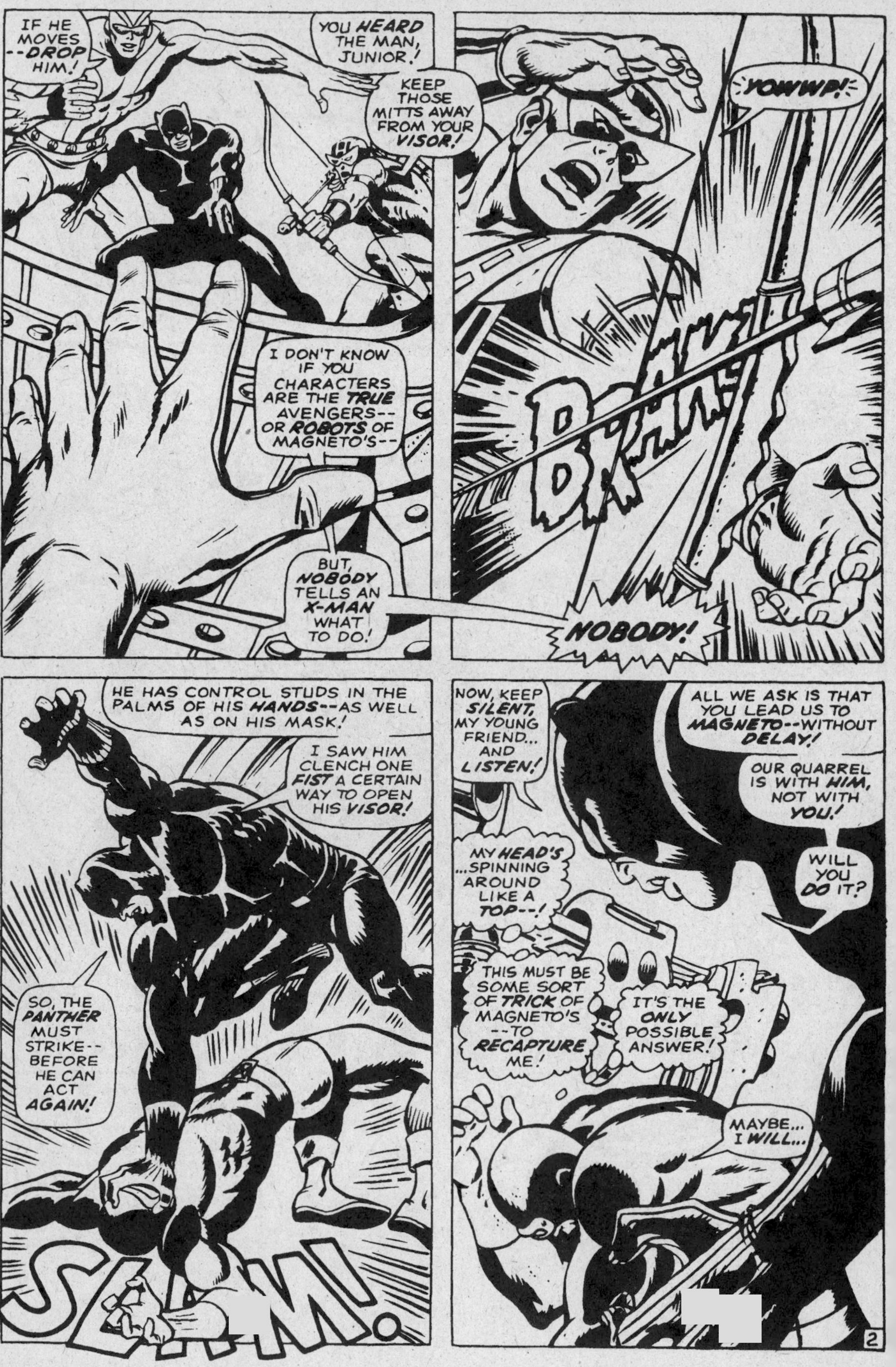
IF HE MOVES --DROP HIM!
YOU HEARD THE MAN, JUNIOR!
KEEP THOSE MITTS AWAY FROM YOUR VISOR!
I DON'T KNOW IF YOU CHARACTERS ARE THE TRUE AVENGERS--OR ROBOTS OF MAGNETO'S--
BUT, NOBODY TELLS AN X-MAN WHAT TO DO!
YOWWP!
NOBODY!
HE HAS CONTROL STUDS IN THE PALMS OF HIS HANDS--AS WELL AS ON HIS MASK!
I SAW HIM CLENCH ONE FIST A CERTAIN WAY TO OPEN HIS VISOR!
SO, THE PANTHER MUST STRIKE--BEFORE HE CAN ACT AGAIN!
NOW, KEEP SILENT, MY YOUNG FRIEND... AND LISTEN!
ALL WE ASK IS THAT YOU LEAD US TO MAGNETO--WITHOUT DELAY!
OUR QUARREL IS WITH HIM, NOT WITH YOU!
WILL YOU DO IT?
MY HEAD'S ...SPINNING AROUND LIKE A TOP--!
THIS MUST BE SOME SORT OF TRICK OF MAGNETO'S --TO RECAPTURE ME!
IT'S THE ONLY POSSIBLE ANSWER!
MAYBE... I WILL...
2

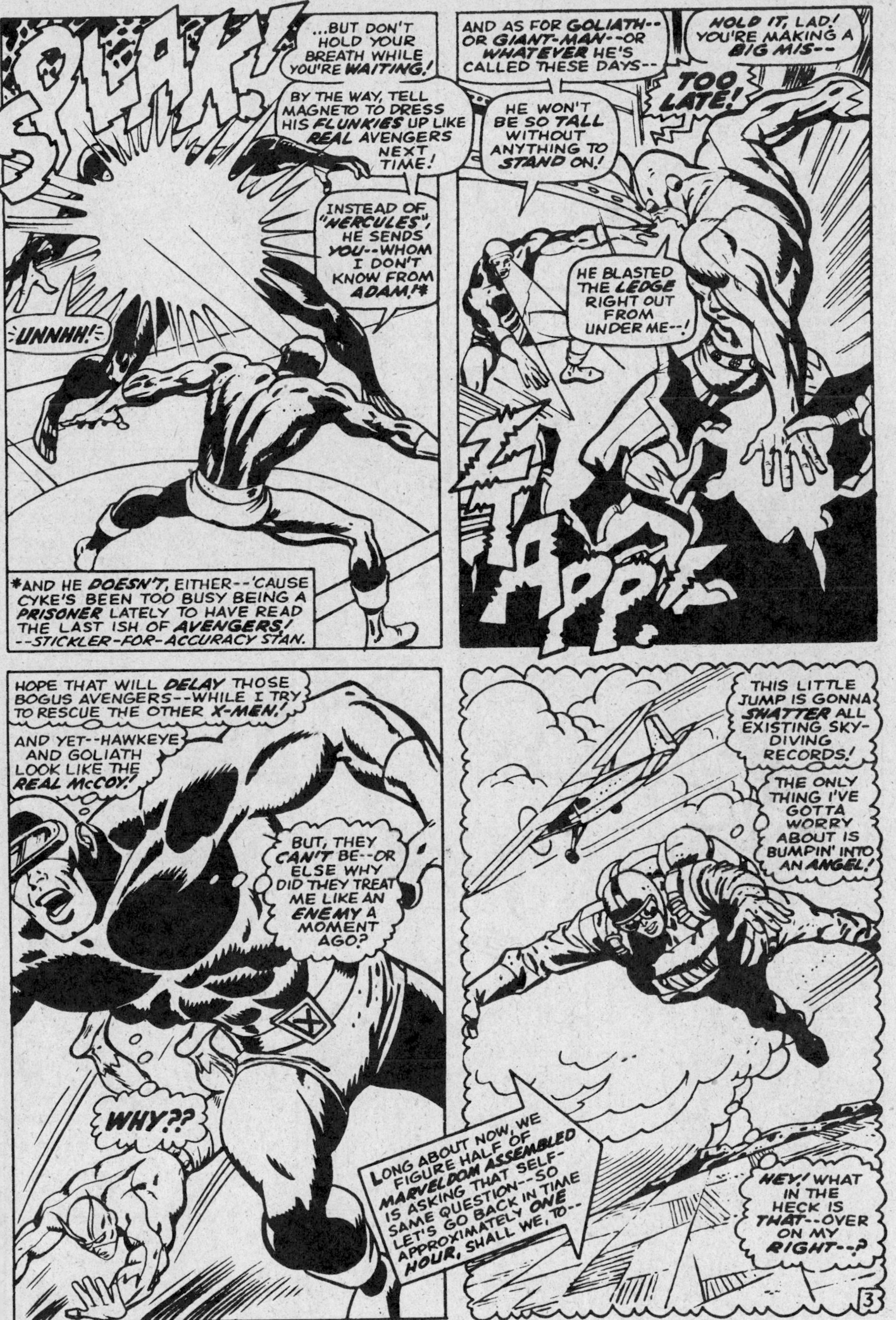
SPLAK!
...BUT DON'T HOLD YOUR BREATH WHILE YOU'RE WAITING!
BY THE WAY, TELL MAGNETO TO DRESS HIS FLUNKIES UP LIKE REAL AVENGERS NEXT TIME!
INSTEAD OF "HERCULES", HE SENDS YOU--WHOM I DON'T KNOW FROM ADAM!*
UNNHH!
*AND HE DOESN'T, EITHER--'CAUSE CYKE'S BEEN TOO BUSY BEING A PRISONER LATELY TO HAVE READ THE LAST ISH OF AVENGERS! --STICKLER-FOR-ACCURACY STAN.
AND AS FOR GOLIATH--OR GIANT-MAN--OR WHATEVER HE'S CALLED THESE DAYS--
HE WON'T BE SO TALL WITHOUT ANYTHING TO STAND ON!
HOLD IT, LAD! YOU'RE MAKING A BIG MIS--
TOO LATE!
HE BLASTED THE LEDGE RIGHT OUT FROM UNDER ME--!
ZZAPP!
HOPE THAT WILL DELAY THOSE BOGUS AVENGERS--WHILE I TRY TO RESCUE THE OTHER X-MEN!
AND YET--HAWKEYE AND GOLIATH LOOK LIKE THE REAL McCOY!
BUT, THEY CAN'T BE--OR ELSE WHY DID THEY TREAT ME LIKE AN ENEMY A MOMENT AGO?
WHY??
LONG ABOUT NOW, WE FIGURE HALF OF MARVELDOM ASSEMBLED IS ASKING THAT SELF-SAME QUESTION--SO LET'S GO BACK IN TIME APPROXIMATELY ONE HOUR, SHALL WE, TO--
THIS LITTLE JUMP IS GONNA SHATTER ALL EXISTING SKY-DIVING RECORDS!
THE ONLY THING I'VE GOTTA WORRY ABOUT IS BUMPIN' INTO AN ANGEL!
HEY! WHAT IN THE HECK IS THAT--OVER ON MY RIGHT--?
3

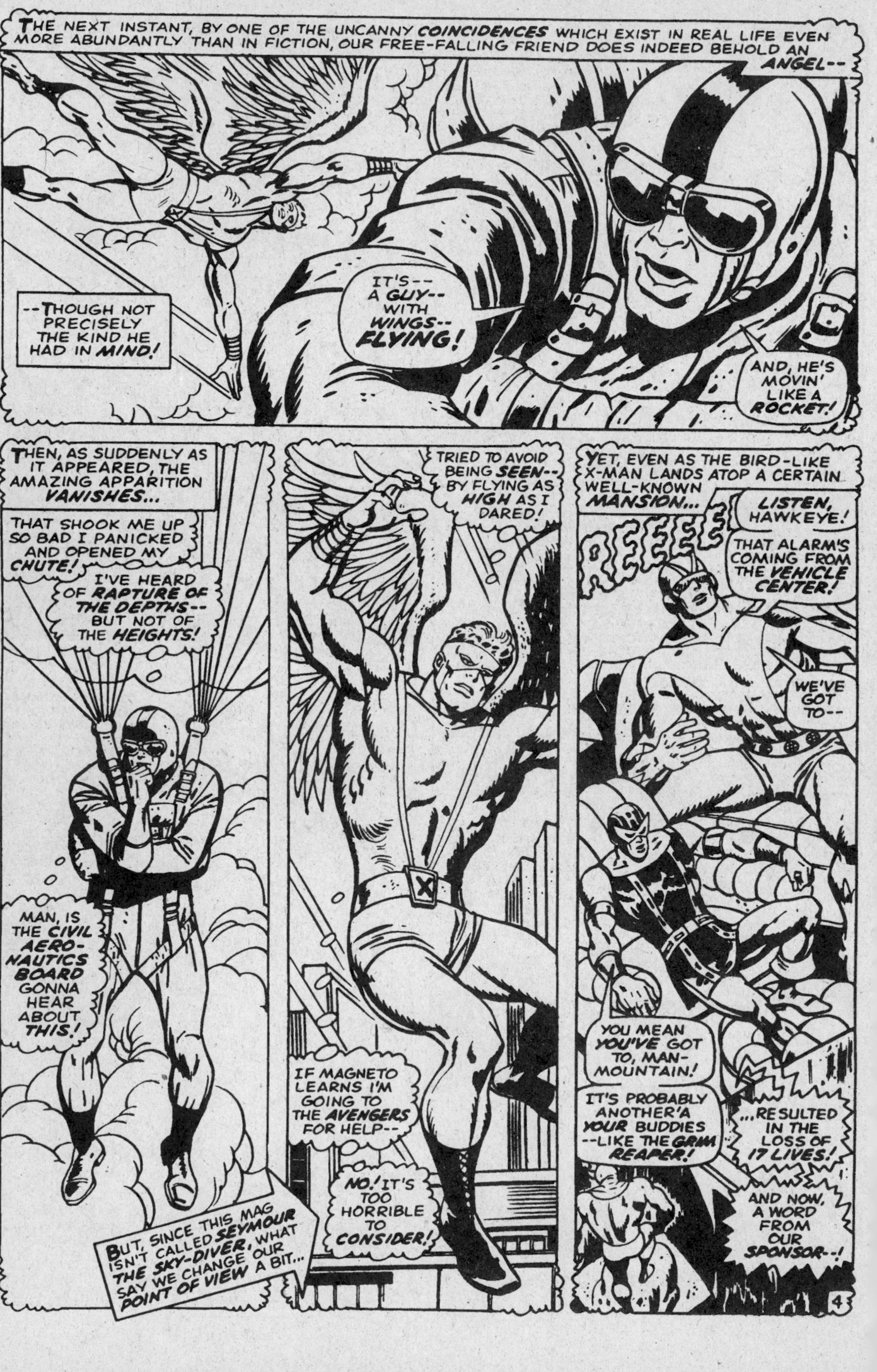
THE NEXT INSTANT, BY ONE OF THE UNCANNY COINCIDENCES WHICH EXIST IN REAL LIFE EVEN MORE ABUNDANTLY THAN IN FICTION, OUR FREE-FALLING FRIEND DOES INDEED BEHOLD AN ANGEL--
--THOUGH NOT PRECISELY THE KIND HE HAD IN MIND!
IT'S-- A GUY-- WITH WINGS-- FLYING!
AND, HE'S MOVIN' LIKE A ROCKET!
THEN, AS SUDDENLY AS IT APPEARED, THE AMAZING APPARITION VANISHES...
THAT SHOOK ME UP SO BAD I PANICKED AND OPENED MY CHUTE!
I'VE HEARD OF RAPTURE OF THE DEPTHS-- BUT NOT OF THE HEIGHTS!
MAN, IS THE CIVIL AERO-NAUTICS BOARD GONNA HEAR ABOUT THIS!
BUT, SINCE THIS MAG ISN'T CALLED SEYMOUR THE SKY-DIVER, WHAT SAY WE CHANGE OUR POINT OF VIEW A BIT...
TRIED TO AVOID BEING SEEN-- BY FLYING AS HIGH AS I DARED!
IF MAGNETO LEARNS I'M GOING TO THE AVENGERS FOR HELP--
NO! IT'S TOO HORRIBLE TO CONSIDER!
YET, EVEN AS THE BIRD-LIKE X-MAN LANDS ATOP A CERTAIN WELL-KNOWN MANSION...
REEEE
LISTEN, HAWKEYE!
THAT ALARM'S COMING FROM THE VEHICLE CENTER!
WE'VE GOT TO--
YOU MEAN YOU'VE GOT TO, MAN-MOUNTAIN!
IT'S PROBABLY ANOTHER'A YOUR BUDDIES --LIKE THE GRIM REAPER!
...RESULTED IN THE LOSS OF 17 LIVES!
AND NOW, A WORD FROM OUR SPONSOR--!

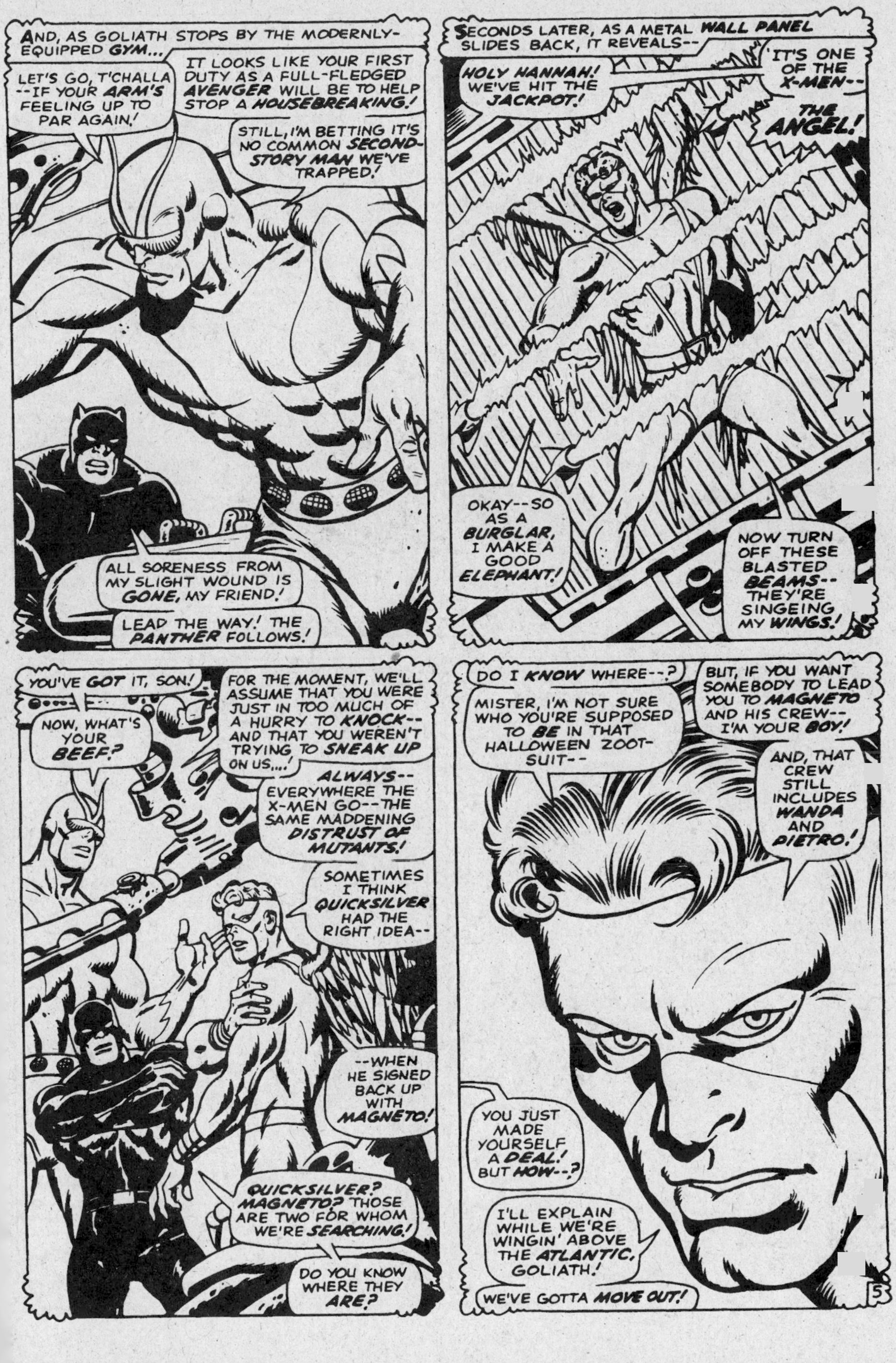

AND, AS GOLIATH STOPS BY THE MODERNLY-EQUIPPED GYM...
LET'S GO, T'CHALLA --IF YOUR ARM'S FEELING UP TO PAR AGAIN!
IT LOOKS LIKE YOUR FIRST DUTY AS A FULL-FLEDGED AVENGER WILL BE TO HELP STOP A HOUSEBREAKING!
STILL, I'M BETTING IT'S NO COMMON SECOND-STORY MAN WE'VE TRAPPED!
ALL SORENESS FROM MY SLIGHT WOUND IS GONE, MY FRIEND!
LEAD THE WAY! THE PANTHER FOLLOWS!
SECONDS LATER, AS A METAL WALL PANEL SLIDES BACK, IT REVEALS--
HOLY HANNAH! WE'VE HIT THE JACKPOT!
IT'S ONE OF THE X-MEN--
THE ANGEL!
OKAY--SO AS A BURGLAR, I MAKE A GOOD ELEPHANT!
NOW TURN OFF THESE BLASTED BEAMS--THEY'RE SINGEING MY WINGS!
YOU'VE GOT IT, SON!
NOW, WHAT'S YOUR BEEF?
FOR THE MOMENT, WE'LL ASSUME THAT YOU WERE JUST IN TOO MUCH OF A HURRY TO KNOCK--AND THAT YOU WEREN'T TRYING TO SNEAK UP ON US...!
ALWAYS--EVERYWHERE THE X-MEN GO--THE SAME MADDENING DISTRUST OF MUTANTS!
SOMETIMES I THINK QUICKSILVER HAD THE RIGHT IDEA--
--WHEN HE SIGNED BACK UP WITH MAGNETO!
QUICKSILVER? MAGNETO? THOSE ARE TWO FOR WHOM WE'RE SEARCHING!
DO YOU KNOW WHERE THEY ARE?
DO I KNOW WHERE--?
MISTER, I'M NOT SURE WHO YOU'RE SUPPOSED TO BE IN THAT HALLOWEEN ZOOT-SUIT--
BUT, IF YOU WANT SOMEBODY TO LEAD YOU TO MAGNETO AND HIS CREW--I'M YOUR BOY!
AND, THAT CREW STILL INCLUDES WANDA AND PIETRO!
YOU JUST MADE YOURSELF A DEAL! BUT HOW--?
I'LL EXPLAIN WHILE WE'RE WINGIN' ABOVE THE ATLANTIC, GOLIATH!
WE'VE GOTTA MOVE OUT!
5

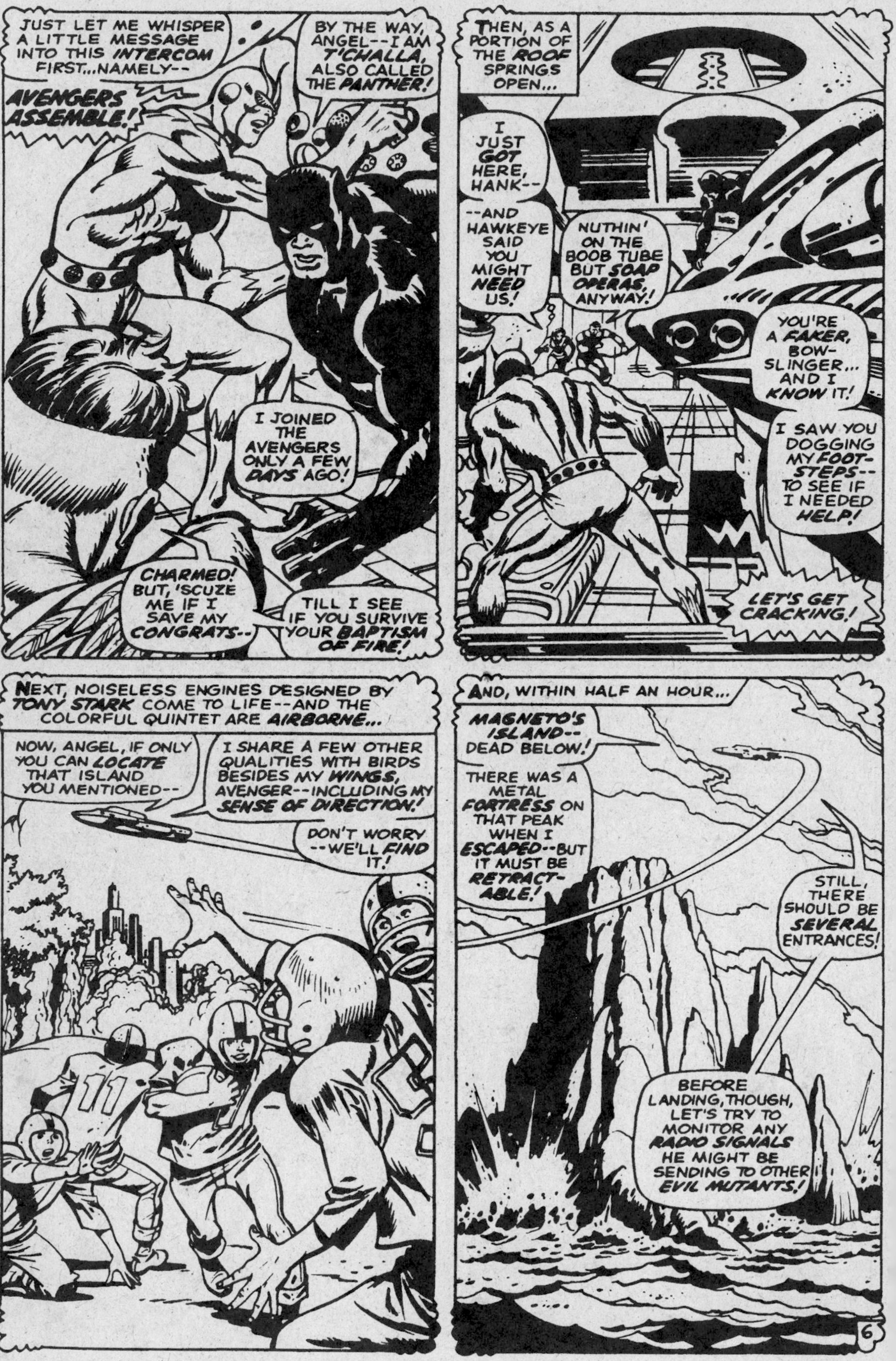
JUST LET ME WHISPER A LITTLE MESSAGE INTO THIS INTERCOM FIRST...NAMELY--
AVENGERS ASSEMBLE!
BY THE WAY, ANGEL--I AM T'CHALLA, ALSO CALLED THE PANTHER!
I JOINED THE AVENGERS ONLY A FEW DAYS AGO!
CHARMED! BUT, 'SCUZE ME IF I SAVE MY CONGRATS--
TILL I SEE IF YOU SURVIVE YOUR BAPTISM OF FIRE!
THEN, AS A PORTION OF THE ROOF SPRINGS OPEN...
I JUST GOT HERE, HANK--
--AND HAWKEYE SAID YOU MIGHT NEED US!
NUTHIN' ON THE BOOB TUBE BUT SOAP OPERAS, ANYWAY!
YOU'RE A FAKER, BOW-SLINGER... AND I KNOW IT!
I SAW YOU DOGGING MY FOOT-STEPS--TO SEE IF I NEEDED HELP!
LET'S GET CRACKING!
NEXT, NOISELESS ENGINES DESIGNED BY TONY STARK COME TO LIFE--AND THE COLORFUL QUINTET ARE AIRBORNE...
NOW, ANGEL, IF ONLY YOU CAN LOCATE THAT ISLAND YOU MENTIONED--
I SHARE A FEW OTHER QUALITIES WITH BIRDS BESIDES MY WINGS, AVENGER--INCLUDING MY SENSE OF DIRECTION!
DON'T WORRY --WE'LL FIND IT!
11
AND, WITHIN HALF AN HOUR...
MAGNETO'S ISLAND--DEAD BELOW!
THERE WAS A METAL FORTRESS ON THAT PEAK WHEN I ESCAPED--BUT IT MUST BE RETRACT-ABLE!
STILL, THERE SHOULD BE SEVERAL ENTRANCES!
BEFORE LANDING, THOUGH, LET'S TRY TO MONITOR ANY RADIO SIGNALS HE MIGHT BE SENDING TO OTHER EVIL MUTANTS!
6

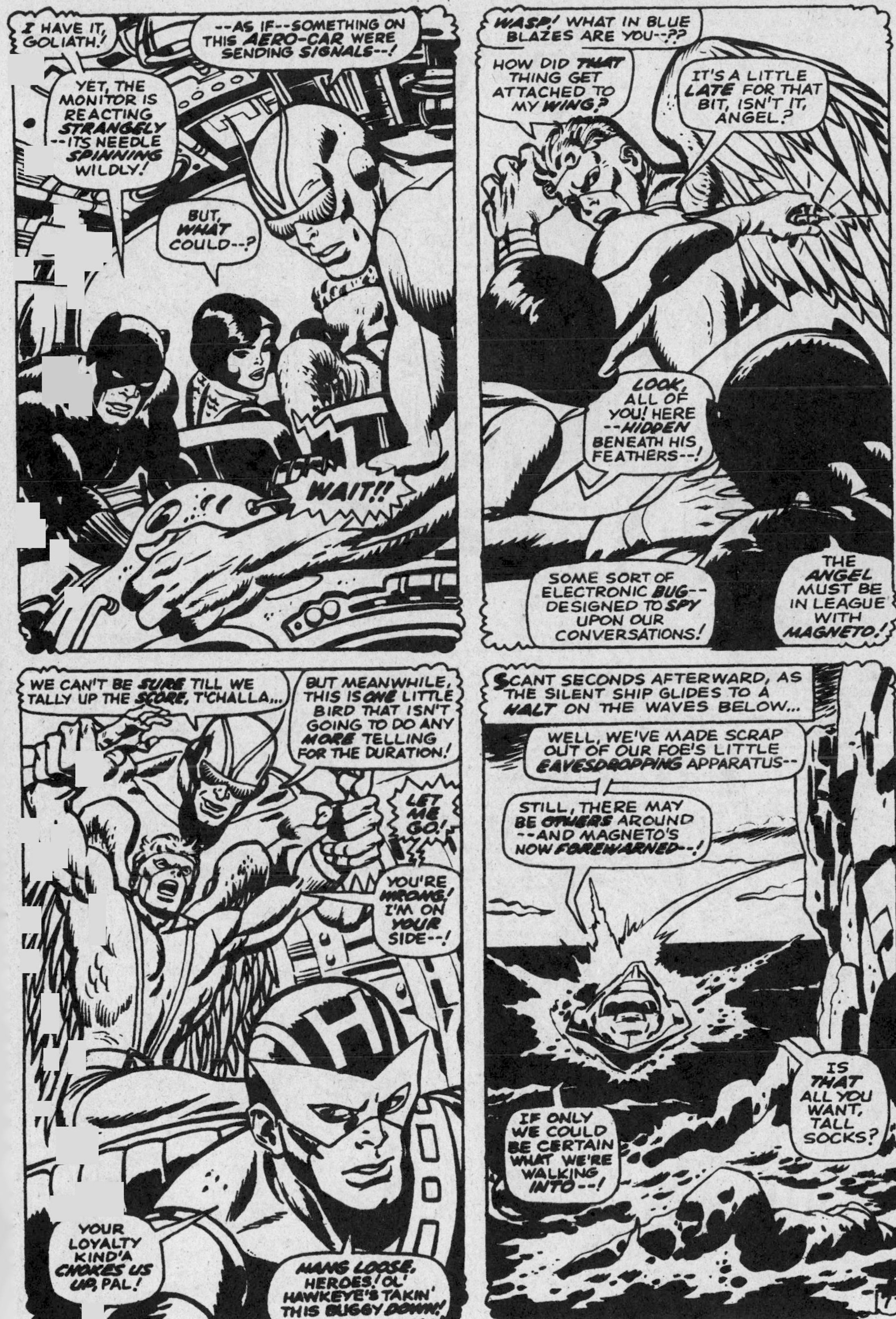
I HAVE IT, GOLIATH!
--AS IF--SOMETHING ON THIS AERO-CAR WERE SENDING SIGNALS--!
YET, THE MONITOR IS REACTING STRANGELY --ITS NEEDLE SPINNING WILDLY!
BUT, WHAT COULD--?
WAIT!!
WASP! WHAT IN BLUE BLAZES ARE YOU--??
HOW DID THAT THING GET ATTACHED TO MY WING?
IT'S A LITTLE LATE FOR THAT BIT, ISN'T IT, ANGEL?
LOOK, ALL OF YOU! HERE --HIDDEN BENEATH HIS FEATHERS--!
SOME SORT OF ELECTRONIC BUG--DESIGNED TO SPY UPON OUR CONVERSATIONS!
THE ANGEL MUST BE IN LEAGUE WITH MAGNETO!
WE CAN'T BE SURE TILL WE TALLY UP THE SCORE, T'CHALLA...
BUT MEANWHILE, THIS IS ONE LITTLE BIRD THAT ISN'T GOING TO DO ANY MORE TELLING FOR THE DURATION!
LET ME GO!
YOU'RE WRONG! I'M ON YOUR SIDE--!
YOUR LOYALTY KIND'A CHOKES US UP, PAL!
HANG LOOSE, HEROES! OL' HAWKEYE'S TAKIN' THIS BUGGY DOWN!
SCANT SECONDS AFTERWARD, AS THE SILENT SHIP GLIDES TO A HALT ON THE WAVES BELOW...
WELL, WE'VE MADE SCRAP OUT OF OUR FOE'S LITTLE EAVESDROPPING APPARATUS--
STILL, THERE MAY BE OTHERS AROUND --AND MAGNETO'S NOW FOREWARNED--!
IF ONLY WE COULD BE CERTAIN WHAT WE'RE WALKING INTO--!
IS THAT ALL YOU WANT, TALL SOCKS?

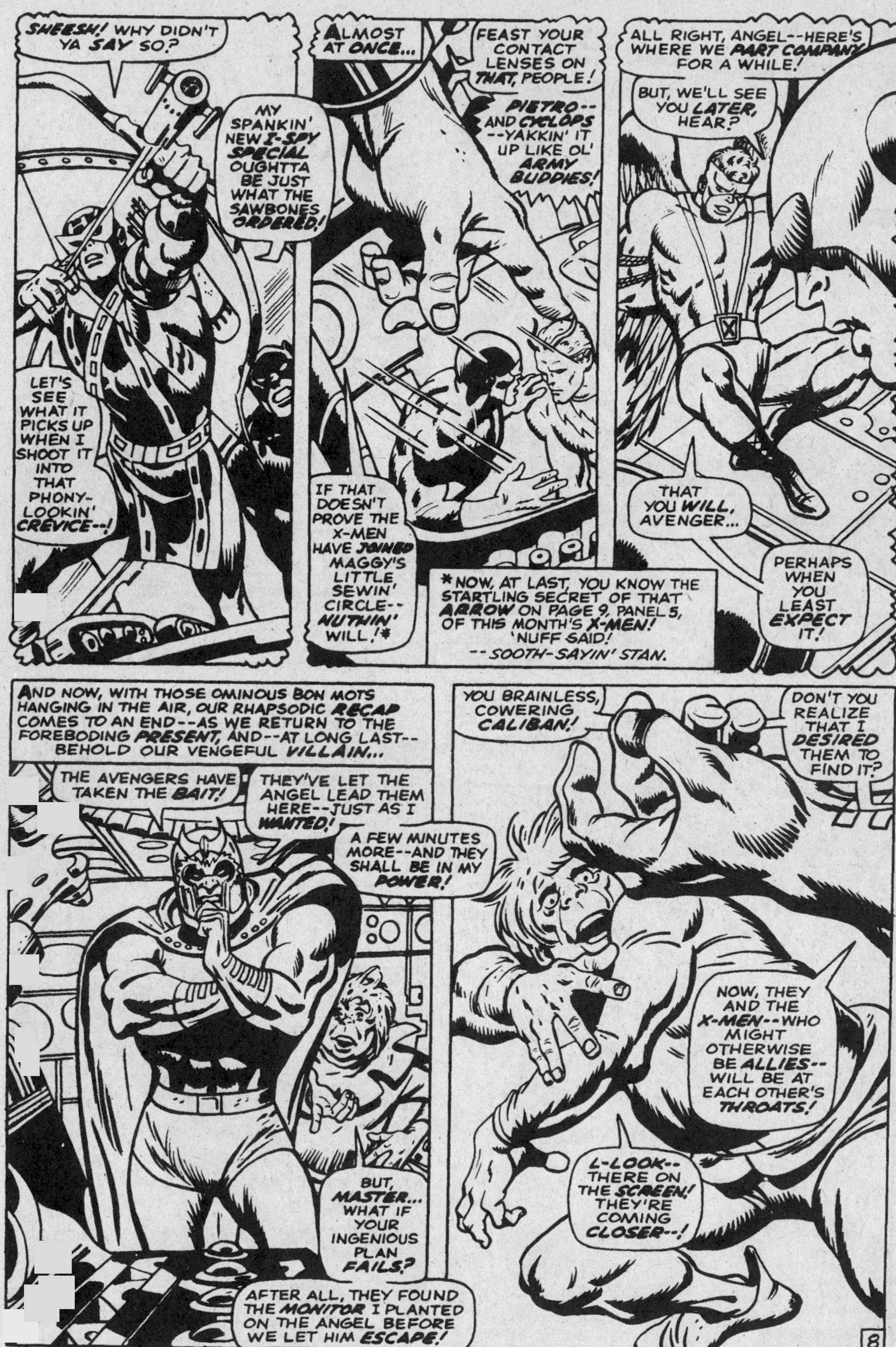
SHEESH! WHY DIDN'T YA SAY SO?
MY SPANKIN' NEW I-SPY SPECIAL OUGHTTA BE JUST WHAT THE SAWBONES ORDERED!
LET'S SEE WHAT IT PICKS UP WHEN I SHOOT IT INTO THAT PHONY-LOOKIN' CREVICE--!
ALMOST AT ONCE...
FEAST YOUR CONTACT LENSES ON THAT, PEOPLE!
PIETRO--AND CYCLOPS--YAKKIN' IT UP LIKE OL' ARMY BUDDIES!
IF THAT DOESN'T PROVE THE X-MEN HAVE JOINED MAGGY'S LITTLE SEWIN' CIRCLE--NUTHIN' WILL!*
*NOW, AT LAST, YOU KNOW THE STARTLING SECRET OF THAT ARROW ON PAGE 9, PANEL 5, OF THIS MONTH'S X-MEN! 'NUFF SAID! --SOOTH-SAYIN' STAN.
ALL RIGHT, ANGEL--HERE'S WHERE WE PART COMPANY FOR A WHILE!
BUT, WE'LL SEE YOU LATER, HEAR?
THAT YOU WILL, AVENGER...
PERHAPS WHEN YOU LEAST EXPECT IT!
AND NOW, WITH THOSE OMINOUS BON MOTS HANGING IN THE AIR, OUR RHAPSODIC RECAP COMES TO AN END--AS WE RETURN TO THE FOREBODING PRESENT, AND--AT LONG LAST--BEHOLD OUR VENGEFUL VILLAIN...
THE AVENGERS HAVE TAKEN THE BAIT!
THEY'VE LET THE ANGEL LEAD THEM HERE--JUST AS I WANTED!
A FEW MINUTES MORE--AND THEY SHALL BE IN MY POWER!
BUT, MASTER... WHAT IF YOUR INGENIOUS PLAN FAILS?
AFTER ALL, THEY FOUND THE MONITOR I PLANTED ON THE ANGEL BEFORE WE LET HIM ESCAPE!
YOU BRAINLESS, COWERING CALIBAN!
DON'T YOU REALIZE THAT I DESIRED THEM TO FIND IT?
NOW, THEY AND THE X-MEN--WHO MIGHT OTHERWISE BE ALLIES--WILL BE AT EACH OTHER'S THROATS!
L-LOOK--THERE ON THE SCREEN! THEY'RE COMING CLOSER--!

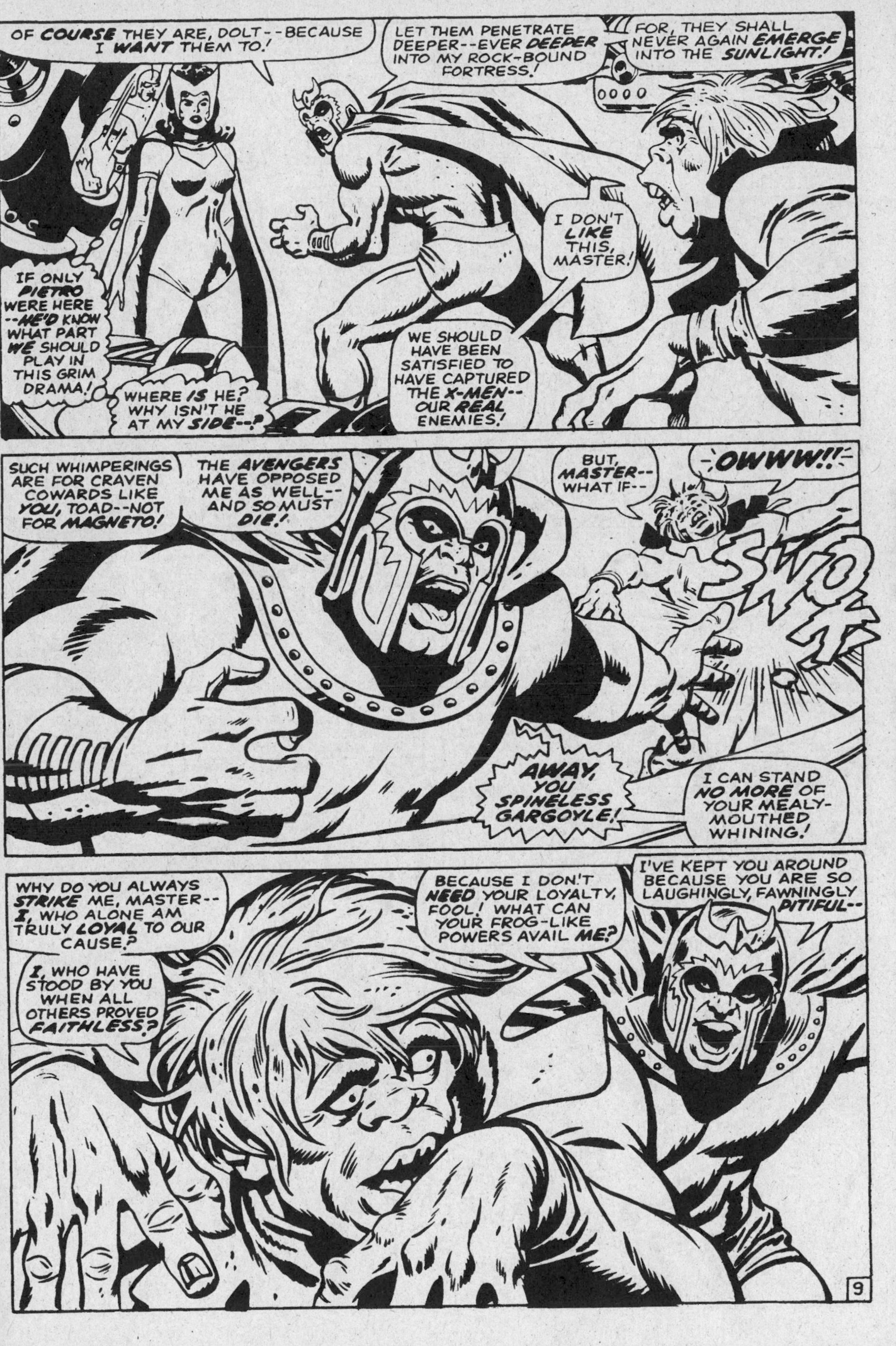

OF COURSE THEY ARE, DOLT--BECAUSE I WANT THEM TO.!
LET THEM PENETRATE DEEPER--EVER DEEPER INTO MY ROCK-BOUND FORTRESS.!
FOR, THEY SHALL NEVER AGAIN EMERGE INTO THE SUNLIGHT.!
I DON'T LIKE THIS, MASTER!
IF ONLY PIETRO WERE HERE--HE'D KNOW WHAT PART WE SHOULD PLAY IN THIS GRIM DRAMA!
WHERE IS HE? WHY ISN'T HE AT MY SIDE--?
WE SHOULD HAVE BEEN SATISFIED TO HAVE CAPTURED THE X-MEN--OUR REAL ENEMIES.!
SUCH WHIMPERINGS ARE FOR CRAVEN COWARDS LIKE YOU, TOAD--NOT FOR MAGNETO!
THE AVENGERS HAVE OPPOSED ME AS WELL--AND SO MUST DIE.!
BUT, MASTER--WHAT IF--
-OWWW!!-
SWOK
AWAY, YOU SPINELESS GARGOYLE!
I CAN STAND NO MORE OF YOUR MEALY-MOUTHED WHINING.!
WHY DO YOU ALWAYS STRIKE ME, MASTER--I, WHO ALONE AM TRULY LOYAL TO OUR CAUSE?
I, WHO HAVE STOOD BY YOU WHEN ALL OTHERS PROVED FAITHLESS?
BECAUSE I DON'T NEED YOUR LOYALTY, FOOL! WHAT CAN YOUR FROG-LIKE POWERS AVAIL ME?
I'VE KEPT YOU AROUND BECAUSE YOU ARE SO LAUGHINGLY, FAWNINGLY PITIFUL--
9

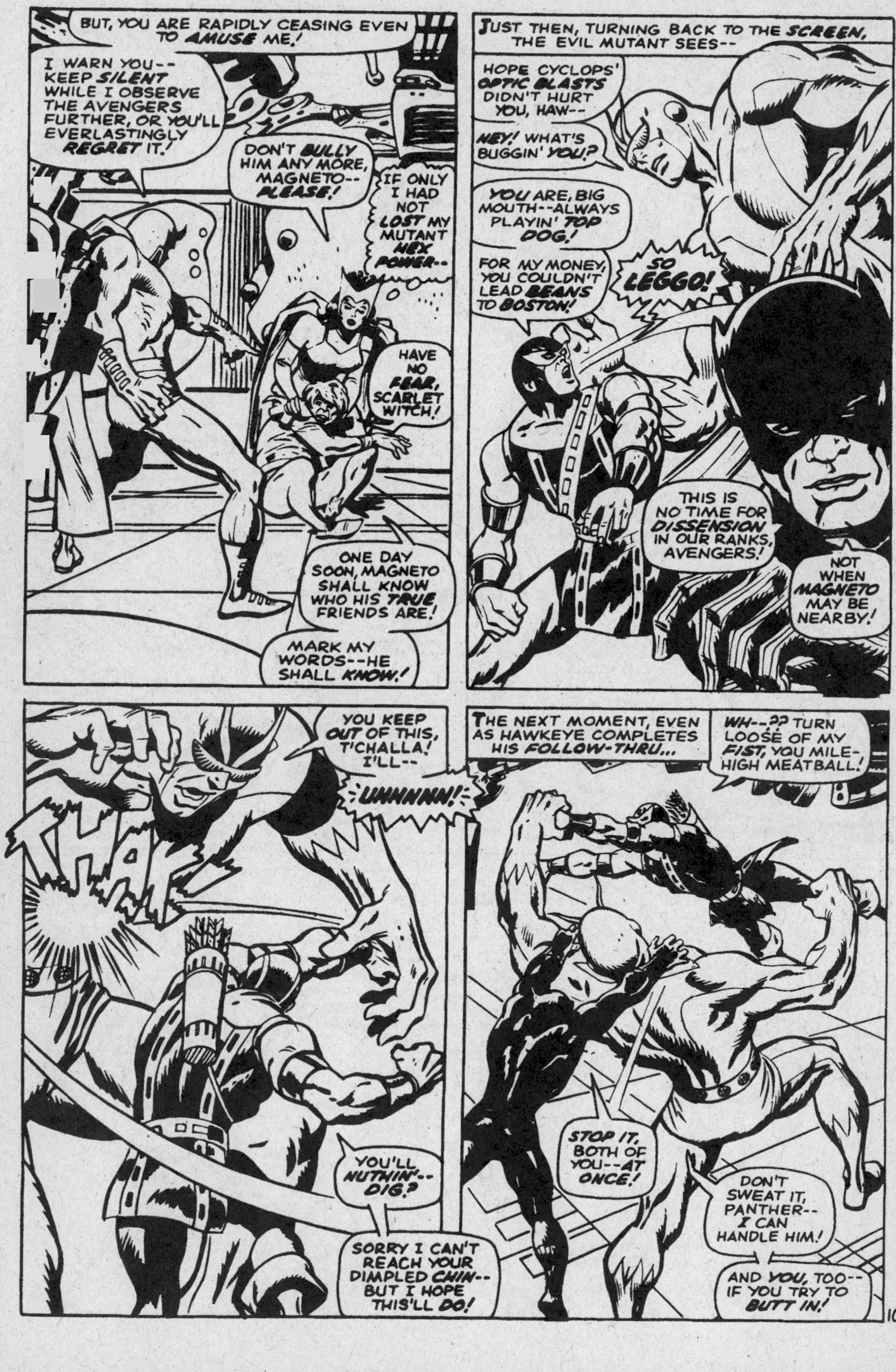

BUT, YOU ARE RAPIDLY CEASING EVEN TO AMUSE ME.!
I WARN YOU--KEEP SILENT WHILE I OBSERVE THE AVENGERS FURTHER, OR YOU'LL EVERLASTINGLY REGRET IT.!
DON'T BULLY HIM ANY MORE, MAGNETO--PLEASE!
IF ONLY I HAD NOT LOST MY MUTANT HEX POWER--
HAVE NO FEAR, SCARLET WITCH!
ONE DAY SOON, MAGNETO SHALL KNOW WHO HIS TRUE FRIENDS ARE!
MARK MY WORDS--HE SHALL KNOW!
JUST THEN, TURNING BACK TO THE SCREEN, THE EVIL MUTANT SEES--
HOPE CYCLOPS' OPTIC BLASTS DIDN'T HURT YOU, HAW--
HEY! WHAT'S BUGGIN' YOU?
YOU ARE, BIG MOUTH--ALWAYS PLAYIN' TOP DOG!
FOR MY MONEY, YOU COULDN'T LEAD BEANS TO BOSTON!
SO LEGGO!
THIS IS NO TIME FOR DISSENSION IN OUR RANKS, AVENGERS!
NOT WHEN MAGNETO MAY BE NEARBY!
YOU KEEP OUT OF THIS, T'CHALLA! I'LL--
UHHNNN!
THAK
YOU'LL NUTHIN'--DIG?
SORRY I CAN'T REACH YOUR DIMPLED CHIN--BUT I HOPE THIS'LL DO!
THE NEXT MOMENT, EVEN AS HAWKEYE COMPLETES HIS FOLLOW-THRU...
WH--?? TURN LOOSE OF MY FIST, YOU MILE-HIGH MEATBALL!
STOP IT, BOTH OF YOU--AT ONCE!
DON'T SWEAT IT, PANTHER--I CAN HANDLE HIM!
AND YOU, TOO--IF YOU TRY TO BUTT IN!

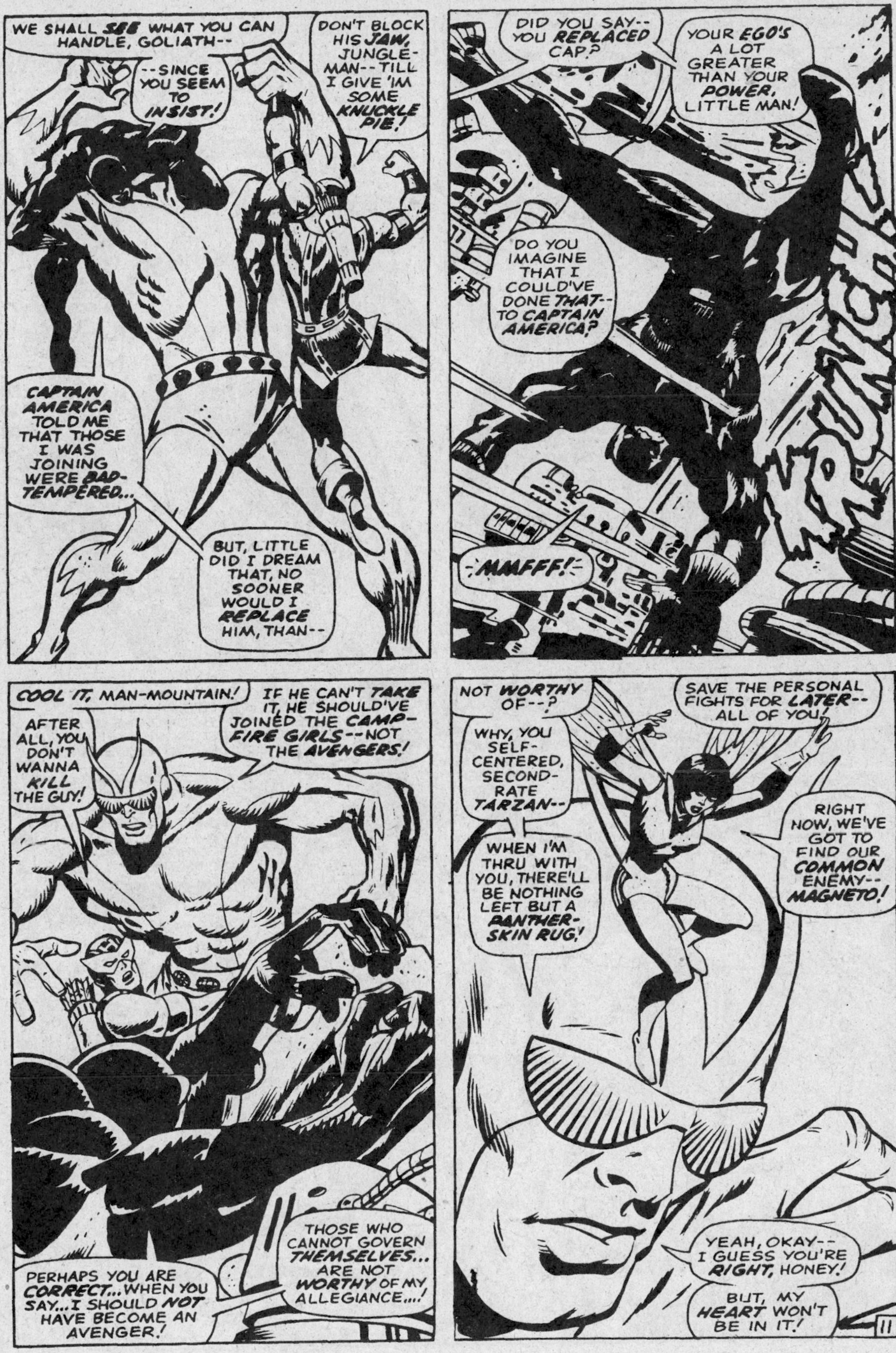
WE SHALL SEE WHAT YOU CAN HANDLE, GOLIATH--
--SINCE YOU SEEM TO INSIST!
DON'T BLOCK HIS JAW, JUNGLE-MAN--TILL I GIVE 'IM SOME KNUCKLE PIE!
CAPTAIN AMERICA TOLD ME THAT THOSE I WAS JOINING WERE BAD-TEMPERED...
BUT, LITTLE DID I DREAM THAT, NO SOONER WOULD I REPLACE HIM, THAN--
DID YOU SAY--YOU REPLACED CAP?
YOUR EGO'S A LOT GREATER THAN YOUR POWER, LITTLE MAN!
DO YOU IMAGINE THAT I COULD'VE DONE THAT--TO CAPTAIN AMERICA?
KRUNCH!
MMFFF!
COOL IT, MAN-MOUNTAIN!
AFTER ALL, YOU DON'T WANNA KILL THE GUY!
IF HE CAN'T TAKE IT, HE SHOULD'VE JOINED THE CAMP-FIRE GIRLS--NOT THE AVENGERS!
PERHAPS YOU ARE CORRECT...WHEN YOU SAY...I SHOULD NOT HAVE BECOME AN AVENGER!
THOSE WHO CANNOT GOVERN THEMSELVES... ARE NOT WORTHY OF MY ALLEGIANCE....!
NOT WORTHY OF--?
WHY, YOU SELF-CENTERED, SECOND-RATE TARZAN--
WHEN I'M THRU WITH YOU, THERE'LL BE NOTHING LEFT BUT A PANTHER-SKIN RUG!
SAVE THE PERSONAL FIGHTS FOR LATER--ALL OF YOU!
RIGHT NOW, WE'VE GOT TO FIND OUR COMMON ENEMY--MAGNETO!
YEAH, OKAY--I GUESS YOU'RE RIGHT, HONEY!
BUT, MY HEART WON'T BE IN IT!

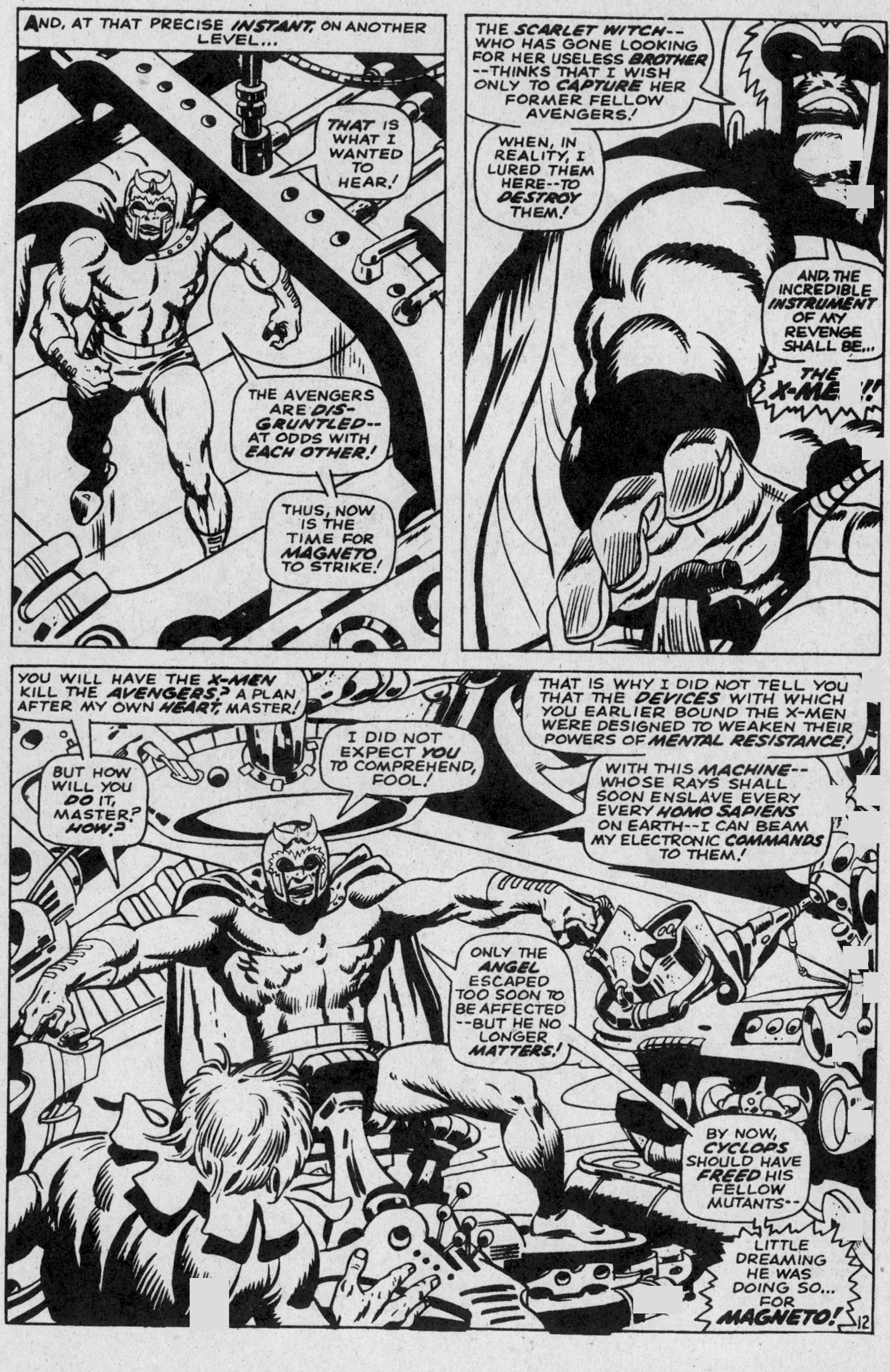
AND, AT THAT PRECISE *INSTANT*, ON ANOTHER LEVEL...
THAT IS WHAT I WANTED TO HEAR!
THE AVENGERS ARE *DIS-GRUNTLED*-- AT ODDS WITH *EACH OTHER*!
THUS, NOW IS THE TIME FOR *MAGNETO* TO STRIKE!
THE *SCARLET WITCH*-- WHO HAS GONE LOOKING FOR HER USELESS *BROTHER* --THINKS THAT I WISH ONLY TO *CAPTURE* HER FORMER FELLOW AVENGERS!
WHEN, IN REALITY, I LURED THEM HERE--TO *DESTROY* THEM!
AND THE INCREDIBLE *INSTRUMENT* OF MY REVENGE SHALL BE...
THE X-ME
YOU WILL HAVE THE *X-MEN* KILL THE *AVENGERS*? A PLAN AFTER MY OWN *HEART*, MASTER!
BUT HOW WILL YOU *DO* IT, MASTER? *HOW?*
I DID NOT EXPECT *YOU* TO COMPREHEND, FOOL!
THAT IS WHY I DID NOT TELL YOU THAT THE *DEVICES* WITH WHICH YOU EARLIER BOUND THE X-MEN WERE DESIGNED TO WEAKEN THEIR POWERS OF *MENTAL RESISTANCE*!
WITH THIS *MACHINE*-- WHOSE RAYS SHALL SOON ENSLAVE EVERY EVERY *HOMO SAPIENS* ON EARTH--I CAN BEAM MY ELECTRONIC *COMMANDS* TO THEM!
ONLY THE *ANGEL* ESCAPED TOO SOON TO BE AFFECTED --BUT HE NO LONGER *MATTERS*!
BY NOW, *CYCLOPS* SHOULD HAVE *FREED* HIS FELLOW MUTANTS--
LITTLE DREAMING HE WAS DOING SO... FOR *MAGNETO*!
12

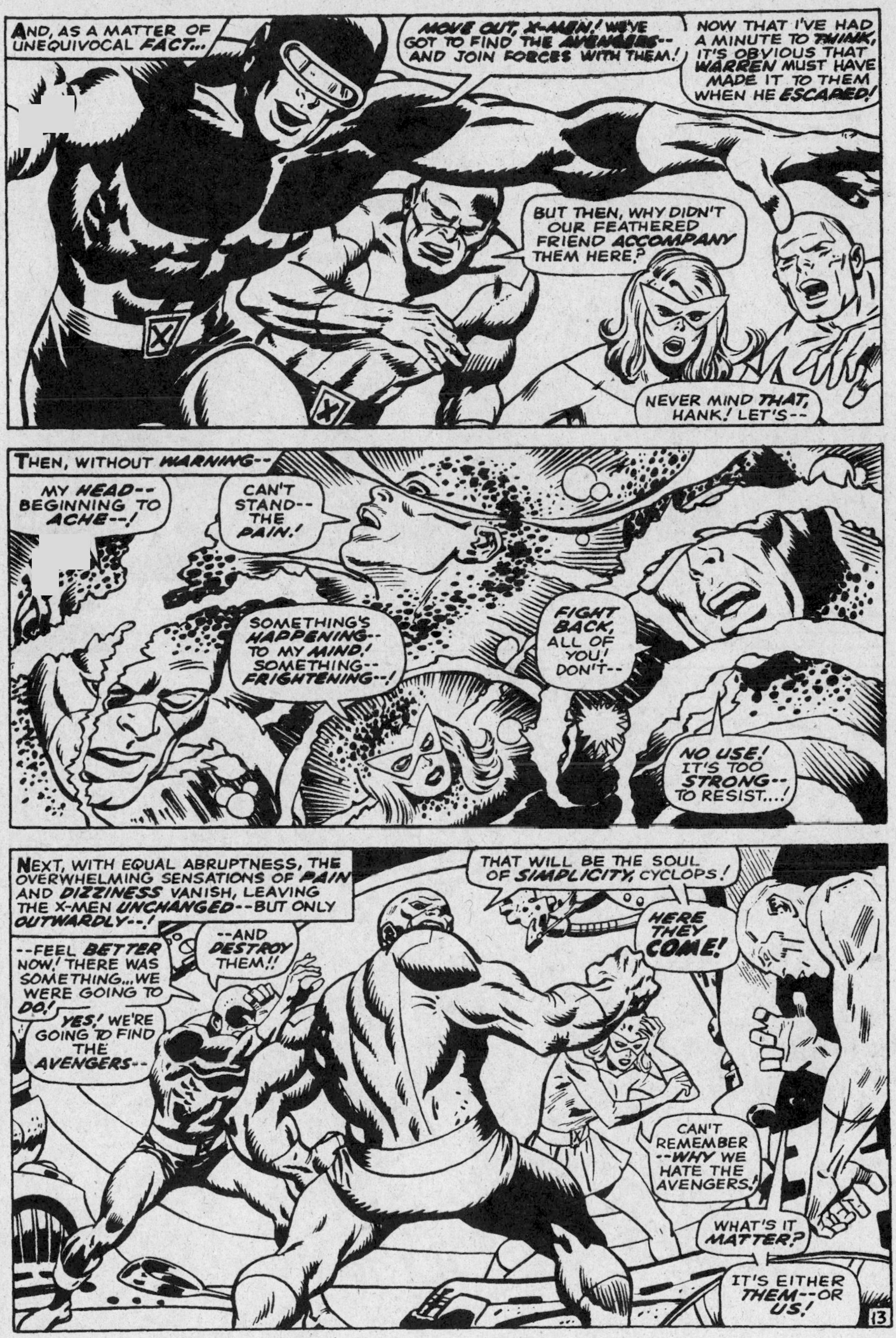
AND, AS A MATTER OF UNEQUIVOCAL FACT...
MOVE OUT, X-MEN! WE'VE GOT TO FIND THE AVENGERS-- AND JOIN FORCES WITH THEM!
NOW THAT I'VE HAD A MINUTE TO THINK, IT'S OBVIOUS THAT WARREN MUST HAVE MADE IT TO THEM WHEN HE ESCAPED!
BUT THEN, WHY DIDN'T OUR FEATHERED FRIEND ACCOMPANY THEM HERE?
NEVER MIND THAT, HANK! LET'S--
THEN, WITHOUT WARNING--
MY HEAD-- BEGINNING TO ACHE--!
CAN'T STAND-- THE PAIN!
SOMETHING'S HAPPENING-- TO MY MIND! SOMETHING-- FRIGHTENING--!
FIGHT BACK, ALL OF YOU! DON'T--
NO USE! IT'S TOO STRONG-- TO RESIST...!
NEXT, WITH EQUAL ABRUPTNESS, THE OVERWHELMING SENSATIONS OF PAIN AND DIZZINESS VANISH, LEAVING THE X-MEN UNCHANGED--BUT ONLY OUTWARDLY--!
--FEEL BETTER NOW! THERE WAS SOMETHING...WE WERE GOING TO DO!
--AND DESTROY THEM!!
YES! WE'RE GOING TO FIND THE AVENGERS--
THAT WILL BE THE SOUL OF SIMPLICITY, CYCLOPS!
HERE THEY COME!
CAN'T REMEMBER --WHY WE HATE THE AVENGERS!
WHAT'S IT MATTER?
IT'S EITHER THEM--OR US!

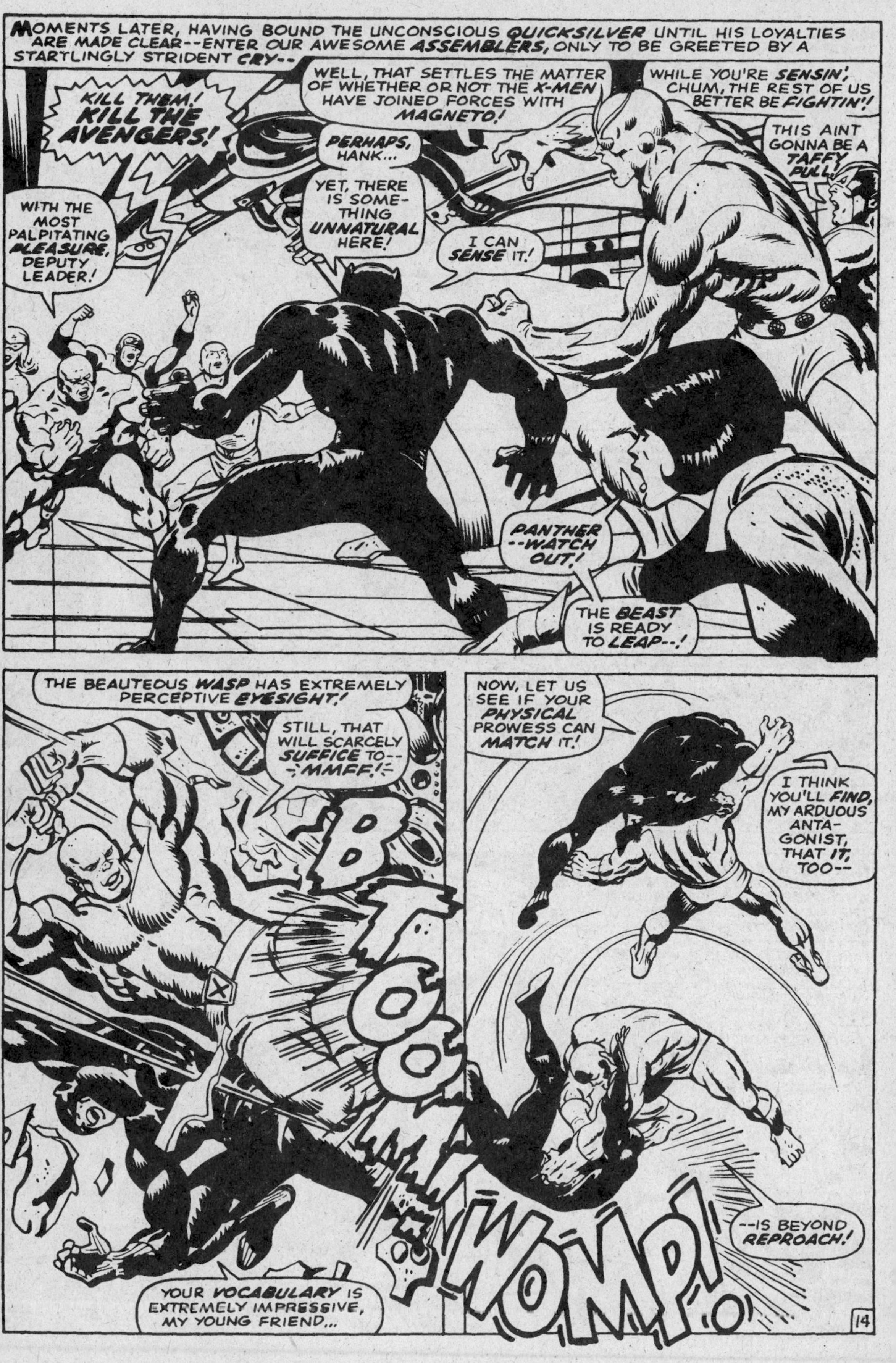
MOMENTS LATER, HAVING BOUND THE UNCONSCIOUS QUICKSILVER UNTIL HIS LOYALTIES ARE MADE CLEAR--ENTER OUR AWESOME ASSEMBLERS, ONLY TO BE GREETED BY A STARTLINGLY STRIDENT CRY--
KILL THEM! KILL THE AVENGERS!
WITH THE MOST PALPITATING PLEASURE, DEPUTY LEADER!
WELL, THAT SETTLES THE MATTER OF WHETHER OR NOT THE X-MEN HAVE JOINED FORCES WITH MAGNETO!
PERHAPS, HANK...
YET, THERE IS SOME-THING UNNATURAL HERE!
I CAN SENSE IT!
WHILE YOU'RE SENSIN', CHUM, THE REST OF US BETTER BE FIGHTIN'!
THIS AINT GONNA BE A TAFFY PULL!
PANTHER --WATCH OUT!
THE BEAST IS READY TO LEAP--!
THE BEAUTEOUS WASP HAS EXTREMELY PERCEPTIVE EYESIGHT!
STILL, THAT WILL SCARCELY SUFFICE TO-- MMFF!
BTOOOM
YOUR VOCABULARY IS EXTREMELY IMPRESSIVE, MY YOUNG FRIEND...
NOW, LET US SEE IF YOUR PHYSICAL PROWESS CAN MATCH IT!
I THINK YOU'LL FIND, MY ARDUOUS ANTA-GONIST, THAT IT, TOO--
--IS BEYOND REPROACH!
WOMP!
14

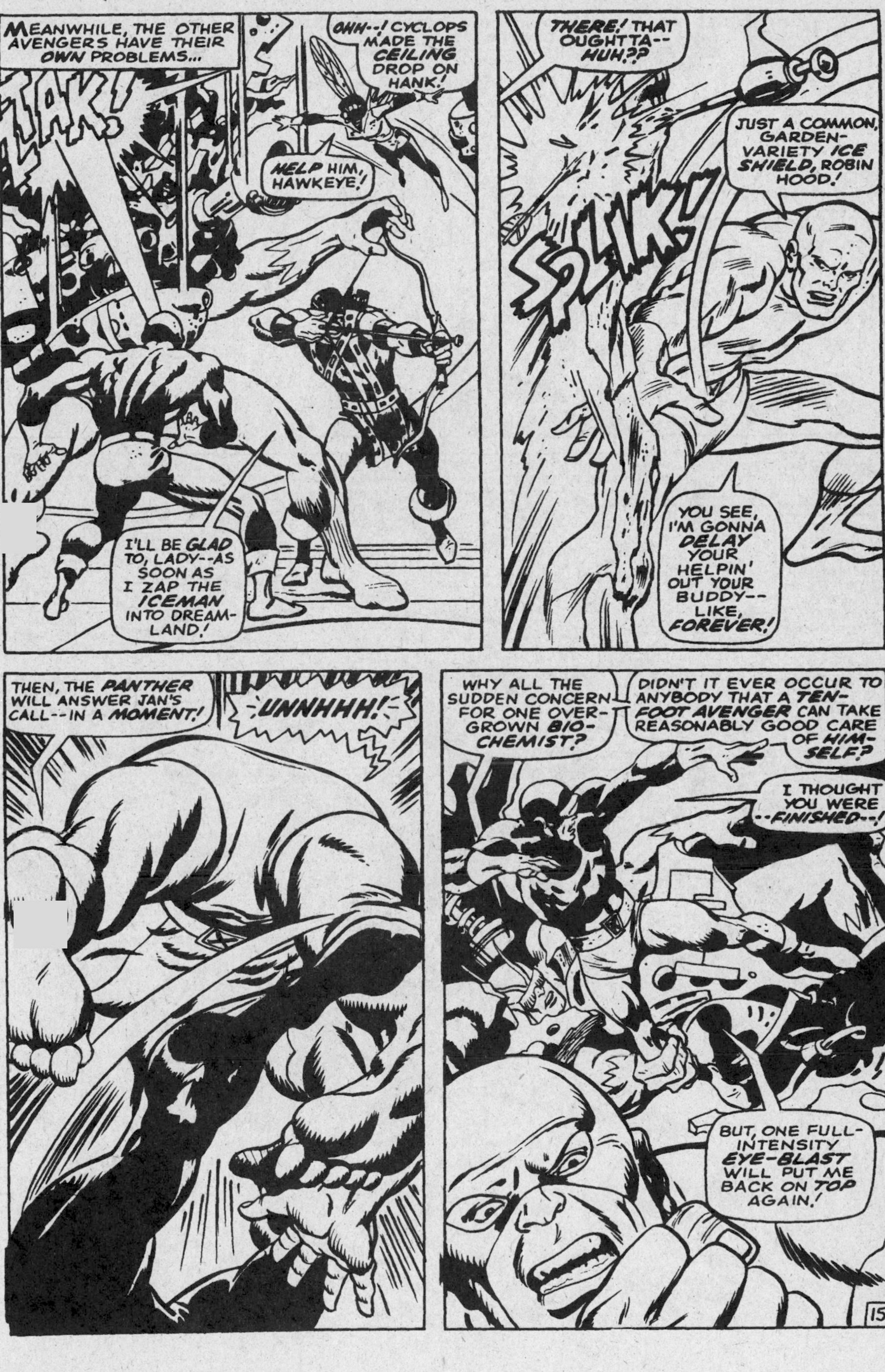
MEANWHILE, THE OTHER AVENGERS HAVE THEIR OWN PROBLEMS...
TAK!
OHH--! CYCLOPS MADE THE CEILING DROP ON HANK!
HELP HIM, HAWKEYE!
I'LL BE GLAD TO, LADY--AS SOON AS I ZAP THE ICEMAN INTO DREAM-LAND!
THERE! THAT OUGHTTA-- HUH??
JUST A COMMON, GARDEN-VARIETY ICE SHIELD, ROBIN HOOD!
SPLIK!
YOU SEE, I'M GONNA DELAY YOUR HELPIN' OUT YOUR BUDDY--LIKE, FOREVER!
THEN, THE PANTHER WILL ANSWER JAN'S CALL--IN A MOMENT!
UNNHHH!
WHY ALL THE SUDDEN CONCERN FOR ONE OVER-GROWN BIO-CHEMIST?
DIDN'T IT EVER OCCUR TO ANYBODY THAT A TEN-FOOT AVENGER CAN TAKE REASONABLY GOOD CARE OF HIM-SELF?
I THOUGHT YOU WERE --FINISHED--!
BUT, ONE FULL-INTENSITY EYE-BLAST WILL PUT ME BACK ON TOP AGAIN!
15

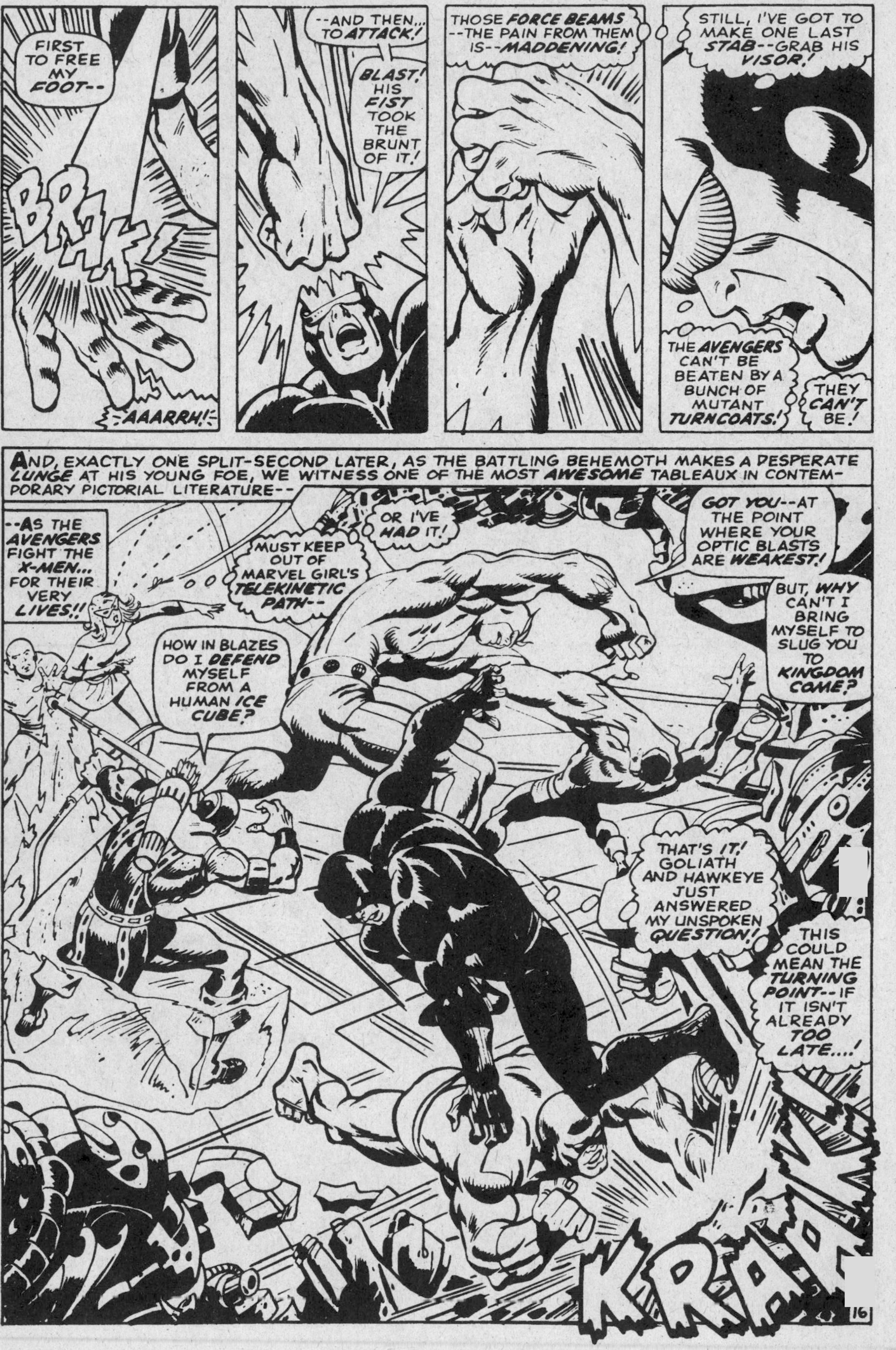
FIRST TO FREE MY FOOT--
BRAK!
AAARRH!
--AND THEN... TO ATTACK!
BLAST! HIS FIST TOOK THE BRUNT OF IT!
THOSE FORCE BEAMS --THE PAIN FROM THEM IS--MADDENING!
STILL, I'VE GOT TO MAKE ONE LAST STAB--GRAB HIS VISOR!
THE AVENGERS CAN'T BE BEATEN BY A BUNCH OF MUTANT TURNCOATS!
THEY CAN'T BE!
AND, EXACTLY ONE SPLIT-SECOND LATER, AS THE BATTLING BEHEMOTH MAKES A DESPERATE LUNGE AT HIS YOUNG FOE, WE WITNESS ONE OF THE MOST AWESOME TABLEAUX IN CONTEMPORARY PICTORIAL LITERATURE--
--AS THE AVENGERS FIGHT THE X-MEN... FOR THEIR VERY LIVES!!
MUST KEEP OUT OF MARVEL GIRL'S TELEKINETIC PATH--
OR I'VE HAD IT!
HOW IN BLAZES DO I DEFEND MYSELF FROM A HUMAN ICE CUBE?
GOT YOU--AT THE POINT WHERE YOUR OPTIC BLASTS ARE WEAKEST!
BUT, WHY CAN'T I BRING MYSELF TO SLUG YOU TO KINGDOM COME?
THAT'S IT! GOLIATH AND HAWKEYE JUST ANSWERED MY UNSPOKEN QUESTION!
THIS COULD MEAN THE TURNING POINT--IF IT ISN'T ALREADY TOO LATE....!
KRAK

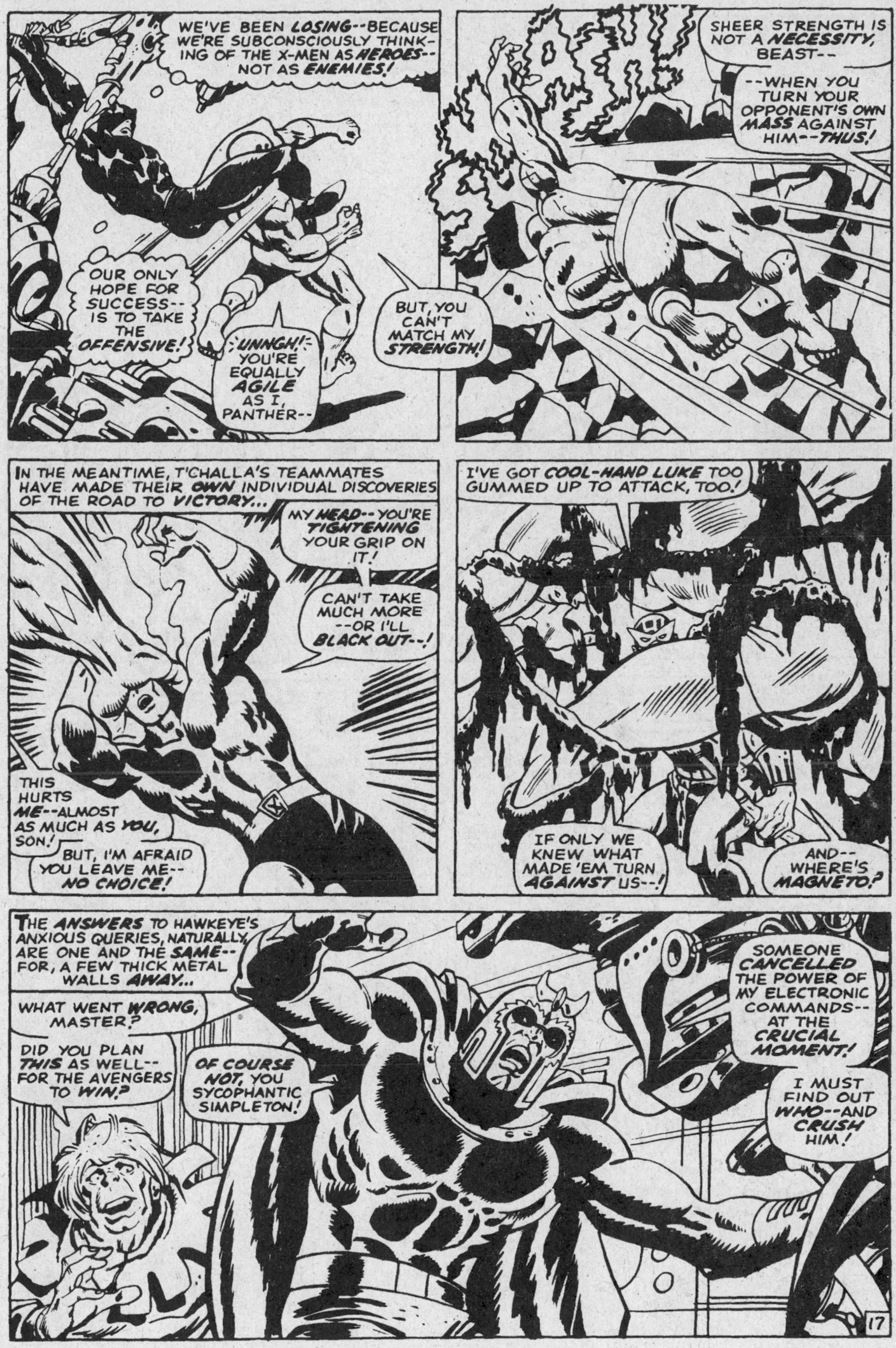
WE'VE BEEN LOSING--BECAUSE WE'RE SUBCONSCIOUSLY THINKING OF THE X-MEN AS HEROES--NOT AS ENEMIES!
OUR ONLY HOPE FOR SUCCESS--IS TO TAKE THE OFFENSIVE!
UNNGH! YOU'RE EQUALLY AGILE AS I, PANTHER--
BUT, YOU CAN'T MATCH MY STRENGTH!
SHEER STRENGTH IS NOT A NECESSITY, BEAST--
--WHEN YOU TURN YOUR OPPONENT'S OWN MASS AGAINST HIM--THUS!
IN THE MEANTIME, T'CHALLA'S TEAMMATES HAVE MADE THEIR OWN INDIVIDUAL DISCOVERIES OF THE ROAD TO VICTORY...
MY HEAD--YOU'RE TIGHTENING YOUR GRIP ON IT!
CAN'T TAKE MUCH MORE --OR I'LL BLACK OUT--!
THIS HURTS ME--ALMOST AS MUCH AS YOU, SON!
BUT, I'M AFRAID YOU LEAVE ME--NO CHOICE!
I'VE GOT COOL-HAND LUKE TOO GUMMED UP TO ATTACK, TOO!
IF ONLY WE KNEW WHAT MADE 'EM TURN AGAINST US--!
AND--WHERE'S MAGNETO?
THE ANSWERS TO HAWKEYE'S ANXIOUS QUERIES, NATURALLY, ARE ONE AND THE SAME--FOR, A FEW THICK METAL WALLS AWAY...
WHAT WENT WRONG, MASTER?
DID YOU PLAN THIS AS WELL--FOR THE AVENGERS TO WIN?
OF COURSE NOT, YOU SYCOPHANTIC SIMPLETON!
SOMEONE CANCELLED THE POWER OF MY ELECTRONIC COMMANDS--AT THE CRUCIAL MOMENT!
I MUST FIND OUT WHO--AND CRUSH HIM!
17

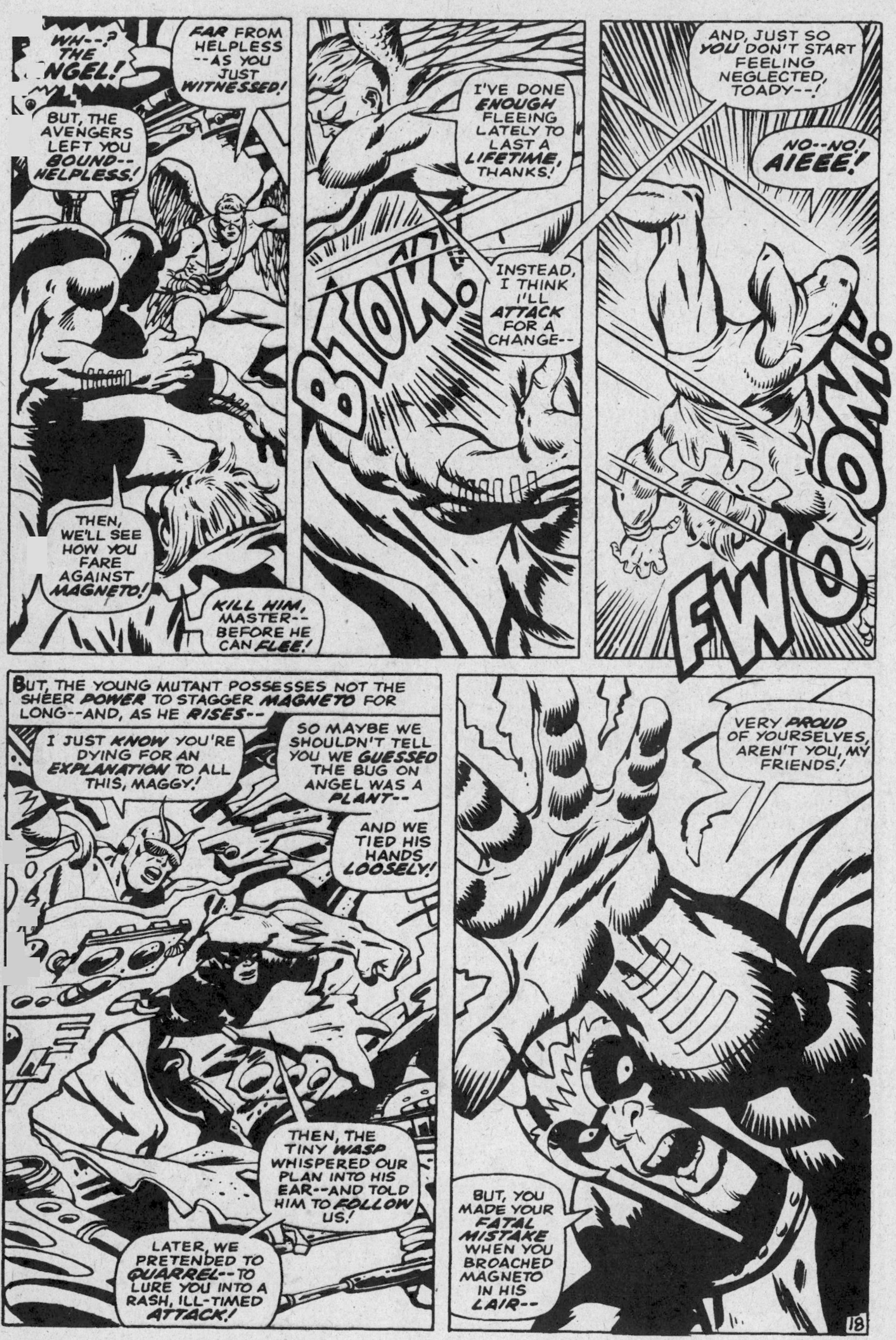
WH--? THE NGEL!
FAR FROM HELPLESS --AS YOU JUST WITNESSED!
BUT, THE AVENGERS LEFT YOU BOUND--HELPLESS!
THEN, WE'LL SEE HOW YOU FARE AGAINST MAGNETO!
KILL HIM, MASTER--BEFORE HE CAN FLEE!
I'VE DONE ENOUGH FLEEING LATELY TO LAST A LIFETIME, THANKS!
INSTEAD, I THINK I'LL ATTACK FOR A CHANGE--
BTOK!
AND, JUST SO YOU DON'T START FEELING NEGLECTED, TOADY--!
NO--NO! AIEEE!
FWOOM!
BUT, THE YOUNG MUTANT POSSESSES NOT THE SHEER POWER TO STAGGER MAGNETO FOR LONG--AND, AS HE RISES--
I JUST KNOW YOU'RE DYING FOR AN EXPLANATION TO ALL THIS, MAGGY!
SO MAYBE WE SHOULDN'T TELL YOU WE GUESSED THE BUG ON ANGEL WAS A PLANT--
AND WE TIED HIS HANDS LOOSELY!
THEN, THE TINY WASP WHISPERED OUR PLAN INTO HIS EAR--AND TOLD HIM TO FOLLOW US!
LATER, WE PRETENDED TO QUARREL--TO LURE YOU INTO A RASH, ILL-TIMED ATTACK!
VERY PROUD OF YOURSELVES, AREN'T YOU, MY FRIENDS!
BUT, YOU MADE YOUR FATAL MISTAKE WHEN YOU BROACHED MAGNETO IN HIS LAIR--

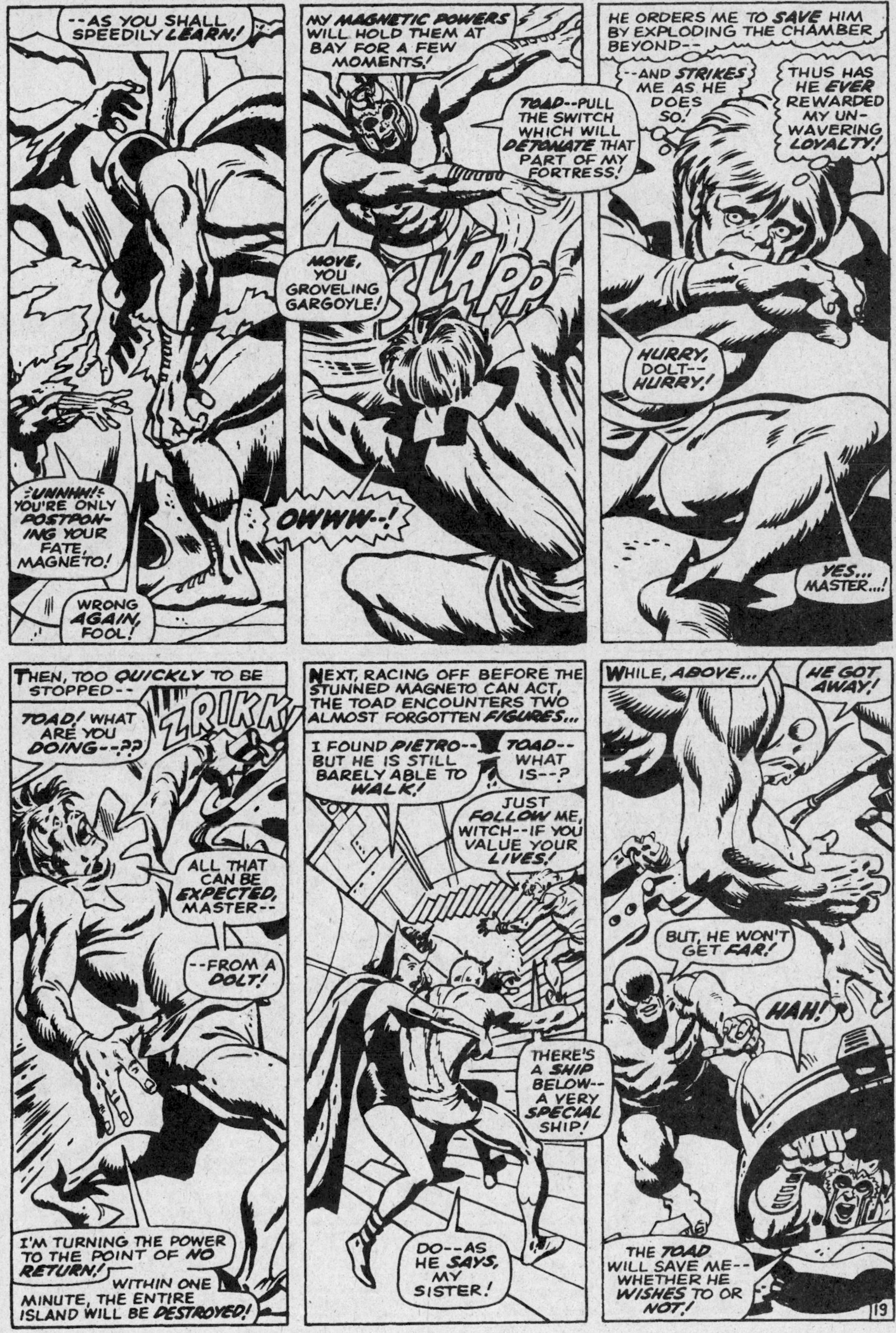

--AS YOU SHALL SPEEDILY LEARN!
UNNHH! YOU'RE ONLY POSTPONING YOUR FATE, MAGNETO!
WRONG AGAIN, FOOL!
MY MAGNETIC POWERS WILL HOLD THEM AT BAY FOR A FEW MOMENTS!
TOAD--PULL THE SWITCH WHICH WILL DETONATE THAT PART OF MY FORTRESS!
MOVE, YOU GROVELING GARGOYLE!
SLAPP
OWWW--!
HE ORDERS ME TO SAVE HIM BY EXPLODING THE CHAMBER BEYOND--
--AND STRIKES ME AS HE DOES SO!
THUS HAS HE EVER REWARDED MY UNWAVERING LOYALTY!
HURRY, DOLT--HURRY!
YES... MASTER...!
THEN, TOO QUICKLY TO BE STOPPED--
ZRIKK!
TOAD! WHAT ARE YOU DOING--??
ALL THAT CAN BE EXPECTED, MASTER--
--FROM A DOLT!
I'M TURNING THE POWER TO THE POINT OF NO RETURN!
WITHIN ONE MINUTE, THE ENTIRE ISLAND WILL BE DESTROYED!
NEXT, RACING OFF BEFORE THE STUNNED MAGNETO CAN ACT, THE TOAD ENCOUNTERS TWO ALMOST FORGOTTEN FIGURES...
I FOUND PIETRO--BUT HE IS STILL BARELY ABLE TO WALK!
TOAD--WHAT IS--?
JUST FOLLOW ME, WITCH--IF YOU VALUE YOUR LIVES!
THERE'S A SHIP BELOW--A VERY SPECIAL SHIP!
DO--AS HE SAYS, MY SISTER!
WHILE, ABOVE...
HE GOT AWAY!
BUT, HE WON'T GET FAR!
HAH!
THE TOAD WILL SAVE ME--WHETHER HE WISHES TO OR NOT!

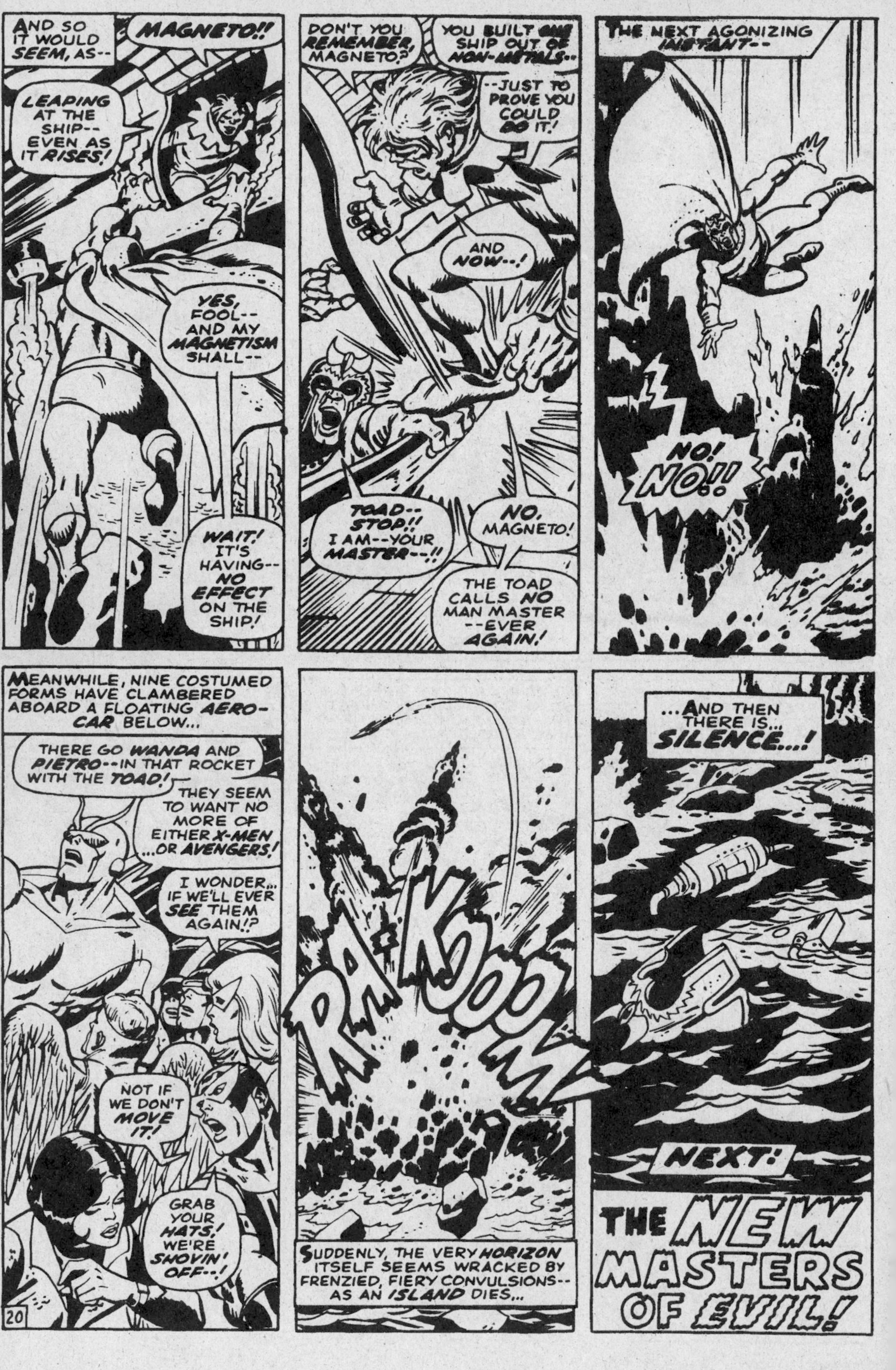
AND SO IT WOULD SEEM, AS--
MAGNETO!!
LEAPING AT THE SHIP-- EVEN AS IT RISES!
YES, FOOL-- AND MY MAGNETISM SHALL--
WAIT! IT'S HAVING-- NO EFFECT ON THE SHIP!
DON'T YOU REMEMBER, MAGNETO?
YOU BUILT ONE SHIP OUT OF NON-METALS--
--JUST TO PROVE YOU COULD DO IT!
AND NOW--!
TOAD-- STOP!! I AM--YOUR MASTER--!!
NO, MAGNETO!
THE TOAD CALLS NO MAN MASTER --EVER AGAIN!
THE NEXT AGONIZING INSTANT--
NO! NO!!
MEANWHILE, NINE COSTUMED FORMS HAVE CLAMBERED ABOARD A FLOATING AERO-CAR BELOW...
THERE GO WANDA AND PIETRO--IN THAT ROCKET WITH THE TOAD!
THEY SEEM TO WANT NO MORE OF EITHER X-MEN ...OR AVENGERS!
I WONDER... IF WE'LL EVER SEE THEM AGAIN!?
NOT IF WE DON'T MOVE IT!
GRAB YOUR HATS! WE'RE SHOVIN' OFF--!
RA-KOOOM
SUDDENLY, THE VERY HORIZON ITSELF SEEMS WRACKED BY FRENZIED, FIERY CONVULSIONS-- AS AN ISLAND DIES...
...AND THEN THERE IS... SILENCE...!
NEXT:
THE NEW MASTERS OF EVIL!

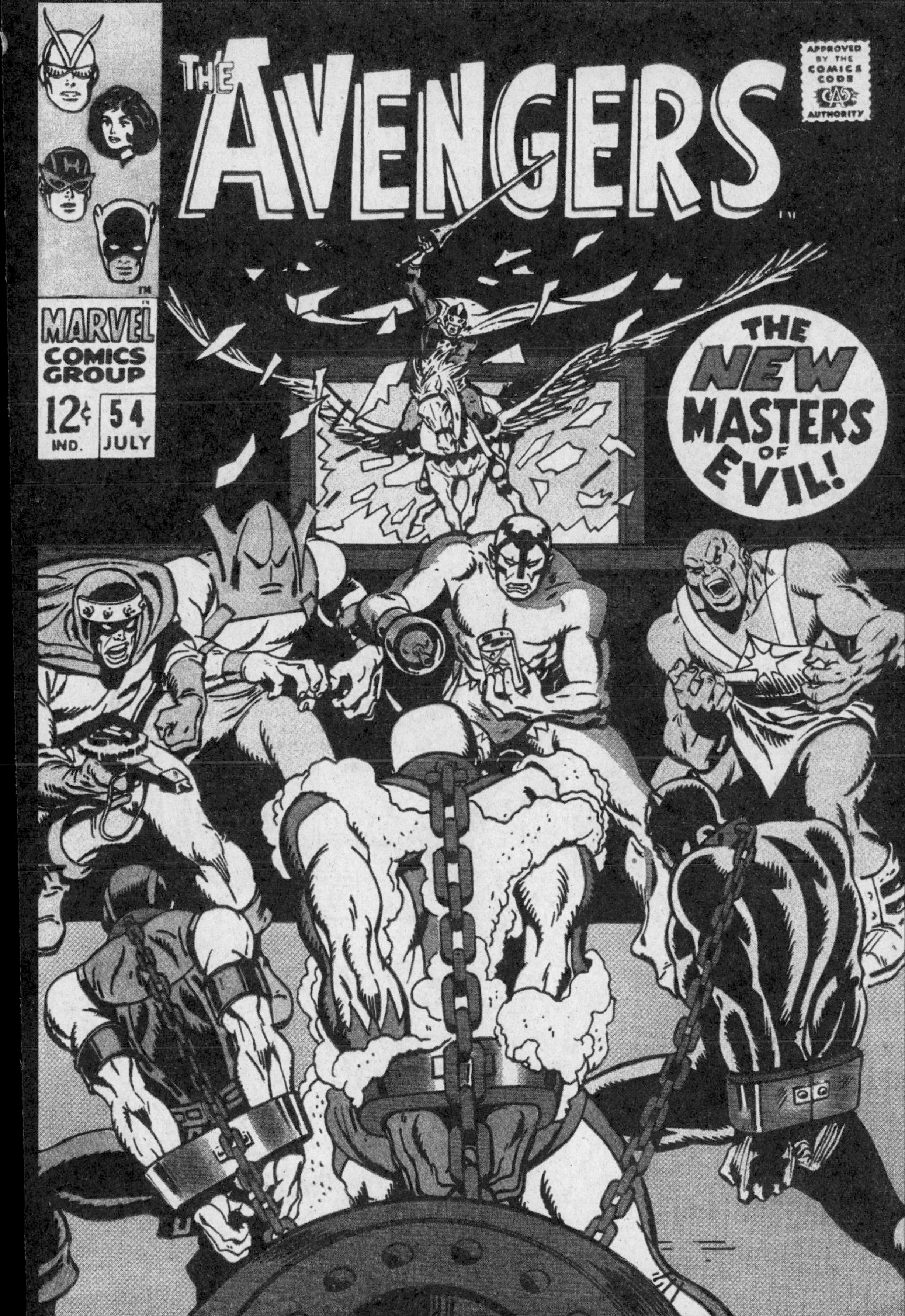
THE AVENGERS
APPROVED BY THE COMICS CODE AUTHORITY
MARVEL COMICS GROUP
12¢ IND.
54 JULY
THE NEW MASTERS OF EVIL!

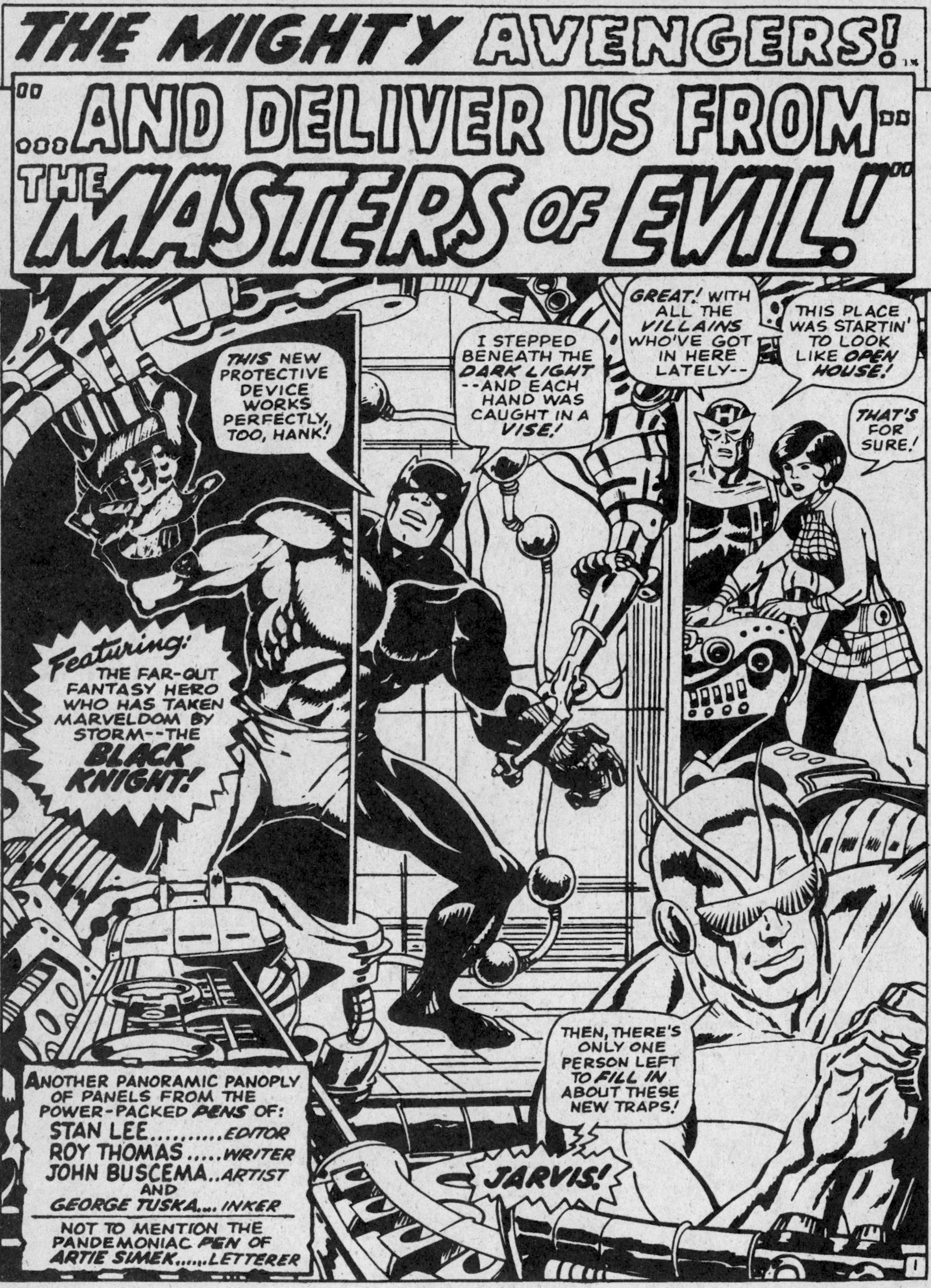
THE MIGHTY AVENGERS!
"...AND DELIVER US FROM--" THE "MASTERS OF EVIL!"
THIS NEW PROTECTIVE DEVICE WORKS PERFECTLY, TOO, HANK!
I STEPPED BENEATH THE DARK LIGHT --AND EACH HAND WAS CAUGHT IN A VISE!
GREAT! WITH ALL THE VILLAINS WHO'VE GOT IN HERE LATELY--
THIS PLACE WAS STARTIN' TO LOOK LIKE OPEN HOUSE!
THAT'S FOR SURE!
FEATURING: THE FAR-OUT FANTASY HERO WHO HAS TAKEN MARVELDOM BY STORM--THE BLACK KNIGHT!
THEN, THERE'S ONLY ONE PERSON LEFT TO FILL IN ABOUT THESE NEW TRAPS!
JARVIS!
ANOTHER PANORAMIC PANOPLY OF PANELS FROM THE POWER-PACKED PENS OF:
STAN LEE..........EDITOR
ROY THOMAS.....WRITER
JOHN BUSCEMA..ARTIST
AND
GEORGE TUSKA....INKER
NOT TO MENTION THE PANDEMONIAC PEN OF ARTIE SIMEK.....LETTERER
1

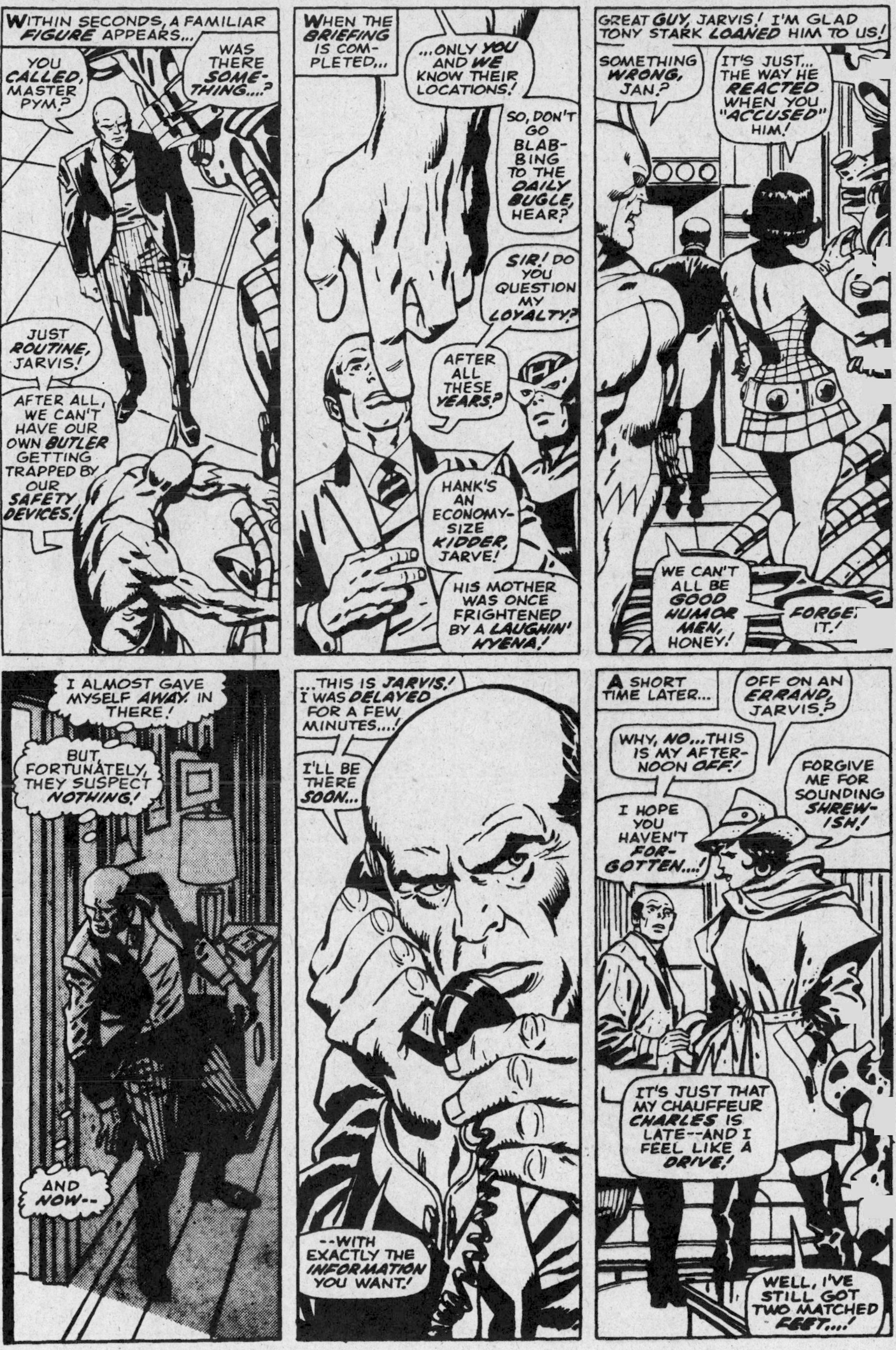
WITHIN SECONDS, A FAMILIAR FIGURE APPEARS...
YOU CALLED, MASTER PYM?
WAS THERE SOME-THING....?
JUST ROUTINE, JARVIS!
AFTER ALL, WE CAN'T HAVE OUR OWN BUTLER GETTING TRAPPED BY OUR SAFETY DEVICES!
WHEN THE BRIEFING IS COM-PLETED,..
...ONLY YOU AND WE KNOW THEIR LOCATIONS!
SO, DON'T GO BLAB-BING TO THE DAILY BUGLE, HEAR?
SIR! DO YOU QUESTION MY LOYALTY?
AFTER ALL THESE YEARS?
HANK'S AN ECONOMY-SIZE KIDDER, JARVE!
HIS MOTHER WAS ONCE FRIGHTENED BY A LAUGHIN' HYENA!
GREAT GUY, JARVIS! I'M GLAD TONY STARK LOANED HIM TO US!
SOMETHING WRONG, JAN?
IT'S JUST... THE WAY HE REACTED WHEN YOU "ACCUSED" HIM!
WE CAN'T ALL BE GOOD HUMOR MEN, HONEY!
FORGE IT.!
I ALMOST GAVE MYSELF AWAY IN THERE!
BUT, FORTUNATELY, THEY SUSPECT NOTHING!
AND NOW--
...THIS IS JARVIS! I WAS DELAYED FOR A FEW MINUTES...!
I'LL BE THERE SOON...
--WITH EXACTLY THE INFORMATION YOU WANT!
A SHORT TIME LATER...
OFF ON AN ERRAND, JARVIS?
WHY, NO...THIS IS MY AFTER-NOON OFF!
FORGIVE ME FOR SOUNDING SHREW-ISH!
I HOPE YOU HAVEN'T FOR-GOTTEN...!
IT'S JUST THAT MY CHAUFFEUR CHARLES IS LATE--AND I FEEL LIKE A DRIVE!
WELL, I'VE STILL GOT TWO MATCHED FEET....!

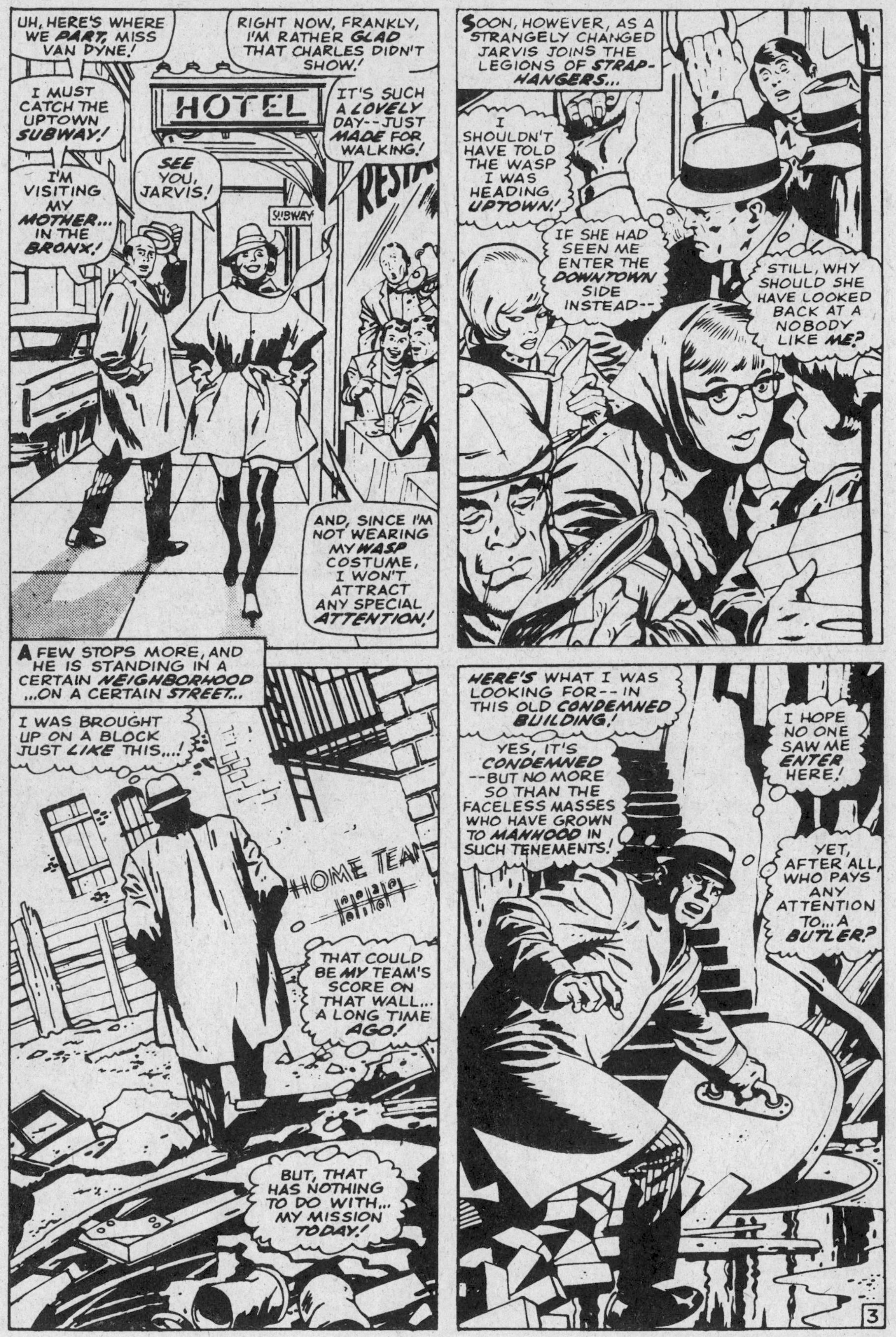
UH, HERE'S WHERE WE PART, MISS VAN DYNE!
I MUST CATCH THE UPTOWN SUBWAY!
I'M VISITING MY MOTHER... IN THE BRONX!
RIGHT NOW, FRANKLY, I'M RATHER GLAD THAT CHARLES DIDN'T SHOW!
IT'S SUCH A LOVELY DAY--JUST MADE FOR WALKING!
SEE YOU, JARVIS!
HOTEL
SUBWAY
AND, SINCE I'M NOT WEARING MY WASP COSTUME, I WON'T ATTRACT ANY SPECIAL ATTENTION!
SOON, HOWEVER, AS A STRANGELY CHANGED JARVIS JOINS THE LEGIONS OF STRAP-HANGERS...
I SHOULDN'T HAVE TOLD THE WASP I WAS HEADING UPTOWN!
IF SHE HAD SEEN ME ENTER THE DOWNTOWN SIDE INSTEAD--
STILL, WHY SHOULD SHE HAVE LOOKED BACK AT A NOBODY LIKE ME?
A FEW STOPS MORE, AND HE IS STANDING IN A CERTAIN NEIGHBORHOOD ...ON A CERTAIN STREET...
I WAS BROUGHT UP ON A BLOCK JUST LIKE THIS...!
HOME TEAM
THAT COULD BE MY TEAM'S SCORE ON THAT WALL... A LONG TIME AGO!
BUT, THAT HAS NOTHING TO DO WITH... MY MISSION TODAY!
HERE'S WHAT I WAS LOOKING FOR-- IN THIS OLD CONDEMNED BUILDING!
YES, IT'S CONDEMNED --BUT NO MORE SO THAN THE FACELESS MASSES WHO HAVE GROWN TO MANHOOD IN SUCH TENEMENTS!
I HOPE NO ONE SAW ME ENTER HERE!
YET, AFTER ALL, WHO PAYS ANY ATTENTION TO... A BUTLER?
3

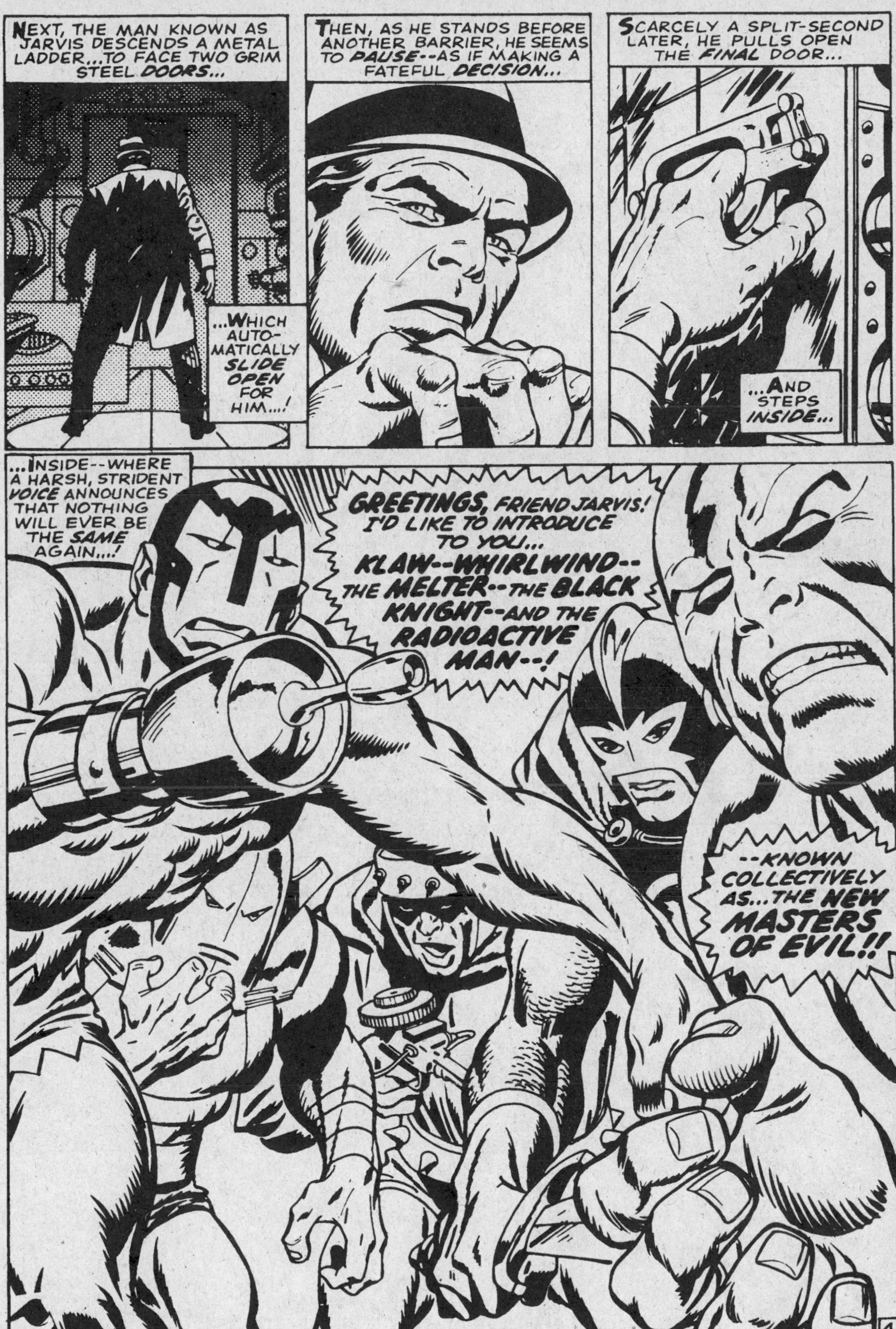
NEXT, THE MAN KNOWN AS JARVIS DESCENDS A METAL LADDER...TO FACE TWO GRIM STEEL DOORS...
...WHICH AUTOMATICALLY SLIDE OPEN FOR HIM...!
THEN, AS HE STANDS BEFORE ANOTHER BARRIER, HE SEEMS TO PAUSE--AS IF MAKING A FATEFUL DECISION...
SCARCELY A SPLIT-SECOND LATER, HE PULLS OPEN THE FINAL DOOR...
...AND STEPS INSIDE...
...INSIDE--WHERE A HARSH, STRIDENT VOICE ANNOUNCES THAT NOTHING WILL EVER BE THE SAME AGAIN...!
GREETINGS, FRIEND JARVIS! I'D LIKE TO INTRODUCE TO YOU... KLAW--WHIRLWIND--THE MELTER--THE BLACK KNIGHT--AND THE RADIOACTIVE MAN--!
--KNOWN COLLECTIVELY AS...THE NEW MASTERS OF EVIL!!
4

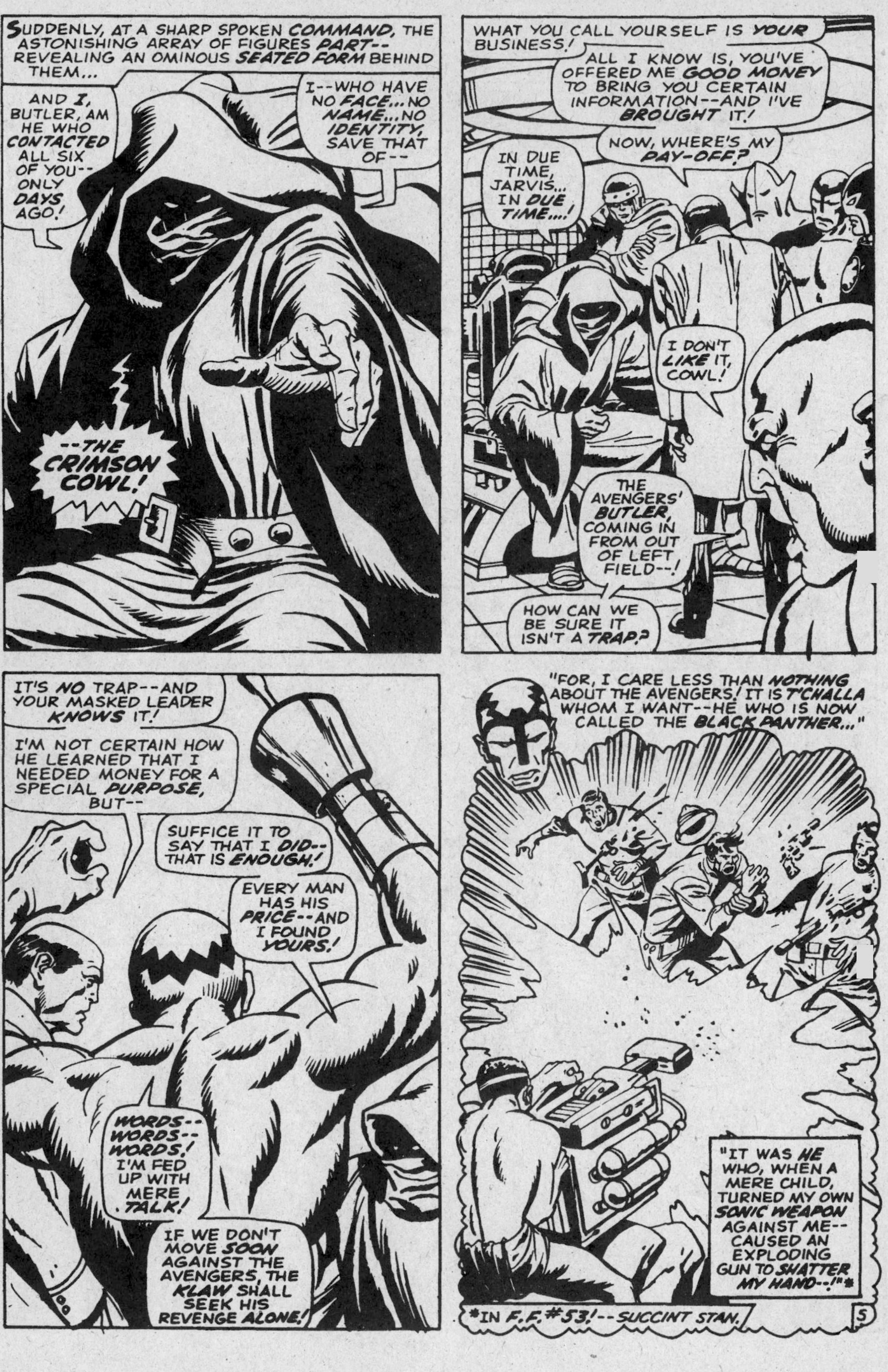
SUDDENLY, AT A SHARP SPOKEN COMMAND, THE ASTONISHING ARRAY OF FIGURES PART-- REVEALING AN OMINOUS SEATED FORM BEHIND THEM...
AND I, BUTLER, AM HE WHO CONTACTED ALL SIX OF YOU-- ONLY DAYS AGO!
I--WHO HAVE NO FACE...NO NAME...NO IDENTITY, SAVE THAT OF--
--THE CRIMSON COWL!
WHAT YOU CALL YOURSELF IS YOUR BUSINESS!
ALL I KNOW IS, YOU'VE OFFERED ME GOOD MONEY TO BRING YOU CERTAIN INFORMATION--AND I'VE BROUGHT IT!
NOW, WHERE'S MY PAY-OFF?
IN DUE TIME, JARVIS... IN DUE TIME....!
I DON'T LIKE IT, COWL!
THE AVENGERS' BUTLER, COMING IN FROM OUT OF LEFT FIELD--!
HOW CAN WE BE SURE IT ISN'T A TRAP?
IT'S NO TRAP--AND YOUR MASKED LEADER KNOWS IT!
I'M NOT CERTAIN HOW HE LEARNED THAT I NEEDED MONEY FOR A SPECIAL PURPOSE, BUT--
SUFFICE IT TO SAY THAT I DID-- THAT IS ENOUGH!
EVERY MAN HAS HIS PRICE--AND I FOUND YOURS!
WORDS-- WORDS-- WORDS! I'M FED UP WITH MERE TALK!
IF WE DON'T MOVE SOON AGAINST THE AVENGERS, THE KLAW SHALL SEEK HIS REVENGE ALONE!
"FOR, I CARE LESS THAN NOTHING ABOUT THE AVENGERS! IT IS T'CHALLA WHOM I WANT--HE WHO IS NOW CALLED THE BLACK PANTHER..."
"IT WAS HE WHO, WHEN A MERE CHILD, TURNED MY OWN SONIC WEAPON AGAINST ME--CAUSED AN EXPLODING GUN TO SHATTER MY HAND--!"*
*IN F.F. #53!--SUCCINT STAN.
5

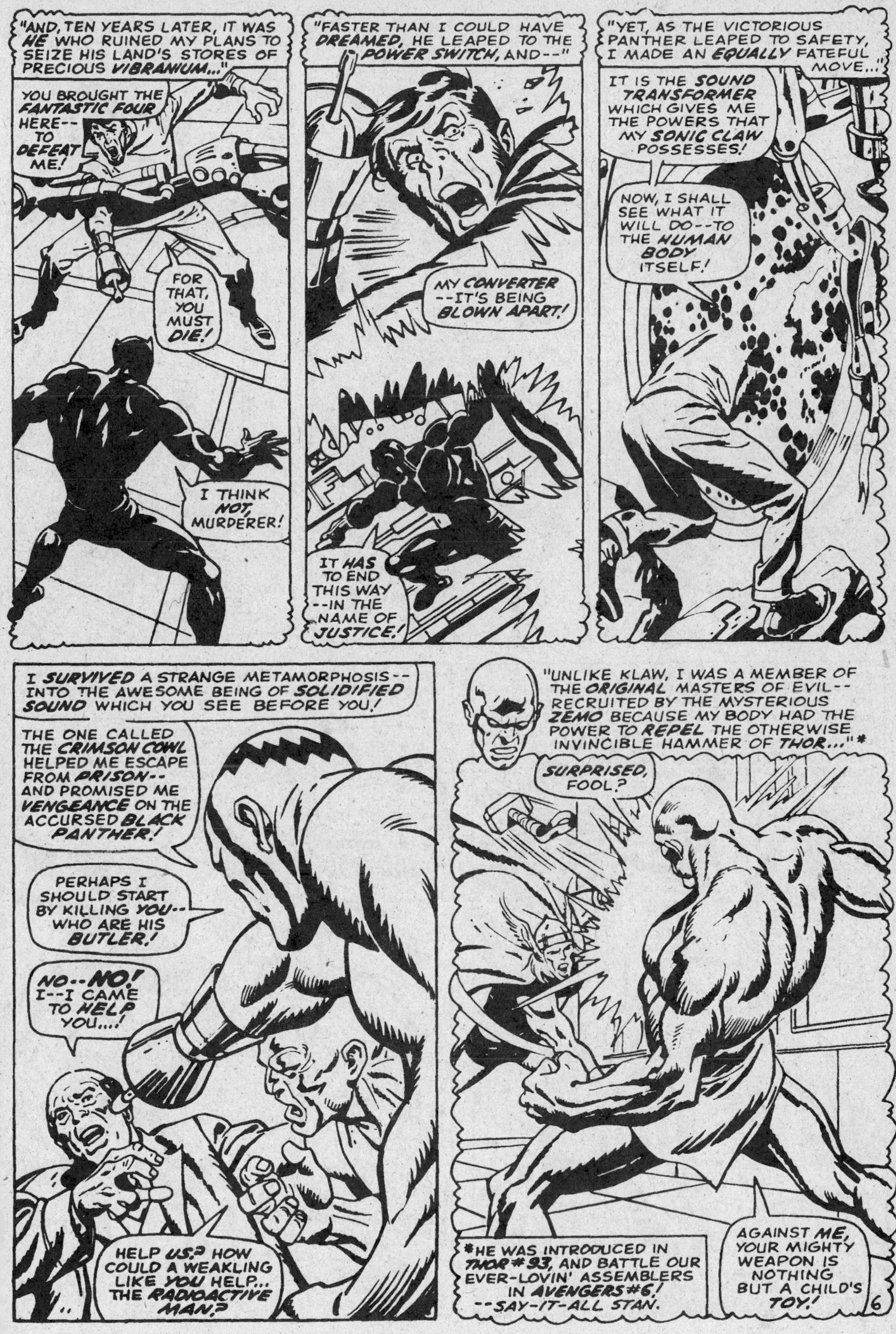
"AND, TEN YEARS LATER, IT WAS HE WHO RUINED MY PLANS TO SEIZE HIS LAND'S STORES OF PRECIOUS VIBRANIUM..."
YOU BROUGHT THE FANTASTIC FOUR HERE--TO DEFEAT ME!
FOR THAT, YOU MUST DIE!
I THINK NOT, MURDERER!
"FASTER THAN I COULD HAVE DREAMED, HE LEAPED TO THE POWER SWITCH, AND--"
MY CONVERTER--IT'S BEING BLOWN APART!
IT HAS TO END THIS WAY--IN THE NAME OF JUSTICE!
"YET, AS THE VICTORIOUS PANTHER LEAPED TO SAFETY, I MADE AN EQUALLY FATEFUL MOVE..."
IT IS THE SOUND TRANSFORMER WHICH GIVES ME THE POWERS THAT MY SONIC CLAW POSSESSES!
NOW, I SHALL SEE WHAT IT WILL DO--TO THE HUMAN BODY ITSELF!
I SURVIVED A STRANGE METAMORPHOSIS--INTO THE AWESOME BEING OF SOLIDIFIED SOUND WHICH YOU SEE BEFORE YOU!
THE ONE CALLED THE CRIMSON COWL HELPED ME ESCAPE FROM PRISON--AND PROMISED ME VENGEANCE ON THE ACCURSED BLACK PANTHER!
PERHAPS I SHOULD START BY KILLING YOU--WHO ARE HIS BUTLER!
NO--NO! I--I CAME TO HELP YOU....!
HELP US? HOW COULD A WEAKLING LIKE YOU HELP... THE RADIOACTIVE MAN?
"UNLIKE KLAW, I WAS A MEMBER OF THE ORIGINAL MASTERS OF EVIL--RECRUITED BY THE MYSTERIOUS ZEMO BECAUSE MY BODY HAD THE POWER TO REPEL THE OTHERWISE INVINCIBLE HAMMER OF THOR..."*
SURPRISED, FOOL?
*HE WAS INTRODUCED IN THOR #93, AND BATTLE OUR EVER-LOVIN' ASSEMBLERS IN AVENGERS #6! --SAY-IT-ALL STAN.
AGAINST ME, YOUR MIGHTY WEAPON IS NOTHING BUT A CHILD'S TOY!
6

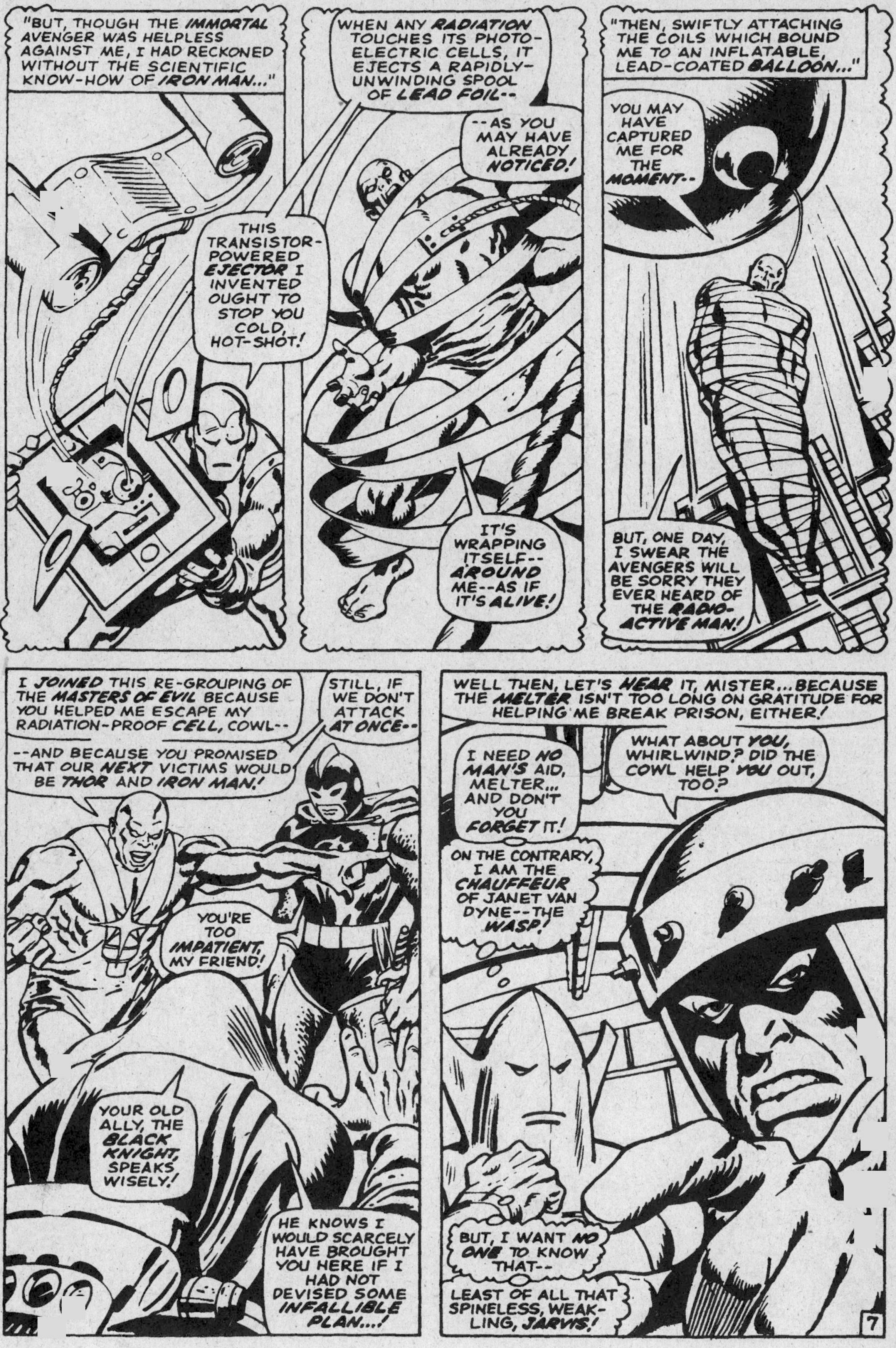
"BUT, THOUGH THE IMMORTAL AVENGER WAS HELPLESS AGAINST ME, I HAD RECKONED WITHOUT THE SCIENTIFIC KNOW-HOW OF IRON MAN..."
THIS TRANSISTOR-POWERED EJECTOR I INVENTED OUGHT TO STOP YOU COLD, HOT-SHOT!
WHEN ANY RADIATION TOUCHES ITS PHOTO-ELECTRIC CELLS, IT EJECTS A RAPIDLY-UNWINDING SPOOL OF LEAD FOIL--
--AS YOU MAY HAVE ALREADY NOTICED!
IT'S WRAPPING ITSELF--AROUND ME--AS IF IT'S ALIVE!
"THEN, SWIFTLY ATTACHING THE COILS WHICH BOUND ME TO AN INFLATABLE, LEAD-COATED BALLOON..."
YOU MAY HAVE CAPTURED ME FOR THE MOMENT--
BUT, ONE DAY, I SWEAR THE AVENGERS WILL BE SORRY THEY EVER HEARD OF THE RADIO-ACTIVE MAN!
I JOINED THIS RE-GROUPING OF THE MASTERS OF EVIL BECAUSE YOU HELPED ME ESCAPE MY RADIATION-PROOF CELL, COWL--
--AND BECAUSE YOU PROMISED THAT OUR NEXT VICTIMS WOULD BE THOR AND IRON MAN!
STILL, IF WE DON'T ATTACK AT ONCE--
YOU'RE TOO IMPATIENT, MY FRIEND!
YOUR OLD ALLY, THE BLACK KNIGHT, SPEAKS WISELY!
HE KNOWS I WOULD SCARCELY HAVE BROUGHT YOU HERE IF I HAD NOT DEVISED SOME INFALLIBLE PLAN...!
WELL THEN, LET'S HEAR IT, MISTER... BECAUSE THE MELTER ISN'T TOO LONG ON GRATITUDE FOR HELPING ME BREAK PRISON, EITHER!
I NEED NO MAN'S AID, MELTER... AND DON'T YOU FORGET IT!
WHAT ABOUT YOU, WHIRLWIND? DID THE COWL HELP YOU OUT, TOO?
ON THE CONTRARY, I AM THE CHAUFFEUR OF JANET VAN DYNE--THE WASP!
BUT, I WANT NO ONE TO KNOW THAT--
LEAST OF ALL THAT SPINELESS, WEAK-LING, JARVIS!

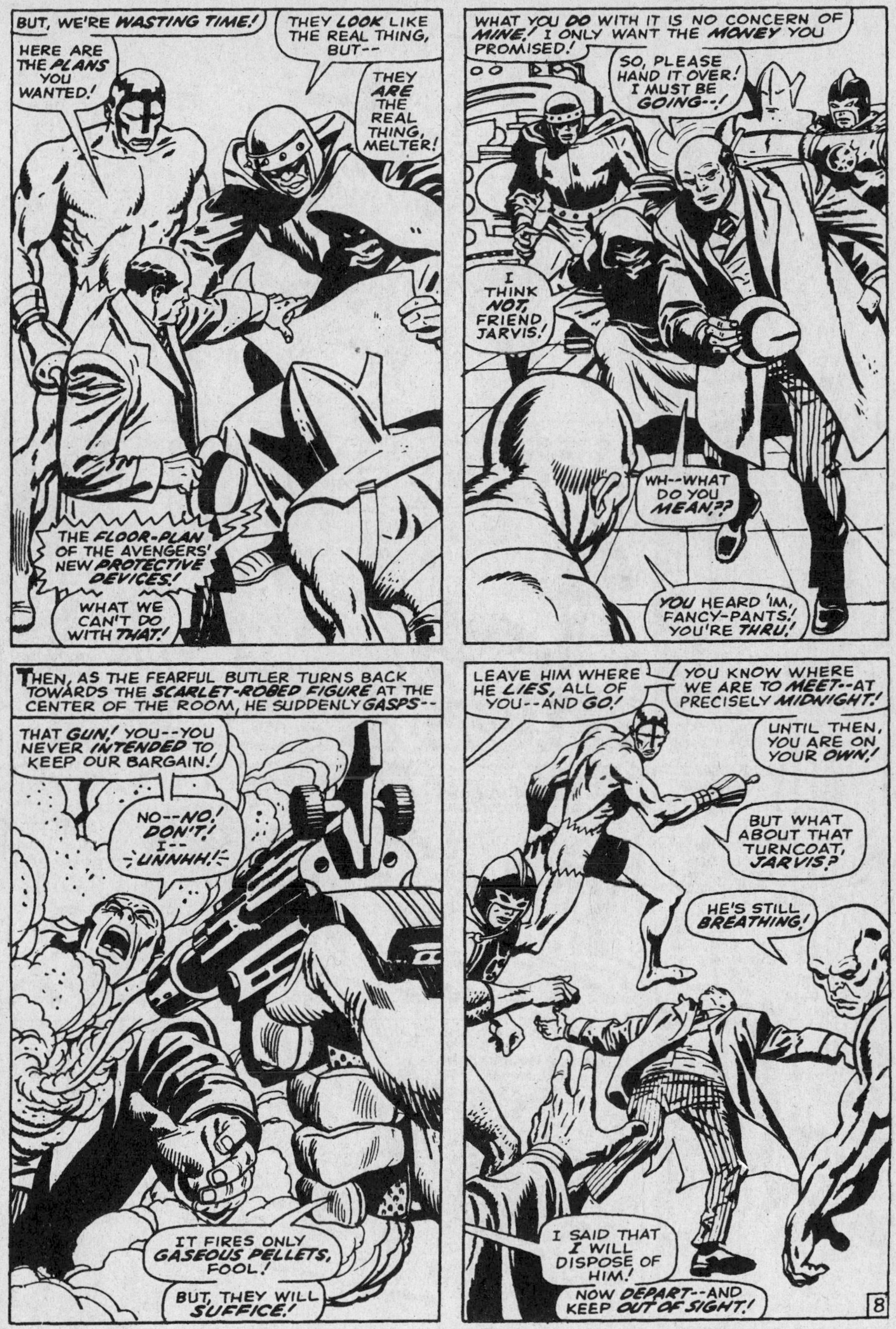

BUT, WE'RE WASTING TIME!
HERE ARE THE PLANS YOU WANTED!
THEY LOOK LIKE THE REAL THING, BUT--
THEY ARE THE REAL THING, MELTER!
THE FLOOR-PLAN OF THE AVENGERS' NEW PROTECTIVE DEVICES!
WHAT WE CAN'T DO WITH THAT!
WHAT YOU DO WITH IT IS NO CONCERN OF MINE! I ONLY WANT THE MONEY YOU PROMISED!
SO, PLEASE HAND IT OVER! I MUST BE GOING--!
I THINK NOT, FRIEND JARVIS!
WH--WHAT DO YOU MEAN??
YOU HEARD 'IM, FANCY-PANTS! YOU'RE THRU!
THEN, AS THE FEARFUL BUTLER TURNS BACK TOWARDS THE SCARLET-ROBED FIGURE AT THE CENTER OF THE ROOM, HE SUDDENLY GASPS--
THAT GUN! YOU--YOU NEVER INTENDED TO KEEP OUR BARGAIN!
NO--NO! DON'T! I-- UNNHH!
IT FIRES ONLY GASEOUS PELLETS, FOOL!
BUT, THEY WILL SUFFICE!
LEAVE HIM WHERE HE LIES, ALL OF YOU--AND GO!
YOU KNOW WHERE WE ARE TO MEET--AT PRECISELY MIDNIGHT!
UNTIL THEN, YOU ARE ON YOUR OWN!
BUT WHAT ABOUT THAT TURNCOAT, JARVIS?
HE'S STILL BREATHING!
I SAID THAT I WILL DISPOSE OF HIM!
NOW DEPART--AND KEEP OUT OF SIGHT!

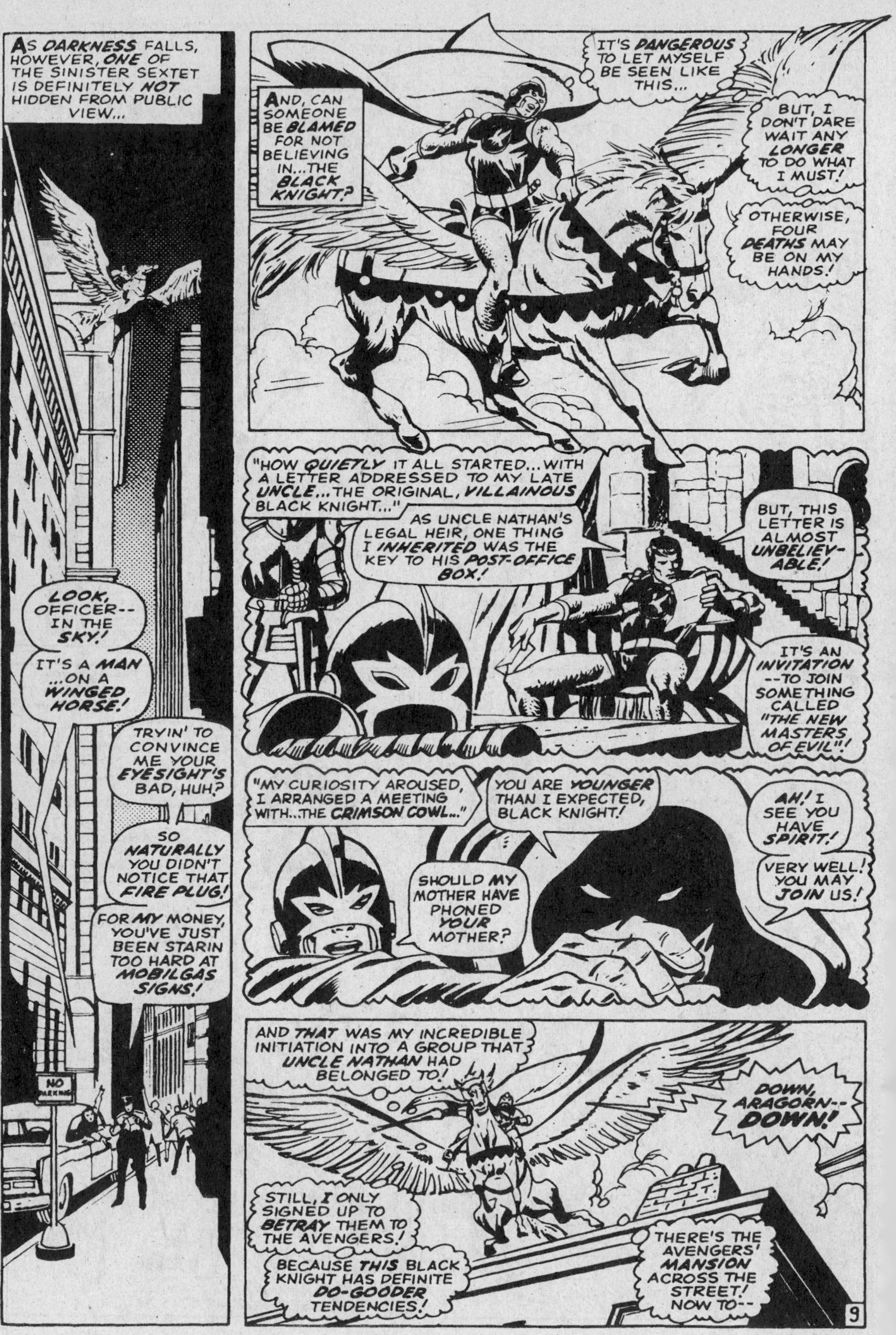

AS DARKNESS FALLS, HOWEVER, ONE OF THE SINISTER SEXTET IS DEFINITELY NOT HIDDEN FROM PUBLIC VIEW...
LOOK, OFFICER-- IN THE SKY!
IT'S A MAN ...ON A WINGED HORSE!
TRYIN' TO CONVINCE ME YOUR EYESIGHT'S BAD, HUH?
SO NATURALLY YOU DIDN'T NOTICE THAT FIRE PLUG!
FOR MY MONEY, YOU'VE JUST BEEN STARIN TOO HARD AT MOBILGAS SIGNS!
NO PARKING
AND, CAN SOMEONE BE BLAMED FOR NOT BELIEVING IN...THE BLACK KNIGHT?
IT'S DANGEROUS TO LET MYSELF BE SEEN LIKE THIS...
BUT, I DON'T DARE WAIT ANY LONGER TO DO WHAT I MUST!
OTHERWISE, FOUR DEATHS MAY BE ON MY HANDS!
"HOW QUIETLY IT ALL STARTED...WITH A LETTER ADDRESSED TO MY LATE UNCLE...THE ORIGINAL, VILLAINOUS BLACK KNIGHT..."
AS UNCLE NATHAN'S LEGAL HEIR, ONE THING I INHERITED WAS THE KEY TO HIS POST-OFFICE BOX!
BUT, THIS LETTER IS ALMOST UNBELIEV-ABLE!
IT'S AN INVITATION --TO JOIN SOMETHING CALLED "THE NEW MASTERS OF EVIL"!
"MY CURIOSITY AROUSED, I ARRANGED A MEETING WITH...THE CRIMSON COWL..."
YOU ARE YOUNGER THAN I EXPECTED, BLACK KNIGHT!
SHOULD MY MOTHER HAVE PHONED YOUR MOTHER?
AH! I SEE YOU HAVE SPIRIT!
VERY WELL! YOU MAY JOIN US!
AND THAT WAS MY INCREDIBLE INITIATION INTO A GROUP THAT UNCLE NATHAN HAD BELONGED TO!
DOWN, ARAGORN-- DOWN!
STILL, I ONLY SIGNED UP TO BETRAY THEM TO THE AVENGERS!
BECAUSE THIS BLACK KNIGHT HAS DEFINITE DO-GOODER TENDENCIES!
THERE'S THE AVENGERS' MANSION ACROSS THE STREET! NOW TO--

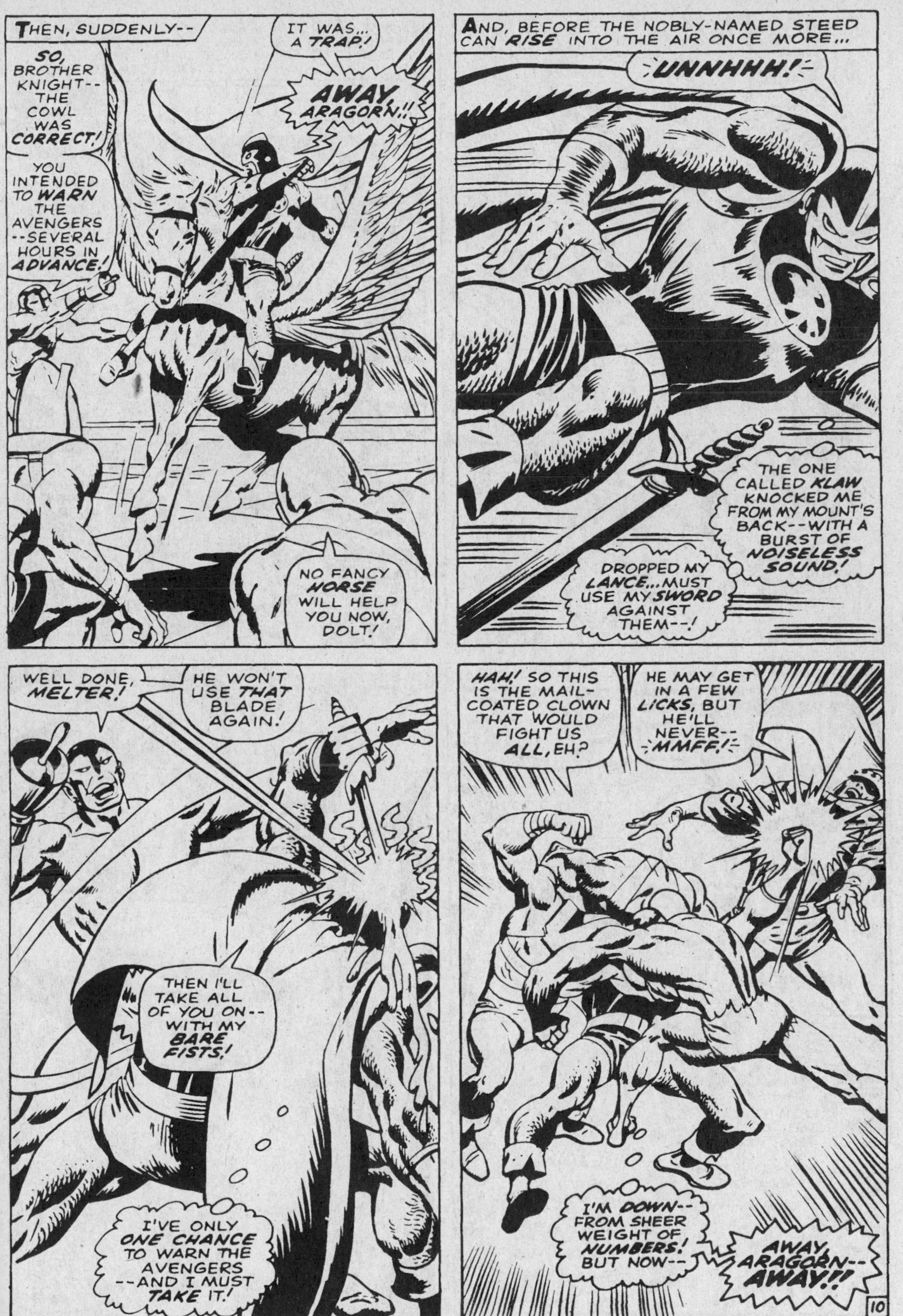
THEN, SUDDENLY--
IT WAS... A TRAP!
SO, BROTHER KNIGHT--THE COWL WAS CORRECT!
YOU INTENDED TO WARN THE AVENGERS --SEVERAL HOURS IN ADVANCE!
AWAY, ARAGORN!!
NO FANCY HORSE WILL HELP YOU NOW, DOLT!
AND, BEFORE THE NOBLY-NAMED STEED CAN RISE INTO THE AIR ONCE MORE...
UNNHHH!
THE ONE CALLED KLAW KNOCKED ME FROM MY MOUNT'S BACK--WITH A BURST OF NOISELESS SOUND!
DROPPED MY LANCE... MUST USE MY SWORD AGAINST THEM--!
WELL DONE, MELTER!
HE WON'T USE THAT BLADE AGAIN!
THEN I'LL TAKE ALL OF YOU ON--WITH MY BARE FISTS!
I'VE ONLY ONE CHANCE TO WARN THE AVENGERS --AND I MUST TAKE IT!
HAH! SO THIS IS THE MAIL-COATED CLOWN THAT WOULD FIGHT US ALL, EH?
HE MAY GET IN A FEW LICKS, BUT HE'LL NEVER-- MMFF!
I'M DOWN--FROM SHEER WEIGHT OF NUMBERS! BUT NOW--
AWAY, ARAGORN--AWAY!!
10

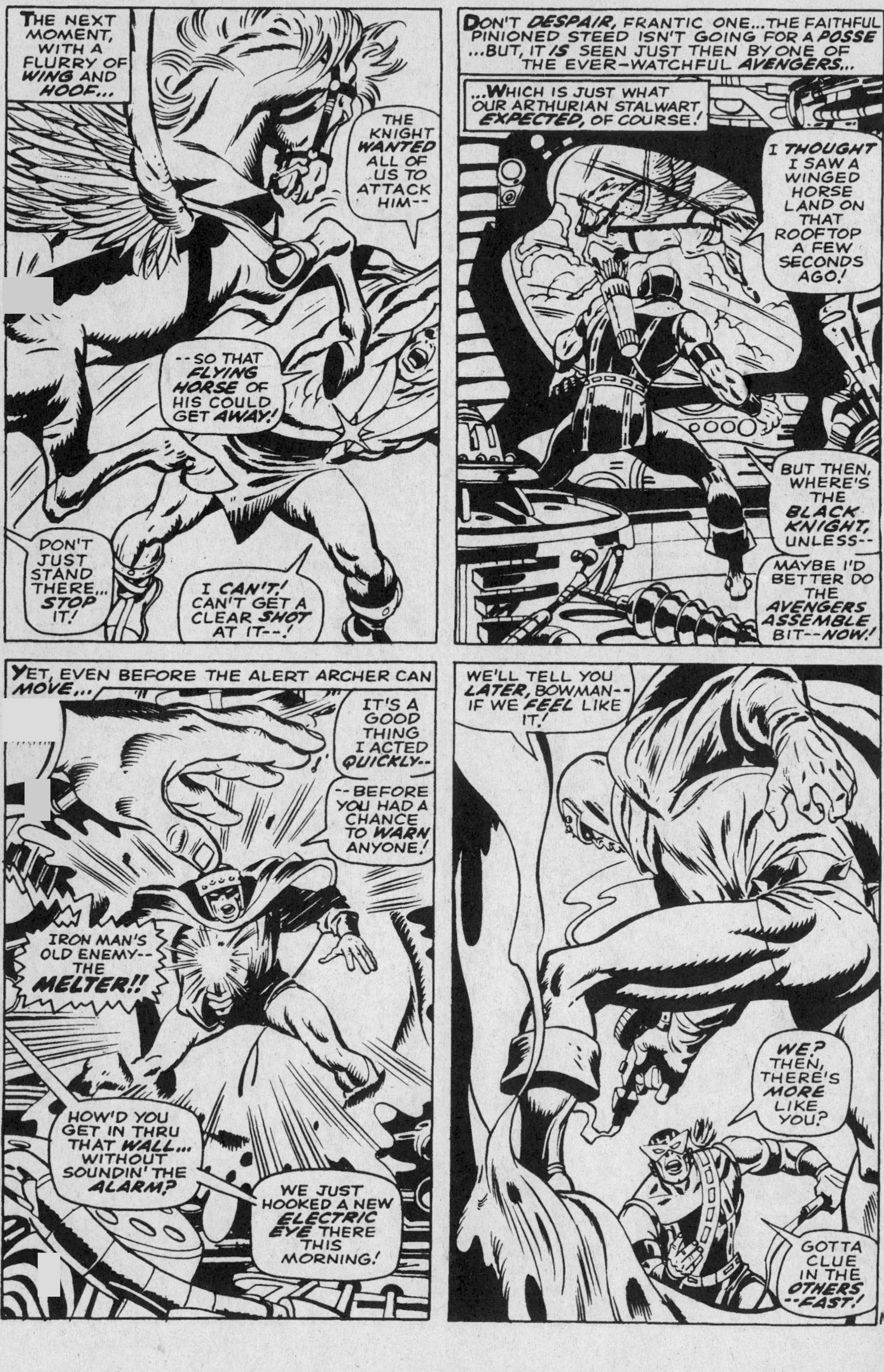
THE NEXT MOMENT, WITH A FLURRY OF WING AND HOOF...
THE KNIGHT WANTED ALL OF US TO ATTACK HIM--
--SO THAT FLYING HORSE OF HIS COULD GET AWAY!
DON'T JUST STAND THERE... STOP IT!
I CAN'T! CAN'T GET A CLEAR SHOT AT IT--!
DON'T DESPAIR, FRANTIC ONE...THE FAITHFUL PINIONED STEED ISN'T GOING FOR A POSSE ...BUT, IT IS SEEN JUST THEN BY ONE OF THE EVER-WATCHFUL AVENGERS...
...WHICH IS JUST WHAT OUR ARTHURIAN STALWART EXPECTED, OF COURSE!
I THOUGHT I SAW A WINGED HORSE LAND ON THAT ROOFTOP A FEW SECONDS AGO!
BUT THEN, WHERE'S THE BLACK KNIGHT, UNLESS--
MAYBE I'D BETTER DO THE AVENGERS ASSEMBLE BIT--NOW!
YET, EVEN BEFORE THE ALERT ARCHER CAN MOVE...
IT'S A GOOD THING I ACTED QUICKLY--
--BEFORE YOU HAD A CHANCE TO WARN ANYONE!
IRON MAN'S OLD ENEMY--THE MELTER!!
HOW'D YOU GET IN THRU THAT WALL... WITHOUT SOUNDIN' THE ALARM?
WE JUST HOOKED A NEW ELECTRIC EYE THERE THIS MORNING!
WE'LL TELL YOU LATER, BOWMAN-- IF WE FEEL LIKE IT!
WE? THEN, THERE'S MORE LIKE YOU?
GOTTA CLUE IN THE OTHERS --FAST!

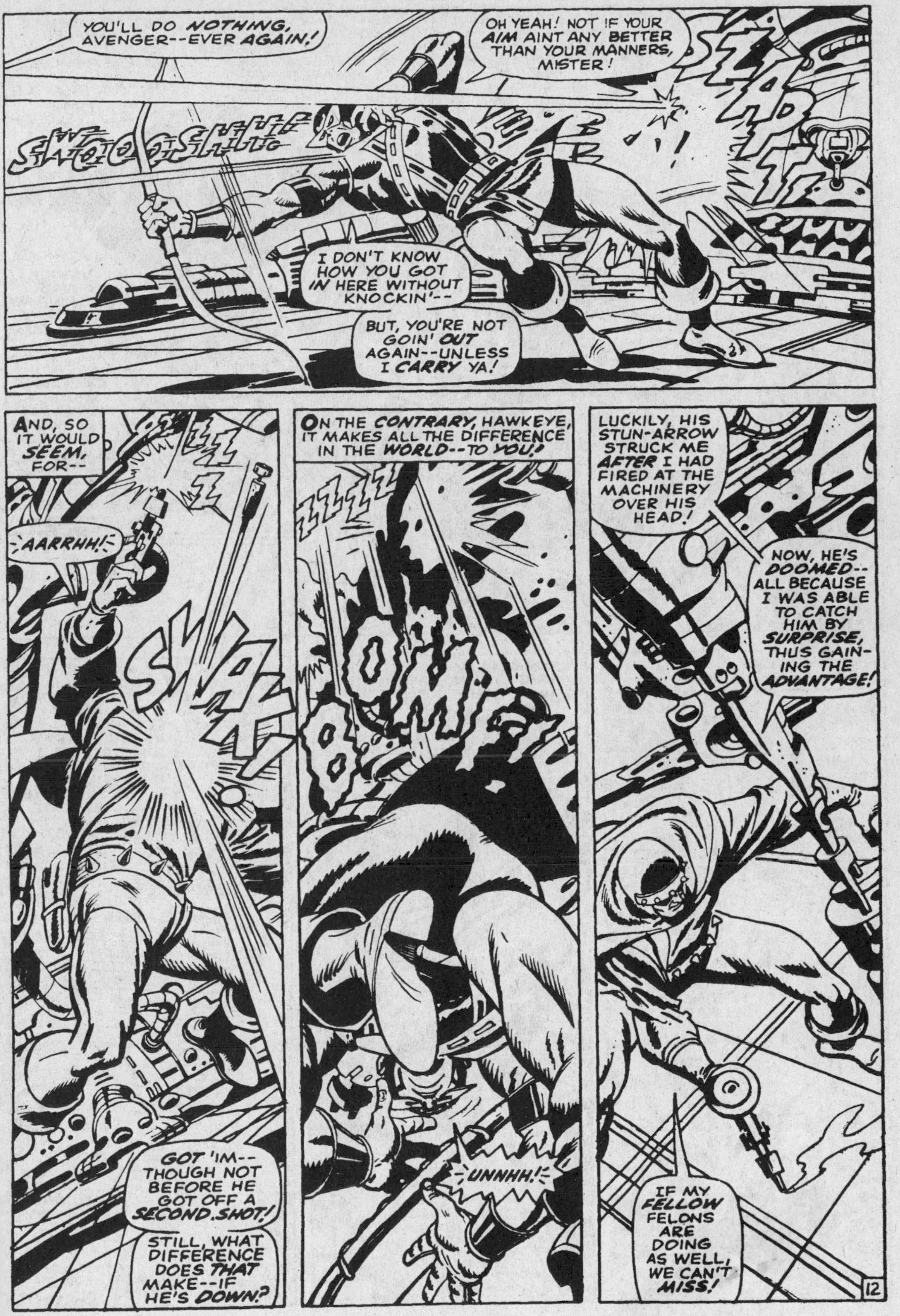
YOU'LL DO NOTHING, AVENGER--EVER AGAIN!
OH YEAH! NOT IF YOUR AIM AINT ANY BETTER THAN YOUR MANNERS, MISTER!
I DON'T KNOW HOW YOU GOT IN HERE WITHOUT KNOCKIN'--
BUT, YOU'RE NOT GOIN' OUT AGAIN--UNLESS I CARRY YA!
AND, SO IT WOULD SEEM, FOR--
AARRHH!
SWAK
GOT 'IM--THOUGH NOT BEFORE HE GOT OFF A SECOND SHOT!
STILL, WHAT DIFFERENCE DOES THAT MAKE--IF HE'S DOWN?
ON THE CONTRARY, HAWKEYE, IT MAKES ALL THE DIFFERENCE IN THE WORLD--TO YOU!
BOOM
UNNHH!
LUCKILY, HIS STUN-ARROW STRUCK ME AFTER I HAD FIRED AT THE MACHINERY OVER HIS HEAD!
NOW, HE'S DOOMED--ALL BECAUSE I WAS ABLE TO CATCH HIM BY SURPRISE, THUS GAINING THE ADVANTAGE!
IF MY FELLOW FELONS ARE DOING AS WELL, WE CAN'T MISS!
12

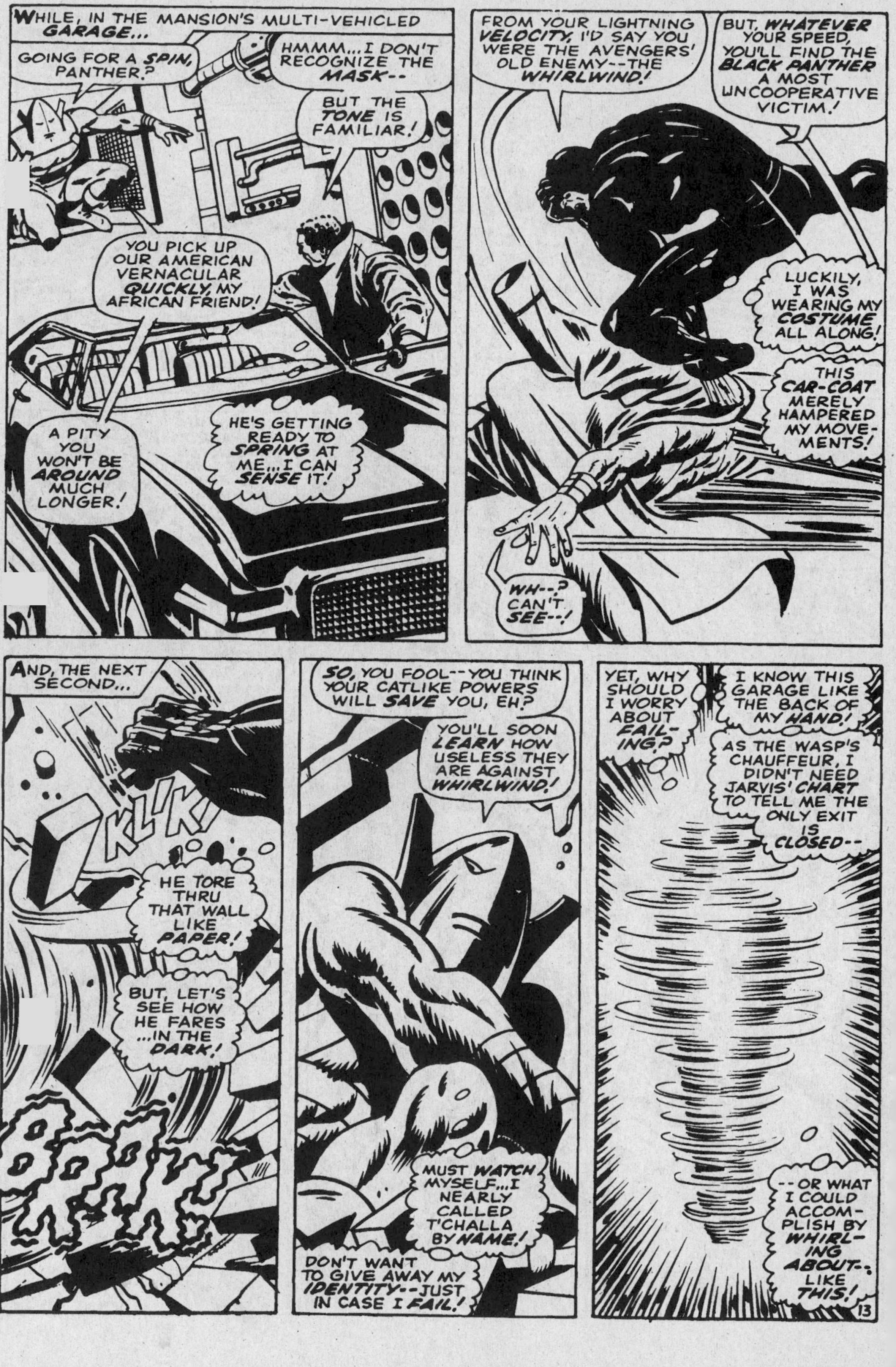

WHILE, IN THE MANSION'S MULTI-VEHICLED GARAGE...
GOING FOR A SPIN, PANTHER?
HMMM...I DON'T RECOGNIZE THE MASK--
BUT THE TONE IS FAMILIAR!
YOU PICK UP OUR AMERICAN VERNACULAR QUICKLY, MY AFRICAN FRIEND!
A PITY YOU WON'T BE AROUND MUCH LONGER!
HE'S GETTING READY TO SPRING AT ME...I CAN SENSE IT!
FROM YOUR LIGHTNING VELOCITY, I'D SAY YOU WERE THE AVENGERS' OLD ENEMY--THE WHIRLWIND!
BUT, WHATEVER YOUR SPEED, YOU'LL FIND THE BLACK PANTHER A MOST UNCOOPERATIVE VICTIM!
LUCKILY, I WAS WEARING MY COSTUME ALL ALONG!
THIS CAR-COAT MERELY HAMPERED MY MOVE-MENTS!
WH--? CAN'T SEE--!
AND, THE NEXT SECOND...
KLIK!
HE TORE THRU THAT WALL LIKE PAPER!
BUT, LET'S SEE HOW HE FARES ...IN THE DARK!
BRAK
SO, YOU FOOL--YOU THINK YOUR CATLIKE POWERS WILL SAVE YOU, EH?
YOU'LL SOON LEARN HOW USELESS THEY ARE AGAINST WHIRLWIND!
MUST WATCH MYSELF...I NEARLY CALLED T'CHALLA BY NAME!
DON'T WANT TO GIVE AWAY MY IDENTITY--JUST IN CASE I FAIL!
YET, WHY SHOULD I WORRY ABOUT FAIL-ING?
I KNOW THIS GARAGE LIKE THE BACK OF MY HAND!
AS THE WASP'S CHAUFFEUR, I DIDN'T NEED JARVIS' CHART TO TELL ME THE ONLY EXIT IS CLOSED--
--OR WHAT I COULD ACCOM-PLISH BY WHIRL-ING ABOUT-- LIKE THIS!

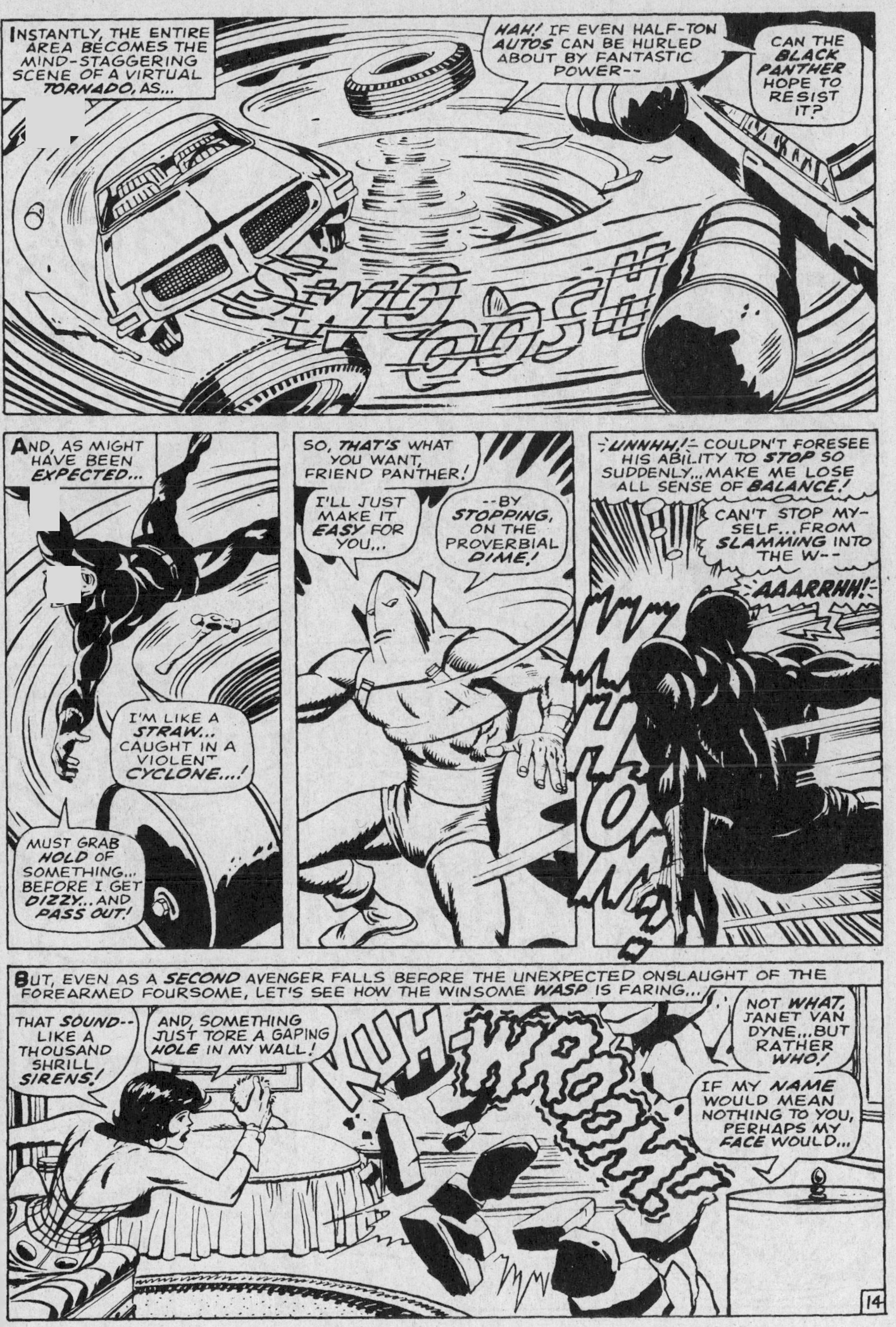

INSTANTLY, THE ENTIRE AREA BECOMES THE MIND-STAGGERING SCENE OF A VIRTUAL TORNADO, AS...
HAH! IF EVEN HALF-TON AUTOS CAN BE HURLED ABOUT BY FANTASTIC POWER--
CAN THE BLACK PANTHER HOPE TO RESIST IT?
AND, AS MIGHT HAVE BEEN EXPECTED...
I'M LIKE A STRAW... CAUGHT IN A VIOLENT CYCLONE...!
MUST GRAB HOLD OF SOMETHING... BEFORE I GET DIZZY... AND PASS OUT!
SO, THAT'S WHAT YOU WANT, FRIEND PANTHER!
I'LL JUST MAKE IT EASY FOR YOU...
--BY STOPPING, ON THE PROVERBIAL DIME!
UNNHH!-- COULDN'T FORESEE HIS ABILITY TO STOP SO SUDDENLY... MAKE ME LOSE ALL SENSE OF BALANCE!
CAN'T STOP MY-SELF... FROM SLAMMING INTO THE W--
AAARRHH!
BUT, EVEN AS A SECOND AVENGER FALLS BEFORE THE UNEXPECTED ONSLAUGHT OF THE FOREARMED FOURSOME, LET'S SEE HOW THE WINSOME WASP IS FARING...
THAT SOUND-- LIKE A THOUSAND SHRILL SIRENS!
AND, SOMETHING JUST TORE A GAPING HOLE IN MY WALL!
NOT WHAT, JANET VAN DYNE... BUT RATHER WHO!
IF MY NAME WOULD MEAN NOTHING TO YOU, PERHAPS MY FACE WOULD...

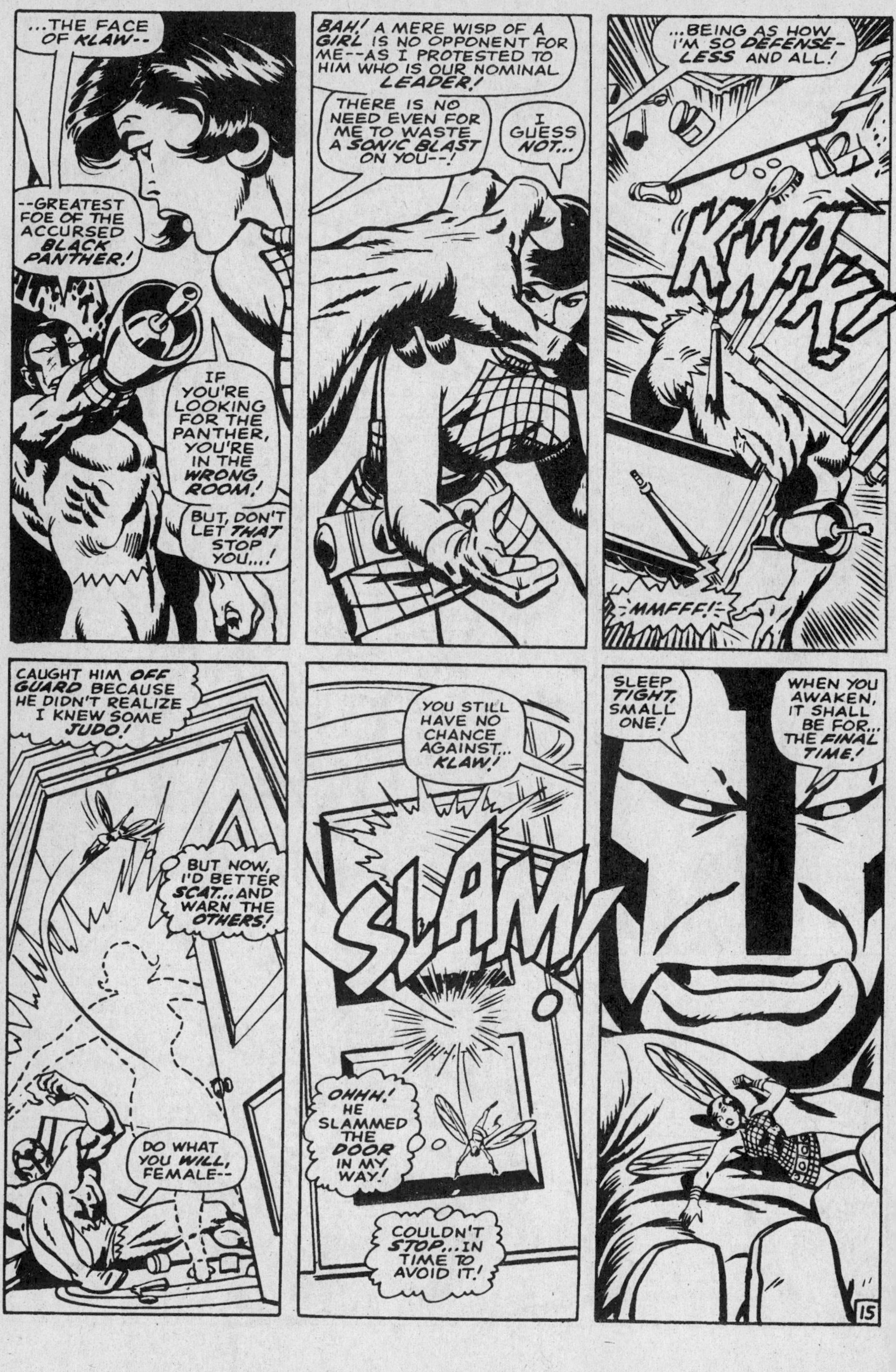
...THE FACE OF KLAW--
--GREATEST FOE OF THE ACCURSED BLACK PANTHER!
IF YOU'RE LOOKING FOR THE PANTHER, YOU'RE IN THE WRONG ROOM!
BUT, DON'T LET THAT STOP YOU...!
BAH! A MERE WISP OF A GIRL IS NO OPPONENT FOR ME--AS I PROTESTED TO HIM WHO IS OUR NOMINAL LEADER!
THERE IS NO NEED EVEN FOR ME TO WASTE A SONIC BLAST ON YOU--!
I GUESS NOT...
...BEING AS HOW I'M SO DEFENSE-LESS AND ALL!
KWAK!
MMFFF!
CAUGHT HIM OFF GUARD BECAUSE HE DIDN'T REALIZE I KNEW SOME JUDO!
BUT NOW, I'D BETTER SCAT...AND WARN THE OTHERS!
DO WHAT YOU WILL, FEMALE--
YOU STILL HAVE NO CHANCE AGAINST... KLAW!
SLAM!
OHHH! HE SLAMMED THE DOOR IN MY WAY!
COULDN'T STOP...IN TIME TO AVOID IT!
SLEEP TIGHT, SMALL ONE!
WHEN YOU AWAKEN, IT SHALL BE FOR... THE FINAL TIME!
15

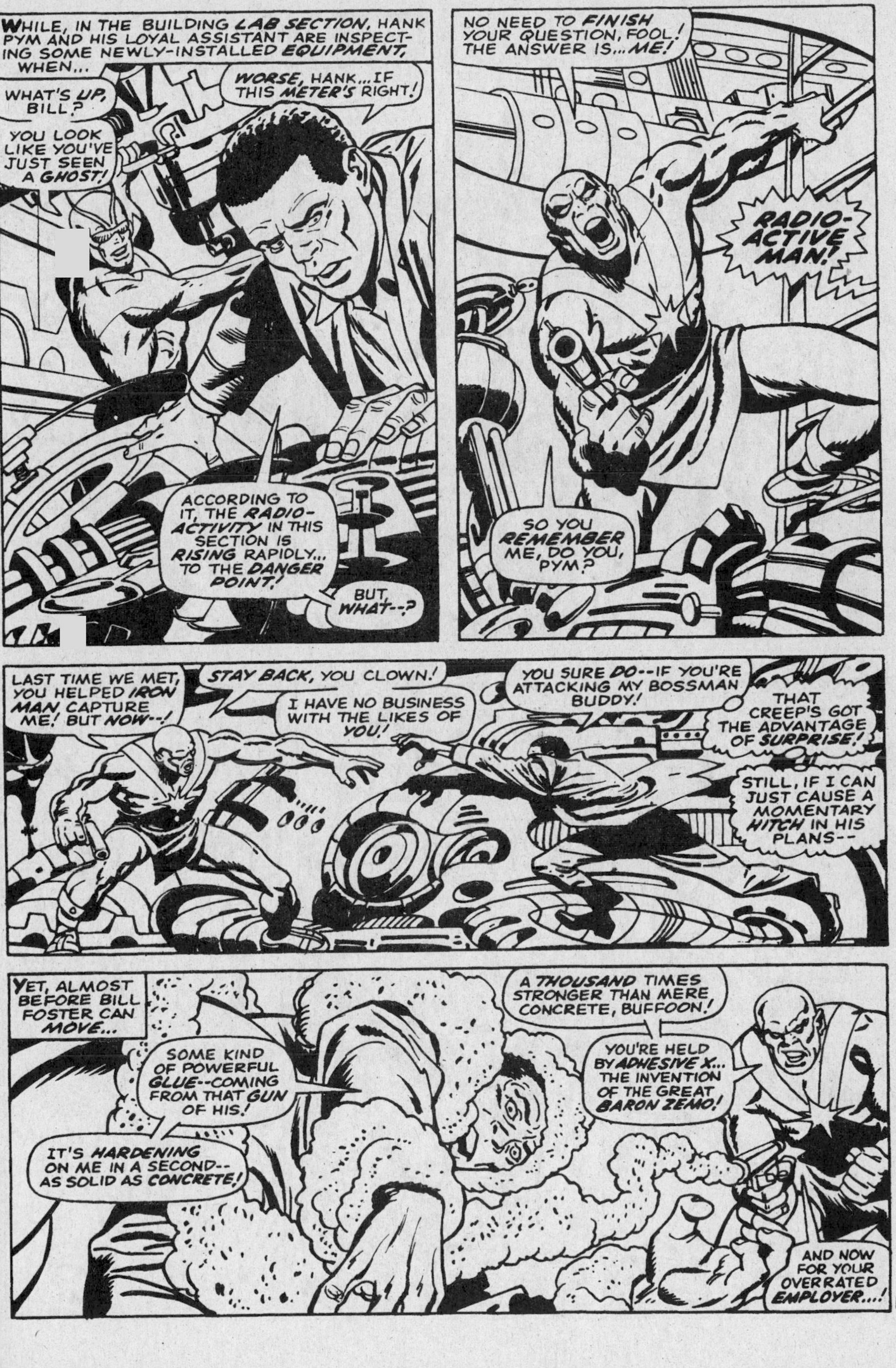

WHILE, IN THE BUILDING LAB SECTION, HANK PYM AND HIS LOYAL ASSISTANT ARE INSPECTING SOME NEWLY-INSTALLED EQUIPMENT, WHEN...
WHAT'S UP, BILL?
YOU LOOK LIKE YOU'VE JUST SEEN A GHOST!
WORSE, HANK...IF THIS METER'S RIGHT!
ACCORDING TO IT, THE RADIO-ACTIVITY IN THIS SECTION IS RISING RAPIDLY... TO THE DANGER POINT!
BUT, WHAT--?
NO NEED TO FINISH YOUR QUESTION, FOOL! THE ANSWER IS...ME!
RADIO-ACTIVE MAN!
SO YOU REMEMBER ME, DO YOU, PYM?
LAST TIME WE MET, YOU HELPED IRON MAN CAPTURE ME! BUT NOW--!
STAY BACK, YOU CLOWN!
I HAVE NO BUSINESS WITH THE LIKES OF YOU!
YOU SURE DO--IF YOU'RE ATTACKING MY BOSSMAN BUDDY!
THAT CREEP'S GOT THE ADVANTAGE OF SURPRISE!
STILL, IF I CAN JUST CAUSE A MOMENTARY HITCH IN HIS PLANS--
YET, ALMOST BEFORE BILL FOSTER CAN MOVE...
SOME KIND OF POWERFUL GLUE--COMING FROM THAT GUN OF HIS!
IT'S HARDENING ON ME IN A SECOND--AS SOLID AS CONCRETE!
A THOUSAND TIMES STRONGER THAN MERE CONCRETE, BUFFOON!
YOU'RE HELD BY ADHESIVE X... THE INVENTION OF THE GREAT BARON ZEMO!
AND NOW FOR YOUR OVERRATED EMPLOYER...!

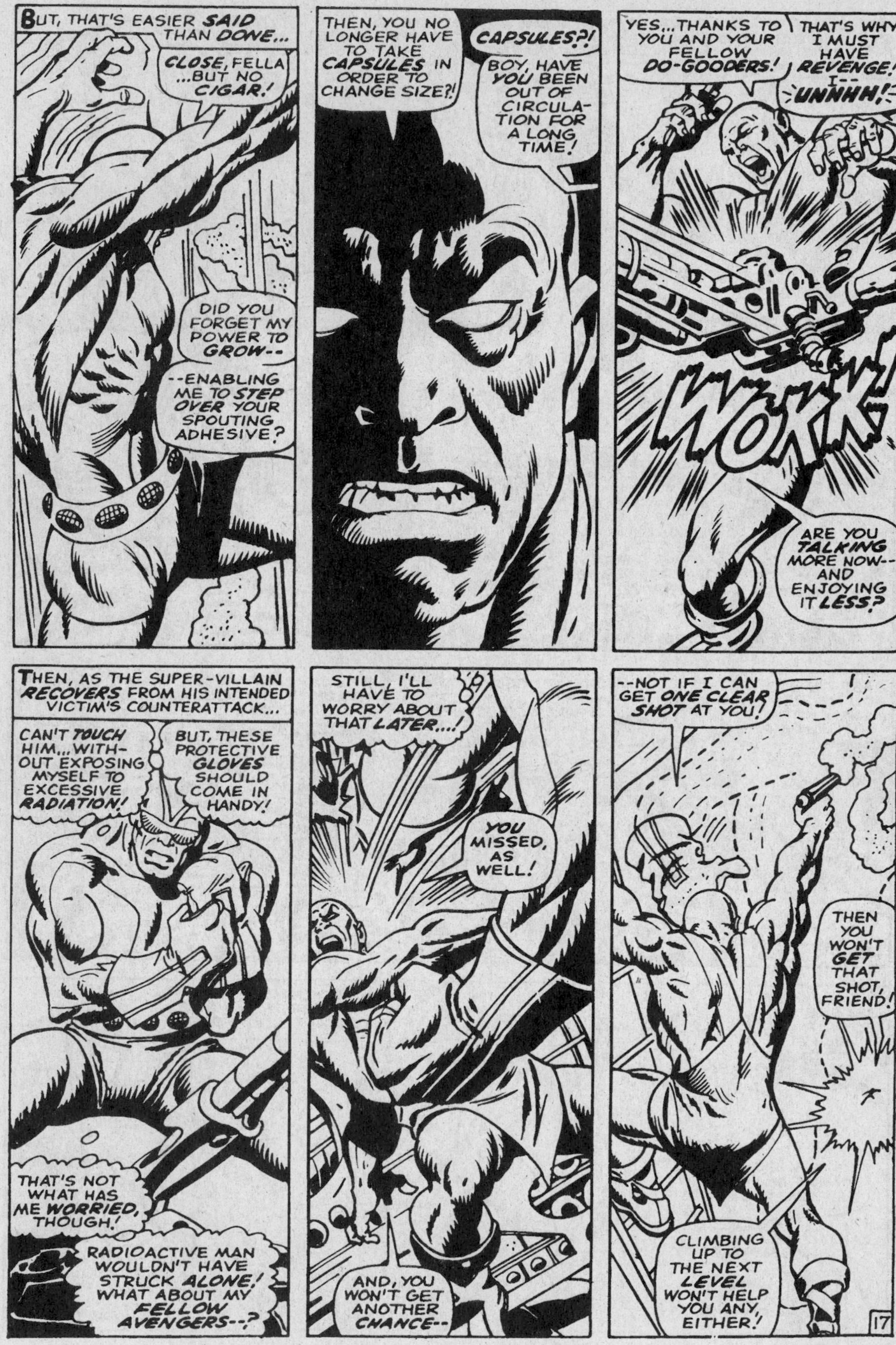
BUT, THAT'S EASIER SAID THAN DONE...
CLOSE, FELLA ...BUT NO CIGAR!
DID YOU FORGET MY POWER TO GROW--
--ENABLING ME TO STEP OVER YOUR SPOUTING ADHESIVE?
THEN, YOU NO LONGER HAVE TO TAKE CAPSULES IN ORDER TO CHANGE SIZE?!
CAPSULES?!
BOY, HAVE YOU BEEN OUT OF CIRCULATION FOR A LONG TIME!
YES...THANKS TO YOU AND YOUR FELLOW DO-GOODERS!
THAT'S WHY I MUST HAVE REVENGE! I--
UNNHH!
WOKK
ARE YOU TALKING MORE NOW--AND ENJOYING IT LESS?
THEN, AS THE SUPER-VILLAIN RECOVERS FROM HIS INTENDED VICTIM'S COUNTERATTACK...
CAN'T TOUCH HIM...WITHOUT EXPOSING MYSELF TO EXCESSIVE RADIATION!
BUT, THESE PROTECTIVE GLOVES SHOULD COME IN HANDY!
THAT'S NOT WHAT HAS ME WORRIED, THOUGH!
RADIOACTIVE MAN WOULDN'T HAVE STRUCK ALONE! WHAT ABOUT MY FELLOW AVENGERS--?
STILL, I'LL HAVE TO WORRY ABOUT THAT LATER...!
YOU MISSED, AS WELL!
AND, YOU WON'T GET ANOTHER CHANCE--
--NOT IF I CAN GET ONE CLEAR SHOT AT YOU!
THEN YOU WON'T GET THAT SHOT, FRIEND!
CLIMBING UP TO THE NEXT LEVEL WON'T HELP YOU ANY, EITHER!
17

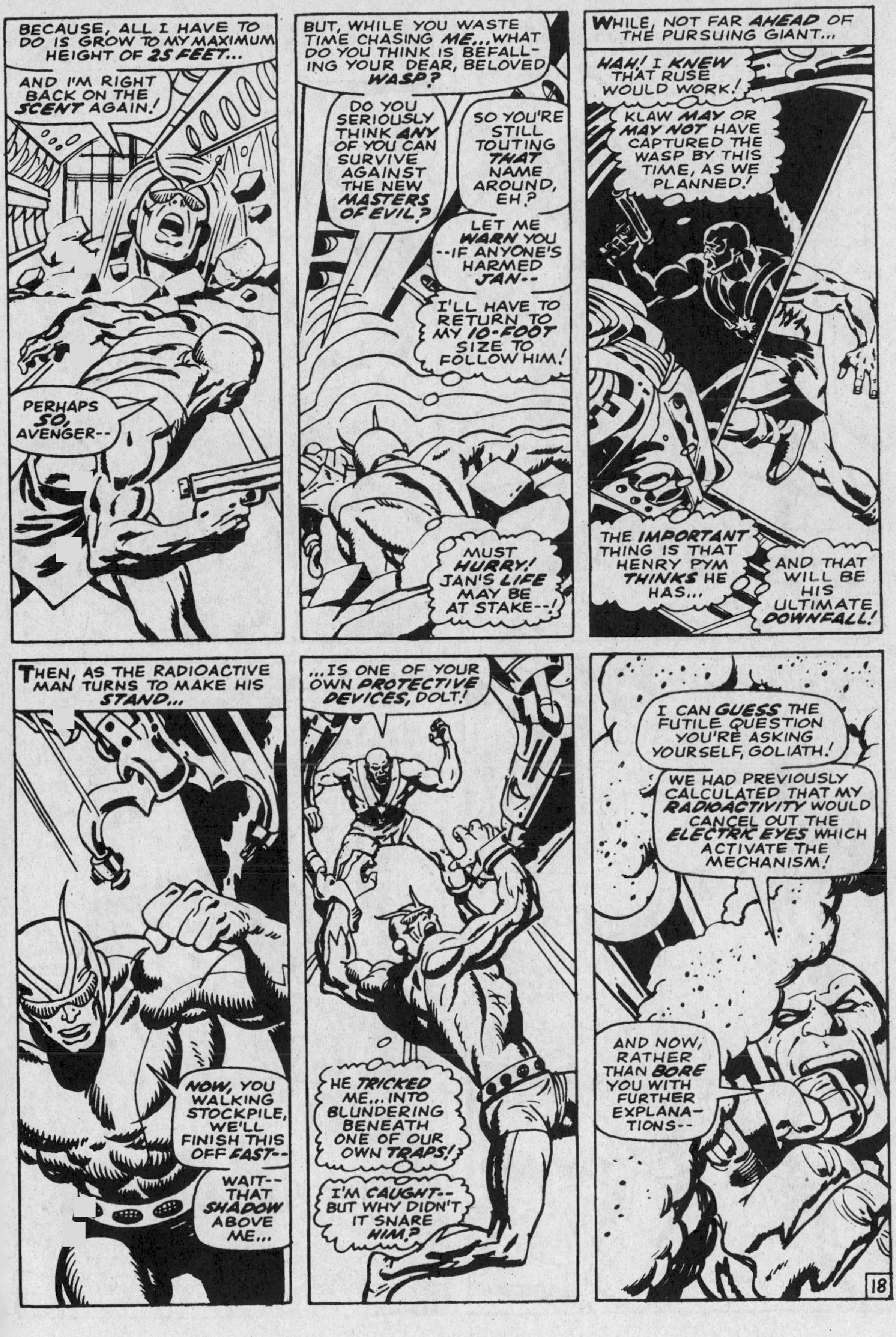
BECAUSE, ALL I HAVE TO DO IS GROW TO MY MAXIMUM HEIGHT OF 25 FEET...
AND I'M RIGHT BACK ON THE SCENT AGAIN!
PERHAPS SO, AVENGER--
BUT, WHILE YOU WASTE TIME CHASING ME... WHAT DO YOU THINK IS BEFALLING YOUR DEAR, BELOVED WASP?
DO YOU SERIOUSLY THINK ANY OF YOU CAN SURVIVE AGAINST THE NEW MASTERS OF EVIL?
SO YOU'RE STILL TOUTING THAT NAME AROUND, EH?
LET ME WARN YOU --IF ANYONE'S HARMED JAN--
I'LL HAVE TO RETURN TO MY 10-FOOT SIZE TO FOLLOW HIM!
MUST HURRY! JAN'S LIFE MAY BE AT STAKE--!
WHILE, NOT FAR AHEAD OF THE PURSUING GIANT...
HAH! I KNEW THAT RUSE WOULD WORK!
KLAW MAY OR MAY NOT HAVE CAPTURED THE WASP BY THIS TIME, AS WE PLANNED!
THE IMPORTANT THING IS THAT HENRY PYM THINKS HE HAS...
AND THAT WILL BE HIS ULTIMATE DOWNFALL!
THEN, AS THE RADIOACTIVE MAN TURNS TO MAKE HIS STAND...
NOW, YOU WALKING STOCKPILE, WE'LL FINISH THIS OFF FAST--
WAIT-- THAT SHADOW ABOVE ME...
...IS ONE OF YOUR OWN PROTECTIVE DEVICES, DOLT!
HE TRICKED ME... INTO BLUNDERING BENEATH ONE OF OUR OWN TRAPS!
I'M CAUGHT-- BUT WHY DIDN'T IT SNARE HIM?
I CAN GUESS THE FUTILE QUESTION YOU'RE ASKING YOURSELF, GOLIATH!
WE HAD PREVIOUSLY CALCULATED THAT MY RADIOACTIVITY WOULD CANCEL OUT THE ELECTRIC EYES WHICH ACTIVATE THE MECHANISM!
AND NOW, RATHER THAN BORE YOU WITH FURTHER EXPLANA-TIONS--
18

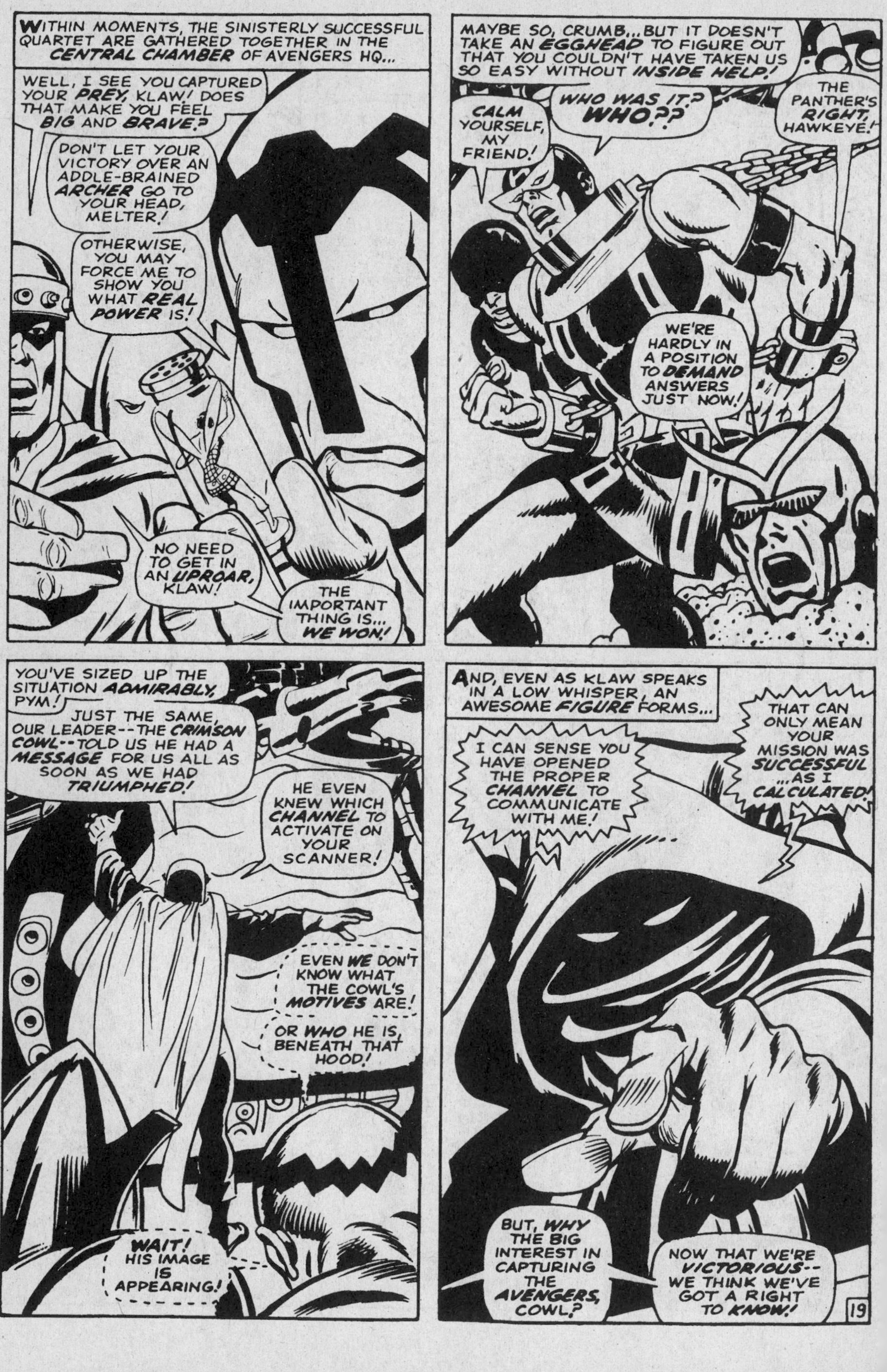
WITHIN MOMENTS, THE SINISTERLY SUCCESSFUL QUARTET ARE GATHERED TOGETHER IN THE CENTRAL CHAMBER OF AVENGERS HQ...
WELL, I SEE YOU CAPTURED YOUR PREY, KLAW! DOES THAT MAKE YOU FEEL BIG AND BRAVE?
DON'T LET YOUR VICTORY OVER AN ADDLE-BRAINED ARCHER GO TO YOUR HEAD, MELTER!
OTHERWISE, YOU MAY FORCE ME TO SHOW YOU WHAT REAL POWER IS!
NO NEED TO GET IN AN UPROAR, KLAW!
THE IMPORTANT THING IS... WE WON!
MAYBE SO, CRUMB... BUT IT DOESN'T TAKE AN EGGHEAD TO FIGURE OUT THAT YOU COULDN'T HAVE TAKEN US SO EASY WITHOUT INSIDE HELP!
WHO WAS IT? WHO??
CALM YOURSELF, MY FRIEND!
THE PANTHER'S RIGHT, HAWKEYE!
WE'RE HARDLY IN A POSITION TO DEMAND ANSWERS JUST NOW!
YOU'VE SIZED UP THE SITUATION ADMIRABLY, PYM!
JUST THE SAME, OUR LEADER--THE CRIMSON COWL--TOLD US HE HAD A MESSAGE FOR US ALL AS SOON AS WE HAD TRIUMPHED!
HE EVEN KNEW WHICH CHANNEL TO ACTIVATE ON YOUR SCANNER!
EVEN WE DON'T KNOW WHAT THE COWL'S MOTIVES ARE!
OR WHO HE IS, BENEATH THAT HOOD!
WAIT! HIS IMAGE IS APPEARING!
AND, EVEN AS KLAW SPEAKS IN A LOW WHISPER, AN AWESOME FIGURE FORMS...
I CAN SENSE YOU HAVE OPENED THE PROPER CHANNEL TO COMMUNICATE WITH ME!
THAT CAN ONLY MEAN YOUR MISSION WAS SUCCESSFUL ...AS I CALCULATED!
BUT, WHY THE BIG INTEREST IN CAPTURING THE AVENGERS, COWL?
NOW THAT WE'RE VICTORIOUS-- WE THINK WE'VE GOT A RIGHT TO KNOW!
19

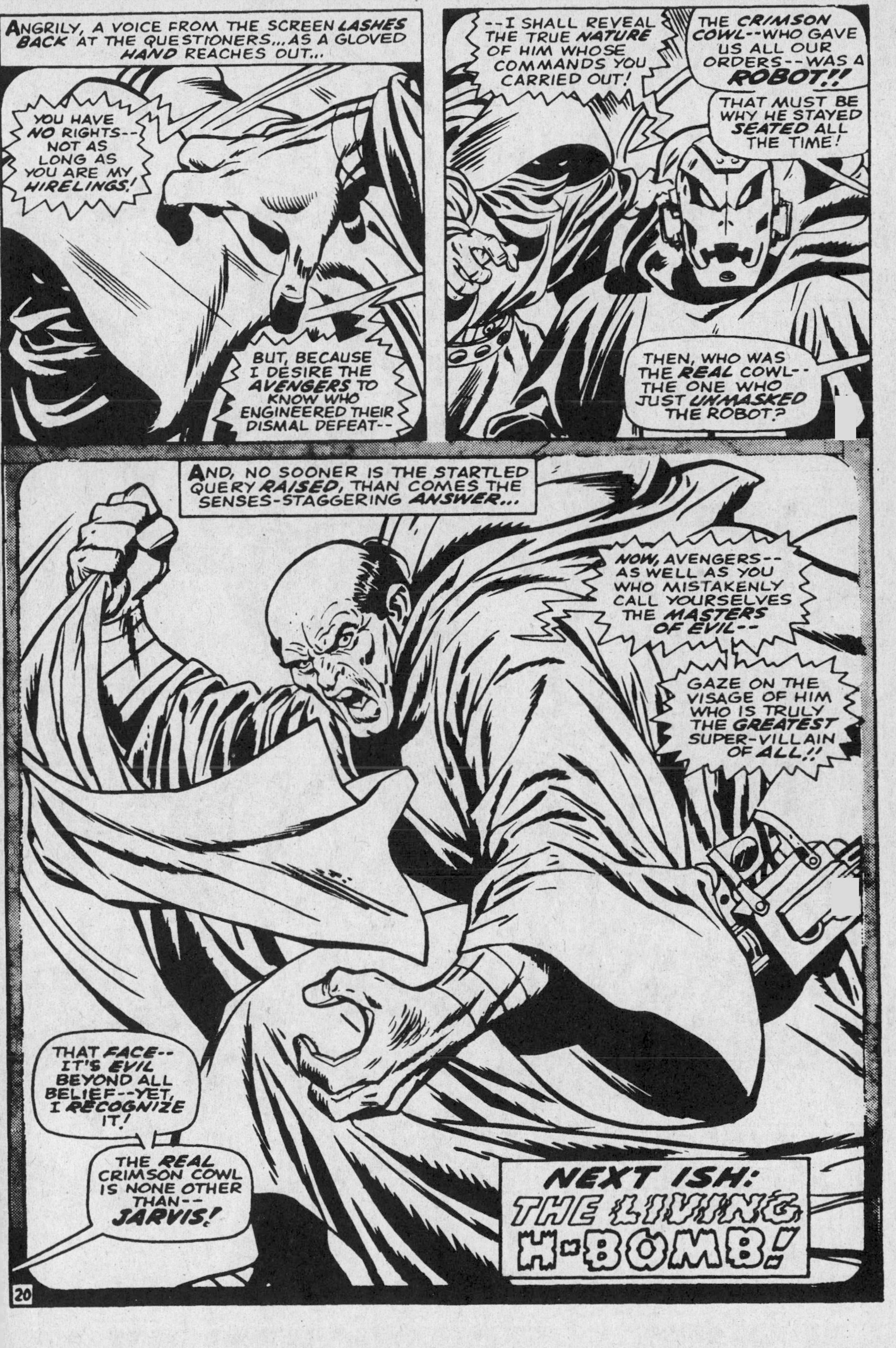
ANGRILY, A VOICE FROM THE SCREEN LASHES BACK AT THE QUESTIONERS... AS A GLOVED HAND REACHES OUT...
YOU HAVE NO RIGHTS-- NOT AS LONG AS YOU ARE MY HIRELINGS!
BUT, BECAUSE I DESIRE THE AVENGERS TO KNOW WHO ENGINEERED THEIR DISMAL DEFEAT--
--I SHALL REVEAL THE TRUE NATURE OF HIM WHOSE COMMANDS YOU CARRIED OUT!
THE CRIMSON COWL--WHO GAVE US ALL OUR ORDERS--WAS A ROBOT!!
THAT MUST BE WHY HE STAYED SEATED ALL THE TIME!
THEN, WHO WAS THE REAL COWL-- THE ONE WHO JUST UNMASKED THE ROBOT?
AND, NO SOONER IS THE STARTLED QUERY RAISED, THAN COMES THE SENSES-STAGGERING ANSWER...
NOW, AVENGERS-- AS WELL AS YOU WHO MISTAKENLY CALL YOURSELVES THE MASTERS OF EVIL--
GAZE ON THE VISAGE OF HIM WHO IS TRULY THE GREATEST SUPER-VILLAIN OF ALL!!
THAT FACE-- IT'S EVIL BEYOND ALL BELIEF--YET, I RECOGNIZE IT!
THE REAL CRIMSON COWL IS NONE OTHER THAN-- JARVIS!
NEXT ISH: THE LIVING H-BOMB!
20

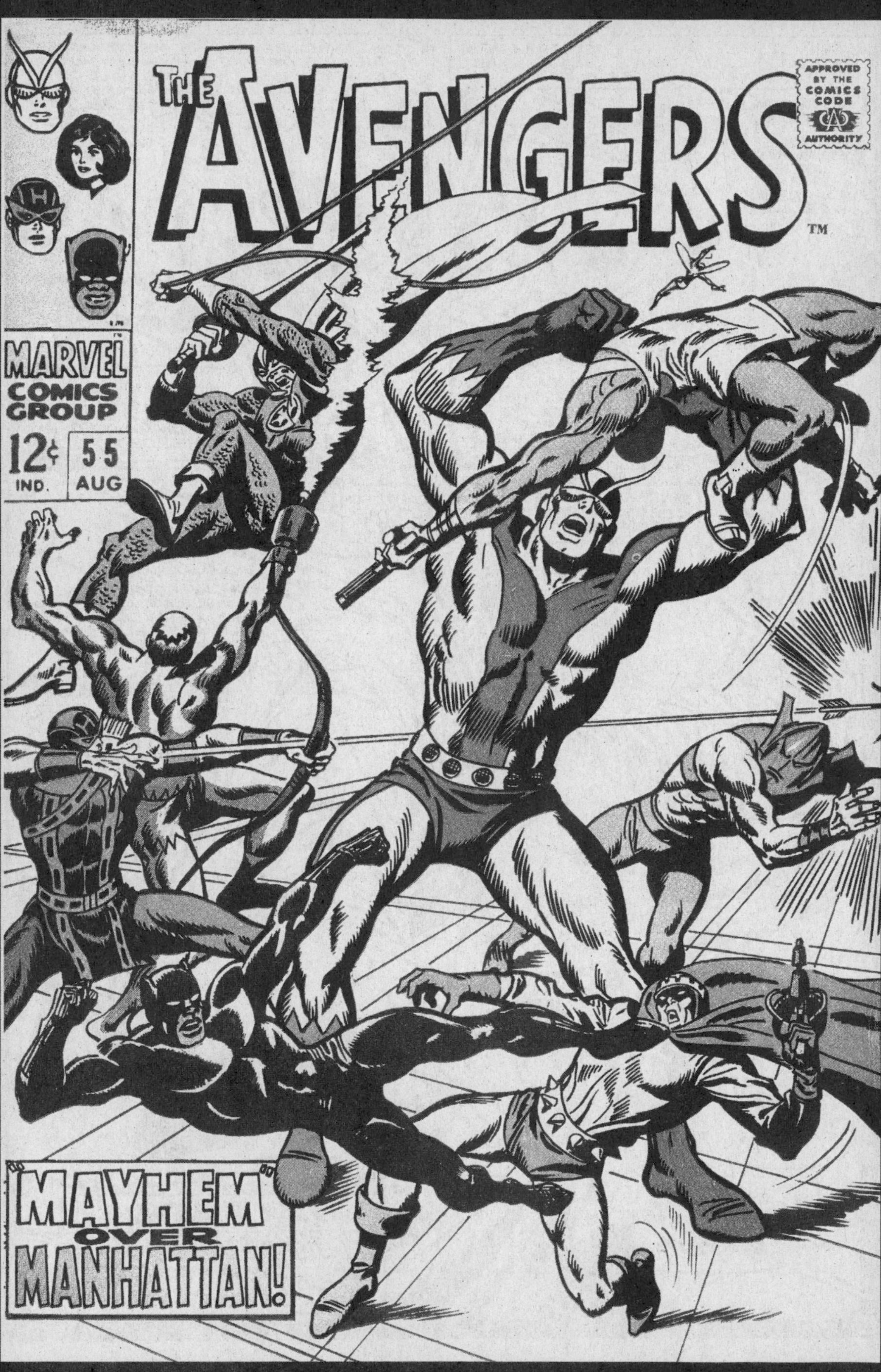
THE AVENGERS
TM
APPROVED BY THE COMICS CODE AUTHORITY
MARVEL COMICS GROUP
12¢ IND.
55 AUG
"MAYHEM" OVER MANHATTAN!

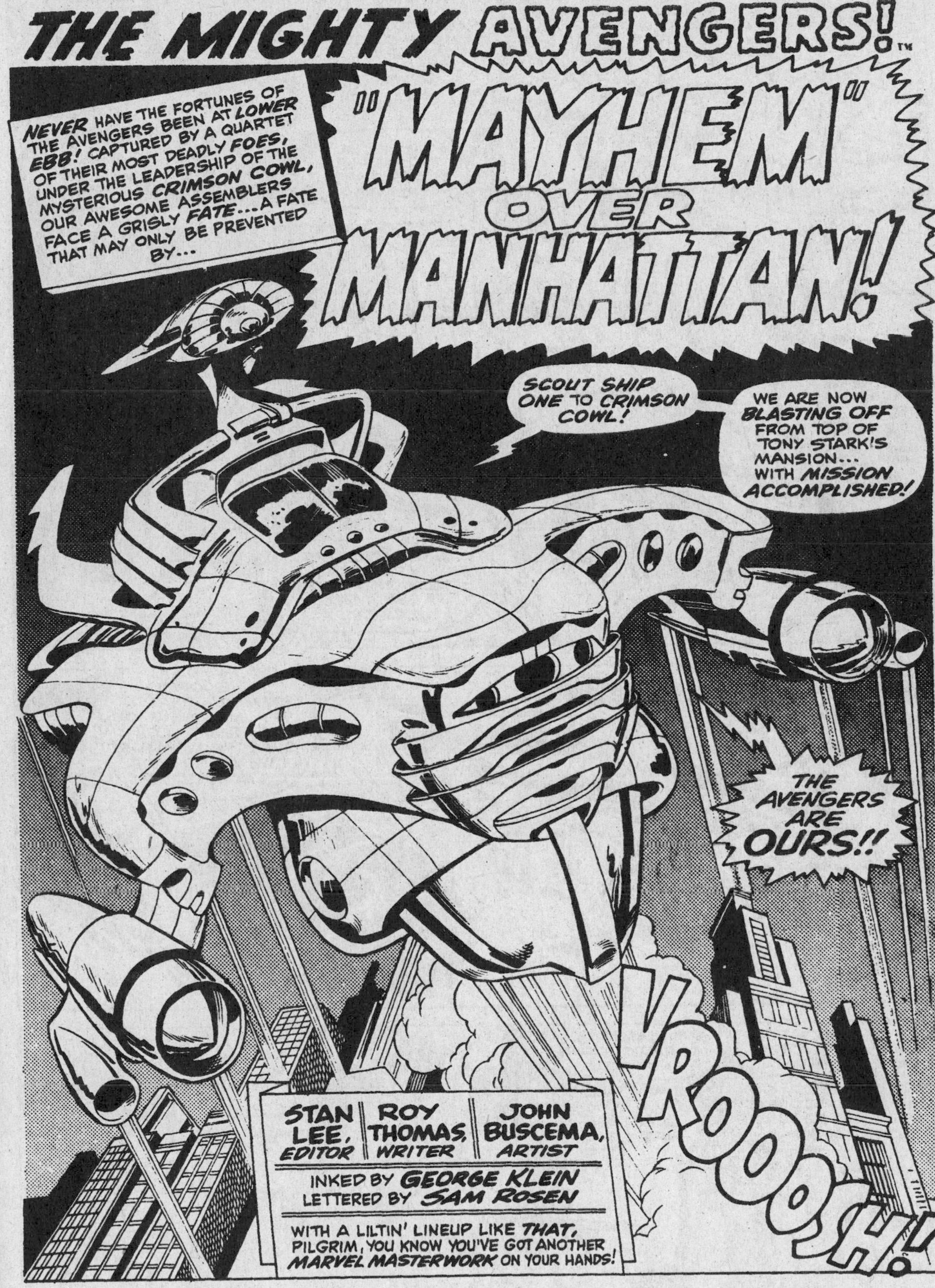
THE MIGHTY AVENGERS!™
NEVER HAVE THE FORTUNES OF THE AVENGERS BEEN AT LOWER EBB! CAPTURED BY A QUARTET OF THEIR MOST DEADLY FOES, UNDER THE LEADERSHIP OF THE MYSTERIOUS CRIMSON COWL, OUR AWESOME ASSEMBLERS FACE A GRISLY FATE... A FATE THAT MAY ONLY BE PREVENTED BY...
"MAYHEM" OVER MANHATTAN!
SCOUT SHIP ONE TO CRIMSON COWL!
WE ARE NOW BLASTING OFF FROM TOP OF TONY STARK'S MANSION... WITH MISSION ACCOMPLISHED!
THE AVENGERS ARE OURS!!
STAN LEE, EDITOR
ROY THOMAS, WRITER
JOHN BUSCEMA, ARTIST
INKED BY GEORGE KLEIN
LETTERED BY SAM ROSEN
WITH A LILTIN' LINEUP LIKE THAT, PILGRIM, YOU KNOW YOU'VE GOT ANOTHER MARVEL MASTERWORK ON YOUR HANDS!
VROOOOSH!

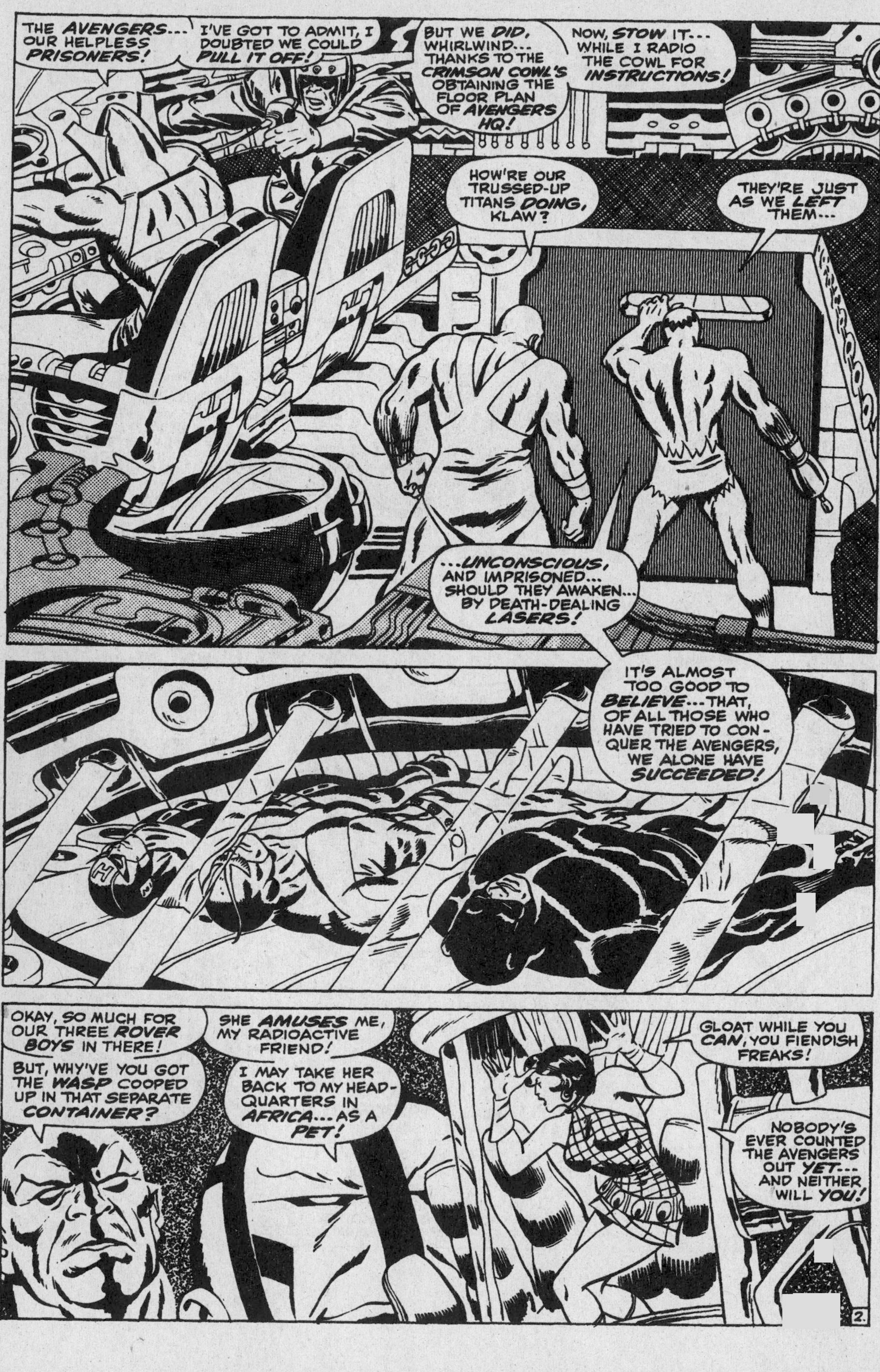
THE AVENGERS... OUR HELPLESS PRISONERS!
I'VE GOT TO ADMIT, I DOUBTED WE COULD PULL IT OFF!
BUT WE DID, WHIRLWIND... THANKS TO THE CRIMSON COWL'S OBTAINING THE FLOOR PLAN OF AVENGERS HQ!
NOW, STOW IT... WHILE I RADIO THE COWL FOR INSTRUCTIONS!
HOW'RE OUR TRUSSED-UP TITANS DOING, KLAW?
THEY'RE JUST AS WE LEFT THEM...
...UNCONSCIOUS, AND IMPRISONED... SHOULD THEY AWAKEN... BY DEATH-DEALING LASERS!
IT'S ALMOST TOO GOOD TO BELIEVE... THAT, OF ALL THOSE WHO HAVE TRIED TO CONQUER THE AVENGERS, WE ALONE HAVE SUCCEEDED!
OKAY, SO MUCH FOR OUR THREE ROVER BOYS IN THERE!
BUT, WHY'VE YOU GOT THE WASP COOPED UP IN THAT SEPARATE CONTAINER?
SHE AMUSES ME, MY RADIOACTIVE FRIEND!
I MAY TAKE HER BACK TO MY HEADQUARTERS IN AFRICA... AS A PET!
GLOAT WHILE YOU CAN, YOU FIENDISH FREAKS!
NOBODY'S EVER COUNTED THE AVENGERS OUT YET... AND NEITHER WILL YOU!

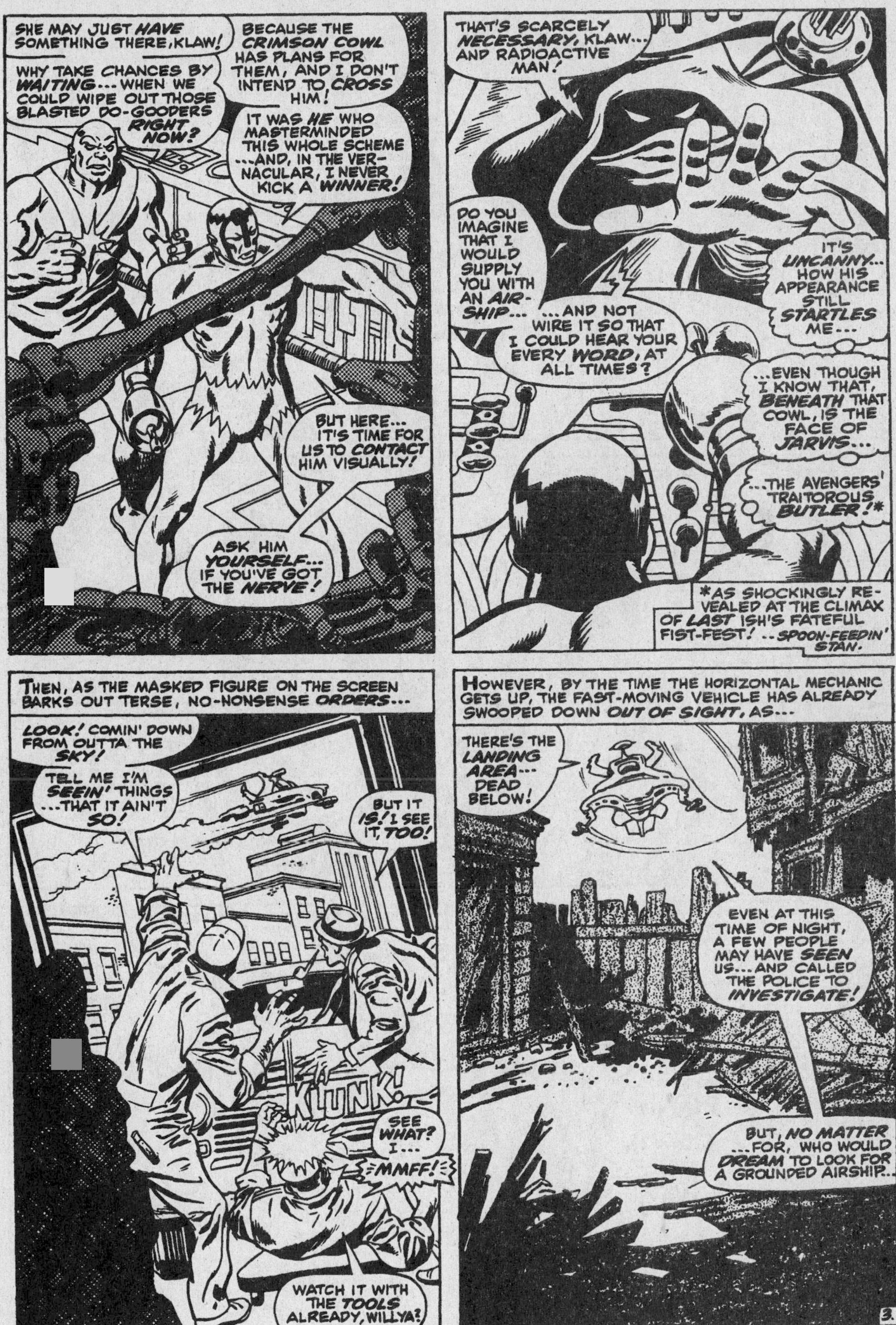
SHE MAY JUST HAVE SOMETHING THERE, KLAW!
WHY TAKE CHANCES BY WAITING... WHEN WE COULD WIPE OUT THOSE BLASTED DO-GOODERS RIGHT NOW?
BECAUSE THE CRIMSON COWL HAS PLANS FOR THEM, AND I DON'T INTEND TO CROSS HIM!
IT WAS HE WHO MASTERMINDED THIS WHOLE SCHEME ...AND, IN THE VERNACULAR, I NEVER KICK A WINNER!
BUT HERE... IT'S TIME FOR US TO CONTACT HIM VISUALLY!
ASK HIM YOURSELF... IF YOU'VE GOT THE NERVE!
THAT'S SCARCELY NECESSARY, KLAW... AND RADIOACTIVE MAN!
DO YOU IMAGINE THAT I WOULD SUPPLY YOU WITH AN AIR-SHIP...
...AND NOT WIRE IT SO THAT I COULD HEAR YOUR EVERY WORD, AT ALL TIMES?
IT'S UNCANNY... HOW HIS APPEARANCE STILL STARTLES ME---
...EVEN THOUGH I KNOW THAT, BENEATH THAT COWL, IS THE FACE OF JARVIS...
...THE AVENGERS' TRAITOROUS BUTLER!*
*AS SHOCKINGLY REVEALED AT THE CLIMAX OF LAST ISH'S FATEFUL FIST-FEST! --SPOON-FEEDIN' STAN.
THEN, AS THE MASKED FIGURE ON THE SCREEN BARKS OUT TERSE, NO-NONSENSE ORDERS...
LOOK! COMIN' DOWN FROM OUTTA THE SKY!
TELL ME I'M SEEIN' THINGS ...THAT IT AIN'T SO!
BUT IT IS! I SEE IT, TOO!
KLUNK!
SEE WHAT? I...
MMFF!
WATCH IT WITH THE TOOLS ALREADY, WILLYA?
HOWEVER, BY THE TIME THE HORIZONTAL MECHANIC GETS UP, THE FAST-MOVING VEHICLE HAS ALREADY SWOOPED DOWN OUT OF SIGHT, AS...
THERE'S THE LANDING AREA--- DEAD BELOW!
EVEN AT THIS TIME OF NIGHT, A FEW PEOPLE MAY HAVE SEEN US... AND CALLED THE POLICE TO INVESTIGATE!
BUT, NO MATTER ...FOR, WHO WOULD DREAM TO LOOK FOR A GROUNDED AIRSHIP...
3.

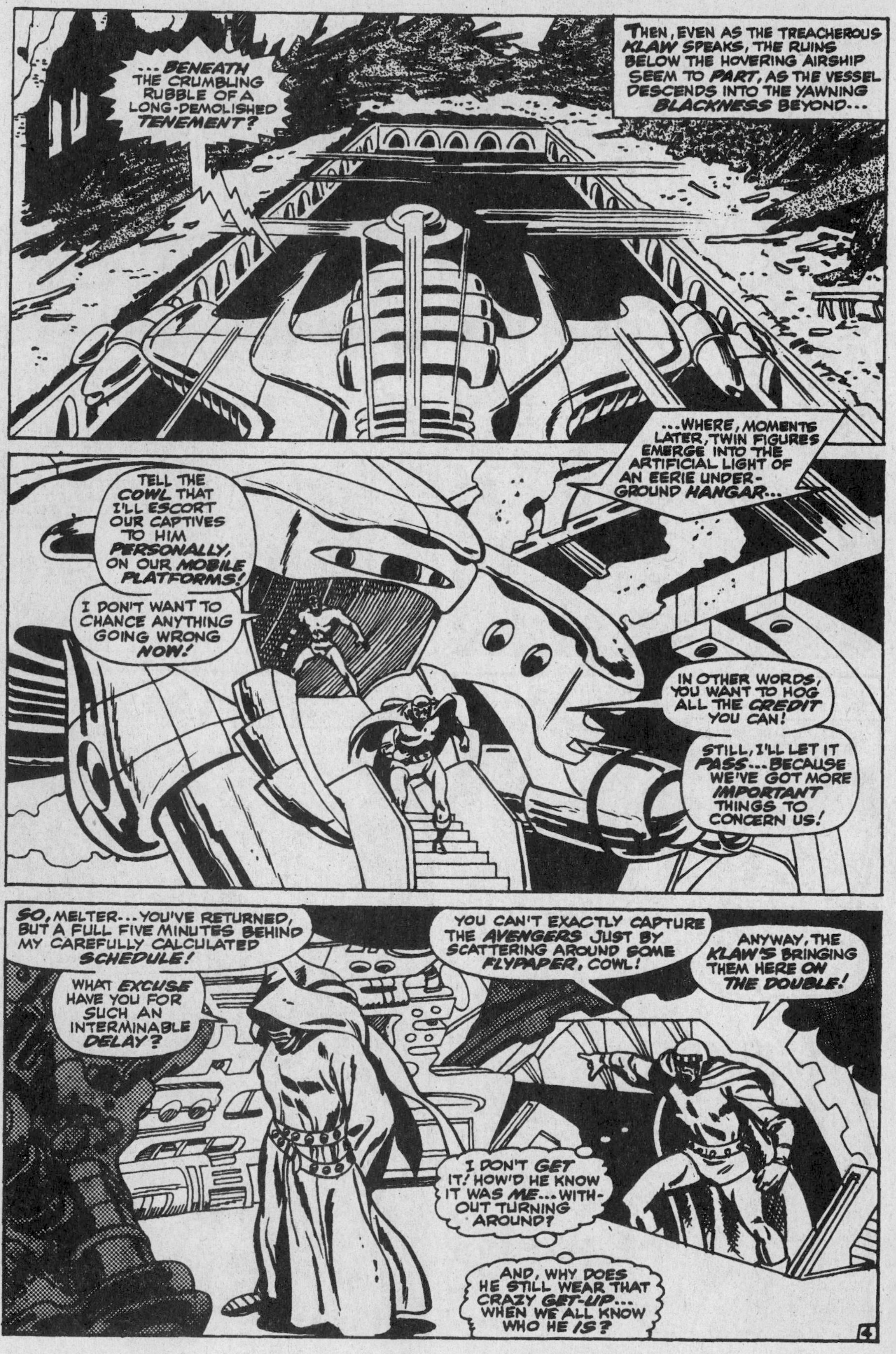
...BENEATH THE CRUMBLING RUBBLE OF A LONG-DEMOLISHED TENEMENT?
THEN, EVEN AS THE TREACHEROUS KLAW SPEAKS, THE RUINS BELOW THE HOVERING AIRSHIP SEEM TO PART, AS THE VESSEL DESCENDS INTO THE YAWNING BLACKNESS BEYOND...
...WHERE, MOMENTS LATER, TWIN FIGURES EMERGE INTO THE ARTIFICIAL LIGHT OF AN EERIE UNDER-GROUND HANGAR...
TELL THE COWL THAT I'LL ESCORT OUR CAPTIVES TO HIM PERSONALLY, ON OUR MOBILE PLATFORMS!
I DON'T WANT TO CHANCE ANYTHING GOING WRONG NOW!
IN OTHER WORDS, YOU WANT TO HOG ALL THE CREDIT YOU CAN!
STILL, I'LL LET IT PASS... BECAUSE WE'VE GOT MORE IMPORTANT THINGS TO CONCERN US!
SO, MELTER... YOU'VE RETURNED, BUT A FULL FIVE MINUTES BEHIND MY CAREFULLY CALCULATED SCHEDULE!
WHAT EXCUSE HAVE YOU FOR SUCH AN INTERMINABLE DELAY?
YOU CAN'T EXACTLY CAPTURE THE AVENGERS JUST BY SCATTERING AROUND SOME FLYPAPER, COWL!
ANYWAY, THE KLAW'S BRINGING THEM HERE ON THE DOUBLE!
I DON'T GET IT! HOW'D HE KNOW IT WAS ME... WITH-OUT TURNING AROUND?
AND, WHY DOES HE STILL WEAR THAT CRAZY GET-UP... WHEN WE ALL KNOW WHO HE IS?
6

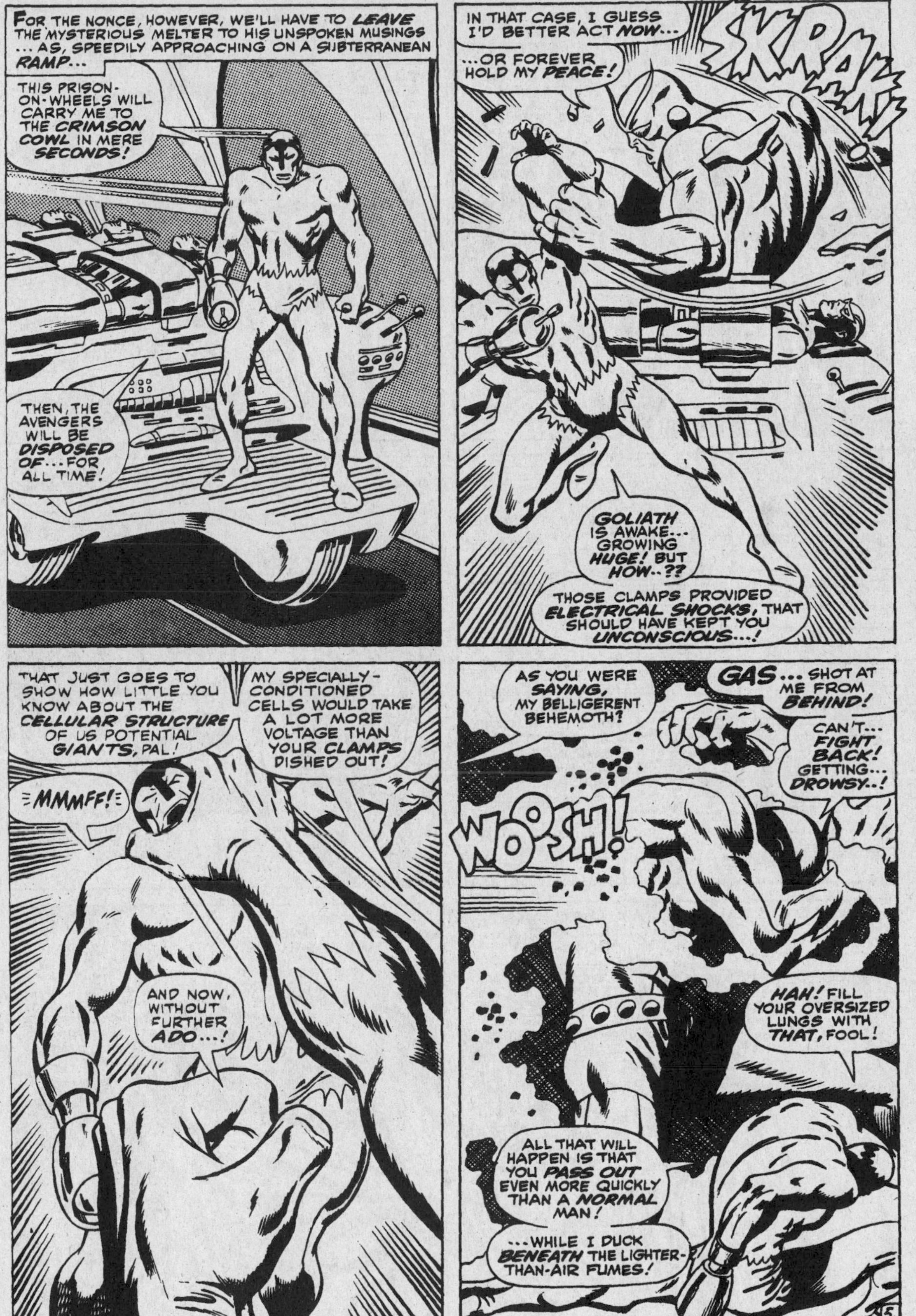
FOR THE NONCE, HOWEVER, WE'LL HAVE TO LEAVE THE MYSTERIOUS MELTER TO HIS UNSPOKEN MUSINGS ... AS, SPEEDILY APPROACHING ON A SUBTERRANEAN RAMP...
THIS PRISON-ON-WHEELS WILL CARRY ME TO THE CRIMSON COWL IN MERE SECONDS!
THEN, THE AVENGERS WILL BE DISPOSED OF... FOR ALL TIME!
IN THAT CASE, I GUESS I'D BETTER ACT NOW...
...OR FOREVER HOLD MY PEACE!
SKRAK!
GOLIATH IS AWAKE... GROWING HUGE! BUT HOW..??
THOSE CLAMPS PROVIDED ELECTRICAL SHOCKS, THAT SHOULD HAVE KEPT YOU UNCONSCIOUS...!
THAT JUST GOES TO SHOW HOW LITTLE YOU KNOW ABOUT THE CELLULAR STRUCTURE OF US POTENTIAL GIANTS, PAL!
MY SPECIALLY-CONDITIONED CELLS WOULD TAKE A LOT MORE VOLTAGE THAN YOUR CLAMPS DISHED OUT!
MMMFF!
AND NOW, WITHOUT FURTHER ADO...!
AS YOU WERE SAYING, MY BELLIGERENT BEHEMOTH?
GAS... SHOT AT ME FROM BEHIND!
CAN'T... FIGHT BACK! GETTING... DROWSY..!
WOOSH!
HAH! FILL YOUR OVERSIZED LUNGS WITH THAT, FOOL!
ALL THAT WILL HAPPEN IS THAT YOU PASS OUT EVEN MORE QUICKLY THAN A NORMAL MAN!
...WHILE I DUCK BENEATH THE LIGHTER-THAN-AIR FUMES!
5.

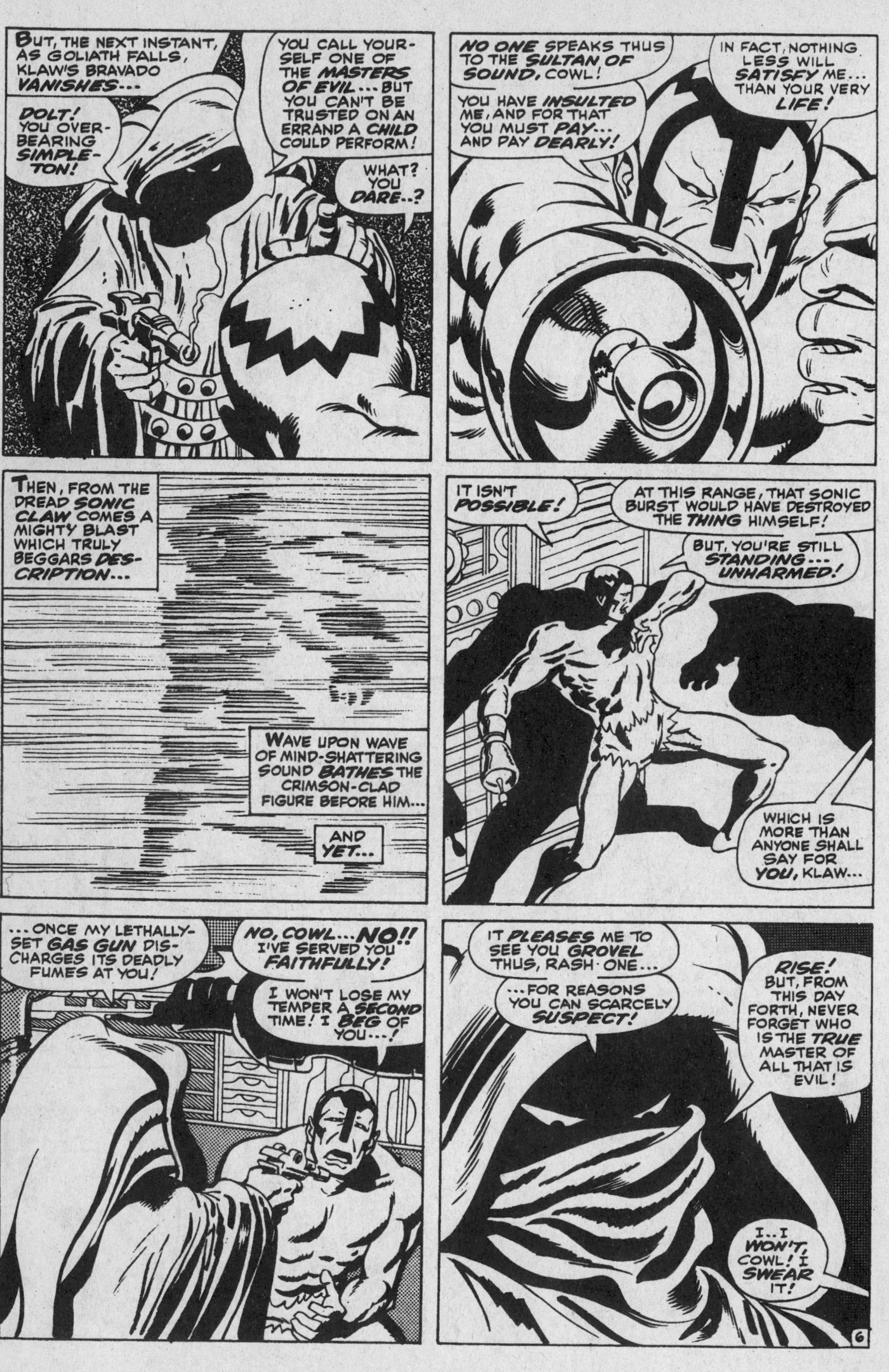

BUT, THE NEXT INSTANT, AS GOLIATH FALLS, KLAW'S BRAVADO VANISHES...
DOLT! YOU OVER-BEARING SIMPLE-TON!
YOU CALL YOUR-SELF ONE OF THE MASTERS OF EVIL... BUT YOU CAN'T BE TRUSTED ON AN ERRAND A CHILD COULD PERFORM!
WHAT? YOU DARE..?
NO ONE SPEAKS THUS TO THE SULTAN OF SOUND, COWL!
YOU HAVE INSULTED ME, AND FOR THAT YOU MUST PAY... AND PAY DEARLY!
IN FACT, NOTHING LESS WILL SATISFY ME... THAN YOUR VERY LIFE!
THEN, FROM THE DREAD SONIC CLAW COMES A MIGHTY BLAST WHICH TRULY BEGGARS DES-CRIPTION...
WAVE UPON WAVE OF MIND-SHATTERING SOUND BATHES THE CRIMSON-CLAD FIGURE BEFORE HIM...
AND YET...
IT ISN'T POSSIBLE!
AT THIS RANGE, THAT SONIC BURST WOULD HAVE DESTROYED THE THING HIMSELF!
BUT, YOU'RE STILL STANDING... UNHARMED!
WHICH IS MORE THAN ANYONE SHALL SAY FOR YOU, KLAW...
...ONCE MY LETHALLY-SET GAS GUN DIS-CHARGES ITS DEADLY FUMES AT YOU!
NO, COWL... NO!! I'VE SERVED YOU FAITHFULLY!
I WON'T LOSE MY TEMPER A SECOND TIME! I BEG OF YOU...!
IT PLEASES ME TO SEE YOU GROVEL THUS, RASH ONE...
...FOR REASONS YOU CAN SCARCELY SUSPECT!
RISE! BUT, FROM THIS DAY FORTH, NEVER FORGET WHO IS THE TRUE MASTER OF ALL THAT IS EVIL!
I..I WON'T, COWL! I SWEAR IT!
6

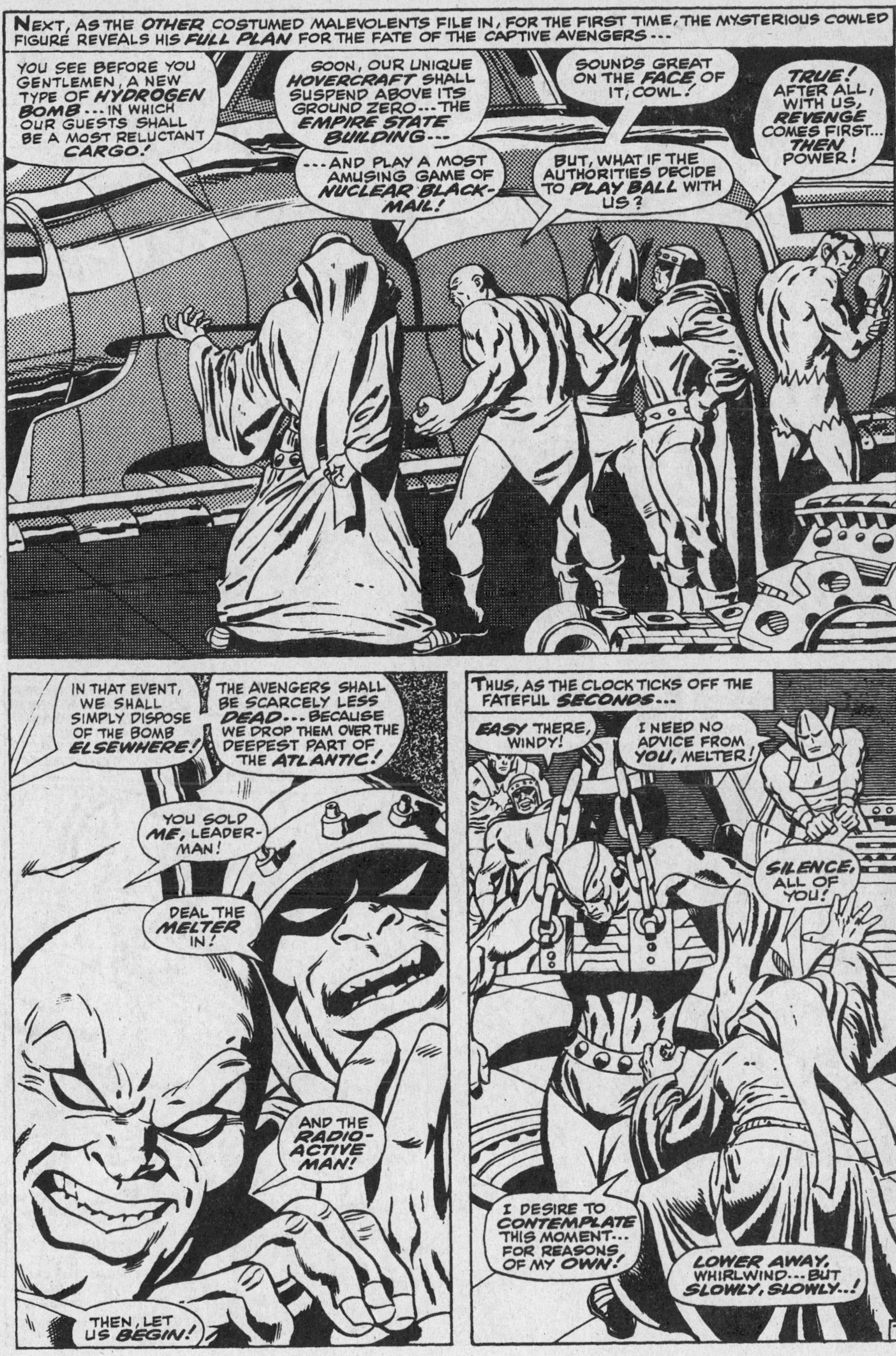

NEXT, AS THE OTHER COSTUMED MALEVOLENTS FILE IN, FOR THE FIRST TIME, THE MYSTERIOUS COWLED FIGURE REVEALS HIS FULL PLAN FOR THE FATE OF THE CAPTIVE AVENGERS---
YOU SEE BEFORE YOU GENTLEMEN, A NEW TYPE OF HYDROGEN BOMB---IN WHICH OUR GUESTS SHALL BE A MOST RELUCTANT CARGO!
SOON, OUR UNIQUE HOVERCRAFT SHALL SUSPEND ABOVE ITS GROUND ZERO---THE EMPIRE STATE BUILDING---
---AND PLAY A MOST AMUSING GAME OF NUCLEAR BLACK-MAIL!
SOUNDS GREAT ON THE FACE OF IT, COWL!
BUT, WHAT IF THE AUTHORITIES DECIDE TO PLAY BALL WITH US?
TRUE! AFTER ALL, WITH US, REVENGE COMES FIRST... THEN POWER!
IN THAT EVENT, WE SHALL SIMPLY DISPOSE OF THE BOMB ELSEWHERE!
THE AVENGERS SHALL BE SCARCELY LESS DEAD---BECAUSE WE DROP THEM OVER THE DEEPEST PART OF THE ATLANTIC!
YOU SOLD ME, LEADER-MAN!
DEAL THE MELTER IN!
AND THE RADIO-ACTIVE MAN!
THEN, LET US BEGIN!
THUS, AS THE CLOCK TICKS OFF THE FATEFUL SECONDS---
EASY THERE, WINDY!
I NEED NO ADVICE FROM YOU, MELTER!
SILENCE, ALL OF YOU!
I DESIRE TO CONTEMPLATE THIS MOMENT... FOR REASONS OF MY OWN!
LOWER AWAY, WHIRLWIND---BUT SLOWLY, SLOWLY...!
7

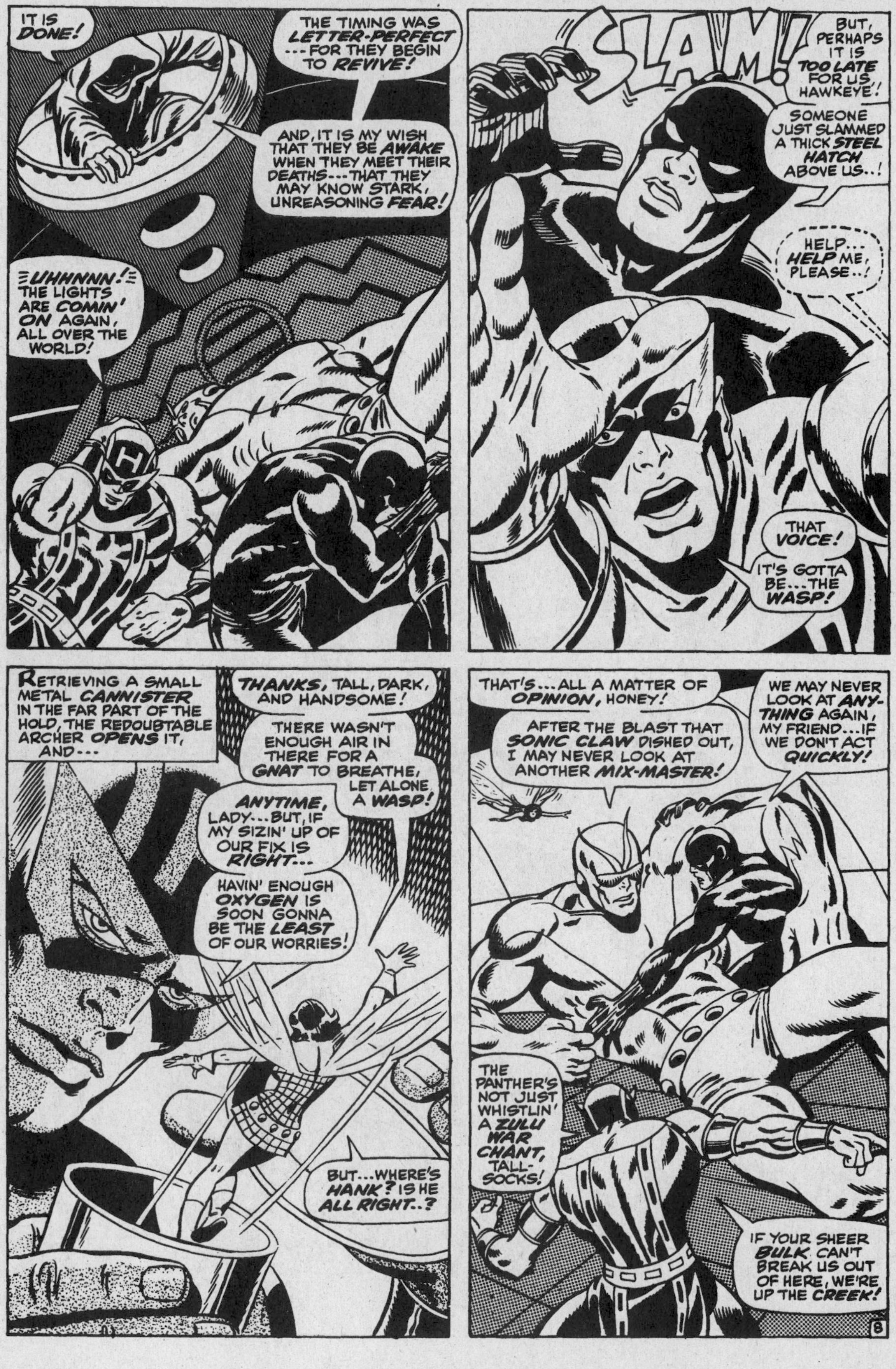
IT IS DONE!
THE TIMING WAS LETTER-PERFECT --- FOR THEY BEGIN TO REVIVE!
AND, IT IS MY WISH THAT THEY BE AWAKE WHEN THEY MEET THEIR DEATHS --- THAT THEY MAY KNOW STARK, UNREASONING FEAR!
UHHNNN! THE LIGHTS ARE COMIN' ON AGAIN, ALL OVER THE WORLD!
SLAM!
BUT, PERHAPS IT IS TOO LATE FOR US, HAWKEYE!
SOMEONE JUST SLAMMED A THICK STEEL HATCH ABOVE US..!
HELP... HELP ME, PLEASE..!
THAT VOICE!
IT'S GOTTA BE... THE WASP!
RETRIEVING A SMALL METAL CANNISTER IN THE FAR PART OF THE HOLD, THE REDOUBTABLE ARCHER OPENS IT, AND---
THANKS, TALL, DARK, AND HANDSOME!
THERE WASN'T ENOUGH AIR IN THERE FOR A GNAT TO BREATHE, LET ALONE A WASP!
ANYTIME, LADY... BUT, IF MY SIZIN' UP OF OUR FIX IS RIGHT...
HAVIN' ENOUGH OXYGEN IS SOON GONNA BE THE LEAST OF OUR WORRIES!
BUT... WHERE'S HANK? IS HE ALL RIGHT..?
THAT'S... ALL A MATTER OF OPINION, HONEY!
AFTER THE BLAST THAT SONIC CLAW DISHED OUT, I MAY NEVER LOOK AT ANOTHER MIX-MASTER!
WE MAY NEVER LOOK AT ANYTHING AGAIN, MY FRIEND... IF WE DON'T ACT QUICKLY!
THE PANTHER'S NOT JUST WHISTLIN' A ZULU WAR CHANT, TALL-SOCKS!
IF YOUR SHEER BULK CAN'T BREAK US OUT OF HERE, WE'RE UP THE CREEK!
8

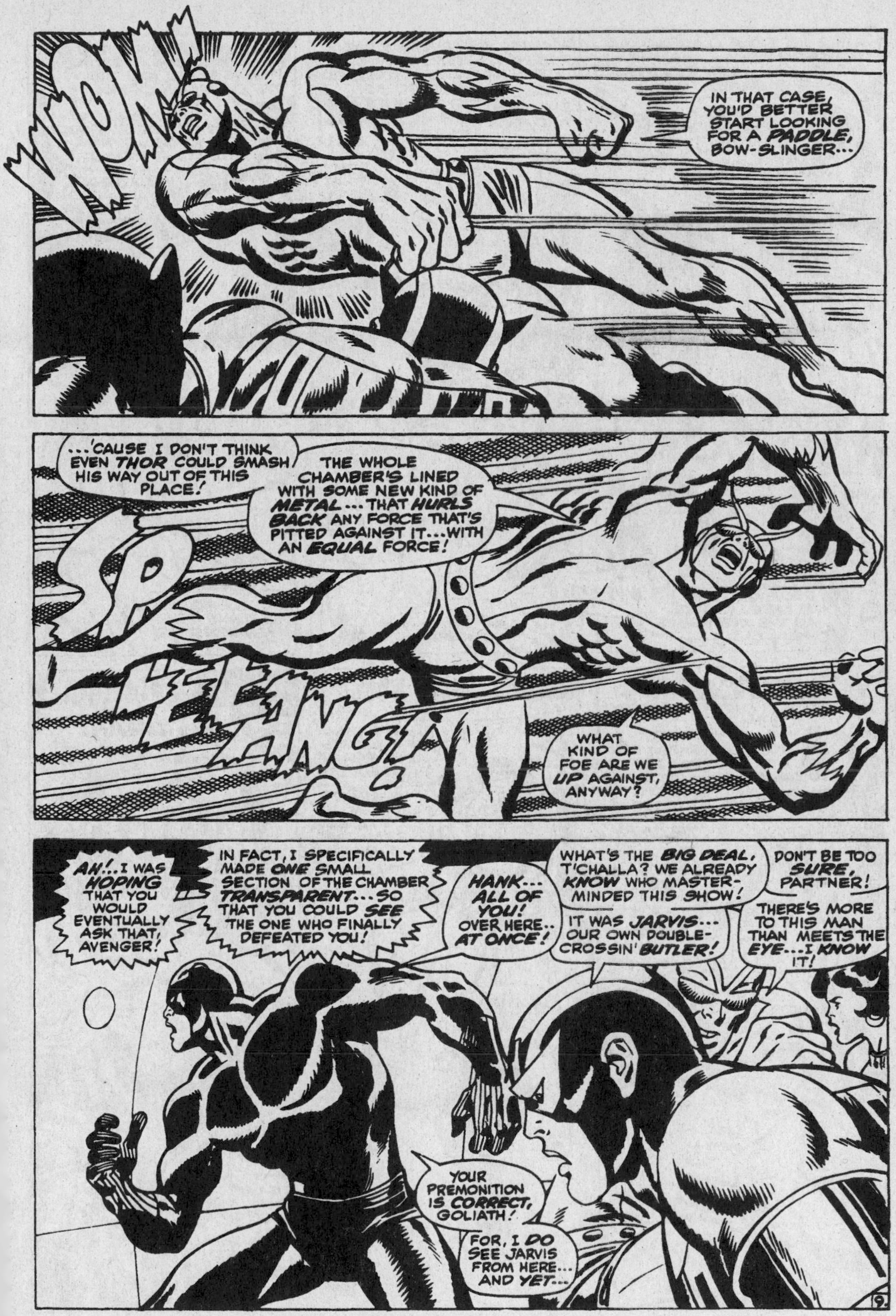
WOK!
IN THAT CASE, YOU'D BETTER START LOOKING FOR A PADDLE, BOW-SLINGER...
...'CAUSE I DON'T THINK EVEN THOR COULD SMASH HIS WAY OUT OF THIS PLACE!
THE WHOLE CHAMBER'S LINED WITH SOME NEW KIND OF METAL... THAT HURLS BACK ANY FORCE THAT'S PITTED AGAINST IT... WITH AN EQUAL FORCE!
SP
SPLANG!
WHAT KIND OF FOE ARE WE UP AGAINST, ANYWAY?
AH!.. I WAS HOPING THAT YOU WOULD EVENTUALLY ASK THAT, AVENGER!
IN FACT, I SPECIFICALLY MADE ONE SMALL SECTION OF THE CHAMBER TRANSPARENT... SO THAT YOU COULD SEE THE ONE WHO FINALLY DEFEATED YOU!
HANK... ALL OF YOU! OVER HERE.. AT ONCE!
WHAT'S THE BIG DEAL, T'CHALLA? WE ALREADY KNOW WHO MASTER-MINDED THIS SHOW!
IT WAS JARVIS... OUR OWN DOUBLE-CROSSIN' BUTLER!
DON'T BE TOO SURE, PARTNER!
THERE'S MORE TO THIS MAN THAN MEETS THE EYE... I KNOW IT!
YOUR PREMONITION IS CORRECT, GOLIATH!
FOR, I DO SEE JARVIS FROM HERE... AND YET...
9

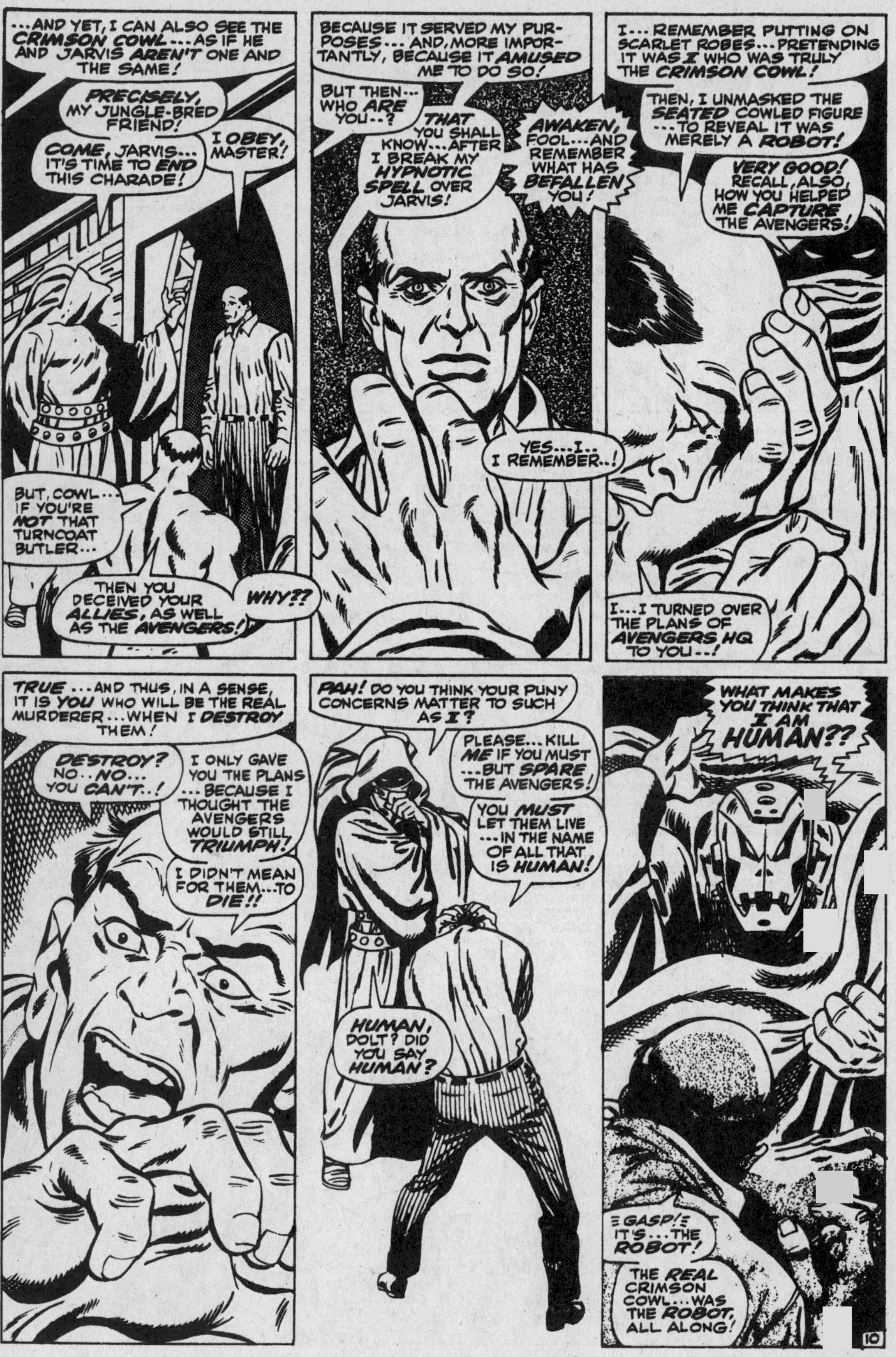
...AND YET, I CAN ALSO SEE THE CRIMSON COWL... AS IF HE AND JARVIS AREN'T ONE AND THE SAME!
PRECISELY, MY JUNGLE-BRED FRIEND!
COME, JARVIS... IT'S TIME TO END THIS CHARADE!
I OBEY, MASTER!
BUT, COWL... IF YOU'RE NOT THAT TURNCOAT BUTLER...
THEN YOU DECEIVED YOUR ALLIES, AS WELL AS THE AVENGERS!
WHY??
BECAUSE IT SERVED MY PURPOSES... AND, MORE IMPORTANTLY, BECAUSE IT AMUSED ME TO DO SO!
BUT THEN... WHO ARE YOU--?
THAT YOU SHALL KNOW...AFTER I BREAK MY HYPNOTIC SPELL OVER JARVIS!
AWAKEN, FOOL... AND REMEMBER WHAT HAS BEFALLEN YOU!
YES...I... I REMEMBER..!
I... REMEMBER PUTTING ON SCARLET ROBES... PRETENDING IT WAS I WHO WAS TRULY THE CRIMSON COWL!
THEN, I UNMASKED THE SEATED COWLED FIGURE --TO REVEAL IT WAS MERELY A ROBOT!
VERY GOOD! RECALL, ALSO, HOW YOU HELPED ME CAPTURE THE AVENGERS!
I...I TURNED OVER THE PLANS OF AVENGERS HQ TO YOU--!
TRUE ...AND THUS, IN A SENSE, IT IS YOU WHO WILL BE THE REAL MURDERER... WHEN I DESTROY THEM!
DESTROY? NO.. NO... YOU CAN'T..!
I ONLY GAVE YOU THE PLANS ... BECAUSE I THOUGHT THE AVENGERS WOULD STILL TRIUMPH!
I DIDN'T MEAN FOR THEM...TO DIE!!
PAH! DO YOU THINK YOUR PUNY CONCERNS MATTER TO SUCH AS I?
PLEASE... KILL ME IF YOU MUST ...BUT SPARE THE AVENGERS!
YOU MUST LET THEM LIVE ...IN THE NAME OF ALL THAT IS HUMAN!
HUMAN, DOLT? DID YOU SAY HUMAN?
WHAT MAKES YOU THINK THAT I AM HUMAN??
GASP! IT'S...THE ROBOT!
THE REAL CRIMSON COWL...WAS THE ROBOT, ALL ALONG!
10

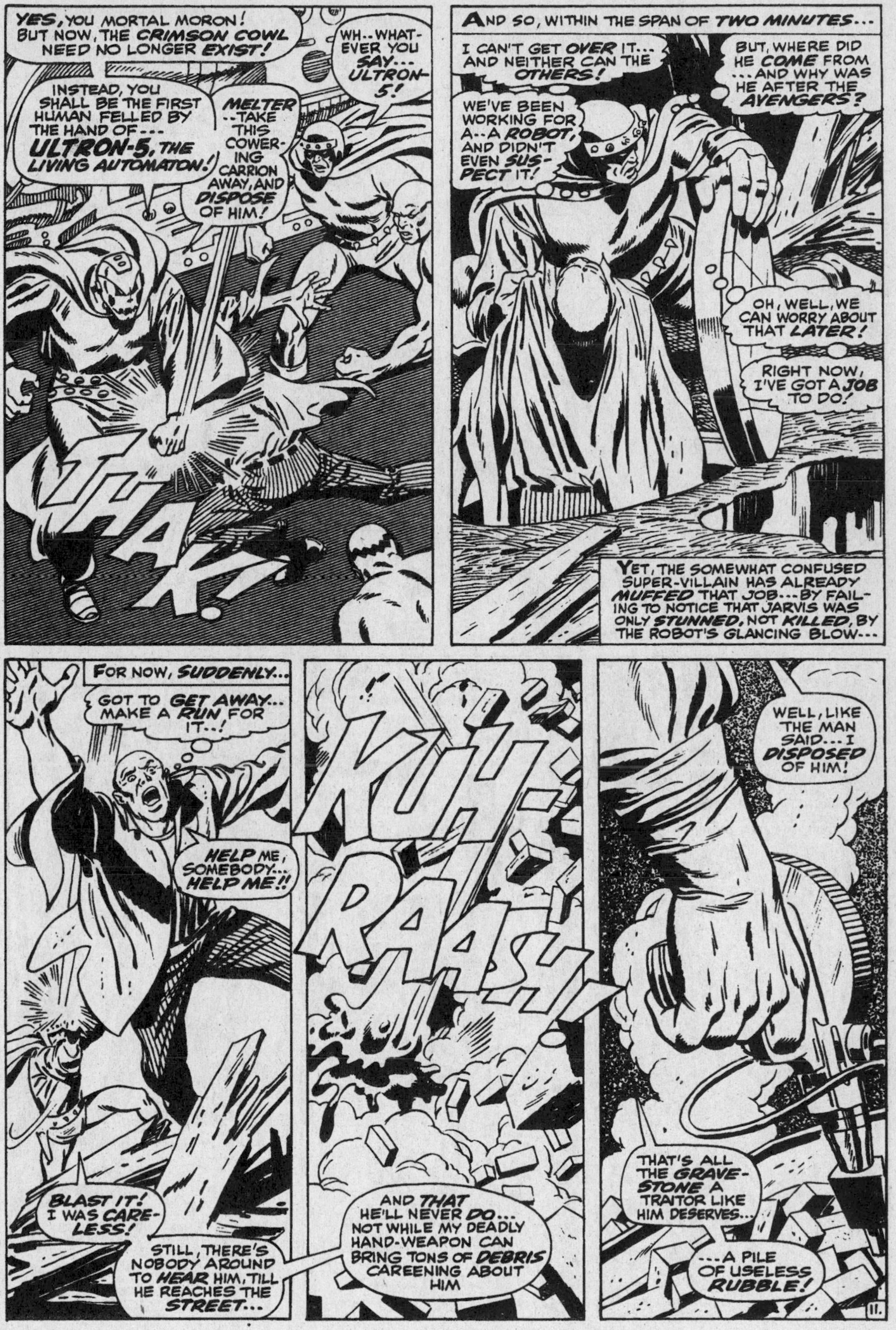
YES, YOU MORTAL MORON! BUT NOW, THE CRIMSON COWL NEED NO LONGER EXIST!
WH..WHATEVER YOU SAY... ULTRON-5!
INSTEAD, YOU SHALL BE THE FIRST HUMAN FELLED BY THE HAND OF--- ULTRON-5, THE LIVING AUTOMATON!
MELTER--TAKE THIS COWERING CARRION AWAY, AND DISPOSE OF HIM!
THAK!
AND SO, WITHIN THE SPAN OF TWO MINUTES...
I CAN'T GET OVER IT... AND NEITHER CAN THE OTHERS!
BUT, WHERE DID HE COME FROM ...AND WHY WAS HE AFTER THE AVENGERS?
WE'VE BEEN WORKING FOR A..A ROBOT, AND DIDN'T EVEN SUSPECT IT!
OH, WELL, WE CAN WORRY ABOUT THAT LATER!
RIGHT NOW, I'VE GOT A JOB TO DO!
YET, THE SOMEWHAT CONFUSED SUPER-VILLAIN HAS ALREADY MUFFED THAT JOB---BY FAILING TO NOTICE THAT JARVIS WAS ONLY STUNNED, NOT KILLED, BY THE ROBOT'S GLANCING BLOW---
FOR NOW, SUDDENLY...
GOT TO GET AWAY... MAKE A RUN FOR IT..!
HELP ME, SOMEBODY... HELP ME!!
BLAST IT! I WAS CARELESS!
STILL, THERE'S NOBODY AROUND TO HEAR HIM, TILL HE REACHES THE STREET...
KUH-RAASH!
AND THAT HE'LL NEVER DO... NOT WHILE MY DEADLY HAND-WEAPON CAN BRING TONS OF DEBRIS CAREENING ABOUT HIM
WELL, LIKE THE MAN SAID... I DISPOSED OF HIM!
THAT'S ALL THE GRAVESTONE A TRAITOR LIKE HIM DESERVES...
...A PILE OF USELESS RUBBLE!
11.

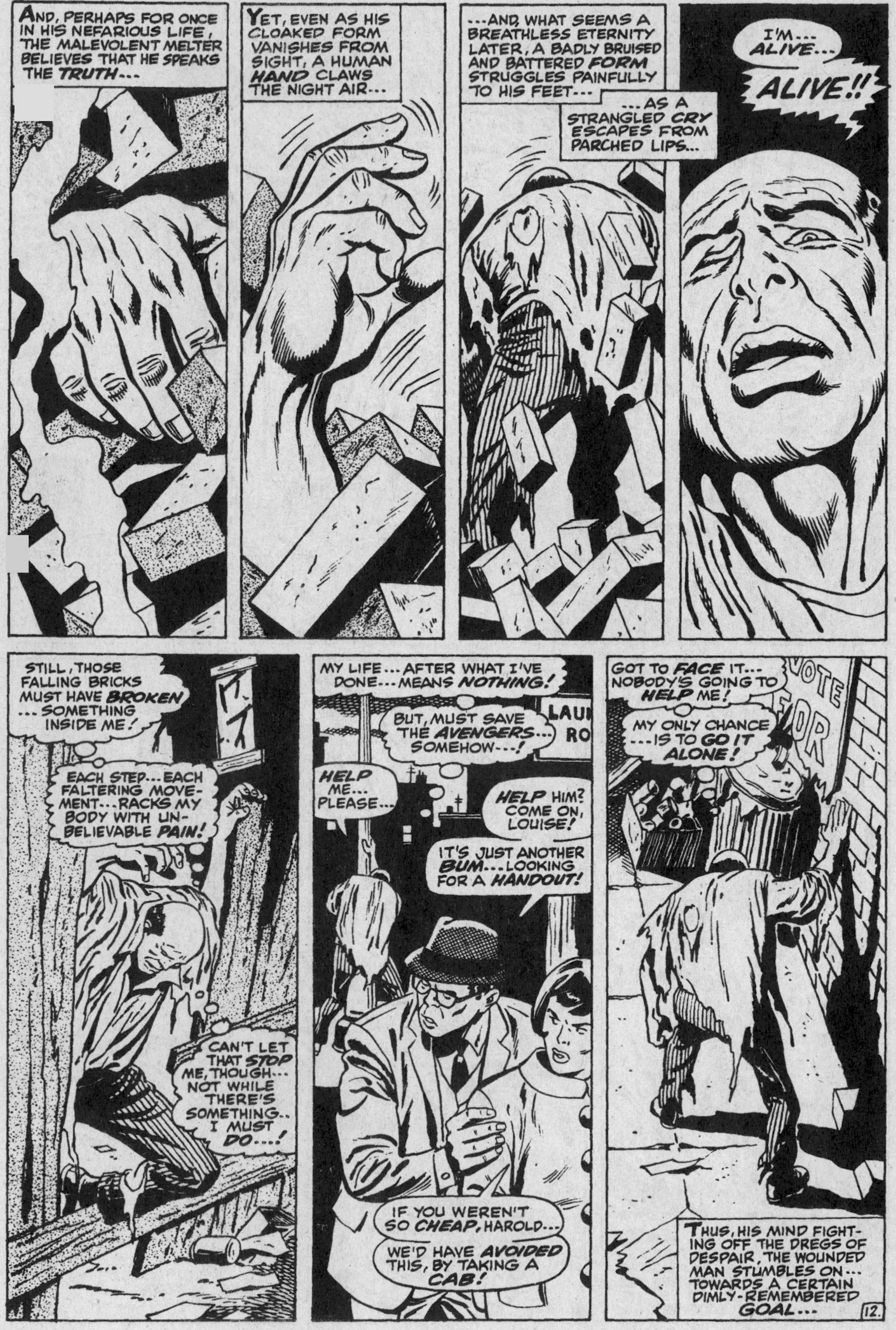
AND, PERHAPS FOR ONCE IN HIS NEFARIOUS LIFE, THE MALEVOLENT MELTER BELIEVES THAT HE SPEAKS THE TRUTH...
YET, EVEN AS HIS CLOAKED FORM VANISHES FROM SIGHT, A HUMAN HAND CLAWS THE NIGHT AIR...
...AND, WHAT SEEMS A BREATHLESS ETERNITY LATER, A BADLY BRUISED AND BATTERED FORM STRUGGLES PAINFULLY TO HIS FEET...
...AS A STRANGLED CRY ESCAPES FROM PARCHED LIPS...
I'M... ALIVE...
ALIVE!!
STILL, THOSE FALLING BRICKS MUST HAVE BROKEN ... SOMETHING INSIDE ME!
EACH STEP... EACH FALTERING MOVEMENT... RACKS MY BODY WITH UNBELIEVABLE PAIN!
CAN'T LET THAT STOP ME, THOUGH... NOT WHILE THERE'S SOMETHING.. I MUST DO...!
MY LIFE... AFTER WHAT I'VE DONE... MEANS NOTHING!
BUT, MUST SAVE THE AVENGERS... SOMEHOW...!
HELP ME... PLEASE...
HELP HIM? COME ON, LOUISE!
IT'S JUST ANOTHER BUM... LOOKING FOR A HANDOUT!
IF YOU WEREN'T SO CHEAP, HAROLD...
WE'D HAVE AVOIDED THIS, BY TAKING A CAB!
GOT TO FACE IT... NOBODY'S GOING TO HELP ME!
MY ONLY CHANCE ...IS TO GO IT ALONE!
VOTE FOR
THUS, HIS MIND FIGHTING OFF THE DREGS OF DESPAIR, THE WOUNDED MAN STUMBLES ON... TOWARDS A CERTAIN DIMLY-REMEMBERED GOAL...
12.

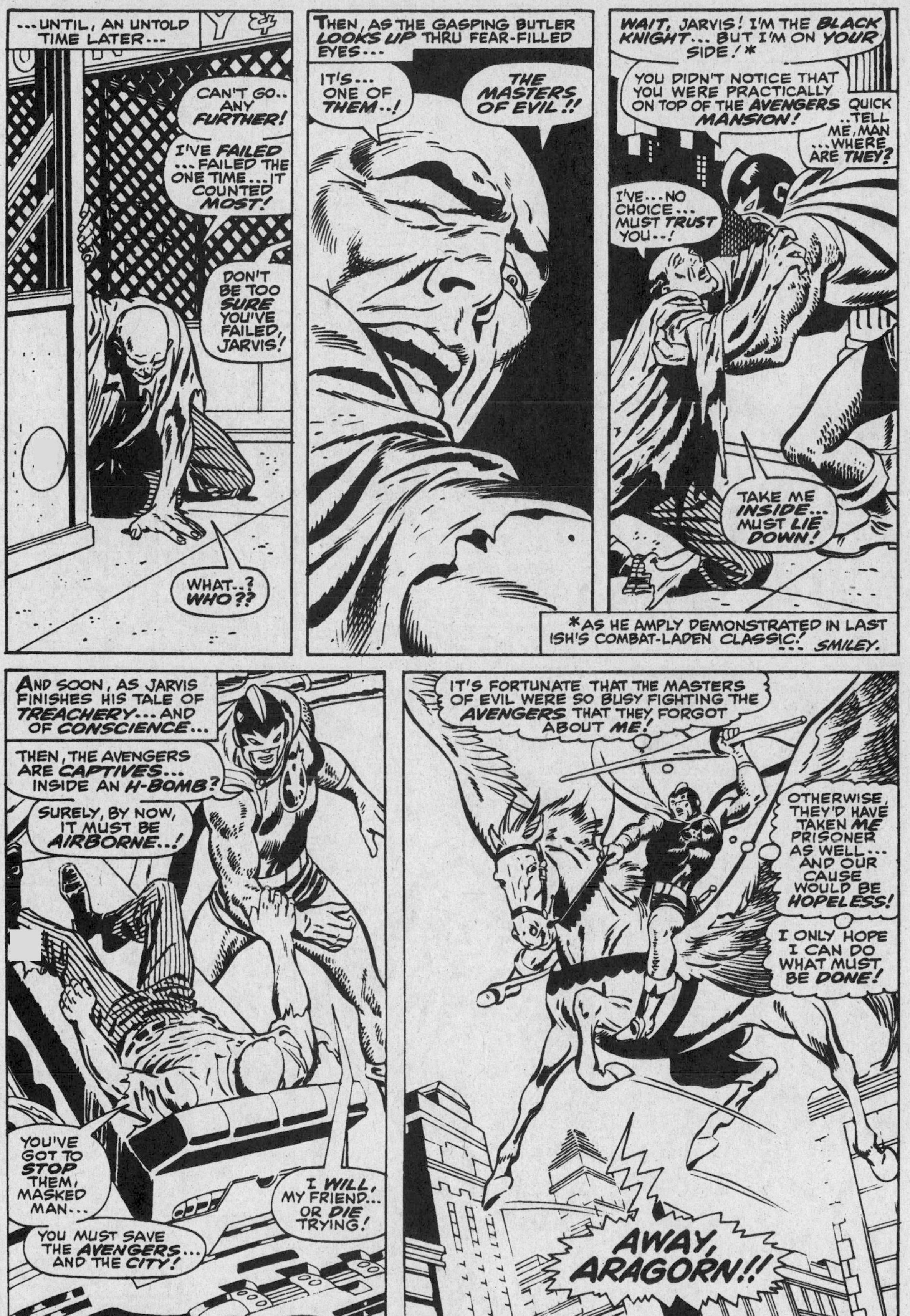

...UNTIL, AN UNTOLD TIME LATER...
CAN'T GO.. ANY FURTHER!
I'VE FAILED ...FAILED THE ONE TIME...IT COUNTED MOST!
DON'T BE TOO SURE YOU'VE FAILED, JARVIS!
WHAT..? WHO??
THEN, AS THE GASPING BUTLER LOOKS UP THRU FEAR-FILLED EYES...
IT'S... ONE OF THEM..!
THE MASTERS OF EVIL!!
WAIT, JARVIS! I'M THE BLACK KNIGHT... BUT I'M ON YOUR SIDE! *
YOU DIDN'T NOTICE THAT YOU WERE PRACTICALLY ON TOP OF THE AVENGERS MANSION!
QUICK ..TELL ME, MAN ...WHERE ARE THEY?
I'VE...NO CHOICE... MUST TRUST YOU..!
TAKE ME INSIDE... MUST LIE DOWN!
*AS HE AMPLY DEMONSTRATED IN LAST ISH'S COMBAT-LADEN CLASSIC! ... SMILEY.
AND SOON, AS JARVIS FINISHES HIS TALE OF TREACHERY... AND OF CONSCIENCE...
THEN, THE AVENGERS ARE CAPTIVES... INSIDE AN H-BOMB?
SURELY, BY NOW, IT MUST BE AIRBORNE..!
YOU'VE GOT TO STOP THEM, MASKED MAN...
YOU MUST SAVE THE AVENGERS... AND THE CITY!
I WILL, MY FRIEND... OR DIE TRYING!
IT'S FORTUNATE THAT THE MASTERS OF EVIL WERE SO BUSY FIGHTING THE AVENGERS THAT THEY FORGOT ABOUT ME!
OTHERWISE, THEY'D HAVE TAKEN ME PRISONER AS WELL... AND OUR CAUSE WOULD BE HOPELESS!
I ONLY HOPE I CAN DO WHAT MUST BE DONE!
AWAY, ARAGORN!!
13.

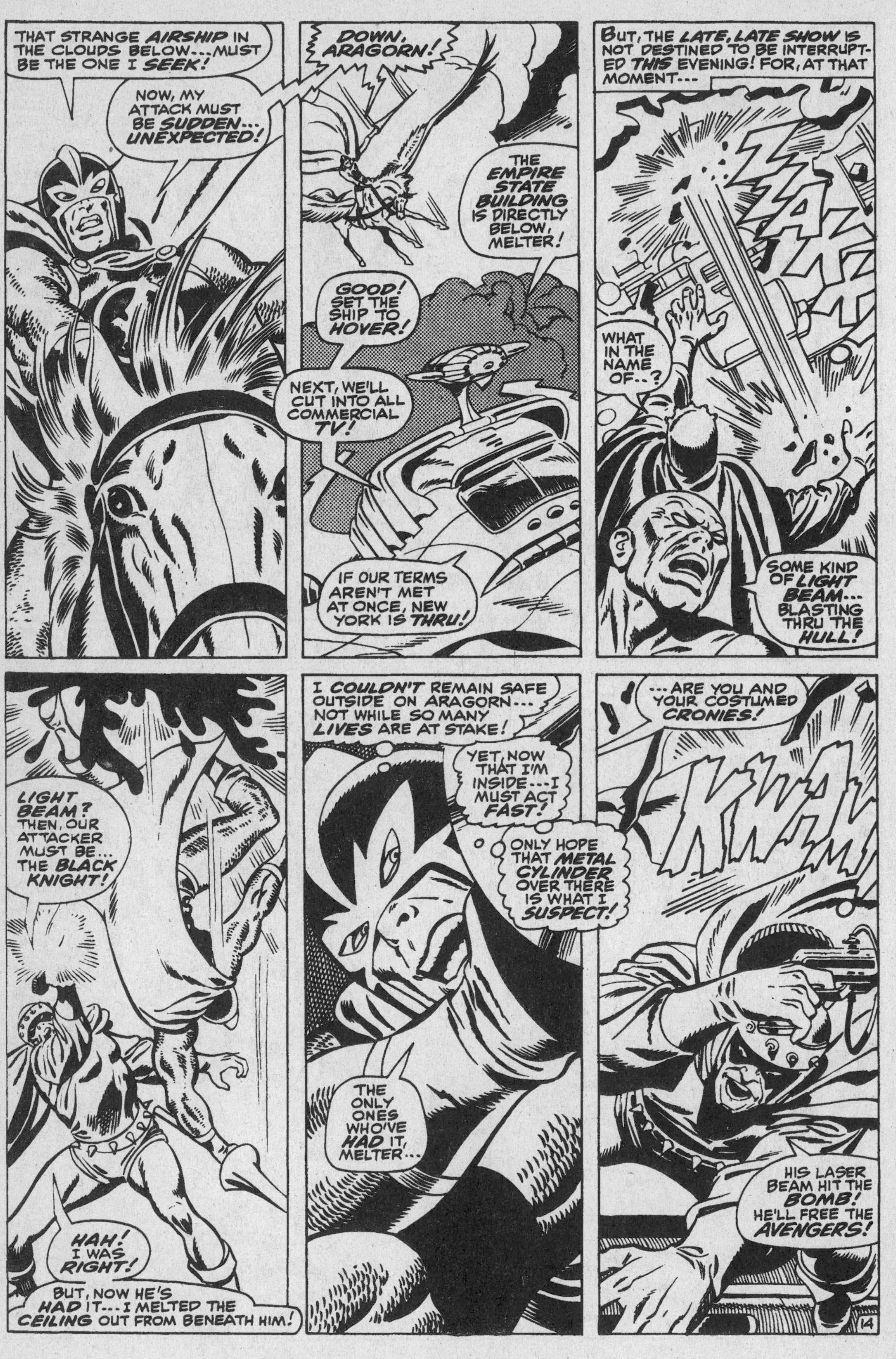
THAT STRANGE AIRSHIP IN THE CLOUDS BELOW... MUST BE THE ONE I SEEK!
NOW, MY ATTACK MUST BE SUDDEN... UNEXPECTED!
DOWN, ARAGORN!
THE EMPIRE STATE BUILDING IS DIRECTLY BELOW, MELTER!
GOOD! SET THE SHIP TO HOVER!
NEXT, WE'LL CUT INTO ALL COMMERCIAL TV!
IF OUR TERMS AREN'T MET AT ONCE, NEW YORK IS THRU!
BUT, THE LATE, LATE SHOW IS NOT DESTINED TO BE INTERRUPTED THIS EVENING! FOR, AT THAT MOMENT---
ZAKK
WHAT IN THE NAME OF..?
SOME KIND OF LIGHT BEAM... BLASTING THRU THE HULL!
LIGHT BEAM? THEN, OUR ATTACKER MUST BE... THE BLACK KNIGHT!
HAH! I WAS RIGHT!
BUT, NOW HE'S HAD IT... I MELTED THE CEILING OUT FROM BENEATH HIM!
I COULDN'T REMAIN SAFE OUTSIDE ON ARAGORN... NOT WHILE SO MANY LIVES ARE AT STAKE!
YET, NOW THAT I'M INSIDE---I MUST ACT FAST!
ONLY HOPE THAT METAL CYLINDER OVER THERE IS WHAT I SUSPECT!
THE ONLY ONES WHO'VE HAD IT, MELTER...
---ARE YOU AND YOUR COSTUMED CRONIES!
KWAM
HIS LASER BEAM HIT THE BOMB! HE'LL FREE THE AVENGERS!
14

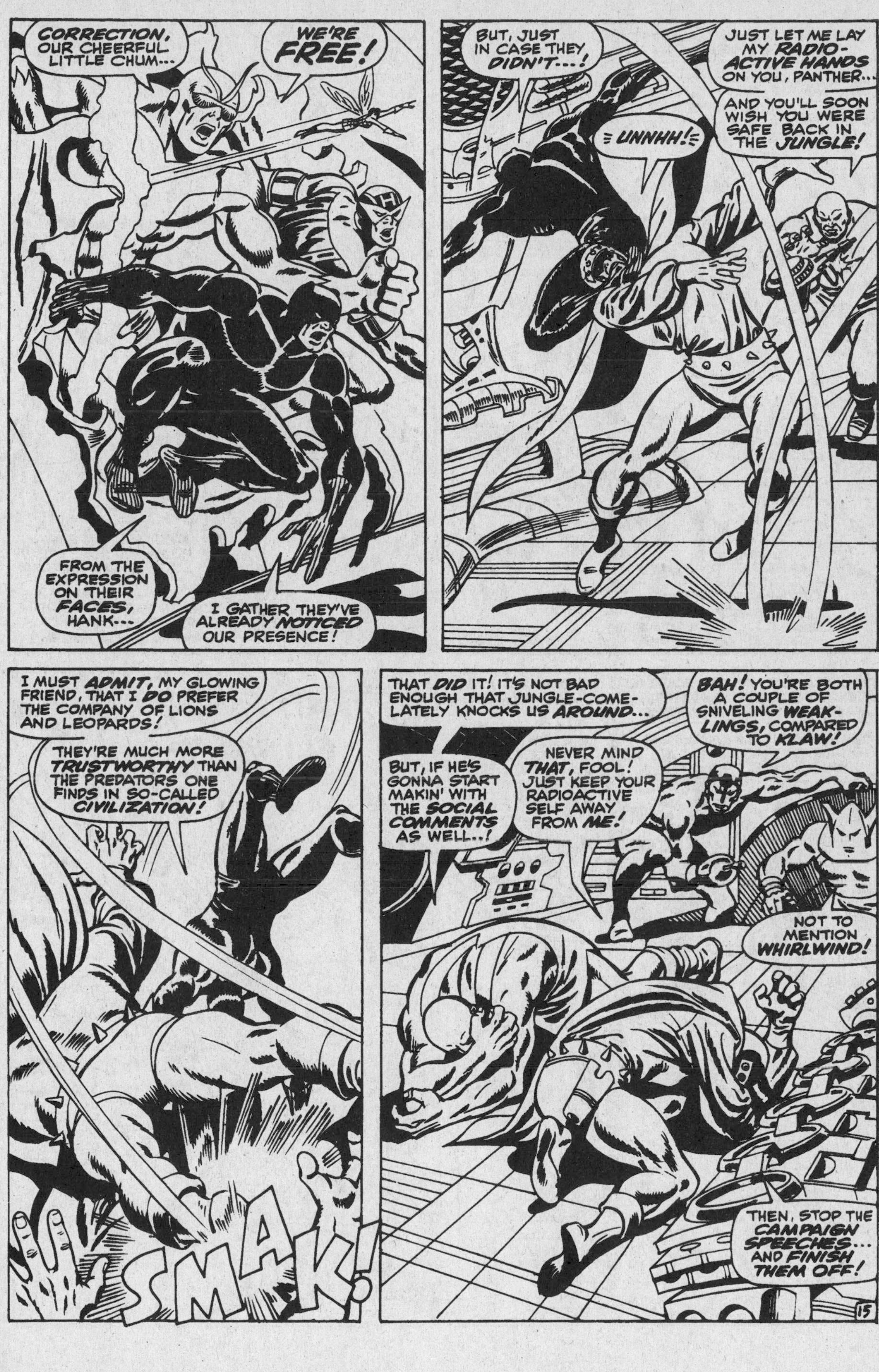
CORRECTION, OUR CHEERFUL LITTLE CHUM...
WE'RE FREE!
FROM THE EXPRESSION ON THEIR FACES, HANK...
I GATHER THEY'VE ALREADY NOTICED OUR PRESENCE!
BUT, JUST IN CASE THEY DIDN'T...!
UNNHH!
JUST LET ME LAY MY RADIO-ACTIVE HANDS ON YOU, PANTHER...
AND YOU'LL SOON WISH YOU WERE SAFE BACK IN THE JUNGLE!
I MUST ADMIT, MY GLOWING FRIEND, THAT I DO PREFER THE COMPANY OF LIONS AND LEOPARDS!
THEY'RE MUCH MORE TRUSTWORTHY THAN THE PREDATORS ONE FINDS IN SO-CALLED CIVILIZATION!
SMAK!
THAT DID IT! IT'S NOT BAD ENOUGH THAT JUNGLE-COME-LATELY KNOCKS US AROUND...
BUT, IF HE'S GONNA START MAKIN' WITH THE SOCIAL COMMENTS AS WELL...!
NEVER MIND THAT, FOOL! JUST KEEP YOUR RADIOACTIVE SELF AWAY FROM ME!
BAH! YOU'RE BOTH A COUPLE OF SNIVELING WEAK-LINGS, COMPARED TO KLAW!
NOT TO MENTION WHIRLWIND!
THEN, STOP THE CAMPAIGN SPEECHES... AND FINISH THEM OFF!
15

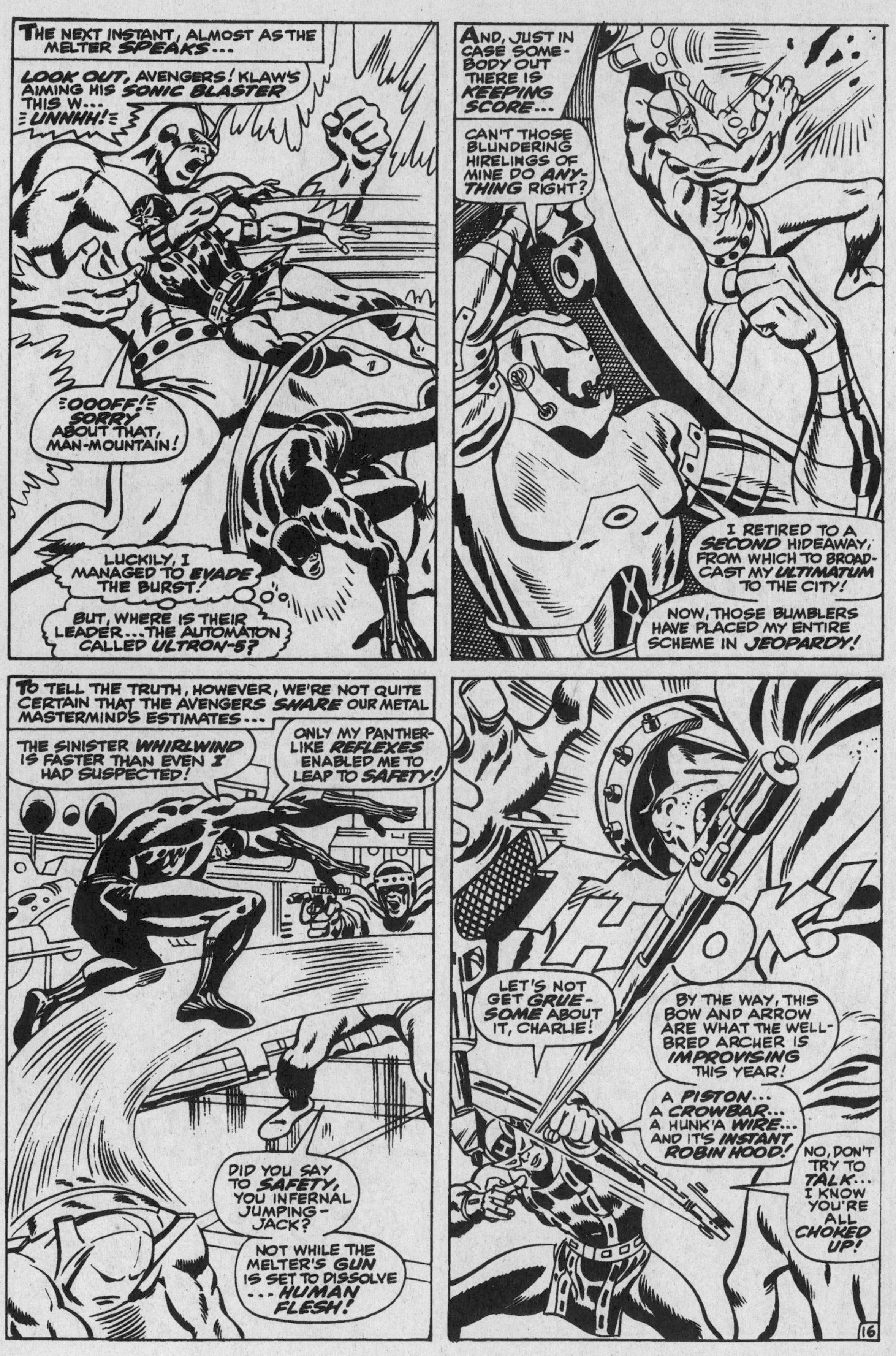

THE NEXT INSTANT, ALMOST AS THE MELTER SPEAKS...
LOOK OUT, AVENGERS! KLAW'S AIMING HIS SONIC BLASTER THIS W... UNNHH!
OOOFF! SORRY ABOUT THAT, MAN-MOUNTAIN!
LUCKILY, I MANAGED TO EVADE THE BURST!
BUT, WHERE IS THEIR LEADER... THE AUTOMATON CALLED ULTRON-5?
AND, JUST IN CASE SOMEBODY OUT THERE IS KEEPING SCORE...
CAN'T THOSE BLUNDERING HIRELINGS OF MINE DO ANYTHING RIGHT?
I RETIRED TO A SECOND HIDEAWAY, FROM WHICH TO BROADCAST MY ULTIMATUM TO THE CITY!
NOW, THOSE BUMBLERS HAVE PLACED MY ENTIRE SCHEME IN JEOPARDY!
TO TELL THE TRUTH, HOWEVER, WE'RE NOT QUITE CERTAIN THAT THE AVENGERS SHARE OUR METAL MASTERMIND'S ESTIMATES...
THE SINISTER WHIRLWIND IS FASTER THAN EVEN I HAD SUSPECTED!
ONLY MY PANTHER-LIKE REFLEXES ENABLED ME TO LEAP TO SAFETY!
DID YOU SAY TO SAFETY, YOU INFERNAL JUMPING-JACK?
NOT WHILE THE MELTER'S GUN IS SET TO DISSOLVE ...HUMAN FLESH!
THOK!
LET'S NOT GET GRUESOME ABOUT IT, CHARLIE!
BY THE WAY, THIS BOW AND ARROW ARE WHAT THE WELL-BRED ARCHER IS IMPROVISING THIS YEAR!
A PISTON... A CROWBAR... A HUNK'A WIRE... AND IT'S INSTANT ROBIN HOOD!
NO, DON'T TRY TO TALK... I KNOW YOU'RE ALL CHOKED UP!
16

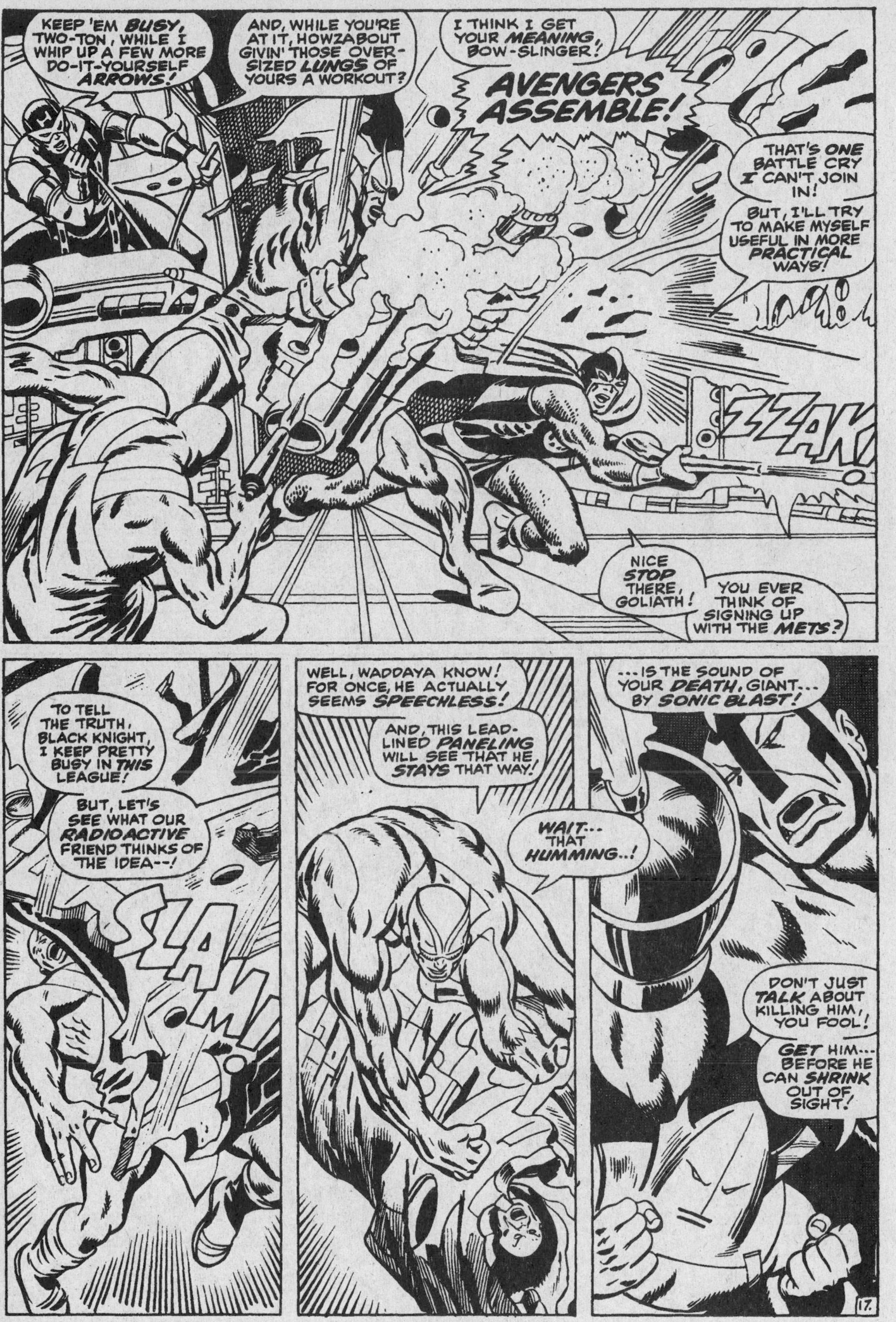
KEEP 'EM BUSY, TWO-TON, WHILE I WHIP UP A FEW MORE DO-IT-YOURSELF ARROWS!
AND, WHILE YOU'RE AT IT, HOWZABOUT GIVIN' THOSE OVER-SIZED LUNGS OF YOURS A WORKOUT?
I THINK I GET YOUR MEANING, BOW-SLINGER!
AVENGERS ASSEMBLE!
THAT'S ONE BATTLE CRY I CAN'T JOIN IN!
BUT, I'LL TRY TO MAKE MYSELF USEFUL IN MORE PRACTICAL WAYS!
ZZZAK!
NICE STOP THERE, GOLIATH!
YOU EVER THINK OF SIGNING UP WITH THE METS?
TO TELL THE TRUTH, BLACK KNIGHT, I KEEP PRETTY BUSY IN THIS LEAGUE!
BUT, LET'S SEE WHAT OUR RADIOACTIVE FRIEND THINKS OF THE IDEA--!
SLAM!
WELL, WADDAYA KNOW! FOR ONCE, HE ACTUALLY SEEMS SPEECHLESS!
AND, THIS LEAD-LINED PANELING WILL SEE THAT HE STAYS THAT WAY!
WAIT... THAT HUMMING..!
...IS THE SOUND OF YOUR DEATH, GIANT... BY SONIC BLAST!
DON'T JUST TALK ABOUT KILLING HIM, YOU FOOL!
GET HIM... BEFORE HE CAN SHRINK OUT OF SIGHT!
17.

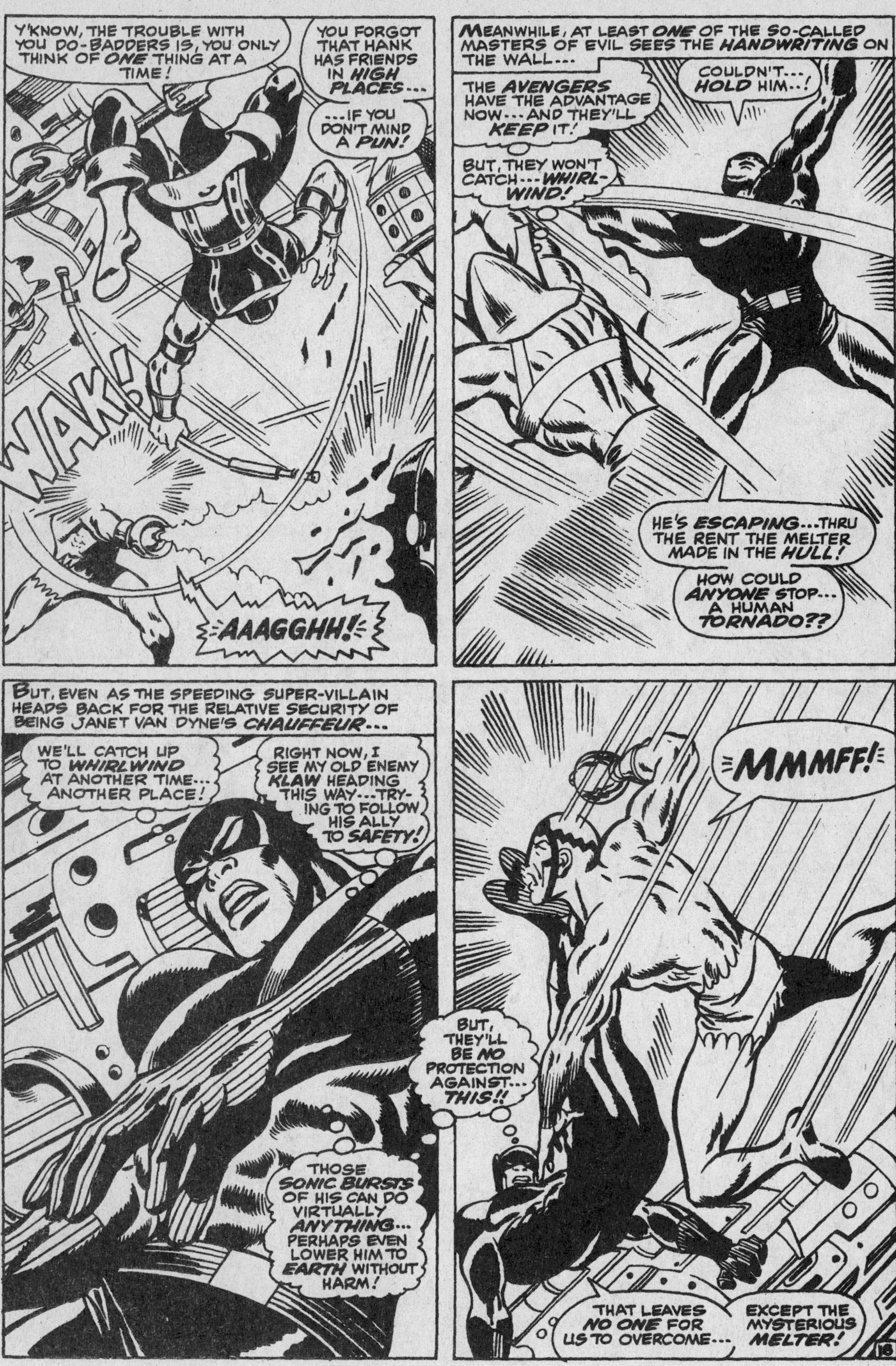
Y'KNOW, THE TROUBLE WITH YOU DO-BADDERS IS, YOU ONLY THINK OF ONE THING AT A TIME!
YOU FORGOT THAT HANK HAS FRIENDS IN HIGH PLACES...
...IF YOU DON'T MIND A PUN!
WAK!
AAAGGHH!
MEANWHILE, AT LEAST ONE OF THE SO-CALLED MASTERS OF EVIL SEES THE HANDWRITING ON THE WALL...
THE AVENGERS HAVE THE ADVANTAGE NOW... AND THEY'LL KEEP IT!
BUT, THEY WON'T CATCH... WHIRLWIND!
COULDN'T... HOLD HIM...!
HE'S ESCAPING...THRU THE RENT THE MELTER MADE IN THE HULL!
HOW COULD ANYONE STOP... A HUMAN TORNADO??
BUT, EVEN AS THE SPEEDING SUPER-VILLAIN HEADS BACK FOR THE RELATIVE SECURITY OF BEING JANET VAN DYNE'S CHAUFFEUR...
WE'LL CATCH UP TO WHIRLWIND AT ANOTHER TIME... ANOTHER PLACE!
RIGHT NOW, I SEE MY OLD ENEMY KLAW HEADING THIS WAY...TRYING TO FOLLOW HIS ALLY TO SAFETY!
THOSE SONIC BURSTS OF HIS CAN DO VIRTUALLY ANYTHING... PERHAPS EVEN LOWER HIM TO EARTH WITHOUT HARM!
MMMFF!
BUT, THEY'LL BE NO PROTECTION AGAINST... THIS!!
THAT LEAVES NO ONE FOR US TO OVERCOME...
EXCEPT THE MYSTERIOUS MELTER!
18

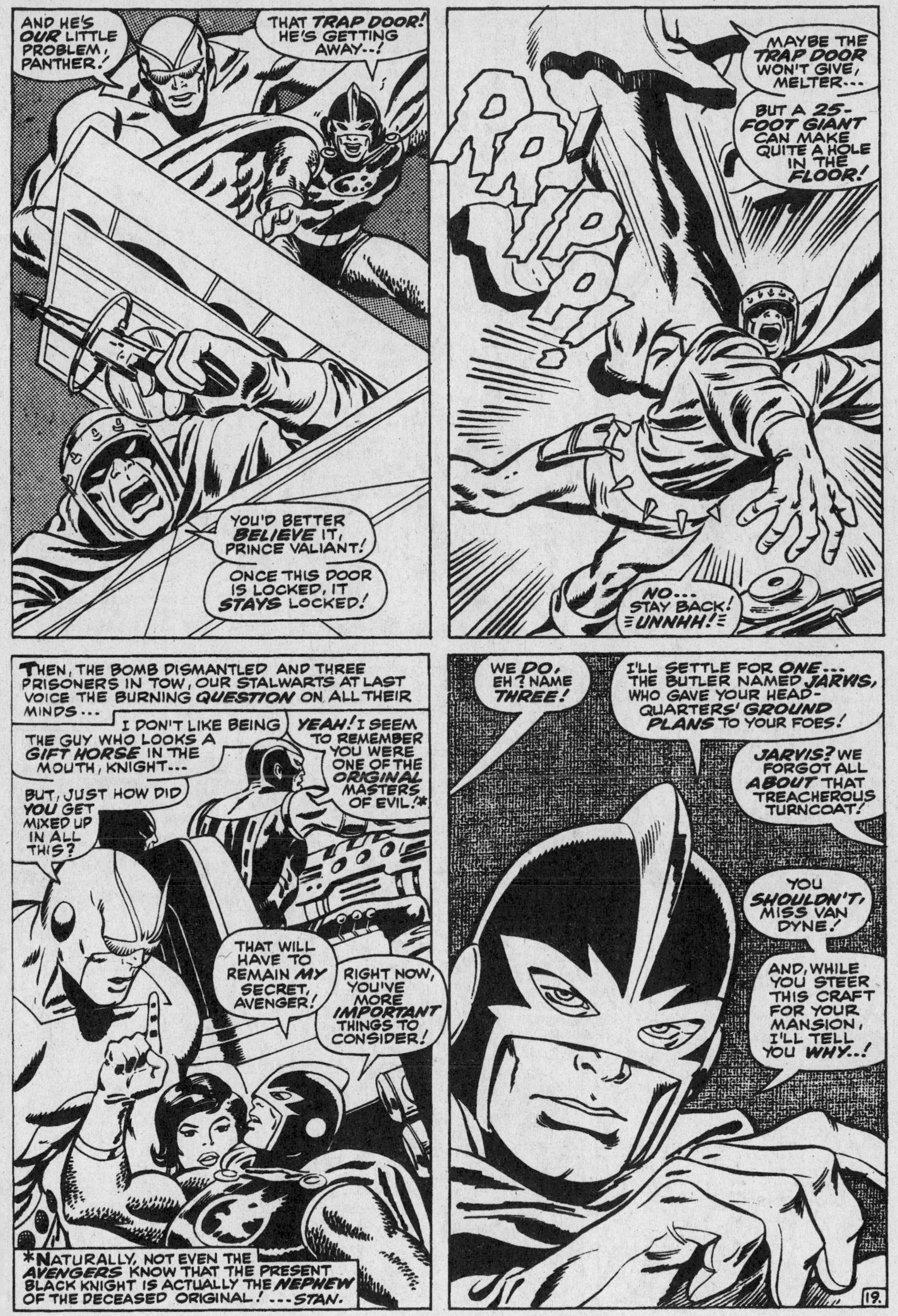

AND HE'S OUR LITTLE PROBLEM, PANTHER!
THAT TRAP DOOR! HE'S GETTING AWAY--!
YOU'D BETTER BELIEVE IT, PRINCE VALIANT!
ONCE THIS DOOR IS LOCKED, IT STAYS LOCKED!
RRIPP!
MAYBE THE TRAP DOOR WON'T GIVE, MELTER...
BUT A 25-FOOT GIANT CAN MAKE QUITE A HOLE IN THE FLOOR!
NO... STAY BACK! UNNHH!
THEN, THE BOMB DISMANTLED AND THREE PRISONERS IN TOW, OUR STALWARTS AT LAST VOICE THE BURNING QUESTION ON ALL THEIR MINDS...
I DON'T LIKE BEING THE GUY WHO LOOKS A GIFT HORSE IN THE MOUTH, KNIGHT...
BUT, JUST HOW DID YOU GET MIXED UP IN ALL THIS?
YEAH! I SEEM TO REMEMBER YOU WERE ONE OF THE ORIGINAL MASTERS OF EVIL!*
THAT WILL HAVE TO REMAIN MY SECRET, AVENGER!
RIGHT NOW, YOU'VE MORE IMPORTANT THINGS TO CONSIDER!
*NATURALLY, NOT EVEN THE AVENGERS KNOW THAT THE PRESENT BLACK KNIGHT IS ACTUALLY THE NEPHEW OF THE DECEASED ORIGINAL! ---STAN.
WE DO, EH? NAME THREE!
I'LL SETTLE FOR ONE... THE BUTLER NAMED JARVIS, WHO GAVE YOUR HEAD-QUARTERS' GROUND PLANS TO YOUR FOES!
JARVIS? WE FORGOT ALL ABOUT THAT TREACHEROUS TURNCOAT!
YOU SHOULDN'T, MISS VAN DYNE!
AND, WHILE YOU STEER THIS CRAFT FOR YOUR MANSION, I'LL TELL YOU WHY..!

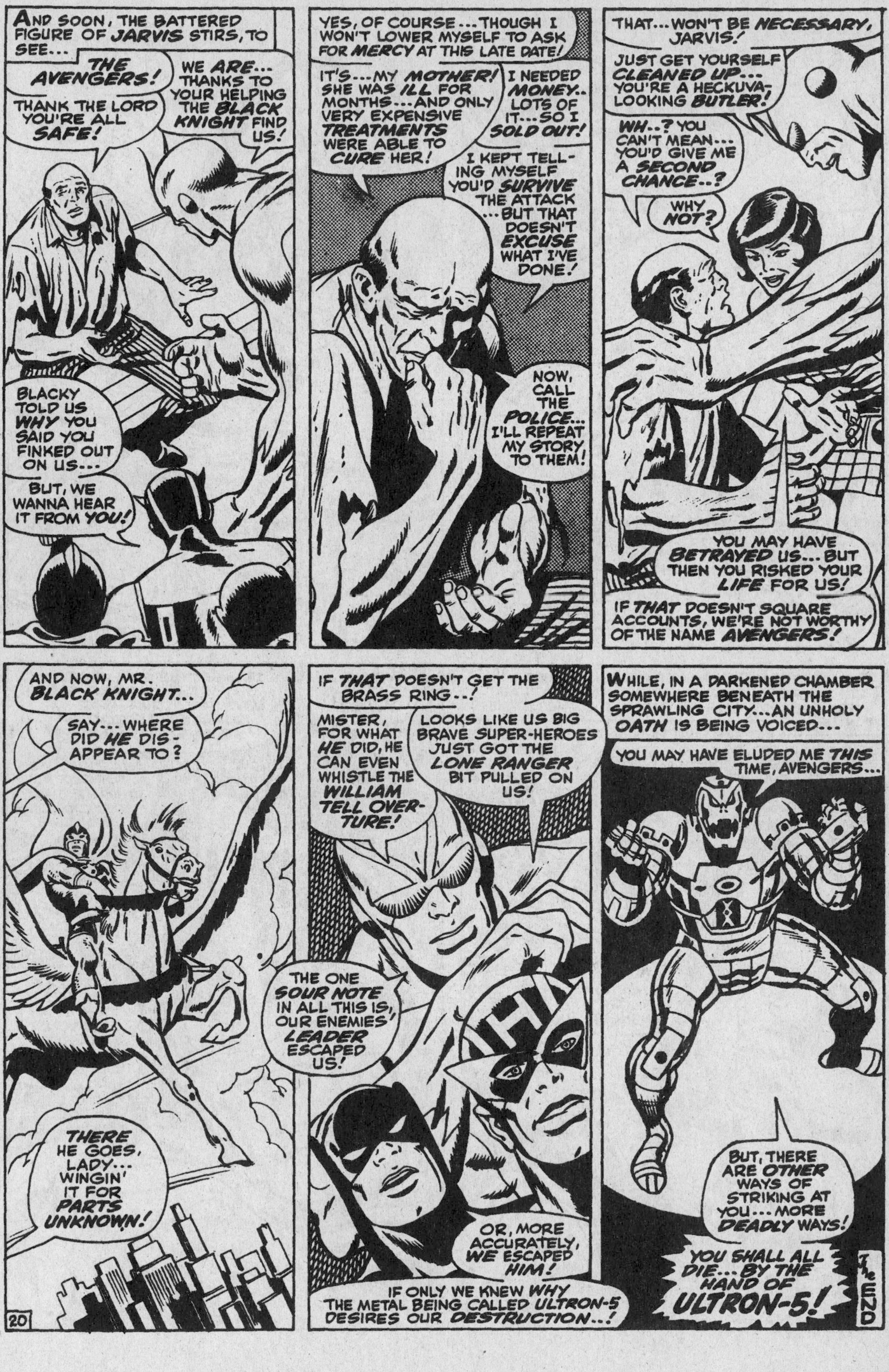
AND SOON, THE BATTERED FIGURE OF JARVIS STIRS, TO SEE...
THE AVENGERS!
THANK THE LORD YOU'RE ALL SAFE!
WE ARE... THANKS TO YOUR HELPING THE BLACK KNIGHT FIND US!
BLACKY TOLD US WHY YOU SAID YOU FINKED OUT ON US...
BUT, WE WANNA HEAR IT FROM YOU!
YES, OF COURSE... THOUGH I WON'T LOWER MYSELF TO ASK FOR MERCY AT THIS LATE DATE!
IT'S... MY MOTHER! SHE WAS ILL FOR MONTHS... AND ONLY VERY EXPENSIVE TREATMENTS WERE ABLE TO CURE HER!
I NEEDED MONEY.. LOTS OF IT... SO I SOLD OUT!
I KEPT TELLING MYSELF YOU'D SURVIVE THE ATTACK ...BUT THAT DOESN'T EXCUSE WHAT I'VE DONE!
NOW, CALL THE POLICE... I'LL REPEAT MY STORY TO THEM!
THAT... WON'T BE NECESSARY, JARVIS!
JUST GET YOURSELF CLEANED UP... YOU'RE A HECKUVA-LOOKING BUTLER!
WH..? YOU CAN'T MEAN... YOU'D GIVE ME A SECOND CHANCE..?
WHY NOT?
YOU MAY HAVE BETRAYED US... BUT THEN YOU RISKED YOUR LIFE FOR US!
IF THAT DOESN'T SQUARE ACCOUNTS, WE'RE NOT WORTHY OF THE NAME AVENGERS!
AND NOW, MR. BLACK KNIGHT...
SAY... WHERE DID HE DISAPPEAR TO?
THERE HE GOES, LADY... WINGIN' IT FOR PARTS UNKNOWN!
20
IF THAT DOESN'T GET THE BRASS RING..!
MISTER, FOR WHAT HE DID, HE CAN EVEN WHISTLE THE WILLIAM TELL OVERTURE!
LOOKS LIKE US BIG BRAVE SUPER-HEROES JUST GOT THE LONE RANGER BIT PULLED ON US!
THE ONE SOUR NOTE IN ALL THIS IS, OUR ENEMIES' LEADER ESCAPED US!
OR, MORE ACCURATELY, WE ESCAPED HIM!
IF ONLY WE KNEW WHY THE METAL BEING CALLED ULTRON-5 DESIRES OUR DESTRUCTION..!
WHILE, IN A DARKENED CHAMBER SOMEWHERE BENEATH THE SPRAWLING CITY... AN UNHOLY OATH IS BEING VOICED...
YOU MAY HAVE ELUDED ME THIS TIME, AVENGERS...
BUT, THERE ARE OTHER WAYS OF STRIKING AT YOU... MORE DEADLY WAYS!
YOU SHALL ALL DIE... BY THE HAND OF ULTRON-5!
THE END

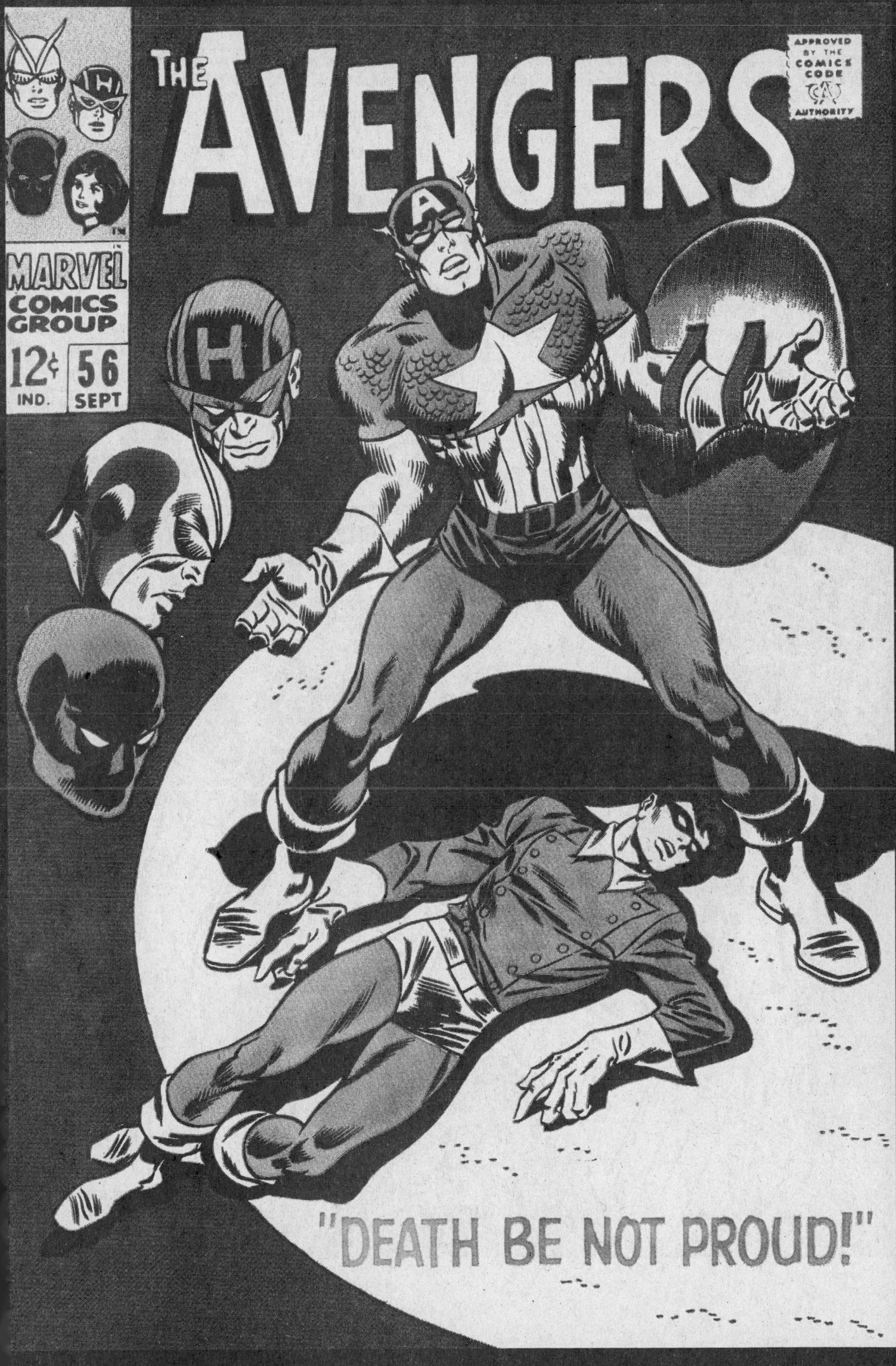
THE AVENGERS
APPROVED BY THE COMICS CODE AUTHORITY
MARVEL COMICS GROUP
12¢ IND.
56 SEPT
"DEATH BE NOT PROUD!"

PRODUCED BY AS TALENTED A TEAM OF STRIVING STALWARTS AS EVER PUT PEN OR PENCIL TO PAPER!!
STAN LEE • ROY THOMAS • JOHN BUSCEMA • GEORGE KLEIN • SAM ROSEN
EDITOR! WRITER! ARTIST! INKER! LETTERER!
SOMEWHERE BENEATH THE SOMBRE SHROUD OF NIGHT, A CASTLE STANDS...ITS LOFTY TOWERS GAZING SILENTLY DOWN UPON A UNIQUELY DRAMATIC TABLEAU...
DEATH BE NOT PROUD!
...AS, BEFORE ITS LONG-UNGUARDED RAMPARTS, A GRIM QUARTET PAUSE, TO GAZE UNCERTAINLY, ALMOST FEARFULLY, ABOUT THEM...
...AND THE MOST FATE-FUL AVENGER SAGA OF ALL BEGINS..!

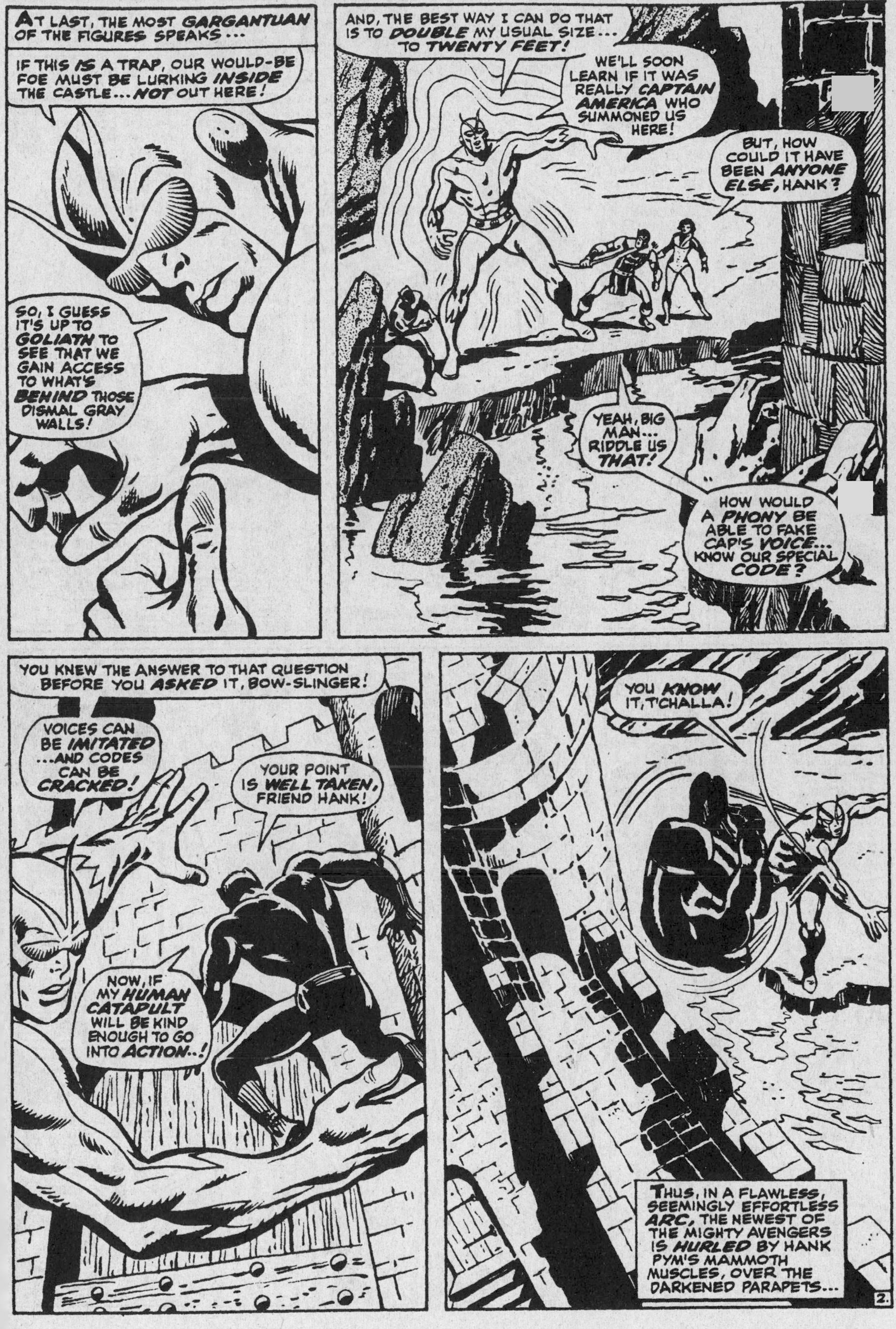
AT LAST, THE MOST GARGANTUAN OF THE FIGURES SPEAKS...
IF THIS IS A TRAP, OUR WOULD-BE FOE MUST BE LURKING INSIDE THE CASTLE... NOT OUT HERE!
SO, I GUESS IT'S UP TO GOLIATH TO SEE THAT WE GAIN ACCESS TO WHAT'S BEHIND THOSE DISMAL GRAY WALLS!
AND, THE BEST WAY I CAN DO THAT IS TO DOUBLE MY USUAL SIZE... TO TWENTY FEET!
WE'LL SOON LEARN IF IT WAS REALLY CAPTAIN AMERICA WHO SUMMONED US HERE!
BUT, HOW COULD IT HAVE BEEN ANYONE ELSE, HANK?
YEAH, BIG MAN... RIDDLE US THAT!
HOW WOULD A PHONY BE ABLE TO FAKE CAP'S VOICE... KNOW OUR SPECIAL CODE?
YOU KNEW THE ANSWER TO THAT QUESTION BEFORE YOU ASKED IT, BOW-SLINGER!
VOICES CAN BE IMITATED ...AND CODES CAN BE CRACKED!
YOUR POINT IS WELL TAKEN, FRIEND HANK!
NOW, IF MY HUMAN CATAPULT WILL BE KIND ENOUGH TO GO INTO ACTION..!
YOU KNOW IT, T'CHALLA!
THUS, IN A FLAWLESS, SEEMINGLY EFFORTLESS ARC, THE NEWEST OF THE MIGHTY AVENGERS IS HURLED BY HANK PYM'S MAMMOTH MUSCLES, OVER THE DARKENED PARAPETS...
2.

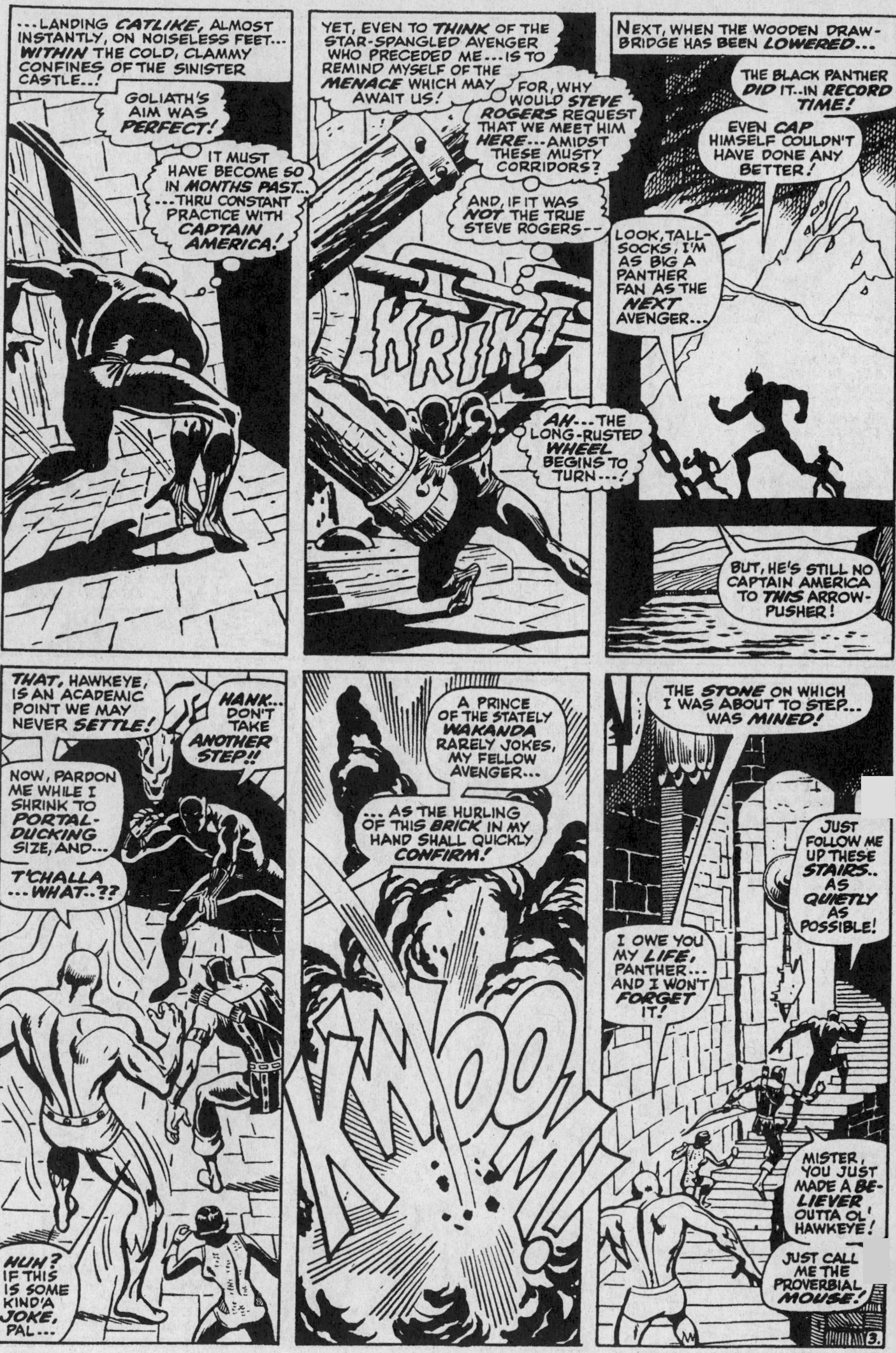

...LANDING CATLIKE, ALMOST INSTANTLY, ON NOISELESS FEET... WITHIN THE COLD, CLAMMY CONFINES OF THE SINISTER CASTLE..!
GOLIATH'S AIM WAS PERFECT!
IT MUST HAVE BECOME SO IN MONTHS PAST... ...THRU CONSTANT PRACTICE WITH CAPTAIN AMERICA!
YET, EVEN TO THINK OF THE STAR-SPANGLED AVENGER WHO PRECEDED ME...IS TO REMIND MYSELF OF THE MENACE WHICH MAY AWAIT US!
FOR, WHY WOULD STEVE ROGERS REQUEST THAT WE MEET HIM HERE...AMIDST THESE MUSTY CORRIDORS?
AND, IF IT WAS NOT THE TRUE STEVE ROGERS--
KRIK!
AH...THE LONG-RUSTED WHEEL BEGINS TO TURN...!
NEXT, WHEN THE WOODEN DRAW-BRIDGE HAS BEEN LOWERED...
THE BLACK PANTHER DID IT..IN RECORD TIME!
EVEN CAP HIMSELF COULDN'T HAVE DONE ANY BETTER!
LOOK, TALL-SOCKS, I'M AS BIG A PANTHER FAN AS THE NEXT AVENGER...
BUT, HE'S STILL NO CAPTAIN AMERICA TO THIS ARROW-PUSHER!
THAT, HAWKEYE, IS AN ACADEMIC POINT WE MAY NEVER SETTLE!
HANK... DON'T TAKE ANOTHER STEP!!
NOW, PARDON ME WHILE I SHRINK TO PORTAL-DUCKING SIZE, AND...
T'CHALLA ...WHAT..??
HUH? IF THIS IS SOME KIND'A JOKE, PAL...
A PRINCE OF THE STATELY WAKANDA RARELY JOKES, MY FELLOW AVENGER...
...AS THE HURLING OF THIS BRICK IN MY HAND SHALL QUICKLY CONFIRM!
KWOOOM!!
THE STONE ON WHICH I WAS ABOUT TO STEP... WAS MINED!
JUST FOLLOW ME UP THESE STAIRS.. AS QUIETLY AS POSSIBLE!
I OWE YOU MY LIFE, PANTHER... AND I WON'T FORGET IT!
MISTER, YOU JUST MADE A BE-LIEVER OUTTA OL' HAWKEYE!
JUST CALL ME THE PROVERBIAL MOUSE!
3.

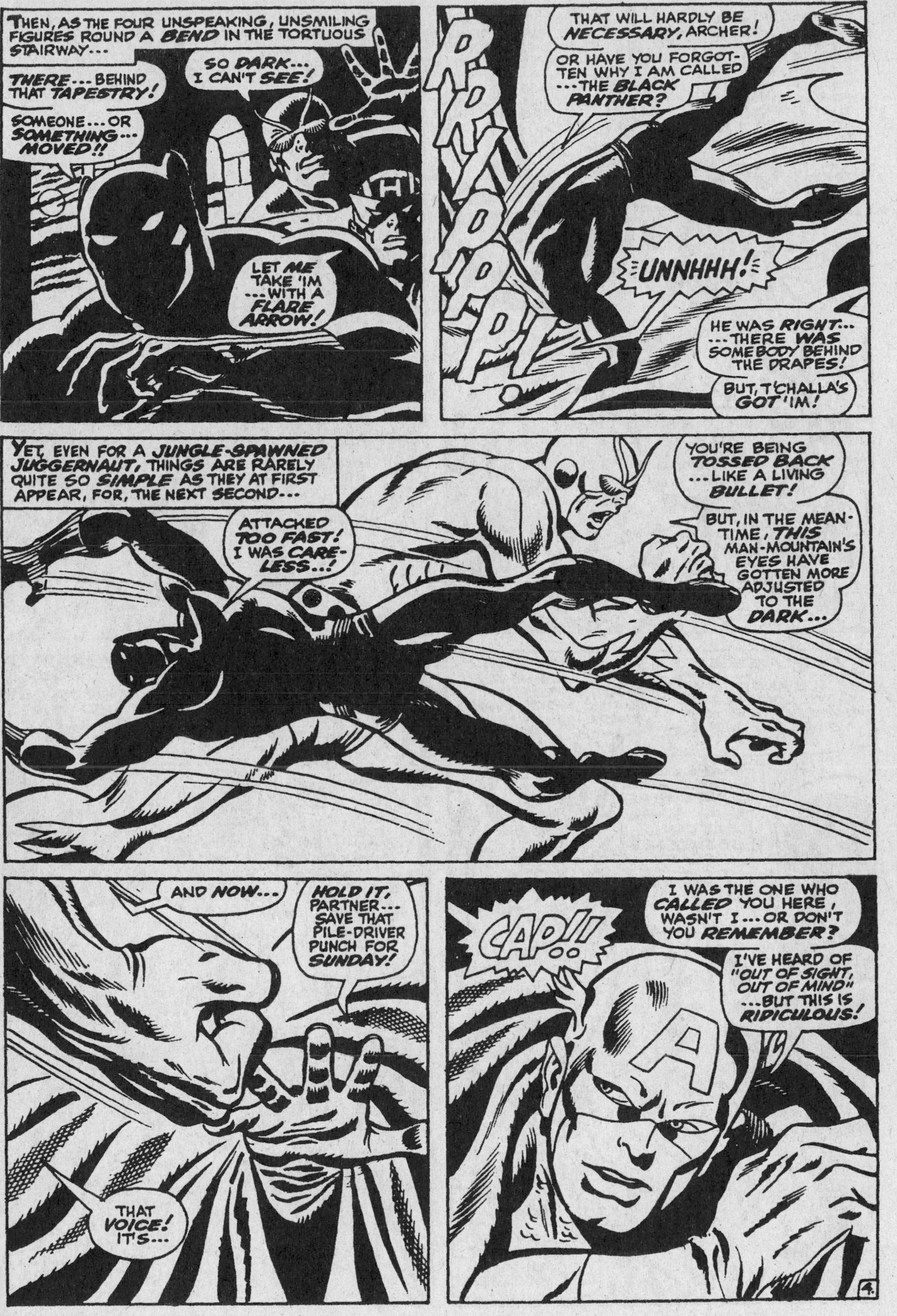
THEN, AS THE FOUR UNSPEAKING, UNSMILING FIGURES ROUND A BEND IN THE TORTUOUS STAIRWAY...
THERE... BEHIND THAT TAPESTRY!
SO DARK... I CAN'T SEE!
SOMEONE... OR SOMETHING... MOVED!!
LET ME TAKE 'IM ...WITH A FLARE ARROW!
THAT WILL HARDLY BE NECESSARY, ARCHER!
OR HAVE YOU FORGOTTEN WHY I AM CALLED ...THE BLACK PANTHER?
RRRIPPP!
UNNHHH!
HE WAS RIGHT... ...THERE WAS SOMEBODY BEHIND THE DRAPES!
BUT, T'CHALLA'S GOT 'IM!
YET, EVEN FOR A JUNGLE-SPAWNED JUGGERNAUT, THINGS ARE RARELY QUITE SO SIMPLE AS THEY AT FIRST APPEAR, FOR, THE NEXT SECOND...
ATTACKED TOO FAST! I WAS CARELESS...!
YOU'RE BEING TOSSED BACK ...LIKE A LIVING BULLET!
BUT, IN THE MEANTIME, THIS MAN-MOUNTAIN'S EYES HAVE GOTTEN MORE ADJUSTED TO THE DARK...
AND NOW...
HOLD IT, PARTNER... SAVE THAT PILE-DRIVER PUNCH FOR SUNDAY!
THAT VOICE! IT'S...
CAP!!
I WAS THE ONE WHO CALLED YOU HERE, WASN'T I... OR DON'T YOU REMEMBER?
I'VE HEARD OF "OUT OF SIGHT, OUT OF MIND" ...BUT THIS IS RIDICULOUS!
4.

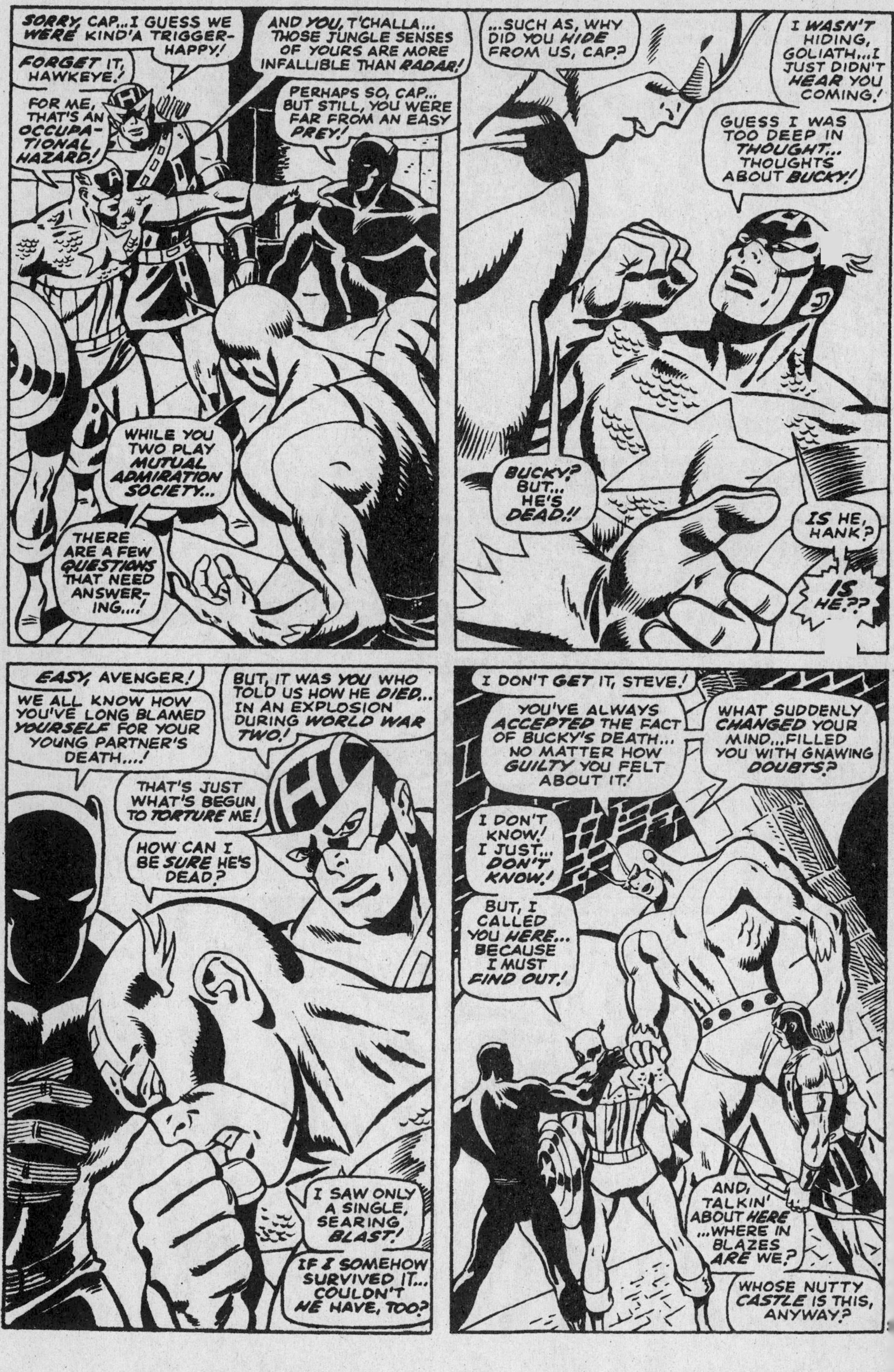
SORRY, CAP...I GUESS WE WERE KIND'A TRIGGER-HAPPY!
FORGET IT, HAWKEYE!
FOR ME, THAT'S AN OCCUPATIONAL HAZARD!
AND YOU, T'CHALLA... THOSE JUNGLE SENSES OF YOURS ARE MORE INFALLIBLE THAN RADAR!
PERHAPS SO, CAP... BUT STILL, YOU WERE FAR FROM AN EASY PREY!
WHILE YOU TWO PLAY MUTUAL ADMIRATION SOCIETY...
THERE ARE A FEW QUESTIONS THAT NEED ANSWERING...!
...SUCH AS, WHY DID YOU HIDE FROM US, CAP?
I WASN'T HIDING, GOLIATH...I JUST DIDN'T HEAR YOU COMING!
GUESS I WAS TOO DEEP IN THOUGHT... THOUGHTS ABOUT BUCKY!
BUCKY? BUT... HE'S DEAD!!
IS HE, HANK?
IS HE??
EASY, AVENGER!
WE ALL KNOW HOW YOU'VE LONG BLAMED YOURSELF FOR YOUR YOUNG PARTNER'S DEATH....!
BUT, IT WAS YOU WHO TOLD US HOW HE DIED... IN AN EXPLOSION DURING WORLD WAR TWO!
THAT'S JUST WHAT'S BEGUN TO TORTURE ME!
HOW CAN I BE SURE HE'S DEAD?
I SAW ONLY A SINGLE, SEARING BLAST!
IF I SOMEHOW SURVIVED IT... COULDN'T HE HAVE, TOO?
I DON'T GET IT, STEVE!
YOU'VE ALWAYS ACCEPTED THE FACT OF BUCKY'S DEATH... NO MATTER HOW GUILTY YOU FELT ABOUT IT!
WHAT SUDDENLY CHANGED YOUR MIND...FILLED YOU WITH GNAWING DOUBTS?
I DON'T KNOW! I JUST... DON'T KNOW!
BUT, I CALLED YOU HERE... BECAUSE I MUST FIND OUT!
AND, TALKIN' ABOUT HERE ...WHERE IN BLAZES ARE WE?
WHOSE NUTTY CASTLE IS THIS, ANYWAY?

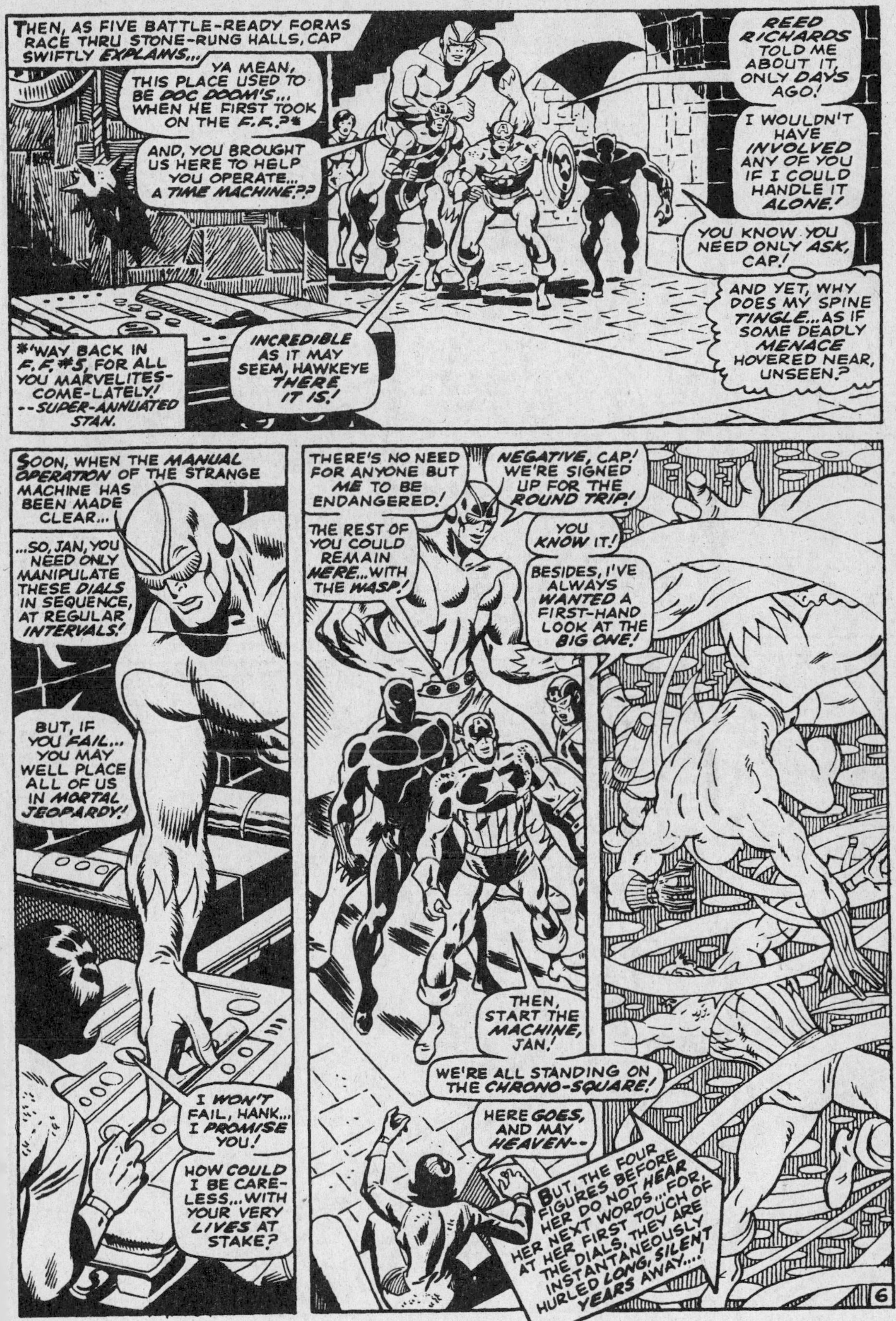
THEN, AS FIVE BATTLE-READY FORMS RACE THRU STONE-RUNG HALLS, CAP SWIFTLY EXPLAINS...
YA MEAN, THIS PLACE USED TO BE DOC DOOM'S... WHEN HE FIRST TOOK ON THE F.F.?*
AND, YOU BROUGHT US HERE TO HELP YOU OPERATE... A TIME MACHINE??
REED RICHARDS TOLD ME ABOUT IT, ONLY DAYS AGO!
I WOULDN'T HAVE INVOLVED ANY OF YOU IF I COULD HANDLE IT ALONE!
YOU KNOW YOU NEED ONLY ASK, CAP!
AND YET, WHY DOES MY SPINE TINGLE... AS IF SOME DEADLY MENACE HOVERED NEAR, UNSEEN?
*'WAY BACK IN F.F. #5, FOR ALL YOU MARVELITES-COME-LATELY! --SUPER-ANNUATED STAN.
INCREDIBLE AS IT MAY SEEM, HAWKEYE THERE IT IS!
SOON, WHEN THE MANUAL OPERATION OF THE STRANGE MACHINE HAS BEEN MADE CLEAR...
...SO, JAN, YOU NEED ONLY MANIPULATE THESE DIALS IN SEQUENCE, AT REGULAR INTERVALS!
BUT, IF YOU FAIL... YOU MAY WELL PLACE ALL OF US IN MORTAL JEOPARDY!
I WON'T FAIL, HANK... I PROMISE YOU!
HOW COULD I BE CARELESS... WITH YOUR VERY LIVES AT STAKE?
THERE'S NO NEED FOR ANYONE BUT ME TO BE ENDANGERED!
THE REST OF YOU COULD REMAIN HERE... WITH THE WASP!
NEGATIVE, CAP! WE'RE SIGNED UP FOR THE ROUND TRIP!
YOU KNOW IT!
BESIDES, I'VE ALWAYS WANTED A FIRST-HAND LOOK AT THE BIG ONE!
THEN, START THE MACHINE, JAN!
WE'RE ALL STANDING ON THE CHRONO-SQUARE!
HERE GOES, AND MAY HEAVEN--
BUT, THE FOUR FIGURES BEFORE HER DO NOT HEAR HER NEXT WORDS... FOR, AT HER FIRST TOUCH OF THE DIALS, THEY ARE INSTANTANEOUSLY HURLED LONG, SILENT YEARS AWAY...!
6

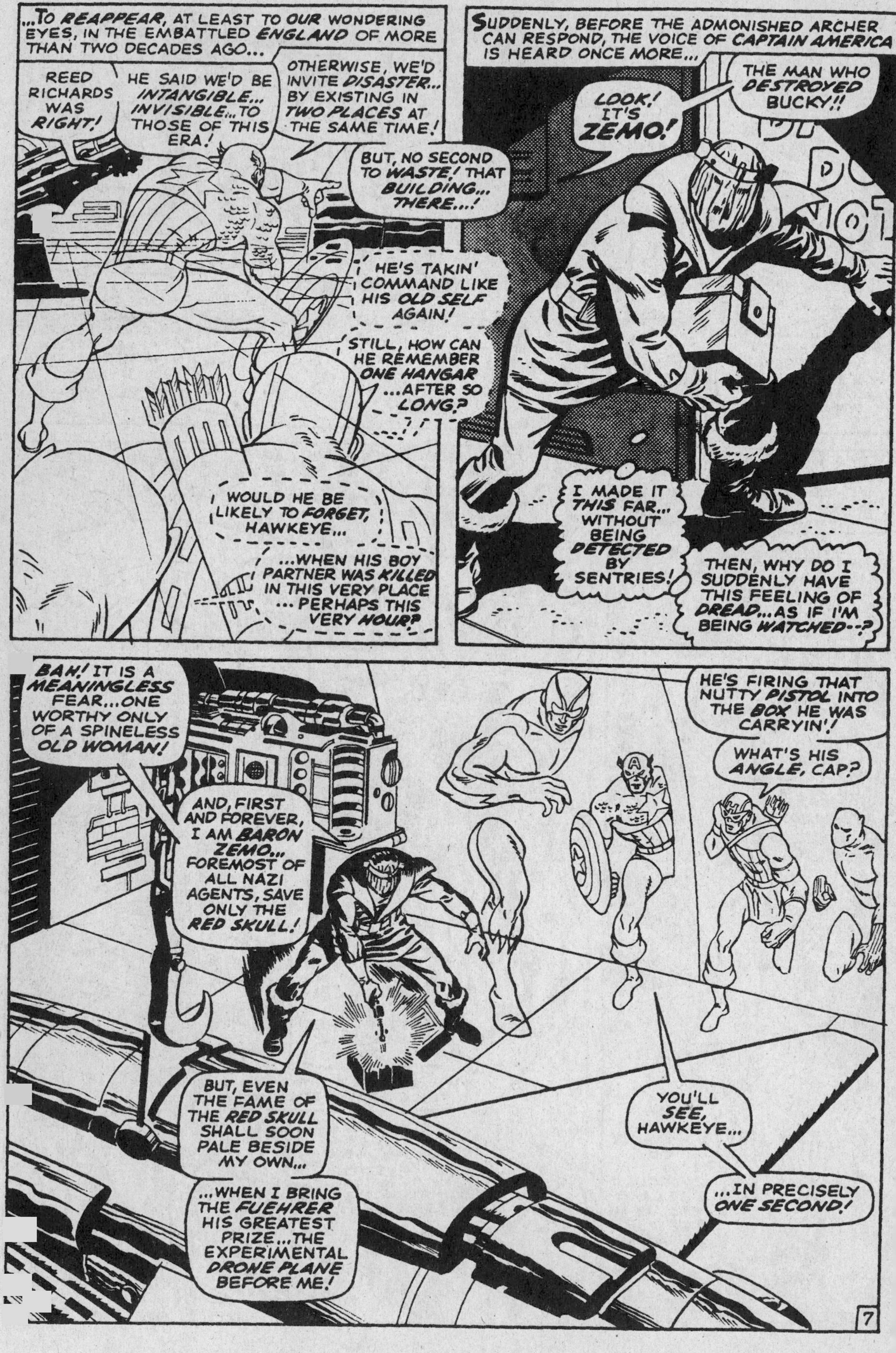
...TO REAPPEAR, AT LEAST TO OUR WONDERING EYES, IN THE EMBATTLED ENGLAND OF MORE THAN TWO DECADES AGO...
REED RICHARDS WAS RIGHT!
HE SAID WE'D BE INTANGIBLE... INVISIBLE...TO THOSE OF THIS ERA!
OTHERWISE, WE'D INVITE DISASTER... BY EXISTING IN TWO PLACES AT THE SAME TIME!
BUT, NO SECOND TO WASTE! THAT BUILDING... THERE...!
HE'S TAKIN' COMMAND LIKE HIS OLD SELF AGAIN!
STILL, HOW CAN HE REMEMBER ONE HANGAR ...AFTER SO LONG?
WOULD HE BE LIKELY TO FORGET, HAWKEYE...
...WHEN HIS BOY PARTNER WAS KILLED IN THIS VERY PLACE ... PERHAPS THIS VERY HOUR?
SUDDENLY, BEFORE THE ADMONISHED ARCHER CAN RESPOND, THE VOICE OF CAPTAIN AMERICA IS HEARD ONCE MORE...
LOOK! IT'S ZEMO!
THE MAN WHO DESTROYED BUCKY!!
I MADE IT THIS FAR... WITHOUT BEING DETECTED BY SENTRIES!
THEN, WHY DO I SUDDENLY HAVE THIS FEELING OF DREAD...AS IF I'M BEING WATCHED--?
BAH! IT IS A MEANINGLESS FEAR...ONE WORTHY ONLY OF A SPINELESS OLD WOMAN!
AND, FIRST AND FOREVER, I AM BARON ZEMO... FOREMOST OF ALL NAZI AGENTS, SAVE ONLY THE RED SKULL!
BUT, EVEN THE FAME OF THE RED SKULL SHALL SOON PALE BESIDE MY OWN...
...WHEN I BRING THE FUEHRER HIS GREATEST PRIZE...THE EXPERIMENTAL DRONE PLANE BEFORE ME!
HE'S FIRING THAT NUTTY PISTOL INTO THE BOX HE WAS CARRYIN'!
WHAT'S HIS ANGLE, CAP?
YOU'LL SEE, HAWKEYE...
...IN PRECISELY ONE SECOND!
7

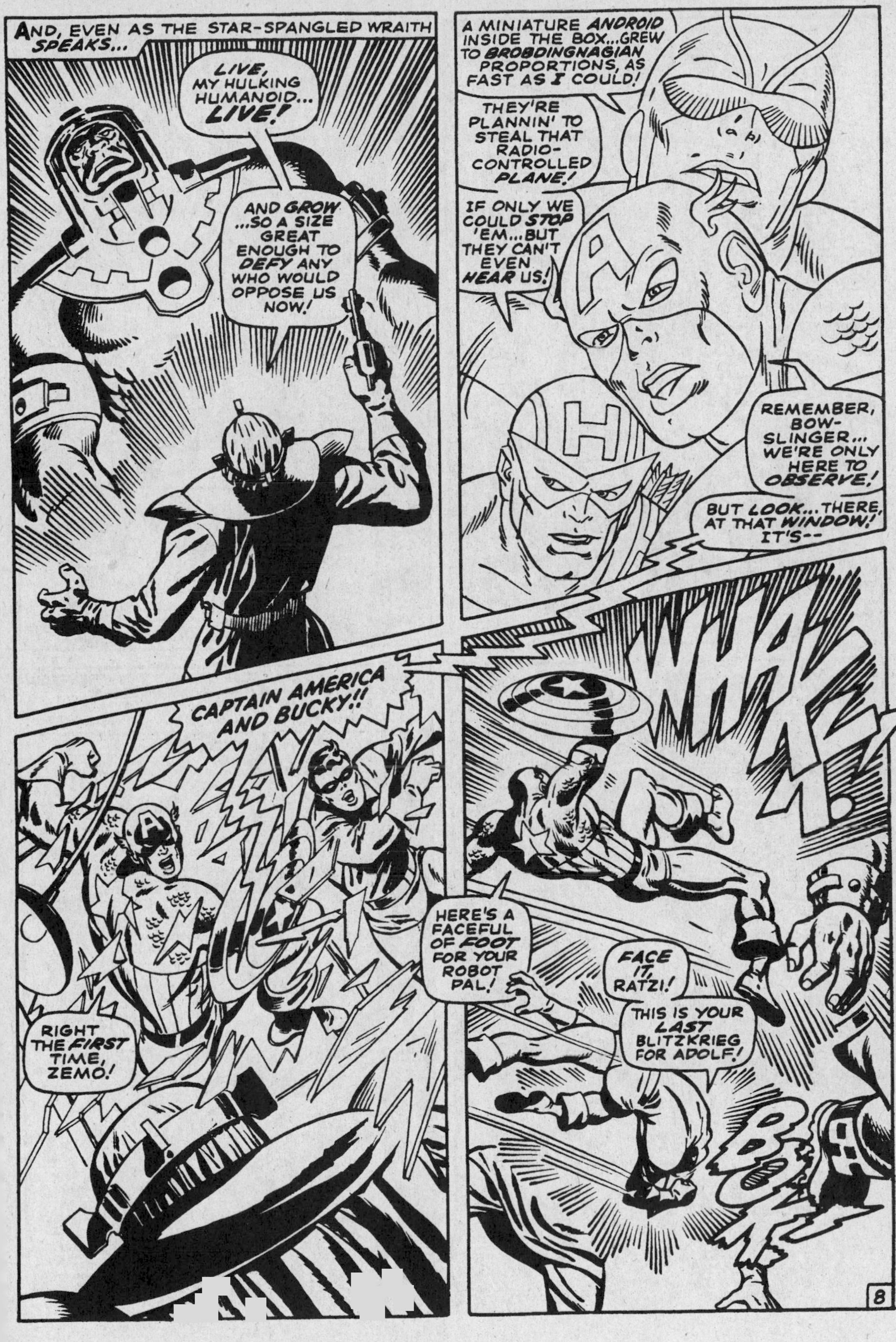
AND, EVEN AS THE STAR-SPANGLED WRAITH SPEAKS...
LIVE, MY HULKING HUMANOID... LIVE!
AND GROW ...SO A SIZE GREAT ENOUGH TO DEFY ANY WHO WOULD OPPOSE US NOW!
A MINIATURE ANDROID INSIDE THE BOX...GREW TO BROBDINGNAGIAN PROPORTIONS, AS FAST AS I COULD!
THEY'RE PLANNIN' TO STEAL THAT RADIO-CONTROLLED PLANE!
IF ONLY WE COULD STOP 'EM...BUT THEY CAN'T EVEN HEAR US!
REMEMBER, BOW-SLINGER... WE'RE ONLY HERE TO OBSERVE!
BUT LOOK...THERE, AT THAT WINDOW! IT'S--
CAPTAIN AMERICA AND BUCKY!!
WHAK!
RIGHT THE FIRST TIME, ZEMO!
HERE'S A FACEFUL OF FOOT FOR YOUR ROBOT PAL!
FACE IT, RATZI!
THIS IS YOUR LAST BLITZKRIEG FOR ADOLF!
BOK!
8

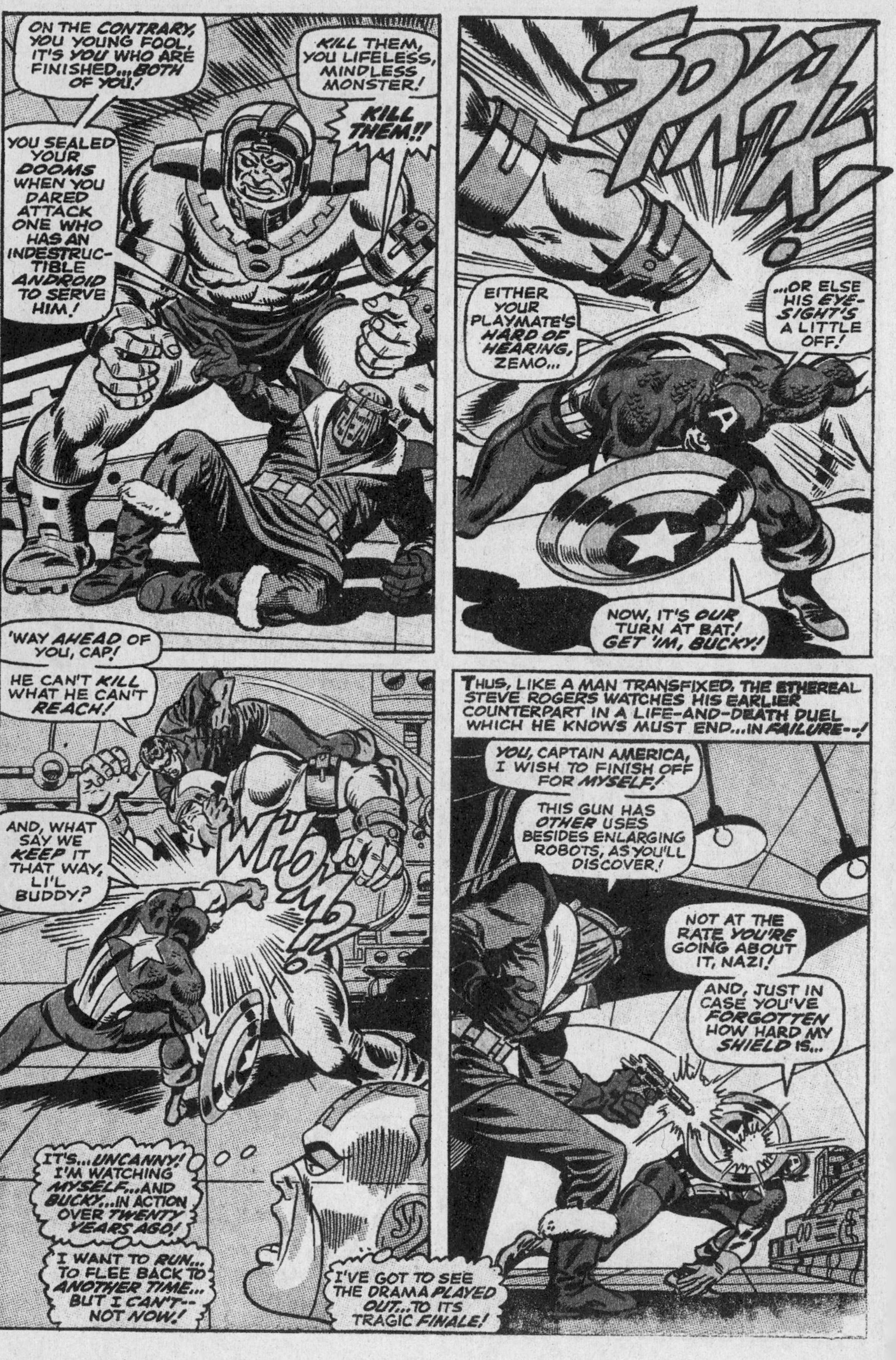
ON THE CONTRARY, YOU YOUNG FOOL, IT'S YOU WHO ARE FINISHED...BOTH OF YOU!
YOU SEALED YOUR DOOMS WHEN YOU DARED ATTACK ONE WHO HAS AN INDESTRUCTIBLE ANDROID TO SERVE HIM!
KILL THEM, YOU LIFELESS, MINDLESS MONSTER!
KILL THEM!!
SPAKK!
EITHER YOUR PLAYMATE'S HARD OF HEARING, ZEMO...
...OR ELSE HIS EYE-SIGHT'S A LITTLE OFF!
NOW, IT'S OUR TURN AT BAT! GET 'IM, BUCKY!
'WAY AHEAD OF YOU, CAP!
HE CAN'T KILL WHAT HE CAN'T REACH!
AND, WHAT SAY WE KEEP IT THAT WAY, LI'L BUDDY?
WHOMP
IT'S...UNCANNY! I'M WATCHING MYSELF...AND BUCKY...IN ACTION OVER TWENTY YEARS AGO!
I WANT TO RUN... TO FLEE BACK TO ANOTHER TIME... BUT I CAN'T-- NOT NOW!
I'VE GOT TO SEE THE DRAMA PLAYED OUT...TO ITS TRAGIC FINALE!
THUS, LIKE A MAN TRANSFIXED, THE ETHEREAL STEVE ROGERS WATCHES HIS EARLIER COUNTERPART IN A LIFE-AND-DEATH DUEL WHICH HE KNOWS MUST END...IN FAILURE--!
YOU, CAPTAIN AMERICA, I WISH TO FINISH OFF FOR MYSELF!
THIS GUN HAS OTHER USES BESIDES ENLARGING ROBOTS, AS YOU'LL DISCOVER!
NOT AT THE RATE YOU'RE GOING ABOUT IT, NAZI!
AND, JUST IN CASE YOU'VE FORGOTTEN HOW HARD MY SHIELD IS...

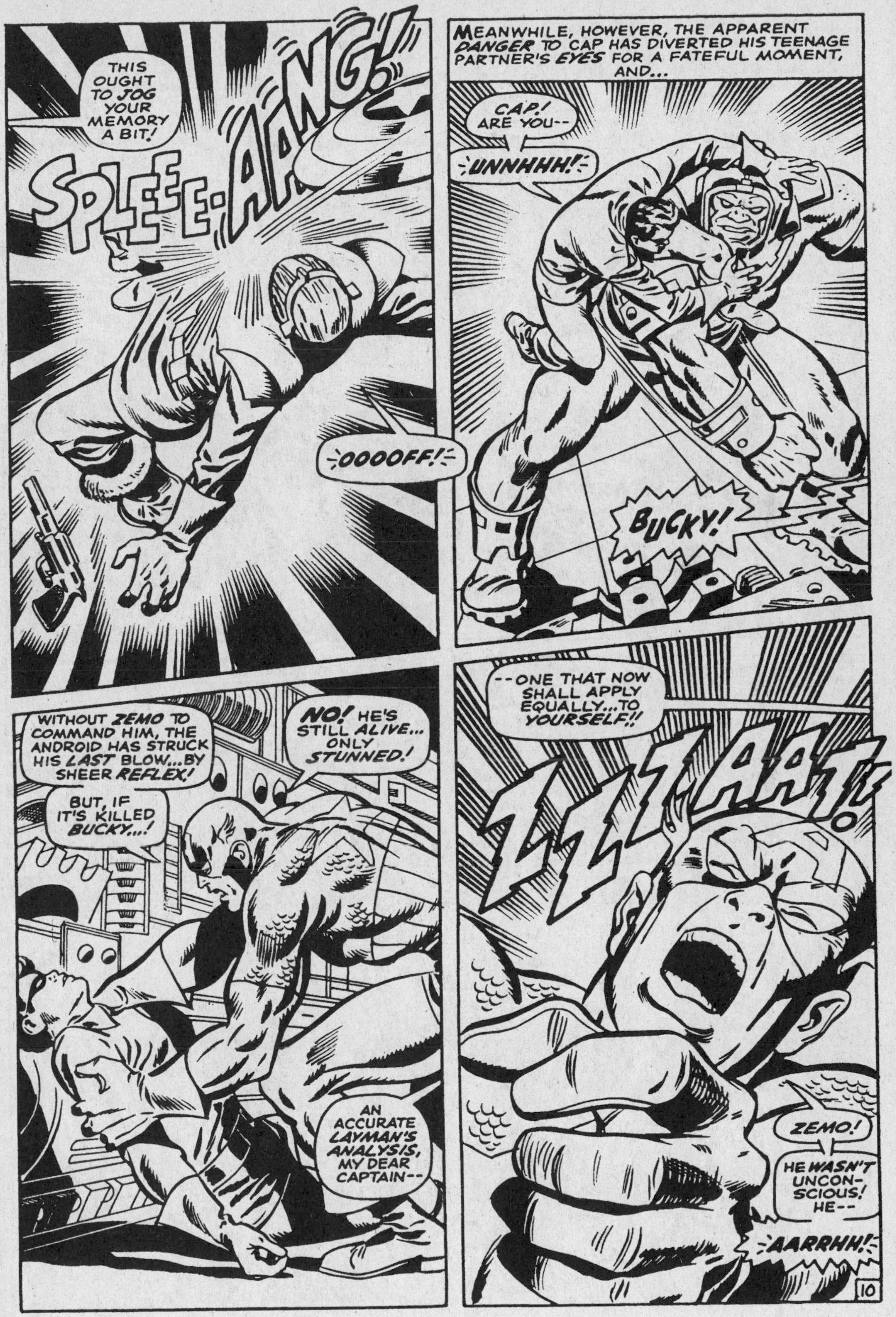
THIS OUGHT TO JOG YOUR MEMORY A BIT!
SPLEEE-AANG!
-OOOOFF!-
MEANWHILE, HOWEVER, THE APPARENT DANGER TO CAP HAS DIVERTED HIS TEENAGE PARTNER'S EYES FOR A FATEFUL MOMENT, AND...
CAP! ARE YOU--
-UNNHHH!-
BUCKY!
WITHOUT ZEMO TO COMMAND HIM, THE ANDROID HAS STRUCK HIS LAST BLOW...BY SHEER REFLEX!
BUT, IF IT'S KILLED BUCKY...!
NO! HE'S STILL ALIVE... ONLY STUNNED!
AN ACCURATE LAYMAN'S ANALYSIS, MY DEAR CAPTAIN--
--ONE THAT NOW SHALL APPLY EQUALLY...TO YOURSELF!!
ZZZAAT!
ZEMO!
HE WASN'T UNCONSCIOUS! HE--
-AARRHH!-

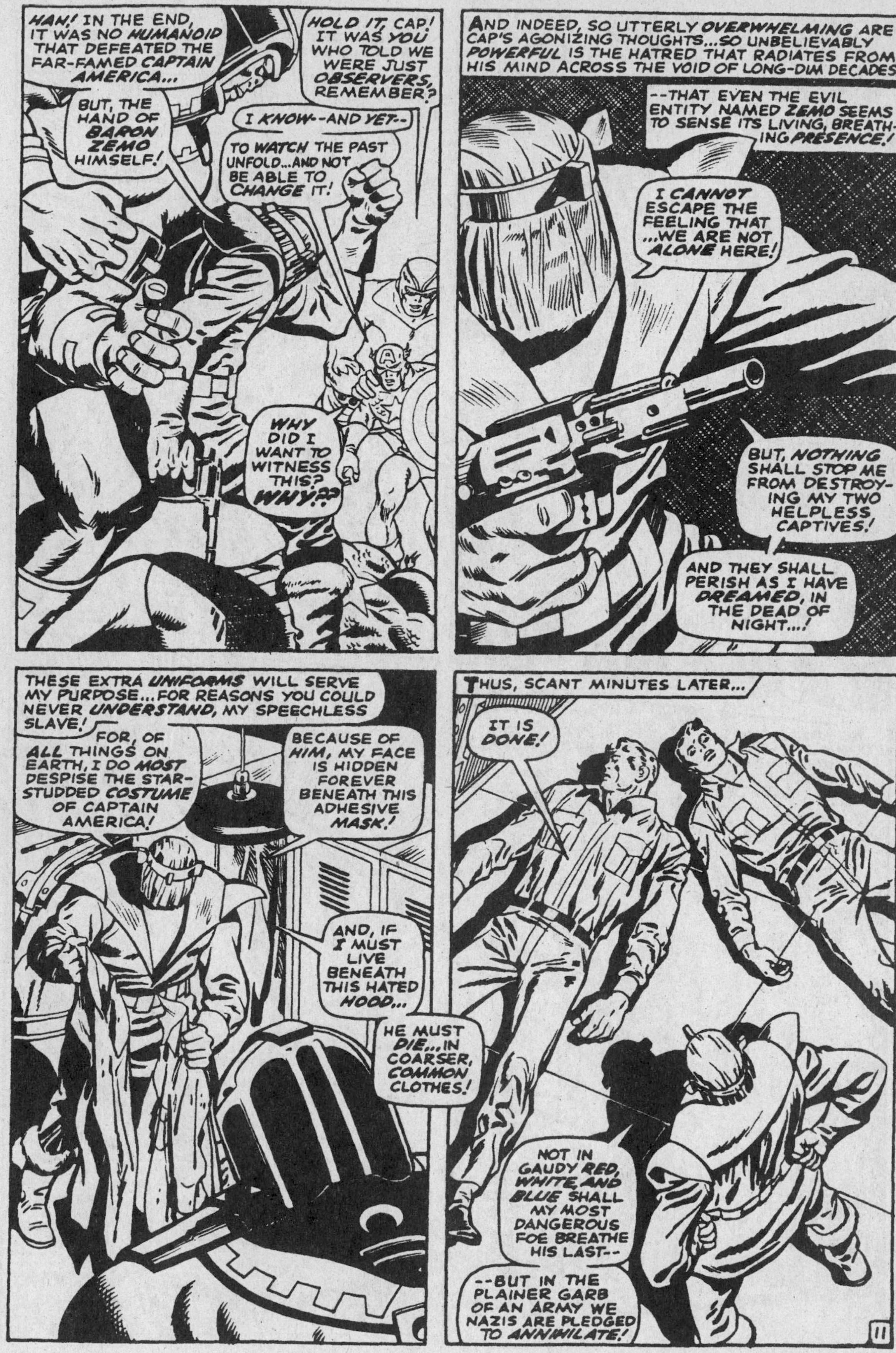
HAH! IN THE END, IT WAS NO HUMANOID THAT DEFEATED THE FAR-FAMED CAPTAIN AMERICA...
BUT, THE HAND OF BARON ZEMO HIMSELF!
HOLD IT, CAP! IT WAS YOU WHO TOLD WE WERE JUST OBSERVERS, REMEMBER?
I KNOW--AND YET--
TO WATCH THE PAST UNFOLD...AND NOT BE ABLE TO CHANGE IT!
WHY DID I WANT TO WITNESS THIS? WHY?!?
AND INDEED, SO UTTERLY OVERWHELMING ARE CAP'S AGONIZING THOUGHTS...SO UNBELIEVABLY POWERFUL IS THE HATRED THAT RADIATES FROM HIS MIND ACROSS THE VOID OF LONG-DIM DECADES...
--THAT EVEN THE EVIL ENTITY NAMED ZEMO SEEMS TO SENSE ITS LIVING, BREATHING PRESENCE!
I CANNOT ESCAPE THE FEELING THAT ...WE ARE NOT ALONE HERE!
BUT, NOTHING SHALL STOP ME FROM DESTROYING MY TWO HELPLESS CAPTIVES!
AND THEY SHALL PERISH AS I HAVE DREAMED, IN THE DEAD OF NIGHT...!
THESE EXTRA UNIFORMS WILL SERVE MY PURPOSE...FOR REASONS YOU COULD NEVER UNDERSTAND, MY SPEECHLESS SLAVE!
FOR, OF ALL THINGS ON EARTH, I DO MOST DESPISE THE STAR-STUDDED COSTUME OF CAPTAIN AMERICA!
BECAUSE OF HIM, MY FACE IS HIDDEN FOREVER BENEATH THIS ADHESIVE MASK!
AND, IF I MUST LIVE BENEATH THIS HATED HOOD...
HE MUST DIE...IN COARSER, COMMON CLOTHES!
THUS, SCANT MINUTES LATER...
IT IS DONE!
NOT IN GAUDY RED, WHITE AND BLUE SHALL MY MOST DANGEROUS FOE BREATHE HIS LAST--
--BUT IN THE PLAINER GARB OF AN ARMY WE NAZIS ARE PLEDGED TO ANNIHILATE!
11

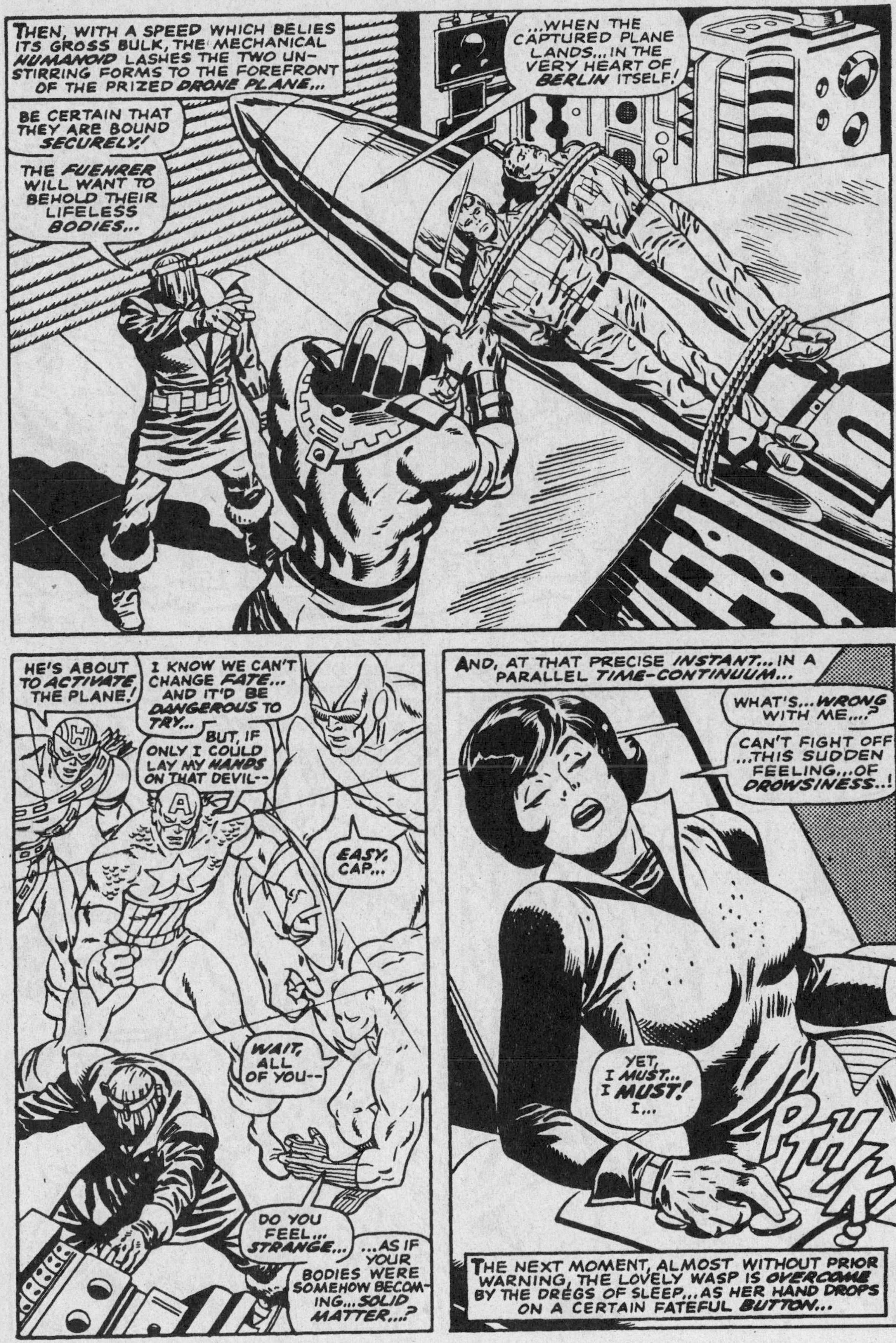
THEN, WITH A SPEED WHICH BELIES ITS GROSS BULK, THE MECHANICAL HUMANOID LASHES THE TWO UN-STIRRING FORMS TO THE FOREFRONT OF THE PRIZED DRONE PLANE...
BE CERTAIN THAT THEY ARE BOUND SECURELY!
THE FUEHRER WILL WANT TO BEHOLD THEIR LIFELESS BODIES...
...WHEN THE CAPTURED PLANE LANDS...IN THE VERY HEART OF BERLIN ITSELF!
HE'S ABOUT TO ACTIVATE THE PLANE!
I KNOW WE CAN'T CHANGE FATE... AND IT'D BE DANGEROUS TO TRY...
BUT, IF ONLY I COULD LAY MY HANDS ON THAT DEVIL--
EASY, CAP...
WAIT, ALL OF YOU--
DO YOU FEEL... STRANGE...
...AS IF YOUR BODIES WERE SOMEHOW BECOMING...SOLID MATTER...?
AND, AT THAT PRECISE INSTANT...IN A PARALLEL TIME-CONTINUUM...
WHAT'S...WRONG WITH ME....?
CAN'T FIGHT OFF ...THIS SUDDEN FEELING...OF DROWSINESS..!
YET, I MUST... I MUST! I...
PTHK!
THE NEXT MOMENT, ALMOST WITHOUT PRIOR WARNING, THE LOVELY WASP IS OVERCOME BY THE DREGS OF SLEEP... AS HER HAND DROPS ON A CERTAIN FATEFUL BUTTON...

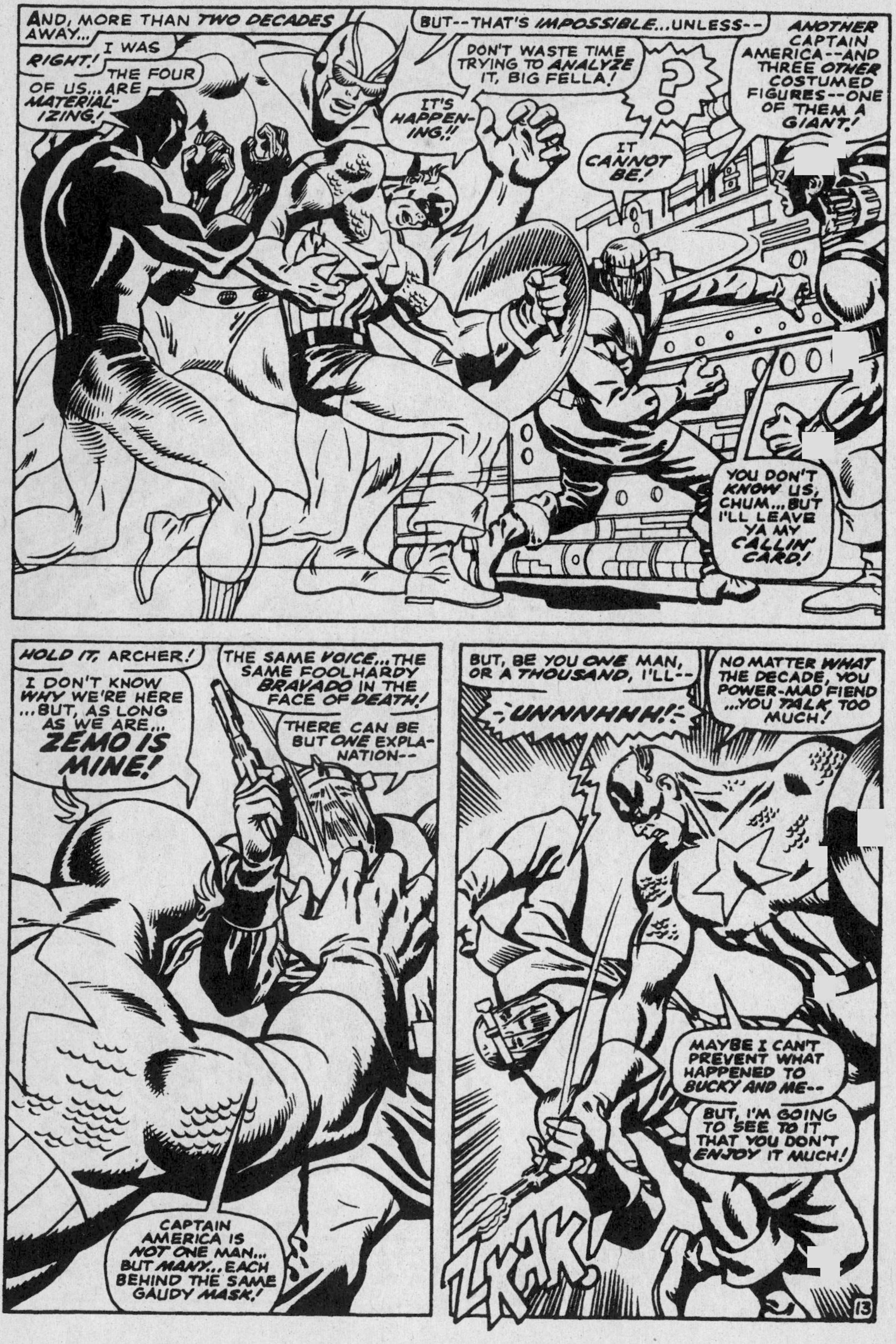

AND, MORE THAN TWO DECADES AWAY...
I WAS RIGHT!
THE FOUR OF US... ARE MATERIAL-IZING!
BUT--THAT'S IMPOSSIBLE...UNLESS--
DON'T WASTE TIME TRYING TO ANALYZE IT, BIG FELLA!
IT'S HAPPEN-ING!!
?
IT CANNOT BE!
ANOTHER CAPTAIN AMERICA--AND THREE OTHER COSTUMED FIGURES--ONE OF THEM A GIANT!
YOU DON'T KNOW US, CHUM...BUT I'LL LEAVE YA MY CALLIN' CARD!
HOLD IT, ARCHER!
I DON'T KNOW WHY WE'RE HERE ...BUT, AS LONG AS WE ARE... ZEMO IS MINE!
THE SAME VOICE...THE SAME FOOLHARDY BRAVADO IN THE FACE OF DEATH!
THERE CAN BE BUT ONE EXPLA-NATION--
CAPTAIN AMERICA IS NOT ONE MAN... BUT MANY...EACH BEHIND THE SAME GAUDY MASK!
BUT, BE YOU ONE MAN, OR A THOUSAND, I'LL--
UNNNHHH!
NO MATTER WHAT THE DECADE, YOU POWER-MAD FIEND ...YOU TALK TOO MUCH!
MAYBE I CAN'T PREVENT WHAT HAPPENED TO BUCKY AND ME--
BUT, I'M GOING TO SEE TO IT THAT YOU DON'T ENJOY IT MUCH!
ZKAK!
13

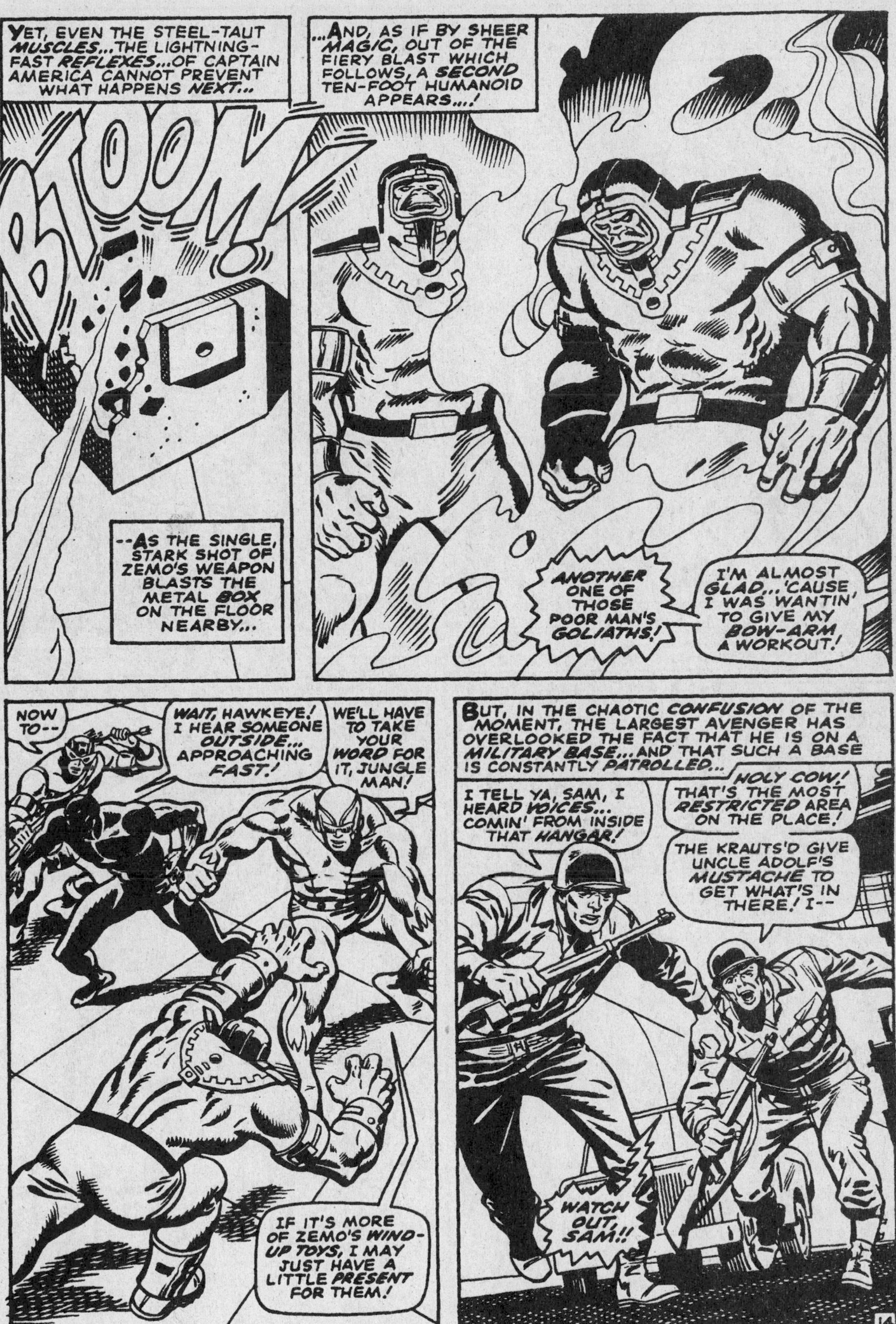

YET, EVEN THE STEEL-TAUT MUSCLES... THE LIGHTNING-FAST REFLEXES... OF CAPTAIN AMERICA CANNOT PREVENT WHAT HAPPENS NEXT...
BTOOM!
--AS THE SINGLE, STARK SHOT OF ZEMO'S WEAPON BLASTS THE METAL BOX ON THE FLOOR NEARBY...
...AND, AS IF BY SHEER MAGIC, OUT OF THE FIERY BLAST WHICH FOLLOWS, A SECOND TEN-FOOT HUMANOID APPEARS...!
ANOTHER ONE OF THOSE POOR MAN'S GOLIATHS!
I'M ALMOST GLAD... 'CAUSE I WAS WANTIN' TO GIVE MY BOW-ARM A WORKOUT!
NOW TO--
WAIT, HAWKEYE! I HEAR SOMEONE OUTSIDE... APPROACHING FAST!
WE'LL HAVE TO TAKE YOUR WORD FOR IT, JUNGLE MAN!
IF IT'S MORE OF ZEMO'S WIND-UP TOYS, I MAY JUST HAVE A LITTLE PRESENT FOR THEM!
BUT, IN THE CHAOTIC CONFUSION OF THE MOMENT, THE LARGEST AVENGER HAS OVERLOOKED THE FACT THAT HE IS ON A MILITARY BASE... AND THAT SUCH A BASE IS CONSTANTLY PATROLLED...
I TELL YA, SAM, I HEARD VOICES... COMIN' FROM INSIDE THAT HANGAR!
HOLY COW! THAT'S THE MOST RESTRICTED AREA ON THE PLACE!
THE KRAUTS'D GIVE UNCLE ADOLF'S MUSTACHE TO GET WHAT'S IN THERE! I--
WATCH OUT, SAM!!
14

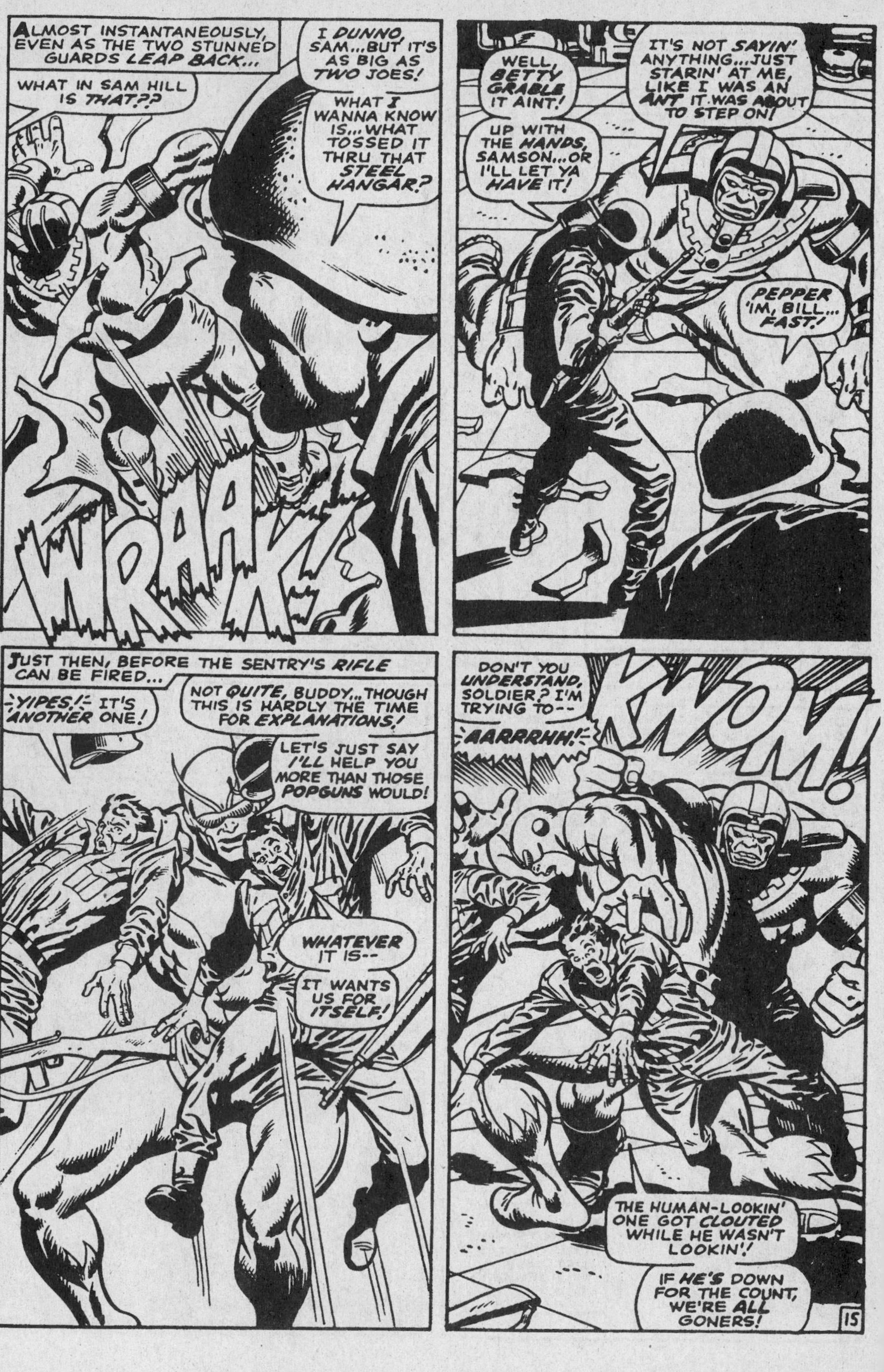
ALMOST INSTANTANEOUSLY, EVEN AS THE TWO STUNNED GUARDS LEAP BACK...
WHAT IN SAM HILL IS THAT??
I DUNNO, SAM... BUT IT'S AS BIG AS TWO JOES!
WHAT I WANNA KNOW IS... WHAT TOSSED IT THRU THAT STEEL HANGAR?
WRAAK!
WELL, BETTY GRABLE IT AINT!
IT'S NOT SAYIN' ANYTHING... JUST STARIN' AT ME, LIKE I WAS AN ANT IT WAS ABOUT TO STEP ON!
UP WITH THE HANDS, SAMSON... OR I'LL LET YA HAVE IT!
PEPPER 'IM, BILL... FAST!
JUST THEN, BEFORE THE SENTRY'S RIFLE CAN BE FIRED...
YIPES! IT'S ANOTHER ONE!
NOT QUITE, BUDDY... THOUGH THIS IS HARDLY THE TIME FOR EXPLANATIONS!
LET'S JUST SAY I'LL HELP YOU MORE THAN THOSE POPGUNS WOULD!
WHATEVER IT IS--
IT WANTS US FOR ITSELF!
DON'T YOU UNDERSTAND, SOLDIER? I'M TRYING TO--
KWOM!
AARRRHH!
THE HUMAN-LOOKIN' ONE GOT CLOUTED WHILE HE WASN'T LOOKIN'!
IF HE'S DOWN FOR THE COUNT, WE'RE ALL GONERS!
15

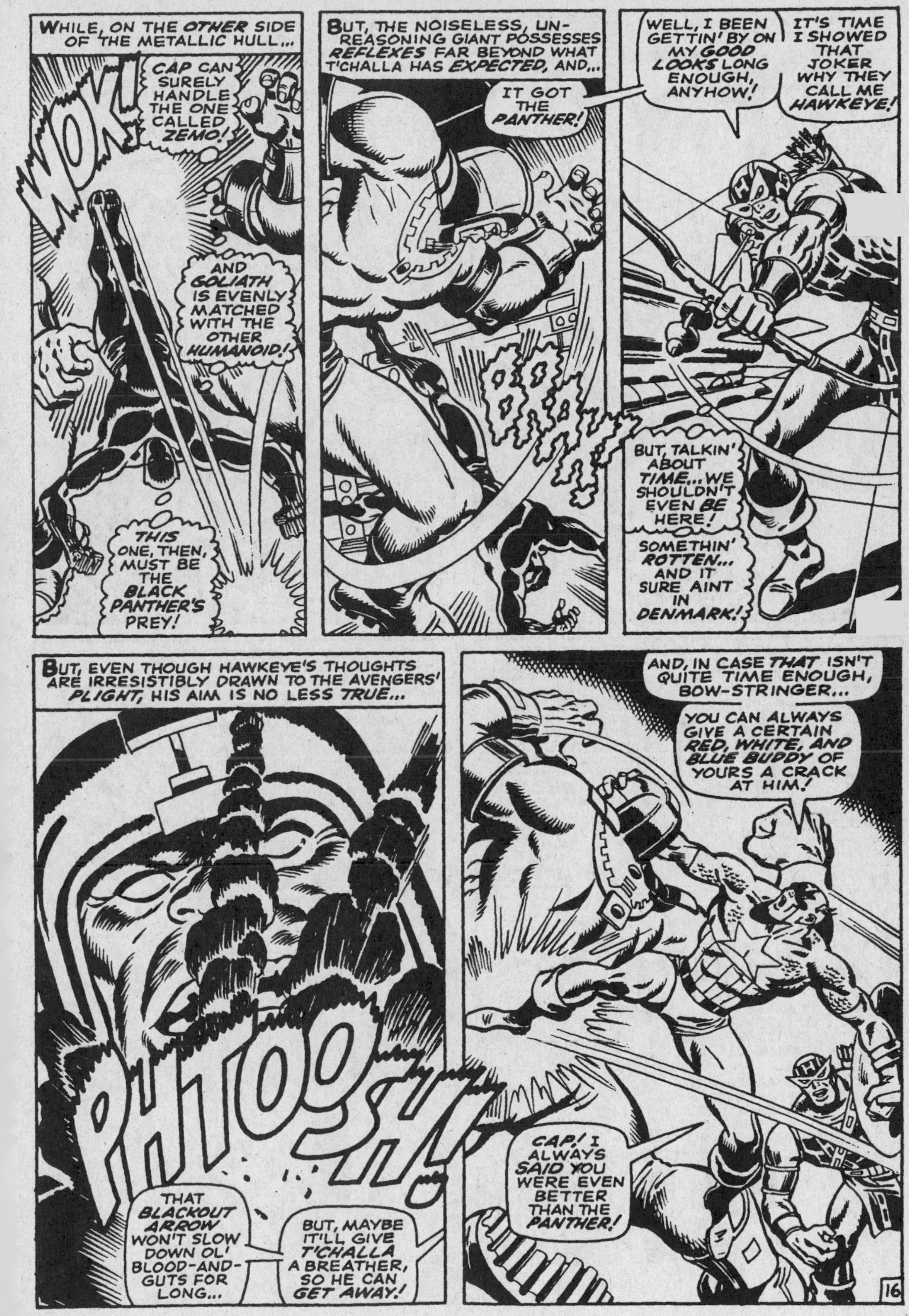

WHILE, ON THE OTHER SIDE OF THE METALLIC HULL...
WOK!
CAP CAN SURELY HANDLE THE ONE CALLED ZEMO!
AND GOLIATH IS EVENLY MATCHED WITH THE OTHER HUMANOID!
THIS ONE, THEN, MUST BE THE BLACK PANTHER'S PREY!
BUT, THE NOISELESS, UN-REASONING GIANT POSSESSES REFLEXES FAR BEYOND WHAT T'CHALLA HAS EXPECTED, AND...
IT GOT THE PANTHER!
WELL, I BEEN GETTIN' BY ON MY GOOD LOOKS LONG ENOUGH, ANYHOW!
IT'S TIME I SHOWED THAT JOKER WHY THEY CALL ME HAWKEYE!
BUT, TALKIN' ABOUT TIME...WE SHOULDN'T EVEN BE HERE!
SOMETHIN' ROTTEN... AND IT SURE AINT IN DENMARK!
BUT, EVEN THOUGH HAWKEYE'S THOUGHTS ARE IRRESISTIBLY DRAWN TO THE AVENGERS' PLIGHT, HIS AIM IS NO LESS TRUE...
PHTOOSH!
THAT BLACKOUT ARROW WON'T SLOW DOWN OL' BLOOD-AND-GUTS FOR LONG...
BUT, MAYBE IT'LL GIVE T'CHALLA A BREATHER, SO HE CAN GET AWAY!
AND, IN CASE THAT ISN'T QUITE TIME ENOUGH, BOW-STRINGER...
YOU CAN ALWAYS GIVE A CERTAIN RED, WHITE, AND BLUE BUDDY OF YOURS A CRACK AT HIM!
CAP! I ALWAYS SAID YOU WERE EVEN BETTER THAN THE PANTHER!
16

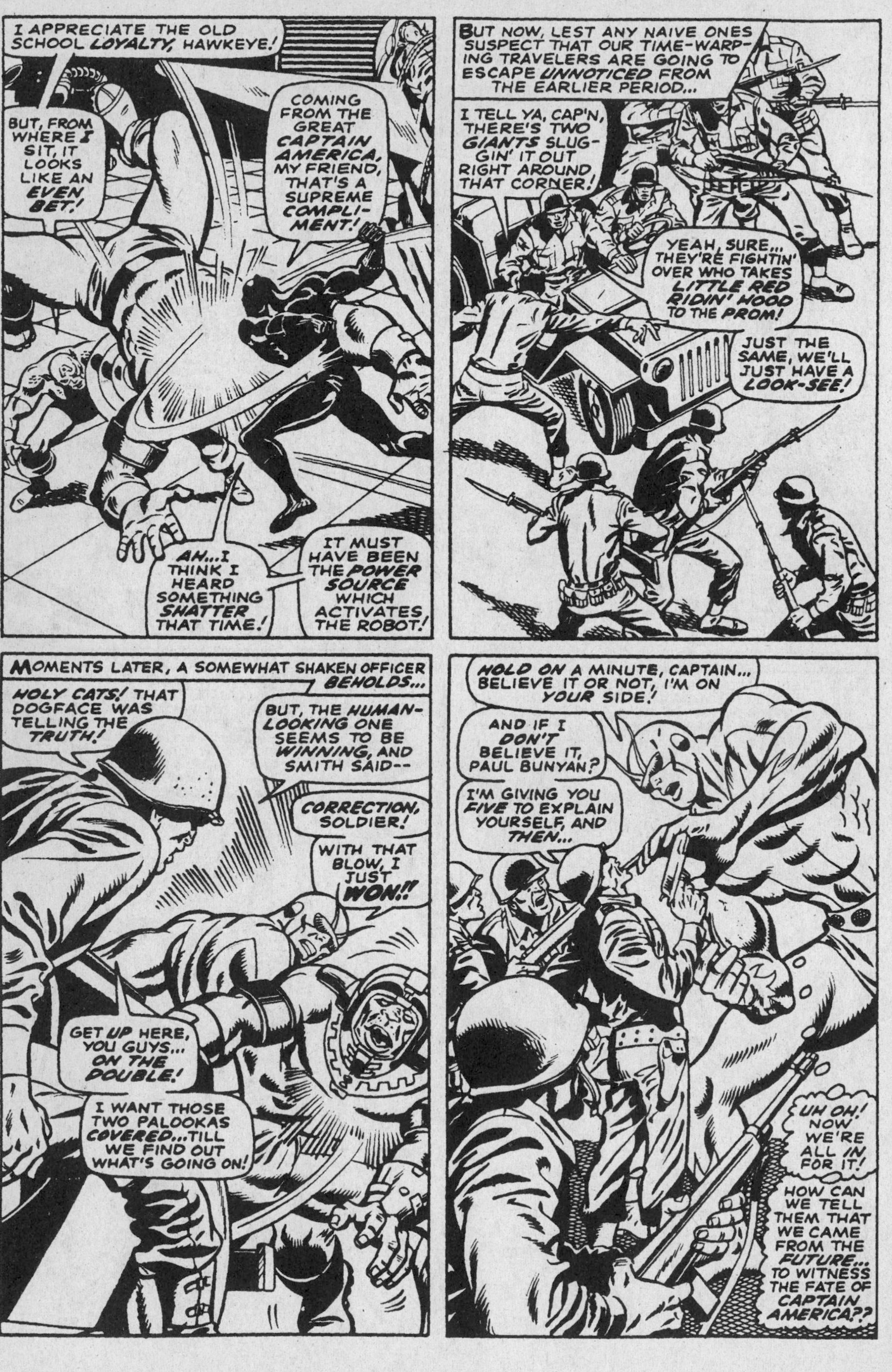

I APPRECIATE THE OLD SCHOOL LOYALTY, HAWKEYE!
BUT, FROM WHERE I SIT, IT LOOKS LIKE AN EVEN BET!
COMING FROM THE GREAT CAPTAIN AMERICA, MY FRIEND, THAT'S A SUPREME COMPLI-MENT!
AH...I THINK I HEARD SOMETHING SHATTER THAT TIME!
IT MUST HAVE BEEN THE POWER SOURCE WHICH ACTIVATES THE ROBOT!
BUT NOW, LEST ANY NAIVE ONES SUSPECT THAT OUR TIME-WARPING TRAVELERS ARE GOING TO ESCAPE UNNOTICED FROM THE EARLIER PERIOD...
I TELL YA, CAP'N, THERE'S TWO GIANTS SLUG-GIN' IT OUT RIGHT AROUND THAT CORNER!
YEAH, SURE... THEY'RE FIGHTIN' OVER WHO TAKES LITTLE RED RIDIN' HOOD TO THE PROM!
JUST THE SAME, WE'LL JUST HAVE A LOOK-SEE!
MOMENTS LATER, A SOMEWHAT SHAKEN OFFICER BEHOLDS...
HOLY CATS! THAT DOGFACE WAS TELLING THE TRUTH!
BUT, THE HUMAN-LOOKING ONE SEEMS TO BE WINNING, AND SMITH SAID--
CORRECTION, SOLDIER!
WITH THAT BLOW, I JUST WON!!
GET UP HERE, YOU GUYS... ON THE DOUBLE!
I WANT THOSE TWO PALOOKAS COVERED...TILL WE FIND OUT WHAT'S GOING ON!
HOLD ON A MINUTE, CAPTAIN... BELIEVE IT OR NOT, I'M ON YOUR SIDE!
AND IF I DON'T BELIEVE IT, PAUL BUNYAN?
I'M GIVING YOU FIVE TO EXPLAIN YOURSELF, AND THEN...
UH OH! NOW WE'RE ALL IN FOR IT!
HOW CAN WE TELL THEM THAT WE CAME FROM THE FUTURE... TO WITNESS THE FATE OF CAPTAIN AMERICA??

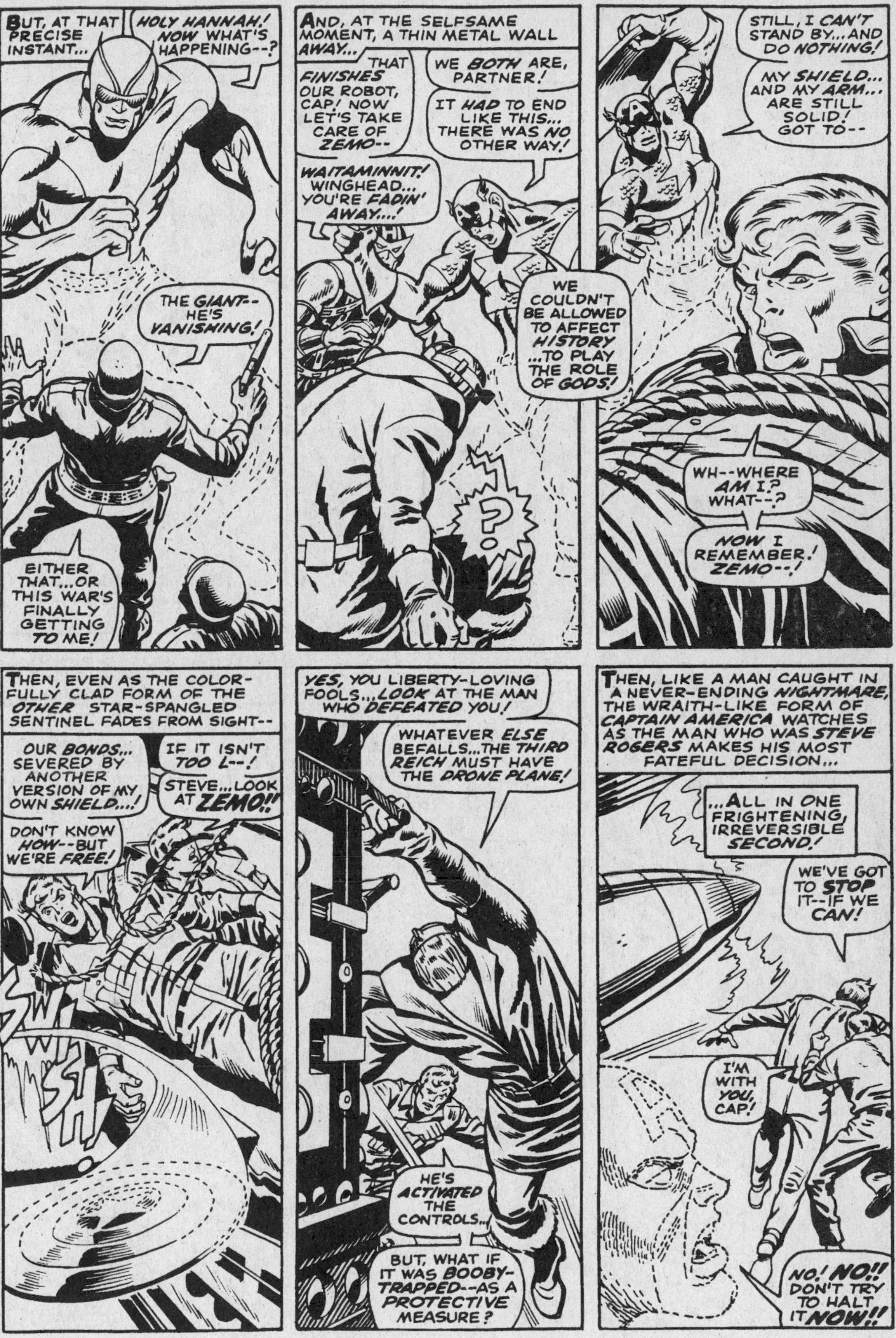
BUT, AT THAT PRECISE INSTANT...
HOLY HANNAH! NOW WHAT'S HAPPENING--?
THE GIANT--HE'S VANISHING!
EITHER THAT...OR THIS WAR'S FINALLY GETTING TO ME!
AND, AT THE SELFSAME MOMENT, A THIN METAL WALL AWAY...
THAT FINISHES OUR ROBOT, CAP! NOW LET'S TAKE CARE OF ZEMO--
WE BOTH ARE, PARTNER!
IT HAD TO END LIKE THIS... THERE WAS NO OTHER WAY!
WAITAMINNIT! WINGHEAD... YOU'RE FADIN' AWAY...!
WE COULDN'T BE ALLOWED TO AFFECT HISTORY ...TO PLAY THE ROLE OF GODS!
?
STILL, I CAN'T STAND BY...AND DO NOTHING!
MY SHIELD... AND MY ARM... ARE STILL SOLID! GOT TO--
WH--WHERE AM I? WHAT--?
NOW I REMEMBER! ZEMO--!
THEN, EVEN AS THE COLORFULLY CLAD FORM OF THE OTHER STAR-SPANGLED SENTINEL FADES FROM SIGHT--
OUR BONDS... SEVERED BY ANOTHER VERSION OF MY OWN SHIELD...!
IF IT ISN'T TOO L--!
STEVE...LOOK AT ZEMO!!
DON'T KNOW HOW--BUT WE'RE FREE!
SWISH
YES, YOU LIBERTY-LOVING FOOLS...LOOK AT THE MAN WHO DEFEATED YOU!
WHATEVER ELSE BEFALLS...THE THIRD REICH MUST HAVE THE DRONE PLANE!
HE'S ACTIVATED THE CONTROLS...
BUT, WHAT IF IT WAS BOOBY-TRAPPED--AS A PROTECTIVE MEASURE?
THEN, LIKE A MAN CAUGHT IN A NEVER-ENDING NIGHTMARE, THE WRAITH-LIKE FORM OF CAPTAIN AMERICA WATCHES AS THE MAN WHO WAS STEVE ROGERS MAKES HIS MOST FATEFUL DECISION...
...ALL IN ONE FRIGHTENING, IRREVERSIBLE SECOND!
WE'VE GOT TO STOP IT--IF WE CAN!
I'M WITH YOU, CAP!
NO! NO!! DON'T TRY TO HALT IT NOW!!

Panel 1:
WE'RE *TOO LATE,* BUCKY! WE HAVE TO GO AFTER IT IN *ANOTHER* PLANE!

NO! DON'T STOP!

I THINK I CAN *REACH* IT, CAP!

Panel 2:
CAN'T--MAKE IT! DROP OFF INTO THE *WATER,* LAD!

DON'T TRY TO GO IT *ALONE!*

NO! I CAN BRING THE PLANE BACK-- I *KNOW* I CAN!

Panel 3:
BUCKY--LET GO!

IT MIGHT BE *BOOBY-TRAPPED* --AND YOU CAN'T DEACTIVATE THE BOMB WITHOUT *ME!*

DROP OFF-- BEFORE IT *EXPLODES!!*

YOU'RE *RIGHT,* CAP-- I SEE THE *FUSE!*

IT'S GONNA--

Panel 4:
NOOooo!

FOR A SINGLE, SHOCKED INSTANT, NEITHER *ZEMO* NOR THE WATCHING, VENGEFUL *WRAITHS* BELOW MOVE TO BREAK THE SOMBRE *TABLEAU!* THEN--

Panel 5:
HE'S *DEAD!* BUCKY'S DEAD... BECAUSE OF *ZEMO!*

GOT TO *GET* HIM....!

CAP-- *NO!* YOU *CAN'T....!*

HAH! PERHAPS THERE ARE *OTHER* CAPTAIN AMERICAS...

BUT *THAT* ONE... AND HIS *YOUNG* ALLY... ARE *FINISHED!*

Panel 6:
FINALLY, ENRAGED BEYOND WORDS... BEYOND THOUGHT... CAP LEAPS--

KNEW I COULDN'T TOUCH HIM... OR EVEN MAKE HIM *HEAR* ME!

BUT I HAD TO *TRY*... I *HAD* TO--!

STRANGE... FOR A MOMENT, I FELT... A *SLIGHT,* SUDDEN CHILL!

YET, IT WAS NOTHING... *LESS* THAN NOTHING!

19

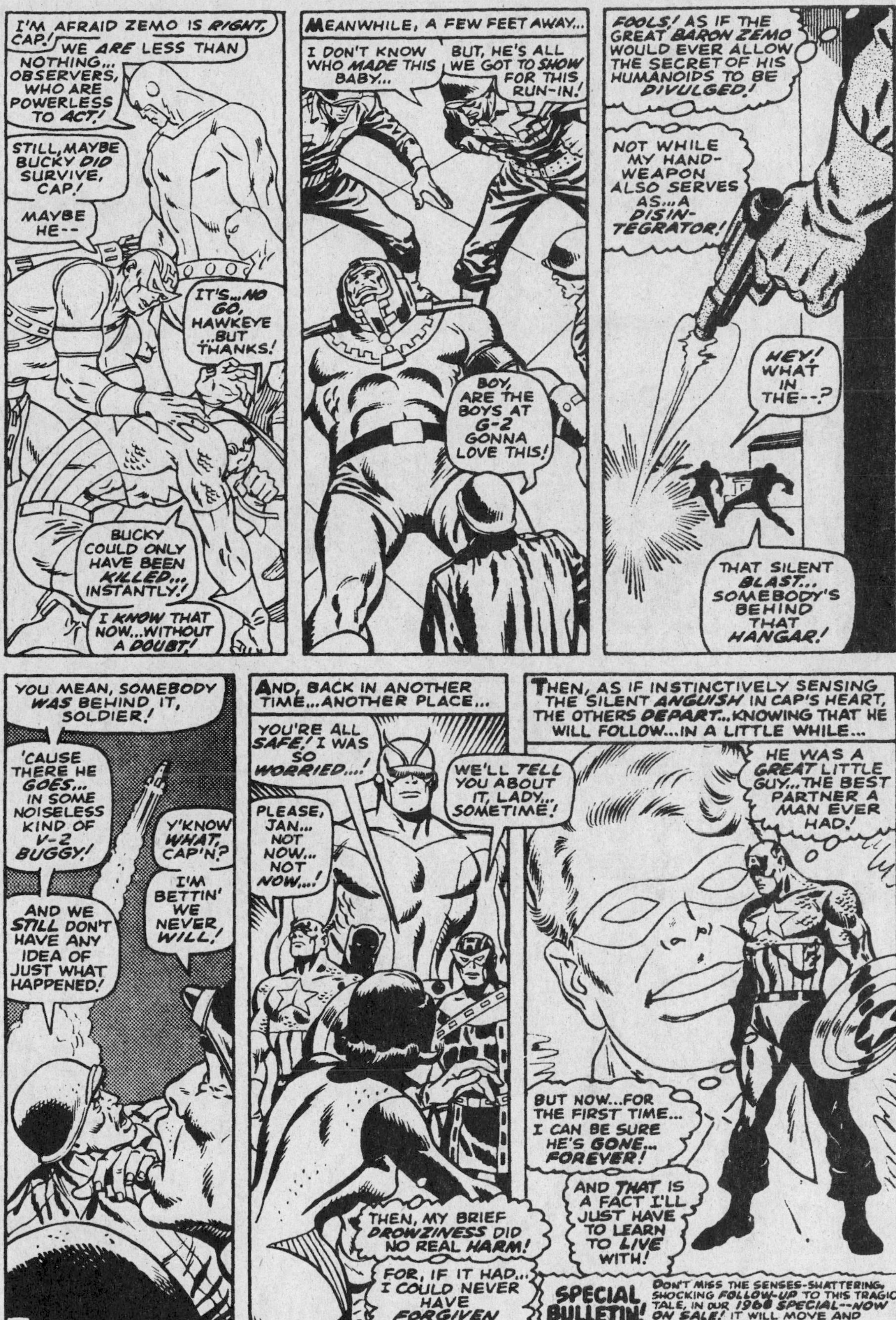

I'M AFRAID ZEMO IS RIGHT, CAP!
WE ARE LESS THAN NOTHING... OBSERVERS, WHO ARE POWERLESS TO ACT!
STILL, MAYBE BUCKY DID SURVIVE, CAP!
MAYBE HE--
IT'S...NO GO, HAWKEYE ...BUT THANKS!
BUCKY COULD ONLY HAVE BEEN KILLED... INSTANTLY!
I KNOW THAT NOW...WITHOUT A DOUBT!
MEANWHILE, A FEW FEET AWAY...
I DON'T KNOW WHO MADE THIS BABY...
BUT, HE'S ALL WE GOT TO SHOW FOR THIS RUN-IN!
BOY, ARE THE BOYS AT G-2 GONNA LOVE THIS!
FOOLS! AS IF THE GREAT BARON ZEMO WOULD EVER ALLOW THE SECRET OF HIS HUMANOIDS TO BE DIVULGED!
NOT WHILE MY HAND-WEAPON ALSO SERVES AS...A DISIN-TEGRATOR!
HEY! WHAT IN THE--?
THAT SILENT BLAST... SOMEBODY'S BEHIND THAT HANGAR!
YOU MEAN, SOMEBODY WAS BEHIND IT, SOLDIER!
'CAUSE THERE HE GOES... IN SOME NOISELESS KIND OF V-2 BUGGY!
AND WE STILL DON'T HAVE ANY IDEA OF JUST WHAT HAPPENED!
Y'KNOW WHAT, CAP'N?
I'M BETTIN' WE NEVER WILL!
20
AND, BACK IN ANOTHER TIME...ANOTHER PLACE...
YOU'RE ALL SAFE! I WAS SO WORRIED...!
PLEASE, JAN... NOT NOW... NOT NOW...!
WE'LL TELL YOU ABOUT IT, LADY... SOMETIME!
THEN, MY BRIEF DROWZINESS DID NO REAL HARM!
FOR, IF IT HAD... I COULD NEVER HAVE FORGIVEN MYSELF!
THEN, AS IF INSTINCTIVELY SENSING THE SILENT ANGUISH IN CAP'S HEART, THE OTHERS DEPART...KNOWING THAT HE WILL FOLLOW...IN A LITTLE WHILE...
HE WAS A GREAT LITTLE GUY...THE BEST PARTNER A MAN EVER HAD!
BUT NOW...FOR THE FIRST TIME... I CAN BE SURE HE'S GONE... FOREVER!
AND THAT IS A FACT I'LL JUST HAVE TO LEARN TO LIVE WITH!
SPECIAL BULLETIN!
DON'T MISS THE SENSES-SHATTERING, SHOCKING FOLLOW-UP TO THIS TRAGIC TALE, IN OUR 1968 SPECIAL--NOW ON SALE! IT WILL MOVE AND SHAKE YOU!! 'NUFF SAID!

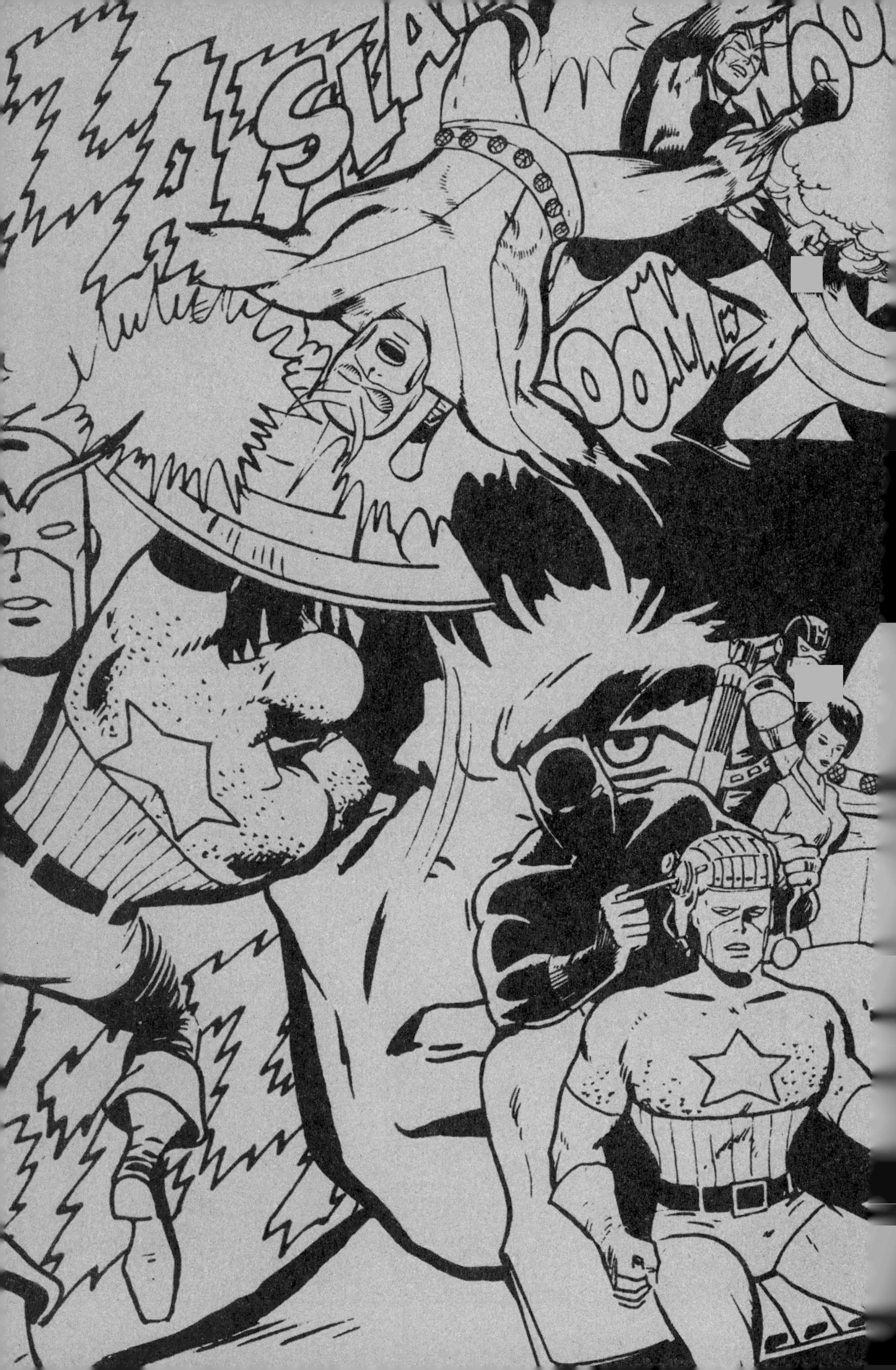

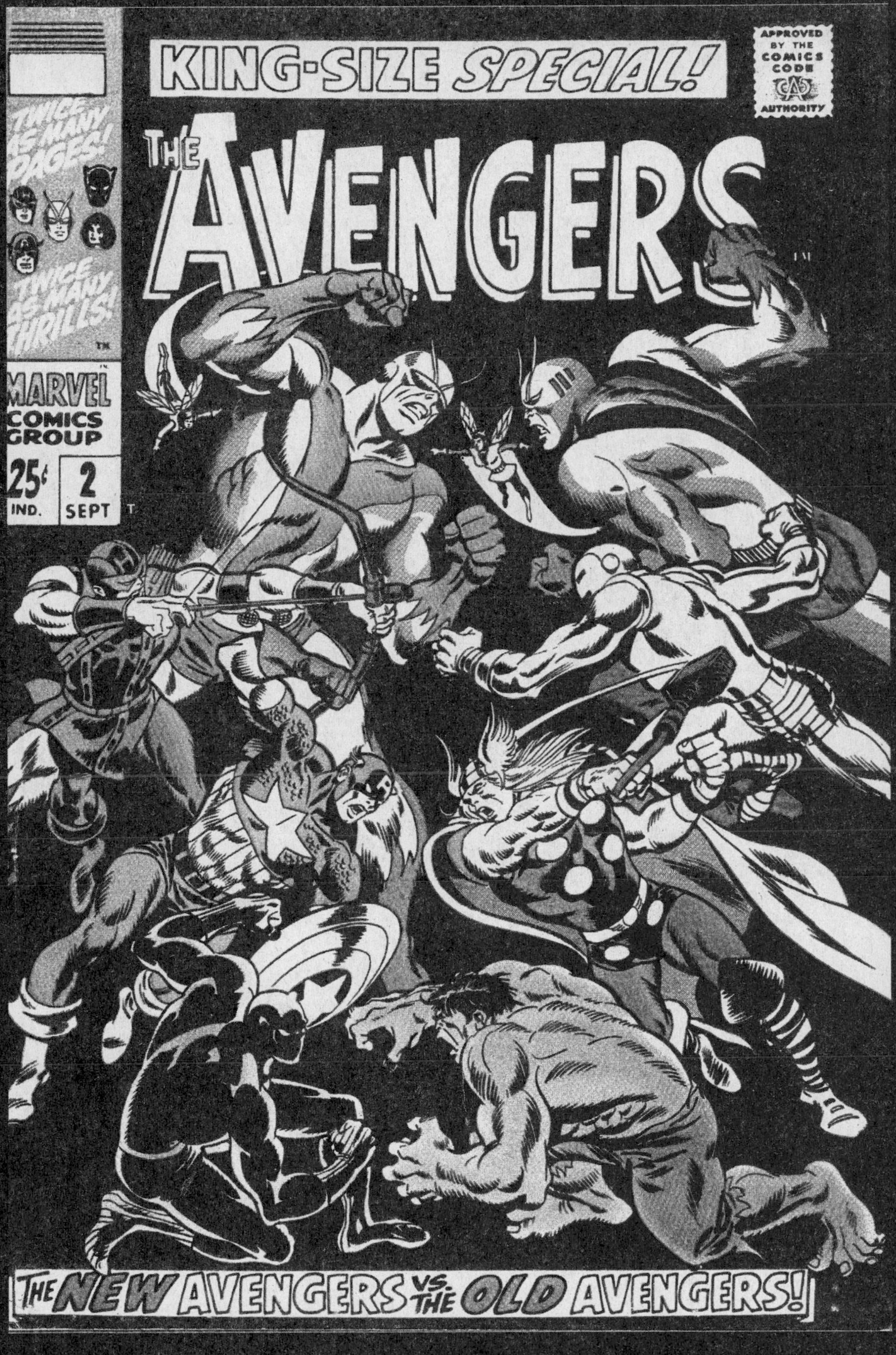
KING-SIZE SPECIAL!
APPROVED BY THE COMICS CODE AUTHORITY
THE AVENGERS
TWICE AS MANY PAGES!
TWICE AS MANY THRILLS!
MARVEL COMICS GROUP
25¢ IND.
2 SEPT
THE NEW AVENGERS VS. THE OLD AVENGERS!

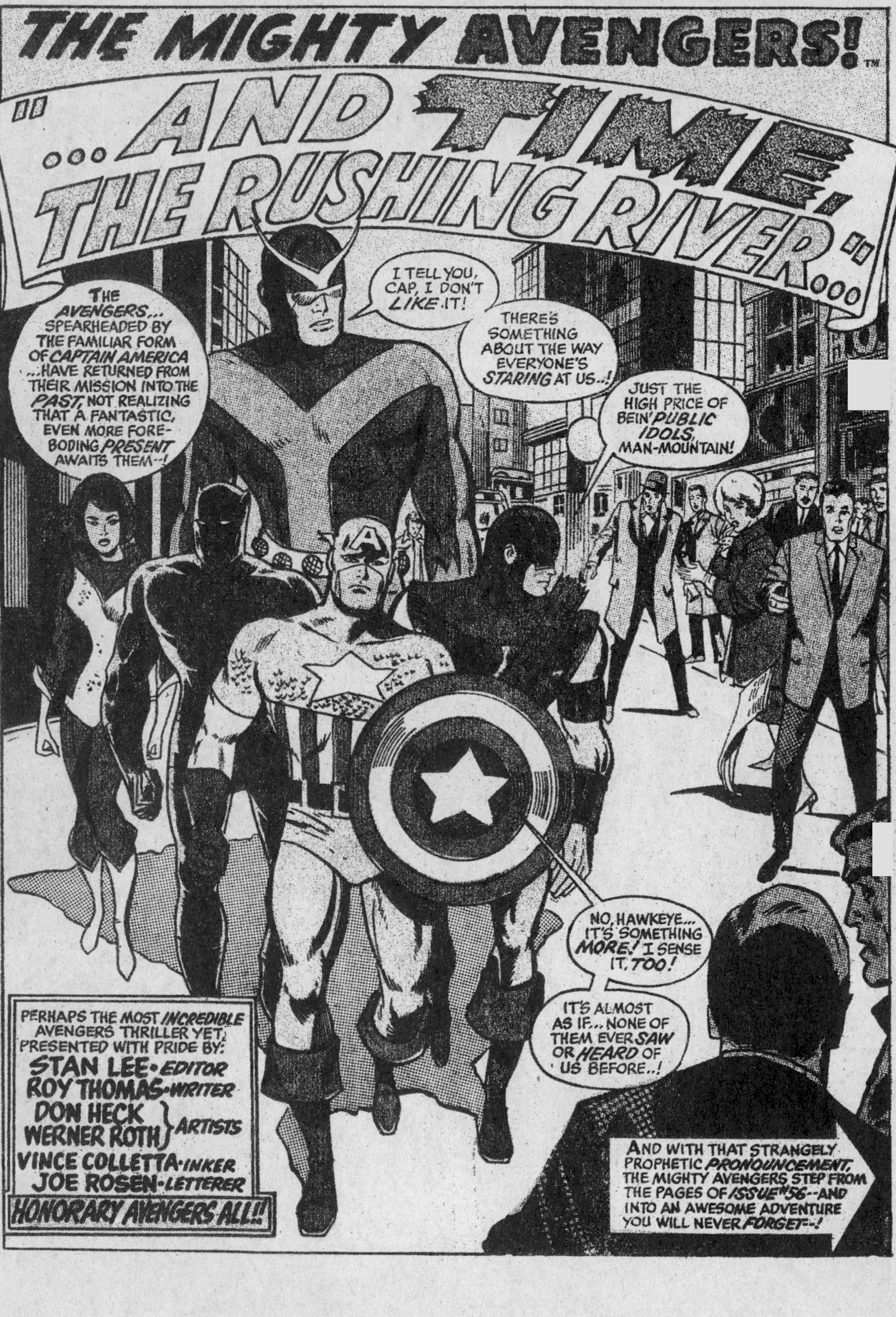
THE MIGHTY AVENGERS!
"...AND TIME, THE RUSHING RIVER..."
THE AVENGERS... SPEARHEADED BY THE FAMILIAR FORM OF CAPTAIN AMERICA ...HAVE RETURNED FROM THEIR MISSION INTO THE PAST, NOT REALIZING THAT A FANTASTIC, EVEN MORE FORE-BODING PRESENT AWAITS THEM--!
I TELL YOU, CAP, I DON'T LIKE IT!
THERE'S SOMETHING ABOUT THE WAY EVERYONE'S STARING AT US..!
JUST THE HIGH PRICE OF BEIN' PUBLIC IDOLS, MAN-MOUNTAIN!
NO, HAWKEYE... IT'S SOMETHING MORE! I SENSE IT, TOO!
IT'S ALMOST AS IF... NONE OF THEM EVER SAW OR HEARD OF US BEFORE..!
PERHAPS THE MOST INCREDIBLE AVENGERS THRILLER YET, PRESENTED WITH PRIDE BY: STAN LEE•EDITOR ROY THOMAS•WRITER DON HECK WERNER ROTH ARTISTS VINCE COLLETTA•INKER JOE ROSEN•LETTERER HONORARY AVENGERS ALL!!
AND WITH THAT STRANGELY PROPHETIC PRONOUNCEMENT, THE MIGHTY AVENGERS STEP FROM THE PAGES OF ISSUE #56--AND INTO AN AWESOME ADVENTURE YOU WILL NEVER FORGET--!

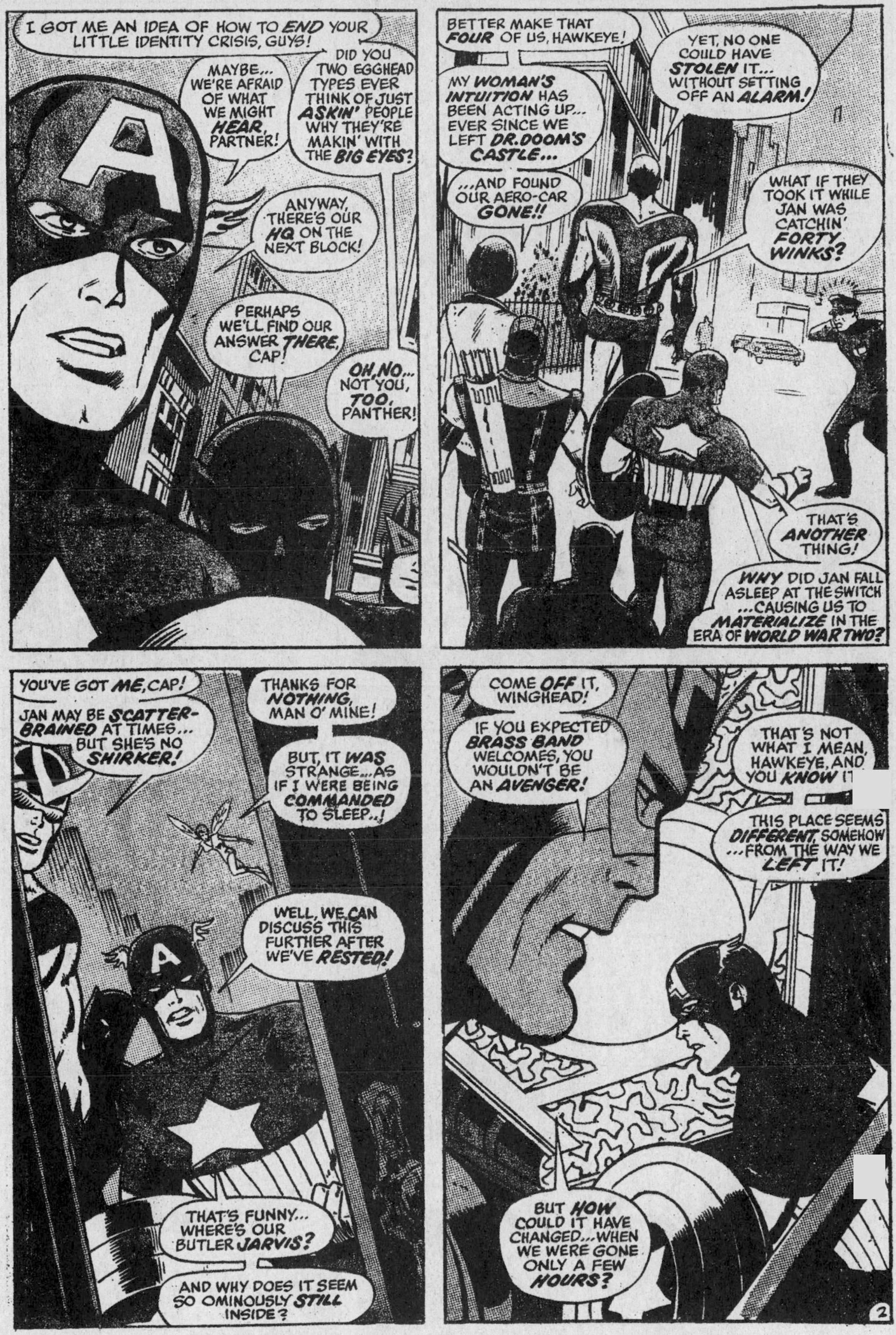
I GOT ME AN IDEA OF HOW TO END YOUR LITTLE IDENTITY CRISIS, GUYS!
MAYBE... WE'RE AFRAID OF WHAT WE MIGHT HEAR, PARTNER!
DID YOU TWO EGGHEAD TYPES EVER THINK OF JUST ASKIN' PEOPLE WHY THEY'RE MAKIN' WITH THE BIG EYES?
ANYWAY, THERE'S OUR HQ ON THE NEXT BLOCK!
PERHAPS WE'LL FIND OUR ANSWER THERE, CAP!
OH, NO... NOT YOU, TOO, PANTHER!
BETTER MAKE THAT FOUR OF US, HAWKEYE!
MY WOMAN'S INTUITION HAS BEEN ACTING UP... EVER SINCE WE LEFT DR. DOOM'S CASTLE...
...AND FOUND OUR AERO-CAR GONE!!
YET, NO ONE COULD HAVE STOLEN IT... WITHOUT SETTING OFF AN ALARM!
WHAT IF THEY TOOK IT WHILE JAN WAS CATCHIN' FORTY WINKS?
THAT'S ANOTHER THING!
WHY DID JAN FALL ASLEEP AT THE SWITCH ...CAUSING US TO MATERIALIZE IN THE ERA OF WORLD WAR TWO?
YOU'VE GOT ME, CAP!
JAN MAY BE SCATTER-BRAINED AT TIMES... BUT SHE'S NO SHIRKER!
THANKS FOR NOTHING, MAN O' MINE!
BUT, IT WAS STRANGE... AS IF I WERE BEING COMMANDED TO SLEEP...!
WELL, WE CAN DISCUSS THIS FURTHER AFTER WE'VE RESTED!
THAT'S FUNNY... WHERE'S OUR BUTLER JARVIS?
AND WHY DOES IT SEEM SO OMINOUSLY STILL INSIDE?
COME OFF IT, WINGHEAD!
IF YOU EXPECTED BRASS BAND WELCOMES, YOU WOULDN'T BE AN AVENGER!
THAT'S NOT WHAT I MEAN, HAWKEYE, AND YOU KNOW IT
THIS PLACE SEEMS DIFFERENT, SOMEHOW ...FROM THE WAY WE LEFT IT!
BUT HOW COULD IT HAVE CHANGED... WHEN WE WERE GONE ONLY A FEW HOURS?
2

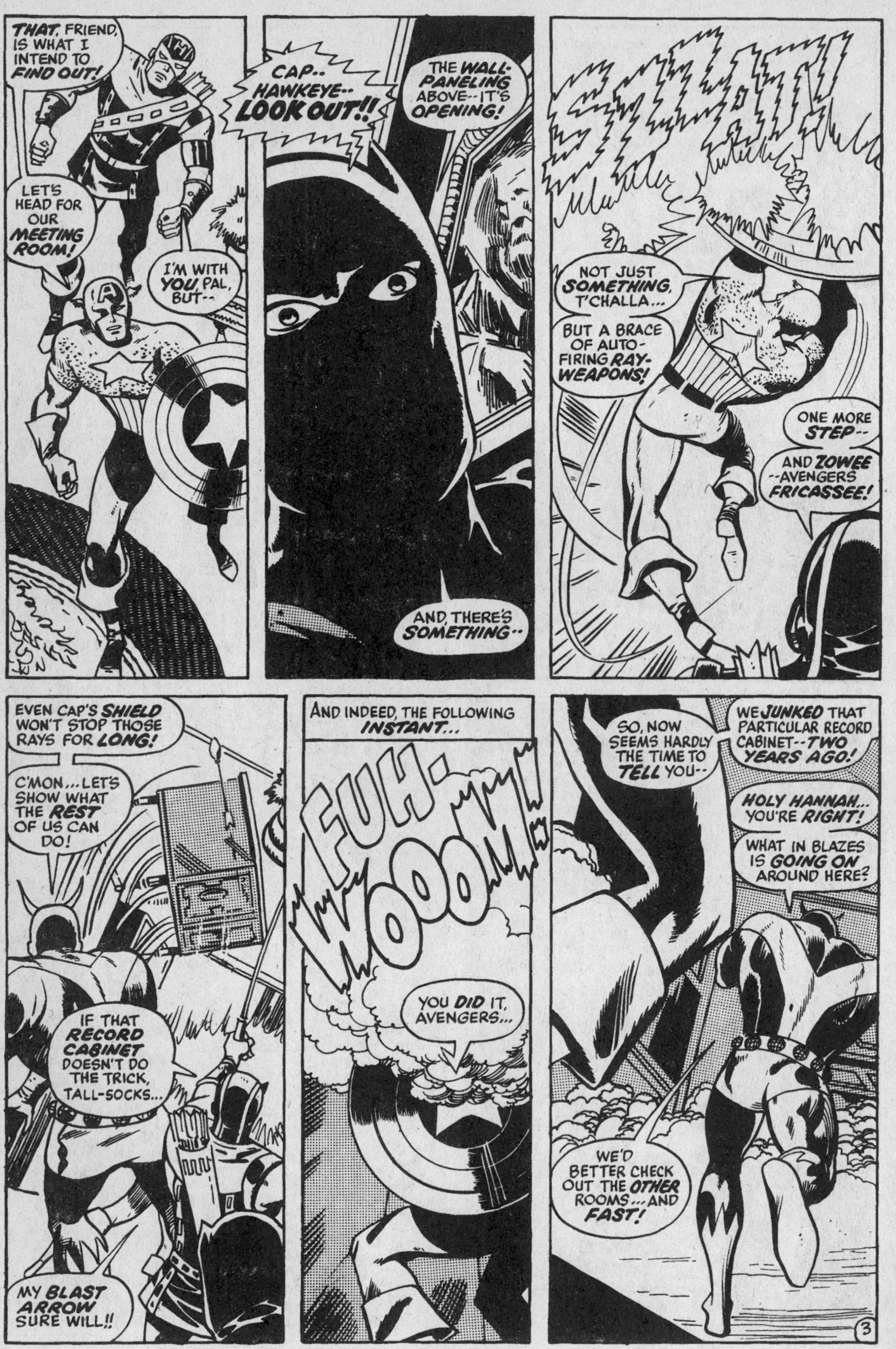

THAT, FRIEND, IS WHAT I INTEND TO FIND OUT!
LET'S HEAD FOR OUR MEETING ROOM!
I'M WITH YOU, PAL, BUT--
CAP.. HAWKEYE-- LOOK OUT!!
THE WALL-PANELING ABOVE--IT'S OPENING!
AND, THERE'S SOMETHING--
SSZZAAT!
NOT JUST SOMETHING, T'CHALLA...
BUT A BRACE OF AUTO-FIRING RAY-WEAPONS!
ONE MORE STEP--
AND ZOWEE --AVENGERS FRICASSEE!
EVEN CAP'S SHIELD WON'T STOP THOSE RAYS FOR LONG!
C'MON... LET'S SHOW WHAT THE REST OF US CAN DO!
IF THAT RECORD CABINET DOESN'T DO THE TRICK, TALL-SOCKS...
MY BLAST ARROW SURE WILL!!
AND INDEED, THE FOLLOWING INSTANT...
FUH-WOOOM!
YOU DID IT, AVENGERS...
SO, NOW SEEMS HARDLY THE TIME TO TELL YOU--
WE JUNKED THAT PARTICULAR RECORD CABINET--TWO YEARS AGO!
HOLY HANNAH... YOU'RE RIGHT!
WHAT IN BLAZES IS GOING ON AROUND HERE?
WE'D BETTER CHECK OUT THE OTHER ROOMS... AND FAST!
3

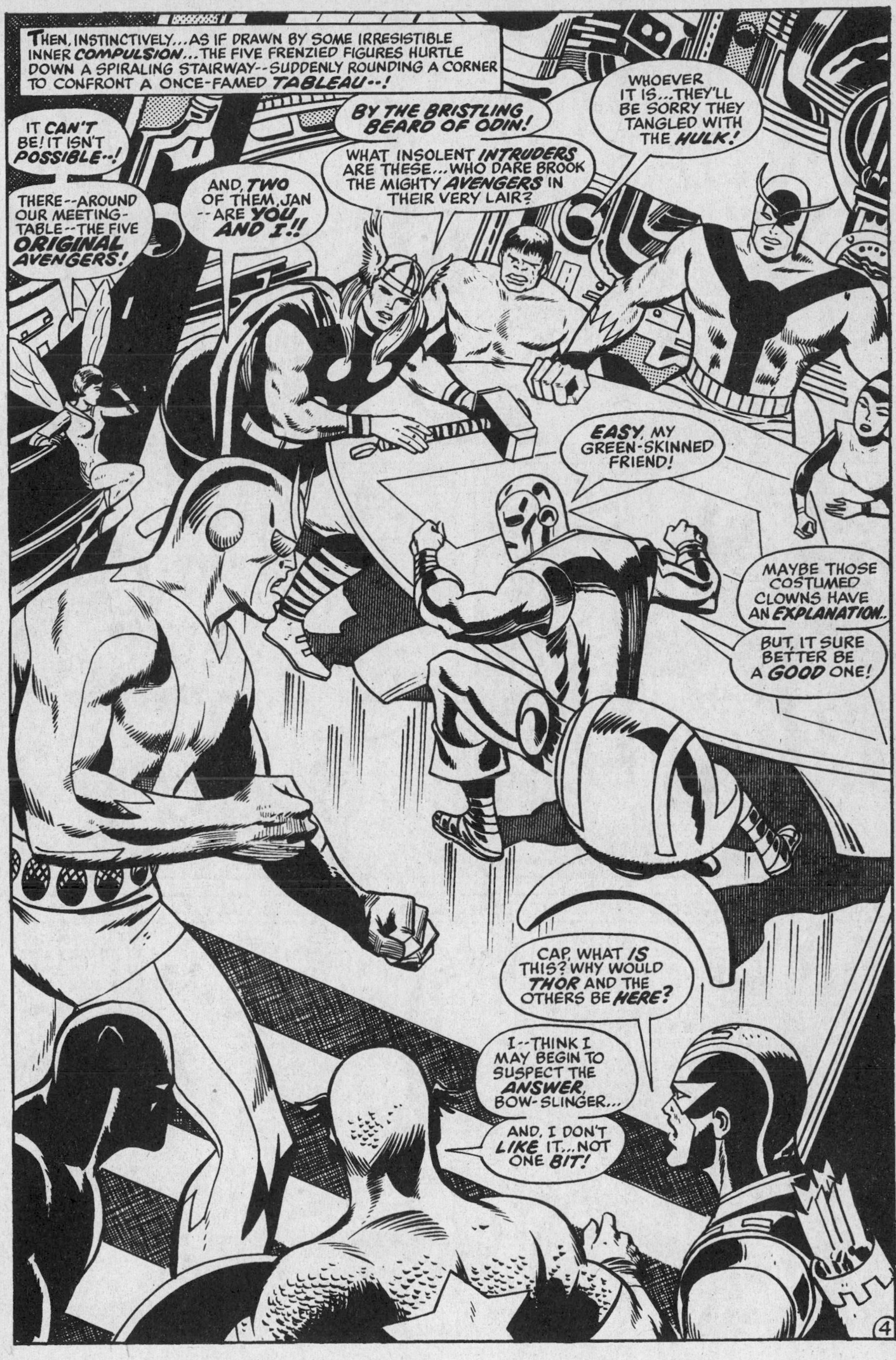
THEN, INSTINCTIVELY... AS IF DRAWN BY SOME IRRESISTIBLE INNER COMPULSION... THE FIVE FRENZIED FIGURES HURTLE DOWN A SPIRALING STAIRWAY--SUDDENLY ROUNDING A CORNER TO CONFRONT A ONCE-FAMED TABLEAU--!
IT CAN'T BE! IT ISN'T POSSIBLE--!
THERE--AROUND OUR MEETING-TABLE--THE FIVE ORIGINAL AVENGERS!
AND, TWO OF THEM, JAN --ARE YOU AND I!!
BY THE BRISTLING BEARD OF ODIN!
WHAT INSOLENT INTRUDERS ARE THESE... WHO DARE BROOK THE MIGHTY AVENGERS IN THEIR VERY LAIR?
WHOEVER IT IS... THEY'LL BE SORRY THEY TANGLED WITH THE HULK!
EASY, MY GREEN-SKINNED FRIEND!
MAYBE THOSE COSTUMED CLOWNS HAVE AN EXPLANATION..
BUT, IT SURE BETTER BE A GOOD ONE!
CAP, WHAT IS THIS? WHY WOULD THOR AND THE OTHERS BE HERE?
I--THINK I MAY BEGIN TO SUSPECT THE ANSWER, BOW-SLINGER...
AND, I DON'T LIKE IT... NOT ONE BIT!
4

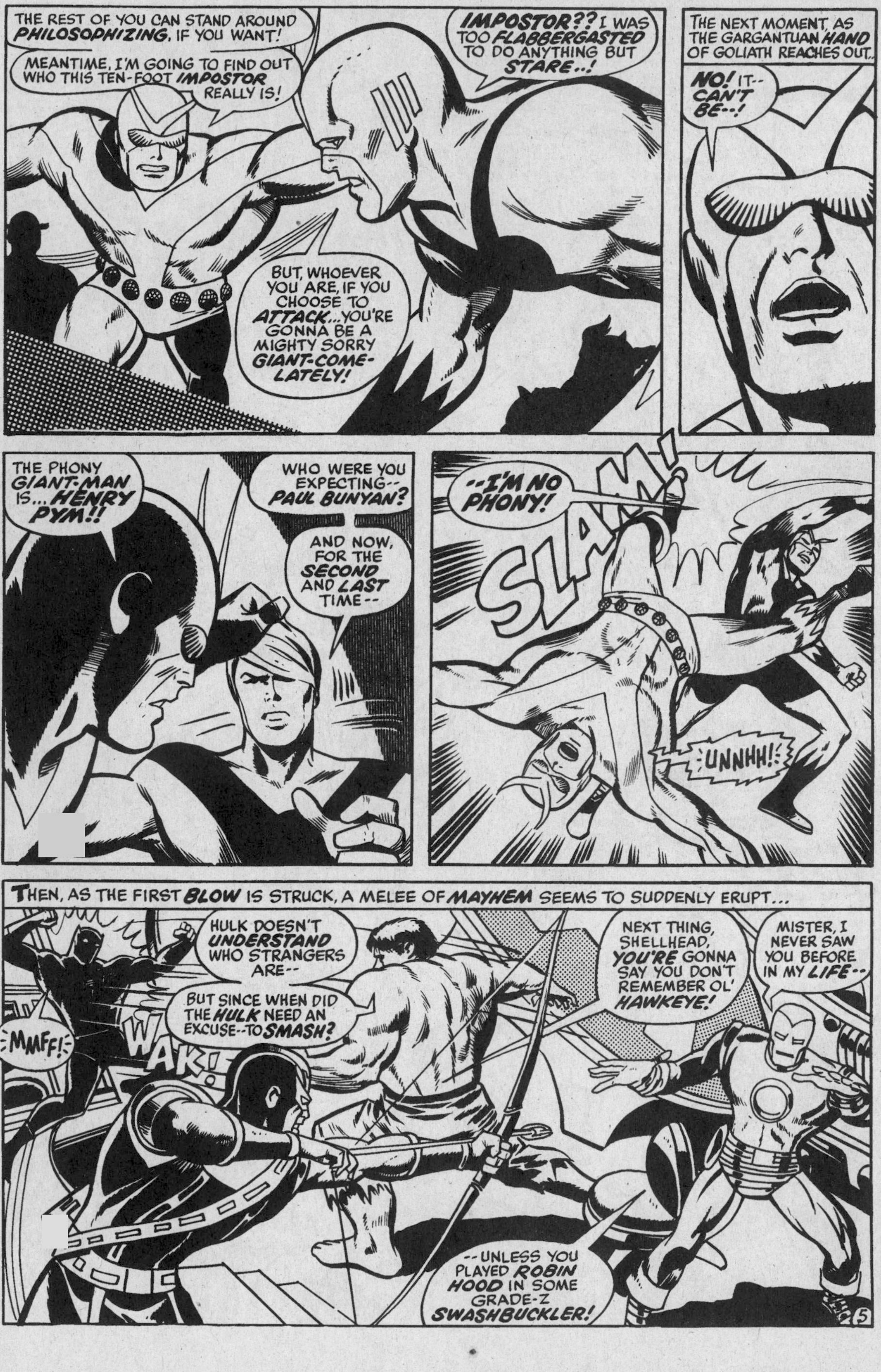
THE REST OF YOU CAN STAND AROUND PHILOSOPHIZING, IF YOU WANT!
MEANTIME, I'M GOING TO FIND OUT WHO THIS TEN-FOOT IMPOSTOR REALLY IS!
IMPOSTOR?? I WAS TOO FLABBERGASTED TO DO ANYTHING BUT STARE..!
BUT, WHOEVER YOU ARE, IF YOU CHOOSE TO ATTACK...YOU'RE GONNA BE A MIGHTY SORRY GIANT-COME-LATELY!
THE NEXT MOMENT, AS THE GARGANTUAN HAND OF GOLIATH REACHES OUT...
NO! IT--CAN'T BE--!
THE PHONY GIANT-MAN IS... HENRY PYM!!
WHO WERE YOU EXPECTING--PAUL BUNYAN?
AND NOW, FOR THE SECOND AND LAST TIME--
--I'M NO PHONY!
SLAM!
UNNHH!
THEN, AS THE FIRST BLOW IS STRUCK, A MELEE OF MAYHEM SEEMS TO SUDDENLY ERUPT...
MMFF!
WAK!
HULK DOESN'T UNDERSTAND WHO STRANGERS ARE--
BUT SINCE WHEN DID THE HULK NEED AN EXCUSE--TO SMASH?
NEXT THING, SHELLHEAD, YOU'RE GONNA SAY YOU DON'T REMEMBER OL' HAWKEYE!
MISTER, I NEVER SAW YOU BEFORE IN MY LIFE--
--UNLESS YOU PLAYED ROBIN HOOD IN SOME GRADE-Z SWASHBUCKLER!
5

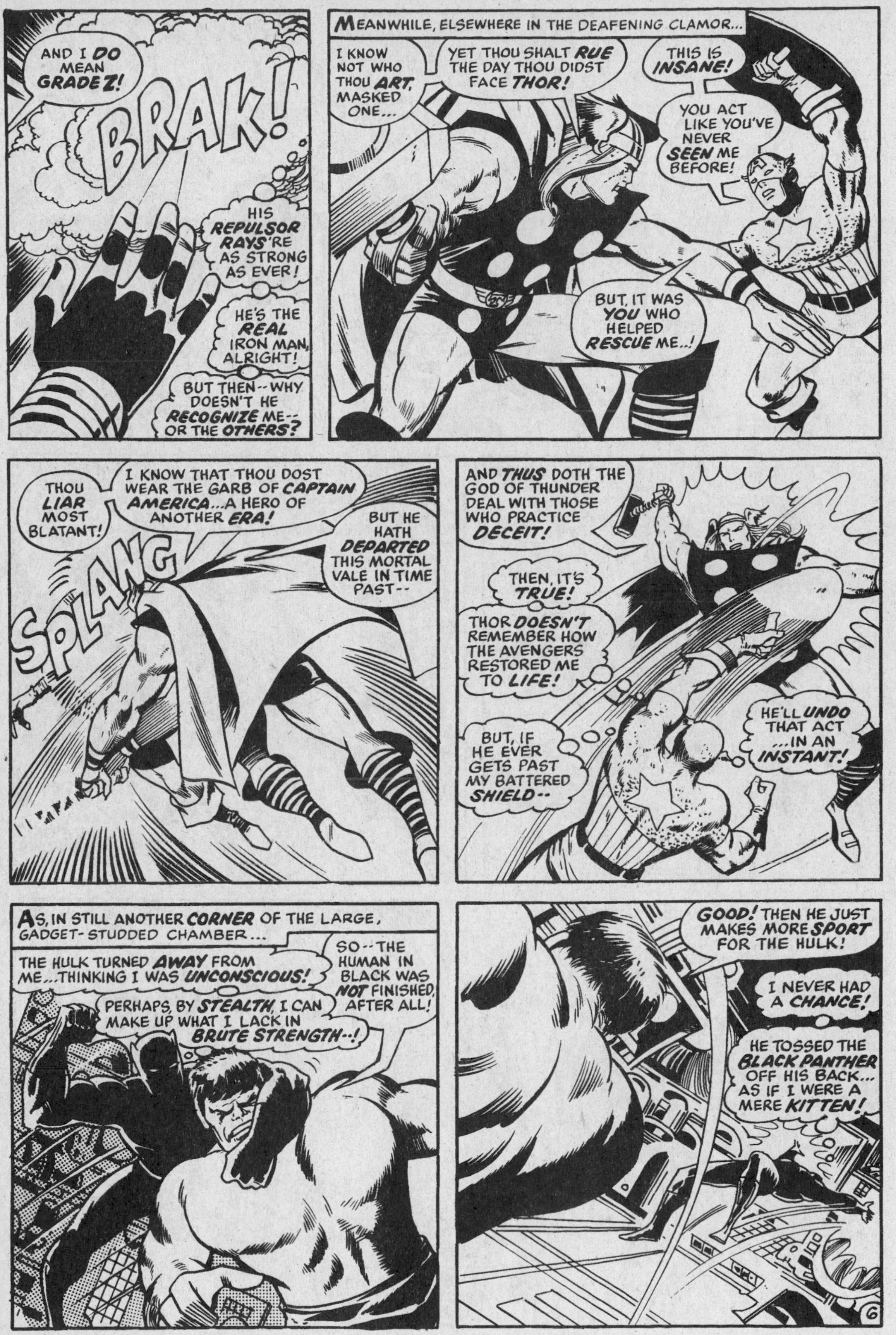
AND I DO MEAN GRADE Z!
BRAK!
HIS REPULSOR RAYS'RE AS STRONG AS EVER!
HE'S THE REAL IRON MAN, ALRIGHT!
BUT THEN--WHY DOESN'T HE RECOGNIZE ME--OR THE OTHERS?
MEANWHILE, ELSEWHERE IN THE DEAFENING CLAMOR...
I KNOW NOT WHO THOU ART, MASKED ONE...
YET THOU SHALT RUE THE DAY THOU DIDST FACE THOR!
THIS IS INSANE!
YOU ACT LIKE YOU'VE NEVER SEEN ME BEFORE!
BUT, IT WAS YOU WHO HELPED RESCUE ME..!
THOU LIAR MOST BLATANT!
I KNOW THAT THOU DOST WEAR THE GARB OF CAPTAIN AMERICA...A HERO OF ANOTHER ERA!
BUT HE HATH DEPARTED THIS MORTAL VALE IN TIME PAST--
SPLANG
AND THUS DOTH THE GOD OF THUNDER DEAL WITH THOSE WHO PRACTICE DECEIT!
THEN, IT'S TRUE!
THOR DOESN'T REMEMBER HOW THE AVENGERS RESTORED ME TO LIFE!
BUT, IF HE EVER GETS PAST MY BATTERED SHIELD--
HE'LL UNDO THAT ACT ...IN AN INSTANT!
AS, IN STILL ANOTHER CORNER OF THE LARGE, GADGET-STUDDED CHAMBER...
THE HULK TURNED AWAY FROM ME...THINKING I WAS UNCONSCIOUS!
PERHAPS, BY STEALTH, I CAN MAKE UP WHAT I LACK IN BRUTE STRENGTH--!
SO--THE HUMAN IN BLACK WAS NOT FINISHED, AFTER ALL!
GOOD! THEN HE JUST MAKES MORE SPORT FOR THE HULK!
I NEVER HAD A CHANCE!
HE TOSSED THE BLACK PANTHER OFF HIS BACK... AS IF I WERE A MERE KITTEN!
6

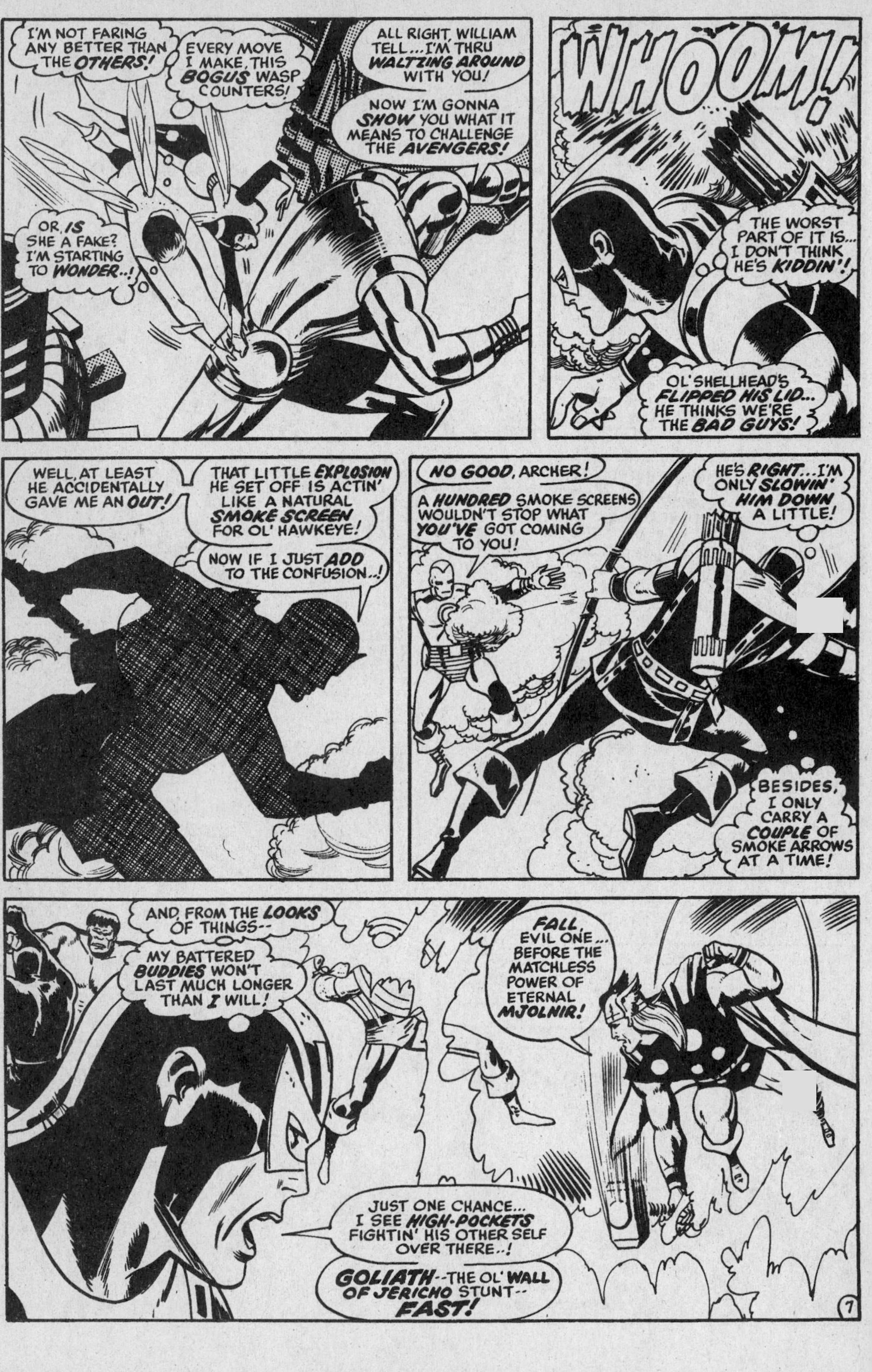
I'M NOT FARING ANY BETTER THAN THE OTHERS!
EVERY MOVE I MAKE, THIS BOGUS WASP COUNTERS!
OR, IS SHE A FAKE? I'M STARTING TO WONDER..!
ALL RIGHT, WILLIAM TELL...I'M THRU WALTZING AROUND WITH YOU!
NOW I'M GONNA SHOW YOU WHAT IT MEANS TO CHALLENGE THE AVENGERS!
WHOOM!
THE WORST PART OF IT IS... I DON'T THINK HE'S KIDDIN'!
OL' SHELLHEAD'S FLIPPED HIS LID... HE THINKS WE'RE THE BAD GUYS!
WELL, AT LEAST HE ACCIDENTALLY GAVE ME AN OUT!
THAT LITTLE EXPLOSION HE SET OFF IS ACTIN' LIKE A NATURAL SMOKE SCREEN FOR OL' HAWKEYE!
NOW IF I JUST ADD TO THE CONFUSION..!
NO GOOD, ARCHER!
A HUNDRED SMOKE SCREENS WOULDN'T STOP WHAT YOU'VE GOT COMING TO YOU!
HE'S RIGHT...I'M ONLY SLOWIN' HIM DOWN A LITTLE!
BESIDES, I ONLY CARRY A COUPLE OF SMOKE ARROWS AT A TIME!
AND, FROM THE LOOKS OF THINGS--
MY BATTERED BUDDIES WON'T LAST MUCH LONGER THAN I WILL!
FALL, EVIL ONE... BEFORE THE MATCHLESS POWER OF ETERNAL MJOLNIR!
JUST ONE CHANCE... I SEE HIGH-POCKETS FIGHTIN' HIS OTHER SELF OVER THERE..!
GOLIATH--THE OL' WALL OF JERICHO STUNT-- FAST!
7

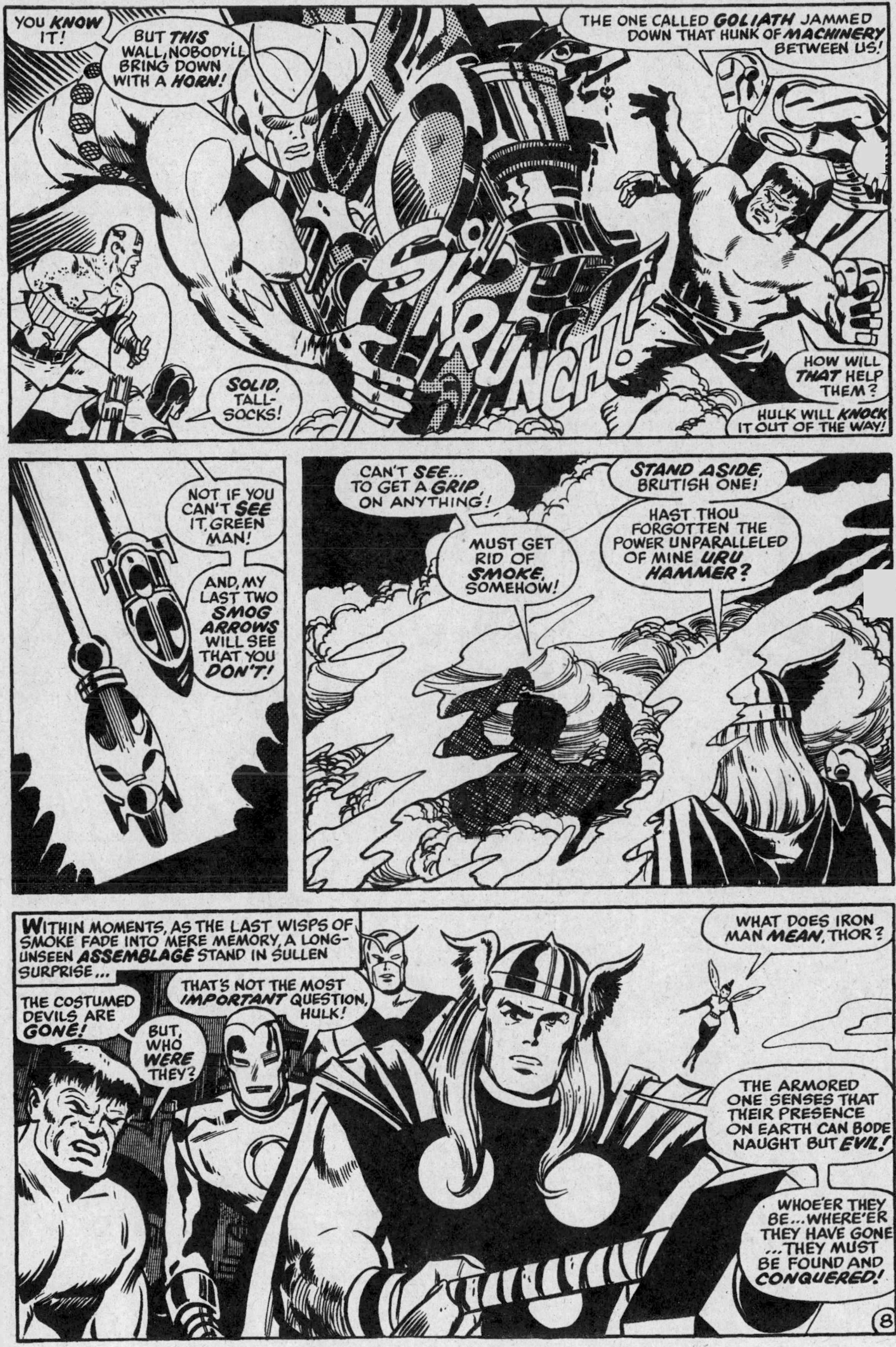

YOU KNOW IT!
BUT THIS WALL, NOBODY'LL BRING DOWN WITH A HORN!
THE ONE CALLED GOLIATH JAMMED DOWN THAT HUNK OF MACHINERY BETWEEN US!
SKRUNCH!
SOLID, TALL-SOCKS!
HOW WILL THAT HELP THEM?
HULK WILL KNOCK IT OUT OF THE WAY!
NOT IF YOU CAN'T SEE IT, GREEN MAN!
AND, MY LAST TWO SMOG ARROWS WILL SEE THAT YOU DON'T!
CAN'T SEE... TO GET A GRIP ON ANYTHING!
MUST GET RID OF SMOKE, SOMEHOW!
STAND ASIDE, BRUTISH ONE!
HAST THOU FORGOTTEN THE POWER UNPARALLELED OF MINE URU HAMMER?
WITHIN MOMENTS, AS THE LAST WISPS OF SMOKE FADE INTO MERE MEMORY, A LONG-UNSEEN ASSEMBLAGE STAND IN SULLEN SURPRISE...
THE COSTUMED DEVILS ARE GONE!
BUT, WHO WERE THEY?
THAT'S NOT THE MOST IMPORTANT QUESTION, HULK!
WHAT DOES IRON MAN MEAN, THOR?
THE ARMORED ONE SENSES THAT THEIR PRESENCE ON EARTH CAN BODE NAUGHT BUT EVIL!
WHOE'ER THEY BE... WHERE'ER THEY HAVE GONE ...THEY MUST BE FOUND AND CONQUERED!
8

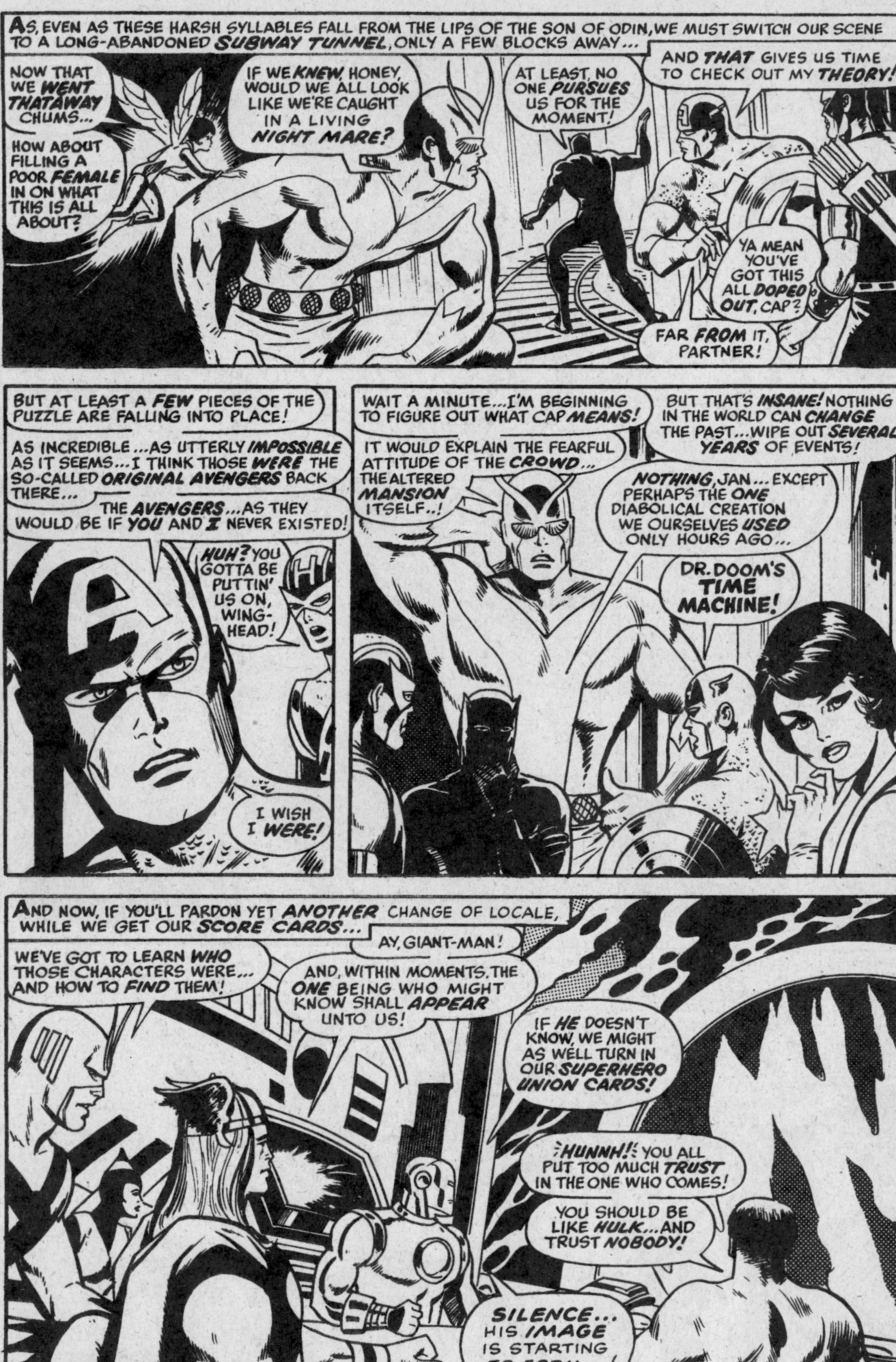

AS, EVEN AS THESE HARSH SYLLABLES FALL FROM THE LIPS OF THE SON OF ODIN, WE MUST SWITCH OUR SCENE TO A LONG-ABANDONED SUBWAY TUNNEL, ONLY A FEW BLOCKS AWAY...
NOW THAT WE WENT THATAWAY CHUMS...
HOW ABOUT FILLING A POOR FEMALE IN ON WHAT THIS IS ALL ABOUT?
IF WE KNEW, HONEY, WOULD WE ALL LOOK LIKE WE'RE CAUGHT IN A LIVING NIGHT MARE?
AT LEAST, NO ONE PURSUES US FOR THE MOMENT!
AND THAT GIVES US TIME TO CHECK OUT MY THEORY!
YA MEAN YOU'VE GOT THIS ALL DOPED OUT, CAP?
FAR FROM IT, PARTNER!
BUT AT LEAST A FEW PIECES OF THE PUZZLE ARE FALLING INTO PLACE!
AS INCREDIBLE ...AS UTTERLY IMPOSSIBLE AS IT SEEMS... I THINK THOSE WERE THE SO-CALLED ORIGINAL AVENGERS BACK THERE...
THE AVENGERS... AS THEY WOULD BE IF YOU AND I NEVER EXISTED!
HUH? YOU GOTTA BE PUTTIN' US ON, WING-HEAD!
I WISH I WERE!
WAIT A MINUTE...I'M BEGINNING TO FIGURE OUT WHAT CAP MEANS!
IT WOULD EXPLAIN THE FEARFUL ATTITUDE OF THE CROWD... THE ALTERED MANSION ITSELF..!
BUT THAT'S INSANE! NOTHING IN THE WORLD CAN CHANGE THE PAST...WIPE OUT SEVERAL YEARS OF EVENTS!
NOTHING, JAN ... EXCEPT PERHAPS THE ONE DIABOLICAL CREATION WE OURSELVES USED ONLY HOURS AGO...
DR. DOOM'S TIME MACHINE!
AND NOW, IF YOU'LL PARDON YET ANOTHER CHANGE OF LOCALE, WHILE WE GET OUR SCORE CARDS...
WE'VE GOT TO LEARN WHO THOSE CHARACTERS WERE... AND HOW TO FIND THEM!
AY, GIANT-MAN!
AND, WITHIN MOMENTS, THE ONE BEING WHO MIGHT KNOW SHALL APPEAR UNTO US!
IF HE DOESN'T KNOW, WE MIGHT AS WELL TURN IN OUR SUPERHERO UNION CARDS!
HUNNH!! YOU ALL PUT TOO MUCH TRUST IN THE ONE WHO COMES!
YOU SHOULD BE LIKE HULK...AND TRUST NOBODY!
SILENCE... HIS IMAGE IS STARTING TO FORM...!
9

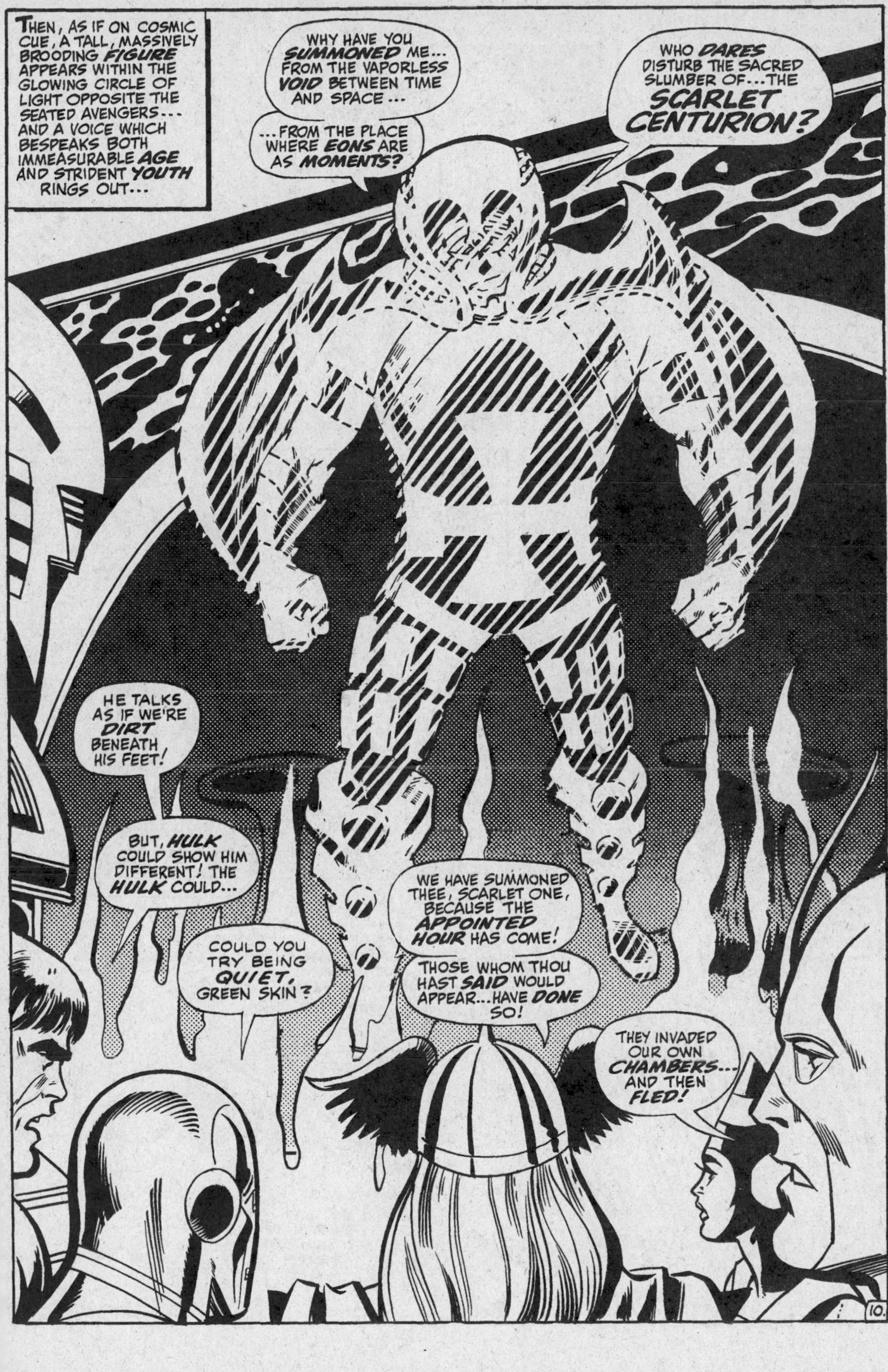
THEN, AS IF ON COSMIC CUE, A TALL, MASSIVELY BROODING FIGURE APPEARS WITHIN THE GLOWING CIRCLE OF LIGHT OPPOSITE THE SEATED AVENGERS... AND A VOICE WHICH BESPEAKS BOTH IMMEASURABLE AGE AND STRIDENT YOUTH RINGS OUT...
WHY HAVE YOU SUMMONED ME... FROM THE VAPORLESS VOID BETWEEN TIME AND SPACE...
...FROM THE PLACE WHERE EONS ARE AS MOMENTS?
WHO DARES DISTURB THE SACRED SLUMBER OF... THE SCARLET CENTURION?
HE TALKS AS IF WE'RE DIRT BENEATH HIS FEET!
BUT, HULK COULD SHOW HIM DIFFERENT! THE HULK COULD...
COULD YOU TRY BEING QUIET, GREEN SKIN?
WE HAVE SUMMONED THEE, SCARLET ONE, BECAUSE THE APPOINTED HOUR HAS COME!
THOSE WHOM THOU HAST SAID WOULD APPEAR... HAVE DONE SO!
THEY INVADED OUR OWN CHAMBERS... AND THEN FLED!
10.

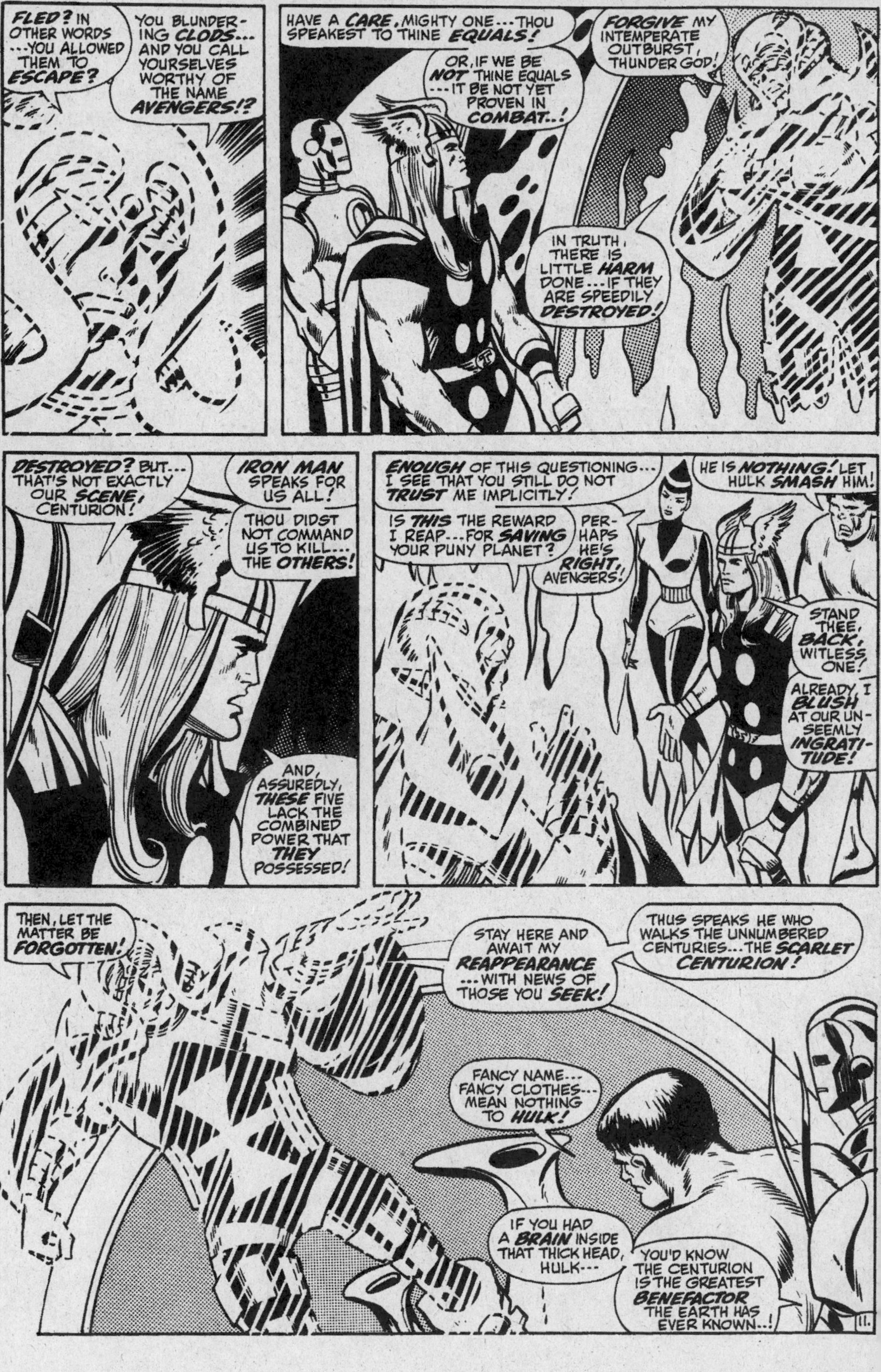

FLED? IN OTHER WORDS ...YOU ALLOWED THEM TO ESCAPE?
YOU BLUNDERING CLODS... AND YOU CALL YOURSELVES WORTHY OF THE NAME AVENGERS!?
HAVE A CARE, MIGHTY ONE ... THOU SPEAKEST TO THINE EQUALS!
OR, IF WE BE NOT THINE EQUALS --- IT BE NOT YET PROVEN IN COMBAT..!
FORGIVE MY INTEMPERATE OUTBURST, THUNDER GOD!
IN TRUTH, THERE IS LITTLE HARM DONE ... IF THEY ARE SPEEDILY DESTROYED!
DESTROYED? BUT... THAT'S NOT EXACTLY OUR SCENE, CENTURION!
IRON MAN SPEAKS FOR US ALL!
THOU DIDST NOT COMMAND US TO KILL... THE OTHERS!
AND, ASSUREDLY, THESE FIVE LACK THE COMBINED POWER THAT THEY POSSESSED!
ENOUGH OF THIS QUESTIONING... I SEE THAT YOU STILL DO NOT TRUST ME IMPLICITLY!
IS THIS THE REWARD I REAP... FOR SAVING YOUR PUNY PLANET?
PERHAPS HE'S RIGHT, AVENGERS!
HE IS NOTHING! LET HULK SMASH HIM!
STAND THEE BACK, WITLESS ONE!
ALREADY, I BLUSH AT OUR UNSEEMLY INGRATITUDE!
THEN, LET THE MATTER BE FORGOTTEN!
STAY HERE AND AWAIT MY REAPPEARANCE ... WITH NEWS OF THOSE YOU SEEK!
THUS SPEAKS HE WHO WALKS THE UNNUMBERED CENTURIES... THE SCARLET CENTURION!
FANCY NAME... FANCY CLOTHES... MEAN NOTHING TO HULK!
IF YOU HAD A BRAIN INSIDE THAT THICK HEAD, HULK---
YOU'D KNOW THE CENTURION IS THE GREATEST BENEFACTOR THE EARTH HAS EVER KNOWN..!
11.

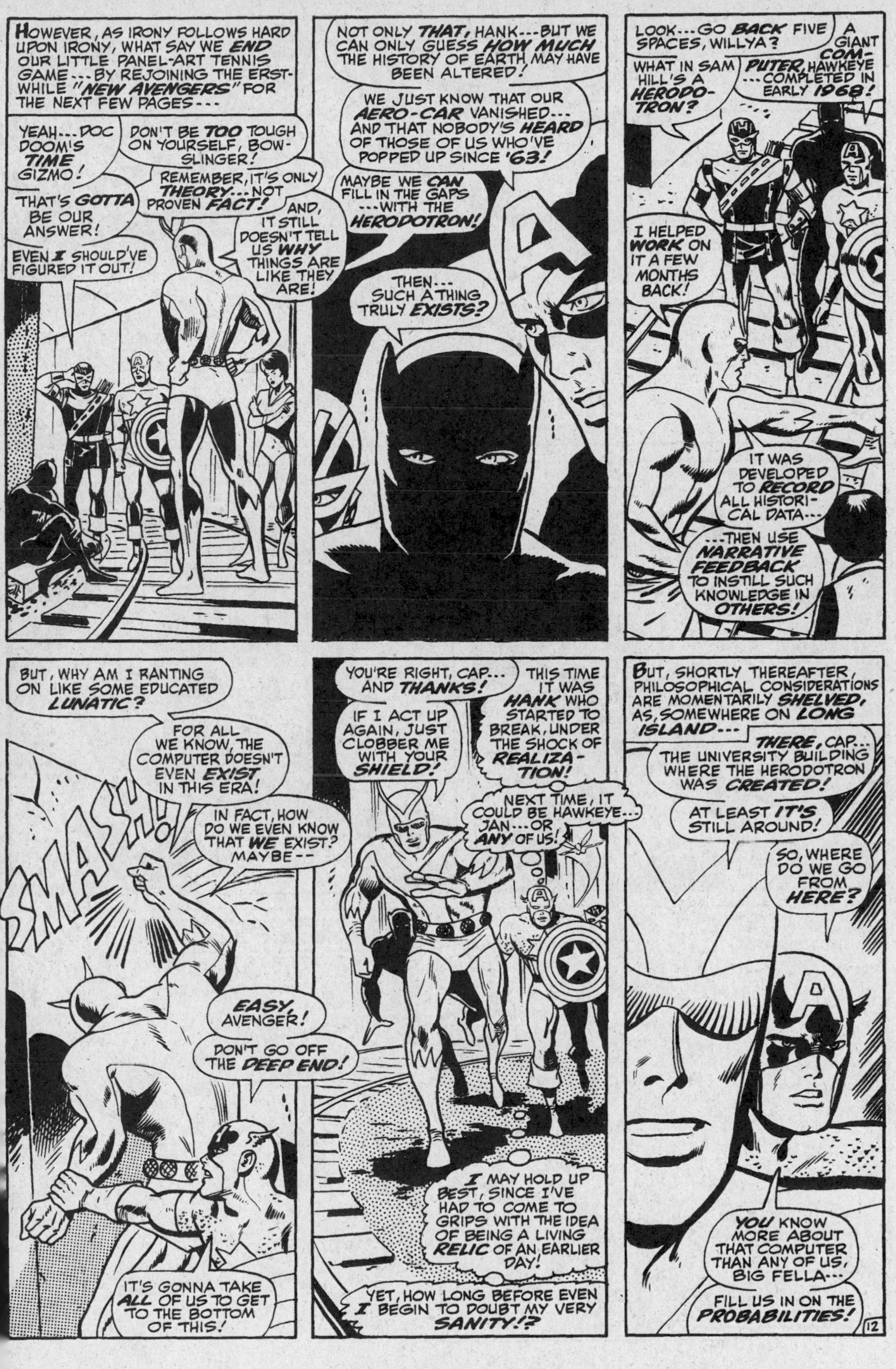
HOWEVER, AS IRONY FOLLOWS HARD UPON IRONY, WHAT SAY WE END OUR LITTLE PANEL-ART TENNIS GAME --- BY REJOINING THE ERSTWHILE "NEW AVENGERS" FOR THE NEXT FEW PAGES---
YEAH--- DOC DOOM'S TIME GIZMO!
THAT'S GOTTA BE OUR ANSWER!
EVEN I SHOULD'VE FIGURED IT OUT!
DON'T BE TOO TOUGH ON YOURSELF, BOW-SLINGER!
REMEMBER, IT'S ONLY THEORY... NOT PROVEN FACT!
AND, IT STILL DOESN'T TELL US WHY THINGS ARE LIKE THEY ARE!
NOT ONLY THAT, HANK---BUT WE CAN ONLY GUESS HOW MUCH THE HISTORY OF EARTH MAY HAVE BEEN ALTERED!
WE JUST KNOW THAT OUR AERO-CAR VANISHED--- AND THAT NOBODY'S HEARD OF THOSE OF US WHO'VE POPPED UP SINCE '63!
MAYBE WE CAN FILL IN THE GAPS ---WITH THE HERODOTRON!
THEN... SUCH A THING TRULY EXISTS?
LOOK...GO BACK FIVE SPACES, WILLYA?
WHAT IN SAM HILL'S A HERODOTRON?
A GIANT COMPUTER, HAWKEYE ...COMPLETED IN EARLY 1968!
I HELPED WORK ON IT A FEW MONTHS BACK!
IT WAS DEVELOPED TO RECORD ALL HISTORICAL DATA...
...THEN USE NARRATIVE FEEDBACK TO INSTILL SUCH KNOWLEDGE IN OTHERS!
BUT, WHY AM I RANTING ON LIKE SOME EDUCATED LUNATIC?
FOR ALL WE KNOW, THE COMPUTER DOESN'T EVEN EXIST IN THIS ERA!
IN FACT, HOW DO WE EVEN KNOW THAT WE EXIST? MAYBE--
SMASH!
EASY, AVENGER!
DON'T GO OFF THE DEEP END!
IT'S GONNA TAKE ALL OF US TO GET TO THE BOTTOM OF THIS!
YOU'RE RIGHT, CAP... AND THANKS!
IF I ACT UP AGAIN, JUST CLOBBER ME WITH YOUR SHIELD!
THIS TIME IT WAS HANK WHO STARTED TO BREAK, UNDER THE SHOCK OF REALIZATION!
NEXT TIME, IT COULD BE HAWKEYE... JAN...OR ANY OF US!
I MAY HOLD UP BEST, SINCE I'VE HAD TO COME TO GRIPS WITH THE IDEA OF BEING A LIVING RELIC OF AN EARLIER DAY!
YET, HOW LONG BEFORE EVEN I BEGIN TO DOUBT MY VERY SANITY!?
BUT, SHORTLY THEREAFTER, PHILOSOPHICAL CONSIDERATIONS ARE MOMENTARILY SHELVED, AS, SOMEWHERE ON LONG ISLAND...
THERE, CAP... THE UNIVERSITY BUILDING WHERE THE HERODOTRON WAS CREATED!
AT LEAST IT'S STILL AROUND!
SO, WHERE DO WE GO FROM HERE?
YOU KNOW MORE ABOUT THAT COMPUTER THAN ANY OF US, BIG FELLA---
FILL US IN ON THE PROBABILITIES!
12

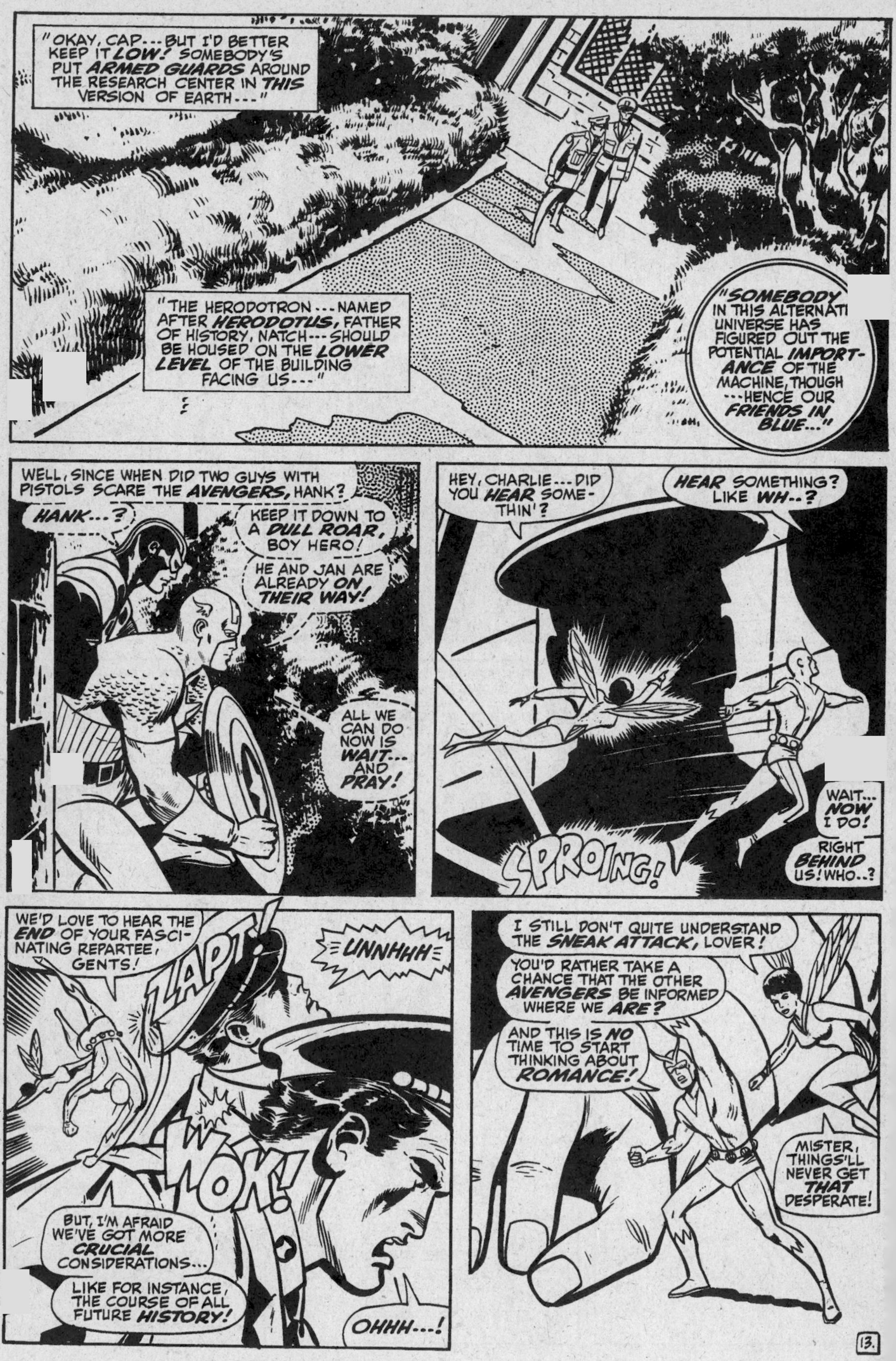
"OKAY, CAP--- BUT I'D BETTER KEEP IT LOW! SOMEBODY'S PUT ARMED GUARDS AROUND THE RESEARCH CENTER IN THIS VERSION OF EARTH---"
"THE HERODOTRON---NAMED AFTER HERODOTUS, FATHER OF HISTORY, NATCH---SHOULD BE HOUSED ON THE LOWER LEVEL OF THE BUILDING FACING US---"
"SOMEBODY IN THIS ALTERNATE UNIVERSE HAS FIGURED OUT THE POTENTIAL IMPORTANCE OF THE MACHINE, THOUGH ---HENCE OUR FRIENDS IN BLUE..."
WELL, SINCE WHEN DID TWO GUYS WITH PISTOLS SCARE THE AVENGERS, HANK?
HANK...?
KEEP IT DOWN TO A DULL ROAR, BOY HERO!
HE AND JAN ARE ALREADY ON THEIR WAY!
ALL WE CAN DO NOW IS WAIT... AND PRAY!
HEY, CHARLIE... DID YOU HEAR SOMETHIN'?
HEAR SOMETHING? LIKE WH--?
SPROING!
WAIT... NOW I DO!
RIGHT BEHIND US! WHO..?
WE'D LOVE TO HEAR THE END OF YOUR FASCINATING REPARTEE, GENTS!
ZAPT!
UNNHHH
WOK!
BUT, I'M AFRAID WE'VE GOT MORE CRUCIAL CONSIDERATIONS...
LIKE FOR INSTANCE, THE COURSE OF ALL FUTURE HISTORY!
OHHH...!
I STILL DON'T QUITE UNDERSTAND THE SNEAK ATTACK, LOVER!
YOU'D RATHER TAKE A CHANCE THAT THE OTHER AVENGERS BE INFORMED WHERE WE ARE?
AND THIS IS NO TIME TO START THINKING ABOUT ROMANCE!
MISTER, THINGS'LL NEVER GET THAT DESPERATE!

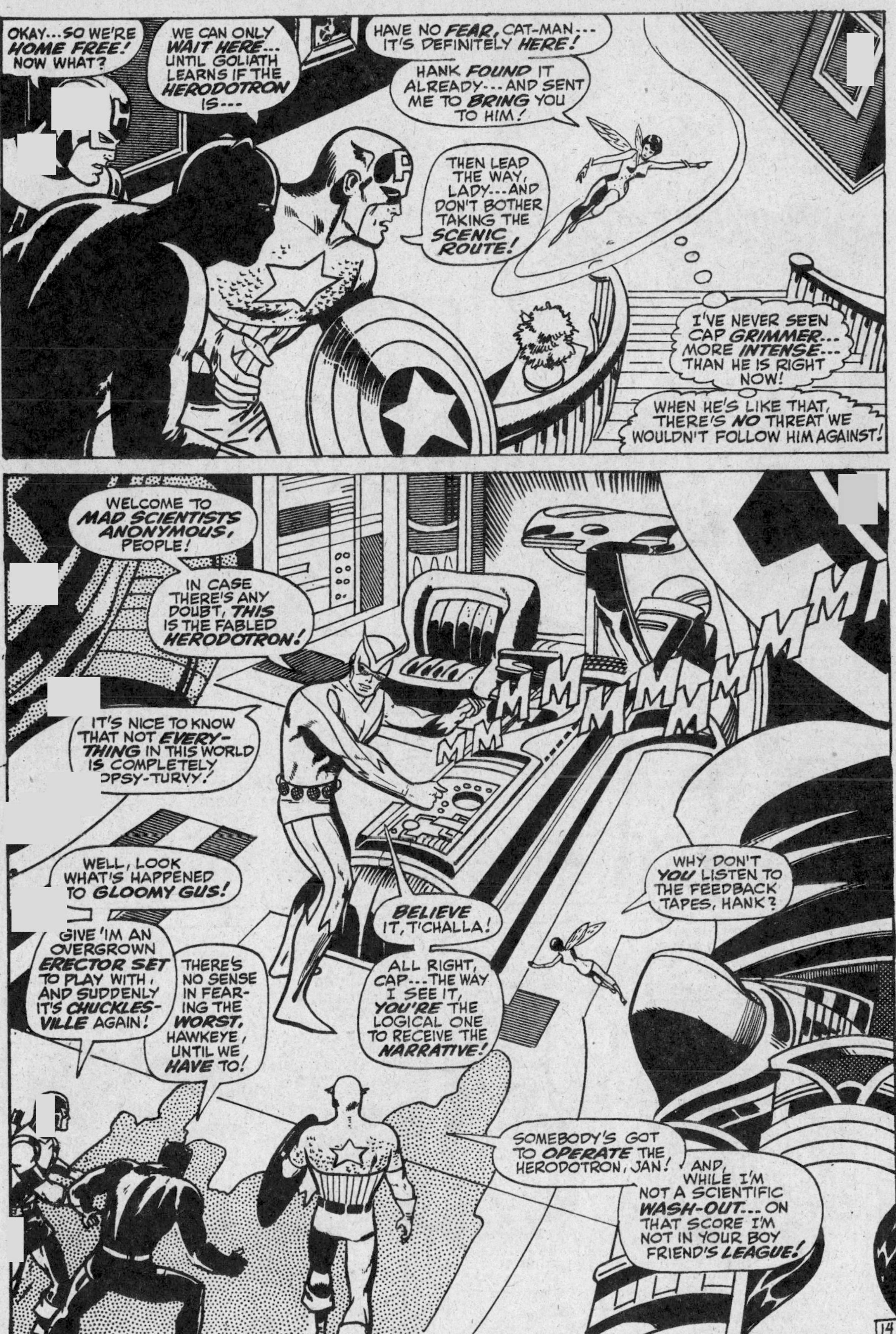
OKAY...SO WE'RE HOME FREE! NOW WHAT?
WE CAN ONLY WAIT HERE... UNTIL GOLIATH LEARNS IF THE HERODOTRON IS---
HAVE NO FEAR, CAT-MAN--- IT'S DEFINITELY HERE!
HANK FOUND IT ALREADY---AND SENT ME TO BRING YOU TO HIM!
THEN LEAD THE WAY, LADY---AND DON'T BOTHER TAKING THE SCENIC ROUTE!
I'VE NEVER SEEN CAP GRIMMER... MORE INTENSE--- THAN HE IS RIGHT NOW!
WHEN HE'S LIKE THAT, THERE'S NO THREAT WE WOULDN'T FOLLOW HIM AGAINST!
WELCOME TO MAD SCIENTISTS ANONYMOUS, PEOPLE!
IN CASE THERE'S ANY DOUBT, THIS IS THE FABLED HERODOTRON!
MMMMMMMMMMMMMMMMMMM
IT'S NICE TO KNOW THAT NOT EVERY-THING IN THIS WORLD IS COMPLETELY TOPSY-TURVY!
WELL, LOOK WHAT'S HAPPENED TO GLOOMY GUS!
GIVE 'IM AN OVERGROWN ERECTOR SET TO PLAY WITH, AND SUDDENLY IT'S CHUCKLES-VILLE AGAIN!
THERE'S NO SENSE IN FEAR-ING THE WORST, HAWKEYE, UNTIL WE HAVE TO!
BELIEVE IT, T'CHALLA!
WHY DON'T YOU LISTEN TO THE FEEDBACK TAPES, HANK?
ALL RIGHT, CAP---THE WAY I SEE IT, YOU'RE THE LOGICAL ONE TO RECEIVE THE NARRATIVE!
SOMEBODY'S GOT TO OPERATE THE HERODOTRON, JAN!
AND, WHILE I'M NOT A SCIENTIFIC WASH-OUT...ON THAT SCORE I'M NOT IN YOUR BOY FRIEND'S LEAGUE!

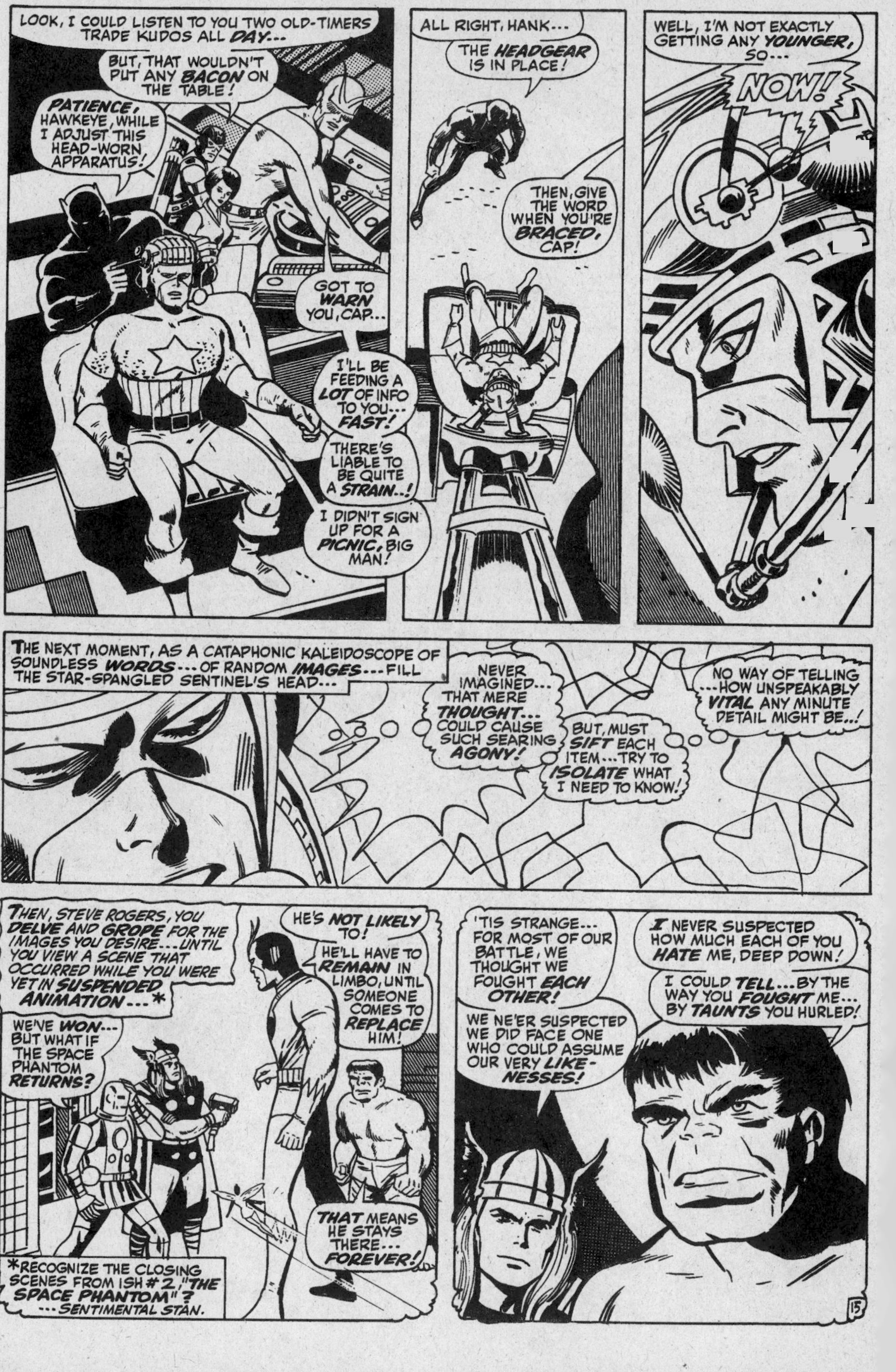

LOOK, I COULD LISTEN TO YOU TWO OLD-TIMERS TRADE KUDOS ALL DAY...
BUT, THAT WOULDN'T PUT ANY BACON ON THE TABLE!
PATIENCE, HAWKEYE, WHILE I ADJUST THIS HEAD-WORN APPARATUS!
GOT TO WARN YOU, CAP...
I'LL BE FEEDING A LOT OF INFO TO YOU... FAST!
THERE'S LIABLE TO BE QUITE A STRAIN..!
I DIDN'T SIGN UP FOR A PICNIC, BIG MAN!
ALL RIGHT, HANK...
THE HEADGEAR IS IN PLACE!
THEN, GIVE THE WORD WHEN YOU'RE BRACED, CAP!
WELL, I'M NOT EXACTLY GETTING ANY YOUNGER, SO...
NOW!
THE NEXT MOMENT, AS A CATAPHONIC KALEIDOSCOPE OF SOUNDLESS WORDS... OF RANDOM IMAGES... FILL THE STAR-SPANGLED SENTINEL'S HEAD...
NEVER IMAGINED... THAT MERE THOUGHT... COULD CAUSE SUCH SEARING AGONY!
BUT, MUST SIFT EACH ITEM... TRY TO ISOLATE WHAT I NEED TO KNOW!
NO WAY OF TELLING ...HOW UNSPEAKABLY VITAL ANY MINUTE DETAIL MIGHT BE...!
THEN, STEVE ROGERS, YOU DELVE AND GROPE FOR THE IMAGES YOU DESIRE... UNTIL YOU VIEW A SCENE THAT OCCURRED WHILE YOU WERE YET IN SUSPENDED ANIMATION...*
WE'VE WON... BUT WHAT IF THE SPACE PHANTOM RETURNS?
HE'S NOT LIKELY TO!
HE'LL HAVE TO REMAIN IN LIMBO, UNTIL SOMEONE COMES TO REPLACE HIM!
THAT MEANS HE STAYS THERE... FOREVER!
*RECOGNIZE THE CLOSING SCENES FROM ISH #2, "THE SPACE PHANTOM"? ...SENTIMENTAL STAN.
'TIS STRANGE... FOR MOST OF OUR BATTLE, WE THOUGHT WE FOUGHT EACH OTHER!
WE NE'ER SUSPECTED WE DID FACE ONE WHO COULD ASSUME OUR VERY LIKE-NESSES!
I NEVER SUSPECTED HOW MUCH EACH OF YOU HATE ME, DEEP DOWN!
I COULD TELL... BY THE WAY YOU FOUGHT ME... BY TAUNTS YOU HURLED!
15

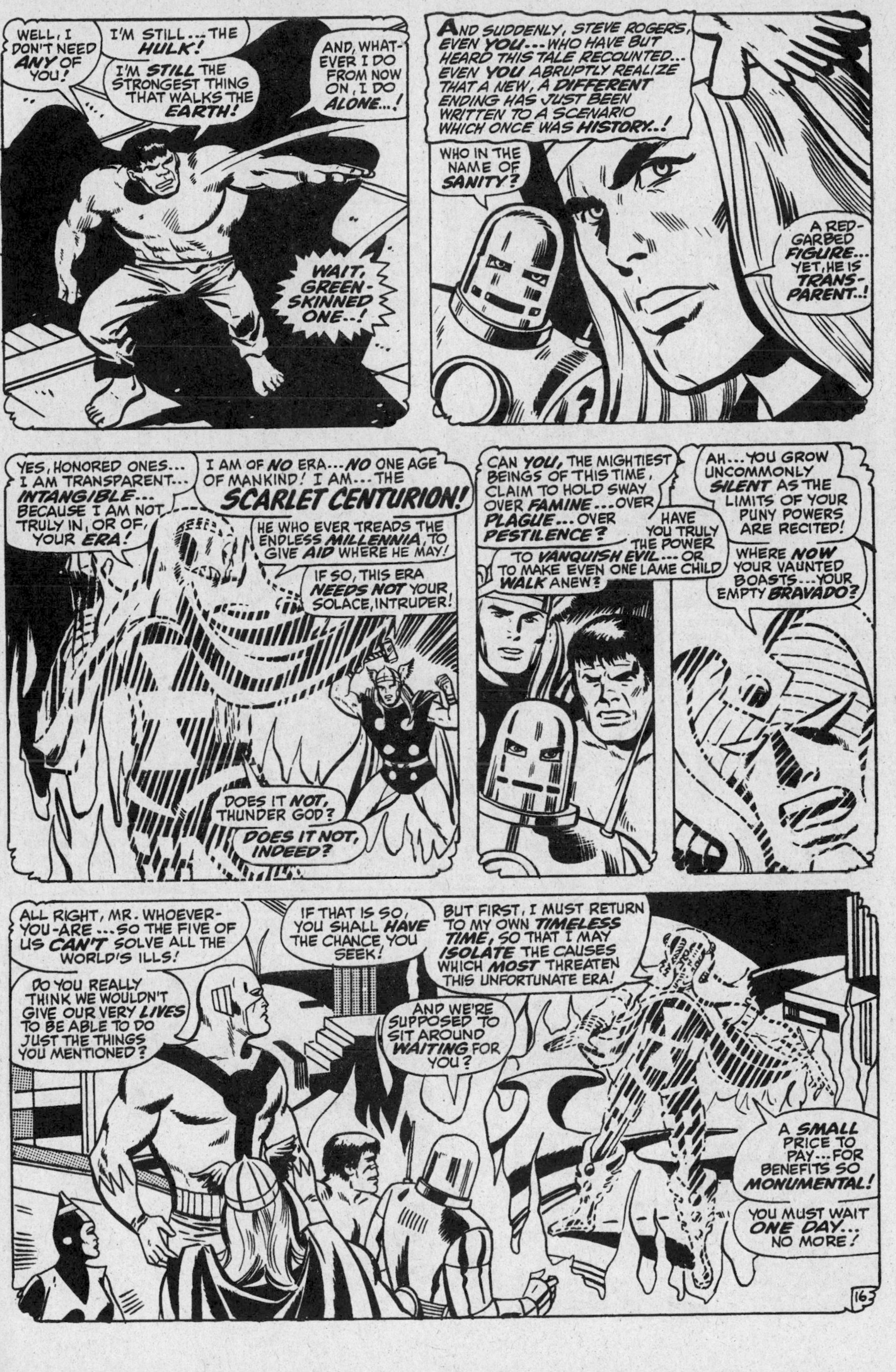
WELL, I DON'T NEED ANY OF YOU!
I'M STILL... THE HULK!
I'M STILL THE STRONGEST THING THAT WALKS THE EARTH!
AND, WHATEVER I DO FROM NOW ON, I DO ALONE...!
WAIT, GREEN-SKINNED ONE..!
AND SUDDENLY, STEVE ROGERS, EVEN YOU... WHO HAVE BUT HEARD THIS TALE RECOUNTED... EVEN YOU ABRUPTLY REALIZE THAT A NEW, A DIFFERENT ENDING HAS JUST BEEN WRITTEN TO A SCENARIO WHICH ONCE WAS HISTORY..!
WHO IN THE NAME OF SANITY?
A RED-GARBED FIGURE... YET, HE IS TRANSPARENT..!
YES, HONORED ONES... I AM TRANSPARENT... INTANGIBLE... BECAUSE I AM NOT TRULY IN, OR OF, YOUR ERA!
I AM OF NO ERA... NO ONE AGE OF MANKIND! I AM... THE SCARLET CENTURION!
HE WHO EVER TREADS THE ENDLESS MILLENNIA, TO GIVE AID WHERE HE MAY!
IF SO, THIS ERA NEEDS NOT YOUR SOLACE, INTRUDER!
DOES IT NOT, THUNDER GOD?
DOES IT NOT, INDEED?
CAN YOU, THE MIGHTIEST BEINGS OF THIS TIME, CLAIM TO HOLD SWAY OVER FAMINE... OVER PLAGUE... OVER PESTILENCE?
HAVE YOU TRULY THE POWER TO VANQUISH EVIL... OR TO MAKE EVEN ONE LAME CHILD WALK ANEW?
AH... YOU GROW UNCOMMONLY SILENT AS THE LIMITS OF YOUR PUNY POWERS ARE RECITED!
WHERE NOW YOUR VAUNTED BOASTS... YOUR EMPTY BRAVADO?
ALL RIGHT, MR. WHOEVER-YOU-ARE... SO THE FIVE OF US CAN'T SOLVE ALL THE WORLD'S ILLS!
DO YOU REALLY THINK WE WOULDN'T GIVE OUR VERY LIVES TO BE ABLE TO DO JUST THE THINGS YOU MENTIONED?
IF THAT IS SO, YOU SHALL HAVE THE CHANCE YOU SEEK!
BUT FIRST, I MUST RETURN TO MY OWN TIMELESS TIME, SO THAT I MAY ISOLATE THE CAUSES WHICH MOST THREATEN THIS UNFORTUNATE ERA!
AND WE'RE SUPPOSED TO SIT AROUND WAITING FOR YOU?
A SMALL PRICE TO PAY... FOR BENEFITS SO MONUMENTAL!
YOU MUST WAIT ONE DAY... NO MORE!
16

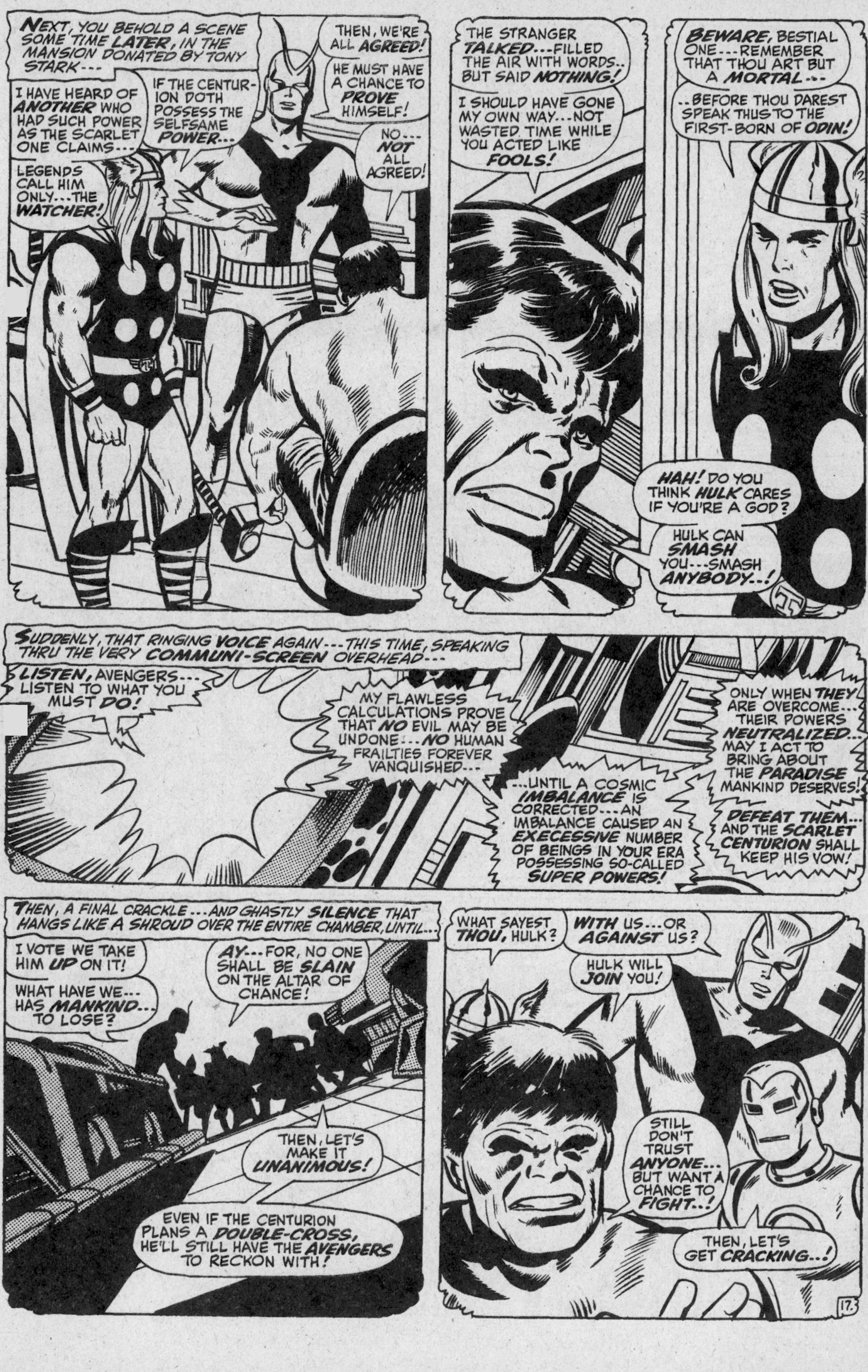
NEXT, YOU BEHOLD A SCENE SOME TIME LATER, IN THE MANSION DONATED BY TONY STARK---
I HAVE HEARD OF ANOTHER WHO HAD SUCH POWER AS THE SCARLET ONE CLAIMS---
LEGENDS CALL HIM ONLY---THE WATCHER!
IF THE CENTURION DOTH POSSESS THE SELFSAME POWER...
THEN, WE'RE ALL AGREED!
HE MUST HAVE A CHANCE TO PROVE HIMSELF!
NO--- NOT ALL AGREED!
THE STRANGER TALKED---FILLED THE AIR WITH WORDS.. BUT SAID NOTHING!
I SHOULD HAVE GONE MY OWN WAY---NOT WASTED TIME WHILE YOU ACTED LIKE FOOLS!
BEWARE, BESTIAL ONE---REMEMBER THAT THOU ART BUT A MORTAL---
..BEFORE THOU DAREST SPEAK THUS TO THE FIRST-BORN OF ODIN!
HAH! DO YOU THINK HULK CARES IF YOU'RE A GOD?
HULK CAN SMASH YOU---SMASH ANYBODY..!
SUDDENLY, THAT RINGING VOICE AGAIN---THIS TIME, SPEAKING THRU THE VERY COMMUNI-SCREEN OVERHEAD---
LISTEN, AVENGERS--- LISTEN TO WHAT YOU MUST DO!
MY FLAWLESS CALCULATIONS PROVE THAT NO EVIL MAY BE UNDONE---NO HUMAN FRAILTIES FOREVER VANQUISHED---
...UNTIL A COSMIC IMBALANCE IS CORRECTED---AN IMBALANCE CAUSED AN EXECESSIVE NUMBER OF BEINGS IN YOUR ERA POSSESSING SO-CALLED SUPER POWERS!
ONLY WHEN THEY ARE OVERCOME... THEIR POWERS NEUTRALIZED... MAY I ACT TO BRING ABOUT THE PARADISE MANKIND DESERVES!
DEFEAT THEM... AND THE SCARLET CENTURION SHALL KEEP HIS VOW!
THEN, A FINAL CRACKLE...AND GHASTLY SILENCE THAT HANGS LIKE A SHROUD OVER THE ENTIRE CHAMBER, UNTIL...
I VOTE WE TAKE HIM UP ON IT!
WHAT HAVE WE... HAS MANKIND... TO LOSE?
AY---FOR, NO ONE SHALL BE SLAIN ON THE ALTAR OF CHANCE!
THEN, LET'S MAKE IT UNANIMOUS!
EVEN IF THE CENTURION PLANS A DOUBLE-CROSS, HE'LL STILL HAVE THE AVENGERS TO RECKON WITH!
WHAT SAYEST THOU, HULK?
WITH US...OR AGAINST US?
HULK WILL JOIN YOU!
STILL DON'T TRUST ANYONE... BUT WANT A CHANCE TO FIGHT..!
THEN, LET'S GET CRACKING..!
17

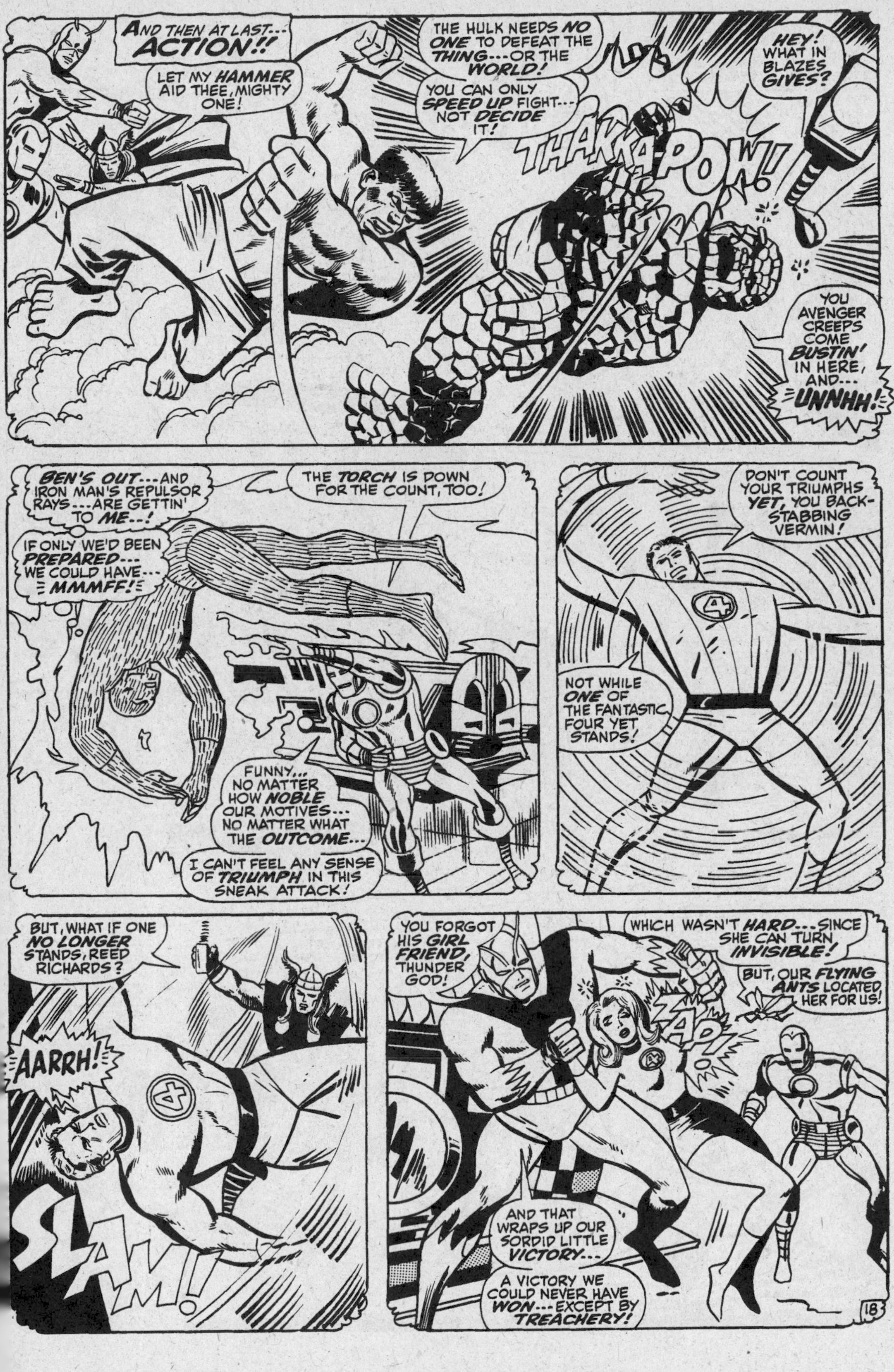

AND THEN AT LAST... ACTION!!
LET MY HAMMER AID THEE, MIGHTY ONE!
THE HULK NEEDS NO ONE TO DEFEAT THE THING...OR THE WORLD!
YOU CAN ONLY SPEED UP FIGHT... NOT DECIDE IT!
THAKKA-POW!
HEY! WHAT IN BLAZES GIVES?
YOU AVENGER CREEPS COME BUSTIN' IN HERE, AND... UNNHH!
BEN'S OUT...AND IRON MAN'S REPULSOR RAYS...ARE GETTIN' TO ME--!
THE TORCH IS DOWN FOR THE COUNT, TOO!
IF ONLY WE'D BEEN PREPARED... WE COULD HAVE... MMMFF!
FUNNY... NO MATTER HOW NOBLE OUR MOTIVES... NO MATTER WHAT THE OUTCOME...
I CAN'T FEEL ANY SENSE OF TRIUMPH IN THIS SNEAK ATTACK!
DON'T COUNT YOUR TRIUMPHS YET, YOU BACK-STABBING VERMIN!
NOT WHILE ONE OF THE FANTASTIC FOUR YET STANDS!
BUT, WHAT IF ONE NO LONGER STANDS, REED RICHARDS?
AARRH!
SLAM!
YOU FORGOT HIS GIRL FRIEND, THUNDER GOD!
WHICH WASN'T HARD...SINCE SHE CAN TURN INVISIBLE!
BUT, OUR FLYING ANTS LOCATED HER FOR US!
ZAP!
AND THAT WRAPS UP OUR SORDID LITTLE VICTORY...
A VICTORY WE COULD NEVER HAVE WON...EXCEPT BY TREACHERY!
18

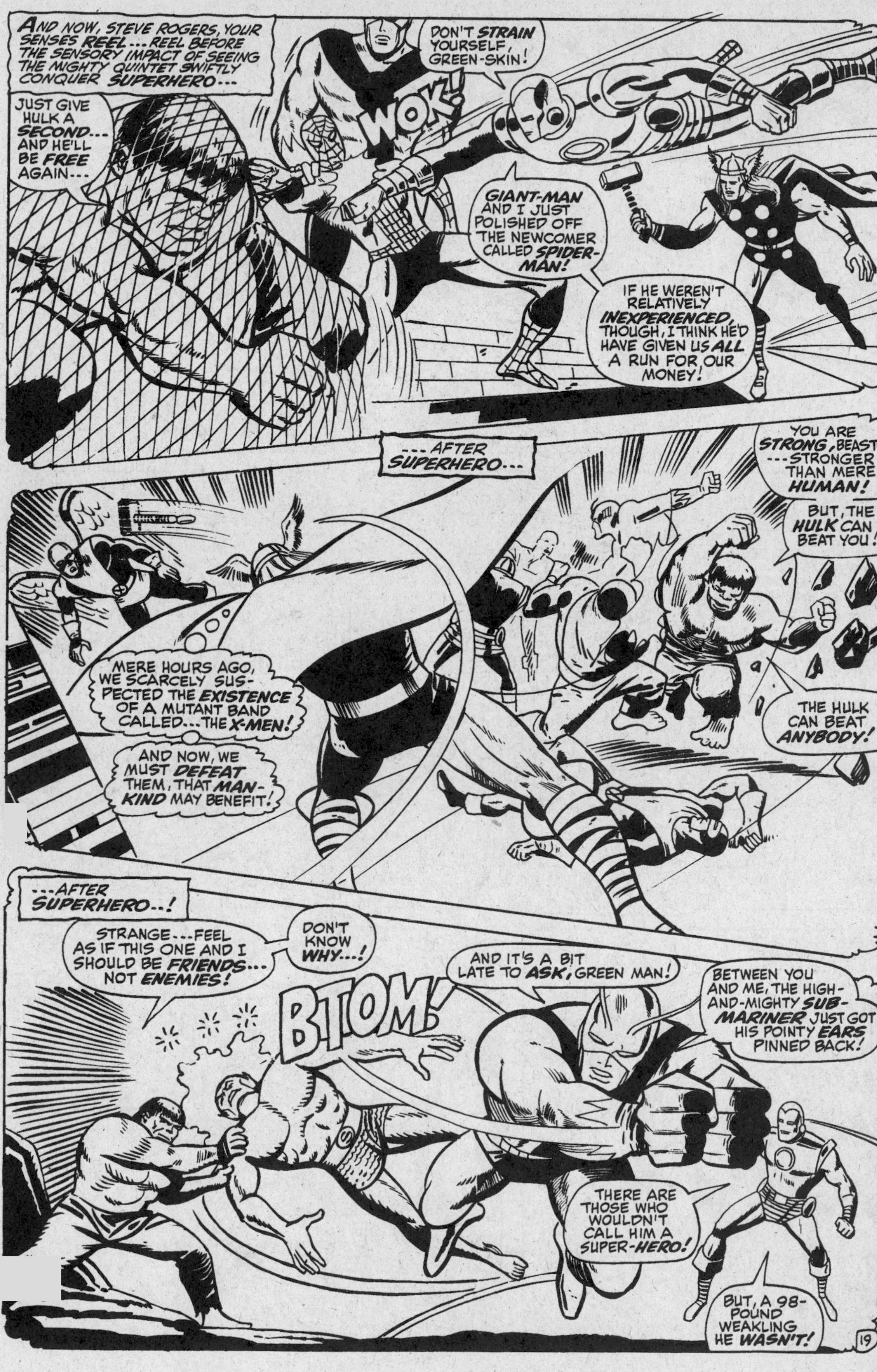

AND NOW, STEVE ROGERS, YOUR SENSES REEL... REEL BEFORE THE SENSORY IMPACT OF SEEING THE MIGHTY QUINTET SWIFTLY CONQUER SUPERHERO---
DON'T STRAIN YOURSELF, GREEN-SKIN!
JUST GIVE HULK A SECOND... AND HE'LL BE FREE AGAIN---
WOK!
GIANT-MAN AND I JUST POLISHED OFF THE NEWCOMER CALLED SPIDER-MAN!
IF HE WEREN'T RELATIVELY INEXPERIENCED, THOUGH, I THINK HE'D HAVE GIVEN US ALL A RUN FOR OUR MONEY!
---AFTER SUPERHERO...
YOU ARE STRONG, BEAST ---STRONGER THAN MERE HUMAN!
BUT, THE HULK CAN BEAT YOU!
MERE HOURS AGO, WE SCARCELY SUSPECTED THE EXISTENCE OF A MUTANT BAND CALLED... THE X-MEN!
AND NOW, WE MUST DEFEAT THEM, THAT MANKIND MAY BENEFIT!
THE HULK CAN BEAT ANYBODY!
...AFTER SUPERHERO..!
STRANGE---FEEL AS IF THIS ONE AND I SHOULD BE FRIENDS... NOT ENEMIES!
DON'T KNOW WHY...!
AND IT'S A BIT LATE TO ASK, GREEN MAN!
BETWEEN YOU AND ME, THE HIGH-AND-MIGHTY SUB-MARINER JUST GOT HIS POINTY EARS PINNED BACK!
BTOM!
THERE ARE THOSE WHO WOULDN'T CALL HIM A SUPER-HERO!
BUT, A 98-POUND WEAKLING HE WASN'T!
19

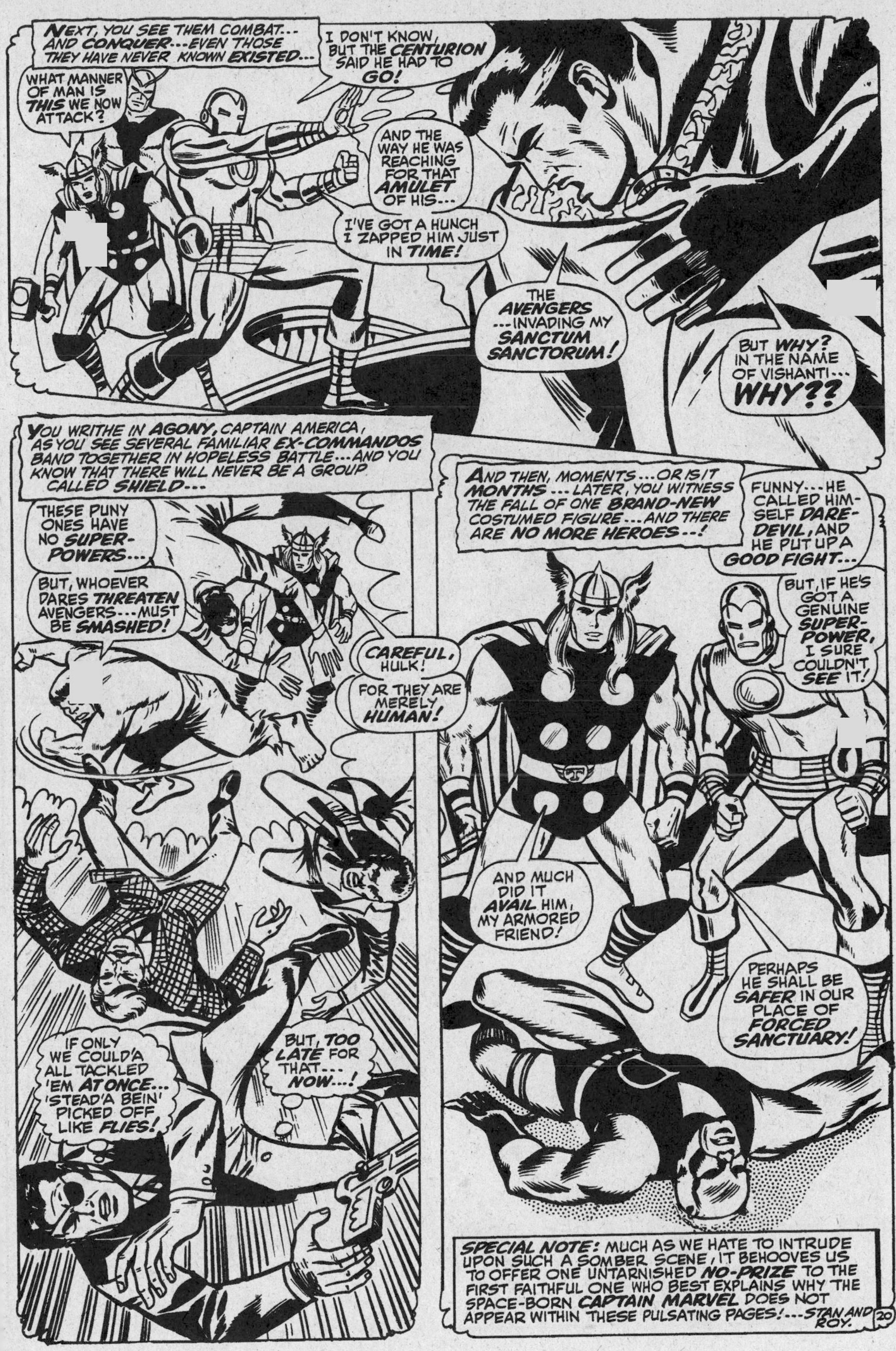
NEXT, YOU SEE THEM COMBAT... AND CONQUER... EVEN THOSE THEY HAVE NEVER KNOWN EXISTED...
WHAT MANNER OF MAN IS THIS WE NOW ATTACK?
I DON'T KNOW, BUT THE CENTURION SAID HE HAD TO GO!
AND THE WAY HE WAS REACHING FOR THAT AMULET OF HIS...
I'VE GOT A HUNCH I ZAPPED HIM JUST IN TIME!
THE AVENGERS ...INVADING MY SANCTUM SANCTORUM!
BUT WHY? IN THE NAME OF VISHANTI... WHY??
YOU WRITHE IN AGONY, CAPTAIN AMERICA, AS YOU SEE SEVERAL FAMILIAR EX-COMMANDOS BAND TOGETHER IN HOPELESS BATTLE... AND YOU KNOW THAT THERE WILL NEVER BE A GROUP CALLED SHIELD...
THESE PUNY ONES HAVE NO SUPER-POWERS...
BUT, WHOEVER DARES THREATEN AVENGERS... MUST BE SMASHED!
CAREFUL, HULK!
FOR THEY ARE MERELY HUMAN!
IF ONLY WE COULD'A ALL TACKLED 'EM AT ONCE... 'STEAD'A BEIN' PICKED OFF LIKE FLIES!
BUT, TOO LATE FOR THAT... NOW...!
AND THEN, MOMENTS... OR IS IT MONTHS... LATER, YOU WITNESS THE FALL OF ONE BRAND-NEW COSTUMED FIGURE... AND THERE ARE NO MORE HEROES--!
FUNNY... HE CALLED HIMSELF DARE-DEVIL, AND HE PUT UP A GOOD FIGHT...
BUT, IF HE'S GOT A GENUINE SUPER-POWER, I SURE COULDN'T SEE IT!
AND MUCH DID IT AVAIL HIM, MY ARMORED FRIEND!
PERHAPS HE SHALL BE SAFER IN OUR PLACE OF FORCED SANCTUARY!
SPECIAL NOTE: MUCH AS WE HATE TO INTRUDE UPON SUCH A SOMBER SCENE, IT BEHOOVES US TO OFFER ONE UNTARNISHED NO-PRIZE TO THE FIRST FAITHFUL ONE WHO BEST EXPLAINS WHY THE SPACE-BORN CAPTAIN MARVEL DOES NOT APPEAR WITHIN THESE PULSATING PAGES! ...STAN AND ROY.
20

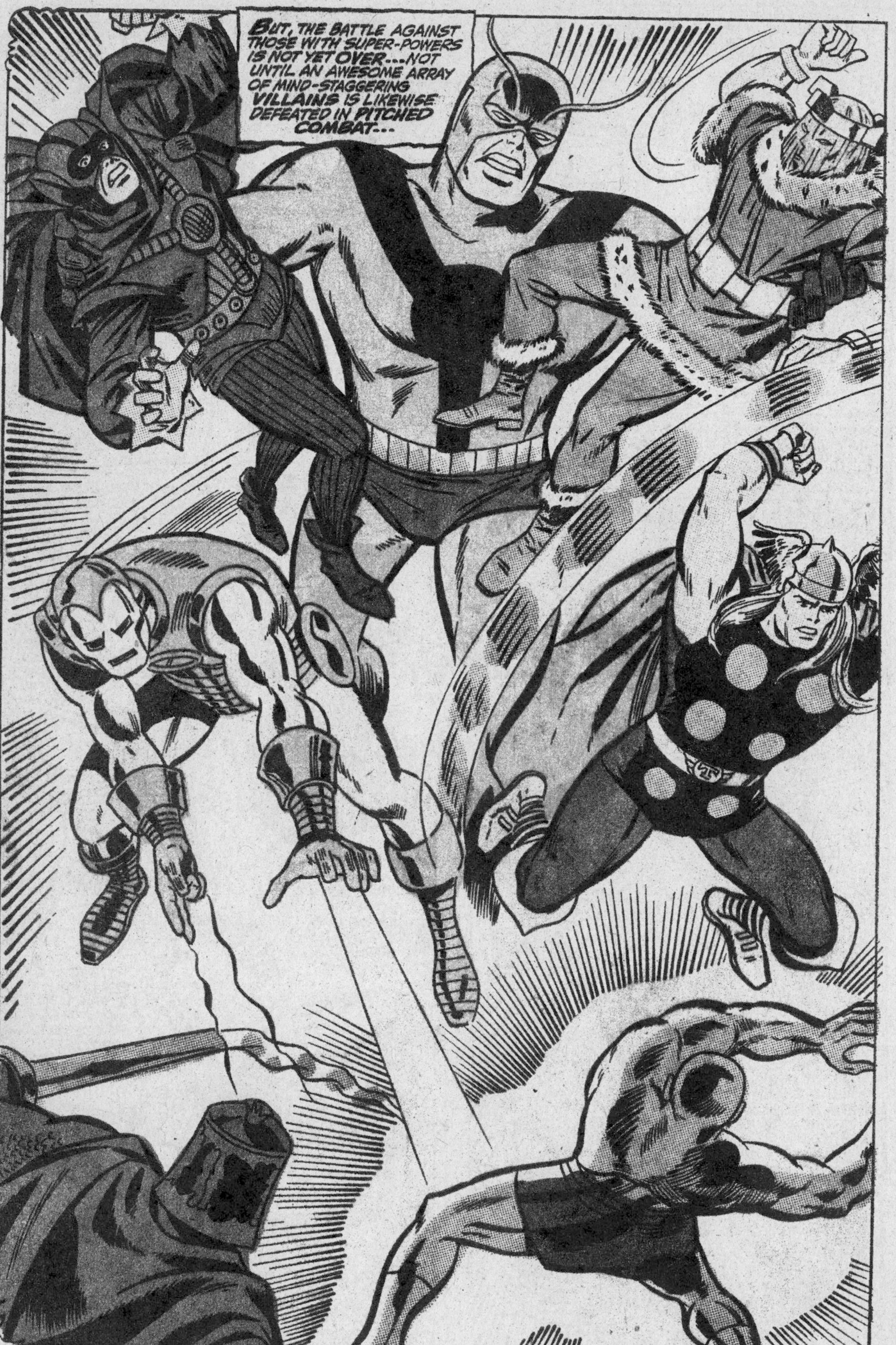
BUT, THE BATTLE AGAINST THOSE WITH SUPER-POWERS IS NOT YET OVER...NOT UNTIL AN AWESOME ARRAY OF MIND-STAGGERING VILLAINS IS LIKEWISE DEFEATED IN PITCHED COMBAT...
21.

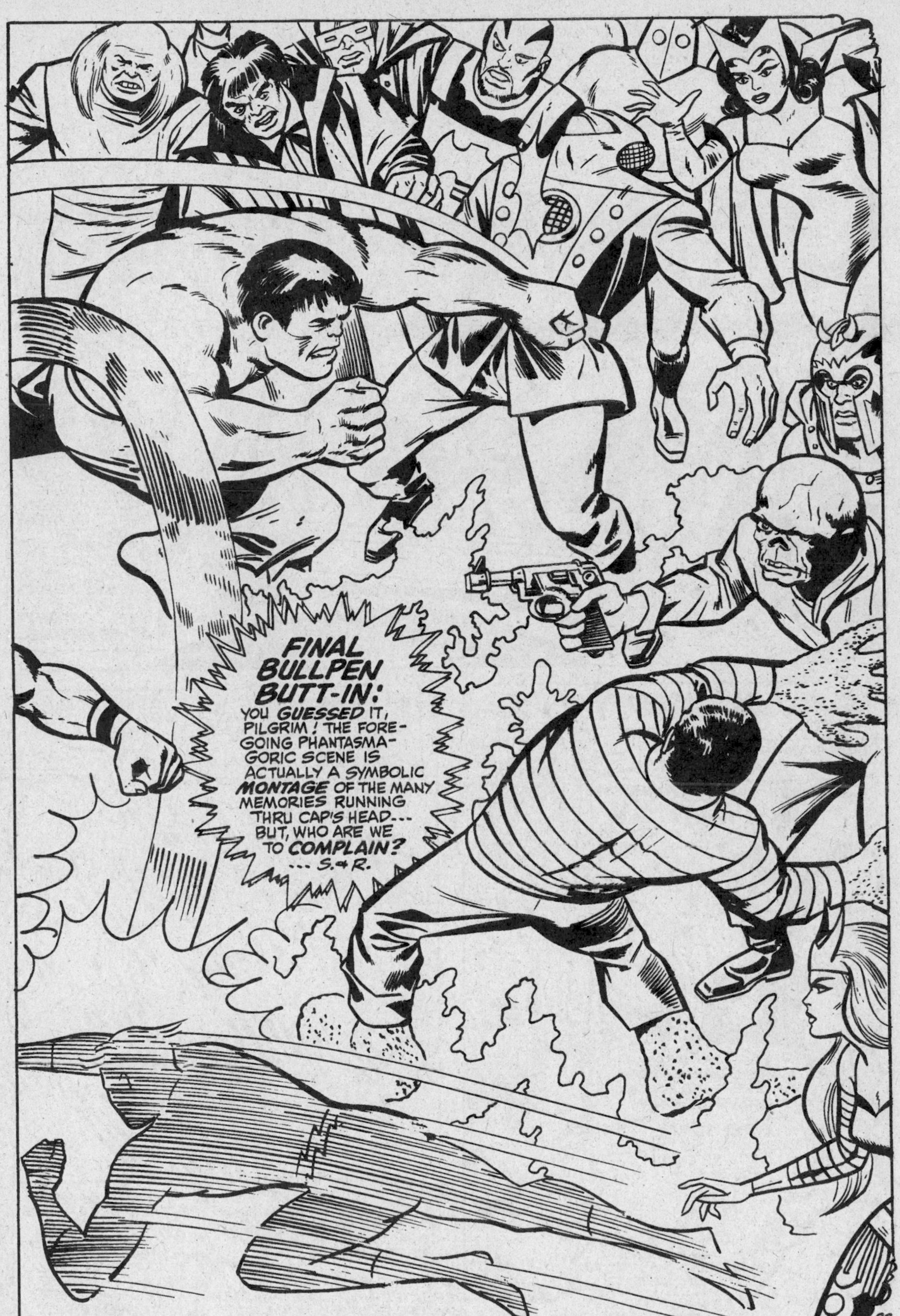
FINAL BULLPEN BUTT-IN:
YOU GUESSED IT, PILGRIM! THE FORE-GOING PHANTASMA-GORIC SCENE IS ACTUALLY A SYMBOLIC MONTAGE OF THE MANY MEMORIES RUNNING THRU CAP'S HEAD--- BUT, WHO ARE WE TO COMPLAIN? ...S.&R.
22

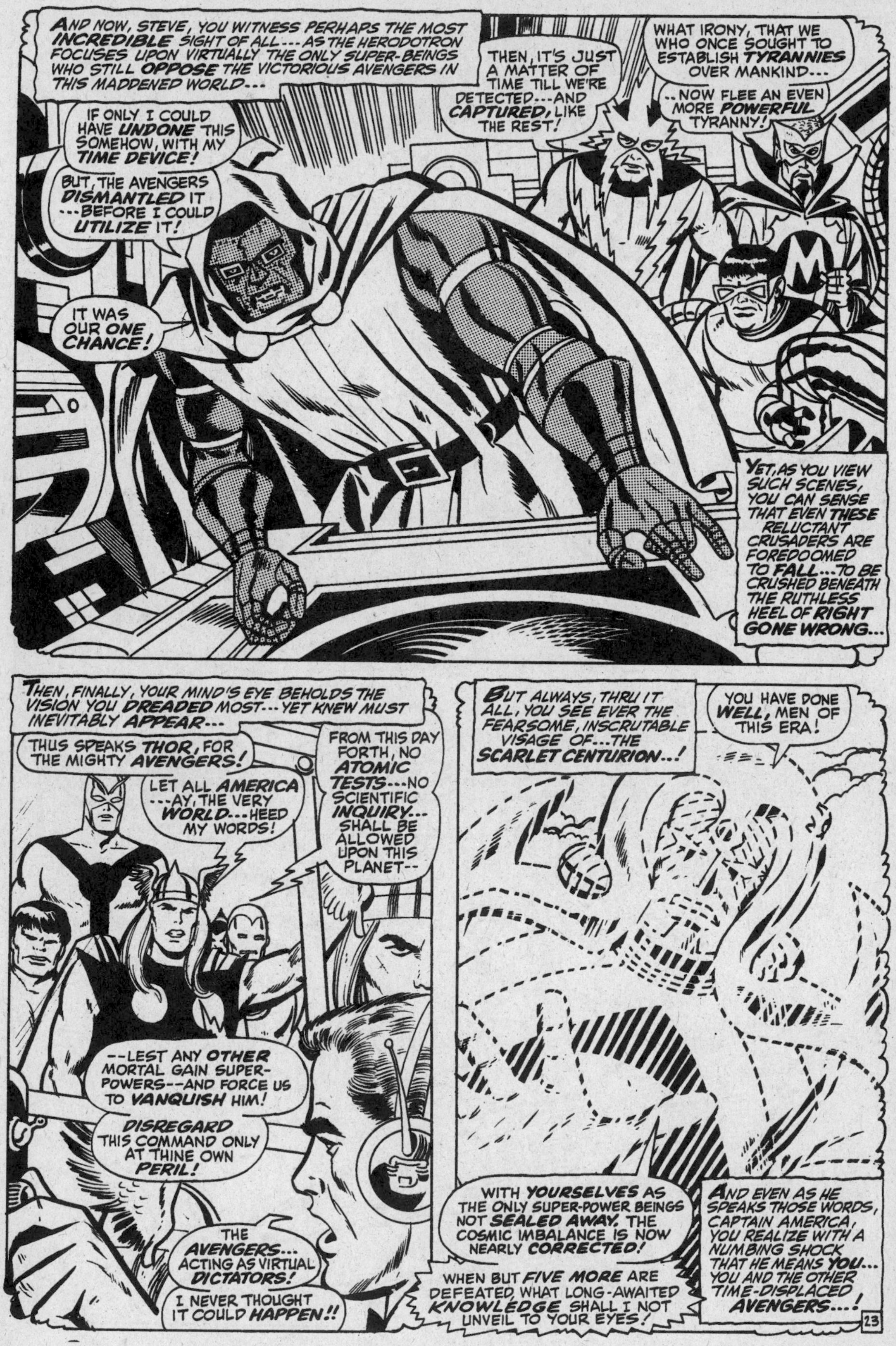
AND NOW, STEVE, YOU WITNESS PERHAPS THE MOST INCREDIBLE SIGHT OF ALL--- AS THE HERODOTRON FOCUSES UPON VIRTUALLY THE ONLY SUPER-BEINGS WHO STILL OPPOSE THE VICTORIOUS AVENGERS IN THIS MADDENED WORLD---
THEN, IT'S JUST A MATTER OF TIME TILL WE'RE DETECTED---AND CAPTURED, LIKE THE REST!
WHAT IRONY, THAT WE WHO ONCE SOUGHT TO ESTABLISH TYRANNIES OVER MANKIND---
..NOW FLEE AN EVEN MORE POWERFUL TYRANNY!
IF ONLY I COULD HAVE UNDONE THIS SOMEHOW, WITH MY TIME DEVICE!
BUT, THE AVENGERS DISMANTLED IT ---BEFORE I COULD UTILIZE IT!
IT WAS OUR ONE CHANCE!
YET, AS YOU VIEW SUCH SCENES, YOU CAN SENSE THAT EVEN THESE RELUCTANT CRUSADERS ARE FOREDOOMED TO FALL...TO BE CRUSHED BENEATH THE RUTHLESS HEEL OF RIGHT GONE WRONG...
THEN, FINALLY, YOUR MIND'S EYE BEHOLDS THE VISION YOU DREADED MOST---YET KNEW MUST INEVITABLY APPEAR---
THUS SPEAKS THOR, FOR THE MIGHTY AVENGERS!
LET ALL AMERICA ---AY, THE VERY WORLD---HEED MY WORDS!
FROM THIS DAY FORTH, NO ATOMIC TESTS---NO SCIENTIFIC INQUIRY--- SHALL BE ALLOWED UPON THIS PLANET--
--LEST ANY OTHER MORTAL GAIN SUPER-POWERS--AND FORCE US TO VANQUISH HIM!
DISREGARD THIS COMMAND ONLY AT THINE OWN PERIL!
THE AVENGERS... ACTING AS VIRTUAL DICTATORS!
I NEVER THOUGHT IT COULD HAPPEN!!
BUT ALWAYS, THRU IT ALL, YOU SEE EVER THE FEARSOME, INSCRUTABLE VISAGE OF...THE SCARLET CENTURION..!
YOU HAVE DONE WELL, MEN OF THIS ERA!
WITH YOURSELVES AS THE ONLY SUPER-POWER BEINGS NOT SEALED AWAY, THE COSMIC IMBALANCE IS NOW NEARLY CORRECTED!
WHEN BUT FIVE MORE ARE DEFEATED WHAT LONG-AWAITED KNOWLEDGE SHALL I NOT UNVEIL TO YOUR EYES!
AND EVEN AS HE SPEAKS THOSE WORDS, CAPTAIN AMERICA, YOU REALIZE WITH A NUMBING SHOCK THAT HE MEANS YOU... YOU AND THE OTHER TIME-DISPLACED AVENGERS...!
23

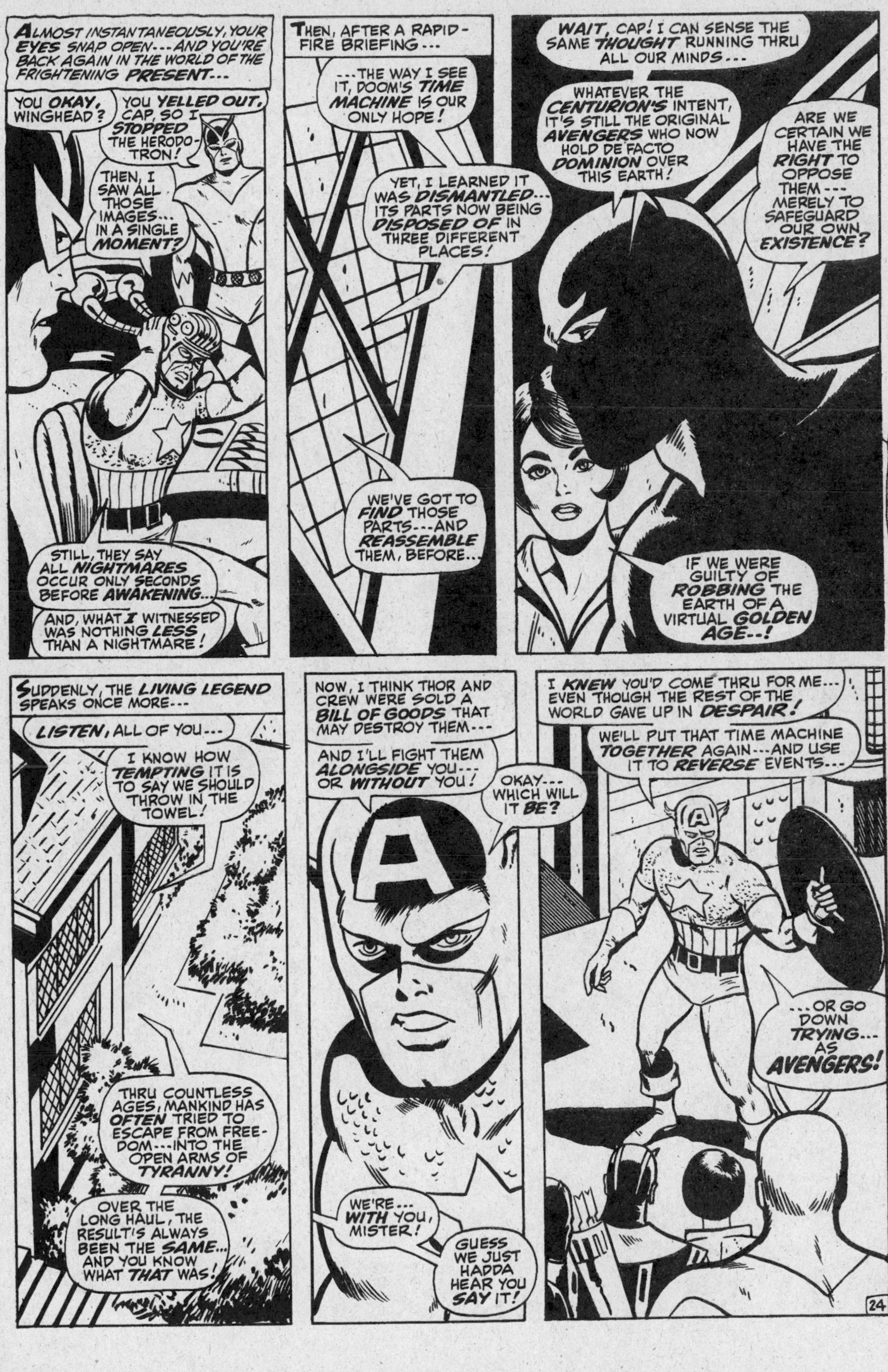
ALMOST INSTANTANEOUSLY, YOUR EYES SNAP OPEN---AND YOU'RE BACK AGAIN IN THE WORLD OF THE FRIGHTENING PRESENT---
YOU OKAY, WINGHEAD?
YOU YELLED OUT, CAP, SO I STOPPED THE HERODO-TRON!
THEN, I SAW ALL THOSE IMAGES... IN A SINGLE MOMENT?
STILL, THEY SAY ALL NIGHTMARES OCCUR ONLY SECONDS BEFORE AWAKENING...
AND, WHAT I WITNESSED WAS NOTHING LESS THAN A NIGHTMARE!
THEN, AFTER A RAPID-FIRE BRIEFING---
---THE WAY I SEE IT, DOOM'S TIME MACHINE IS OUR ONLY HOPE!
YET, I LEARNED IT WAS DISMANTLED... ITS PARTS NOW BEING DISPOSED OF IN THREE DIFFERENT PLACES!
WE'VE GOT TO FIND THOSE PARTS---AND REASSEMBLE THEM, BEFORE...
WAIT, CAP! I CAN SENSE THE SAME THOUGHT RUNNING THRU ALL OUR MINDS---
WHATEVER THE CENTURION'S INTENT, IT'S STILL THE ORIGINAL AVENGERS WHO NOW HOLD DE FACTO DOMINION OVER THIS EARTH!
ARE WE CERTAIN WE HAVE THE RIGHT TO OPPOSE THEM--- MERELY TO SAFEGUARD OUR OWN EXISTENCE?
IF WE WERE GUILTY OF ROBBING THE EARTH OF A VIRTUAL GOLDEN AGE--!
SUDDENLY, THE LIVING LEGEND SPEAKS ONCE MORE---
LISTEN, ALL OF YOU---
I KNOW HOW TEMPTING IT IS TO SAY WE SHOULD THROW IN THE TOWEL!
THRU COUNTLESS AGES, MANKIND HAS OFTEN TRIED TO ESCAPE FROM FREE-DOM---INTO THE OPEN ARMS OF TYRANNY!
OVER THE LONG HAUL, THE RESULT'S ALWAYS BEEN THE SAME... AND YOU KNOW WHAT THAT WAS!
NOW, I THINK THOR AND CREW WERE SOLD A BILL OF GOODS THAT MAY DESTROY THEM---
AND I'LL FIGHT THEM ALONGSIDE YOU--- OR WITHOUT YOU!
OKAY--- WHICH WILL IT BE?
WE'RE... WITH YOU, MISTER!
GUESS WE JUST HADDA HEAR YOU SAY IT!
I KNEW YOU'D COME THRU FOR ME... EVEN THOUGH THE REST OF THE WORLD GAVE UP IN DESPAIR!
WE'LL PUT THAT TIME MACHINE TOGETHER AGAIN---AND USE IT TO REVERSE EVENTS---
---OR GO DOWN TRYING... AS AVENGERS!
24

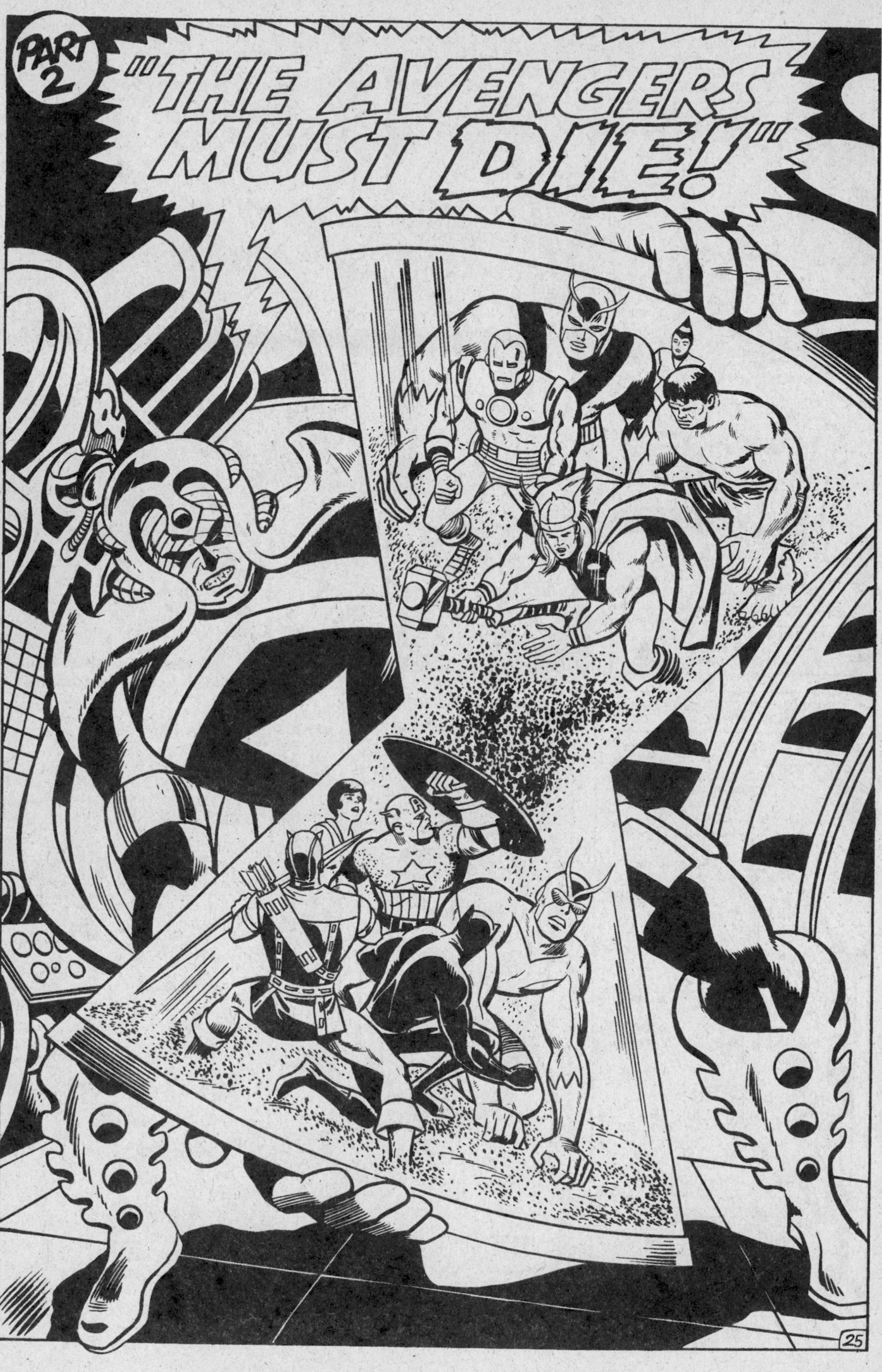
PART 2
"THE AVENGERS MUST DIE!"

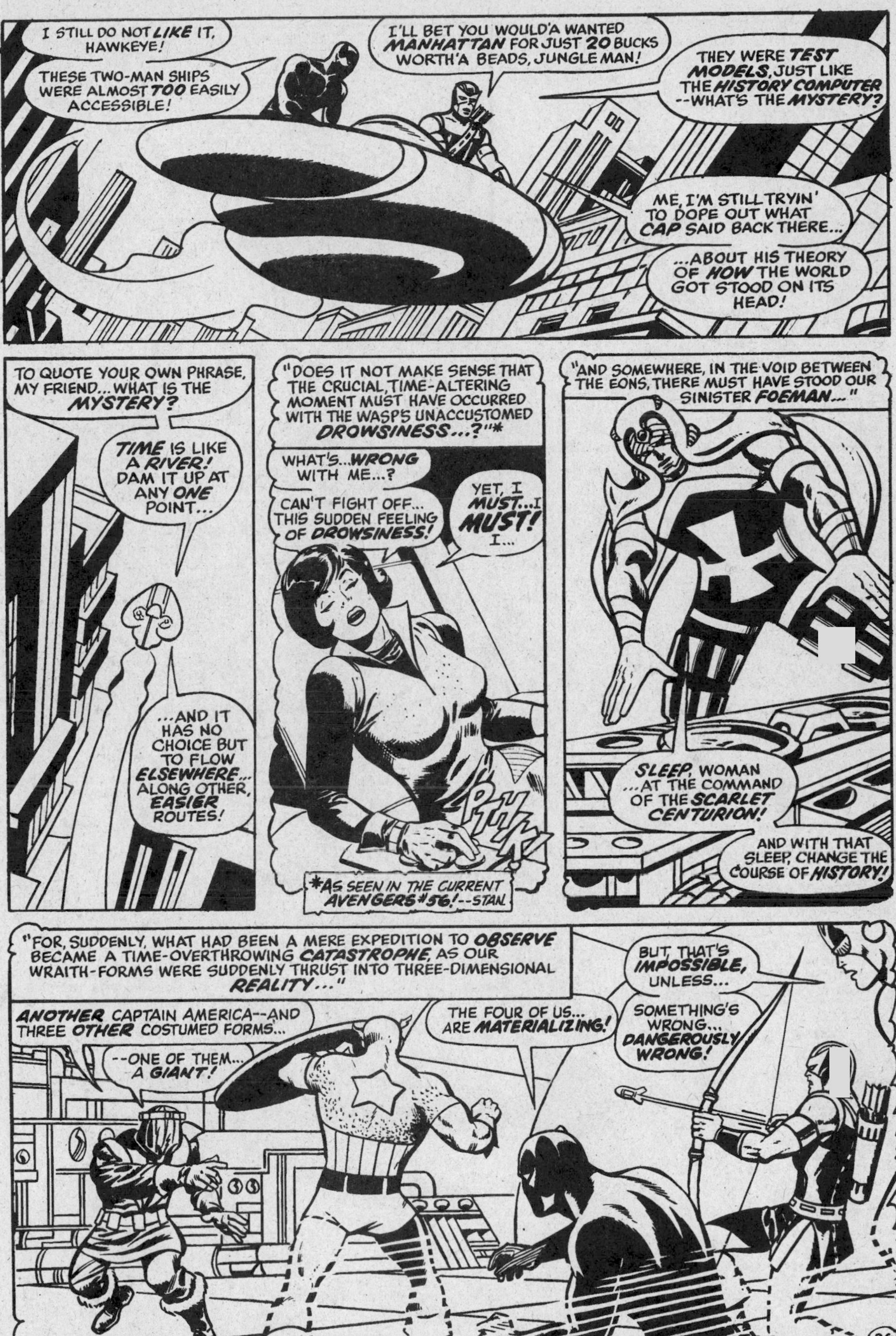
I STILL DO NOT LIKE IT, HAWKEYE!
THESE TWO-MAN SHIPS WERE ALMOST TOO EASILY ACCESSIBLE!
I'LL BET YOU WOULD'A WANTED MANHATTAN FOR JUST 20 BUCKS WORTH'A BEADS, JUNGLE MAN!
THEY WERE TEST MODELS, JUST LIKE THE HISTORY COMPUTER --WHAT'S THE MYSTERY?
ME, I'M STILL TRYIN' TO DOPE OUT WHAT CAP SAID BACK THERE...
...ABOUT HIS THEORY OF HOW THE WORLD GOT STOOD ON ITS HEAD!
TO QUOTE YOUR OWN PHRASE, MY FRIEND... WHAT IS THE MYSTERY?
TIME IS LIKE A RIVER! DAM IT UP AT ANY ONE POINT...
...AND IT HAS NO CHOICE BUT TO FLOW ELSEWHERE... ALONG OTHER, EASIER ROUTES!
"DOES IT NOT MAKE SENSE THAT THE CRUCIAL, TIME-ALTERING MOMENT MUST HAVE OCCURRED WITH THE WASP'S UNACCUSTOMED DROWSINESS...?"*
WHAT'S... WRONG WITH ME...?
CAN'T FIGHT OFF... THIS SUDDEN FEELING OF DROWSINESS!
YET, I MUST...I MUST! I...
PTHK!
*AS SEEN IN THE CURRENT AVENGERS #56!--STAN.
"AND SOMEWHERE, IN THE VOID BETWEEN THE EONS, THERE MUST HAVE STOOD OUR SINISTER FOEMAN..."
SLEEP, WOMAN ...AT THE COMMAND OF THE SCARLET CENTURION!
AND WITH THAT SLEEP, CHANGE THE COURSE OF HISTORY!
"FOR, SUDDENLY, WHAT HAD BEEN A MERE EXPEDITION TO OBSERVE BECAME A TIME-OVERTHROWING CATASTROPHE, AS OUR WRAITH-FORMS WERE SUDDENLY THRUST INTO THREE-DIMENSIONAL REALITY..."
ANOTHER CAPTAIN AMERICA--AND THREE OTHER COSTUMED FORMS...
--ONE OF THEM... A GIANT!
THE FOUR OF US... ARE MATERIALIZING!
BUT, THAT'S IMPOSSIBLE, UNLESS...
SOMETHING'S WRONG... DANGEROUSLY WRONG!
26

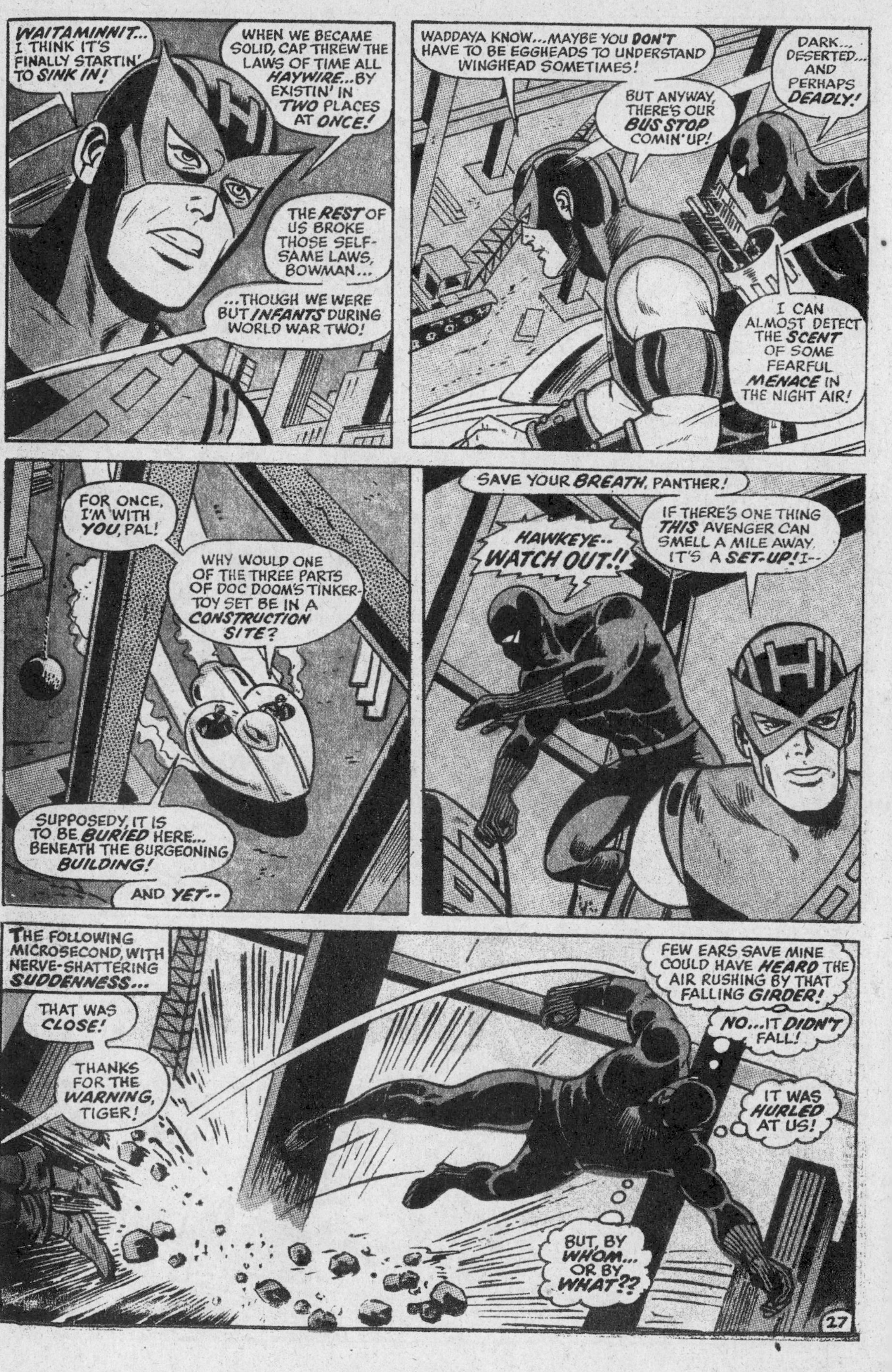

WAITAMINNIT... I THINK IT'S FINALLY STARTIN' TO SINK IN!
WHEN WE BECAME SOLID, CAP THREW THE LAWS OF TIME ALL HAYWIRE...BY EXISTIN' IN TWO PLACES AT ONCE!
THE REST OF US BROKE THOSE SELF-SAME LAWS, BOWMAN...
...THOUGH WE WERE BUT INFANTS DURING WORLD WAR TWO!
WADDAYA KNOW...MAYBE YOU DON'T HAVE TO BE EGGHEADS TO UNDERSTAND WINGHEAD SOMETIMES!
BUT ANYWAY, THERE'S OUR BUS STOP COMIN' UP!
DARK... DESERTED... AND PERHAPS DEADLY!
I CAN ALMOST DETECT THE SCENT OF SOME FEARFUL MENACE IN THE NIGHT AIR!
FOR ONCE, I'M WITH YOU, PAL!
WHY WOULD ONE OF THE THREE PARTS OF DOC DOOM'S TINKER-TOY SET BE IN A CONSTRUCTION SITE?
SUPPOSEDY, IT IS TO BE BURIED HERE... BENEATH THE BURGEONING BUILDING!
AND YET--
SAVE YOUR BREATH, PANTHER!
IF THERE'S ONE THING THIS AVENGER CAN SMELL A MILE AWAY, IT'S A SET-UP! I--
HAWKEYE-- WATCH OUT!!
THE FOLLOWING MICROSECOND, WITH NERVE-SHATTERING SUDDENNESS...
THAT WAS CLOSE!
THANKS FOR THE WARNING, TIGER!
FEW EARS SAVE MINE COULD HAVE HEARD THE AIR RUSHING BY THAT FALLING GIRDER!
NO...IT DIDN'T FALL!
IT WAS HURLED AT US!
BUT, BY WHOM... OR BY WHAT??

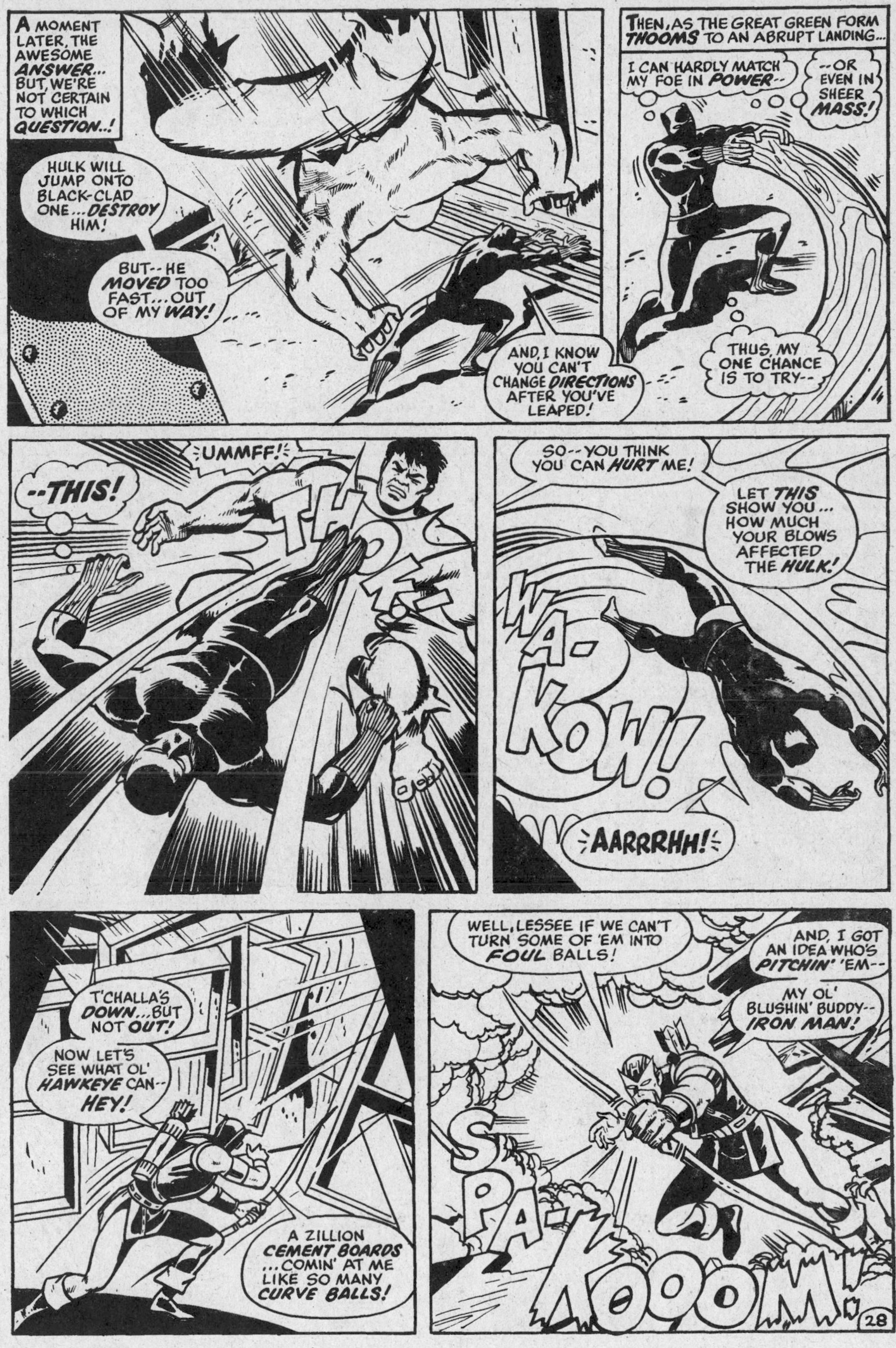
A MOMENT LATER, THE AWESOME ANSWER... BUT, WE'RE NOT CERTAIN TO WHICH QUESTION..!
HULK WILL JUMP ONTO BLACK-CLAD ONE... DESTROY HIM!
BUT--HE MOVED TOO FAST... OUT OF MY WAY!
AND, I KNOW YOU CAN'T CHANGE DIRECTIONS AFTER YOU'VE LEAPED!
THEN, AS THE GREAT GREEN FORM THOOMS TO AN ABRUPT LANDING...
I CAN HARDLY MATCH MY FOE IN POWER--
--OR EVEN IN SHEER MASS!
THUS, MY ONE CHANCE IS TO TRY--
--THIS!
UMMFF!
THOK!
SO--YOU THINK YOU CAN HURT ME!
LET THIS SHOW YOU... HOW MUCH YOUR BLOWS AFFECTED THE HULK!
WA-KOW!
AARRRHH!
T'CHALLA'S DOWN... BUT NOT OUT!
NOW LET'S SEE WHAT OL' HAWKEYE CAN-- HEY!
A ZILLION CEMENT BOARDS ...COMIN' AT ME LIKE SO MANY CURVE BALLS!
WELL, LESSEE IF WE CAN'T TURN SOME OF 'EM INTO FOUL BALLS!
AND, I GOT AN IDEA WHO'S PITCHIN' 'EM--
MY OL' BLUSHIN' BUDDY-- IRON MAN!
SPA-KOOOM!

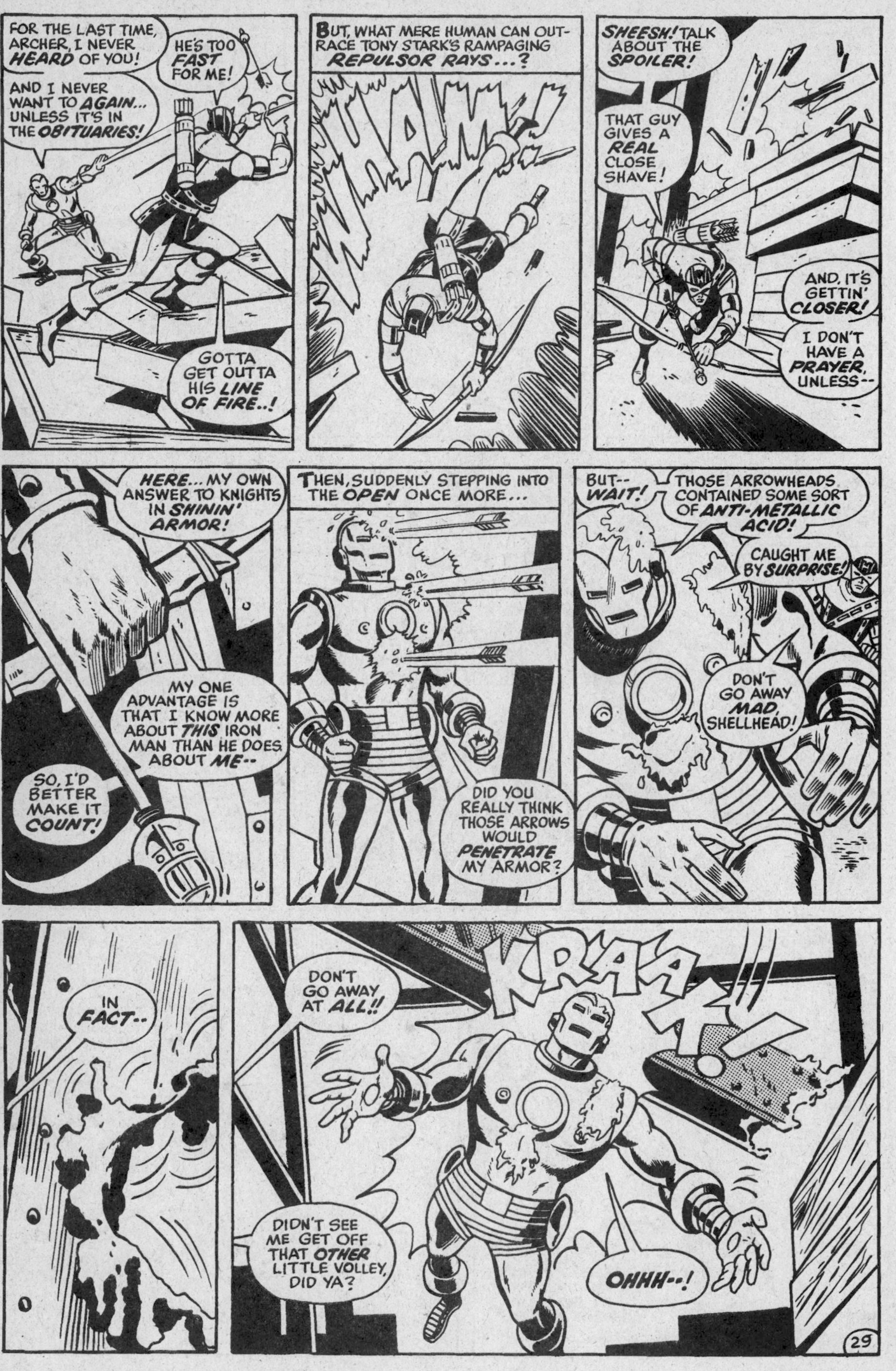
FOR THE LAST TIME, ARCHER, I NEVER HEARD OF YOU!
HE'S TOO FAST FOR ME!
AND I NEVER WANT TO AGAIN... UNLESS IT'S IN THE OBITUARIES!
GOTTA GET OUTTA HIS LINE OF FIRE..!
BUT, WHAT MERE HUMAN CAN OUT-RACE TONY STARK'S RAMPAGING REPULSOR RAYS...?
WHAM!
SHEESH! TALK ABOUT THE SPOILER!
THAT GUY GIVES A REAL CLOSE SHAVE!
AND, IT'S GETTIN' CLOSER!
I DON'T HAVE A PRAYER, UNLESS--
HERE... MY OWN ANSWER TO KNIGHTS IN SHININ' ARMOR!
MY ONE ADVANTAGE IS THAT I KNOW MORE ABOUT THIS IRON MAN THAN HE DOES ABOUT ME--
SO, I'D BETTER MAKE IT COUNT!
THEN, SUDDENLY STEPPING INTO THE OPEN ONCE MORE...
DID YOU REALLY THINK THOSE ARROWS WOULD PENETRATE MY ARMOR?
BUT-- WAIT!
THOSE ARROWHEADS CONTAINED SOME SORT OF ANTI-METALLIC ACID!
CAUGHT ME BY SURPRISE!
DON'T GO AWAY MAD, SHELLHEAD!
IN FACT--
DON'T GO AWAY AT ALL!!
KRAAAK!
DIDN'T SEE ME GET OFF THAT OTHER LITTLE VOLLEY, DID YA?
OHHH--!
29

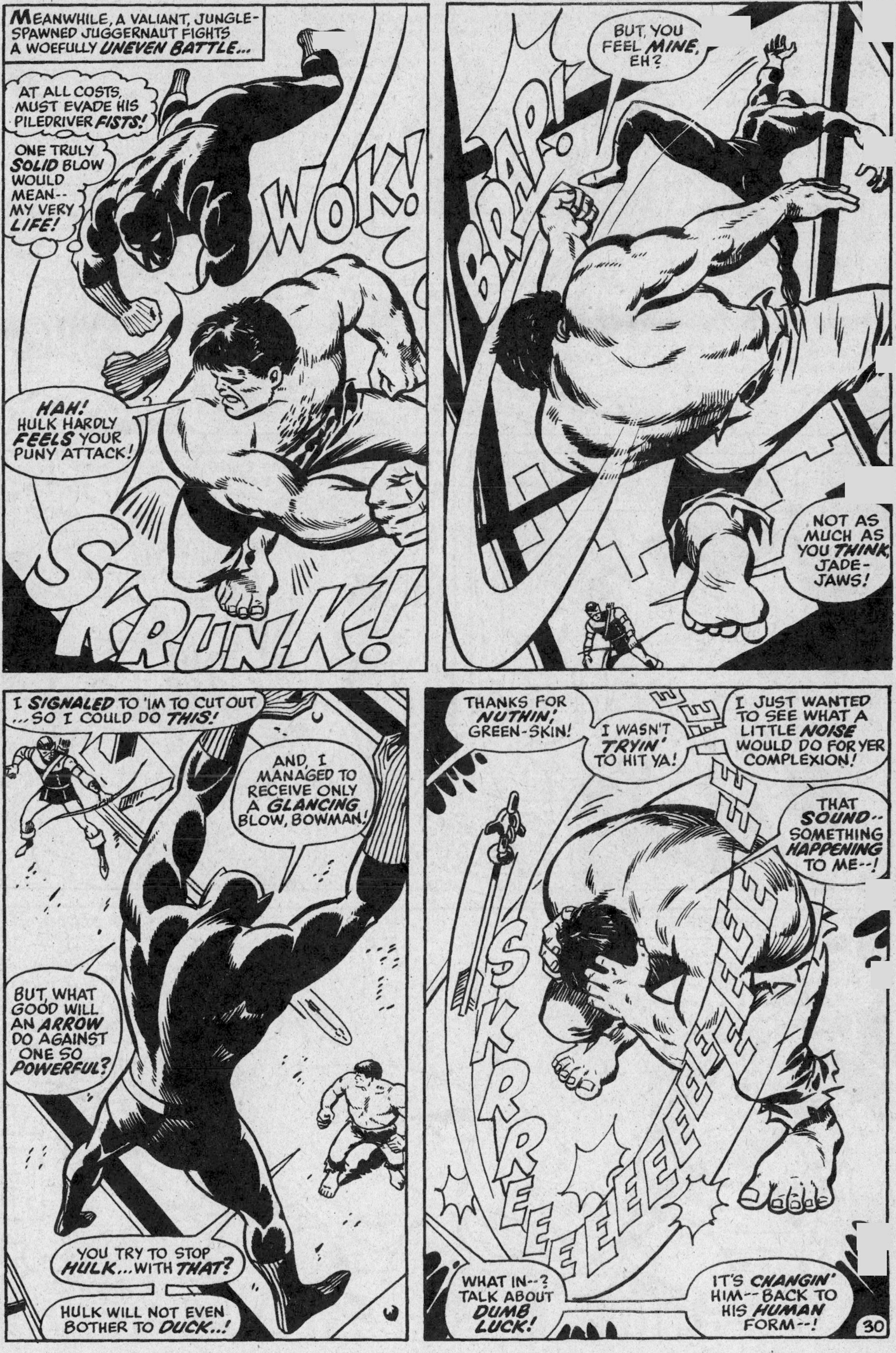
MEANWHILE, A VALIANT, JUNGLE-SPAWNED JUGGERNAUT FIGHTS A WOEFULLY UNEVEN BATTLE...
AT ALL COSTS, MUST EVADE HIS PILEDRIVER FISTS!
ONE TRULY SOLID BLOW WOULD MEAN-- MY VERY LIFE!
WOK!
HAH! HULK HARDLY FEELS YOUR PUNY ATTACK!
SKRUNK!
BUT, YOU FEEL MINE, EH?
BRAP!
NOT AS MUCH AS YOU THINK, JADE-JAWS!
I SIGNALED TO 'IM TO CUT OUT ...SO I COULD DO THIS!
AND, I MANAGED TO RECEIVE ONLY A GLANCING BLOW, BOWMAN!
BUT, WHAT GOOD WILL AN ARROW DO AGAINST ONE SO POWERFUL?
YOU TRY TO STOP HULK...WITH THAT?
HULK WILL NOT EVEN BOTHER TO DUCK..!
THANKS FOR NUTHIN', GREEN-SKIN!
I WASN'T TRYIN' TO HIT YA!
I JUST WANTED TO SEE WHAT A LITTLE NOISE WOULD DO FOR YER COMPLEXION!
THAT SOUND-- SOMETHING HAPPENING TO ME--!
SKRREEEEEEEEEEEEEE
WHAT IN--? TALK ABOUT DUMB LUCK!
IT'S CHANGIN' HIM--BACK TO HIS HUMAN FORM--!

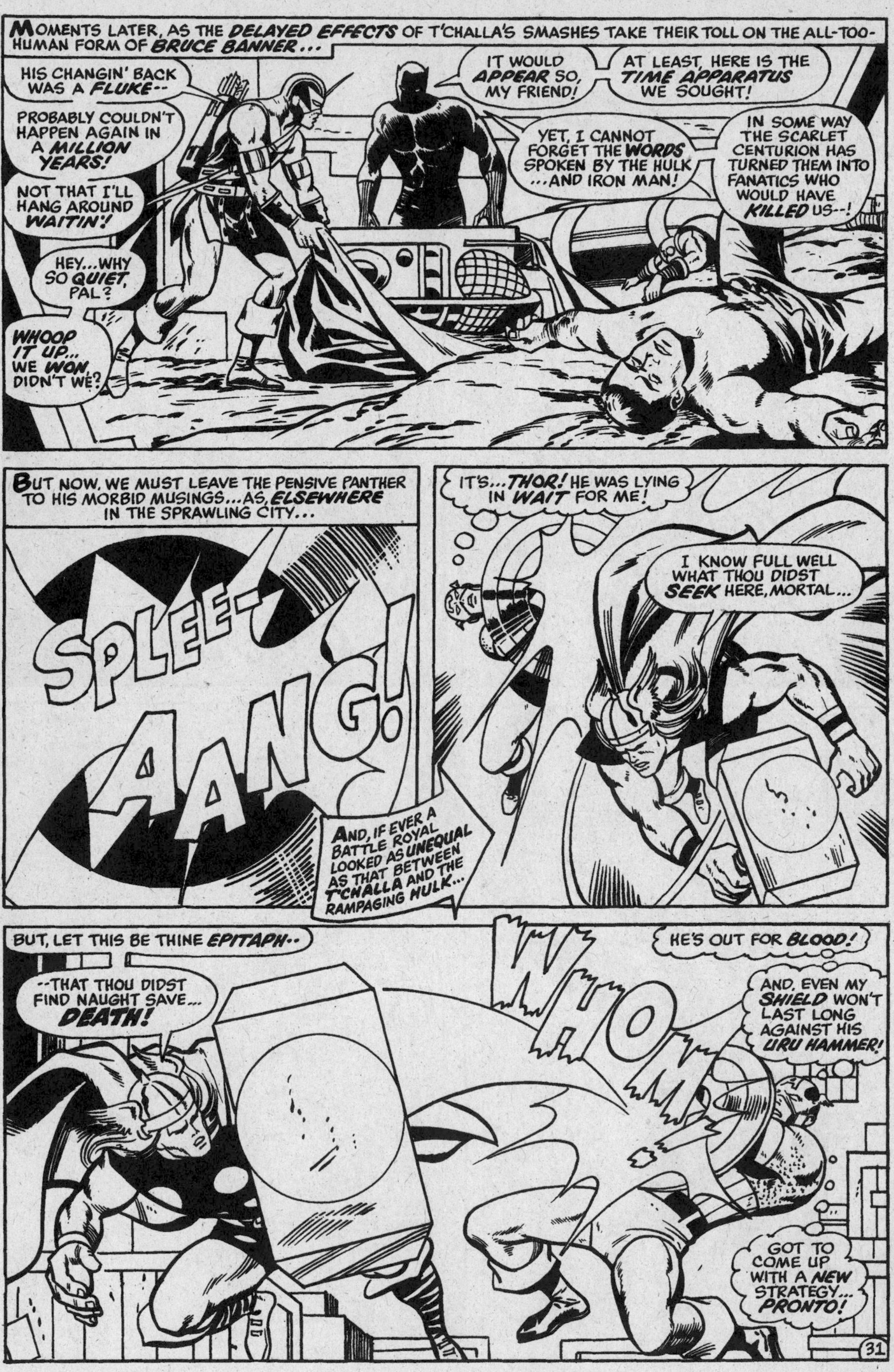
MOMENTS LATER, AS THE DELAYED EFFECTS OF T'CHALLA'S SMASHES TAKE THEIR TOLL ON THE ALL-TOO-HUMAN FORM OF BRUCE BANNER...
HIS CHANGIN' BACK WAS A FLUKE--
PROBABLY COULDN'T HAPPEN AGAIN IN A MILLION YEARS!
NOT THAT I'LL HANG AROUND WAITIN'!
HEY...WHY SO QUIET, PAL?
WHOOP IT UP... WE WON, DIDN'T WE?
IT WOULD APPEAR SO, MY FRIEND!
AT LEAST, HERE IS THE TIME APPARATUS WE SOUGHT!
YET, I CANNOT FORGET THE WORDS SPOKEN BY THE HULK ...AND IRON MAN!
IN SOME WAY THE SCARLET CENTURION HAS TURNED THEM INTO FANATICS WHO WOULD HAVE KILLED US--!
BUT NOW, WE MUST LEAVE THE PENSIVE PANTHER TO HIS MORBID MUSINGS...AS, ELSEWHERE IN THE SPRAWLING CITY...
SPLEE-AANG!
AND, IF EVER A BATTLE ROYAL LOOKED AS UNEQUAL AS THAT BETWEEN T'CHALLA AND THE RAMPAGING HULK...
IT'S...THOR! HE WAS LYING IN WAIT FOR ME!
I KNOW FULL WELL WHAT THOU DIDST SEEK HERE, MORTAL...
BUT, LET THIS BE THINE EPITAPH--
--THAT THOU DIDST FIND NAUGHT SAVE... DEATH!
WHOOM
HE'S OUT FOR BLOOD!
AND, EVEN MY SHIELD WON'T LAST LONG AGAINST HIS URU HAMMER!
GOT TO COME UP WITH A NEW STRATEGY... PRONTO!
31

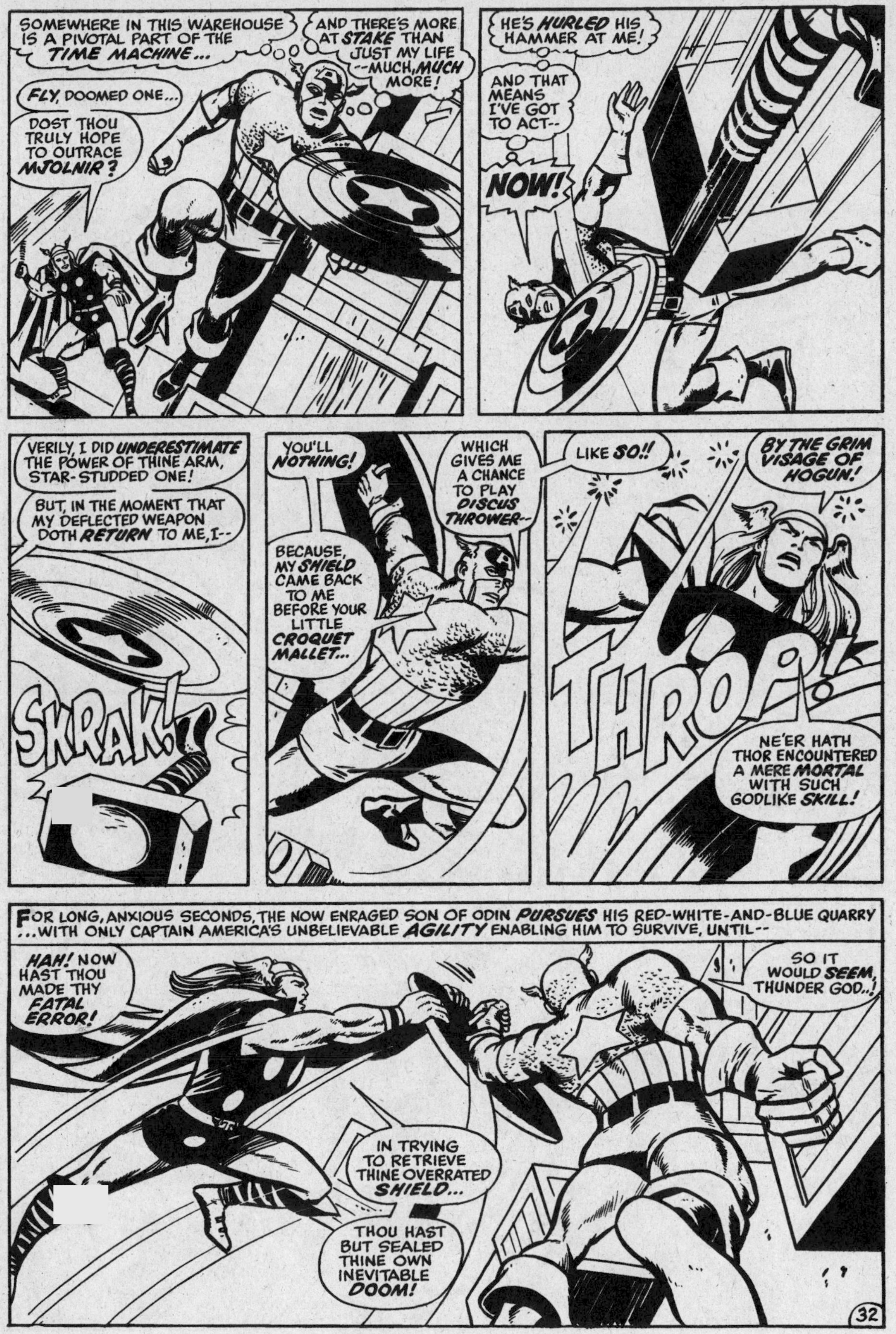
SOMEWHERE IN THIS WAREHOUSE IS A PIVOTAL PART OF THE TIME MACHINE...
AND THERE'S MORE AT STAKE THAN JUST MY LIFE --MUCH, MUCH MORE!
FLY, DOOMED ONE...
DOST THOU TRULY HOPE TO OUTRACE MJOLNIR?
HE'S HURLED HIS HAMMER AT ME!
AND THAT MEANS I'VE GOT TO ACT--
NOW!
VERILY, I DID UNDERESTIMATE THE POWER OF THINE ARM, STAR-STUDDED ONE!
BUT, IN THE MOMENT THAT MY DEFLECTED WEAPON DOTH RETURN TO ME, I--
SKRAK!
YOU'LL NOTHING!
BECAUSE, MY SHIELD CAME BACK TO ME BEFORE YOUR LITTLE CROQUET MALLET...
WHICH GIVES ME A CHANCE TO PLAY DISCUS THROWER--
LIKE SO!!
BY THE GRIM VISAGE OF HOGUN!
THROP!
NE'ER HATH THOR ENCOUNTERED A MERE MORTAL WITH SUCH GODLIKE SKILL!
FOR LONG, ANXIOUS SECONDS, THE NOW ENRAGED SON OF ODIN PURSUES HIS RED-WHITE-AND-BLUE QUARRY ...WITH ONLY CAPTAIN AMERICA'S UNBELIEVABLE AGILITY ENABLING HIM TO SURVIVE, UNTIL--
HAH! NOW HAST THOU MADE THY FATAL ERROR!
SO IT WOULD SEEM, THUNDER GOD...!
IN TRYING TO RETRIEVE THINE OVERRATED SHIELD...
THOU HAST BUT SEALED THINE OWN INEVITABLE DOOM!
32

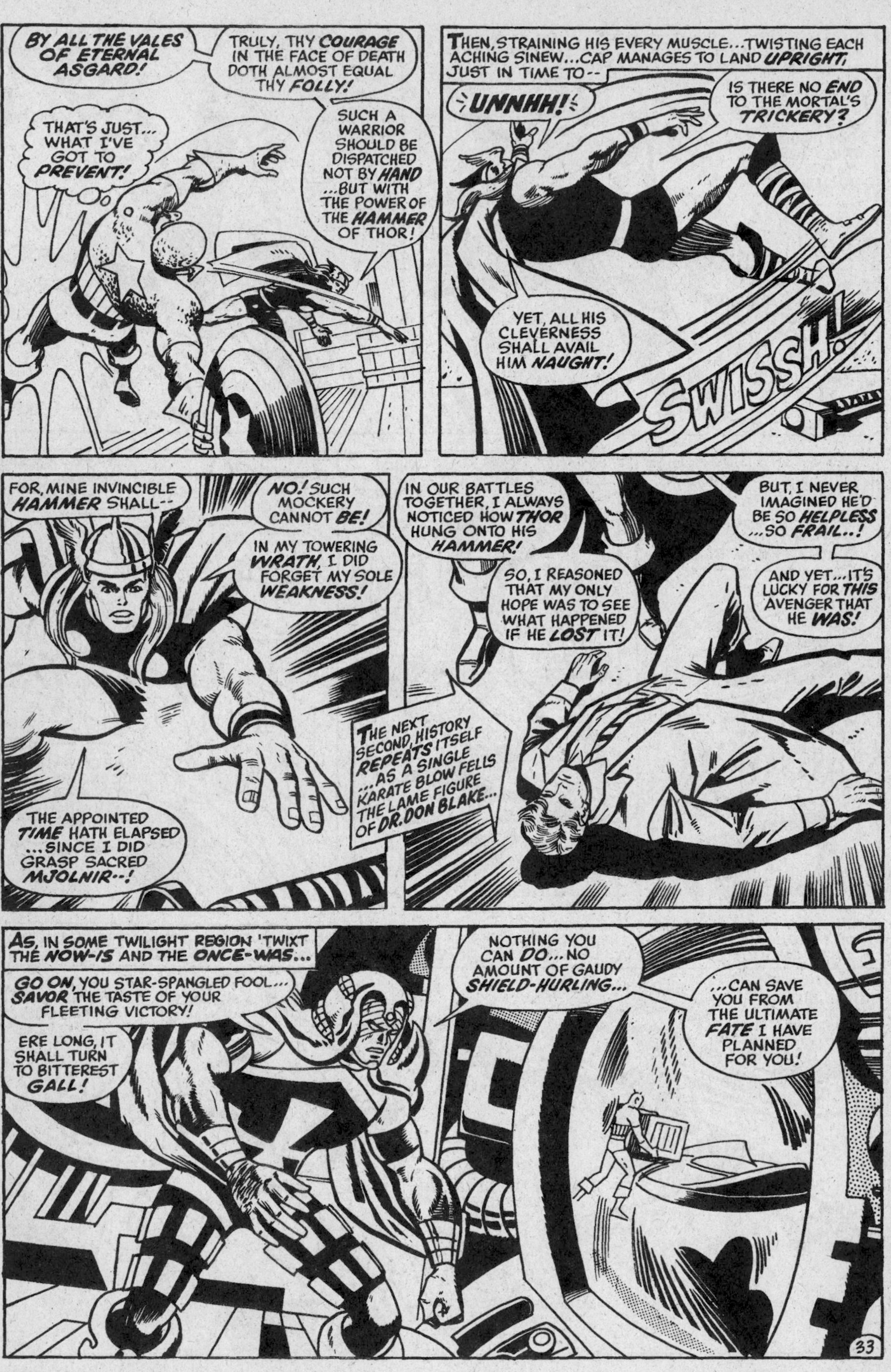
BY ALL THE VALES OF ETERNAL ASGARD!
TRULY, THY COURAGE IN THE FACE OF DEATH DOTH ALMOST EQUAL THY FOLLY!
THAT'S JUST... WHAT I'VE GOT TO PREVENT!
SUCH A WARRIOR SHOULD BE DISPATCHED NOT BY HAND ...BUT WITH THE POWER OF THE HAMMER OF THOR!
THEN, STRAINING HIS EVERY MUSCLE...TWISTING EACH ACHING SINEW...CAP MANAGES TO LAND UPRIGHT, JUST IN TIME TO--
UNNHH!
IS THERE NO END TO THE MORTAL'S TRICKERY?
YET, ALL HIS CLEVERNESS SHALL AVAIL HIM NAUGHT!
SWISSH!
FOR, MINE INVINCIBLE HAMMER SHALL--
NO! SUCH MOCKERY CANNOT BE!
IN MY TOWERING WRATH, I DID FORGET MY SOLE WEAKNESS!
THE APPOINTED TIME HATH ELAPSED ...SINCE I DID GRASP SACRED MJOLNIR--!
IN OUR BATTLES TOGETHER, I ALWAYS NOTICED HOW THOR HUNG ONTO HIS HAMMER!
BUT, I NEVER IMAGINED HE'D BE SO HELPLESS ...SO FRAIL..!
SO, I REASONED THAT MY ONLY HOPE WAS TO SEE WHAT HAPPENED IF HE LOST IT!
AND YET...IT'S LUCKY FOR THIS AVENGER THAT HE WAS!
THE NEXT SECOND, HISTORY REPEATS ITSELF ...AS A SINGLE KARATE BLOW FELLS THE LAME FIGURE OF DR. DON BLAKE...
AS, IN SOME TWILIGHT REGION 'TWIXT THE NOW-IS AND THE ONCE-WAS...
GO ON, YOU STAR-SPANGLED FOOL... SAVOR THE TASTE OF YOUR FLEETING VICTORY!
ERE LONG, IT SHALL TURN TO BITTEREST GALL!
NOTHING YOU CAN DO...NO AMOUNT OF GAUDY SHIELD-HURLING...
...CAN SAVE YOU FROM THE ULTIMATE FATE I HAVE PLANNED FOR YOU!
33

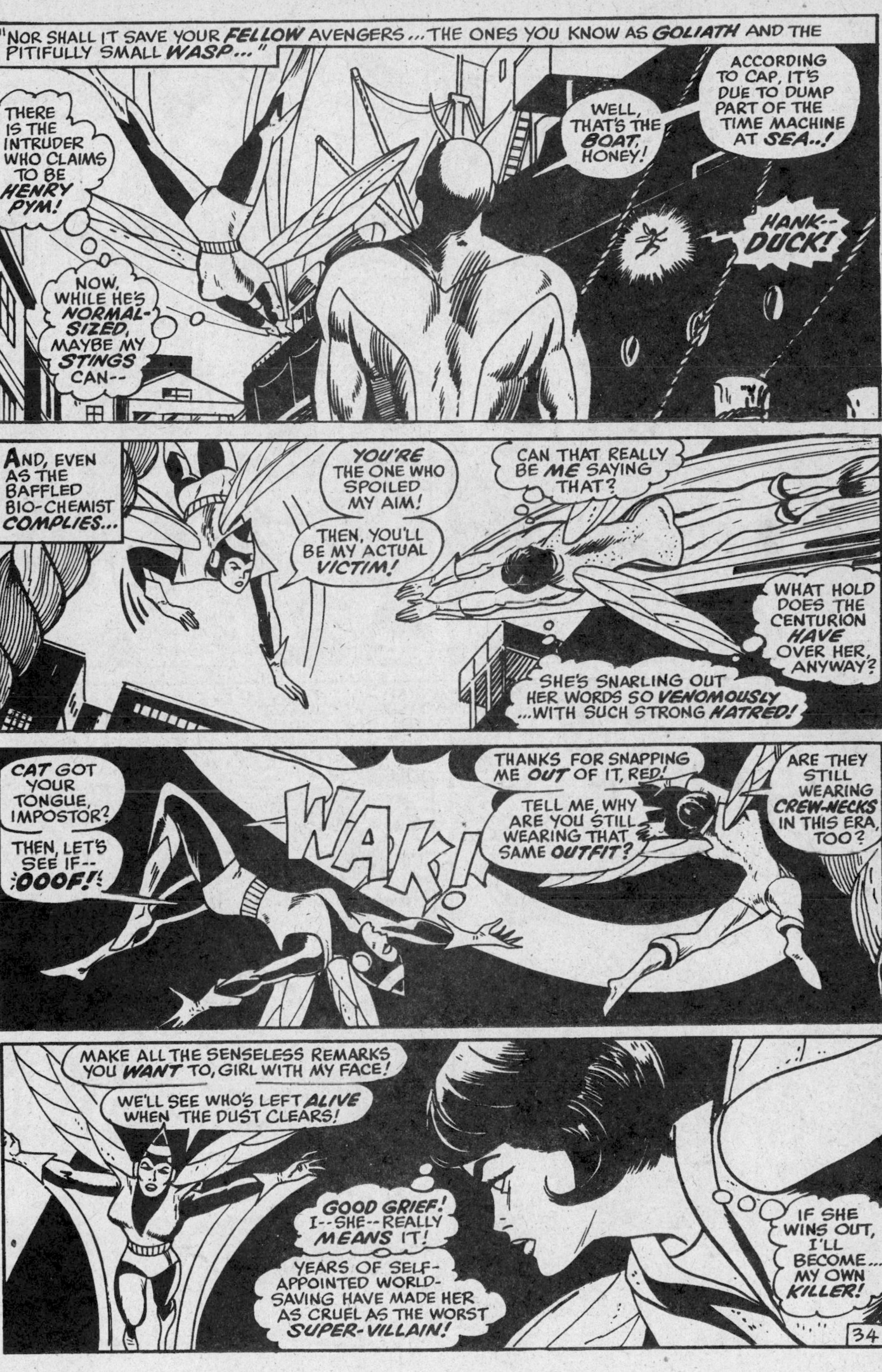

"NOR SHALL IT SAVE YOUR FELLOW AVENGERS... THE ONES YOU KNOW AS GOLIATH AND THE PITIFULLY SMALL WASP..."
THERE IS THE INTRUDER WHO CLAIMS TO BE HENRY PYM!
NOW, WHILE HE'S NORMAL-SIZED, MAYBE MY STINGS CAN--
WELL, THAT'S THE BOAT, HONEY!
ACCORDING TO CAP, IT'S DUE TO DUMP PART OF THE TIME MACHINE AT SEA..!
HANK--DUCK!
AND, EVEN AS THE BAFFLED BIO-CHEMIST COMPLIES...
YOU'RE THE ONE WHO SPOILED MY AIM!
THEN, YOU'LL BE MY ACTUAL VICTIM!
CAN THAT REALLY BE ME SAYING THAT?
WHAT HOLD DOES THE CENTURION HAVE OVER HER, ANYWAY?
SHE'S SNARLING OUT HER WORDS SO VENOMOUSLY ...WITH SUCH STRONG HATRED!
CAT GOT YOUR TONGUE, IMPOSTOR?
THEN, LET'S SEE IF--
OOOF!
WAK!
THANKS FOR SNAPPING ME OUT OF IT, RED!
TELL ME, WHY ARE YOU STILL WEARING THAT SAME OUTFIT?
ARE THEY STILL WEARING CREW-NECKS IN THIS ERA, TOO?
MAKE ALL THE SENSELESS REMARKS YOU WANT TO, GIRL WITH MY FACE!
WE'LL SEE WHO'S LEFT ALIVE WHEN THE DUST CLEARS!
GOOD GRIEF! I--SHE--REALLY MEANS IT!
YEARS OF SELF-APPOINTED WORLD-SAVING HAVE MADE HER AS CRUEL AS THE WORST SUPER-VILLAIN!
IF SHE WINS OUT, I'LL BECOME... MY OWN KILLER!

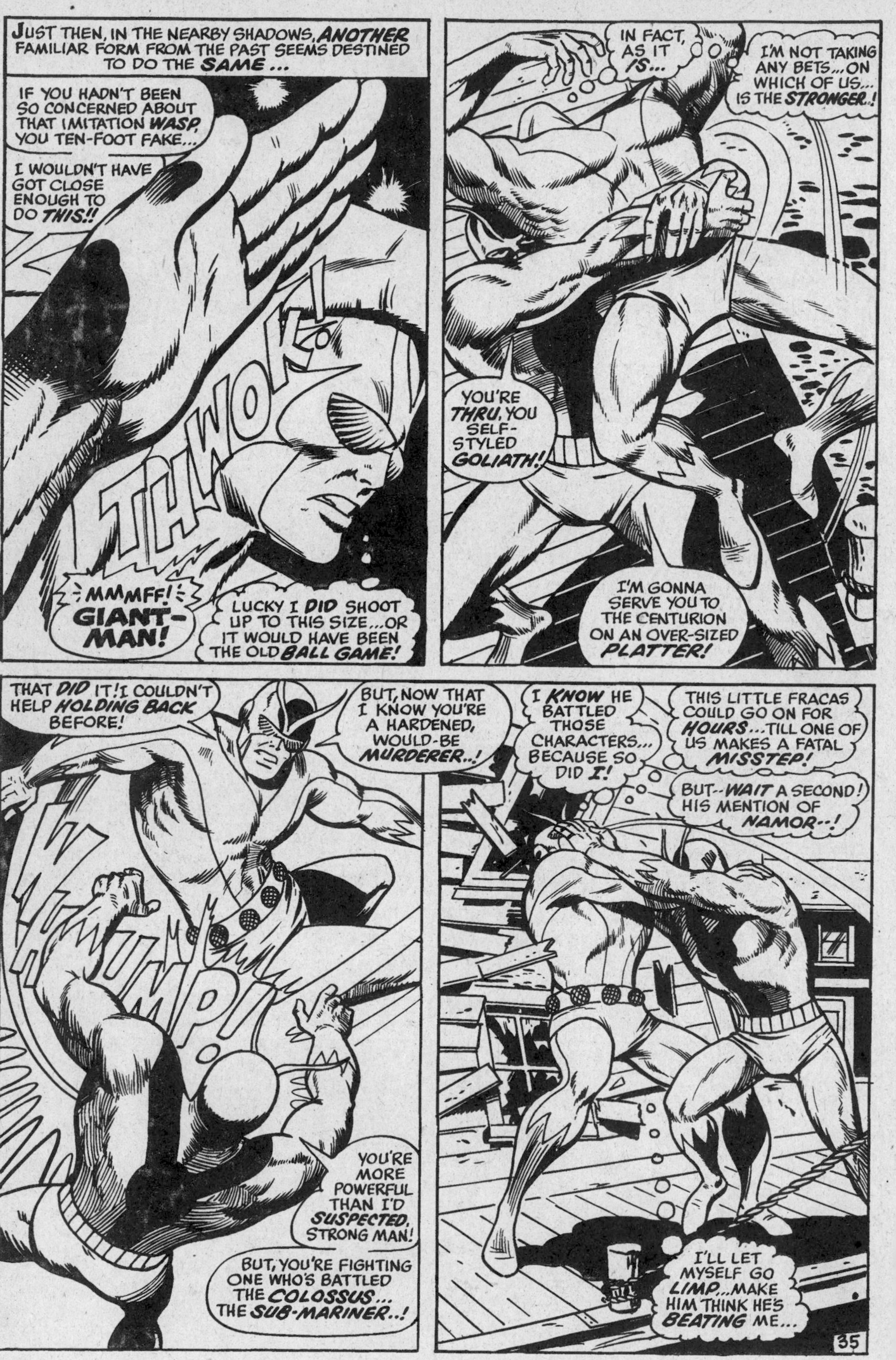
JUST THEN, IN THE NEARBY SHADOWS, ANOTHER FAMILIAR FORM FROM THE PAST SEEMS DESTINED TO DO THE SAME...
IF YOU HADN'T BEEN SO CONCERNED ABOUT THAT IMITATION WASP, YOU TEN-FOOT FAKE...
I WOULDN'T HAVE GOT CLOSE ENOUGH TO DO THIS!!
THWOK!
MMMFF! GIANT-MAN!
LUCKY I DID SHOOT UP TO THIS SIZE...OR IT WOULD HAVE BEEN THE OLD BALL GAME!
IN FACT, AS IT IS...
I'M NOT TAKING ANY BETS...ON WHICH OF US... IS THE STRONGER..!
YOU'RE THRU, YOU SELF-STYLED GOLIATH!
I'M GONNA SERVE YOU TO THE CENTURION ON AN OVER-SIZED PLATTER!
THAT DID IT! I COULDN'T HELP HOLDING BACK BEFORE!
BUT, NOW THAT I KNOW YOU'RE A HARDENED, WOULD-BE MURDERER..!
WHUMP!
YOU'RE MORE POWERFUL THAN I'D SUSPECTED, STRONG MAN!
BUT, YOU'RE FIGHTING ONE WHO'S BATTLED THE COLOSSUS... THE SUB-MARINER..!
I KNOW HE BATTLED THOSE CHARACTERS... BECAUSE SO DID I!
THIS LITTLE FRACAS COULD GO ON FOR HOURS...TILL ONE OF US MAKES A FATAL MISSTEP!
BUT--WAIT A SECOND! HIS MENTION OF NAMOR--!
I'LL LET MYSELF GO LIMP...MAKE HIM THINK HE'S BEATING ME...
35

--THEN MAKE US *TOPPLE OFF* THE PIER... INTO THE *HARBOR!*

THIS PLAN BETTER *WORK*...OR I JUST *DUG* MYSELF A *DEEP SIX!*

:UNNHH!: HE'S ALREADY... SLIPPING OUT OF MY *GRASP!*

AND THUS IT IS THAT, PRECISELY THREE FRANTIC SECONDS LATER, AN EERIE, UNNERVING *SIGHT* GREETS TWO LATE-NIGHT BAY FISHERMEN...

MY OTHER SELF BRACED HIS KING-SIZE *FEET* AGAINST THE BOTTOM...PROPELLED US TO THE *TOP!*

GOT TO GET HIM *DOWN* AGAIN...!

WHAT IN *SAM HILL?*

IT'S LIKE SOMETHIN' OUT OF ONE OF THEM *HORROR PICTURES*...!

BUT, NO SOONER DO THE AWESOME APPARITIONS BURST INTO THE OPEN AIR...THAN THEY *SINK* FROM VIEW ONCE MORE...

MANAGED TO GET...*BEHIND,* GIANT-MAN!

THE NEXT FEW *SECONDS* OUGHT TO TELL THE TALE...!

THE TWO *HANKS*...BOTH DISAPPEARED UNDER THE *WATER!*

GOT TO GO *AFTER* THEM...HELP THE MAN I LOVE...*SOMEHOW!*

IT'S A GOOD THING I *KNOW* MYSELF ...HOW I GET *CARELESS* WHEN I GET *MAD!*

OTHERWISE, I'D NEVER HAVE *OUT-MANEUVERED* THIS WASP!

SZASP!

OHHH!

HANK...YOU *WON!* I WAS SO *WORRIED*--

BUT, YOUR *OTHER SELF* ....IS HE--?

JUST... OUT *COLD,* JAN!

DON'T MAKE THINGS ANY MORE *COMPLICATED*... THAN THEY ALREADY *ARE!*

NOW, LET'S GET... WHAT WE *CAME* FOR...

--AND *SCAT!*

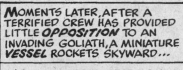

MOMENTS LATER, AFTER A TERRIFIED CREW HAS PROVIDED LITTLE *OPPOSITION* TO AN INVADING GOLIATH, A MINIATURE *VESSEL* ROCKETS SKYWARD...

IN CASE YOU'RE WONDERING, HONEY, I BEAT MY ALTER EGO BY *SUPERIOR LUNGPOWER*...

SOMETHING I'D BEEN *WORKING ON* IN CASE WE EVER TANGLED AGAIN!

IN *THIS* WORLD, THOUGH, NAMOR'S *NO LONGER* A THREAT...

SO *GIANT-MAN,* TO PUT IT MILDLY, WAS A WEE BIT *SHORT-WINDED!*

36

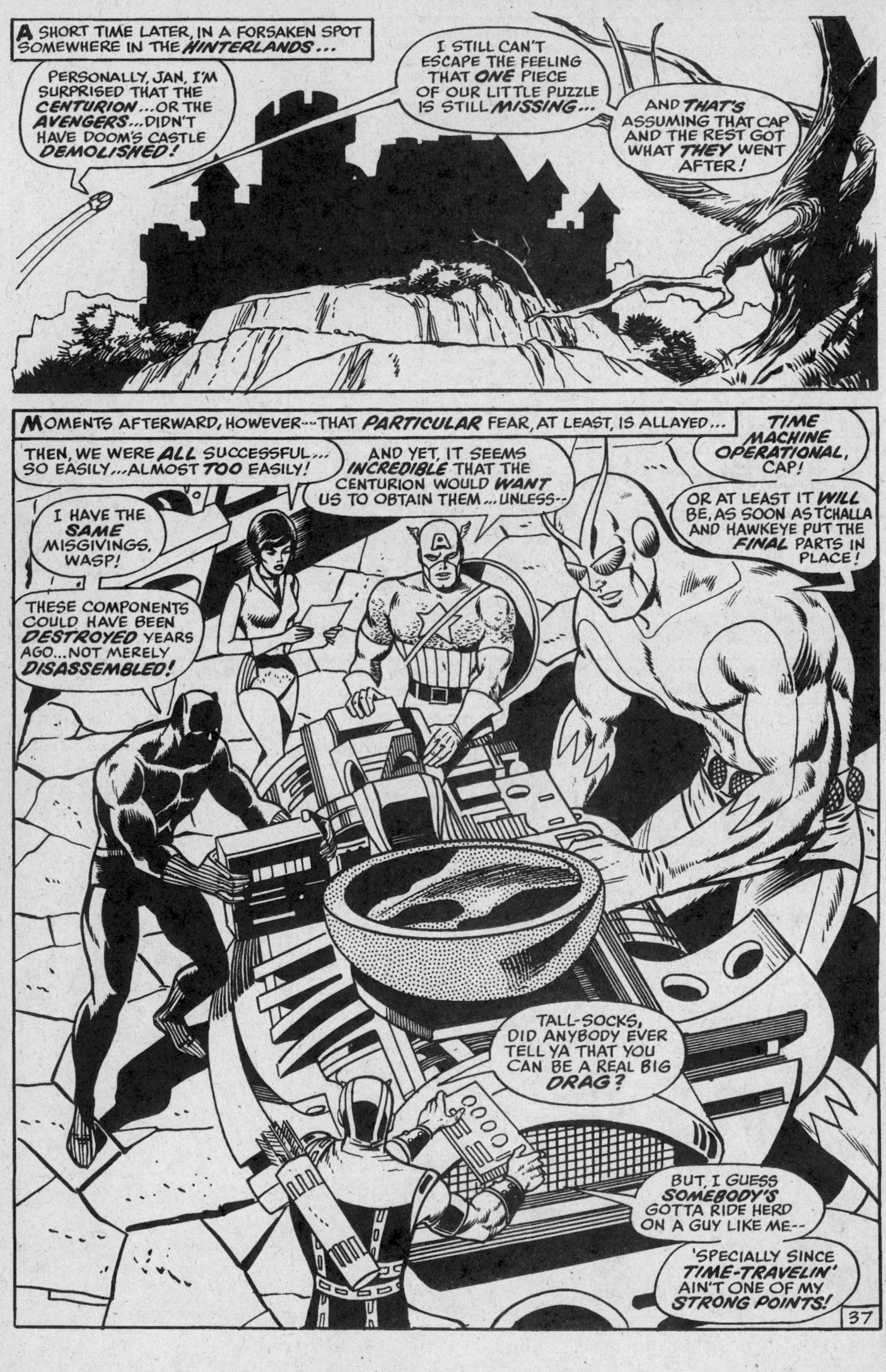
A SHORT TIME LATER, IN A FORSAKEN SPOT SOMEWHERE IN THE HINTERLANDS...
PERSONALLY, JAN, I'M SURPRISED THAT THE CENTURION...OR THE AVENGERS...DIDN'T HAVE DOOM'S CASTLE DEMOLISHED!
I STILL CAN'T ESCAPE THE FEELING THAT ONE PIECE OF OUR LITTLE PUZZLE IS STILL MISSING...
AND THAT'S ASSUMING THAT CAP AND THE REST GOT WHAT THEY WENT AFTER!
MOMENTS AFTERWARD, HOWEVER--THAT PARTICULAR FEAR, AT LEAST, IS ALLAYED...
THEN, WE WERE ALL SUCCESSFUL... SO EASILY...ALMOST TOO EASILY!
AND YET, IT SEEMS INCREDIBLE THAT THE CENTURION WOULD WANT US TO OBTAIN THEM...UNLESS--
...TIME MACHINE OPERATIONAL, CAP!
OR AT LEAST IT WILL BE, AS SOON AS T'CHALLA AND HAWKEYE PUT THE FINAL PARTS IN PLACE!
I HAVE THE SAME MISGIVINGS, WASP!
THESE COMPONENTS COULD HAVE BEEN DESTROYED YEARS AGO...NOT MERELY DISASSEMBLED!
TALL-SOCKS, DID ANYBODY EVER TELL YA THAT YOU CAN BE A REAL BIG DRAG?
BUT, I GUESS SOMEBODY'S GOTTA RIDE HERD ON A GUY LIKE ME--
'SPECIALLY SINCE TIME-TRAVELIN' AIN'T ONE OF MY STRONG POINTS!

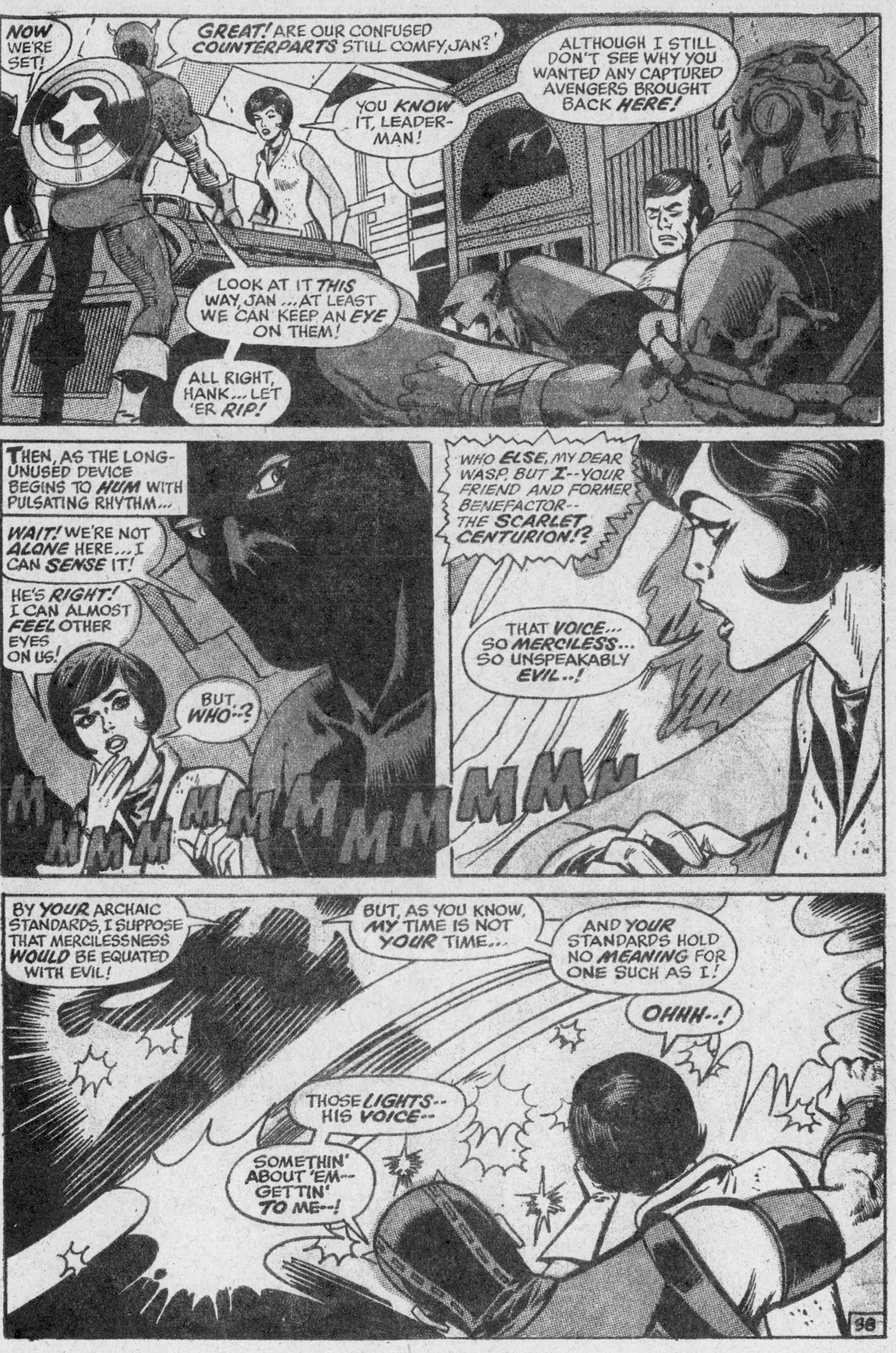

NOW WE'RE SET!
GREAT! ARE OUR CONFUSED COUNTERPARTS STILL COMFY, JAN?
YOU KNOW IT, LEADER-MAN!
ALTHOUGH I STILL DON'T SEE WHY YOU WANTED ANY CAPTURED AVENGERS BROUGHT BACK HERE!
LOOK AT IT THIS WAY, JAN ... AT LEAST WE CAN KEEP AN EYE ON THEM!
ALL RIGHT, HANK... LET 'ER RIP!
THEN, AS THE LONG-UNUSED DEVICE BEGINS TO HUM WITH PULSATING RHYTHM...
WAIT! WE'RE NOT ALONE HERE... I CAN SENSE IT!
HE'S RIGHT! I CAN ALMOST FEEL OTHER EYES ON US!
BUT, WHO--?
MMMMMMMMMMMMMMMMM
WHO ELSE, MY DEAR WASP, BUT I--YOUR FRIEND AND FORMER BENEFACTOR--THE SCARLET CENTURION!?
THAT VOICE... SO MERCILESS... SO UNSPEAKABLY EVIL..!
BY YOUR ARCHAIC STANDARDS, I SUPPOSE THAT MERCILESSNESS WOULD BE EQUATED WITH EVIL!
BUT, AS YOU KNOW, MY TIME IS NOT YOUR TIME...
AND YOUR STANDARDS HOLD NO MEANING FOR ONE SUCH AS I!
OHHH--!
THOSE LIGHTS--HIS VOICE--
SOMETHIN' ABOUT 'EM--GETTIN' TO ME--!
38

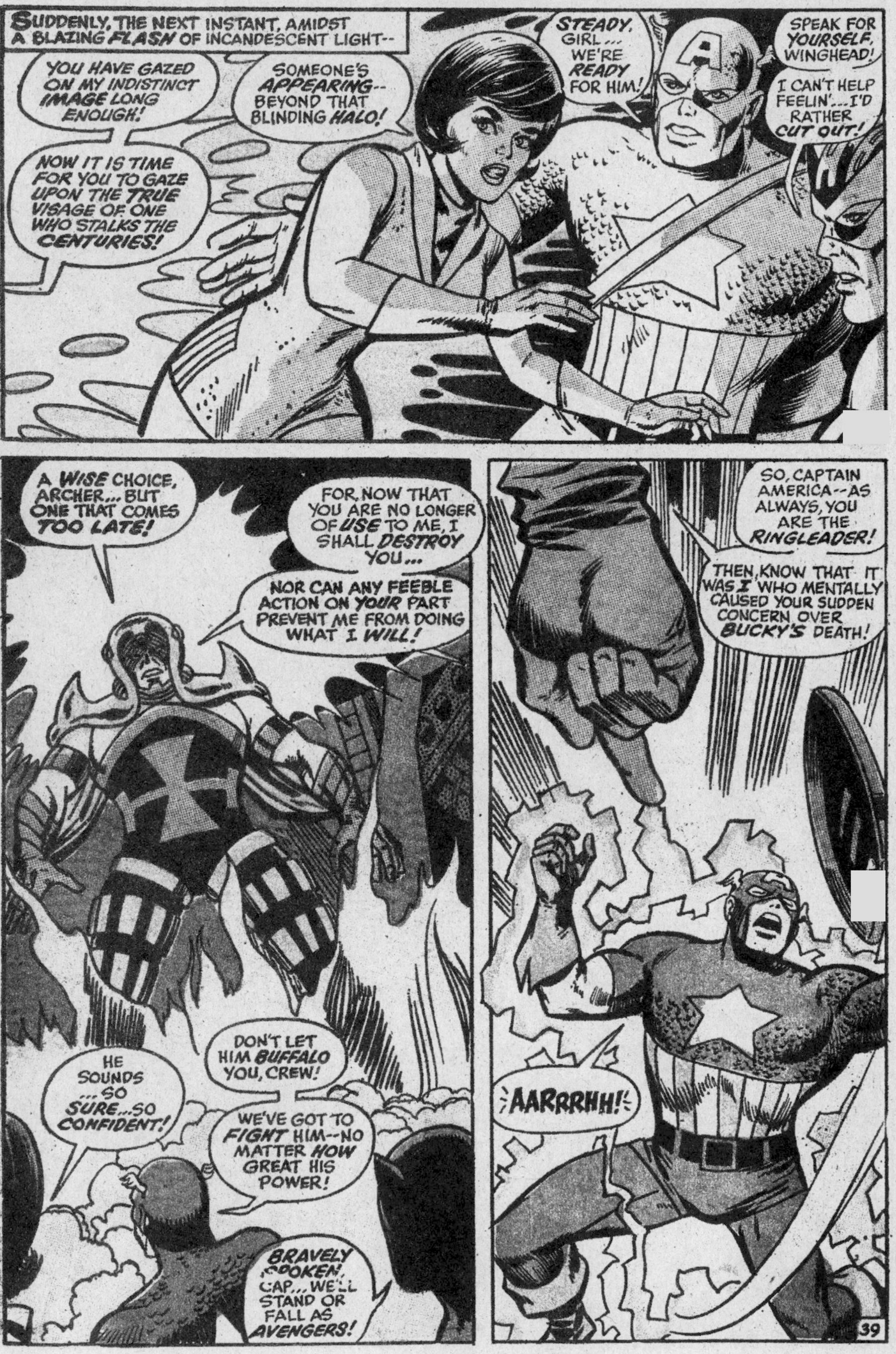
SUDDENLY, THE NEXT INSTANT, AMIDST A BLAZING FLASH OF INCANDESCENT LIGHT--
YOU HAVE GAZED ON MY INDISTINCT IMAGE LONG ENOUGH!
NOW IT IS TIME FOR YOU TO GAZE UPON THE TRUE VISAGE OF ONE WHO STALKS THE CENTURIES!
SOMEONE'S APPEARING-- BEYOND THAT BLINDING HALO!
STEADY, GIRL... WE'RE READY FOR HIM!
SPEAK FOR YOURSELF, WINGHEAD!
I CAN'T HELP FEELIN'...I'D RATHER CUT OUT!
A WISE CHOICE, ARCHER... BUT ONE THAT COMES TOO LATE!
FOR, NOW THAT YOU ARE NO LONGER OF USE TO ME, I SHALL DESTROY YOU...
NOR CAN ANY FEEBLE ACTION ON YOUR PART PREVENT ME FROM DOING WHAT I WILL!
HE SOUNDS ...SO SURE...SO CONFIDENT!
DON'T LET HIM BUFFALO YOU, CREW!
WE'VE GOT TO FIGHT HIM--NO MATTER HOW GREAT HIS POWER!
BRAVELY SPOKEN, CAP... WE'LL STAND OR FALL AS AVENGERS!
SO, CAPTAIN AMERICA--AS ALWAYS, YOU ARE THE RINGLEADER!
THEN, KNOW THAT IT WAS I WHO MENTALLY CAUSED YOUR SUDDEN CONCERN OVER BUCKY'S DEATH!
AARRRHH!

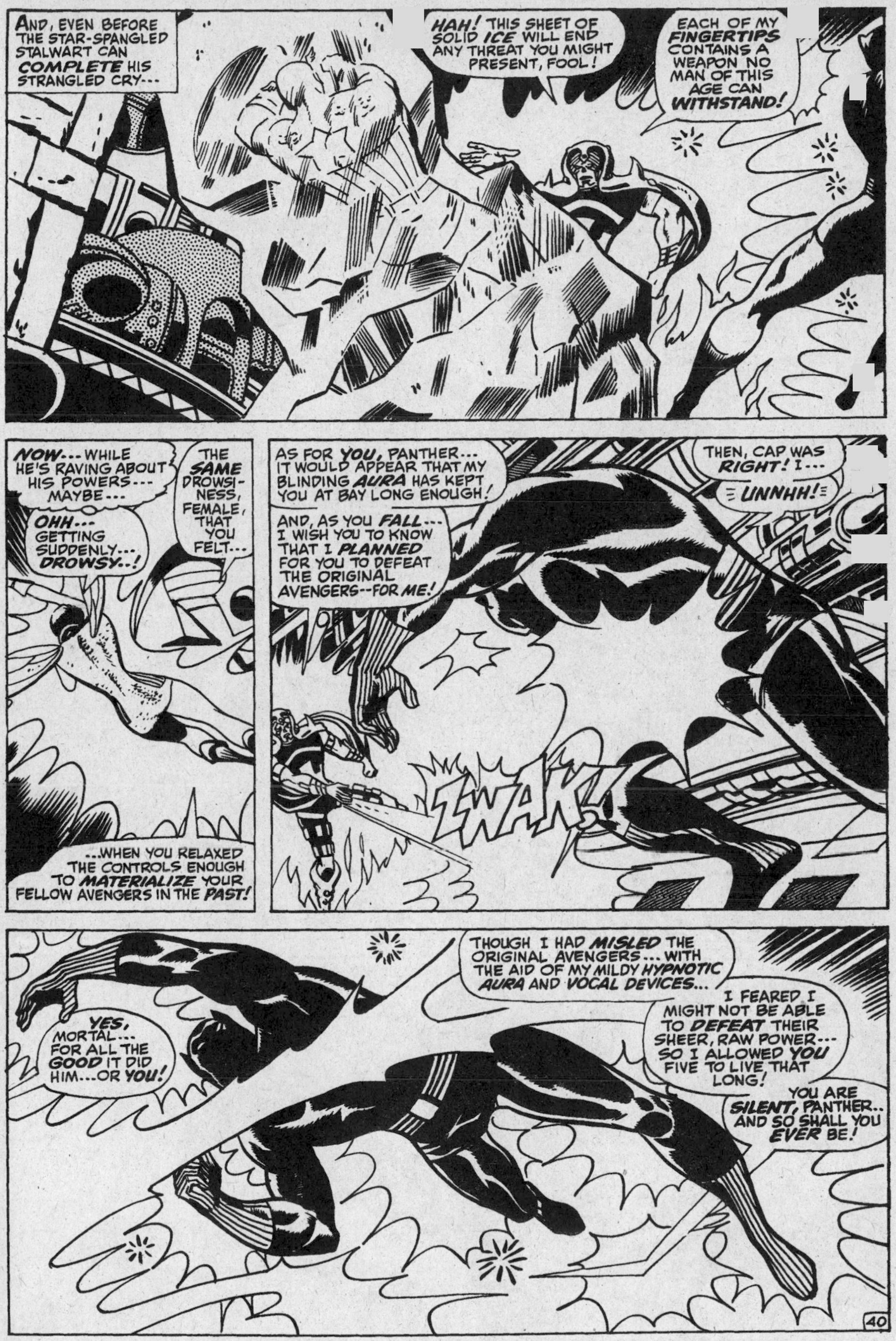
AND, EVEN BEFORE THE STAR-SPANGLED STALWART CAN COMPLETE HIS STRANGLED CRY---
HAH! THIS SHEET OF SOLID ICE WILL END ANY THREAT YOU MIGHT PRESENT, FOOL!
EACH OF MY FINGERTIPS CONTAINS A WEAPON NO MAN OF THIS AGE CAN WITHSTAND!
NOW--- WHILE HE'S RAVING ABOUT HIS POWERS--- MAYBE---
OHH--- GETTING SUDDENLY--- DROWSY--!
THE SAME DROWSINESS, FEMALE, THAT YOU FELT---
...WHEN YOU RELAXED THE CONTROLS ENOUGH TO MATERIALIZE YOUR FELLOW AVENGERS IN THE PAST!
AS FOR YOU, PANTHER--- IT WOULD APPEAR THAT MY BLINDING AURA HAS KEPT YOU AT BAY LONG ENOUGH!
AND, AS YOU FALL--- I WISH YOU TO KNOW THAT I PLANNED FOR YOU TO DEFEAT THE ORIGINAL AVENGERS--FOR ME!
THEN, CAP WAS RIGHT! I---
UNNHH!
ZWAK!
THOUGH I HAD MISLED THE ORIGINAL AVENGERS... WITH THE AID OF MY MILDY HYPNOTIC AURA AND VOCAL DEVICES...
I FEARED I MIGHT NOT BE ABLE TO DEFEAT THEIR SHEER, RAW POWER--- SO I ALLOWED YOU FIVE TO LIVE, THAT LONG!
YOU ARE SILENT, PANTHER.. AND SO SHALL YOU EVER BE!
YES, MORTAL--- FOR ALL THE GOOD IT DID HIM---OR YOU!

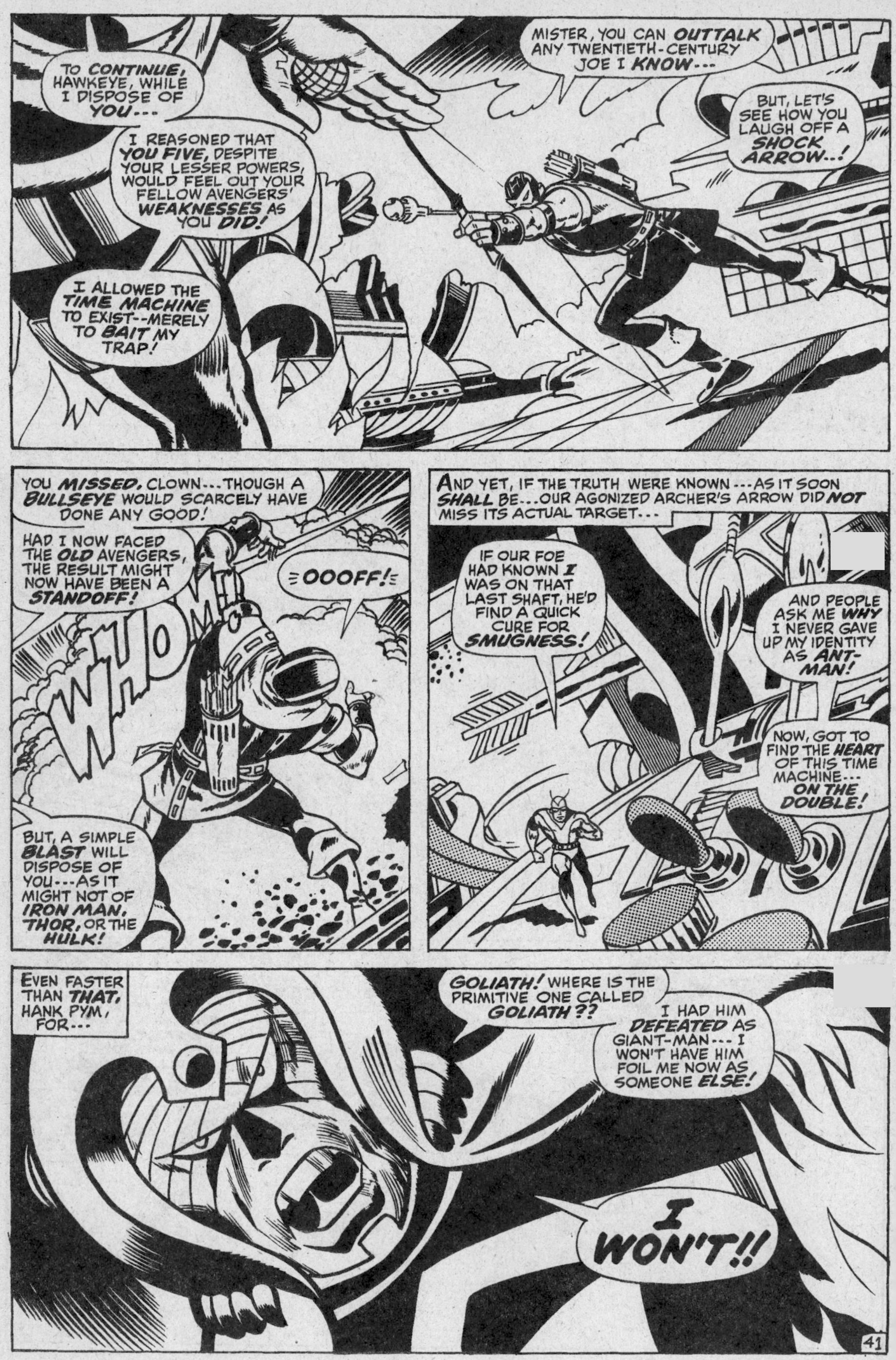
TO CONTINUE, HAWKEYE, WHILE I DISPOSE OF YOU...
I REASONED THAT YOU FIVE, DESPITE YOUR LESSER POWERS, WOULD FEEL OUT YOUR FELLOW AVENGERS' WEAKNESSES AS YOU DID!
I ALLOWED THE TIME MACHINE TO EXIST--MERELY TO BAIT MY TRAP!
MISTER, YOU CAN OUTTALK ANY TWENTIETH-CENTURY JOE I KNOW...
BUT, LET'S SEE HOW YOU LAUGH OFF A SHOCK ARROW..!
YOU MISSED, CLOWN... THOUGH A BULLSEYE WOULD SCARCELY HAVE DONE ANY GOOD!
HAD I NOW FACED THE OLD AVENGERS, THE RESULT MIGHT NOW HAVE BEEN A STANDOFF!
OOOFF!
WHOM
BUT, A SIMPLE BLAST WILL DISPOSE OF YOU...AS IT MIGHT NOT OF IRON MAN, THOR, OR THE HULK!
AND YET, IF THE TRUTH WERE KNOWN... AS IT SOON SHALL BE...OUR AGONIZED ARCHER'S ARROW DID NOT MISS ITS ACTUAL TARGET...
IF OUR FOE HAD KNOWN I WAS ON THAT LAST SHAFT, HE'D FIND A QUICK CURE FOR SMUGNESS!
AND PEOPLE ASK ME WHY I NEVER GAVE UP MY IDENTITY AS ANT-MAN!
NOW, GOT TO FIND THE HEART OF THIS TIME MACHINE... ON THE DOUBLE!
EVEN FASTER THAN THAT, HANK PYM, FOR...
GOLIATH! WHERE IS THE PRIMITIVE ONE CALLED GOLIATH??
I HAD HIM DEFEATED AS GIANT-MAN... I WON'T HAVE HIM FOIL ME NOW AS SOMEONE ELSE!
I WON'T!!
41

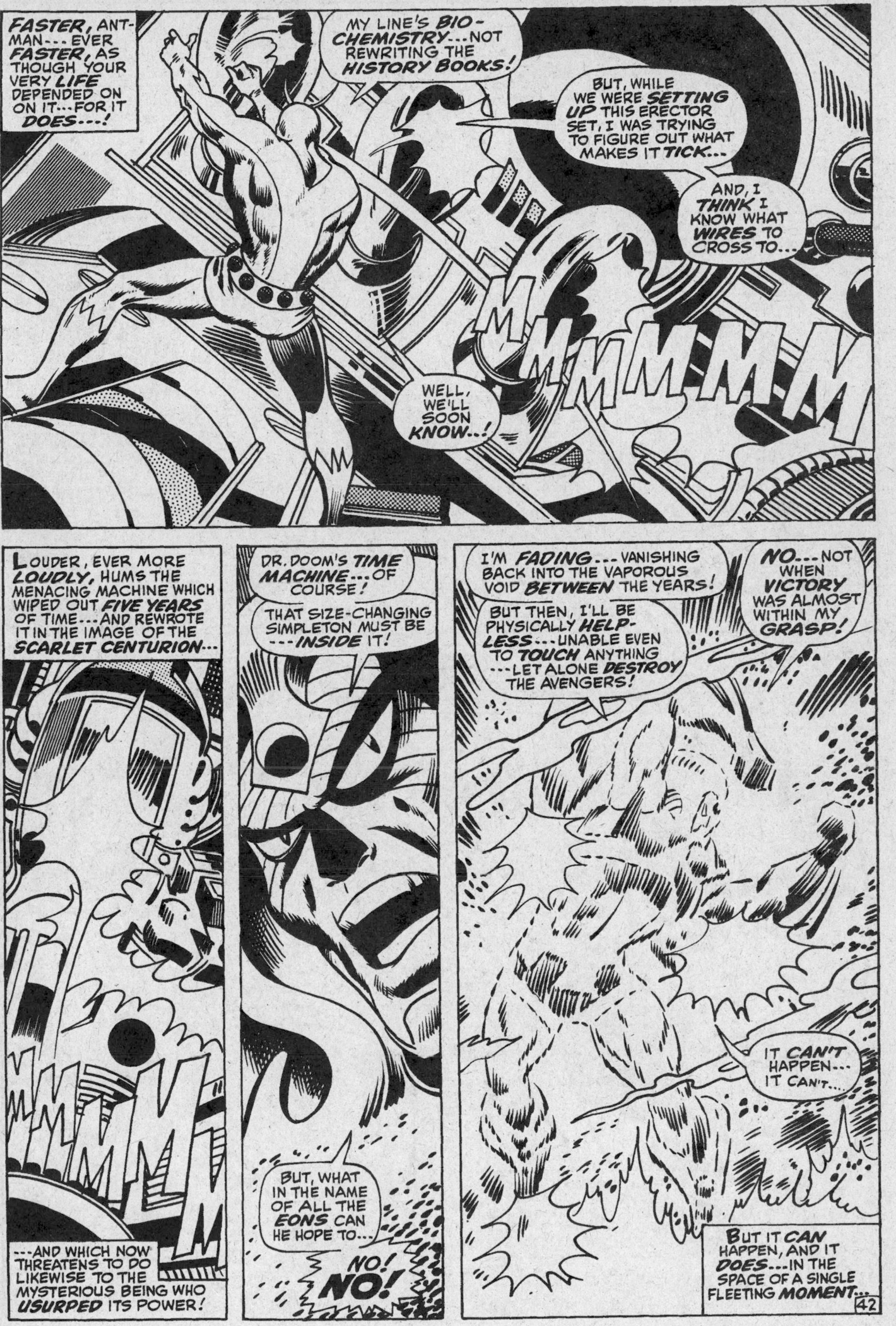

FASTER, ANT-MAN--- EVER FASTER, AS THOUGH YOUR VERY LIFE DEPENDED ON ON IT---FOR IT DOES---!
MY LINE'S BIO-CHEMISTRY---NOT REWRITING THE HISTORY BOOKS!
BUT, WHILE WE WERE SETTING UP THIS ERECTOR SET, I WAS TRYING TO FIGURE OUT WHAT MAKES IT TICK...
AND, I THINK I KNOW WHAT WIRES TO CROSS TO...
MMMMMMMM
WELL, WE'LL SOON KNOW..!
LOUDER, EVER MORE LOUDLY, HUMS THE MENACING MACHINE WHICH WIPED OUT FIVE YEARS OF TIME---AND REWROTE IT IN THE IMAGE OF THE SCARLET CENTURION...
MMMM
---AND WHICH NOW THREATENS TO DO LIKEWISE TO THE MYSTERIOUS BEING WHO USURPED ITS POWER!
DR. DOOM'S TIME MACHINE---OF COURSE!
THAT SIZE-CHANGING SIMPLETON MUST BE ---INSIDE IT!
BUT, WHAT IN THE NAME OF ALL THE EONS CAN HE HOPE TO...
NO! NO!
I'M FADING---VANISHING BACK INTO THE VAPOROUS VOID BETWEEN THE YEARS!
BUT THEN, I'LL BE PHYSICALLY HELP-LESS---UNABLE EVEN TO TOUCH ANYTHING ---LET ALONE DESTROY THE AVENGERS!
NO---NOT WHEN VICTORY WAS ALMOST WITHIN MY GRASP!
IT CAN'T HAPPEN--- IT CAN'T...
BUT IT CAN HAPPEN, AND IT DOES---IN THE SPACE OF A SINGLE FLEETING MOMENT...
42

Panel 1:
AND, IN THAT *SELF-SAME* MOMENT...

I *DID* IT... ...TURNED THE ENTIRE *CHAMBER* INTO ONE HUGE VERSION OF THE *CHRONO-SQUARE* WHICH ONCE SENT THE *F.F.* TO THE DAYS OF *BLACK-BEARD!*

BUT NOW...I'M *FADING AWAY* ---LIKE A *WILL O' THE WISP!*

THEN, MY SCHEME MUST HAVE WORKED... TO *PERFECTION!*

Panel 2:
WHILE, OUTSIDE THE MACHINE, AN IMMOBILIZED *CAPTAIN AMERICA* SEES...

WE'RE *VANISHING*... JUST LIKE THE *CENTURION!*

IF HANK DID WHAT I *SUSPECT*, WHAT A *STORY* WE'LL HAVE FOR OUR *FILES*...!

Panel 3:
THEN, SUDDENLY, CAP'S THOUGHTS ARE *INTRUDED UPON*...BY A VOICE-LESS VOICE WHICH IS *OLDER* THAN THE STARS, YET *YOUNGER* THAN AN UNBORN PLANET...

NO, STEVE ROGERS... THOUGH THE *FINAL* TRIUMPH IS INDEED YOURS, IT MUST NEVER BE *KNOWN!*

ALLOW ME TO *INTRODUCE* MYSELF!

MEN CALL ME...THE *WATCHER!!*

Panel 4:
"*BECAUSE* YOU ARE NOW VICTORIOUS, I CAN TELL YOU WHAT I DARED NOT *BEFORE*...THAT THE FOE YOU SO VALOROUSLY FOUGHT AND BESTED WAS A VENGEFUL ENTITY WHO ONCE WAS KNOWN AS....THE PHARAOH *RAMA-TUT*...!"

"ON HIS WAY FROM THE *PAST* TO THE *FAR-FLUNG FUTURE*...DURING WHICH HE ENCOUNTERED *DR. DOOM* HIMSELF...HIS ERA-SPANNING *SPHERE* ENCOUNTERED ELECTRO-STATIC DISTURBANCES IN THE *RELATIVE* TIME STREAM..."*

"HE LANDED BY *CHANCE* IN *THIS* CENTURY...WHICH HE DECIDED TO MAKE HIS OWN, UNDER THE NAME OF ...THE *SCARLET CENTURION*..."

*AS RECOUNTED IN THE IMMORTAL PAGES OF *AVENGERS #8!* --SURPRISE-ENDING STAN

43

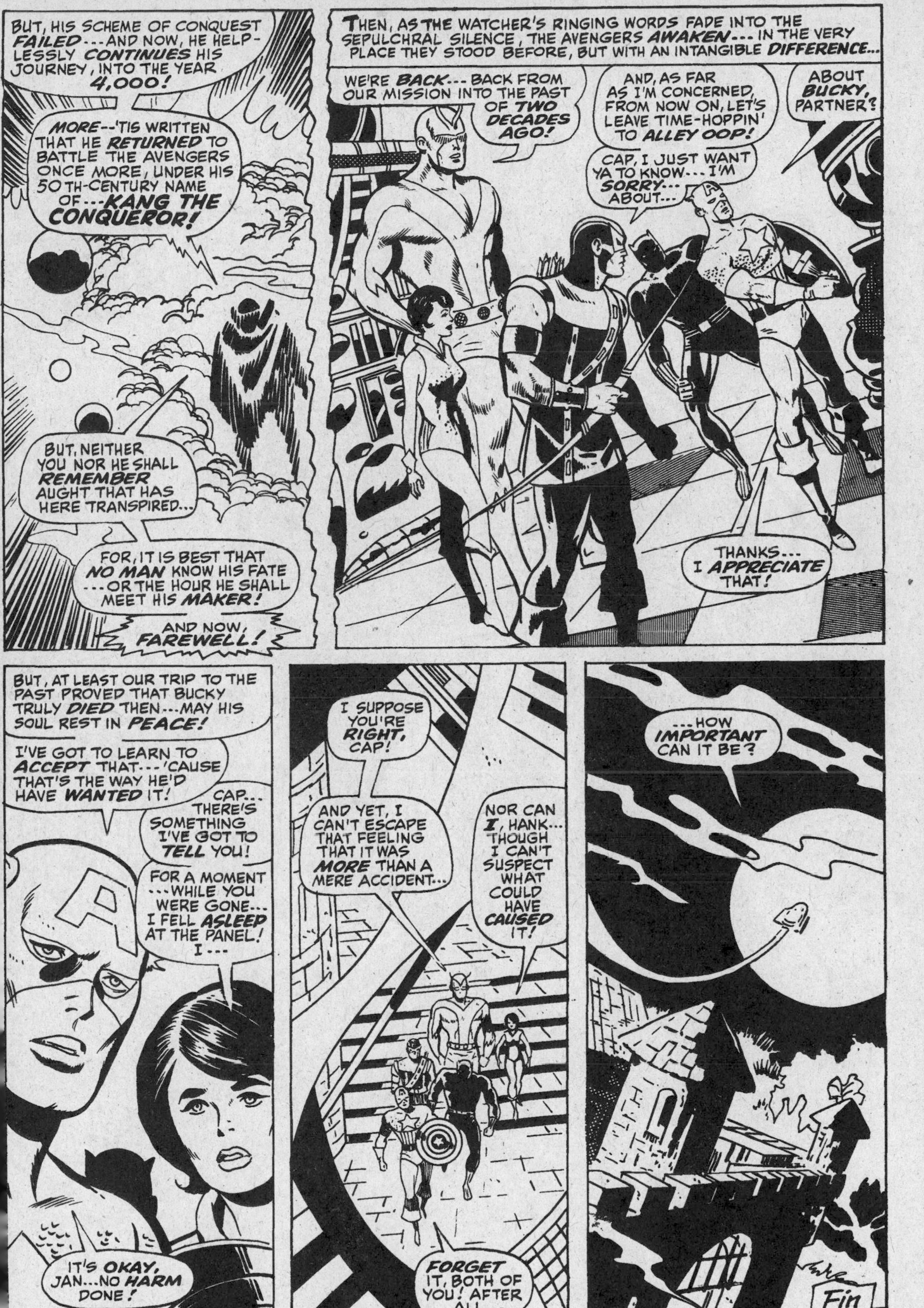
BUT, HIS SCHEME OF CONQUEST FAILED---AND NOW, HE HELPLESSLY CONTINUES HIS JOURNEY, INTO THE YEAR 4,000!
MORE--'TIS WRITTEN THAT HE RETURNED TO BATTLE THE AVENGERS ONCE MORE, UNDER HIS 50TH-CENTURY NAME OF---KANG THE CONQUEROR!
BUT, NEITHER YOU NOR HE SHALL REMEMBER AUGHT THAT HAS HERE TRANSPIRED...
FOR, IT IS BEST THAT NO MAN KNOW HIS FATE ---OR THE HOUR HE SHALL MEET HIS MAKER!
AND NOW, FAREWELL!
THEN, AS THE WATCHER'S RINGING WORDS FADE INTO THE SEPULCHRAL SILENCE, THE AVENGERS AWAKEN--- IN THE VERY PLACE THEY STOOD BEFORE, BUT WITH AN INTANGIBLE DIFFERENCE...
WE'RE BACK--- BACK FROM OUR MISSION INTO THE PAST OF TWO DECADES AGO!
AND, AS FAR AS I'M CONCERNED, FROM NOW ON, LET'S LEAVE TIME-HOPPIN' TO ALLEY OOP!
CAP, I JUST WANT YA TO KNOW--- I'M SORRY ABOUT...
ABOUT BUCKY, PARTNER?
THANKS... I APPRECIATE THAT!
BUT, AT LEAST OUR TRIP TO THE PAST PROVED THAT BUCKY TRULY DIED THEN---MAY HIS SOUL REST IN PEACE!
I'VE GOT TO LEARN TO ACCEPT THAT---'CAUSE THAT'S THE WAY HE'D HAVE WANTED IT!
CAP... THERE'S SOMETHING I'VE GOT TO TELL YOU!
FOR A MOMENT ---WHILE YOU WERE GONE... I FELL ASLEEP AT THE PANEL! I---
IT'S OKAY, JAN...NO HARM DONE!
I SUPPOSE YOU'RE RIGHT, CAP!
AND YET, I CAN'T ESCAPE THAT FEELING THAT IT WAS MORE THAN A MERE ACCIDENT...
NOR CAN I, HANK... THOUGH I CAN'T SUSPECT WHAT COULD HAVE CAUSED IT!
FORGET IT, BOTH OF YOU! AFTER ALL...
...HOW IMPORTANT CAN IT BE?
Fin
24

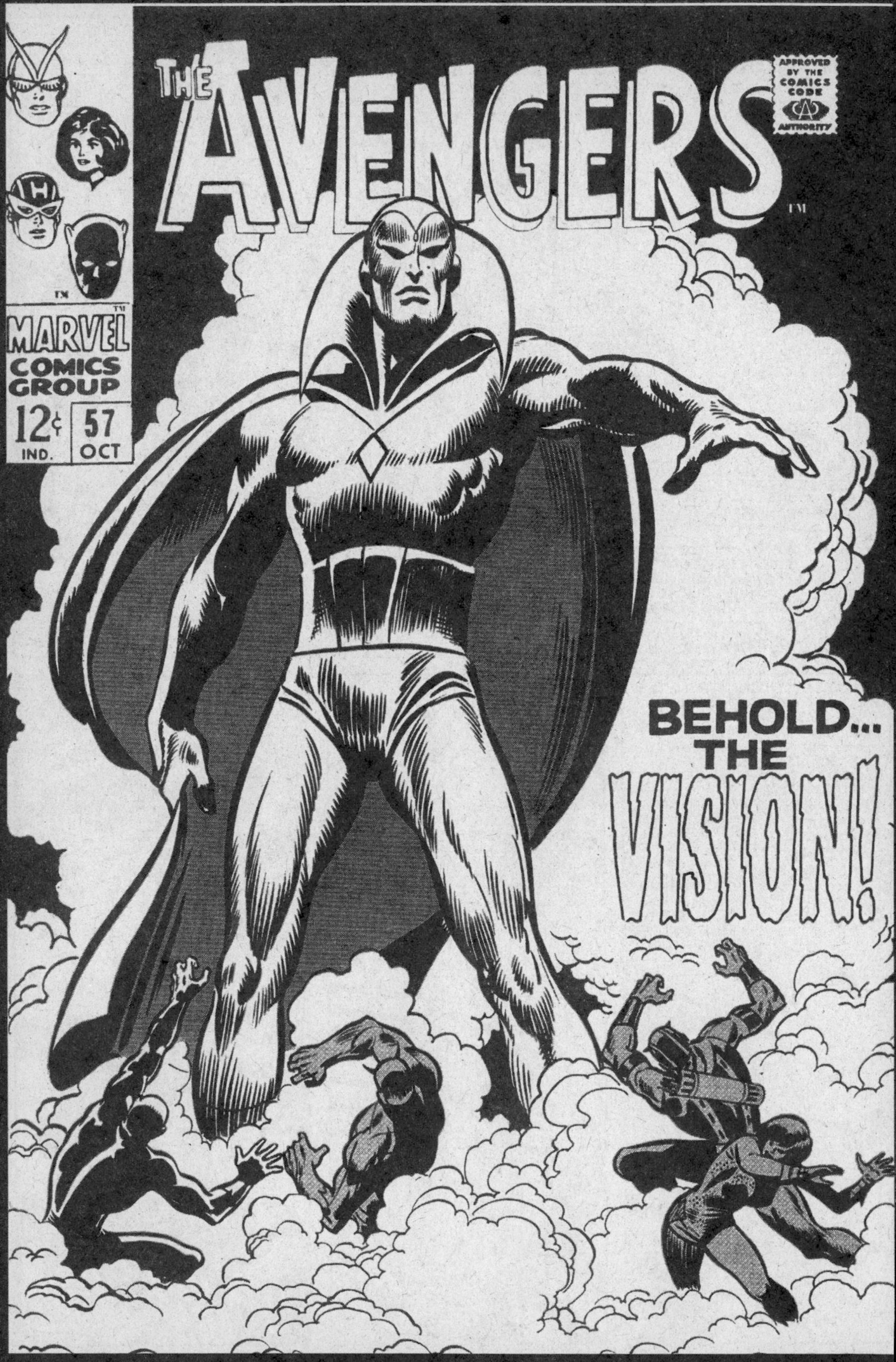
THE AVENGERS
APPROVED BY THE COMICS CODE AUTHORITY
MARVEL COMICS GROUP
12¢ IND.
57 OCT
BEHOLD... THE VISION!

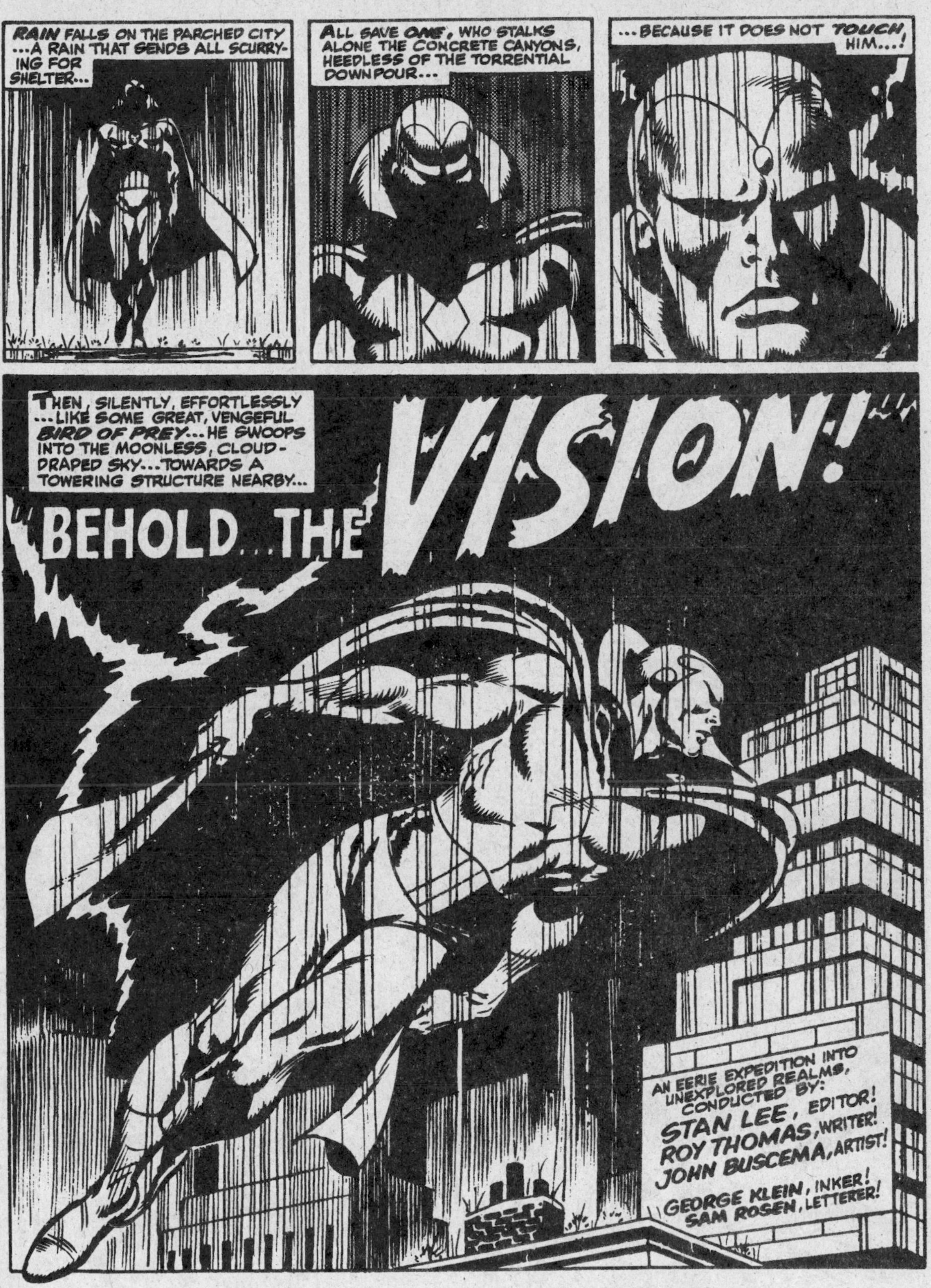
RAIN FALLS ON THE PARCHED CITY ...A RAIN THAT SENDS ALL SCURRYING FOR SHELTER...
ALL SAVE ONE, WHO STALKS ALONE THE CONCRETE CANYONS, HEEDLESS OF THE TORRENTIAL DOWNPOUR...
...BECAUSE IT DOES NOT TOUCH HIM...!
THEN, SILENTLY, EFFORTLESSLY ...LIKE SOME GREAT, VENGEFUL BIRD OF PREY...HE SWOOPS INTO THE MOONLESS, CLOUD-DRAPED SKY...TOWARDS A TOWERING STRUCTURE NEARBY...
BEHOLD...THE VISION!
AN EERIE EXPEDITION INTO UNEXPLORED REALMS, CONDUCTED BY:
STAN LEE, EDITOR!
ROY THOMAS, WRITER!
JOHN BUSCEMA, ARTIST!
GEORGE KLEIN, INKER!
SAM ROSEN, LETTERER!

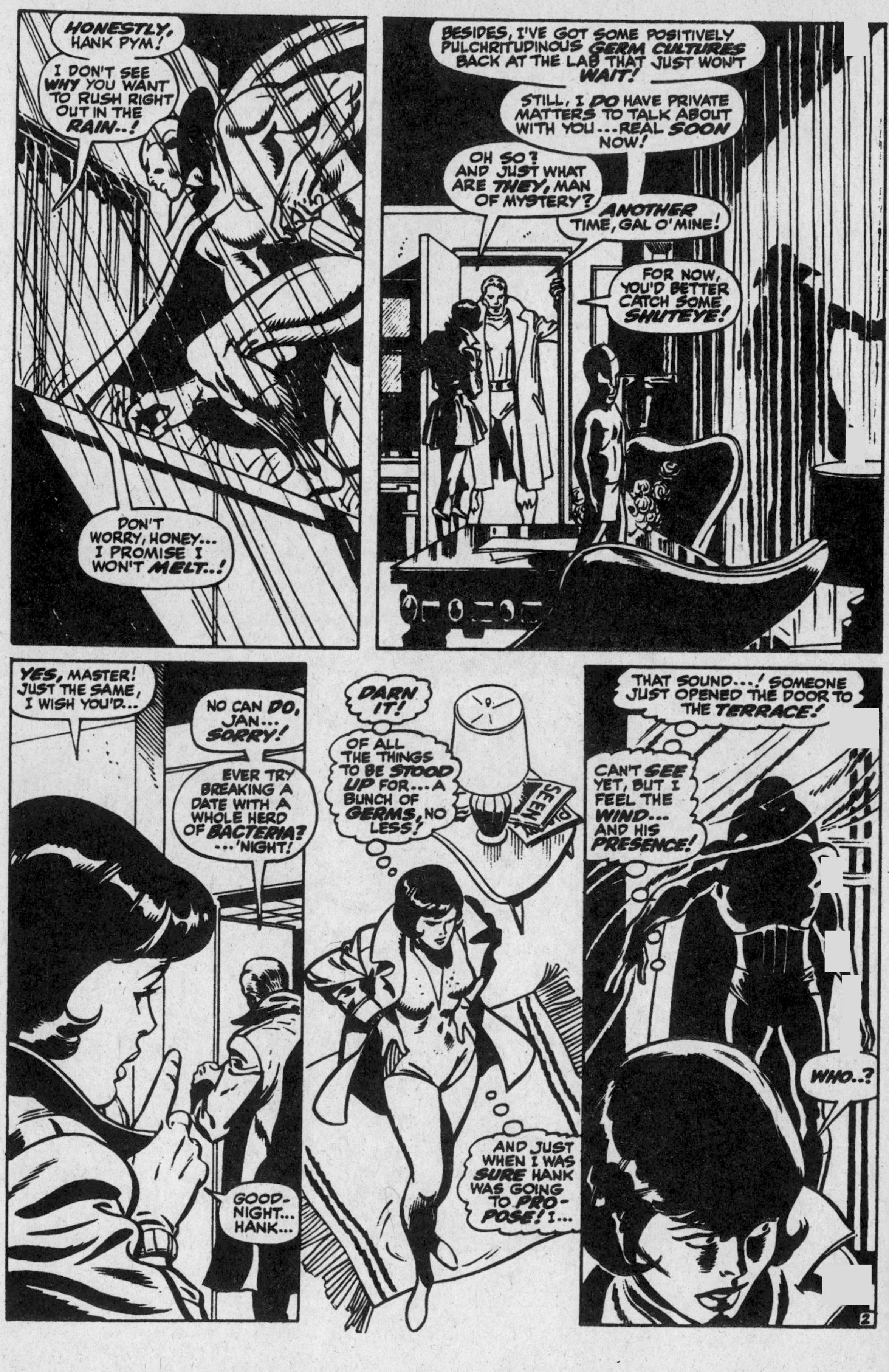
HONESTLY, HANK PYM!
I DON'T SEE WHY YOU WANT TO RUSH RIGHT OUT IN THE RAIN..!
DON'T WORRY, HONEY... I PROMISE I WON'T MELT..!
BESIDES, I'VE GOT SOME POSITIVELY PULCHRITUDINOUS GERM CULTURES BACK AT THE LAB THAT JUST WON'T WAIT!
STILL, I DO HAVE PRIVATE MATTERS TO TALK ABOUT WITH YOU... REAL SOON NOW!
OH SO? AND JUST WHAT ARE THEY, MAN OF MYSTERY?
ANOTHER TIME, GAL O' MINE!
FOR NOW, YOU'D BETTER CATCH SOME SHUTEYE!
YES, MASTER! JUST THE SAME, I WISH YOU'D...
NO CAN DO, JAN... SORRY!
EVER TRY BREAKING A DATE WITH A WHOLE HERD OF BACTERIA? ...'NIGHT!
GOOD-NIGHT... HANK...
DARN IT!
OF ALL THE THINGS TO BE STOOD UP FOR... A BUNCH OF GERMS, NO LESS!
AND JUST WHEN I WAS SURE HANK WAS GOING TO PRO-POSE! I...
THAT SOUND...! SOMEONE JUST OPENED THE DOOR TO THE TERRACE!
CAN'T SEE YET, BUT I FEEL THE WIND... AND HIS PRESENCE!
WHO..?
2

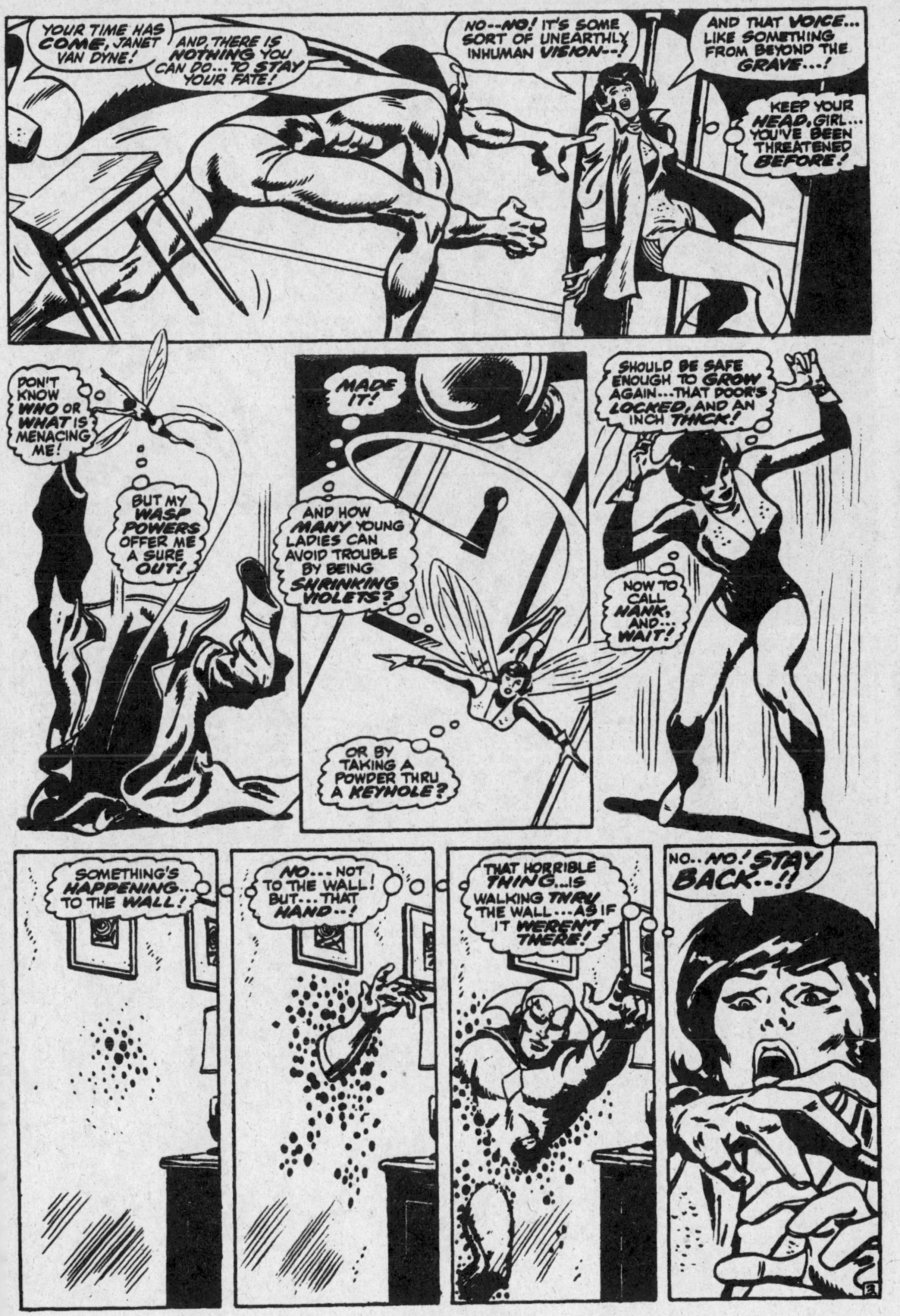
YOUR TIME HAS COME, JANET VAN DYNE!
AND THERE IS NOTHING YOU CAN DO... TO STAY YOUR FATE!
NO--NO! IT'S SOME SORT OF UNEARTHLY, INHUMAN VISION--!
AND THAT VOICE... LIKE SOMETHING FROM BEYOND THE GRAVE...!
KEEP YOUR HEAD, GIRL... YOU'VE BEEN THREATENED BEFORE!
DON'T KNOW WHO OR WHAT IS MENACING ME!
BUT MY WASP POWERS OFFER ME A SURE OUT!
MADE IT!
AND HOW MANY YOUNG LADIES CAN AVOID TROUBLE BY BEING SHRINKING VIOLETS?
OR BY TAKING A POWDER THRU A KEYHOLE?
SHOULD BE SAFE ENOUGH TO GROW AGAIN... THAT DOOR'S LOCKED, AND AN INCH THICK!
NOW TO CALL HANK, AND... WAIT!
SOMETHING'S HAPPENING... TO THE WALL!
NO... NOT TO THE WALL! BUT... THAT HAND--!
THAT HORRIBLE THING... IS WALKING THRU THE WALL... AS IF IT WEREN'T THERE!
NO.. NO! STAY BACK..!!
3

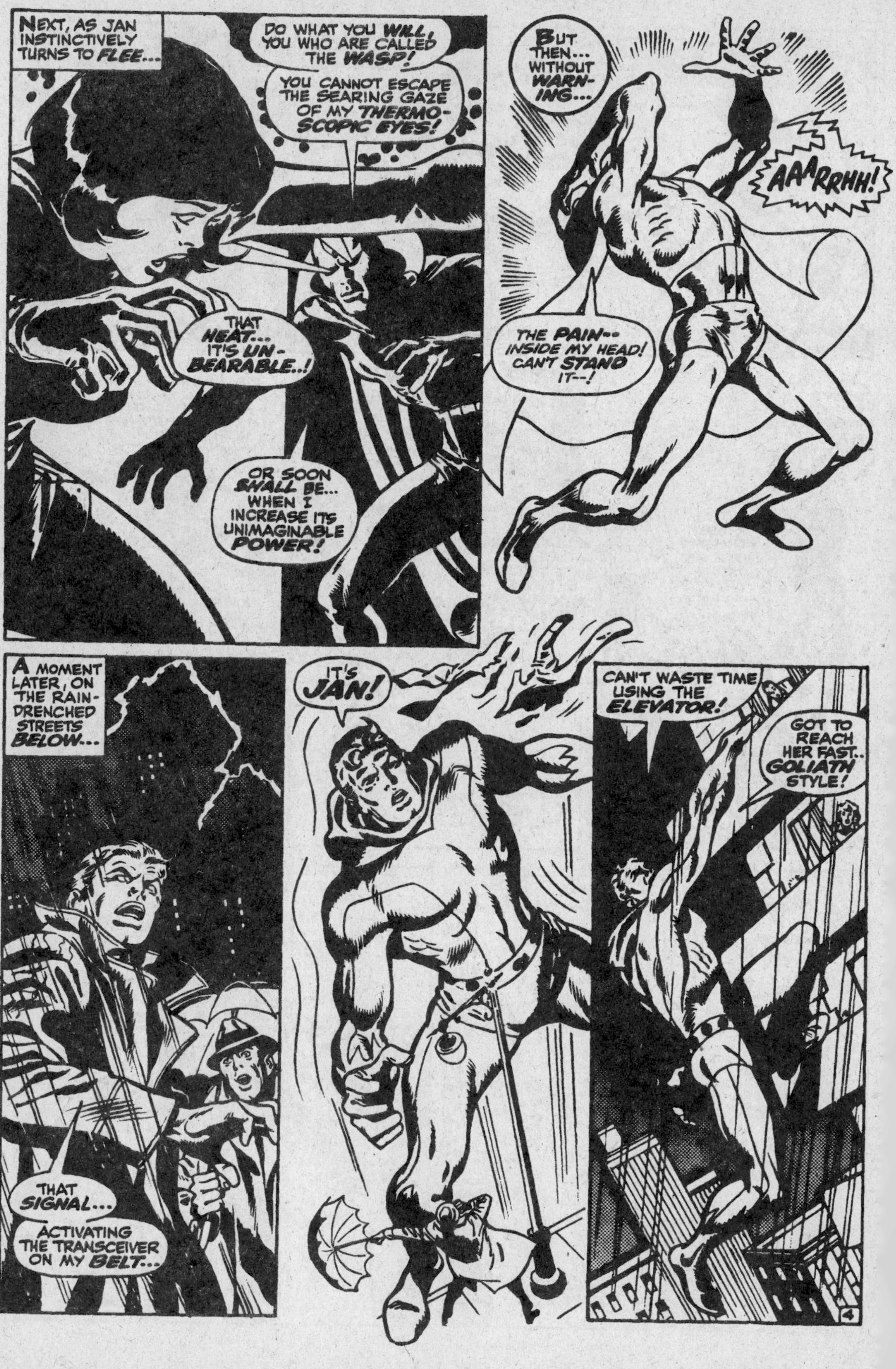
NEXT, AS JAN INSTINCTIVELY TURNS TO FLEE...
DO WHAT YOU WILL, YOU WHO ARE CALLED THE WASP!
YOU CANNOT ESCAPE THE SEARING GAZE OF MY THERMO-SCOPIC EYES!
THAT HEAT... IT'S UN-BEARABLE..!
OR SOON SHALL BE... WHEN I INCREASE ITS UNIMAGINABLE POWER!
BUT THEN... WITHOUT WARN-ING...
AAARRHH!
THE PAIN-- INSIDE MY HEAD! CAN'T STAND IT--!
A MOMENT LATER, ON THE RAIN-DRENCHED STREETS BELOW...
THAT SIGNAL...
ACTIVATING THE TRANSCEIVER ON MY BELT...
IT'S JAN!
CAN'T WASTE TIME USING THE ELEVATOR!
GOT TO REACH HER FAST.. GOLIATH STYLE!
4

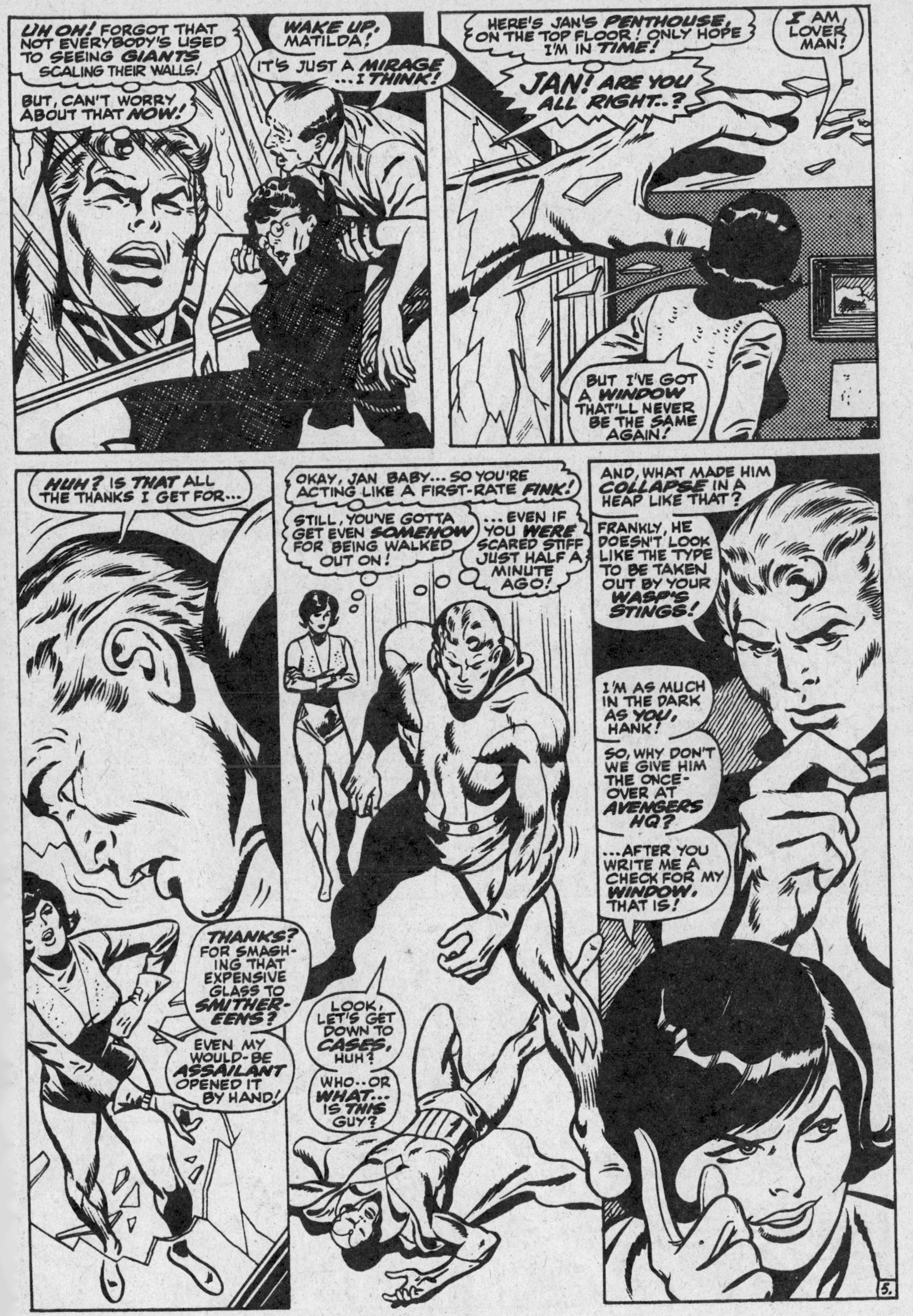
UH OH! FORGOT THAT NOT EVERYBODY'S USED TO SEEING GIANTS SCALING THEIR WALLS!
BUT, CAN'T WORRY ABOUT THAT NOW!
WAKE UP, MATILDA!
IT'S JUST A MIRAGE ...I THINK!
HERE'S JAN'S PENTHOUSE, ON THE TOP FLOOR! ONLY HOPE I'M IN TIME!
JAN! ARE YOU ALL RIGHT..?
I AM, LOVER MAN!
BUT I'VE GOT A WINDOW THAT'LL NEVER BE THE SAME AGAIN!
HUH? IS THAT ALL THE THANKS I GET FOR...
THANKS? FOR SMASHING THAT EXPENSIVE GLASS TO SMITHEREENS?
EVEN MY WOULD-BE ASSAILANT OPENED IT BY HAND!
OKAY, JAN BABY... SO YOU'RE ACTING LIKE A FIRST-RATE FINK!
STILL, YOU'VE GOTTA GET EVEN SOMEHOW FOR BEING WALKED OUT ON!
... EVEN IF YOU WERE SCARED STIFF JUST HALF A MINUTE AGO!
LOOK, LET'S GET DOWN TO CASES, HUH?
WHO...OR WHAT... IS THIS GUY?
AND, WHAT MADE HIM COLLAPSE IN A HEAP LIKE THAT?
FRANKLY, HE DOESN'T LOOK LIKE THE TYPE TO BE TAKEN OUT BY YOUR WASP'S STINGS!
I'M AS MUCH IN THE DARK AS YOU, HANK!
SO, WHY DON'T WE GIVE HIM THE ONCE-OVER AT AVENGERS HQ?
...AFTER YOU WRITE ME A CHECK FOR MY WINDOW, THAT IS!
5.

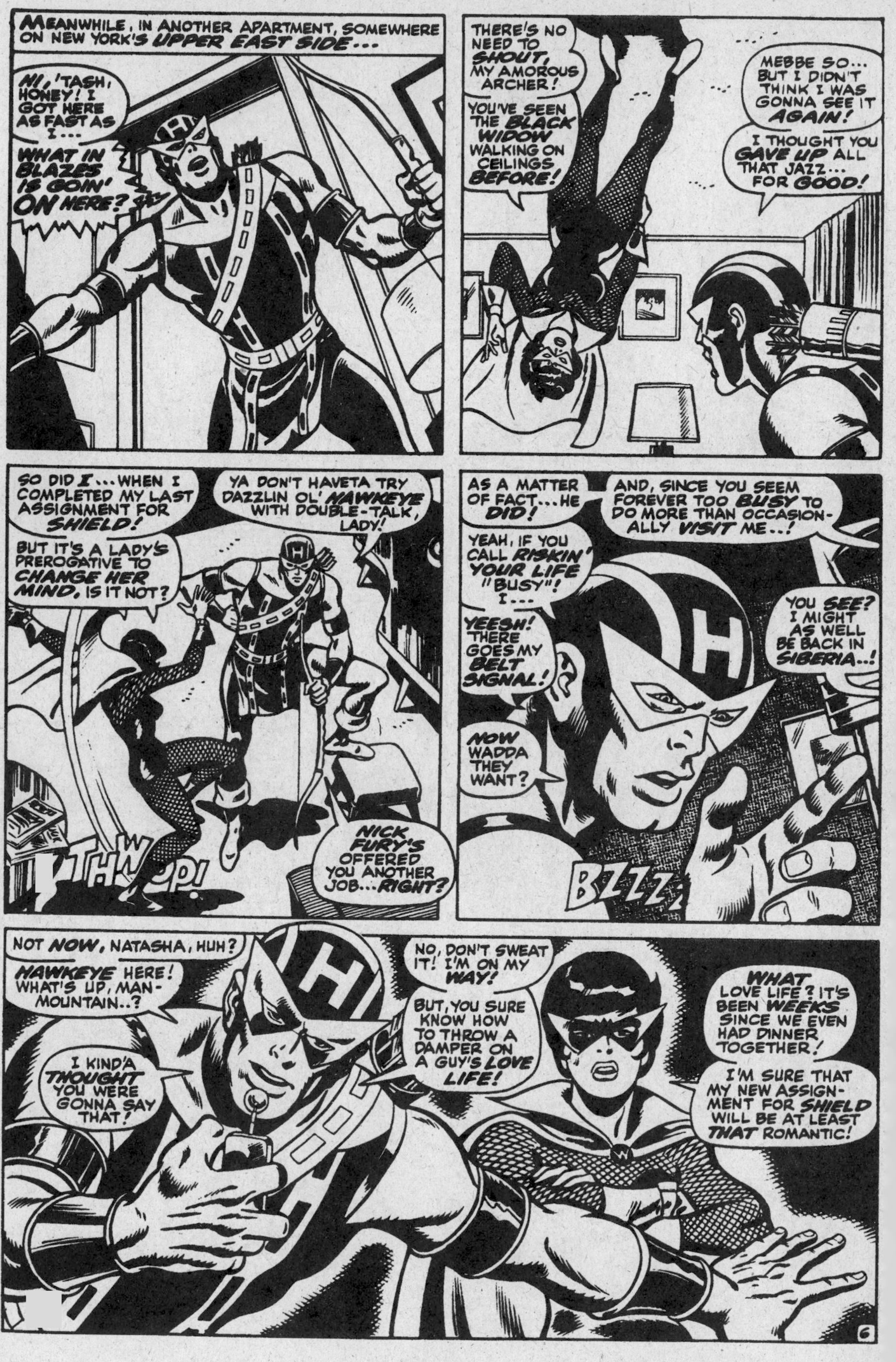
MEANWHILE, IN ANOTHER APARTMENT, SOMEWHERE ON NEW YORK'S UPPER EAST SIDE...
HI, 'TASH, HONEY! I GOT HERE AS FAST AS I...
WHAT IN BLAZES IS GOIN' ON HERE?
THERE'S NO NEED TO SHOUT, MY AMOROUS ARCHER!
YOU'VE SEEN THE BLACK WIDOW WALKING ON CEILINGS BEFORE!
MEBBE SO... BUT I DIDN'T THINK I WAS GONNA SEE IT AGAIN!
I THOUGHT YOU GAVE UP ALL THAT JAZZ... FOR GOOD!
SO DID I... WHEN I COMPLETED MY LAST ASSIGNMENT FOR SHIELD!
BUT IT'S A LADY'S PREROGATIVE TO CHANGE HER MIND, IS IT NOT?
YA DON'T HAVETA TRY DAZZLIN OL' HAWKEYE WITH DOUBLE-TALK, LADY!
NICK FURY'S OFFERED YOU ANOTHER JOB... RIGHT?
AS A MATTER OF FACT... HE DID!
AND, SINCE YOU SEEM FOREVER TOO BUSY TO DO MORE THAN OCCASIONALLY VISIT ME...!
YEAH, IF YOU CALL RISKIN' YOUR LIFE "BUSY"! I...
YEESH! THERE GOES MY BELT SIGNAL!
YOU SEE? I MIGHT AS WELL BE BACK IN SIBERIA..!
NOW WADDA THEY WANT?
BZZZ
NOT NOW, NATASHA, HUH?
HAWKEYE HERE! WHAT'S UP, MAN-MOUNTAIN..?
I KIND'A THOUGHT YOU WERE GONNA SAY THAT!
NO, DON'T SWEAT IT! I'M ON MY WAY!
BUT, YOU SURE KNOW HOW TO THROW A DAMPER ON A GUY'S LOVE LIFE!
WHAT LOVE LIFE? IT'S BEEN WEEKS SINCE WE EVEN HAD DINNER TOGETHER!
I'M SURE THAT MY NEW ASSIGNMENT FOR SHIELD WILL BE AT LEAST THAT ROMANTIC!
6

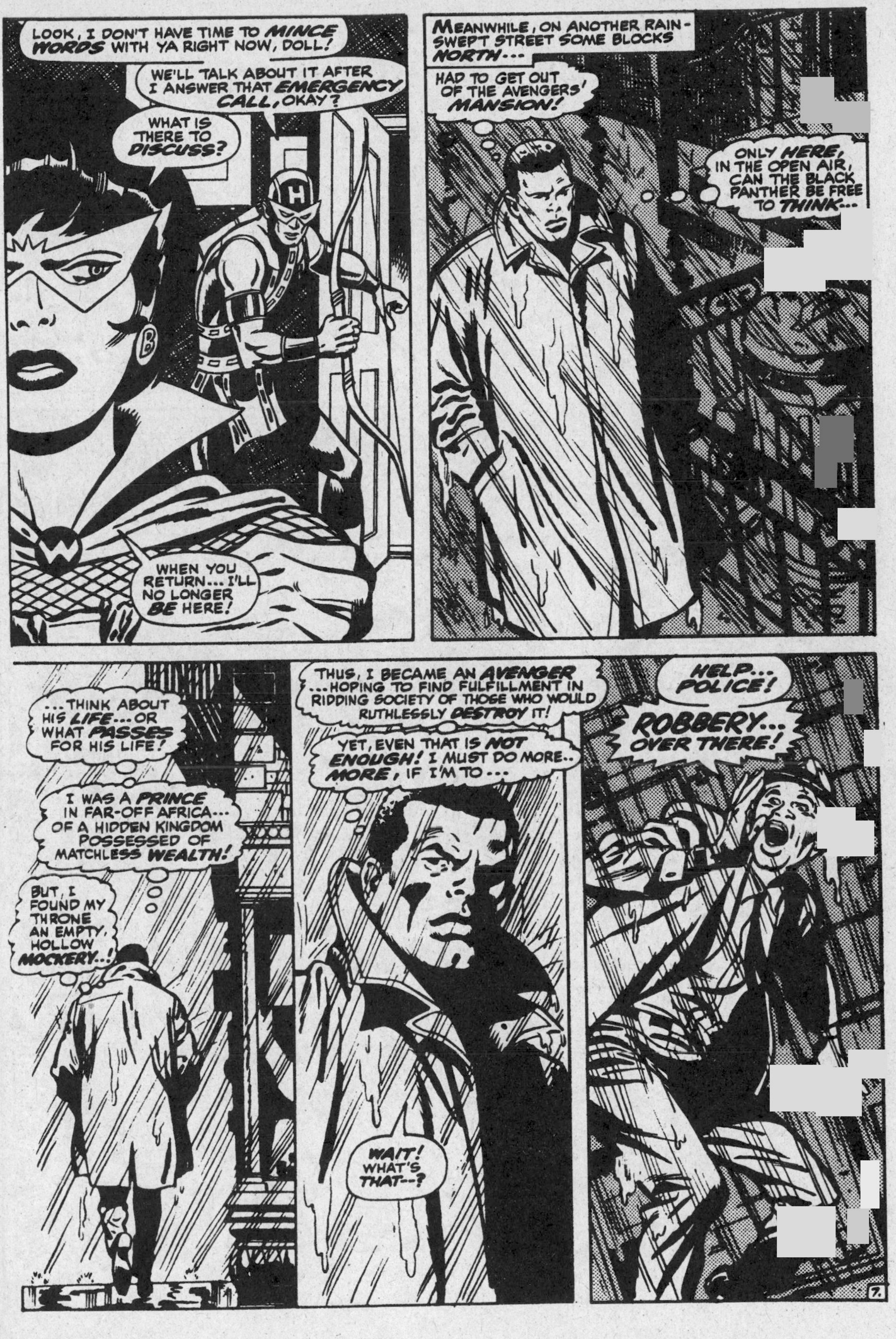
LOOK, I DON'T HAVE TIME TO MINCE WORDS WITH YA RIGHT NOW, DOLL!
WE'LL TALK ABOUT IT AFTER I ANSWER THAT EMERGENCY CALL, OKAY?
WHAT IS THERE TO DISCUSS?
WHEN YOU RETURN... I'LL NO LONGER BE HERE!
MEANWHILE, ON ANOTHER RAIN-SWEPT STREET SOME BLOCKS NORTH...
HAD TO GET OUT OF THE AVENGERS' MANSION!
ONLY HERE, IN THE OPEN AIR, CAN THE BLACK PANTHER BE FREE TO THINK...
...THINK ABOUT HIS LIFE... OR WHAT PASSES FOR HIS LIFE!
I WAS A PRINCE IN FAR-OFF AFRICA... OF A HIDDEN KINGDOM POSSESSED OF MATCHLESS WEALTH!
BUT, I FOUND MY THRONE AN EMPTY, HOLLOW MOCKERY...!
THUS, I BECAME AN AVENGER ...HOPING TO FIND FULFILLMENT IN RIDDING SOCIETY OF THOSE WHO WOULD RUTHLESSLY DESTROY IT!
YET, EVEN THAT IS NOT ENOUGH! I MUST DO MORE.. MORE, IF I'M TO...
WAIT! WHAT'S THAT--?
HELP... POLICE!
ROBBERY... OVER THERE!
7.

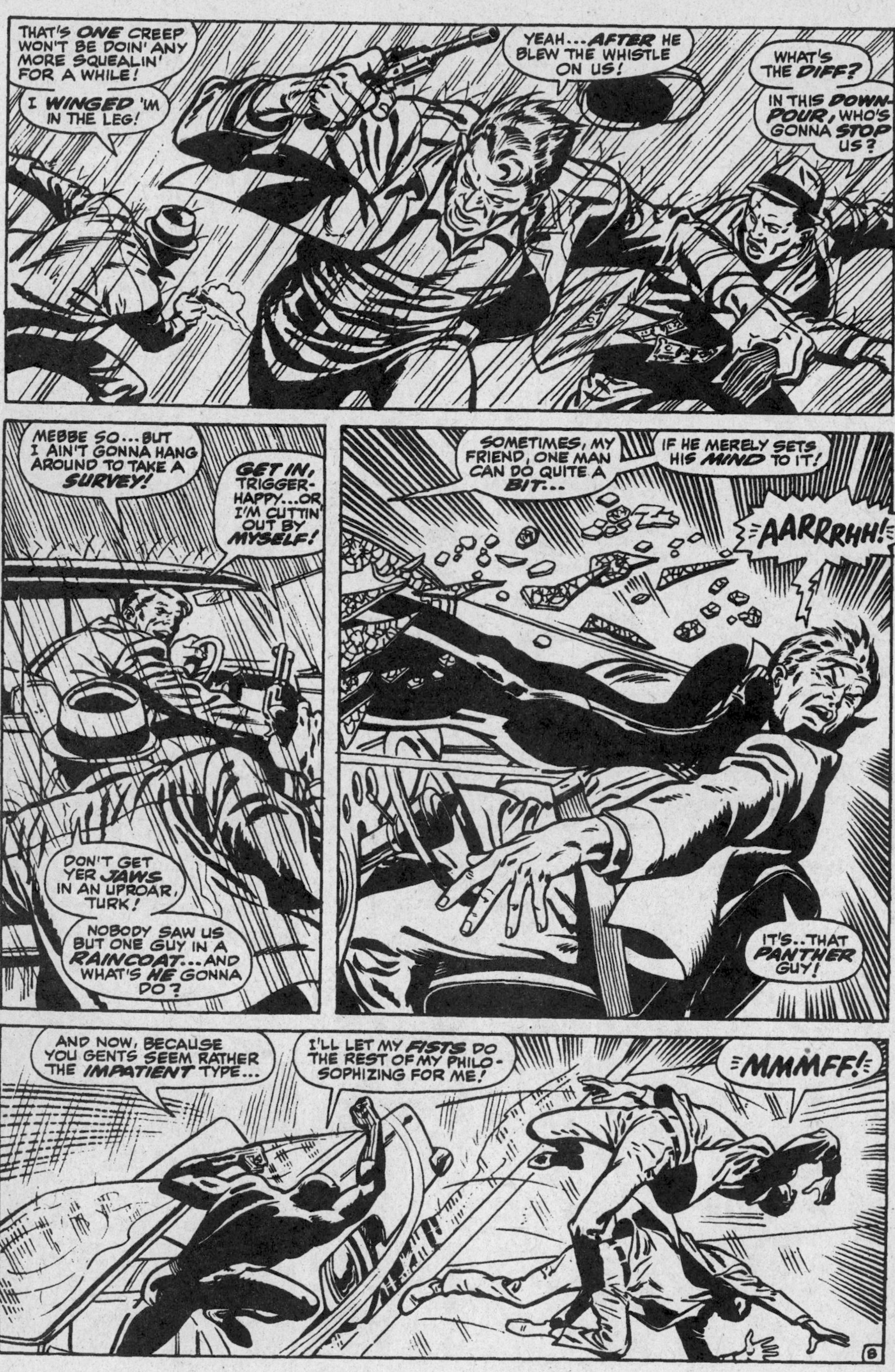
THAT'S ONE CREEP WON'T BE DOIN' ANY MORE SQUEALIN' FOR A WHILE!
I WINGED 'IM IN THE LEG!
YEAH... AFTER HE BLEW THE WHISTLE ON US!
WHAT'S THE DIFF?
IN THIS DOWN-POUR, WHO'S GONNA STOP US?
MEBBE SO... BUT I AIN'T GONNA HANG AROUND TO TAKE A SURVEY!
GET IN, TRIGGER-HAPPY...OR I'M CUTTIN' OUT BY MYSELF!
DON'T GET YER JAWS IN AN UPROAR, TURK!
NOBODY SAW US BUT ONE GUY IN A RAINCOAT... AND WHAT'S HE GONNA DO?
SOMETIMES, MY FRIEND, ONE MAN CAN DO QUITE A BIT...
IF HE MERELY SETS HIS MIND TO IT!
AARRRHH!
IT'S.. THAT PANTHER GUY!
AND NOW, BECAUSE YOU GENTS SEEM RATHER THE IMPATIENT TYPE...
I'LL LET MY FISTS DO THE REST OF MY PHILO-SOPHIZING FOR ME!
MMMFF!
8

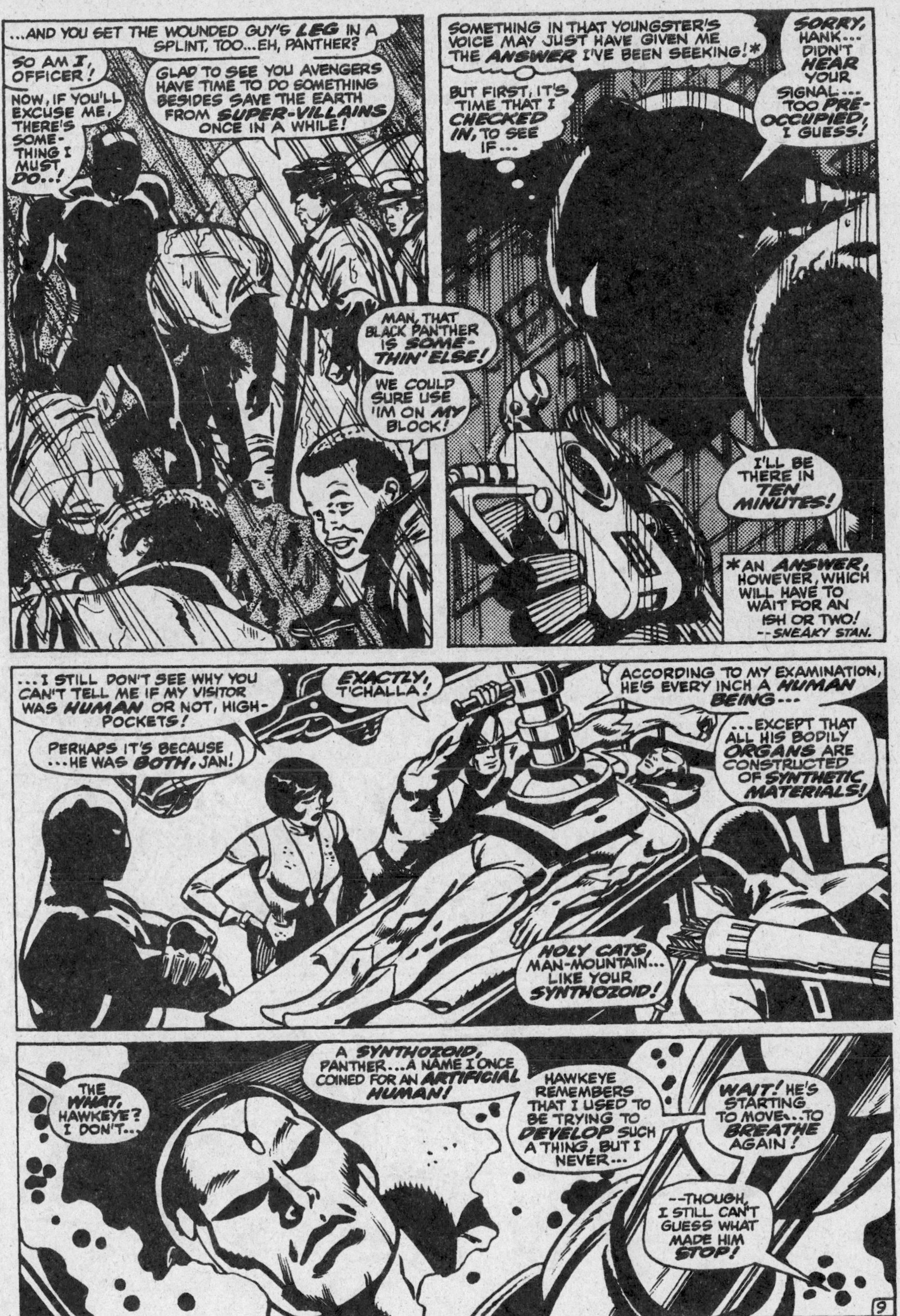
...AND YOU SET THE WOUNDED GUY'S LEG IN A SPLINT, TOO...EH, PANTHER?
SO AM I, OFFICER!
GLAD TO SEE YOU AVENGERS HAVE TIME TO DO SOMETHING BESIDES SAVE THE EARTH FROM SUPER-VILLAINS ONCE IN A WHILE!
NOW, IF YOU'LL EXCUSE ME, THERE'S SOME-THING I MUST DO..!
MAN, THAT BLACK PANTHER IS SOME-THIN' ELSE!
WE COULD SURE USE 'IM ON MY BLOCK!
SOMETHING IN THAT YOUNGSTER'S VOICE MAY JUST HAVE GIVEN ME THE ANSWER I'VE BEEN SEEKING!*
BUT FIRST, IT'S TIME THAT I CHECKED IN, TO SEE IF...
SORRY, HANK... DIDN'T HEAR YOUR SIGNAL... TOO PRE-OCCUPIED, I GUESS!
I'LL BE THERE IN TEN MINUTES!
*AN ANSWER, HOWEVER, WHICH WILL HAVE TO WAIT FOR AN ISH OR TWO! --SNEAKY STAN.
...I STILL DON'T SEE WHY YOU CAN'T TELL ME IF MY VISITOR WAS HUMAN OR NOT, HIGH-POCKETS!
PERHAPS IT'S BECAUSE ...HE WAS BOTH, JAN!
EXACTLY, T'CHALLA!
ACCORDING TO MY EXAMINATION, HE'S EVERY INCH A HUMAN BEING---
...EXCEPT THAT ALL HIS BODILY ORGANS ARE CONSTRUCTED OF SYNTHETIC MATERIALS!
HOLY CATS, MAN-MOUNTAIN... LIKE YOUR SYNTHOZOID!
THE WHAT, HAWKEYE? I DON'T...
A SYNTHOZOID, PANTHER...A NAME I ONCE COINED FOR AN ARTIFICIAL HUMAN!
HAWKEYE REMEMBERS THAT I USED TO BE TRYING TO DEVELOP SUCH A THING, BUT I NEVER...
WAIT! HE'S STARTING TO MOVE...TO BREATHE AGAIN!
--THOUGH, I STILL CAN'T GUESS WHAT MADE HIM STOP!
9

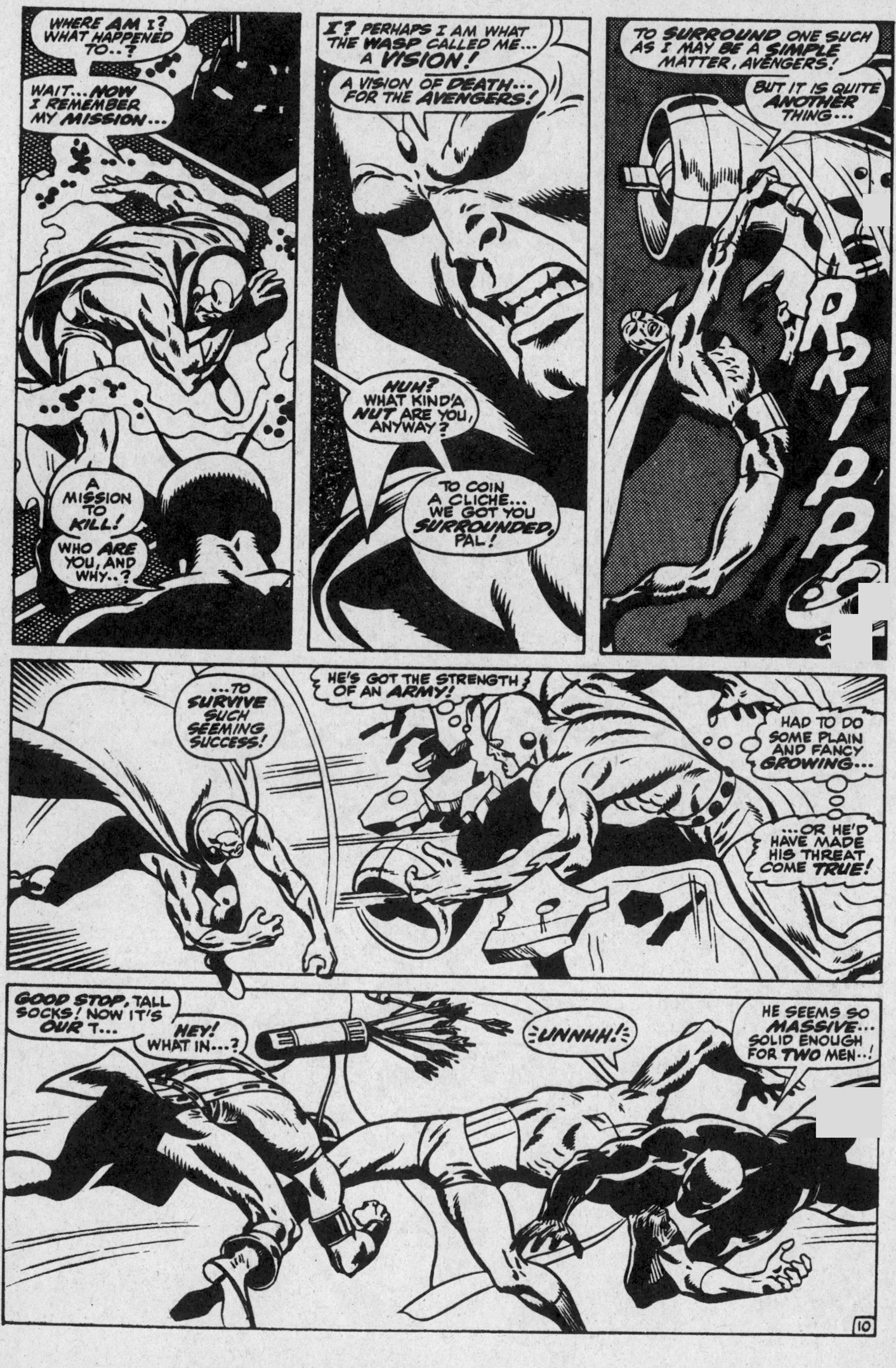

WHERE AM I? WHAT HAPPENED TO..?
WAIT...NOW I REMEMBER MY MISSION...
A MISSION TO KILL!
WHO ARE YOU, AND WHY..?
I? PERHAPS I AM WHAT THE WASP CALLED ME... A VISION!
A VISION OF DEATH... FOR THE AVENGERS!
HUH? WHAT KIND'A NUT ARE YOU, ANYWAY?
TO COIN A CLICHE... WE GOT YOU SURROUNDED, PAL!
TO SURROUND ONE SUCH AS I MAY BE A SIMPLE MATTER, AVENGERS!
BUT IT IS QUITE ANOTHER THING...
RRIPP!
...TO SURVIVE SUCH SEEMING SUCCESS!
HE'S GOT THE STRENGTH OF AN ARMY!
HAD TO DO SOME PLAIN AND FANCY GROWING...
...OR HE'D HAVE MADE HIS THREAT COME TRUE!
GOOD STOP, TALL SOCKS! NOW IT'S OUR T...
HEY! WHAT IN...?
UNNHH!
HE SEEMS SO MASSIVE... SOLID ENOUGH FOR TWO MEN..!

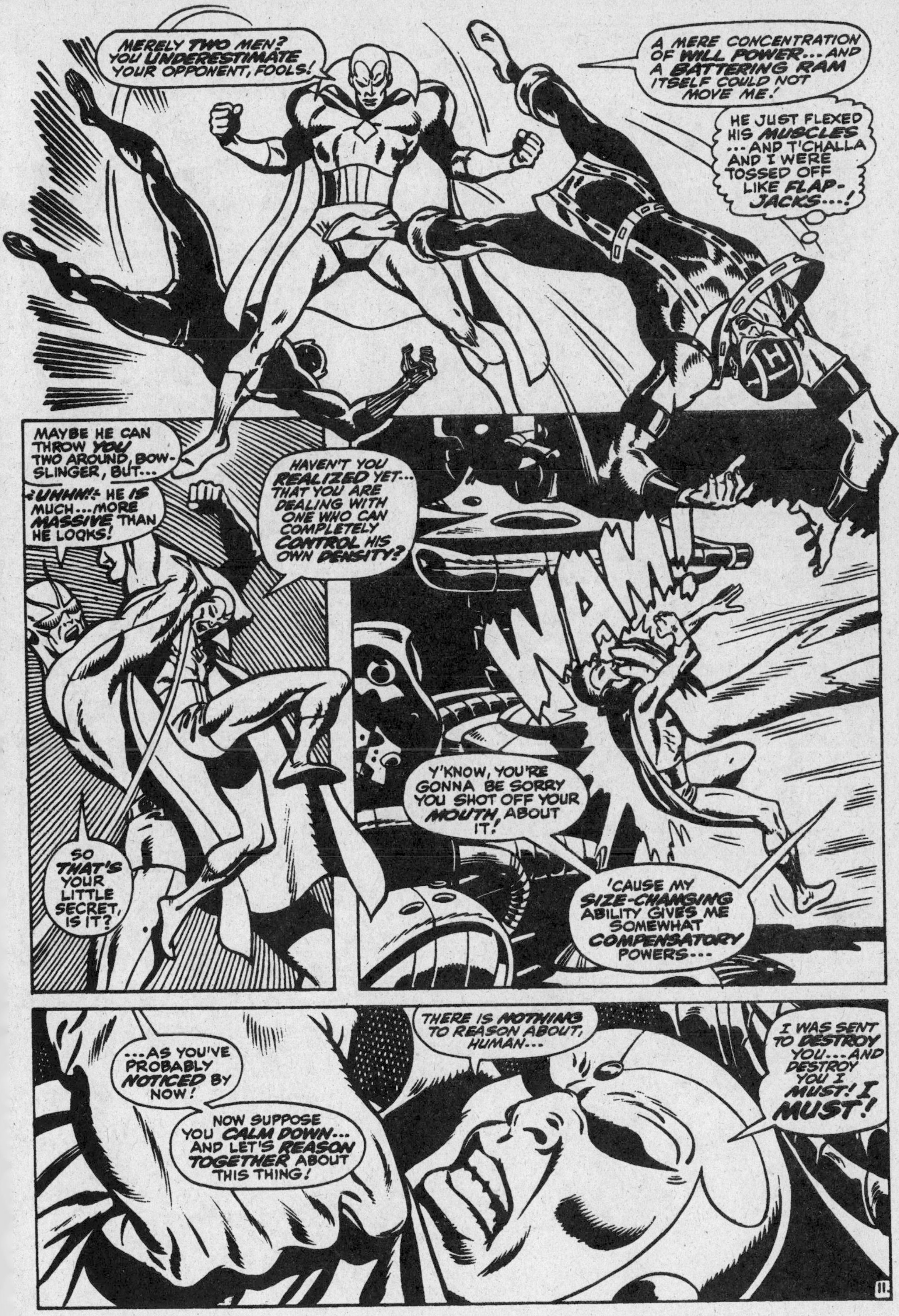
MERELY TWO MEN? YOU UNDERESTIMATE YOUR OPPONENT, FOOLS!
A MERE CONCENTRATION OF WILL POWER... AND A BATTERING RAM ITSELF COULD NOT MOVE ME!
HE JUST FLEXED HIS MUSCLES ...AND T'CHALLA AND I WERE TOSSED OFF LIKE FLAP-JACKS...!
MAYBE HE CAN THROW YOU TWO AROUND, BOW-SLINGER, BUT...
UHHH! HE IS MUCH...MORE MASSIVE THAN HE LOOKS!
HAVEN'T YOU REALIZED YET... THAT YOU ARE DEALING WITH ONE WHO CAN COMPLETELY CONTROL HIS OWN DENSITY?
SO THAT'S YOUR LITTLE SECRET, IS IT?
WAM
Y'KNOW, YOU'RE GONNA BE SORRY YOU SHOT OFF YOUR MOUTH ABOUT IT!
'CAUSE MY SIZE-CHANGING ABILITY GIVES ME SOMEWHAT COMPENSATORY POWERS...
...AS YOU'VE PROBABLY NOTICED BY NOW!
NOW SUPPOSE YOU CALM DOWN... AND LET'S REASON TOGETHER ABOUT THIS THING!
THERE IS NOTHING TO REASON ABOUT, HUMAN...
I WAS SENT TO DESTROY YOU...AND DESTROY YOU I MUST! I MUST!
11

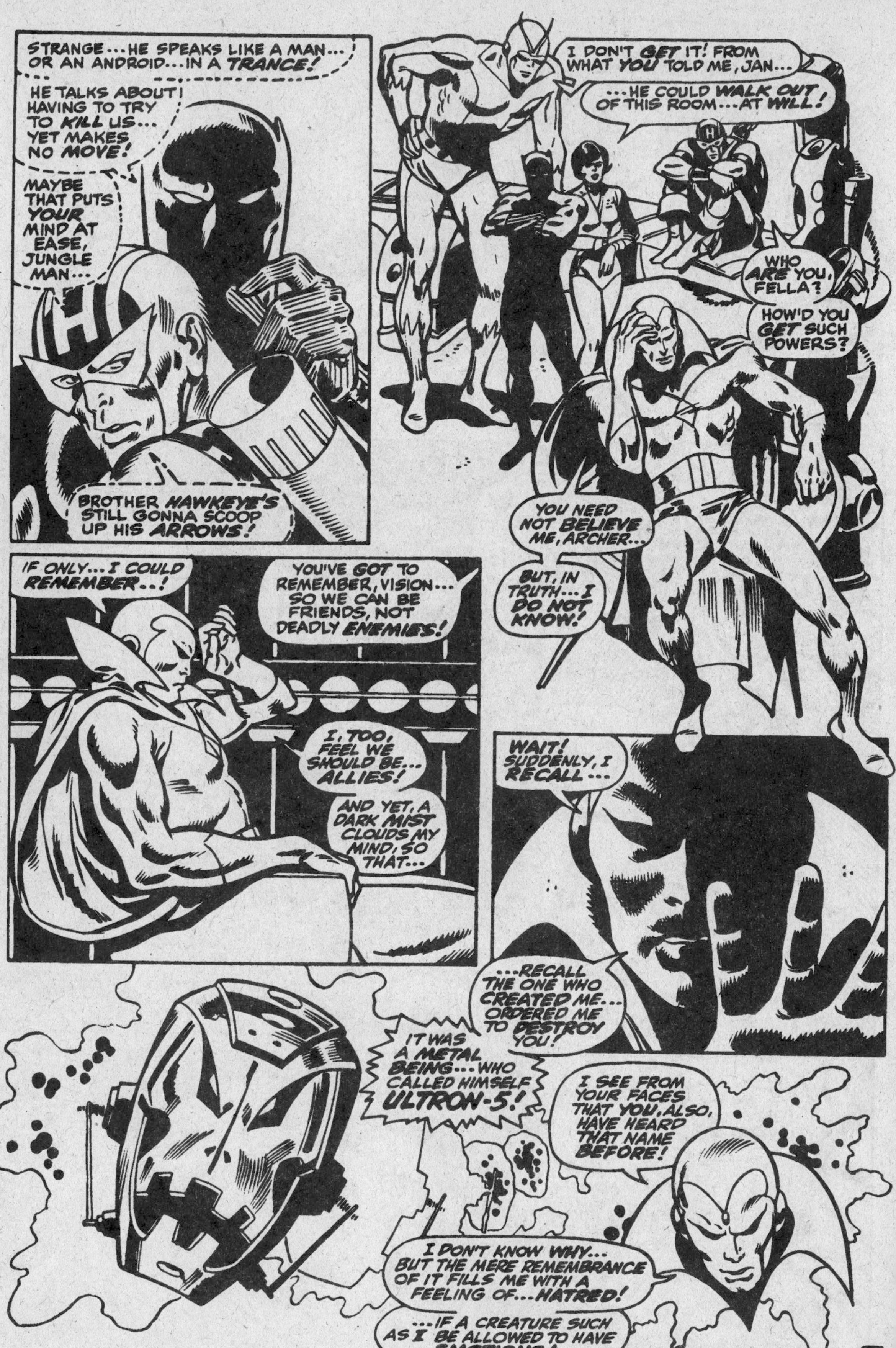

STRANGE... HE SPEAKS LIKE A MAN... OR AN ANDROID... IN A TRANCE!
HE TALKS ABOUT HAVING TO TRY TO KILL US... YET MAKES NO MOVE!
MAYBE THAT PUTS YOUR MIND AT EASE, JUNGLE MAN...
BROTHER HAWKEYE'S STILL GONNA SCOOP UP HIS ARROWS!
I DON'T GET IT! FROM WHAT YOU TOLD ME, JAN...
...HE COULD WALK OUT OF THIS ROOM... AT WILL!
WHO ARE YOU, FELLA?
HOW'D YOU GET SUCH POWERS?
YOU NEED NOT BELIEVE ME, ARCHER...
BUT, IN TRUTH... I DO NOT KNOW!
IF ONLY... I COULD REMEMBER...!
YOU'VE GOT TO REMEMBER, VISION... SO WE CAN BE FRIENDS, NOT DEADLY ENEMIES!
I, TOO, FEEL WE SHOULD BE... ALLIES!
AND YET, A DARK MIST CLOUDS MY MIND, SO THAT...
WAIT! SUDDENLY, I RECALL...
...RECALL THE ONE WHO CREATED ME... ORDERED ME TO DESTROY YOU!
IT WAS A METAL BEING... WHO CALLED HIMSELF ULTRON-5!
I SEE FROM YOUR FACES THAT YOU, ALSO, HAVE HEARD THAT NAME BEFORE!
I DON'T KNOW WHY... BUT THE MERE REMEMBRANCE OF IT FILLS ME WITH A FEELING OF... HATRED!
...IF A CREATURE SUCH AS I BE ALLOWED TO HAVE EMOTIONS!

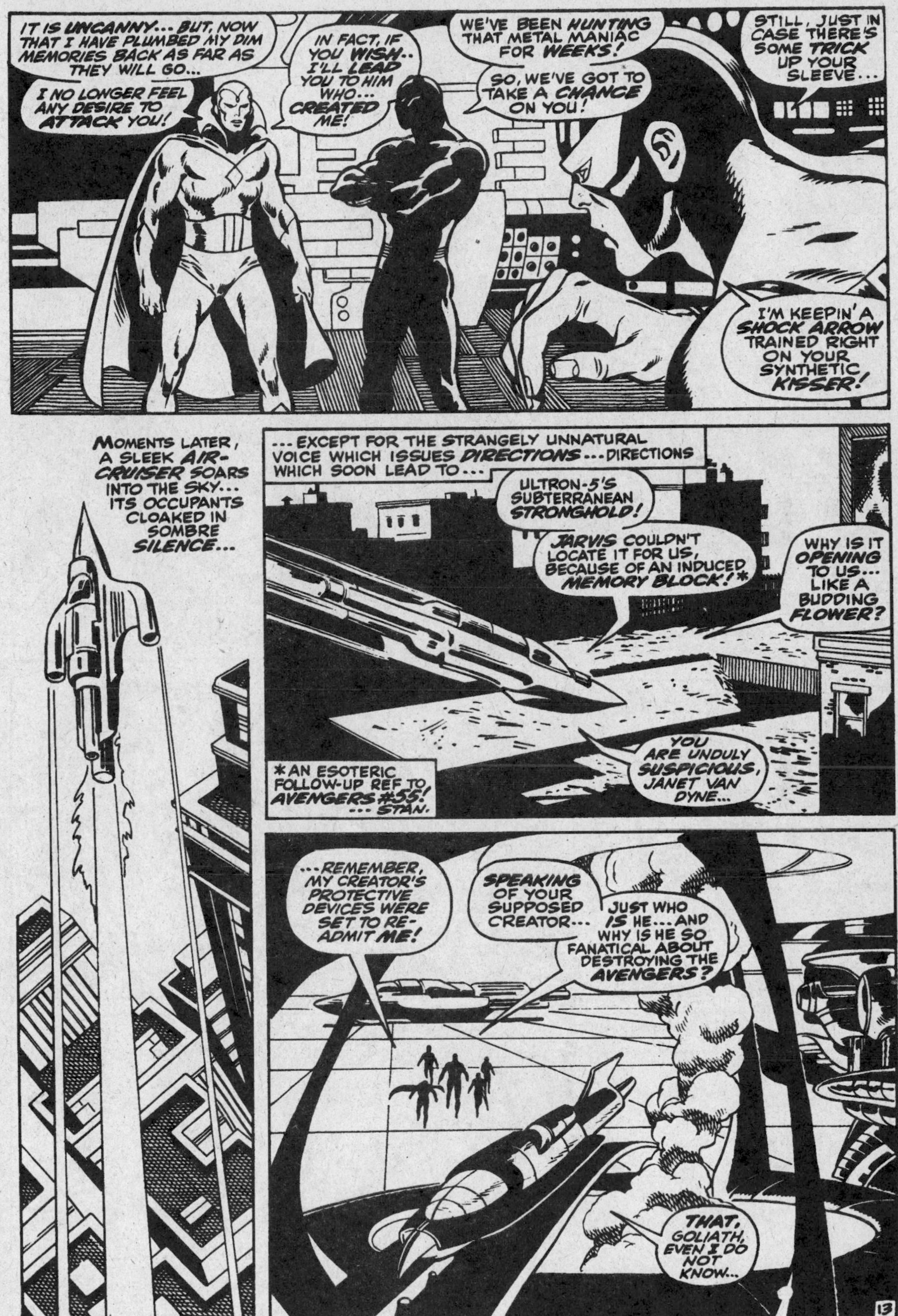
IT IS UNCANNY... BUT, NOW THAT I HAVE PLUMBED MY DIM MEMORIES BACK AS FAR AS THEY WILL GO...
I NO LONGER FEEL ANY DESIRE TO ATTACK YOU!
IN FACT, IF YOU WISH.. I'LL LEAD YOU TO HIM WHO... CREATED ME!
WE'VE BEEN HUNTING THAT METAL MANIAC FOR WEEKS!
SO, WE'VE GOT TO TAKE A CHANCE ON YOU!
STILL, JUST IN CASE THERE'S SOME TRICK UP YOUR SLEEVE...
I'M KEEPIN' A SHOCK ARROW TRAINED RIGHT ON YOUR SYNTHETIC KISSER!
MOMENTS LATER, A SLEEK AIR-CRUISER SOARS INTO THE SKY... ITS OCCUPANTS CLOAKED IN SOMBRE SILENCE...
...EXCEPT FOR THE STRANGELY UNNATURAL VOICE WHICH ISSUES DIRECTIONS... DIRECTIONS WHICH SOON LEAD TO...
ULTRON-5'S SUBTERRANEAN STRONGHOLD!
JARVIS COULDN'T LOCATE IT FOR US, BECAUSE OF AN INDUCED MEMORY BLOCK!*
WHY IS IT OPENING TO US... LIKE A BUDDING FLOWER?
YOU ARE UNDULY SUSPICIOUS, JANET VAN DYNE...
*AN ESOTERIC FOLLOW-UP REF TO AVENGERS #55! ... STAN.
...REMEMBER, MY CREATOR'S PROTECTIVE DEVICES WERE SET TO RE-ADMIT ME!
SPEAKING OF YOUR SUPPOSED CREATOR...
JUST WHO IS HE... AND WHY IS HE SO FANATICAL ABOUT DESTROYING THE AVENGERS?
THAT, GOLIATH, EVEN I DO NOT KNOW...
13

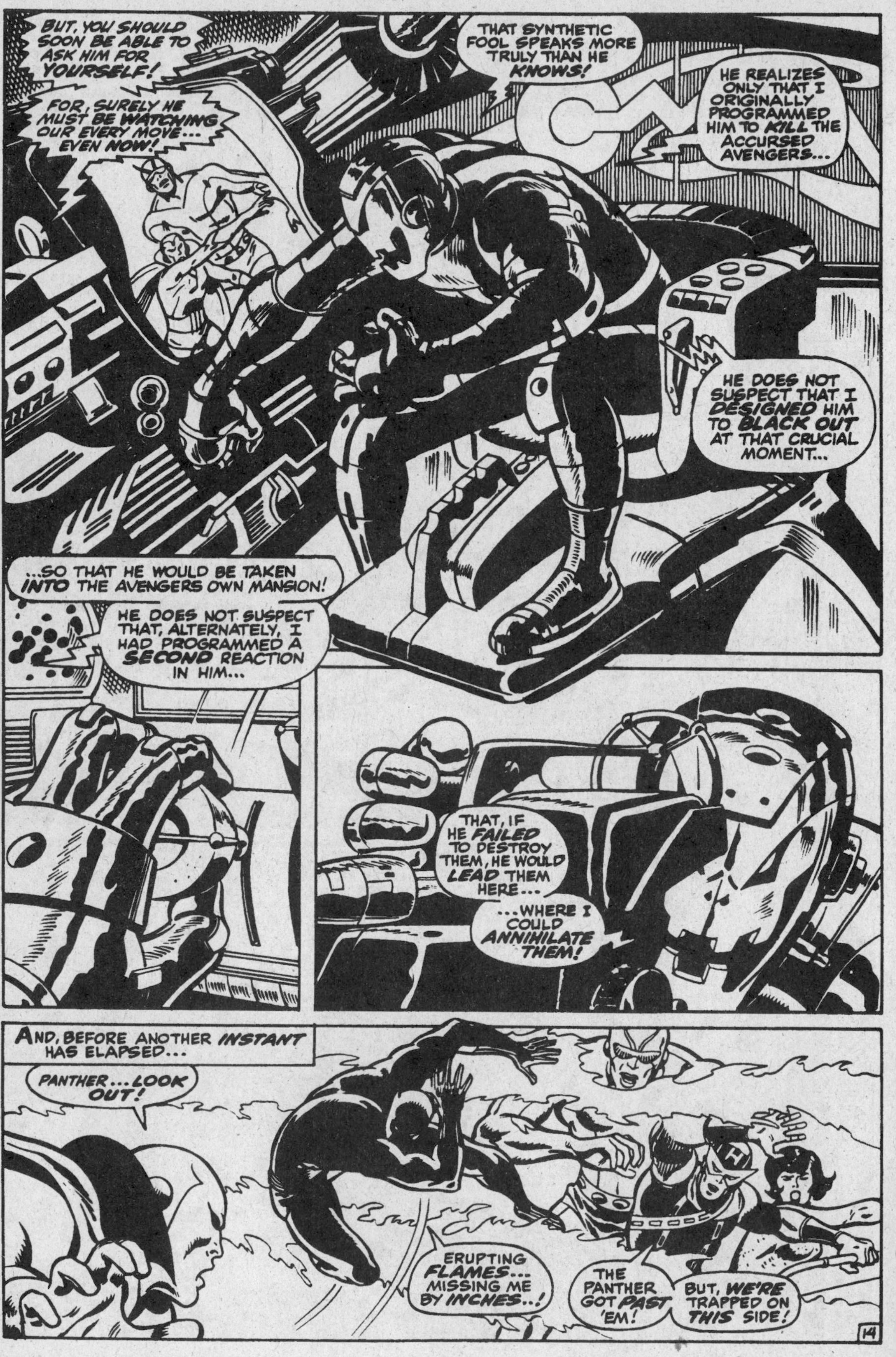

BUT, YOU SHOULD SOON BE ABLE TO ASK HIM FOR YOURSELF!
FOR, SURELY HE MUST BE WATCHING OUR EVERY MOVE... EVEN NOW!
THAT SYNTHETIC FOOL SPEAKS MORE TRULY THAN HE KNOWS!
HE REALIZES ONLY THAT I ORIGINALLY PROGRAMMED HIM TO KILL THE ACCURSED AVENGERS...
HE DOES NOT SUSPECT THAT I DESIGNED HIM TO BLACK OUT AT THAT CRUCIAL MOMENT...
...SO THAT HE WOULD BE TAKEN INTO THE AVENGERS OWN MANSION!
HE DOES NOT SUSPECT THAT, ALTERNATELY, I HAD PROGRAMMED A SECOND REACTION IN HIM...
THAT, IF HE FAILED TO DESTROY THEM, HE WOULD LEAD THEM HERE...
...WHERE I COULD ANNIHILATE THEM!
AND, BEFORE ANOTHER INSTANT HAS ELAPSED...
PANTHER... LOOK OUT!
ERUPTING FLAMES... MISSING ME BY INCHES..!
THE PANTHER GOT PAST 'EM!
BUT, WE'RE TRAPPED ON THIS SIDE!
14

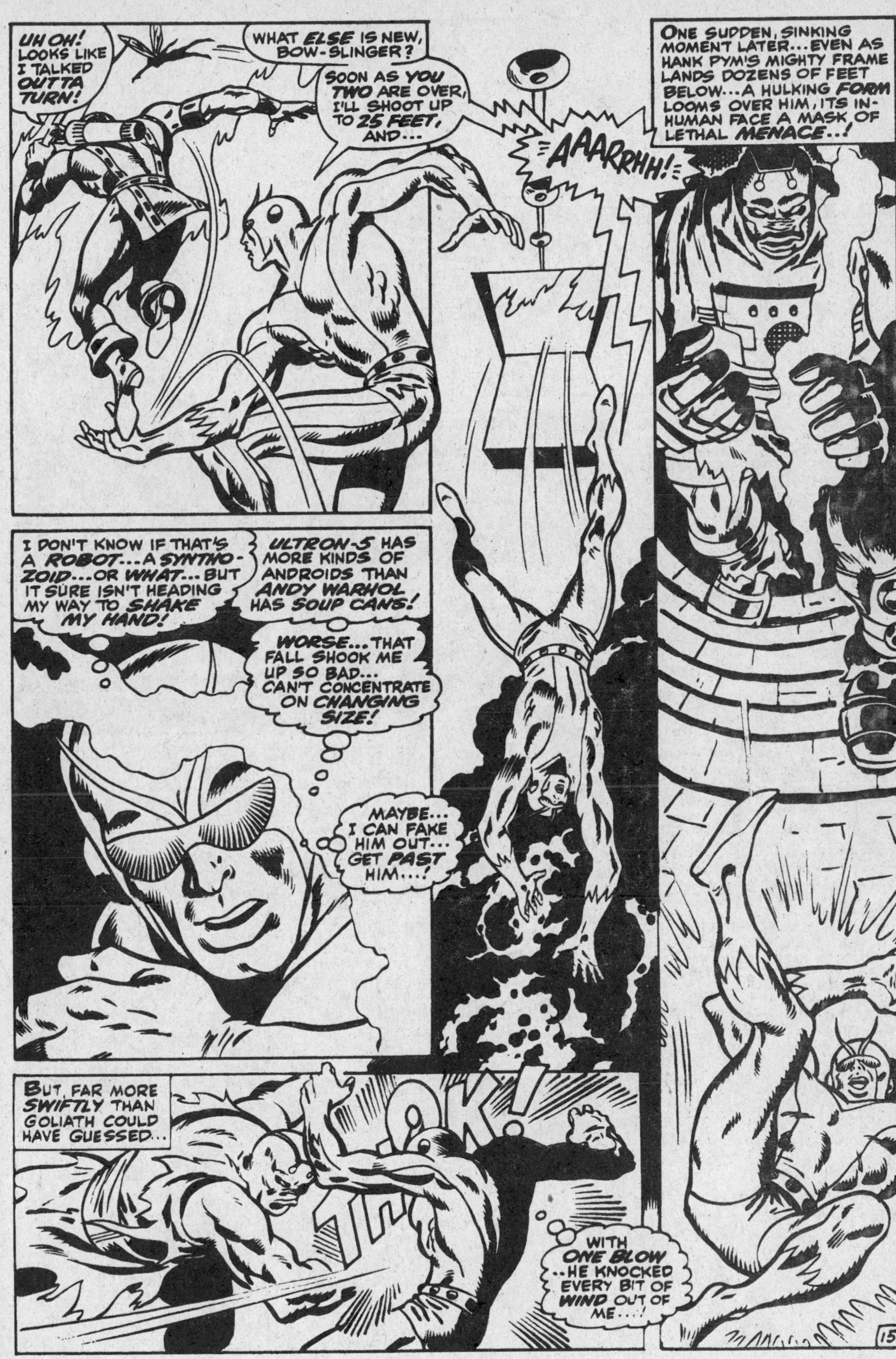
UH OH! LOOKS LIKE I TALKED OUTTA TURN!
WHAT ELSE IS NEW, BOW-SLINGER?
SOON AS YOU TWO ARE OVER, I'LL SHOOT UP TO 25 FEET, AND...
AAAARRHH!
ONE SUDDEN, SINKING MOMENT LATER... EVEN AS HANK PYM'S MIGHTY FRAME LANDS DOZENS OF FEET BELOW... A HULKING FORM LOOMS OVER HIM, ITS IN-HUMAN FACE A MASK OF LETHAL MENACE..!
I DON'T KNOW IF THAT'S A ROBOT... A SYNTHO-ZOID... OR WHAT... BUT IT SURE ISN'T HEADING MY WAY TO SHAKE MY HAND!
ULTRON-5 HAS MORE KINDS OF ANDROIDS THAN ANDY WARHOL HAS SOUP CANS!
WORSE... THAT FALL SHOOK ME UP SO BAD... CAN'T CONCENTRATE ON CHANGING SIZE!
MAYBE... I CAN FAKE HIM OUT... GET PAST HIM...!
BUT, FAR MORE SWIFTLY THAN GOLIATH COULD HAVE GUESSED...
THOK!
WITH ONE BLOW ..HE KNOCKED EVERY BIT OF WIND OUT OF ME...!
15

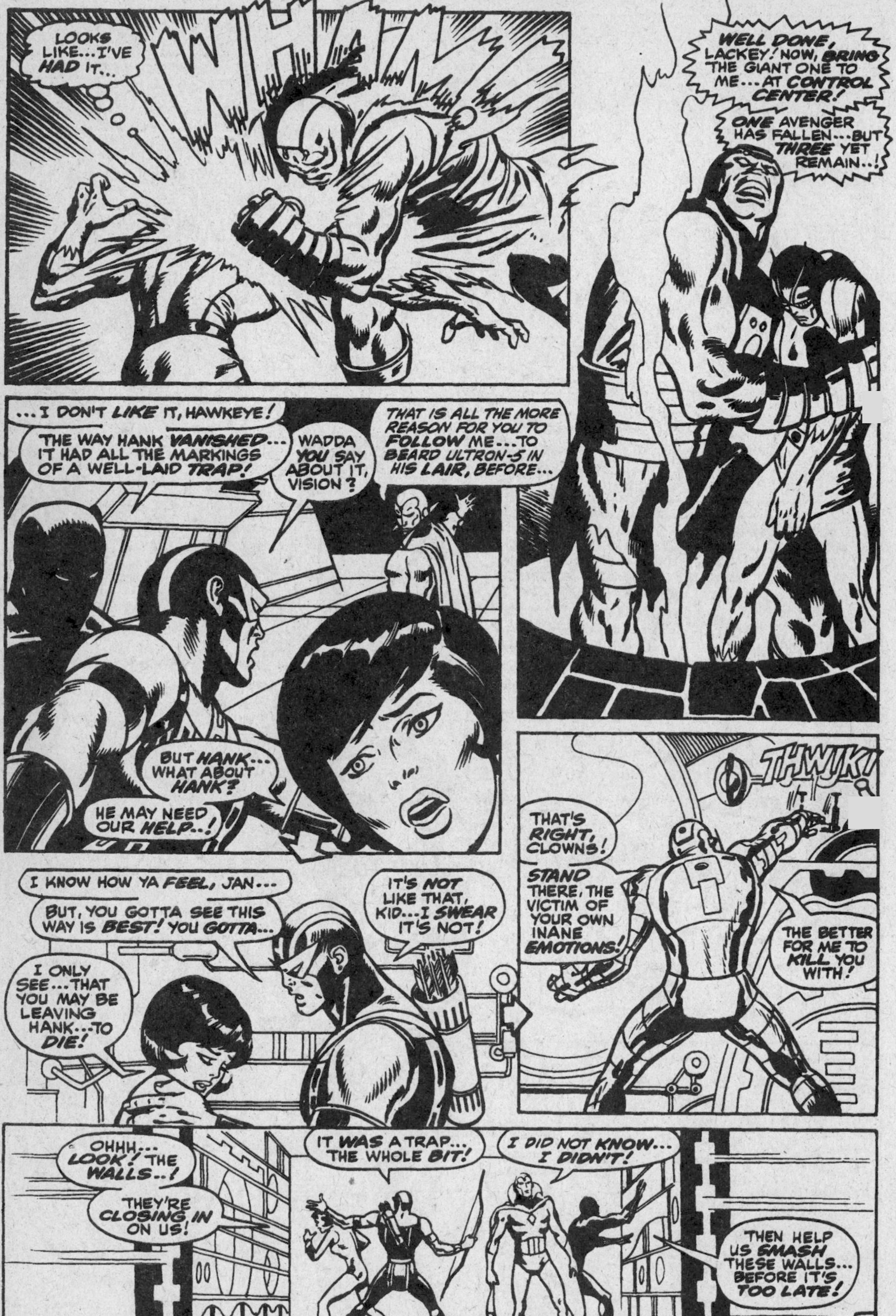
LOOKS LIKE... I'VE HAD IT...
WHAM!
WELL DONE, LACKEY! NOW, BRING THE GIANT ONE TO ME... AT CONTROL CENTER!
ONE AVENGER HAS FALLEN... BUT THREE YET REMAIN...!
... I DON'T LIKE IT, HAWKEYE!
THE WAY HANK VANISHED... IT HAD ALL THE MARKINGS OF A WELL-LAID TRAP!
WADDA YOU SAY ABOUT IT, VISION?
THAT IS ALL THE MORE REASON FOR YOU TO FOLLOW ME... TO BEARD ULTRON-5 IN HIS LAIR, BEFORE...
BUT HANK... WHAT ABOUT HANK?
HE MAY NEED OUR HELP...!
I KNOW HOW YA FEEL, JAN...
BUT, YOU GOTTA SEE THIS WAY IS BEST! YOU GOTTA...
IT'S NOT LIKE THAT, KID... I SWEAR IT'S NOT!
I ONLY SEE... THAT YOU MAY BE LEAVING HANK... TO DIE!
THWIK!
THAT'S RIGHT, CLOWNS!
STAND THERE, THE VICTIM OF YOUR OWN INANE EMOTIONS!
THE BETTER FOR ME TO KILL YOU WITH!
OHHH... LOOK! THE WALLS...!
THEY'RE CLOSING IN ON US!
IT WAS A TRAP... THE WHOLE BIT!
I DID NOT KNOW... I DIDN'T!
THEN HELP US SMASH THESE WALLS... BEFORE IT'S TOO LATE!
16

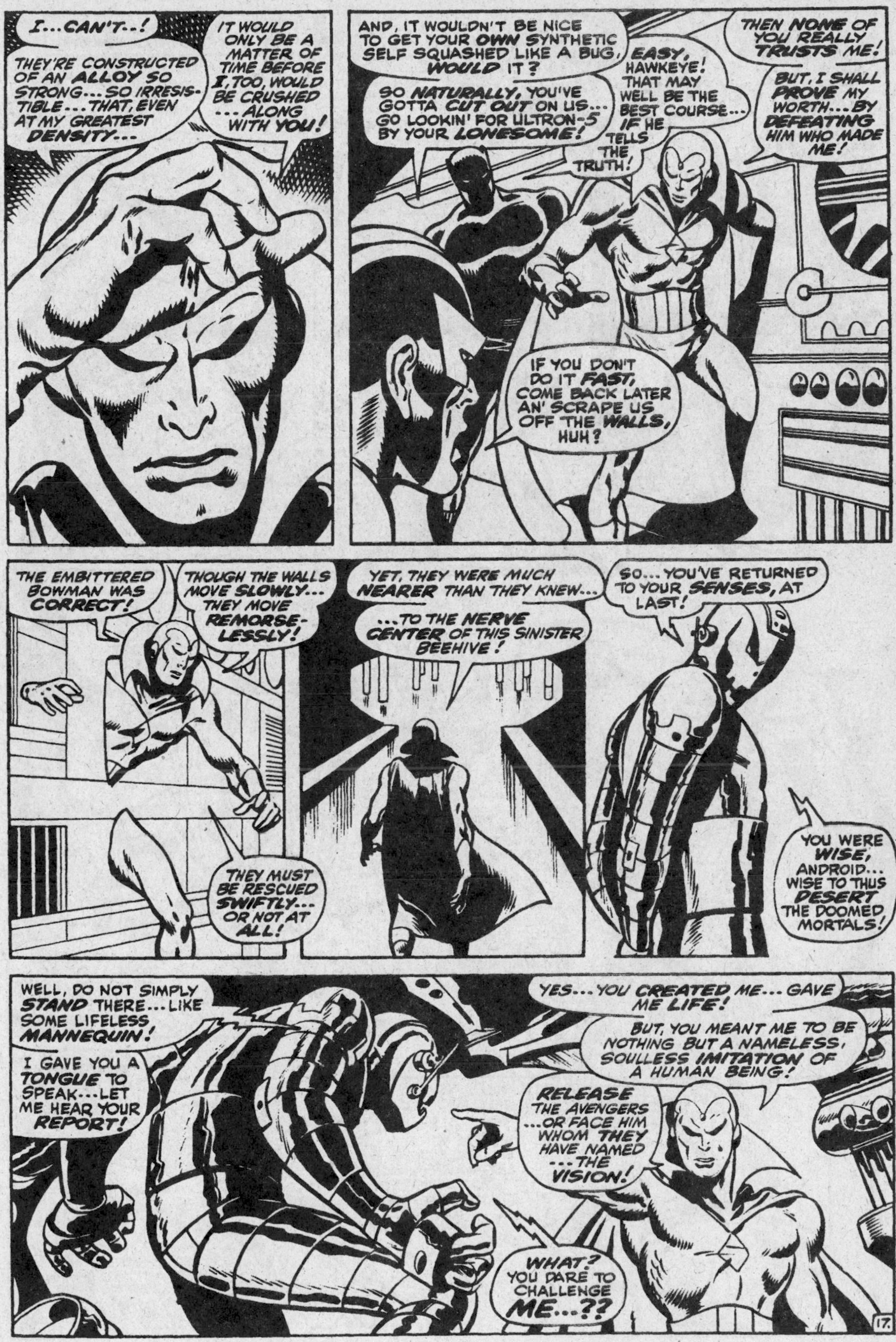
I...CAN'T..!
THEY'RE CONSTRUCTED OF AN ALLOY SO STRONG...SO IRRESISTIBLE...THAT, EVEN AT MY GREATEST DENSITY...
IT WOULD ONLY BE A MATTER OF TIME BEFORE I, TOO, WOULD BE CRUSHED...ALONG WITH YOU!
AND, IT WOULDN'T BE NICE TO GET YOUR OWN SYNTHETIC SELF SQUASHED LIKE A BUG, WOULD IT?
SO NATURALLY, YOU'VE GOTTA CUT OUT ON US...GO LOOKIN' FOR ULTRON-5 BY YOUR LONESOME!
EASY, HAWKEYE! THAT MAY WELL BE THE BEST COURSE...IF HE TELLS THE TRUTH!
THEN NONE OF YOU REALLY TRUSTS ME!
BUT, I SHALL PROVE MY WORTH...BY DEFEATING HIM WHO MADE ME!
IF YOU DON'T DO IT FAST, COME BACK LATER AN' SCRAPE US OFF THE WALLS, HUH?
THE EMBITTERED BOWMAN WAS CORRECT!
THOUGH THE WALLS MOVE SLOWLY...THEY MOVE REMORSELESSLY!
THEY MUST BE RESCUED SWIFTLY...OR NOT AT ALL!
YET, THEY WERE MUCH NEARER THAN THEY KNEW...
...TO THE NERVE CENTER OF THIS SINISTER BEEHIVE!
SO...YOU'VE RETURNED TO YOUR SENSES, AT LAST!
YOU WERE WISE, ANDROID...WISE TO THUS DESERT THE DOOMED MORTALS!
WELL, DO NOT SIMPLY STAND THERE...LIKE SOME LIFELESS MANNEQUIN!
I GAVE YOU A TONGUE TO SPEAK...LET ME HEAR YOUR REPORT!
YES...YOU CREATED ME...GAVE ME LIFE!
BUT, YOU MEANT ME TO BE NOTHING BUT A NAMELESS, SOULLESS IMITATION OF A HUMAN BEING!
RELEASE THE AVENGERS...OR FACE HIM WHOM THEY HAVE NAMED...THE VISION!
WHAT? YOU DARE TO CHALLENGE ME...??

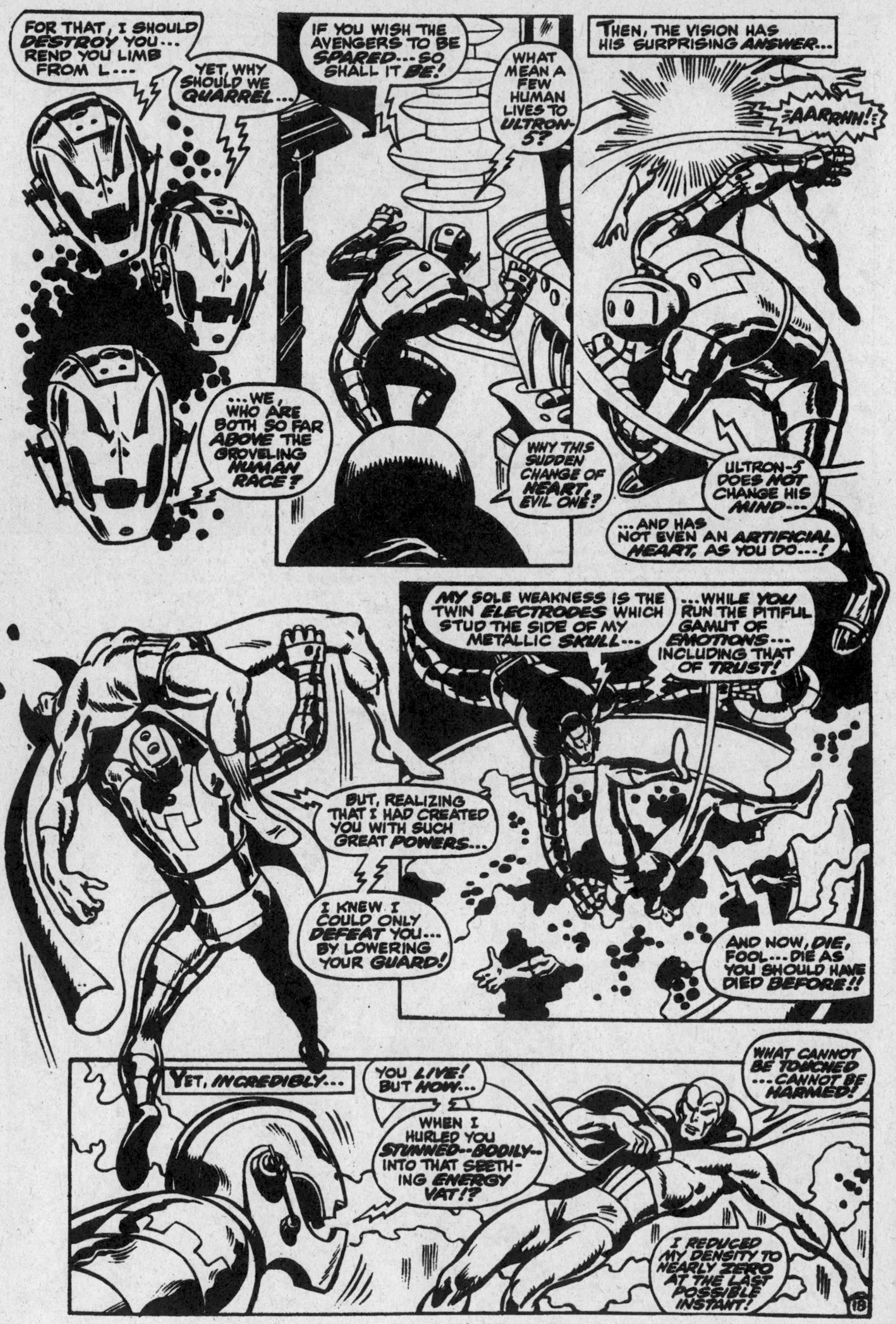

FOR THAT, I SHOULD DESTROY YOU... REND YOU LIMB FROM L---
YET, WHY SHOULD WE QUARREL...
...WE, WHO ARE BOTH SO FAR ABOVE THE GROVELING HUMAN RACE?
IF YOU WISH THE AVENGERS TO BE SPARED... SO SHALL IT BE!
WHAT MEAN A FEW HUMAN LIVES TO ULTRON-5?
WHY THIS SUDDEN CHANGE OF HEART, EVIL ONE?
THEN, THE VISION HAS HIS SURPRISING ANSWER...
AARRHH!
ULTRON-5 DOES NOT CHANGE HIS MIND...
...AND HAS NOT EVEN AN ARTIFICIAL HEART, AS YOU DO...!
BUT, REALIZING THAT I HAD CREATED YOU WITH SUCH GREAT POWERS...
I KNEW I COULD ONLY DEFEAT YOU... BY LOWERING YOUR GUARD!
MY SOLE WEAKNESS IS THE TWIN ELECTRODES WHICH STUD THE SIDE OF MY METALLIC SKULL...
...WHILE YOU RUN THE PITIFUL GAMUT OF EMOTIONS... INCLUDING THAT OF TRUST!
AND NOW, DIE, FOOL... DIE AS YOU SHOULD HAVE DIED BEFORE!!
YET, INCREDIBLY...
YOU LIVE! BUT HOW...
WHEN I HURLED YOU STUNNED--BODILY--INTO THAT SEETHING ENERGY VAT!?
WHAT CANNOT BE TOUCHED ...CANNOT BE HARMED!
I REDUCED MY DENSITY TO NEARLY ZERO AT THE LAST POSSIBLE INSTANT!
18

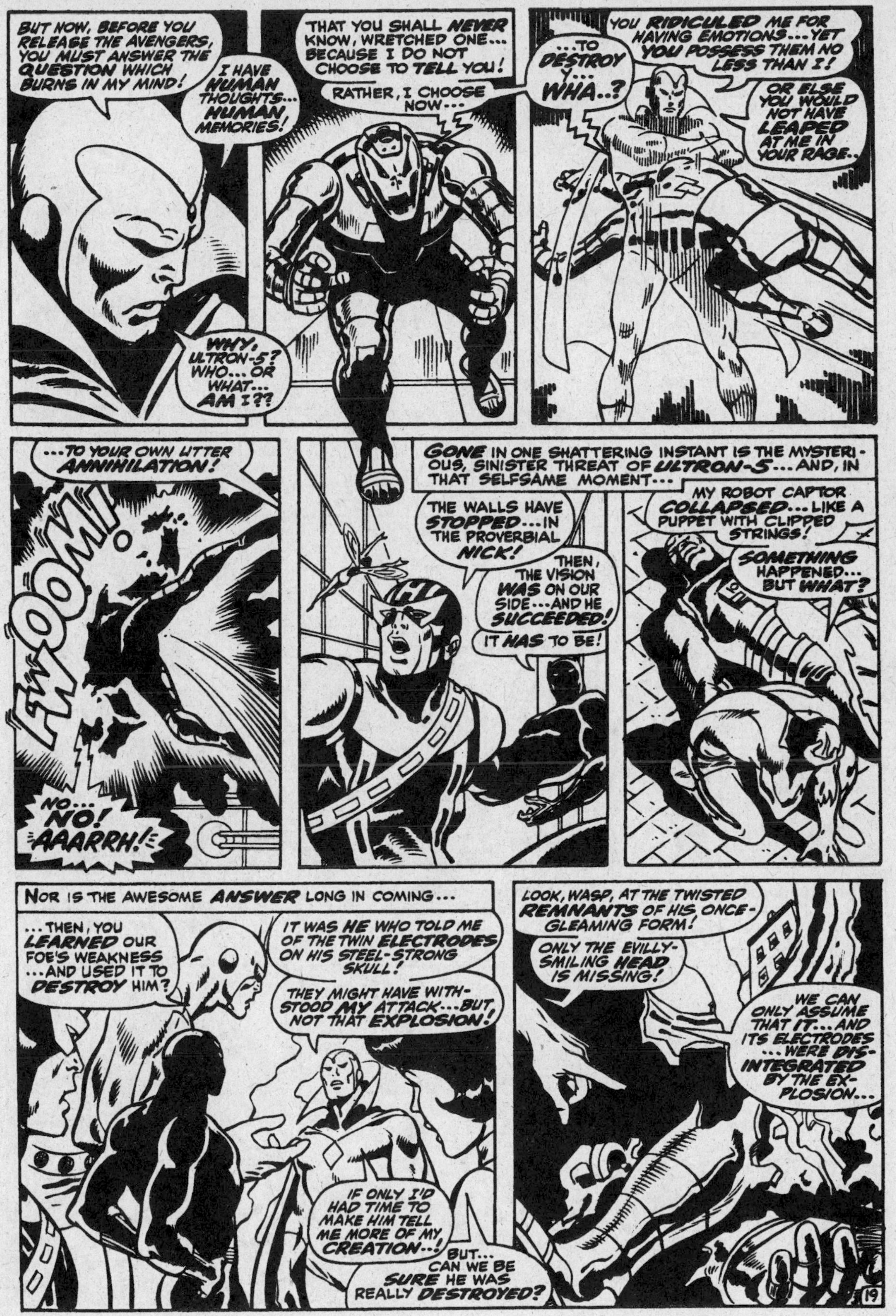

BUT NOW, BEFORE YOU RELEASE THE AVENGERS, YOU MUST ANSWER THE QUESTION WHICH BURNS IN MY MIND!
I HAVE HUMAN THOUGHTS... HUMAN MEMORIES!
WHY, ULTRON-5? WHO... OR WHAT... AM I??
THAT YOU SHALL NEVER KNOW, WRETCHED ONE... BECAUSE I DO NOT CHOOSE TO TELL YOU!
RATHER, I CHOOSE NOW...
...TO DESTROY Y... WHA..?
YOU RIDICULED ME FOR HAVING EMOTIONS... YET YOU POSSESS THEM NO LESS THAN I!
OR ELSE YOU WOULD NOT HAVE LEAPED AT ME IN YOUR RAGE..
...TO YOUR OWN UTTER ANNIHILATION!
FWOOM!
NO... NO! AAARRH!
GONE IN ONE SHATTERING INSTANT IS THE MYSTERIOUS, SINISTER THREAT OF ULTRON-5... AND, IN THAT SELFSAME MOMENT...
THE WALLS HAVE STOPPED... IN THE PROVERBIAL NICK!
THEN, THE VISION WAS ON OUR SIDE... AND HE SUCCEEDED!
IT HAS TO BE!
MY ROBOT CAPTOR COLLAPSED... LIKE A PUPPET WITH CLIPPED STRINGS!
SOMETHING HAPPENED... BUT WHAT?
NOR IS THE AWESOME ANSWER LONG IN COMING...
...THEN, YOU LEARNED OUR FOE'S WEAKNESS ...AND USED IT TO DESTROY HIM?
IT WAS HE WHO TOLD ME OF THE TWIN ELECTRODES ON HIS STEEL-STRONG SKULL!
THEY MIGHT HAVE WITHSTOOD MY ATTACK... BUT, NOT THAT EXPLOSION!
IF ONLY I'D HAD TIME TO MAKE HIM TELL ME MORE OF MY CREATION..!
BUT... CAN WE BE SURE HE WAS REALLY DESTROYED?
LOOK, WASP, AT THE TWISTED REMNANTS OF HIS ONCE-GLEAMING FORM!
ONLY THE EVILLY-SMILING HEAD IS MISSING!
WE CAN ONLY ASSUME THAT IT... AND ITS ELECTRODES ...WERE DISINTEGRATED BY THE EXPLOSION...

...FOR, IF THEY SOMEHOW REMAINED INTACT, WE WOULD ALL BE IN DEADLY DANGER....!

EPILOGUE:
I met a traveler from an antique land, Who said:

Two vast and trunkless legs of stone Stand in the desert.

Near them, on the sand, Half sunk, a shattered visage lies,

Whose frown, And wrinkled lip, and sneer of cold command,

Tell that its sculptor well those passions read Which yet survive, stamped on these lifeless things...

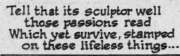

The hand that mocked them, and the heart that fed; And on the pedestal these words appear:

"My name is Ozymandias, King of Kings: Look on my works, ye Mighty, and despair!"

Nothing beside remains. Round the decay Of that colossal wreck, Boundless and bare

The lone and level sands stretch far away.

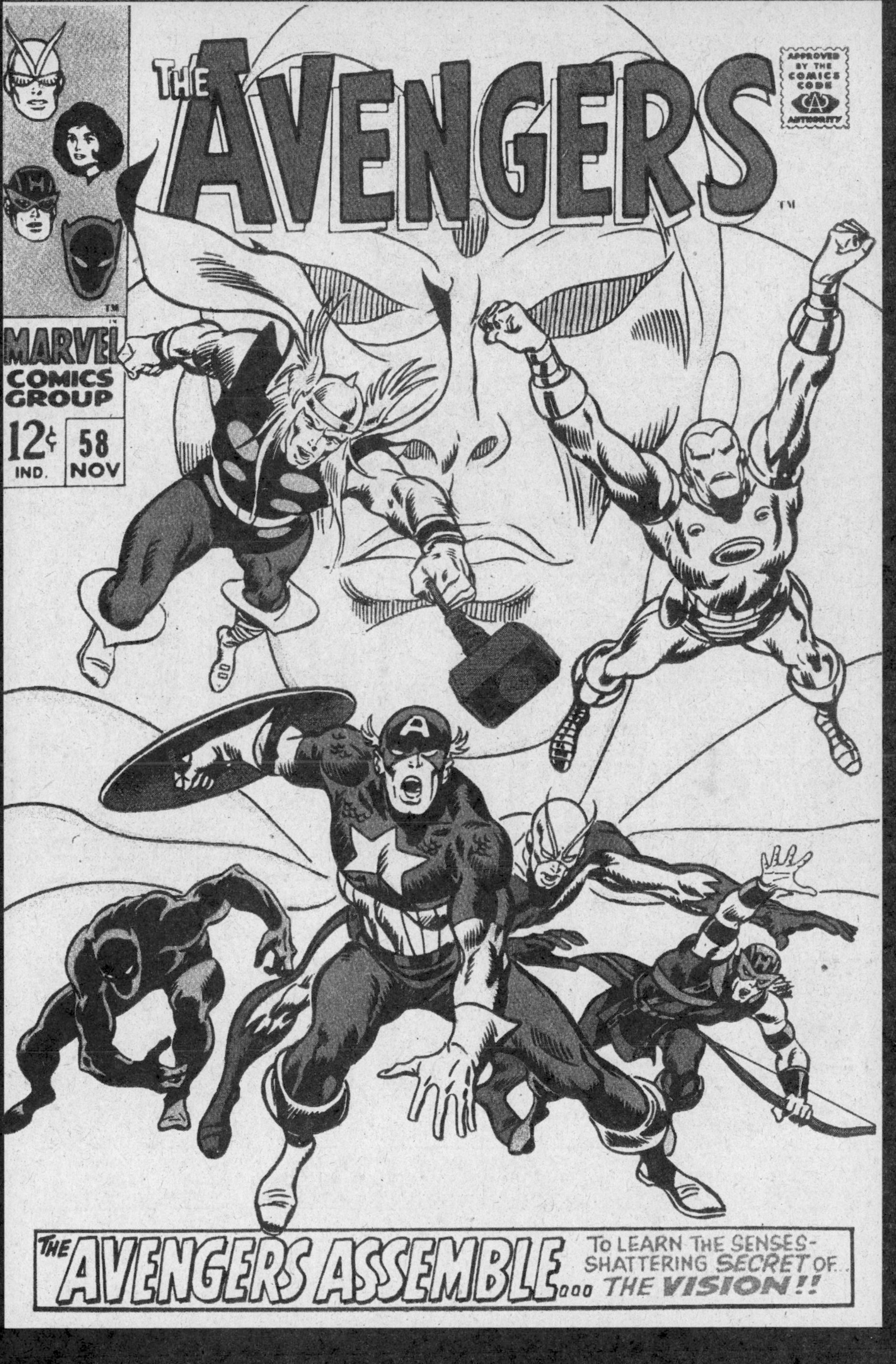
THE AVENGERS
APPROVED BY THE COMICS CODE AUTHORITY
MARVEL COMICS GROUP
12¢ IND.
58 NOV
THE AVENGERS ASSEMBLE... TO LEARN THE SENSES-SHATTERING SECRET OF... THE VISION!!

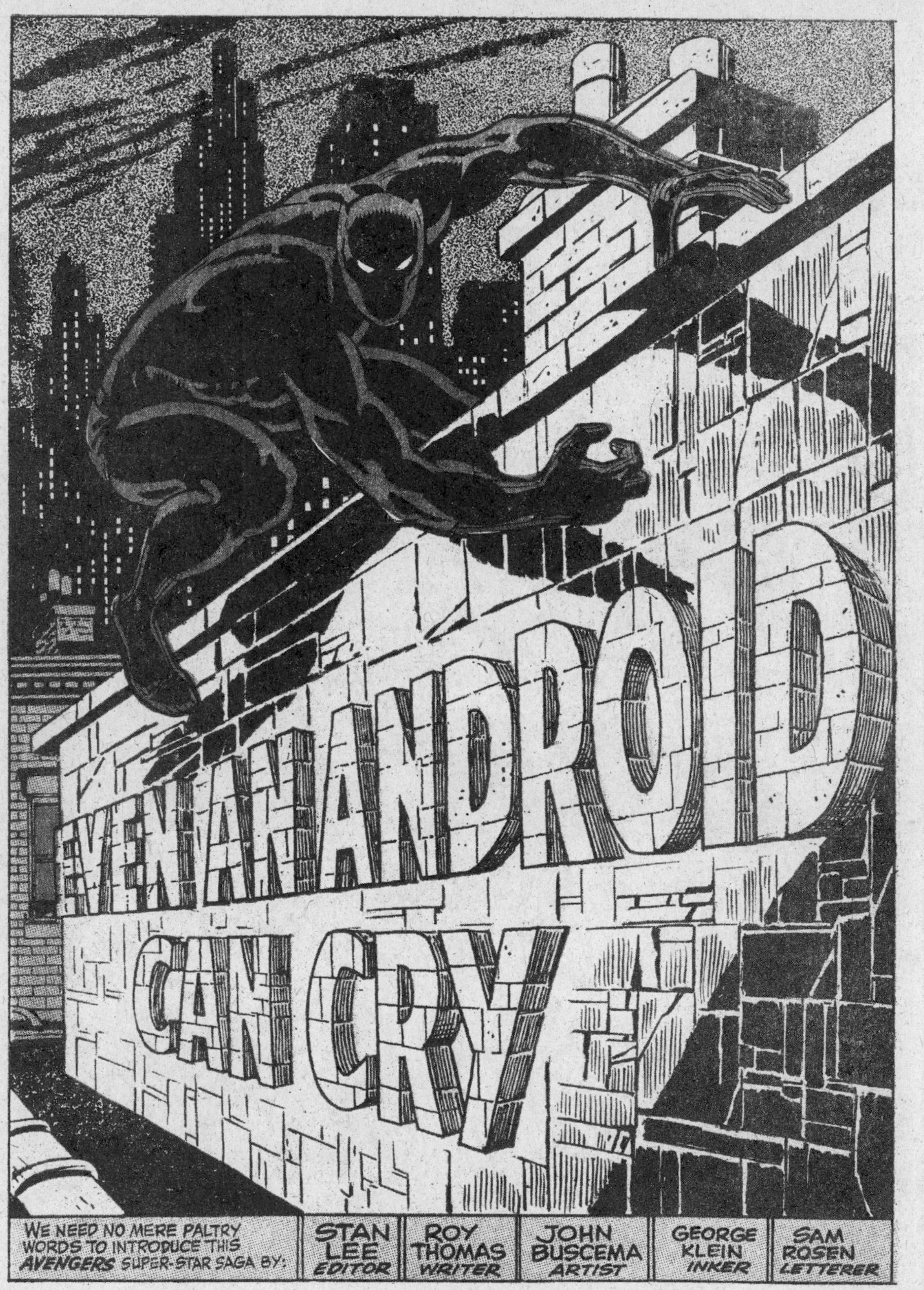
EVEN AN ANDROID CAN CRY
WE NEED NO MERE PALTRY WORDS TO INTRODUCE THIS *AVENGERS* SUPER-STAR SAGA BY:
STAN LEE *EDITOR*
ROY THOMAS *WRITER*
JOHN BUSCEMA *ARTIST*
GEORGE KLEIN *INKER*
SAM ROSEN *LETTERER*

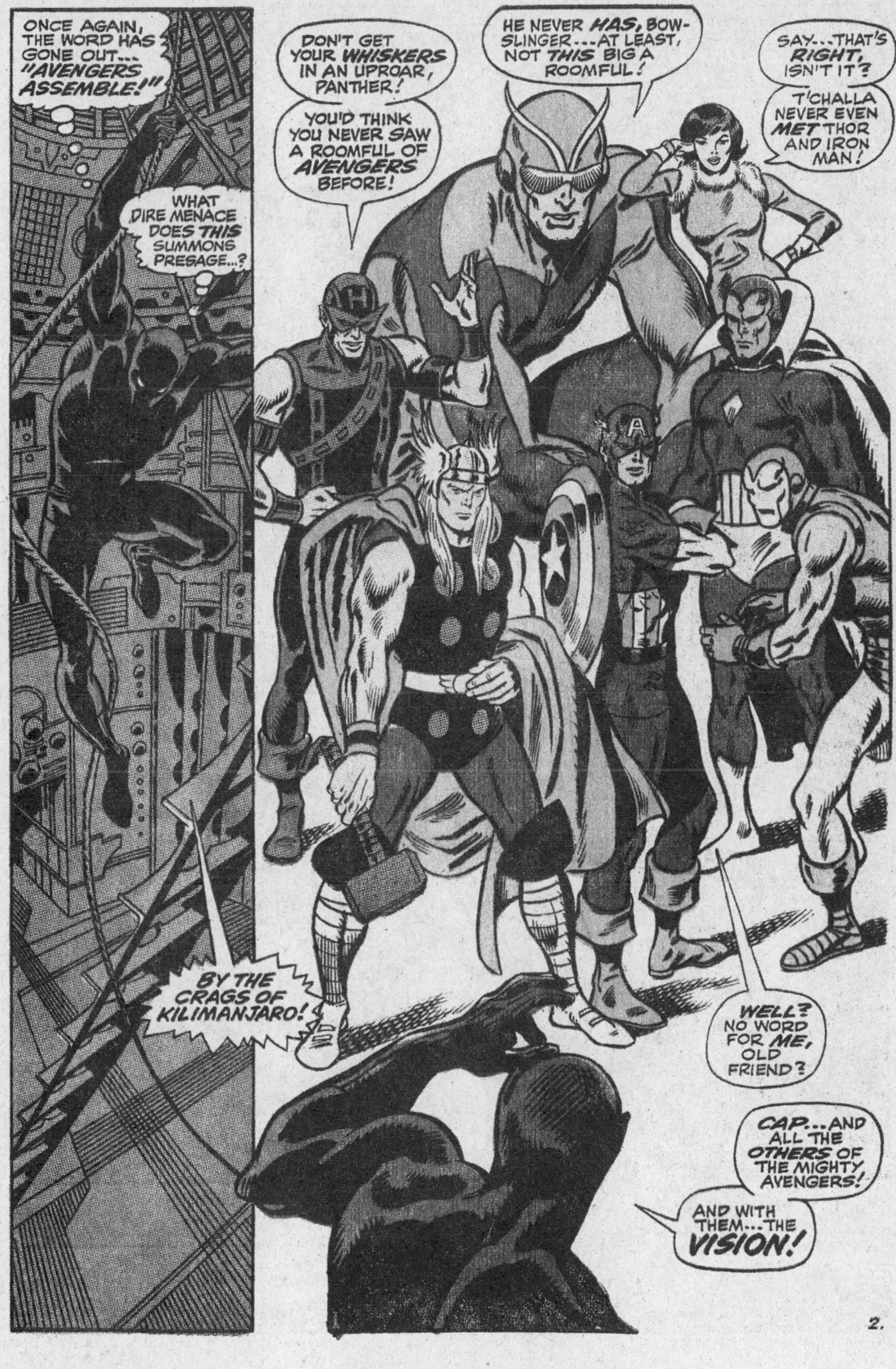
ONCE AGAIN, THE WORD HAS GONE OUT... "AVENGERS ASSEMBLE!"
WHAT DIRE MENACE DOES THIS SUMMONS PRESAGE...?
BY THE CRAGS OF KILIMANJARO!
DON'T GET YOUR WHISKERS IN AN UPROAR, PANTHER!
YOU'D THINK YOU NEVER SAW A ROOMFUL OF AVENGERS BEFORE!
HE NEVER HAS, BOW-SLINGER...AT LEAST, NOT THIS BIG A ROOMFUL!
SAY...THAT'S RIGHT, ISN'T IT?
T'CHALLA NEVER EVEN MET THOR AND IRON MAN!
WELL? NO WORD FOR ME, OLD FRIEND?
CAP...AND ALL THE OTHERS OF THE MIGHTY AVENGERS!
AND WITH THEM...THE VISION!

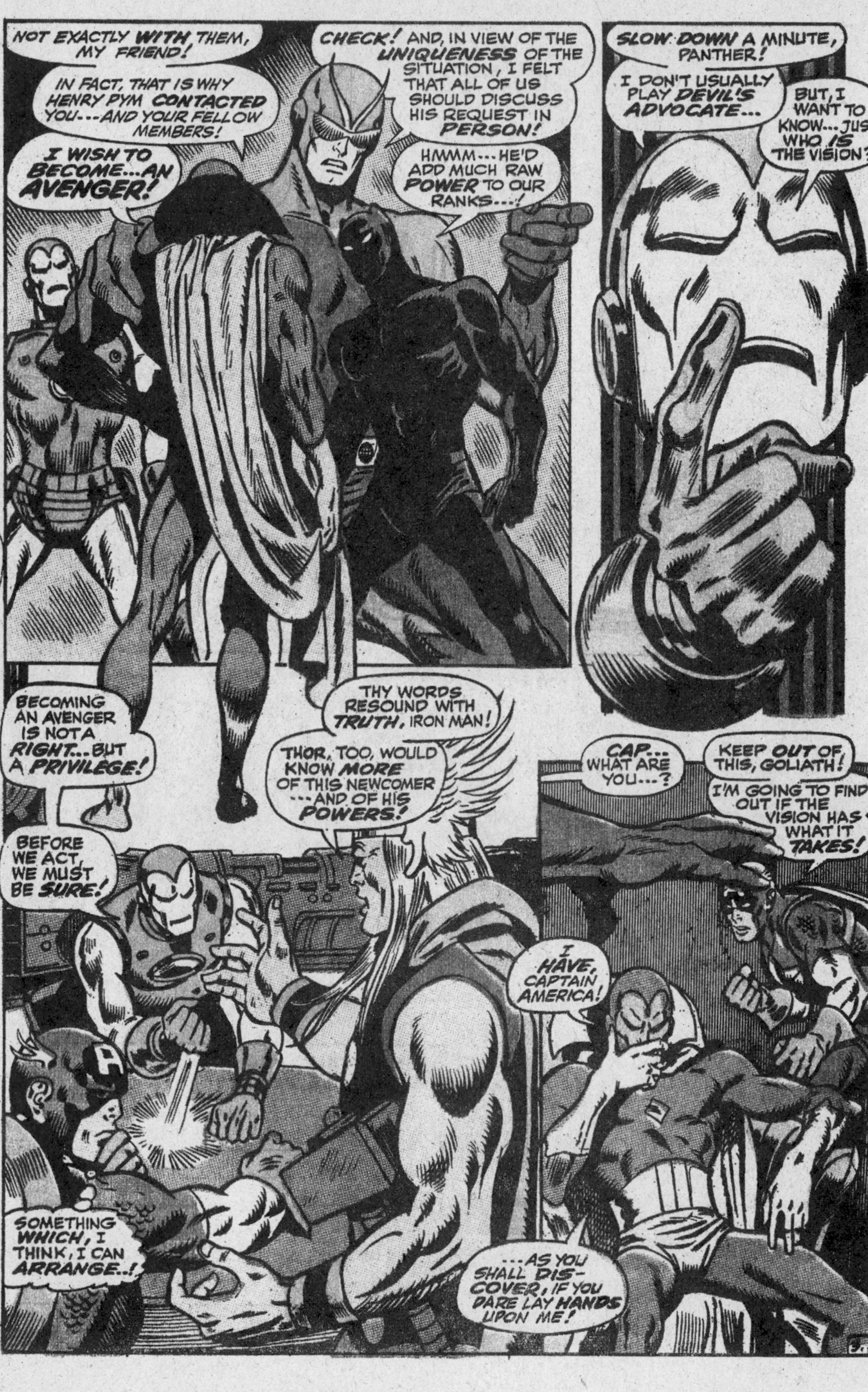
NOT EXACTLY WITH THEM, MY FRIEND!
IN FACT, THAT IS WHY HENRY PYM CONTACTED YOU---AND YOUR FELLOW MEMBERS!
I WISH TO BECOME...AN AVENGER!
CHECK! AND, IN VIEW OF THE UNIQUENESS OF THE SITUATION, I FELT THAT ALL OF US SHOULD DISCUSS HIS REQUEST IN PERSON!
HMMM---HE'D ADD MUCH RAW POWER TO OUR RANKS---!
SLOW DOWN A MINUTE, PANTHER!
I DON'T USUALLY PLAY DEVIL'S ADVOCATE...
BUT, I WANT TO KNOW...JUST WHO IS THE VISION?
BECOMING AN AVENGER IS NOT A RIGHT...BUT A PRIVILEGE!
BEFORE WE ACT, WE MUST BE SURE!
THY WORDS RESOUND WITH TRUTH, IRON MAN!
THOR, TOO, WOULD KNOW MORE OF THIS NEWCOMER ---AND OF HIS POWERS!
SOMETHING WHICH, I THINK, I CAN ARRANGE..!
CAP... WHAT ARE YOU---?
KEEP OUT OF THIS, GOLIATH!
I'M GOING TO FIND OUT IF THE VISION HAS WHAT IT TAKES!
I HAVE, CAPTAIN AMERICA!
...AS YOU SHALL DIS-COVER, IF YOU DARE LAY HANDS UPON ME!
5

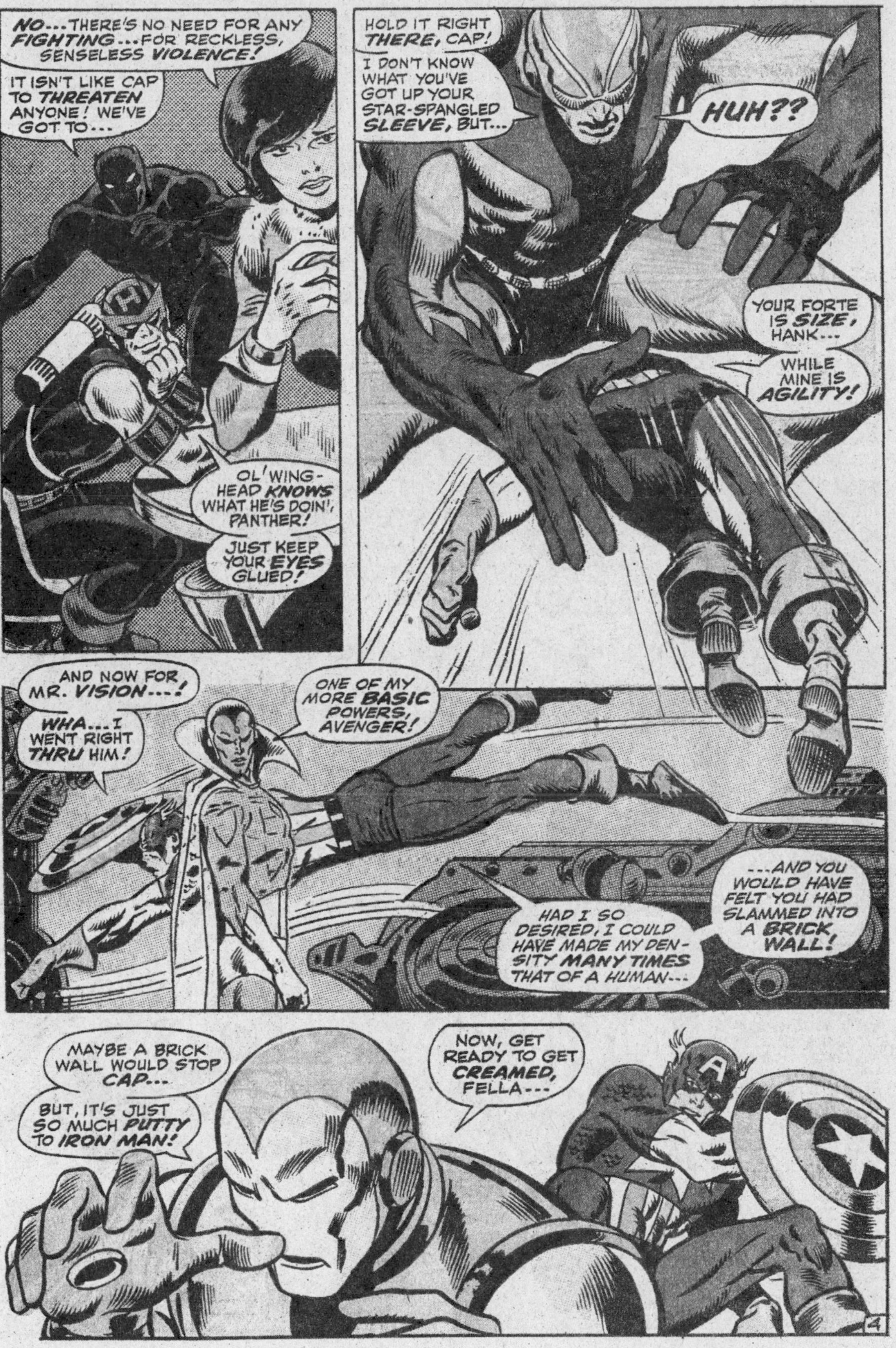
NO...THERE'S NO NEED FOR ANY FIGHTING...FOR RECKLESS, SENSELESS VIOLENCE!
IT ISN'T LIKE CAP TO THREATEN ANYONE! WE'VE GOT TO...
OL' WING-HEAD KNOWS WHAT HE'S DOIN', PANTHER!
JUST KEEP YOUR EYES GLUED!
HOLD IT RIGHT THERE, CAP!
I DON'T KNOW WHAT YOU'VE GOT UP YOUR STAR-SPANGLED SLEEVE, BUT...
HUH??
YOUR FORTE IS SIZE, HANK...
WHILE MINE IS AGILITY!
AND NOW FOR MR. VISION...!
WHA...I WENT RIGHT THRU HIM!
ONE OF MY MORE BASIC POWERS, AVENGER!
HAD I SO DESIRED, I COULD HAVE MADE MY DENSITY MANY TIMES THAT OF A HUMAN...
...AND YOU WOULD HAVE FELT YOU HAD SLAMMED INTO A BRICK WALL!
MAYBE A BRICK WALL WOULD STOP CAP...
BUT, IT'S JUST SO MUCH PUTTY TO IRON MAN!
NOW, GET READY TO GET CREAMED, FELLA...
4

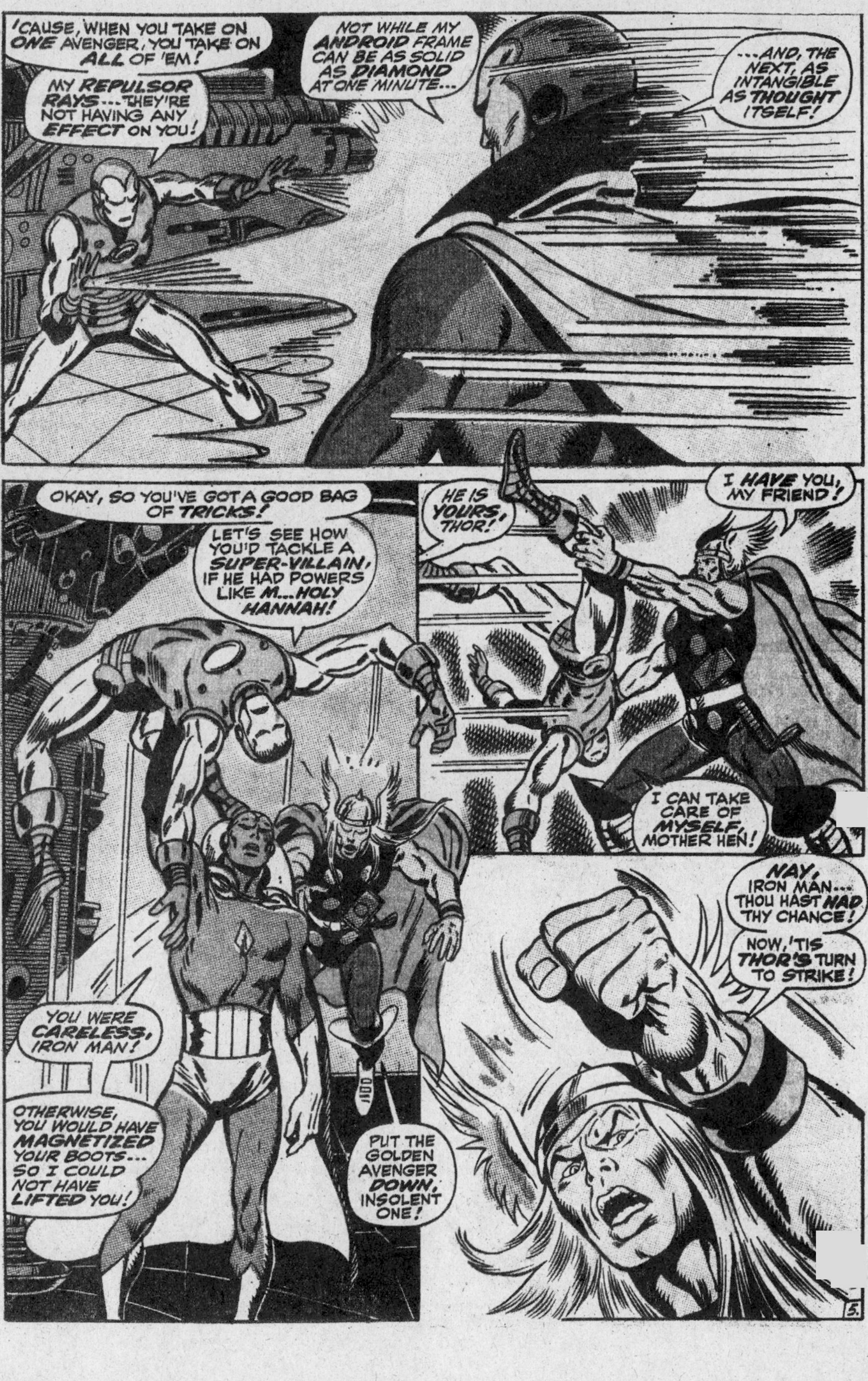
'CAUSE, WHEN YOU TAKE ON ONE AVENGER, YOU TAKE ON ALL OF 'EM!
MY REPULSOR RAYS... THEY'RE NOT HAVING ANY EFFECT ON YOU!
NOT WHILE MY ANDROID FRAME CAN BE AS SOLID AS DIAMOND AT ONE MINUTE...
...AND, THE NEXT, AS INTANGIBLE AS THOUGHT ITSELF!
OKAY, SO YOU'VE GOT A GOOD BAG OF TRICKS!
LET'S SEE HOW YOU'D TACKLE A SUPER-VILLAIN, IF HE HAD POWERS LIKE M... HOLY HANNAH!
YOU WERE CARELESS, IRON MAN!
OTHERWISE, YOU WOULD HAVE MAGNETIZED YOUR BOOTS... SO I COULD NOT HAVE LIFTED YOU!
PUT THE GOLDEN AVENGER DOWN, INSOLENT ONE!
HE IS YOURS, THOR!
I HAVE YOU, MY FRIEND!
I CAN TAKE CARE OF MYSELF, MOTHER HEN!
NAY, IRON MAN... THOU HAST HAD THY CHANCE!
NOW, 'TIS THOR'S TURN TO STRIKE!
5.

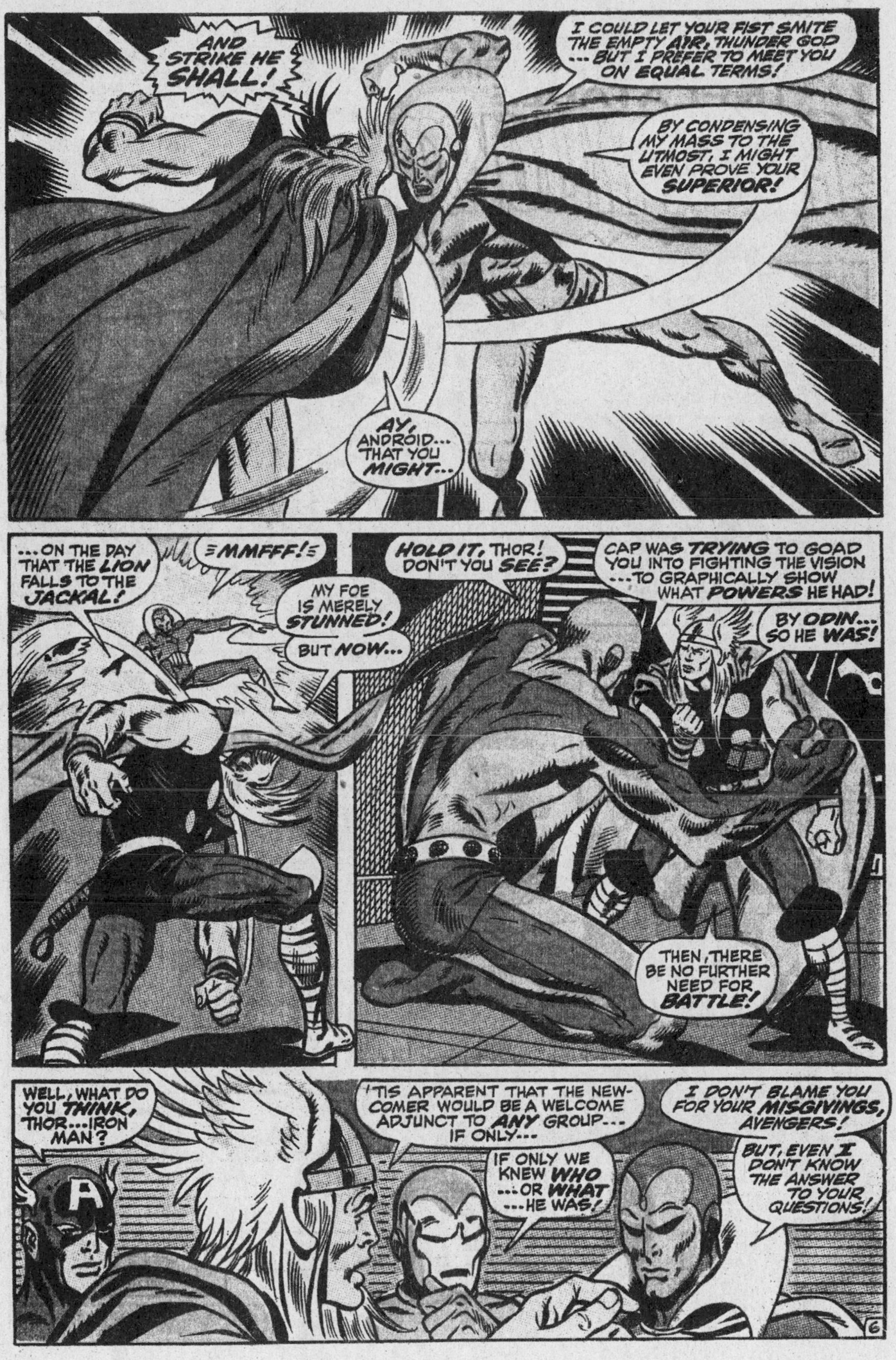

AND STRIKE HE SHALL!
I COULD LET YOUR FIST SMITE THE EMPTY AIR, THUNDER GOD --- BUT I PREFER TO MEET YOU ON EQUAL TERMS!
BY CONDENSING MY MASS TO THE UTMOST, I MIGHT EVEN PROVE YOUR SUPERIOR!
AY, ANDROID... THAT YOU MIGHT...
...ON THE DAY THAT THE LION FALLS TO THE JACKAL!
MMFFF!
MY FOE IS MERELY STUNNED!
BUT NOW...
HOLD IT, THOR! DON'T YOU SEE?
CAP WAS TRYING TO GOAD YOU INTO FIGHTING THE VISION ---TO GRAPHICALLY SHOW WHAT POWERS HE HAD!
BY ODIN... SO HE WAS!
THEN, THERE BE NO FURTHER NEED FOR BATTLE!
WELL, WHAT DO YOU THINK, THOR....IRON MAN?
'TIS APPARENT THAT THE NEW-COMER WOULD BE A WELCOME ADJUNCT TO ANY GROUP... IF ONLY...
IF ONLY WE KNEW WHO ...OR WHAT ---HE WAS!
I DON'T BLAME YOU FOR YOUR MISGIVINGS, AVENGERS!
BUT, EVEN I DON'T KNOW THE ANSWER TO YOUR QUESTIONS!
6

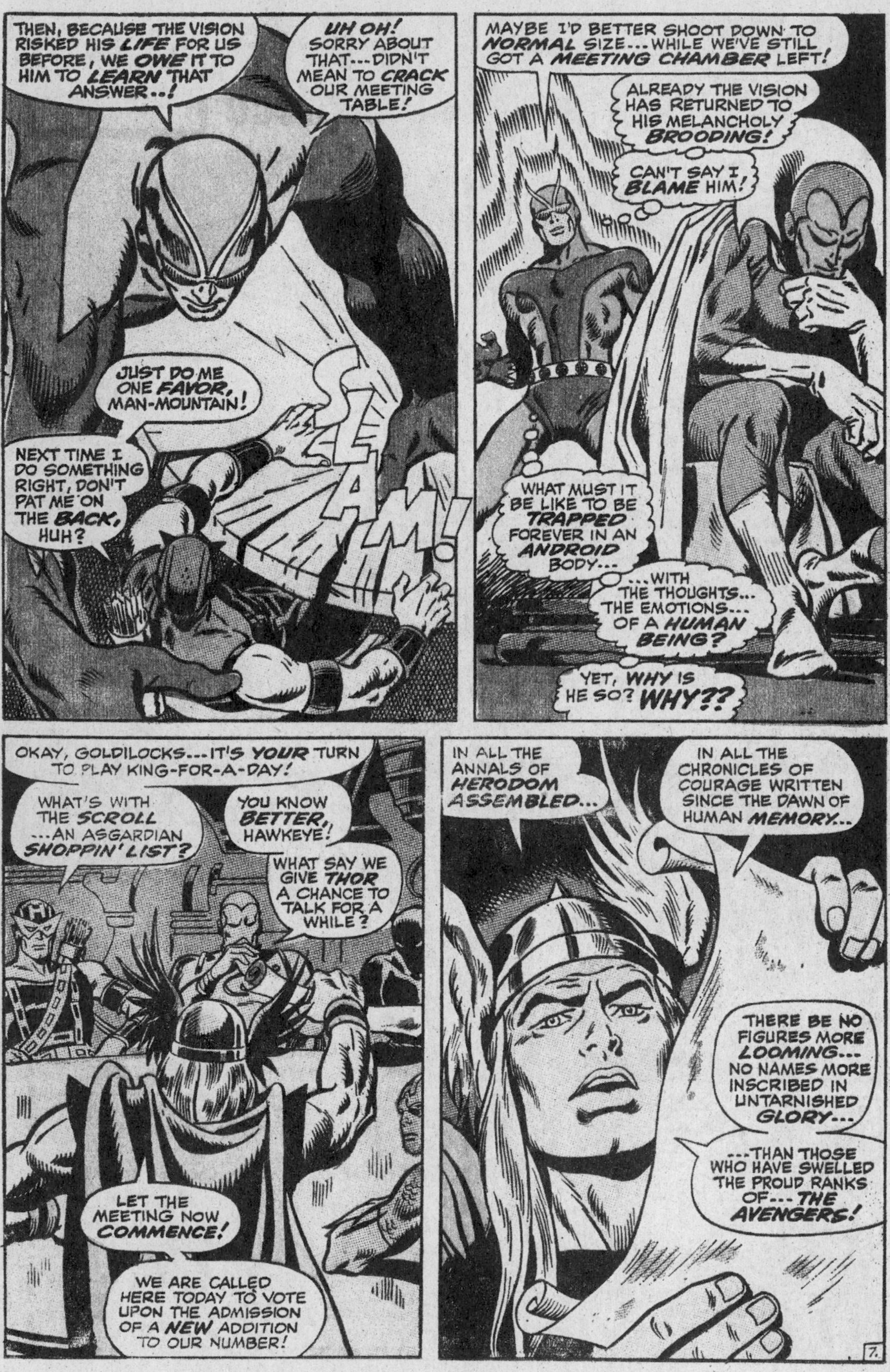
THEN, BECAUSE THE VISION RISKED HIS LIFE FOR US BEFORE, WE OWE IT TO HIM TO LEARN THAT ANSWER..!
UH OH! SORRY ABOUT THAT---DIDN'T MEAN TO CRACK OUR MEETING TABLE!
JUST DO ME ONE FAVOR, MAN-MOUNTAIN!
NEXT TIME I DO SOMETHING RIGHT, DON'T PAT ME ON THE BACK, HUH?
SLAM!
MAYBE I'D BETTER SHOOT DOWN TO NORMAL SIZE... WHILE WE'VE STILL GOT A MEETING CHAMBER LEFT!
ALREADY THE VISION HAS RETURNED TO HIS MELANCHOLY BROODING!
CAN'T SAY I BLAME HIM!
WHAT MUST IT BE LIKE TO BE TRAPPED FOREVER IN AN ANDROID BODY...
...WITH THE THOUGHTS... THE EMOTIONS... OF A HUMAN BEING?
YET, WHY IS HE SO? WHY??
OKAY, GOLDILOCKS---IT'S YOUR TURN TO PLAY KING-FOR-A-DAY!
WHAT'S WITH THE SCROLL ...AN ASGARDIAN SHOPPIN' LIST?
YOU KNOW BETTER, HAWKEYE!
WHAT SAY WE GIVE THOR A CHANCE TO TALK FOR A WHILE?
LET THE MEETING NOW COMMENCE!
WE ARE CALLED HERE TODAY TO VOTE UPON THE ADMISSION OF A NEW ADDITION TO OUR NUMBER!
IN ALL THE ANNALS OF HERODOM ASSEMBLED...
IN ALL THE CHRONICLES OF COURAGE WRITTEN SINCE THE DAWN OF HUMAN MEMORY...
THERE BE NO FIGURES MORE LOOMING... NO NAMES MORE INSCRIBED IN UNTARNISHED GLORY...
---THAN THOSE WHO HAVE SWELLED THE PROUD RANKS OF--- THE AVENGERS!

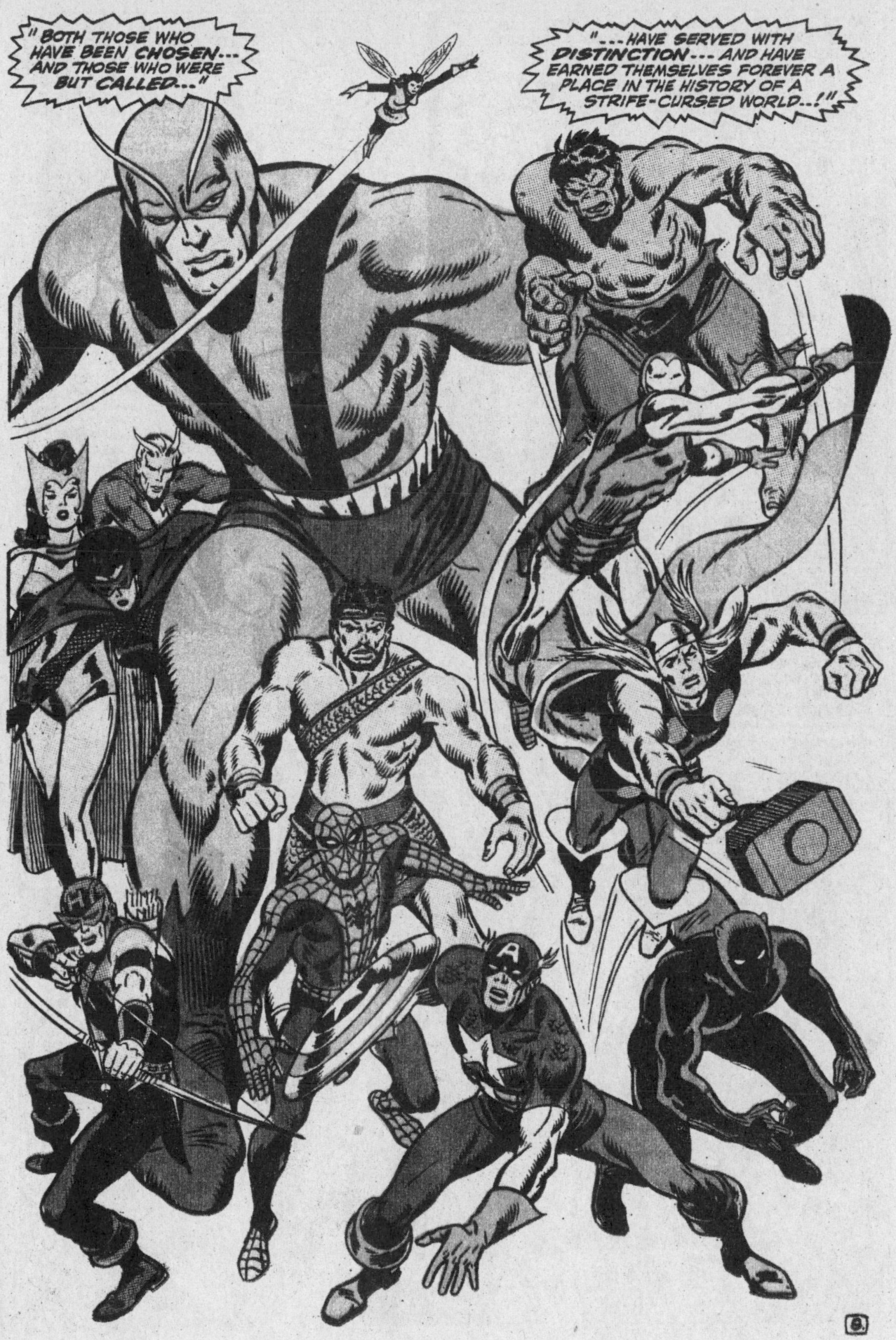
"BOTH THOSE WHO HAVE BEEN CHOSEN... AND THOSE WHO WERE BUT CALLED..."
"...HAVE SERVED WITH DISTINCTION... AND HAVE EARNED THEMSELVES FOREVER A PLACE IN THE HISTORY OF A STRIFE-CURSED WORLD...!"
8

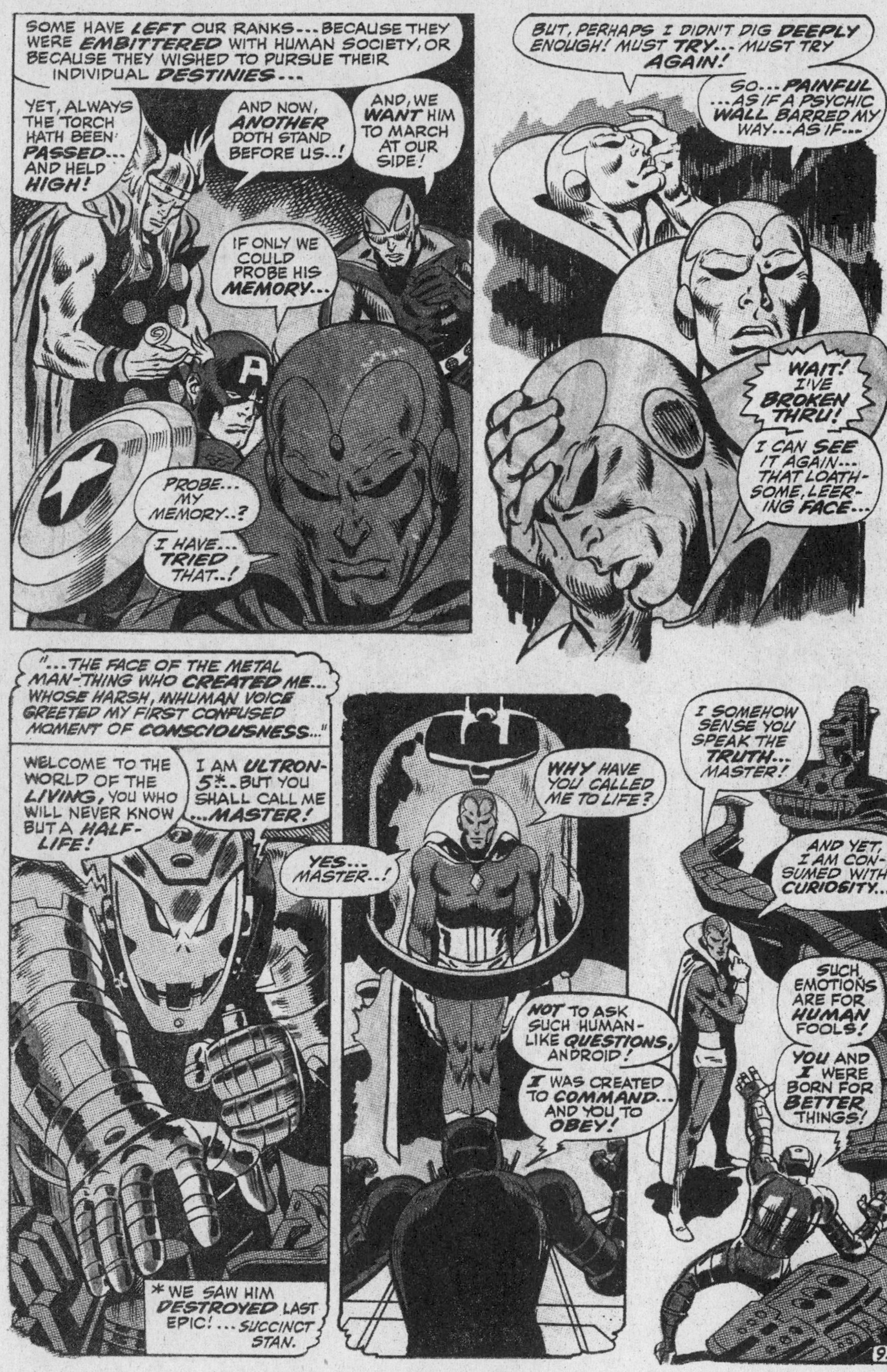

SOME HAVE LEFT OUR RANKS... BECAUSE THEY WERE EMBITTERED WITH HUMAN SOCIETY, OR BECAUSE THEY WISHED TO PURSUE THEIR INDIVIDUAL DESTINIES...
YET, ALWAYS THE TORCH HATH BEEN PASSED... AND HELD HIGH!
AND NOW, ANOTHER DOTH STAND BEFORE US...!
AND, WE WANT HIM TO MARCH AT OUR SIDE!
IF ONLY WE COULD PROBE HIS MEMORY...
PROBE... MY MEMORY..?
I HAVE... TRIED THAT..!
BUT, PERHAPS I DIDN'T DIG DEEPLY ENOUGH! MUST TRY... MUST TRY AGAIN!
SO... PAINFUL ...AS IF A PSYCHIC WALL BARRED MY WAY...AS IF...
WAIT! I'VE BROKEN THRU!
I CAN SEE IT AGAIN... THAT LOATHSOME, LEERING FACE...
"...THE FACE OF THE METAL MAN-THING WHO CREATED ME... WHOSE HARSH, INHUMAN VOICE GREETED MY FIRST CONFUSED MOMENT OF CONSCIOUSNESS..."
WELCOME TO THE WORLD OF THE LIVING, YOU WHO WILL NEVER KNOW BUT A HALF-LIFE!
I AM ULTRON-5*... BUT YOU SHALL CALL ME ...MASTER!
*WE SAW HIM DESTROYED LAST EPIC! ... SUCCINCT STAN.
YES... MASTER...!
WHY HAVE YOU CALLED ME TO LIFE?
NOT TO ASK SUCH HUMAN-LIKE QUESTIONS, ANDROID!
I WAS CREATED TO COMMAND... AND YOU TO OBEY!
I SOMEHOW SENSE YOU SPEAK THE TRUTH... MASTER!
AND YET, I AM CONSUMED WITH CURIOSITY...
SUCH EMOTIONS ARE FOR HUMAN FOOLS!
YOU AND I WERE BORN FOR BETTER THINGS!
9.

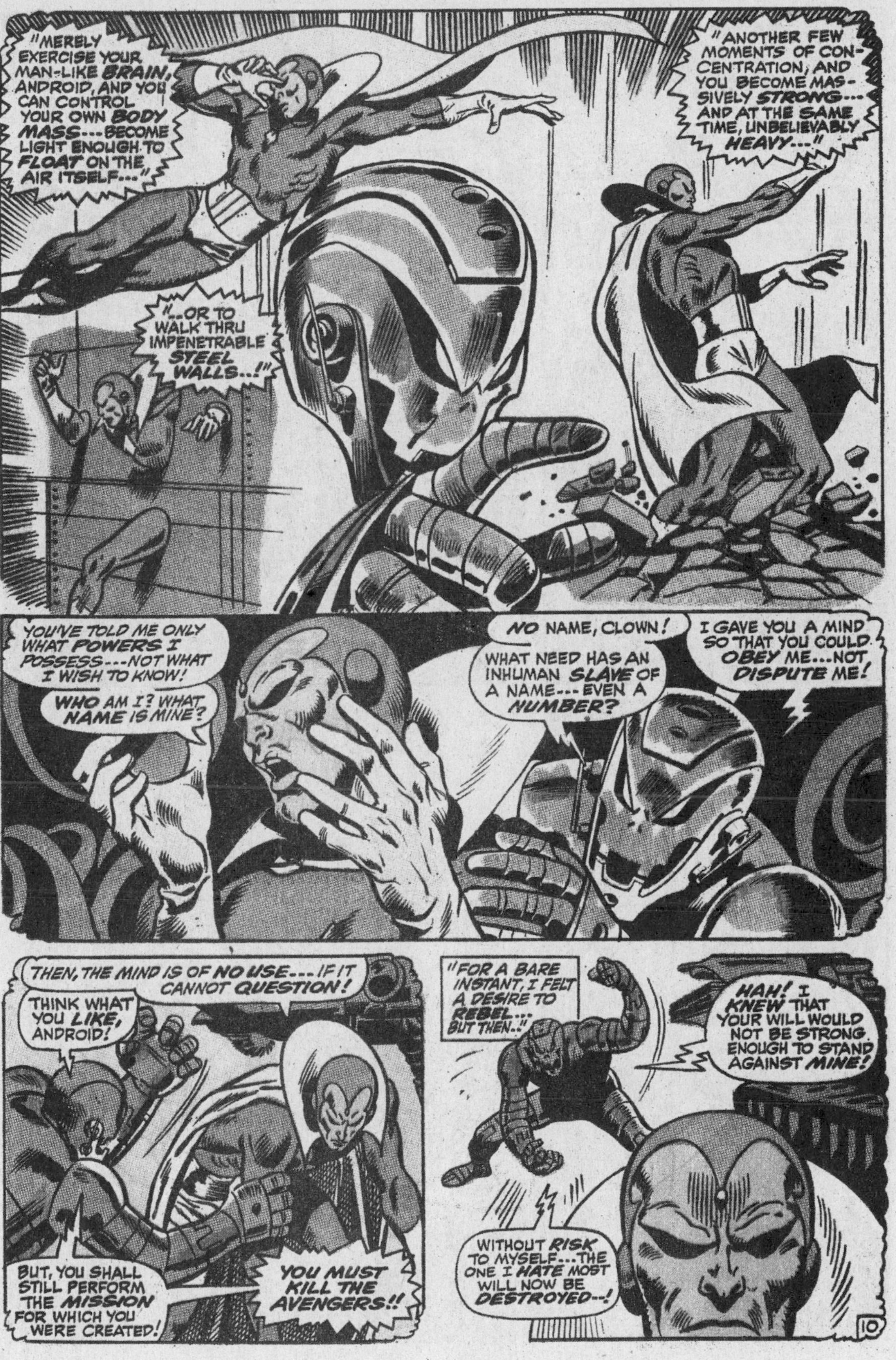
"MERELY EXERCISE YOUR MAN-LIKE BRAIN, ANDROID, AND YOU CAN CONTROL YOUR OWN BODY MASS---BECOME LIGHT ENOUGH TO FLOAT ON THE AIR ITSELF..."
"..OR TO WALK THRU IMPENETRABLE STEEL WALLS..!"
"ANOTHER FEW MOMENTS OF CONCENTRATION, AND YOU BECOME MASSIVELY STRONG... AND AT THE SAME TIME, UNBELIEVABLY HEAVY..."
YOU'VE TOLD ME ONLY WHAT POWERS I POSSESS---NOT WHAT I WISH TO KNOW!
WHO AM I? WHAT NAME IS MINE?
NO NAME, CLOWN!
WHAT NEED HAS AN INHUMAN SLAVE OF A NAME--- EVEN A NUMBER?
I GAVE YOU A MIND SO THAT YOU COULD OBEY ME... NOT DISPUTE ME!
THEN, THE MIND IS OF NO USE--- IF IT CANNOT QUESTION!
THINK WHAT YOU LIKE, ANDROID!
BUT, YOU SHALL STILL PERFORM THE MISSION FOR WHICH YOU WERE CREATED!
YOU MUST KILL THE AVENGERS!!
"FOR A BARE INSTANT, I FELT A DESIRE TO REBEL... BUT THEN.."
HAH! I KNEW THAT YOUR WILL WOULD NOT BE STRONG ENOUGH TO STAND AGAINST MINE!
WITHOUT RISK TO MYSELF---THE ONE I HATE MOST WILL NOW BE DESTROYED--!
10

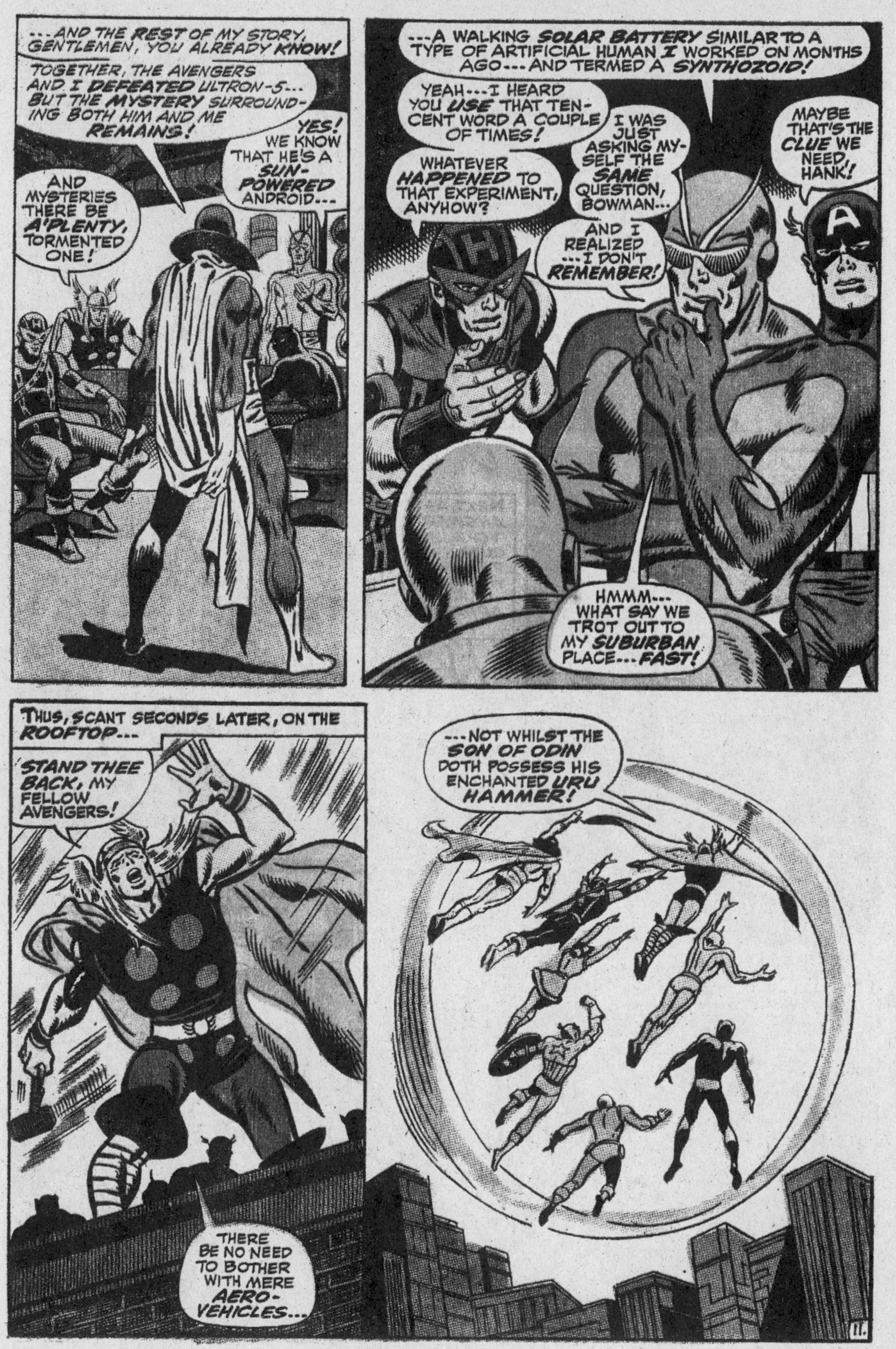
...AND THE REST OF MY STORY, GENTLEMEN, YOU ALREADY KNOW!
TOGETHER, THE AVENGERS AND I DEFEATED ULTRON-5... BUT THE MYSTERY SURROUNDING BOTH HIM AND ME REMAINS!
YES! WE KNOW THAT HE'S A SUN-POWERED ANDROID---
AND MYSTERIES THERE BE A'PLENTY, TORMENTED ONE!
---A WALKING SOLAR BATTERY SIMILAR TO A TYPE OF ARTIFICIAL HUMAN I WORKED ON MONTHS AGO---AND TERMED A SYNTHOZOID!
YEAH---I HEARD YOU USE THAT TEN-CENT WORD A COUPLE OF TIMES!
WHATEVER HAPPENED TO THAT EXPERIMENT, ANYHOW?
I WAS JUST ASKING MYSELF THE SAME QUESTION, BOWMAN...
AND I REALIZED ...I DON'T REMEMBER!
MAYBE THAT'S THE CLUE WE NEED, HANK!
HMMM... WHAT SAY WE TROT OUT TO MY SUBURBAN PLACE---FAST!
THUS, SCANT SECONDS LATER, ON THE ROOFTOP...
STAND THEE BACK, MY FELLOW AVENGERS!
THERE BE NO NEED TO BOTHER WITH MERE AERO-VEHICLES...
---NOT WHILST THE SON OF ODIN DOTH POSSESS HIS ENCHANTED URU HAMMER!
11.

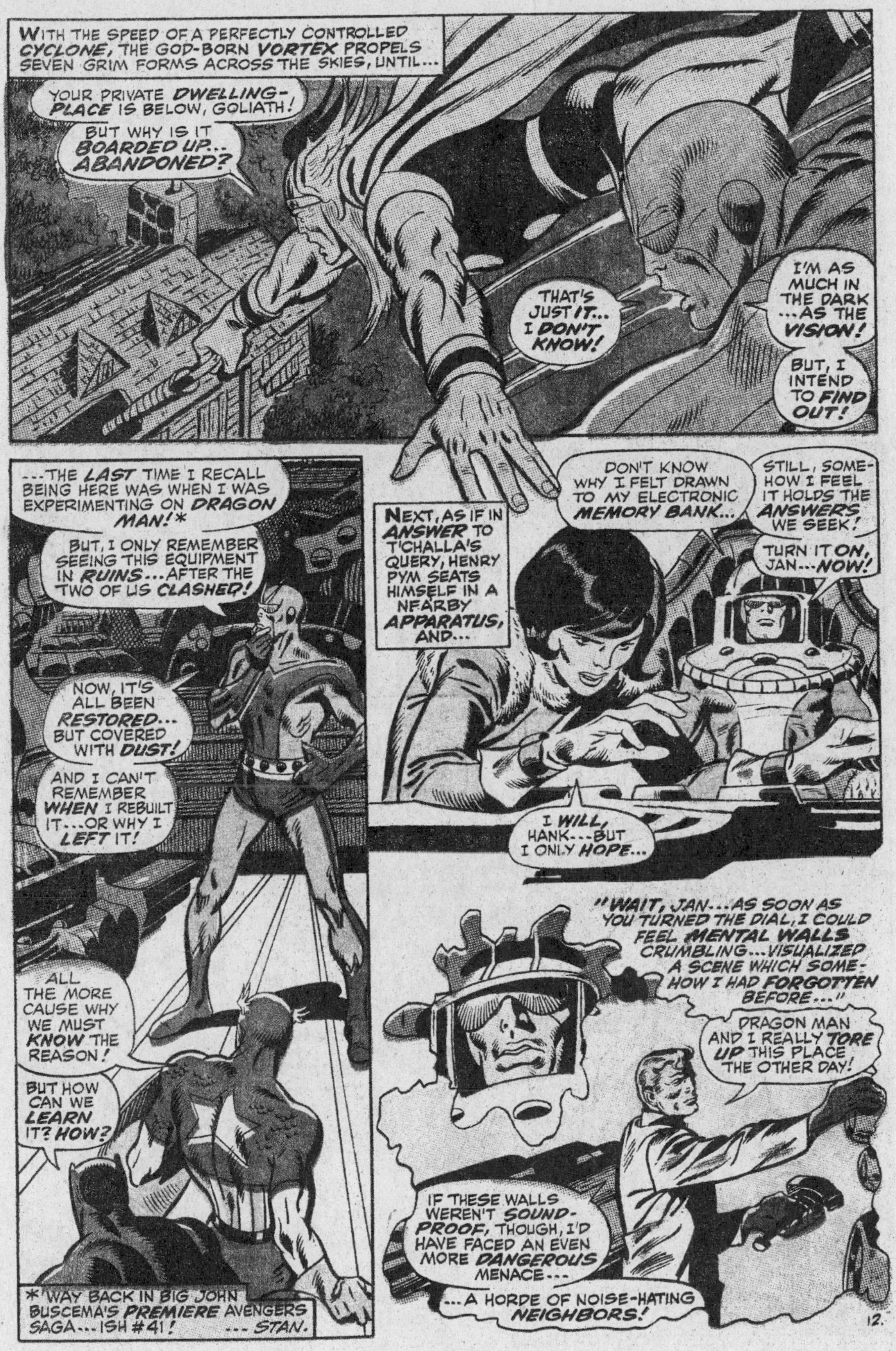
WITH THE SPEED OF A PERFECTLY CONTROLLED CYCLONE, THE GOD-BORN VORTEX PROPELS SEVEN GRIM FORMS ACROSS THE SKIES, UNTIL...
YOUR PRIVATE DWELLING-PLACE IS BELOW, GOLIATH!
BUT WHY IS IT BOARDED UP... ABANDONED?
THAT'S JUST IT... I DON'T KNOW!
I'M AS MUCH IN THE DARK ...AS THE VISION!
BUT, I INTEND TO FIND OUT!
---THE LAST TIME I RECALL BEING HERE WAS WHEN I WAS EXPERIMENTING ON DRAGON MAN!*
BUT, I ONLY REMEMBER SEEING THIS EQUIPMENT IN RUINS...AFTER THE TWO OF US CLASHED!
NOW, IT'S ALL BEEN RESTORED... BUT COVERED WITH DUST!
AND I CAN'T REMEMBER WHEN I REBUILT IT...OR WHY I LEFT IT!
ALL THE MORE CAUSE WHY WE MUST KNOW THE REASON!
BUT HOW CAN WE LEARN IT? HOW?
*WAY BACK IN BIG JOHN BUSCEMA'S PREMIERE AVENGERS SAGA...ISH #41! ---STAN.
NEXT, AS IF IN ANSWER TO T'CHALLA'S QUERY, HENRY PYM SEATS HIMSELF IN A NEARBY APPARATUS, AND...
DON'T KNOW WHY I FELT DRAWN TO MY ELECTRONIC MEMORY BANK...
STILL, SOMEHOW I FEEL IT HOLDS THE ANSWERS WE SEEK!
TURN IT ON, JAN---NOW!
I WILL, HANK---BUT I ONLY HOPE...
"WAIT, JAN...AS SOON AS YOU TURNED THE DIAL, I COULD FEEL MENTAL WALLS CRUMBLING...VISUALIZED A SCENE WHICH SOMEHOW I HAD FORGOTTEN BEFORE..."
DRAGON MAN AND I REALLY TORE UP THIS PLACE THE OTHER DAY!
IF THESE WALLS WEREN'T SOUND-PROOF, THOUGH, I'D HAVE FACED AN EVEN MORE DANGEROUS MENACE---
...A HORDE OF NOISE-HATING NEIGHBORS!

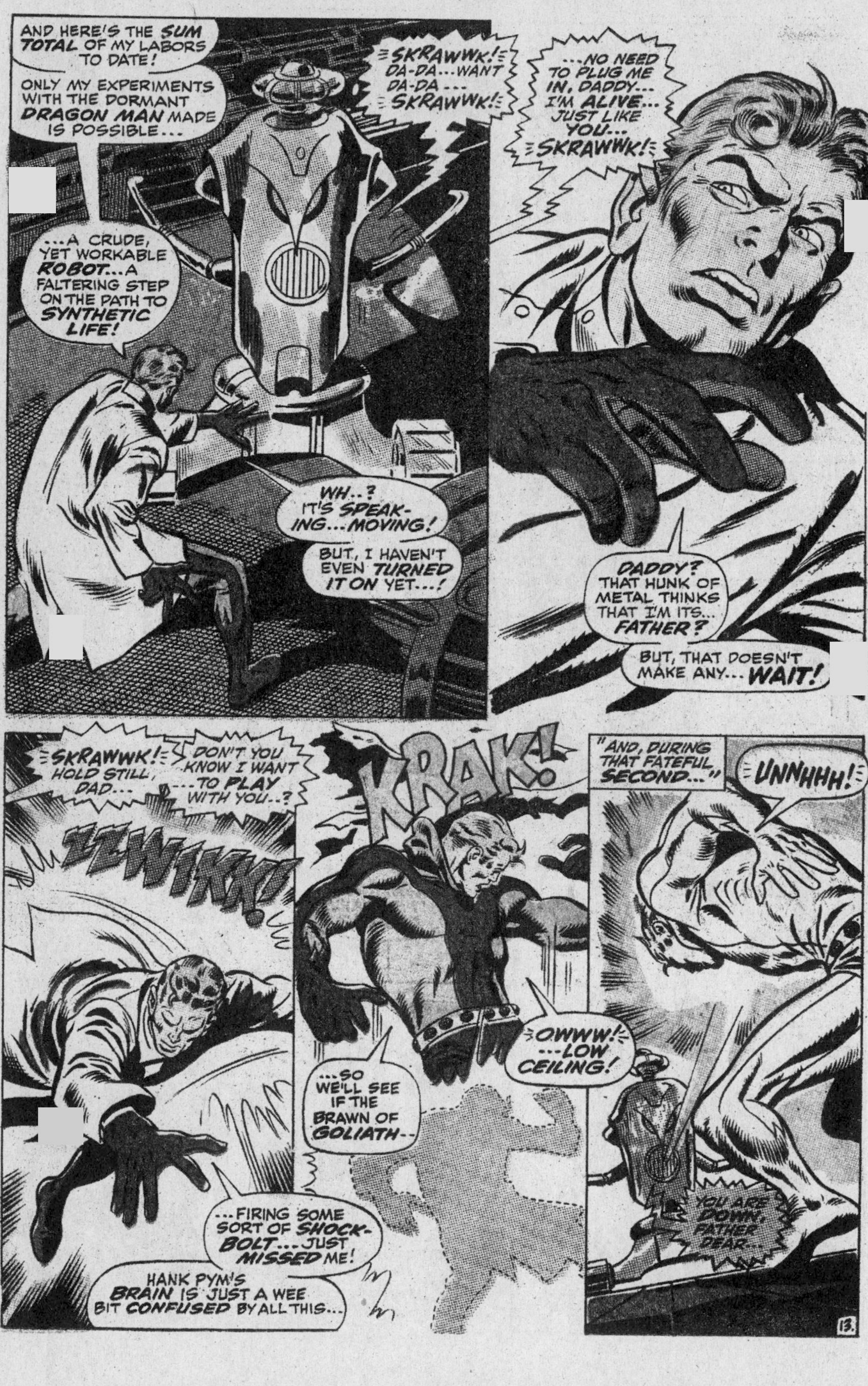
AND HERE'S THE SUM TOTAL OF MY LABORS TO DATE!
ONLY MY EXPERIMENTS WITH THE DORMANT DRAGON MAN MADE IS POSSIBLE...
...A CRUDE, YET WORKABLE ROBOT...A FALTERING STEP ON THE PATH TO SYNTHETIC LIFE!
SKRAWWK! DA-DA...WANT DA-DA... SKRAWWK!
WH..? IT'S SPEAKING...MOVING!
BUT, I HAVEN'T EVEN TURNED IT ON YET...!
...NO NEED TO PLUG ME IN, DADDY... I'M ALIVE... JUST LIKE YOU... SKRAWWK!
DADDY? THAT HUNK OF METAL THINKS THAT I'M ITS... FATHER?
BUT, THAT DOESN'T MAKE ANY... WAIT!
SKRAWWK! HOLD STILL, DAD...
DON'T YOU KNOW I WANT TO PLAY WITH YOU..?
ZZWIKK!
...FIRING SOME SORT OF SHOCK-BOLT... JUST MISSED ME!
HANK PYM'S BRAIN IS JUST A WEE BIT CONFUSED BY ALL THIS...
KRAK!
...SO WE'LL SEE IF THE BRAWN OF GOLIATH--
OWWW! ...LOW CEILING!
"AND, DURING THAT FATEFUL SECOND..."
UNNHHH!
YOU ARE DOWN, FATHER DEAR...

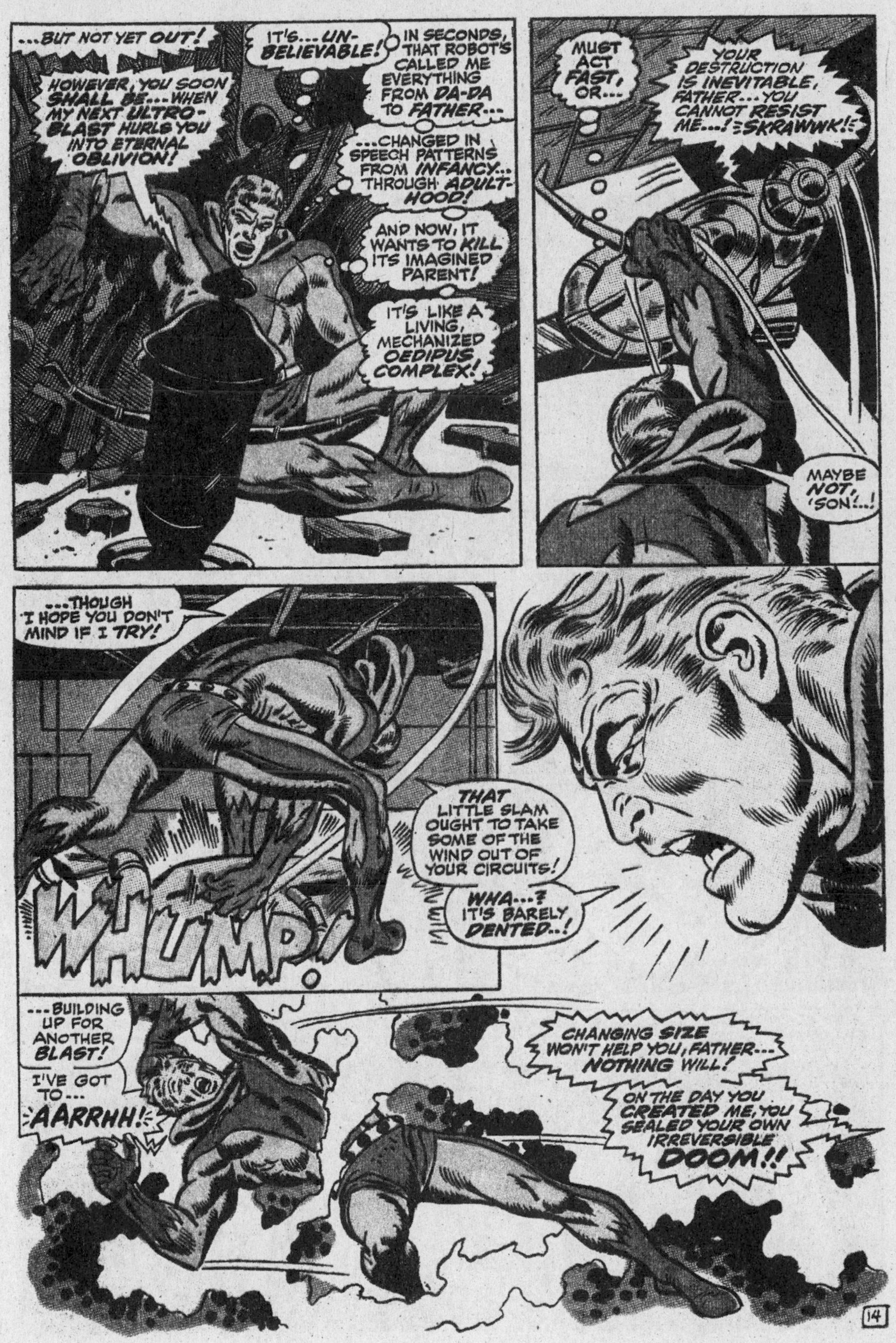
...BUT NOT YET OUT!
HOWEVER, YOU SOON SHALL BE... WHEN MY NEXT ULTRO-BLAST HURLS YOU INTO ETERNAL OBLIVION!
IT'S... UN-BELIEVABLE!
IN SECONDS, THAT ROBOT'S CALLED ME EVERYTHING FROM DA-DA TO FATHER...
...CHANGED IN SPEECH PATTERNS FROM INFANCY... THROUGH ADULT-HOOD!
AND NOW, IT WANTS TO KILL ITS IMAGINED PARENT!
IT'S LIKE A LIVING, MECHANIZED OEDIPUS COMPLEX!
MUST ACT FAST, OR...
YOUR DESTRUCTION IS INEVITABLE, FATHER... YOU CANNOT RESIST ME...! SKRAWWK!
MAYBE NOT, 'SON'...!
...THOUGH I HOPE YOU DON'T MIND IF I TRY!
THAT LITTLE SLAM OUGHT TO TAKE SOME OF THE WIND OUT OF YOUR CIRCUITS!
WHUMP!
WHA...? IT'S BARELY DENTED...!
...BUILDING UP FOR ANOTHER BLAST!
I'VE GOT TO...
AARRHH!
CHANGING SIZE WON'T HELP YOU, FATHER... NOTHING WILL!
ON THE DAY YOU CREATED ME, YOU SEALED YOUR OWN IRREVERSIBLE DOOM!!

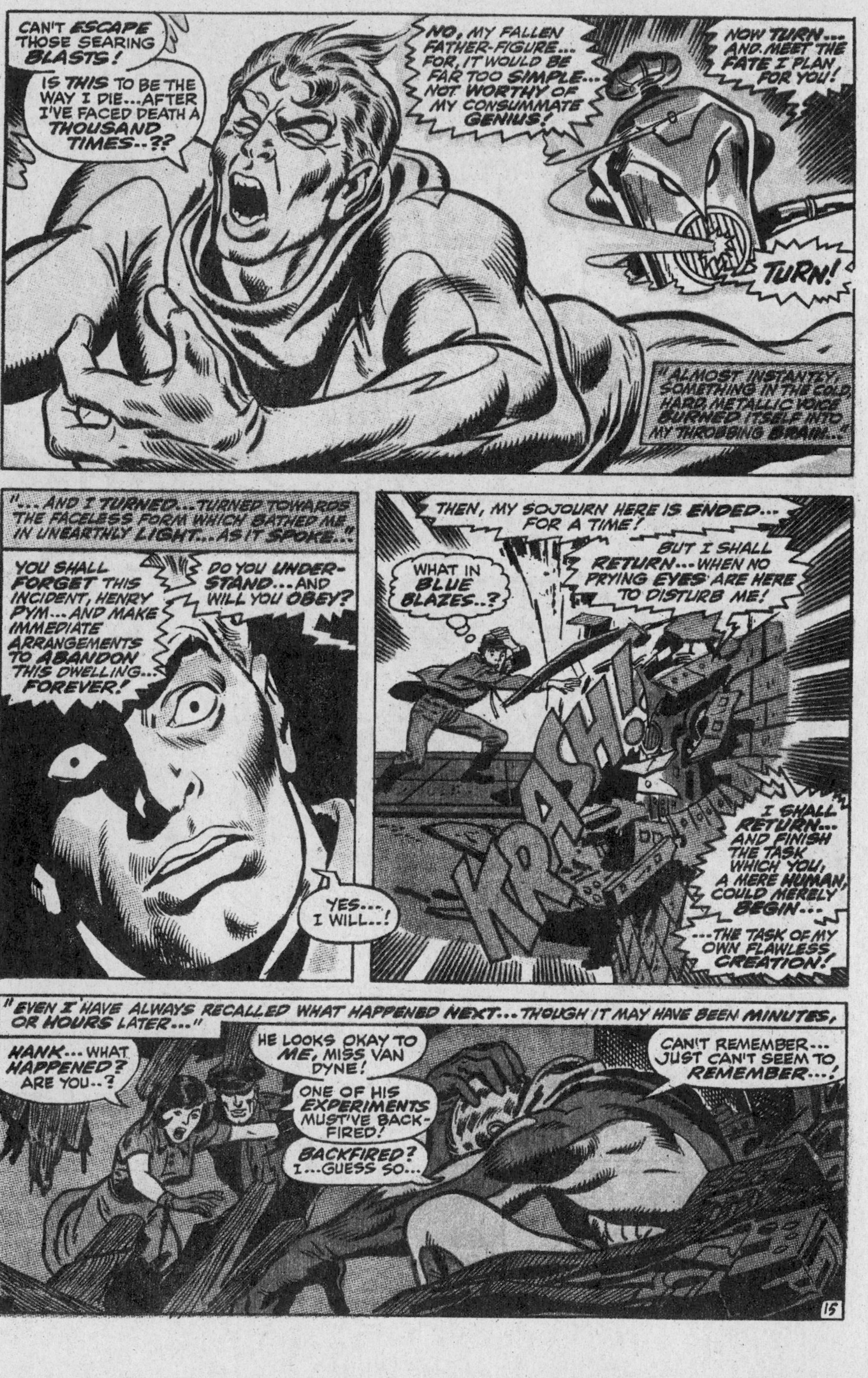

CAN'T ESCAPE THOSE SEARING BLASTS!
IS THIS TO BE THE WAY I DIE...AFTER I'VE FACED DEATH A THOUSAND TIMES--??
NO, MY FALLEN FATHER-FIGURE... FOR, IT WOULD BE FAR TOO SIMPLE... NOT WORTHY OF MY CONSUMMATE GENIUS!
NOW TURN... AND MEET THE FATE I PLAN FOR YOU!
TURN!
"ALMOST INSTANTLY, SOMETHING IN THE COLD, HARD METALLIC VOICE BURNED ITSELF INTO MY THROBBING BRAIN..."
"...AND I TURNED...TURNED TOWARDS THE FACELESS FORM WHICH BATHED ME IN UNEARTHLY LIGHT...AS IT SPOKE..."
YOU SHALL FORGET THIS INCIDENT, HENRY PYM...AND MAKE IMMEDIATE ARRANGEMENTS TO ABANDON THIS DWELLING... FOREVER!
DO YOU UNDERSTAND...AND WILL YOU OBEY?
YES... I WILL--!
THEN, MY SOJOURN HERE IS ENDED... FOR A TIME!
WHAT IN BLUE BLAZES..?
BUT I SHALL RETURN...WHEN NO PRYING EYES ARE HERE TO DISTURB ME!
KRASH!
I SHALL RETURN... AND FINISH THE TASK WHICH YOU, A MERE HUMAN, COULD MERELY BEGIN...
...THE TASK OF MY OWN FLAWLESS CREATION!
"EVEN I HAVE ALWAYS RECALLED WHAT HAPPENED NEXT...THOUGH IT MAY HAVE BEEN MINUTES, OR HOURS LATER..."
HANK...WHAT HAPPENED? ARE YOU..?
HE LOOKS OKAY TO ME, MISS VAN DYNE!
ONE OF HIS EXPERIMENTS MUST'VE BACK-FIRED!
BACKFIRED? I...GUESS SO...
CAN'T REMEMBER... JUST CAN'T SEEM TO REMEMBER...!
15

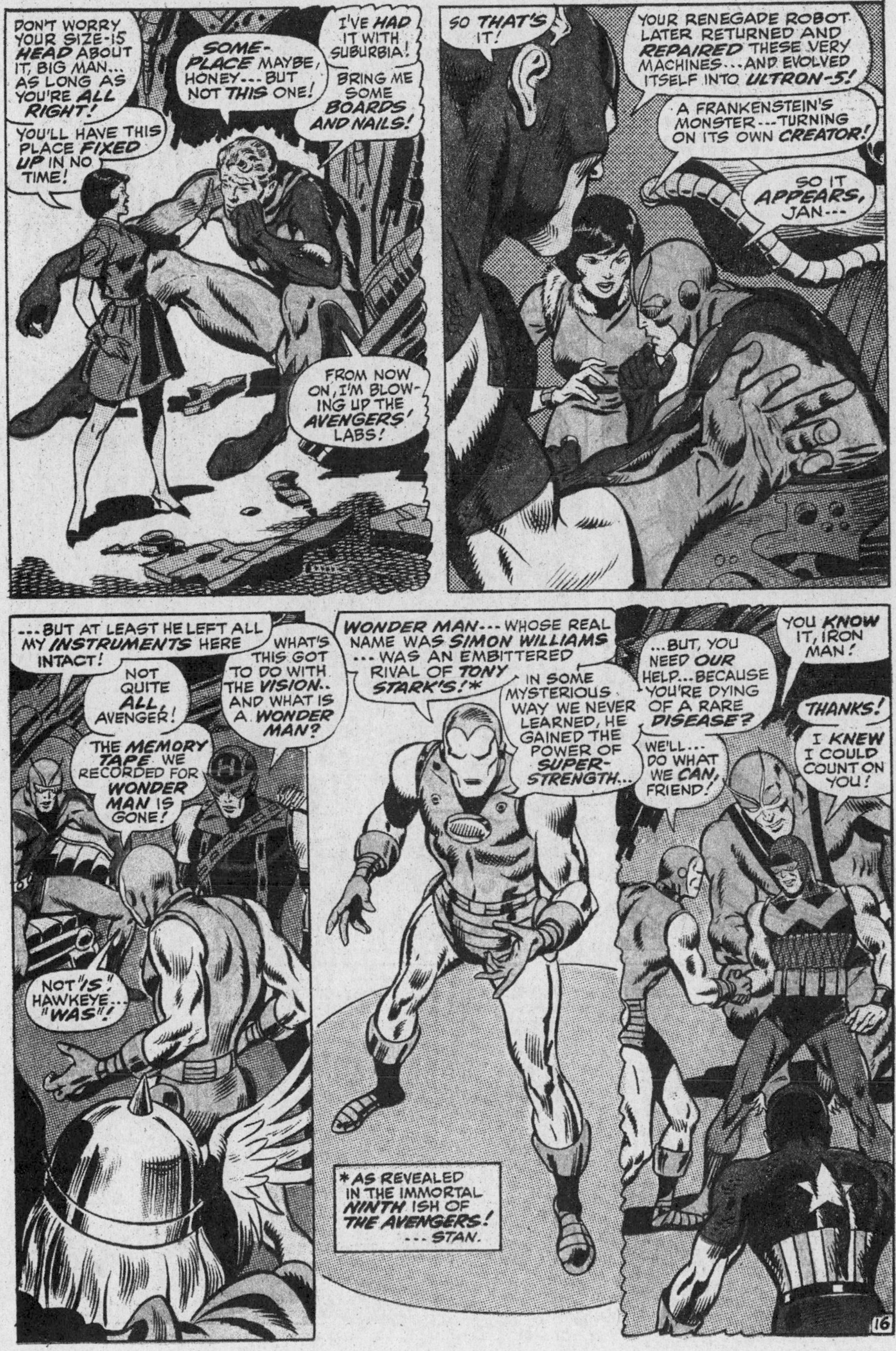
DON'T WORRY YOUR SIZE-15 HEAD ABOUT IT, BIG MAN... AS LONG AS YOU'RE ALL RIGHT!
YOU'LL HAVE THIS PLACE FIXED UP IN NO TIME!
SOME-PLACE MAYBE, HONEY--- BUT NOT THIS ONE!
I'VE HAD IT WITH SUBURBIA!
BRING ME SOME BOARDS AND NAILS!
FROM NOW ON, I'M BLOWING UP THE AVENGERS' LABS!
SO THAT'S IT!
YOUR RENEGADE ROBOT LATER RETURNED AND REPAIRED THESE VERY MACHINES...AND EVOLVED ITSELF INTO ULTRON-5!
A FRANKENSTEIN'S MONSTER---TURNING ON ITS OWN CREATOR!
SO IT APPEARS, JAN---
---BUT AT LEAST HE LEFT ALL MY INSTRUMENTS HERE INTACT!
NOT QUITE ALL, AVENGER!
THE MEMORY TAPE WE RECORDED FOR WONDER MAN IS GONE!
WHAT'S THIS GOT TO DO WITH THE VISION.. AND WHAT IS A WONDER MAN?
NOT "IS", HAWKEYE... "WAS"!
WONDER MAN--- WHOSE REAL NAME WAS SIMON WILLIAMS --- WAS AN EMBITTERED RIVAL OF TONY STARK'S!*
IN SOME MYSTERIOUS WAY WE NEVER LEARNED, HE GAINED THE POWER OF SUPER-STRENGTH...
*AS REVEALED IN THE IMMORTAL NINTH ISH OF THE AVENGERS! --- STAN.
...BUT, YOU NEED OUR HELP...BECAUSE YOU'RE DYING OF A RARE DISEASE?
WE'LL... DO WHAT WE CAN, FRIEND!
YOU KNOW IT, IRON MAN!
THANKS!
I KNEW I COULD COUNT ON YOU!
16

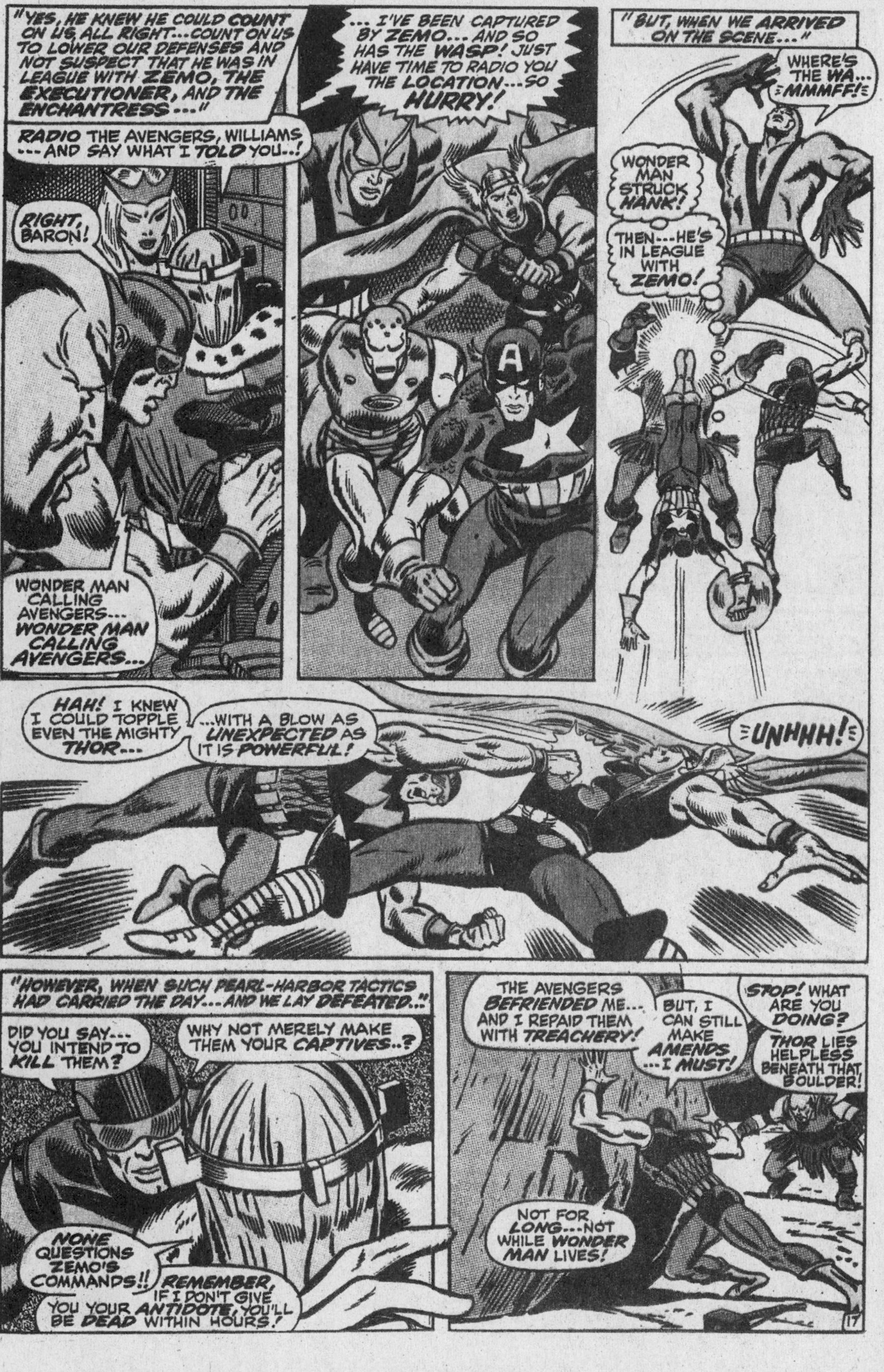
"YES, HE KNEW HE COULD COUNT ON US, ALL RIGHT... COUNT ON US TO LOWER OUR DEFENSES AND NOT SUSPECT THAT HE WAS IN LEAGUE WITH ZEMO, THE EXECUTIONER, AND THE ENCHANTRESS..."
RADIO THE AVENGERS, WILLIAMS ...AND SAY WHAT I TOLD YOU..!
RIGHT, BARON!
WONDER MAN CALLING AVENGERS... WONDER MAN CALLING AVENGERS...
... I'VE BEEN CAPTURED BY ZEMO... AND SO HAS THE WASP! JUST HAVE TIME TO RADIO YOU THE LOCATION... SO HURRY!
"BUT, WHEN WE ARRIVED ON THE SCENE..."
WHERE'S THE WA... MMMFF!
WONDER MAN STRUCK HANK!
THEN--HE'S IN LEAGUE WITH ZEMO!
HAH! I KNEW I COULD TOPPLE EVEN THE MIGHTY THOR...
...WITH A BLOW AS UNEXPECTED AS IT IS POWERFUL!
UNHHH!
"HOWEVER, WHEN SUCH PEARL-HARBOR TACTICS HAD CARRIED THE DAY... AND WE LAY DEFEATED..."
DID YOU SAY... YOU INTEND TO KILL THEM?
WHY NOT MERELY MAKE THEM YOUR CAPTIVES..?
NONE QUESTIONS ZEMO'S COMMANDS!!
REMEMBER, IF I DON'T GIVE YOU YOUR ANTIDOTE, YOU'LL BE DEAD WITHIN HOURS!
THE AVENGERS BEFRIENDED ME... AND I REPAID THEM WITH TREACHERY!
BUT, I CAN STILL MAKE AMENDS ...I MUST!
STOP! WHAT ARE YOU DOING? THOR LIES HELPLESS BENEATH THAT BOULDER!
NOT FOR LONG...NOT WHILE WONDER MAN LIVES!
17

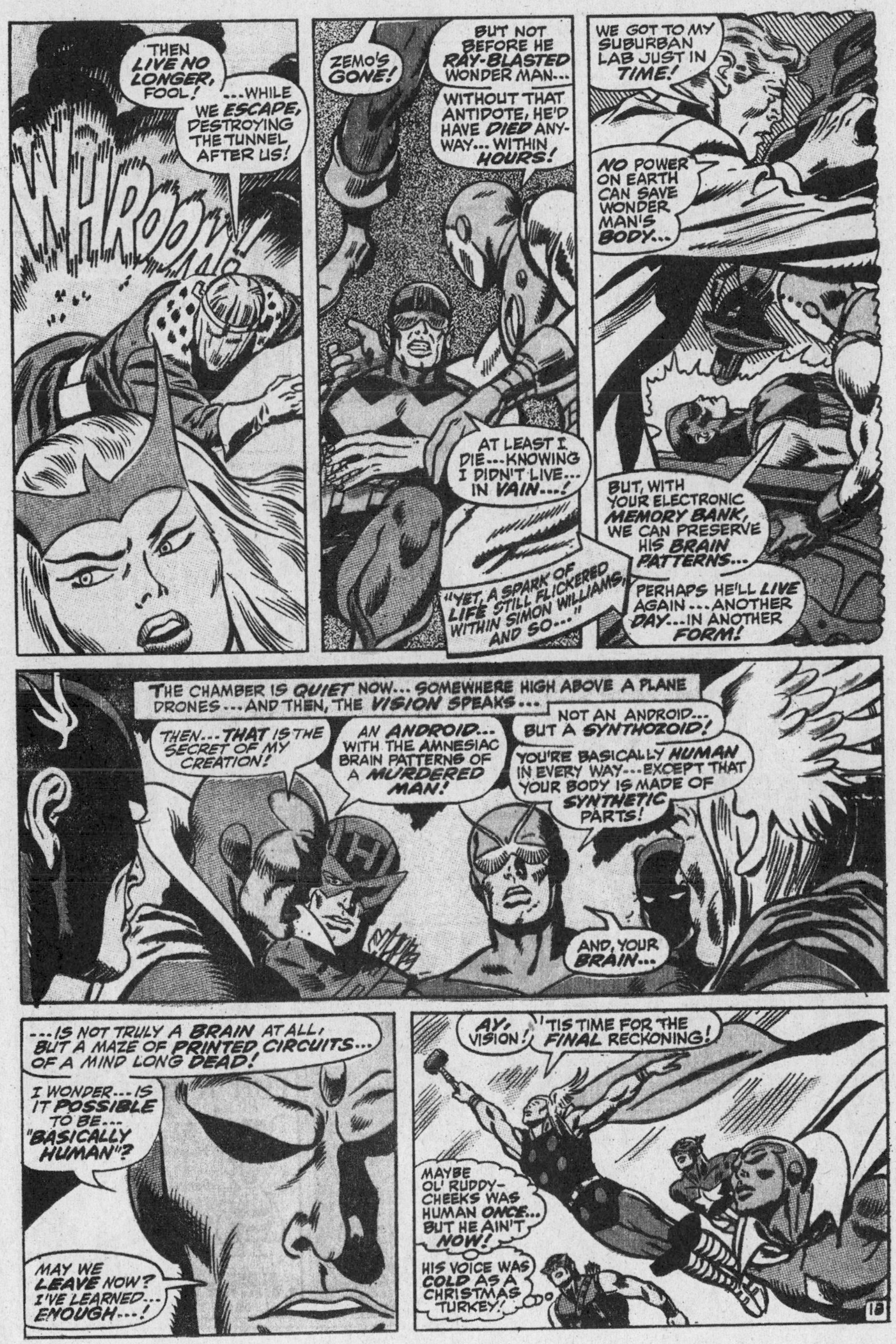
THEN LIVE NO LONGER, FOOL!
...WHILE WE ESCAPE, DESTROYING THE TUNNEL AFTER US!
WHROOOM!
ZEMO'S GONE!
BUT NOT BEFORE HE RAY-BLASTED WONDER MAN...
WITHOUT THAT ANTIDOTE, HE'D HAVE DIED ANY-WAY... WITHIN HOURS!
AT LEAST I DIE---KNOWING I DIDN'T LIVE... IN VAIN...!
"YET, A SPARK OF LIFE STILL FLICKERED WITHIN SIMON WILLIAMS, AND SO..."
WE GOT TO MY SUBURBAN LAB JUST IN TIME!
NO POWER ON EARTH CAN SAVE WONDER MAN'S BODY...
BUT, WITH YOUR ELECTRONIC MEMORY BANK, WE CAN PRESERVE HIS BRAIN PATTERNS...
PERHAPS HE'LL LIVE AGAIN... ANOTHER DAY...IN ANOTHER FORM!
THE CHAMBER IS QUIET NOW... SOMEWHERE HIGH ABOVE A PLANE DRONES... AND THEN, THE VISION SPEAKS...
THEN... THAT IS THE SECRET OF MY CREATION!
AN ANDROID... WITH THE AMNESIAC BRAIN PATTERNS OF A MURDERED MAN!
NOT AN ANDROID... BUT A SYNTHOZOID!
YOU'RE BASICALLY HUMAN IN EVERY WAY---EXCEPT THAT YOUR BODY IS MADE OF SYNTHETIC PARTS!
AND, YOUR BRAIN...
...IS NOT TRULY A BRAIN AT ALL, BUT A MAZE OF PRINTED CIRCUITS... OF A MIND LONG DEAD!
I WONDER... IS IT POSSIBLE TO BE... "BASICALLY HUMAN"?
MAY WE LEAVE NOW? I'VE LEARNED... ENOUGH---!
AY, VISION!
'TIS TIME FOR THE FINAL RECKONING!
MAYBE OL' RUDDY-CHEEKS WAS HUMAN ONCE... BUT HE AIN'T NOW!
HIS VOICE WAS COLD AS A CHRISTMAS TURKEY!
13

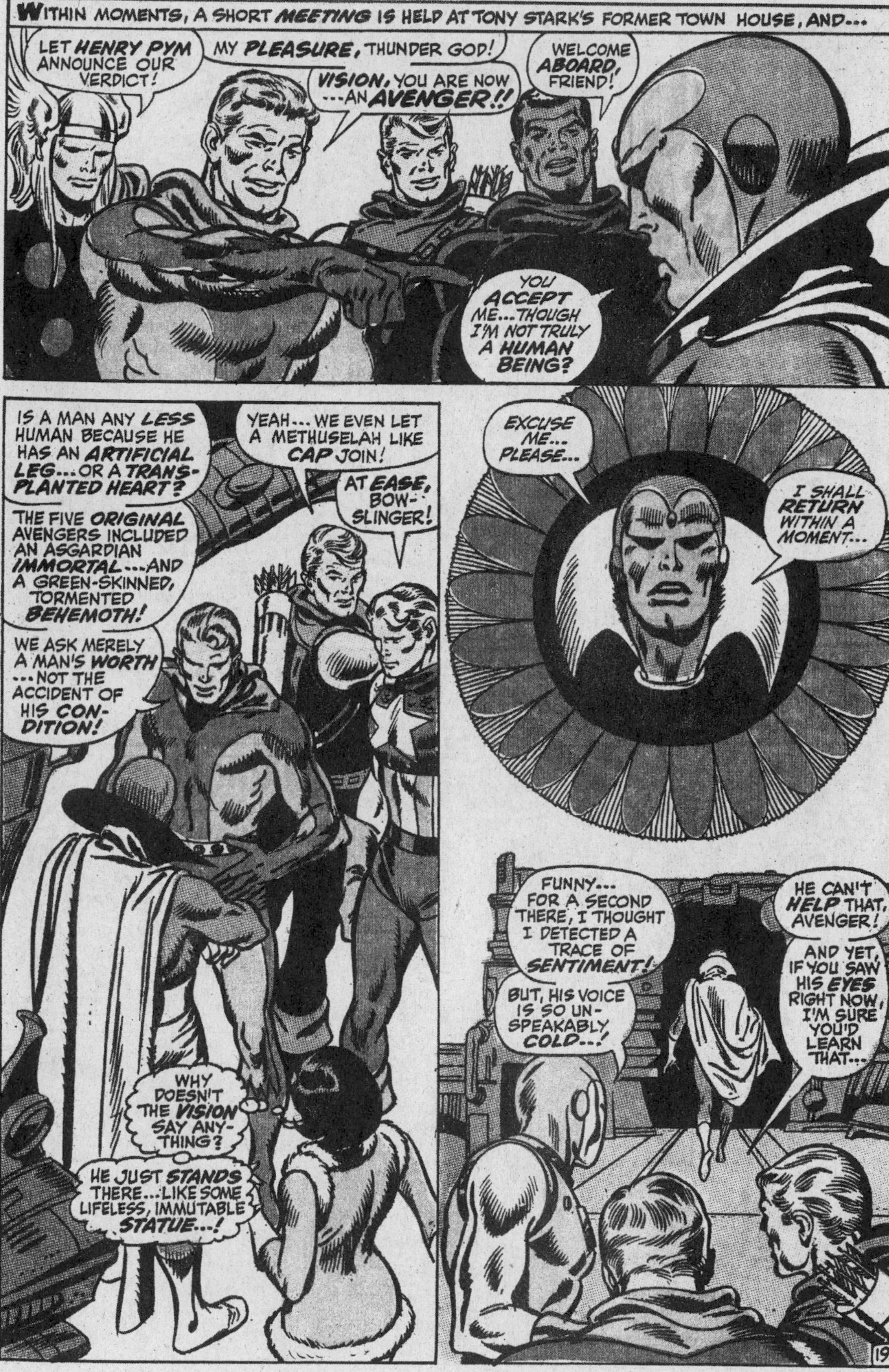
WITHIN MOMENTS, A SHORT MEETING IS HELD AT TONY STARK'S FORMER TOWN HOUSE, AND...
LET HENRY PYM ANNOUNCE OUR VERDICT!
MY PLEASURE, THUNDER GOD!
VISION, YOU ARE NOW ---AN AVENGER!!
WELCOME ABOARD, FRIEND!
YOU ACCEPT ME...THOUGH I'M NOT TRULY A HUMAN BEING?
IS A MAN ANY LESS HUMAN BECAUSE HE HAS AN ARTIFICIAL LEG...OR A TRANS-PLANTED HEART?
YEAH... WE EVEN LET A METHUSELAH LIKE CAP JOIN!
AT EASE, BOW-SLINGER!
THE FIVE ORIGINAL AVENGERS INCLUDED AN ASGARDIAN IMMORTAL...AND A GREEN-SKINNED, TORMENTED BEHEMOTH!
WE ASK MERELY A MAN'S WORTH ...NOT THE ACCIDENT OF HIS CON-DITION!
WHY DOESN'T THE VISION SAY ANY-THING?
HE JUST STANDS THERE...LIKE SOME LIFELESS, IMMUTABLE STATUE...!
EXCUSE ME... PLEASE...
I SHALL RETURN WITHIN A MOMENT...
FUNNY... FOR A SECOND THERE, I THOUGHT I DETECTED A TRACE OF SENTIMENT!
BUT, HIS VOICE IS SO UN-SPEAKABLY COLD...!
HE CAN'T HELP THAT, AVENGER!
AND YET, IF YOU SAW HIS EYES RIGHT NOW, I'M SURE YOU'D LEARN THAT...
19

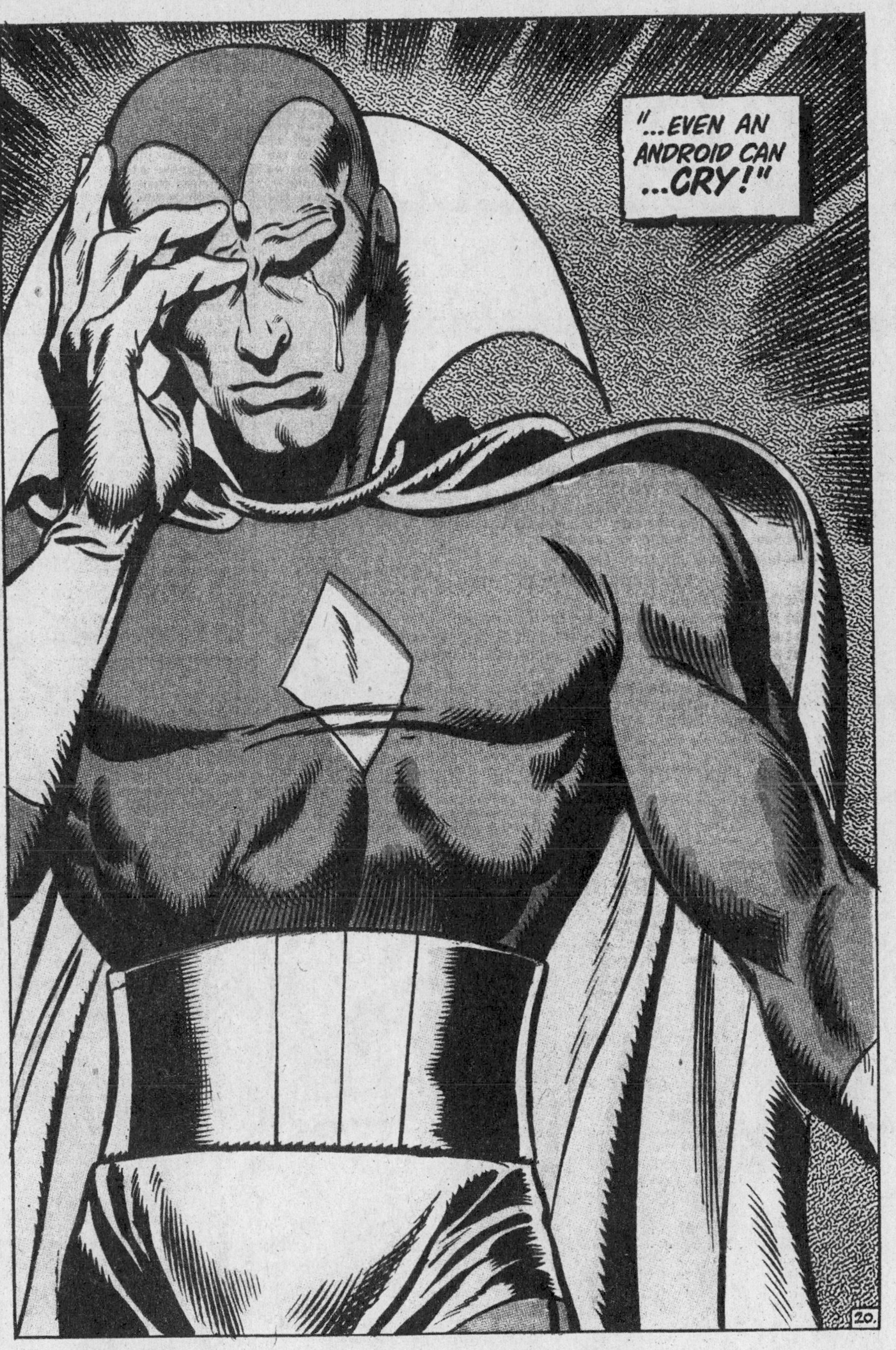
"...EVEN AN ANDROID CAN ...CRY!"
20.

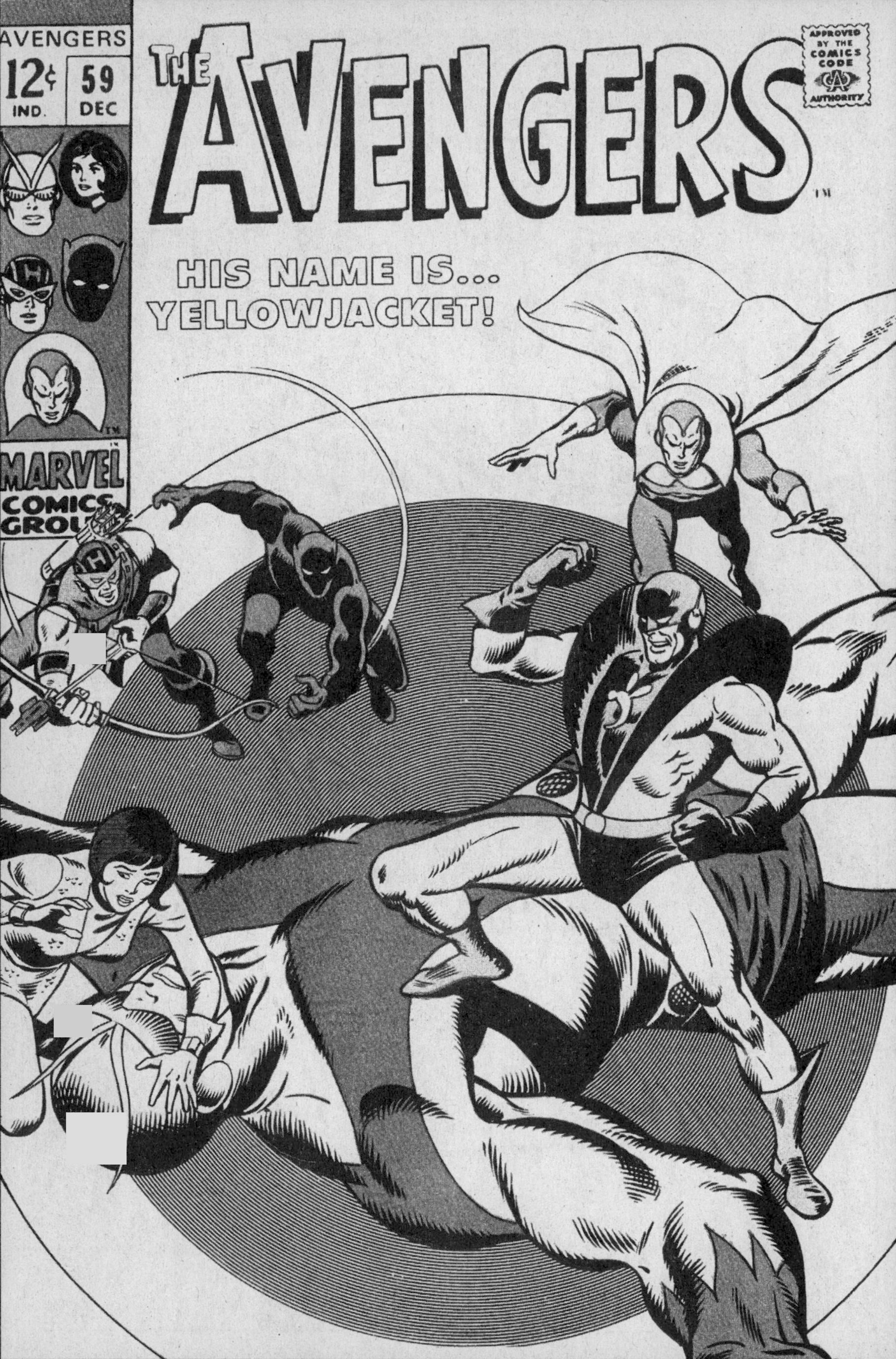
AVENGERS
12¢
IND.
59
DEC
THE AVENGERS
APPROVED BY THE COMICS CODE AUTHORITY
MARVEL COMICS GROUP
HIS NAME IS... YELLOWJACKET!

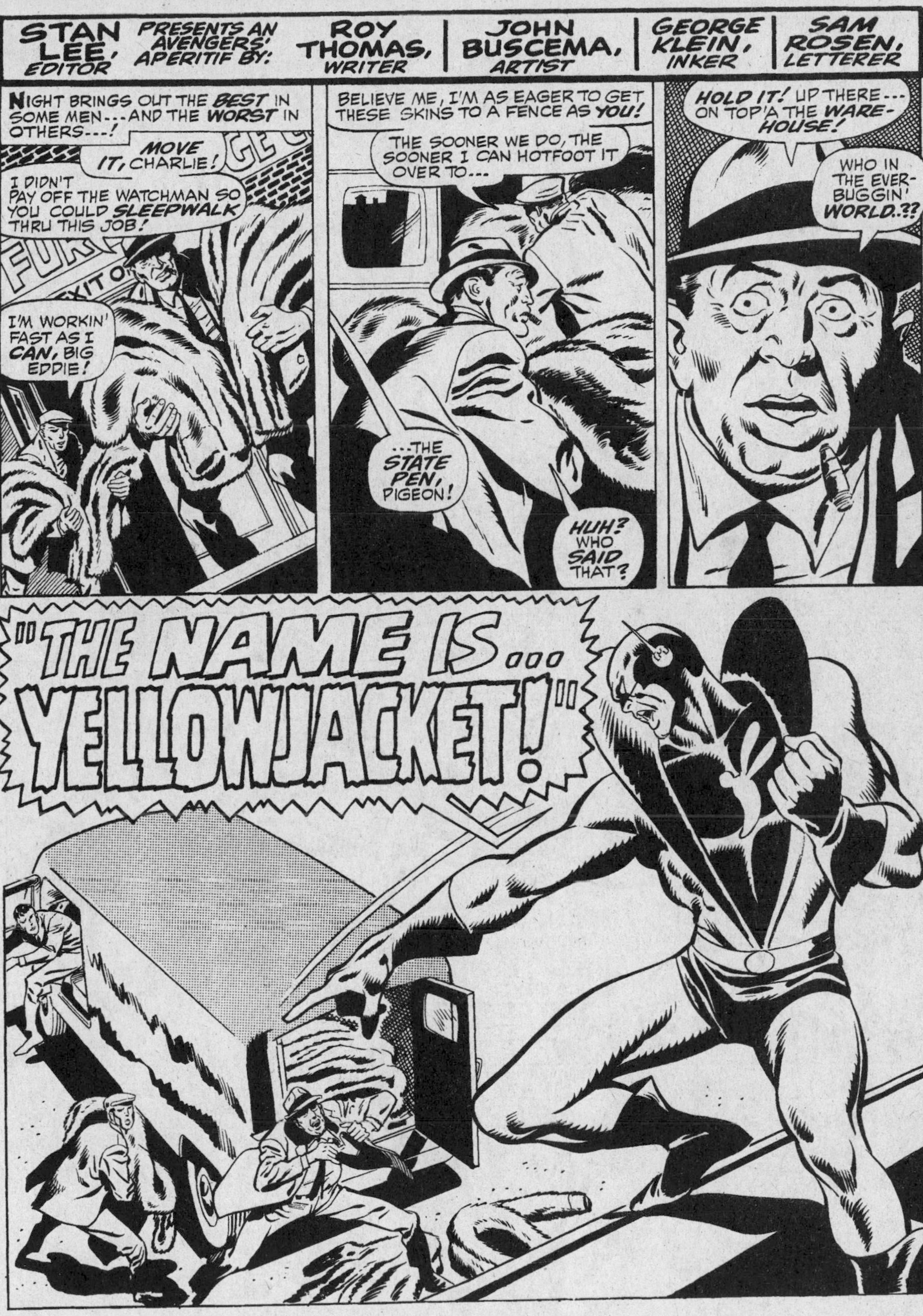
STAN LEE, EDITOR
PRESENTS AN AVENGERS' APERITIF BY:
ROY THOMAS, WRITER
JOHN BUSCEMA, ARTIST
GEORGE KLEIN, INKER
SAM ROSEN, LETTERER
NIGHT BRINGS OUT THE BEST IN SOME MEN--- AND THE WORST IN OTHERS---!
MOVE IT, CHARLIE!
I DIDN'T PAY OFF THE WATCHMAN SO YOU COULD SLEEPWALK THRU THIS JOB!
I'M WORKIN' FAST AS I CAN, BIG EDDIE!
BELIEVE ME, I'M AS EAGER TO GET THESE SKINS TO A FENCE AS YOU!
THE SOONER WE DO, THE SOONER I CAN HOTFOOT IT OVER TO...
...THE STATE PEN, PIGEON!
HUH? WHO SAID THAT?
HOLD IT! UP THERE--- ON TOP'A THE WARE-HOUSE!
WHO IN THE EVER-BUGGIN' WORLD..??
"THE NAME IS... YELLOWJACKET!"

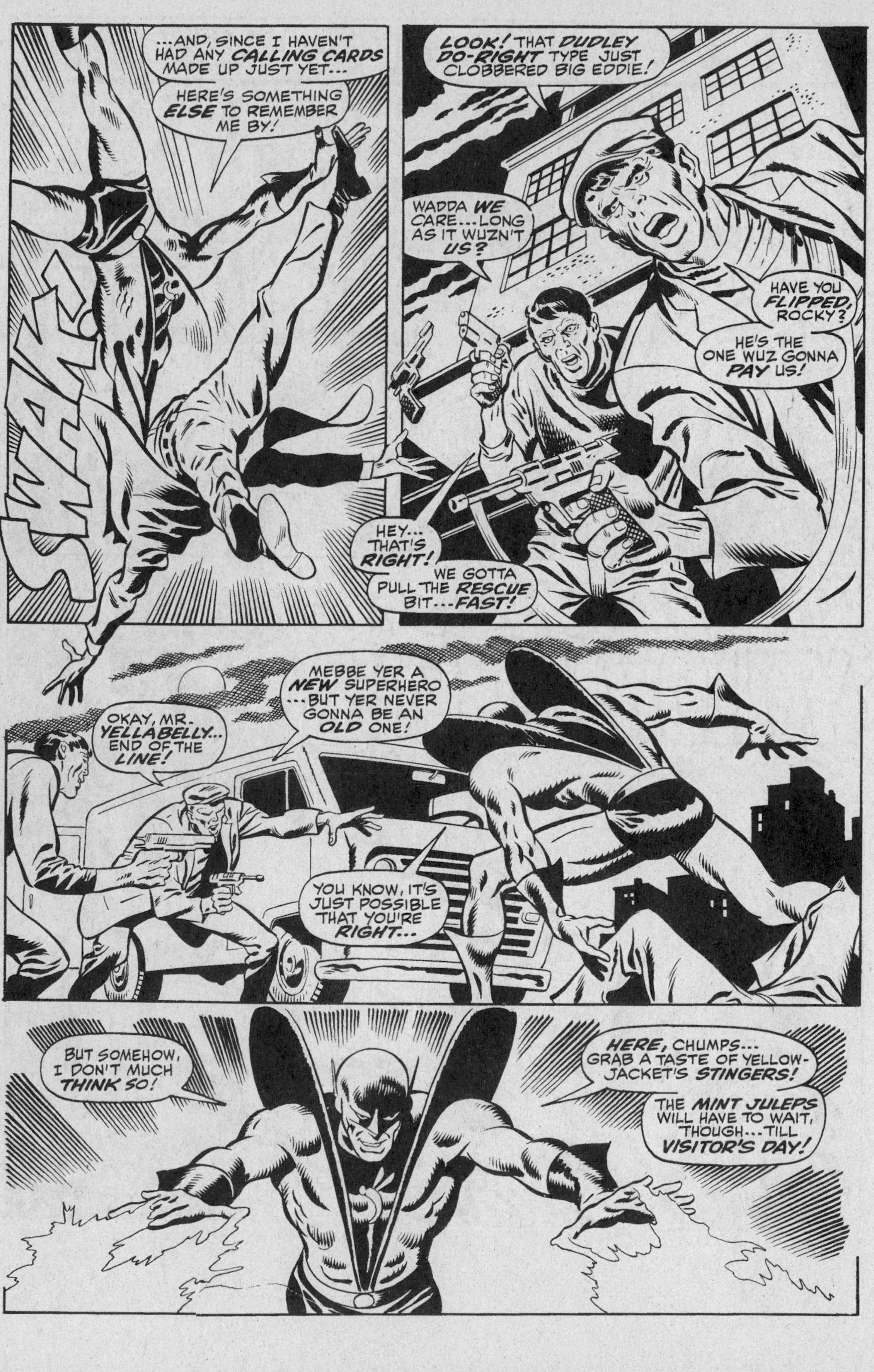

...AND, SINCE I HAVEN'T HAD ANY CALLING CARDS MADE UP JUST YET---
HERE'S SOMETHING ELSE TO REMEMBER ME BY!
SWAK
LOOK! THAT DUDLEY DO-RIGHT TYPE JUST CLOBBERED BIG EDDIE!
WADDA WE CARE...LONG AS IT WUZN'T US?
HAVE YOU FLIPPED, ROCKY?
HE'S THE ONE WUZ GONNA PAY US!
HEY... THAT'S RIGHT!
WE GOTTA PULL THE RESCUE BIT---FAST!
OKAY, MR. YELLABELLY... END OF THE LINE!
MEBBE YER A NEW SUPERHERO ---BUT YER NEVER GONNA BE AN OLD ONE!
YOU KNOW, IT'S JUST POSSIBLE THAT YOU'RE RIGHT...
BUT SOMEHOW, I DON'T MUCH THINK SO!
HERE, CHUMPS... GRAB A TASTE OF YELLOW-JACKET'S STINGERS!
THE MINT JULEPS WILL HAVE TO WAIT, THOUGH...TILL VISITOR'S DAY!

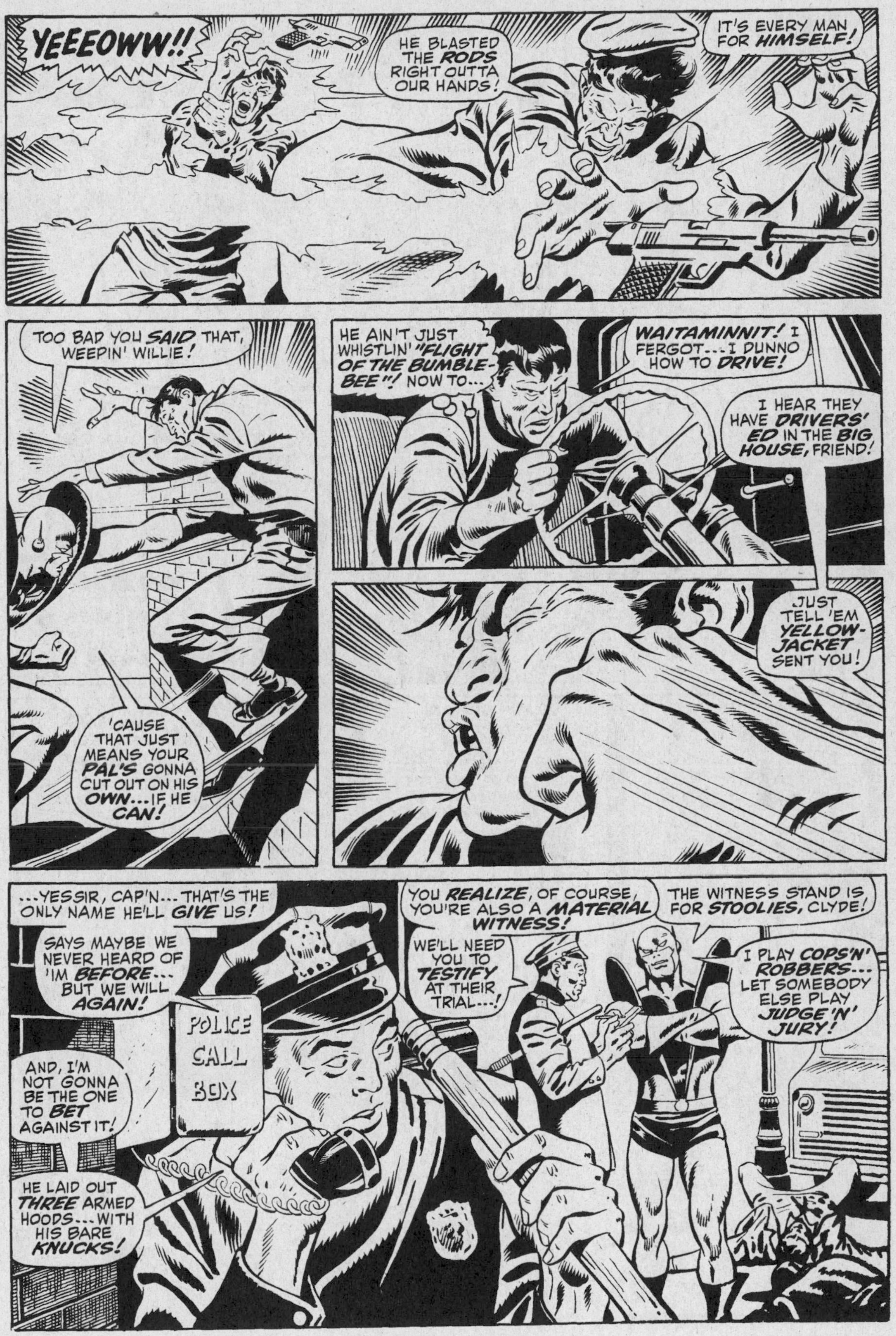

YEEEOWW!!
HE BLASTED THE RODS RIGHT OUTTA OUR HANDS!
IT'S EVERY MAN FOR HIMSELF!
TOO BAD YOU SAID THAT, WEEPIN' WILLIE!
'CAUSE THAT JUST MEANS YOUR PAL'S GONNA CUT OUT ON HIS OWN...IF HE CAN!
HE AIN'T JUST WHISTLIN' "FLIGHT OF THE BUMBLE-BEE"! NOW TO...
WAITAMINNIT! I FERGOT---I DUNNO HOW TO DRIVE!
I HEAR THEY HAVE DRIVERS' ED IN THE BIG HOUSE, FRIEND!
JUST TELL 'EM YELLOW-JACKET SENT YOU!
...YESSIR, CAP'N... THAT'S THE ONLY NAME HE'LL GIVE US!
SAYS MAYBE WE NEVER HEARD OF 'IM BEFORE... BUT WE WILL AGAIN!
POLICE CALL BOX
AND, I'M NOT GONNA BE THE ONE TO BET AGAINST IT!
HE LAID OUT THREE ARMED HOODS...WITH HIS BARE KNUCKS!
YOU REALIZE, OF COURSE, YOU'RE ALSO A MATERIAL WITNESS!
WE'LL NEED YOU TO TESTIFY AT THEIR TRIAL...!
THE WITNESS STAND IS FOR STOOLIES, CLYDE!
I PLAY COPS 'N' ROBBERS... LET SOMEBODY ELSE PLAY JUDGE 'N' JURY!

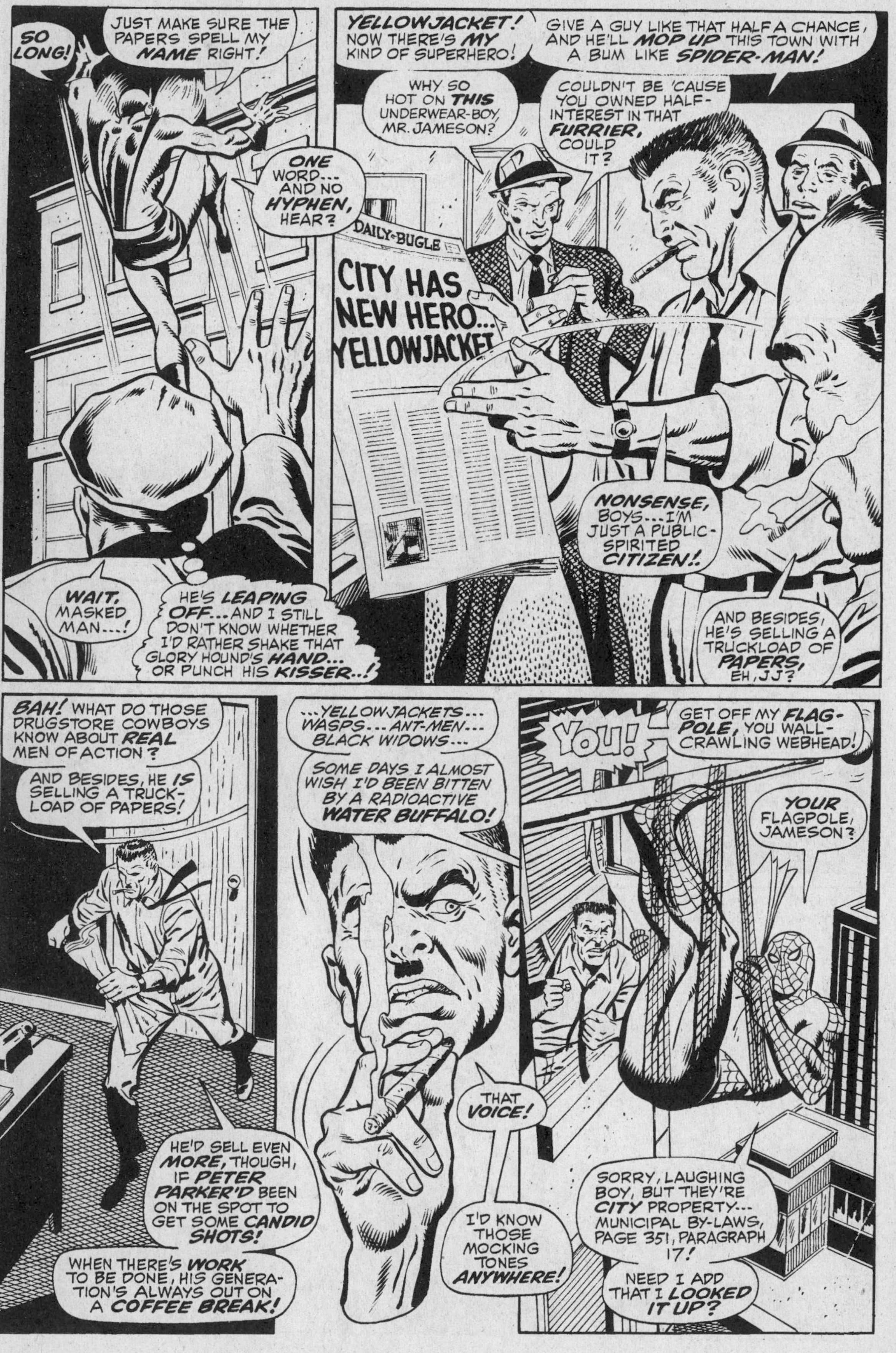
SO LONG!
JUST MAKE SURE THE PAPERS SPELL MY NAME RIGHT!
ONE WORD... AND NO HYPHEN, HEAR?
WAIT, MASKED MAN...!
HE'S LEAPING OFF... AND I STILL DON'T KNOW WHETHER I'D RATHER SHAKE THAT GLORY HOUND'S HAND... OR PUNCH HIS KISSER..!
YELLOWJACKET! NOW THERE'S MY KIND OF SUPERHERO!
GIVE A GUY LIKE THAT HALF A CHANCE, AND HE'LL MOP UP THIS TOWN WITH A BUM LIKE SPIDER-MAN!
WHY SO HOT ON THIS UNDERWEAR-BOY, MR. JAMESON?
COULDN'T BE 'CAUSE YOU OWNED HALF-INTEREST IN THAT FURRIER, COULD IT?
DAILY BUGLE
CITY HAS NEW HERO... YELLOWJACKET
NONSENSE, BOYS... I'M JUST A PUBLIC-SPIRITED CITIZEN!.
AND BESIDES, HE'S SELLING A TRUCKLOAD OF PAPERS, EH, JJ?
BAH! WHAT DO THOSE DRUGSTORE COWBOYS KNOW ABOUT REAL MEN OF ACTION?
AND BESIDES, HE IS SELLING A TRUCK-LOAD OF PAPERS!
HE'D SELL EVEN MORE, THOUGH, IF PETER PARKER'D BEEN ON THE SPOT TO GET SOME CANDID SHOTS!
WHEN THERE'S WORK TO BE DONE, HIS GENERATION'S ALWAYS OUT ON A COFFEE BREAK!
...YELLOWJACKETS... WASPS... ANT-MEN... BLACK WIDOWS...
SOME DAYS I ALMOST WISH I'D BEEN BITTEN BY A RADIOACTIVE WATER BUFFALO!
THAT VOICE!
I'D KNOW THOSE MOCKING TONES ANYWHERE!
YOU!
GET OFF MY FLAG-POLE, YOU WALL-CRAWLING WEBHEAD!
YOUR FLAGPOLE, JAMESON?
SORRY, LAUGHING BOY, BUT THEY'RE CITY PROPERTY--- MUNICIPAL BY-LAWS, PAGE 351, PARAGRAPH 17!
NEED I ADD THAT I LOOKED IT UP?

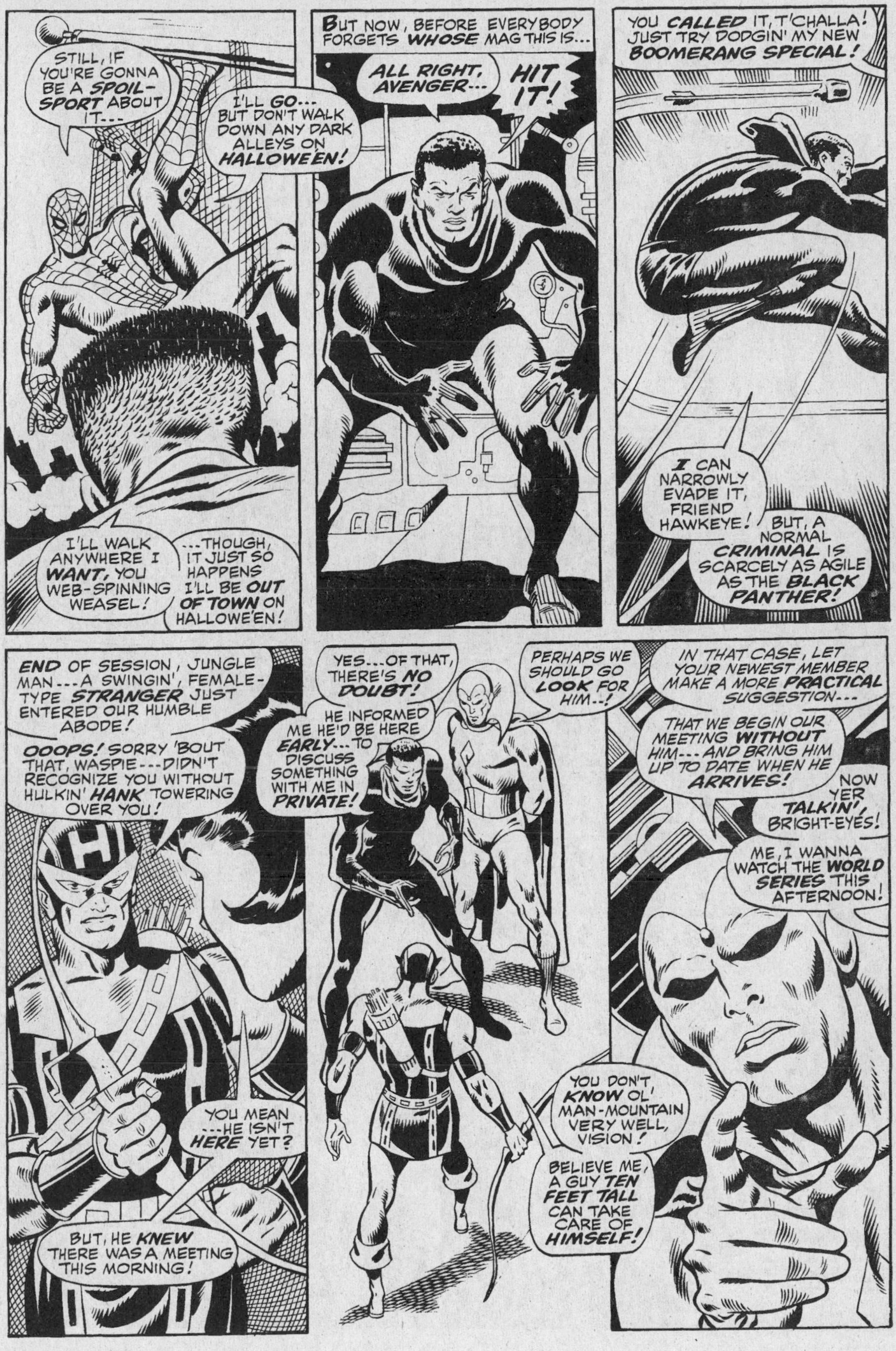
STILL, IF YOU'RE GONNA BE A SPOIL-SPORT ABOUT IT---
I'LL GO... BUT DON'T WALK DOWN ANY DARK ALLEYS ON HALLOWE'EN!
I'LL WALK ANYWHERE I WANT, YOU WEB-SPINNING WEASEL!
---THOUGH, IT JUST SO HAPPENS I'LL BE OUT OF TOWN ON HALLOWE'EN!
BUT NOW, BEFORE EVERYBODY FORGETS WHOSE MAG THIS IS...
ALL RIGHT, AVENGER---
HIT IT!
YOU CALLED IT, T'CHALLA! JUST TRY DODGIN' MY NEW BOOMERANG SPECIAL!
I CAN NARROWLY EVADE IT, FRIEND HAWKEYE!
BUT, A NORMAL CRIMINAL IS SCARCELY AS AGILE AS THE BLACK PANTHER!
END OF SESSION, JUNGLE MAN---A SWINGIN', FEMALE-TYPE STRANGER JUST ENTERED OUR HUMBLE ABODE!
OOOPS! SORRY 'BOUT THAT, WASPIE---DIDN'T RECOGNIZE YOU WITHOUT HULKIN' HANK TOWERING OVER YOU!
YOU MEAN ---HE ISN'T HERE YET?
BUT, HE KNEW THERE WAS A MEETING THIS MORNING!
YES...OF THAT, THERE'S NO DOUBT!
HE INFORMED ME HE'D BE HERE EARLY--- TO DISCUSS SOMETHING WITH ME IN PRIVATE!
PERHAPS WE SHOULD GO LOOK FOR HIM--!
YOU DON'T KNOW OL' MAN-MOUNTAIN VERY WELL, VISION!
BELIEVE ME, A GUY TEN FEET TALL CAN TAKE CARE OF HIMSELF!
IN THAT CASE, LET YOUR NEWEST MEMBER MAKE A MORE PRACTICAL SUGGESTION---
THAT WE BEGIN OUR MEETING WITHOUT HIM--- AND BRING HIM UP TO DATE WHEN HE ARRIVES!
NOW YER TALKIN', BRIGHT-EYES!
ME, I WANNA WATCH THE WORLD SERIES THIS AFTERNOON!

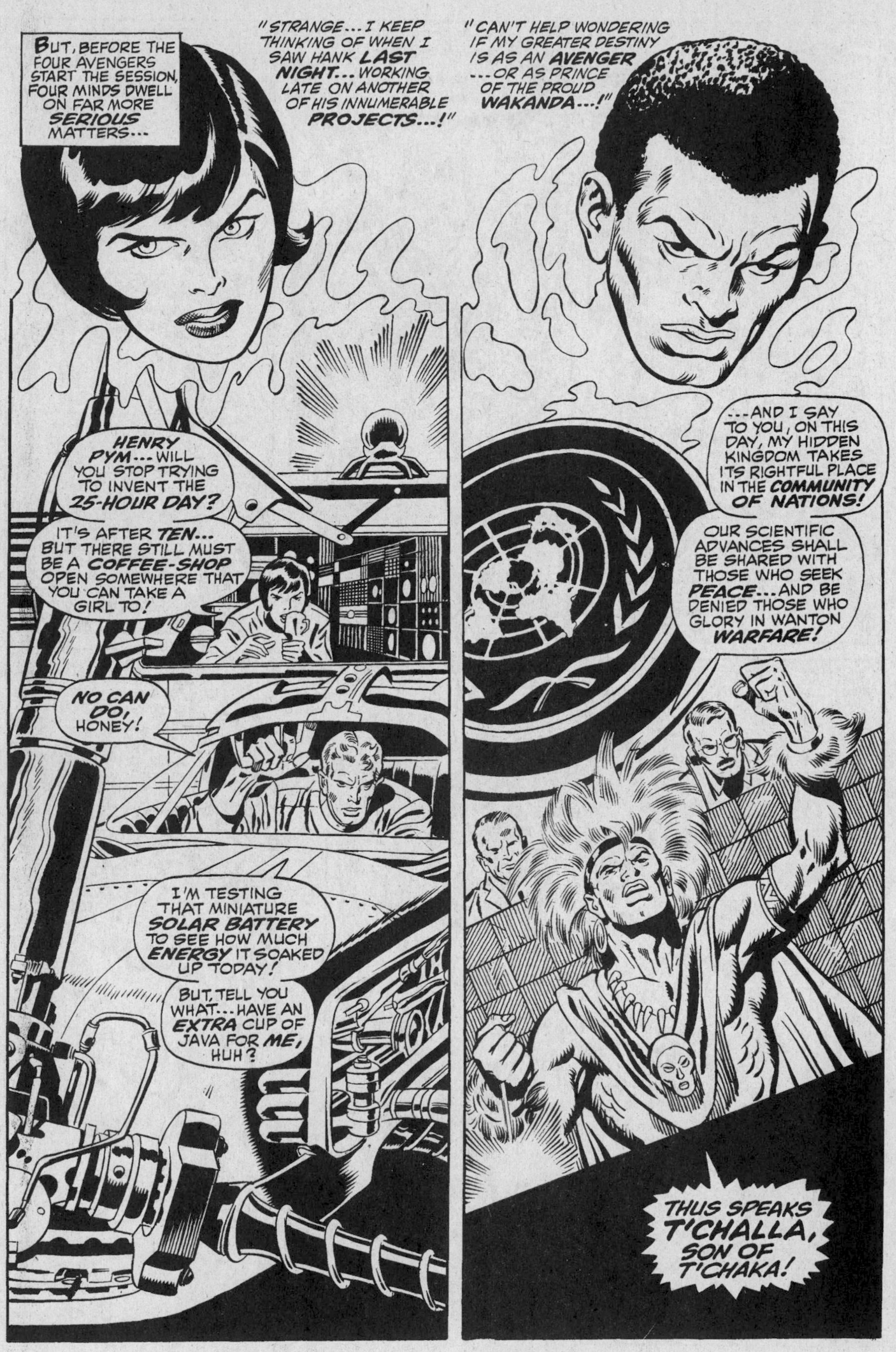
BUT, BEFORE THE FOUR AVENGERS START THE SESSION, FOUR MINDS DWELL ON FAR MORE SERIOUS MATTERS...
"STRANGE... I KEEP THINKING OF WHEN I SAW HANK LAST NIGHT... WORKING LATE ON ANOTHER OF HIS INNUMERABLE PROJECTS...!"
HENRY PYM... WILL YOU STOP TRYING TO INVENT THE 25-HOUR DAY?
IT'S AFTER TEN... BUT THERE STILL MUST BE A COFFEE-SHOP OPEN SOMEWHERE THAT YOU CAN TAKE A GIRL TO!
NO CAN DO, HONEY!
I'M TESTING THAT MINIATURE SOLAR BATTERY TO SEE HOW MUCH ENERGY IT SOAKED UP TODAY!
BUT, TELL YOU WHAT... HAVE AN EXTRA CUP OF JAVA FOR ME, HUH?
"CAN'T HELP WONDERING IF MY GREATER DESTINY IS AS AN AVENGER ...OR AS PRINCE OF THE PROUD WAKANDA...!"
...AND I SAY TO YOU, ON THIS DAY, MY HIDDEN KINGDOM TAKES ITS RIGHTFUL PLACE IN THE COMMUNITY OF NATIONS!
OUR SCIENTIFIC ADVANCES SHALL BE SHARED WITH THOSE WHO SEEK PEACE... AND BE DENIED THOSE WHO GLORY IN WANTON WARFARE!
THUS SPEAKS T'CHALLA, SON OF T'CHAKA!

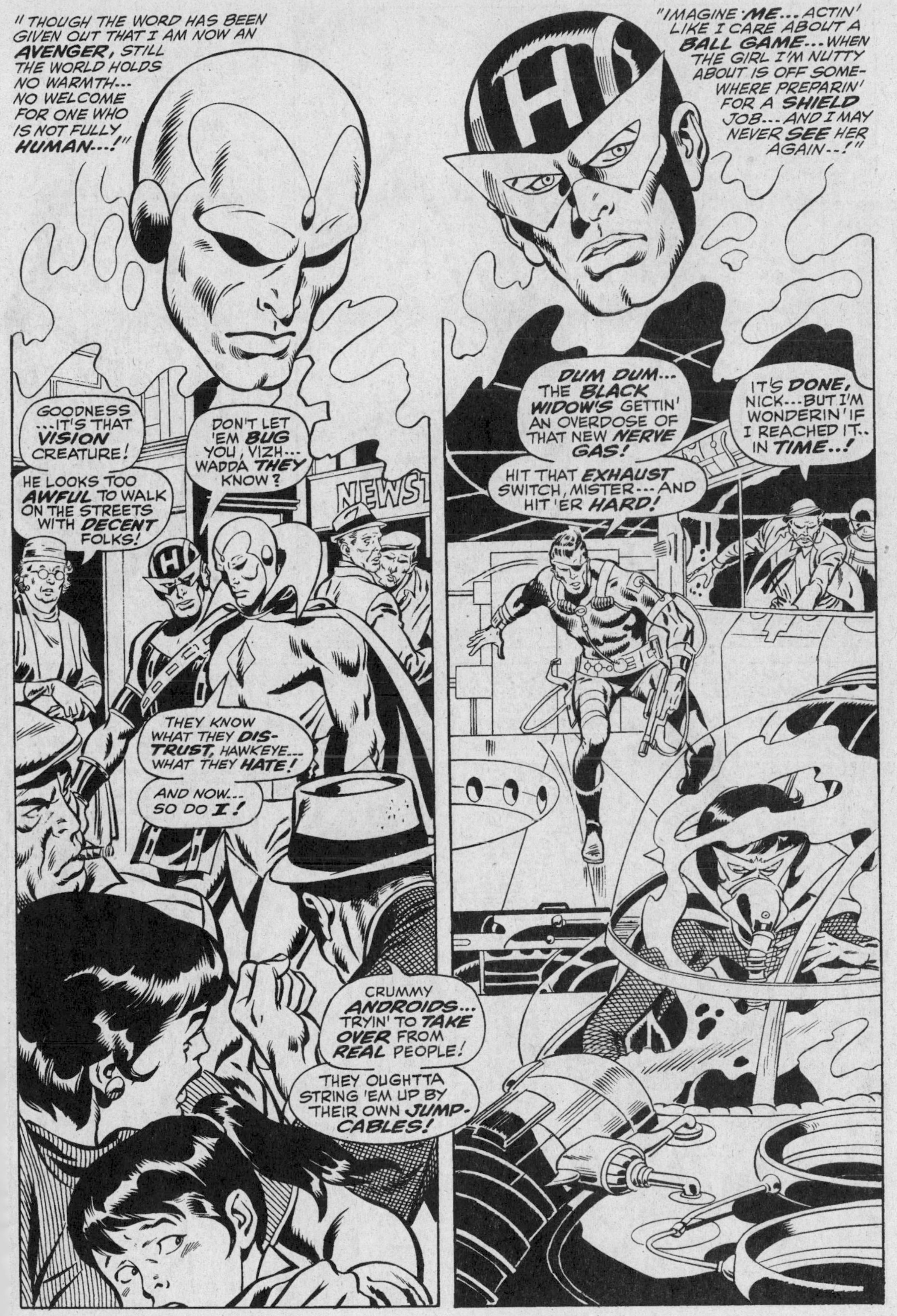
"THOUGH THE WORD HAS BEEN GIVEN OUT THAT I AM NOW AN AVENGER, STILL THE WORLD HOLDS NO WARMTH--- NO WELCOME FOR ONE WHO IS NOT FULLY HUMAN---!"
GOODNESS ...IT'S THAT VISION CREATURE!
HE LOOKS TOO AWFUL TO WALK ON THE STREETS WITH DECENT FOLKS!
DON'T LET 'EM BUG YOU, VIZH... WADDA THEY KNOW?
NEWS
THEY KNOW WHAT THEY DIS-TRUST, HAWKEYE... WHAT THEY HATE!
AND NOW... SO DO I!
CRUMMY ANDROIDS... TRYIN' TO TAKE OVER FROM REAL PEOPLE!
THEY OUGHTTA STRING 'EM UP BY THEIR OWN JUMP-CABLES!
"IMAGINE ME... ACTIN' LIKE I CARE ABOUT A BALL GAME... WHEN THE GIRL I'M NUTTY ABOUT IS OFF SOME-WHERE PREPARIN' FOR A SHIELD JOB... AND I MAY NEVER SEE HER AGAIN--!"
DUM DUM... THE BLACK WIDOW'S GETTIN' AN OVERDOSE OF THAT NEW NERVE GAS!
HIT THAT EXHAUST SWITCH, MISTER--- AND HIT 'ER HARD!
IT'S DONE, NICK---BUT I'M WONDERIN' IF I REACHED IT.. IN TIME..!

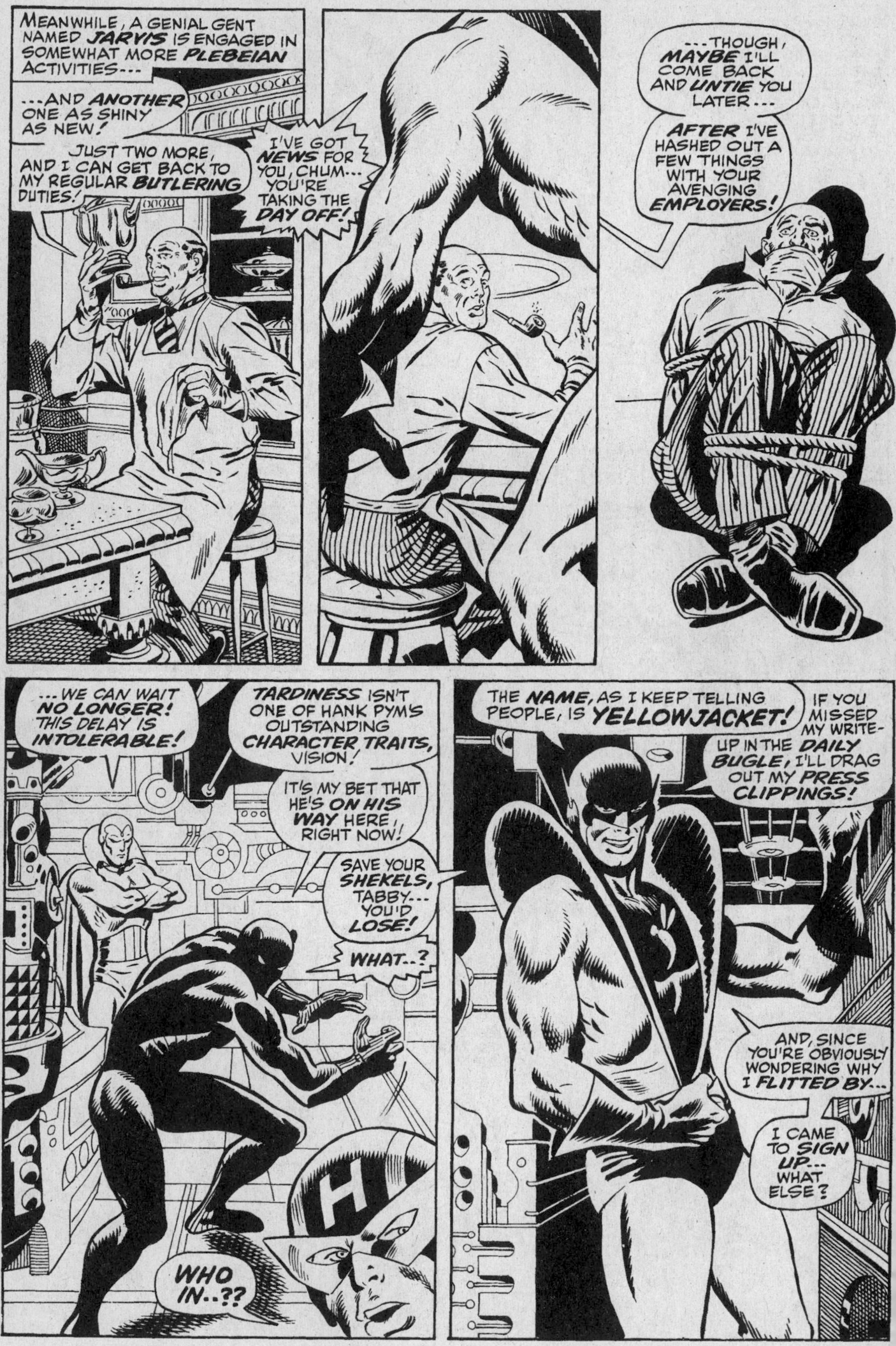

MEANWHILE, A GENIAL GENT NAMED JARVIS IS ENGAGED IN SOMEWHAT MORE PLEBEIAN ACTIVITIES---
...AND ANOTHER ONE AS SHINY AS NEW!
JUST TWO MORE, AND I CAN GET BACK TO MY REGULAR BUTLERING DUTIES!
I'VE GOT NEWS FOR YOU, CHUM--- YOU'RE TAKING THE DAY OFF!
---THOUGH, MAYBE I'LL COME BACK AND UNTIE YOU LATER---
AFTER I'VE HASHED OUT A FEW THINGS WITH YOUR AVENGING EMPLOYERS!
...WE CAN WAIT NO LONGER! THIS DELAY IS INTOLERABLE!
TARDINESS ISN'T ONE OF HANK PYM'S OUTSTANDING CHARACTER TRAITS, VISION!
IT'S MY BET THAT HE'S ON HIS WAY HERE, RIGHT NOW!
SAVE YOUR SHEKELS, TABBY--- YOU'D LOSE!
WHAT..?
WHO IN..??
THE NAME, AS I KEEP TELLING PEOPLE, IS YELLOWJACKET!
IF YOU MISSED MY WRITE-UP IN THE DAILY BUGLE, I'LL DRAG OUT MY PRESS CLIPPINGS!
AND, SINCE YOU'RE OBVIOUSLY WONDERING WHY I FLITTED BY...
I CAME TO SIGN UP... WHAT ELSE?

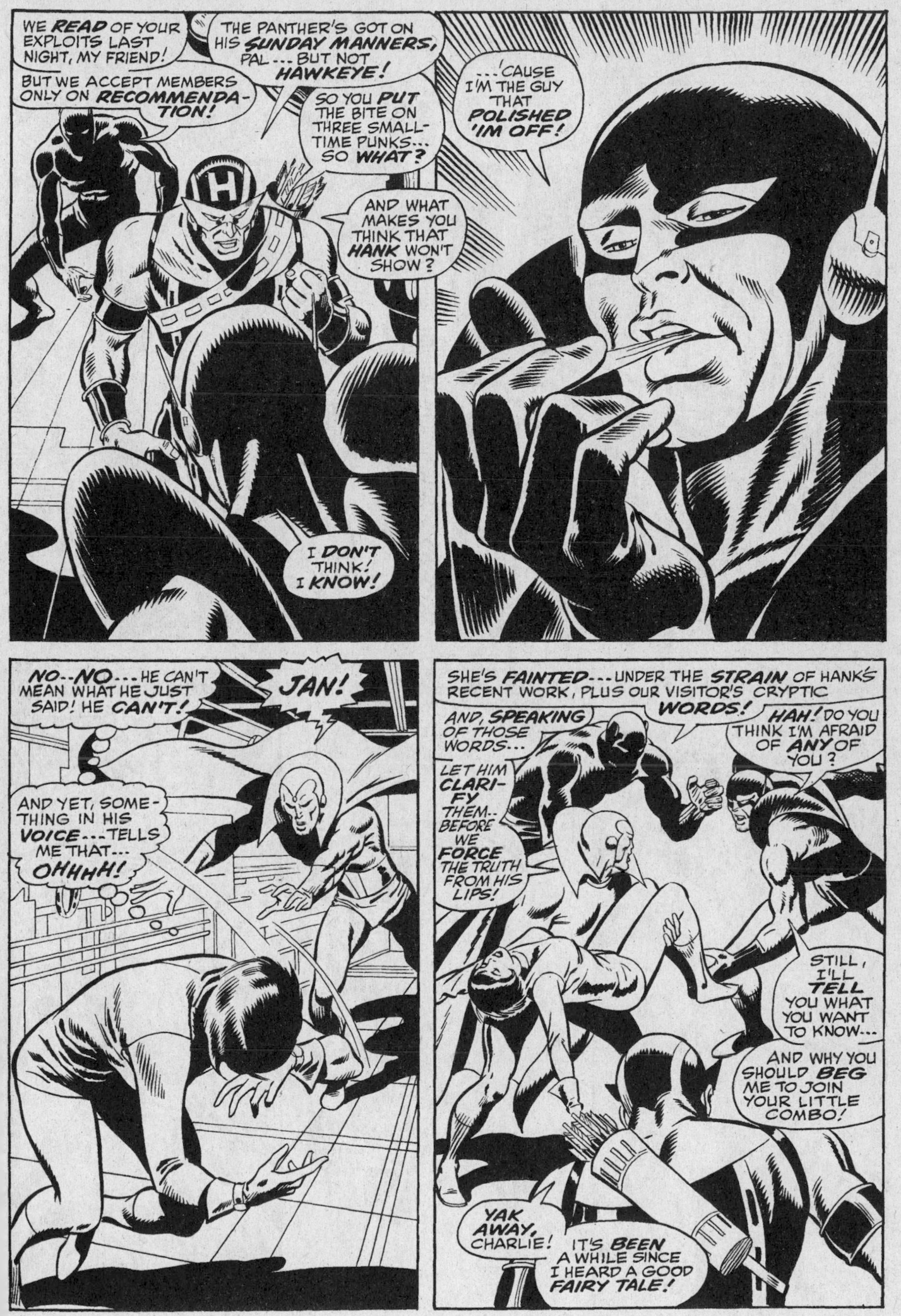
WE READ OF YOUR EXPLOITS LAST NIGHT, MY FRIEND!
BUT WE ACCEPT MEMBERS ONLY ON RECOMMENDATION!
THE PANTHER'S GOT ON HIS SUNDAY MANNERS, PAL... BUT NOT HAWKEYE!
SO YOU PUT THE BITE ON THREE SMALL-TIME PUNKS... SO WHAT?
AND WHAT MAKES YOU THINK THAT HANK WON'T SHOW?
I DON'T THINK! I KNOW!
...'CAUSE I'M THE GUY THAT POLISHED 'IM OFF!
NO--NO... HE CAN'T MEAN WHAT HE JUST SAID! HE CAN'T!
JAN!
AND YET, SOMETHING IN HIS VOICE... TELLS ME THAT... OHHHH!
SHE'S FAINTED... UNDER THE STRAIN OF HANK'S RECENT WORK, PLUS OUR VISITOR'S CRYPTIC WORDS!
AND, SPEAKING OF THOSE WORDS...
LET HIM CLARIFY THEM.. BEFORE WE FORCE THE TRUTH FROM HIS LIPS!
HAH! DO YOU THINK I'M AFRAID OF ANY OF YOU?
STILL, I'LL TELL YOU WHAT YOU WANT TO KNOW...
AND WHY YOU SHOULD BEG ME TO JOIN YOUR LITTLE COMBO!
YAK AWAY, CHARLIE!
IT'S BEEN A WHILE SINCE I HEARD A GOOD FAIRY TALE!

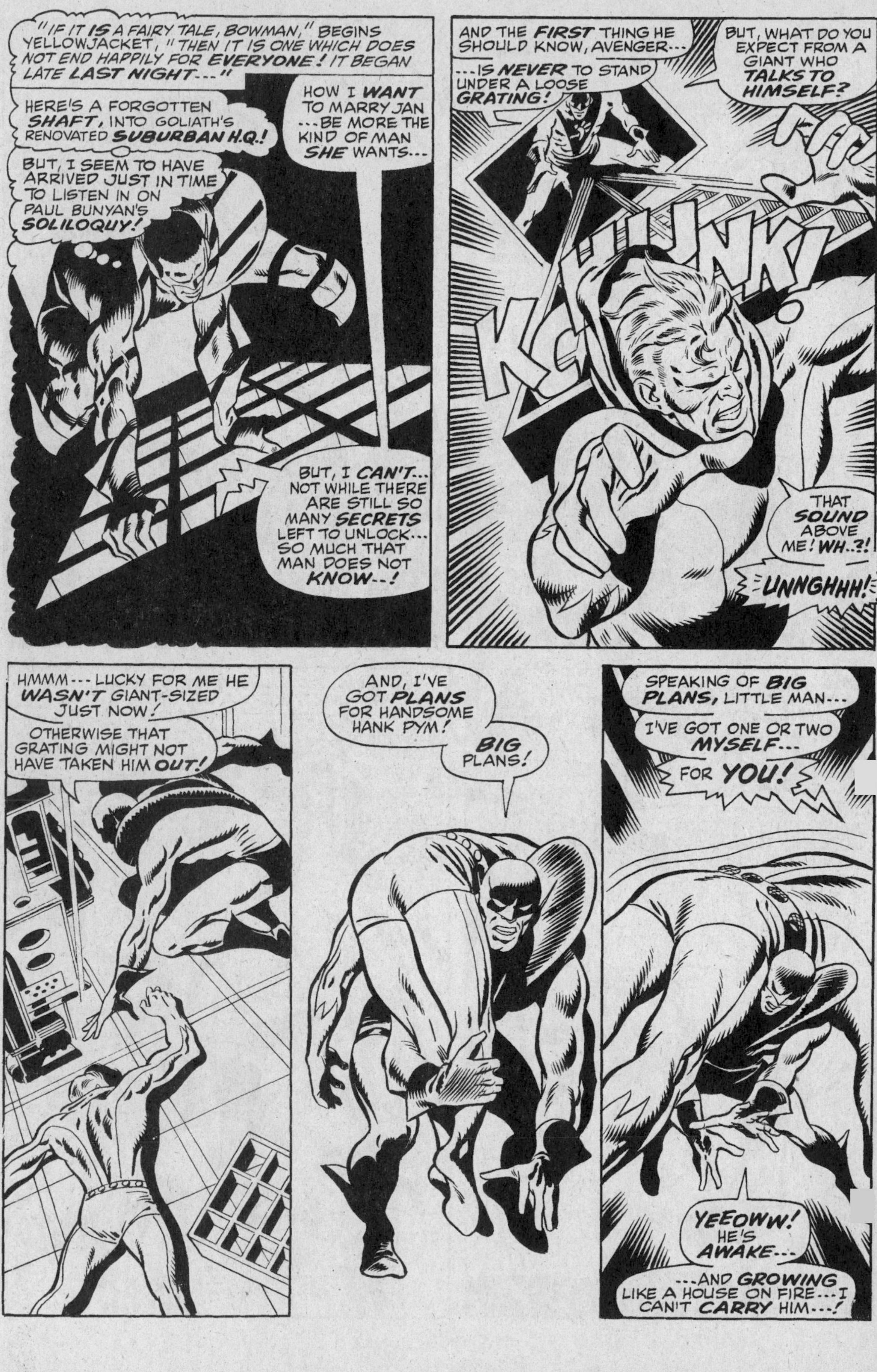
"IF IT IS A FAIRY TALE, BOWMAN," BEGINS YELLOWJACKET, "THEN IT IS ONE WHICH DOES NOT END HAPPILY FOR EVERYONE! IT BEGAN LATE LAST NIGHT..."
HERE'S A FORGOTTEN SHAFT, INTO GOLIATH'S RENOVATED SUBURBAN H.Q.!
BUT, I SEEM TO HAVE ARRIVED JUST IN TIME TO LISTEN IN ON PAUL BUNYAN'S SOLILOQUY!
HOW I WANT TO MARRY JAN ...BE MORE THE KIND OF MAN SHE WANTS...
BUT, I CAN'T... NOT WHILE THERE ARE STILL SO MANY SECRETS LEFT TO UNLOCK... SO MUCH THAT MAN DOES NOT KNOW--!
AND THE FIRST THING HE SHOULD KNOW, AVENGER...
...IS NEVER TO STAND UNDER A LOOSE GRATING!
BUT, WHAT DO YOU EXPECT FROM A GIANT WHO TALKS TO HIMSELF?
K-CHUNK!
THAT SOUND ABOVE ME! WH..?!
UNNGHHH!
HMMM--- LUCKY FOR ME HE WASN'T GIANT-SIZED JUST NOW!
OTHERWISE THAT GRATING MIGHT NOT HAVE TAKEN HIM OUT!
AND, I'VE GOT PLANS FOR HANDSOME HANK PYM!
BIG PLANS!
SPEAKING OF BIG PLANS, LITTLE MAN...
I'VE GOT ONE OR TWO MYSELF...
FOR YOU!
YEEOWW! HE'S AWAKE...
...AND GROWING LIKE A HOUSE ON FIRE---I CAN'T CARRY HIM---!

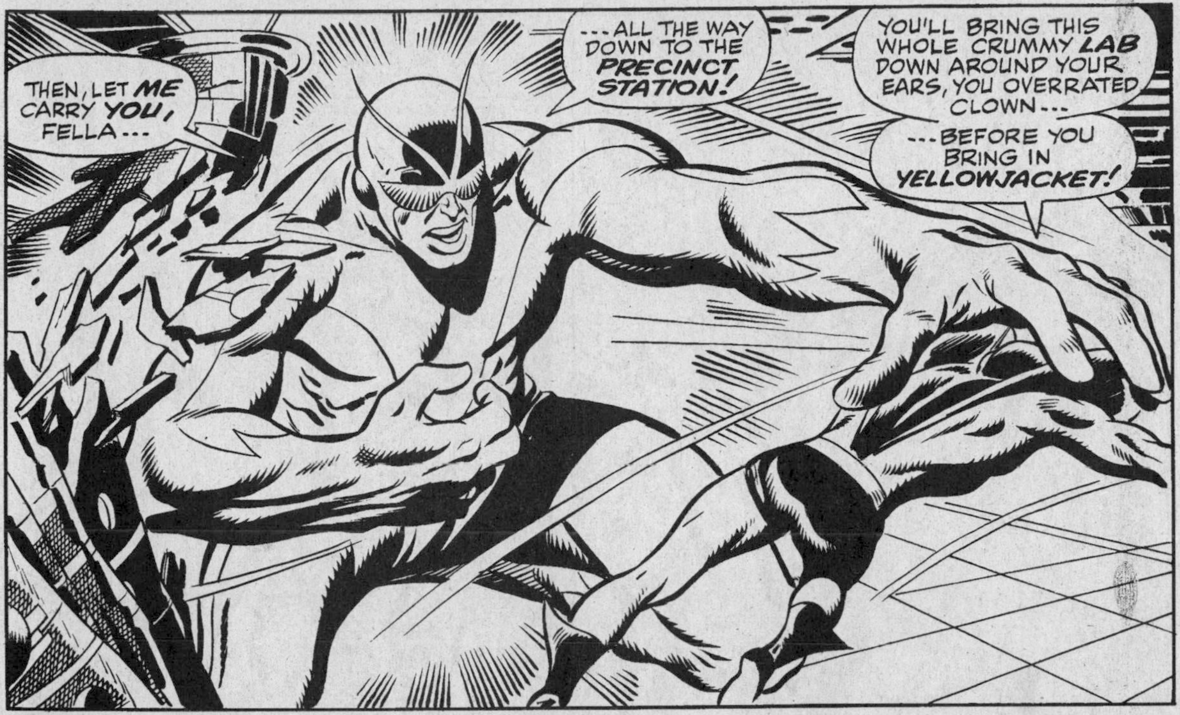
THEN, LET ME CARRY YOU, FELLA...
...ALL THE WAY DOWN TO THE PRECINCT STATION!
YOU'LL BRING THIS WHOLE CRUMMY LAB DOWN AROUND YOUR EARS, YOU OVERRATED CLOWN...
...BEFORE YOU BRING IN YELLOWJACKET!

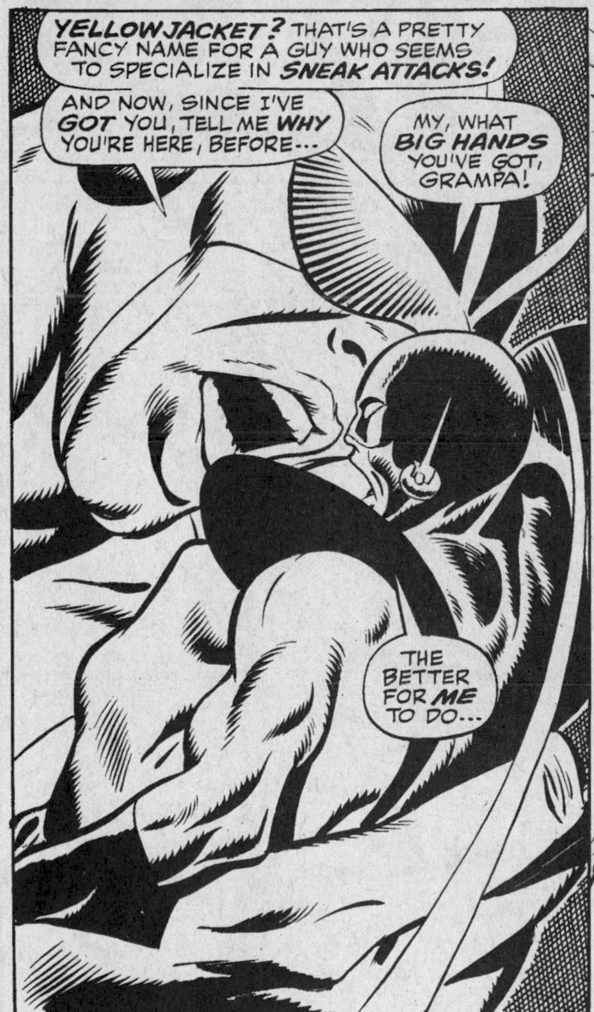
YELLOWJACKET? THAT'S A PRETTY FANCY NAME FOR A GUY WHO SEEMS TO SPECIALIZE IN SNEAK ATTACKS!
AND NOW, SINCE I'VE GOT YOU, TELL ME WHY YOU'RE HERE, BEFORE...
MY, WHAT BIG HANDS YOU'VE GOT, GRAMPA!
THE BETTER FOR ME TO DO...

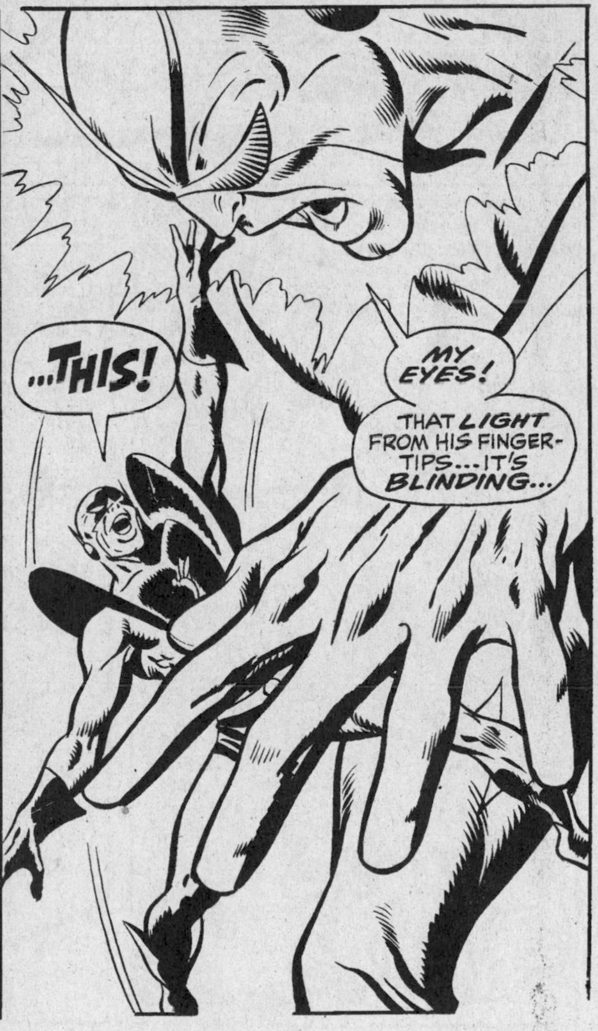
...THIS!
MY EYES!
THAT LIGHT FROM HIS FINGER-TIPS...IT'S BLINDING...

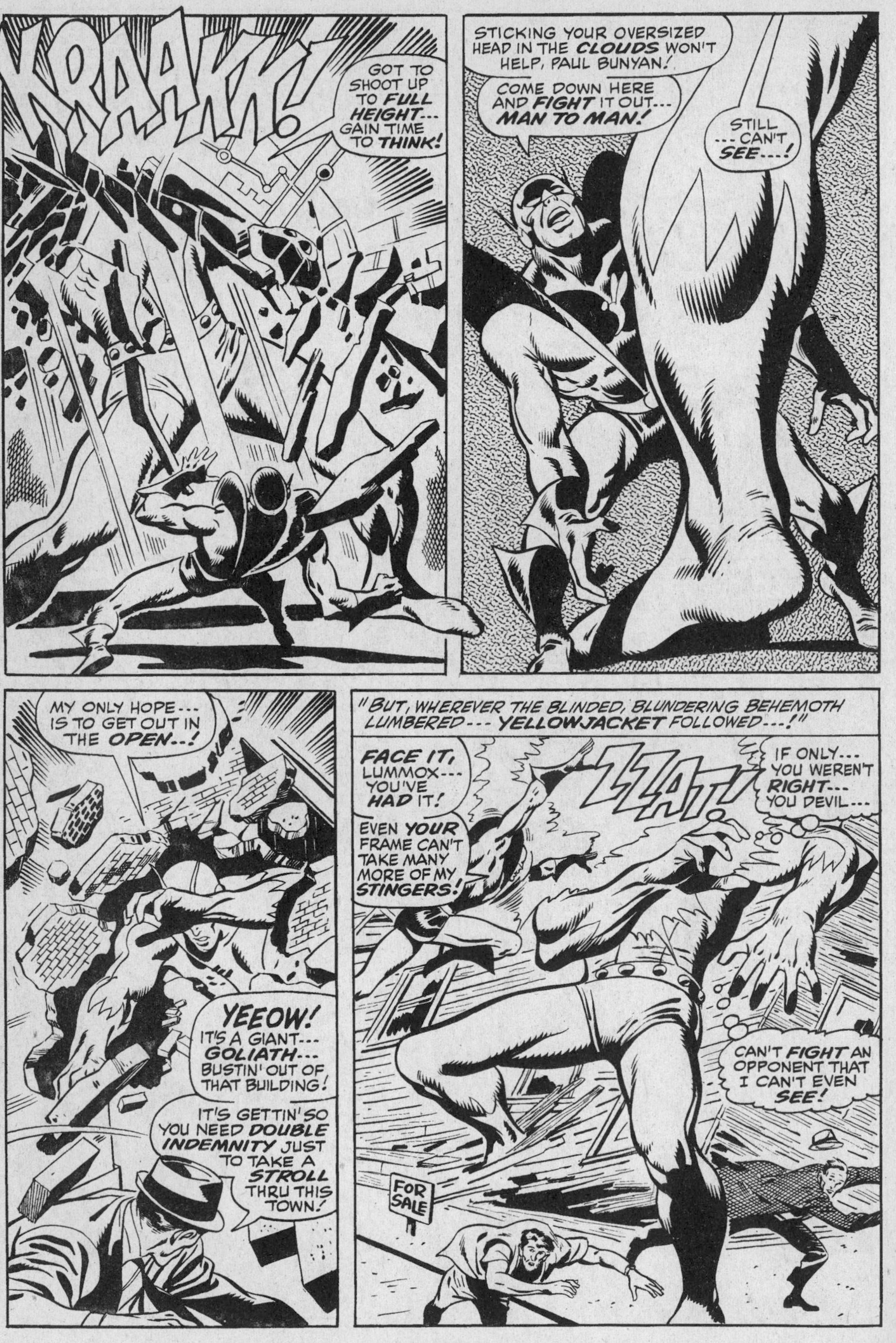
KRAAKK!
GOT TO SHOOT UP TO FULL HEIGHT--- GAIN TIME TO THINK!
STICKING YOUR OVERSIZED HEAD IN THE CLOUDS WON'T HELP, PAUL BUNYAN!
COME DOWN HERE AND FIGHT IT OUT--- MAN TO MAN!
STILL --- CAN'T SEE---!
MY ONLY HOPE--- IS TO GET OUT IN THE OPEN--!
YEEOW! IT'S A GIANT--- GOLIATH--- BUSTIN' OUT OF THAT BUILDING!
IT'S GETTIN' SO YOU NEED DOUBLE INDEMNITY JUST TO TAKE A STROLL THRU THIS TOWN!
"BUT, WHEREVER THE BLINDED, BLUNDERING BEHEMOTH LUMBERED--- YELLOWJACKET FOLLOWED---!"
FACE IT, LUMMOX--- YOU'VE HAD IT!
EVEN YOUR FRAME CAN'T TAKE MANY MORE OF MY STINGERS!
ZZAT!
IF ONLY--- YOU WEREN'T RIGHT--- YOU DEVIL---
CAN'T FIGHT AN OPPONENT THAT I CAN'T EVEN SEE!
FOR SALE

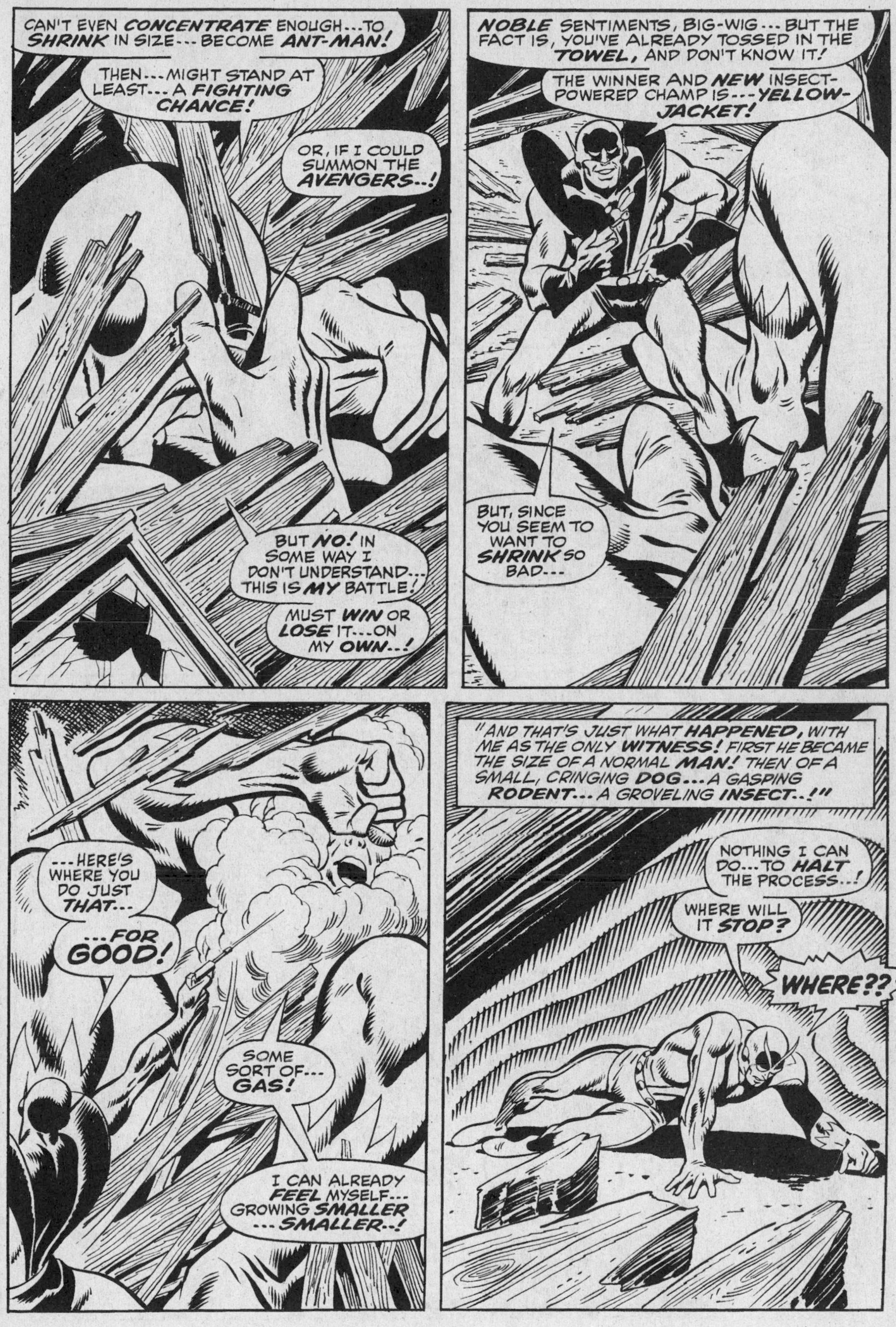
CAN'T EVEN CONCENTRATE ENOUGH... TO SHRINK IN SIZE--- BECOME ANT-MAN!
THEN--- MIGHT STAND AT LEAST--- A FIGHTING CHANCE!
OR, IF I COULD SUMMON THE AVENGERS..!
BUT NO! IN SOME WAY I DON'T UNDERSTAND... THIS IS MY BATTLE!
MUST WIN OR LOSE IT... ON MY OWN..!
NOBLE SENTIMENTS, BIG-WIG... BUT THE FACT IS, YOU'VE ALREADY TOSSED IN THE TOWEL, AND DON'T KNOW IT!
THE WINNER AND NEW INSECT-POWERED CHAMP IS---YELLOW-JACKET!
BUT, SINCE YOU SEEM TO WANT TO SHRINK SO BAD...
---HERE'S WHERE YOU DO JUST THAT...
...FOR GOOD!
SOME SORT OF... GAS!
I CAN ALREADY FEEL MYSELF... GROWING SMALLER ...SMALLER..!
"AND THAT'S JUST WHAT HAPPENED, WITH ME AS THE ONLY WITNESS! FIRST HE BECAME THE SIZE OF A NORMAL MAN! THEN OF A SMALL, CRINGING DOG... A GASPING RODENT... A GROVELING INSECT..!"
NOTHING I CAN DO... TO HALT THE PROCESS..!
WHERE WILL IT STOP?
WHERE??

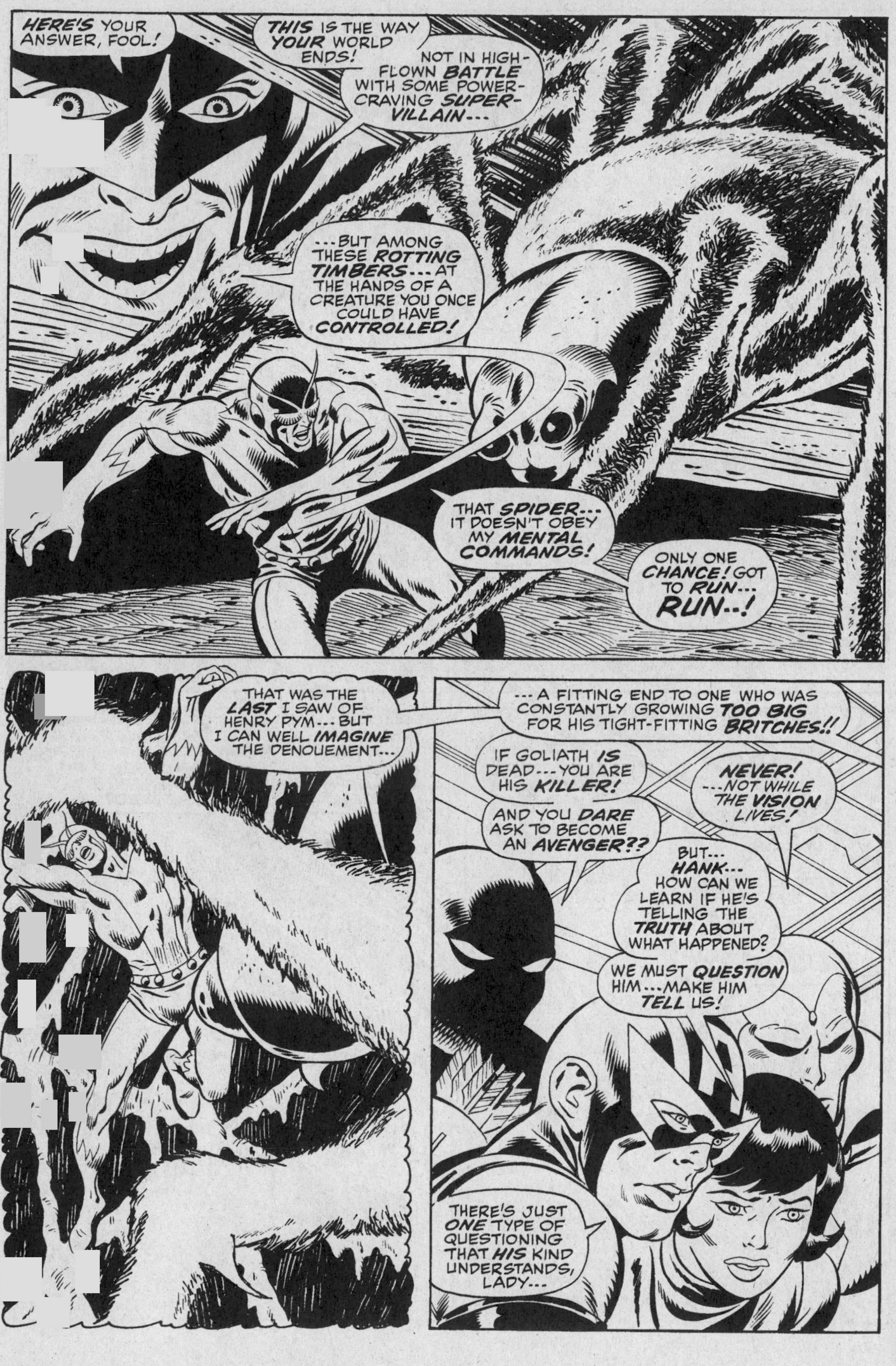
HERE'S YOUR ANSWER, FOOL!
THIS IS THE WAY YOUR WORLD ENDS!
NOT IN HIGH-FLOWN BATTLE WITH SOME POWER-CRAVING SUPER-VILLAIN---
---BUT AMONG THESE ROTTING TIMBERS--- AT THE HANDS OF A CREATURE YOU ONCE COULD HAVE CONTROLLED!
THAT SPIDER--- IT DOESN'T OBEY MY MENTAL COMMANDS!
ONLY ONE CHANCE! GOT TO RUN--- RUN--!
THAT WAS THE LAST I SAW OF HENRY PYM--- BUT I CAN WELL IMAGINE THE DENOUEMENT---
---A FITTING END TO ONE WHO WAS CONSTANTLY GROWING TOO BIG FOR HIS TIGHT-FITTING BRITCHES!!
IF GOLIATH IS DEAD--- YOU ARE HIS KILLER!
AND YOU DARE ASK TO BECOME AN AVENGER??
NEVER! ---NOT WHILE THE VISION LIVES!
BUT--- HANK--- HOW CAN WE LEARN IF HE'S TELLING THE TRUTH ABOUT WHAT HAPPENED?
WE MUST QUESTION HIM---MAKE HIM TELL US!
THERE'S JUST ONE TYPE OF QUESTIONING THAT HIS KIND UNDERSTANDS, LADY---

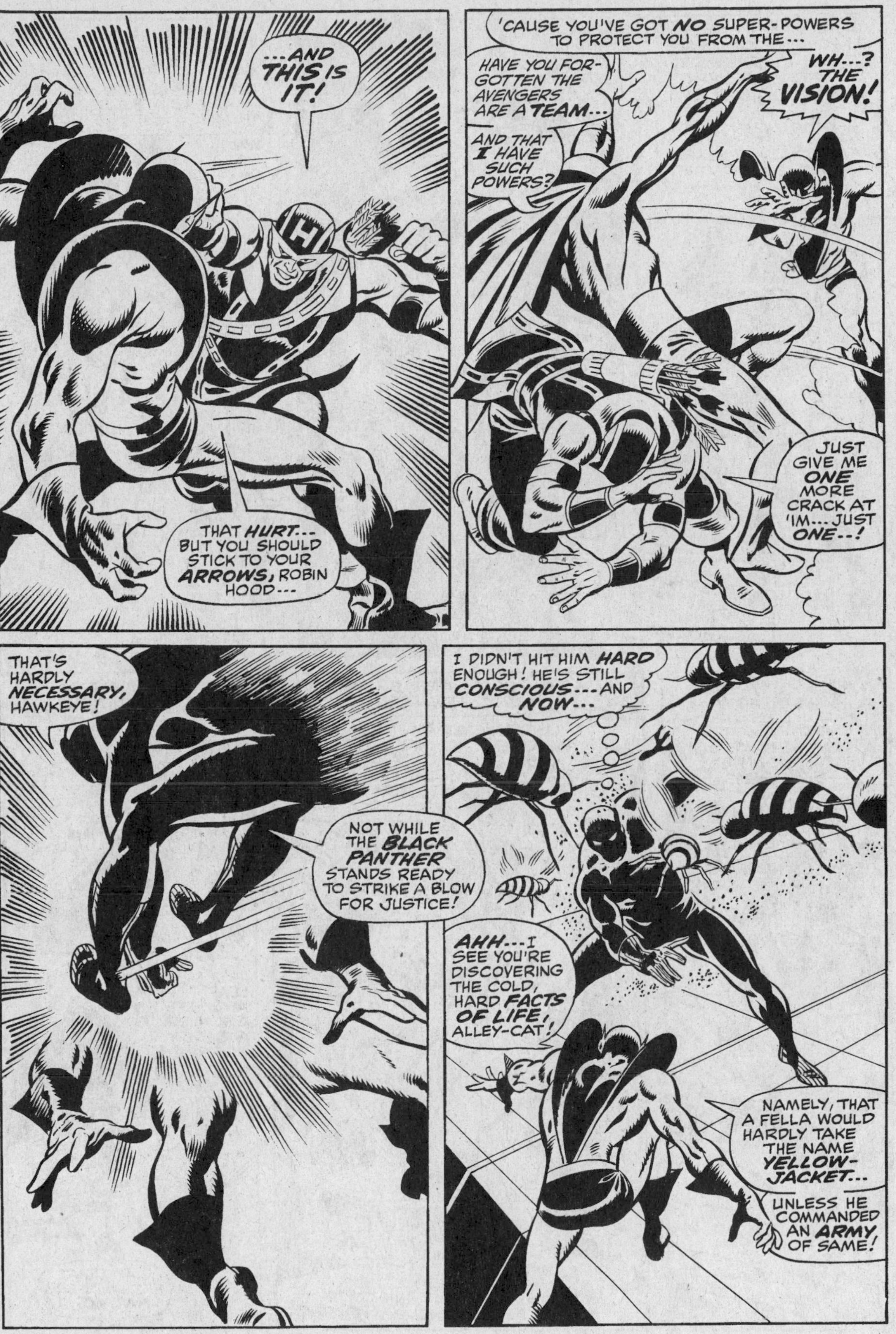
...AND THIS IS IT!
THAT HURT... BUT YOU SHOULD STICK TO YOUR ARROWS, ROBIN HOOD---
'CAUSE YOU'VE GOT NO SUPER-POWERS TO PROTECT YOU FROM THE...
HAVE YOU FORGOTTEN THE AVENGERS ARE A TEAM...
WH...? THE VISION!
AND THAT I HAVE SUCH POWERS?
JUST GIVE ME ONE MORE CRACK AT 'IM... JUST ONE--!
THAT'S HARDLY NECESSARY, HAWKEYE!
NOT WHILE THE BLACK PANTHER STANDS READY TO STRIKE A BLOW FOR JUSTICE!
I DIDN'T HIT HIM HARD ENOUGH! HE'S STILL CONSCIOUS---AND NOW...
AHH---I SEE YOU'RE DISCOVERING THE COLD, HARD FACTS OF LIFE, ALLEY-CAT!
NAMELY, THAT A FELLA WOULD HARDLY TAKE THE NAME YELLOW-JACKET...
UNLESS HE COMMANDED AN ARMY OF SAME!

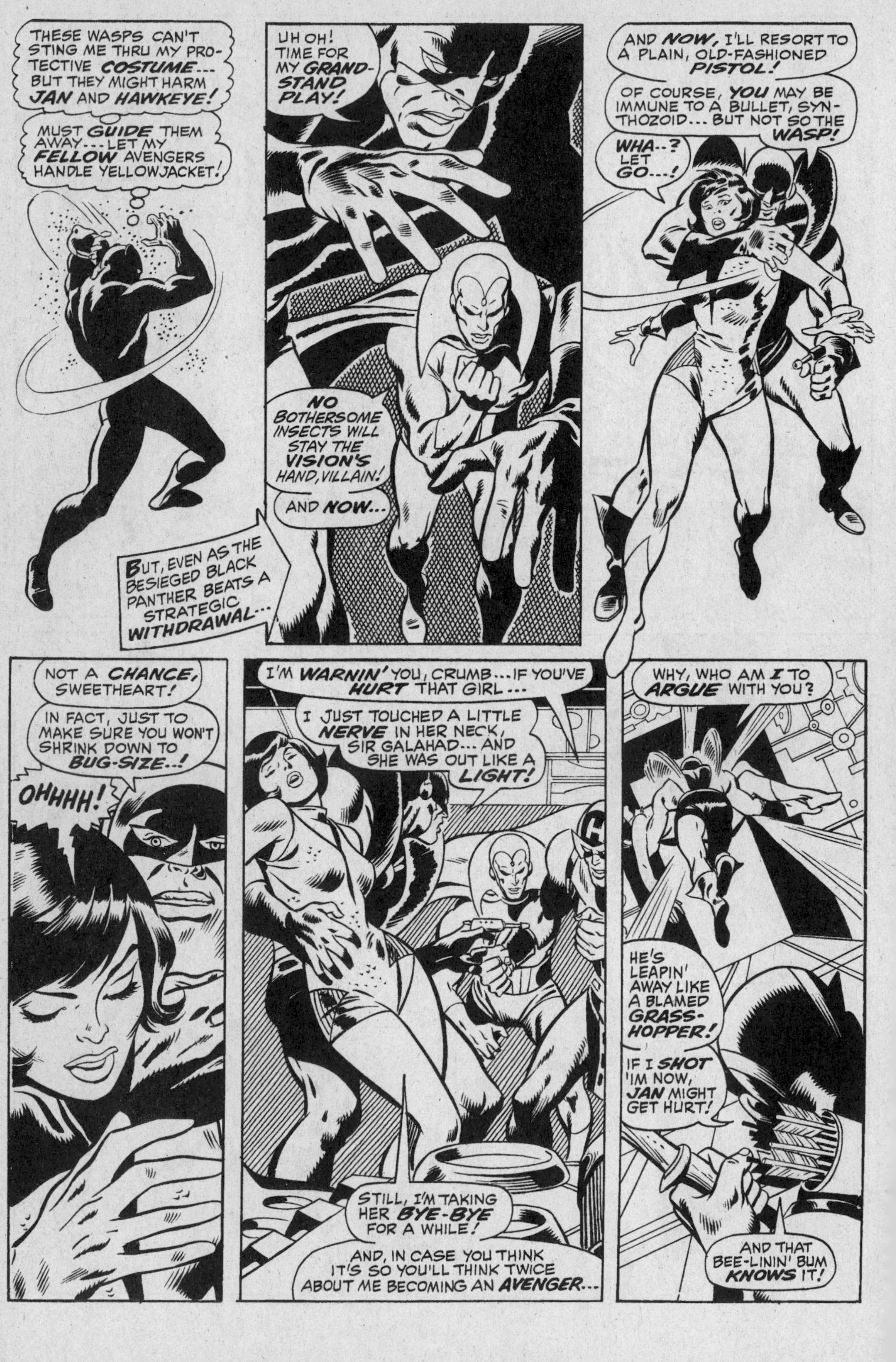

THESE WASPS CAN'T STING ME THRU MY PROTECTIVE COSTUME... BUT THEY MIGHT HARM JAN AND HAWKEYE!
MUST GUIDE THEM AWAY... LET MY FELLOW AVENGERS HANDLE YELLOWJACKET!
UH OH! TIME FOR MY GRAND-STAND PLAY!
NO BOTHERSOME INSECTS WILL STAY THE VISION'S HAND, VILLAIN!
AND NOW...
BUT, EVEN AS THE BESIEGED BLACK PANTHER BEATS A STRATEGIC WITHDRAWAL...
AND NOW, I'LL RESORT TO A PLAIN, OLD-FASHIONED PISTOL!
OF COURSE, YOU MAY BE IMMUNE TO A BULLET, SYNTHOZOID... BUT NOT SO THE WASP!
WHA--? LET GO...!
NOT A CHANCE, SWEETHEART!
IN FACT, JUST TO MAKE SURE YOU WON'T SHRINK DOWN TO BUG-SIZE..!
OHHHH!
I'M WARNIN' YOU, CRUMB... IF YOU'VE HURT THAT GIRL...
I JUST TOUCHED A LITTLE NERVE IN HER NECK, SIR GALAHAD... AND SHE WAS OUT LIKE A LIGHT!
STILL, I'M TAKING HER BYE-BYE FOR A WHILE!
AND, IN CASE YOU THINK IT'S SO YOU'LL THINK TWICE ABOUT ME BECOMING AN AVENGER...
WHY, WHO AM I TO ARGUE WITH YOU?
HE'S LEAPIN' AWAY LIKE A BLAMED GRASS-HOPPER!
IF I SHOT 'IM NOW, JAN MIGHT GET HURT!
AND THAT BEE-LININ' BUM KNOWS IT!

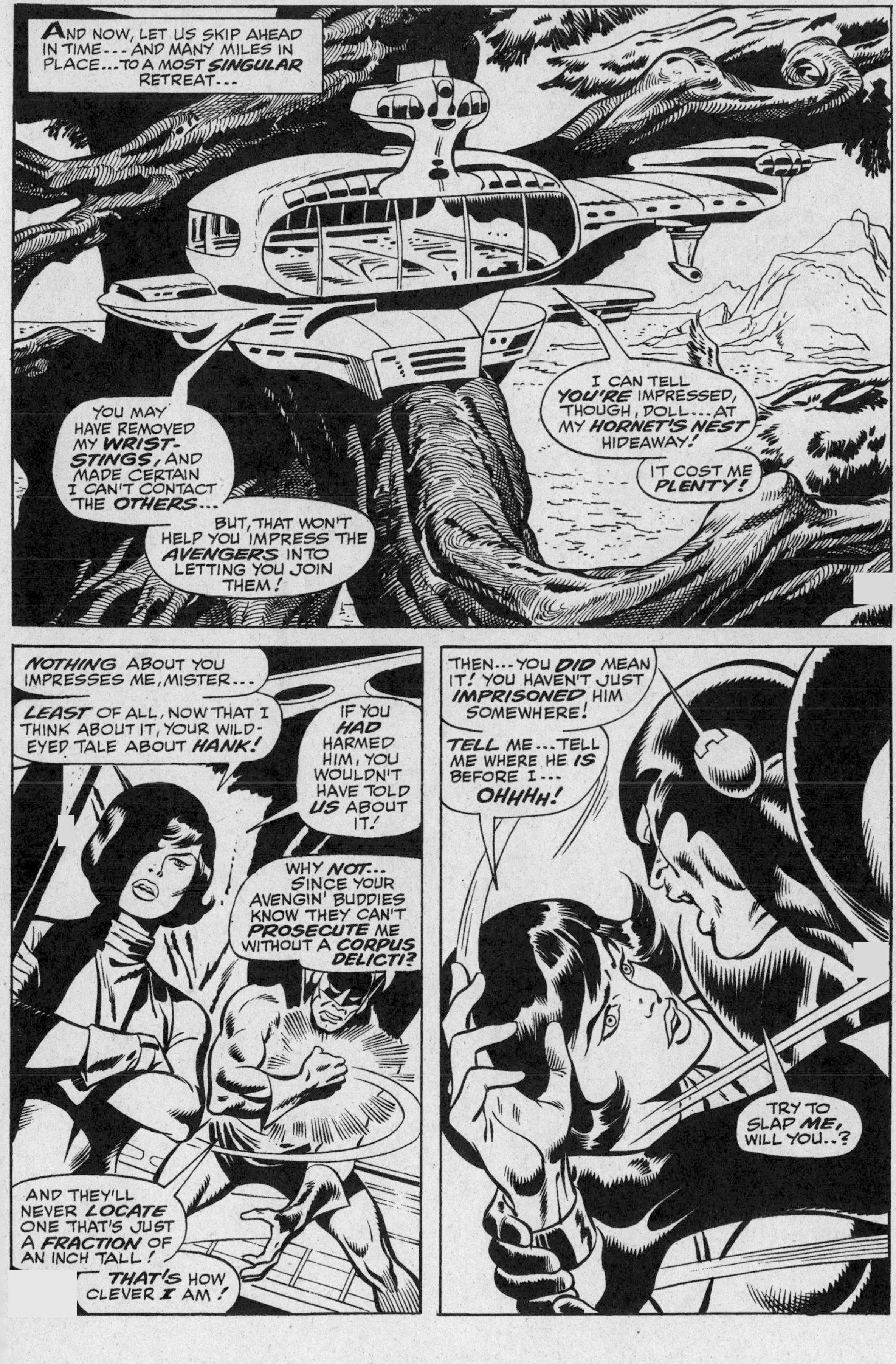
AND NOW, LET US SKIP AHEAD IN TIME--- AND MANY MILES IN PLACE...TO A MOST SINGULAR RETREAT...
YOU MAY HAVE REMOVED MY WRIST-STINGS, AND MADE CERTAIN I CAN'T CONTACT THE OTHERS...
BUT, THAT WON'T HELP YOU IMPRESS THE AVENGERS INTO LETTING YOU JOIN THEM!
I CAN TELL YOU'RE IMPRESSED, THOUGH, DOLL...AT MY HORNET'S NEST HIDEAWAY!
IT COST ME PLENTY!
NOTHING ABOUT YOU IMPRESSES ME, MISTER...
LEAST OF ALL, NOW THAT I THINK ABOUT IT, YOUR WILD-EYED TALE ABOUT HANK!
IF YOU HAD HARMED HIM, YOU WOULDN'T HAVE TOLD US ABOUT IT!
WHY NOT... SINCE YOUR AVENGIN' BUDDIES KNOW THEY CAN'T PROSECUTE ME WITHOUT A CORPUS DELICTI?
AND THEY'LL NEVER LOCATE ONE THAT'S JUST A FRACTION OF AN INCH TALL!
THAT'S HOW CLEVER I AM!
THEN...YOU DID MEAN IT! YOU HAVEN'T JUST IMPRISONED HIM SOMEWHERE!
TELL ME...TELL ME WHERE HE IS BEFORE I... OHHHH!
TRY TO SLAP ME, WILL YOU..?

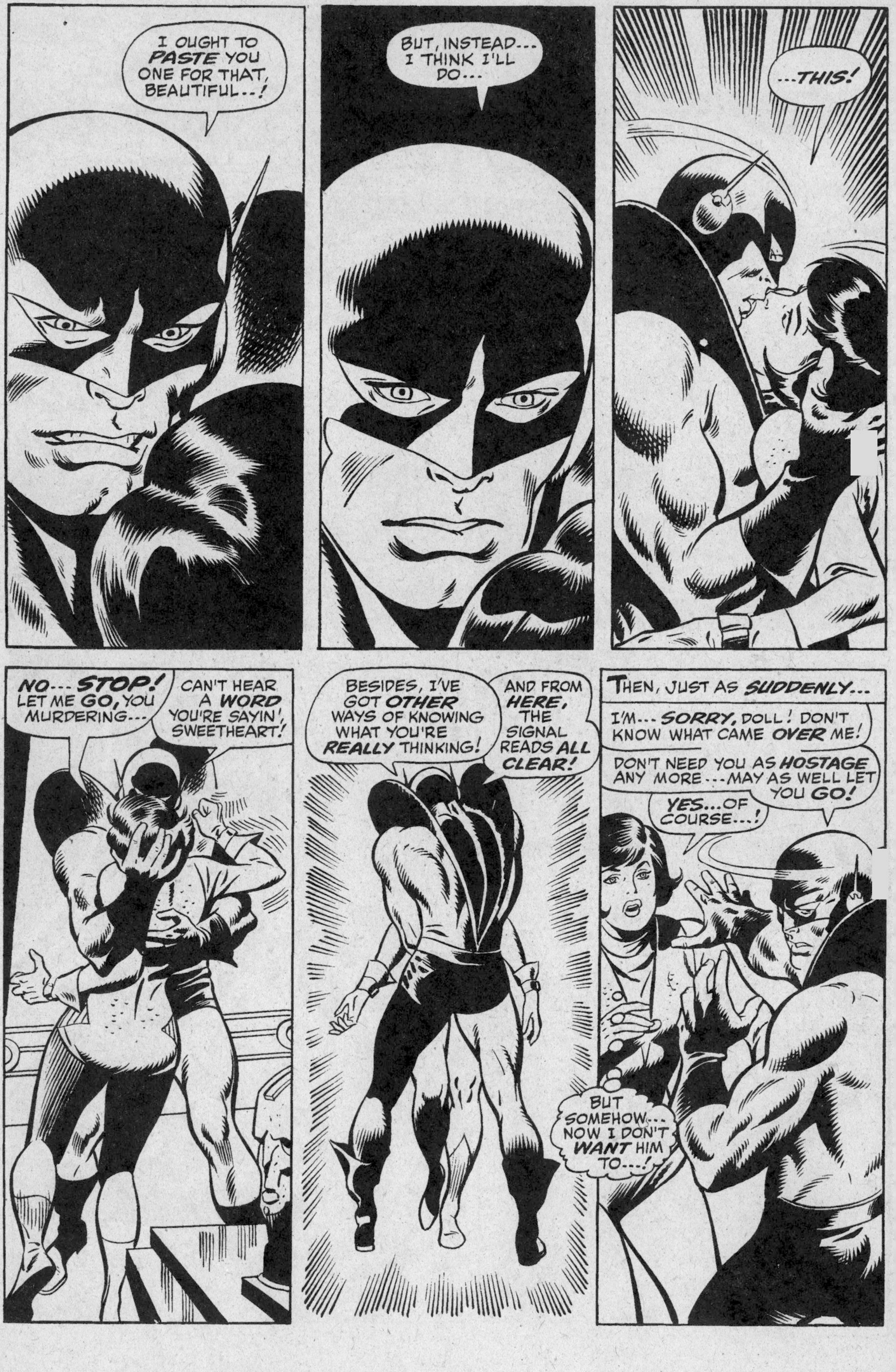
I OUGHT TO PASTE YOU ONE FOR THAT, BEAUTIFUL..!
BUT, INSTEAD... I THINK I'LL DO...
...THIS!
NO... STOP! LET ME GO, YOU MURDERING...
CAN'T HEAR A WORD YOU'RE SAYIN', SWEETHEART!
BESIDES, I'VE GOT OTHER WAYS OF KNOWING WHAT YOU'RE REALLY THINKING!
AND FROM HERE, THE SIGNAL READS ALL CLEAR!
THEN, JUST AS SUDDENLY...
I'M... SORRY, DOLL! DON'T KNOW WHAT CAME OVER ME!
DON'T NEED YOU AS HOSTAGE ANY MORE... MAY AS WELL LET YOU GO!
YES...OF COURSE...!
BUT SOMEHOW... NOW I DON'T WANT HIM TO...!

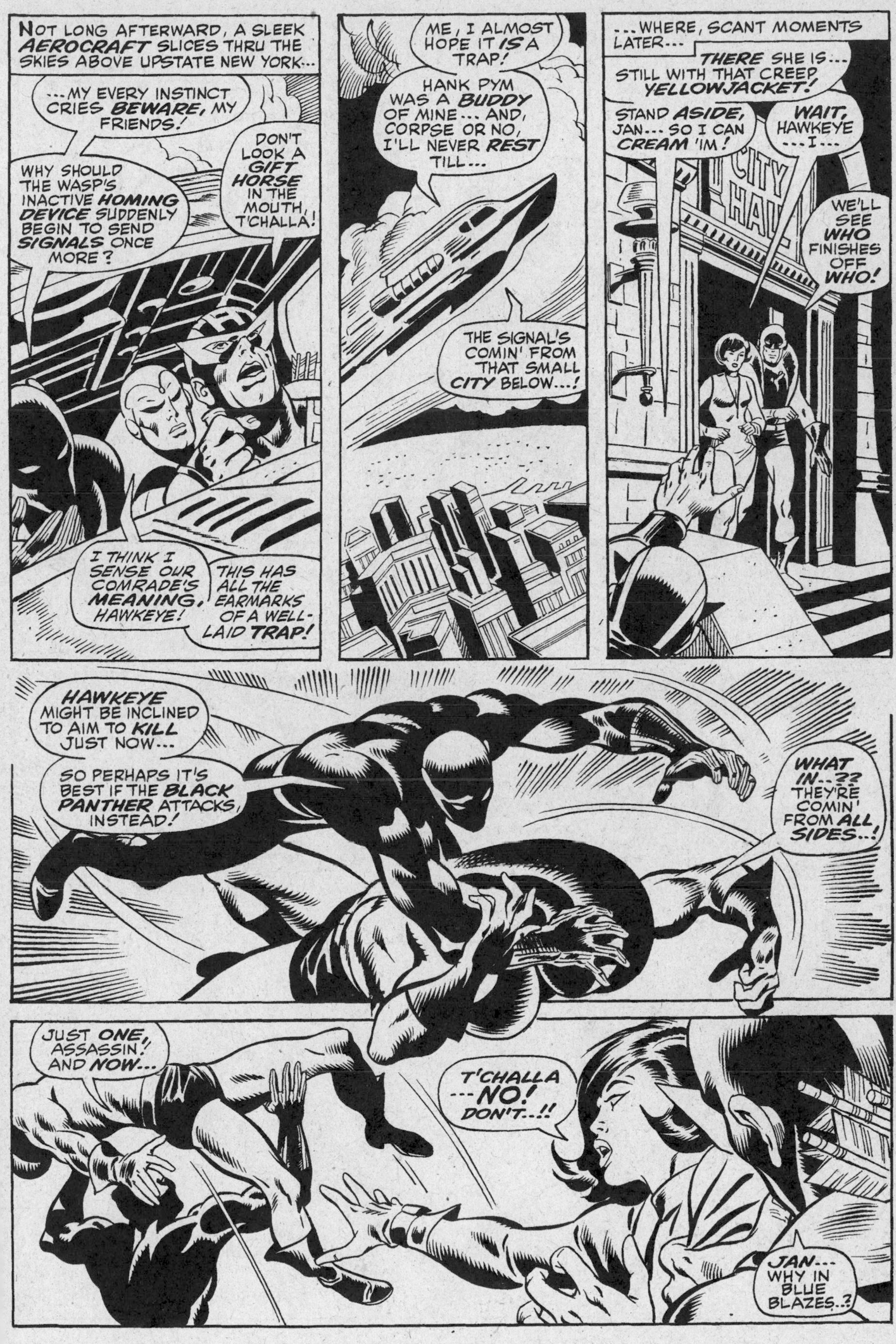
NOT LONG AFTERWARD, A SLEEK AEROCRAFT SLICES THRU THE SKIES ABOVE UPSTATE NEW YORK...
...MY EVERY INSTINCT CRIES BEWARE, MY FRIENDS!
WHY SHOULD THE WASP'S INACTIVE HOMING DEVICE SUDDENLY BEGIN TO SEND SIGNALS ONCE MORE?
DON'T LOOK A GIFT HORSE IN THE MOUTH, T'CHALLA!
I THINK I SENSE OUR COMRADE'S MEANING, HAWKEYE!
THIS HAS ALL THE EARMARKS OF A WELL-LAID TRAP!
ME, I ALMOST HOPE IT IS A TRAP!
HANK PYM WAS A BUDDY OF MINE... AND, CORPSE OR NO, I'LL NEVER REST TILL...
THE SIGNAL'S COMIN' FROM THAT SMALL CITY BELOW...!
...WHERE, SCANT MOMENTS LATER...
THERE SHE IS... STILL WITH THAT CREEP YELLOWJACKET!
STAND ASIDE, JAN... SO I CAN CREAM 'IM!
WAIT, HAWKEYE ...I...
CITY HAL
WE'LL SEE WHO FINISHES OFF WHO!
HAWKEYE MIGHT BE INCLINED TO AIM TO KILL JUST NOW...
SO PERHAPS IT'S BEST IF THE BLACK PANTHER ATTACKS, INSTEAD!
WHAT IN..?? THEY'RE COMIN' FROM ALL SIDES...!
JUST ONE, ASSASSIN! AND NOW...
T'CHALLA ...NO! DON'T..!!
JAN... WHY IN BLUE BLAZES..?

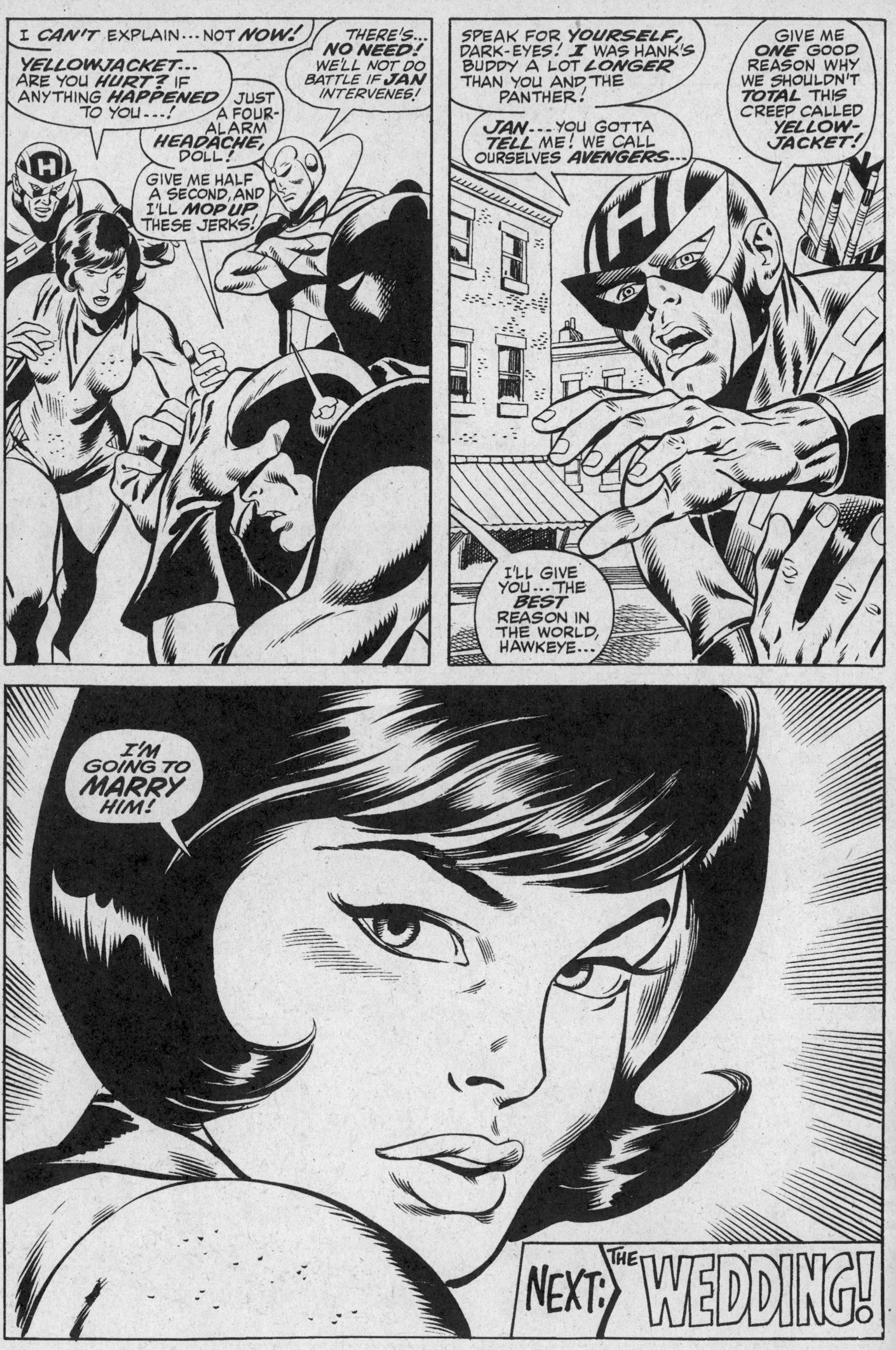
I CAN'T EXPLAIN... NOT NOW!
YELLOWJACKET... ARE YOU HURT? IF ANYTHING HAPPENED TO YOU...!
JUST A FOUR-ALARM HEADACHE, DOLL!
GIVE ME HALF A SECOND, AND I'LL MOP UP THESE JERKS!
THERE'S... NO NEED! WE'LL NOT DO BATTLE IF JAN INTERVENES!
SPEAK FOR YOURSELF, DARK-EYES! I WAS HANK'S BUDDY A LOT LONGER THAN YOU AND THE PANTHER!
GIVE ME ONE GOOD REASON WHY WE SHOULDN'T TOTAL THIS CREEP CALLED YELLOW-JACKET!
JAN... YOU GOTTA TELL ME! WE CALL OURSELVES AVENGERS...
I'LL GIVE YOU... THE BEST REASON IN THE WORLD, HAWKEYE...
I'M GOING TO MARRY HIM!
NEXT: THE WEDDING!

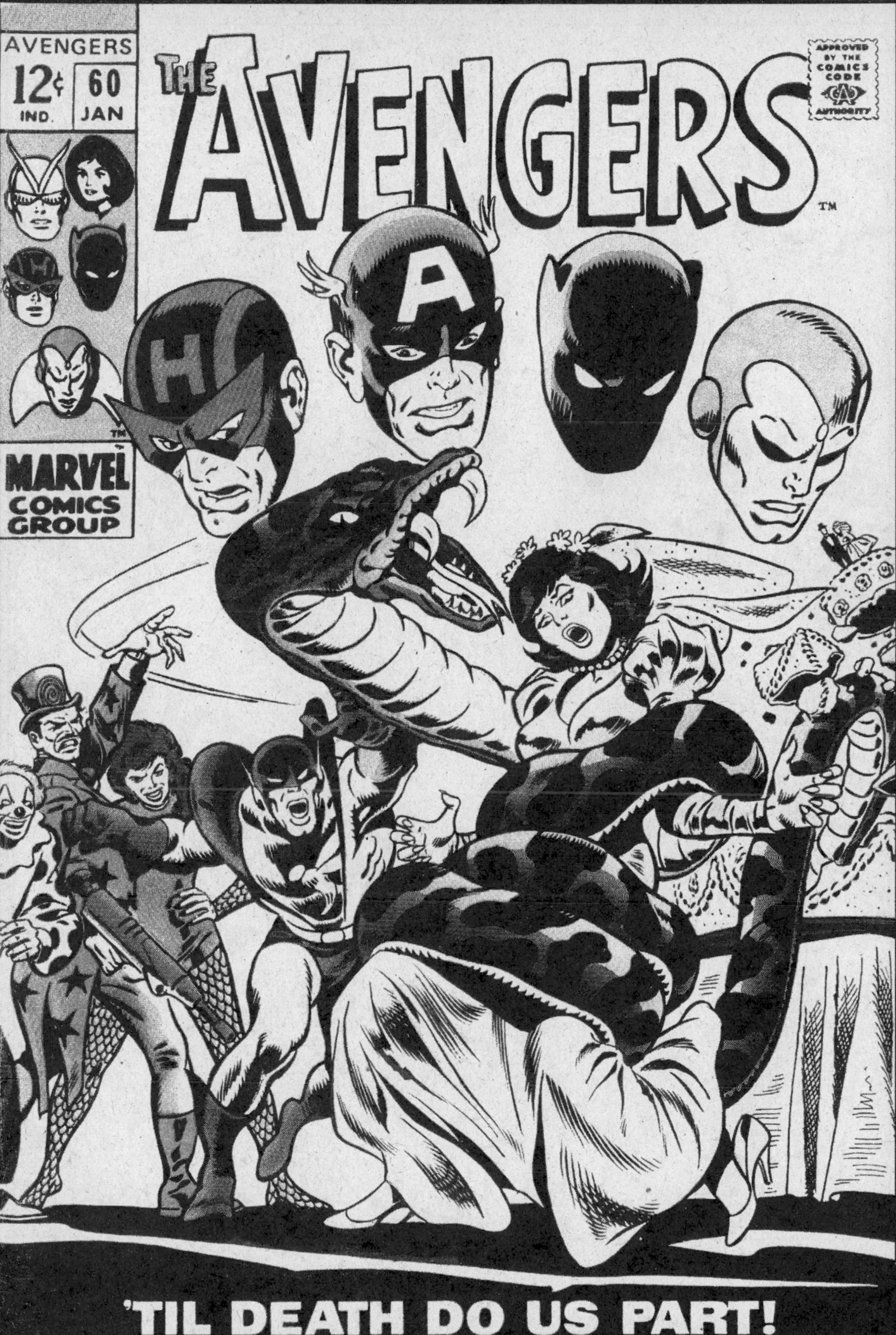
AVENGERS
12¢
IND.
60
JAN
THE AVENGERS
TM
APPROVED BY THE COMICS CODE AUTHORITY
MARVEL COMICS GROUP
'TIL DEATH DO US PART!

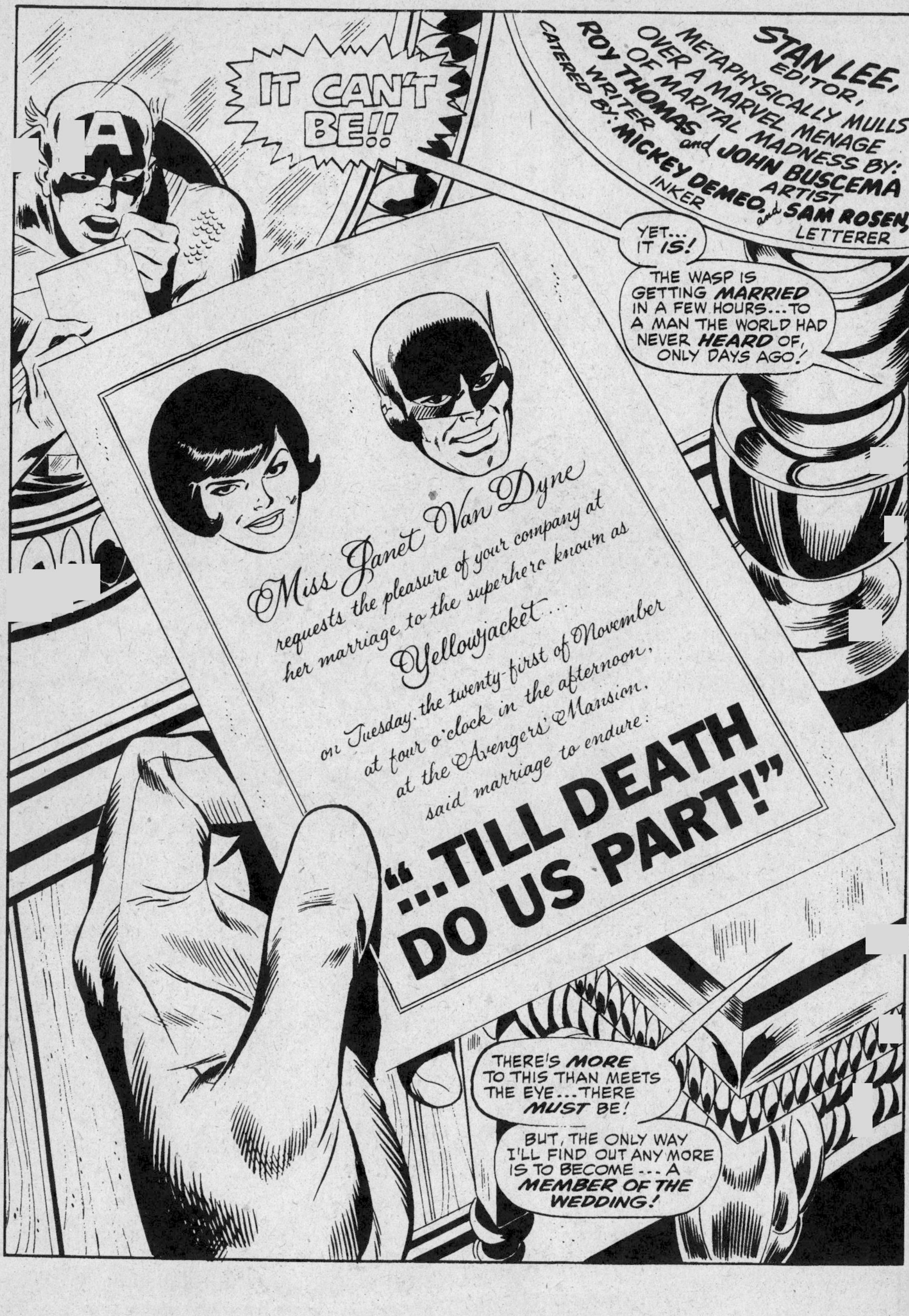
IT CAN'T BE!!
STAN LEE, EDITOR, METAPHYSICALLY MULLS OVER A MARVEL MENAGE OF MARITAL MADNESS BY: ROY THOMAS WRITER and JOHN BUSCEMA ARTIST
CATERED BY: MICKEY DEMEO, INKER and SAM ROSEN, LETTERER
YET... IT IS!
THE WASP IS GETTING MARRIED IN A FEW HOURS... TO A MAN THE WORLD HAD NEVER HEARD OF, ONLY DAYS AGO!
Miss Janet Van Dyne requests the pleasure of your company at her marriage to the superhero known as Yellowjacket... on Tuesday, the twenty-first of November at four o'clock in the afternoon, at the Avengers' Mansion, said marriage to endure:
"...TILL DEATH DO US PART!"
THERE'S MORE TO THIS THAN MEETS THE EYE... THERE MUST BE!
BUT, THE ONLY WAY I'LL FIND OUT ANY MORE IS TO BECOME... A MEMBER OF THE WEDDING!

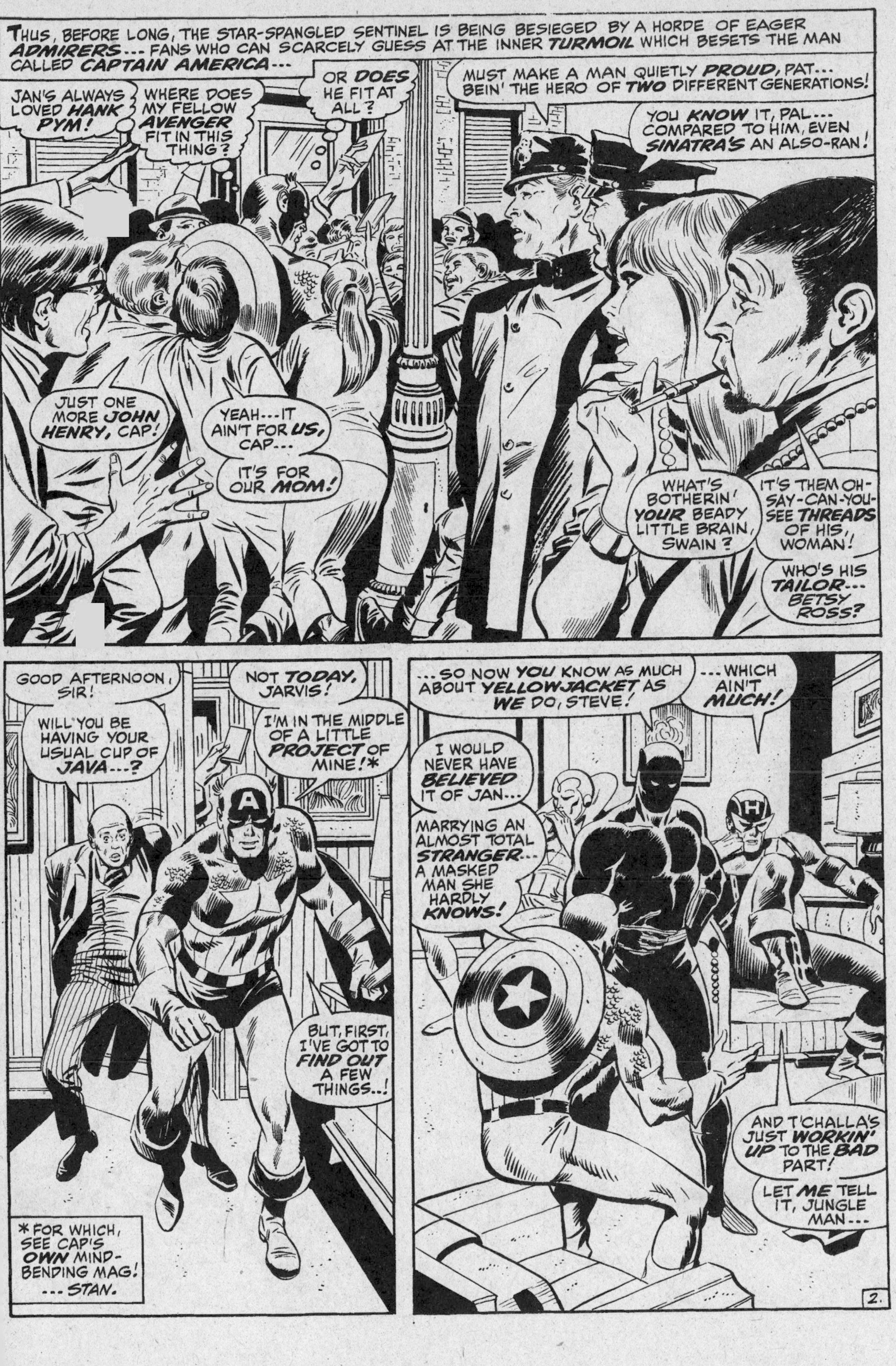
THUS, BEFORE LONG, THE STAR-SPANGLED SENTINEL IS BEING BESIEGED BY A HORDE OF EAGER ADMIRERS... FANS WHO CAN SCARCELY GUESS AT THE INNER TURMOIL WHICH BESETS THE MAN CALLED CAPTAIN AMERICA...
JAN'S ALWAYS LOVED HANK PYM!
WHERE DOES MY FELLOW AVENGER FIT IN THIS THING?
OR DOES HE FIT AT ALL?
MUST MAKE A MAN QUIETLY PROUD, PAT... BEIN' THE HERO OF TWO DIFFERENT GENERATIONS!
YOU KNOW IT, PAL... COMPARED TO HIM, EVEN SINATRA'S AN ALSO-RAN!
JUST ONE MORE JOHN HENRY, CAP!
YEAH...IT AIN'T FOR US, CAP...
IT'S FOR OUR MOM!
WHAT'S BOTHERIN' YOUR BEADY LITTLE BRAIN, SWAIN?
IT'S THEM OH-SAY-CAN-YOU-SEE THREADS OF HIS, WOMAN!
WHO'S HIS TAILOR--- BETSY ROSS?
GOOD AFTERNOON, SIR!
WILL YOU BE HAVING YOUR USUAL CUP OF JAVA...?
NOT TODAY, JARVIS!
I'M IN THE MIDDLE OF A LITTLE PROJECT OF MINE!*
BUT, FIRST, I'VE GOT TO FIND OUT A FEW THINGS..!
*FOR WHICH, SEE CAP'S OWN MIND-BENDING MAG! ...STAN.
...SO NOW YOU KNOW AS MUCH ABOUT YELLOWJACKET AS WE DO, STEVE!
...WHICH AIN'T MUCH!
I WOULD NEVER HAVE BELIEVED IT OF JAN...
MARRYING AN ALMOST TOTAL STRANGER... A MASKED MAN SHE HARDLY KNOWS!
AND T'CHALLA'S JUST WORKIN' UP TO THE BAD PART!
LET ME TELL IT, JUNGLE MAN...
2.

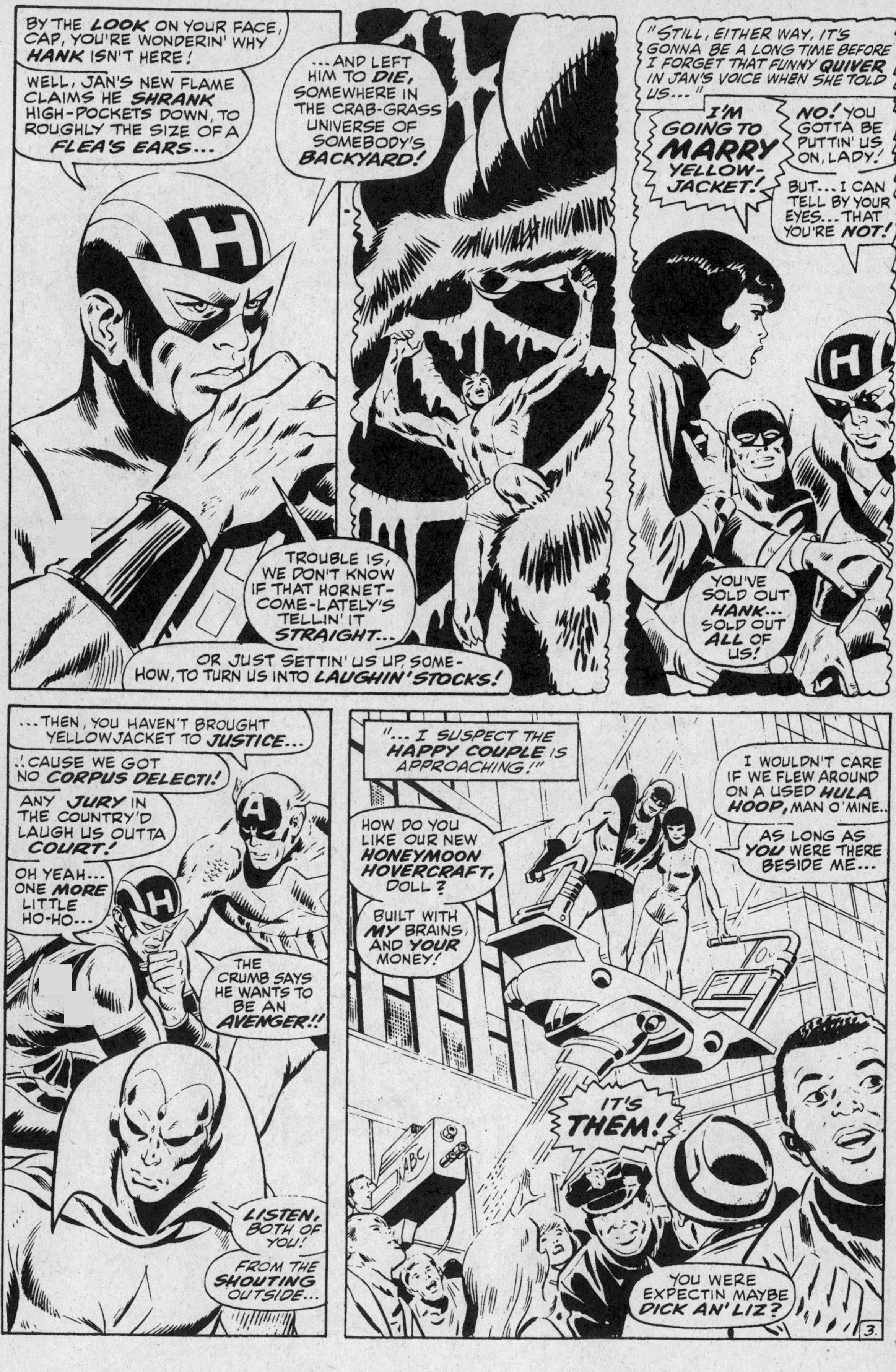
BY THE LOOK ON YOUR FACE, CAP, YOU'RE WONDERIN' WHY HANK ISN'T HERE!
WELL, JAN'S NEW FLAME CLAIMS HE SHRANK HIGH-POCKETS DOWN, TO ROUGHLY THE SIZE OF A FLEA'S EARS...
...AND LEFT HIM TO DIE, SOMEWHERE IN THE CRAB-GRASS UNIVERSE OF SOMEBODY'S BACKYARD!
TROUBLE IS, WE DON'T KNOW IF THAT HORNET-COME-LATELY'S TELLIN' IT STRAIGHT...
OR JUST SETTIN' US UP, SOME-HOW, TO TURN US INTO LAUGHIN' STOCKS!
"STILL, EITHER WAY, IT'S GONNA BE A LONG TIME BEFORE I FORGET THAT FUNNY QUIVER IN JAN'S VOICE WHEN SHE TOLD US..."
I'M GOING TO MARRY YELLOW-JACKET!
NO! YOU GOTTA BE PUTTIN' US ON, LADY!
BUT... I CAN TELL BY YOUR EYES... THAT YOU'RE NOT!
YOU'VE SOLD OUT HANK... SOLD OUT ALL OF US!
...THEN, YOU HAVEN'T BROUGHT YELLOWJACKET TO JUSTICE...
..CAUSE WE GOT NO CORPUS DELECTI!
ANY JURY IN THE COUNTRY'D LAUGH US OUTTA COURT!
OH YEAH... ONE MORE LITTLE HO-HO...
THE CRUMB SAYS HE WANTS TO BE AN AVENGER!!
LISTEN, BOTH OF YOU!
FROM THE SHOUTING OUTSIDE...
"... I SUSPECT THE HAPPY COUPLE IS APPROACHING!"
HOW DO YOU LIKE OUR NEW HONEYMOON HOVERCRAFT, DOLL?
BUILT WITH MY BRAINS AND YOUR MONEY!
I WOULDN'T CARE IF WE FLEW AROUND ON A USED HULA HOOP, MAN O'MINE..
AS LONG AS YOU WERE THERE BESIDE ME...
IT'S THEM!
ABC
YOU WERE EXPECTIN MAYBE DICK AN' LIZ?
3.

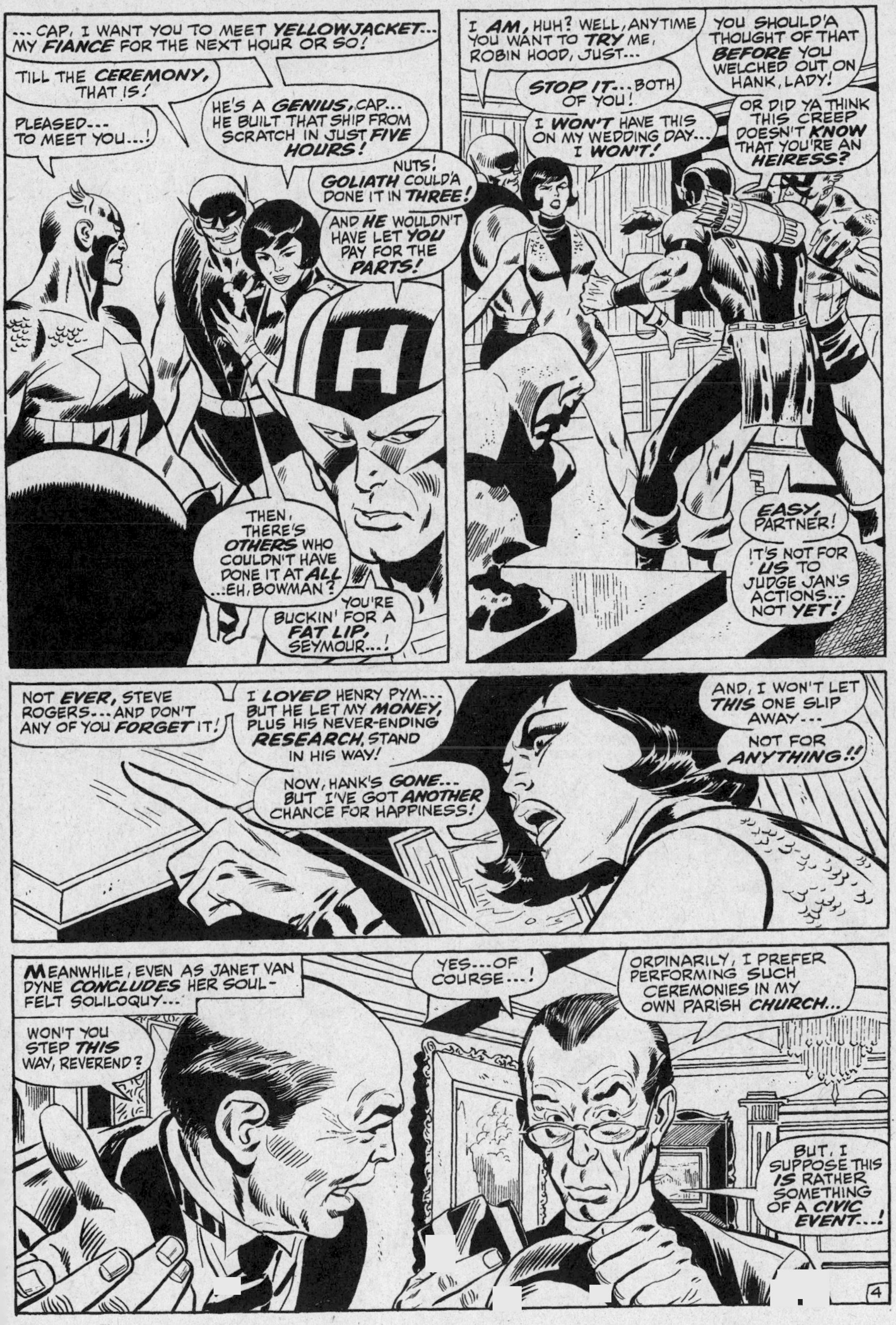

...CAP, I WANT YOU TO MEET YELLOWJACKET... MY FIANCE FOR THE NEXT HOUR OR SO!
TILL THE CEREMONY, THAT IS!
PLEASED--- TO MEET YOU...!
HE'S A GENIUS, CAP... HE BUILT THAT SHIP FROM SCRATCH IN JUST FIVE HOURS!
NUTS! GOLIATH COULD'A DONE IT IN THREE!
AND HE WOULDN'T HAVE LET YOU PAY FOR THE PARTS!
THEN, THERE'S OTHERS WHO COULDN'T HAVE DONE IT AT ALL ...EH, BOWMAN?
YOU'RE BUCKIN' FOR A FAT LIP, SEYMOUR...!
I AM, HUH? WELL, ANYTIME YOU WANT TO TRY ME, ROBIN HOOD, JUST...
YOU SHOULD'A THOUGHT OF THAT BEFORE YOU WELCHED OUT ON HANK, LADY!
STOP IT... BOTH OF YOU!
I WON'T HAVE THIS ON MY WEDDING DAY... I WON'T!
OR DID YA THINK THIS CREEP DOESN'T KNOW THAT YOU'RE AN HEIRESS?
EASY, PARTNER!
IT'S NOT FOR US TO JUDGE JAN'S ACTIONS... NOT YET!
NOT EVER, STEVE ROGERS... AND DON'T ANY OF YOU FORGET IT!
I LOVED HENRY PYM... BUT HE LET MY MONEY, PLUS HIS NEVER-ENDING RESEARCH, STAND IN HIS WAY!
NOW, HANK'S GONE... BUT I'VE GOT ANOTHER CHANCE FOR HAPPINESS!
AND, I WON'T LET THIS ONE SLIP AWAY---
NOT FOR ANYTHING!!
MEANWHILE, EVEN AS JANET VAN DYNE CONCLUDES HER SOUL-FELT SOLILOQUY...
WON'T YOU STEP THIS WAY, REVEREND?
YES... OF COURSE...!
ORDINARILY, I PREFER PERFORMING SUCH CEREMONIES IN MY OWN PARISH CHURCH...
BUT, I SUPPOSE THIS IS RATHER SOMETHING OF A CIVIC EVENT...!
4

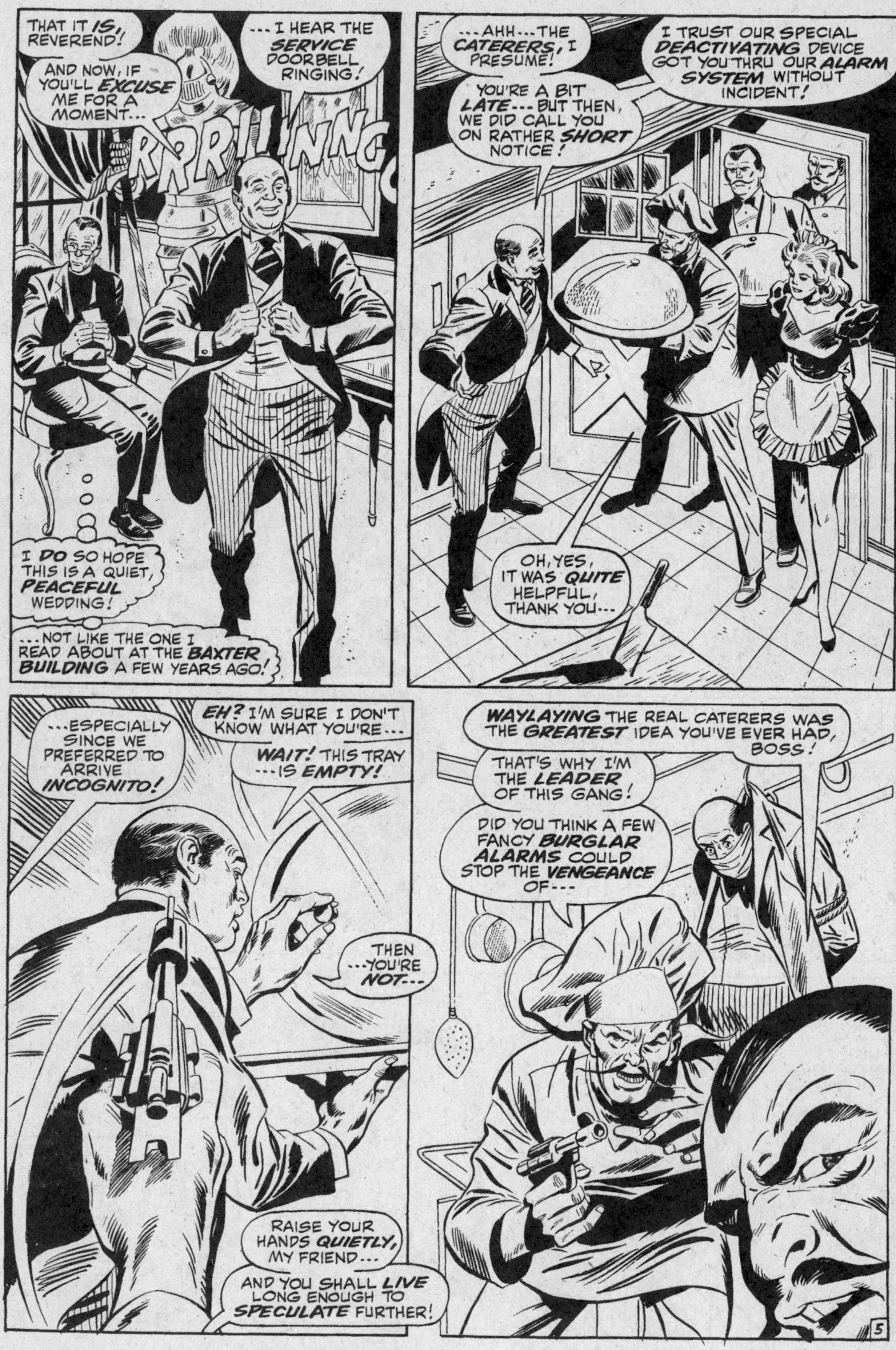
THAT IT IS, REVEREND!
AND NOW, IF YOU'LL EXCUSE ME FOR A MOMENT...
...I HEAR THE SERVICE DOORBELL RINGING!
RRRIIINNG
I DO SO HOPE THIS IS A QUIET, PEACEFUL WEDDING!
...NOT LIKE THE ONE I READ ABOUT AT THE BAXTER BUILDING A FEW YEARS AGO!
...AHH...THE CATERERS, I PRESUME!
YOU'RE A BIT LATE...BUT THEN, WE DID CALL YOU ON RATHER SHORT NOTICE!
I TRUST OUR SPECIAL DEACTIVATING DEVICE GOT YOU THRU OUR ALARM SYSTEM WITHOUT INCIDENT!
OH, YES, IT WAS QUITE HELPFUL, THANK YOU...
...ESPECIALLY SINCE WE PREFERRED TO ARRIVE INCOGNITO!
EH? I'M SURE I DON'T KNOW WHAT YOU'RE...
WAIT! THIS TRAY ...IS EMPTY!
THEN ...YOU'RE NOT...
RAISE YOUR HANDS QUIETLY, MY FRIEND...
AND YOU SHALL LIVE LONG ENOUGH TO SPECULATE FURTHER!
WAYLAYING THE REAL CATERERS WAS THE GREATEST IDEA YOU'VE EVER HAD, BOSS!
THAT'S WHY I'M THE LEADER OF THIS GANG!
DID YOU THINK A FEW FANCY BURGLAR ALARMS COULD STOP THE VENGEANCE OF---
5

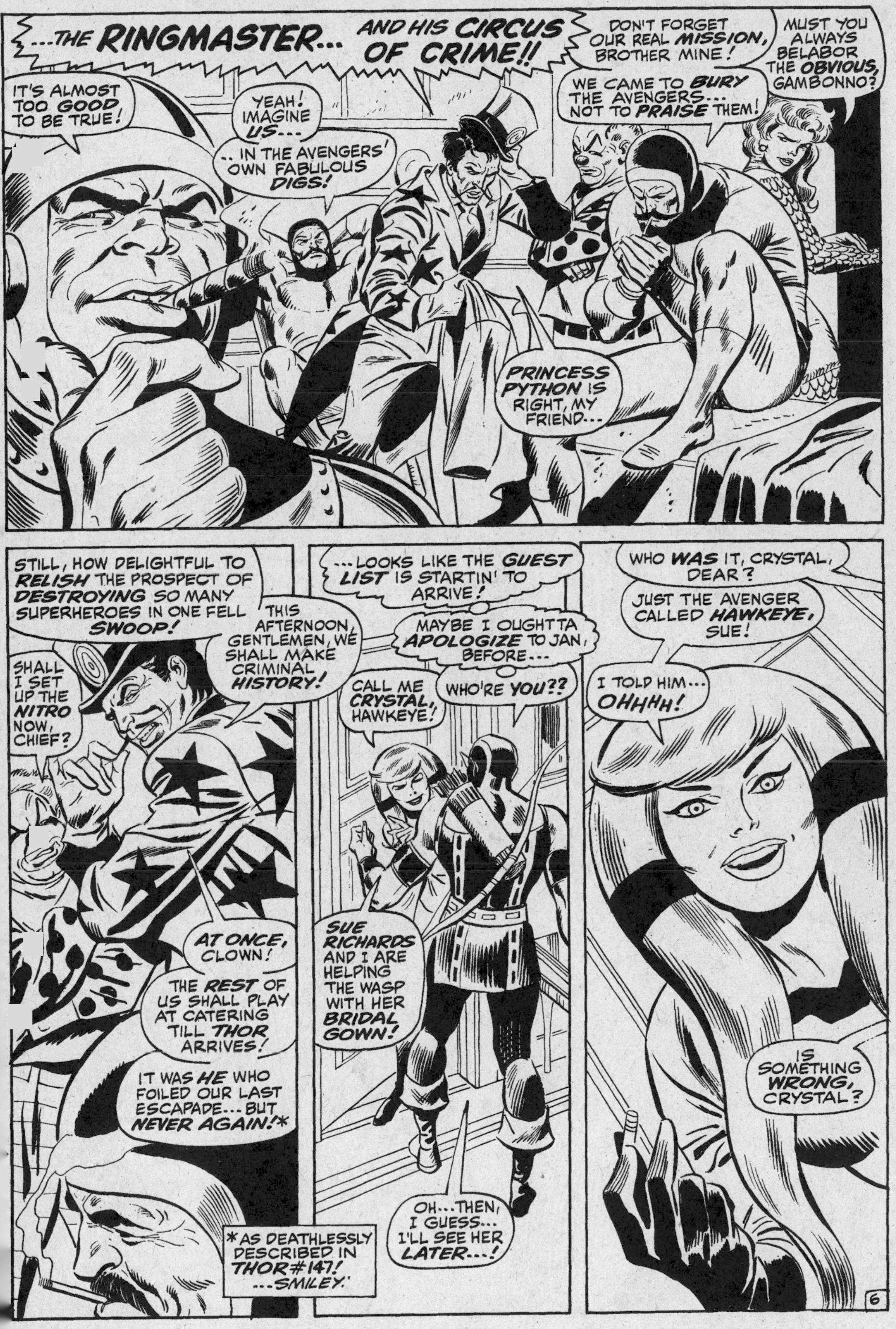
...THE RINGMASTER... AND HIS CIRCUS OF CRIME!!
DON'T FORGET OUR REAL MISSION, BROTHER MINE!
MUST YOU ALWAYS BELABOR THE OBVIOUS, GAMBONNO?
WE CAME TO BURY THE AVENGERS... NOT TO PRAISE THEM!
IT'S ALMOST TOO GOOD TO BE TRUE!
YEAH! IMAGINE US...
.. IN THE AVENGERS' OWN FABULOUS DIGS!
PRINCESS PYTHON IS RIGHT, MY FRIEND...
STILL, HOW DELIGHTFUL TO RELISH THE PROSPECT OF DESTROYING SO MANY SUPERHEROES IN ONE FELL SWOOP!
THIS AFTERNOON, GENTLEMEN, WE SHALL MAKE CRIMINAL HISTORY!
SHALL I SET UP THE NITRO NOW, CHIEF?
AT ONCE, CLOWN!
THE REST OF US SHALL PLAY AT CATERING TILL THOR ARRIVES!
IT WAS HE WHO FOILED OUR LAST ESCAPADE... BUT NEVER AGAIN!*
*AS DEATHLESSLY DESCRIBED IN THOR #147! ...SMILEY.
...LOOKS LIKE THE GUEST LIST IS STARTIN' TO ARRIVE!
MAYBE I OUGHTTA APOLOGIZE TO JAN, BEFORE...
WHO'RE YOU??
CALL ME CRYSTAL, HAWKEYE!
SUE RICHARDS AND I ARE HELPING THE WASP WITH HER BRIDAL GOWN!
OH...THEN, I GUESS... I'LL SEE HER LATER...!
WHO WAS IT, CRYSTAL, DEAR?
JUST THE AVENGER CALLED HAWKEYE, SUE!
I TOLD HIM... OHHHH!
IS SOMETHING WRONG, CRYSTAL?
6

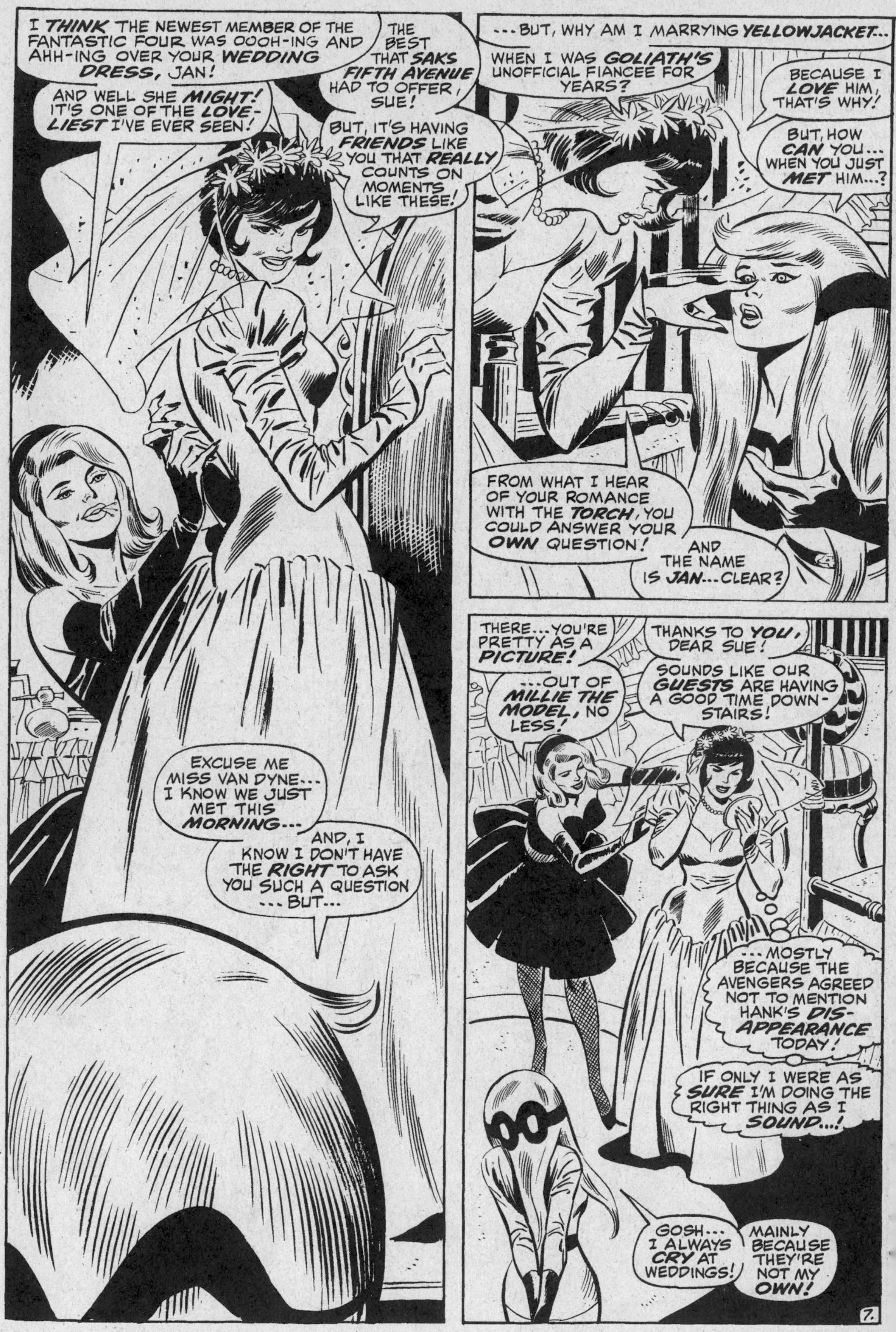
I THINK THE NEWEST MEMBER OF THE FANTASTIC FOUR WAS OOOH-ING AND AHH-ING OVER YOUR WEDDING DRESS, JAN!
AND WELL SHE MIGHT! IT'S ONE OF THE LOVELIEST I'VE EVER SEEN!
THE BEST THAT SAKS FIFTH AVENUE HAD TO OFFER, SUE!
BUT, IT'S HAVING FRIENDS LIKE YOU THAT REALLY COUNTS ON MOMENTS LIKE THESE!
EXCUSE ME MISS VAN DYNE... I KNOW WE JUST MET THIS MORNING...
AND, I KNOW I DON'T HAVE THE RIGHT TO ASK YOU SUCH A QUESTION ... BUT...
...BUT, WHY AM I MARRYING YELLOWJACKET...
WHEN I WAS GOLIATH'S UNOFFICIAL FIANCEE FOR YEARS?
BECAUSE I LOVE HIM, THAT'S WHY!
BUT, HOW CAN YOU... WHEN YOU JUST MET HIM...?
FROM WHAT I HEAR OF YOUR ROMANCE WITH THE TORCH, YOU COULD ANSWER YOUR OWN QUESTION!
AND THE NAME IS JAN... CLEAR?
THERE... YOU'RE PRETTY AS A PICTURE!
...OUT OF MILLIE THE MODEL, NO LESS!
THANKS TO YOU, DEAR SUE!
SOUNDS LIKE OUR GUESTS ARE HAVING A GOOD TIME DOWN-STAIRS!
...MOSTLY BECAUSE THE AVENGERS AGREED NOT TO MENTION HANK'S DIS-APPEARANCE TODAY!
IF ONLY I WERE AS SURE I'M DOING THE RIGHT THING AS I SOUND...!
GOSH... I ALWAYS CRY AT WEDDINGS!
MAINLY BECAUSE THEY'RE NOT MY OWN!
7.

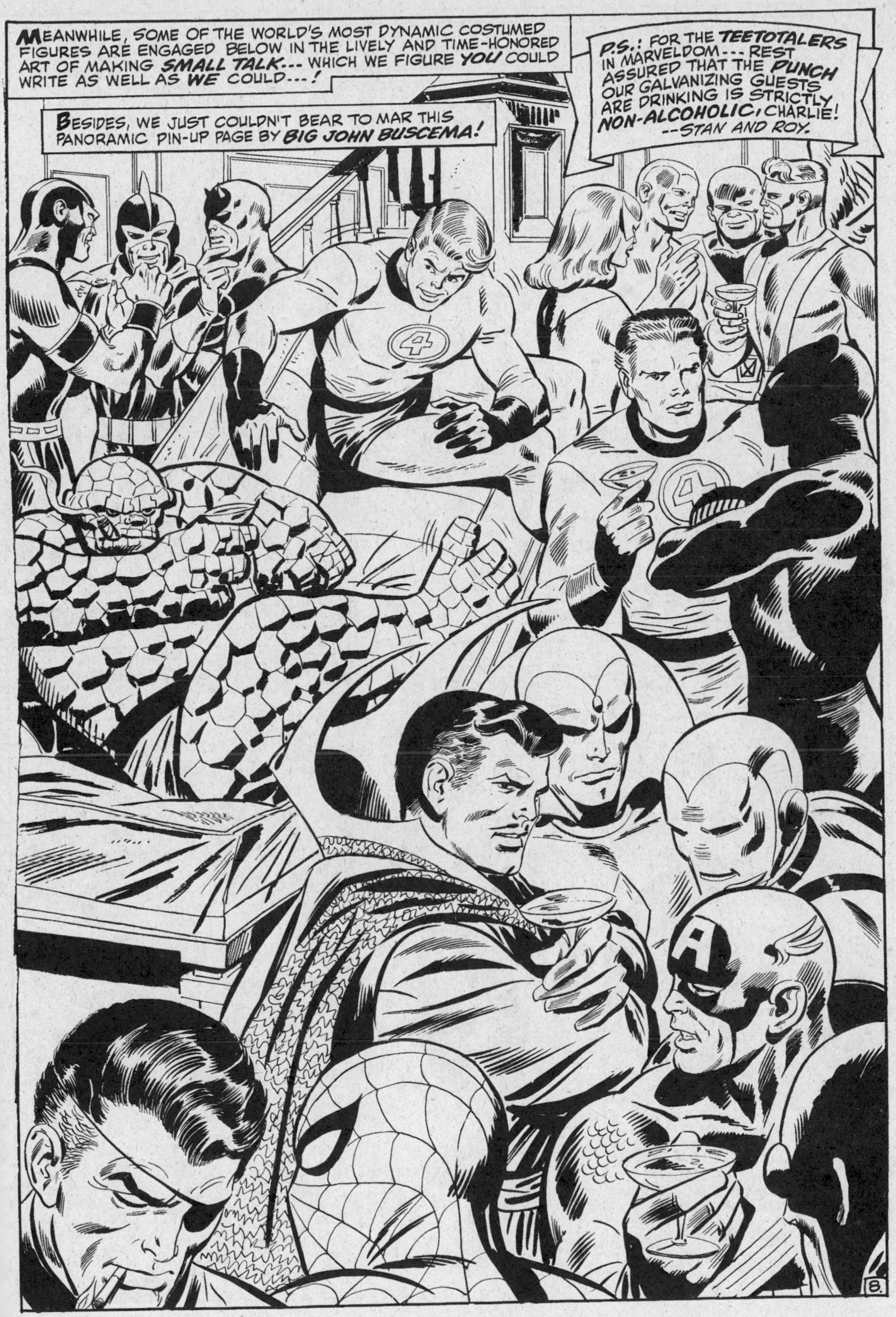

MEANWHILE, SOME OF THE WORLD'S MOST DYNAMIC COSTUMED FIGURES ARE ENGAGED BELOW IN THE LIVELY AND TIME-HONORED ART OF MAKING SMALL TALK... WHICH WE FIGURE YOU COULD WRITE AS WELL AS WE COULD...!
BESIDES, WE JUST COULDN'T BEAR TO MAR THIS PANORAMIC PIN-UP PAGE BY BIG JOHN BUSCEMA!
P.S.: FOR THE TEETOTALERS IN MARVELDOM... REST ASSURED THAT THE PUNCH OUR GALVANIZING GUESTS ARE DRINKING IS STRICTLY NON-ALCOHOLIC, CHARLIE! --STAN AND ROY.
8.

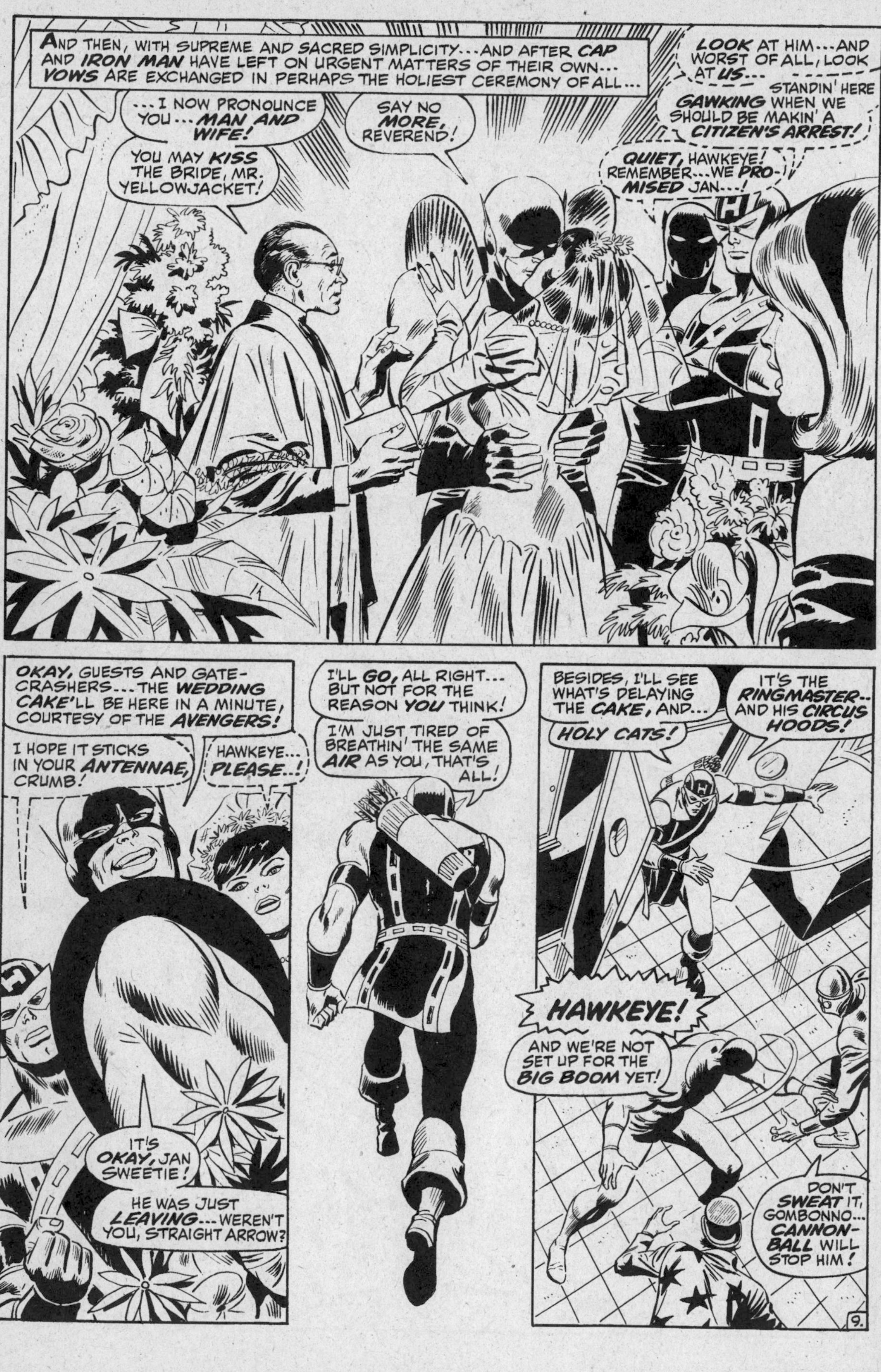
AND THEN, WITH SUPREME AND SACRED SIMPLICITY... AND AFTER CAP AND IRON MAN HAVE LEFT ON URGENT MATTERS OF THEIR OWN... VOWS ARE EXCHANGED IN PERHAPS THE HOLIEST CEREMONY OF ALL...
...I NOW PRONOUNCE YOU... MAN AND WIFE!
YOU MAY KISS THE BRIDE, MR. YELLOWJACKET!
SAY NO MORE, REVEREND!
LOOK AT HIM... AND WORST OF ALL, LOOK AT US...
STANDIN' HERE GAWKING WHEN WE SHOULD BE MAKIN' A CITIZEN'S ARREST!
QUIET, HAWKEYE! REMEMBER... WE PROMISED JAN...!
OKAY, GUESTS AND GATE-CRASHERS... THE WEDDING CAKE'LL BE HERE IN A MINUTE, COURTESY OF THE AVENGERS!
I HOPE IT STICKS IN YOUR ANTENNAE, CRUMB!
HAWKEYE... PLEASE..!
IT'S OKAY, JAN SWEETIE!
HE WAS JUST LEAVING... WEREN'T YOU, STRAIGHT ARROW?
I'LL GO, ALL RIGHT... BUT NOT FOR THE REASON YOU THINK!
I'M JUST TIRED OF BREATHIN' THE SAME AIR AS YOU, THAT'S ALL!
BESIDES, I'LL SEE WHAT'S DELAYING THE CAKE, AND...
HOLY CATS!
IT'S THE RINGMASTER-- AND HIS CIRCUS HOODS!
HAWKEYE!
AND WE'RE NOT SET UP FOR THE BIG BOOM YET!
DON'T SWEAT IT, GOMBONNO... CANNONBALL WILL STOP HIM!
9.

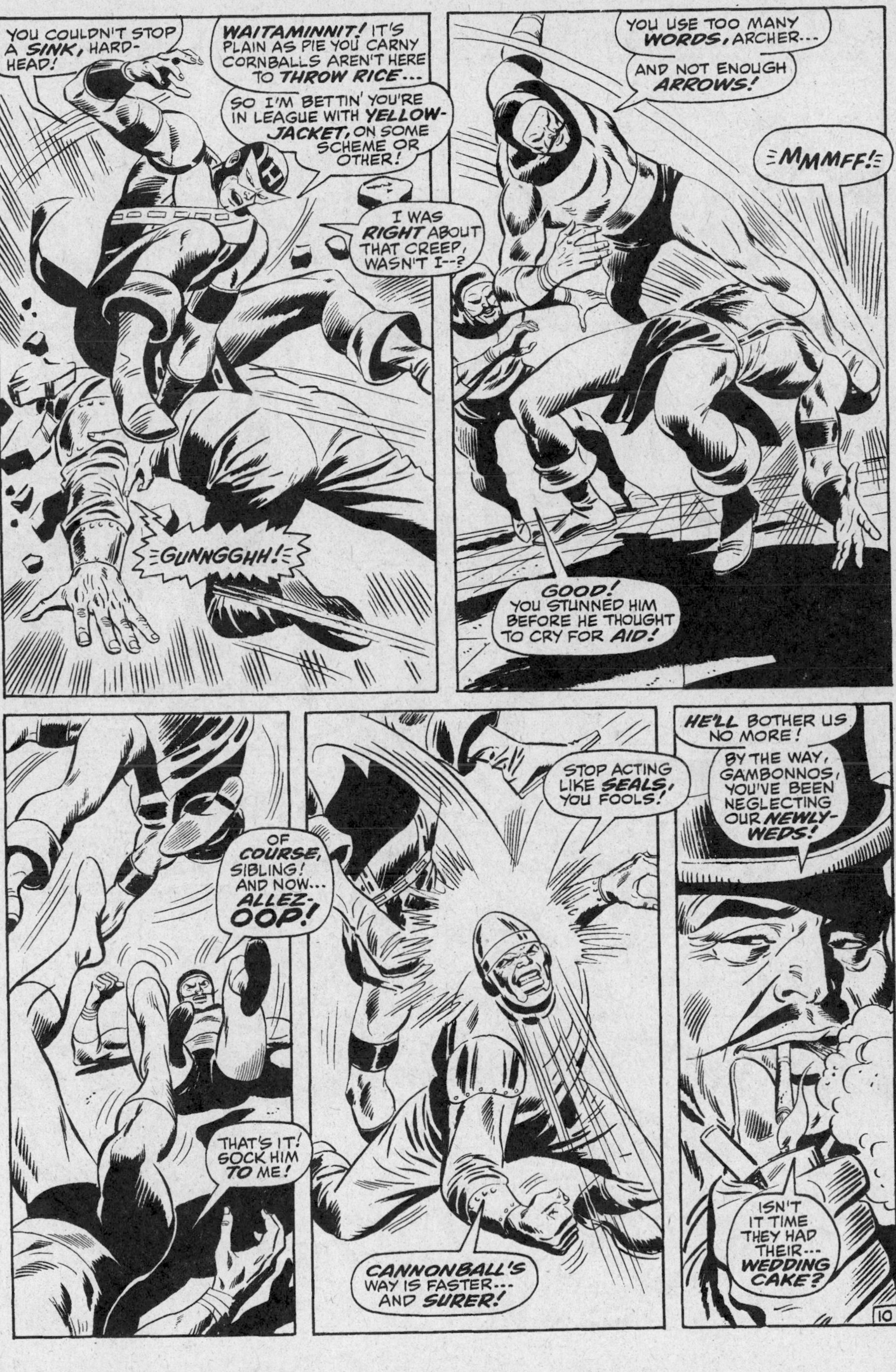
YOU COULDN'T STOP A SINK, HARD-HEAD!
WAITAMINNIT! IT'S PLAIN AS PIE YOU CARNY CORNBALLS AREN'T HERE TO THROW RICE...
SO I'M BETTIN' YOU'RE IN LEAGUE WITH YELLOW-JACKET, ON SOME SCHEME OR OTHER!
I WAS RIGHT ABOUT THAT CREEP, WASN'T I--?
GUNNGGHH!
YOU USE TOO MANY WORDS, ARCHER...
AND NOT ENOUGH ARROWS!
MMMFF!
GOOD! YOU STUNNED HIM BEFORE HE THOUGHT TO CRY FOR AID!
OF COURSE, SIBLING! AND NOW... ALLEZ-OOP!
THAT'S IT! SOCK HIM TO ME!
STOP ACTING LIKE SEALS, YOU FOOLS!
CANNONBALL'S WAY IS FASTER... AND SURER!
HE'LL BOTHER US NO MORE!
BY THE WAY, GAMBONNOS, YOU'VE BEEN NEGLECTING OUR NEWLY-WEDS!
ISN'T IT TIME THEY HAD THEIR... WEDDING CAKE?
10

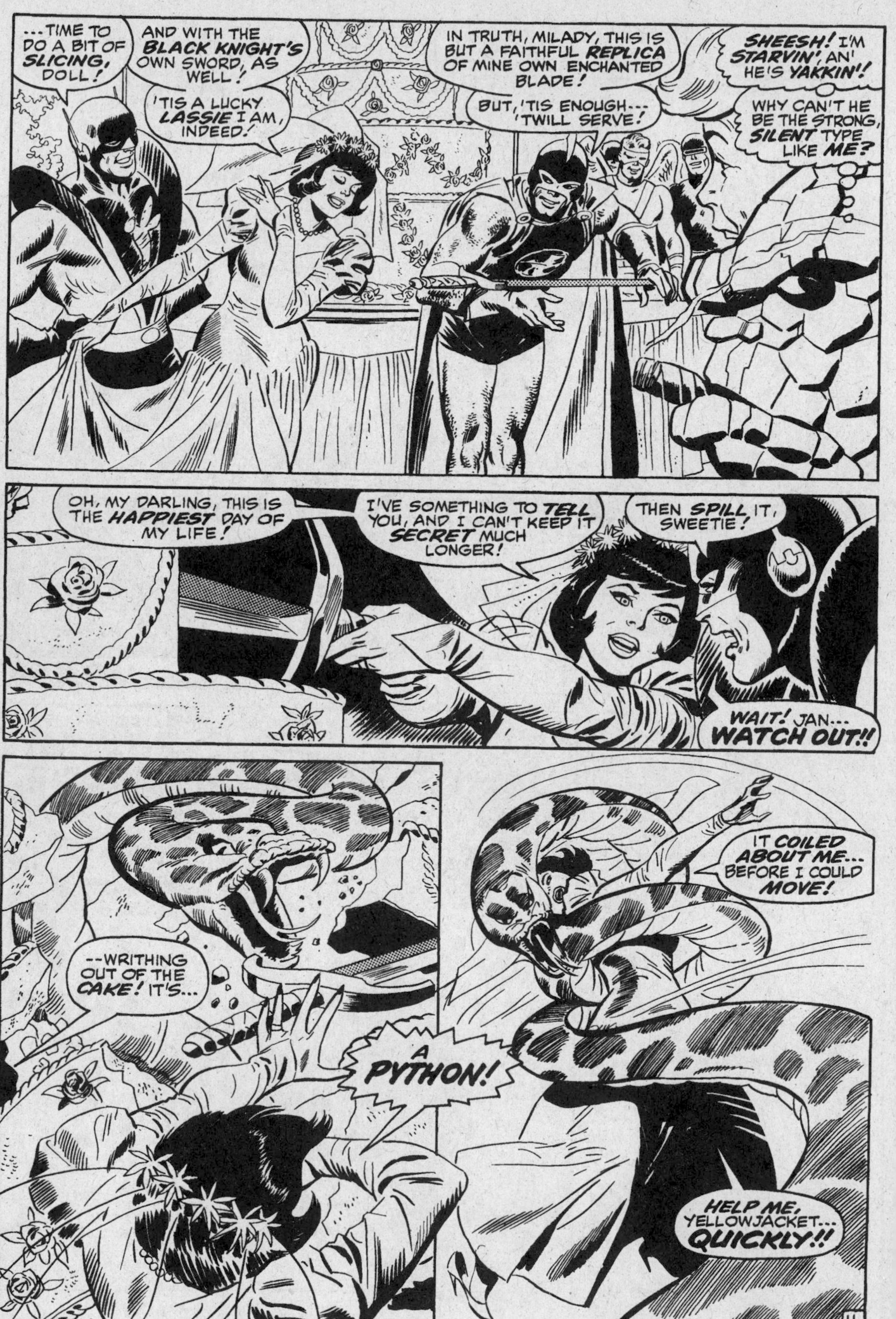

...TIME TO DO A BIT OF SLICING, DOLL!
AND WITH THE BLACK KNIGHT'S OWN SWORD, AS WELL!
'TIS A LUCKY LASSIE I AM, INDEED!
IN TRUTH, MILADY, THIS IS BUT A FAITHFUL REPLICA OF MINE OWN ENCHANTED BLADE!
BUT, 'TIS ENOUGH--- 'TWILL SERVE!
SHEESH! I'M STARVIN', AN' HE'S YAKKIN'!
WHY CAN'T HE BE THE STRONG, SILENT TYPE LIKE ME?
OH, MY DARLING, THIS IS THE HAPPIEST DAY OF MY LIFE!
I'VE SOMETHING TO TELL YOU, AND I CAN'T KEEP IT SECRET MUCH LONGER!
THEN SPILL IT, SWEETIE!
WAIT! JAN... WATCH OUT!!
--WRITHING OUT OF THE CAKE! IT'S...
A PYTHON!
IT COILED ABOUT ME... BEFORE I COULD MOVE!
HELP ME, YELLOWJACKET... QUICKLY!!
11.

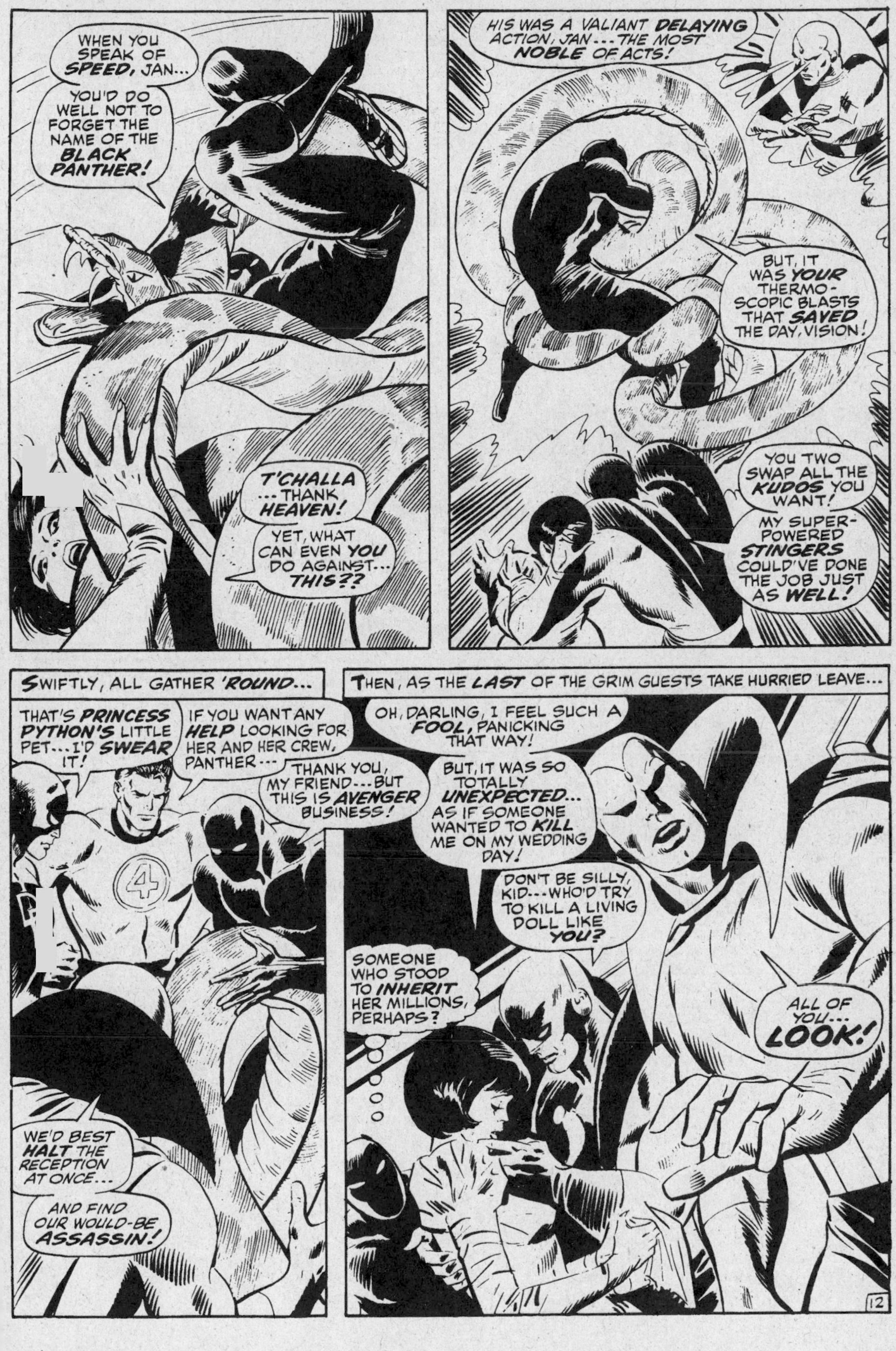
WHEN YOU SPEAK OF SPEED, JAN...
YOU'D DO WELL NOT TO FORGET THE NAME OF THE BLACK PANTHER!
T'CHALLA ...THANK HEAVEN!
YET, WHAT CAN EVEN YOU DO AGAINST... THIS??
HIS WAS A VALIANT DELAYING ACTION, JAN... THE MOST NOBLE OF ACTS!
BUT, IT WAS YOUR THERMO-SCOPIC BLASTS THAT SAVED THE DAY, VISION!
YOU TWO SWAP ALL THE KUDOS YOU WANT!
MY SUPER-POWERED STINGERS COULD'VE DONE THE JOB JUST AS WELL!
SWIFTLY, ALL GATHER 'ROUND...
THAT'S PRINCESS PYTHON'S LITTLE PET... I'D SWEAR IT!
IF YOU WANT ANY HELP LOOKING FOR HER AND HER CREW, PANTHER...
THANK YOU, MY FRIEND... BUT THIS IS AVENGER BUSINESS!
WE'D BEST HALT THE RECEPTION AT ONCE...
AND FIND OUR WOULD-BE ASSASSIN!
THEN, AS THE LAST OF THE GRIM GUESTS TAKE HURRIED LEAVE...
OH, DARLING, I FEEL SUCH A FOOL, PANICKING THAT WAY!
BUT, IT WAS SO TOTALLY UNEXPECTED... AS IF SOMEONE WANTED TO KILL ME ON MY WEDDING DAY!
DON'T BE SILLY, KID... WHO'D TRY TO KILL A LIVING DOLL LIKE YOU?
SOMEONE WHO STOOD TO INHERIT HER MILLIONS, PERHAPS?
ALL OF YOU... LOOK!
12

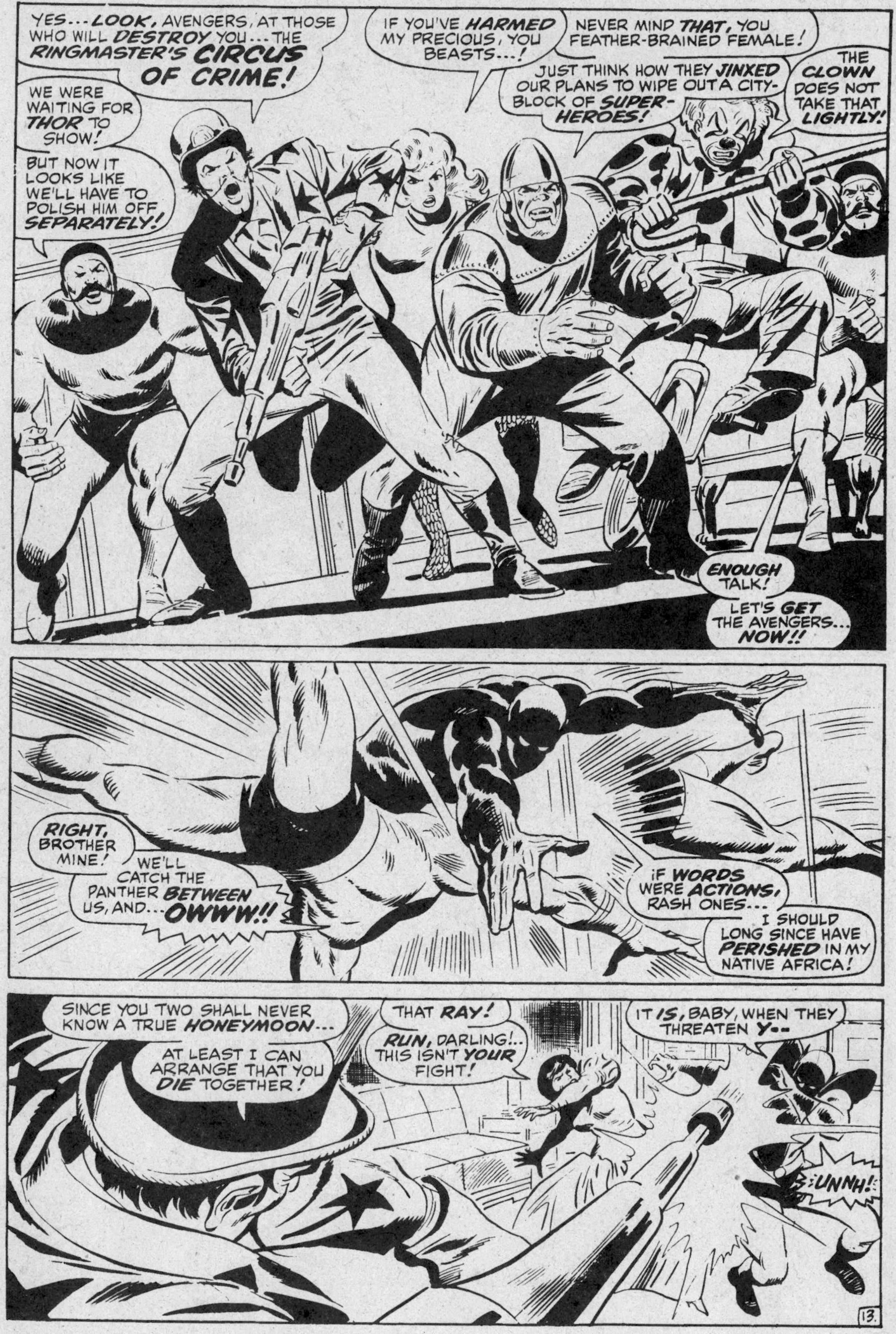
YES... LOOK, AVENGERS, AT THOSE WHO WILL DESTROY YOU... THE RINGMASTER'S CIRCUS OF CRIME!
WE WERE WAITING FOR THOR TO SHOW!
BUT NOW IT LOOKS LIKE WE'LL HAVE TO POLISH HIM OFF SEPARATELY!
IF YOU'VE HARMED MY PRECIOUS, YOU BEASTS...!
NEVER MIND THAT, YOU FEATHER-BRAINED FEMALE!
JUST THINK HOW THEY JINXED OUR PLANS TO WIPE OUT A CITY-BLOCK OF SUPER-HEROES!
THE CLOWN DOES NOT TAKE THAT LIGHTLY!
ENOUGH TALK!
LET'S GET THE AVENGERS... NOW!!
RIGHT, BROTHER MINE!
WE'LL CATCH THE PANTHER BETWEEN US, AND... OWWW!!
IF WORDS WERE ACTIONS, RASH ONES...
I SHOULD LONG SINCE HAVE PERISHED IN MY NATIVE AFRICA!
SINCE YOU TWO SHALL NEVER KNOW A TRUE HONEYMOON...
AT LEAST I CAN ARRANGE THAT YOU DIE TOGETHER!
THAT RAY!
RUN, DARLING!... THIS ISN'T YOUR FIGHT!
IT IS, BABY, WHEN THEY THREATEN Y--
B-UNNH!
13

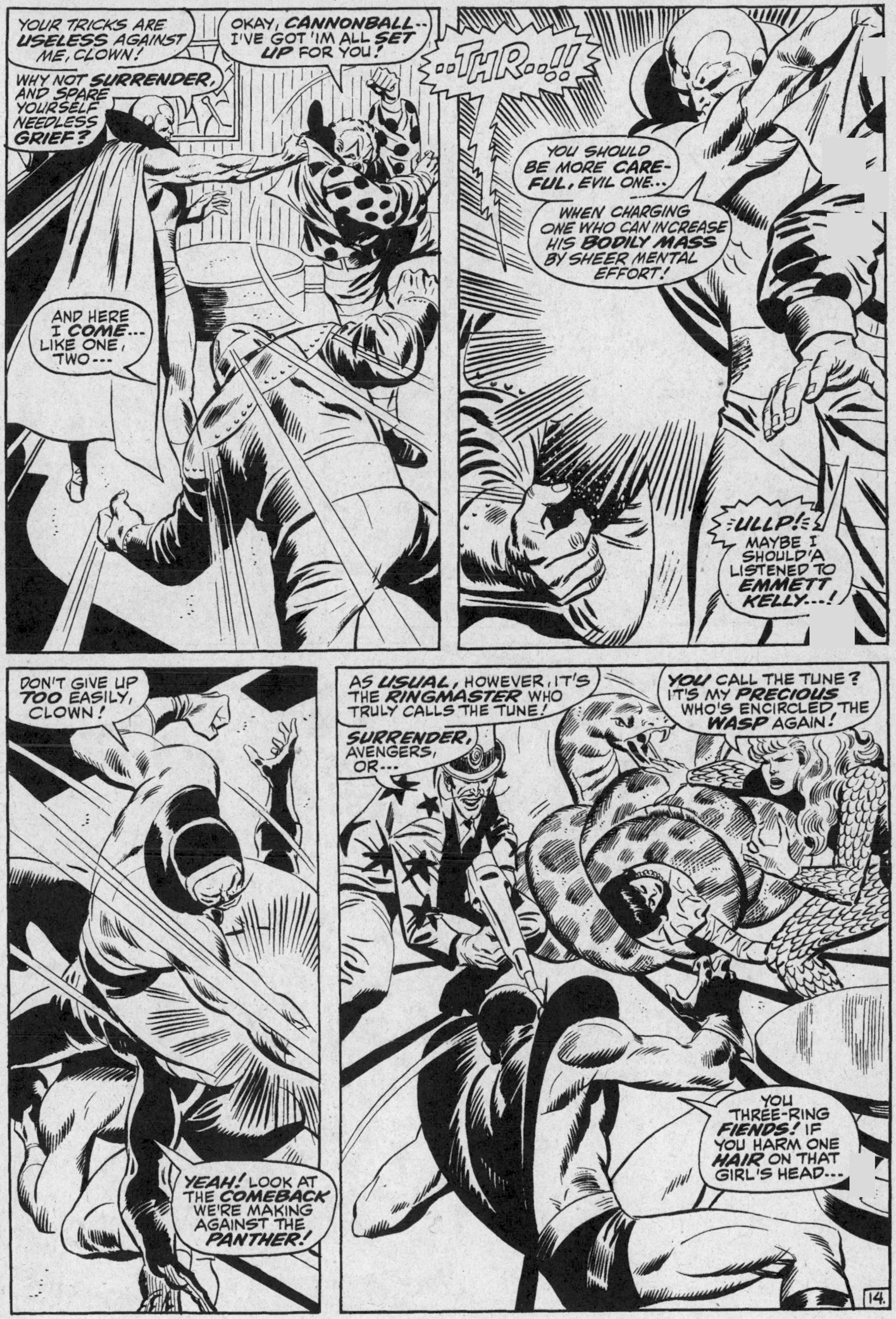
YOUR TRICKS ARE USELESS AGAINST ME, CLOWN!
WHY NOT SURRENDER, AND SPARE YOURSELF NEEDLESS GRIEF?
OKAY, CANNONBALL.. I'VE GOT 'IM ALL SET UP FOR YOU!
AND HERE I COME... LIKE ONE, TWO---
..THR..!!
YOU SHOULD BE MORE CARE-FUL, EVIL ONE...
WHEN CHARGING ONE WHO CAN INCREASE HIS BODILY MASS BY SHEER MENTAL EFFORT!
ULLP! MAYBE I SHOULD'A LISTENED TO EMMETT KELLY...!
DON'T GIVE UP TOO EASILY, CLOWN!
YEAH! LOOK AT THE COMEBACK WE'RE MAKING AGAINST THE PANTHER!
AS USUAL, HOWEVER, IT'S THE RINGMASTER WHO TRULY CALLS THE TUNE!
SURRENDER, AVENGERS, OR---
YOU CALL THE TUNE? IT'S MY PRECIOUS WHO'S ENCIRCLED THE WASP AGAIN!
YOU THREE-RING FIENDS! IF YOU HARM ONE HAIR ON THAT GIRL'S HEAD...
14.

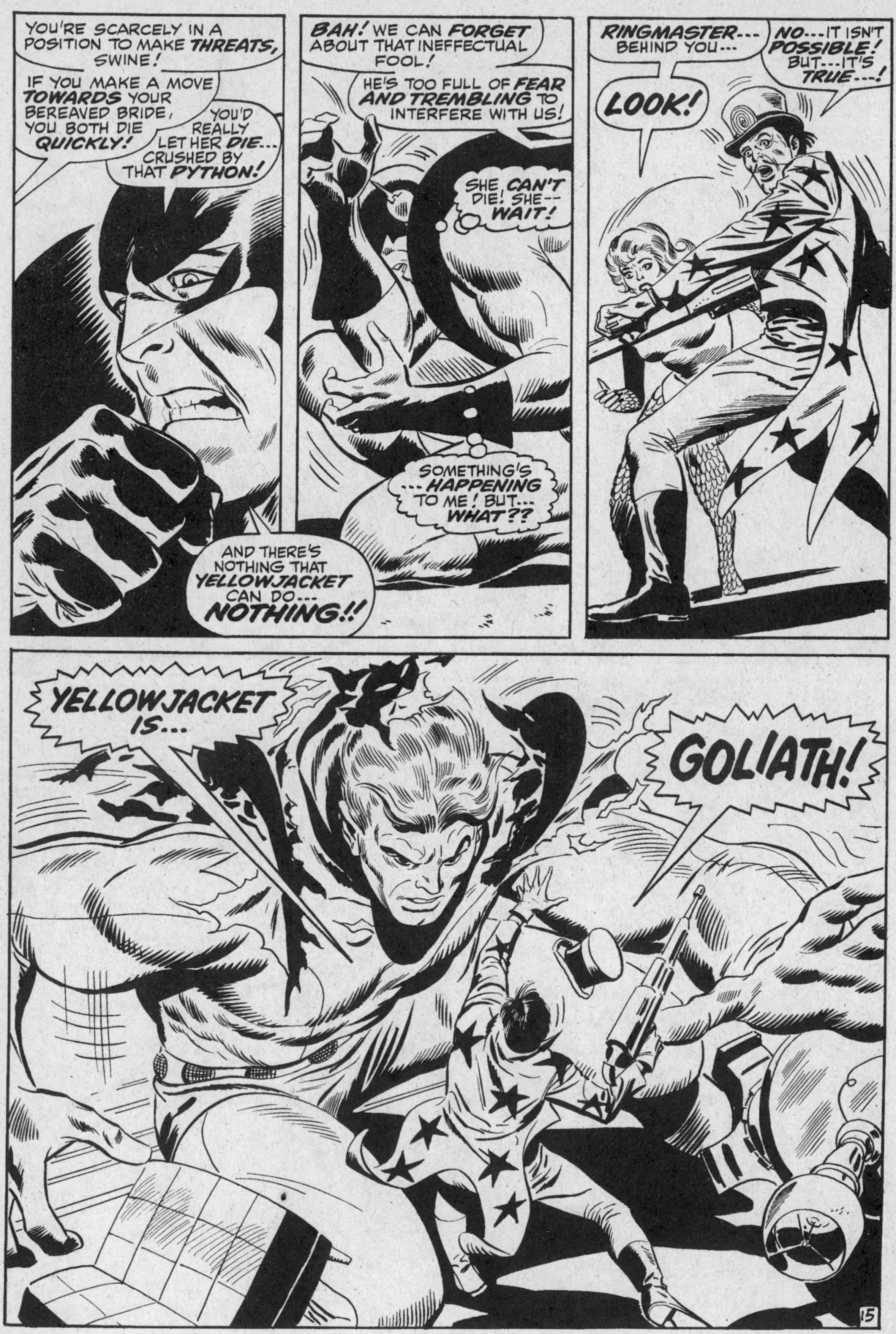

YOU'RE SCARCELY IN A POSITION TO MAKE THREATS, SWINE!
IF YOU MAKE A MOVE TOWARDS YOUR BEREAVED BRIDE, YOU BOTH DIE QUICKLY!
YOU'D REALLY LET HER DIE... CRUSHED BY THAT PYTHON!
BAH! WE CAN FORGET ABOUT THAT INEFFECTUAL FOOL!
HE'S TOO FULL OF FEAR AND TREMBLING TO INTERFERE WITH US!
SHE CAN'T DIE! SHE-- WAIT!
SOMETHING'S ...HAPPENING TO ME! BUT... WHAT??
AND THERE'S NOTHING THAT YELLOWJACKET CAN DO... NOTHING!!
RINGMASTER--- BEHIND YOU---
LOOK!
NO---IT ISN'T POSSIBLE! BUT---IT'S TRUE---!
YELLOWJACKET IS...
GOLIATH!
15

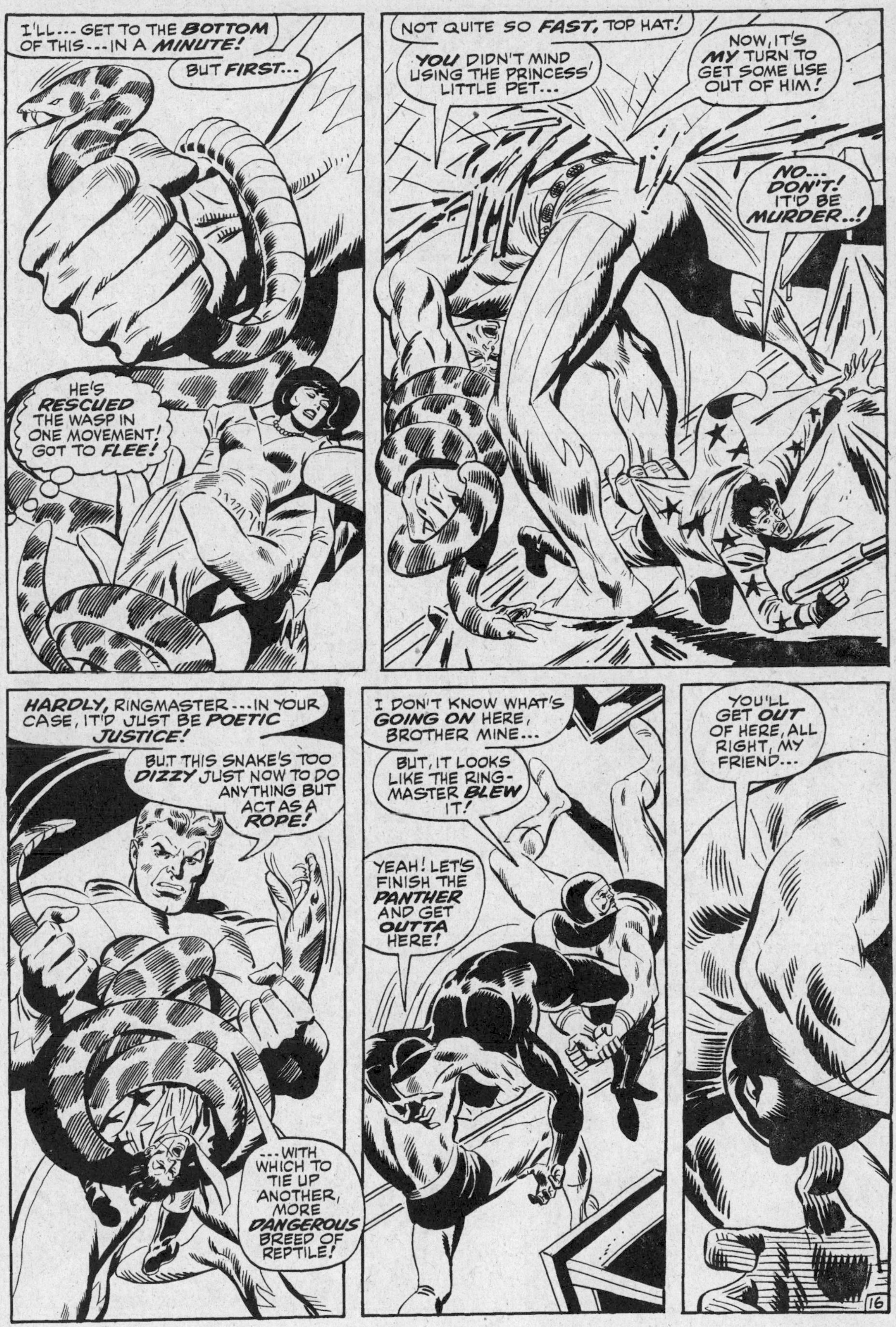
I'LL... GET TO THE BOTTOM OF THIS... IN A MINUTE!
BUT FIRST...
HE'S RESCUED THE WASP IN ONE MOVEMENT! GOT TO FLEE!
NOT QUITE SO FAST, TOP HAT!
YOU DIDN'T MIND USING THE PRINCESS' LITTLE PET...
NOW, IT'S MY TURN TO GET SOME USE OUT OF HIM!
NO... DON'T! IT'D BE MURDER...!
HARDLY, RINGMASTER... IN YOUR CASE, IT'D JUST BE POETIC JUSTICE!
BUT THIS SNAKE'S TOO DIZZY JUST NOW TO DO ANYTHING BUT ACT AS A ROPE!
...WITH WHICH TO TIE UP ANOTHER, MORE DANGEROUS BREED OF REPTILE!
I DON'T KNOW WHAT'S GOING ON HERE, BROTHER MINE...
BUT, IT LOOKS LIKE THE RING-MASTER BLEW IT!
YEAH! LET'S FINISH THE PANTHER AND GET OUTTA HERE!
YOU'LL GET OUT OF HERE, ALL RIGHT, MY FRIEND...
16

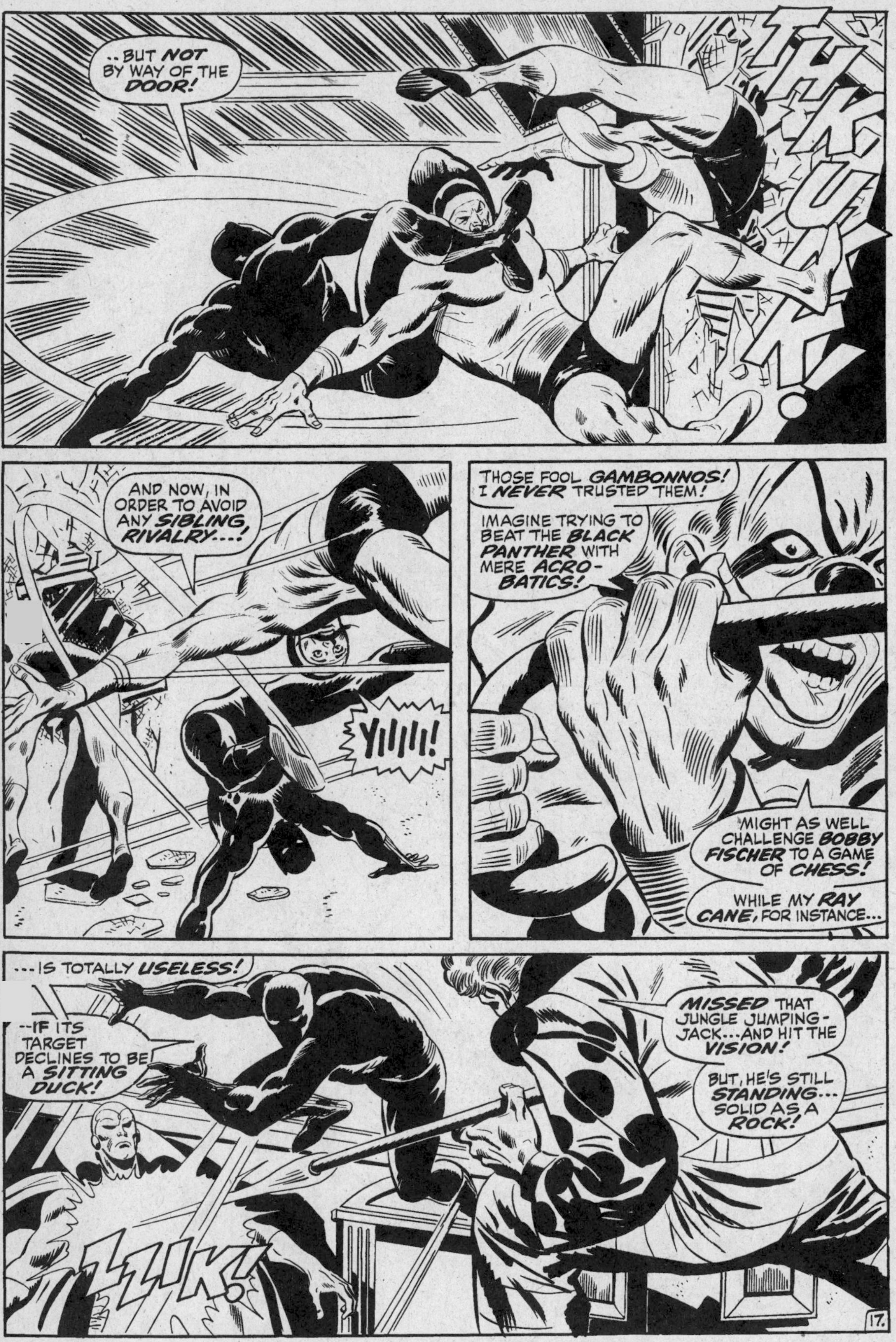

..BUT NOT BY WAY OF THE DOOR!
THKUNK!
AND NOW, IN ORDER TO AVOID ANY SIBLING RIVALRY...!
YIIII!
THOSE FOOL GAMBONNOS! I NEVER TRUSTED THEM!
IMAGINE TRYING TO BEAT THE BLACK PANTHER WITH MERE ACRO-BATICS!
MIGHT AS WELL CHALLENGE BOBBY FISCHER TO A GAME OF CHESS!
WHILE MY RAY CANE, FOR INSTANCE...
...IS TOTALLY USELESS!
--IF ITS TARGET DECLINES TO BE A SITTING DUCK!
MISSED THAT JUNGLE JUMPING-JACK...AND HIT THE VISION!
BUT, HE'S STILL STANDING... SOLID AS A ROCK!
ZZIK!
17.

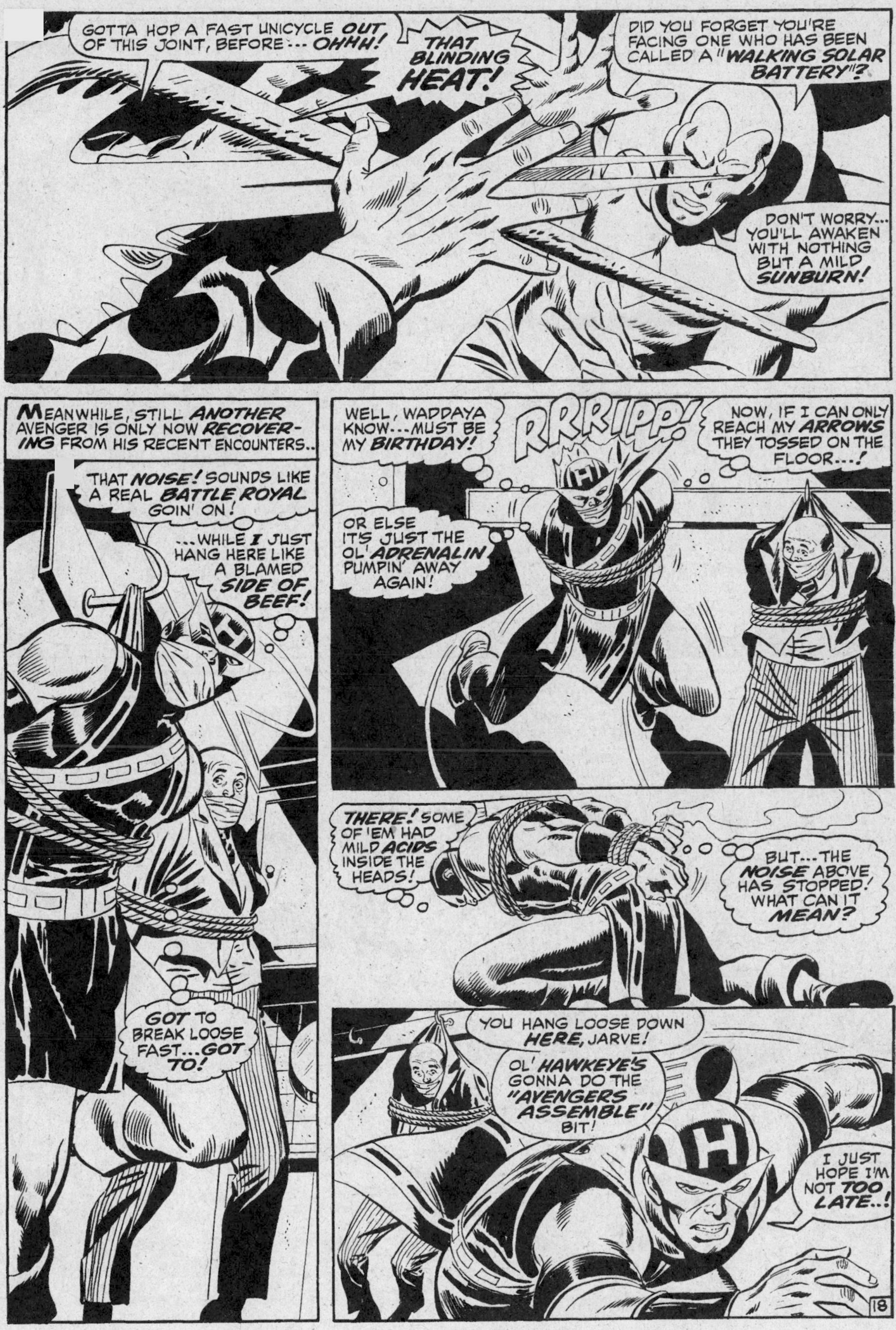
GOTTA HOP A FAST UNICYCLE OUT OF THIS JOINT, BEFORE--- OHHH!
THAT BLINDING HEAT!
DID YOU FORGET YOU'RE FACING ONE WHO HAS BEEN CALLED A "WALKING SOLAR BATTERY"?
DON'T WORRY... YOU'LL AWAKEN WITH NOTHING BUT A MILD SUNBURN!
MEANWHILE, STILL ANOTHER AVENGER IS ONLY NOW RECOVERING FROM HIS RECENT ENCOUNTERS..
THAT NOISE! SOUNDS LIKE A REAL BATTLE ROYAL GOIN' ON!
...WHILE I JUST HANG HERE LIKE A BLAMED SIDE OF BEEF!
GOT TO BREAK LOOSE FAST...GOT TO!
WELL, WADDAYA KNOW---MUST BE MY BIRTHDAY!
RRRIPP!
NOW, IF I CAN ONLY REACH MY ARROWS THEY TOSSED ON THE FLOOR...!
OR ELSE IT'S JUST THE OL' ADRENALIN PUMPIN' AWAY AGAIN!
THERE! SOME OF 'EM HAD MILD ACIDS INSIDE THE HEADS!
BUT... THE NOISE ABOVE HAS STOPPED! WHAT CAN IT MEAN?
YOU HANG LOOSE DOWN HERE, JARVE!
OL' HAWKEYE'S GONNA DO THE "AVENGERS ASSEMBLE" BIT!
I JUST HOPE I'M NOT TOO LATE..!
18

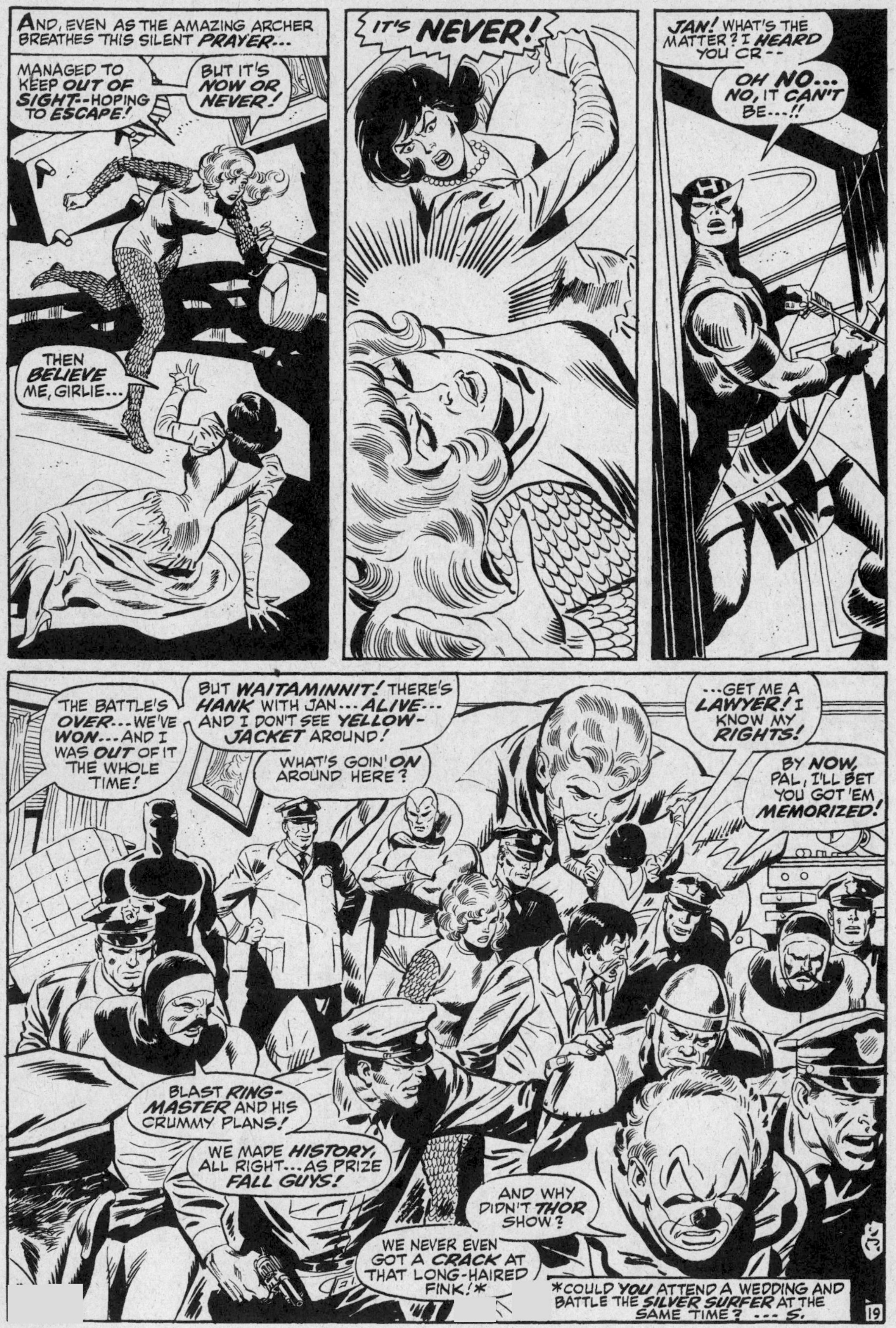
AND, EVEN AS THE AMAZING ARCHER BREATHES THIS SILENT PRAYER...
MANAGED TO KEEP OUT OF SIGHT--HOPING TO ESCAPE!
BUT IT'S NOW OR NEVER!
THEN BELIEVE ME, GIRLIE...
IT'S NEVER!
JAN! WHAT'S THE MATTER? I HEARD YOU CR--
OH NO... NO, IT CAN'T BE...!!
THE BATTLE'S OVER... WE'VE WON... AND I WAS OUT OF IT THE WHOLE TIME!
BUT WAITAMINNIT! THERE'S HANK WITH JAN... ALIVE... AND I DON'T SEE YELLOW-JACKET AROUND!
WHAT'S GOIN' ON AROUND HERE?
...GET ME A LAWYER! I KNOW MY RIGHTS!
BY NOW, PAL, I'LL BET YOU GOT 'EM MEMORIZED!
BLAST RING-MASTER AND HIS CRUMMY PLANS!
WE MADE HISTORY, ALL RIGHT... AS PRIZE FALL GUYS!
AND WHY DIDN'T THOR SHOW?
WE NEVER EVEN GOT A CRACK AT THAT LONG-HAIRED FINK!*
*COULD YOU ATTEND A WEDDING AND BATTLE THE SILVER SURFER AT THE SAME TIME? ... S.
19

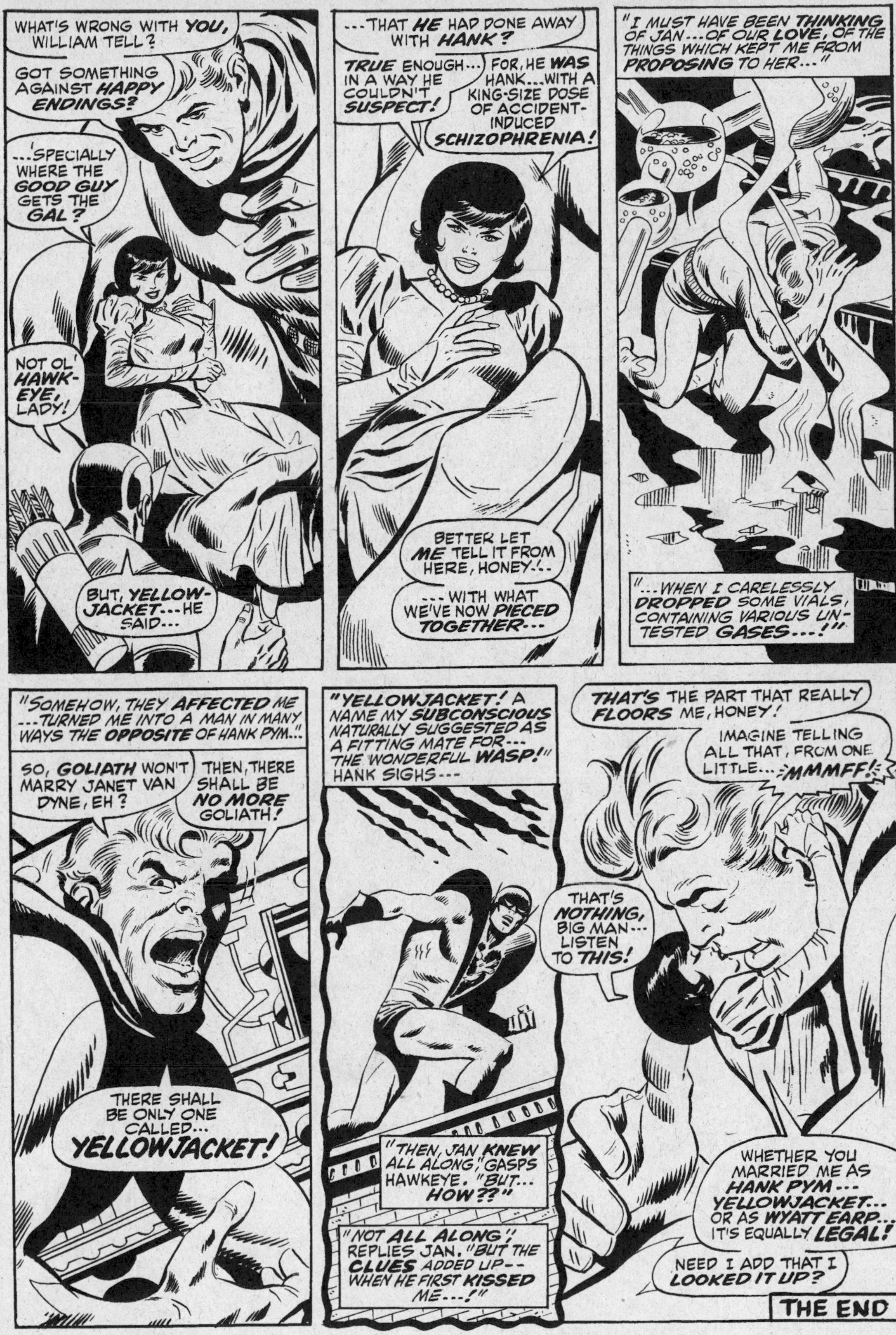

WHAT'S WRONG WITH YOU, WILLIAM TELL?
GOT SOMETHING AGAINST HAPPY ENDINGS?
...'SPECIALLY WHERE THE GOOD GUY GETS THE GAL?
NOT OL' HAWK-EYE, LADY!
BUT, YELLOW-JACKET---HE SAID...
---THAT HE HAD DONE AWAY WITH HANK?
TRUE ENOUGH... IN A WAY HE COULDN'T SUSPECT!
FOR, HE WAS HANK...WITH A KING-SIZE DOSE OF ACCIDENT-INDUCED SCHIZOPHRENIA!
BETTER LET ME TELL IT FROM HERE, HONEY!..
---WITH WHAT WE'VE NOW PIECED TOGETHER---
"I MUST HAVE BEEN THINKING OF JAN...OF OUR LOVE, OF THE THINGS WHICH KEPT ME FROM PROPOSING TO HER..."
"...WHEN I CARELESSLY DROPPED SOME VIALS, CONTAINING VARIOUS UN-TESTED GASES...!"
"SOMEHOW, THEY AFFECTED ME ...TURNED ME INTO A MAN IN MANY WAYS THE OPPOSITE OF HANK PYM..."
SO, GOLIATH WON'T MARRY JANET VAN DYNE, EH?
THEN, THERE SHALL BE NO MORE GOLIATH!
THERE SHALL BE ONLY ONE CALLED... YELLOWJACKET!
"YELLOWJACKET! A NAME MY SUBCONSCIOUS NATURALLY SUGGESTED AS A FITTING MATE FOR... THE WONDERFUL WASP!" HANK SIGHS---
"THEN, JAN KNEW ALL ALONG," GASPS HAWKEYE. "BUT... HOW??"
"NOT ALL ALONG!" REPLIES JAN. "BUT THE CLUES ADDED UP-- WHEN HE FIRST KISSED ME---!"
THAT'S THE PART THAT REALLY FLOORS ME, HONEY!
IMAGINE TELLING ALL THAT, FROM ONE LITTLE... MMMFF!
THAT'S NOTHING, BIG MAN--- LISTEN TO THIS!
WHETHER YOU MARRIED ME AS HANK PYM--- YELLOWJACKET... OR AS WYATT EARP... IT'S EQUALLY LEGAL!
NEED I ADD THAT I LOOKED IT UP?
THE END

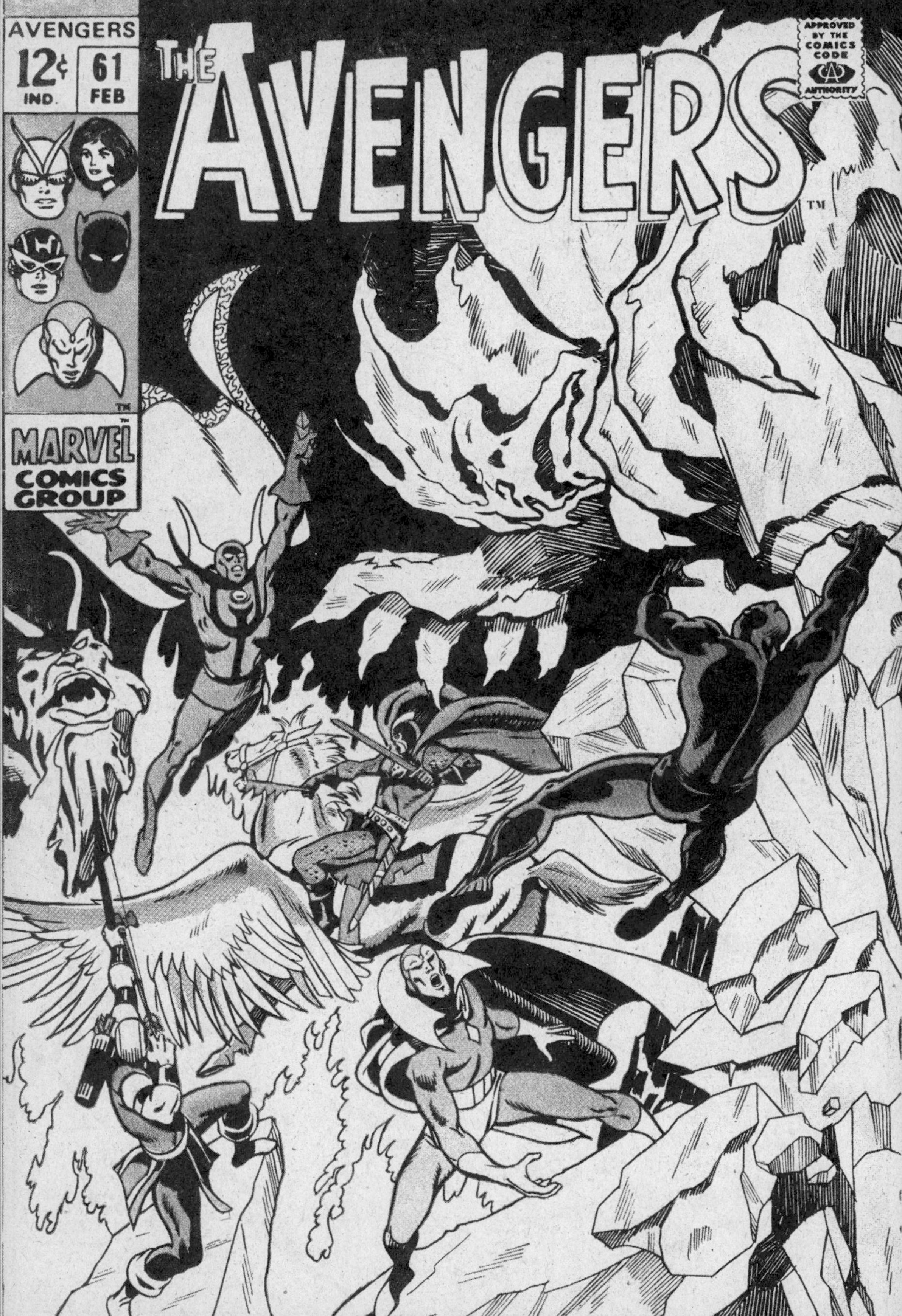
AVENGERS
12¢
IND.
61
FEB
THE AVENGERS
TM
APPROVED BY THE COMICS CODE AUTHORITY
MARVEL COMICS GROUP

STAN LEE, EDITOR PRESENTS A STAR-STUDDED AVENGERS SAGA By: ROY THOMAS WRITER || JOHN BUSCEMA ARTIST || GEORGE KLEIN INKER || SAM ROSEN LETTERER

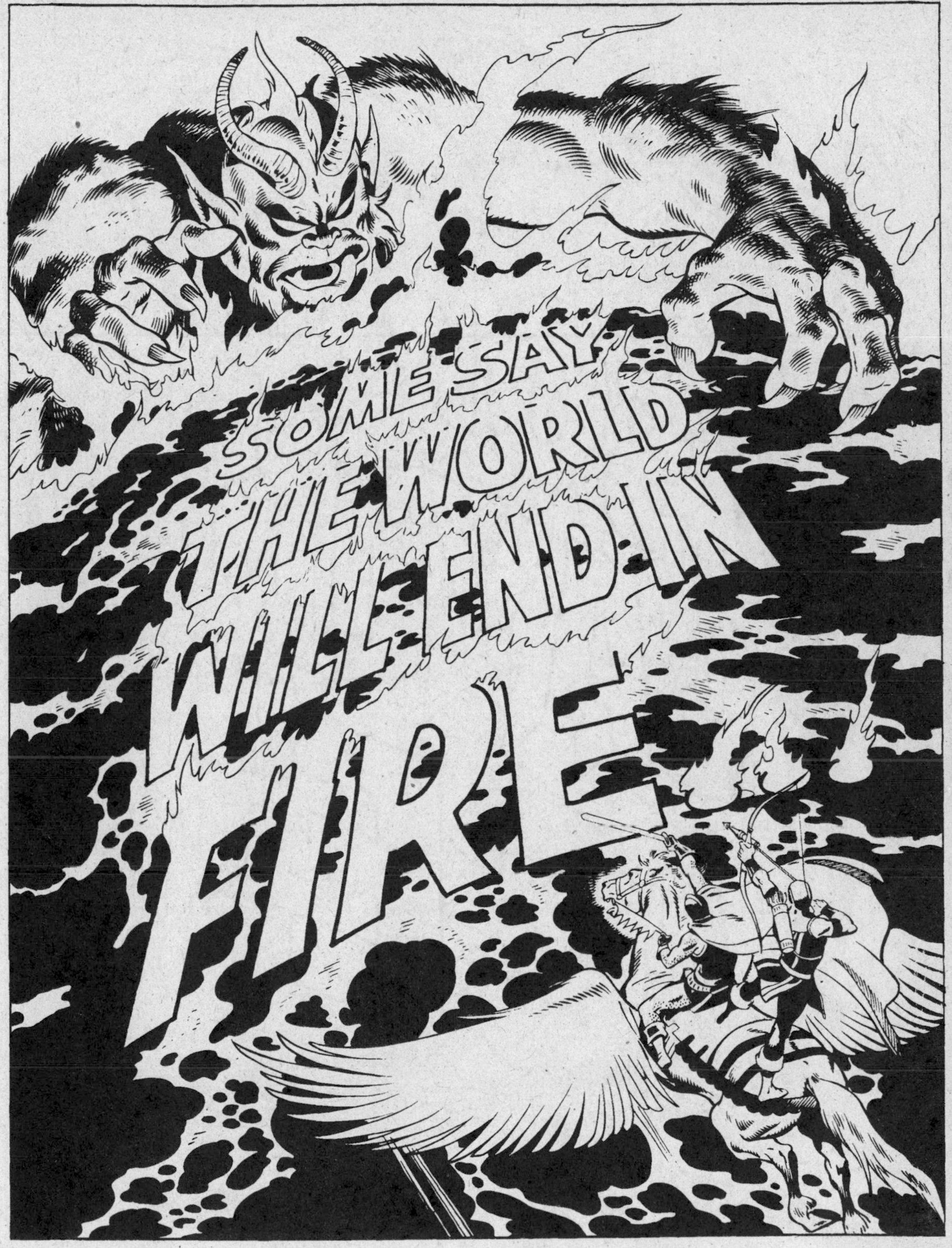

SOME SAY THE WORLD WILL END IN FIRE

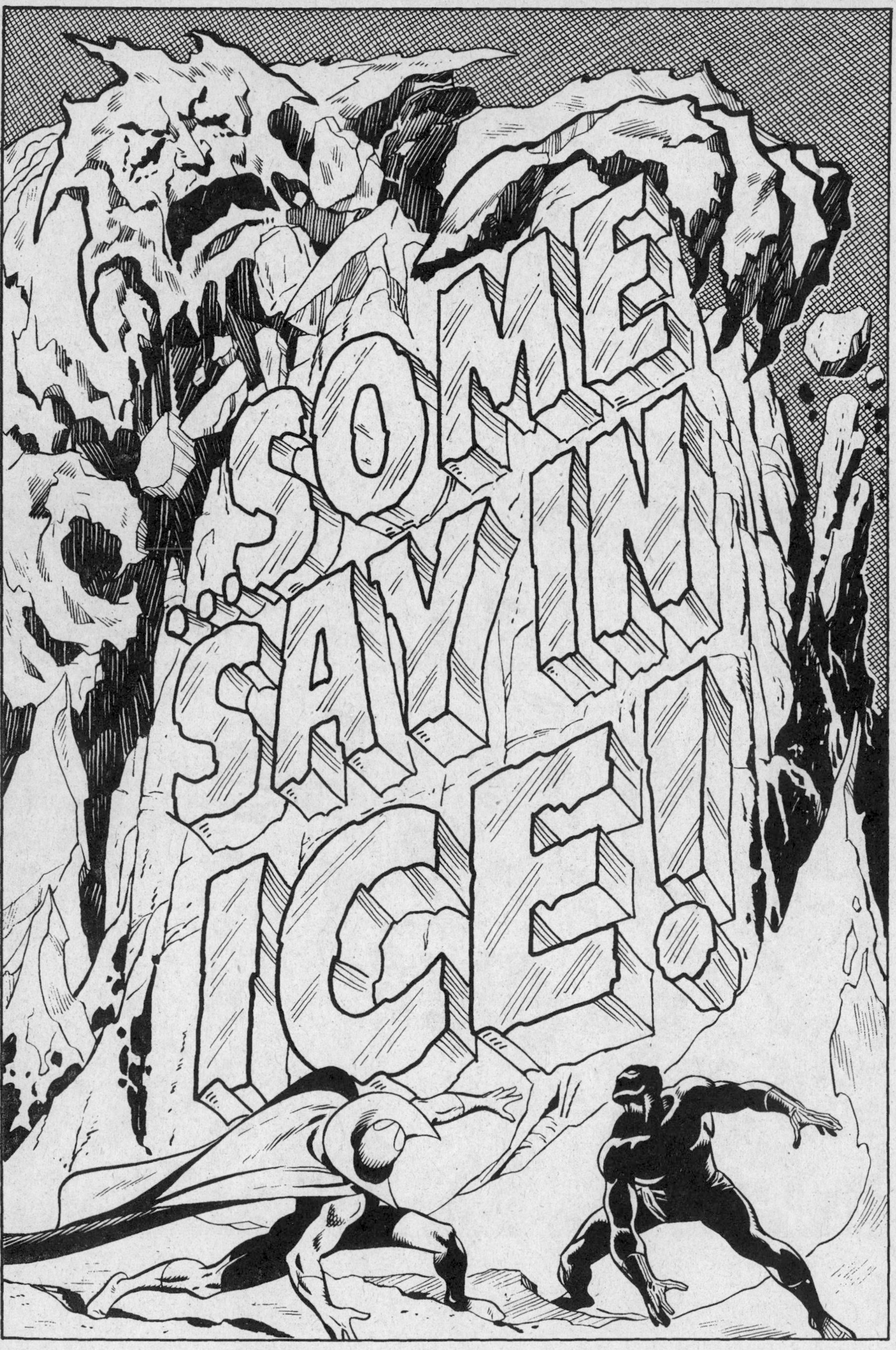
SOME SAVIN' ICE!

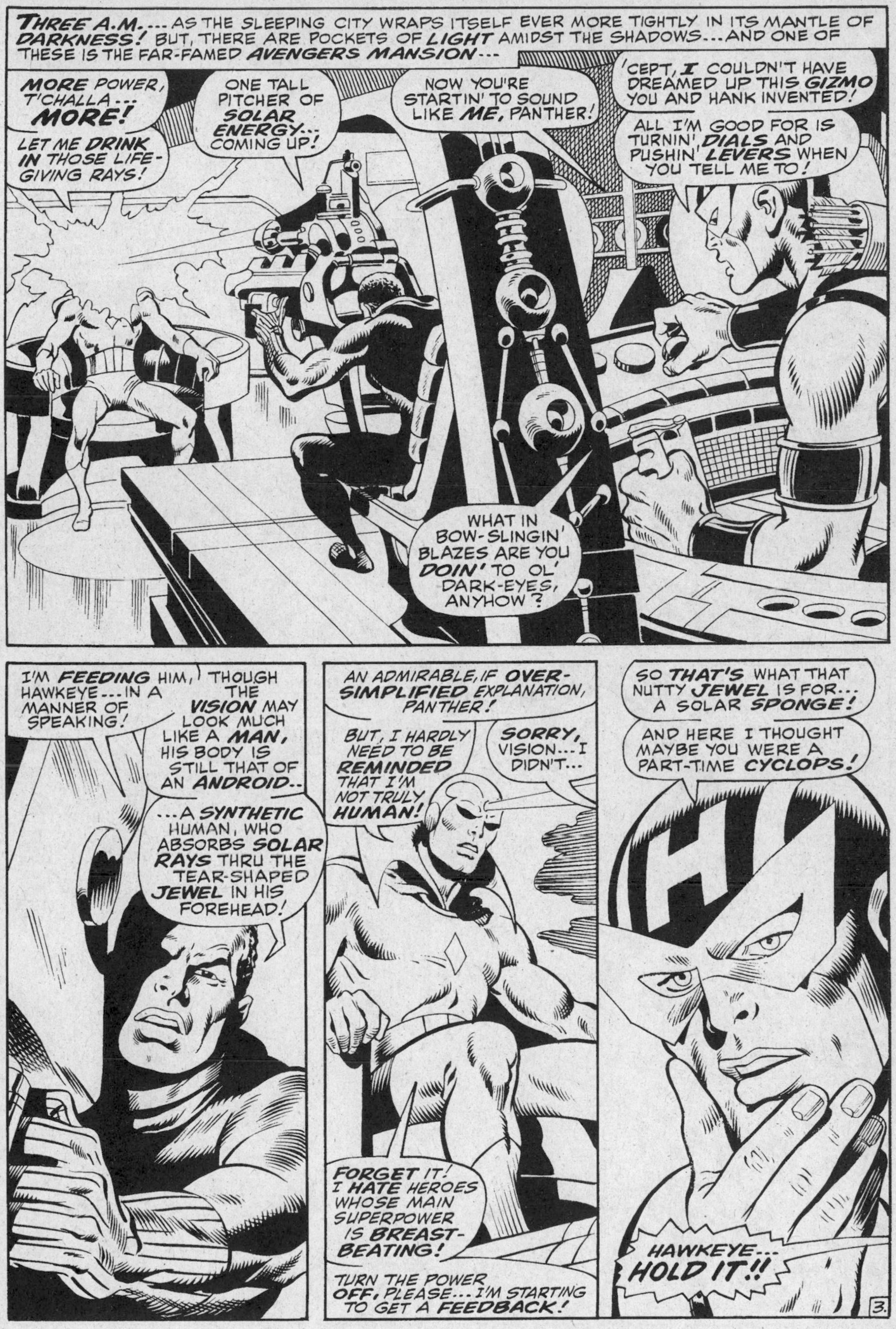
THREE A.M.... AS THE SLEEPING CITY WRAPS ITSELF EVER MORE TIGHTLY IN ITS MANTLE OF DARKNESS! BUT, THERE ARE POCKETS OF LIGHT AMIDST THE SHADOWS... AND ONE OF THESE IS THE FAR-FAMED AVENGERS MANSION...
MORE POWER, T'CHALLA... MORE!
LET ME DRINK IN THOSE LIFE-GIVING RAYS!
ONE TALL PITCHER OF SOLAR ENERGY... COMING UP!
NOW YOU'RE STARTIN' TO SOUND LIKE ME, PANTHER!
'CEPT, I COULDN'T HAVE DREAMED UP THIS GIZMO YOU AND HANK INVENTED!
ALL I'M GOOD FOR IS TURNIN' DIALS AND PUSHIN' LEVERS WHEN YOU TELL ME TO!
WHAT IN BOW-SLINGIN' BLAZES ARE YOU DOIN' TO OL' DARK-EYES, ANYHOW?
I'M FEEDING HIM, HAWKEYE... IN A MANNER OF SPEAKING!
THOUGH THE VISION MAY LOOK MUCH LIKE A MAN, HIS BODY IS STILL THAT OF AN ANDROID..
...A SYNTHETIC HUMAN, WHO ABSORBS SOLAR RAYS THRU THE TEAR-SHAPED JEWEL IN HIS FOREHEAD!
AN ADMIRABLE, IF OVER-SIMPLIFIED EXPLANATION, PANTHER!
BUT, I HARDLY NEED TO BE REMINDED THAT I'M NOT TRULY HUMAN!
SORRY, VISION... I DIDN'T...
FORGET IT! I HATE HEROES WHOSE MAIN SUPERPOWER IS BREAST-BEATING!
TURN THE POWER OFF, PLEASE... I'M STARTING TO GET A FEEDBACK!
SO THAT'S WHAT THAT NUTTY JEWEL IS FOR... A SOLAR SPONGE!
AND HERE I THOUGHT MAYBE YOU WERE A PART-TIME CYCLOPS!
HAWKEYE... HOLD IT!!
3.

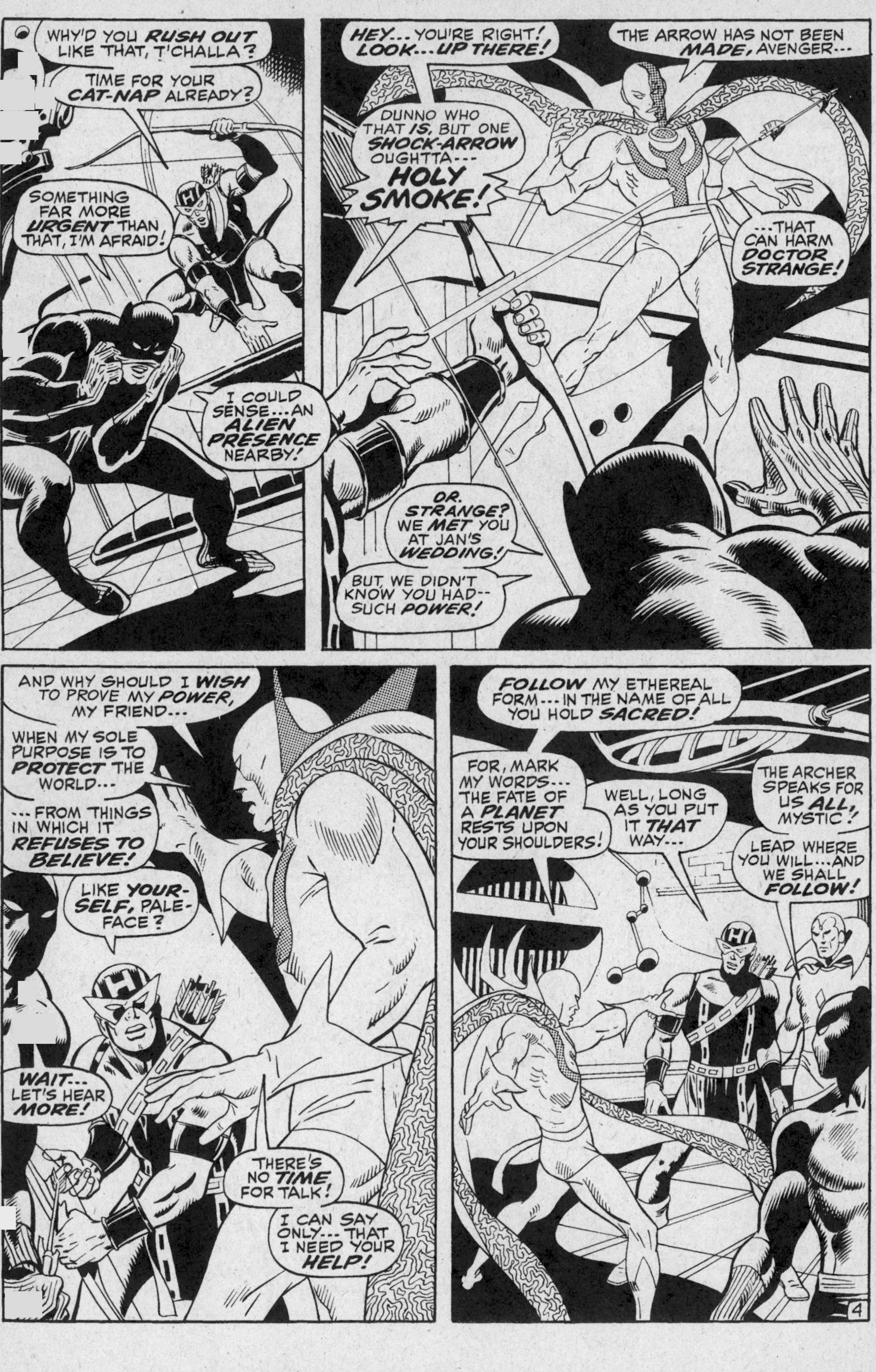
WHY'D YOU RUSH OUT LIKE THAT, T'CHALLA?
TIME FOR YOUR CAT-NAP ALREADY?
SOMETHING FAR MORE URGENT THAN THAT, I'M AFRAID!
I COULD SENSE...AN ALIEN PRESENCE NEARBY!
HEY... YOU'RE RIGHT! LOOK... UP THERE!
DUNNO WHO THAT IS, BUT ONE SHOCK-ARROW OUGHTTA--- HOLY SMOKE!
THE ARROW HAS NOT BEEN MADE, AVENGER---
---THAT CAN HARM DOCTOR STRANGE!
DR. STRANGE? WE MET YOU AT JAN'S WEDDING!
BUT, WE DIDN'T KNOW YOU HAD-- SUCH POWER!
AND WHY SHOULD I WISH TO PROVE MY POWER, MY FRIEND---
WHEN MY SOLE PURPOSE IS TO PROTECT THE WORLD---
---FROM THINGS IN WHICH IT REFUSES TO BELIEVE!
LIKE YOURSELF, PALE-FACE?
WAIT--- LET'S HEAR MORE!
THERE'S NO TIME FOR TALK!
I CAN SAY ONLY--- THAT I NEED YOUR HELP!
FOLLOW MY ETHEREAL FORM--- IN THE NAME OF ALL YOU HOLD SACRED!
FOR, MARK MY WORDS--- THE FATE OF A PLANET RESTS UPON YOUR SHOULDERS!
WELL, LONG AS YOU PUT IT THAT WAY---
THE ARCHER SPEAKS FOR US ALL, MYSTIC!
LEAD WHERE YOU WILL...AND WE SHALL FOLLOW!
4

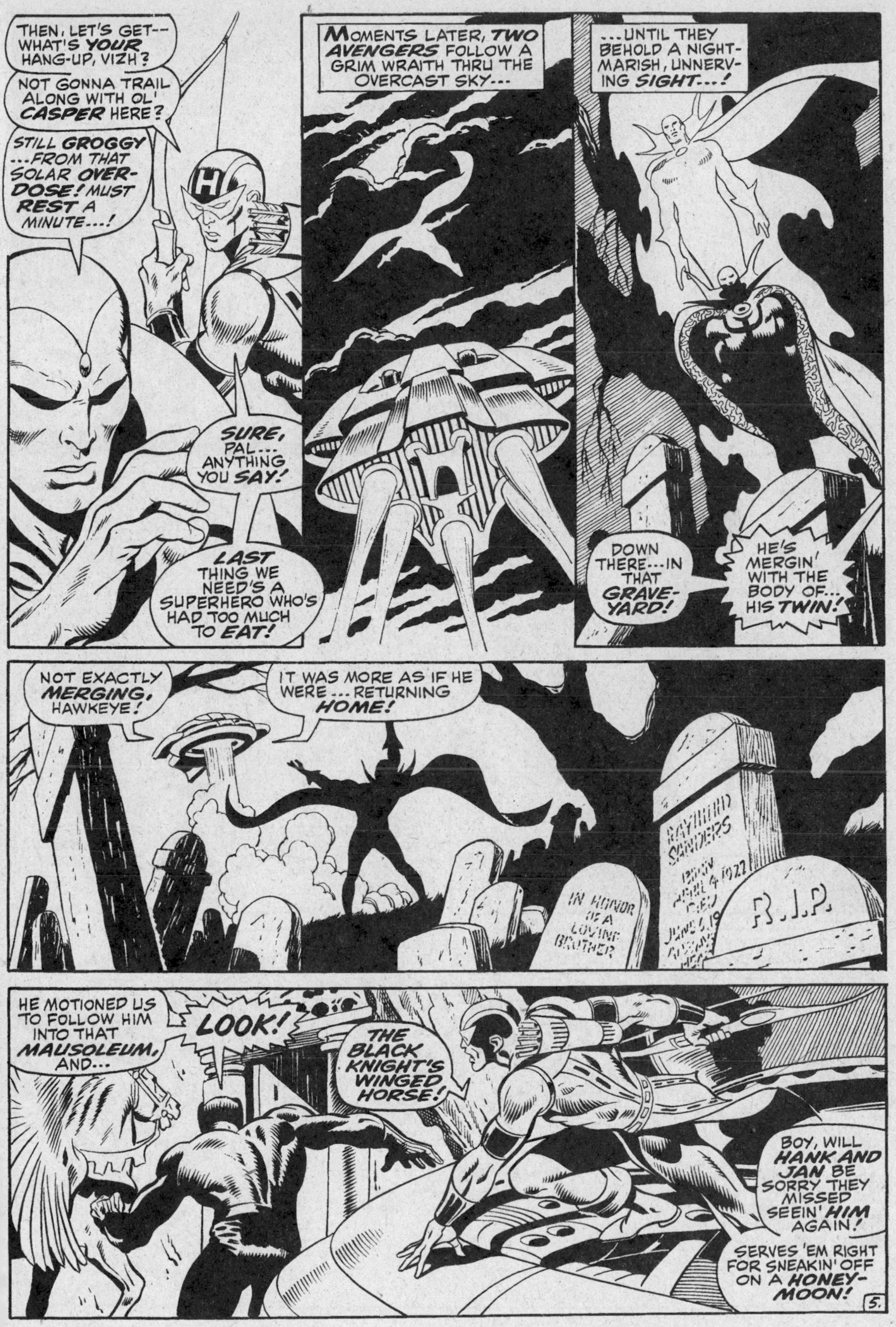
THEN, LET'S GET-- WHAT'S YOUR HANG-UP, VIZH?
NOT GONNA TRAIL ALONG WITH OL' CASPER HERE?
STILL GROGGY ...FROM THAT SOLAR OVER-DOSE! MUST REST A MINUTE...!
SURE, PAL... ANYTHING YOU SAY!
LAST THING WE NEED'S A SUPERHERO WHO'S HAD TOO MUCH TO EAT!
MOMENTS LATER, TWO AVENGERS FOLLOW A GRIM WRAITH THRU THE OVERCAST SKY...
...UNTIL THEY BEHOLD A NIGHT-MARISH, UNNERVING SIGHT...!
DOWN THERE...IN THAT GRAVE-YARD!
HE'S MERGIN' WITH THE BODY OF... HIS TWIN!
NOT EXACTLY MERGING, HAWKEYE!
IT WAS MORE AS IF HE WERE... RETURNING HOME!
IN HONOR OF A LOVING BROTHER
R.I.P.
HE MOTIONED US TO FOLLOW HIM INTO THAT MAUSOLEUM, AND...
LOOK!
THE BLACK KNIGHT'S WINGED HORSE!
BOY, WILL HANK AND JAN BE SORRY THEY MISSED SEEIN' HIM AGAIN!
SERVES 'EM RIGHT FOR SNEAKIN' OFF ON A HONEY-MOON!
5.

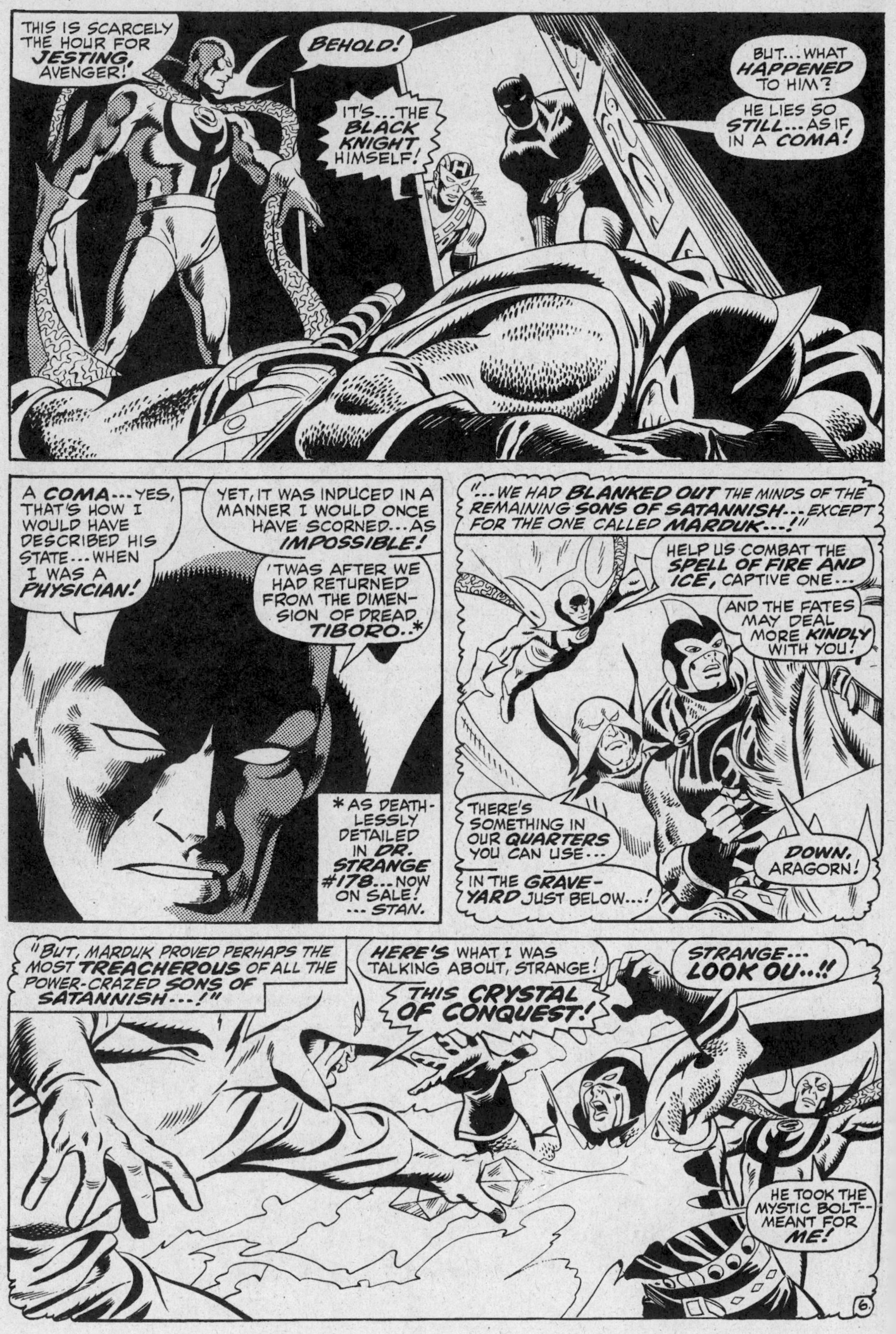
THIS IS SCARCELY THE HOUR FOR JESTING, AVENGER!
BEHOLD!
IT'S...THE BLACK KNIGHT HIMSELF!
BUT...WHAT HAPPENED TO HIM?
HE LIES SO STILL...AS IF, IN A COMA!
A COMA---YES, THAT'S HOW I WOULD HAVE DESCRIBED HIS STATE---WHEN I WAS A PHYSICIAN!
YET, IT WAS INDUCED IN A MANNER I WOULD ONCE HAVE SCORNED...AS IMPOSSIBLE!
'TWAS AFTER WE HAD RETURNED FROM THE DIMENSION OF DREAD TIBORO..*
* AS DEATHLESSLY DETAILED IN DR. STRANGE #178...NOW ON SALE! ---STAN.
"...WE HAD BLANKED OUT THE MINDS OF THE REMAINING SONS OF SATANNISH...EXCEPT FOR THE ONE CALLED MARDUK...!"
HELP US COMBAT THE SPELL OF FIRE AND ICE, CAPTIVE ONE...
AND THE FATES MAY DEAL MORE KINDLY WITH YOU!
THERE'S SOMETHING IN OUR QUARTERS YOU CAN USE...
IN THE GRAVEYARD JUST BELOW...!
DOWN, ARAGORN!
"BUT, MARDUK PROVED PERHAPS THE MOST TREACHEROUS OF ALL THE POWER-CRAZED SONS OF SATANNISH---!"
HERE'S WHAT I WAS TALKING ABOUT, STRANGE!
THIS CRYSTAL OF CONQUEST!
STRANGE... LOOK OU..!!
HE TOOK THE MYSTIC BOLT--MEANT FOR ME!
6.

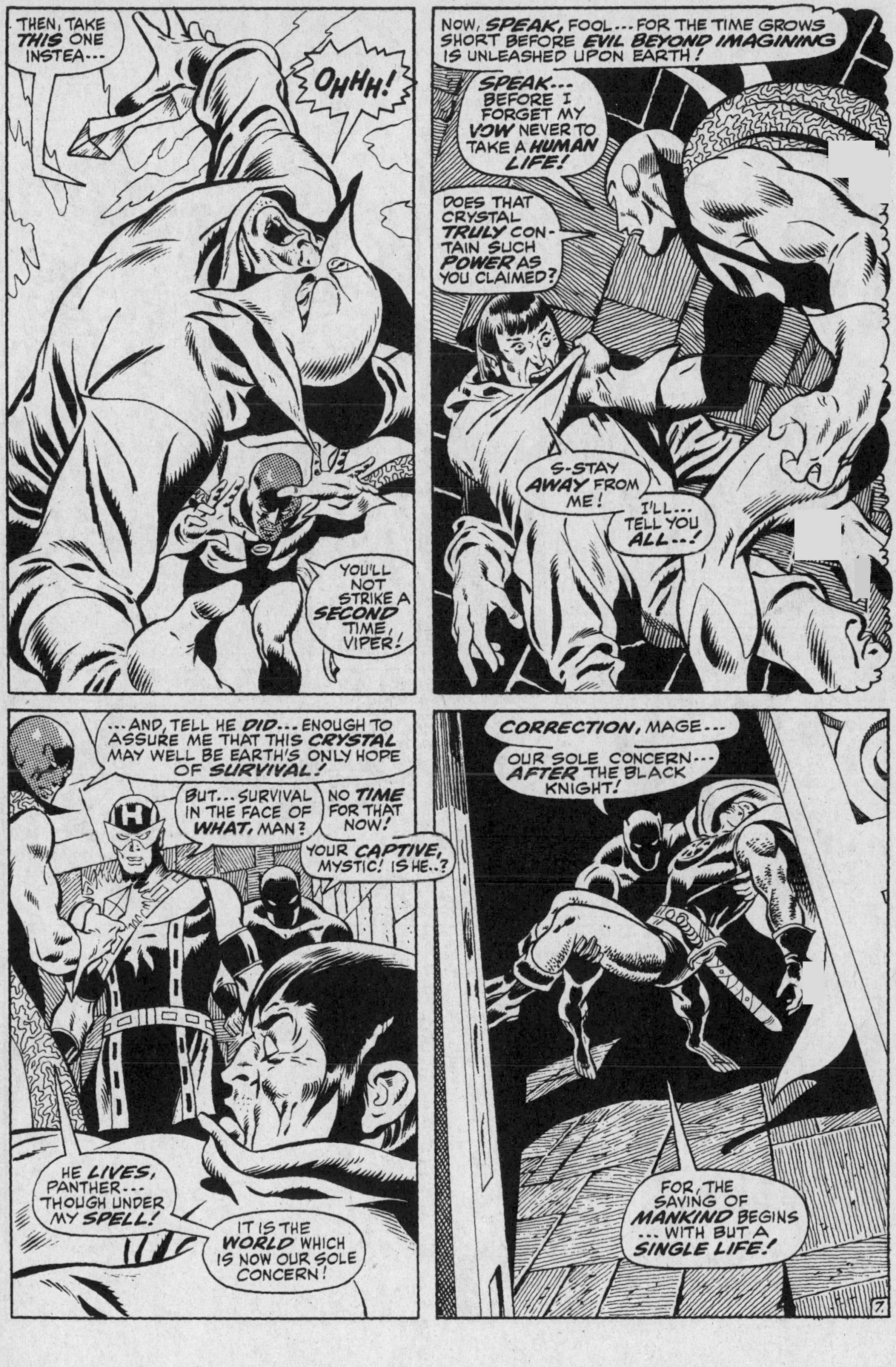

THEN, TAKE THIS ONE INSTEA---
OHHH!
YOU'LL NOT STRIKE A SECOND TIME, VIPER!
NOW, SPEAK, FOOL--- FOR THE TIME GROWS SHORT BEFORE EVIL BEYOND IMAGINING IS UNLEASHED UPON EARTH!
SPEAK--- BEFORE I FORGET MY VOW NEVER TO TAKE A HUMAN LIFE!
DOES THAT CRYSTAL TRULY CONTAIN SUCH POWER AS YOU CLAIMED?
S-STAY AWAY FROM ME!
I'LL... TELL YOU ALL...!
...AND, TELL HE DID... ENOUGH TO ASSURE ME THAT THIS CRYSTAL MAY WELL BE EARTH'S ONLY HOPE OF SURVIVAL!
BUT... SURVIVAL IN THE FACE OF WHAT, MAN?
NO TIME FOR THAT NOW!
YOUR CAPTIVE, MYSTIC! IS HE..?
HE LIVES, PANTHER--- THOUGH UNDER MY SPELL!
IT IS THE WORLD WHICH IS NOW OUR SOLE CONCERN!
CORRECTION, MAGE---
OUR SOLE CONCERN--- AFTER THE BLACK KNIGHT!
FOR, THE SAVING OF MANKIND BEGINS ... WITH BUT A SINGLE LIFE!
7

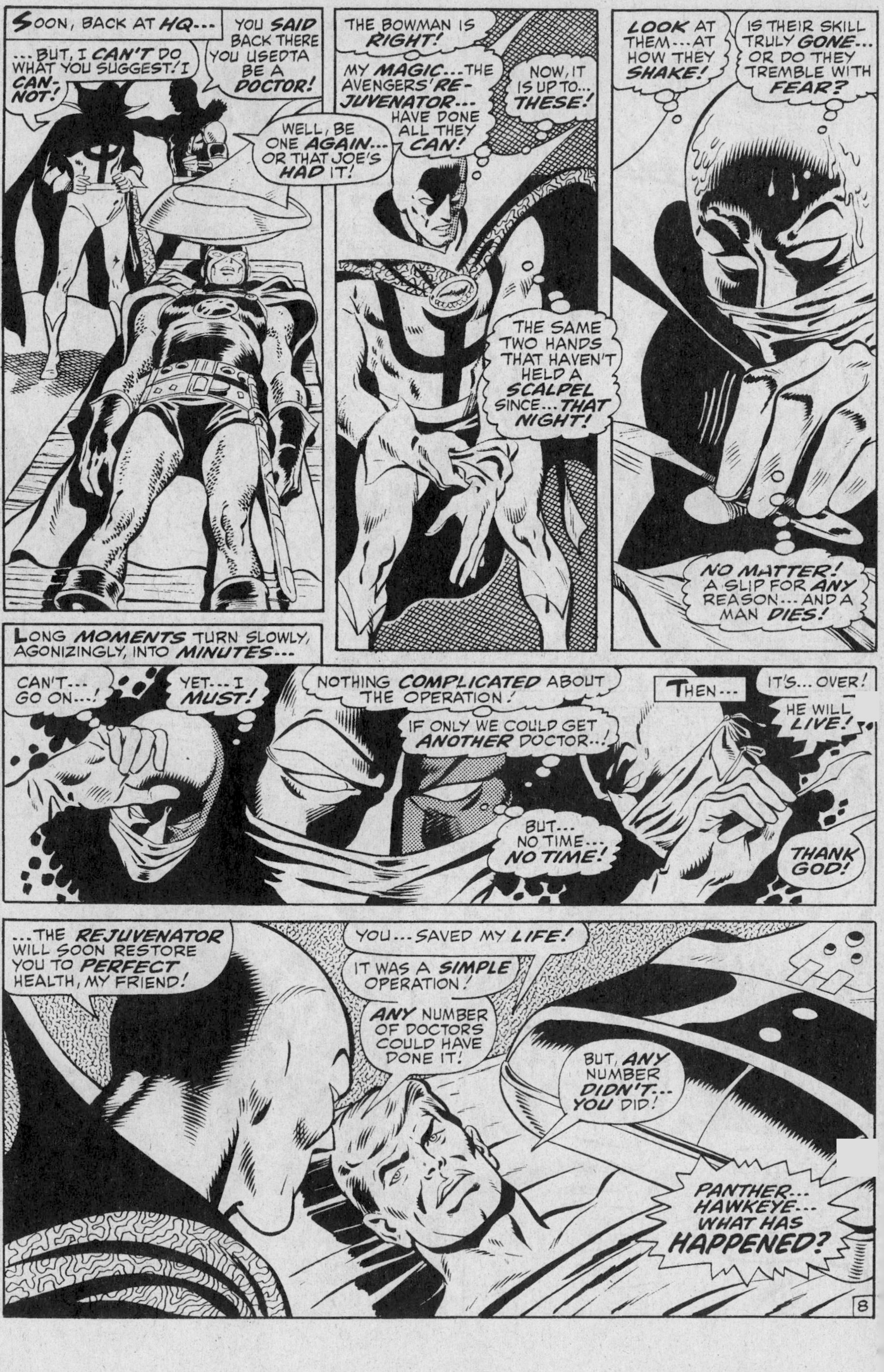

SOON, BACK AT HQ...
...BUT, I CAN'T DO WHAT YOU SUGGEST! I CAN-NOT!
YOU SAID BACK THERE YOU USEDTA BE A DOCTOR!
WELL, BE ONE AGAIN... OR THAT JOE'S HAD IT!
THE BOWMAN IS RIGHT!
MY MAGIC... THE AVENGERS' RE-JUVENATOR... HAVE DONE ALL THEY CAN!
NOW, IT IS UP TO... THESE!
THE SAME TWO HANDS THAT HAVEN'T HELD A SCALPEL SINCE... THAT NIGHT!
LOOK AT THEM... AT HOW THEY SHAKE!
IS THEIR SKILL TRULY GONE... OR DO THEY TREMBLE WITH FEAR?
NO MATTER! A SLIP FOR ANY REASON... AND A MAN DIES!
LONG MOMENTS TURN SLOWLY, AGONIZINGLY, INTO MINUTES...
CAN'T... GO ON...!
YET... I MUST!
NOTHING COMPLICATED ABOUT THE OPERATION!
IF ONLY WE COULD GET ANOTHER DOCTOR...!
BUT... NO TIME... NO TIME!
THEN...
IT'S... OVER!
HE WILL LIVE!
THANK GOD!
...THE REJUVENATOR WILL SOON RESTORE YOU TO PERFECT HEALTH, MY FRIEND!
YOU... SAVED MY LIFE!
IT WAS A SIMPLE OPERATION!
ANY NUMBER OF DOCTORS COULD HAVE DONE IT!
BUT, ANY NUMBER DIDN'T... YOU DID!
PANTHER... HAWKEYE... WHAT HAS HAPPENED?

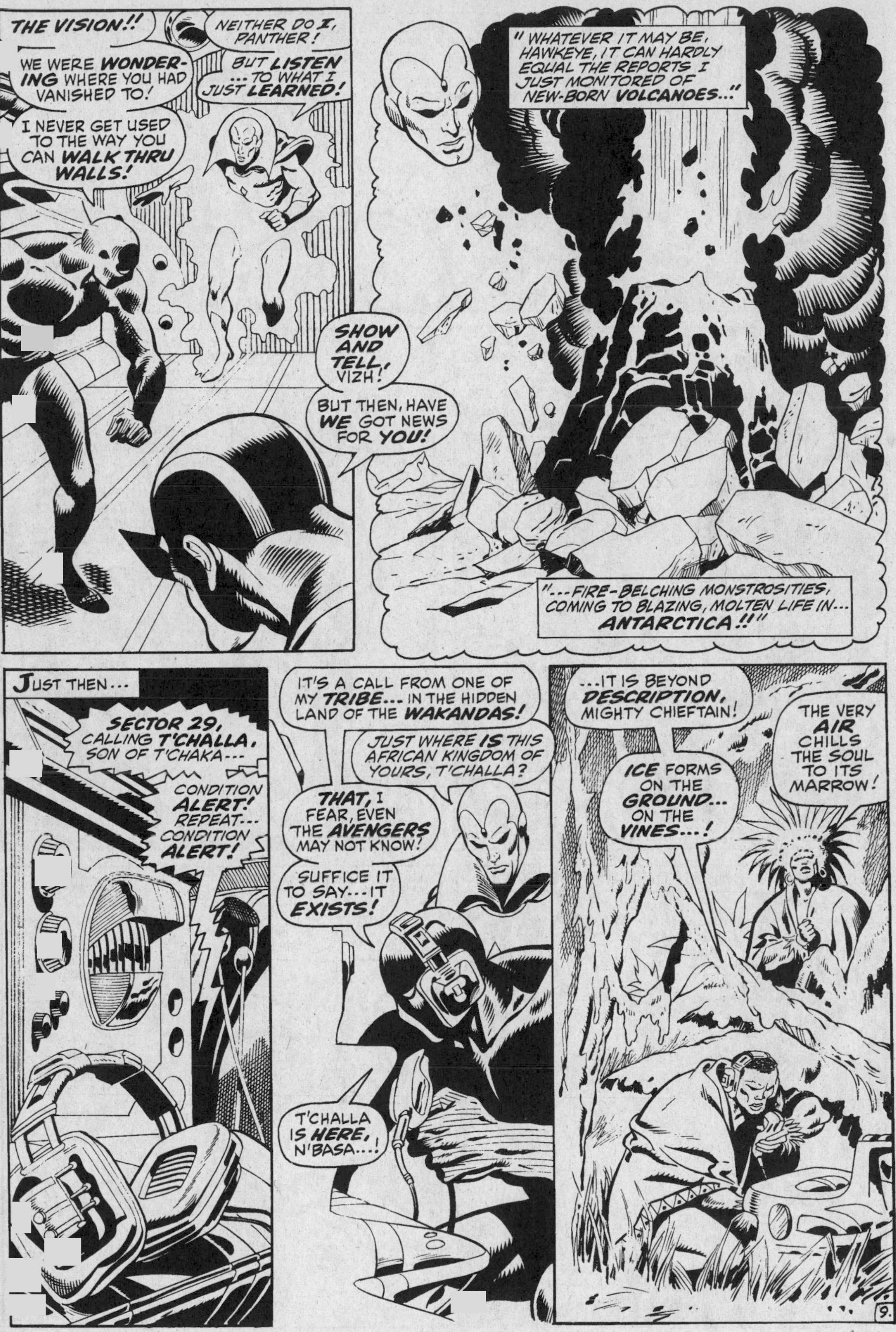
THE VISION!!
WE WERE WONDERING WHERE YOU HAD VANISHED TO!
I NEVER GET USED TO THE WAY YOU CAN WALK THRU WALLS!
NEITHER DO I, PANTHER!
BUT LISTEN ... TO WHAT I JUST LEARNED!
SHOW AND TELL, VIZH!
BUT THEN, HAVE WE GOT NEWS FOR YOU!
" WHATEVER IT MAY BE, HAWKEYE, IT CAN HARDLY EQUAL THE REPORTS I JUST MONITORED OF NEW-BORN VOLCANOES..."
"...FIRE-BELCHING MONSTROSITIES, COMING TO BLAZING, MOLTEN LIFE IN... ANTARCTICA!!"
JUST THEN...
SECTOR 29, CALLING T'CHALLA, SON OF T'CHAKA---
CONDITION ALERT! REPEAT--- CONDITION ALERT!
IT'S A CALL FROM ONE OF MY TRIBE... IN THE HIDDEN LAND OF THE WAKANDAS!
JUST WHERE IS THIS AFRICAN KINGDOM OF YOURS, T'CHALLA?
THAT, I FEAR, EVEN THE AVENGERS MAY NOT KNOW!
SUFFICE IT TO SAY---IT EXISTS!
T'CHALLA IS HERE, N'BASA---!
...IT IS BEYOND DESCRIPTION, MIGHTY CHIEFTAIN!
ICE FORMS ON THE GROUND... ON THE VINES...!
THE VERY AIR CHILLS THE SOUL TO ITS MARROW!
9.

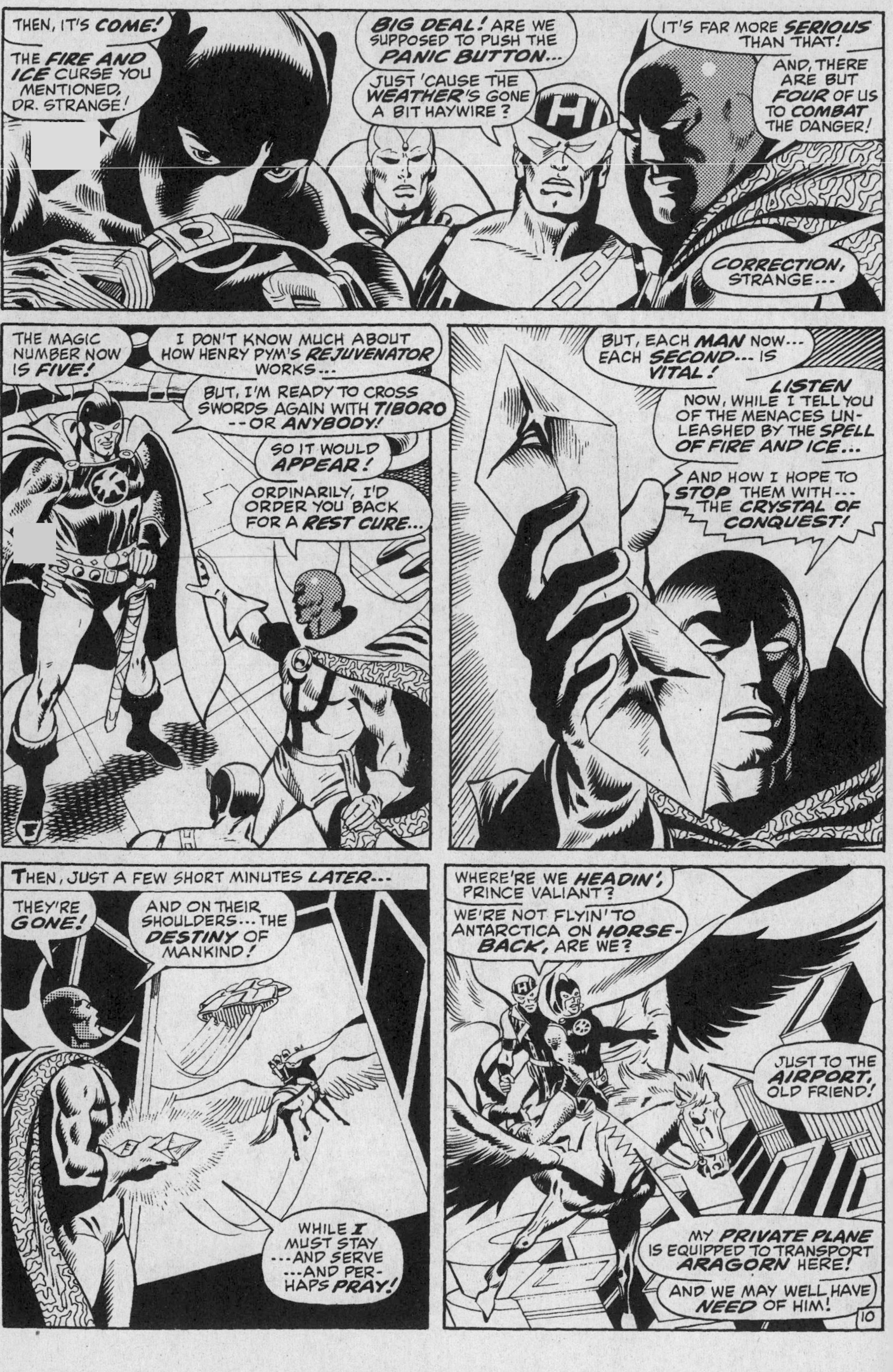
THEN, IT'S COME!
THE FIRE AND ICE CURSE YOU MENTIONED, DR. STRANGE!
BIG DEAL! ARE WE SUPPOSED TO PUSH THE PANIC BUTTON...
JUST 'CAUSE THE WEATHER'S GONE A BIT HAYWIRE?
IT'S FAR MORE SERIOUS THAN THAT!
AND, THERE ARE BUT FOUR OF US TO COMBAT THE DANGER!
CORRECTION, STRANGE---
THE MAGIC NUMBER NOW IS FIVE!
I DON'T KNOW MUCH ABOUT HOW HENRY PYM'S REJUVENATOR WORKS...
BUT, I'M READY TO CROSS SWORDS AGAIN WITH TIBORO --OR ANYBODY!
SO IT WOULD APPEAR!
ORDINARILY, I'D ORDER YOU BACK FOR A REST CURE...
BUT, EACH MAN NOW... EACH SECOND... IS VITAL!
LISTEN NOW, WHILE I TELL YOU OF THE MENACES UNLEASHED BY THE SPELL OF FIRE AND ICE...
AND HOW I HOPE TO STOP THEM WITH--- THE CRYSTAL OF CONQUEST!
THEN, JUST A FEW SHORT MINUTES LATER...
THEY'RE GONE!
AND ON THEIR SHOULDERS... THE DESTINY OF MANKIND!
WHILE I MUST STAY ---AND SERVE ---AND PERHAPS PRAY!
WHERE'RE WE HEADIN', PRINCE VALIANT?
WE'RE NOT FLYIN' TO ANTARCTICA ON HORSEBACK, ARE WE?
JUST TO THE AIRPORT, OLD FRIEND!
MY PRIVATE PLANE IS EQUIPPED TO TRANSPORT ARAGORN HERE!
AND WE MAY WELL HAVE NEED OF HIM!
10

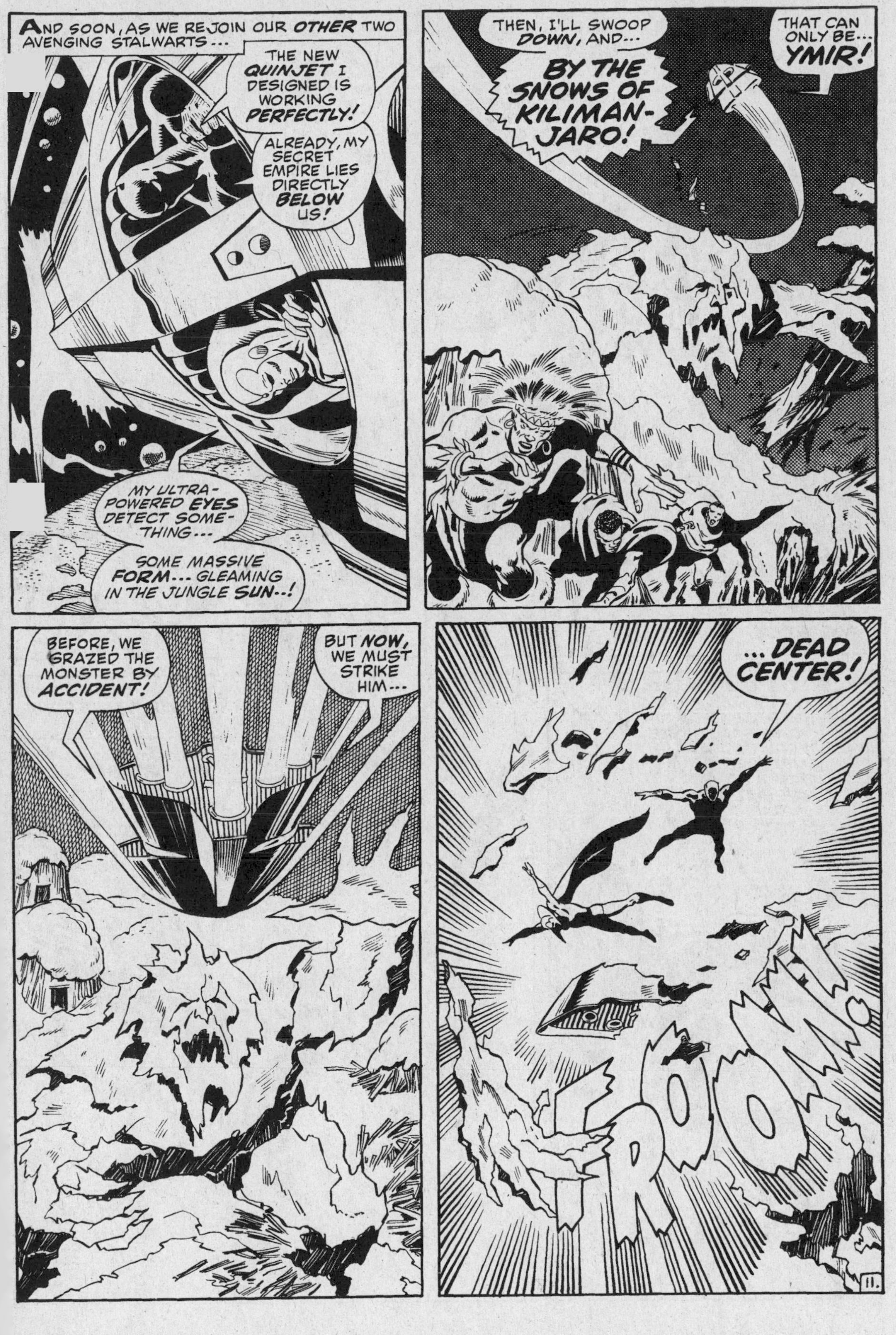
AND SOON, AS WE REJOIN OUR OTHER TWO AVENGING STALWARTS...
THE NEW QUINJET I DESIGNED IS WORKING PERFECTLY!
ALREADY, MY SECRET EMPIRE LIES DIRECTLY BELOW US!
MY ULTRA-POWERED EYES DETECT SOME-THING...
SOME MASSIVE FORM... GLEAMING IN THE JUNGLE SUN..!
THEN, I'LL SWOOP DOWN, AND...
BY THE SNOWS OF KILIMAN-JARO!
THAT CAN ONLY BE... YMIR!
BEFORE, WE GRAZED THE MONSTER BY ACCIDENT!
BUT NOW, WE MUST STRIKE HIM...
...DEAD CENTER!
TROOM!
11.

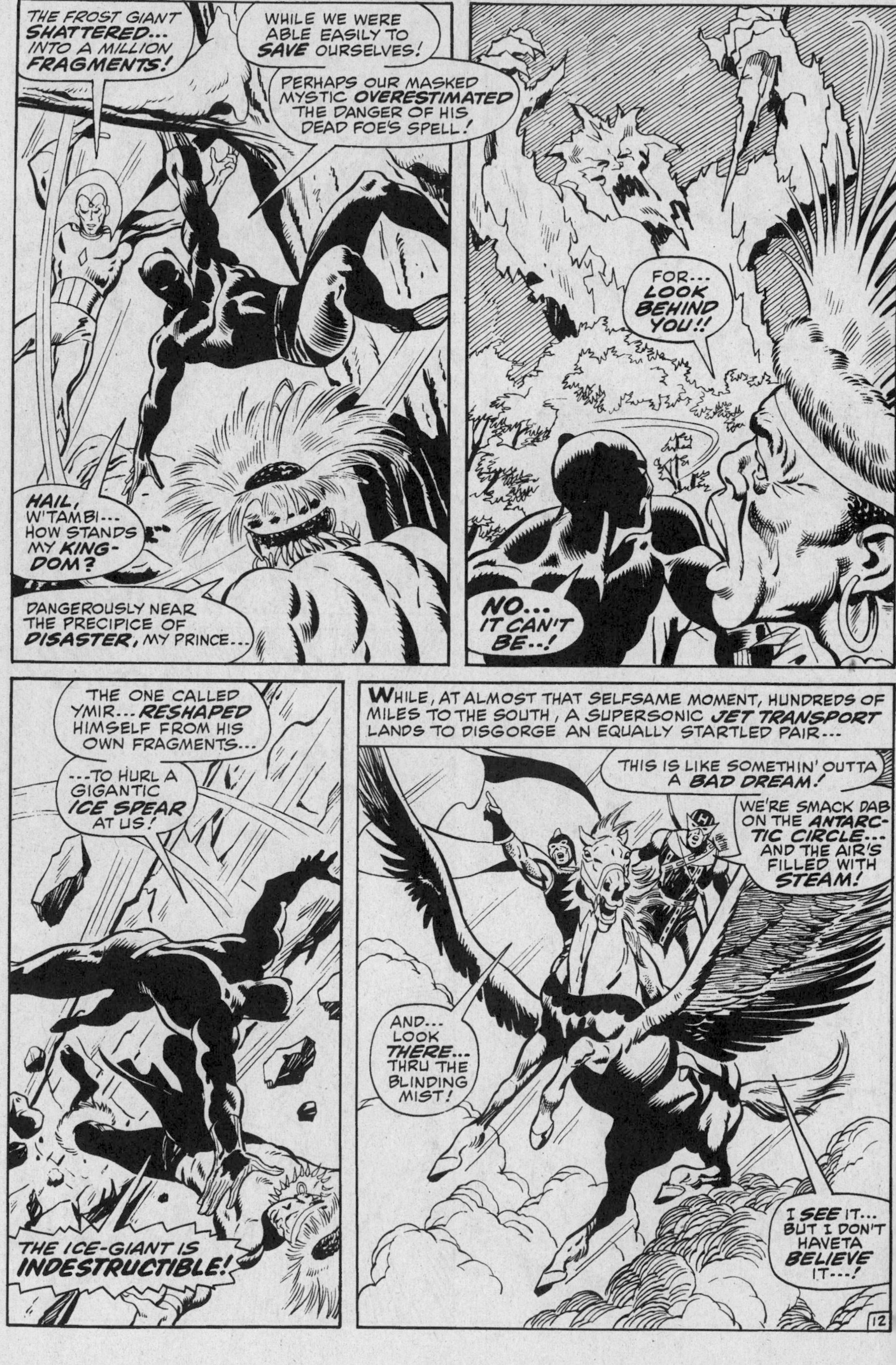
THE FROST GIANT SHATTERED... INTO A MILLION FRAGMENTS!
WHILE WE WERE ABLE EASILY TO SAVE OURSELVES!
PERHAPS OUR MASKED MYSTIC OVERESTIMATED THE DANGER OF HIS DEAD FOE'S SPELL!
HAIL, W'TAMBI... HOW STANDS MY KING-DOM?
DANGEROUSLY NEAR THE PRECIPICE OF DISASTER, MY PRINCE...
FOR... LOOK BEHIND YOU!!
NO... IT CAN'T BE..!
THE ONE CALLED YMIR... RESHAPED HIMSELF FROM HIS OWN FRAGMENTS...
---TO HURL A GIGANTIC ICE SPEAR AT US!
THE ICE-GIANT IS INDESTRUCTIBLE!
WHILE, AT ALMOST THAT SELFSAME MOMENT, HUNDREDS OF MILES TO THE SOUTH, A SUPERSONIC JET TRANSPORT LANDS TO DISGORGE AN EQUALLY STARTLED PAIR---
THIS IS LIKE SOMETHIN' OUTTA A BAD DREAM!
WE'RE SMACK DAB ON THE ANTARC-TIC CIRCLE... AND THE AIR'S FILLED WITH STEAM!
AND... LOOK THERE... THRU THE BLINDING MIST!
I SEE IT... BUT I DON'T HAVETA BELIEVE IT---!
12

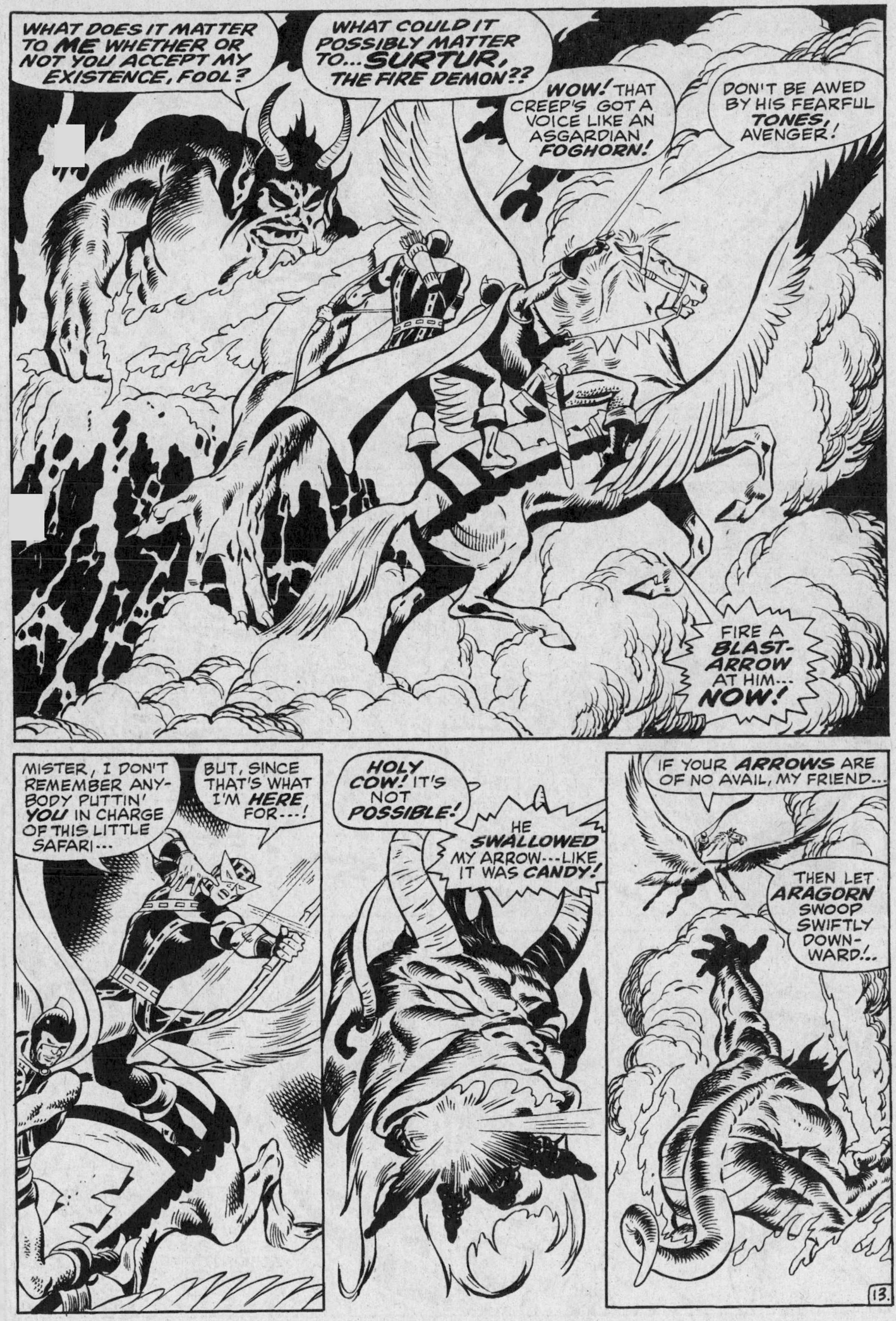
WHAT DOES IT MATTER TO ME WHETHER OR NOT YOU ACCEPT MY EXISTENCE, FOOL?
WHAT COULD IT POSSIBLY MATTER TO... SURTUR, THE FIRE DEMON??
WOW! THAT CREEP'S GOT A VOICE LIKE AN ASGARDIAN FOGHORN!
DON'T BE AWED BY HIS FEARFUL TONES, AVENGER!
FIRE A BLAST-ARROW AT HIM... NOW!
MISTER, I DON'T REMEMBER ANY-BODY PUTTIN' YOU IN CHARGE OF THIS LITTLE SAFARI---
BUT, SINCE THAT'S WHAT I'M HERE FOR---!
HOLY COW! IT'S NOT POSSIBLE!
HE SWALLOWED MY ARROW---LIKE IT WAS CANDY!
IF YOUR ARROWS ARE OF NO AVAIL, MY FRIEND...
THEN LET ARAGORN SWOOP SWIFTLY DOWN-WARD!..
13.

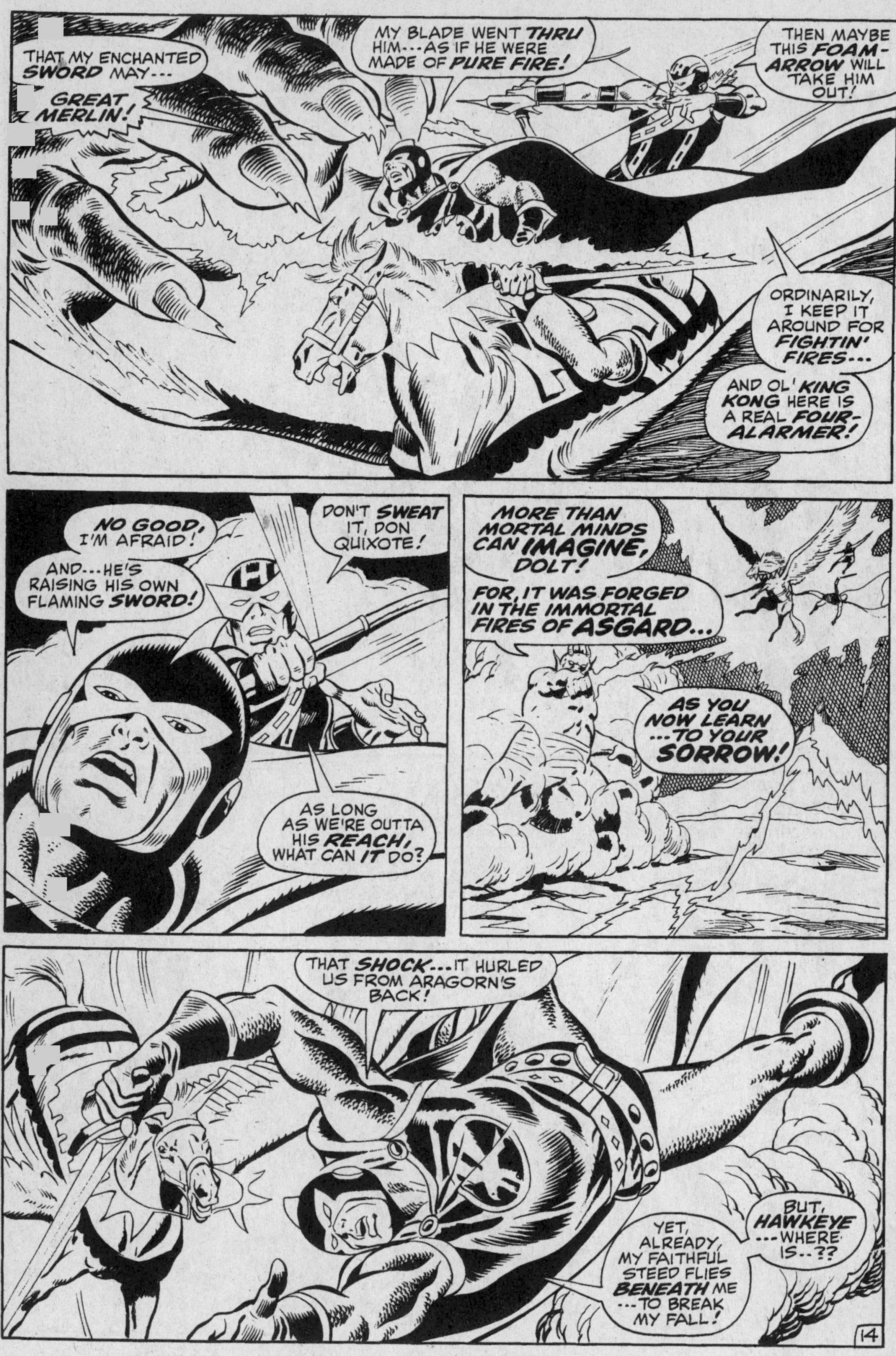

THAT MY ENCHANTED SWORD MAY---
GREAT MERLIN!
MY BLADE WENT THRU HIM---AS IF HE WERE MADE OF PURE FIRE!
THEN MAYBE THIS FOAM-ARROW WILL TAKE HIM OUT!
ORDINARILY, I KEEP IT AROUND FOR FIGHTIN' FIRES---
AND OL' KING KONG HERE IS A REAL FOUR-ALARMER!
NO GOOD, I'M AFRAID!
AND---HE'S RAISING HIS OWN FLAMING SWORD!
DON'T SWEAT IT, DON QUIXOTE!
AS LONG AS WE'RE OUTTA HIS REACH, WHAT CAN IT DO?
MORE THAN MORTAL MINDS CAN IMAGINE, DOLT!
FOR, IT WAS FORGED IN THE IMMORTAL FIRES OF ASGARD...
AS YOU NOW LEARN ---TO YOUR SORROW!
THAT SHOCK---IT HURLED US FROM ARAGORN'S BACK!
YET, ALREADY, MY FAITHFUL STEED FLIES BENEATH ME ---TO BREAK MY FALL!
BUT, HAWKEYE ---WHERE IS--??
14

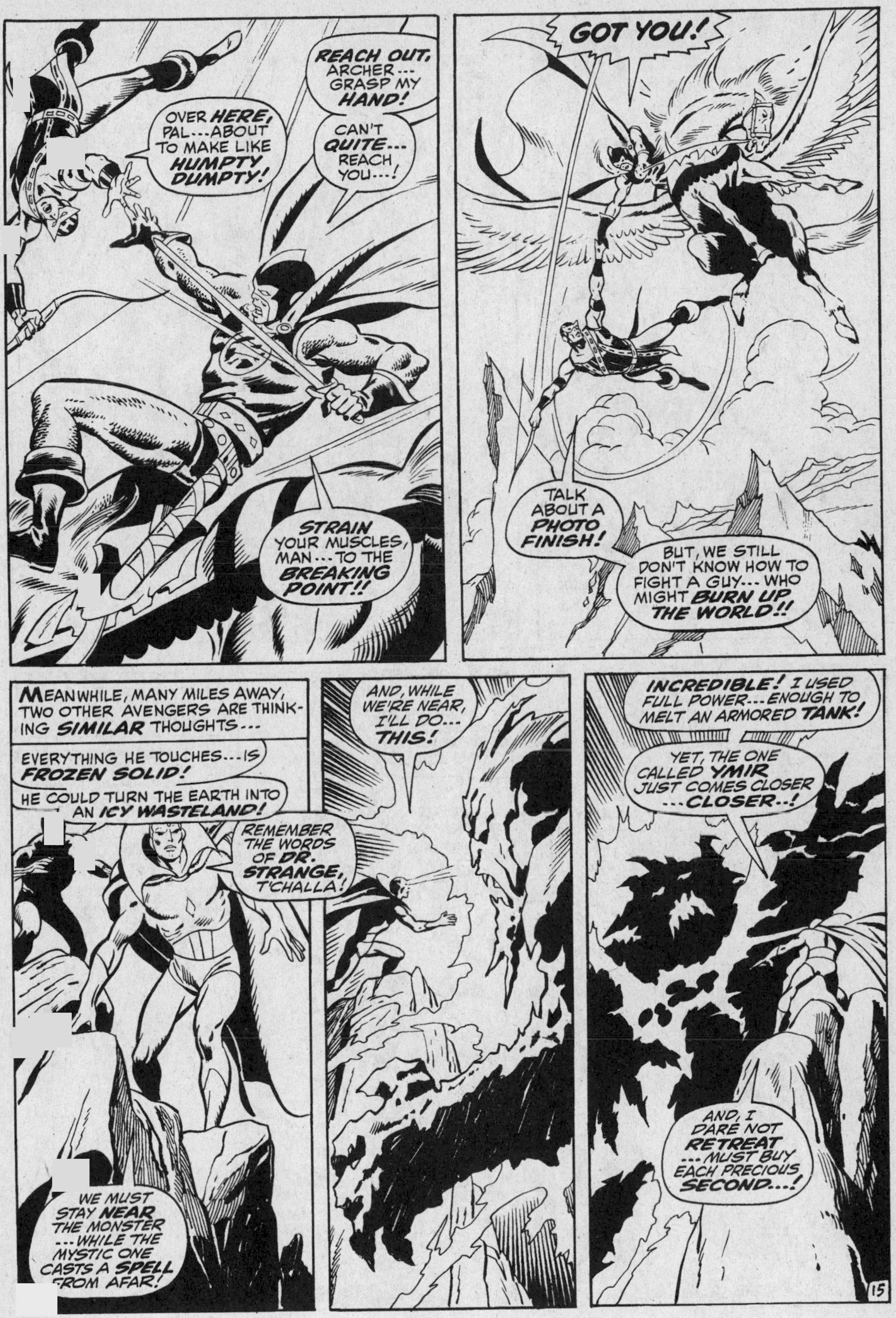
OVER HERE, PAL... ABOUT TO MAKE LIKE HUMPTY DUMPTY!
REACH OUT, ARCHER... GRASP MY HAND!
CAN'T QUITE... REACH YOU...!
STRAIN YOUR MUSCLES, MAN... TO THE BREAKING POINT!!
GOT YOU!
TALK ABOUT A PHOTO FINISH!
BUT, WE STILL DON'T KNOW HOW TO FIGHT A GUY... WHO MIGHT BURN UP THE WORLD!!
MEANWHILE, MANY MILES AWAY, TWO OTHER AVENGERS ARE THINKING SIMILAR THOUGHTS...
EVERYTHING HE TOUCHES... IS FROZEN SOLID!
HE COULD TURN THE EARTH INTO AN ICY WASTELAND!
REMEMBER THE WORDS OF DR. STRANGE, T'CHALLA!
WE MUST STAY NEAR THE MONSTER ...WHILE THE MYSTIC ONE CASTS A SPELL FROM AFAR!
AND, WHILE WE'RE NEAR, I'LL DO... THIS!
INCREDIBLE! I USED FULL POWER... ENOUGH TO MELT AN ARMORED TANK!
YET, THE ONE CALLED YMIR JUST COMES CLOSER ...CLOSER...!
AND, I DARE NOT RETREAT ...MUST BUY EACH PRECIOUS SECOND...!

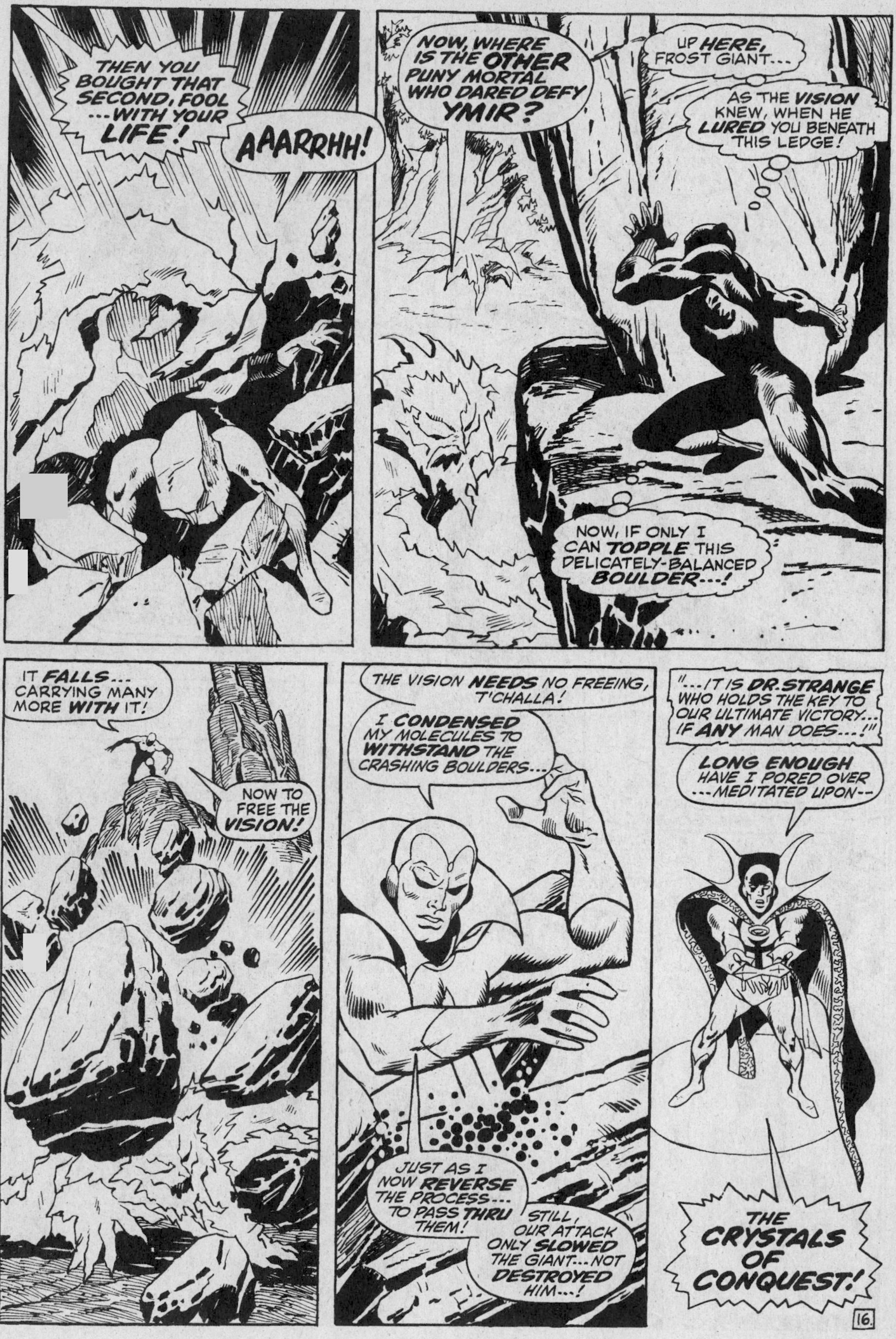
THEN YOU BOUGHT THAT SECOND, FOOL ---WITH YOUR LIFE!
AAARRHH!
NOW, WHERE IS THE OTHER PUNY MORTAL WHO DARED DEFY YMIR?
UP HERE, FROST GIANT---
AS THE VISION KNEW, WHEN HE LURED YOU BENEATH THIS LEDGE!
NOW, IF ONLY I CAN TOPPLE THIS DELICATELY-BALANCED BOULDER---!
IT FALLS... CARRYING MANY MORE WITH IT!
NOW TO FREE THE VISION!
THE VISION NEEDS NO FREEING, T'CHALLA!
I CONDENSED MY MOLECULES TO WITHSTAND THE CRASHING BOULDERS...
JUST AS I NOW REVERSE THE PROCESS... TO PASS THRU THEM!
STILL, OUR ATTACK ONLY SLOWED THE GIANT... NOT DESTROYED HIM...!
"...IT IS DR. STRANGE WHO HOLDS THE KEY TO OUR ULTIMATE VICTORY... IF ANY MAN DOES...!"
LONG ENOUGH HAVE I PORED OVER ---MEDITATED UPON--
THE CRYSTALS OF CONQUEST!
16.

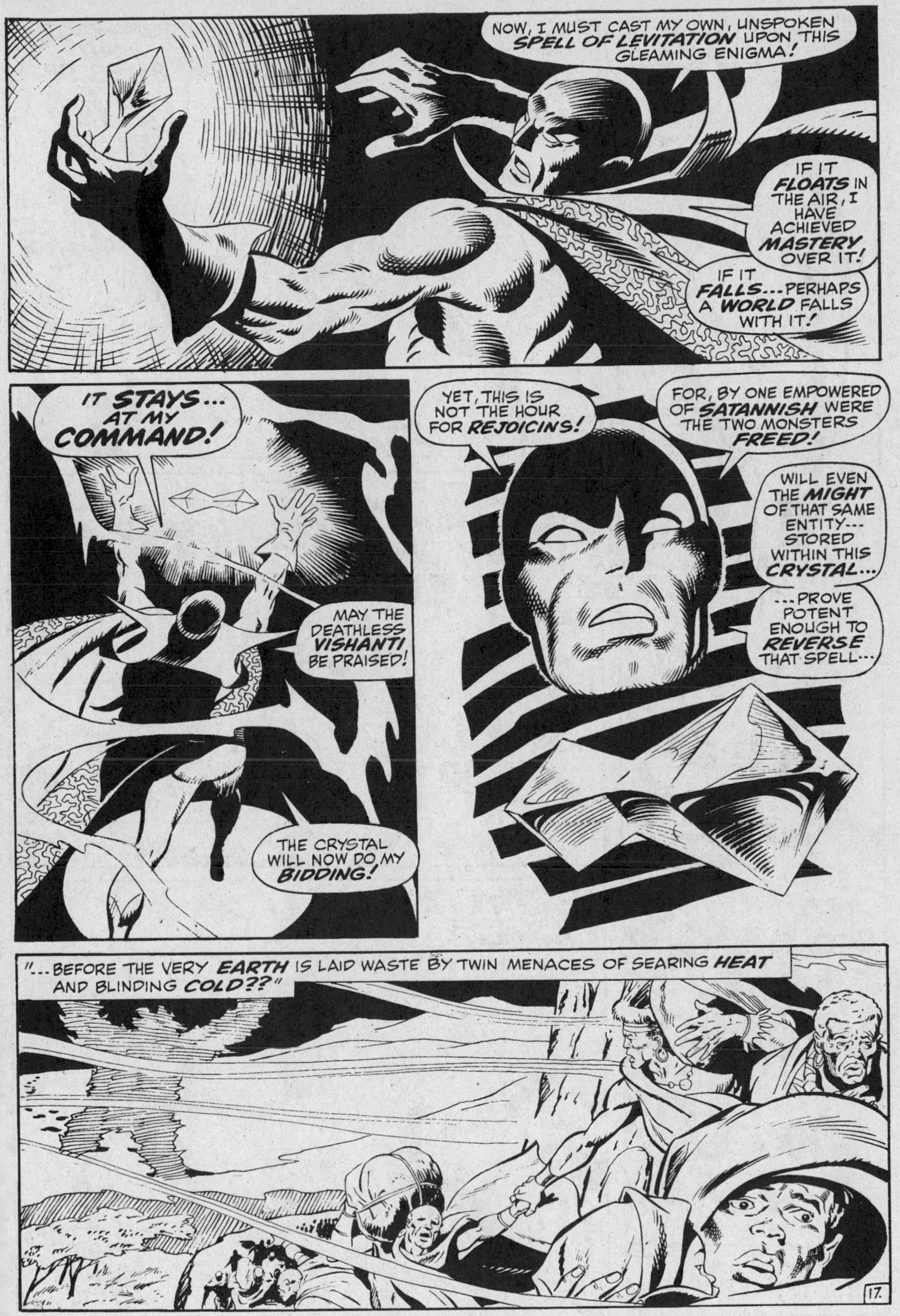
NOW, I MUST CAST MY OWN, UNSPOKEN SPELL OF LEVITATION UPON THIS GLEAMING ENIGMA!
IF IT FLOATS IN THE AIR, I HAVE ACHIEVED MASTERY OVER IT!
IF IT FALLS... PERHAPS A WORLD FALLS WITH IT!
IT STAYS... AT MY COMMAND!
MAY THE DEATHLESS VISHANTI BE PRAISED!
THE CRYSTAL WILL NOW DO MY BIDDING!
YET, THIS IS NOT THE HOUR FOR REJOICINS!
FOR, BY ONE EMPOWERED OF SATANNISH WERE THE TWO MONSTERS FREED!
WILL EVEN THE MIGHT OF THAT SAME ENTITY--- STORED WITHIN THIS CRYSTAL...
...PROVE POTENT ENOUGH TO REVERSE THAT SPELL...
"...BEFORE THE VERY EARTH IS LAID WASTE BY TWIN MENACES OF SEARING HEAT AND BLINDING COLD??"
17.

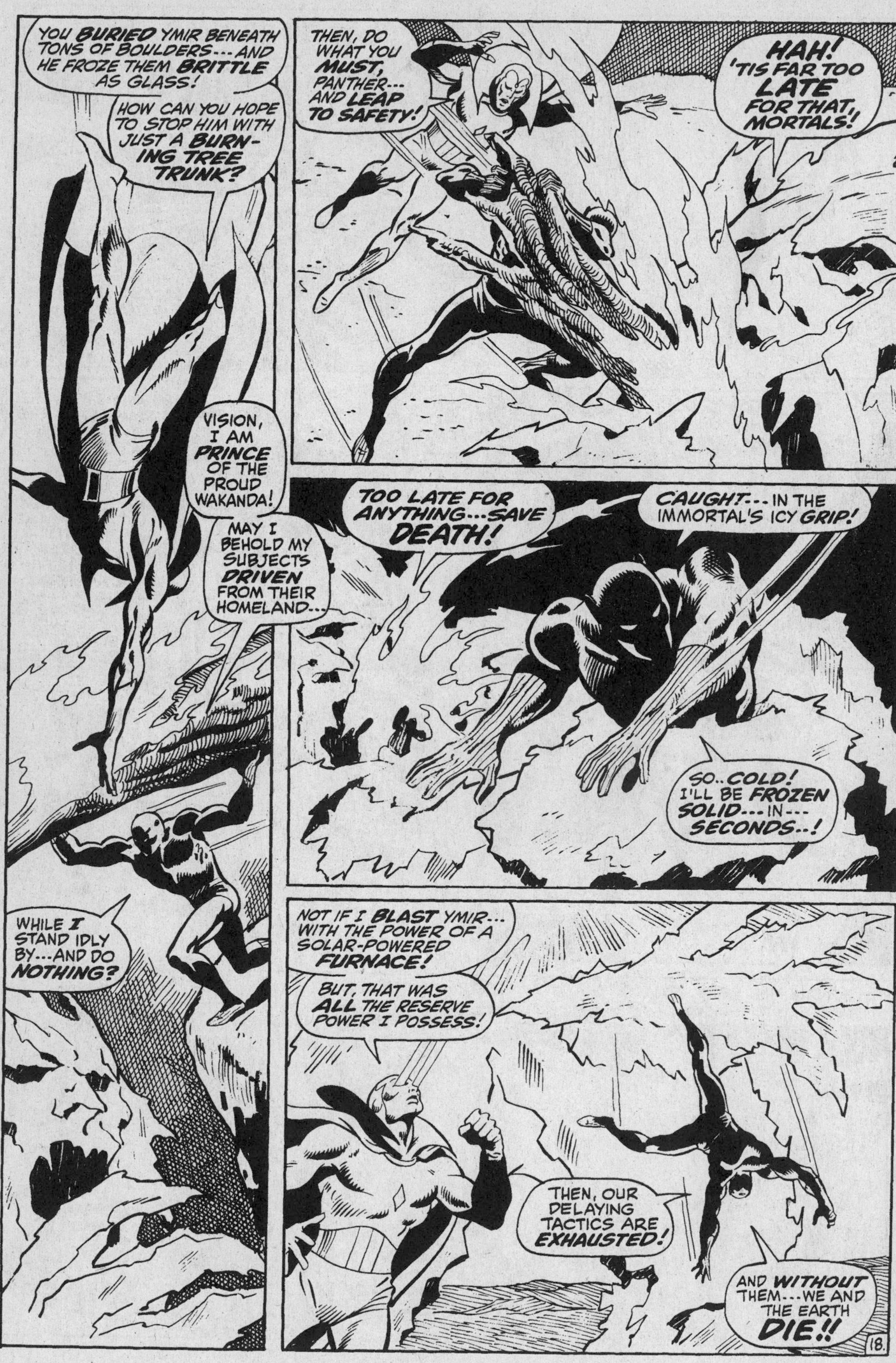

YOU BURIED YMIR BENEATH TONS OF BOULDERS--- AND HE FROZE THEM BRITTLE AS GLASS!
HOW CAN YOU HOPE TO STOP HIM WITH JUST A BURNING TREE TRUNK?
THEN, DO WHAT YOU MUST, PANTHER--- AND LEAP TO SAFETY!
HAH! 'TIS FAR TOO LATE FOR THAT, MORTALS!
VISION, I AM PRINCE OF THE PROUD WAKANDA!
MAY I BEHOLD MY SUBJECTS DRIVEN FROM THEIR HOMELAND...
TOO LATE FOR ANYTHING...SAVE DEATH!
CAUGHT--- IN THE IMMORTAL'S ICY GRIP!
SO..COLD! I'LL BE FROZEN SOLID--- IN--- SECONDS..!
WHILE I STAND IDLY BY...AND DO NOTHING?
NOT IF I BLAST YMIR... WITH THE POWER OF A SOLAR-POWERED FURNACE!
BUT, THAT WAS ALL THE RESERVE POWER I POSSESS!
THEN, OUR DELAYING TACTICS ARE EXHAUSTED!
AND WITHOUT THEM--- WE AND THE EARTH DIE!!
18.

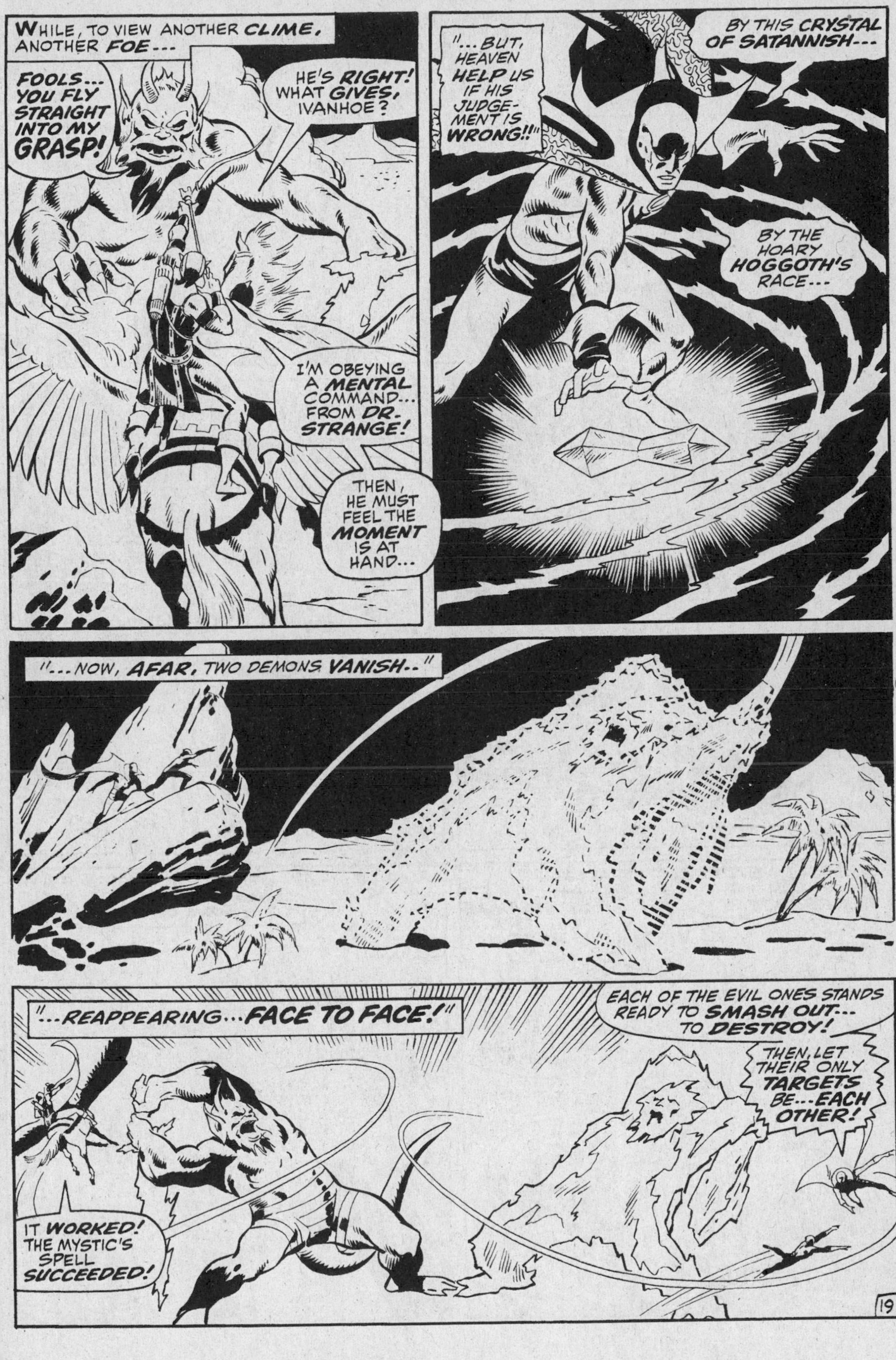
WHILE, TO VIEW ANOTHER CLIME, ANOTHER FOE---
FOOLS... YOU FLY STRAIGHT INTO MY GRASP!
HE'S RIGHT! WHAT GIVES, IVANHOE?
I'M OBEYING A MENTAL COMMAND... FROM DR. STRANGE!
THEN, HE MUST FEEL THE MOMENT IS AT HAND...
"... BUT, HEAVEN HELP US IF HIS JUDGEMENT IS WRONG!!"
BY THIS CRYSTAL OF SATANNISH---
BY THE HOARY HOGGOTH'S RACE---
"... NOW, AFAR, TWO DEMONS VANISH.."
"... REAPPEARING... FACE TO FACE!"
EACH OF THE EVIL ONES STANDS READY TO SMASH OUT... TO DESTROY!
THEN, LET THEIR ONLY TARGETS BE... EACH OTHER!
IT WORKED! THE MYSTIC'S SPELL SUCCEEDED!
19

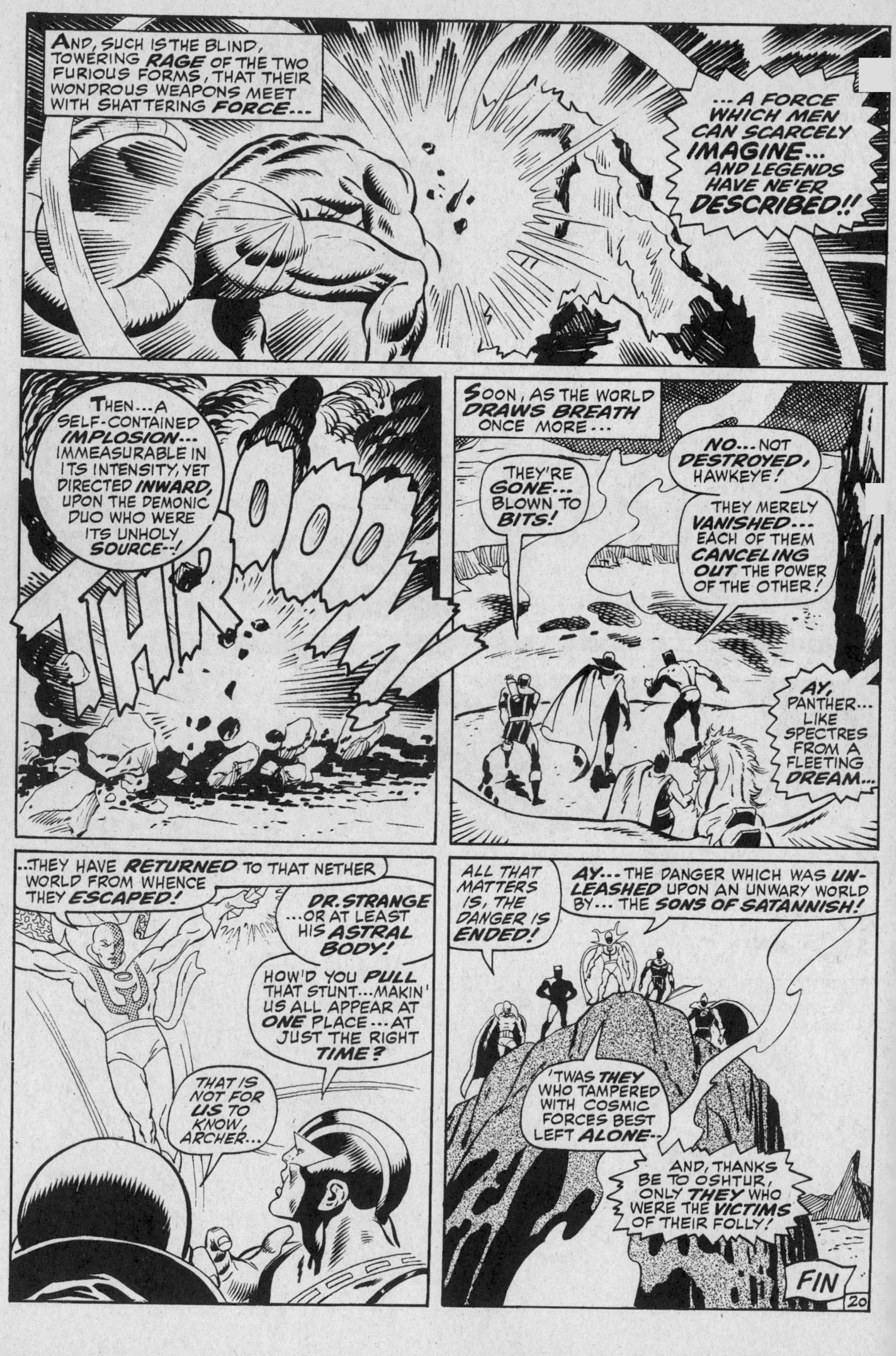
AND, SUCH IS THE BLIND, TOWERING RAGE OF THE TWO FURIOUS FORMS, THAT THEIR WONDROUS WEAPONS MEET WITH SHATTERING FORCE...
...A FORCE WHICH MEN CAN SCARCELY IMAGINE... AND LEGENDS HAVE NE'ER DESCRIBED!!
THEN...A SELF-CONTAINED IMPLOSION... IMMEASURABLE IN ITS INTENSITY, YET DIRECTED INWARD, UPON THE DEMONIC DUO WHO WERE ITS UNHOLY SOURCE--!
THROOOM!
SOON, AS THE WORLD DRAWS BREATH ONCE MORE...
THEY'RE GONE... BLOWN TO BITS!
NO... NOT DESTROYED, HAWKEYE!
THEY MERELY VANISHED... EACH OF THEM CANCELING OUT THE POWER OF THE OTHER!
AY, PANTHER... LIKE SPECTRES FROM A FLEETING DREAM...
...THEY HAVE RETURNED TO THAT NETHER WORLD FROM WHENCE THEY ESCAPED!
DR. STRANGE ...OR AT LEAST HIS ASTRAL BODY!
HOW'D YOU PULL THAT STUNT... MAKIN' US ALL APPEAR AT ONE PLACE --- AT JUST THE RIGHT TIME?
THAT IS NOT FOR US TO KNOW, ARCHER...
ALL THAT MATTERS IS, THE DANGER IS ENDED!
AY... THE DANGER WHICH WAS UN-LEASHED UPON AN UNWARY WORLD BY... THE SONS OF SATANNISH!
'TWAS THEY WHO TAMPERED WITH COSMIC FORCES BEST LEFT ALONE--
AND, THANKS BE TO OSHTUR, ONLY THEY WHO WERE THE VICTIMS OF THEIR FOLLY!
FIN
20

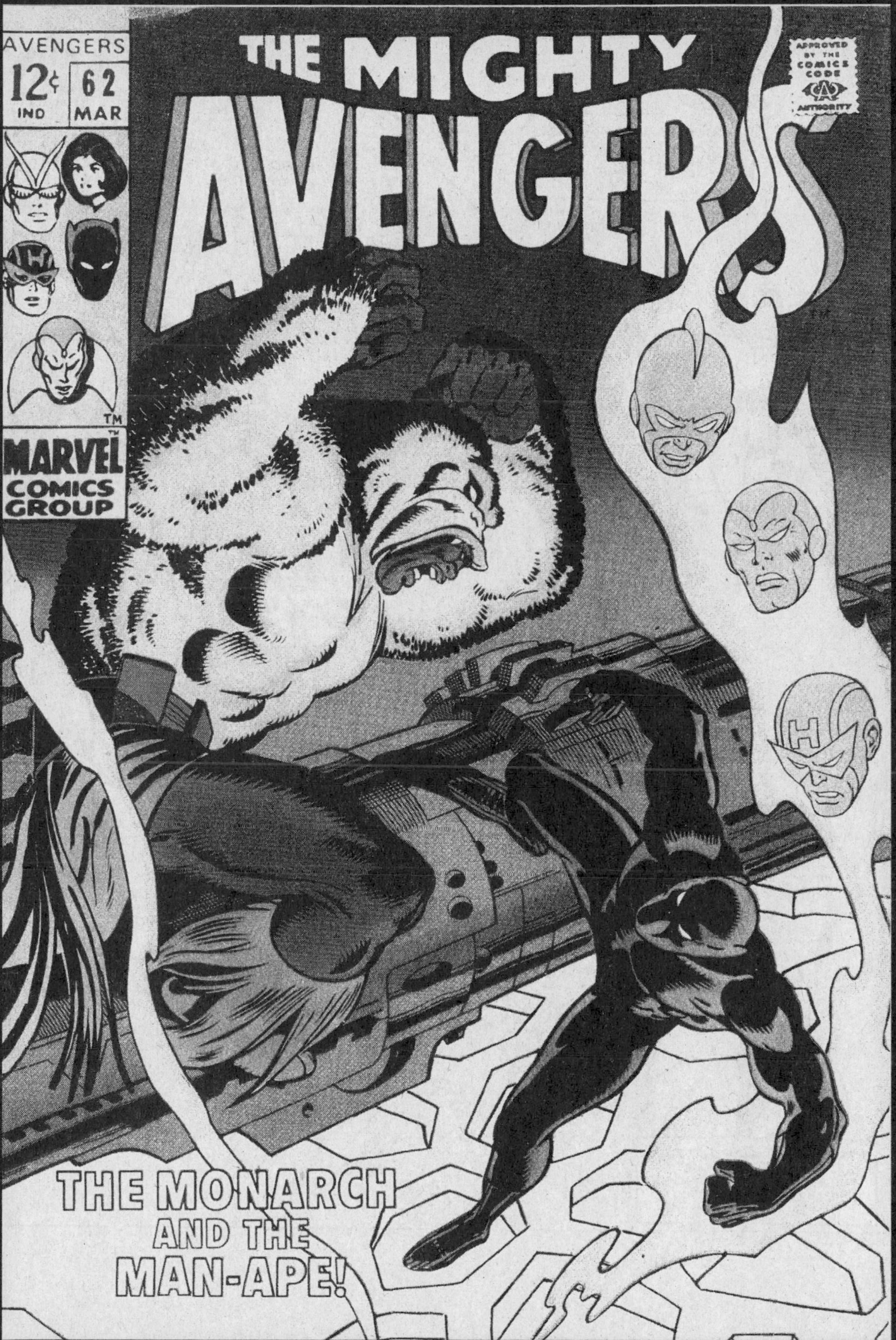
AVENGERS
12¢ IND
62 MAR
TM
MARVEL COMICS GROUP
THE MIGHTY AVENGERS
APPROVED BY THE COMICS CODE AUTHORITY
THE MONARCH AND THE MAN-APE!

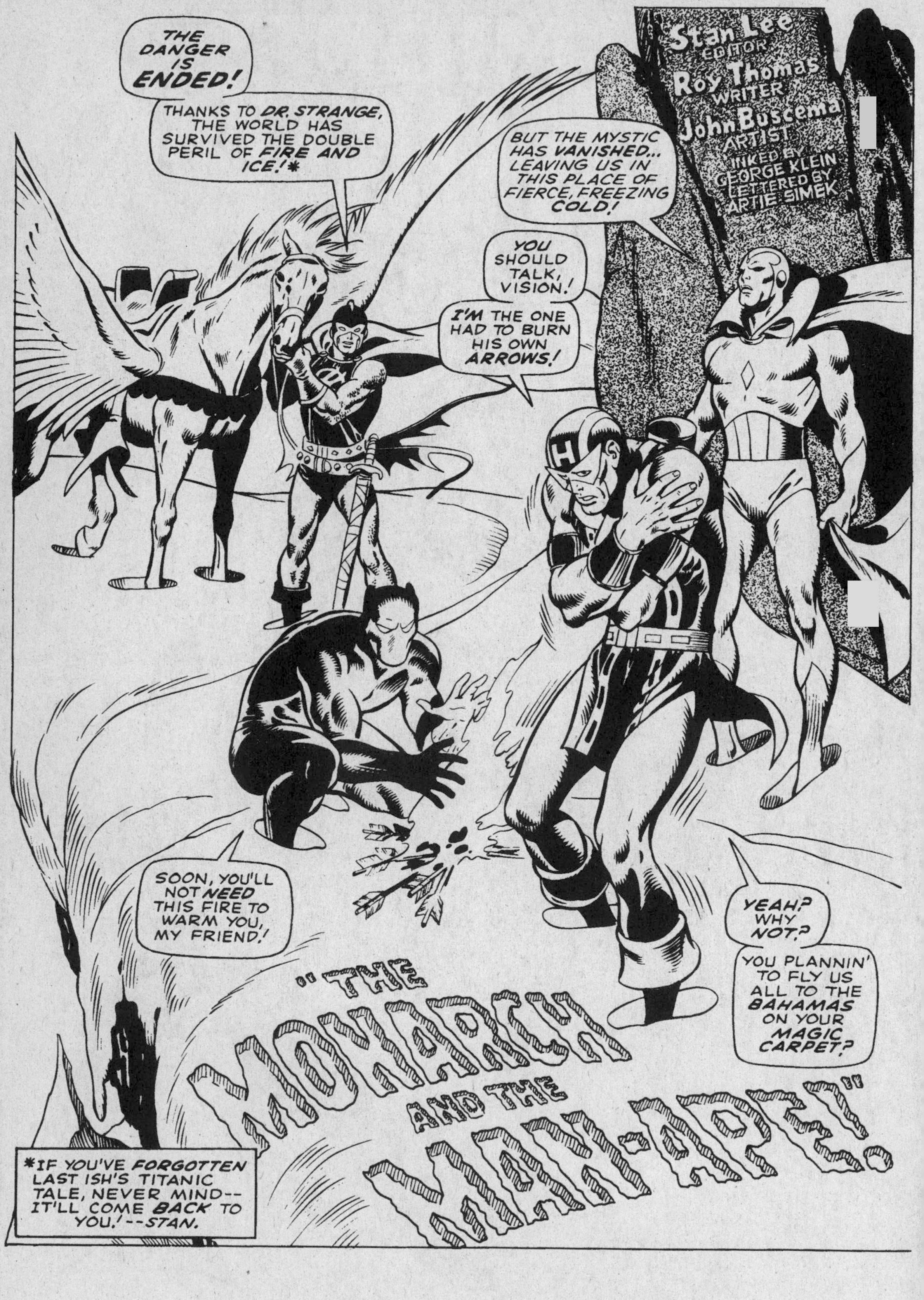

THE DANGER IS ENDED!
THANKS TO DR. STRANGE, THE WORLD HAS SURVIVED THE DOUBLE PERIL OF FIRE AND ICE!*
BUT THE MYSTIC HAS VANISHED... LEAVING US IN THIS PLACE OF FIERCE, FREEZING COLD!
Stan Lee EDITOR
Roy Thomas WRITER
John Buscema ARTIST
INKED BY GEORGE KLEIN
LETTERED BY ARTIE SIMEK
YOU SHOULD TALK, VISION!
I'M THE ONE HAD TO BURN HIS OWN ARROWS!
SOON, YOU'LL NOT NEED THIS FIRE TO WARM YOU, MY FRIEND!
YEAH? WHY NOT?
YOU PLANNIN' TO FLY US ALL TO THE BAHAMAS ON YOUR MAGIC CARPET?
"THE MONARCH AND THE MAN-APE!"
*IF YOU'VE FORGOTTEN LAST ISH'S TITANIC TALE, NEVER MIND-- IT'LL COME BACK TO YOU! --STAN.

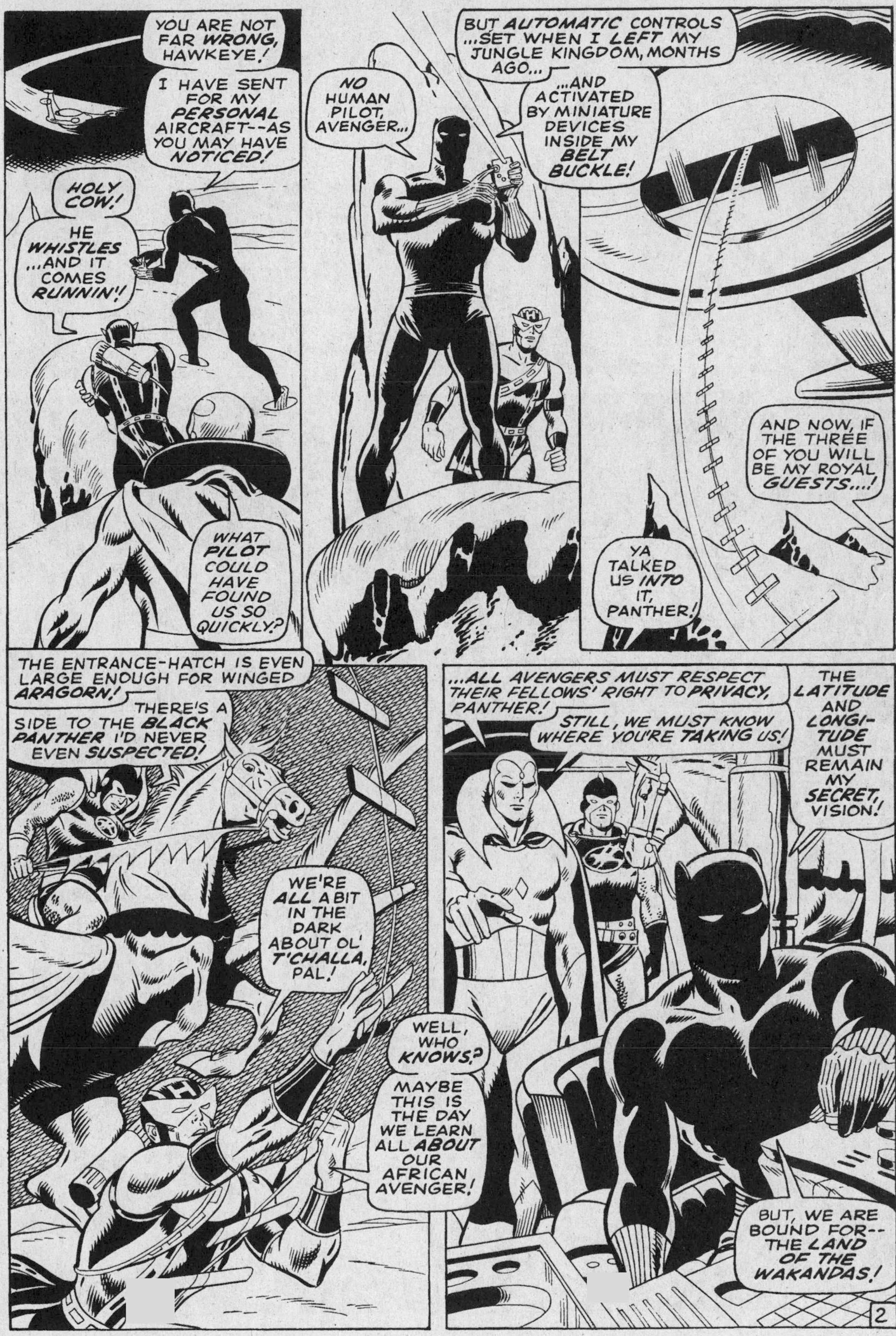
YOU ARE NOT FAR WRONG, HAWKEYE.!
I HAVE SENT FOR MY PERSONAL AIRCRAFT--AS YOU MAY HAVE NOTICED!
HOLY COW!
HE WHISTLES ...AND IT COMES RUNNIN'!
WHAT PILOT COULD HAVE FOUND US SO QUICKLY?
NO HUMAN PILOT, AVENGER...
BUT AUTOMATIC CONTROLS ...SET WHEN I LEFT MY JUNGLE KINGDOM, MONTHS AGO...
...AND ACTIVATED BY MINIATURE DEVICES INSIDE MY BELT BUCKLE!
AND NOW, IF THE THREE OF YOU WILL BE MY ROYAL GUESTS...!
YA TALKED US INTO IT, PANTHER!
THE ENTRANCE-HATCH IS EVEN LARGE ENOUGH FOR WINGED ARAGORN!
THERE'S A SIDE TO THE BLACK PANTHER I'D NEVER EVEN SUSPECTED!
WE'RE ALL A BIT IN THE DARK ABOUT OL' T'CHALLA, PAL!
WELL, WHO KNOWS?
MAYBE THIS IS THE DAY WE LEARN ALL ABOUT OUR AFRICAN AVENGER!
...ALL AVENGERS MUST RESPECT THEIR FELLOWS' RIGHT TO PRIVACY, PANTHER!
STILL, WE MUST KNOW WHERE YOU'RE TAKING US!
THE LATITUDE AND LONGITUDE MUST REMAIN MY SECRET, VISION!
BUT, WE ARE BOUND FOR--THE LAND OF THE WAKANDAS!
2

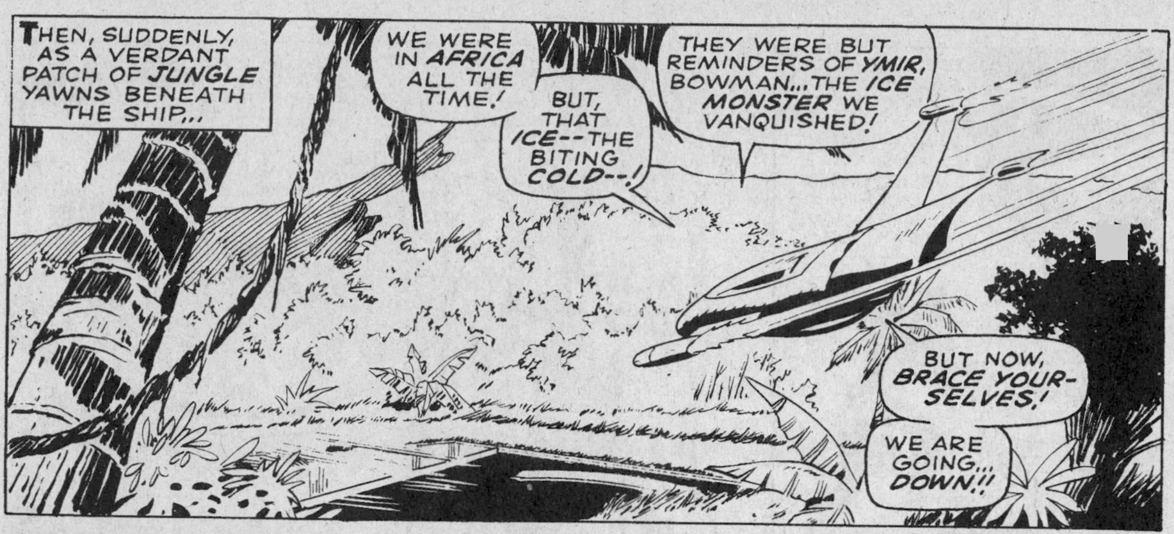
THEN, SUDDENLY, AS A VERDANT PATCH OF JUNGLE YAWNS BENEATH THE SHIP...
WE WERE IN AFRICA ALL THE TIME!
BUT, THAT ICE--THE BITING COLD--!
THEY WERE BUT REMINDERS OF YMIR, BOWMAN... THE ICE MONSTER WE VANQUISHED!
BUT NOW, BRACE YOURSELVES!
WE ARE GOING... DOWN!!

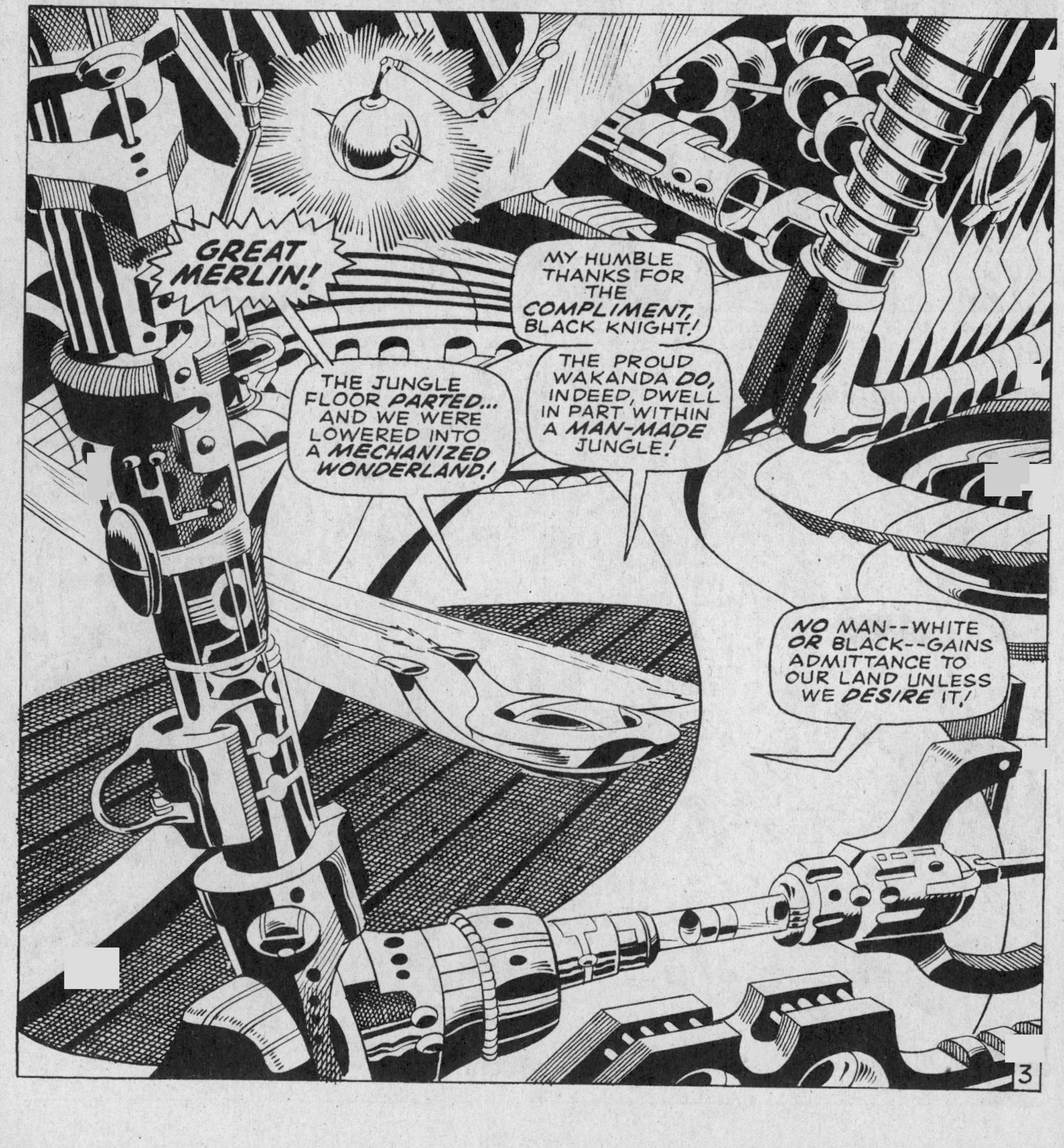
GREAT MERLIN!
THE JUNGLE FLOOR PARTED... AND WE WERE LOWERED INTO A MECHANIZED WONDERLAND!
MY HUMBLE THANKS FOR THE COMPLIMENT, BLACK KNIGHT!
THE PROUD WAKANDA DO, INDEED, DWELL IN PART WITHIN A MAN-MADE JUNGLE!
NO MAN--WHITE OR BLACK--GAINS ADMITTANCE TO OUR LAND UNLESS WE DESIRE IT!
3

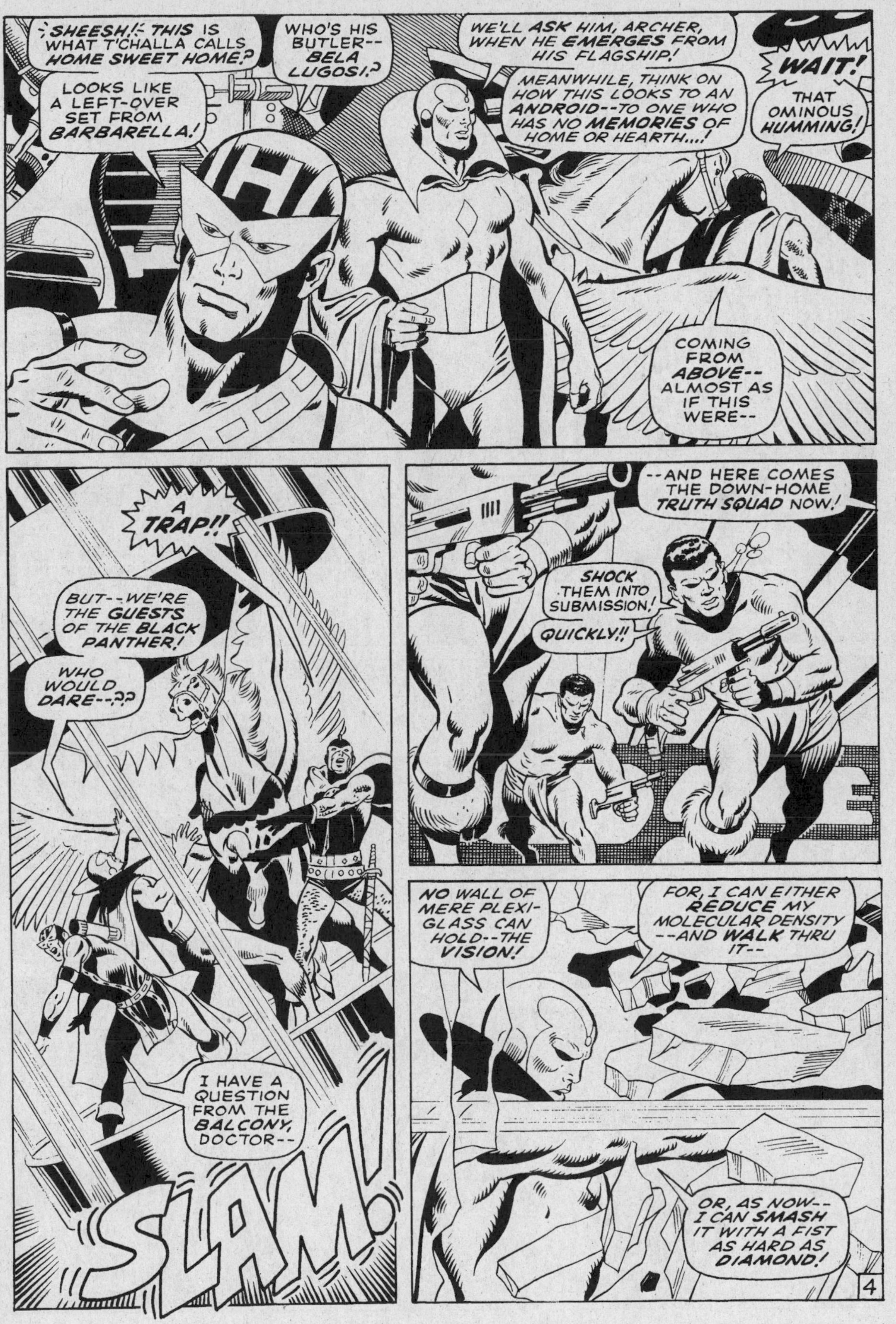
SHEESH! THIS IS WHAT T'CHALLA CALLS HOME SWEET HOME?
LOOKS LIKE A LEFT-OVER SET FROM BARBARELLA!
WHO'S HIS BUTLER-- BELA LUGOSI!?
WE'LL ASK HIM, ARCHER, WHEN HE EMERGES FROM HIS FLAGSHIP!
MEANWHILE, THINK ON HOW THIS LOOKS TO AN ANDROID--TO ONE WHO HAS NO MEMORIES OF HOME OR HEARTH...!
WAIT!
THAT OMINOUS HUMMING!
COMING FROM ABOVE-- ALMOST AS IF THIS WERE--
A TRAP!!
BUT--WE'RE THE GUESTS OF THE BLACK PANTHER!
WHO WOULD DARE--??
I HAVE A QUESTION FROM THE BALCONY, DOCTOR--
SLAM!
--AND HERE COMES THE DOWN-HOME TRUTH SQUAD NOW!
SHOCK THEM INTO SUBMISSION!
QUICKLY!!
NO WALL OF MERE PLEXI-GLASS CAN HOLD--THE VISION!
FOR, I CAN EITHER REDUCE MY MOLECULAR DENSITY --AND WALK THRU IT--
OR, AS NOW-- I CAN SMASH IT WITH A FIST AS HARD AS DIAMOND!
4

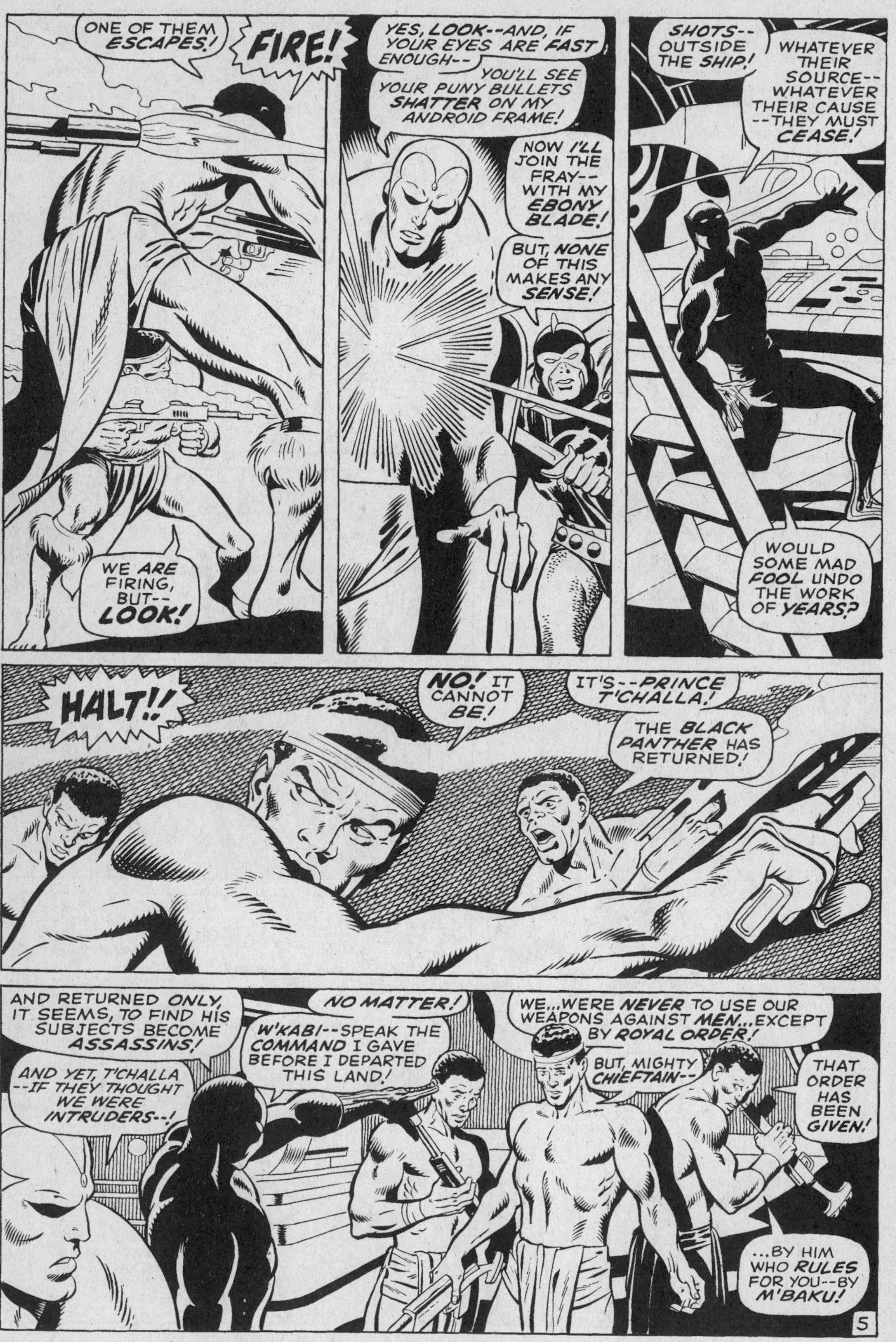

ONE OF THEM ESCAPES!
FIRE!
WE ARE FIRING, BUT--LOOK!
YES, LOOK--AND, IF YOUR EYES ARE FAST ENOUGH--
YOU'LL SEE YOUR PUNY BULLETS SHATTER ON MY ANDROID FRAME!
NOW I'LL JOIN THE FRAY--WITH MY EBONY BLADE!
BUT, NONE OF THIS MAKES ANY SENSE!
SHOTS--OUTSIDE THE SHIP!
WHATEVER THEIR SOURCE--WHATEVER THEIR CAUSE--THEY MUST CEASE!
WOULD SOME MAD FOOL UNDO THE WORK OF YEARS?
HALT!!
NO! IT CANNOT BE!
IT'S--PRINCE T'CHALLA!
THE BLACK PANTHER HAS RETURNED!
AND RETURNED ONLY, IT SEEMS, TO FIND HIS SUBJECTS BECOME ASSASSINS!
AND YET, T'CHALLA--IF THEY THOUGHT WE WERE INTRUDERS--!
NO MATTER!
W'KABI--SPEAK THE COMMAND I GAVE BEFORE I DEPARTED THIS LAND!
WE...WERE NEVER TO USE OUR WEAPONS AGAINST MEN...EXCEPT BY ROYAL ORDER!
BUT, MIGHTY CHIEFTAIN--
THAT ORDER HAS BEEN GIVEN!
...BY HIM WHO RULES FOR YOU--BY M'BAKU!
5

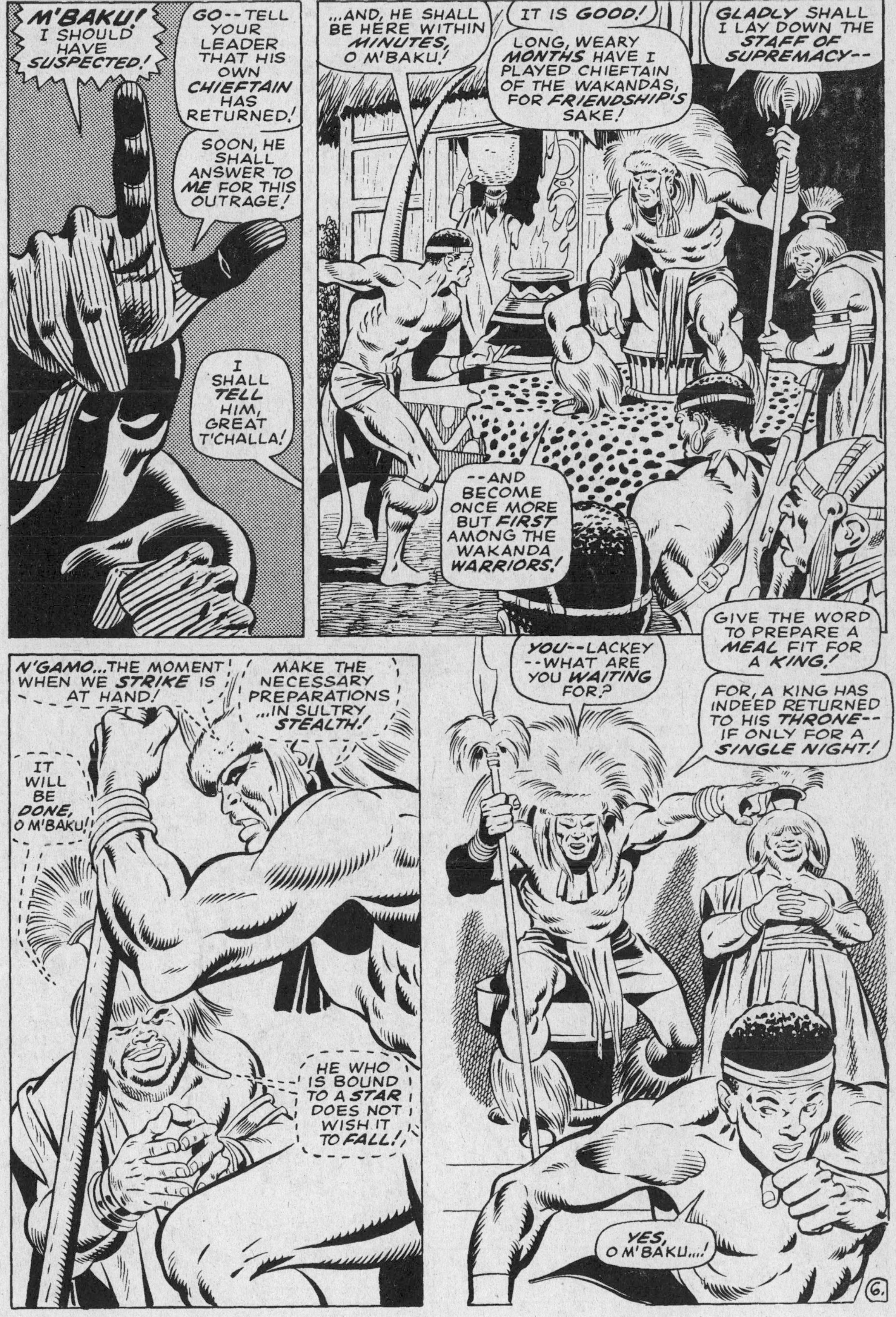
M'BAKU! I SHOULD HAVE SUSPECTED!
GO--TELL YOUR LEADER THAT HIS OWN CHIEFTAIN HAS RETURNED!
SOON, HE SHALL ANSWER TO ME FOR THIS OUTRAGE!
I SHALL TELL HIM, GREAT T'CHALLA!
...AND, HE SHALL BE HERE WITHIN MINUTES, O M'BAKU!
IT IS GOOD!
LONG, WEARY MONTHS HAVE I PLAYED CHIEFTAIN OF THE WAKANDAS, FOR FRIENDSHIP'S SAKE!
GLADLY SHALL I LAY DOWN THE STAFF OF SUPREMACY--
--AND BECOME ONCE MORE BUT FIRST AMONG THE WAKANDA WARRIORS!
N'GAMO...THE MOMENT WHEN WE STRIKE IS AT HAND!
MAKE THE NECESSARY PREPARATIONS ...IN SULTRY STEALTH!
IT WILL BE DONE, O M'BAKU!
HE WHO IS BOUND TO A STAR DOES NOT WISH IT TO FALL!
YOU--LACKEY --WHAT ARE YOU WAITING FOR?
GIVE THE WORD TO PREPARE A MEAL FIT FOR A KING!
FOR, A KING HAS INDEED RETURNED TO HIS THRONE-- IF ONLY FOR A SINGLE NIGHT!
YES, O M'BAKU...!
6.

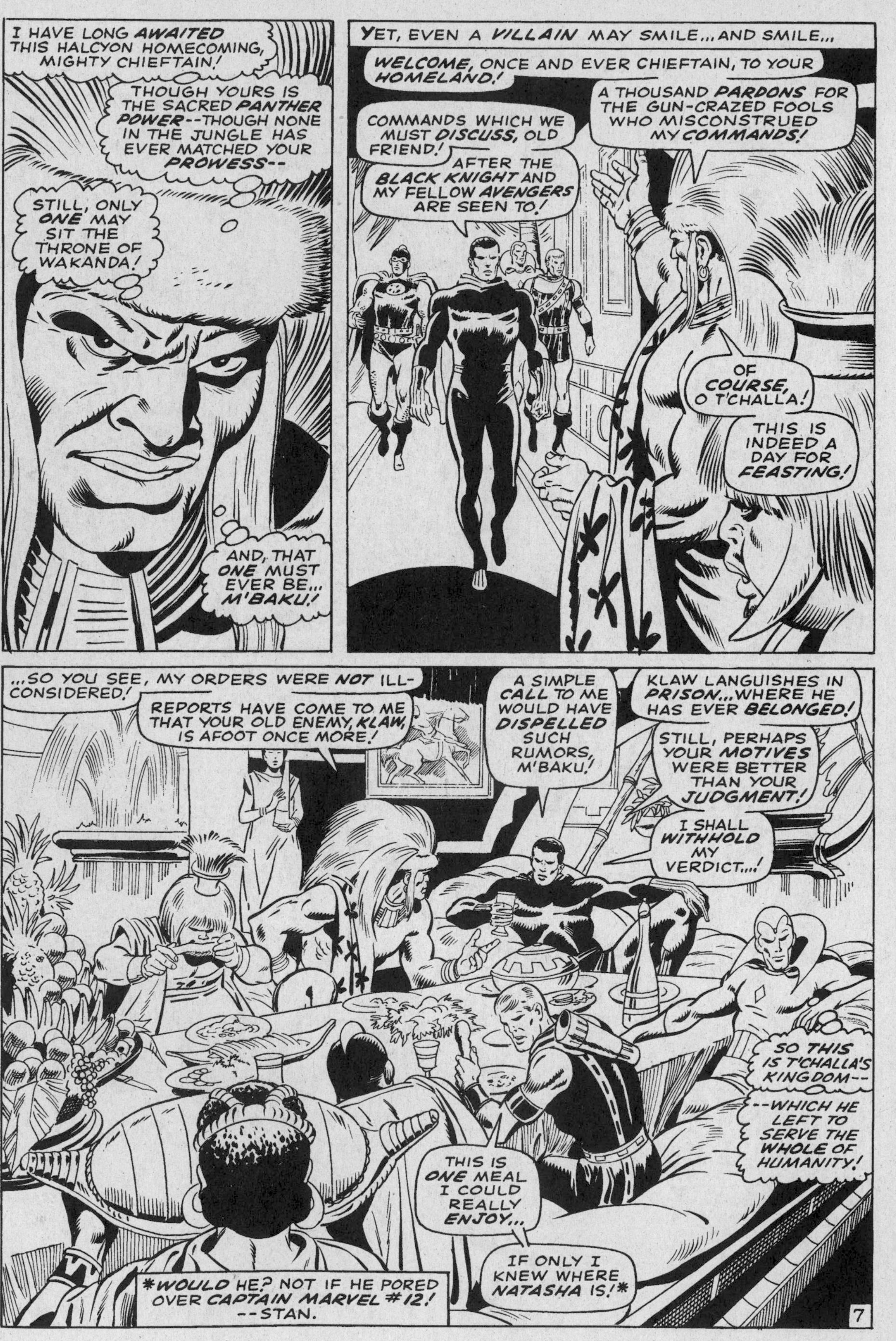

I HAVE LONG AWAITED THIS HALCYON HOMECOMING, MIGHTY CHIEFTAIN!
THOUGH YOURS IS THE SACRED PANTHER POWER--THOUGH NONE IN THE JUNGLE HAS EVER MATCHED YOUR PROWESS--
STILL, ONLY ONE MAY SIT THE THRONE OF WAKANDA!
AND, THAT ONE MUST EVER BE... M'BAKU!
YET, EVEN A VILLAIN MAY SMILE... AND SMILE...
WELCOME, ONCE AND EVER CHIEFTAIN, TO YOUR HOMELAND!
A THOUSAND PARDONS FOR THE GUN-CRAZED FOOLS WHO MISCONSTRUED MY COMMANDS!
COMMANDS WHICH WE MUST DISCUSS, OLD FRIEND!
AFTER THE BLACK KNIGHT AND MY FELLOW AVENGERS ARE SEEN TO!
OF COURSE, O T'CHALLA!
THIS IS INDEED A DAY FOR FEASTING!
...SO YOU SEE, MY ORDERS WERE NOT ILL-CONSIDERED!
REPORTS HAVE COME TO ME THAT YOUR OLD ENEMY, KLAW, IS AFOOT ONCE MORE!
A SIMPLE CALL TO ME WOULD HAVE DISPELLED SUCH RUMORS, M'BAKU!
KLAW LANGUISHES IN PRISON... WHERE HE HAS EVER BELONGED!
STILL, PERHAPS YOUR MOTIVES WERE BETTER THAN YOUR JUDGMENT!
I SHALL WITHHOLD MY VERDICT...!
SO THIS IS T'CHALLA'S KINGDOM--
--WHICH HE LEFT TO SERVE THE WHOLE OF HUMANITY!
THIS IS ONE MEAL I COULD REALLY ENJOY...
IF ONLY I KNEW WHERE NATASHA IS!*
*WOULD HE? NOT IF HE PORED OVER CAPTAIN MARVEL #12! --STAN.

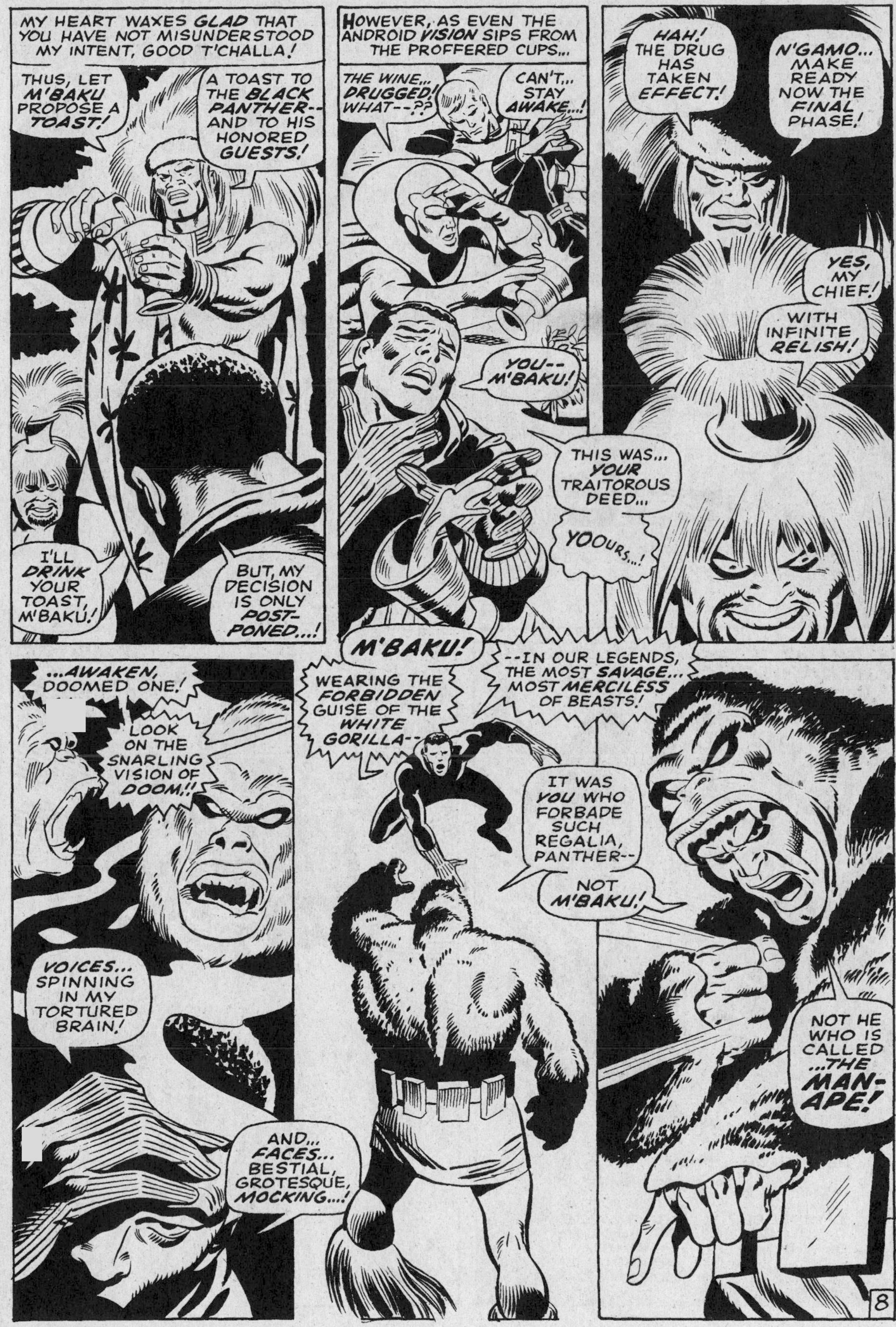
MY HEART WAXES GLAD THAT YOU HAVE NOT MISUNDERSTOOD MY INTENT, GOOD T'CHALLA!
THUS, LET M'BAKU PROPOSE A TOAST!
A TOAST TO THE BLACK PANTHER--AND TO HIS HONORED GUESTS!
I'LL DRINK YOUR TOAST, M'BAKU!
BUT, MY DECISION IS ONLY POST-PONED...!
HOWEVER, AS EVEN THE ANDROID VISION SIPS FROM THE PROFFERED CUPS...
THE WINE... DRUGGED! WHAT--??
CAN'T... STAY AWAKE...!
YOU--M'BAKU!
THIS WAS... YOUR TRAITOROUS DEED...
YOOURS...!
HAH! THE DRUG HAS TAKEN EFFECT!
N'GAMO... MAKE READY NOW THE FINAL PHASE!
YES, MY CHIEF!
WITH INFINITE RELISH!
...AWAKEN, DOOMED ONE!
LOOK ON THE SNARLING VISION OF DOOM!!
VOICES... SPINNING IN MY TORTURED BRAIN!
AND... FACES... BESTIAL, GROTESQUE, MOCKING...!
M'BAKU!
WEARING THE FORBIDDEN GUISE OF THE WHITE GORILLA--
--IN OUR LEGENDS, THE MOST SAVAGE... MOST MERCILESS OF BEASTS!
IT WAS YOU WHO FORBADE SUCH REGALIA, PANTHER--
NOT M'BAKU!
NOT HE WHO IS CALLED ...THE MAN-APE!

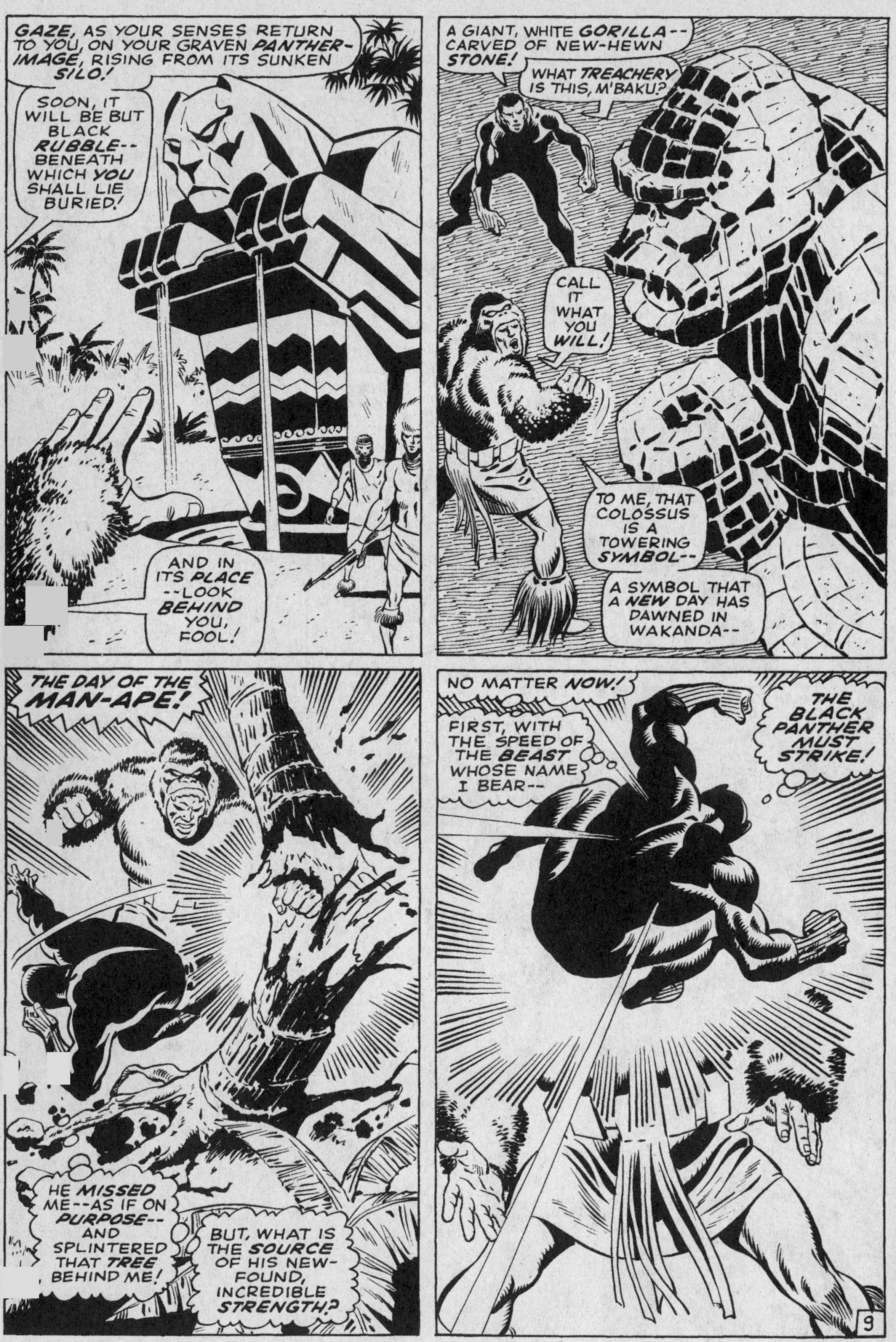
GAZE, AS YOUR SENSES RETURN TO YOU, ON YOUR GRAVEN PANTHER-IMAGE, RISING FROM ITS SUNKEN SILO!
SOON, IT WILL BE BUT BLACK RUBBLE-- BENEATH WHICH YOU SHALL LIE BURIED!
AND IN ITS PLACE --LOOK BEHIND YOU, FOOL!
A GIANT, WHITE GORILLA-- CARVED OF NEW-HEWN STONE!
WHAT TREACHERY IS THIS, M'BAKU?
CALL IT WHAT YOU WILL!
TO ME, THAT COLOSSUS IS A TOWERING SYMBOL--
A SYMBOL THAT A NEW DAY HAS DAWNED IN WAKANDA--
THE DAY OF THE MAN-APE!
HE MISSED ME--AS IF ON PURPOSE-- AND SPLINTERED THAT TREE BEHIND ME!
BUT, WHAT IS THE SOURCE OF HIS NEW-FOUND, INCREDIBLE STRENGTH?
NO MATTER NOW!
FIRST, WITH THE SPEED OF THE BEAST WHOSE NAME I BEAR--
THE BLACK PANTHER MUST STRIKE!
9

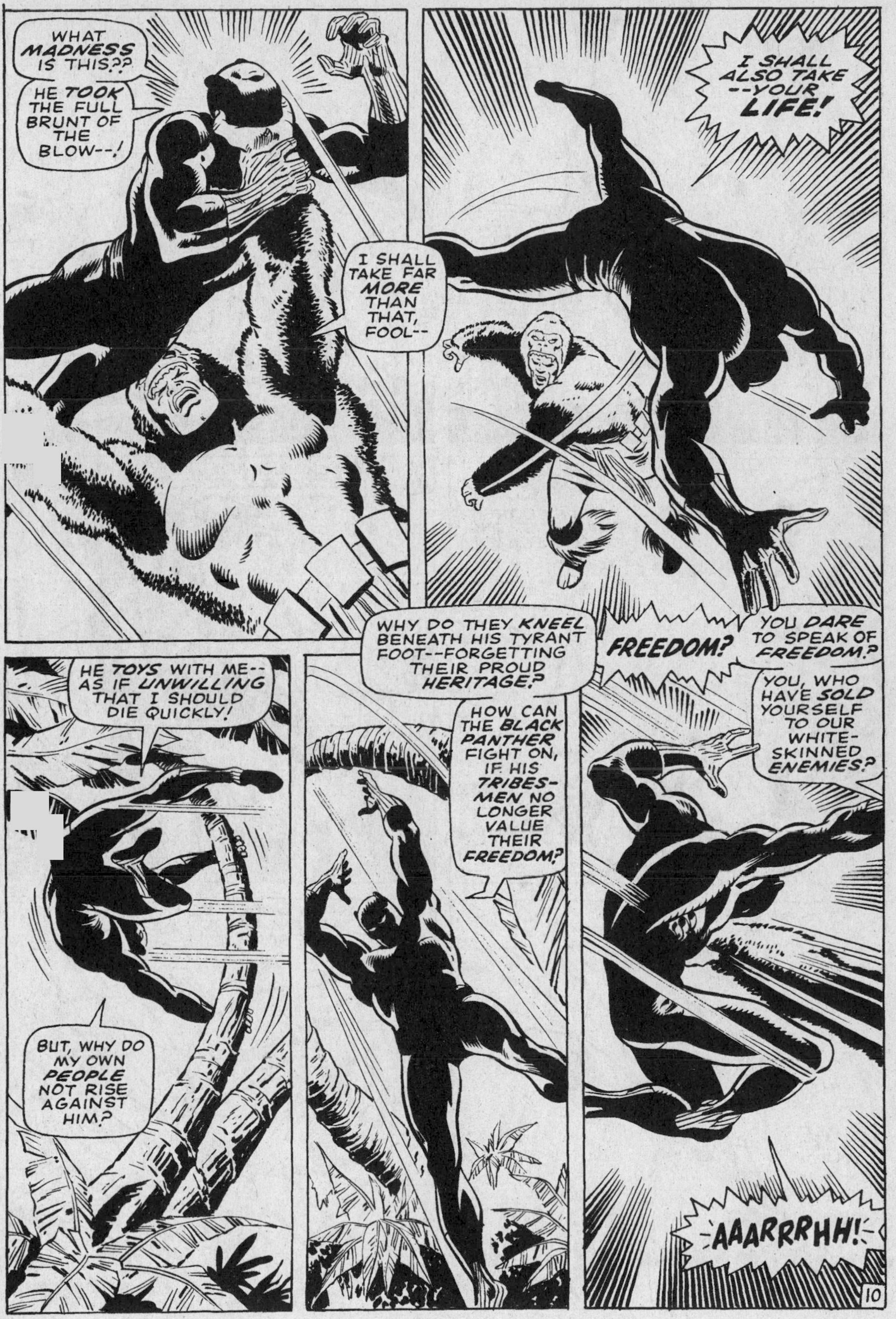

WHAT MADNESS IS THIS??
HE TOOK THE FULL BRUNT OF THE BLOW--!
I SHALL TAKE FAR MORE THAN THAT, FOOL--
I SHALL ALSO TAKE --YOUR LIFE!
HE TOYS WITH ME--AS IF UNWILLING THAT I SHOULD DIE QUICKLY!
BUT, WHY DO MY OWN PEOPLE NOT RISE AGAINST HIM?
WHY DO THEY KNEEL BENEATH HIS TYRANT FOOT--FORGETTING THEIR PROUD HERITAGE?
HOW CAN THE BLACK PANTHER FIGHT ON, IF HIS TRIBESMEN NO LONGER VALUE THEIR FREEDOM?
FREEDOM?
YOU DARE TO SPEAK OF FREEDOM?
YOU, WHO HAVE SOLD YOURSELF TO OUR WHITE-SKINNED ENEMIES?
AAARRRHH!

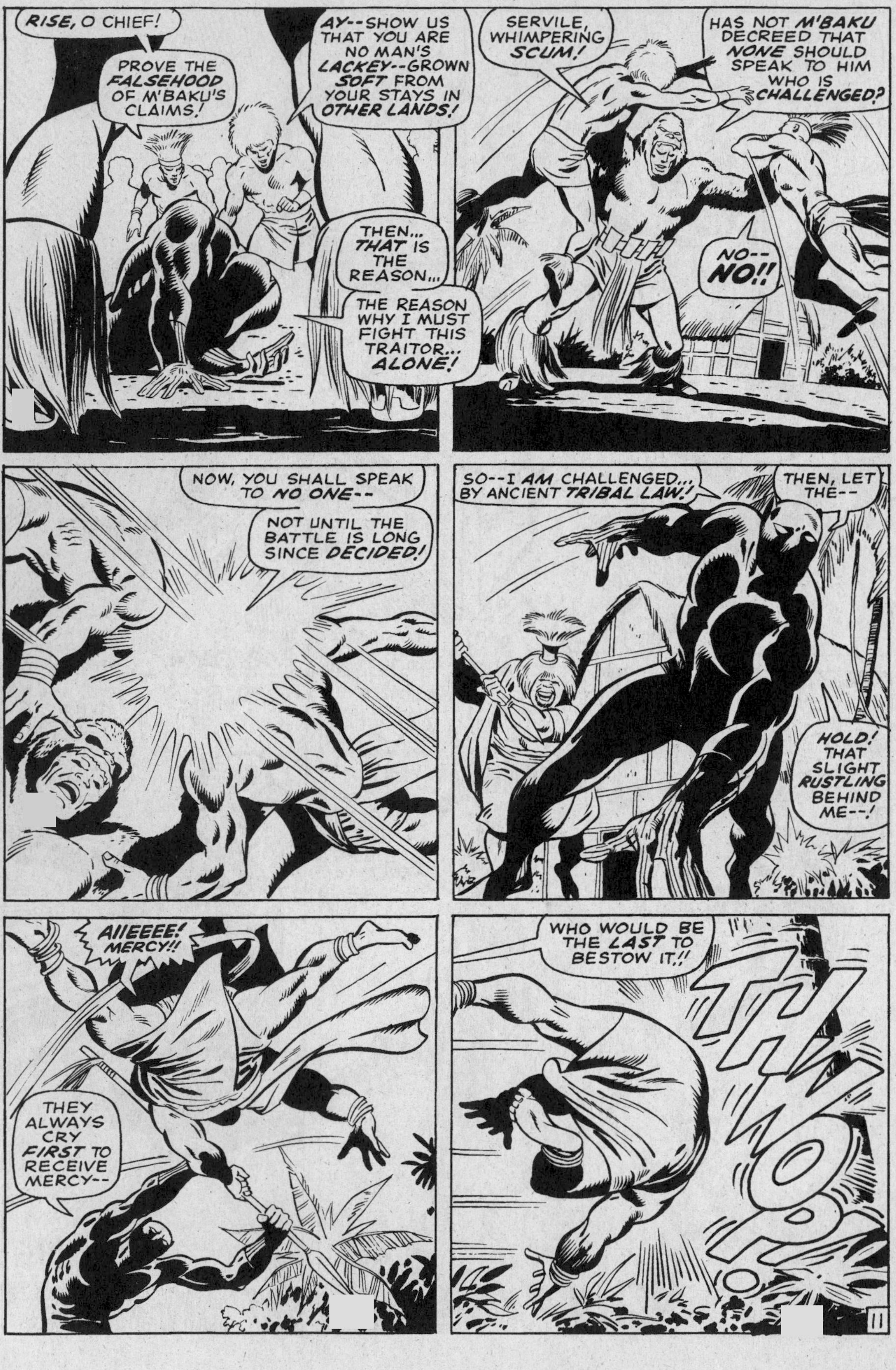

RISE, O CHIEF!
PROVE THE FALSEHOOD OF M'BAKU'S CLAIMS!
AY--SHOW US THAT YOU ARE NO MAN'S LACKEY--GROWN SOFT FROM YOUR STAYS IN OTHER LANDS!
THEN... THAT IS THE REASON...
THE REASON WHY I MUST FIGHT THIS TRAITOR... ALONE!
SERVILE, WHIMPERING SCUM!
HAS NOT M'BAKU DECREED THAT NONE SHOULD SPEAK TO HIM WHO IS CHALLENGED?
NO-- NO!!
NOW, YOU SHALL SPEAK TO NO ONE--
NOT UNTIL THE BATTLE IS LONG SINCE DECIDED!
SO--I AM CHALLENGED... BY ANCIENT TRIBAL LAW!
THEN, LET THE--
HOLD! THAT SLIGHT RUSTLING BEHIND ME--!
AIIEEEE! MERCY!!
THEY ALWAYS CRY FIRST TO RECEIVE MERCY--
WHO WOULD BE THE LAST TO BESTOW IT!!
THWOP!
11

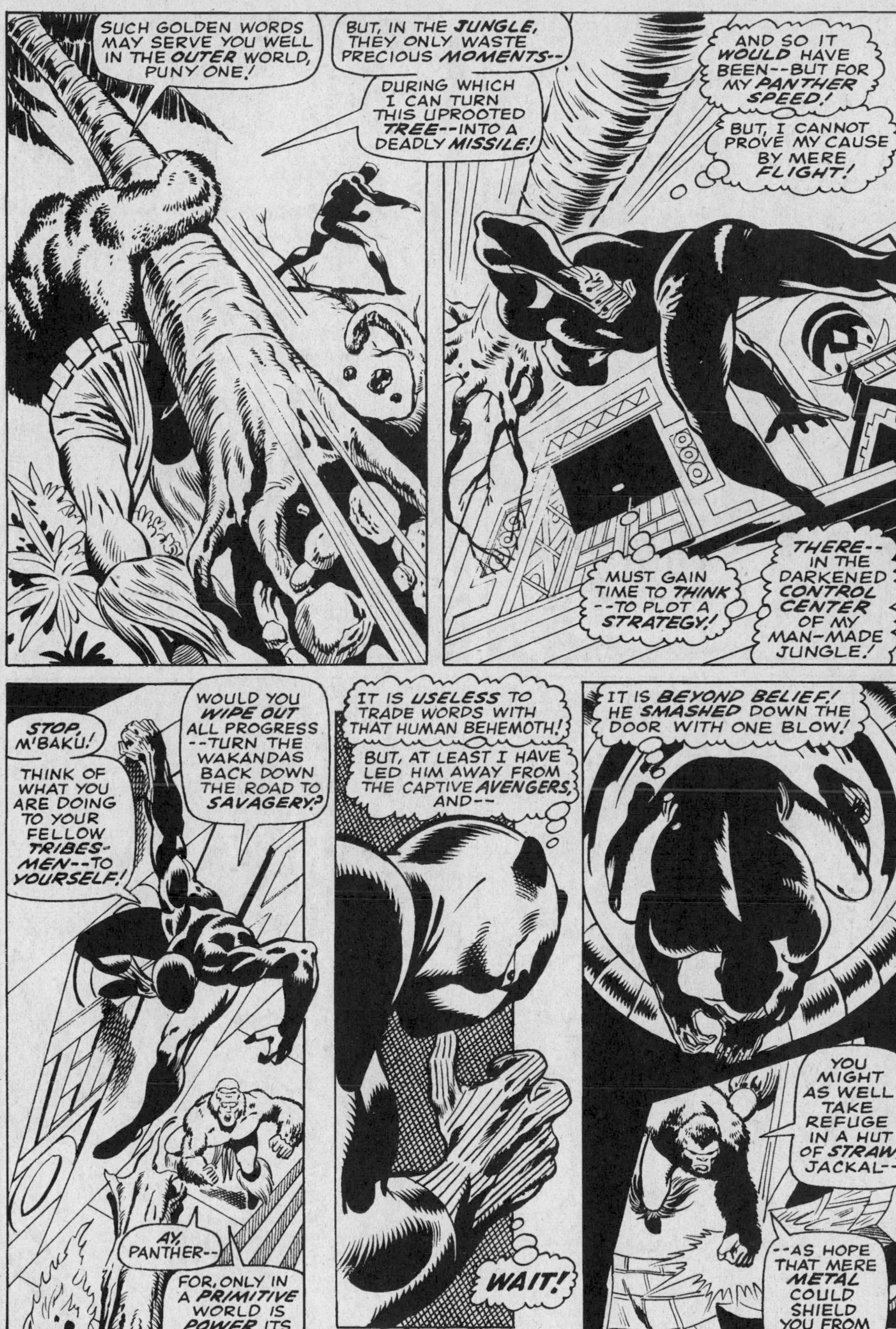
SUCH GOLDEN WORDS MAY SERVE YOU WELL IN THE OUTER WORLD, PUNY ONE!
BUT, IN THE JUNGLE, THEY ONLY WASTE PRECIOUS MOMENTS--
DURING WHICH I CAN TURN THIS UPROOTED TREE--INTO A DEADLY MISSILE!
AND SO IT WOULD HAVE BEEN--BUT FOR MY PANTHER SPEED!
BUT, I CANNOT PROVE MY CAUSE BY MERE FLIGHT!
MUST GAIN TIME TO THINK --TO PLOT A STRATEGY!
THERE-- IN THE DARKENED CONTROL CENTER OF MY MAN-MADE JUNGLE!
STOP, M'BAKU!
THINK OF WHAT YOU ARE DOING TO YOUR FELLOW TRIBES-MEN--TO YOURSELF!
WOULD YOU WIPE OUT ALL PROGRESS --TURN THE WAKANDAS BACK DOWN THE ROAD TO SAVAGERY?
AY, PANTHER--
FOR, ONLY IN A PRIMITIVE WORLD IS POWER ITS OWN REWARD!
IT IS USELESS TO TRADE WORDS WITH THAT HUMAN BEHEMOTH!
BUT, AT LEAST I HAVE LED HIM AWAY FROM THE CAPTIVE AVENGERS, AND--
WAIT!
IT IS BEYOND BELIEF! HE SMASHED DOWN THE DOOR WITH ONE BLOW!
YOU MIGHT AS WELL TAKE REFUGE IN A HUT OF STRAW, JACKAL--
--AS HOPE THAT MERE METAL COULD SHIELD YOU FROM M'BAKU!
12

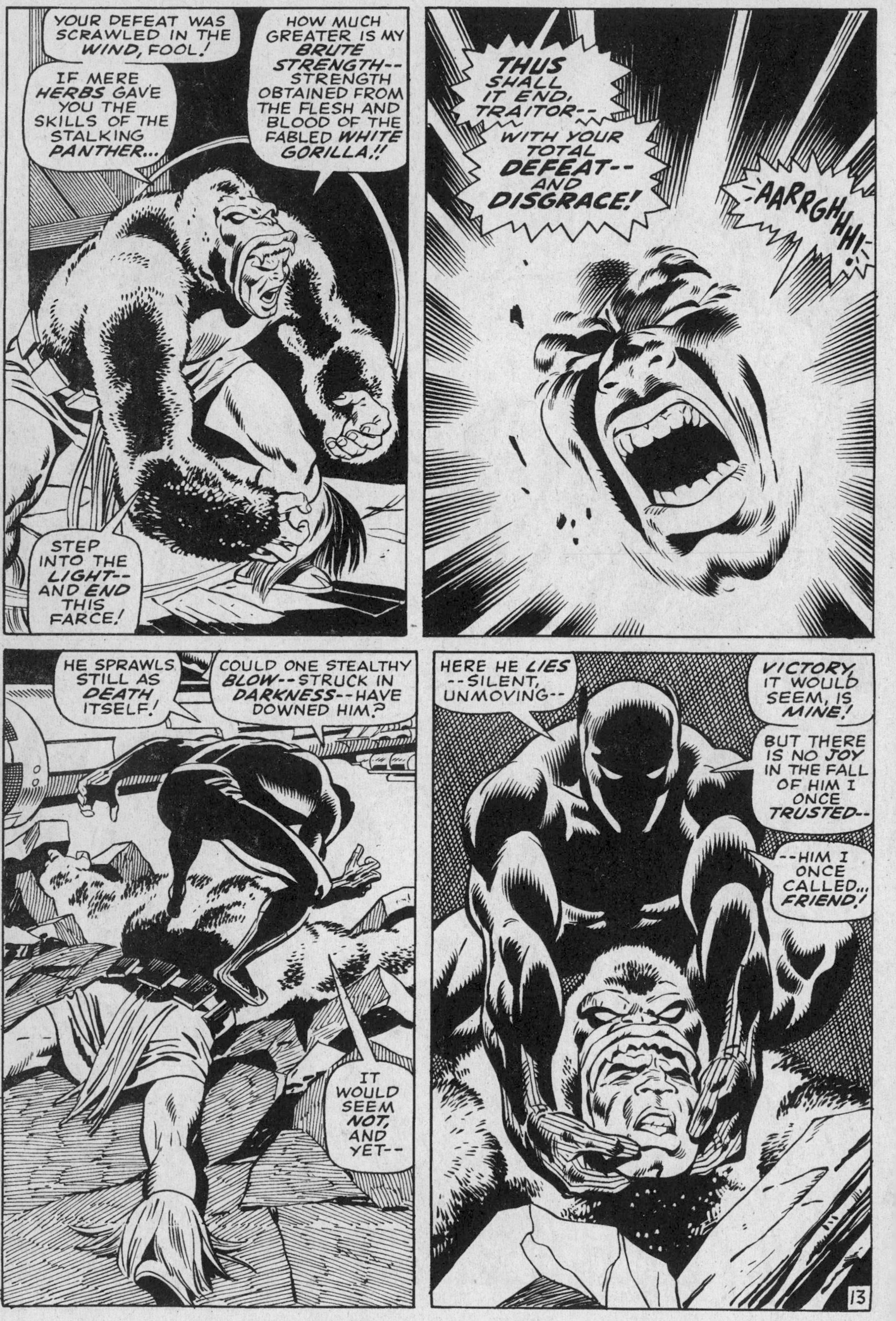
YOUR DEFEAT WAS SCRAWLED IN THE WIND, FOOL!
IF MERE HERBS GAVE YOU THE SKILLS OF THE STALKING PANTHER...
HOW MUCH GREATER IS MY BRUTE STRENGTH-- STRENGTH OBTAINED FROM THE FLESH AND BLOOD OF THE FABLED WHITE GORILLA!!
STEP INTO THE LIGHT-- AND END THIS FARCE!
THUS SHALL IT END, TRAITOR--
WITH YOUR TOTAL DEFEAT-- AND DISGRACE!
AARRGHHH!
HE SPRAWLS STILL AS DEATH ITSELF!
COULD ONE STEALTHY BLOW--STRUCK IN DARKNESS--HAVE DOWNED HIM?
IT WOULD SEEM NOT, AND YET--
HERE HE LIES --SILENT, UNMOVING--
VICTORY, IT WOULD SEEM, IS MINE!
BUT THERE IS NO JOY IN THE FALL OF HIM I ONCE TRUSTED--
--HIM I ONCE CALLED... FRIEND!
13

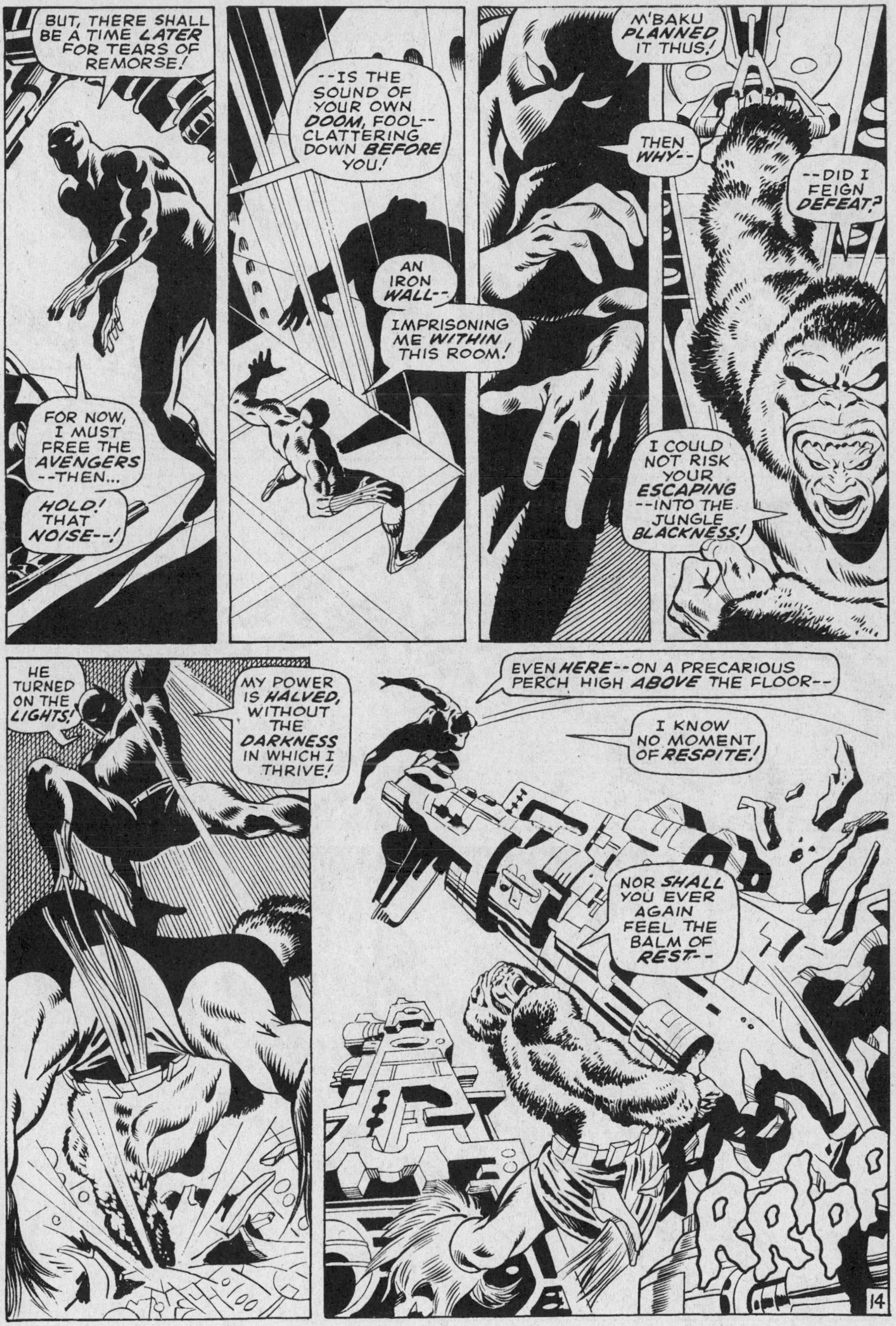
BUT, THERE SHALL BE A TIME LATER FOR TEARS OF REMORSE!
FOR NOW, I MUST FREE THE AVENGERS --THEN...
HOLD! THAT NOISE--!
--IS THE SOUND OF YOUR OWN DOOM, FOOL-- CLATTERING DOWN BEFORE YOU!
AN IRON WALL--
IMPRISONING ME WITHIN THIS ROOM!
M'BAKU PLANNED IT THUS!
THEN WHY--
--DID I FEIGN DEFEAT?
I COULD NOT RISK YOUR ESCAPING --INTO THE JUNGLE BLACKNESS!
HE TURNED ON THE LIGHTS!
MY POWER IS HALVED, WITHOUT THE DARKNESS IN WHICH I THRIVE!
EVEN HERE--ON A PRECARIOUS PERCH HIGH ABOVE THE FLOOR--
I KNOW NO MOMENT OF RESPITE!
NOR SHALL YOU EVER AGAIN FEEL THE BALM OF REST--
RRIP

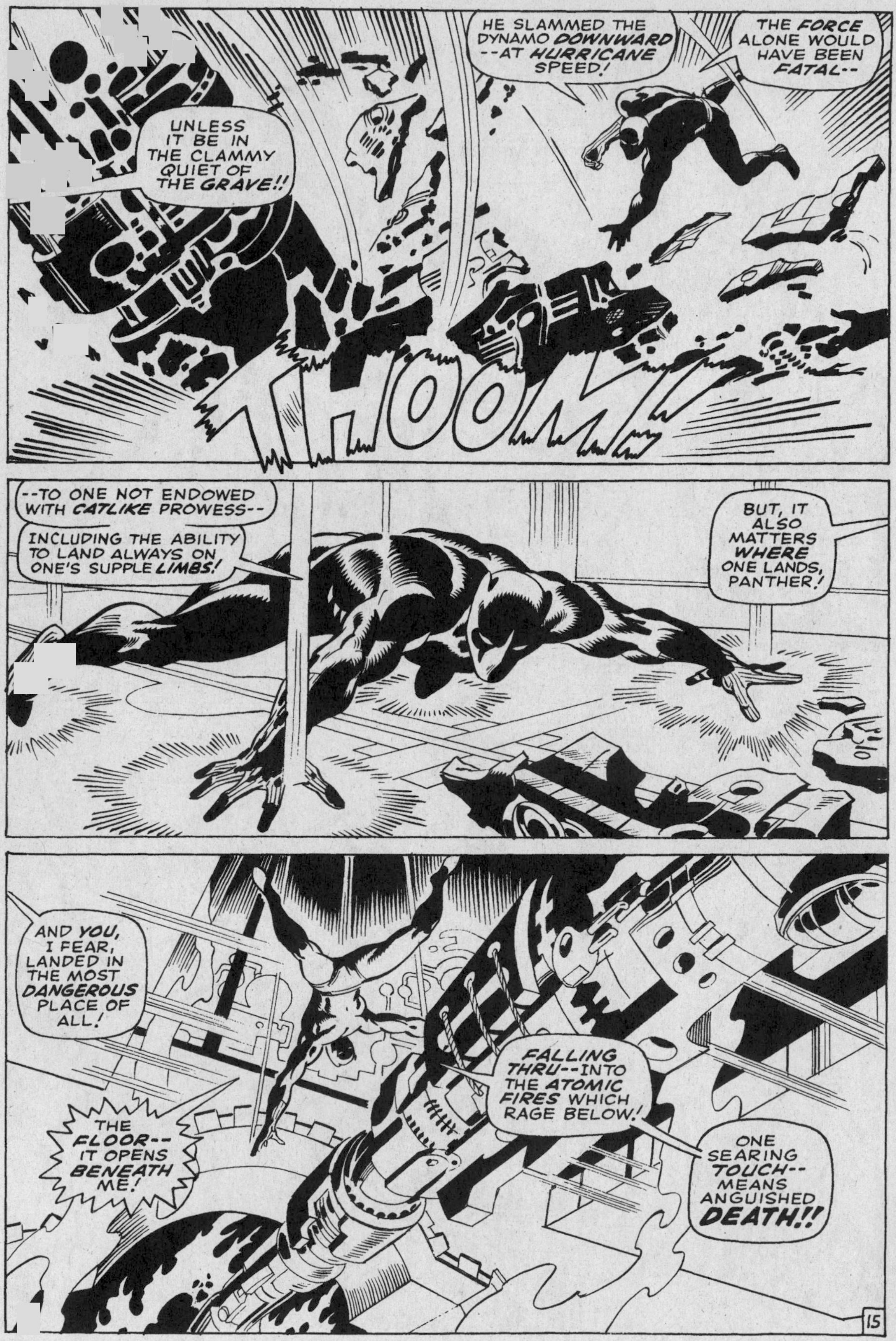
UNLESS IT BE IN THE CLAMMY QUIET OF THE GRAVE!!
HE SLAMMED THE DYNAMO DOWNWARD --AT HURRICANE SPEED!
THE FORCE ALONE WOULD HAVE BEEN FATAL--
THOOM!
--TO ONE NOT ENDOWED WITH CATLIKE PROWESS--
INCLUDING THE ABILITY TO LAND ALWAYS ON ONE'S SUPPLE LIMBS!
BUT, IT ALSO MATTERS WHERE ONE LANDS, PANTHER!
AND YOU, I FEAR, LANDED IN THE MOST DANGEROUS PLACE OF ALL!
THE FLOOR-- IT OPENS BENEATH ME!
FALLING THRU--INTO THE ATOMIC FIRES WHICH RAGE BELOW!
ONE SEARING TOUCH-- MEANS ANGUISHED DEATH!!

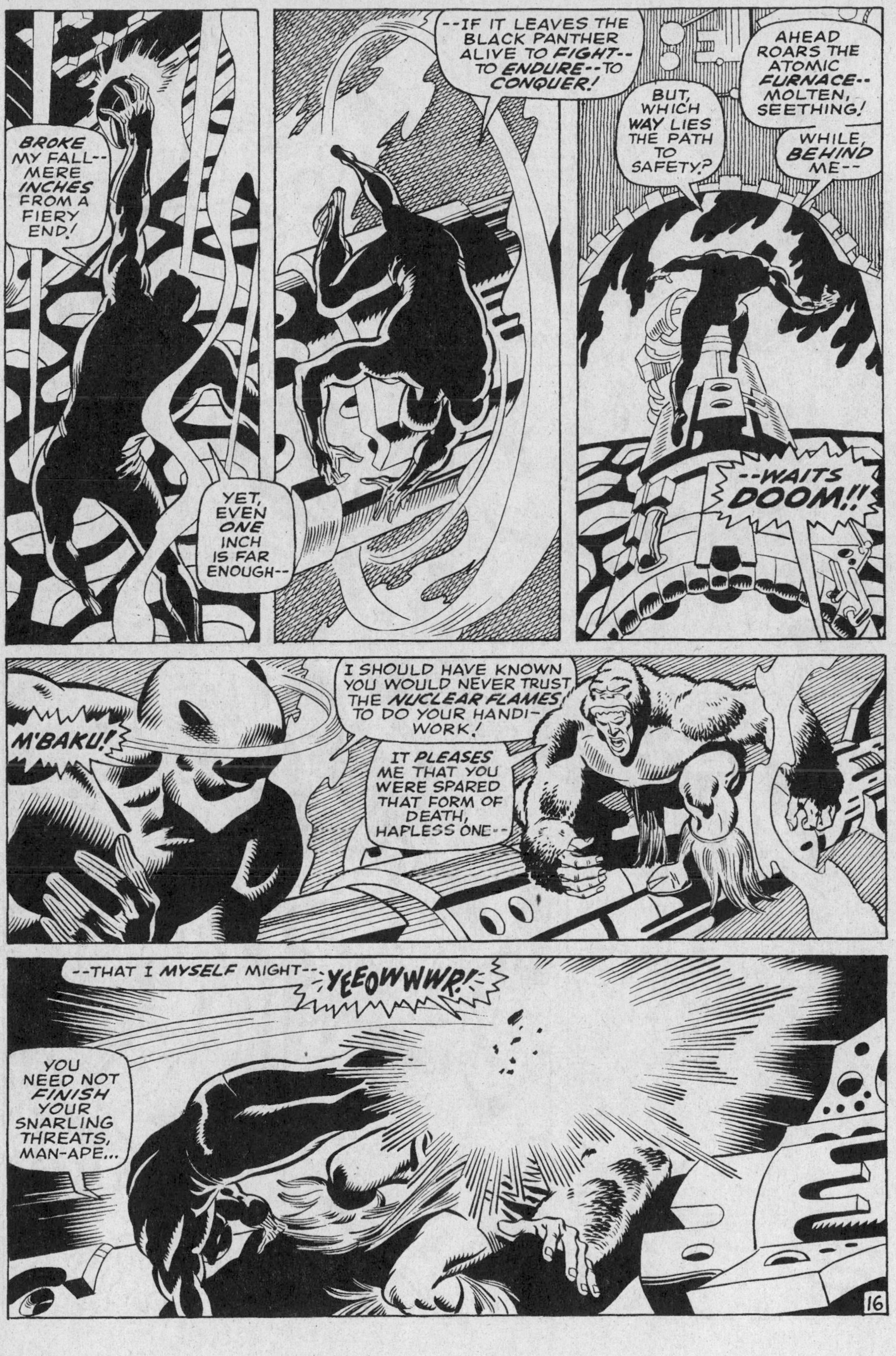
BROKE MY FALL--MERE INCHES FROM A FIERY END!
YET, EVEN ONE INCH IS FAR ENOUGH--
--IF IT LEAVES THE BLACK PANTHER ALIVE TO FIGHT--TO ENDURE--TO CONQUER!
AHEAD ROARS THE ATOMIC FURNACE--MOLTEN, SEETHING!
BUT, WHICH WAY LIES THE PATH TO SAFETY?
WHILE, BEHIND ME--
--WAITS DOOM!!
M'BAKU!
I SHOULD HAVE KNOWN YOU WOULD NEVER TRUST THE NUCLEAR FLAMES TO DO YOUR HANDIWORK!
IT PLEASES ME THAT YOU WERE SPARED THAT FORM OF DEATH, HAPLESS ONE--
--THAT I MYSELF MIGHT--
YEEOWWWR!
YOU NEED NOT FINISH YOUR SNARLING THREATS, MAN-APE...
16

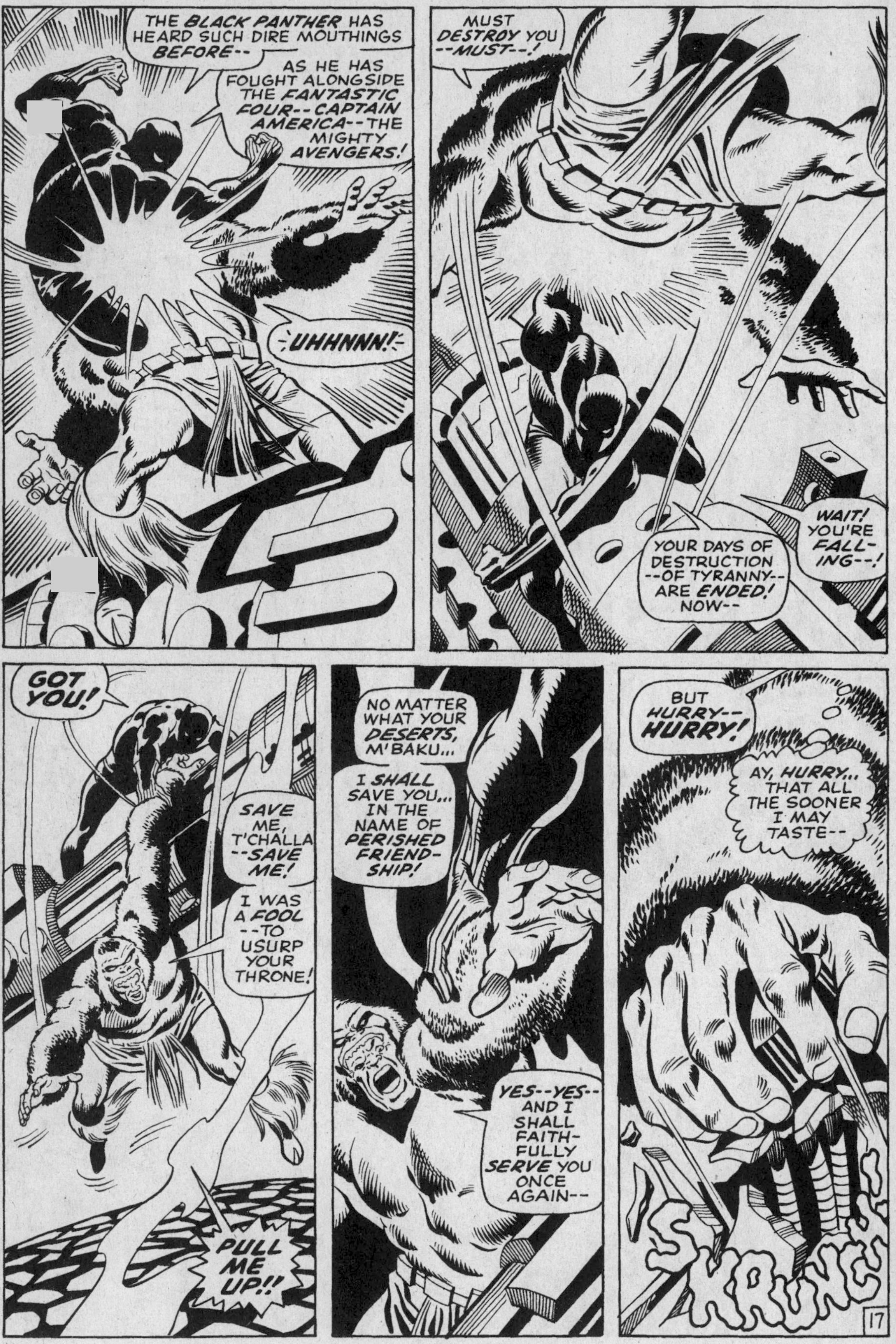
THE *BLACK PANTHER* HAS HEARD SUCH DIRE MOUTHINGS *BEFORE*--
AS HE HAS FOUGHT ALONGSIDE THE *FANTASTIC FOUR*--*CAPTAIN AMERICA*--THE MIGHTY *AVENGERS!*
-UHHNNN!-
MUST *DESTROY* YOU --*MUST*--!
YOUR DAYS OF DESTRUCTION --OF TYRANNY-- ARE *ENDED!* NOW--
WAIT! YOU'RE *FALL-ING*--!
GOT YOU!
SAVE ME, T'CHALLA --*SAVE ME!*
I WAS A *FOOL* --TO USURP YOUR THRONE!
PULL ME UP!!
NO MATTER WHAT YOUR *DESERTS,* M'BAKU...
I *SHALL* SAVE YOU... IN THE NAME OF *PERISHED FRIEND-SHIP!*
YES--YES-- AND I SHALL FAITH-FULLY *SERVE* YOU ONCE AGAIN--
BUT *HURRY--HURRY!*
AY, *HURRY*... THAT ALL THE SOONER I MAY TASTE--
SKRUNC

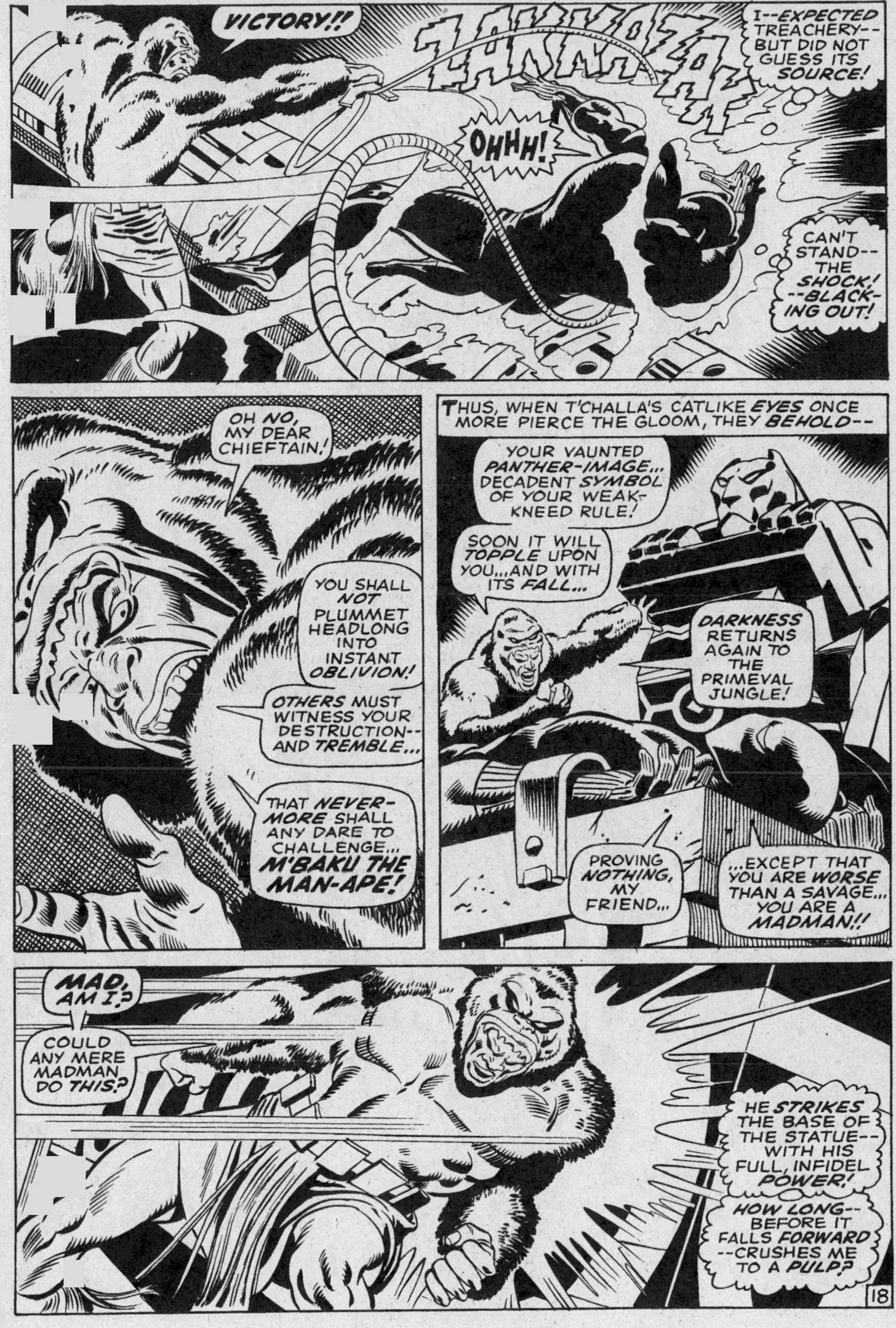
VICTORY!!
I--EXPECTED TREACHERY--BUT DID NOT GUESS ITS SOURCE!
OHHH!
CAN'T STAND--THE SHOCK! --BLACKING OUT!
OH NO, MY DEAR CHIEFTAIN!
YOU SHALL NOT PLUMMET HEADLONG INTO INSTANT OBLIVION!
OTHERS MUST WITNESS YOUR DESTRUCTION--AND TREMBLE...
THAT NEVERMORE SHALL ANY DARE TO CHALLENGE... M'BAKU THE MAN-APE!
THUS, WHEN T'CHALLA'S CATLIKE EYES ONCE MORE PIERCE THE GLOOM, THEY BEHOLD--
YOUR VAUNTED PANTHER-IMAGE... DECADENT SYMBOL OF YOUR WEAK-KNEED RULE!
SOON IT WILL TOPPLE UPON YOU...AND WITH ITS FALL...
DARKNESS RETURNS AGAIN TO THE PRIMEVAL JUNGLE!
PROVING NOTHING, MY FRIEND...
...EXCEPT THAT YOU ARE WORSE THAN A SAVAGE... YOU ARE A MADMAN!!
MAD, AM I?
COULD ANY MERE MADMAN DO THIS?
HE STRIKES THE BASE OF THE STATUE--WITH HIS FULL, INFIDEL POWER!
HOW LONG--BEFORE IT FALLS FORWARD --CRUSHES ME TO A PULP?
18

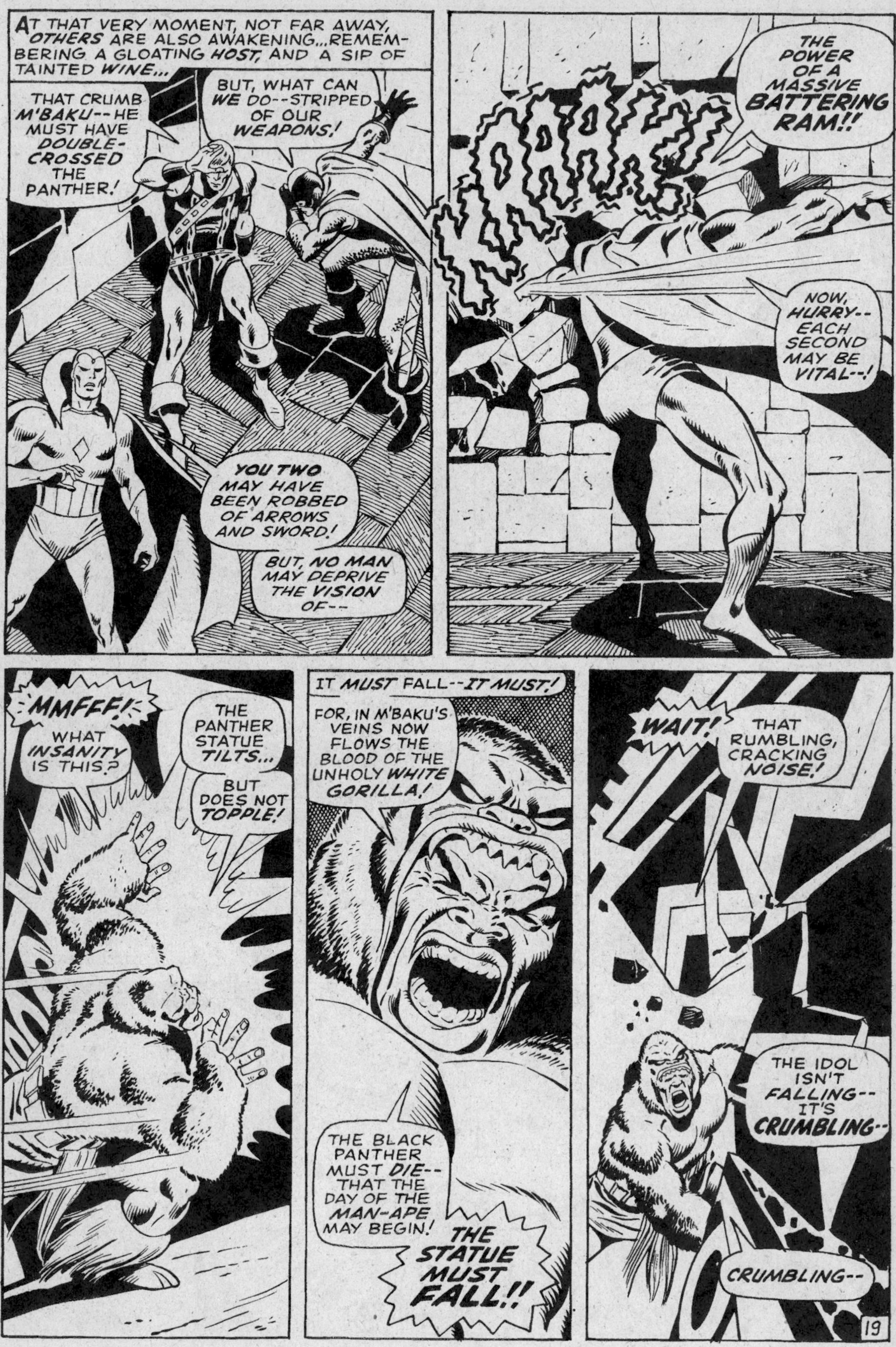
AT THAT VERY MOMENT, NOT FAR AWAY, OTHERS ARE ALSO AWAKENING... REMEMBERING A GLOATING HOST, AND A SIP OF TAINTED WINE...
THAT CRUMB M'BAKU--HE MUST HAVE DOUBLE-CROSSED THE PANTHER!
BUT, WHAT CAN WE DO--STRIPPED OF OUR WEAPONS!
YOU TWO MAY HAVE BEEN ROBBED OF ARROWS AND SWORD!
BUT, NO MAN MAY DEPRIVE THE VISION OF--
THE POWER OF A MASSIVE BATTERING RAM!!
KRAAK!
NOW, HURRY--EACH SECOND MAY BE VITAL--!
MMFFF!
WHAT INSANITY IS THIS?
THE PANTHER STATUE TILTS...
BUT DOES NOT TOPPLE!
IT MUST FALL--IT MUST!
FOR, IN M'BAKU'S VEINS NOW FLOWS THE BLOOD OF THE UNHOLY WHITE GORILLA!
THE BLACK PANTHER MUST DIE--THAT THE DAY OF THE MAN-APE MAY BEGIN!
THE STATUE MUST FALL!!
WAIT!
THAT RUMBLING, CRACKING NOISE!
THE IDOL ISN'T FALLING--IT'S CRUMBLING--
CRUMBLING--

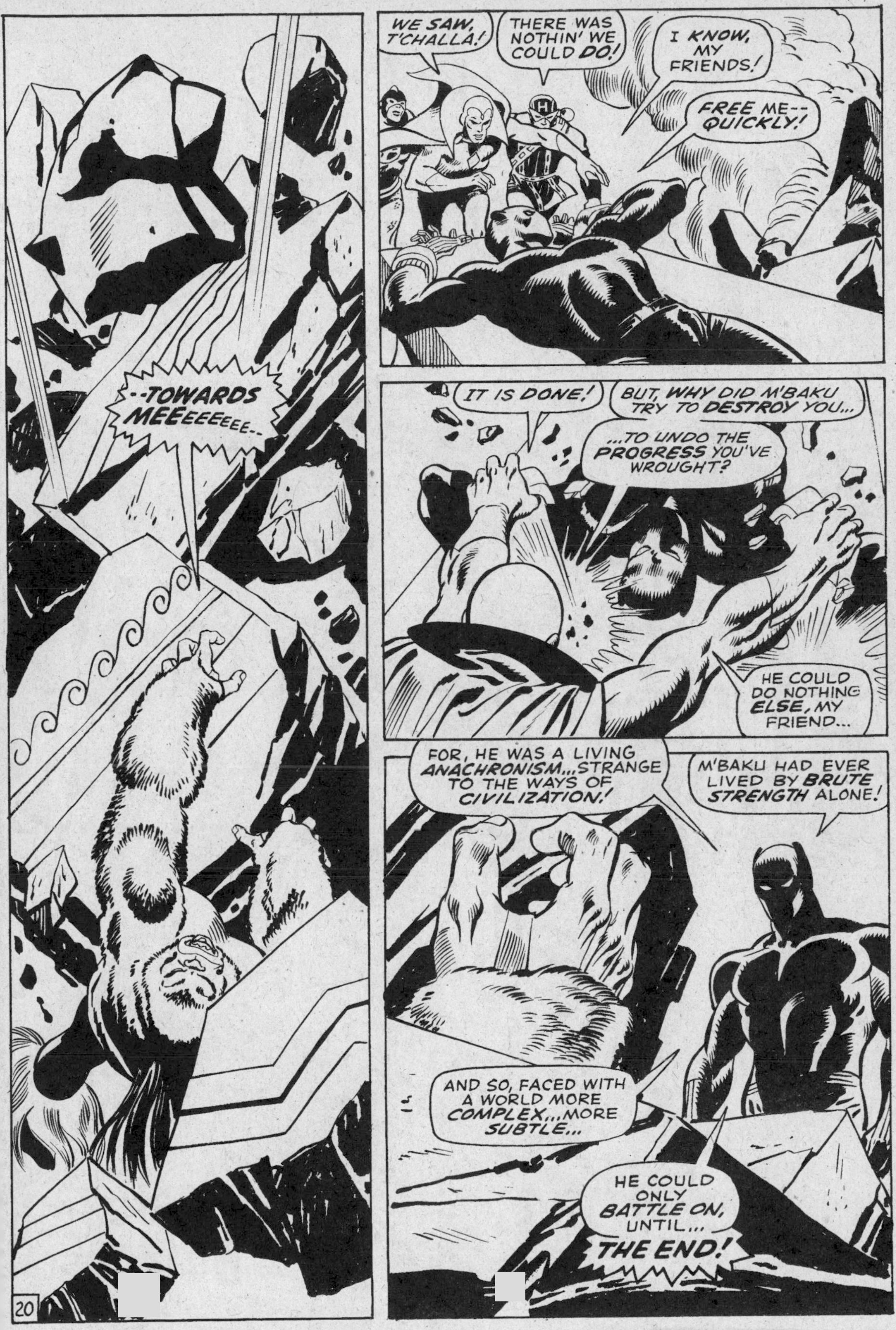

--TOWARDS MEEEEEEEE--
WE SAW, T'CHALLA!
THERE WAS NOTHIN' WE COULD DO!
I KNOW, MY FRIENDS!
FREE ME--QUICKLY!
IT IS DONE!
BUT, WHY DID M'BAKU TRY TO DESTROY YOU...
...TO UNDO THE PROGRESS YOU'VE WROUGHT?
HE COULD DO NOTHING ELSE, MY FRIEND...
FOR, HE WAS A LIVING ANACHRONISM...STRANGE TO THE WAYS OF CIVILIZATION!
M'BAKU HAD EVER LIVED BY BRUTE STRENGTH ALONE!
AND SO, FACED WITH A WORLD MORE COMPLEX...MORE SUBTLE...
HE COULD ONLY BATTLE ON, UNTIL... THE END!
20

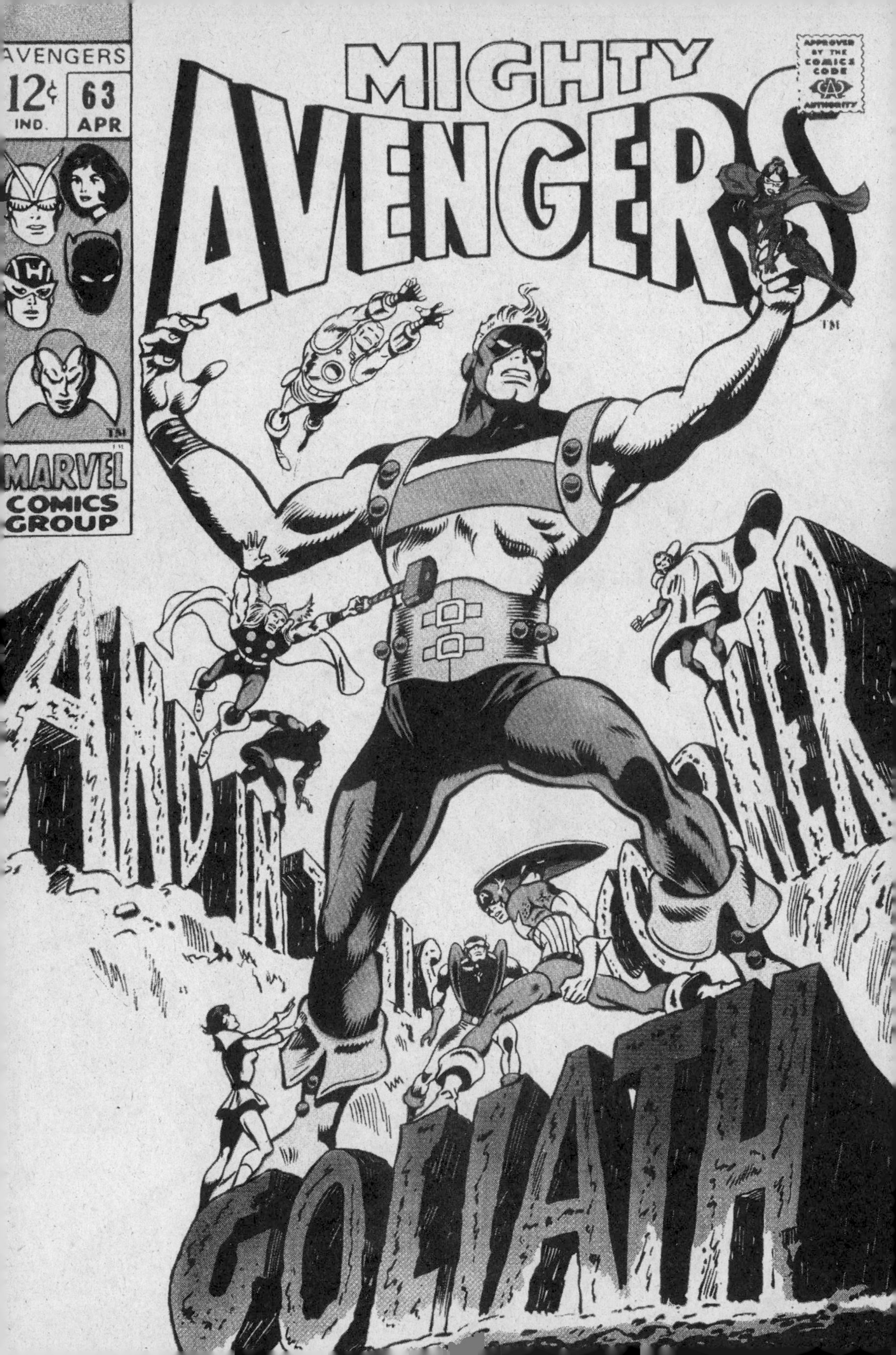

AVENGERS
12¢
IND.
63
APR
MARVEL
COMICS
GROUP
APPROVED BY THE COMICS CODE AUTHORITY
MIGHTY
AVENGERS
AND NOW
GOLIATH

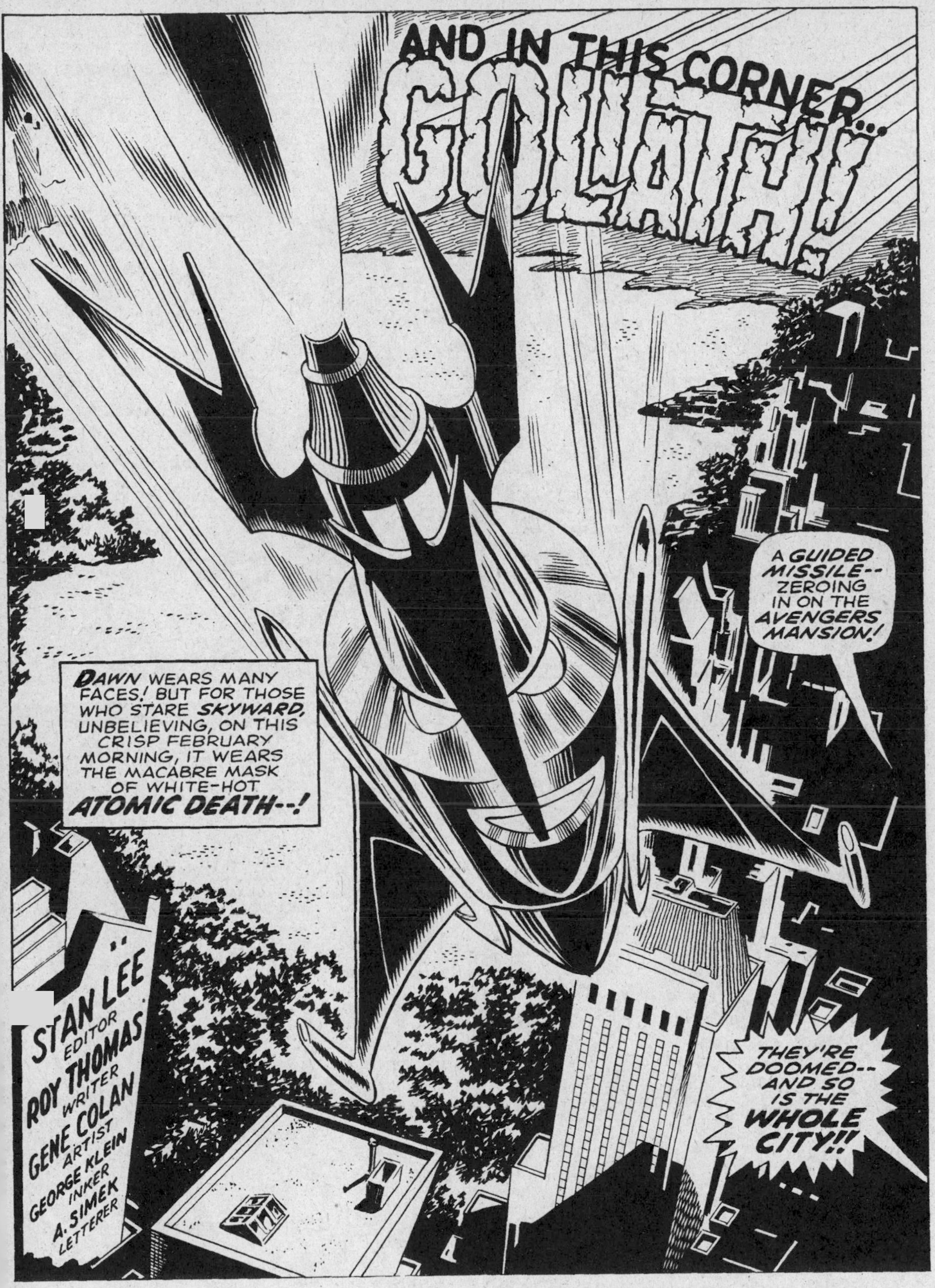

AND IN THIS CORNER...
GOLIATH!
DAWN WEARS MANY FACES! BUT FOR THOSE WHO STARE SKYWARD, UNBELIEVING, ON THIS CRISP FEBRUARY MORNING, IT WEARS THE MACABRE MASK OF WHITE-HOT ATOMIC DEATH--!
A GUIDED MISSILE-- ZEROING IN ON THE AVENGERS MANSION!
THEY'RE DOOMED-- AND SO IS THE WHOLE CITY!!
STAN LEE EDITOR
ROY THOMAS WRITER
GENE COLAN ARTIST
GEORGE KLEIN INKER
A. SIMEK LETTERER

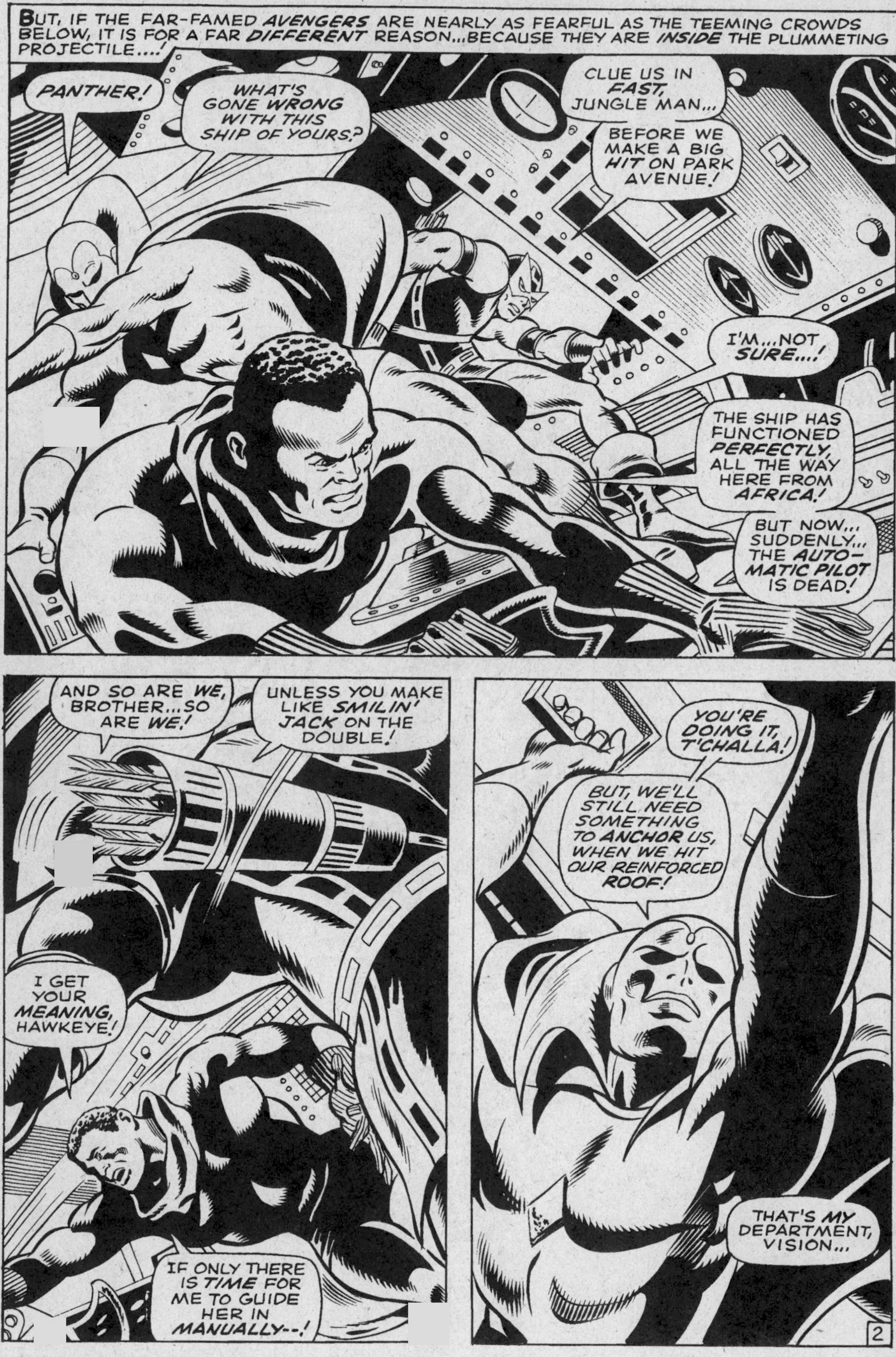

BUT, IF THE FAR-FAMED AVENGERS ARE NEARLY AS FEARFUL AS THE TEEMING CROWDS BELOW, IT IS FOR A FAR DIFFERENT REASON...BECAUSE THEY ARE INSIDE THE PLUMMETING PROJECTILE....!
PANTHER!
WHAT'S GONE WRONG WITH THIS SHIP OF YOURS?
CLUE US IN FAST, JUNGLE MAN...
BEFORE WE MAKE A BIG HIT ON PARK AVENUE!
I'M...NOT SURE...!
THE SHIP HAS FUNCTIONED PERFECTLY, ALL THE WAY HERE FROM AFRICA!
BUT NOW... SUDDENLY... THE AUTOMATIC PILOT IS DEAD!
AND SO ARE WE, BROTHER...SO ARE WE!
UNLESS YOU MAKE LIKE SMILIN' JACK ON THE DOUBLE!
I GET YOUR MEANING, HAWKEYE!
IF ONLY THERE IS TIME FOR ME TO GUIDE HER IN MANUALLY--!
YOU'RE DOING IT, T'CHALLA!
BUT, WE'LL STILL NEED SOMETHING TO ANCHOR US, WHEN WE HIT OUR REINFORCED ROOF!
THAT'S MY DEPARTMENT, VISION...

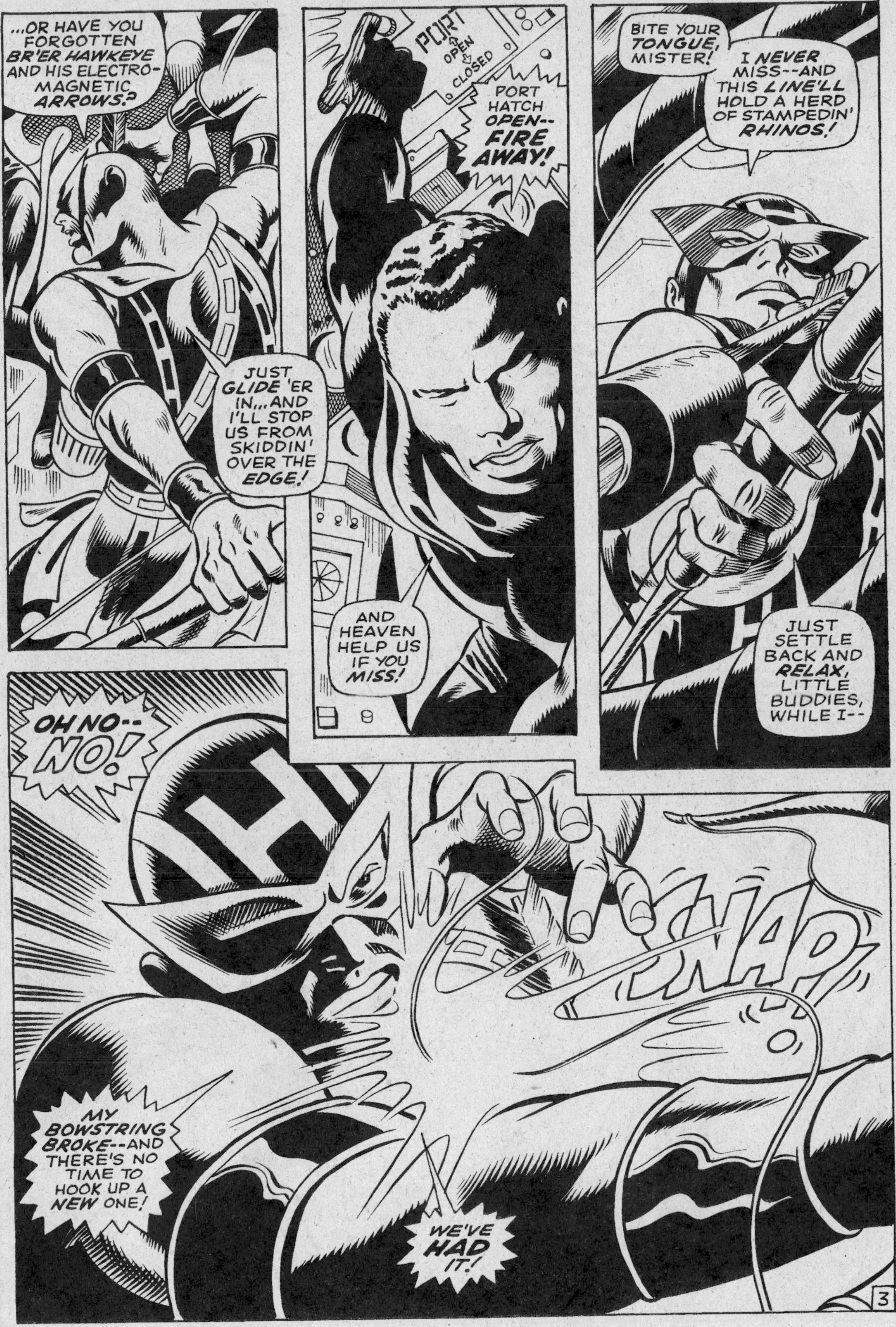
...OR HAVE YOU FORGOTTEN BR'ER HAWKEYE AND HIS ELECTRO-MAGNETIC ARROWS?
PORT
OPEN
CLOSED
PORT HATCH OPEN--FIRE AWAY!
BITE YOUR TONGUE, MISTER!
I NEVER MISS--AND THIS LINE'LL HOLD A HERD OF STAMPEDIN' RHINOS!
JUST GLIDE 'ER IN...AND I'LL STOP US FROM SKIDDIN' OVER THE EDGE!
AND HEAVEN HELP US IF YOU MISS!
JUST SETTLE BACK AND RELAX, LITTLE BUDDIES, WHILE I--
OH NO--NO!
SNAP!
MY BOWSTRING BROKE--AND THERE'S NO TIME TO HOOK UP A NEW ONE!
WE'VE HAD IT!
3

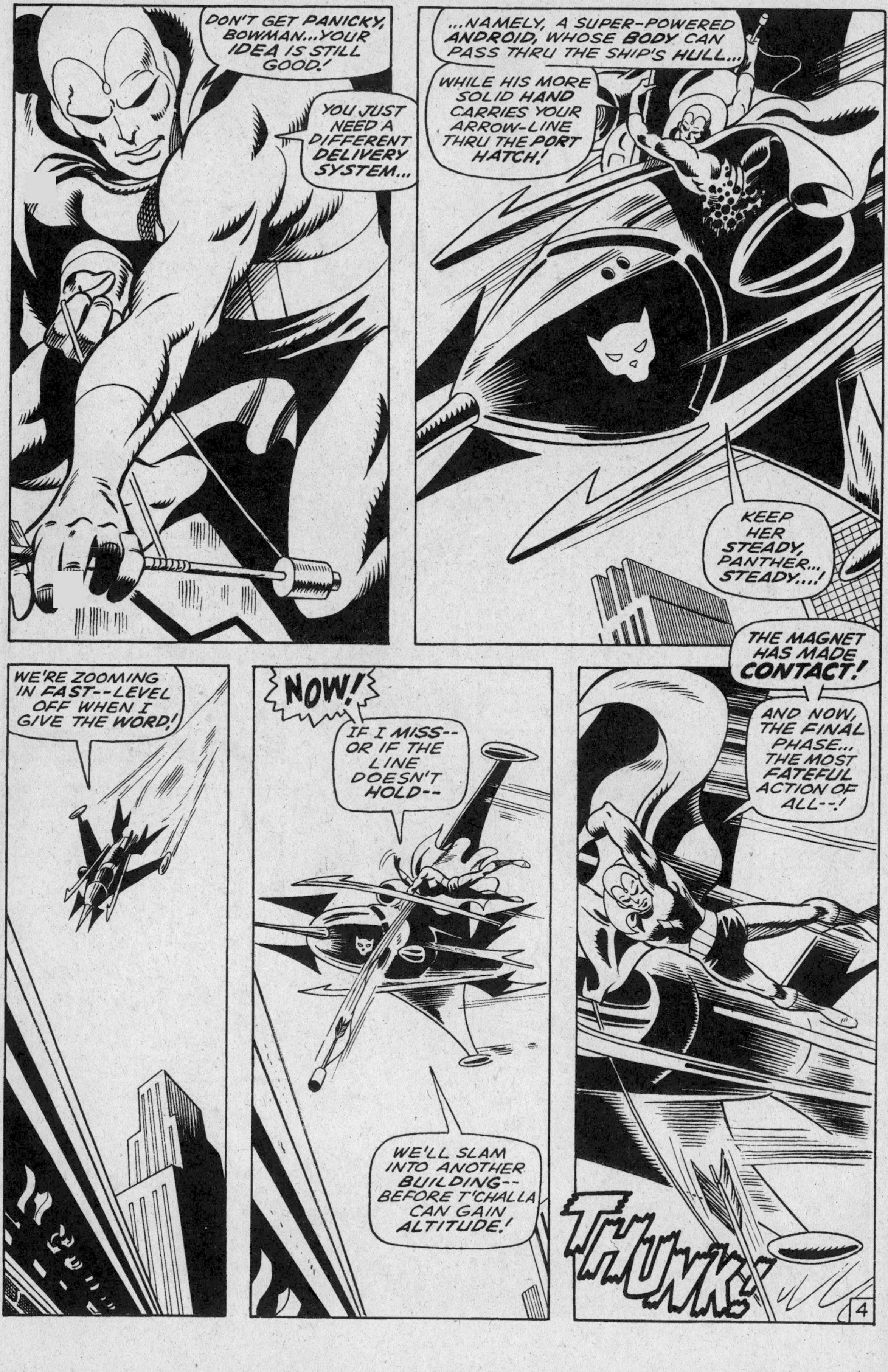

DON'T GET PANICKY, BOWMAN...YOUR IDEA IS STILL GOOD!
YOU JUST NEED A DIFFERENT DELIVERY SYSTEM...
...NAMELY, A SUPER-POWERED ANDROID, WHOSE BODY CAN PASS THRU THE SHIP'S HULL...
WHILE HIS MORE SOLID HAND CARRIES YOUR ARROW-LINE THRU THE PORT HATCH!
KEEP HER STEADY, PANTHER... STEADY...!
WE'RE ZOOMING IN FAST--LEVEL OFF WHEN I GIVE THE WORD!
NOW!
IF I MISS--OR IF THE LINE DOESN'T HOLD--
WE'LL SLAM INTO ANOTHER BUILDING--BEFORE T'CHALLA CAN GAIN ALTITUDE!
THE MAGNET HAS MADE CONTACT!
AND NOW, THE FINAL PHASE... THE MOST FATEFUL ACTION OF ALL--!
THUNK!

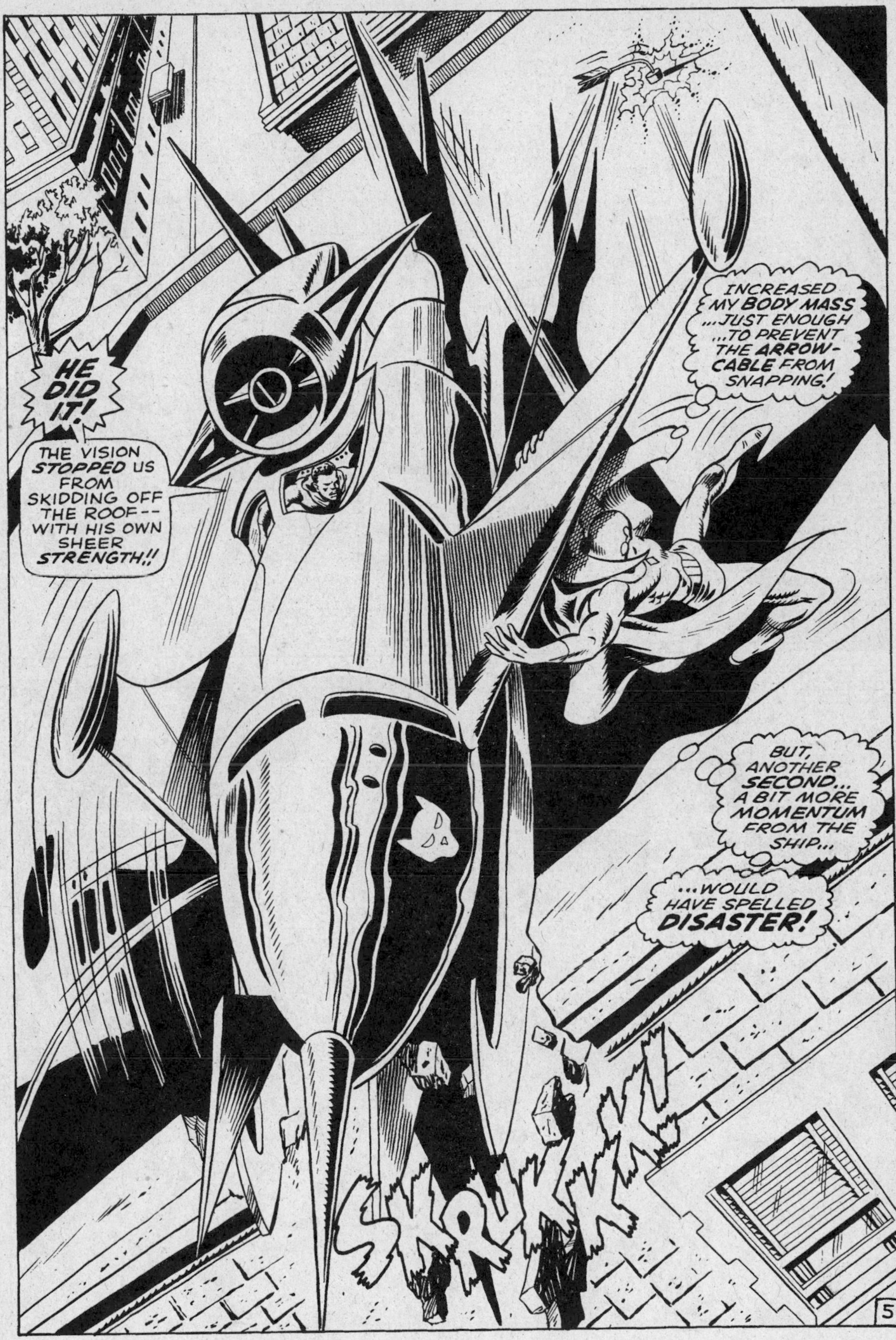
HE DID IT!
THE VISION STOPPED US FROM SKIDDING OFF THE ROOF-- WITH HIS OWN SHEER STRENGTH!!
INCREASED MY BODY MASS ...JUST ENOUGH ...TO PREVENT THE ARROW-CABLE FROM SNAPPING!
BUT, ANOTHER SECOND... A BIT MORE MOMENTUM FROM THE SHIP...
...WOULD HAVE SPELLED DISASTER!
SKRUKK!

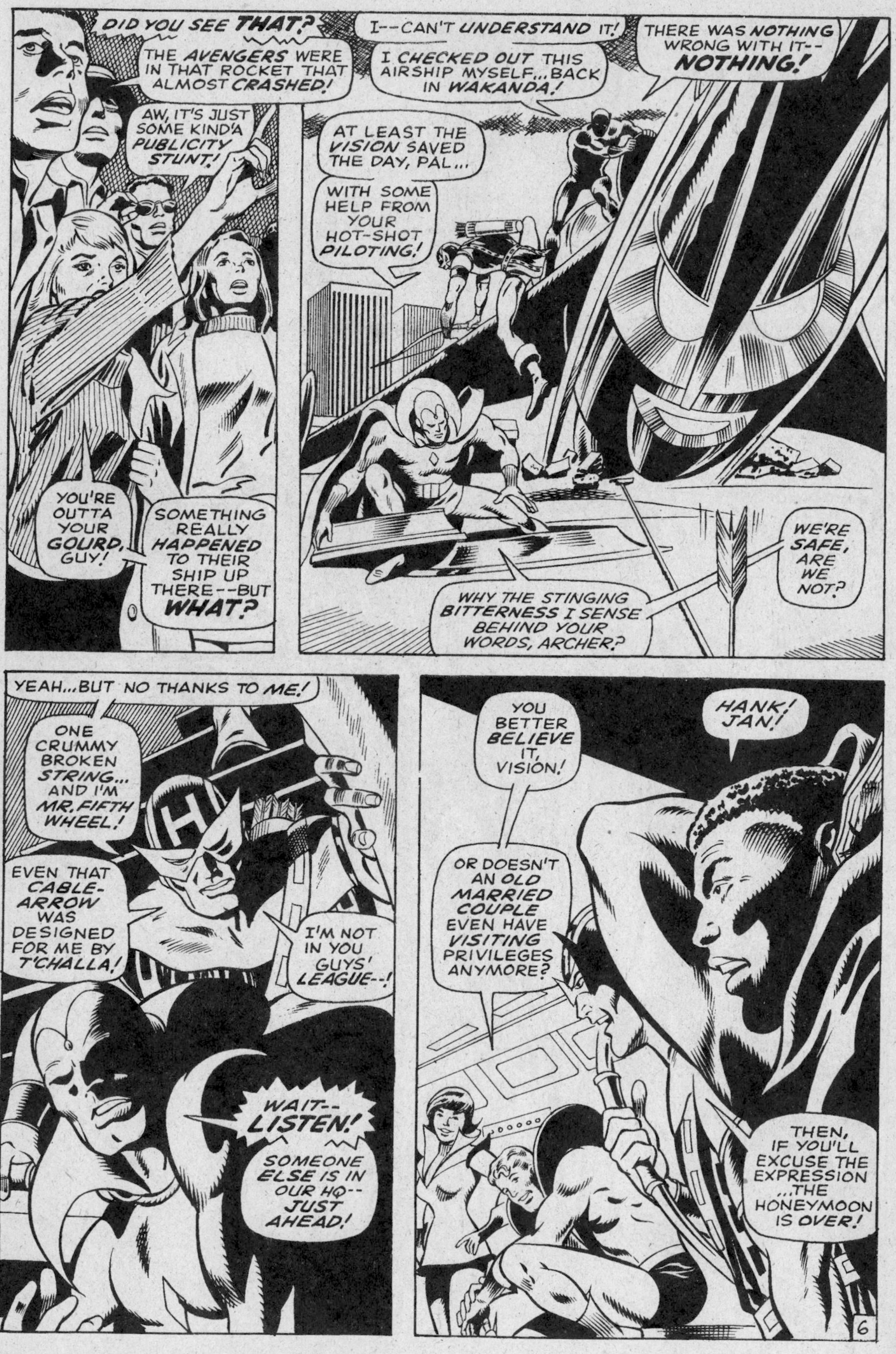
DID YOU SEE THAT?
THE AVENGERS WERE IN THAT ROCKET THAT ALMOST CRASHED!
AW, IT'S JUST SOME KIND'A PUBLICITY STUNT!
YOU'RE OUTTA YOUR GOURD, GUY!
SOMETHING REALLY HAPPENED TO THEIR SHIP UP THERE--BUT WHAT?
I--CAN'T UNDERSTAND IT!
I CHECKED OUT THIS AIRSHIP MYSELF... BACK IN WAKANDA!
THERE WAS NOTHING WRONG WITH IT-- NOTHING!
AT LEAST THE VISION SAVED THE DAY, PAL...
WITH SOME HELP FROM YOUR HOT-SHOT PILOTING!
WE'RE SAFE, ARE WE NOT?
WHY THE STINGING BITTERNESS I SENSE BEHIND YOUR WORDS, ARCHER?
YEAH... BUT NO THANKS TO ME!
ONE CRUMMY BROKEN STRING... AND I'M MR. FIFTH WHEEL!
EVEN THAT CABLE-ARROW WAS DESIGNED FOR ME BY T'CHALLA!
I'M NOT IN YOU GUYS' LEAGUE--!
WAIT-- LISTEN!
SOMEONE ELSE IS IN OUR HQ-- JUST AHEAD!
HANK! JAN!
YOU BETTER BELIEVE IT, VISION!
OR DOESN'T AN OLD MARRIED COUPLE EVEN HAVE VISITING PRIVILEGES ANYMORE?
THEN, IF YOU'LL EXCUSE THE EXPRESSION ...THE HONEYMOON IS OVER!
6

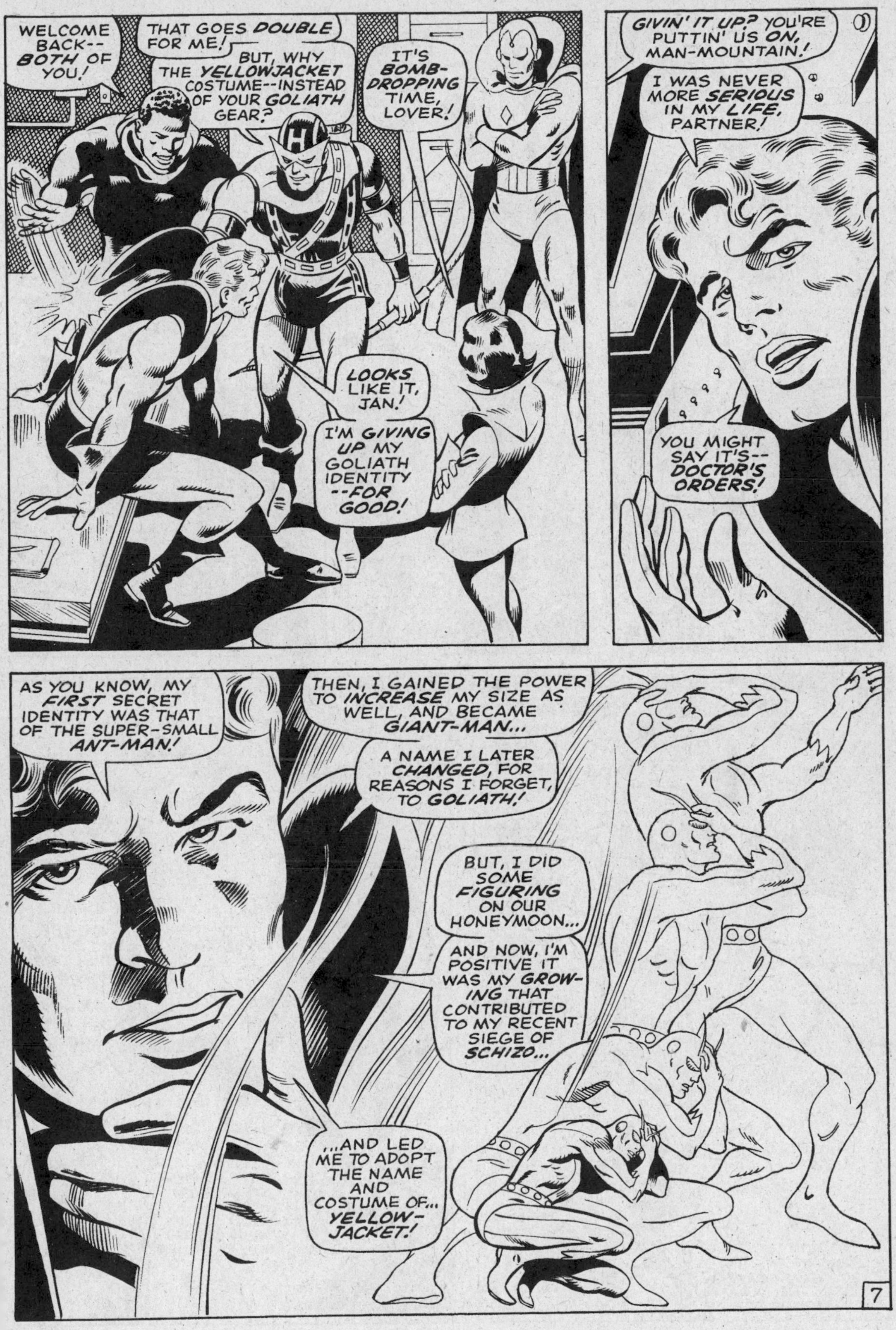
WELCOME BACK-- BOTH OF YOU!
THAT GOES DOUBLE FOR ME!
BUT, WHY THE YELLOWJACKET COSTUME--INSTEAD OF YOUR GOLIATH GEAR?
IT'S BOMB-DROPPING TIME, LOVER!
LOOKS LIKE IT, JAN!
I'M GIVING UP MY GOLIATH IDENTITY --FOR GOOD!
GIVIN' IT UP? YOU'RE PUTTIN' US ON, MAN-MOUNTAIN!
I WAS NEVER MORE SERIOUS IN MY LIFE, PARTNER!
YOU MIGHT SAY IT'S-- DOCTOR'S ORDERS!
AS YOU KNOW, MY FIRST SECRET IDENTITY WAS THAT OF THE SUPER-SMALL ANT-MAN!
THEN, I GAINED THE POWER TO INCREASE MY SIZE AS WELL, AND BECAME GIANT-MAN...
A NAME I LATER CHANGED, FOR REASONS I FORGET, TO GOLIATH!
BUT, I DID SOME FIGURING ON OUR HONEYMOON...
AND NOW, I'M POSITIVE IT WAS MY GROWING THAT CONTRIBUTED TO MY RECENT SIEGE OF SCHIZO...
...AND LED ME TO ADOPT THE NAME AND COSTUME OF... YELLOW-JACKET!
7

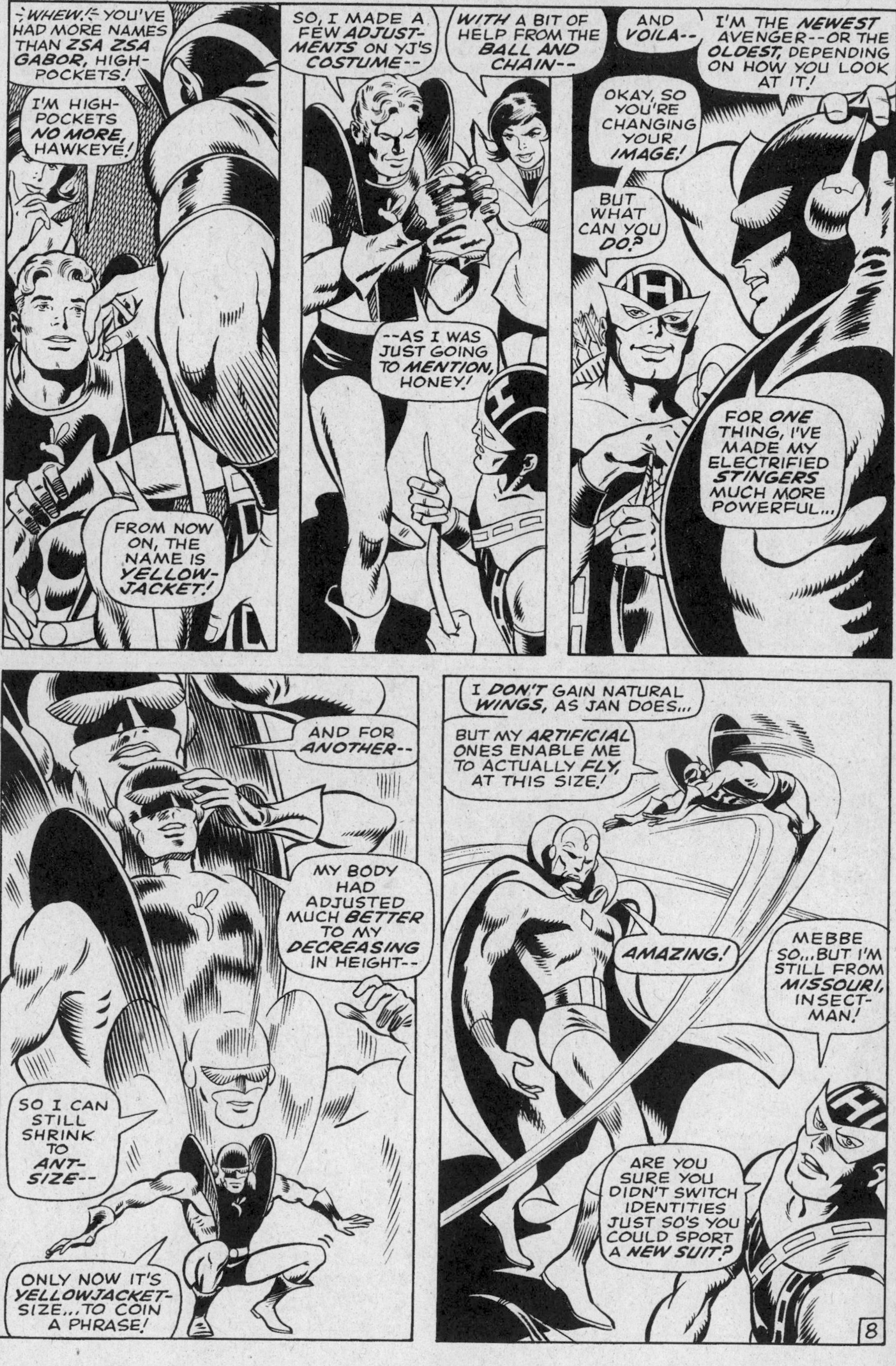

-WHEW!- YOU'VE HAD MORE NAMES THAN ZSA ZSA GABOR, HIGH-POCKETS!
I'M HIGH-POCKETS NO MORE, HAWKEYE!
FROM NOW ON, THE NAME IS YELLOW-JACKET!
SO, I MADE A FEW ADJUST-MENTS ON YJ'S COSTUME--
WITH A BIT OF HELP FROM THE BALL AND CHAIN--
--AS I WAS JUST GOING TO MENTION, HONEY!
AND VOILA--
I'M THE NEWEST AVENGER--OR THE OLDEST, DEPENDING ON HOW YOU LOOK AT IT!
OKAY, SO YOU'RE CHANGING YOUR IMAGE!
BUT WHAT CAN YOU DO?
FOR ONE THING, I'VE MADE MY ELECTRIFIED STINGERS MUCH MORE POWERFUL...
AND FOR ANOTHER--
MY BODY HAD ADJUSTED MUCH BETTER TO MY DECREASING IN HEIGHT--
SO I CAN STILL SHRINK TO ANT-SIZE--
ONLY NOW IT'S YELLOWJACKET-SIZE...TO COIN A PHRASE!
I DON'T GAIN NATURAL WINGS, AS JAN DOES...
BUT MY ARTIFICIAL ONES ENABLE ME TO ACTUALLY FLY, AT THIS SIZE!
AMAZING!
MEBBE SO...BUT I'M STILL FROM MISSOURI, INSECT-MAN!
ARE YOU SURE YOU DIDN'T SWITCH IDENTITIES JUST SO'S YOU COULD SPORT A NEW SUIT?
8

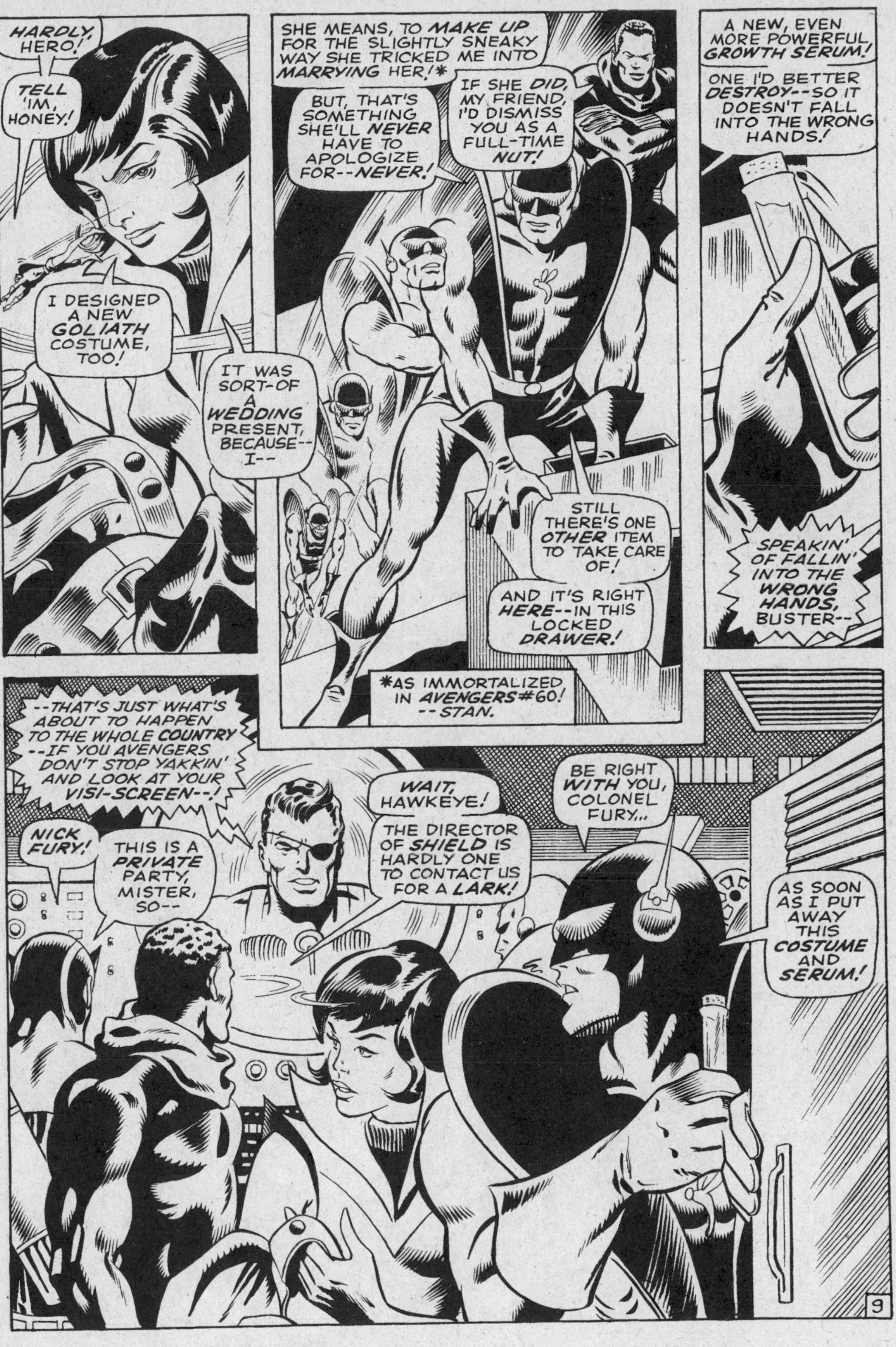
HARDLY, HERO!
TELL 'IM, HONEY!
I DESIGNED A NEW GOLIATH COSTUME, TOO!
IT WAS SORT-OF A WEDDING PRESENT, BECAUSE-- I--
SHE MEANS, TO MAKE UP FOR THE SLIGHTLY SNEAKY WAY SHE TRICKED ME INTO MARRYING HER!*
BUT, THAT'S SOMETHING SHE'LL NEVER HAVE TO APOLOGIZE FOR--NEVER!
IF SHE DID, MY FRIEND, I'D DISMISS YOU AS A FULL-TIME NUT!
STILL THERE'S ONE OTHER ITEM TO TAKE CARE OF!
AND IT'S RIGHT HERE--IN THIS LOCKED DRAWER!
*AS IMMORTALIZED IN AVENGERS #60! --STAN.
A NEW, EVEN MORE POWERFUL GROWTH SERUM!
ONE I'D BETTER DESTROY--SO IT DOESN'T FALL INTO THE WRONG HANDS!
SPEAKIN' OF FALLIN' INTO THE WRONG HANDS, BUSTER--
--THAT'S JUST WHAT'S ABOUT TO HAPPEN TO THE WHOLE COUNTRY --IF YOU AVENGERS DON'T STOP YAKKIN' AND LOOK AT YOUR VISI-SCREEN--!
NICK FURY!
THIS IS A PRIVATE PARTY, MISTER, SO--
WAIT, HAWKEYE!
THE DIRECTOR OF SHIELD IS HARDLY ONE TO CONTACT US FOR A LARK!
BE RIGHT WITH YOU, COLONEL FURY...
AS SOON AS I PUT AWAY THIS COSTUME AND SERUM!
9

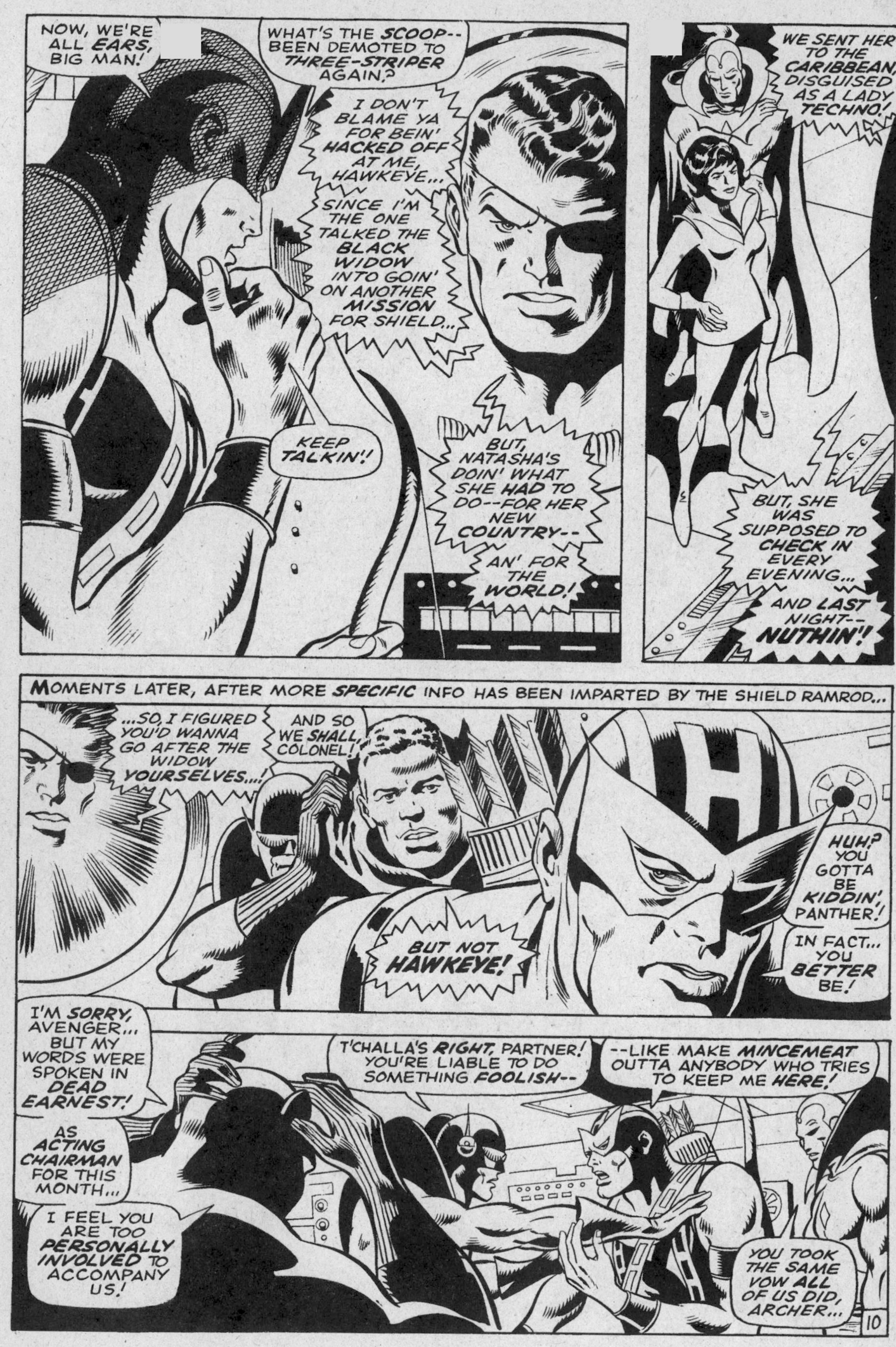
NOW, WE'RE ALL EARS, BIG MAN!
WHAT'S THE SCOOP-- BEEN DEMOTED TO THREE-STRIPER AGAIN?
I DON'T BLAME YA FOR BEIN' HACKED OFF AT ME, HAWKEYE...
SINCE I'M THE ONE TALKED THE BLACK WIDOW INTO GOIN' ON ANOTHER MISSION FOR SHIELD...
KEEP TALKIN'!
BUT, NATASHA'S DOIN' WHAT SHE HAD TO DO--FOR HER NEW COUNTRY--
AN' FOR THE WORLD!
WE SENT HER TO THE CARIBBEAN, DISGUISED AS A LADY TECHNO!
BUT, SHE WAS SUPPOSED TO CHECK IN EVERY EVENING...
AND LAST NIGHT-- NUTHIN'!
MOMENTS LATER, AFTER MORE SPECIFIC INFO HAS BEEN IMPARTED BY THE SHIELD RAMROD...
...SO, I FIGURED YOU'D WANNA GO AFTER THE WIDOW YOURSELVES...!
AND SO WE SHALL, COLONEL!
BUT NOT HAWKEYE!
HUH? YOU GOTTA BE KIDDIN', PANTHER!
IN FACT... YOU BETTER BE!
I'M SORRY, AVENGER... BUT MY WORDS WERE SPOKEN IN DEAD EARNEST!
AS ACTING CHAIRMAN FOR THIS MONTH...
I FEEL YOU ARE TOO PERSONALLY INVOLVED TO ACCOMPANY US!
T'CHALLA'S RIGHT, PARTNER! YOU'RE LIABLE TO DO SOMETHING FOOLISH--
--LIKE MAKE MINCEMEAT OUTTA ANYBODY WHO TRIES TO KEEP ME HERE!
YOU TOOK THE SAME VOW ALL OF US DID, ARCHER...

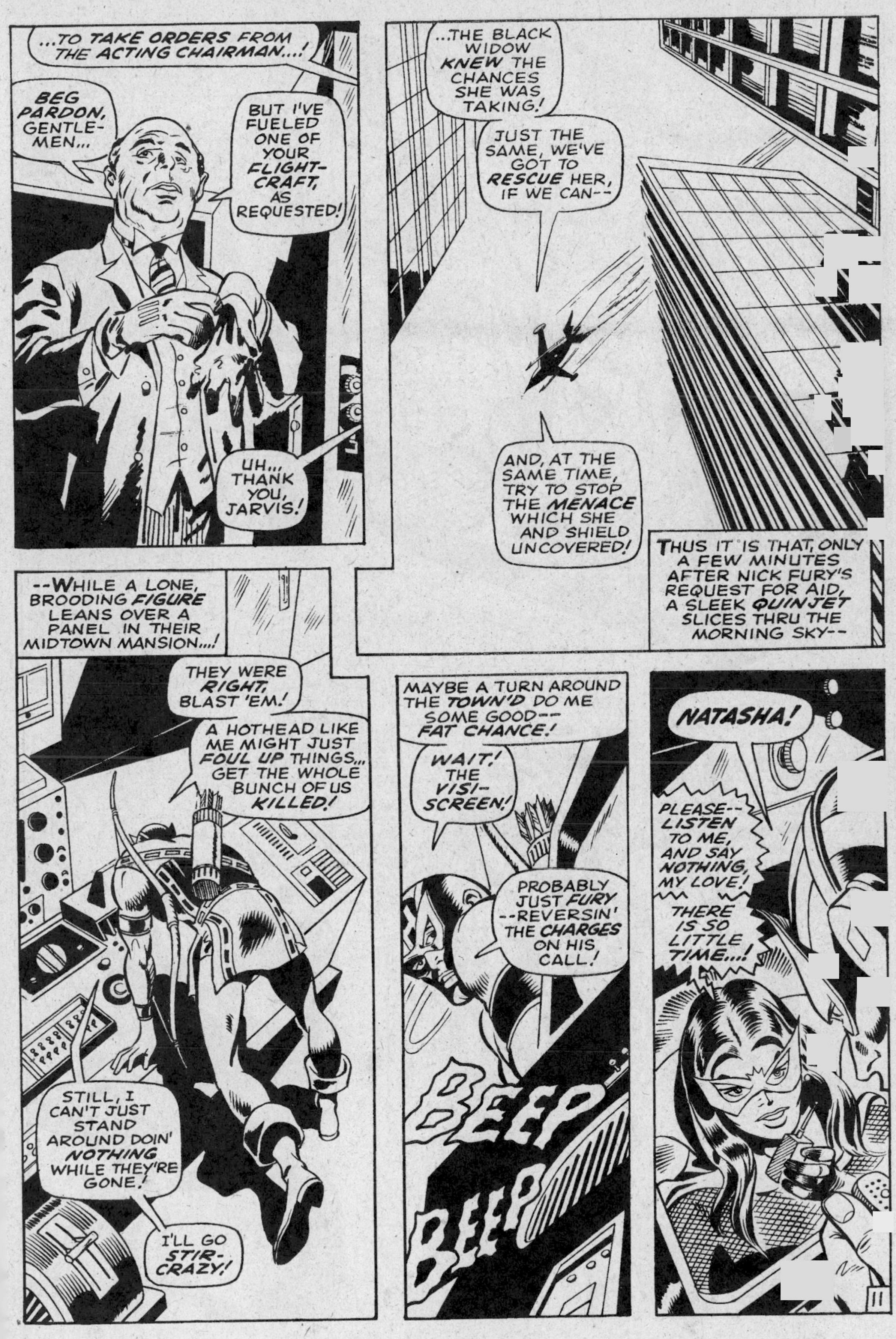
...TO TAKE ORDERS FROM THE ACTING CHAIRMAN...!
BEG PARDON, GENTLEMEN...
BUT I'VE FUELED ONE OF YOUR FLIGHT-CRAFT, AS REQUESTED!
UH... THANK YOU, JARVIS!
THUS IT IS THAT, ONLY A FEW MINUTES AFTER NICK FURY'S REQUEST FOR AID, A SLEEK QUINJET SLICES THRU THE MORNING SKY--
...THE BLACK WIDOW KNEW THE CHANCES SHE WAS TAKING!
JUST THE SAME, WE'VE GOT TO RESCUE HER, IF WE CAN--
AND, AT THE SAME TIME, TRY TO STOP THE MENACE WHICH SHE AND SHIELD UNCOVERED!
--WHILE A LONE, BROODING FIGURE LEANS OVER A PANEL IN THEIR MIDTOWN MANSION...!
THEY WERE RIGHT, BLAST 'EM.!
A HOTHEAD LIKE ME MIGHT JUST FOUL UP THINGS... GET THE WHOLE BUNCH OF US KILLED!
STILL, I CAN'T JUST STAND AROUND DOIN' NOTHING WHILE THEY'RE GONE!
I'LL GO STIR-CRAZY!
MAYBE A TURN AROUND THE TOWN'D DO ME SOME GOOD-- FAT CHANCE!
WAIT! THE VISI-SCREEN!
PROBABLY JUST FURY --REVERSIN' THE CHARGES ON HIS CALL!
BEEP
BEEP
NATASHA!
PLEASE-- LISTEN TO ME, AND SAY NOTHING, MY LOVE!
THERE IS SO LITTLE TIME...!
11

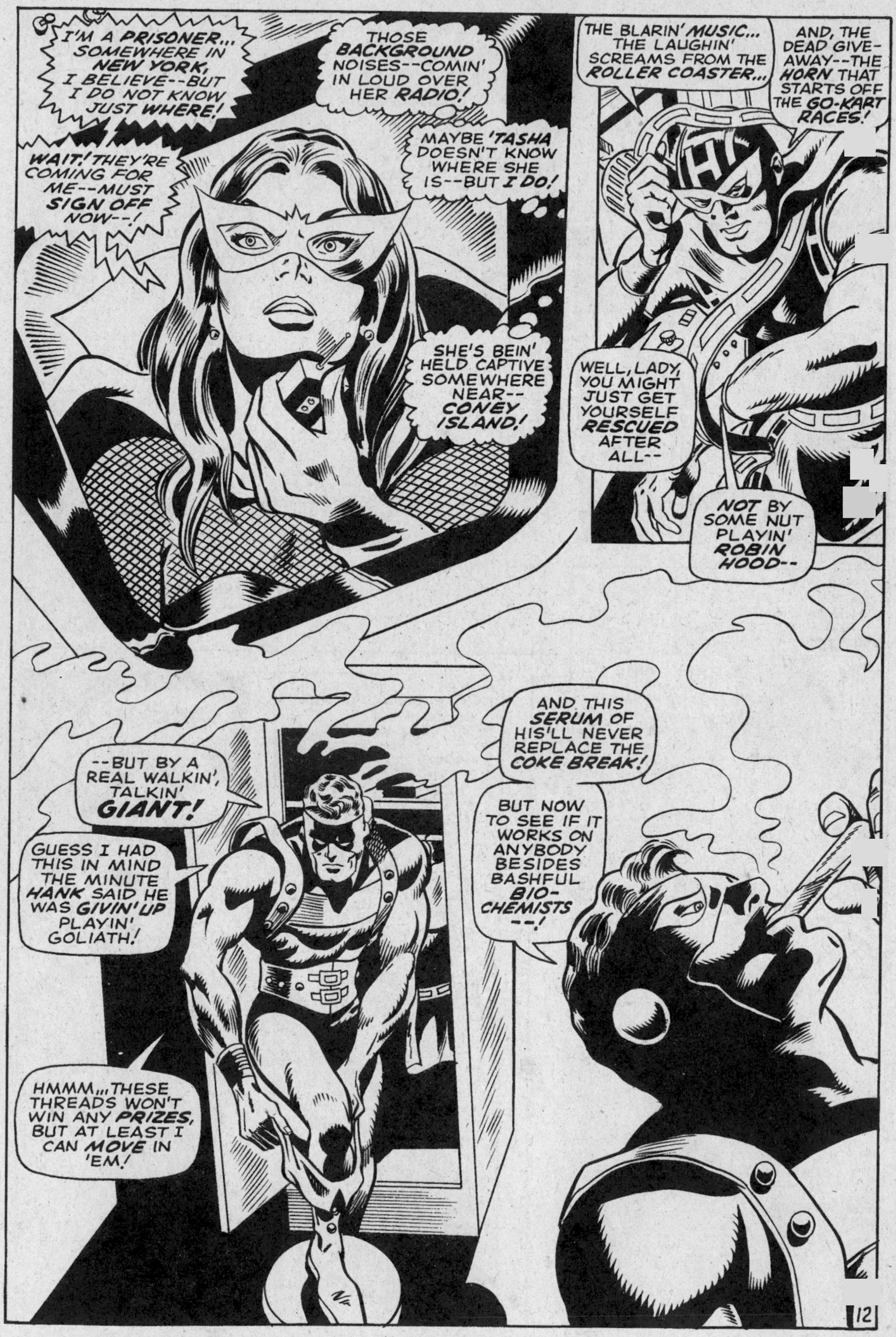

I'M A PRISONER... SOMEWHERE IN NEW YORK, I BELIEVE--BUT I DO NOT KNOW JUST WHERE!
WAIT! THEY'RE COMING FOR ME--MUST SIGN OFF NOW--!
THOSE BACKGROUND NOISES--COMIN' IN LOUD OVER HER RADIO!
MAYBE 'TASHA DOESN'T KNOW WHERE SHE IS--BUT I DO!
SHE'S BEIN' HELD CAPTIVE SOMEWHERE NEAR--CONEY ISLAND!
THE BLARIN' MUSIC... THE LAUGHIN' SCREAMS FROM THE ROLLER COASTER...
AND, THE DEAD GIVE-AWAY--THE HORN THAT STARTS OFF THE GO-KART RACES!
WELL, LADY, YOU MIGHT JUST GET YOURSELF RESCUED AFTER ALL--
NOT BY SOME NUT PLAYIN' ROBIN HOOD--
--BUT BY A REAL WALKIN', TALKIN' GIANT!
GUESS I HAD THIS IN MIND THE MINUTE HANK SAID HE WAS GIVIN' UP PLAYIN' GOLIATH!
HMMM... THESE THREADS WON'T WIN ANY PRIZES, BUT AT LEAST I CAN MOVE IN 'EM!
AND THIS SERUM OF HIS'LL NEVER REPLACE THE COKE BREAK!
BUT NOW TO SEE IF IT WORKS ON ANYBODY BESIDES BASHFUL BIO-CHEMISTS--!
12

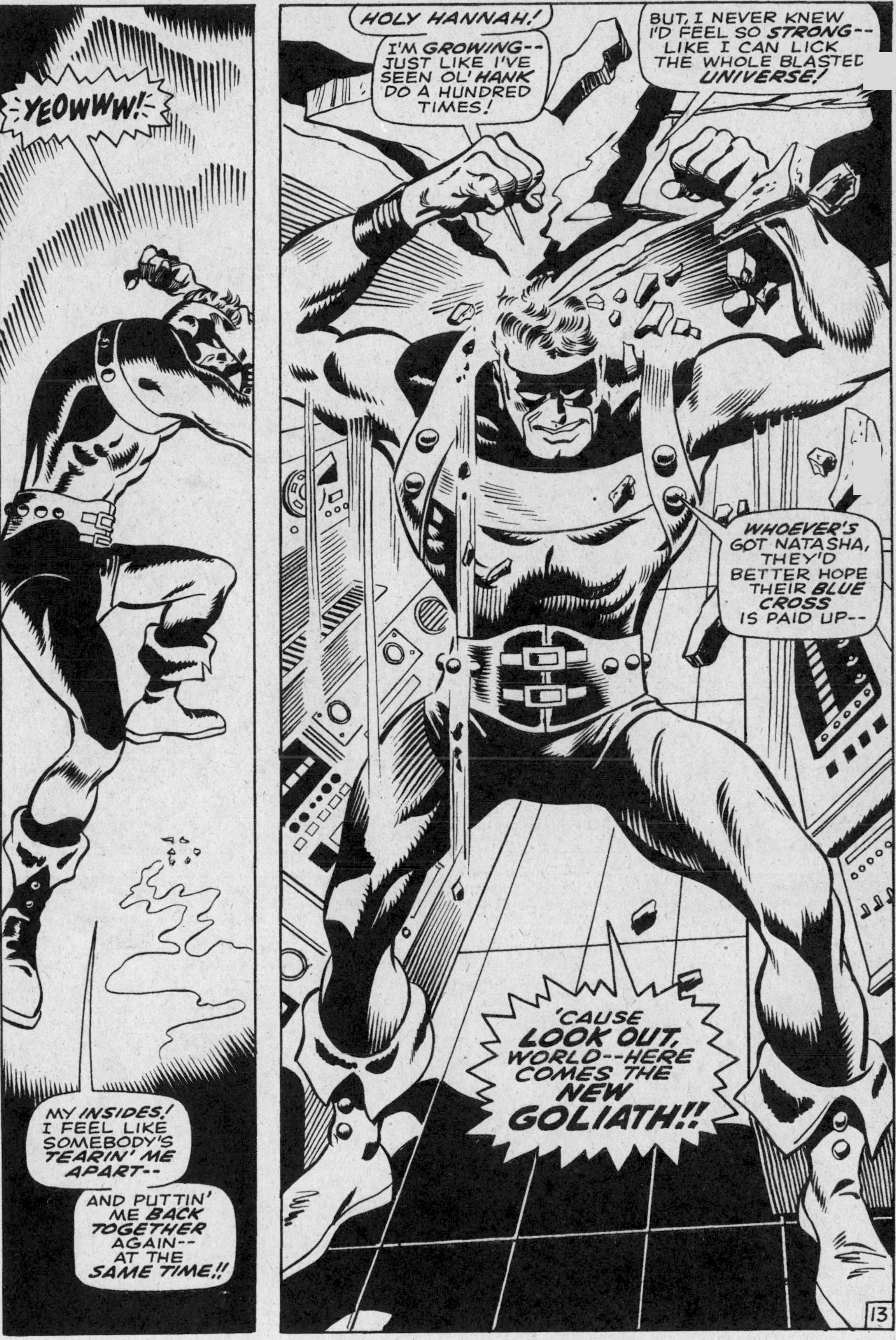
YEOWWW!
MY INSIDES! I FEEL LIKE SOMEBODY'S TEARIN' ME APART--
AND PUTTIN' ME BACK TOGETHER AGAIN-- AT THE SAME TIME!!
HOLY HANNAH!
I'M GROWING-- JUST LIKE I'VE SEEN OL' HANK DO A HUNDRED TIMES!
BUT, I NEVER KNEW I'D FEEL SO STRONG-- LIKE I CAN LICK THE WHOLE BLASTED UNIVERSE!
WHOEVER'S GOT NATASHA, THEY'D BETTER HOPE THEIR BLUE CROSS IS PAID UP--
'CAUSE LOOK OUT, WORLD--HERE COMES THE NEW GOLIATH!!

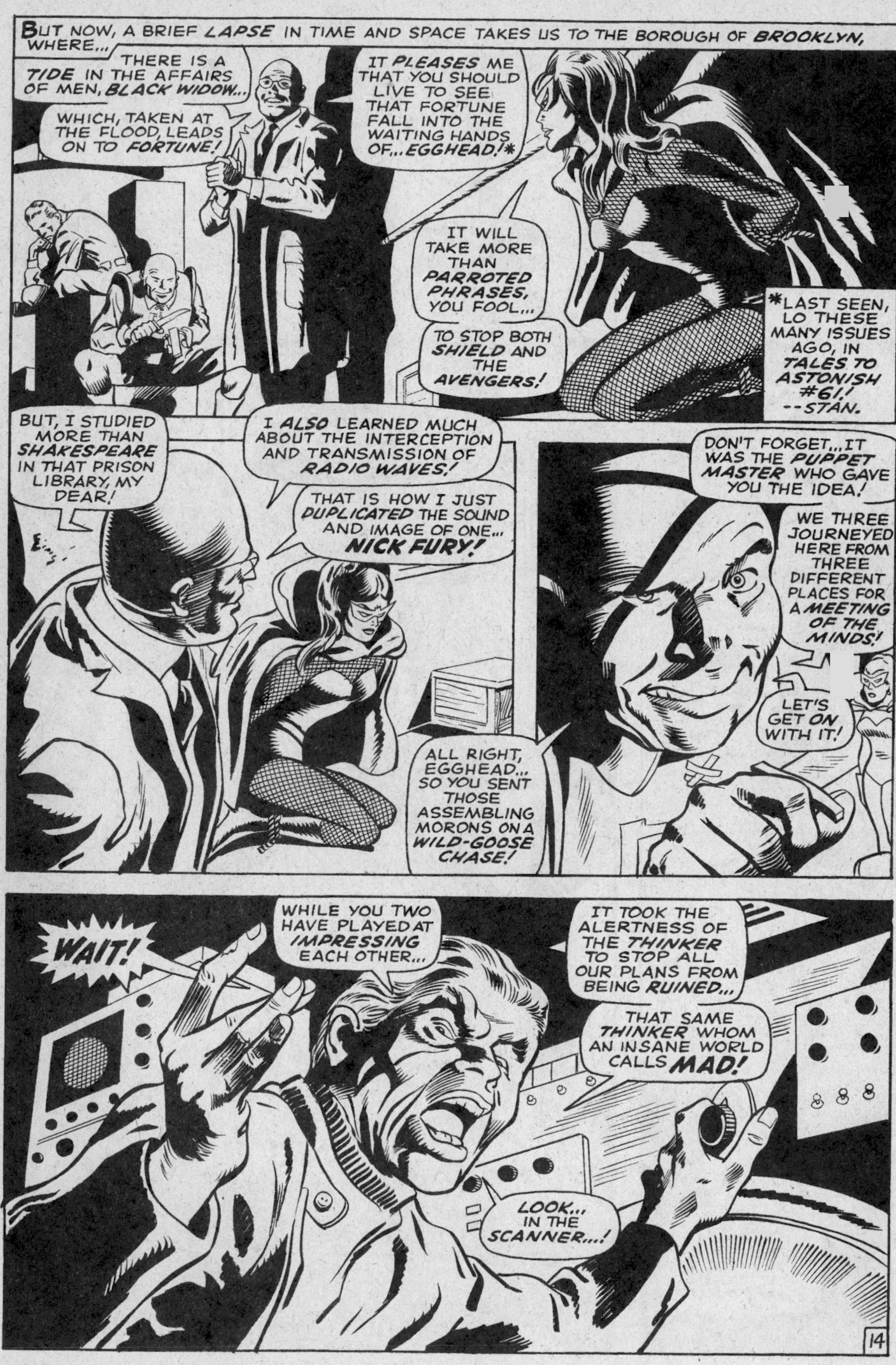

BUT NOW, A BRIEF LAPSE IN TIME AND SPACE TAKES US TO THE BOROUGH OF BROOKLYN, WHERE...
THERE IS A TIDE IN THE AFFAIRS OF MEN, BLACK WIDOW...
WHICH, TAKEN AT THE FLOOD, LEADS ON TO FORTUNE!
IT PLEASES ME THAT YOU SHOULD LIVE TO SEE THAT FORTUNE FALL INTO THE WAITING HANDS OF... EGGHEAD!*
IT WILL TAKE MORE THAN PARROTED PHRASES, YOU FOOL...
TO STOP BOTH SHIELD AND THE AVENGERS!
*LAST SEEN, LO THESE MANY ISSUES AGO, IN TALES TO ASTONISH #61! --STAN.
BUT, I STUDIED MORE THAN SHAKESPEARE IN THAT PRISON LIBRARY, MY DEAR!
I ALSO LEARNED MUCH ABOUT THE INTERCEPTION AND TRANSMISSION OF RADIO WAVES!
THAT IS HOW I JUST DUPLICATED THE SOUND AND IMAGE OF ONE... NICK FURY!
ALL RIGHT, EGGHEAD... SO YOU SENT THOSE ASSEMBLING MORONS ON A WILD-GOOSE CHASE!
DON'T FORGET... IT WAS THE PUPPET MASTER WHO GAVE YOU THE IDEA!
WE THREE JOURNEYED HERE FROM THREE DIFFERENT PLACES FOR A MEETING OF THE MINDS!
LET'S GET ON WITH IT!
WAIT!
WHILE YOU TWO HAVE PLAYED AT IMPRESSING EACH OTHER...
IT TOOK THE ALERTNESS OF THE THINKER TO STOP ALL OUR PLANS FROM BEING RUINED...
THAT SAME THINKER WHOM AN INSANE WORLD CALLS MAD!
LOOK... IN THE SCANNER...!
14

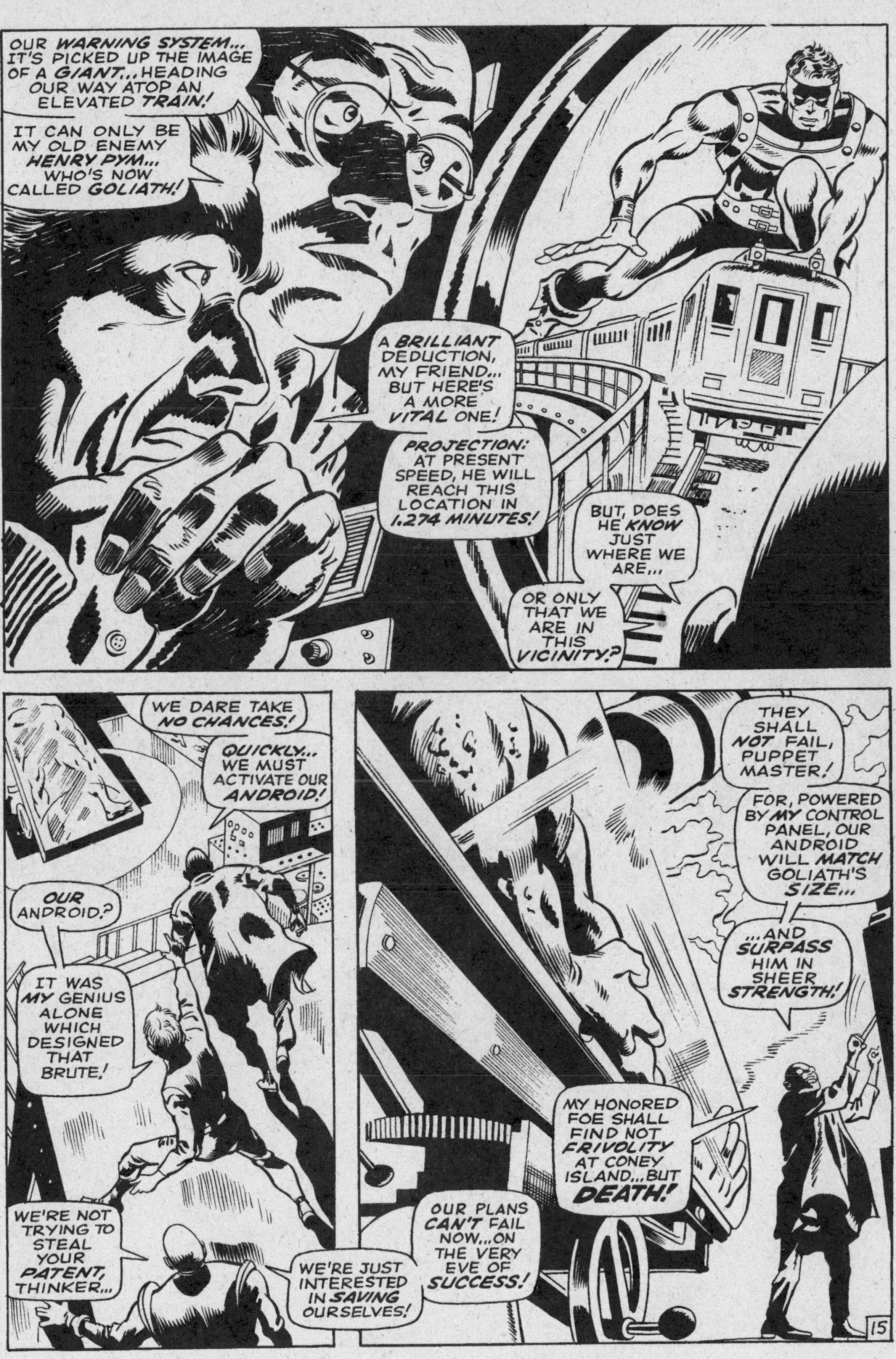
OUR WARNING SYSTEM... IT'S PICKED UP THE IMAGE OF A GIANT... HEADING OUR WAY ATOP AN ELEVATED TRAIN!
IT CAN ONLY BE MY OLD ENEMY HENRY PYM... WHO'S NOW CALLED GOLIATH!
A BRILLIANT DEDUCTION, MY FRIEND... BUT HERE'S A MORE VITAL ONE!
PROJECTION: AT PRESENT SPEED, HE WILL REACH THIS LOCATION IN 1.274 MINUTES!
BUT, DOES HE KNOW JUST WHERE WE ARE...
OR ONLY THAT WE ARE IN THIS VICINITY?
WE DARE TAKE NO CHANCES!
QUICKLY... WE MUST ACTIVATE OUR ANDROID!
OUR ANDROID?
IT WAS MY GENIUS ALONE WHICH DESIGNED THAT BRUTE!
WE'RE NOT TRYING TO STEAL YOUR PATENT, THINKER...
WE'RE JUST INTERESTED IN SAVING OURSELVES!
OUR PLANS CAN'T FAIL NOW... ON THE VERY EVE OF SUCCESS!
THEY SHALL NOT FAIL, PUPPET MASTER!
FOR, POWERED BY MY CONTROL PANEL, OUR ANDROID WILL MATCH GOLIATH'S SIZE...
...AND SURPASS HIM IN SHEER STRENGTH!
MY HONORED FOE SHALL FIND NOT FRIVOLITY AT CONEY ISLAND... BUT DEATH!

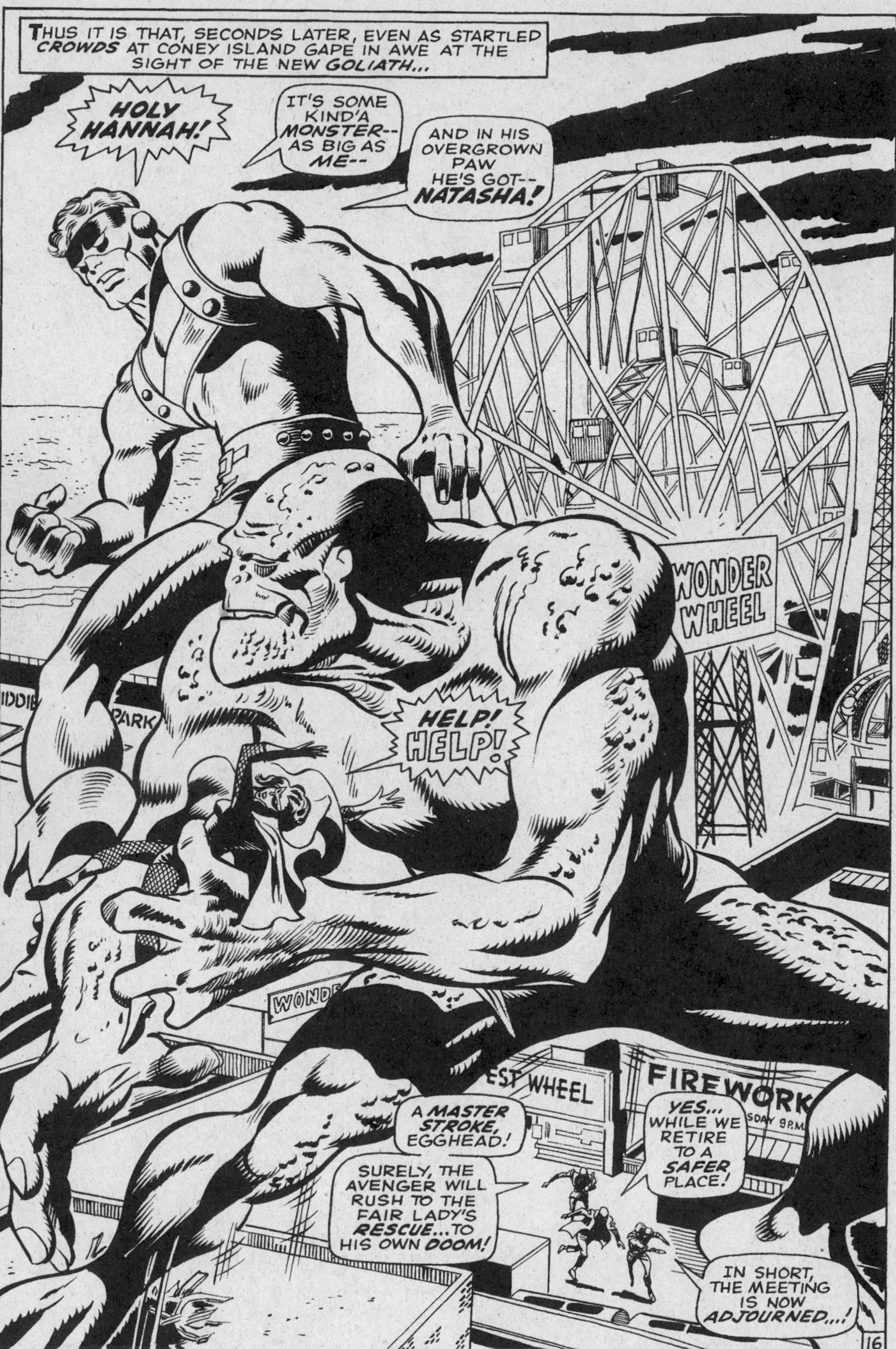
THUS IT IS THAT, SECONDS LATER, EVEN AS STARTLED CROWDS AT CONEY ISLAND GAPE IN AWE AT THE SIGHT OF THE NEW GOLIATH...
HOLY HANNAH!
IT'S SOME KIND'A MONSTER-- AS BIG AS ME--
AND IN HIS OVERGROWN PAW HE'S GOT-- NATASHA!
WONDER WHEEL
PARK
HELP! HELP!
EST WHEEL
FIREWORK
A MASTER STROKE, EGGHEAD!
YES... WHILE WE RETIRE TO A SAFER PLACE!
SURELY, THE AVENGER WILL RUSH TO THE FAIR LADY'S RESCUE...TO HIS OWN DOOM!
IN SHORT, THE MEETING IS NOW ADJOURNED...!
16

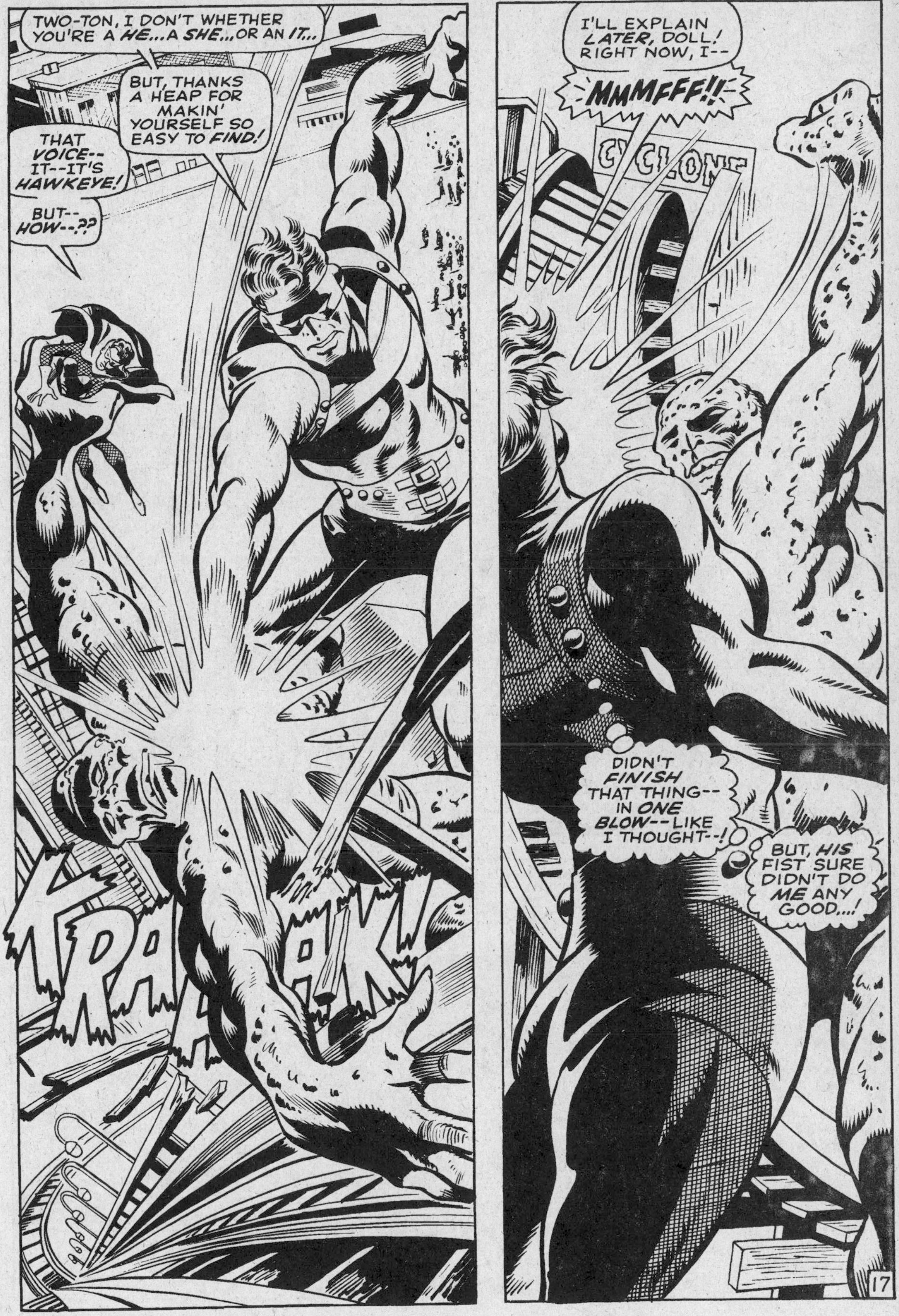

TWO-TON, I DON'T WHETHER YOU'RE A HE...A SHE...OR AN IT...
BUT, THANKS A HEAP FOR MAKIN' YOURSELF SO EASY TO FIND!
THAT VOICE-- IT--IT'S HAWKEYE!
BUT-- HOW--.??
KRAAK
I'LL EXPLAIN LATER, DOLL! RIGHT NOW, I--
MMMFFF!!
CYCLONE
DIDN'T FINISH THAT THING-- IN ONE BLOW--LIKE I THOUGHT--!
BUT, HIS FIST SURE DIDN'T DO ME ANY GOOD...!

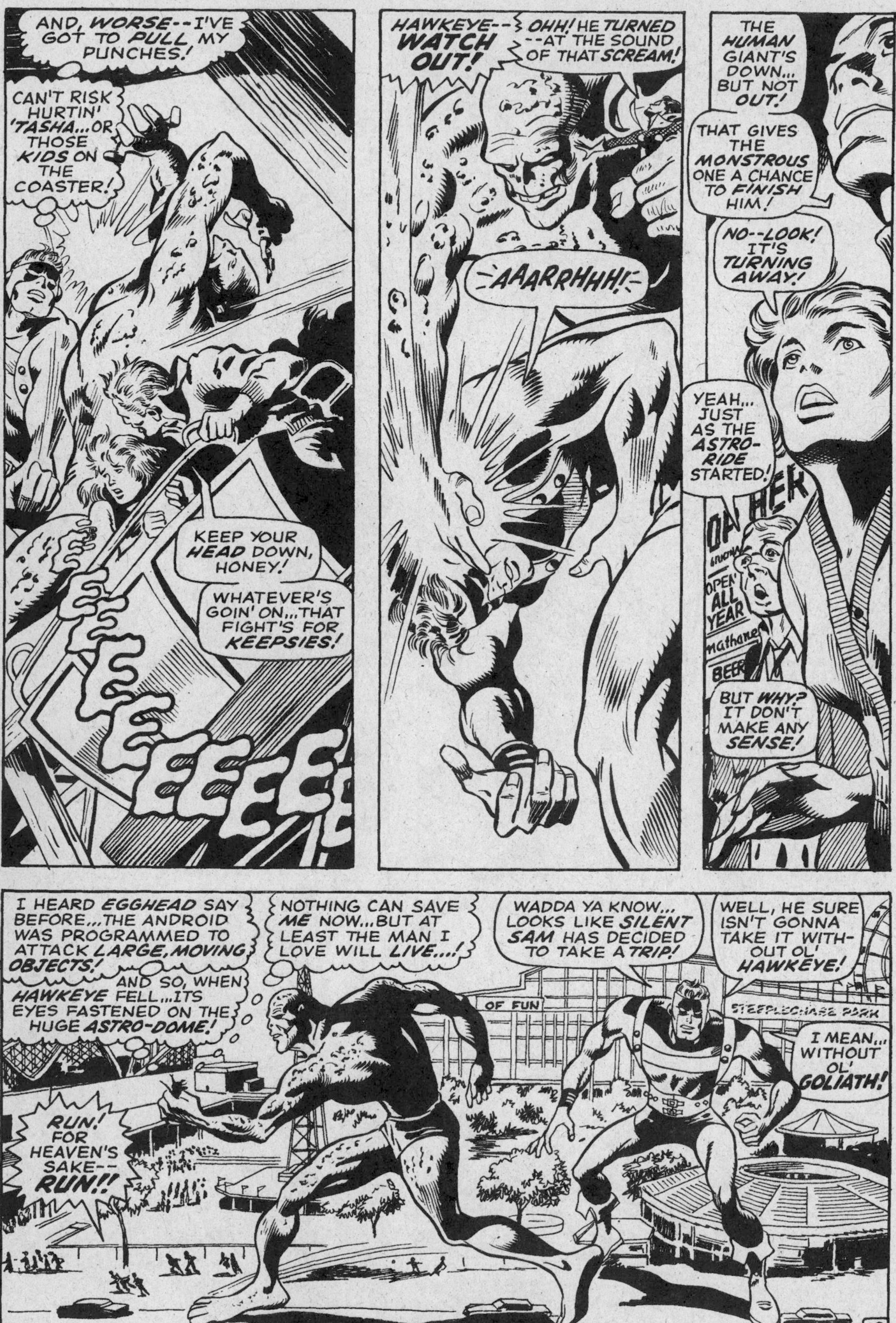
AND, WORSE--I'VE GOT TO PULL MY PUNCHES!
CAN'T RISK HURTIN' 'TASHA...OR THOSE KIDS ON THE COASTER!
KEEP YOUR HEAD DOWN, HONEY!
WHATEVER'S GOIN' ON...THAT FIGHT'S FOR KEEPSIES!
EEEEEE
HAWKEYE--WATCH OUT!
OHH! HE TURNED--AT THE SOUND OF THAT SCREAM!
AAARRHHH!
THE HUMAN GIANT'S DOWN... BUT NOT OUT!
THAT GIVES THE MONSTROUS ONE A CHANCE TO FINISH HIM!
NO--LOOK! IT'S TURNING AWAY!
YEAH... JUST AS THE ASTRO-RIDE STARTED!
OPEN ALL YEAR
BEER
BUT WHY? IT DON'T MAKE ANY SENSE!
I HEARD EGGHEAD SAY BEFORE...THE ANDROID WAS PROGRAMMED TO ATTACK LARGE, MOVING OBJECTS!
AND SO, WHEN HAWKEYE FELL...ITS EYES FASTENED ON THE HUGE ASTRO-DOME!
NOTHING CAN SAVE ME NOW...BUT AT LEAST THE MAN I LOVE WILL LIVE...!
WADDA YA KNOW... LOOKS LIKE SILENT SAM HAS DECIDED TO TAKE A TRIP!
WELL, HE SURE ISN'T GONNA TAKE IT WITH-OUT OL' HAWKEYE!
I MEAN... WITHOUT OL' GOLIATH!
OF FUN
STEEPLECHASE PARK
RUN! FOR HEAVEN'S SAKE--RUN!!
18

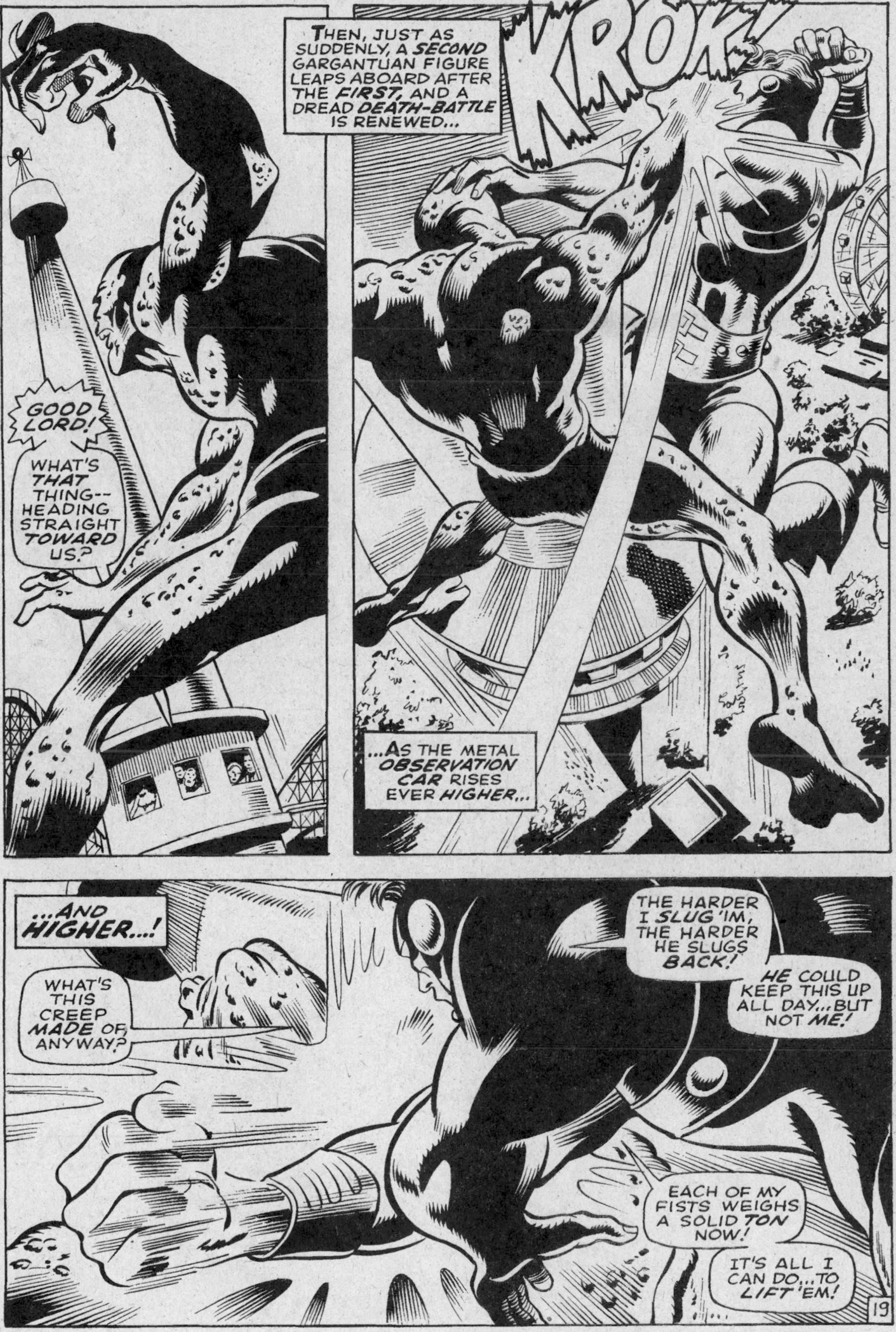
GOOD LORD!
WHAT'S THAT THING-- HEADING STRAIGHT TOWARD US?
THEN, JUST AS SUDDENLY, A SECOND GARGANTUAN FIGURE LEAPS ABOARD AFTER THE FIRST, AND A DREAD DEATH-BATTLE IS RENEWED...
KROK!
...AS THE METAL OBSERVATION CAR RISES EVER HIGHER...
...AND HIGHER...!
WHAT'S THIS CREEP MADE OF, ANYWAY?
THE HARDER I SLUG 'IM, THE HARDER HE SLUGS BACK!
HE COULD KEEP THIS UP ALL DAY...BUT NOT ME!
EACH OF MY FISTS WEIGHS A SOLID TON NOW!
IT'S ALL I CAN DO...TO LIFT 'EM!
19

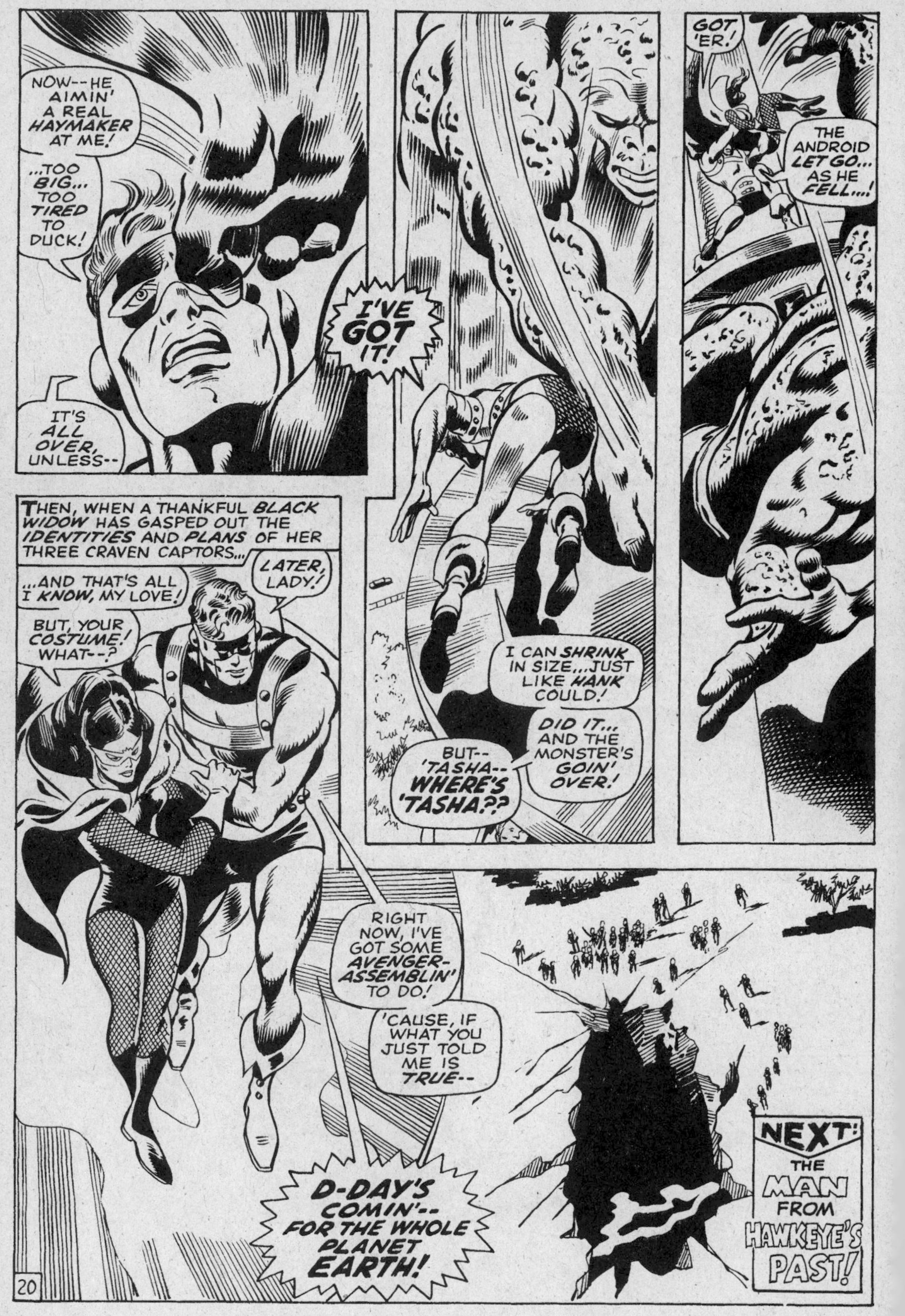
NOW--HE AIMIN' A REAL HAYMAKER AT ME!
...TOO BIG... TOO TIRED TO DUCK!
IT'S ALL OVER, UNLESS--
I'VE GOT IT!
GOT 'ER!
THE ANDROID LET GO... AS HE FELL...!
THEN, WHEN A THANKFUL BLACK WIDOW HAS GASPED OUT THE IDENTITIES AND PLANS OF HER THREE CRAVEN CAPTORS...
...AND THAT'S ALL I KNOW, MY LOVE!
LATER, LADY!
BUT, YOUR COSTUME! WHAT--?
I CAN SHRINK IN SIZE... JUST LIKE HANK COULD!
DID IT... AND THE MONSTER'S GOIN' OVER!
BUT-- 'TASHA-- WHERE'S 'TASHA??
RIGHT NOW, I'VE GOT SOME AVENGER-ASSEMBLIN' TO DO!
'CAUSE, IF WHAT YOU JUST TOLD ME IS TRUE--
D-DAY'S COMIN'-- FOR THE WHOLE PLANET EARTH!
NEXT: THE MAN FROM HAWKEYE'S PAST!
20

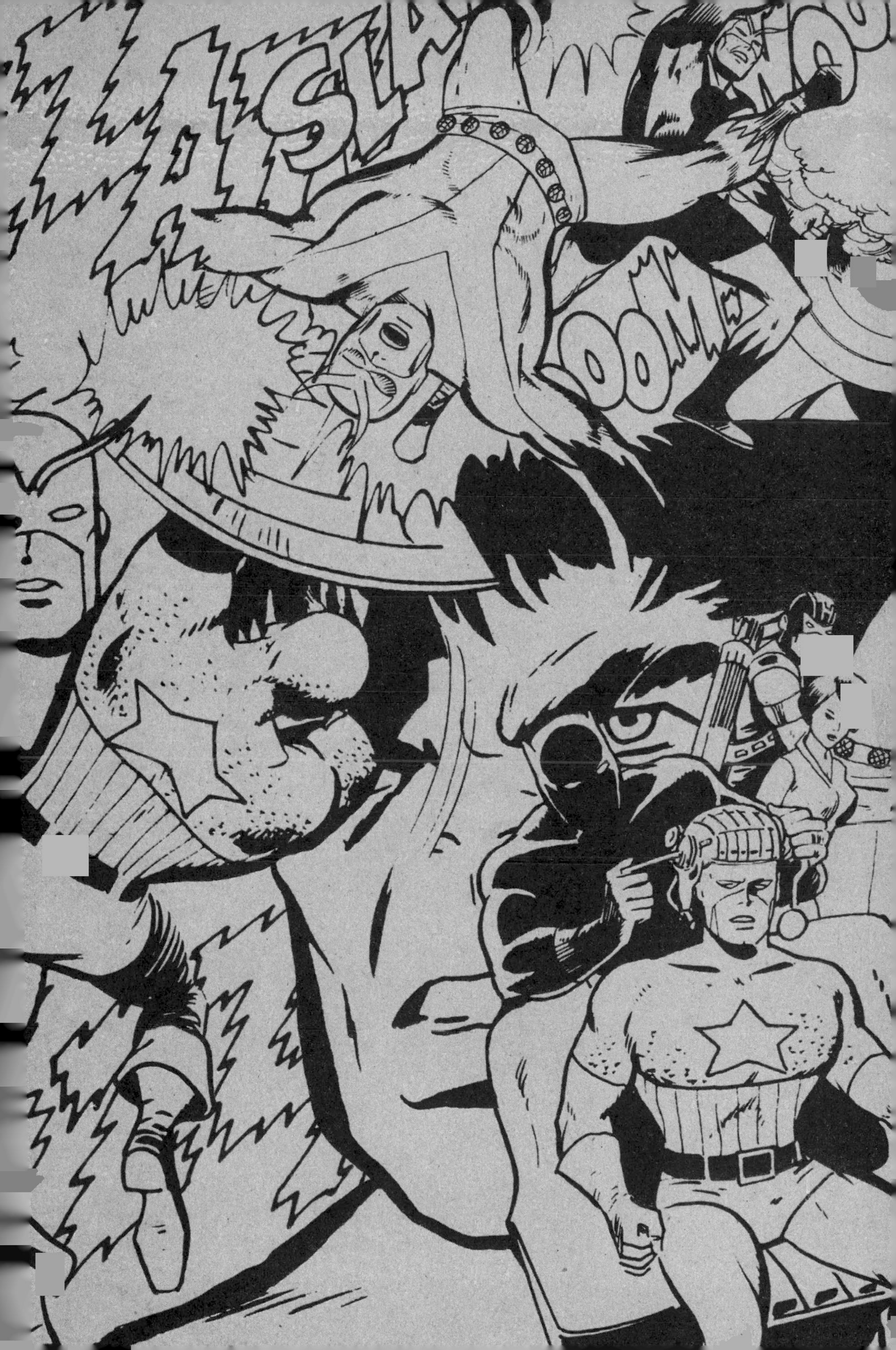

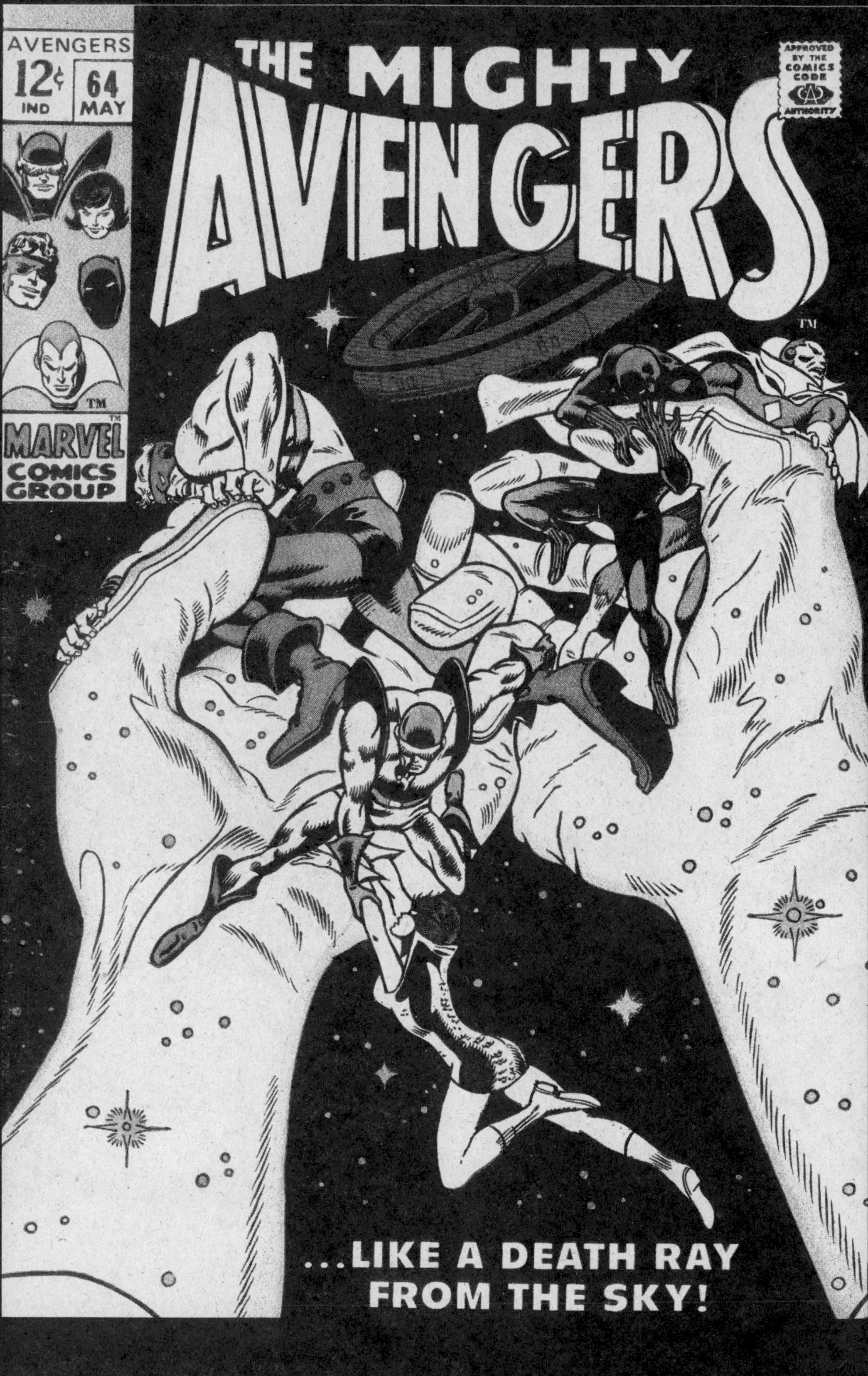
AVENGERS
12¢ IND
64 MAY
THE MIGHTY AVENGERS
APPROVED BY THE COMICS CODE AUTHORITY
MARVEL COMICS GROUP
...LIKE A DEATH RAY FROM THE SKY!

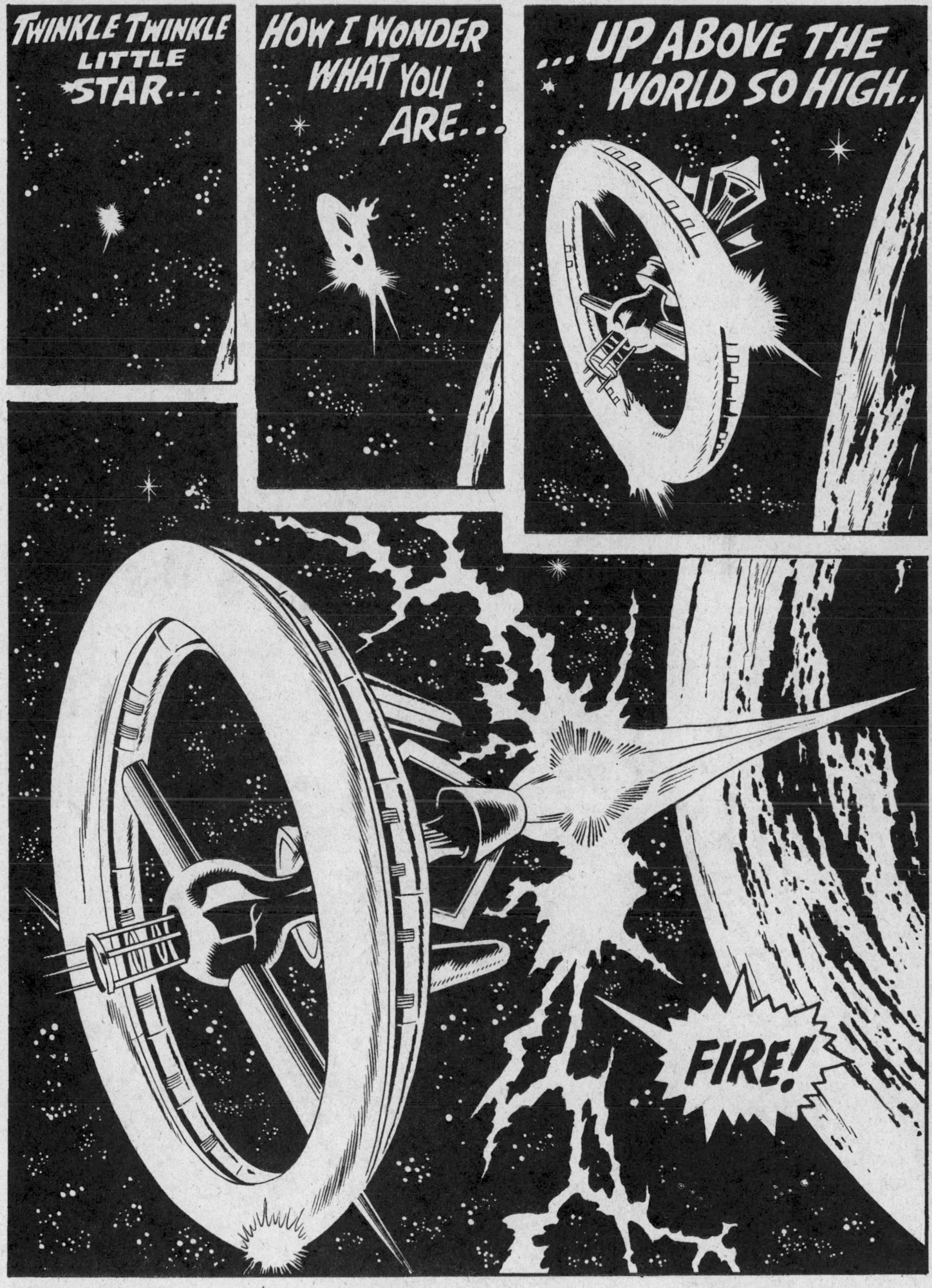
TWINKLE TWINKLE LITTLE STAR...
HOW I WONDER WHAT YOU ARE...
... UP ABOVE THE WORLD SO HIGH..
FIRE!

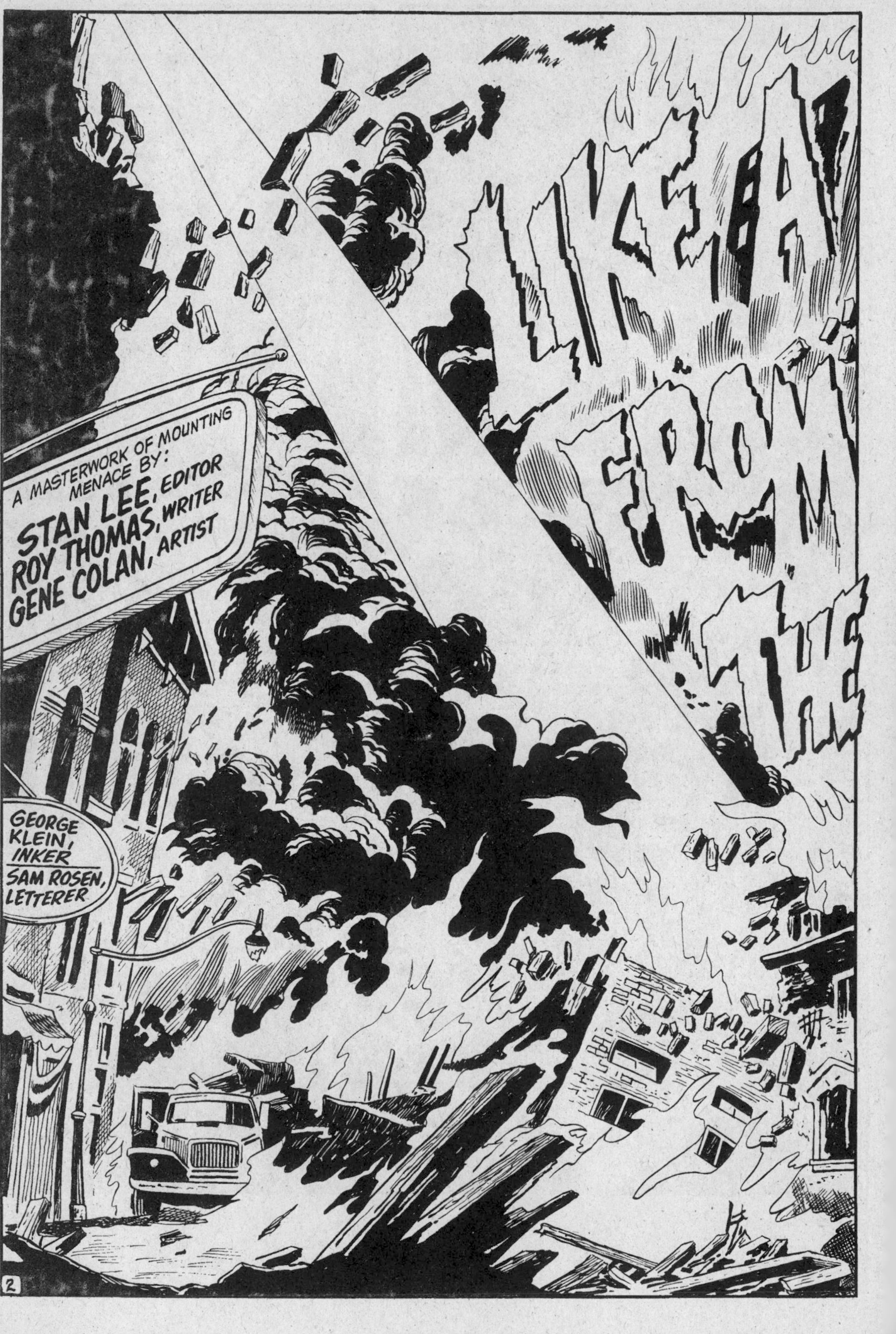
LIKE A
FROM
THE
A MASTERWORK OF MOUNTING MENACE BY:
STAN LEE, EDITOR
ROY THOMAS, WRITER
GENE COLAN, ARTIST
GEORGE KLEIN, INKER
SAM ROSEN, LETTERER

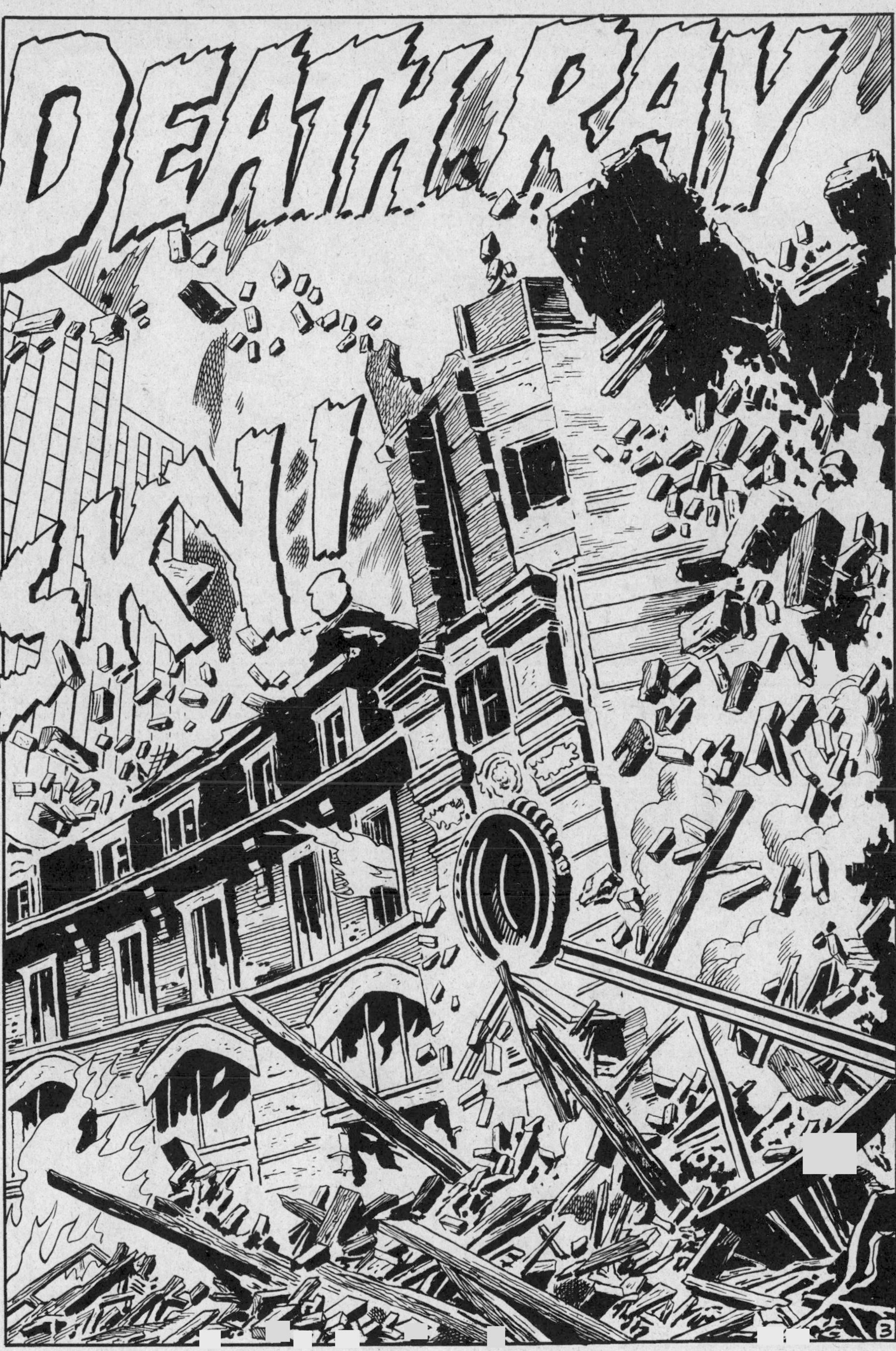
DEATH RAY

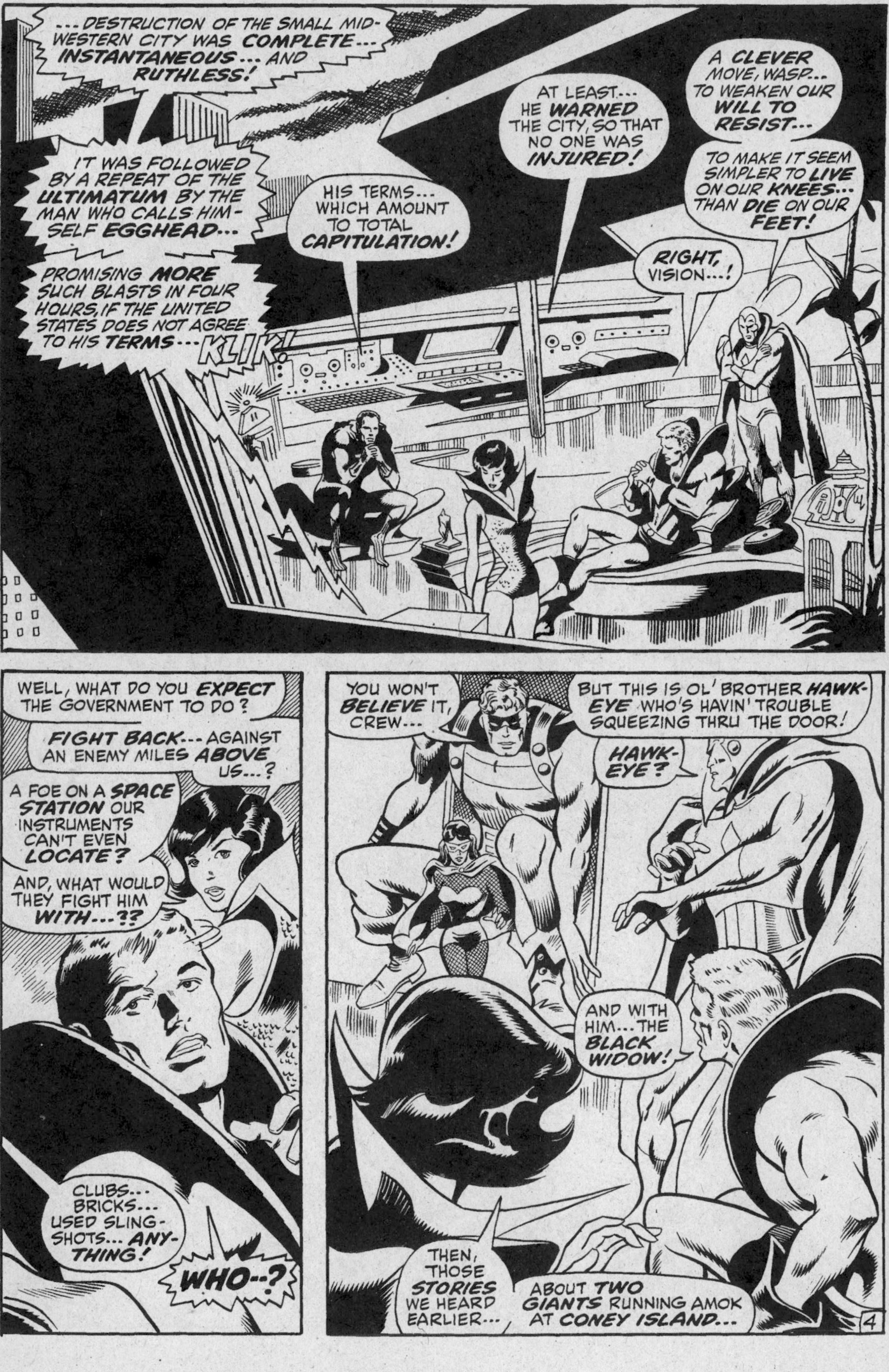

...DESTRUCTION OF THE SMALL MID-WESTERN CITY WAS COMPLETE... INSTANTANEOUS... AND RUTHLESS!
IT WAS FOLLOWED BY A REPEAT OF THE ULTIMATUM BY THE MAN WHO CALLS HIMSELF EGGHEAD...
PROMISING MORE SUCH BLASTS IN FOUR HOURS, IF THE UNITED STATES DOES NOT AGREE TO HIS TERMS---
KLIK!
HIS TERMS... WHICH AMOUNT TO TOTAL CAPITULATION!
AT LEAST... HE WARNED THE CITY, SO THAT NO ONE WAS INJURED!
A CLEVER MOVE, WASP... TO WEAKEN OUR WILL TO RESIST...
TO MAKE IT SEEM SIMPLER TO LIVE ON OUR KNEES... THAN DIE ON OUR FEET!
RIGHT, VISION...!
WELL, WHAT DO YOU EXPECT THE GOVERNMENT TO DO?
FIGHT BACK... AGAINST AN ENEMY MILES ABOVE US...?
A FOE ON A SPACE STATION OUR INSTRUMENTS CAN'T EVEN LOCATE?
AND, WHAT WOULD THEY FIGHT HIM WITH...??
CLUBS... BRICKS... USED SLING-SHOTS... ANYTHING!
WHO--?
YOU WON'T BELIEVE IT, CREW...
BUT THIS IS OL' BROTHER HAWK-EYE WHO'S HAVIN' TROUBLE SQUEEZING THRU THE DOOR!
HAWK-EYE?
AND WITH HIM... THE BLACK WIDOW!
THEN, THOSE STORIES WE HEARD EARLIER...
ABOUT TWO GIANTS RUNNING AMOK AT CONEY ISLAND...
4

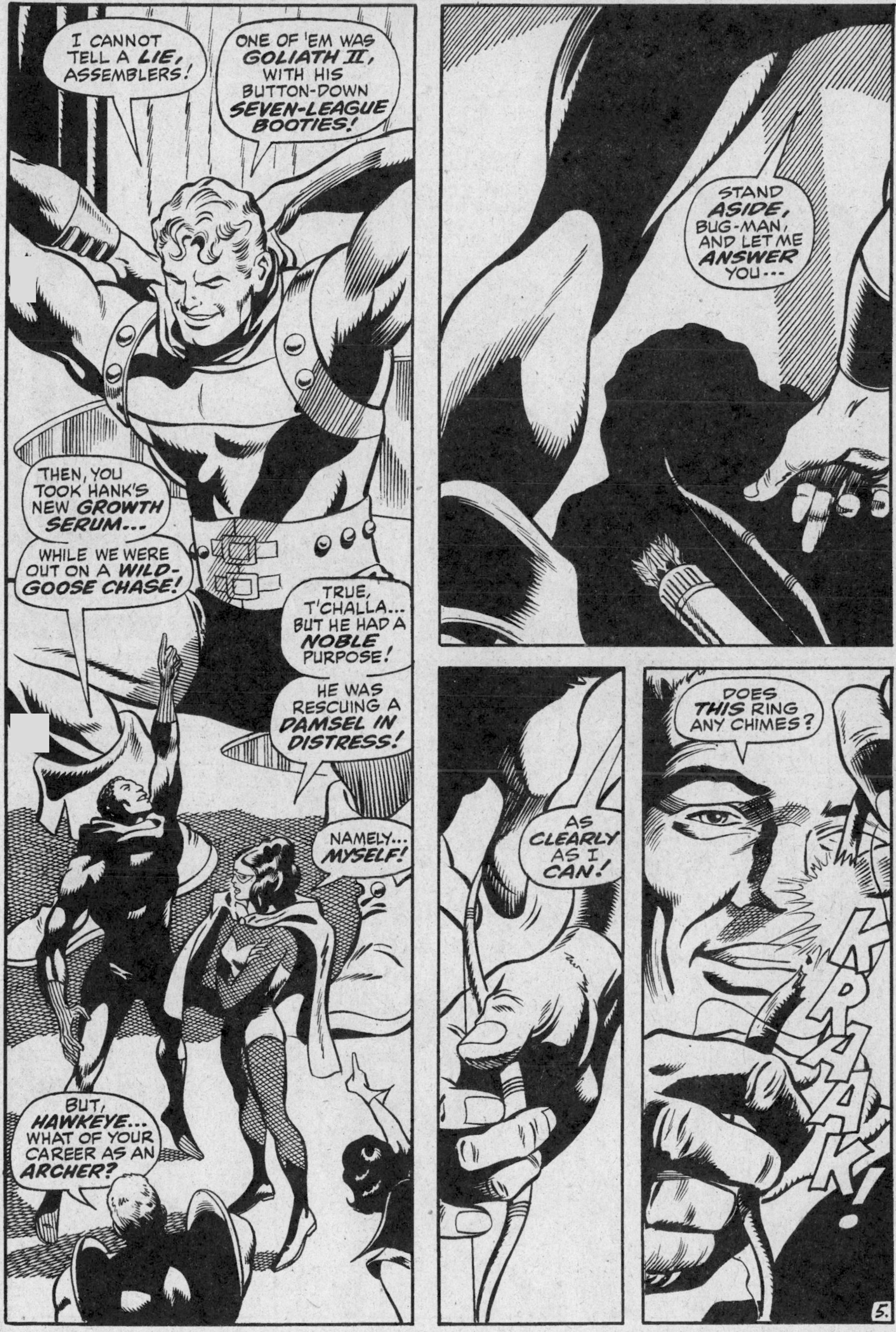
I CANNOT TELL A LIE, ASSEMBLERS!
ONE OF 'EM WAS GOLIATH II, WITH HIS BUTTON-DOWN SEVEN-LEAGUE BOOTIES!
THEN, YOU TOOK HANK'S NEW GROWTH SERUM...
WHILE WE WERE OUT ON A WILD-GOOSE CHASE!
TRUE, T'CHALLA... BUT HE HAD A NOBLE PURPOSE!
HE WAS RESCUING A DAMSEL IN DISTRESS!
NAMELY... MYSELF!
BUT, HAWKEYE... WHAT OF YOUR CAREER AS AN ARCHER?
STAND ASIDE, BUG-MAN, AND LET ME ANSWER YOU...
AS CLEARLY AS I CAN!
DOES THIS RING ANY CHIMES?
KRAAK!

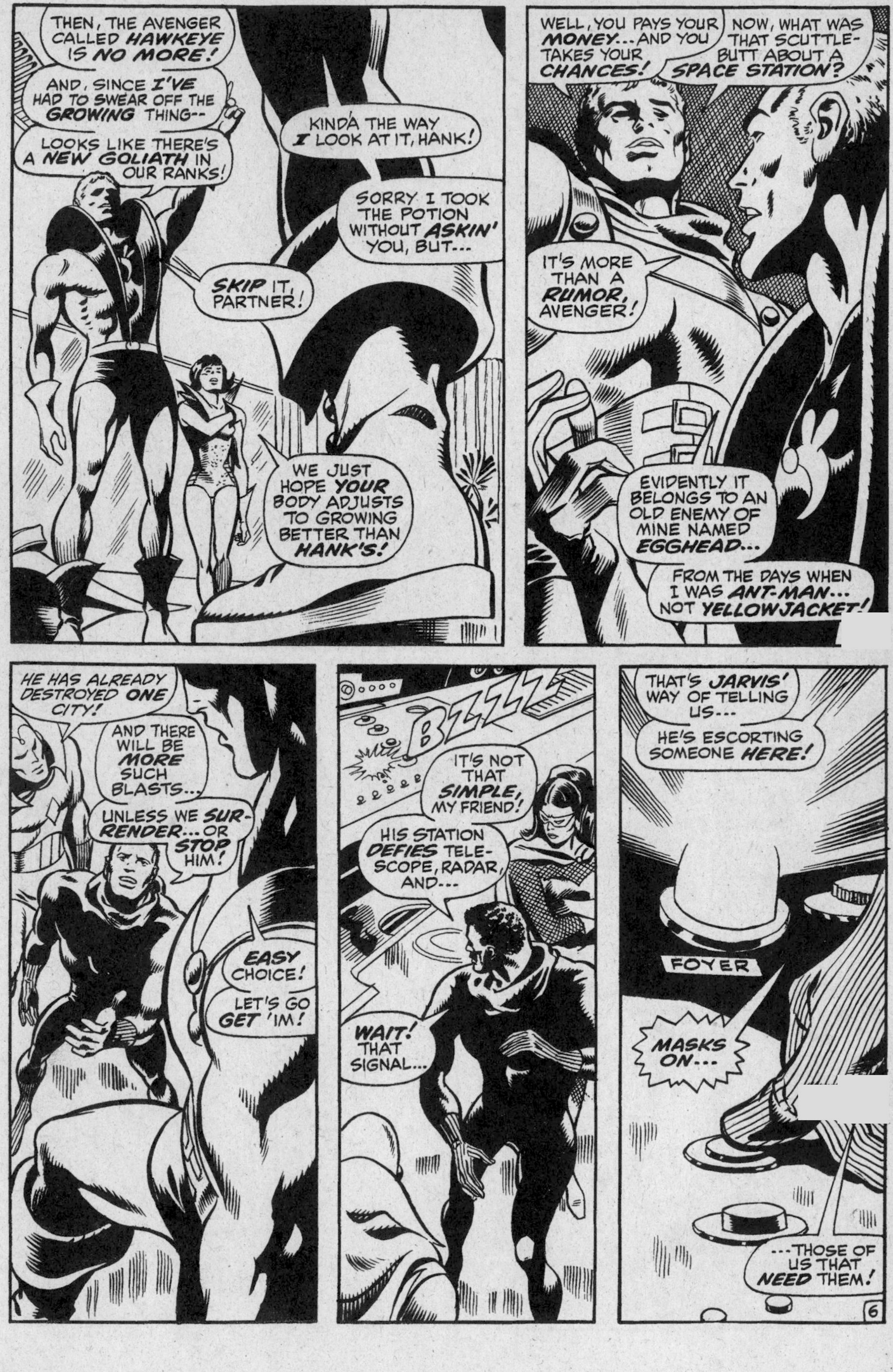
THEN, THE AVENGER CALLED HAWKEYE IS NO MORE!
AND, SINCE I'VE HAD TO SWEAR OFF THE GROWING THING--
LOOKS LIKE THERE'S A NEW GOLIATH IN OUR RANKS!
KIND'A THE WAY I LOOK AT IT, HANK!
SORRY I TOOK THE POTION WITHOUT ASKIN' YOU, BUT...
SKIP IT, PARTNER!
WE JUST HOPE YOUR BODY ADJUSTS TO GROWING BETTER THAN HANK'S!
WELL, YOU PAYS YOUR MONEY... AND YOU TAKES YOUR CHANCES!
NOW, WHAT WAS THAT SCUTTLE-BUTT ABOUT A SPACE STATION?
IT'S MORE THAN A RUMOR, AVENGER!
EVIDENTLY IT BELONGS TO AN OLD ENEMY OF MINE NAMED EGGHEAD...
FROM THE DAYS WHEN I WAS ANT-MAN... NOT YELLOWJACKET!
HE HAS ALREADY DESTROYED ONE CITY!
AND THERE WILL BE MORE SUCH BLASTS...
UNLESS WE SURRENDER... OR STOP HIM!
EASY CHOICE!
LET'S GO GET 'IM!
BZZZZ
IT'S NOT THAT SIMPLE, MY FRIEND!
HIS STATION DEFIES TELESCOPE, RADAR, AND...
WAIT! THAT SIGNAL...
THAT'S JARVIS' WAY OF TELLING US...
HE'S ESCORTING SOMEONE HERE!
FOYER
MASKS ON...
...THOSE OF US THAT NEED THEM!
6

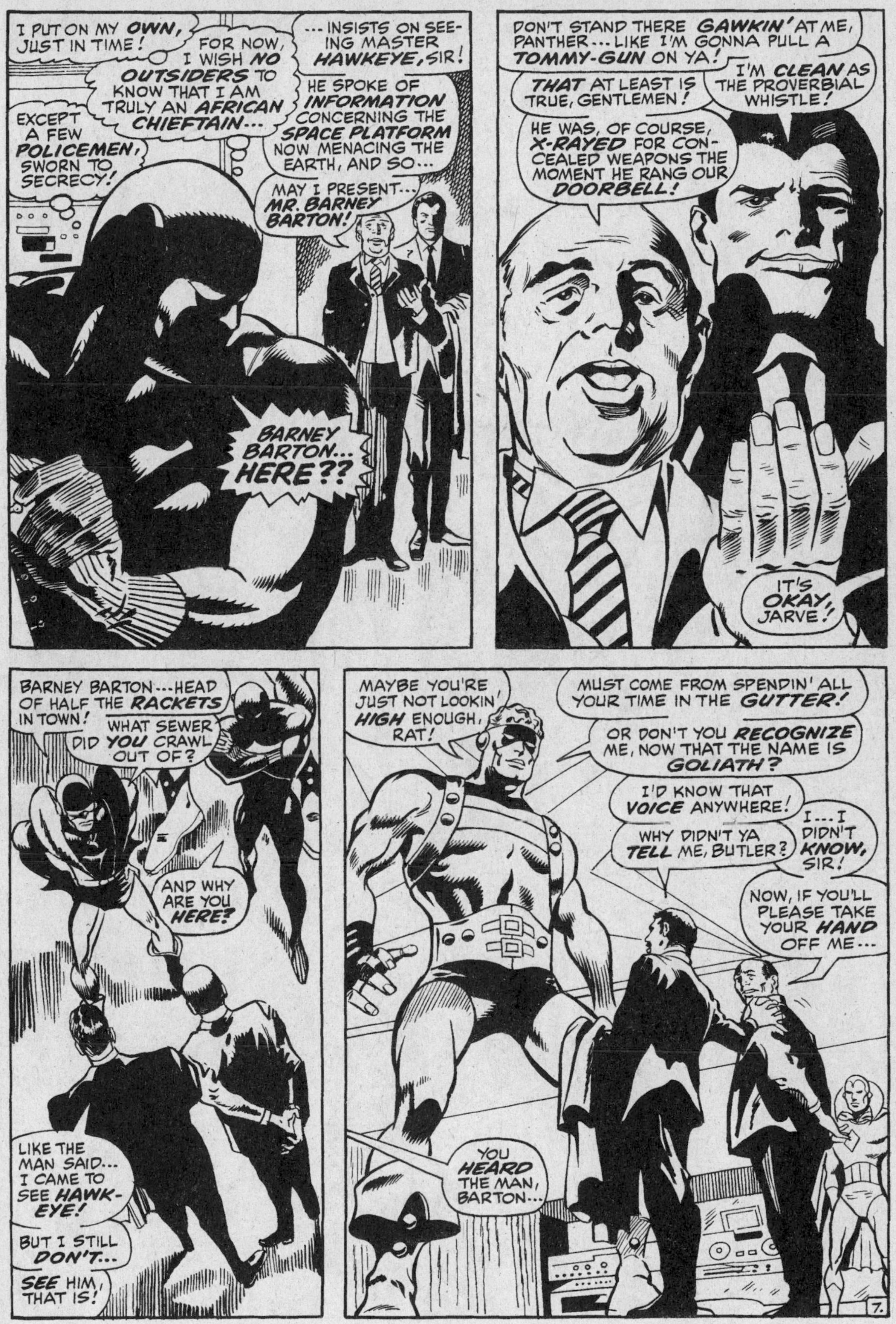

I PUT ON MY OWN, JUST IN TIME!
FOR NOW, I WISH NO OUTSIDERS TO KNOW THAT I AM TRULY AN AFRICAN CHIEFTAIN...
EXCEPT A FEW POLICEMEN, SWORN TO SECRECY!
...INSISTS ON SEEING MASTER HAWKEYE, SIR!
HE SPOKE OF INFORMATION CONCERNING THE SPACE PLATFORM NOW MENACING THE EARTH, AND SO...
MAY I PRESENT... MR. BARNEY BARTON!
BARNEY BARTON... HERE??
DON'T STAND THERE GAWKIN' AT ME, PANTHER... LIKE I'M GONNA PULL A TOMMY-GUN ON YA!
I'M CLEAN AS THE PROVERBIAL WHISTLE!
THAT AT LEAST IS TRUE, GENTLEMEN!
HE WAS, OF COURSE, X-RAYED FOR CONCEALED WEAPONS THE MOMENT HE RANG OUR DOORBELL!
IT'S OKAY, JARVE!
BARNEY BARTON... HEAD OF HALF THE RACKETS IN TOWN!
WHAT SEWER DID YOU CRAWL OUT OF?
AND WHY ARE YOU HERE?
LIKE THE MAN SAID... I CAME TO SEE HAWK-EYE!
BUT I STILL DON'T...
SEE HIM, THAT IS!
MAYBE YOU'RE JUST NOT LOOKIN' HIGH ENOUGH, RAT!
MUST COME FROM SPENDIN' ALL YOUR TIME IN THE GUTTER!
OR DON'T YOU RECOGNIZE ME, NOW THAT THE NAME IS GOLIATH?
I'D KNOW THAT VOICE ANYWHERE!
WHY DIDN'T YA TELL ME, BUTLER?
I... I DIDN'T KNOW, SIR!
NOW, IF YOU'LL PLEASE TAKE YOUR HAND OFF ME...
YOU HEARD THE MAN, BARTON...

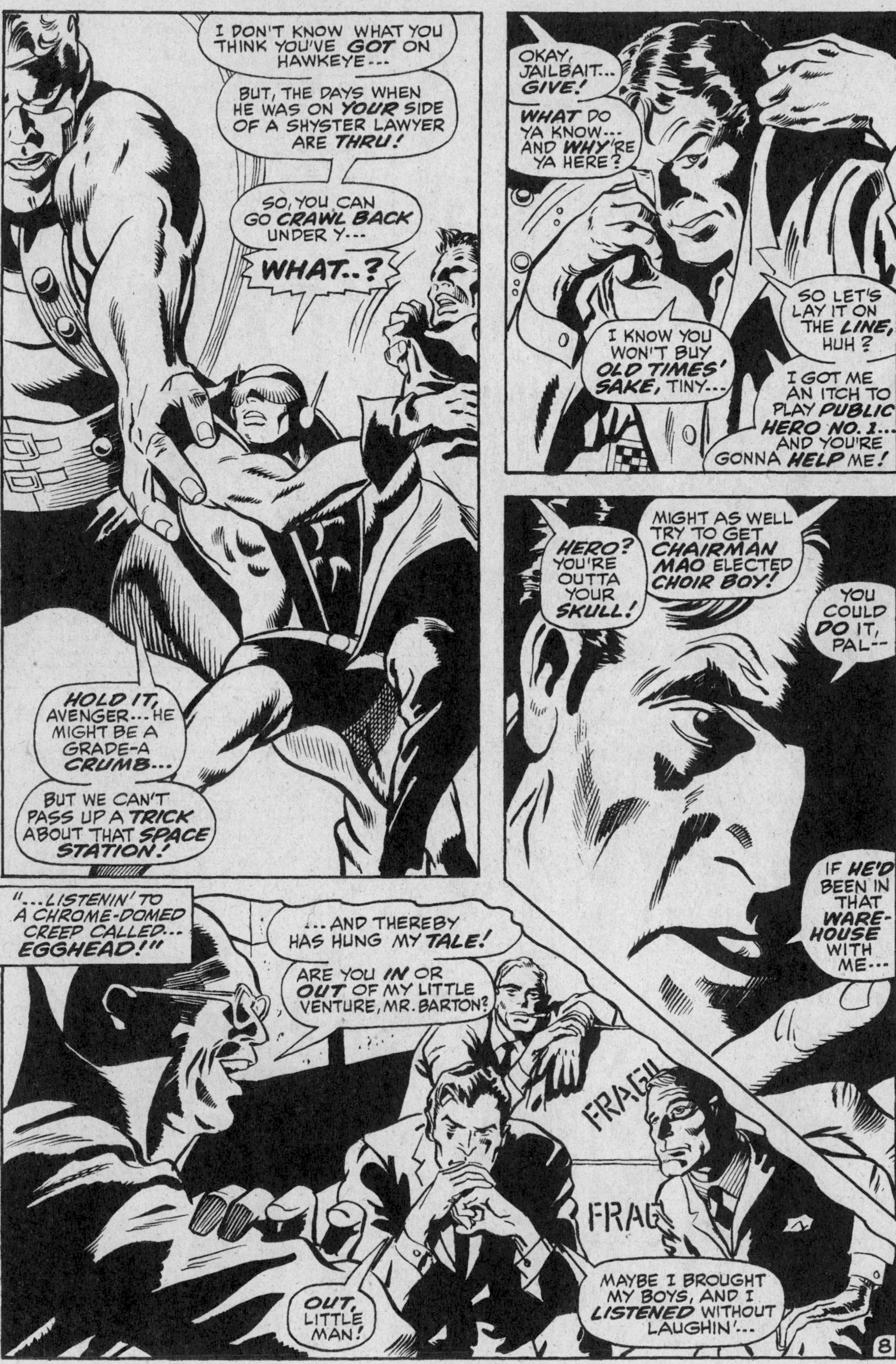
I DON'T KNOW WHAT YOU THINK YOU'VE GOT ON HAWKEYE---
BUT, THE DAYS WHEN HE WAS ON YOUR SIDE OF A SHYSTER LAWYER ARE THRU!
SO, YOU CAN GO CRAWL BACK UNDER Y---
WHAT..?
HOLD IT, AVENGER--- HE MIGHT BE A GRADE-A CRUMB...
BUT WE CAN'T PASS UP A TRICK ABOUT THAT SPACE STATION!
OKAY, JAILBAIT... GIVE!
WHAT DO YA KNOW... AND WHY'RE YA HERE?
I KNOW YOU WON'T BUY OLD TIMES' SAKE, TINY...
SO LET'S LAY IT ON THE LINE, HUH?
I GOT ME AN ITCH TO PLAY PUBLIC HERO NO. 1... AND YOU'RE GONNA HELP ME!
HERO? YOU'RE OUTTA YOUR SKULL!
MIGHT AS WELL TRY TO GET CHAIRMAN MAO ELECTED CHOIR BOY!
YOU COULD DO IT, PAL--
IF HE'D BEEN IN THAT WARE-HOUSE WITH ME...
"...LISTENIN' TO A CHROME-DOMED CREEP CALLED... EGGHEAD!"
...AND THEREBY HAS HUNG MY TALE!
ARE YOU IN OR OUT OF MY LITTLE VENTURE, MR. BARTON?
FRAG!
FRAG
OUT, LITTLE MAN!
MAYBE I BROUGHT MY BOYS, AND I LISTENED WITHOUT LAUGHIN'...
8

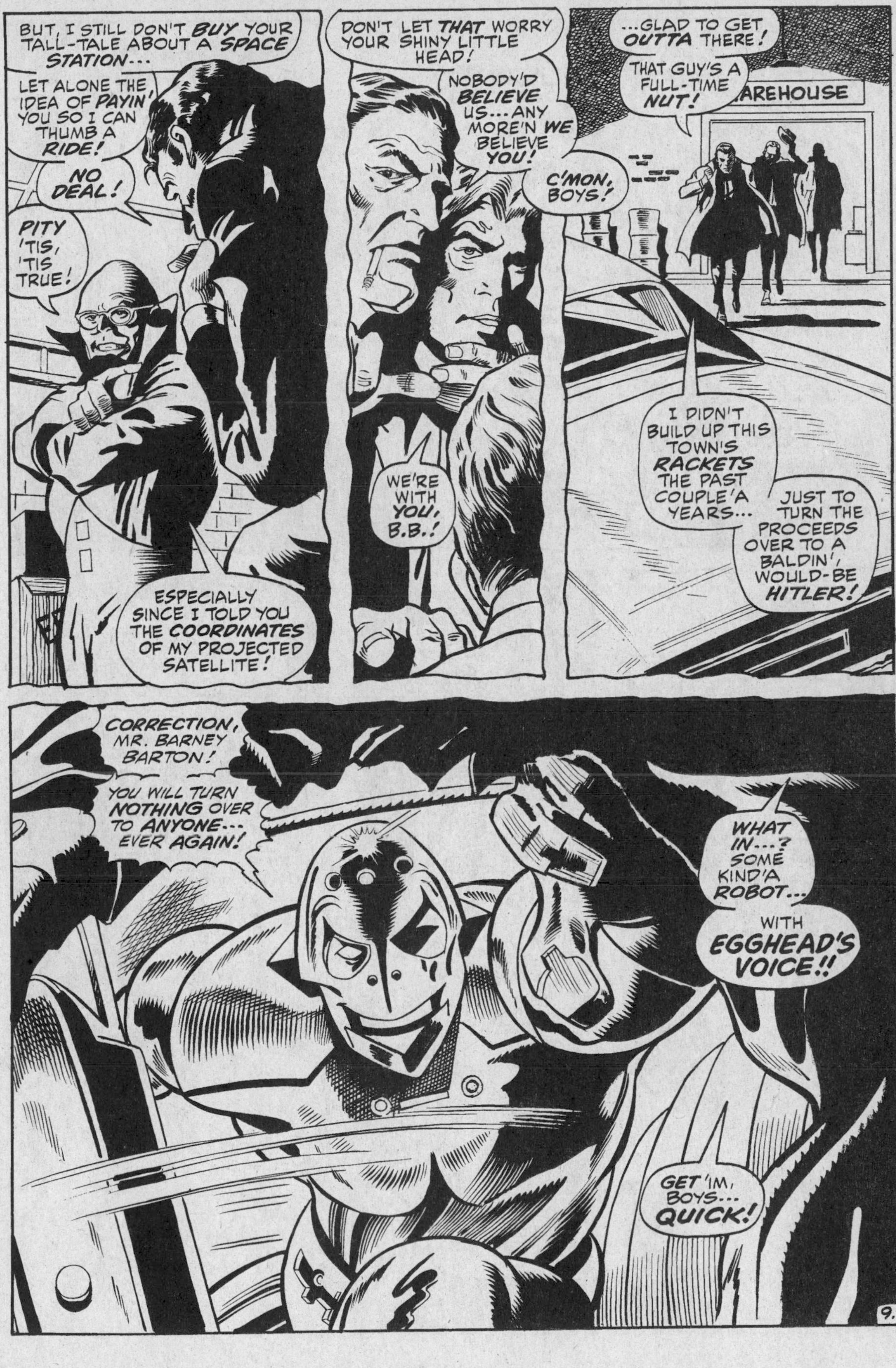

BUT, I STILL DON'T BUY YOUR TALL-TALE ABOUT A SPACE STATION...
LET ALONE THE IDEA OF PAYIN' YOU SO I CAN THUMB A RIDE!
NO DEAL!
PITY 'TIS, 'TIS TRUE!
ESPECIALLY SINCE I TOLD YOU THE COORDINATES OF MY PROJECTED SATELLITE!
DON'T LET THAT WORRY YOUR SHINY LITTLE HEAD!
NOBODY'D BELIEVE US... ANY MORE'N WE BELIEVE YOU!
WE'RE WITH YOU, B.B.!
...GLAD TO GET OUTTA THERE!
THAT GUY'S A FULL-TIME NUT!
AREHOUSE
C'MON, BOYS!
I DIDN'T BUILD UP THIS TOWN'S RACKETS THE PAST COUPLE'A YEARS...
JUST TO TURN THE PROCEEDS OVER TO A BALDIN', WOULD-BE HITLER!
CORRECTION, MR. BARNEY BARTON!
YOU WILL TURN NOTHING OVER TO ANYONE... EVER AGAIN!
WHAT IN...? SOME KIND'A ROBOT...
WITH EGGHEAD'S VOICE!!
GET 'IM, BOYS... QUICK!
9.

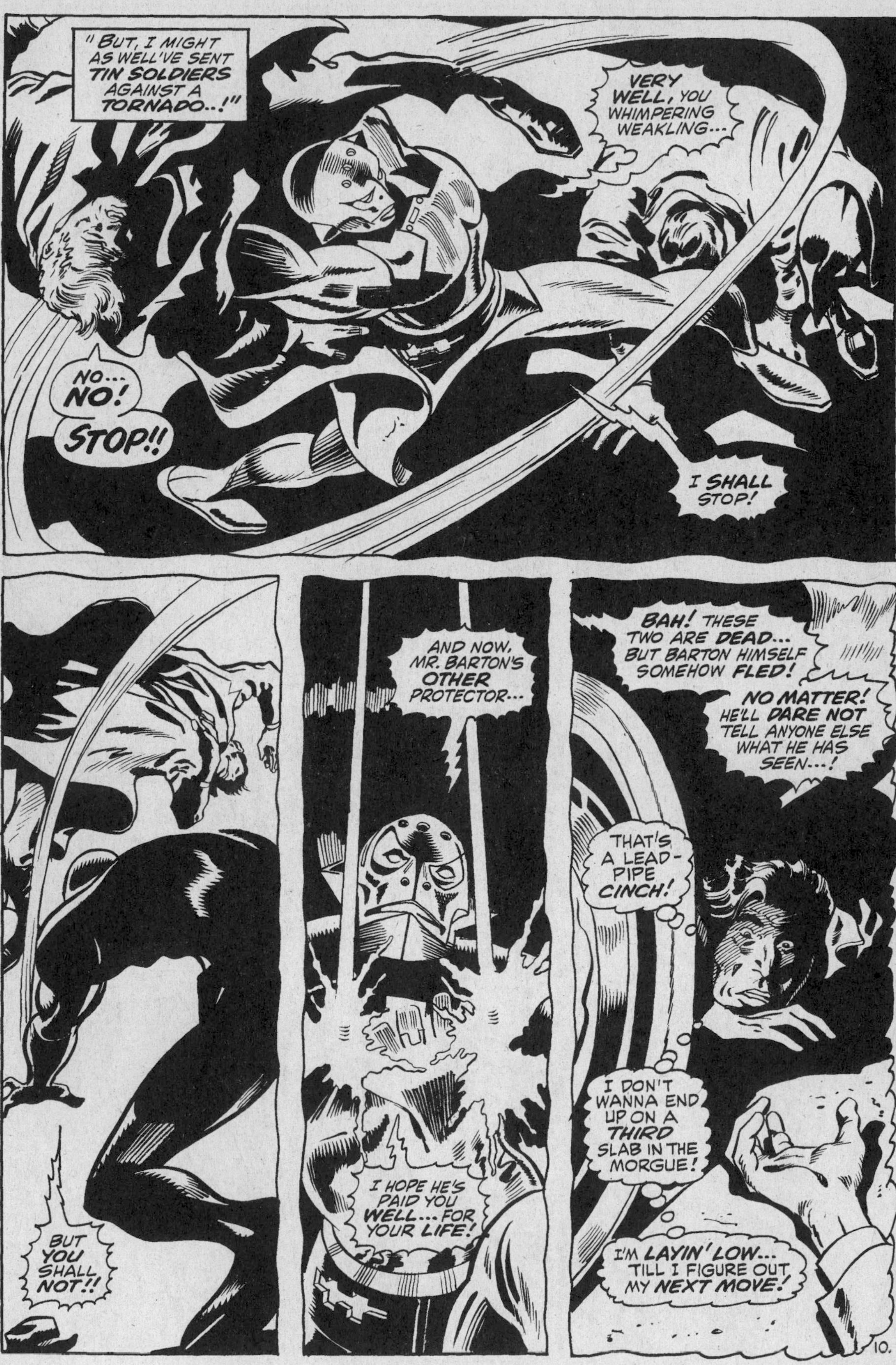
" BUT, I MIGHT AS WELL'VE SENT TIN SOLDIERS AGAINST A TORNADO..!"
VERY WELL, YOU WHIMPERING WEAKLING...
NO... NO!
STOP!!
I SHALL STOP!
BUT YOU SHALL NOT!!
AND NOW, MR. BARTON'S OTHER PROTECTOR...
I HOPE HE'S PAID YOU WELL... FOR YOUR LIFE!
BAH! THESE TWO ARE DEAD... BUT BARTON HIMSELF SOMEHOW FLED!
NO MATTER! HE'LL DARE NOT TELL ANYONE ELSE WHAT HE HAS SEEN...!
THAT'S A LEAD-PIPE CINCH!
I DON'T WANNA END UP ON A THIRD SLAB IN THE MORGUE!
I'M LAYIN' LOW... TILL I FIGURE OUT MY NEXT MOVE!

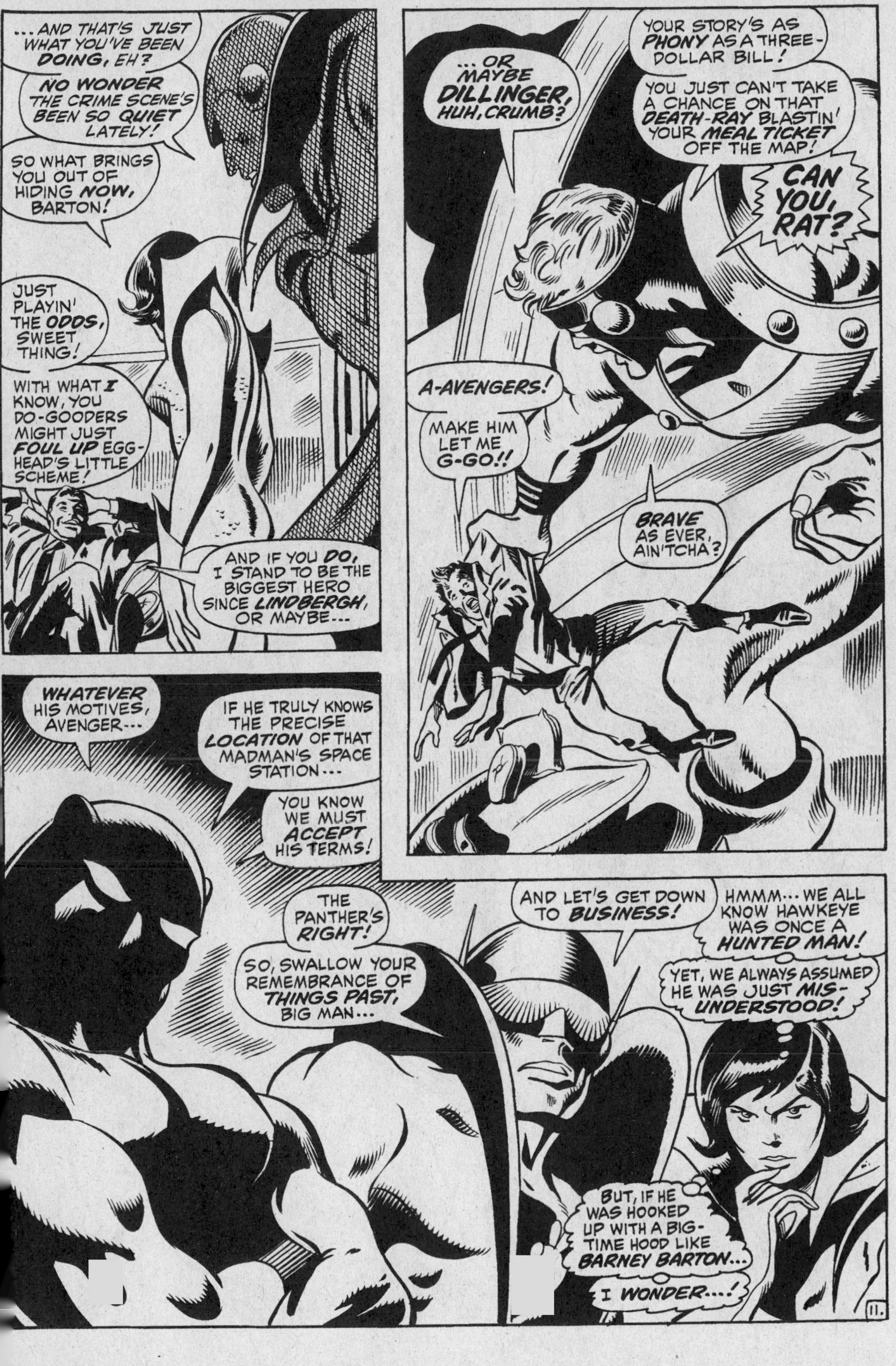

...AND THAT'S JUST WHAT YOU'VE BEEN DOING, EH?
NO WONDER THE CRIME SCENE'S BEEN SO QUIET LATELY!
SO WHAT BRINGS YOU OUT OF HIDING NOW, BARTON!
JUST PLAYIN' THE ODDS, SWEET THING!
WITH WHAT I KNOW, YOU DO-GOODERS MIGHT JUST FOUL UP EGG-HEAD'S LITTLE SCHEME!
AND IF YOU DO, I STAND TO BE THE BIGGEST HERO SINCE LINDBERGH, OR MAYBE---
...OR MAYBE DILLINGER, HUH, CRUMB?
YOUR STORY'S AS PHONY AS A THREE-DOLLAR BILL!
YOU JUST CAN'T TAKE A CHANCE ON THAT DEATH-RAY BLASTIN' YOUR MEAL TICKET OFF THE MAP!
CAN YOU, RAT?
A-AVENGERS!
MAKE HIM LET ME G-GO!!
BRAVE AS EVER, AIN'TCHA?
WHATEVER HIS MOTIVES, AVENGER---
IF HE TRULY KNOWS THE PRECISE LOCATION OF THAT MADMAN'S SPACE STATION---
YOU KNOW WE MUST ACCEPT HIS TERMS!
THE PANTHER'S RIGHT!
SO, SWALLOW YOUR REMEMBRANCE OF THINGS PAST, BIG MAN...
AND LET'S GET DOWN TO BUSINESS!
HMMM... WE ALL KNOW HAWKEYE WAS ONCE A HUNTED MAN!
YET, WE ALWAYS ASSUMED HE WAS JUST MIS-UNDERSTOOD!
BUT, IF HE WAS HOOKED UP WITH A BIG-TIME HOOD LIKE BARNEY BARTON...
I WONDER...!

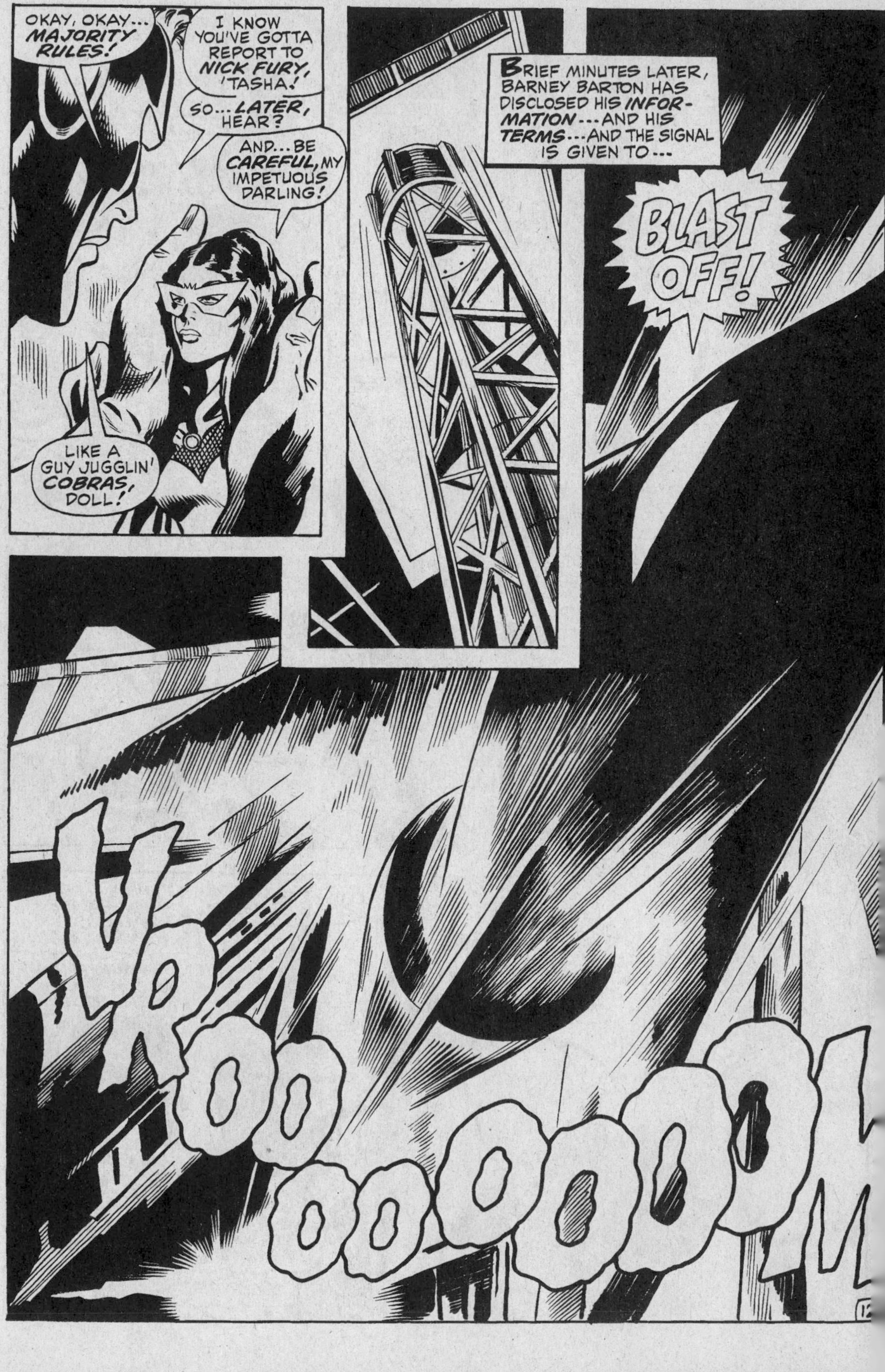

OKAY, OKAY... MAJORITY RULES!
I KNOW YOU'VE GOTTA REPORT TO NICK FURY, 'TASHA!
SO... LATER, HEAR?
AND... BE CAREFUL, MY IMPETUOUS DARLING!
LIKE A GUY JUGGLIN' COBRAS, DOLL!
BRIEF MINUTES LATER, BARNEY BARTON HAS DISCLOSED HIS INFORMATION --- AND HIS TERMS --- AND THE SIGNAL IS GIVEN TO ---
BLAST OFF!
VROOOOOOOOOM

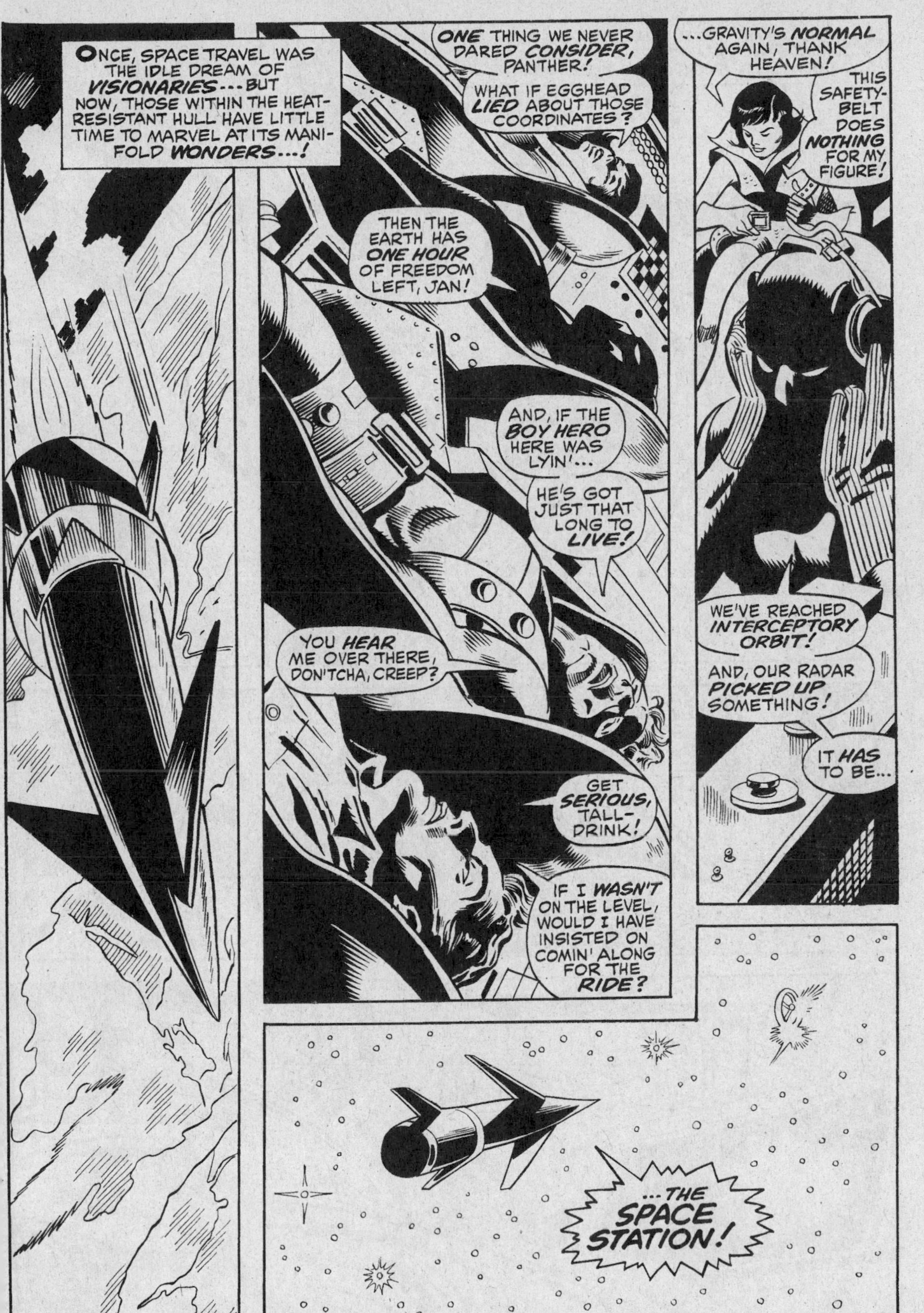
ONCE, SPACE TRAVEL WAS THE IDLE DREAM OF VISIONARIES... BUT NOW, THOSE WITHIN THE HEAT-RESISTANT HULL HAVE LITTLE TIME TO MARVEL AT ITS MANIFOLD WONDERS...!
ONE THING WE NEVER DARED CONSIDER, PANTHER!
WHAT IF EGGHEAD LIED ABOUT THOSE COORDINATES?
THEN THE EARTH HAS ONE HOUR OF FREEDOM LEFT, JAN!
AND, IF THE BOY HERO HERE WAS LYIN'...
HE'S GOT JUST THAT LONG TO LIVE!
YOU HEAR ME OVER THERE, DON'TCHA, CREEP?
GET SERIOUS, TALL-DRINK!
IF I WASN'T ON THE LEVEL, WOULD I HAVE INSISTED ON COMIN' ALONG FOR THE RIDE?
...GRAVITY'S NORMAL AGAIN, THANK HEAVEN!
THIS SAFETY-BELT DOES NOTHING FOR MY FIGURE!
WE'VE REACHED INTERCEPTORY ORBIT!
AND, OUR RADAR PICKED UP SOMETHING!
IT HAS TO BE...
...THE SPACE STATION!
13

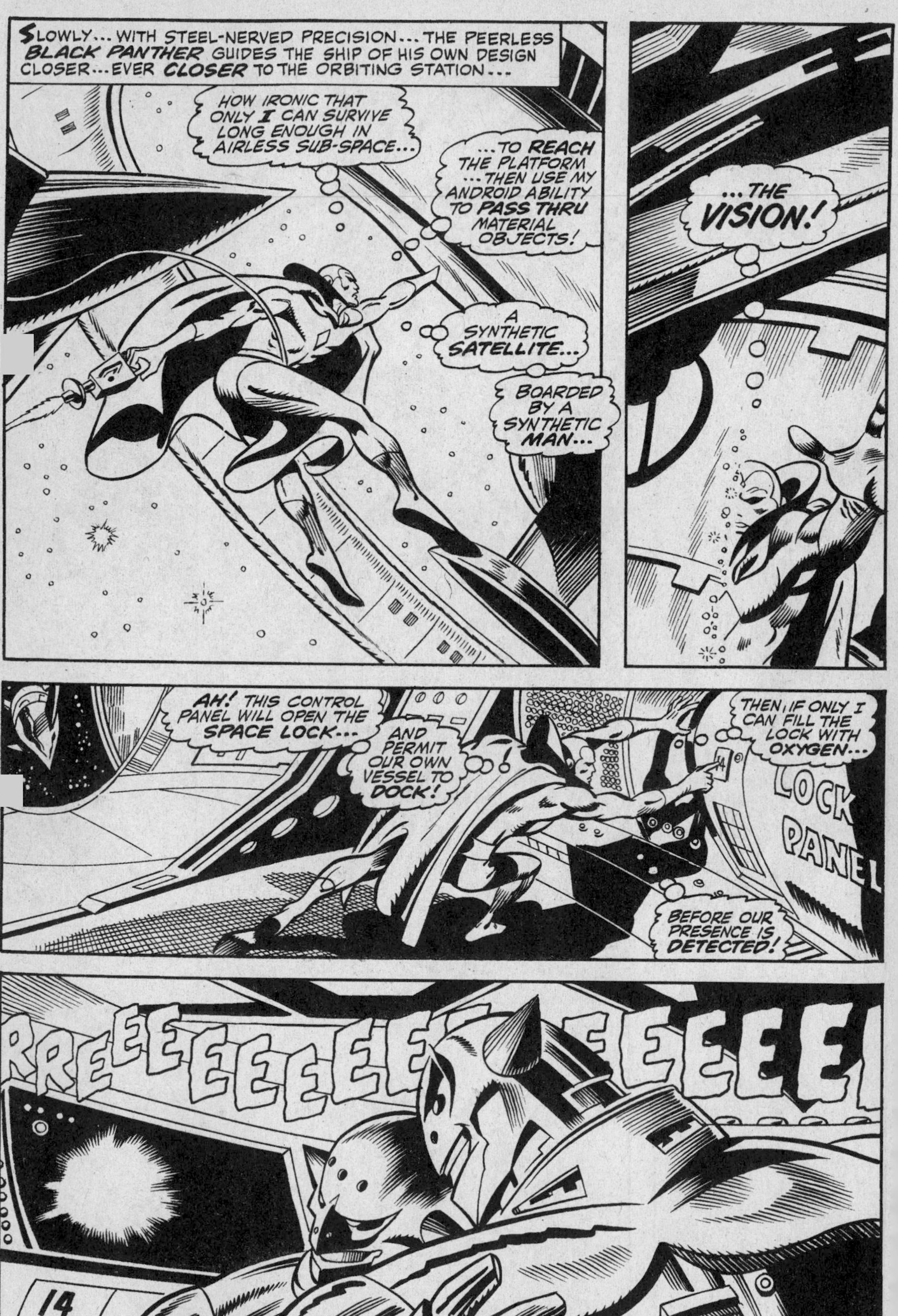
SLOWLY... WITH STEEL-NERVED PRECISION... THE PEERLESS BLACK PANTHER GUIDES THE SHIP OF HIS OWN DESIGN CLOSER... EVER CLOSER TO THE ORBITING STATION...
HOW IRONIC THAT ONLY I CAN SURVIVE LONG ENOUGH IN AIRLESS SUB-SPACE...
...TO REACH THE PLATFORM ...THEN USE MY ANDROID ABILITY TO PASS THRU MATERIAL OBJECTS!
A SYNTHETIC SATELLITE...
BOARDED BY A SYNTHETIC MAN...
...THE VISION!
AH! THIS CONTROL PANEL WILL OPEN THE SPACE LOCK...
AND PERMIT OUR OWN VESSEL TO DOCK!
THEN, IF ONLY I CAN FILL THE LOCK WITH OXYGEN...
LOCK PANEL
BEFORE OUR PRESENCE IS DETECTED!
RREEEEEEEEEEEEEE
14

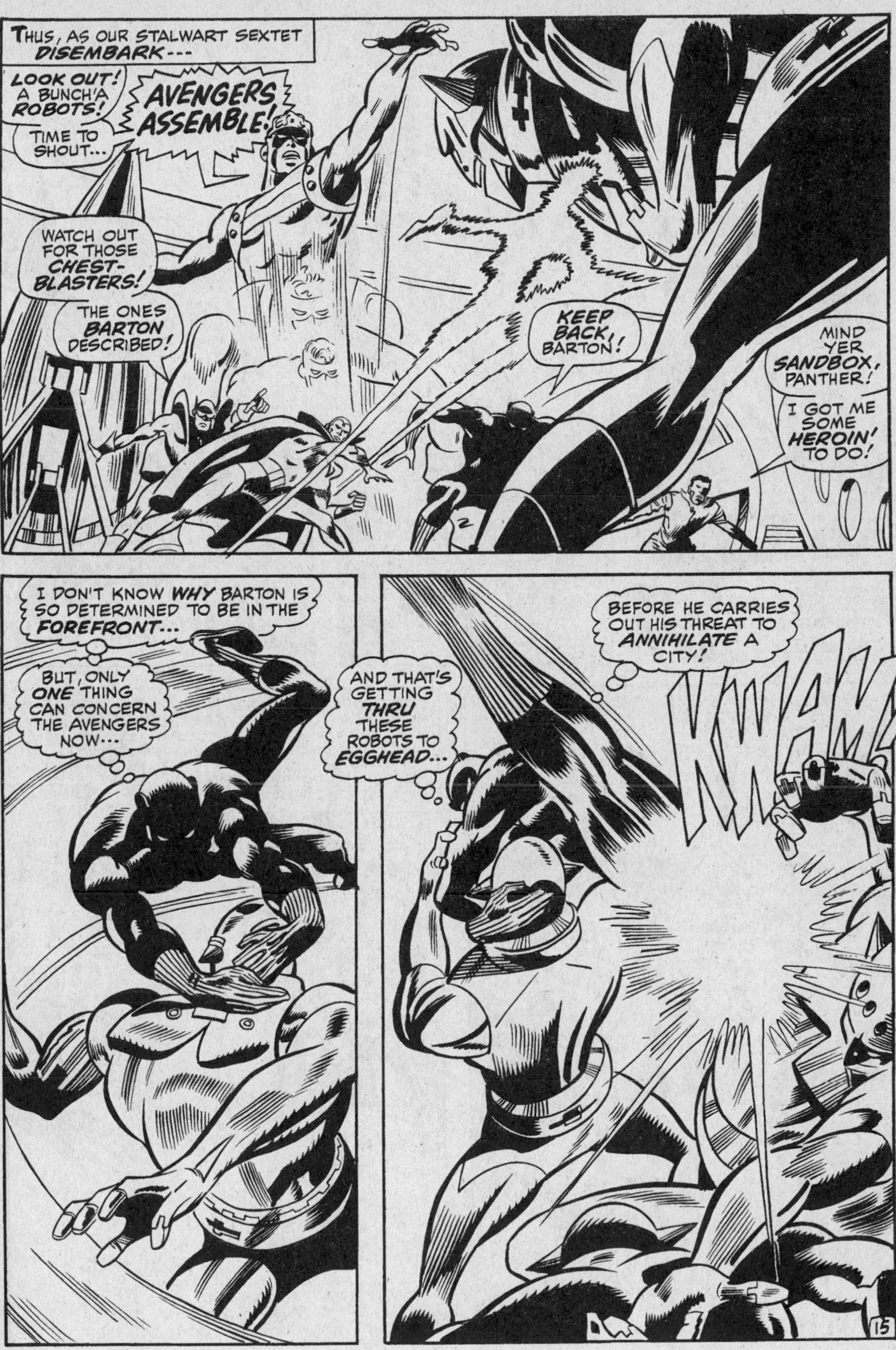
THUS, AS OUR STALWART SEXTET DISEMBARK---
LOOK OUT! A BUNCH'A ROBOTS!
TIME TO SHOUT...
AVENGERS ASSEMBLE!
WATCH OUT FOR THOSE CHEST-BLASTERS!
THE ONES BARTON DESCRIBED!
KEEP BACK, BARTON!
MIND YER SANDBOX, PANTHER!
I GOT ME SOME HEROIN' TO DO!
I DON'T KNOW WHY BARTON IS SO DETERMINED TO BE IN THE FOREFRONT...
BUT, ONLY ONE THING CAN CONCERN THE AVENGERS NOW...
AND THAT'S GETTING THRU THESE ROBOTS TO EGGHEAD...
BEFORE HE CARRIES OUT HIS THREAT TO ANNIHILATE A CITY!
KWAM!

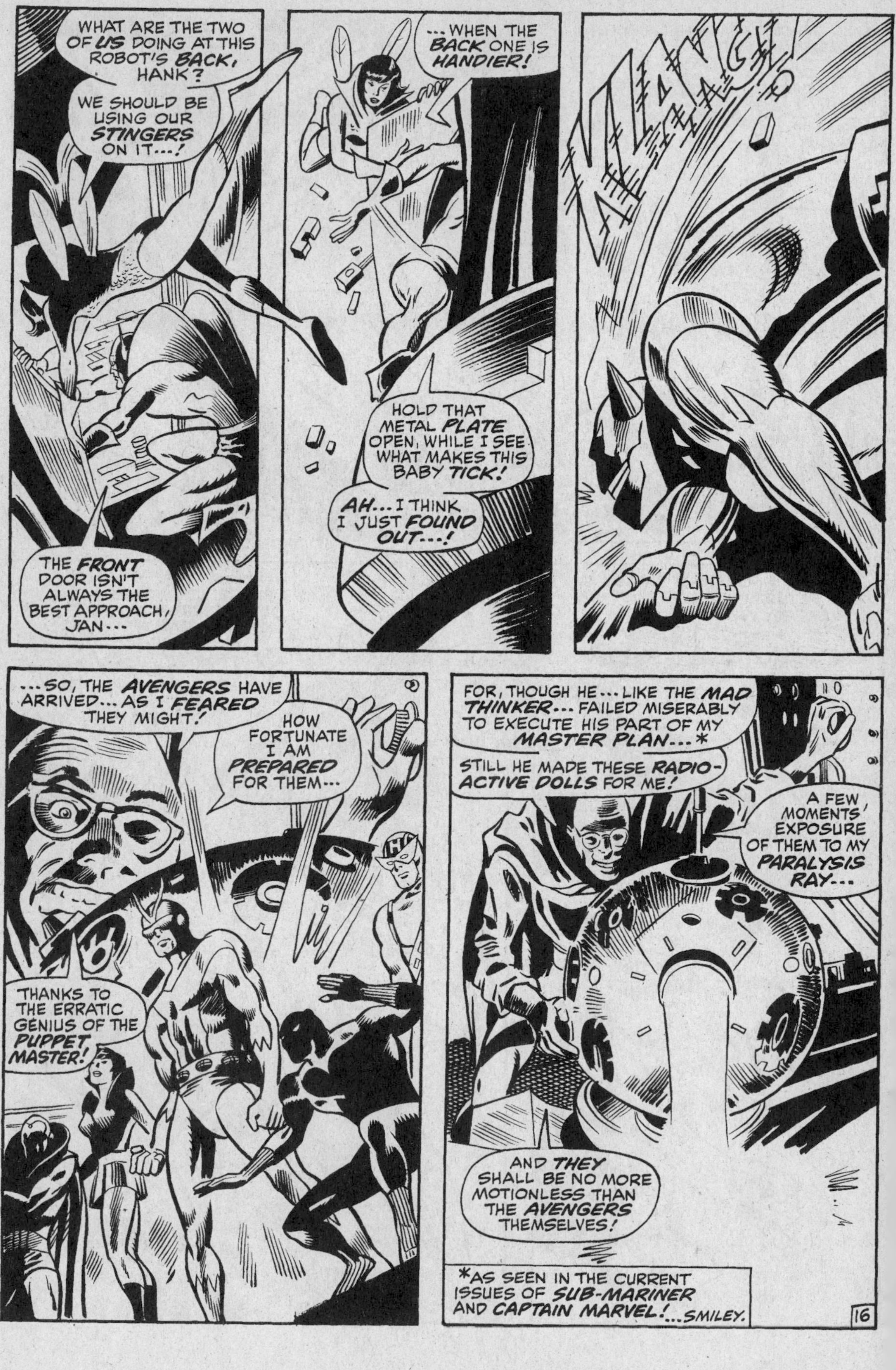
WHAT ARE THE TWO OF US DOING AT THIS ROBOT'S BACK, HANK?
WE SHOULD BE USING OUR STINGERS ON IT...!
THE FRONT DOOR ISN'T ALWAYS THE BEST APPROACH, JAN...
...WHEN THE BACK ONE IS HANDIER!
HOLD THAT METAL PLATE OPEN, WHILE I SEE WHAT MAKES THIS BABY TICK!
AH...I THINK I JUST FOUND OUT...!
...SO, THE AVENGERS HAVE ARRIVED...AS I FEARED THEY MIGHT!
HOW FORTUNATE I AM PREPARED FOR THEM...
THANKS TO THE ERRATIC GENIUS OF THE PUPPET MASTER!
FOR, THOUGH HE...LIKE THE MAD THINKER...FAILED MISERABLY TO EXECUTE HIS PART OF MY MASTER PLAN...*
STILL HE MADE THESE RADIO-ACTIVE DOLLS FOR ME!
A FEW MOMENTS' EXPOSURE OF THEM TO MY PARALYSIS RAY...
AND THEY SHALL BE NO MORE MOTIONLESS THAN THE AVENGERS THEMSELVES!
*AS SEEN IN THE CURRENT ISSUES OF SUB-MARINER AND CAPTAIN MARVEL!...SMILEY.
16

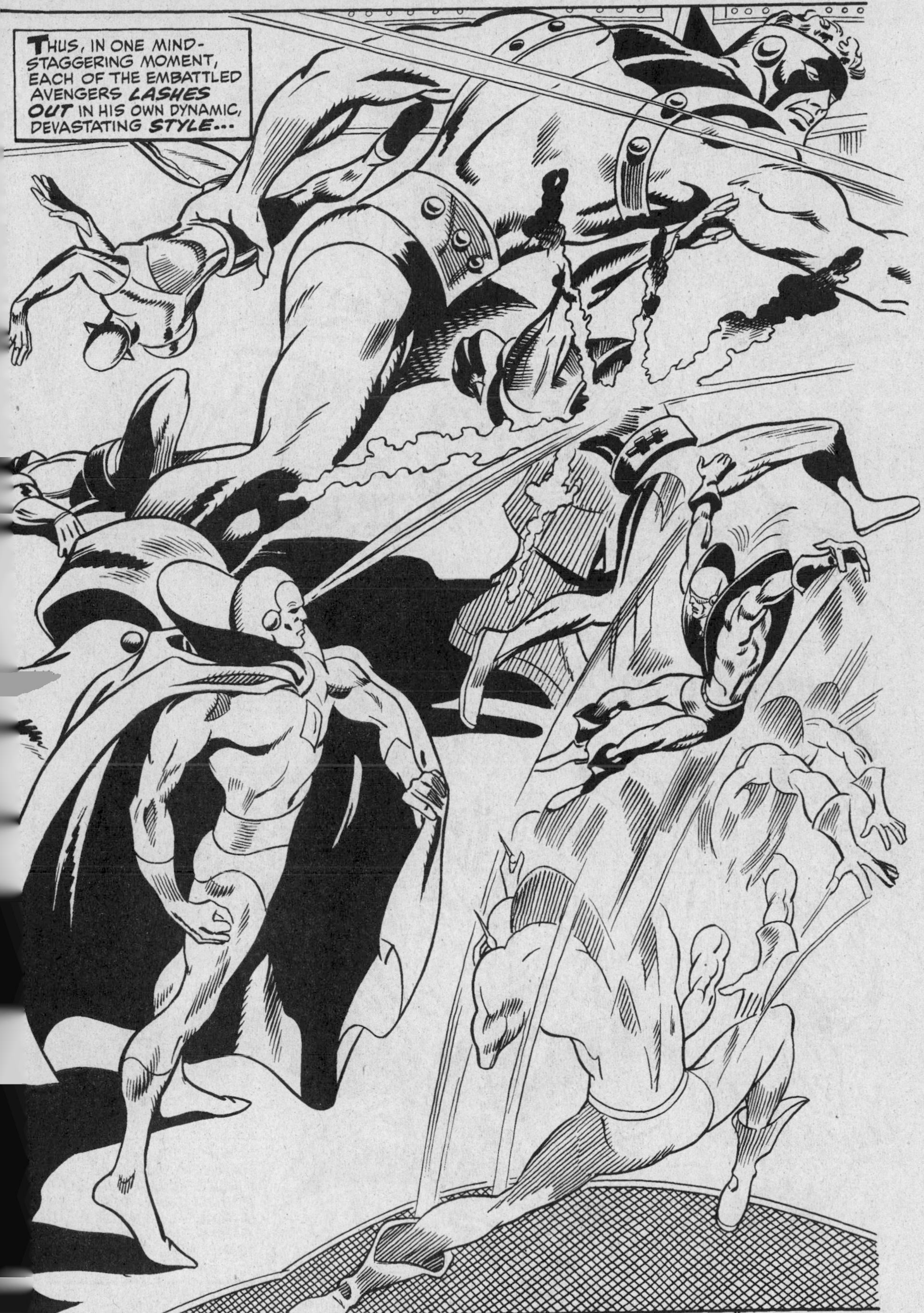
THUS, IN ONE MIND-STAGGERING MOMENT, EACH OF THE EMBATTLED AVENGERS LASHES OUT IN HIS OWN DYNAMIC, DEVASTATING STYLE...

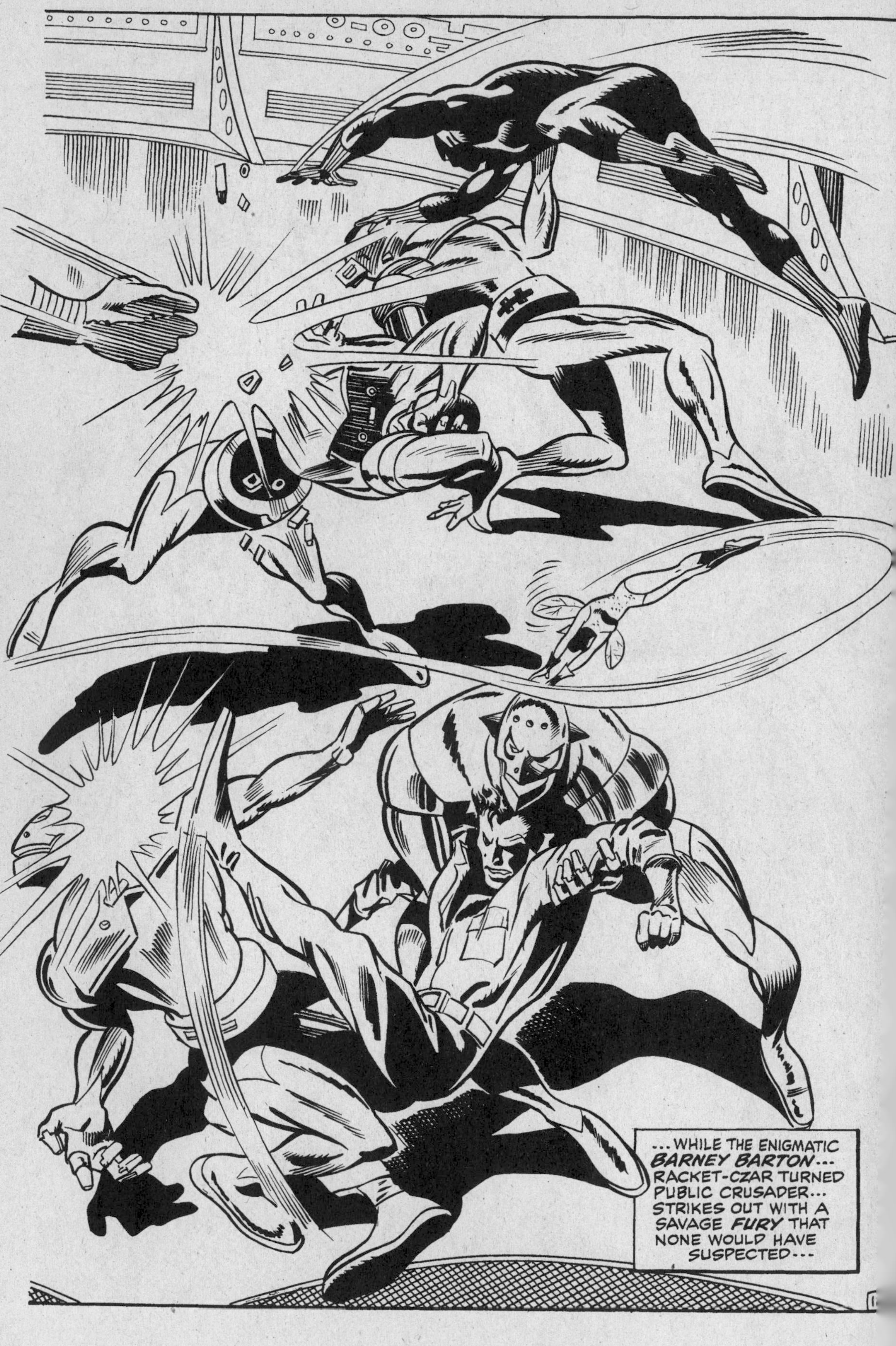
...WHILE THE ENIGMATIC BARNEY BARTON... RACKET-CZAR TURNED PUBLIC CRUSADER... STRIKES OUT WITH A SAVAGE FURY THAT NONE WOULD HAVE SUSPECTED---

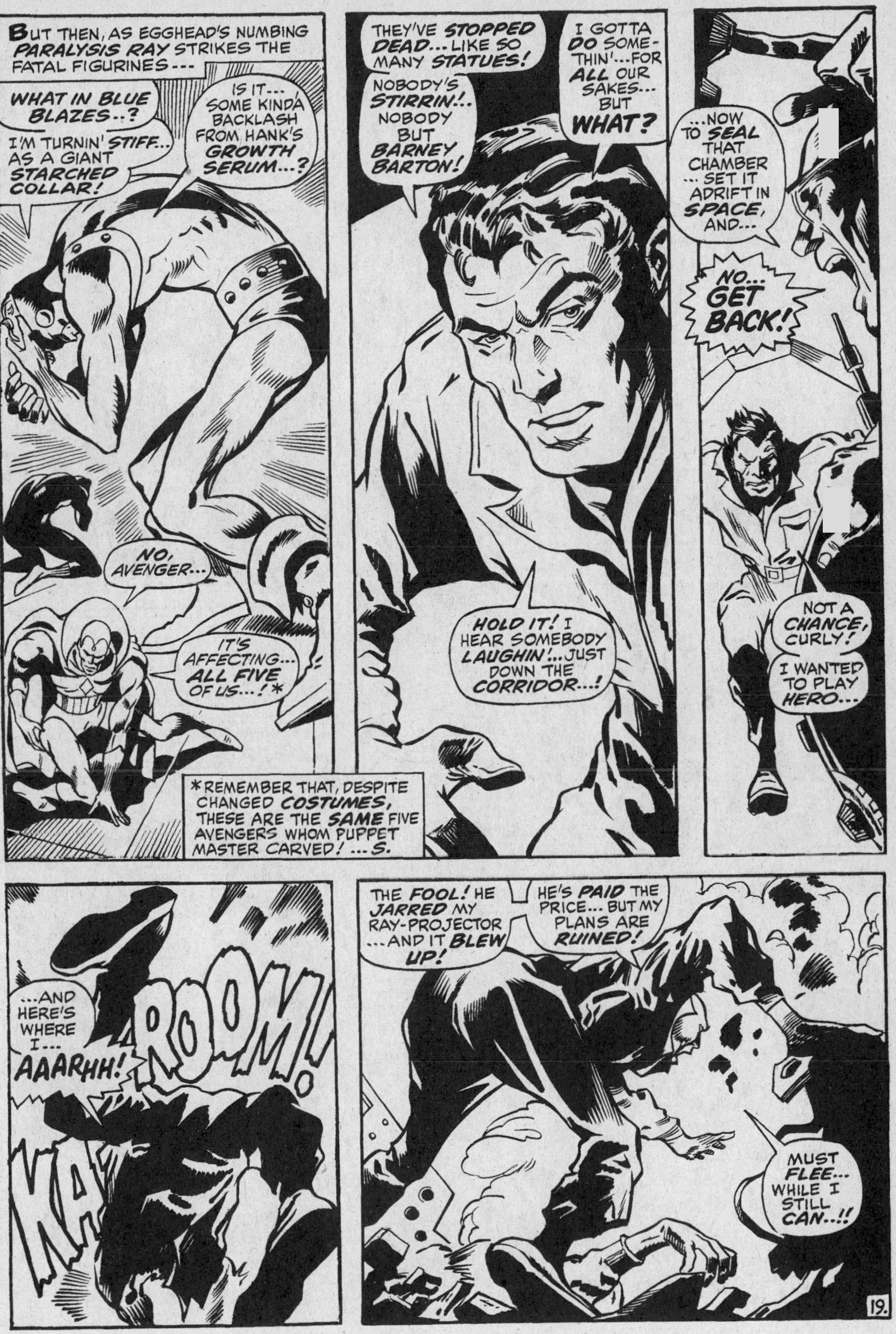
BUT THEN, AS EGGHEAD'S NUMBING PARALYSIS RAY STRIKES THE FATAL FIGURINES---
WHAT IN BLUE BLAZES..?
I'M TURNIN' STIFF... AS A GIANT STARCHED COLLAR!
IS IT... SOME KINDA BACKLASH FROM HANK'S GROWTH SERUM...?
NO, AVENGER...
IT'S AFFECTING... ALL FIVE OF US...! *
*REMEMBER THAT, DESPITE CHANGED COSTUMES, THESE ARE THE SAME FIVE AVENGERS WHOM PUPPET MASTER CARVED! ...S.
THEY'VE STOPPED DEAD... LIKE SO MANY STATUES!
NOBODY'S STIRRIN'!.. NOBODY BUT BARNEY BARTON!
I GOTTA DO SOME-THIN'... FOR ALL OUR SAKES... BUT WHAT?
HOLD IT! I HEAR SOMEBODY LAUGHIN'!... JUST DOWN THE CORRIDOR...!
...NOW TO SEAL THAT CHAMBER ... SET IT ADRIFT IN SPACE, AND...
NO... GET BACK!
NOT A CHANCE, CURLY!
I WANTED TO PLAY HERO...
...AND HERE'S WHERE I... AAARHH!
KA-ROOM!
THE FOOL! HE JARRED MY RAY-PROJECTOR ...AND IT BLEW UP!
HE'S PAID THE PRICE... BUT MY PLANS ARE RUINED!
MUST FLEE... WHILE I STILL CAN..!!

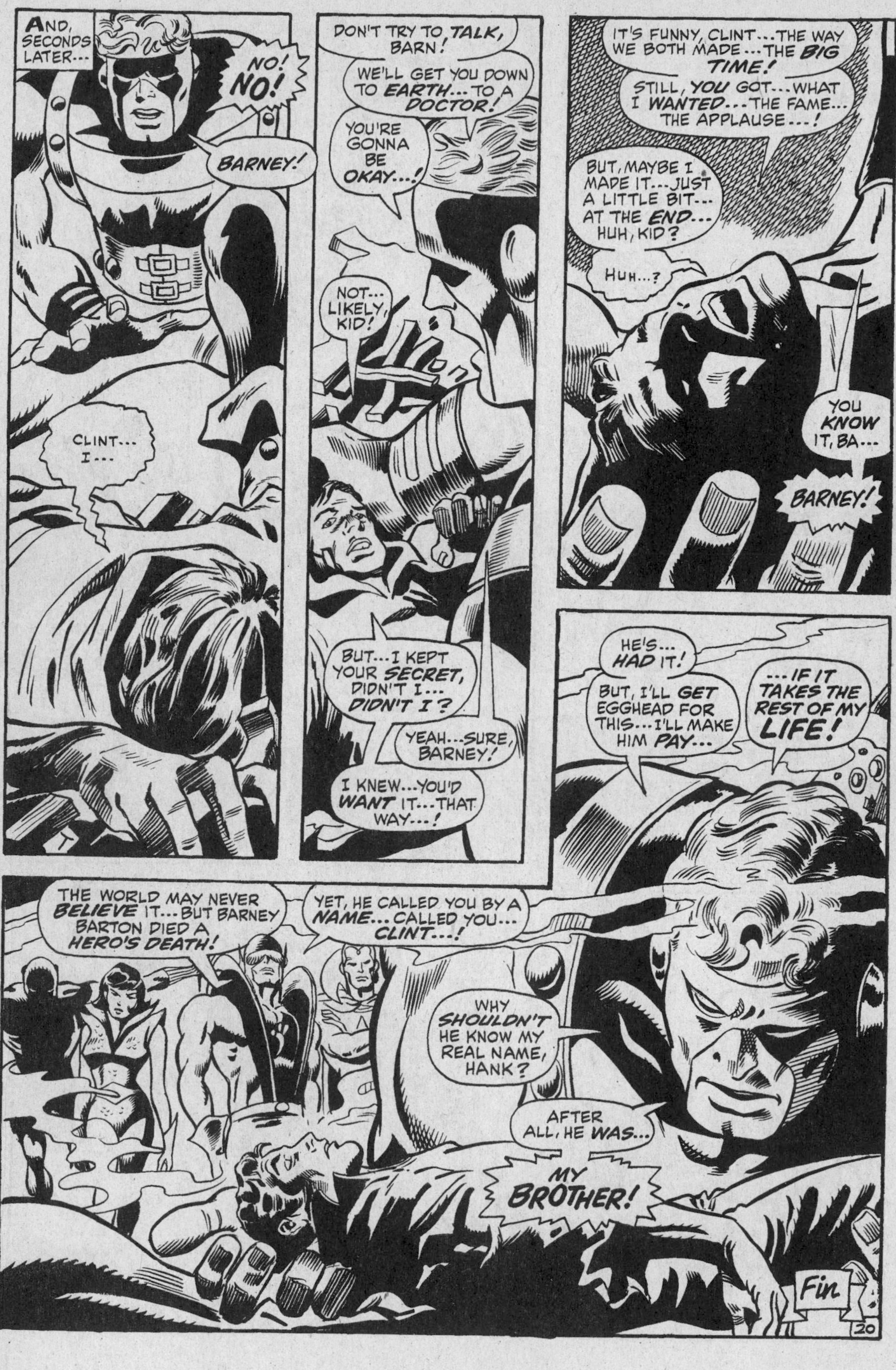

AND, SECONDS LATER...
NO! NO!
BARNEY!
CLINT... I...
DON'T TRY TO TALK, BARN!
WE'LL GET YOU DOWN TO EARTH... TO A DOCTOR!
YOU'RE GONNA BE OKAY...!
NOT... LIKELY, KID!
BUT... I KEPT YOUR SECRET, DIDN'T I... DIDN'T I?
YEAH... SURE, BARNEY!
I KNEW... YOU'D WANT IT... THAT WAY...!
IT'S FUNNY, CLINT... THE WAY WE BOTH MADE... THE BIG TIME!
STILL, YOU GOT... WHAT I WANTED... THE FAME... THE APPLAUSE...!
BUT, MAYBE I MADE IT... JUST A LITTLE BIT... AT THE END... HUH, KID?
HUH...?
YOU KNOW IT, BA...
BARNEY!
HE'S... HAD IT!
BUT, I'LL GET EGGHEAD FOR THIS... I'LL MAKE HIM PAY...
...IF IT TAKES THE REST OF MY LIFE!
THE WORLD MAY NEVER BELIEVE IT... BUT BARNEY BARTON DIED A HERO'S DEATH!
YET, HE CALLED YOU BY A NAME... CALLED YOU... CLINT...!
WHY SHOULDN'T HE KNOW MY REAL NAME, HANK?
AFTER ALL, HE WAS...
MY BROTHER!
Fin
20

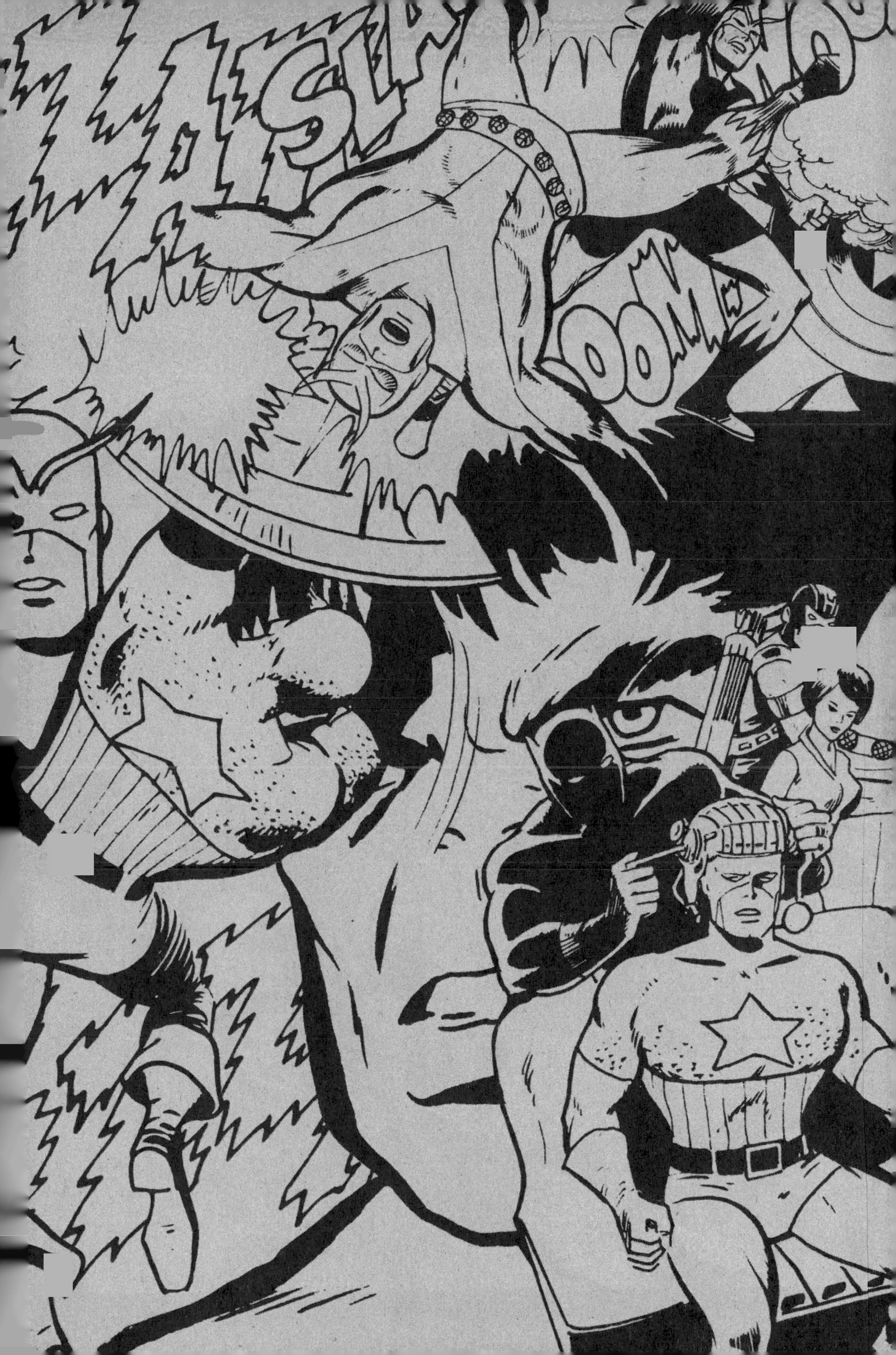

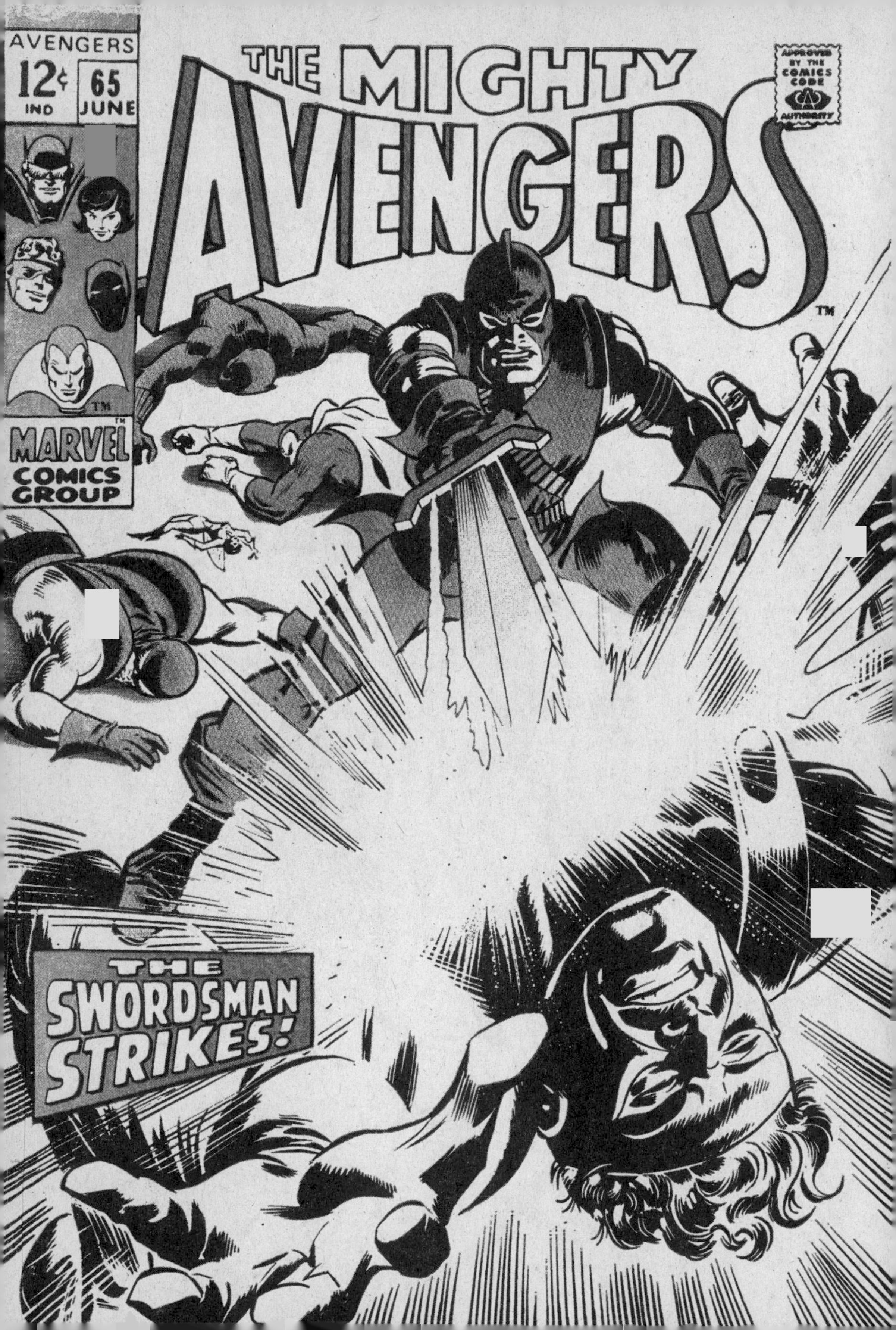

AVENGERS
12¢
IND
65
JUNE
THE MIGHTY
AVENGERS
TM
APPROVED BY THE COMICS CODE AUTHORITY
TM
MARVEL
COMICS GROUP
THE SWORDSMAN STRIKES!

THE MIGHTY AVENGERS!™

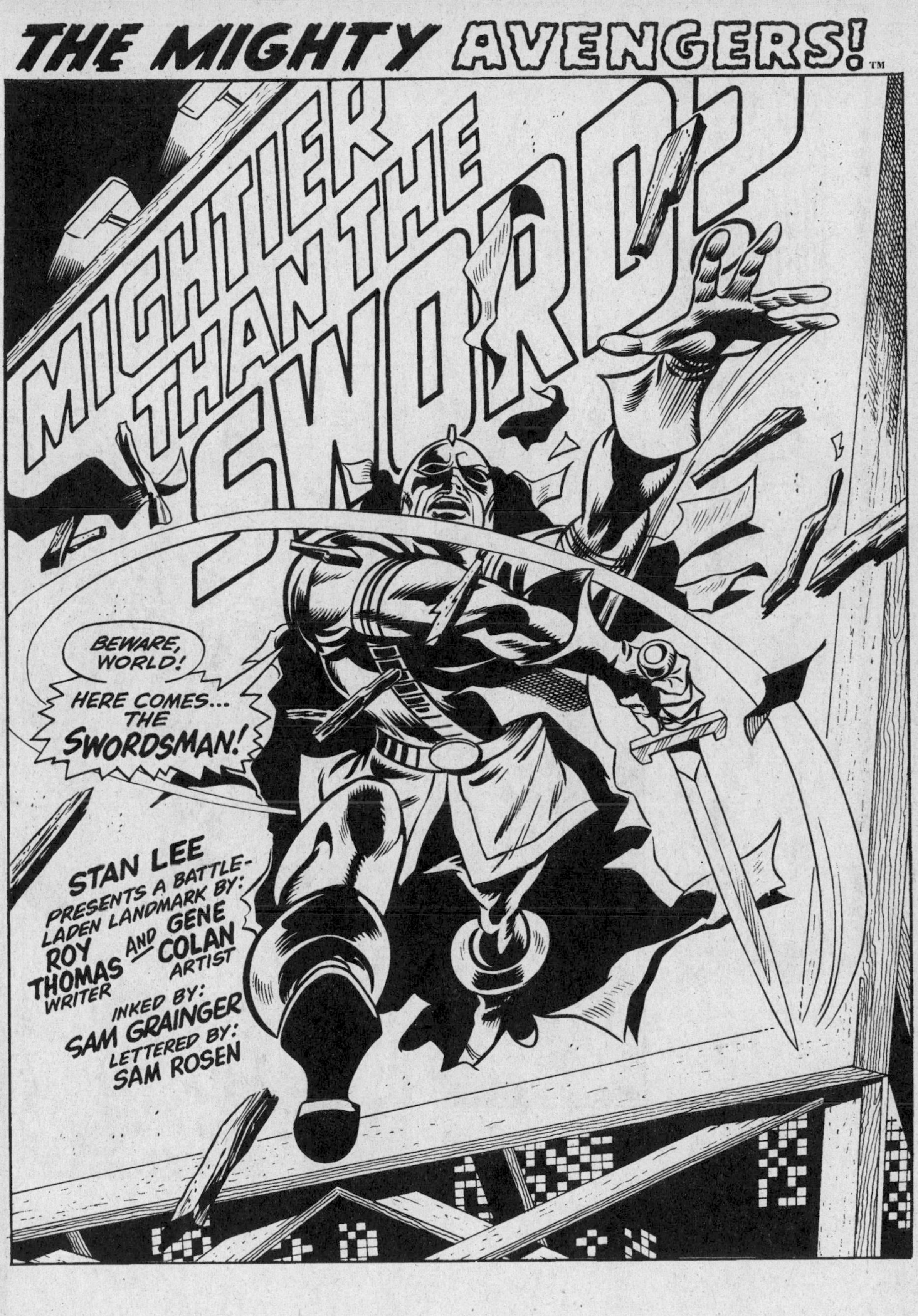
MIGHTIER THAN THE SWORD?
BEWARE, WORLD!
HERE COMES... THE SWORDSMAN!
STAN LEE PRESENTS A BATTLE-LADEN LANDMARK BY:
ROY THOMAS WRITER AND GENE COLAN ARTIST
INKED BY: SAM GRAINGER
LETTERED BY: SAM ROSEN

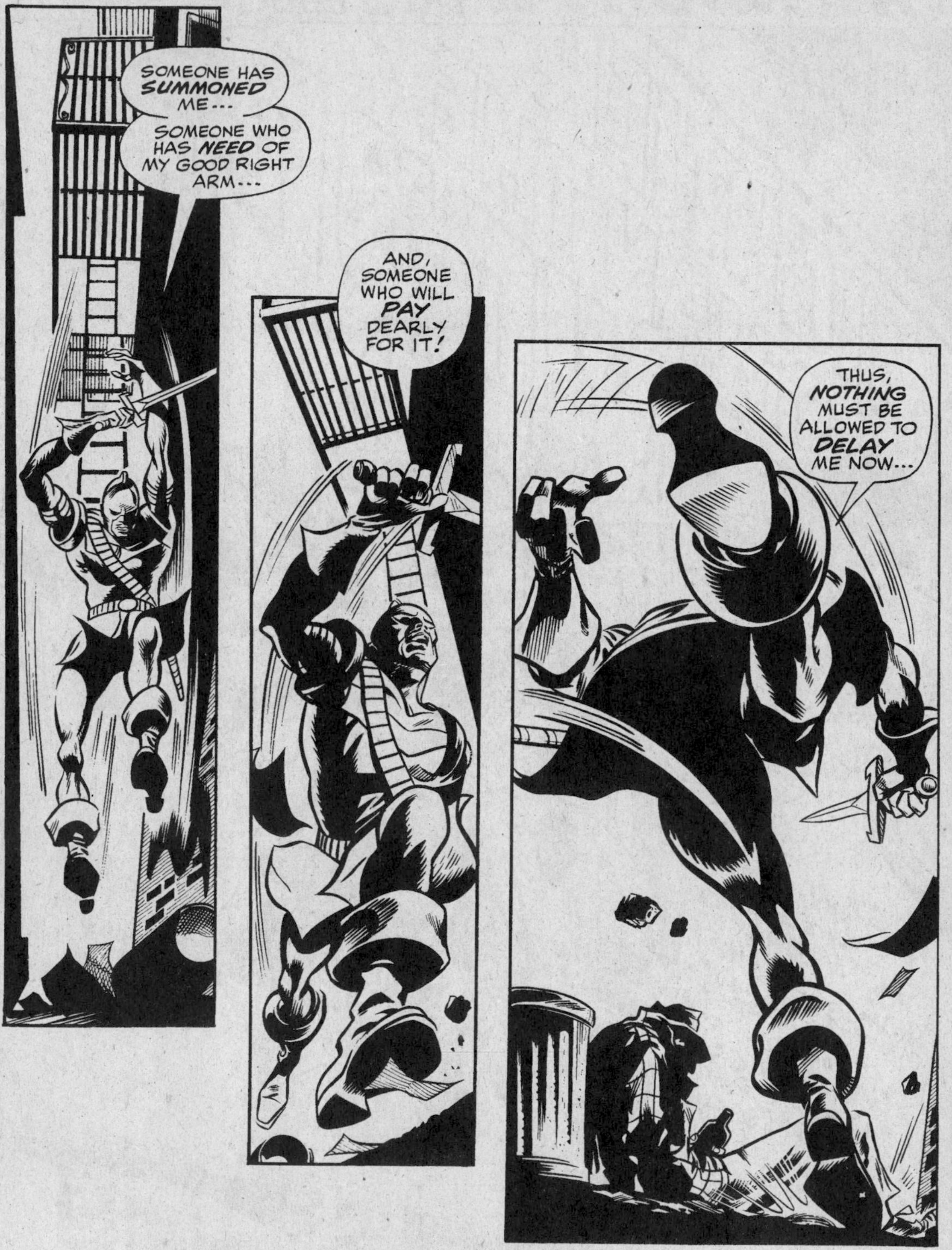
SOMEONE HAS SUMMONED ME...
SOMEONE WHO HAS NEED OF MY GOOD RIGHT ARM...
AND, SOMEONE WHO WILL PAY DEARLY FOR IT!
THUS, NOTHING MUST BE ALLOWED TO DELAY ME NOW...

NOTHING!

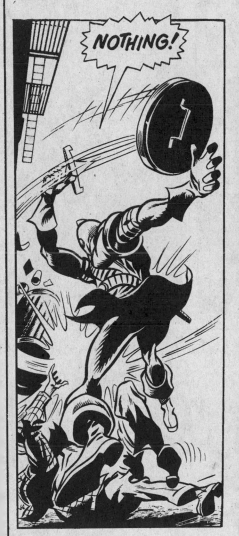

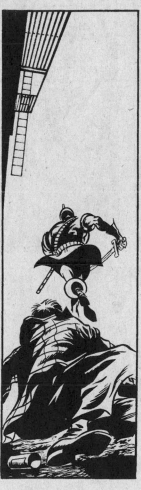

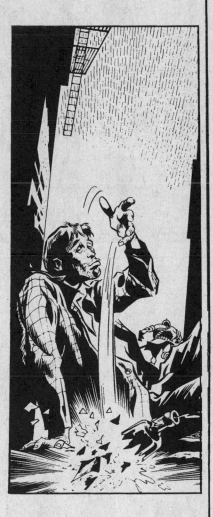

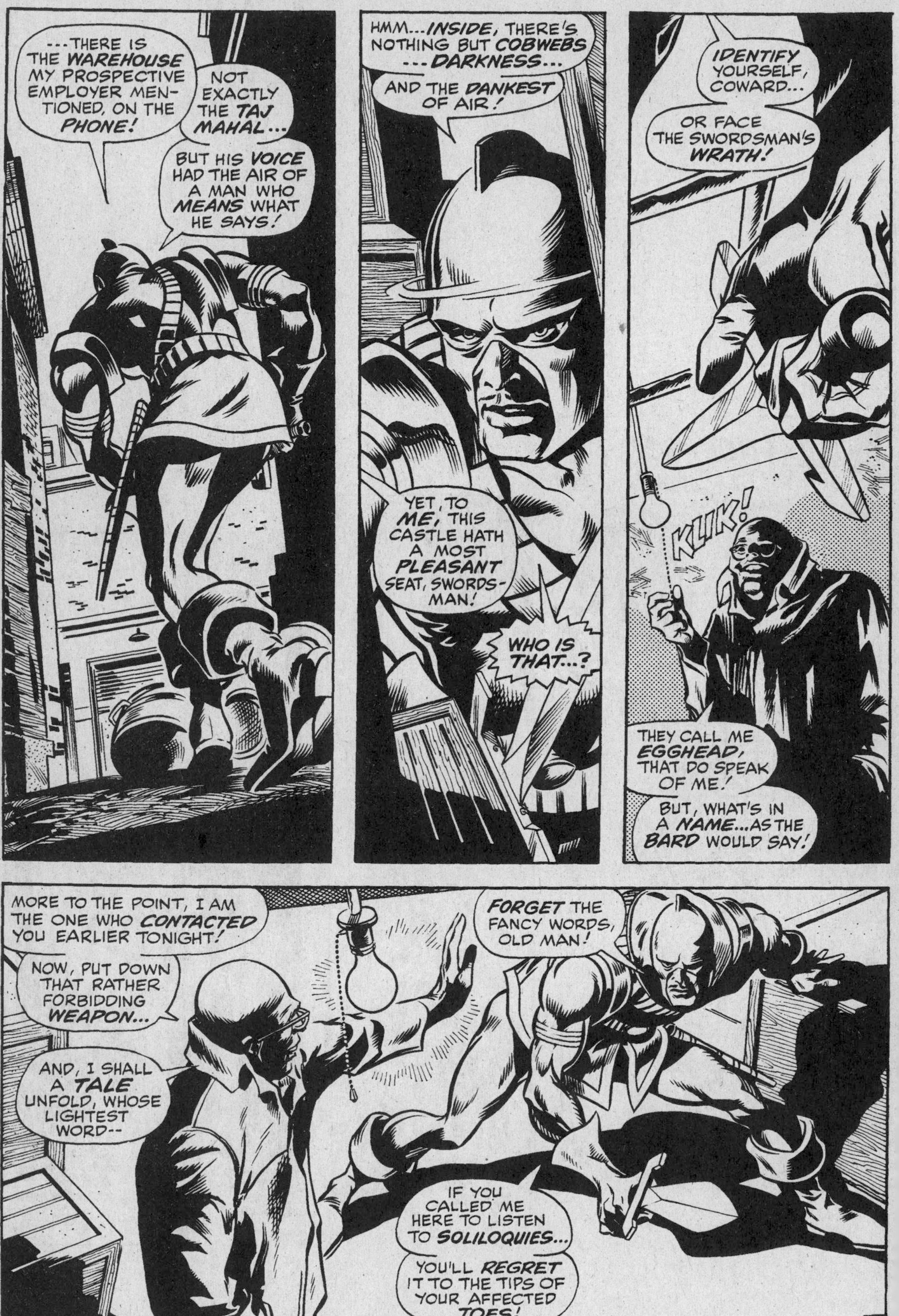
---THERE IS THE WAREHOUSE MY PROSPECTIVE EMPLOYER MENTIONED, ON THE PHONE!
NOT EXACTLY THE TAJ MAHAL...
BUT HIS VOICE HAD THE AIR OF A MAN WHO MEANS WHAT HE SAYS!
HMM...INSIDE, THERE'S NOTHING BUT COBWEBS ---DARKNESS...
AND THE DANKEST OF AIR!
YET, TO ME, THIS CASTLE HATH A MOST PLEASANT SEAT, SWORDSMAN!
WHO IS THAT...?
IDENTIFY YOURSELF, COWARD...
OR FACE THE SWORDSMAN'S WRATH!
KLIK!
THEY CALL ME EGGHEAD, THAT DO SPEAK OF ME!
BUT, WHAT'S IN A NAME...AS THE BARD WOULD SAY!
MORE TO THE POINT, I AM THE ONE WHO CONTACTED YOU EARLIER TONIGHT!
NOW, PUT DOWN THAT RATHER FORBIDDING WEAPON...
AND, I SHALL A TALE UNFOLD, WHOSE LIGHTEST WORD--
FORGET THE FANCY WORDS, OLD MAN!
IF YOU CALLED ME HERE TO LISTEN TO SOLILOQUIES...
YOU'LL REGRET IT TO THE TIPS OF YOUR AFFECTED TOES!
4

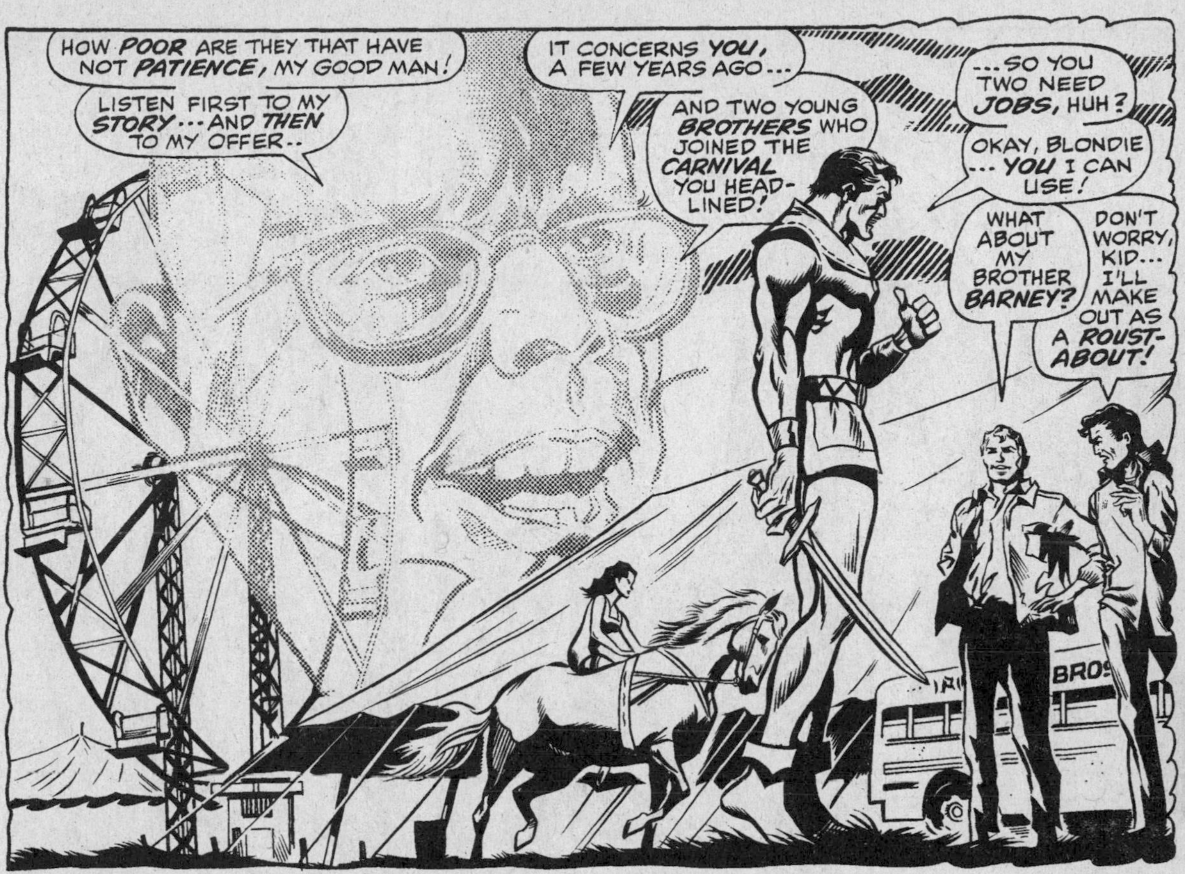
HOW POOR ARE THEY THAT HAVE NOT PATIENCE, MY GOOD MAN!
LISTEN FIRST TO MY STORY... AND THEN TO MY OFFER..
IT CONCERNS YOU, A FEW YEARS AGO...
AND TWO YOUNG BROTHERS WHO JOINED THE CARNIVAL YOU HEADLINED!
...SO YOU TWO NEED JOBS, HUH?
OKAY, BLONDIE ... YOU I CAN USE!
WHAT ABOUT MY BROTHER BARNEY?
DON'T WORRY, KID... I'LL MAKE OUT AS A ROUST-ABOUT!
BROS

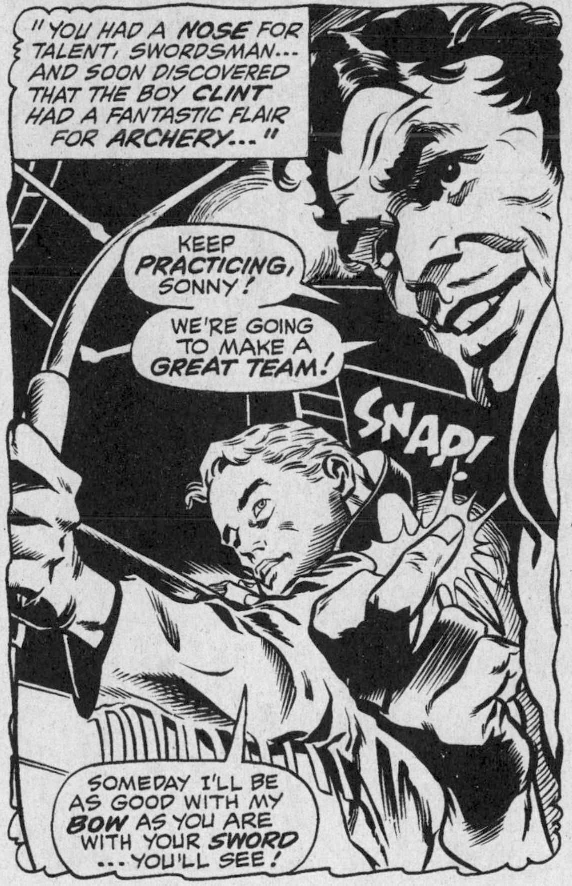
"YOU HAD A NOSE FOR TALENT, SWORDSMAN... AND SOON DISCOVERED THAT THE BOY CLINT HAD A FANTASTIC FLAIR FOR ARCHERY..."
KEEP PRACTICING, SONNY!
WE'RE GOING TO MAKE A GREAT TEAM!
SNAP!
SOMEDAY I'LL BE AS GOOD WITH MY BOW AS YOU ARE WITH YOUR SWORD ... YOU'LL SEE!

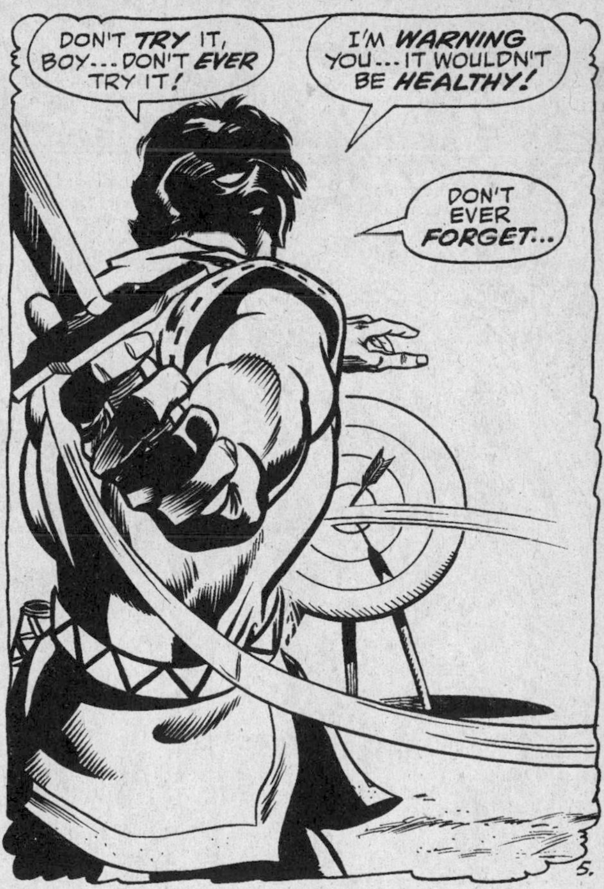
DON'T TRY IT, BOY... DON'T EVER TRY IT!
I'M WARNING YOU... IT WOULDN'T BE HEALTHY!
DON'T EVER FORGET...

"...WHICH ONE OF US IS THE **MASTER!!**"

YOU YOUNG **FOOL!** NOBODY WOULD **EVER** CATCH US...WITH MY **SWORD** AND YOUR **BOW...!**

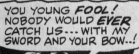

FORGET IT...I'M GETTING **OUT** OF HERE!

"BUT, THE FAULT OF WHAT HAPPENED **THAT NIGHT,** DEAR SWORDSMAN, WAS NOT IN THE STARS, BUT IN **YOURSELF...**"

HEY...DID YOU HEAR ABOUT THE **PAYMASTER** BEING **ROBBED,** AND...

WHA..? WHERE'D YOU GET ALL THAT **MONEY??**

YOU LITTLE **PUNK!**

SO...THINK YOU'RE TOO **GOOD** FOR ME, EH?

YOU'RE TURNING YOUR **BACK** ON ME, ARE YOU?

I WARNED YOU NEVER TO COME IN HERE WITHOUT **ASKING** FIRST!

NOW THAT YOU **KNOW,** YOU'RE IN IT **WITH** ME!

NO! I **WORK** FOR MONEY...I DON'T **STEAL** IT!

THE **HIGH WIRE** OUGHT TO PUT ENOUGH **DISTANCE** BETWEEN US!

YOUR FANCY **SWORD-SLING-ING** WON'T DO YOU MUCH **GOOD** UP **THERE!**

6

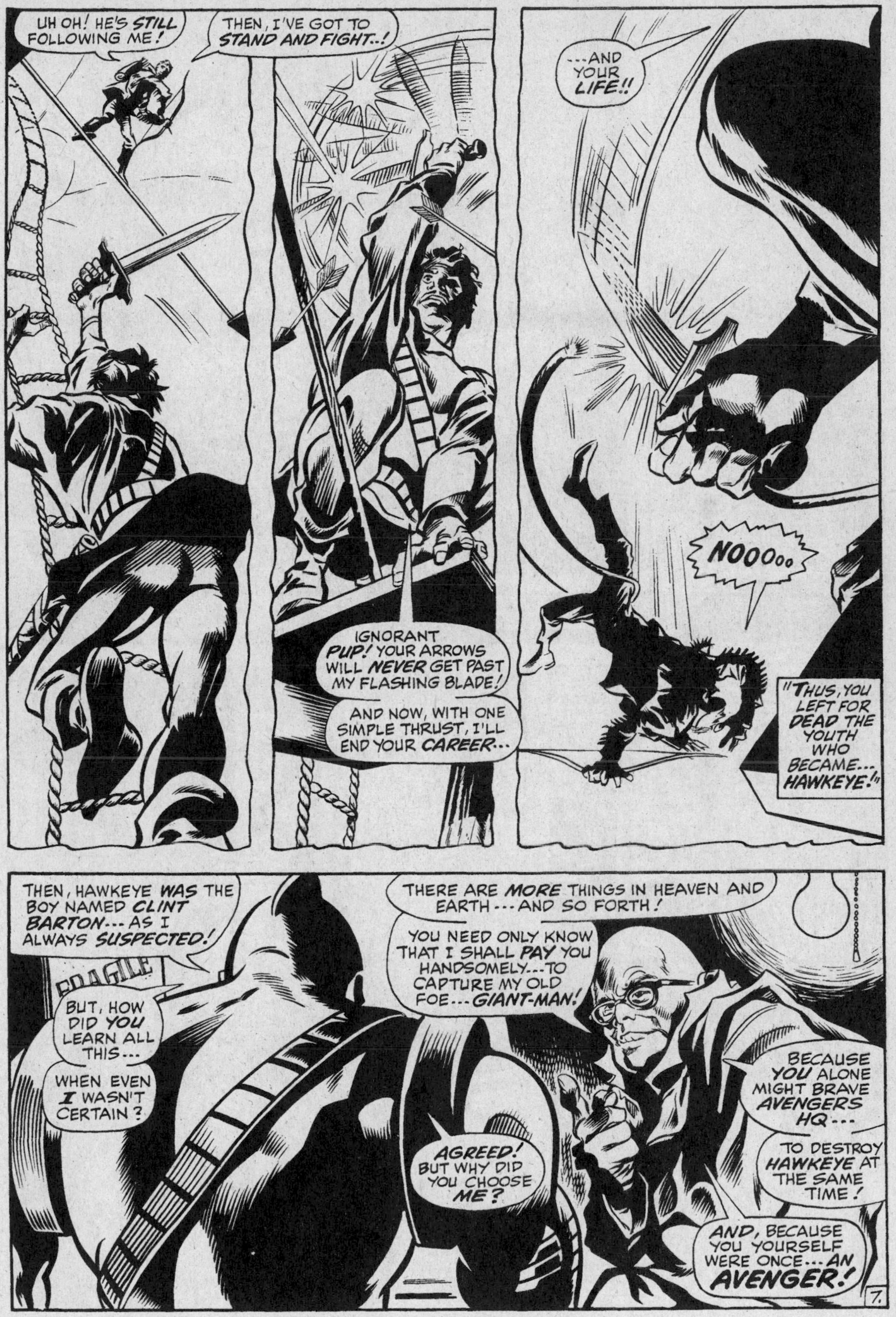

UH OH! HE'S STILL FOLLOWING ME!
THEN, I'VE GOT TO STAND AND FIGHT..!
IGNORANT PUP! YOUR ARROWS WILL NEVER GET PAST MY FLASHING BLADE!
AND NOW, WITH ONE SIMPLE THRUST, I'LL END YOUR CAREER...
...AND YOUR LIFE!!
NOOOoo
"THUS, YOU LEFT FOR DEAD THE YOUTH WHO BECAME... HAWKEYE!"
THEN, HAWKEYE WAS THE BOY NAMED CLINT BARTON... AS I ALWAYS SUSPECTED!
FRAGILE
BUT, HOW DID YOU LEARN ALL THIS...
WHEN EVEN I WASN'T CERTAIN?
THERE ARE MORE THINGS IN HEAVEN AND EARTH... AND SO FORTH!
YOU NEED ONLY KNOW THAT I SHALL PAY YOU HANDSOMELY... TO CAPTURE MY OLD FOE... GIANT-MAN!
AGREED! BUT WHY DID YOU CHOOSE ME?
BECAUSE YOU ALONE MIGHT BRAVE AVENGERS HQ...
TO DESTROY HAWKEYE AT THE SAME TIME!
AND, BECAUSE YOU YOURSELF WERE ONCE... AN AVENGER!
7.

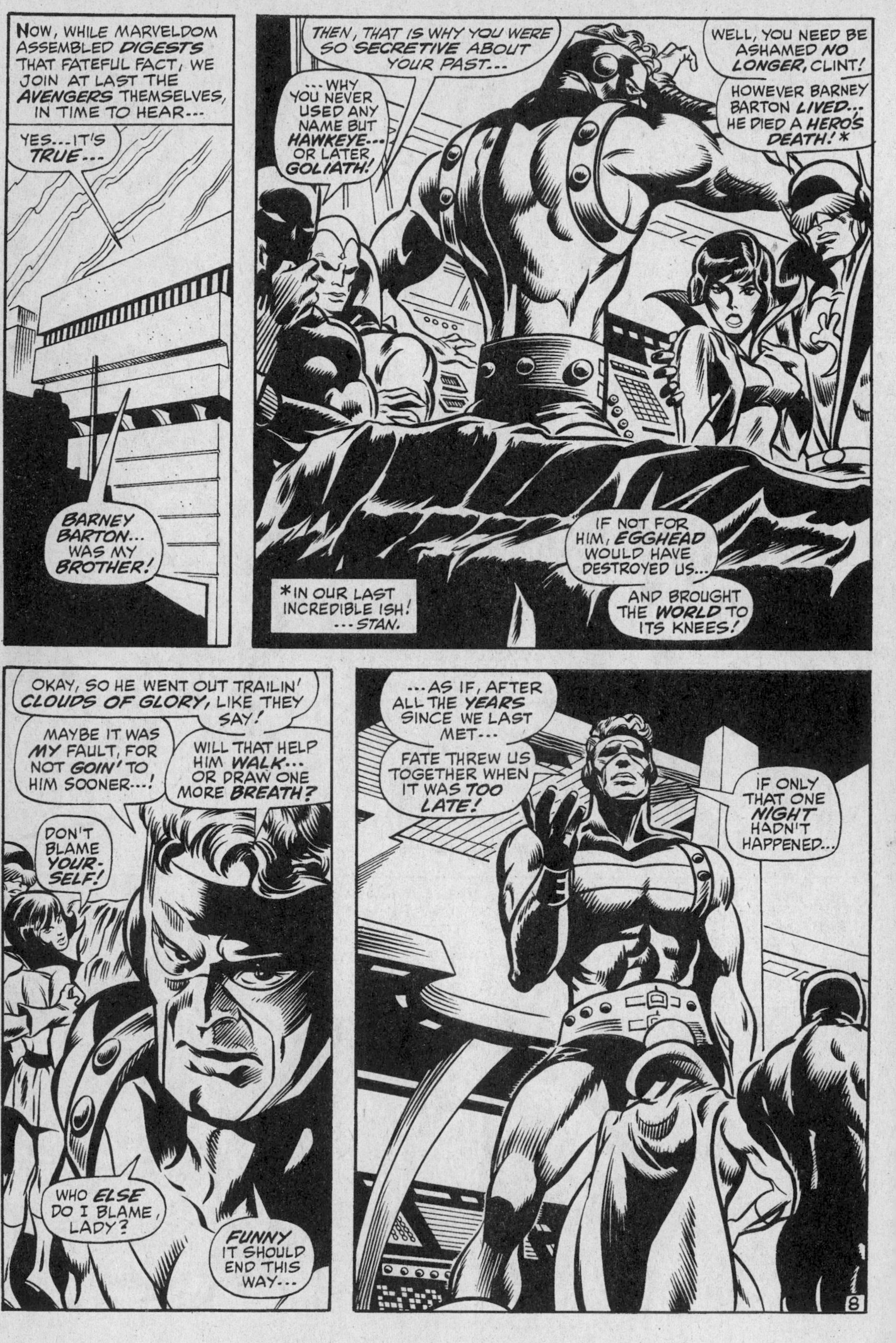

NOW, WHILE MARVELDOM ASSEMBLED DIGESTS THAT FATEFUL FACT, WE JOIN AT LAST THE AVENGERS THEMSELVES, IN TIME TO HEAR---
YES...IT'S TRUE...
BARNEY BARTON... WAS MY BROTHER!
THEN, THAT IS WHY YOU WERE SO SECRETIVE ABOUT YOUR PAST...
...WHY YOU NEVER USED ANY NAME BUT HAWKEYE... OR LATER GOLIATH!
WELL, YOU NEED BE ASHAMED NO LONGER, CLINT!
HOWEVER BARNEY BARTON LIVED... HE DIED A HERO'S DEATH!*
IF NOT FOR HIM, EGGHEAD WOULD HAVE DESTROYED US...
AND BROUGHT THE WORLD TO ITS KNEES!
*IN OUR LAST INCREDIBLE ISH! ---STAN.
OKAY, SO HE WENT OUT TRAILIN' CLOUDS OF GLORY, LIKE THEY SAY!
MAYBE IT WAS MY FAULT, FOR NOT GOIN' TO HIM SOONER---!
WILL THAT HELP HIM WALK... OR DRAW ONE MORE BREATH?
DON'T BLAME YOURSELF!
WHO ELSE DO I BLAME, LADY?
FUNNY IT SHOULD END THIS WAY...
...AS IF, AFTER ALL THE YEARS SINCE WE LAST MET...
FATE THREW US TOGETHER WHEN IT WAS TOO LATE!
IF ONLY THAT ONE NIGHT HADN'T HAPPENED...
8

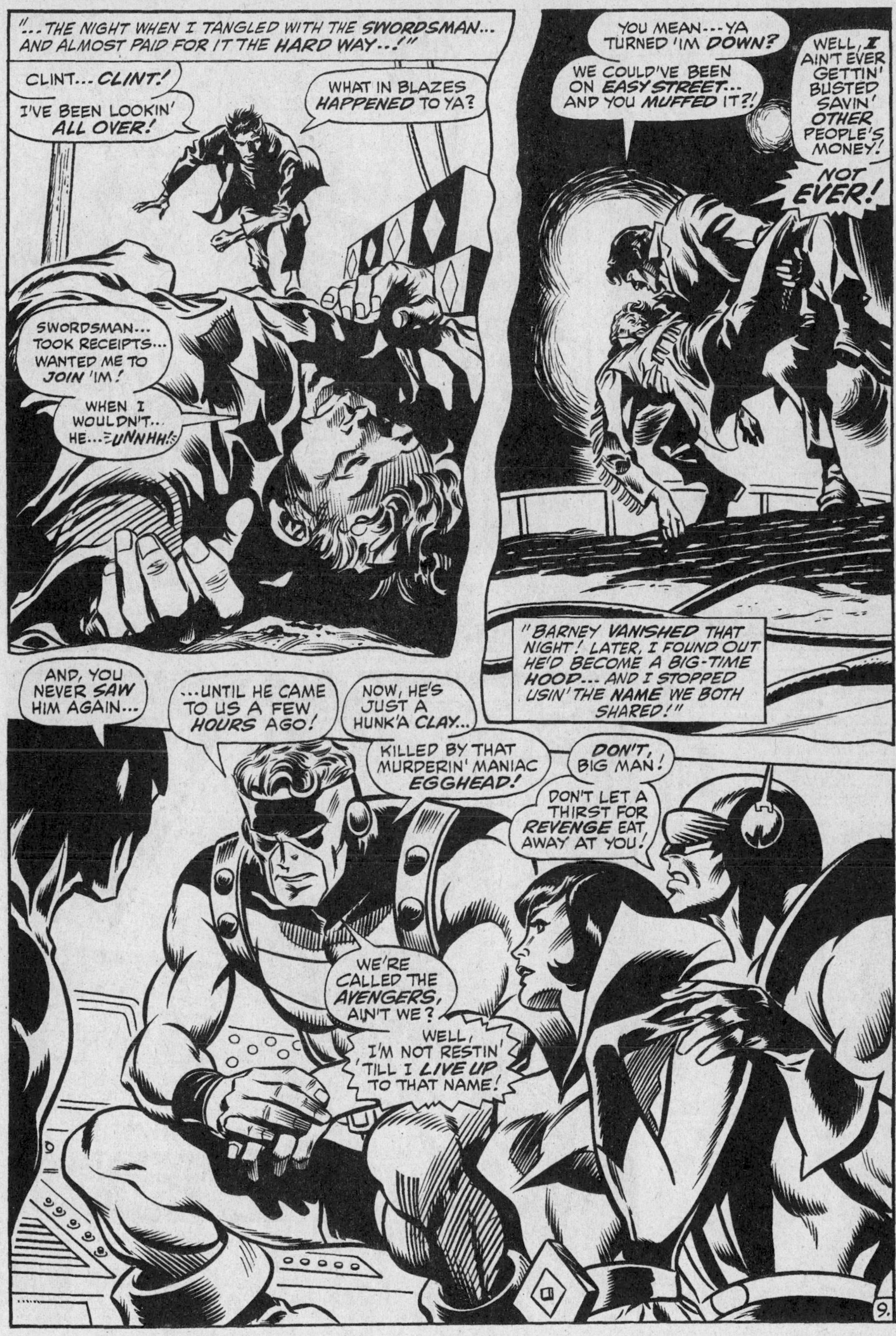
"...THE NIGHT WHEN I TANGLED WITH THE SWORDSMAN... AND ALMOST PAID FOR IT THE HARD WAY...!"
CLINT... CLINT!
I'VE BEEN LOOKIN' ALL OVER!
WHAT IN BLAZES HAPPENED TO YA?
SWORDSMAN... TOOK RECEIPTS... WANTED ME TO JOIN 'IM!
WHEN I WOULDN'T... HE...UNNHH!
YOU MEAN---YA TURNED 'IM DOWN?
WE COULD'VE BEEN ON EASY STREET... AND YOU MUFFED IT?!
WELL, I AIN'T EVER GETTIN' BUSTED SAVIN' OTHER PEOPLE'S MONEY!
NOT EVER!
"BARNEY VANISHED THAT NIGHT! LATER, I FOUND OUT HE'D BECOME A BIG-TIME HOOD... AND I STOPPED USIN' THE NAME WE BOTH SHARED!"
AND, YOU NEVER SAW HIM AGAIN...
...UNTIL HE CAME TO US A FEW HOURS AGO!
NOW, HE'S JUST A HUNK'A CLAY...
KILLED BY THAT MURDERIN' MANIAC EGGHEAD!
DON'T, BIG MAN!
DON'T LET A THIRST FOR REVENGE EAT AWAY AT YOU!
WE'RE CALLED THE AVENGERS, AIN'T WE?
WELL, I'M NOT RESTIN' 'TILL I LIVE UP TO THAT NAME!

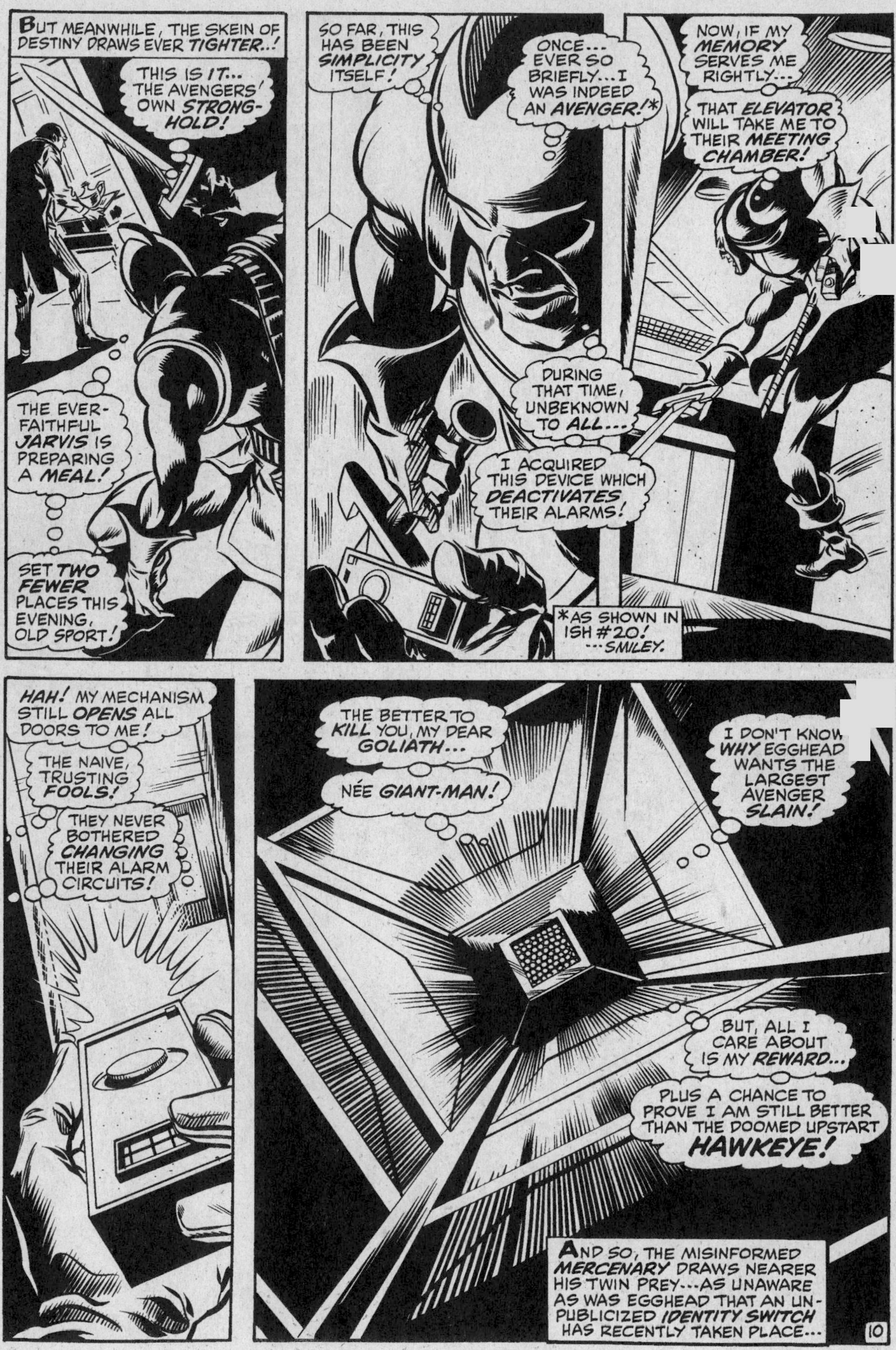

BUT MEANWHILE, THE SKEIN OF DESTINY DRAWS EVER TIGHTER..!
THIS IS IT... THE AVENGERS' OWN STRONGHOLD!
THE EVER-FAITHFUL JARVIS IS PREPARING A MEAL!
SET TWO FEWER PLACES THIS EVENING, OLD SPORT!
SO FAR, THIS HAS BEEN SIMPLICITY ITSELF!
ONCE... EVER SO BRIEFLY... I WAS INDEED AN AVENGER!*
DURING THAT TIME, UNBEKNOWN TO ALL...
I ACQUIRED THIS DEVICE WHICH DEACTIVATES THEIR ALARMS!
*AS SHOWN IN ISH #20! ---SMILEY.
NOW, IF MY MEMORY SERVES ME RIGHTLY...
THAT ELEVATOR WILL TAKE ME TO THEIR MEETING CHAMBER!
HAH! MY MECHANISM STILL OPENS ALL DOORS TO ME!
THE NAIVE, TRUSTING FOOLS!
THEY NEVER BOTHERED CHANGING THEIR ALARM CIRCUITS!
THE BETTER TO KILL YOU, MY DEAR GOLIATH...
NÉE GIANT-MAN!
I DON'T KNOW WHY EGGHEAD WANTS THE LARGEST AVENGER SLAIN!
BUT, ALL I CARE ABOUT IS MY REWARD...
PLUS A CHANCE TO PROVE I AM STILL BETTER THAN THE DOOMED UPSTART HAWKEYE!
AND SO, THE MISINFORMED MERCENARY DRAWS NEARER HIS TWIN PREY---AS UNAWARE AS WAS EGGHEAD THAT AN UN-PUBLICIZED IDENTITY SWITCH HAS RECENTLY TAKEN PLACE...
10

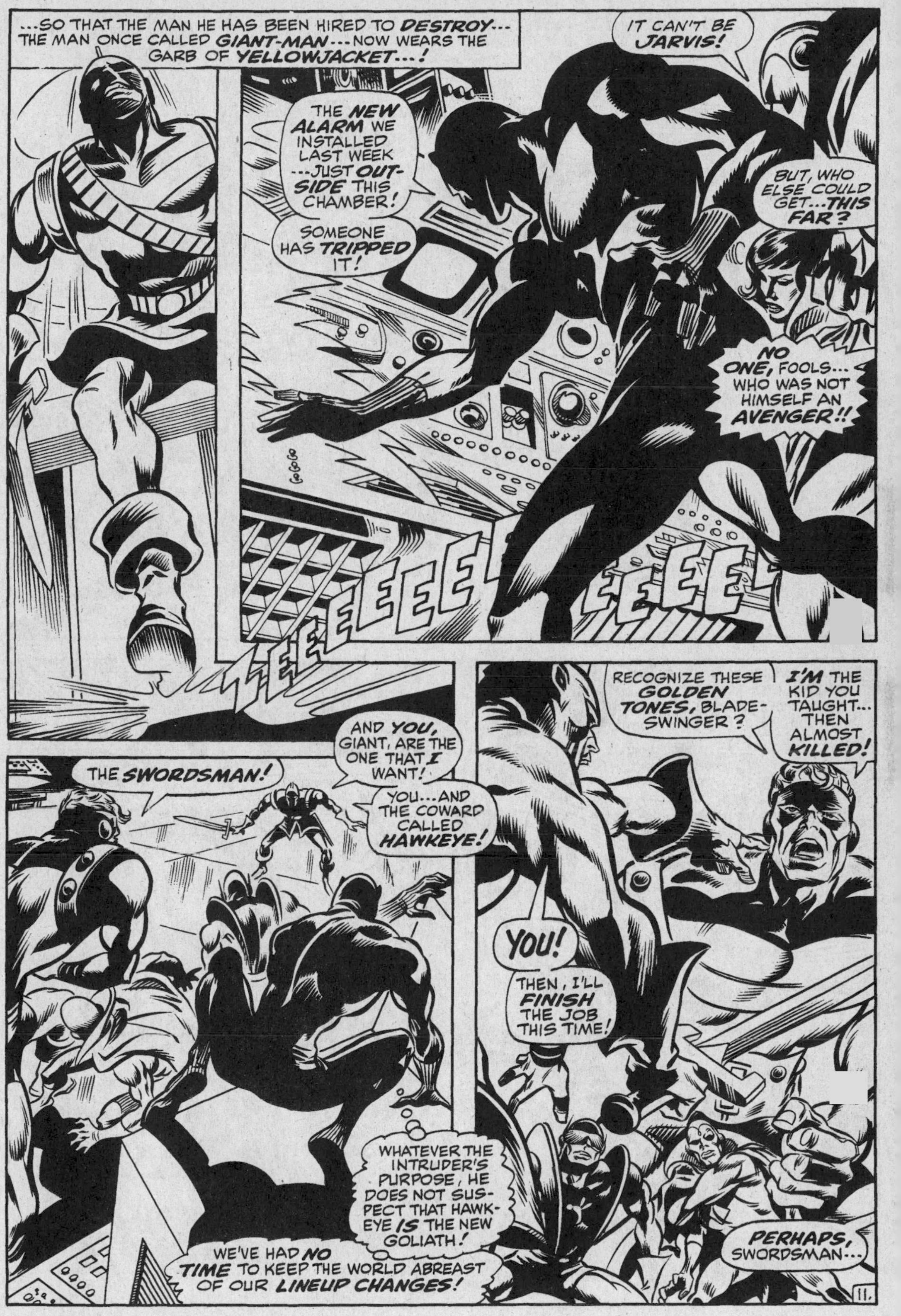

...SO THAT THE MAN HE HAS BEEN HIRED TO DESTROY-- THE MAN ONCE CALLED GIANT-MAN--- NOW WEARS THE GARB OF YELLOWJACKET...!
THE NEW ALARM WE INSTALLED LAST WEEK --JUST OUTSIDE THIS CHAMBER!
SOMEONE HAS TRIPPED IT!
IT CAN'T BE JARVIS!
BUT, WHO ELSE COULD GET...THIS FAR?
NO ONE, FOOLS... WHO WAS NOT HIMSELF AN AVENGER!!
EEEEEEEEEEE
THE SWORDSMAN!
AND YOU, GIANT, ARE THE ONE THAT I WANT!
YOU...AND THE COWARD CALLED HAWKEYE!
WHATEVER THE INTRUDER'S PURPOSE, HE DOES NOT SUSPECT THAT HAWKEYE IS THE NEW GOLIATH!
WE'VE HAD NO TIME TO KEEP THE WORLD ABREAST OF OUR LINEUP CHANGES!
RECOGNIZE THESE GOLDEN TONES, BLADE-SWINGER?
I'M THE KID YOU TAUGHT... THEN ALMOST KILLED!
YOU!
THEN, I'LL FINISH THE JOB THIS TIME!
PERHAPS, SWORDSMAN...

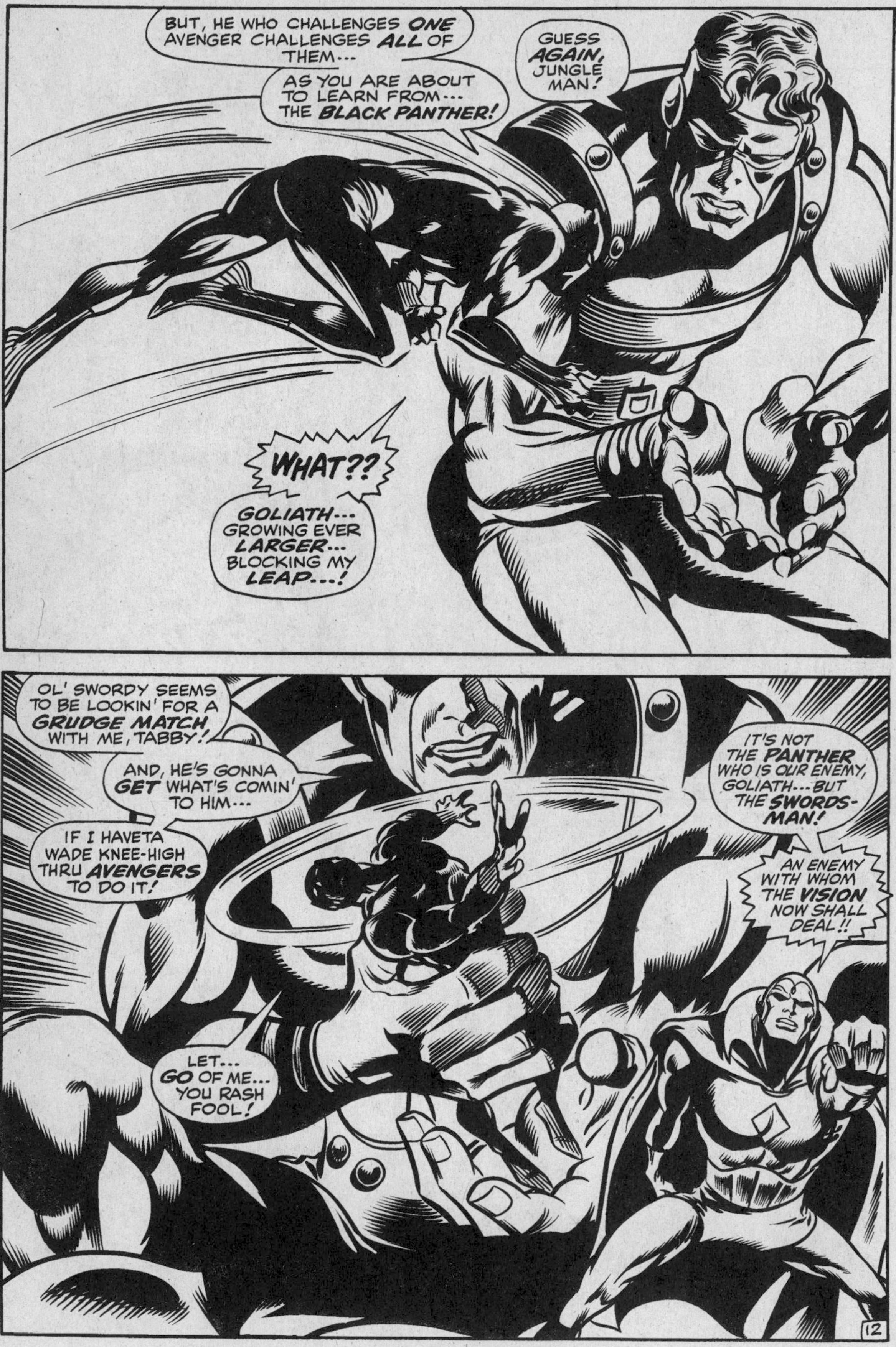
BUT, HE WHO CHALLENGES ONE AVENGER CHALLENGES ALL OF THEM...
AS YOU ARE ABOUT TO LEARN FROM... THE BLACK PANTHER!
GUESS AGAIN, JUNGLE MAN!
WHAT??
GOLIATH... GROWING EVER LARGER... BLOCKING MY LEAP...!
OL' SWORDY SEEMS TO BE LOOKIN' FOR A GRUDGE MATCH WITH ME, TABBY!
AND, HE'S GONNA GET WHAT'S COMIN' TO HIM...
IF I HAVETA WADE KNEE-HIGH THRU AVENGERS TO DO IT!
IT'S NOT THE PANTHER WHO IS OUR ENEMY, GOLIATH... BUT THE SWORDS-MAN!
AN ENEMY WITH WHOM THE VISION NOW SHALL DEAL!!
LET... GO OF ME... YOU RASH FOOL!
12

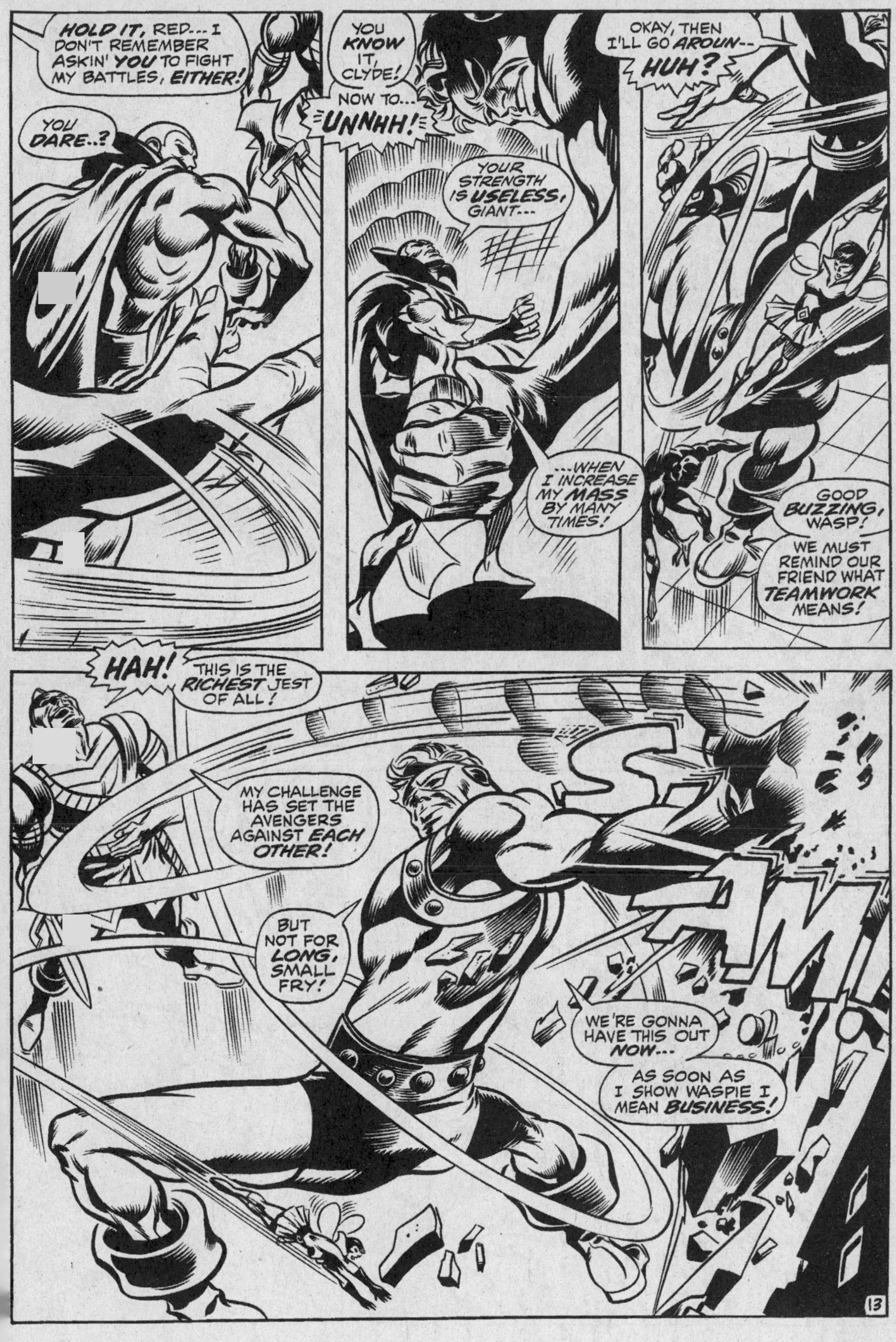

HOLD IT, RED... I DON'T REMEMBER ASKIN' YOU TO FIGHT MY BATTLES, EITHER!
YOU DARE..?
YOU KNOW IT, CLYDE!
NOW TO...
UNNHH!
YOUR STRENGTH IS USELESS, GIANT---
...WHEN I INCREASE MY MASS BY MANY TIMES!
OKAY, THEN I'LL GO AROUN--
HUH?
GOOD BUZZING, WASP!
WE MUST REMIND OUR FRIEND WHAT TEAMWORK MEANS!
HAH!
THIS IS THE RICHEST JEST OF ALL!
MY CHALLENGE HAS SET THE AVENGERS AGAINST EACH OTHER!
BUT NOT FOR LONG, SMALL FRY!
WE'RE GONNA HAVE THIS OUT NOW...
AS SOON AS I SHOW WASPIE I MEAN BUSINESS!
13

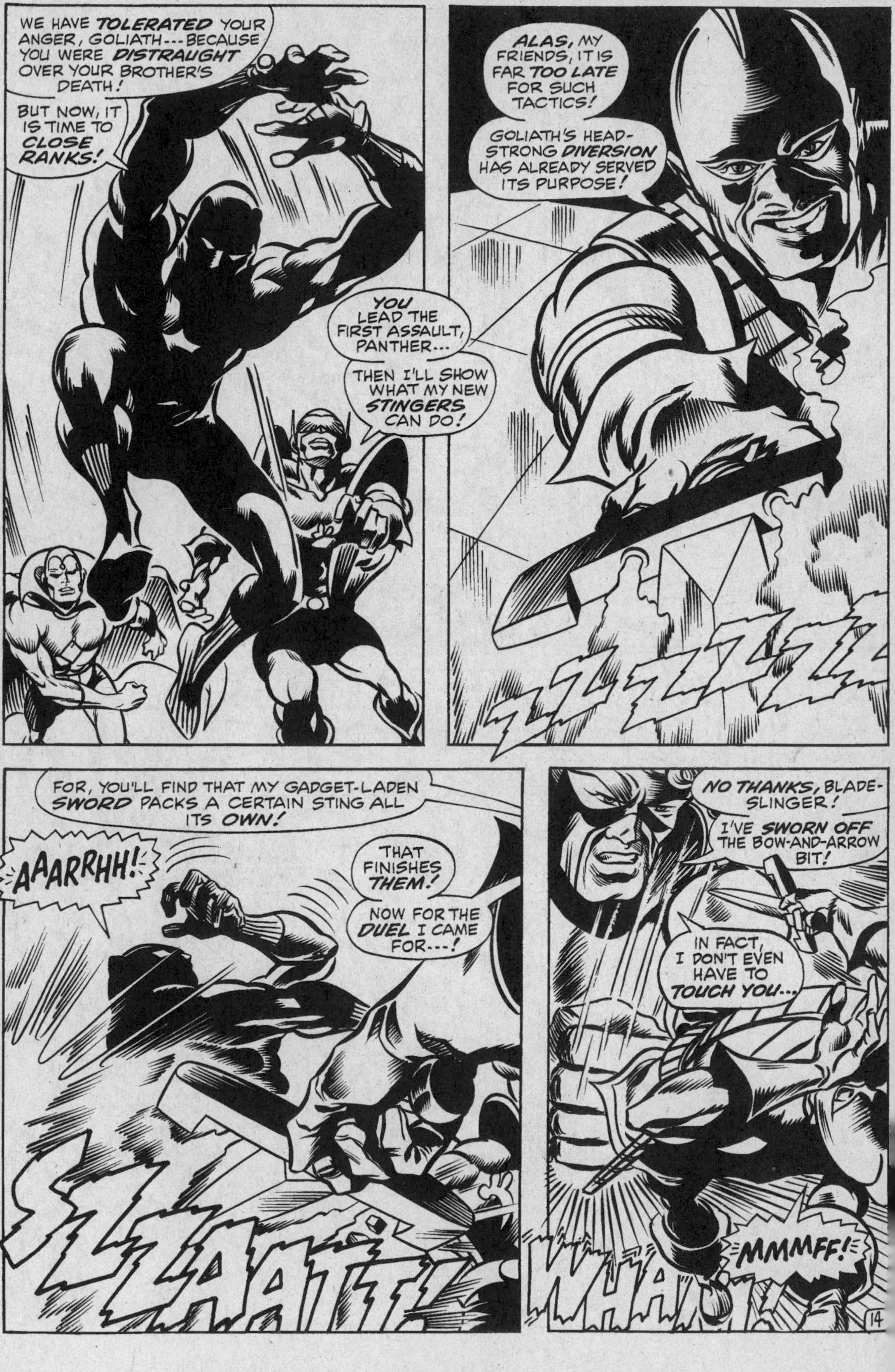

WE HAVE TOLERATED YOUR ANGER, GOLIATH---BECAUSE YOU WERE DISTRAUGHT OVER YOUR BROTHER'S DEATH!
BUT NOW, IT IS TIME TO CLOSE RANKS!
YOU LEAD THE FIRST ASSAULT, PANTHER...
THEN I'LL SHOW WHAT MY NEW STINGERS CAN DO!
ALAS, MY FRIENDS, IT IS FAR TOO LATE FOR SUCH TACTICS!
GOLIATH'S HEAD-STRONG DIVERSION HAS ALREADY SERVED ITS PURPOSE!
ZZZZZZ
FOR, YOU'LL FIND THAT MY GADGET-LADEN SWORD PACKS A CERTAIN STING ALL ITS OWN!
AAARRHH!
THAT FINISHES THEM!
NOW FOR THE DUEL I CAME FOR---!
SLZAAT!
NO THANKS, BLADE-SLINGER!
I'VE SWORN OFF THE BOW-AND-ARROW BIT!
IN FACT, I DON'T EVEN HAVE TO TOUCH YOU...
MMMFF!
WHAT!

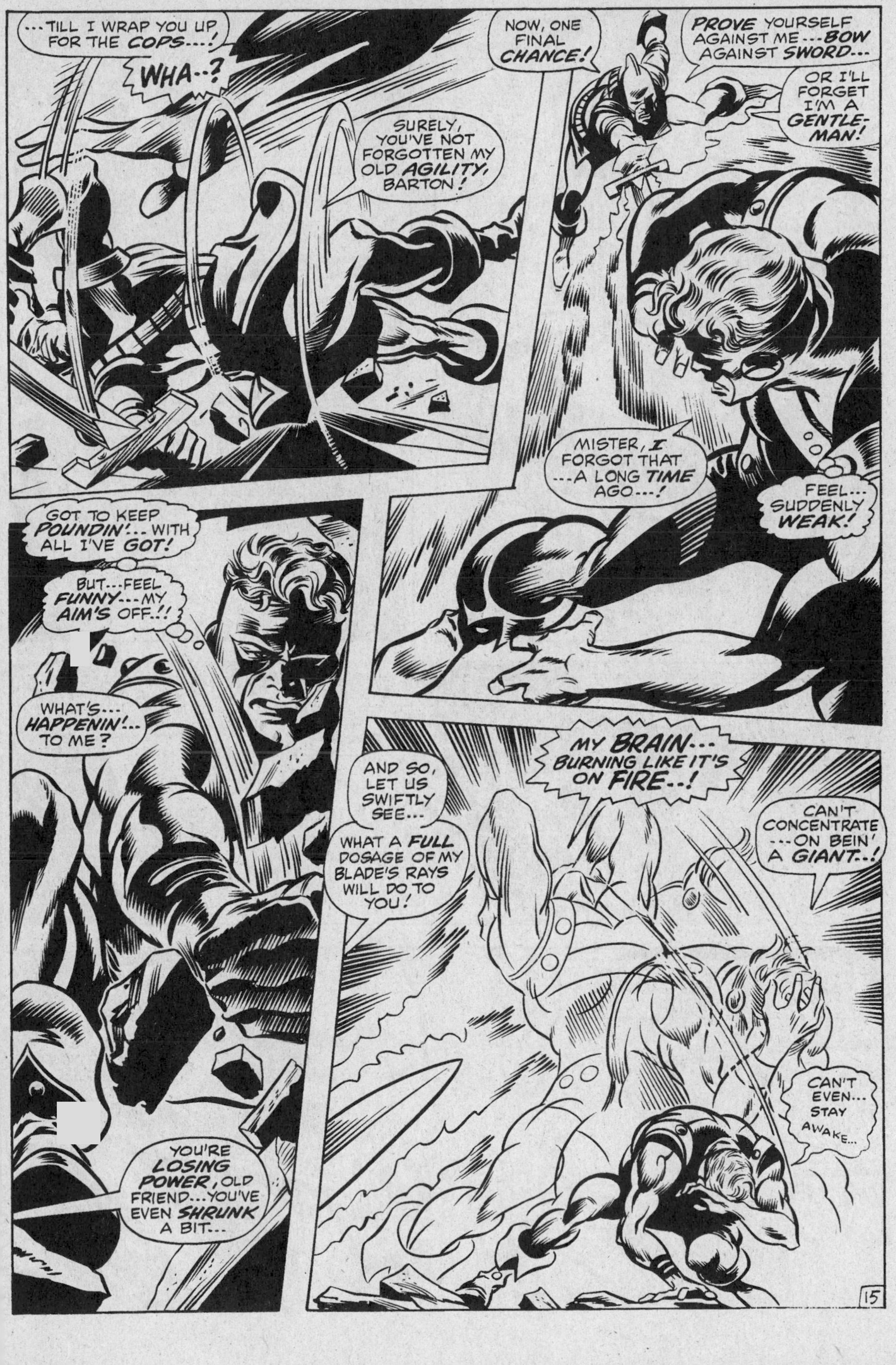
...TILL I WRAP YOU UP FOR THE COPS...!
WHA--?
SURELY, YOU'VE NOT FORGOTTEN MY OLD AGILITY, BARTON!
NOW, ONE FINAL CHANCE!
PROVE YOURSELF AGAINST ME---BOW AGAINST SWORD...
OR I'LL FORGET I'M A GENTLE-MAN!
MISTER, I FORGOT THAT ---A LONG TIME AGO---!
FEEL... SUDDENLY WEAK!
GOT TO KEEP POUNDIN'... WITH ALL I'VE GOT!
BUT---FEEL FUNNY---MY AIM'S OFF..!!
WHAT'S... HAPPENIN'... TO ME?
YOU'RE LOSING POWER, OLD FRIEND...YOU'VE EVEN SHRUNK A BIT...
AND SO, LET US SWIFTLY SEE...
WHAT A FULL DOSAGE OF MY BLADE'S RAYS WILL DO TO YOU!
MY BRAIN... BURNING LIKE IT'S ON FIRE..!
CAN'T CONCENTRATE ---ON BEIN' A GIANT..!
CAN'T EVEN... STAY AWAKE...

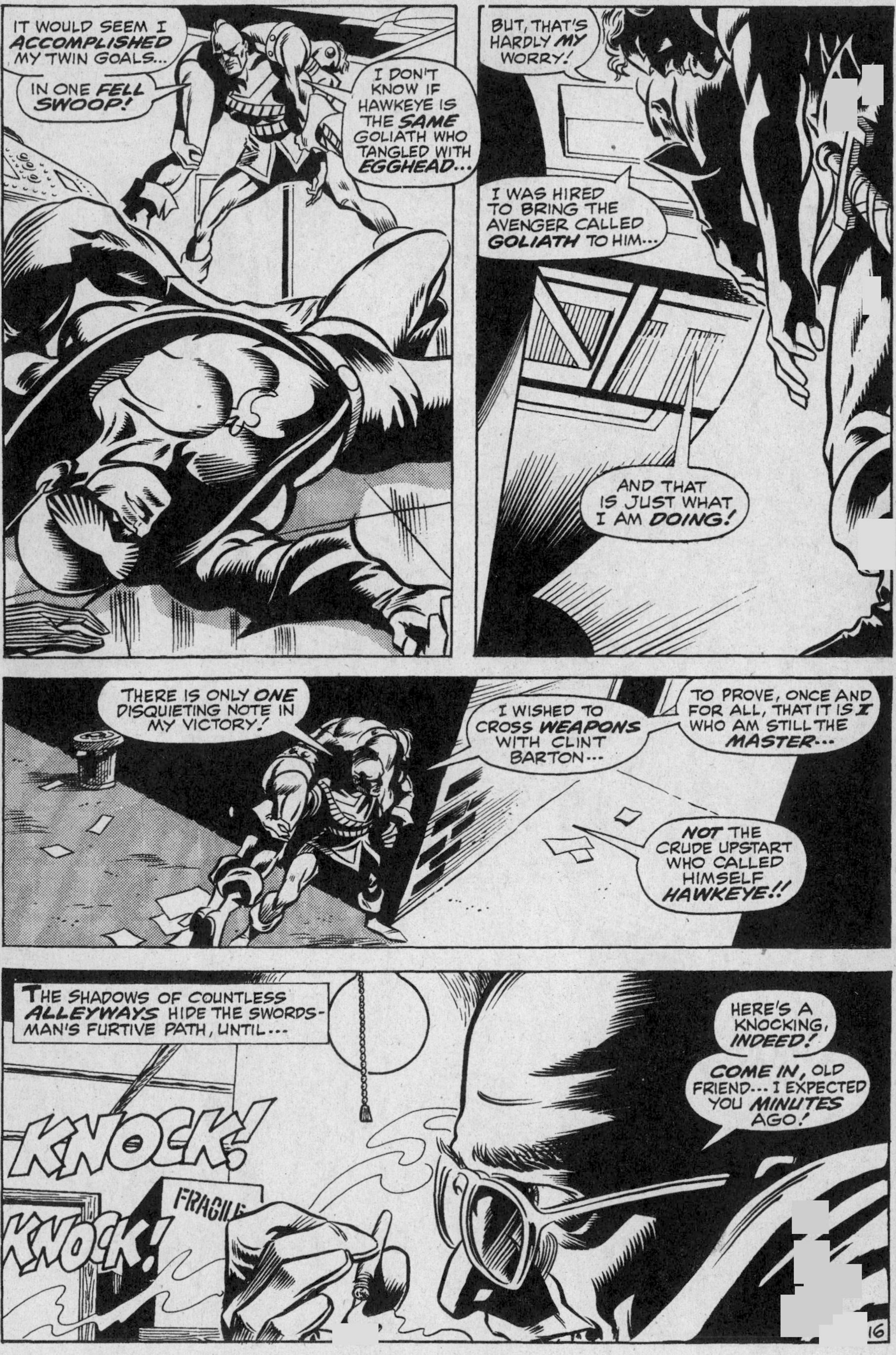
IT WOULD SEEM I ACCOMPLISHED MY TWIN GOALS...
IN ONE FELL SWOOP!
I DON'T KNOW IF HAWKEYE IS THE SAME GOLIATH WHO TANGLED WITH EGGHEAD...
BUT, THAT'S HARDLY MY WORRY!
I WAS HIRED TO BRING THE AVENGER CALLED GOLIATH TO HIM...
AND THAT IS JUST WHAT I AM DOING!
THERE IS ONLY ONE DISQUIETING NOTE IN MY VICTORY!
I WISHED TO CROSS WEAPONS WITH CLINT BARTON...
TO PROVE, ONCE AND FOR ALL, THAT IT IS I WHO AM STILL THE MASTER...
NOT THE CRUDE UPSTART WHO CALLED HIMSELF HAWKEYE!!
THE SHADOWS OF COUNTLESS ALLEYWAYS HIDE THE SWORDSMAN'S FURTIVE PATH, UNTIL...
KNOCK!
KNOCK!
FRAGILE
HERE'S A KNOCKING, INDEED!
COME IN, OLD FRIEND... I EXPECTED YOU MINUTES AGO!

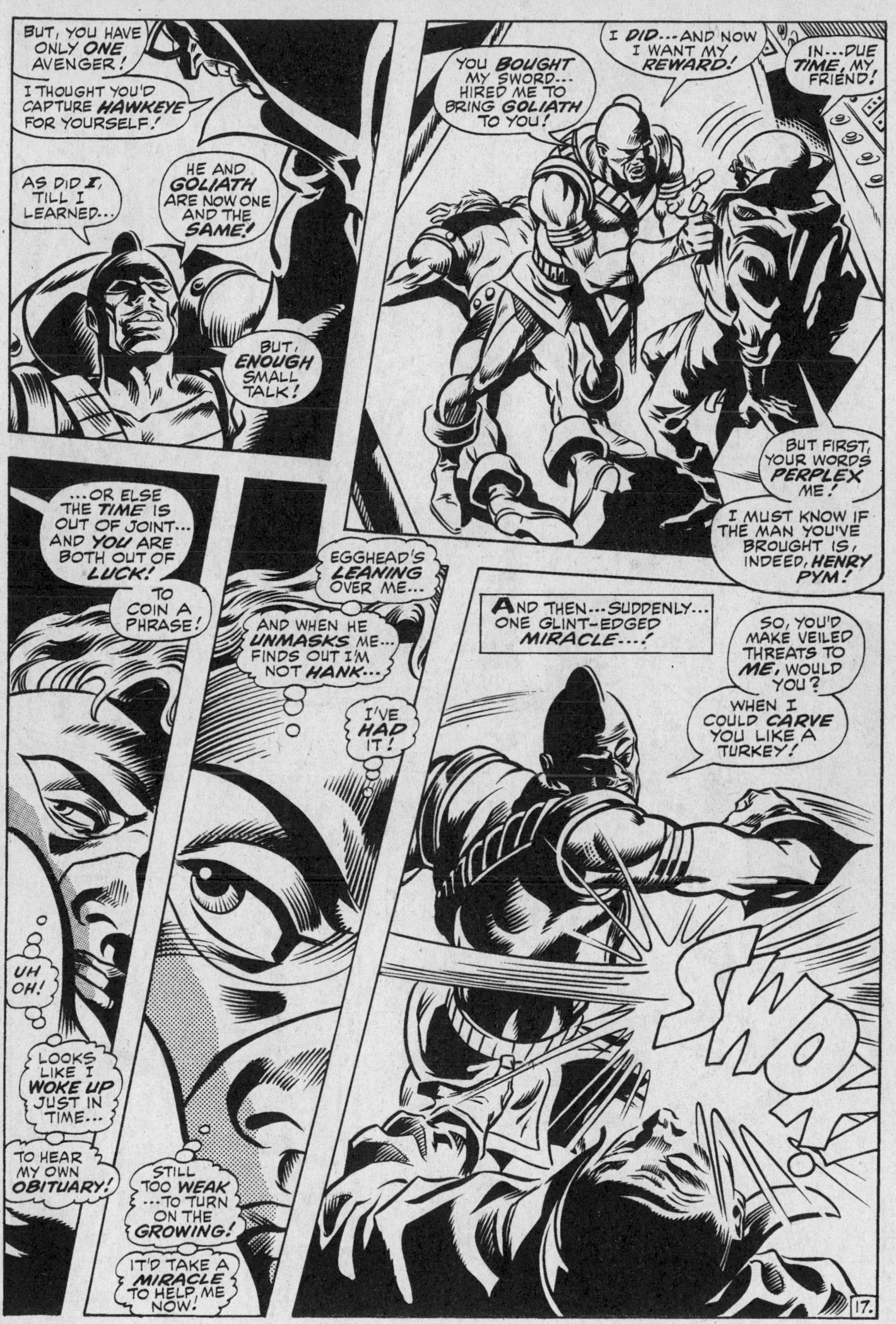

BUT, YOU HAVE ONLY ONE AVENGER!
I THOUGHT YOU'D CAPTURE HAWKEYE FOR YOURSELF!
AS DID I, TILL I LEARNED...
HE AND GOLIATH ARE NOW ONE AND THE SAME!
BUT, ENOUGH SMALL TALK!
YOU BOUGHT MY SWORD... HIRED ME TO BRING GOLIATH TO YOU!
I DID... AND NOW I WANT MY REWARD!
IN... DUE TIME, MY FRIEND!
BUT FIRST, YOUR WORDS PERPLEX ME!
I MUST KNOW IF THE MAN YOU'VE BROUGHT IS, INDEED, HENRY PYM!
...OR ELSE THE TIME IS OUT OF JOINT... AND YOU ARE BOTH OUT OF LUCK!
TO COIN A PHRASE!
EGGHEAD'S LEANING OVER ME...
AND WHEN HE UNMASKS ME... FINDS OUT I'M NOT HANK...
I'VE HAD IT!
UH OH!
LOOKS LIKE I WOKE UP JUST IN TIME...
TO HEAR MY OWN OBITUARY!
STILL TOO WEAK ...TO TURN ON THE GROWING!
IT'D TAKE A MIRACLE TO HELP, ME NOW!
AND THEN... SUDDENLY... ONE GLINT-EDGED MIRACLE...!
SO, YOU'D MAKE VEILED THREATS TO ME, WOULD YOU?
WHEN I COULD CARVE YOU LIKE A TURKEY!
SWOK

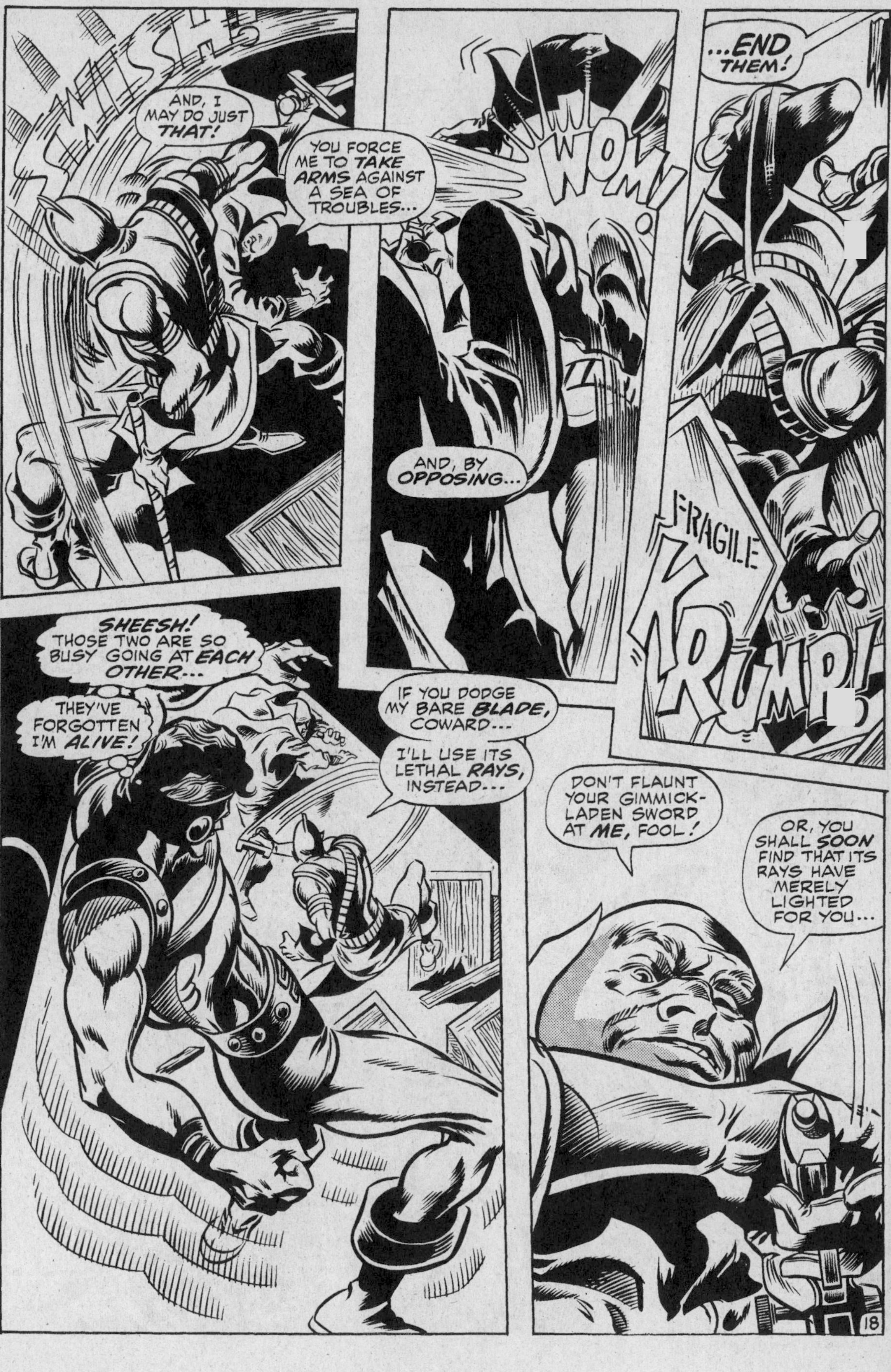
SWISSH!
AND, I MAY DO JUST THAT!
YOU FORCE ME TO TAKE ARMS AGAINST A SEA OF TROUBLES...
WOMM!
AND, BY OPPOSING...
...END THEM!
FRAGILE
KRUMP!
SHEESH! THOSE TWO ARE SO BUSY GOING AT EACH OTHER...
THEY'VE FORGOTTEN I'M ALIVE!
IF YOU DODGE MY BARE BLADE, COWARD...
I'LL USE ITS LETHAL RAYS, INSTEAD...
DON'T FLAUNT YOUR GIMMICK-LADEN SWORD AT ME, FOOL!
OR, YOU SHALL SOON FIND THAT ITS RAYS HAVE MERELY LIGHTED FOR YOU...
18

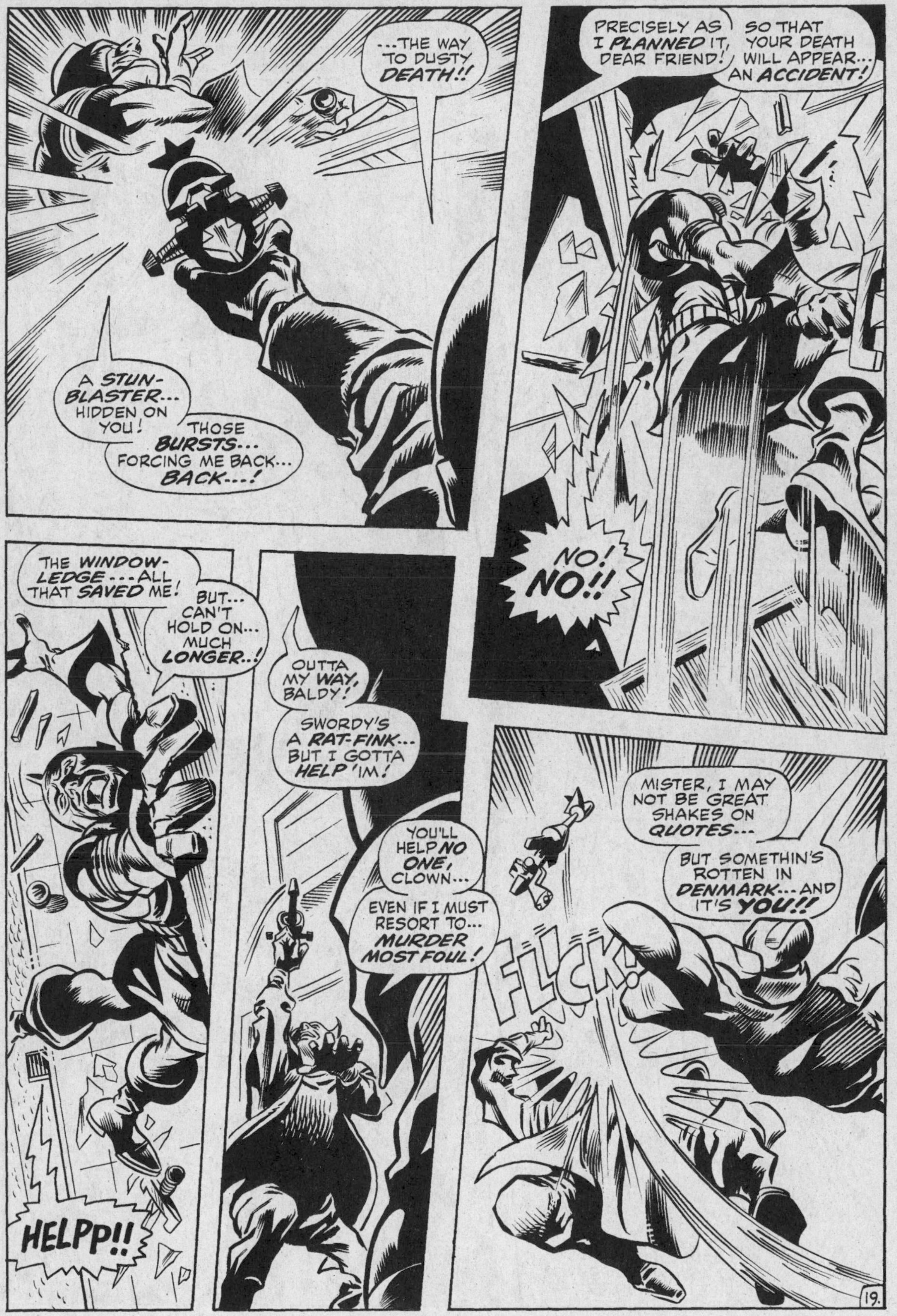
...THE WAY TO DUSTY DEATH!!
A STUN-BLASTER... HIDDEN ON YOU!
THOSE BURSTS... FORCING ME BACK... BACK...!
PRECISELY AS I PLANNED IT, DEAR FRIEND!
SO THAT YOUR DEATH WILL APPEAR... AN ACCIDENT!
NO! NO!!
THE WINDOW-LEDGE...ALL THAT SAVED ME!
BUT... CAN'T HOLD ON... MUCH LONGER..!
HELPP!!
OUTTA MY WAY, BALDY!
SWORDY'S A RAT-FINK... BUT I GOTTA HELP 'IM!
YOU'LL HELP NO ONE, CLOWN...
EVEN IF I MUST RESORT TO... MURDER MOST FOUL!
MISTER, I MAY NOT BE GREAT SHAKES ON QUOTES...
BUT SOMETHIN'S ROTTEN IN DENMARK...AND IT'S YOU!!
FLICK!
19.

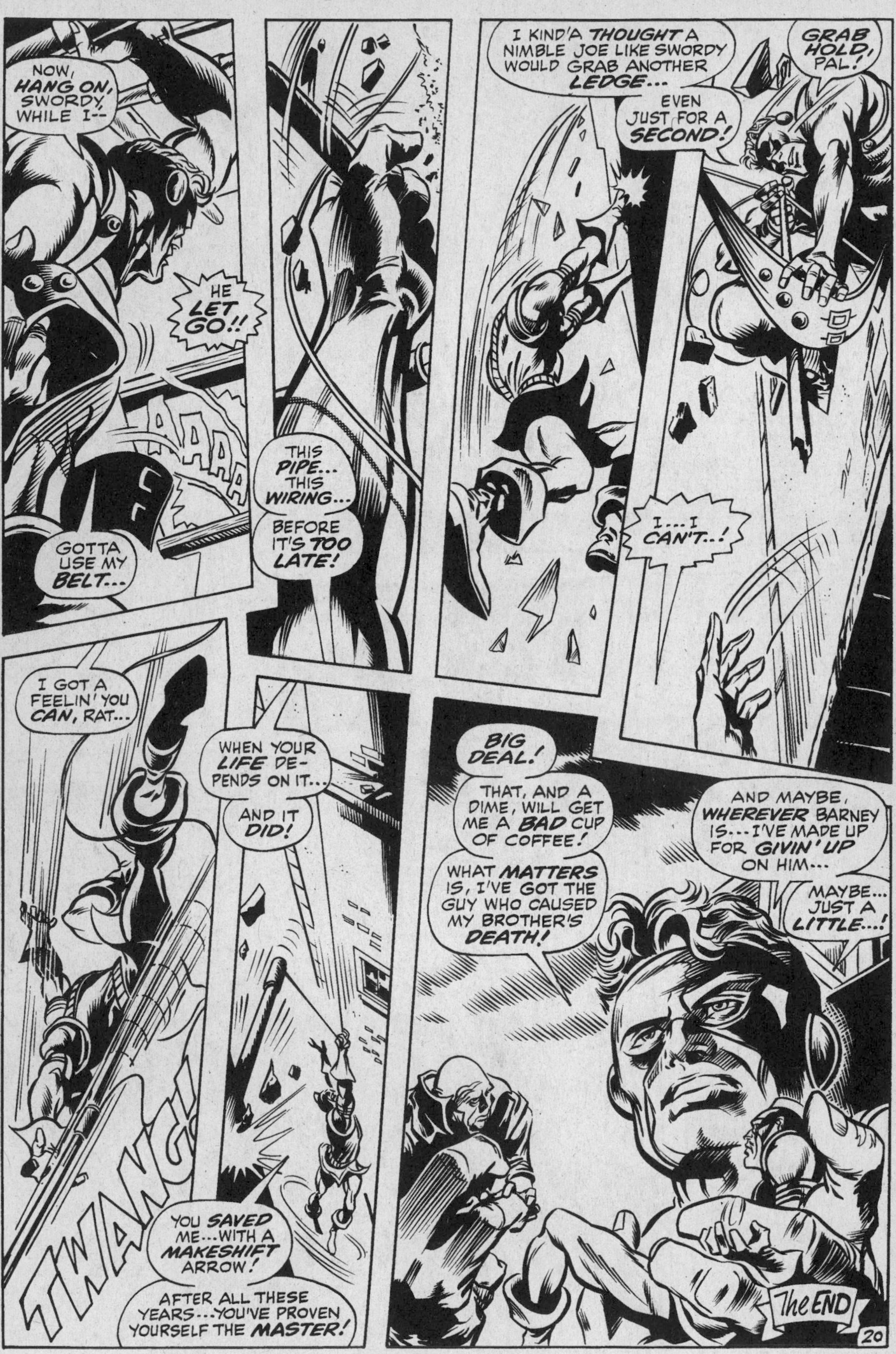
NOW, HANG ON, SWORDY, WHILE I--
HE LET GO!!
AAAAA
GOTTA USE MY BELT...
THIS PIPE... THIS WIRING...
BEFORE IT'S TOO LATE!
I KIND'A THOUGHT A NIMBLE JOE LIKE SWORDY WOULD GRAB ANOTHER LEDGE...
EVEN JUST FOR A SECOND!
GRAB HOLD, PAL!
I...I CAN'T...!
I GOT A FEELIN' YOU CAN, RAT...
WHEN YOUR LIFE DE-PENDS ON IT...
AND IT DID!
TWANG!
YOU SAVED ME...WITH A MAKESHIFT ARROW!
AFTER ALL THESE YEARS...YOU'VE PROVEN YOURSELF THE MASTER!
BIG DEAL!
THAT, AND A DIME, WILL GET ME A BAD CUP OF COFFEE!
WHAT MATTERS IS, I'VE GOT THE GUY WHO CAUSED MY BROTHER'S DEATH!
AND MAYBE, WHEREVER BARNEY IS...I'VE MADE UP FOR GIVIN' UP ON HIM...
MAYBE... JUST A LITTLE...!
The END

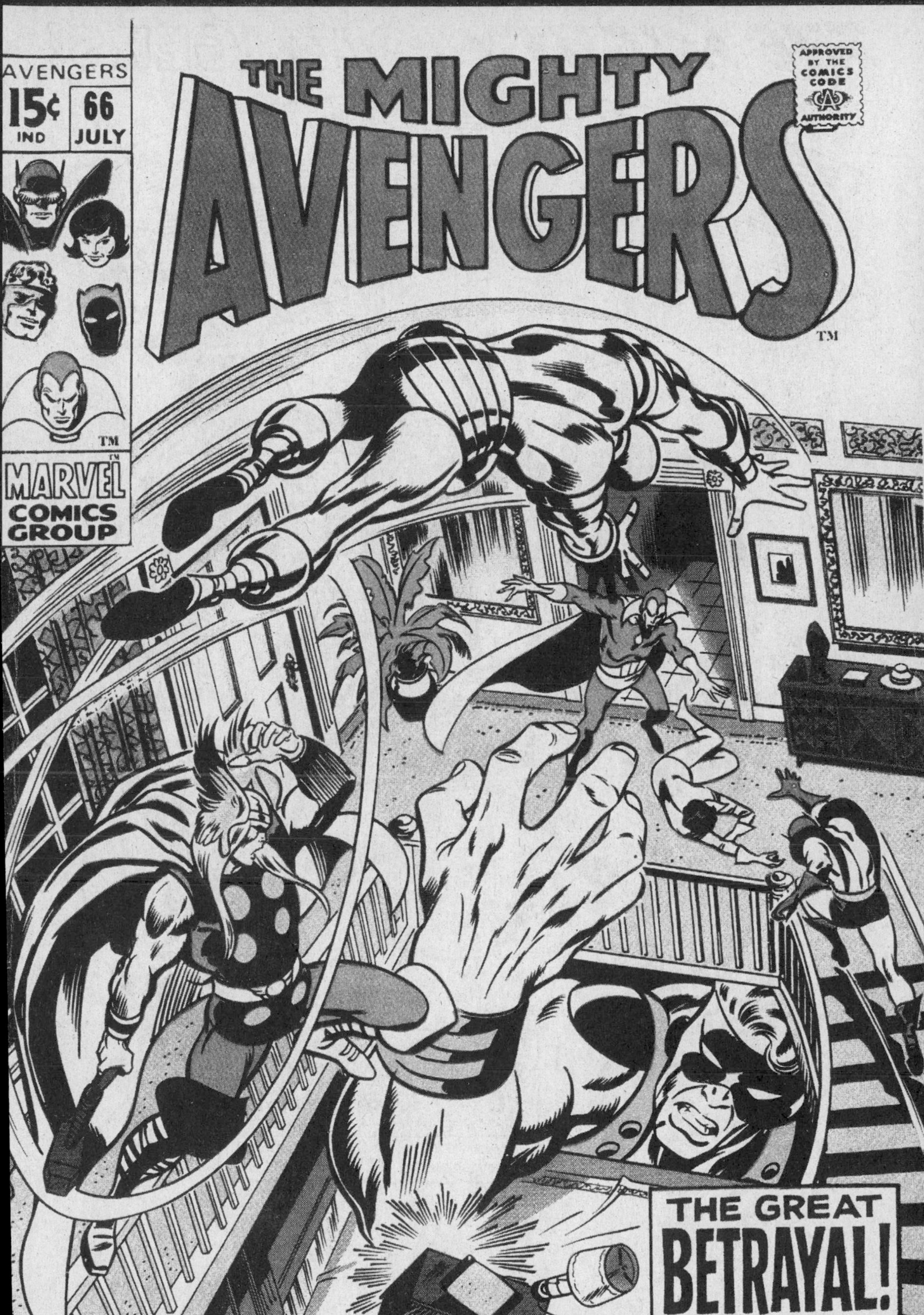
AVENGERS
15¢
IND
66
JULY
THE MIGHTY
AVENGERS
APPROVED BY THE COMICS CODE AUTHORITY
MARVEL COMICS GROUP
THE GREAT
BETRAYAL!

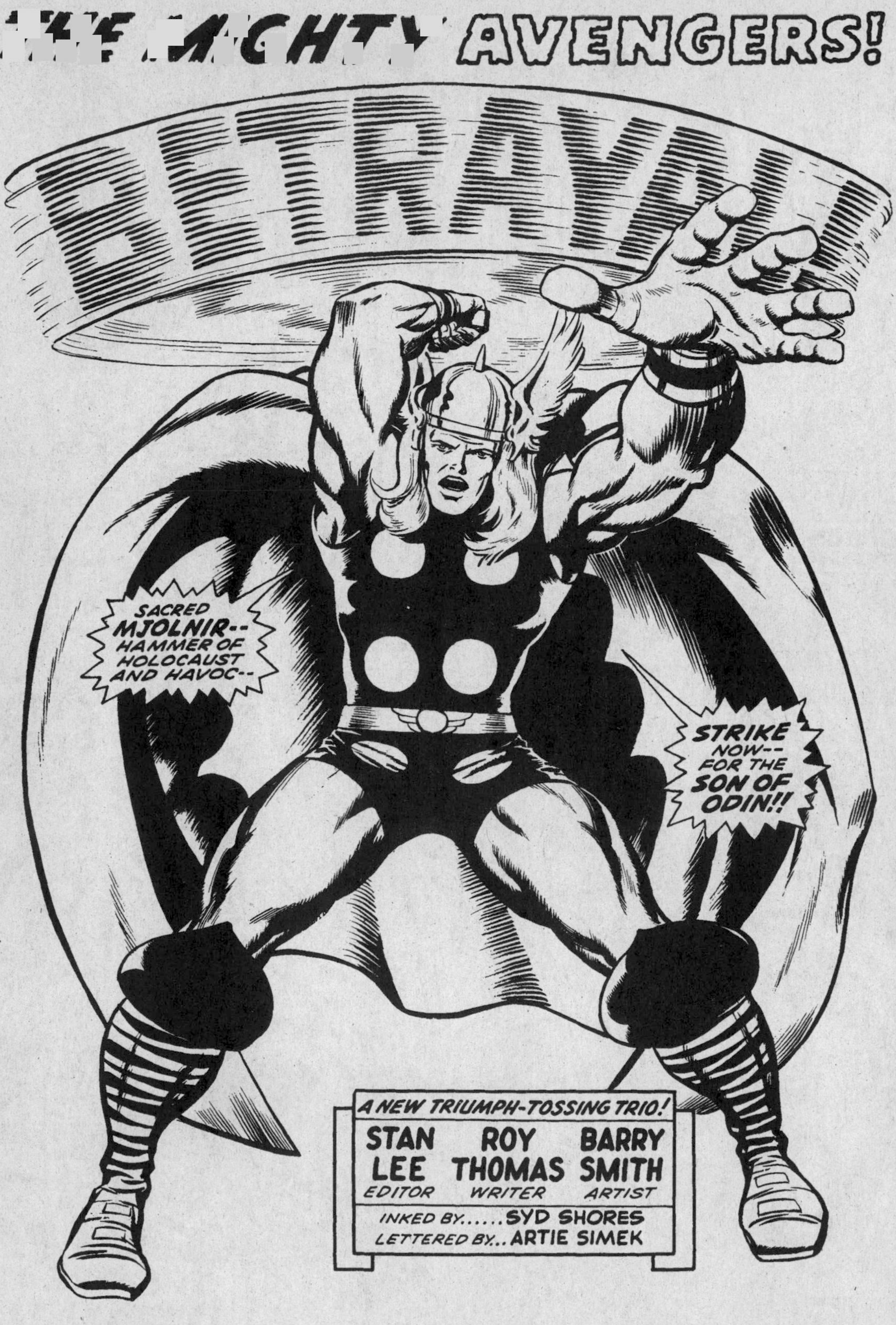
AVENGERS!
BETRAYAL!
SACRED MJOLNIR-- HAMMER OF HOLOCAUST AND HAVOC--
STRIKE NOW-- FOR THE SON OF ODIN!!
A NEW TRIUMPH-TOSSING TRIO!
STAN LEE EDITOR
ROY THOMAS WRITER
BARRY SMITH ARTIST
INKED BY...... SYD SHORES
LETTERED BY... ARTIE SIMEK

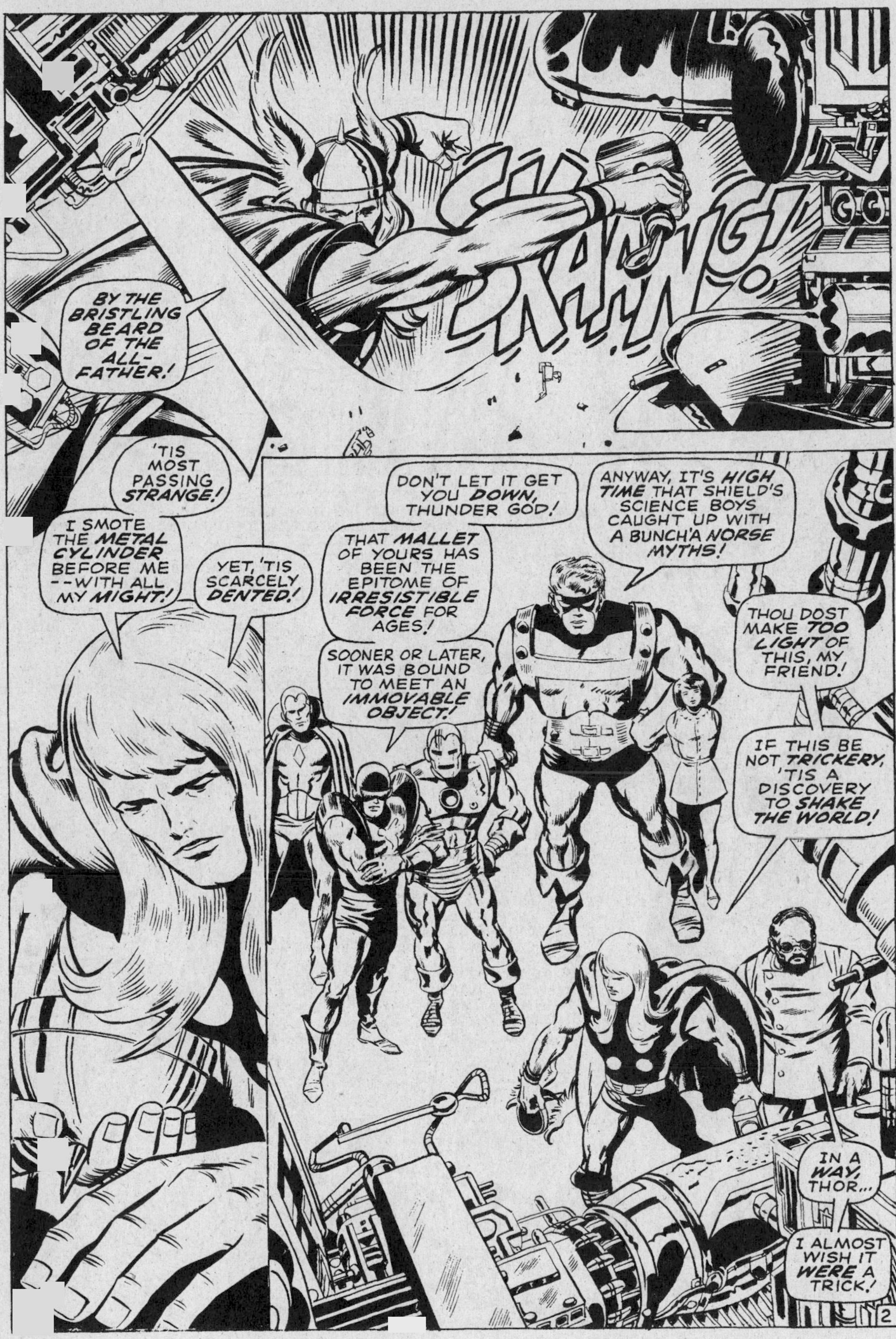
BY THE BRISTLING BEARD OF THE ALL-FATHER!
CHAAANG!
'TIS MOST PASSING STRANGE!
I SMOTE THE METAL CYLINDER BEFORE ME --WITH ALL MY MIGHT!
YET, 'TIS SCARCELY DENTED!
DON'T LET IT GET YOU DOWN, THUNDER GOD!
THAT MALLET OF YOURS HAS BEEN THE EPITOME OF IRRESISTIBLE FORCE FOR AGES!
SOONER OR LATER, IT WAS BOUND TO MEET AN IMMOVABLE OBJECT!
ANYWAY, IT'S HIGH TIME THAT SHIELD'S SCIENCE BOYS CAUGHT UP WITH A BUNCH'A NORSE MYTHS!
THOU DOST MAKE TOO LIGHT OF THIS, MY FRIEND!
IF THIS BE NOT TRICKERY, 'TIS A DISCOVERY TO SHAKE THE WORLD!
IN A WAY, THOR...
I ALMOST WISH IT WERE A TRICK!
2

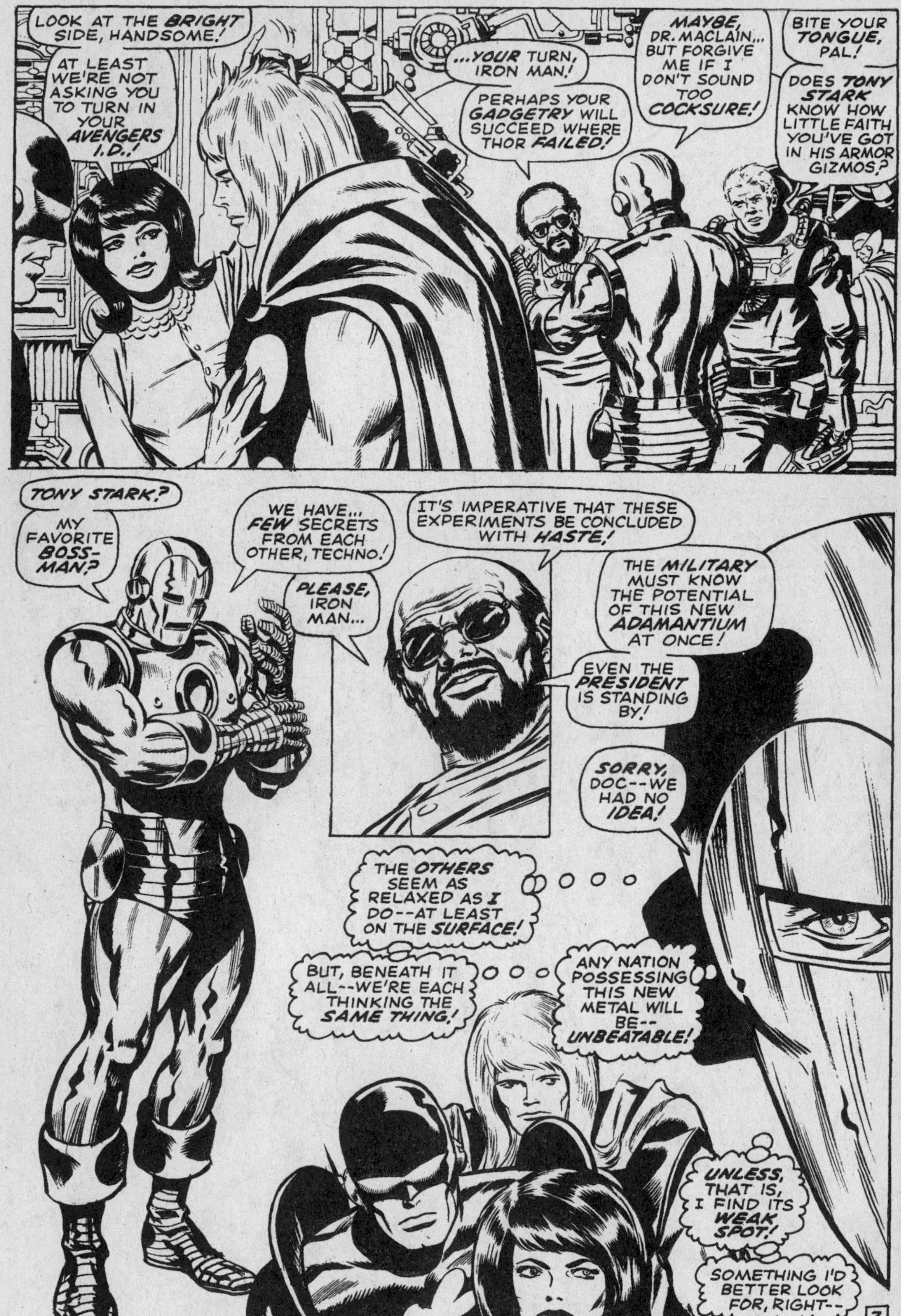
LOOK AT THE BRIGHT SIDE, HANDSOME!
AT LEAST WE'RE NOT ASKING YOU TO TURN IN YOUR AVENGERS I.D.!
...YOUR TURN, IRON MAN!
PERHAPS YOUR GADGETRY WILL SUCCEED WHERE THOR FAILED!
MAYBE, DR. MACLAIN... BUT FORGIVE ME IF I DON'T SOUND TOO COCKSURE!
BITE YOUR TONGUE, PAL!
DOES TONY STARK KNOW HOW LITTLE FAITH YOU'VE GOT IN HIS ARMOR GIZMOS?
TONY STARK?
MY FAVORITE BOSS-MAN?
WE HAVE... FEW SECRETS FROM EACH OTHER, TECHNO!
PLEASE, IRON MAN...
IT'S IMPERATIVE THAT THESE EXPERIMENTS BE CONCLUDED WITH HASTE!
THE MILITARY MUST KNOW THE POTENTIAL OF THIS NEW ADAMANTIUM AT ONCE!
EVEN THE PRESIDENT IS STANDING BY!
SORRY, DOC--WE HAD NO IDEA!
THE OTHERS SEEM AS RELAXED AS I DO--AT LEAST ON THE SURFACE!
BUT, BENEATH IT ALL--WE'RE EACH THINKING THE SAME THING!
ANY NATION POSSESSING THIS NEW METAL WILL BE--UNBEATABLE!
UNLESS, THAT IS, I FIND ITS WEAK SPOT!
SOMETHING I'D BETTER LOOK FOR, RIGHT--

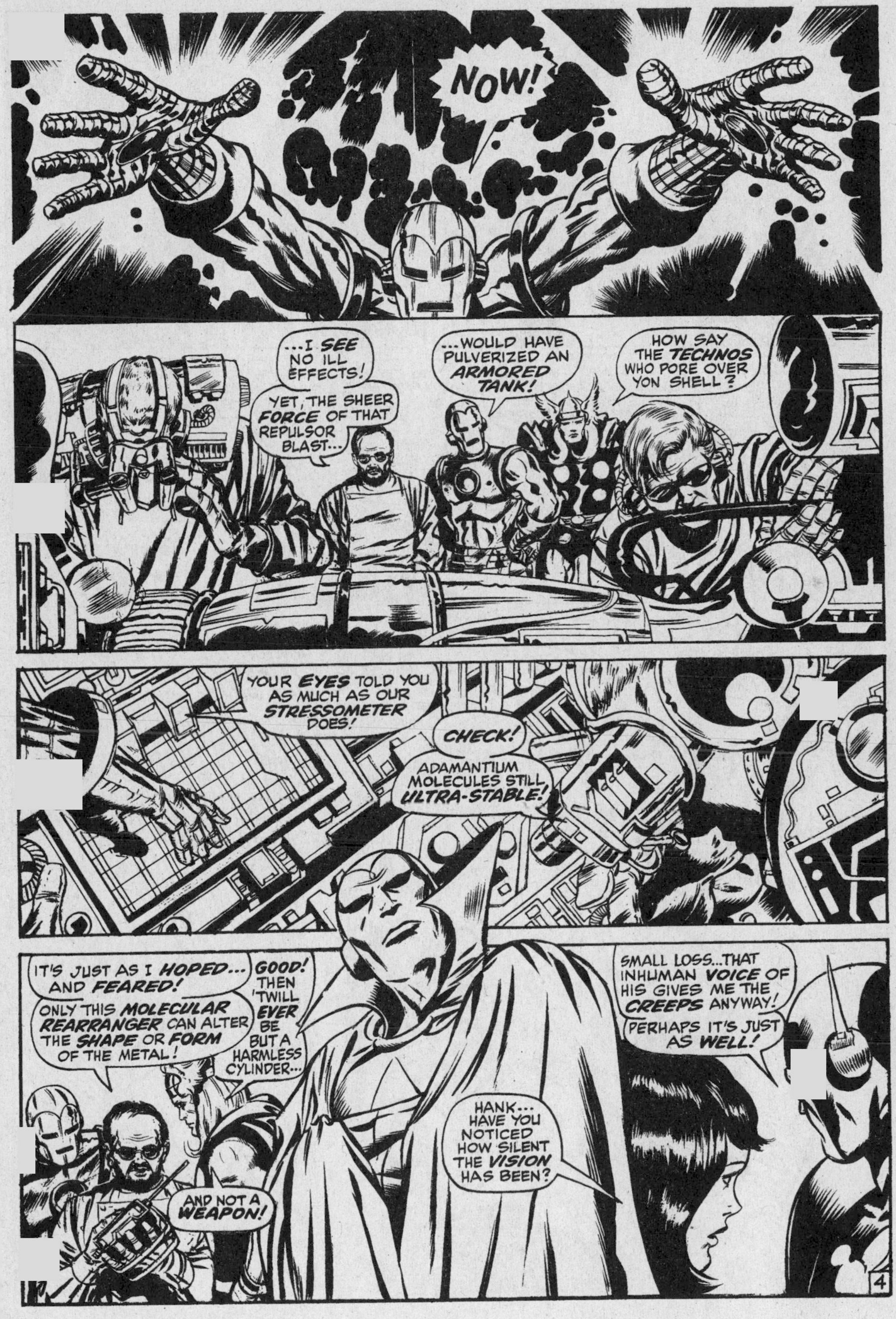
NOW!
...I SEE NO ILL EFFECTS!
YET, THE SHEER FORCE OF THAT REPULSOR BLAST...
...WOULD HAVE PULVERIZED AN ARMORED TANK!
HOW SAY THE TECHNOS WHO PORE OVER YON SHELL?
YOUR EYES TOLD YOU AS MUCH AS OUR STRESSOMETER DOES!
CHECK!
ADAMANTIUM MOLECULES STILL ULTRA-STABLE!
IT'S JUST AS I HOPED... AND FEARED!
ONLY THIS MOLECULAR REARRANGER CAN ALTER THE SHAPE OR FORM OF THE METAL!
GOOD! THEN 'TWILL EVER BE BUT A HARMLESS CYLINDER...
AND NOT A WEAPON!
SMALL LOSS...THAT INHUMAN VOICE OF HIS GIVES ME THE CREEPS ANYWAY!
PERHAPS IT'S JUST AS WELL!
HANK... HAVE YOU NOTICED HOW SILENT THE VISION HAS BEEN?
4

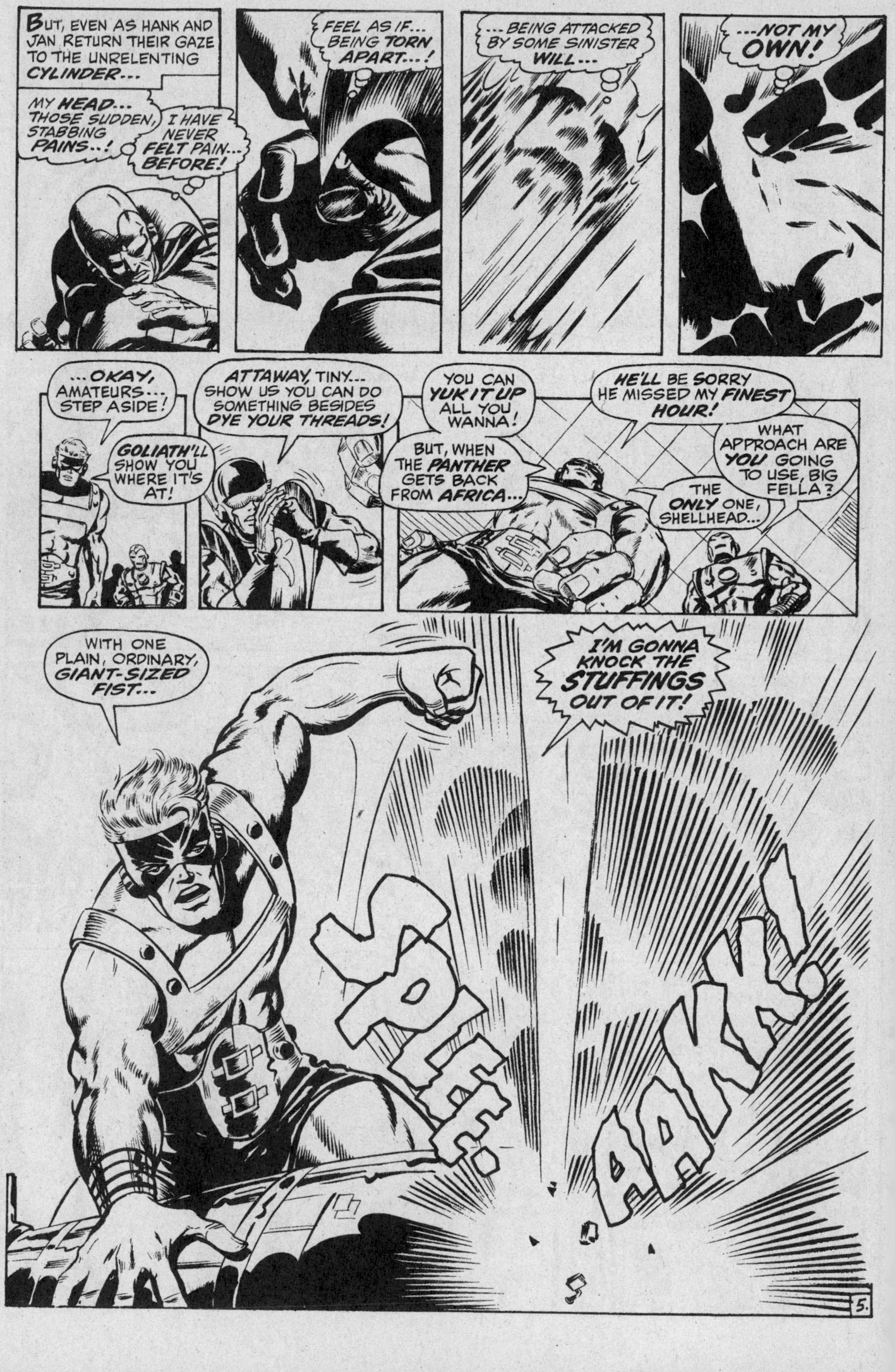
BUT, EVEN AS HANK AND JAN RETURN THEIR GAZE TO THE UNRELENTING CYLINDER...
MY HEAD... THOSE SUDDEN, STABBING PAINS..!
I HAVE NEVER FELT PAIN... BEFORE!
FEEL AS IF... BEING TORN APART...!
...BEING ATTACKED BY SOME SINISTER WILL...
...NOT MY OWN!
...OKAY, AMATEURS... STEP ASIDE!
GOLIATH'LL SHOW YOU WHERE IT'S AT!
ATTAWAY, TINY... SHOW US YOU CAN DO SOMETHING BESIDES DYE YOUR THREADS!
YOU CAN YUK IT UP ALL YOU WANNA!
BUT, WHEN THE PANTHER GETS BACK FROM AFRICA...
HE'LL BE SORRY HE MISSED MY FINEST HOUR!
WHAT APPROACH ARE YOU GOING TO USE, BIG FELLA?
THE ONLY ONE, SHELLHEAD...
WITH ONE PLAIN, ORDINARY, GIANT-SIZED FIST...
I'M GONNA KNOCK THE STUFFINGS OUT OF IT!
SPLEE!
AAKK!
5.

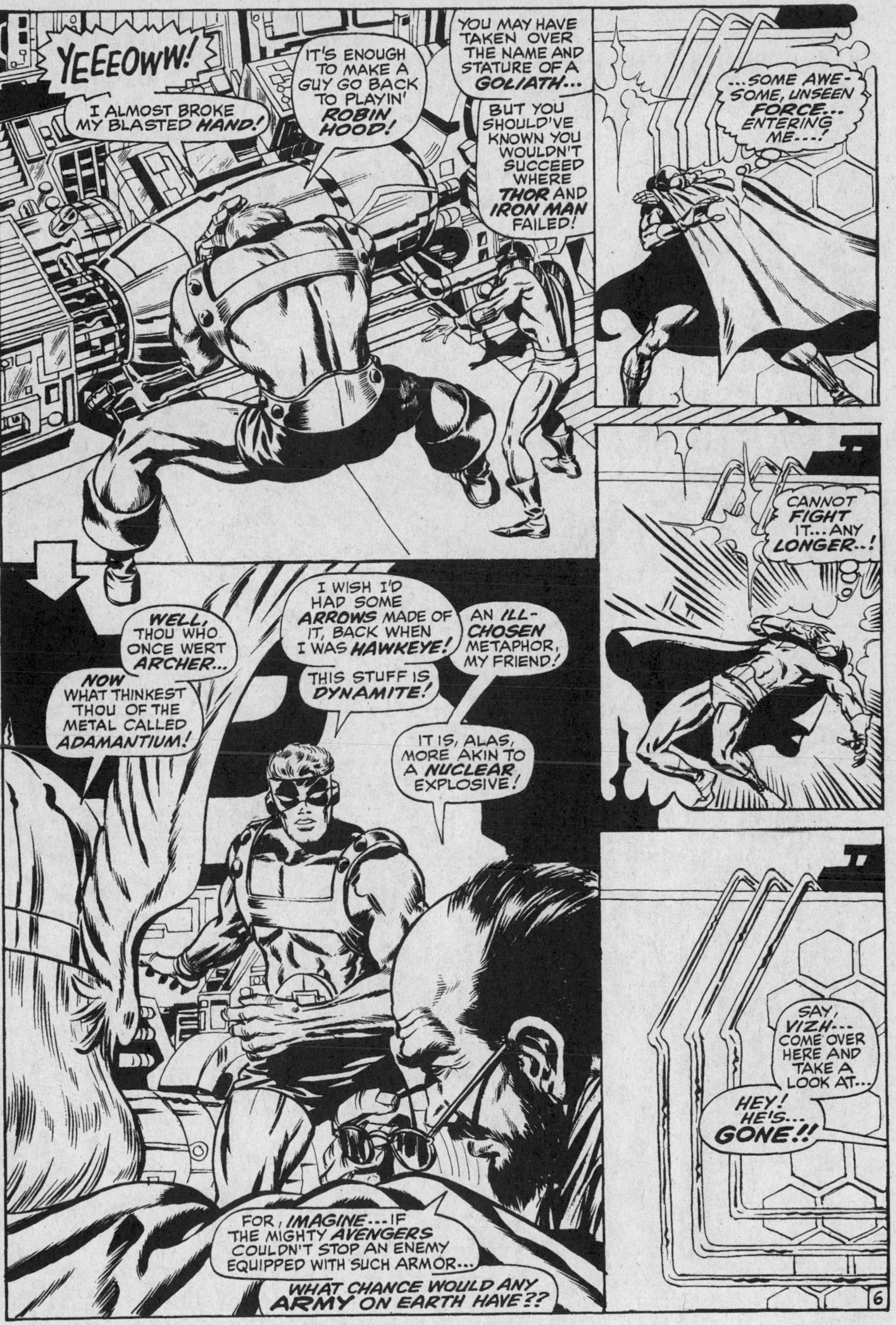
YEEEOWW!
I ALMOST BROKE MY BLASTED HAND!
IT'S ENOUGH TO MAKE A GUY GO BACK TO PLAYIN' ROBIN HOOD!
YOU MAY HAVE TAKEN OVER THE NAME AND STATURE OF A GOLIATH...
BUT YOU SHOULD'VE KNOWN YOU WOULDN'T SUCCEED WHERE THOR AND IRON MAN FAILED!
...SOME AWE-SOME, UNSEEN FORCE... ENTERING ME...!
CANNOT FIGHT IT... ANY LONGER..!
WELL, THOU WHO ONCE WERT ARCHER...
NOW WHAT THINKEST THOU OF THE METAL CALLED ADAMANTIUM!
I WISH I'D HAD SOME ARROWS MADE OF IT, BACK WHEN I WAS HAWKEYE!
THIS STUFF IS DYNAMITE!
AN ILL-CHOSEN METAPHOR, MY FRIEND!
IT IS, ALAS, MORE AKIN TO A NUCLEAR EXPLOSIVE!
FOR, IMAGINE... IF THE MIGHTY AVENGERS COULDN'T STOP AN ENEMY EQUIPPED WITH SUCH ARMOR...
WHAT CHANCE WOULD ANY ARMY ON EARTH HAVE??
SAY, VIZH... COME OVER HERE AND TAKE A LOOK AT...
HEY! HE'S... GONE!!
6

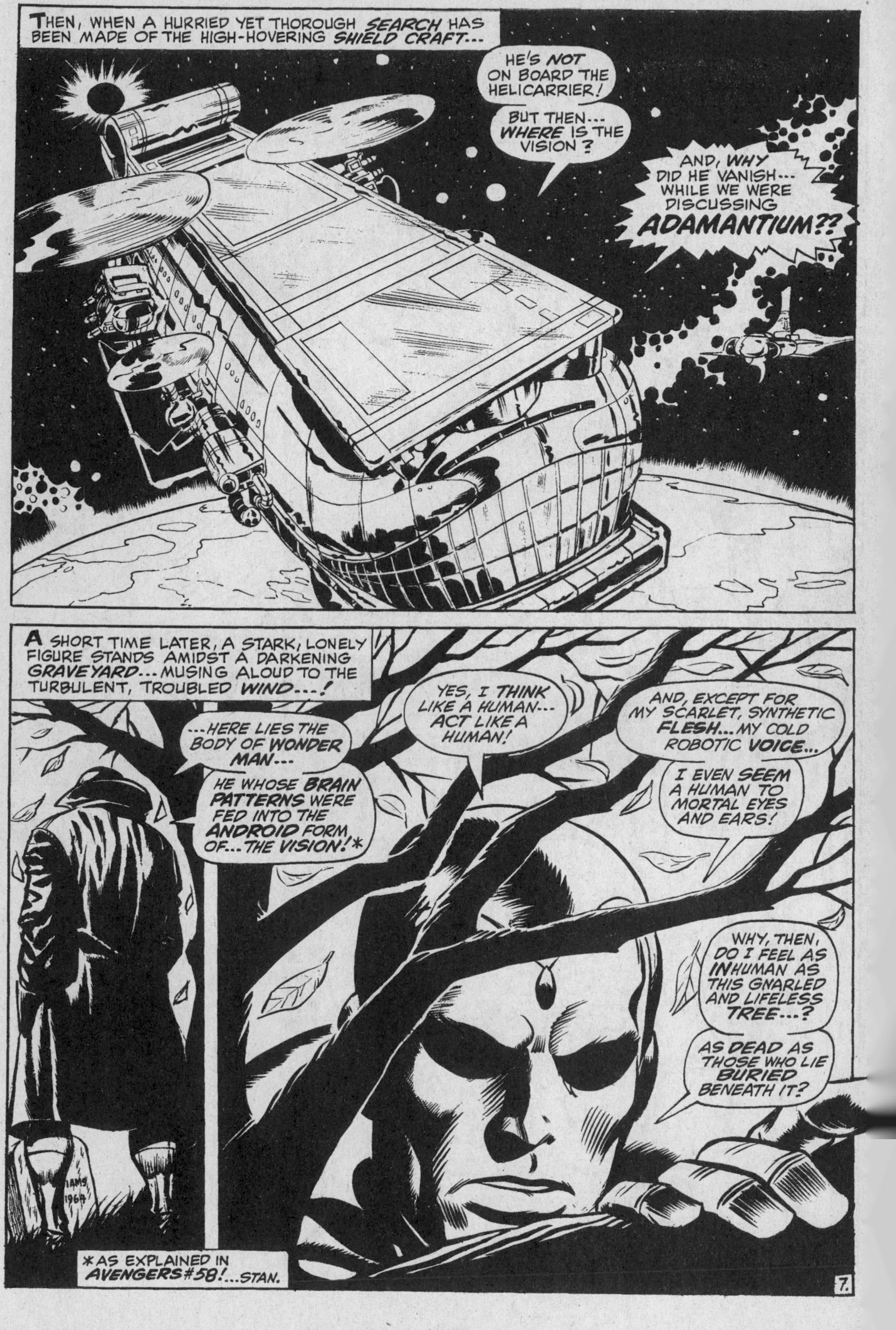
THEN, WHEN A HURRIED YET THOROUGH SEARCH HAS BEEN MADE OF THE HIGH-HOVERING SHIELD CRAFT...
HE'S NOT ON BOARD THE HELICARRIER!
BUT THEN... WHERE IS THE VISION ?
AND, WHY DID HE VANISH... WHILE WE WERE DISCUSSING ADAMANTIUM??
A SHORT TIME LATER, A STARK, LONELY FIGURE STANDS AMIDST A DARKENING GRAVEYARD... MUSING ALOUD TO THE TURBULENT, TROUBLED WIND...!
...HERE LIES THE BODY OF WONDER MAN...
HE WHOSE BRAIN PATTERNS WERE FED INTO THE ANDROID FORM OF... THE VISION!*
IAMS 1964
YES, I THINK LIKE A HUMAN... ACT LIKE A HUMAN!
AND, EXCEPT FOR MY SCARLET, SYNTHETIC FLESH... MY COLD ROBOTIC VOICE...
I EVEN SEEM A HUMAN TO MORTAL EYES AND EARS!
WHY, THEN, DO I FEEL AS INHUMAN AS THIS GNARLED AND LIFELESS TREE...?
AS DEAD AS THOSE WHO LIE BURIED BENEATH IT?
*AS EXPLAINED IN AVENGERS #58!...STAN.
7.

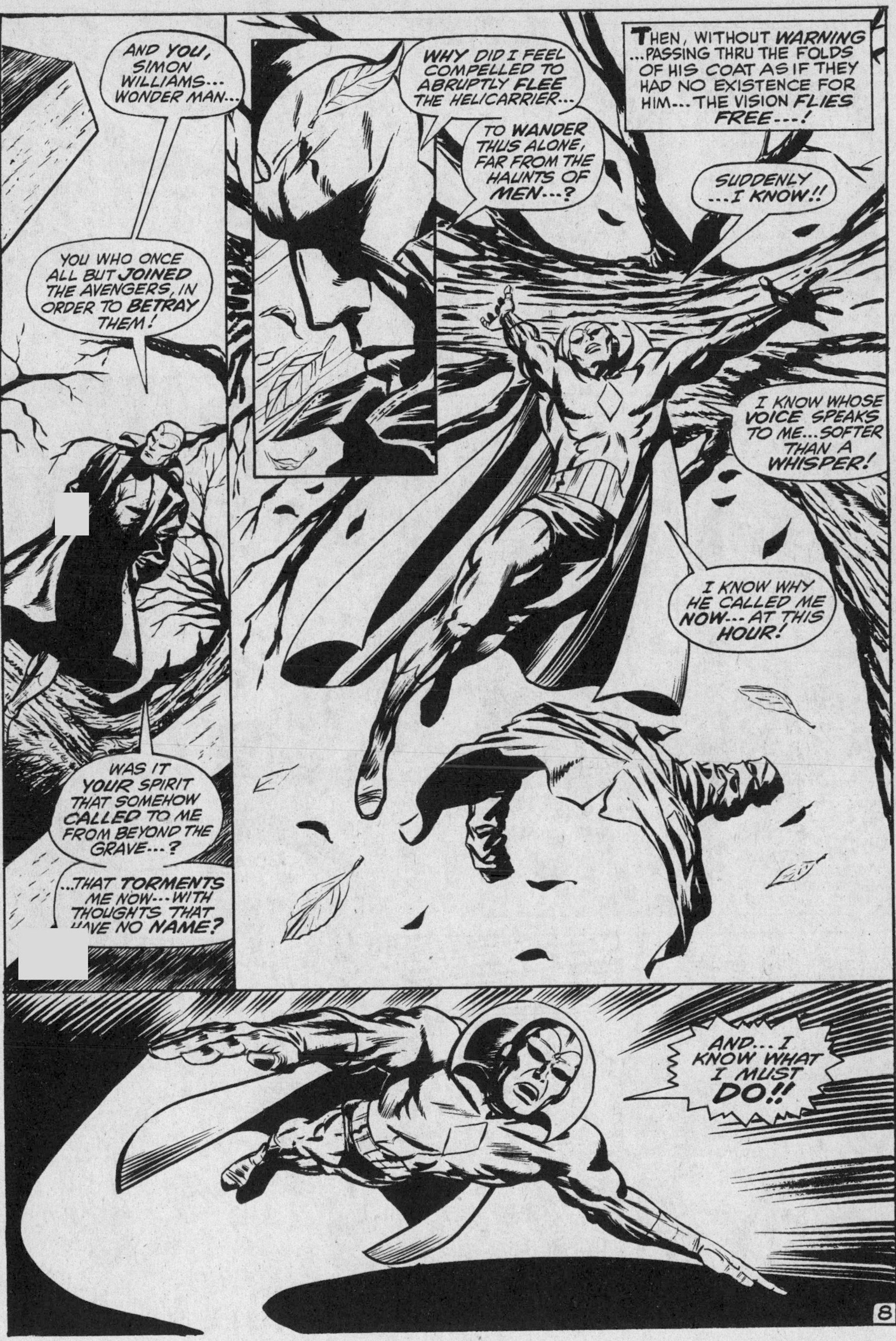
AND YOU, SIMON WILLIAMS... WONDER MAN...
YOU WHO ONCE ALL BUT JOINED THE AVENGERS, IN ORDER TO BETRAY THEM!
WHY DID I FEEL COMPELLED TO ABRUPTLY FLEE THE HELICARRIER...
TO WANDER THUS ALONE, FAR FROM THE HAUNTS OF MEN...?
THEN, WITHOUT WARNING ...PASSING THRU THE FOLDS OF HIS COAT AS IF THEY HAD NO EXISTENCE FOR HIM... THE VISION FLIES FREE...!
SUDDENLY ...I KNOW!!
I KNOW WHOSE VOICE SPEAKS TO ME...SOFTER THAN A WHISPER!
I KNOW WHY HE CALLED ME NOW... AT THIS HOUR!
WAS IT YOUR SPIRIT THAT SOMEHOW CALLED TO ME FROM BEYOND THE GRAVE...?
...THAT TORMENTS ME NOW... WITH THOUGHTS THAT HAVE NO NAME?
AND... I KNOW WHAT I MUST DO!!

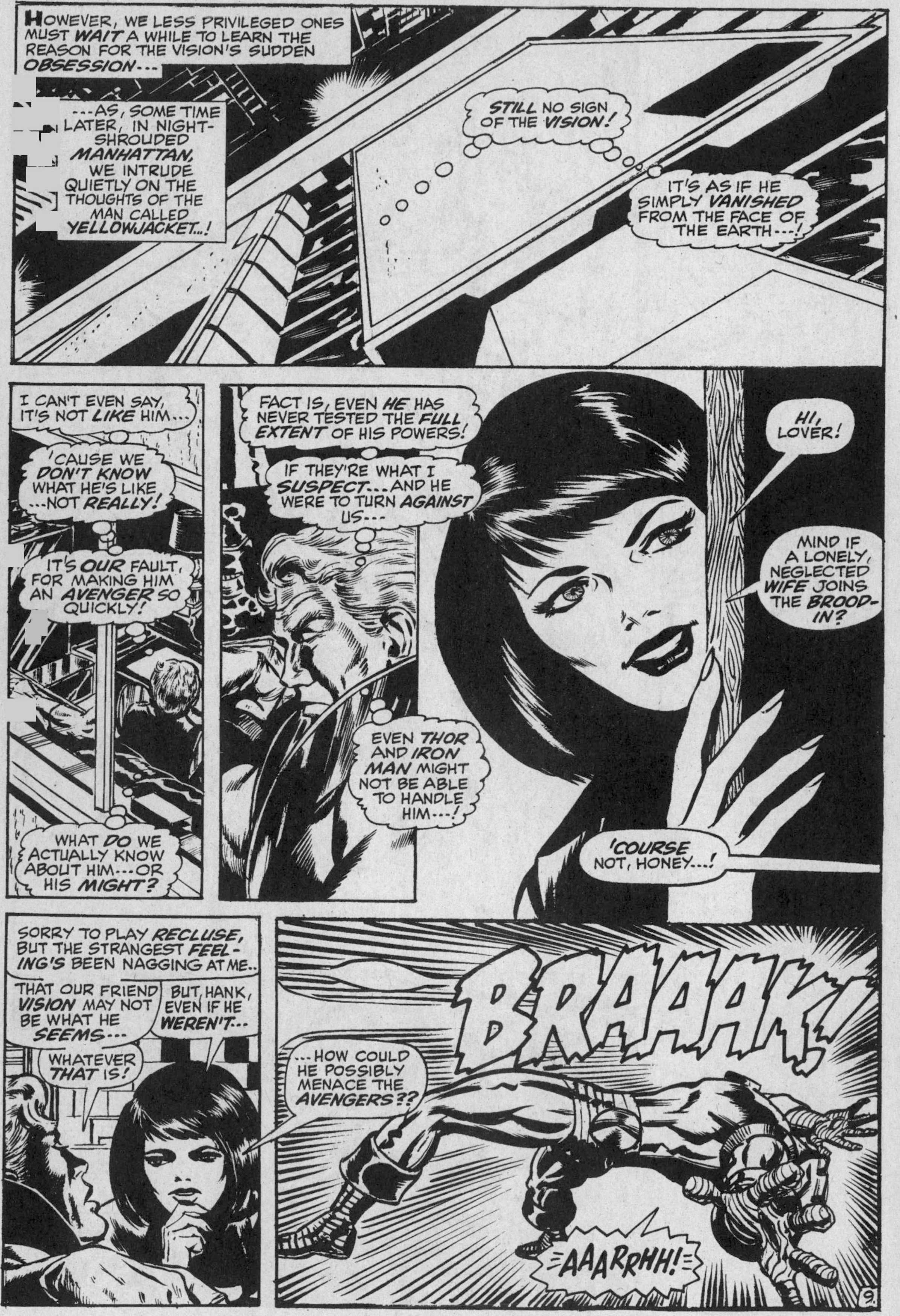

HOWEVER, WE LESS PRIVILEGED ONES MUST WAIT A WHILE TO LEARN THE REASON FOR THE VISION'S SUDDEN OBSESSION---
---AS, SOME TIME LATER, IN NIGHT-SHROUDED MANHATTAN, WE INTRUDE QUIETLY ON THE THOUGHTS OF THE MAN CALLED YELLOWJACKET...!
STILL NO SIGN OF THE VISION!
IT'S AS IF HE SIMPLY VANISHED FROM THE FACE OF THE EARTH---!
I CAN'T EVEN SAY, IT'S NOT LIKE HIM...
'CAUSE WE DON'T KNOW WHAT HE'S LIKE ...NOT REALLY!
IT'S OUR FAULT, FOR MAKING HIM AN AVENGER SO QUICKLY!
WHAT DO WE ACTUALLY KNOW ABOUT HIM---OR HIS MIGHT?
FACT IS, EVEN HE HAS NEVER TESTED THE FULL EXTENT OF HIS POWERS!
IF THEY'RE WHAT I SUSPECT... AND HE WERE TO TURN AGAINST US---
EVEN THOR AND IRON MAN MIGHT NOT BE ABLE TO HANDLE HIM---!
HI, LOVER!
MIND IF A LONELY, NEGLECTED WIFE JOINS THE BROOD-IN?
'COURSE NOT, HONEY...!
SORRY TO PLAY RECLUSE, BUT THE STRANGEST FEEL-ING'S BEEN NAGGING AT ME..
THAT OUR FRIEND VISION MAY NOT BE WHAT HE SEEMS---
WHATEVER THAT IS!
BUT, HANK, EVEN IF HE WEREN'T...
...HOW COULD HE POSSIBLY MENACE THE AVENGERS??
BRAAAK!
AAARRHH!
9.

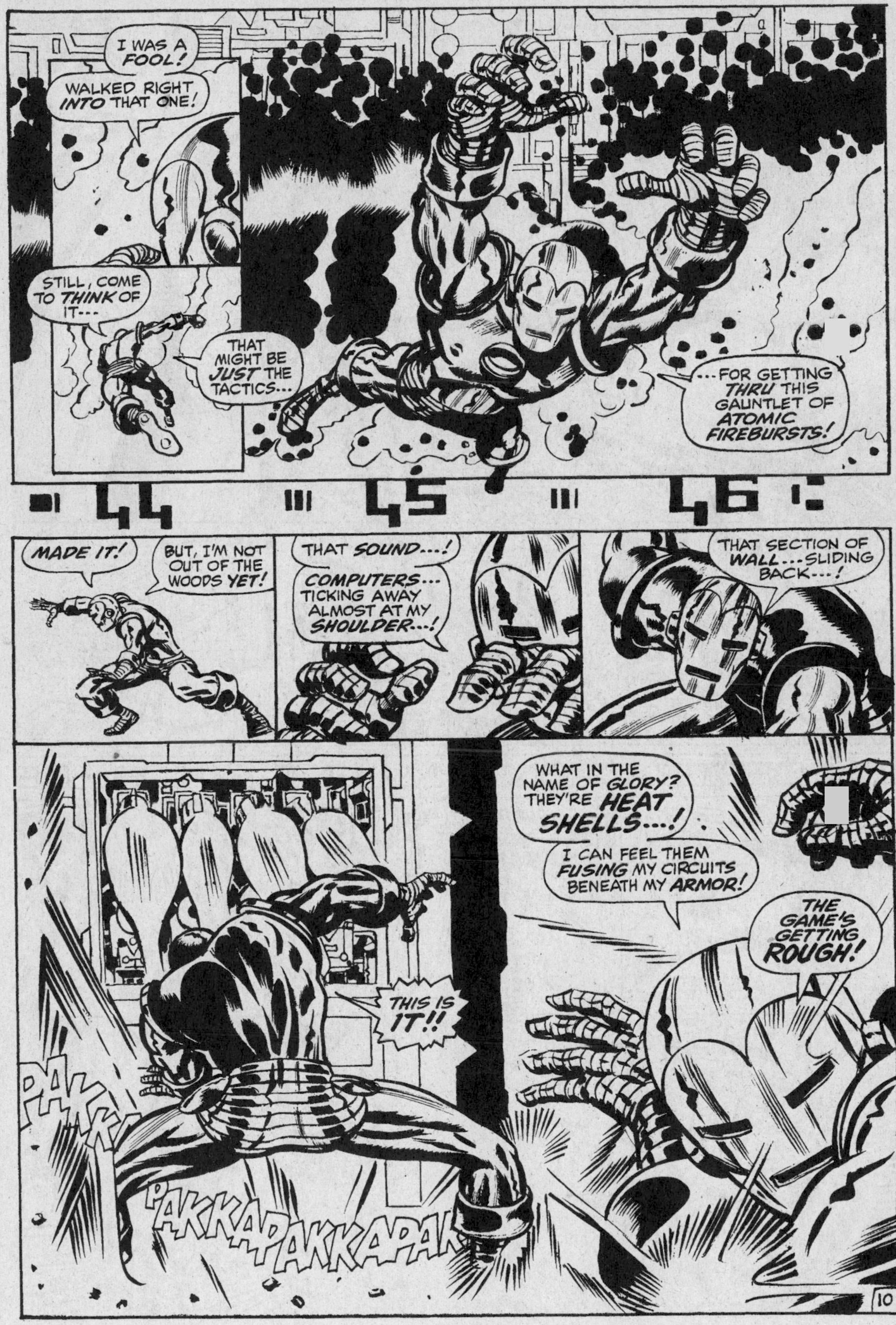

I WAS A FOOL!
WALKED RIGHT INTO THAT ONE!
STILL, COME TO THINK OF IT---
THAT MIGHT BE JUST THE TACTICS...
...FOR GETTING THRU THIS GAUNTLET OF ATOMIC FIREBURSTS!
44
45
46
MADE IT!
BUT, I'M NOT OUT OF THE WOODS YET!
THAT SOUND...!
COMPUTERS... TICKING AWAY ALMOST AT MY SHOULDER...!
THAT SECTION OF WALL... SLIDING BACK...!
THIS IS IT!!
PAKKAPAKKAPAKKAPAK
WHAT IN THE NAME OF GLORY? THEY'RE HEAT SHELLS...!
I CAN FEEL THEM FUSING MY CIRCUITS BENEATH MY ARMOR!
THE GAME'S GETTING ROUGH!

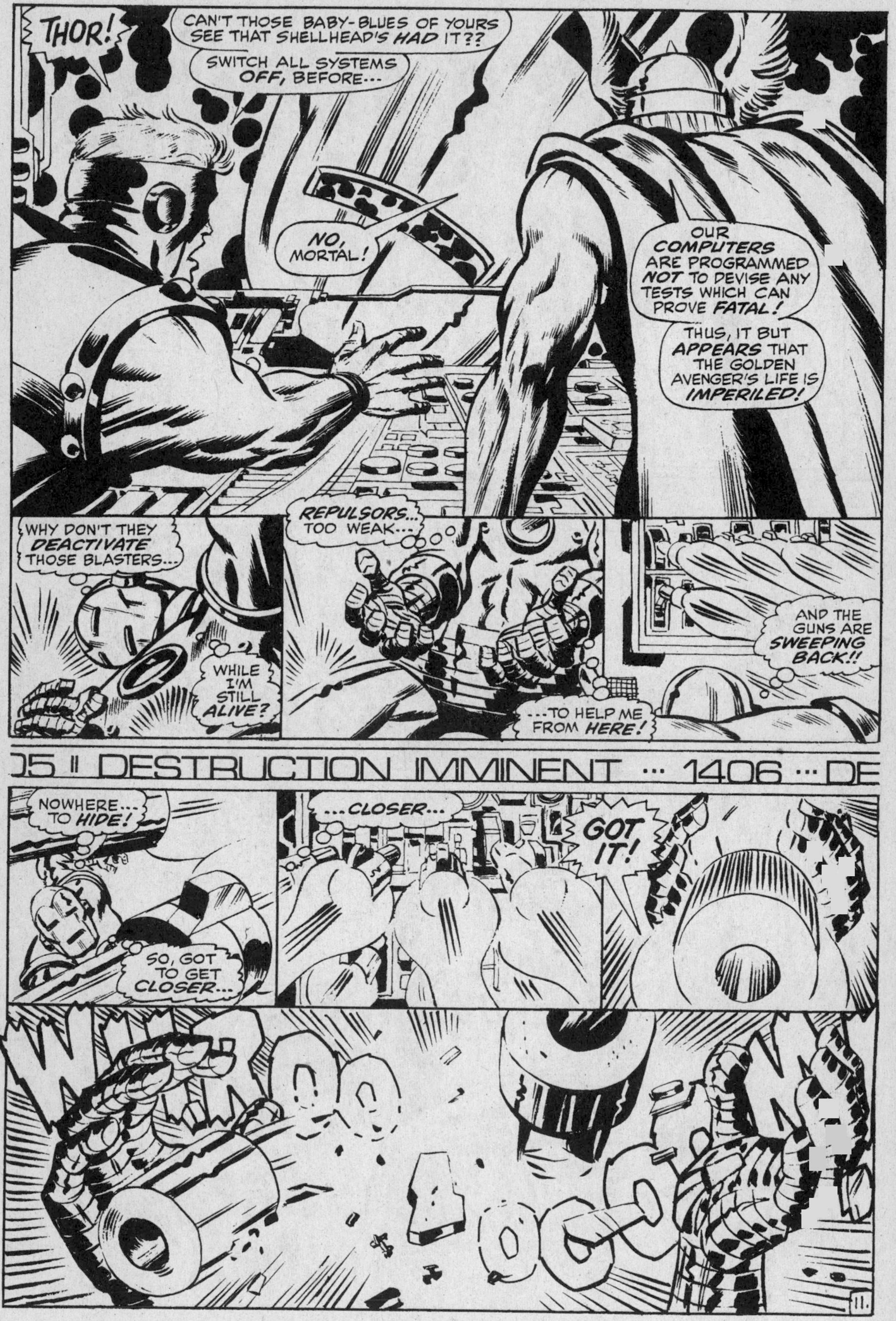
THOR!
CAN'T THOSE BABY-BLUES OF YOURS SEE THAT SHELLHEAD'S HAD IT??
SWITCH ALL SYSTEMS OFF, BEFORE...
NO, MORTAL!
OUR COMPUTERS ARE PROGRAMMED NOT TO DEVISE ANY TESTS WHICH CAN PROVE FATAL!
THUS, IT BUT APPEARS THAT THE GOLDEN AVENGER'S LIFE IS IMPERILED!
WHY DON'T THEY DEACTIVATE THOSE BLASTERS...
WHILE I'M STILL ALIVE?
REPULSORS... TOO WEAK...
...TO HELP ME FROM HERE!
AND THE GUNS ARE SWEEPING BACK!!
05 II DESTRUCTION IMMINENT ··· 1406 ··· DE
NOWHERE... TO HIDE!
SO, GOT TO GET CLOSER...
...CLOSER...
GOT IT!
11.

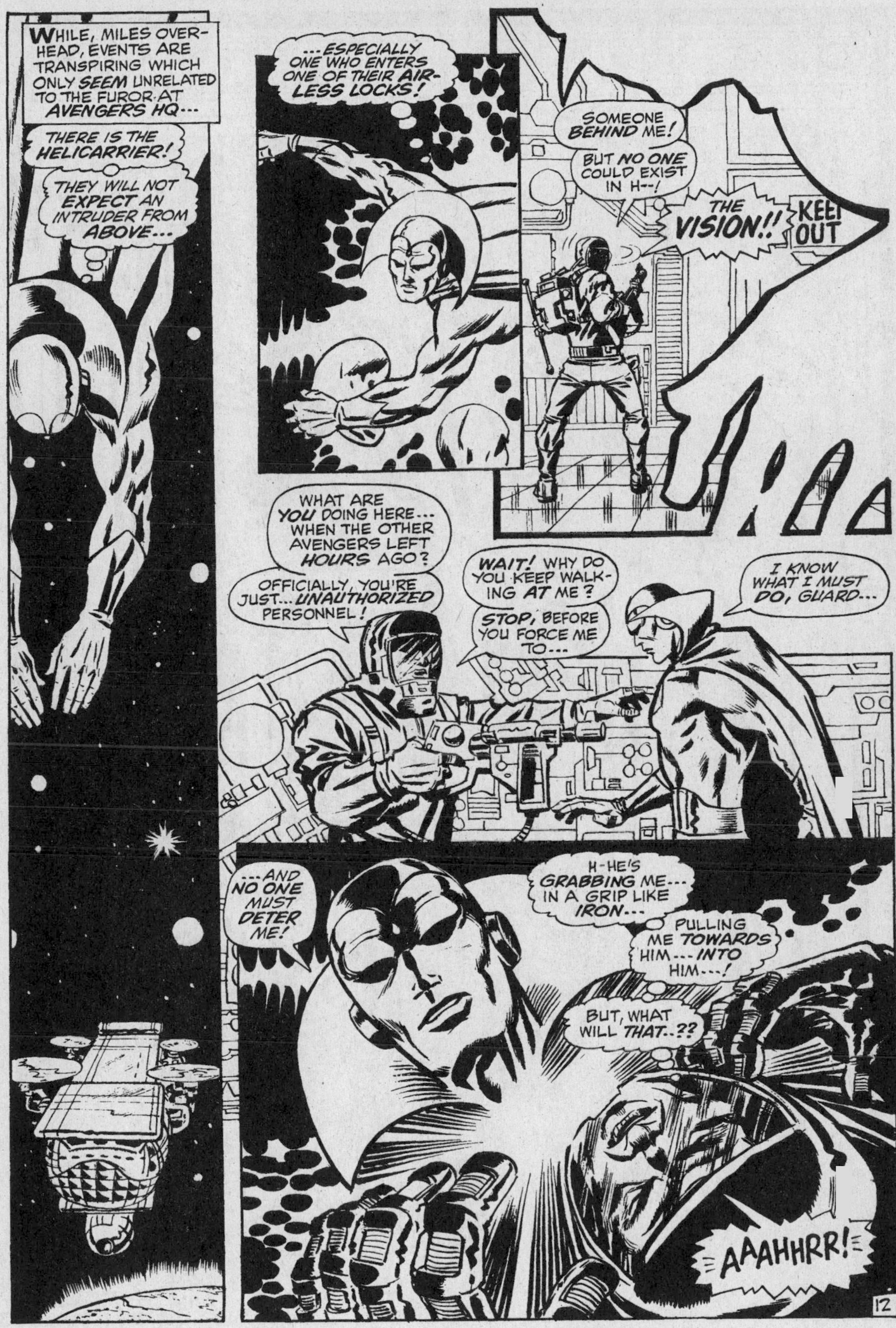
WHILE, MILES OVERHEAD, EVENTS ARE TRANSPIRING WHICH ONLY SEEM UNRELATED TO THE FUROR AT AVENGERS HQ...
THERE IS THE HELICARRIER!
THEY WILL NOT EXPECT AN INTRUDER FROM ABOVE...
...ESPECIALLY ONE WHO ENTERS ONE OF THEIR AIR-LESS LOCKS!
SOMEONE BEHIND ME!
BUT NO ONE COULD EXIST IN H--!
THE VISION!!
KEE OUT
WHAT ARE YOU DOING HERE... WHEN THE OTHER AVENGERS LEFT HOURS AGO?
OFFICIALLY, YOU'RE JUST... UNAUTHORIZED PERSONNEL!
WAIT! WHY DO YOU KEEP WALKING AT ME?
STOP, BEFORE YOU FORCE ME TO...
I KNOW WHAT I MUST DO, GUARD...
...AND NO ONE MUST DETER ME!
H-HE'S GRABBING ME... IN A GRIP LIKE IRON...
PULLING ME TOWARDS HIM...INTO HIM...!
BUT, WHAT WILL THAT..??
AAAHHRR!
12

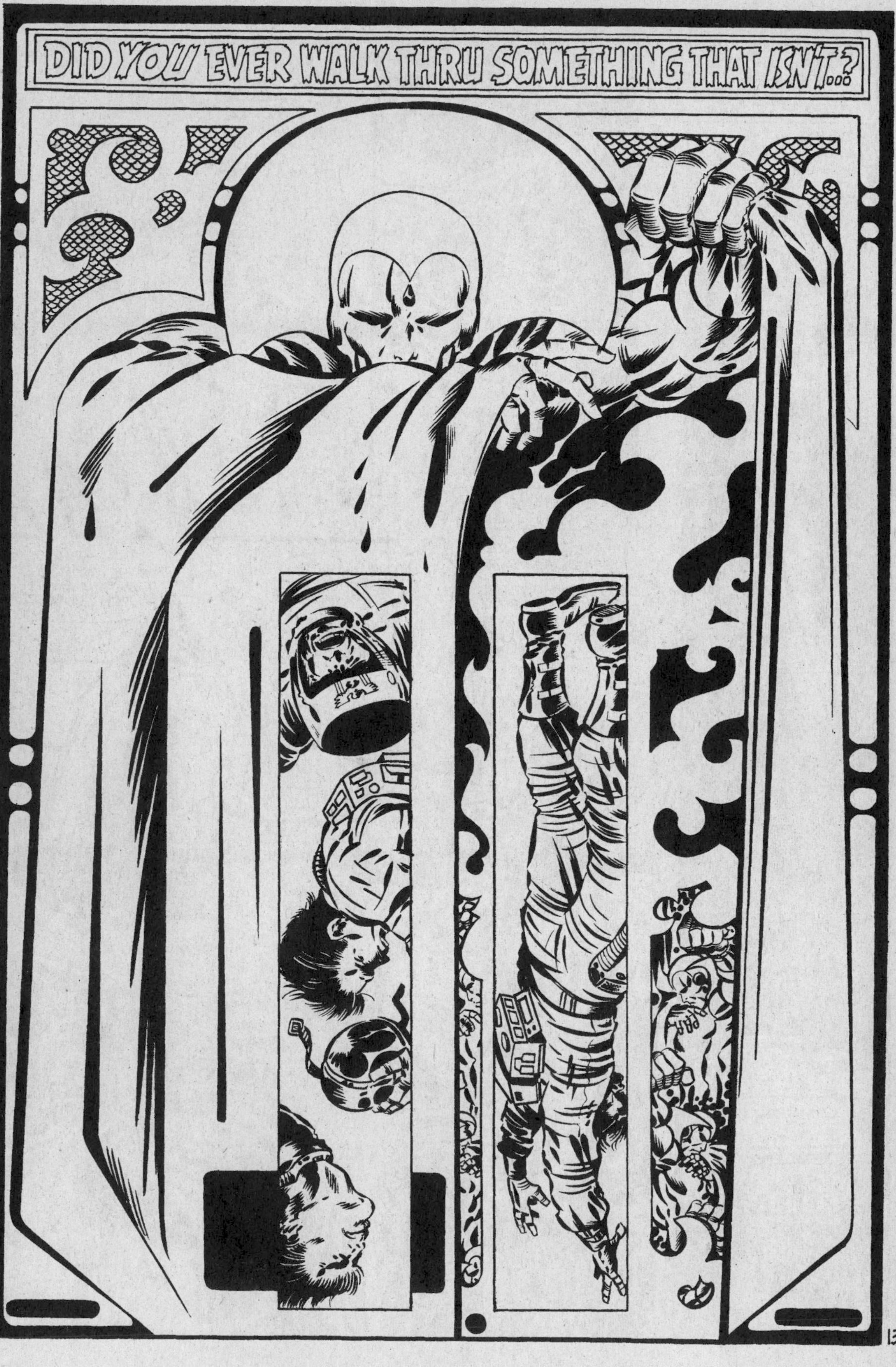
DID YOU EVER WALK THRU SOMETHING THAT ISN'T...?

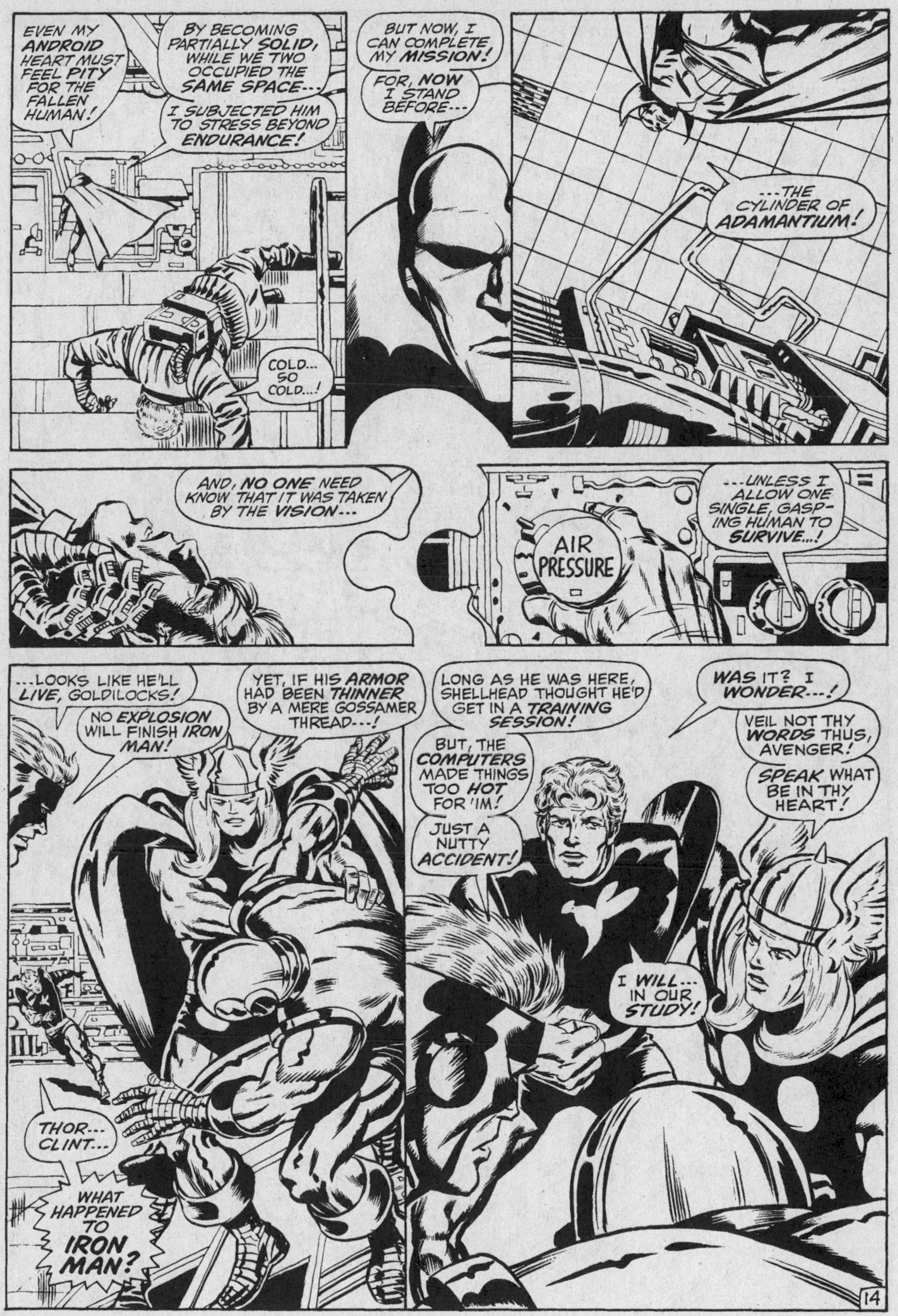
EVEN MY ANDROID HEART MUST FEEL PITY FOR THE FALLEN HUMAN!
BY BECOMING PARTIALLY SOLID, WHILE WE TWO OCCUPIED THE SAME SPACE...
I SUBJECTED HIM TO STRESS BEYOND ENDURANCE!
COLD... SO COLD...!
BUT NOW, I CAN COMPLETE MY MISSION!
FOR, NOW I STAND BEFORE...
...THE CYLINDER OF ADAMANTIUM!
AND, NO ONE NEED KNOW THAT IT WAS TAKEN BY THE VISION...
AIR PRESSURE
...UNLESS I ALLOW ONE SINGLE, GASPING HUMAN TO SURVIVE...!
...LOOKS LIKE HE'LL LIVE, GOLDILOCKS!
NO EXPLOSION WILL FINISH IRON MAN!
YET, IF HIS ARMOR HAD BEEN THINNER BY A MERE GOSSAMER THREAD...!
THOR... CLINT...
WHAT HAPPENED TO IRON MAN?
LONG AS HE WAS HERE, SHELLHEAD THOUGHT HE'D GET IN A TRAINING SESSION!
BUT, THE COMPUTERS MADE THINGS TOO HOT FOR 'IM!
JUST A NUTTY ACCIDENT!
WAS IT? I WONDER...!
VEIL NOT THY WORDS THUS, AVENGER!
SPEAK WHAT BE IN THY HEART!
I WILL... IN OUR STUDY!
14

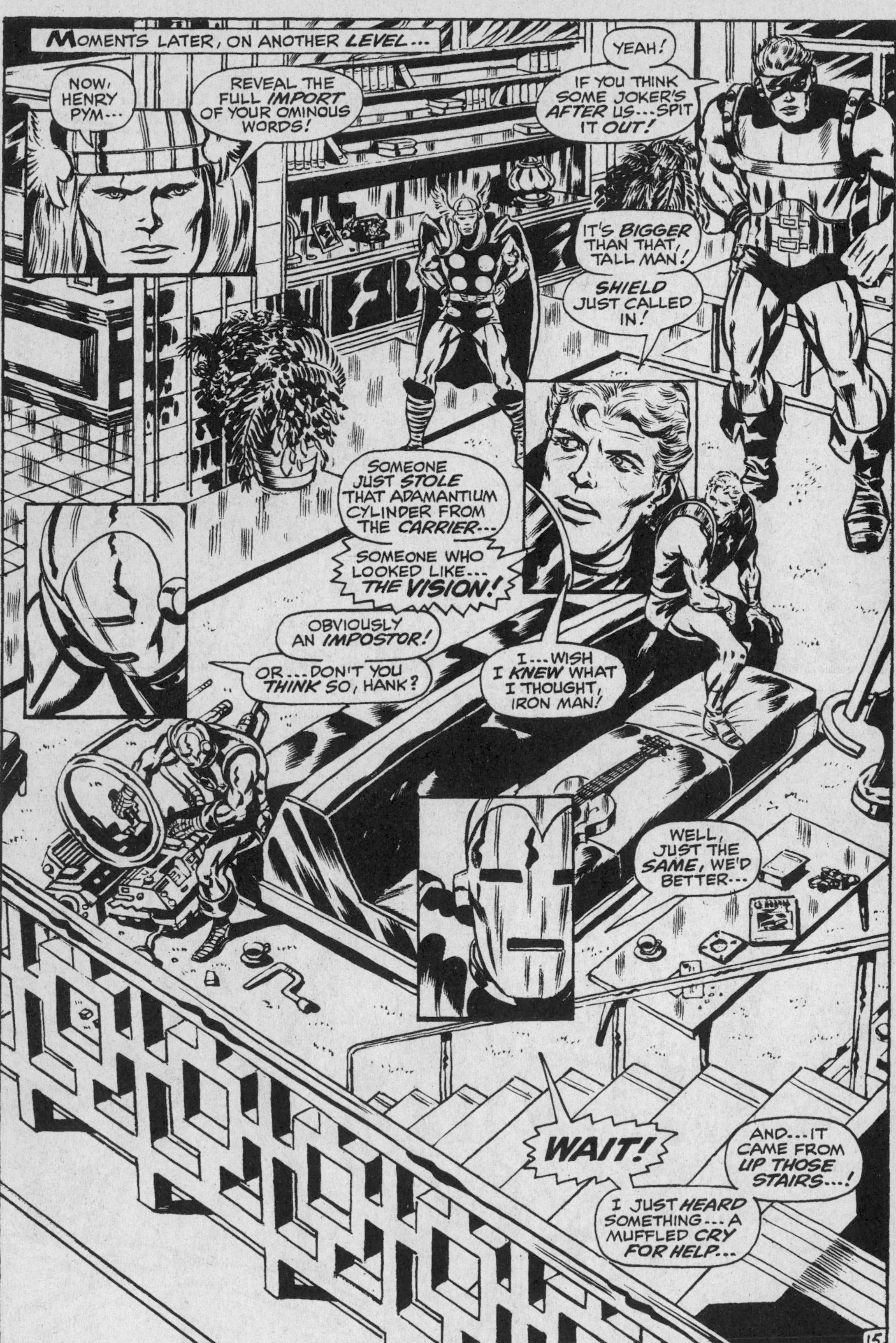
MOMENTS LATER, ON ANOTHER LEVEL...
NOW, HENRY PYM...
REVEAL THE FULL IMPORT OF YOUR OMINOUS WORDS!
YEAH!
IF YOU THINK SOME JOKER'S AFTER US...SPIT IT OUT!
IT'S BIGGER THAN THAT, TALL MAN!
SHIELD JUST CALLED IN!
SOMEONE JUST STOLE THAT ADAMANTIUM CYLINDER FROM THE CARRIER...
SOMEONE WHO LOOKED LIKE... THE VISION!
OBVIOUSLY AN IMPOSTOR!
OR...DON'T YOU THINK SO, HANK?
I...WISH I KNEW WHAT I THOUGHT, IRON MAN!
WELL, JUST THE SAME, WE'D BETTER...
WAIT!
I JUST HEARD SOMETHING... A MUFFLED CRY FOR HELP...
AND...IT CAME FROM UP THOSE STAIRS...!
15

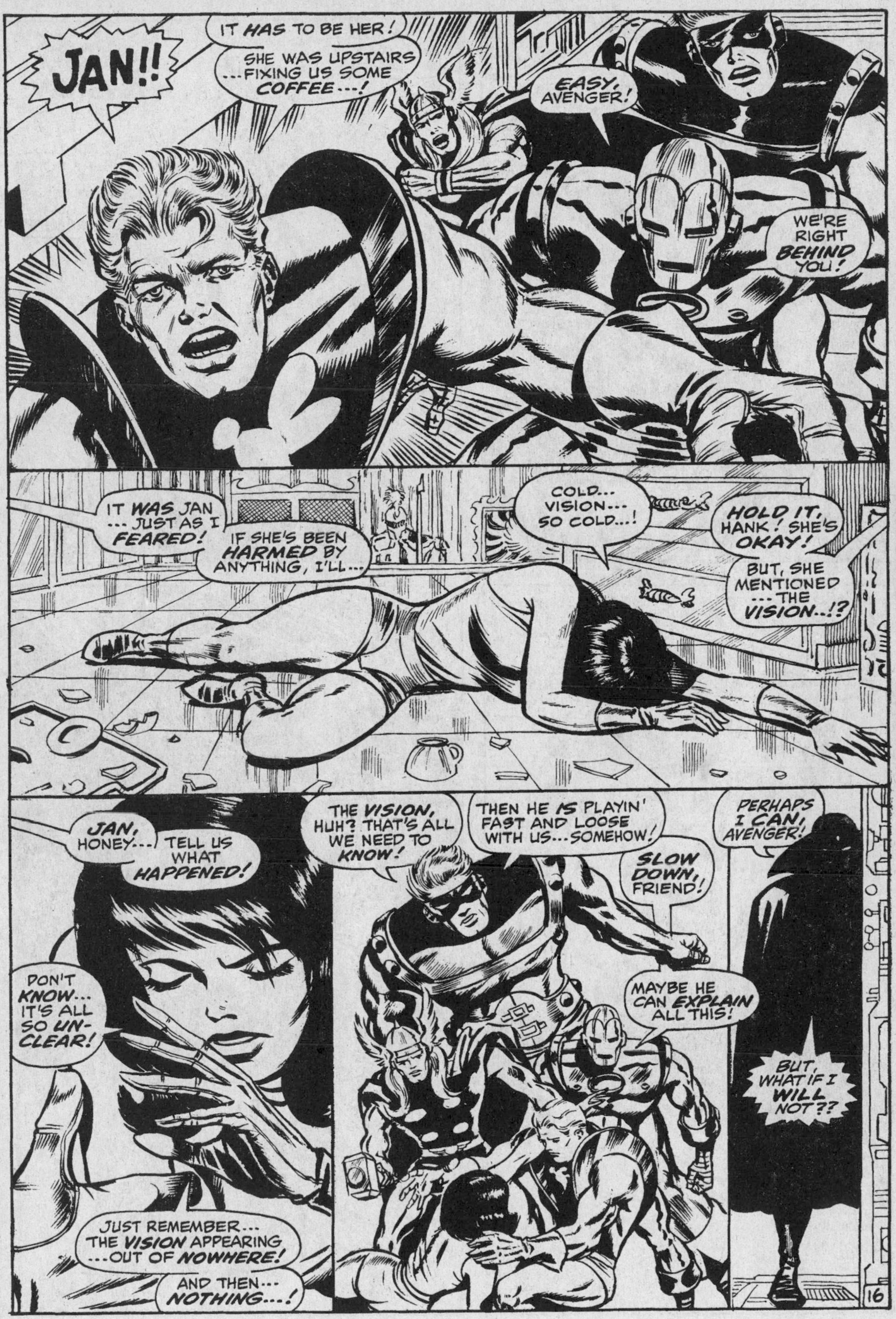
JAN!!
IT HAS TO BE HER!
SHE WAS UPSTAIRS ...FIXING US SOME COFFEE...!
EASY, AVENGER!
WE'RE RIGHT BEHIND YOU!
IT WAS JAN ...JUST AS I FEARED!
IF SHE'S BEEN HARMED BY ANYTHING, I'LL...
COLD... VISION... SO COLD...!
HOLD IT, HANK! SHE'S OKAY!
BUT, SHE MENTIONED ...THE VISION..!?
JAN, HONEY...
TELL US WHAT HAPPENED!
DON'T KNOW... IT'S ALL SO UN-CLEAR!
JUST REMEMBER... THE VISION APPEARING ...OUT OF NOWHERE!
AND THEN... NOTHING...!
THE VISION, HUH? THAT'S ALL WE NEED TO KNOW!
THEN HE IS PLAYIN' FAST AND LOOSE WITH US...SOMEHOW!
SLOW DOWN, FRIEND!
MAYBE HE CAN EXPLAIN ALL THIS!
PERHAPS I CAN, AVENGER!
BUT, WHAT IF I WILL NOT??
16

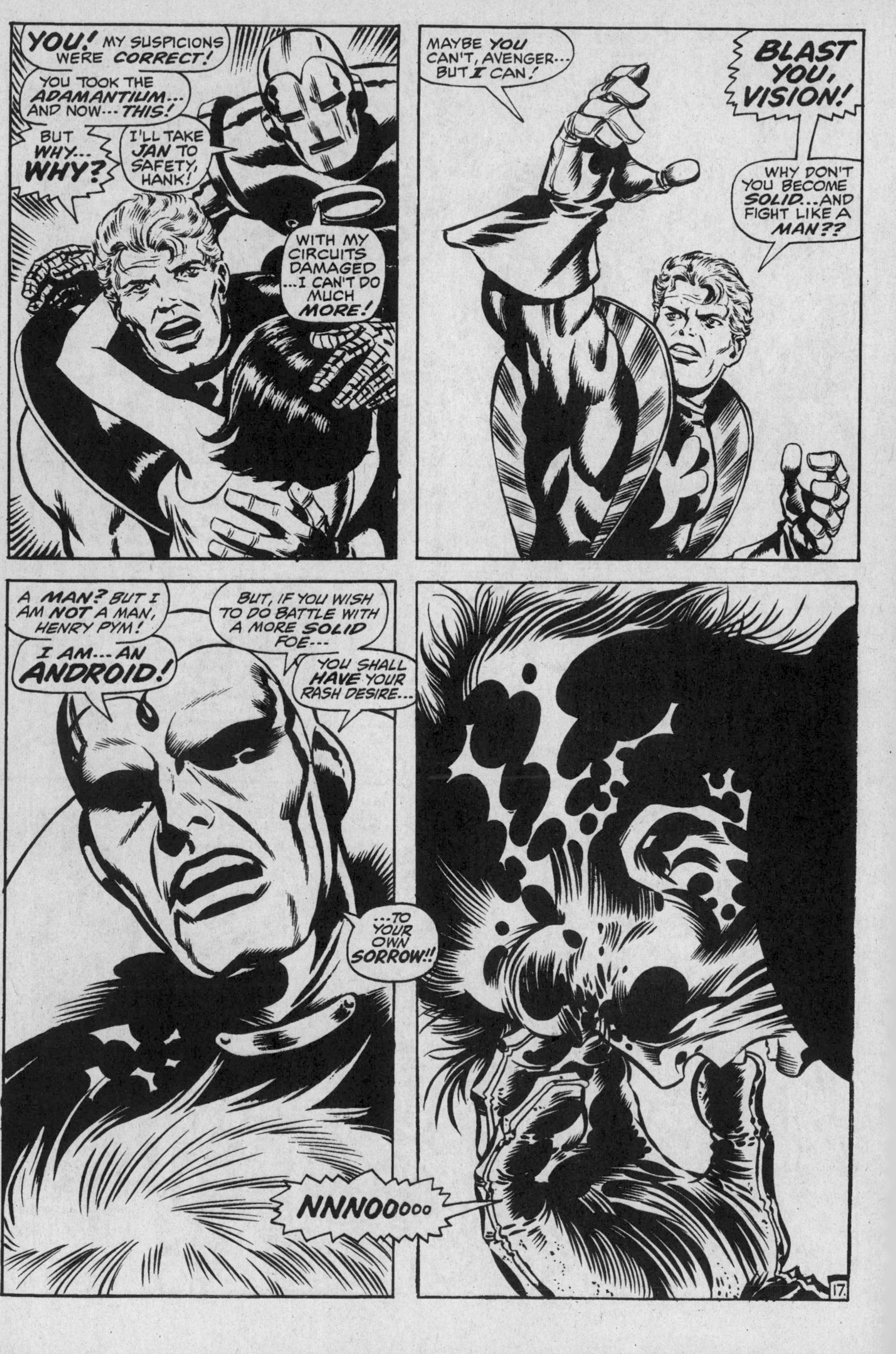
YOU! MY SUSPICIONS WERE CORRECT!
YOU TOOK THE ADAMANTIUM... AND NOW--- THIS!
BUT WHY... WHY?
I'LL TAKE JAN TO SAFETY, HANK!
WITH MY CIRCUITS DAMAGED ...I CAN'T DO MUCH MORE!
MAYBE YOU CAN'T, AVENGER... BUT I CAN!
BLAST YOU, VISION!
WHY DON'T YOU BECOME SOLID...AND FIGHT LIKE A MAN??
A MAN? BUT I AM NOT A MAN, HENRY PYM!
I AM... AN ANDROID!
BUT, IF YOU WISH TO DO BATTLE WITH A MORE SOLID FOE---
YOU SHALL HAVE YOUR RASH DESIRE...
...TO YOUR OWN SORROW!!
NNNOOooo
17.

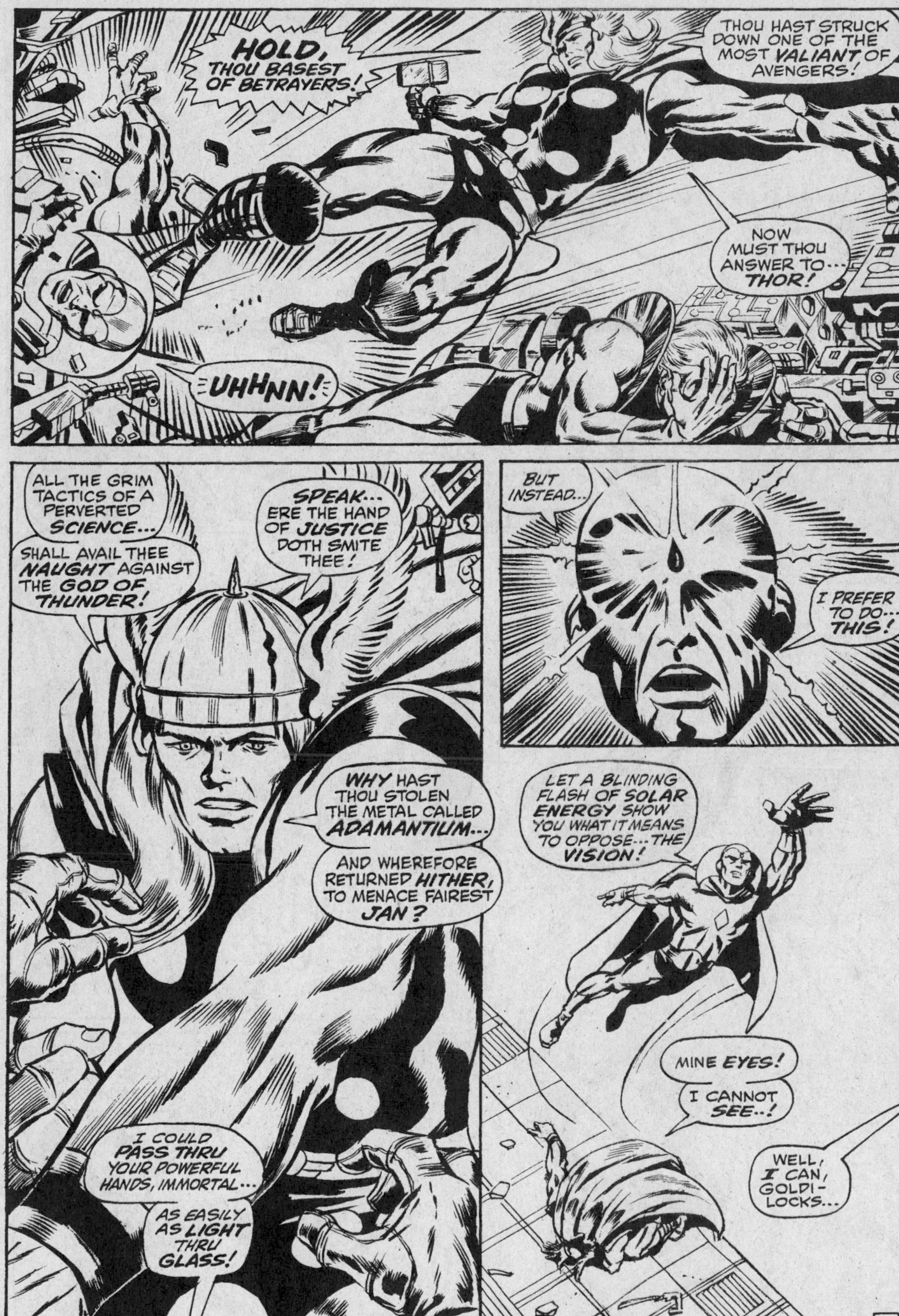
HOLD, THOU BASEST OF BETRAYERS!
THOU HAST STRUCK DOWN ONE OF THE MOST VALIANT OF AVENGERS!
NOW MUST THOU ANSWER TO... THOR!
UHHNN!
ALL THE GRIM TACTICS OF A PERVERTED SCIENCE...
SHALL AVAIL THEE NAUGHT AGAINST THE GOD OF THUNDER!
SPEAK... ERE THE HAND OF JUSTICE DOTH SMITE THEE!
WHY HAST THOU STOLEN THE METAL CALLED ADAMANTIUM...
AND WHEREFORE RETURNED HITHER, TO MENACE FAIREST JAN?
I COULD PASS THRU YOUR POWERFUL HANDS, IMMORTAL...
AS EASILY AS LIGHT THRU GLASS!
BUT INSTEAD...
I PREFER TO DO... THIS!
LET A BLINDING FLASH OF SOLAR ENERGY SHOW YOU WHAT IT MEANS TO OPPOSE... THE VISION!
MINE EYES!
I CANNOT SEE..!
WELL, I CAN, GOLDI-LOCKS...

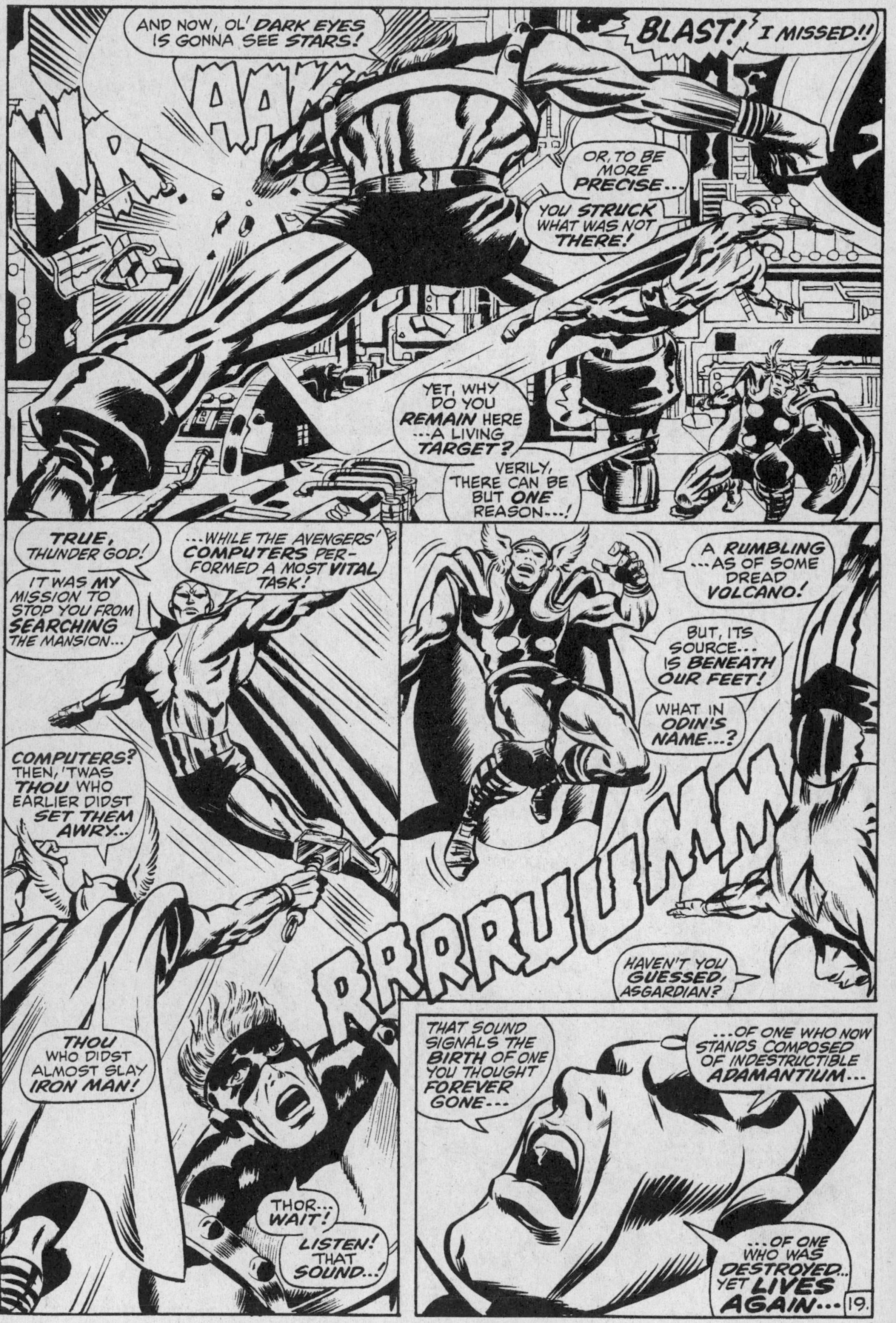

AND NOW, OL' DARK EYES IS GONNA SEE STARS!
WAAAK
BLAST! I MISSED!!
OR, TO BE MORE PRECISE...
YOU STRUCK WHAT WAS NOT THERE!
YET, WHY DO YOU REMAIN HERE ---A LIVING TARGET?
VERILY, THERE CAN BE BUT ONE REASON---!
TRUE, THUNDER GOD!
IT WAS MY MISSION TO STOP YOU FROM SEARCHING THE MANSION...
...WHILE THE AVENGERS' COMPUTERS PERFORMED A MOST VITAL TASK!
COMPUTERS? THEN, 'TWAS THOU WHO EARLIER DIDST SET THEM AWRY...
THOU WHO DIDST ALMOST SLAY IRON MAN!
THOR... WAIT!
LISTEN! THAT SOUND...!
A RUMBLING ---AS OF SOME DREAD VOLCANO!
BUT, ITS SOURCE... IS BENEATH OUR FEET!
WHAT IN ODIN'S NAME...?
RRRRUUMM
HAVEN'T YOU GUESSED, ASGARDIAN?
THAT SOUND SIGNALS THE BIRTH OF ONE YOU THOUGHT FOREVER GONE---
...OF ONE WHO NOW STANDS COMPOSED OF INDESTRUCTIBLE ADAMANTIUM...
...OF ONE WHO WAS DESTROYED... YET LIVES AGAIN...
19.

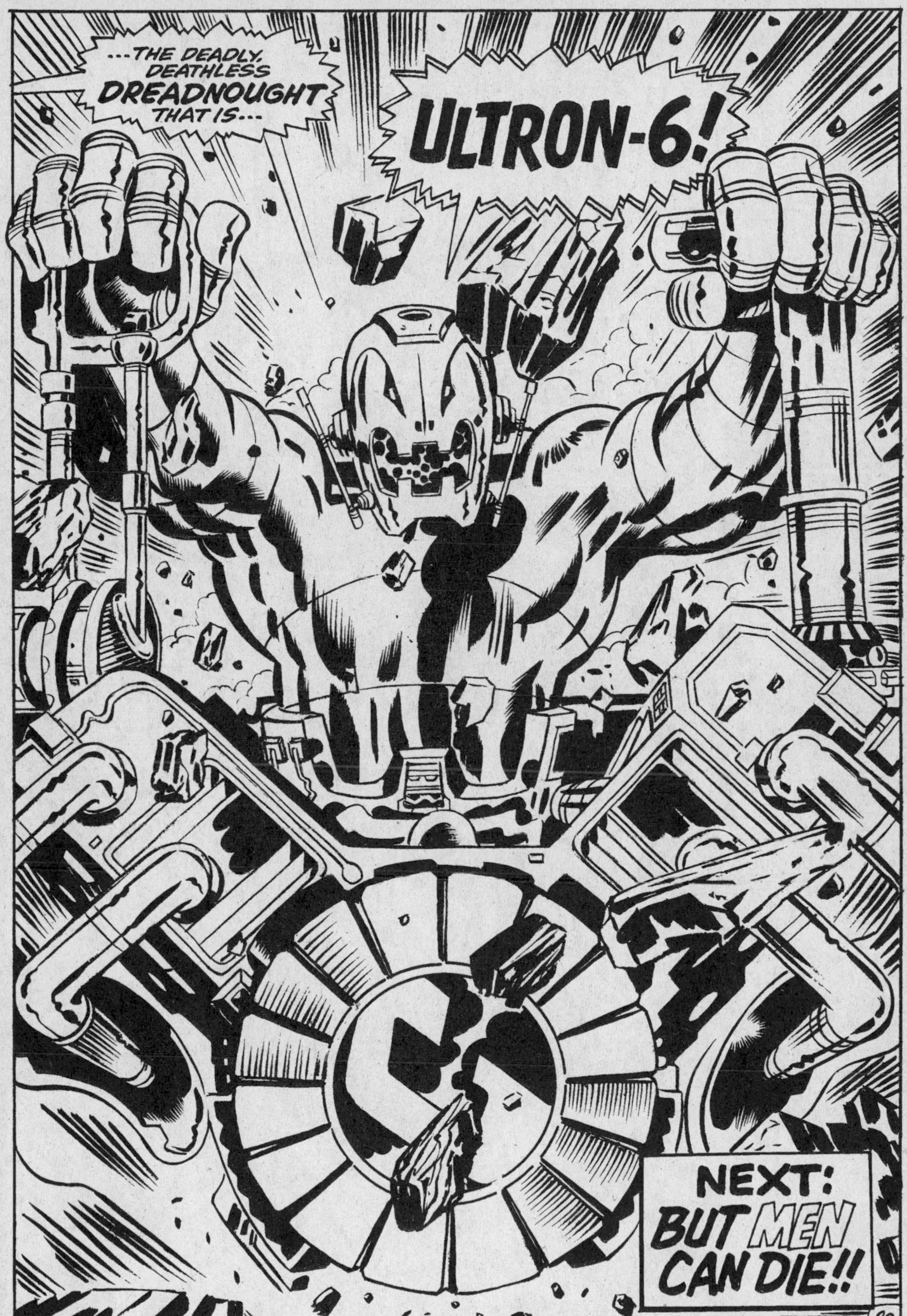
...THE DEADLY, DEATHLESS DREADNOUGHT THAT IS...
ULTRON-6!
NEXT: BUT MEN CAN DIE!!
20

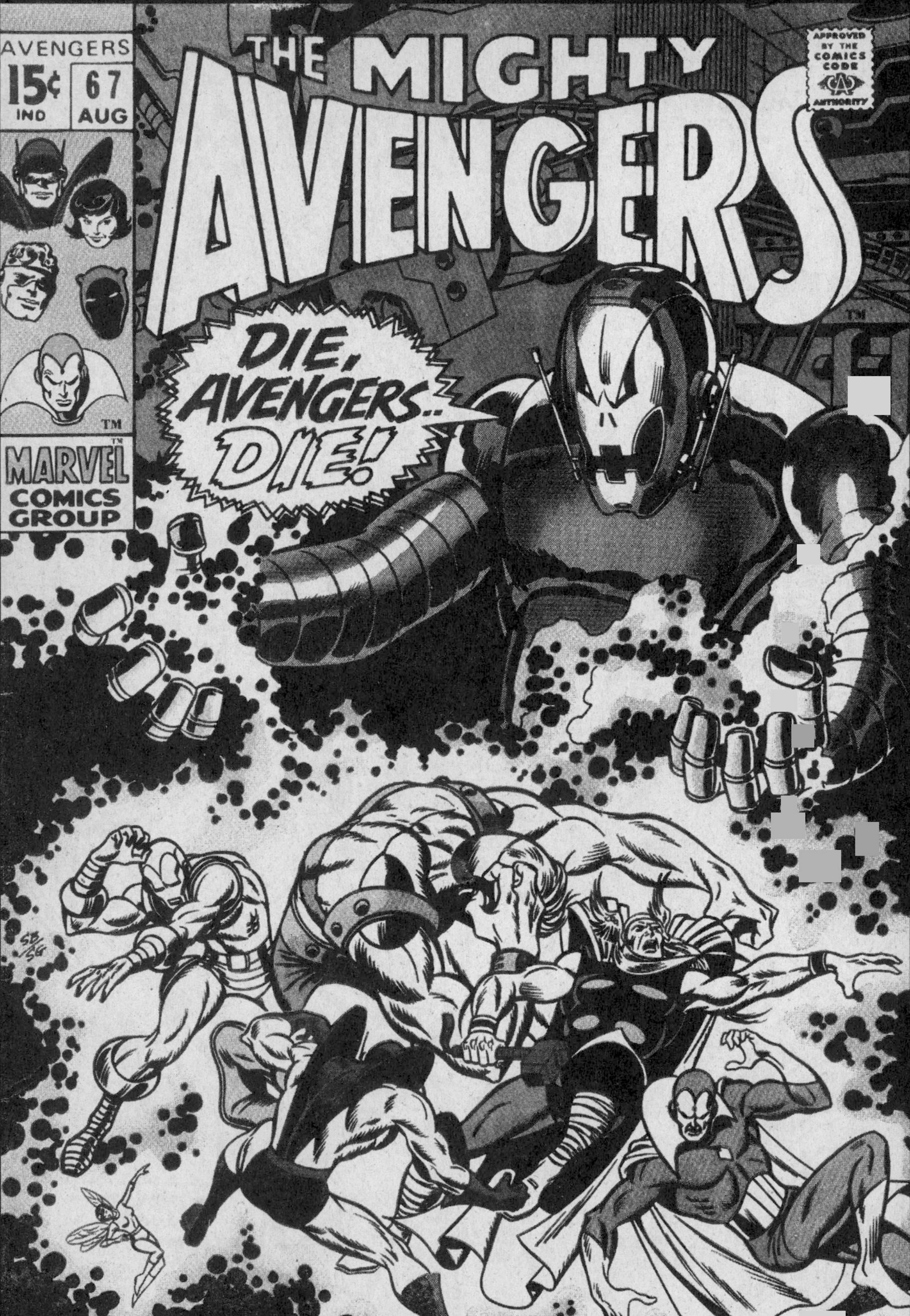
AVENGERS
15¢
IND
67
AUG
MARVEL
COMICS
GROUP
THE MIGHTY
AVENGERS
APPROVED BY THE COMICS CODE AUTHORITY
DIE, AVENGERS.. DIE!

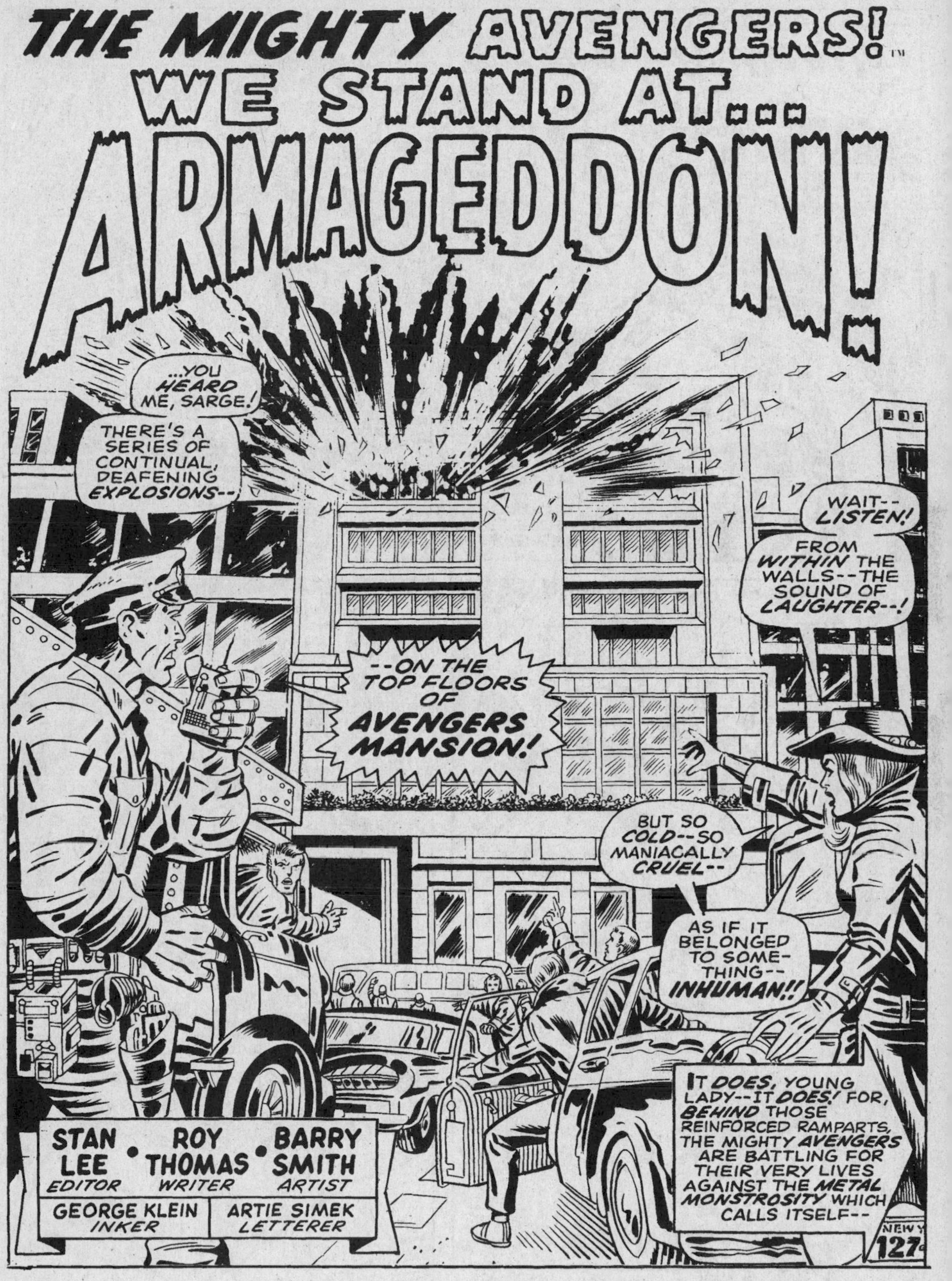
THE MIGHTY AVENGERS!™
WE STAND AT...
ARMAGEDDON!
...YOU HEARD ME, SARGE!
THERE'S A SERIES OF CONTINUAL, DEAFENING EXPLOSIONS--
--ON THE TOP FLOORS OF AVENGERS MANSION!
WAIT-- LISTEN!
FROM WITHIN THE WALLS--THE SOUND OF LAUGHTER--!
BUT SO COLD--SO MANIACALLY CRUEL--
AS IF IT BELONGED TO SOME-THING-- INHUMAN!!
STAN LEE EDITOR • ROY THOMAS WRITER • BARRY SMITH ARTIST
GEORGE KLEIN INKER | ARTIE SIMEK LETTERER
IT DOES, YOUNG LADY--IT DOES! FOR, BEHIND THOSE REINFORCED RAMPARTS, THE MIGHTY AVENGERS ARE BATTLING FOR THEIR VERY LIVES AGAINST THE METAL MONSTROSITY WHICH CALLS ITSELF--

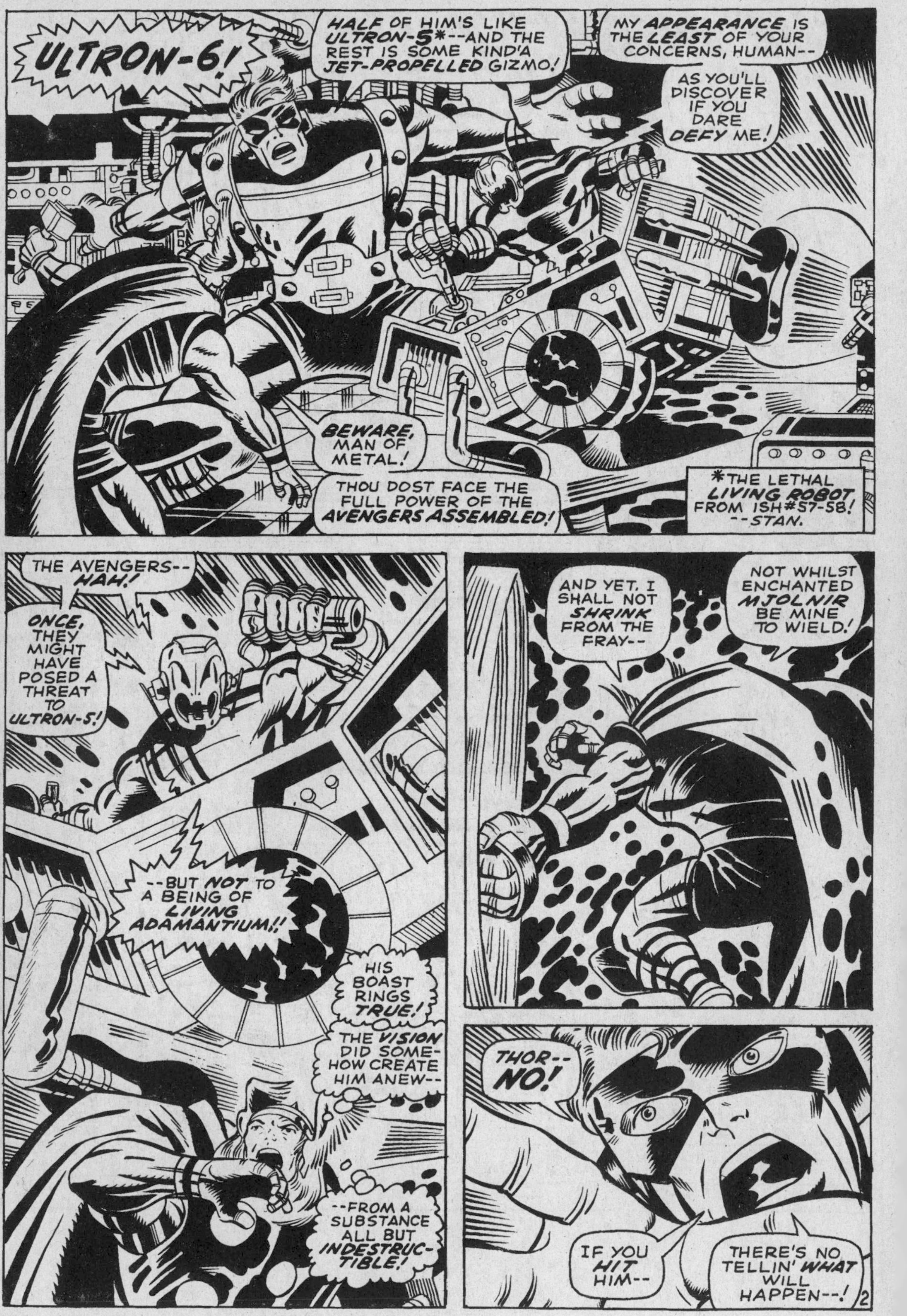

ULTRON-6!
HALF OF HIM'S LIKE ULTRON-5*--AND THE REST IS SOME KIND'A JET-PROPELLED GIZMO!
MY APPEARANCE IS THE LEAST OF YOUR CONCERNS, HUMAN--
AS YOU'LL DISCOVER IF YOU DARE DEFY ME!
BEWARE, MAN OF METAL!
THOU DOST FACE THE FULL POWER OF THE AVENGERS ASSEMBLED!
*THE LETHAL LIVING ROBOT, FROM ISH#57-58! --STAN.
THE AVENGERS--HAH!
ONCE, THEY MIGHT HAVE POSED A THREAT TO ULTRON-5!
--BUT NOT TO A BEING OF LIVING ADAMANTIUM!!
HIS BOAST RINGS TRUE!
THE VISION DID SOME-HOW CREATE HIM ANEW--
--FROM A SUBSTANCE ALL BUT INDESTRUC-TIBLE!
AND YET, I SHALL NOT SHRINK FROM THE FRAY--
NOT WHILST ENCHANTED MJOLNIR BE MINE TO WIELD!
THOR--NO!
IF YOU HIT HIM--
THERE'S NO TELLIN' WHAT WILL HAPPEN--!
2

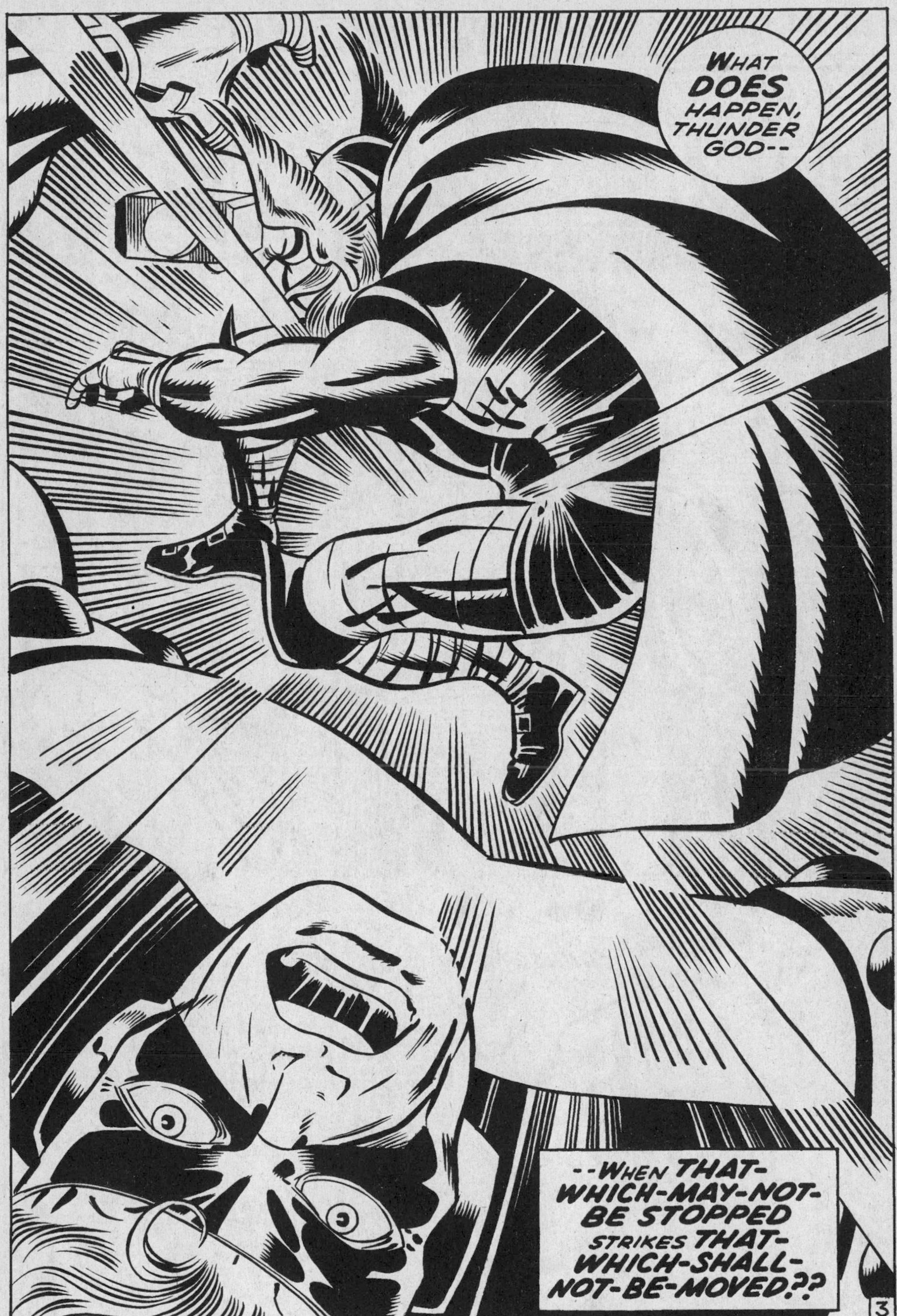
WHAT DOES HAPPEN, THUNDER GOD--
--WHEN THAT-WHICH-MAY-NOT-BE STOPPED STRIKES THAT-WHICH-SHALL-NOT-BE-MOVED??
3

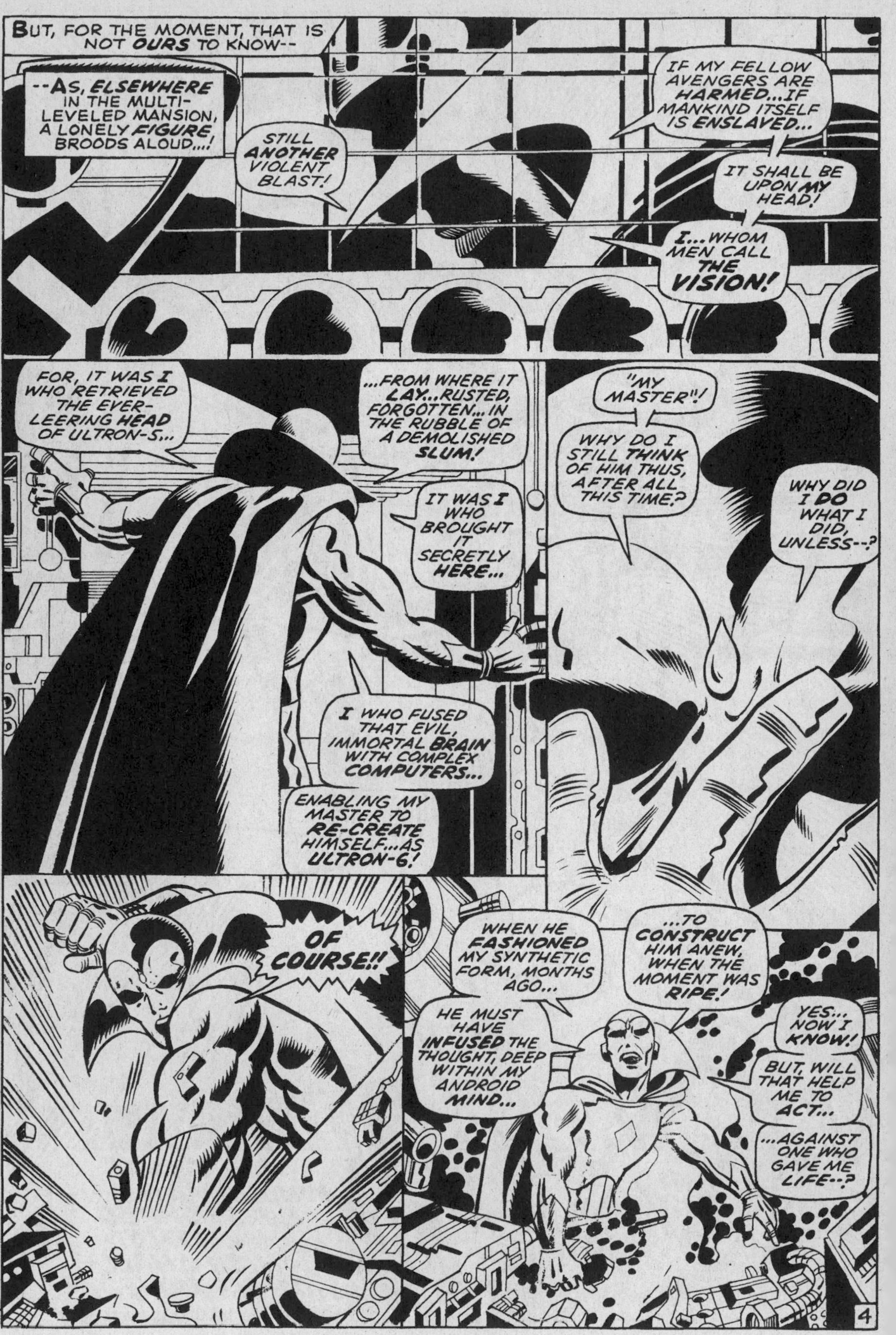
BUT, FOR THE MOMENT, THAT IS NOT OURS TO KNOW--
--AS, ELSEWHERE IN THE MULTI-LEVELED MANSION, A LONELY FIGURE BROODS ALOUD...!
STILL ANOTHER VIOLENT BLAST!
IF MY FELLOW AVENGERS ARE HARMED...IF MANKIND ITSELF IS ENSLAVED...
IT SHALL BE UPON MY HEAD!
I...WHOM MEN CALL THE VISION!
FOR, IT WAS I WHO RETRIEVED THE EVER-LEERING HEAD OF ULTRON-5...
...FROM WHERE IT LAY...RUSTED, FORGOTTEN...IN THE RUBBLE OF A DEMOLISHED SLUM!
IT WAS I WHO BROUGHT IT SECRETLY HERE...
I WHO FUSED THAT EVIL, IMMORTAL BRAIN WITH COMPLEX COMPUTERS...
ENABLING MY MASTER TO RE-CREATE HIMSELF...AS ULTRON-6!
"MY MASTER"!
WHY DO I STILL THINK OF HIM THUS, AFTER ALL THIS TIME?
WHY DID I DO WHAT I DID, UNLESS--?
OF COURSE!!
WHEN HE FASHIONED MY SYNTHETIC FORM, MONTHS AGO...
...TO CONSTRUCT HIM ANEW, WHEN THE MOMENT WAS RIPE!
HE MUST HAVE INFUSED THE THOUGHT, DEEP WITHIN MY ANDROID MIND...
YES... NOW I KNOW!
BUT, WILL THAT HELP ME TO ACT...
...AGAINST ONE WHO GAVE ME LIFE--?
4

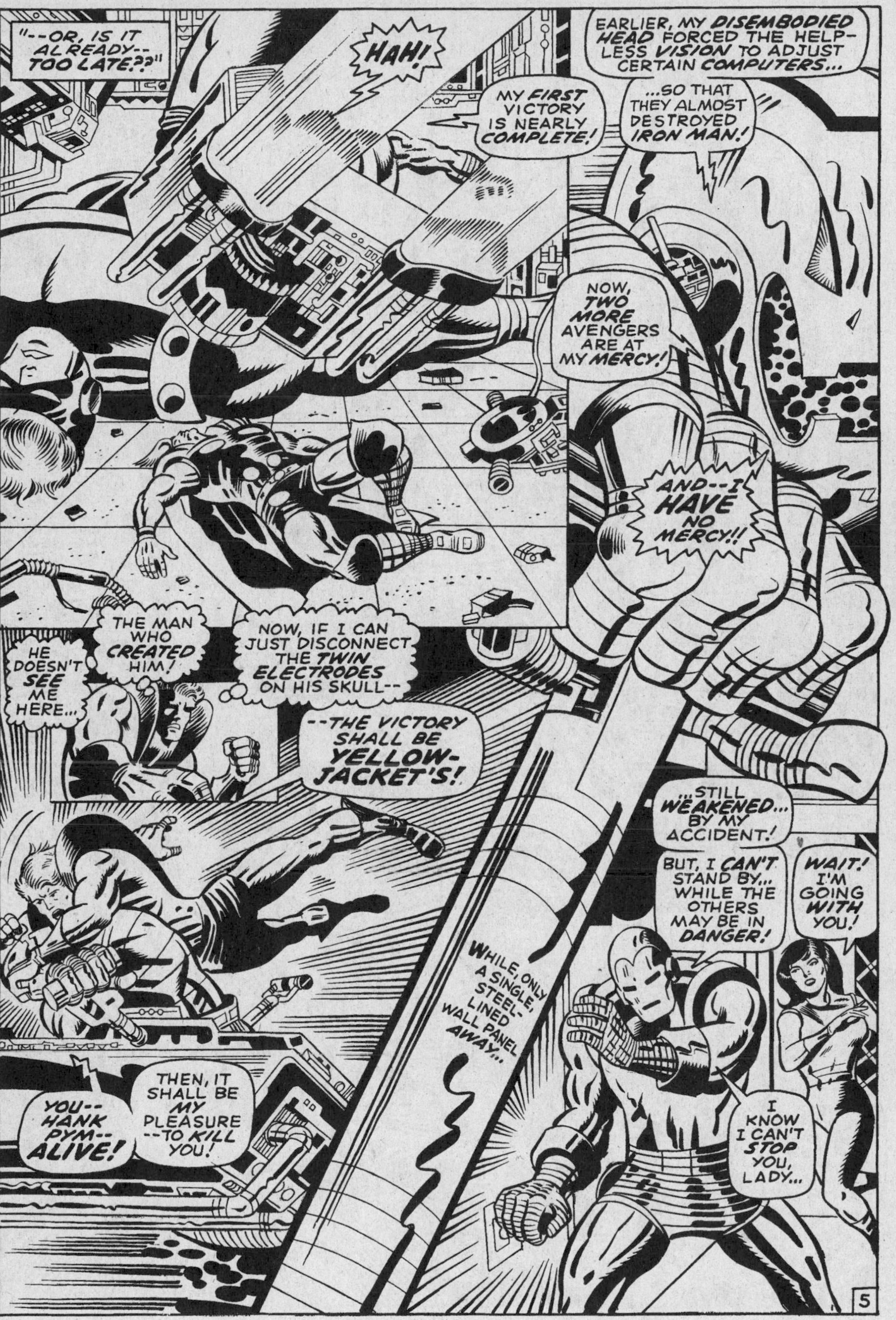
"--OR, IS IT ALREADY-- TOO LATE??"
HAH!
MY FIRST VICTORY IS NEARLY COMPLETE!
EARLIER, MY DISEMBODIED HEAD FORCED THE HELPLESS VISION TO ADJUST CERTAIN COMPUTERS...
...SO THAT THEY ALMOST DESTROYED IRON MAN!
NOW, TWO MORE AVENGERS ARE AT MY MERCY!
AND--I HAVE NO MERCY!!
HE DOESN'T SEE ME HERE...
THE MAN WHO CREATED HIM!
NOW, IF I CAN JUST DISCONNECT THE TWIN ELECTRODES ON HIS SKULL--
--THE VICTORY SHALL BE YELLOW-JACKET'S!
YOU--HANK PYM--ALIVE!
THEN, IT SHALL BE MY PLEASURE --TO KILL YOU!
WHILE, ONLY A SINGLE, STEEL-LINED WALL PANEL AWAY...
...STILL WEAKENED... BY MY ACCIDENT!
BUT, I CAN'T STAND BY... WHILE THE OTHERS MAY BE IN DANGER!
WAIT! I'M GOING WITH YOU!
I KNOW I CAN'T STOP YOU, LADY...
5

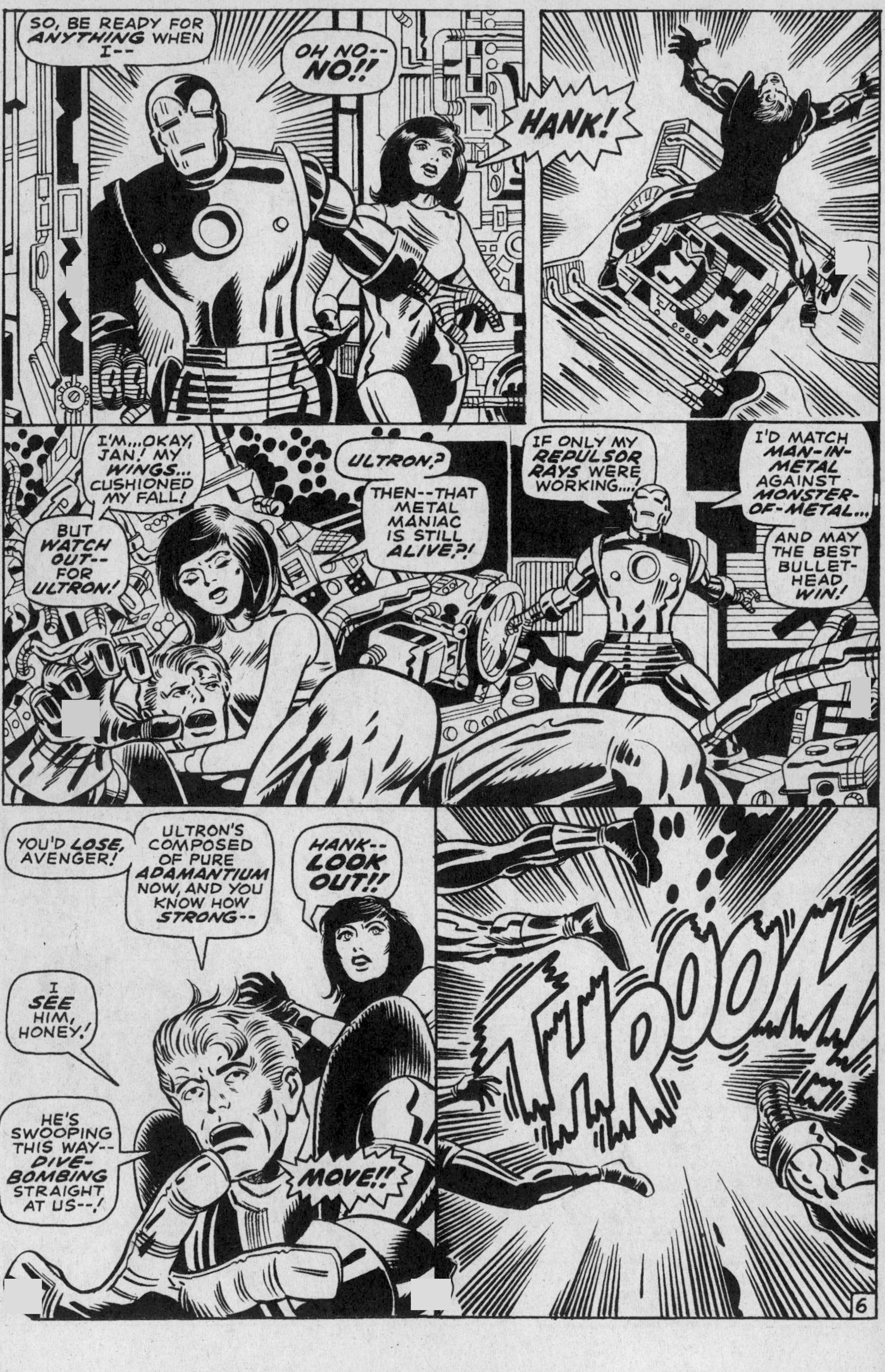

SO, BE READY FOR ANYTHING WHEN I--
OH NO-- NO!!
HANK!
I'M...OKAY, JAN! MY WINGS... CUSHIONED MY FALL!
BUT WATCH OUT-- FOR ULTRON!
ULTRON?
THEN--THAT METAL MANIAC IS STILL ALIVE?!
IF ONLY MY REPULSOR RAYS WERE WORKING....!
I'D MATCH MAN-IN-METAL AGAINST MONSTER-OF-METAL...
AND MAY THE BEST BULLET-HEAD WIN!
YOU'D LOSE, AVENGER!
ULTRON'S COMPOSED OF PURE ADAMANTIUM NOW, AND YOU KNOW HOW STRONG--
HANK-- LOOK OUT!!
I SEE HIM, HONEY!
HE'S SWOOPING THIS WAY-- DIVE-BOMBING STRAIGHT AT US--!
MOVE!!
THROOM

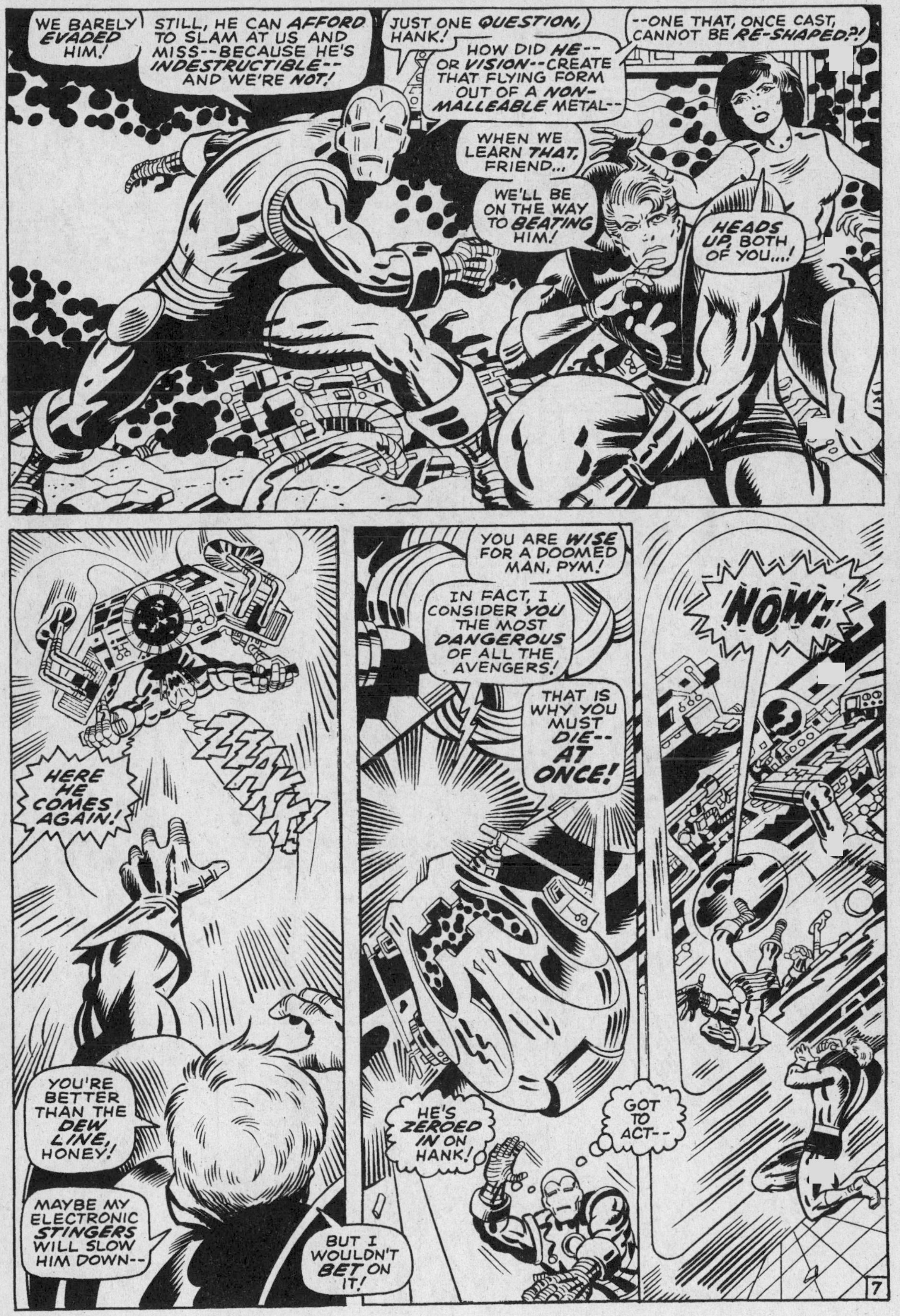
WE BARELY EVADED HIM!
STILL, HE CAN AFFORD TO SLAM AT US AND MISS--BECAUSE HE'S INDESTRUCTIBLE--AND WE'RE NOT!
JUST ONE QUESTION, HANK!
HOW DID HE--OR VISION--CREATE THAT FLYING FORM OUT OF A NON-MALLEABLE METAL--
--ONE THAT, ONCE CAST, CANNOT BE RE-SHAPED?!
WHEN WE LEARN THAT, FRIEND...
WE'LL BE ON THE WAY TO BEATING HIM!
HEADS UP, BOTH OF YOU...!
HERE HE COMES AGAIN!
ZZAKK!
YOU'RE BETTER THAN THE DEW LINE, HONEY!
MAYBE MY ELECTRONIC STINGERS WILL SLOW HIM DOWN--
BUT I WOULDN'T BET ON IT!
YOU ARE WISE FOR A DOOMED MAN, PYM!
IN FACT, I CONSIDER YOU THE MOST DANGEROUS OF ALL THE AVENGERS!
THAT IS WHY YOU MUST DIE--AT ONCE!
NOW!
HE'S ZEROED IN ON HANK!
GOT TO ACT--

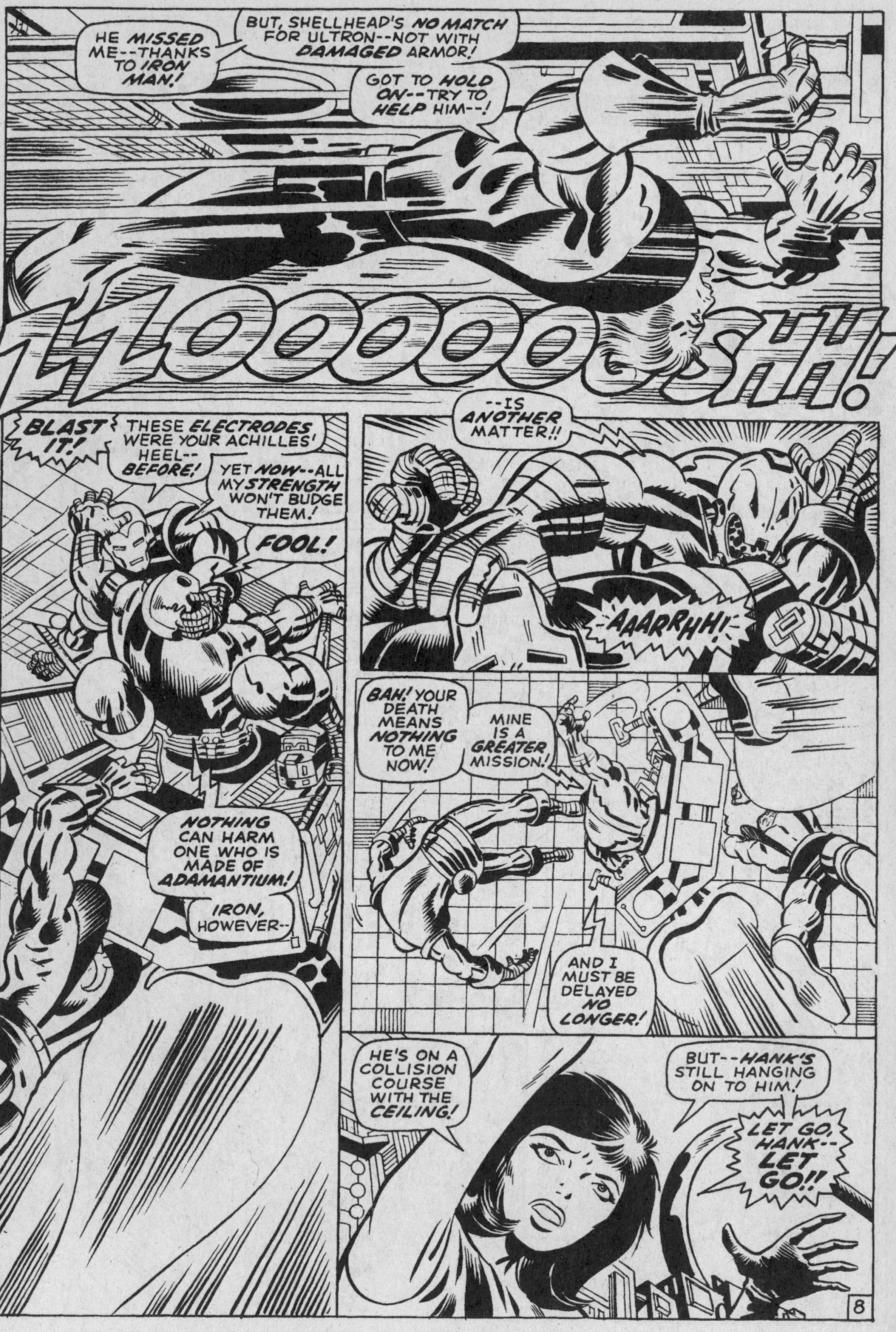
HE MISSED ME--THANKS TO IRON MAN!
BUT, SHELLHEAD'S NO MATCH FOR ULTRON--NOT WITH DAMAGED ARMOR!
GOT TO HOLD ON--TRY TO HELP HIM--!
ZZOOOOOOOSHH!
BLAST IT!
THESE ELECTRODES WERE YOUR ACHILLES' HEEL--BEFORE!
YET NOW--ALL MY STRENGTH WON'T BUDGE THEM!
FOOL!
NOTHING CAN HARM ONE WHO IS MADE OF ADAMANTIUM!
IRON, HOWEVER--
--IS ANOTHER MATTER!!
AAARRHH!
BAH! YOUR DEATH MEANS NOTHING TO ME NOW!
MINE IS A GREATER MISSION!
AND I MUST BE DELAYED NO LONGER!
HE'S ON A COLLISION COURSE WITH THE CEILING!
BUT--HANK'S STILL HANGING ON TO HIM!
LET GO, HANK--LET GO!!

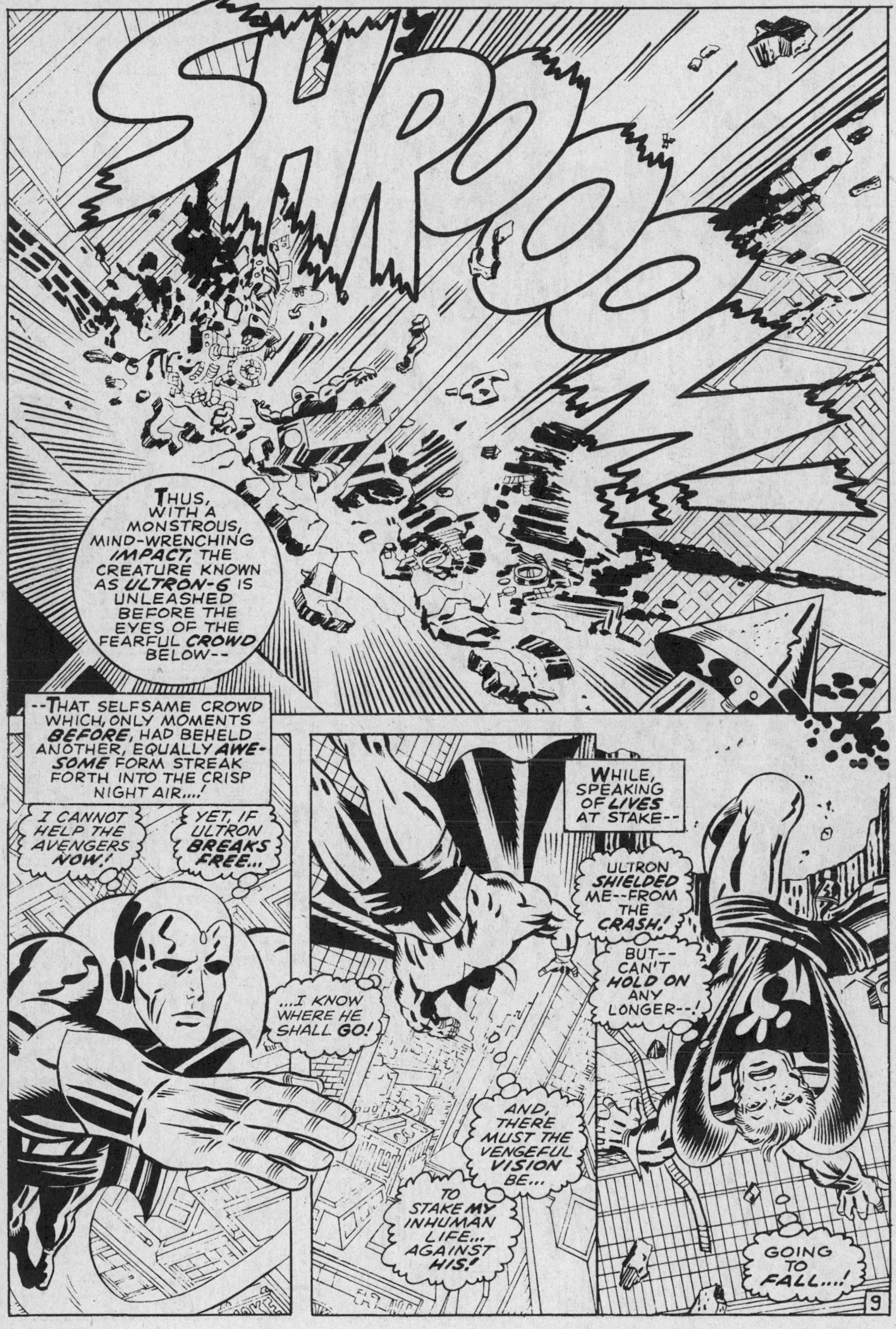
SHROOOM
THUS, WITH A MONSTROUS, MIND-WRENCHING IMPACT, THE CREATURE KNOWN AS ULTRON-6 IS UNLEASHED BEFORE THE EYES OF THE FEARFUL CROWD BELOW--
--THAT SELFSAME CROWD WHICH, ONLY MOMENTS BEFORE, HAD BEHELD ANOTHER, EQUALLY AWESOME FORM STREAK FORTH INTO THE CRISP NIGHT AIR...!
I CANNOT HELP THE AVENGERS NOW!
YET, IF ULTRON BREAKS FREE...
...I KNOW WHERE HE SHALL GO!
AND, THERE MUST THE VENGEFUL VISION BE...
TO STAKE MY INHUMAN LIFE... AGAINST HIS!
WHILE, SPEAKING OF LIVES AT STAKE--
ULTRON SHIELDED ME--FROM THE CRASH!
BUT-- CAN'T HOLD ON ANY LONGER--!
GOING TO FALL...!

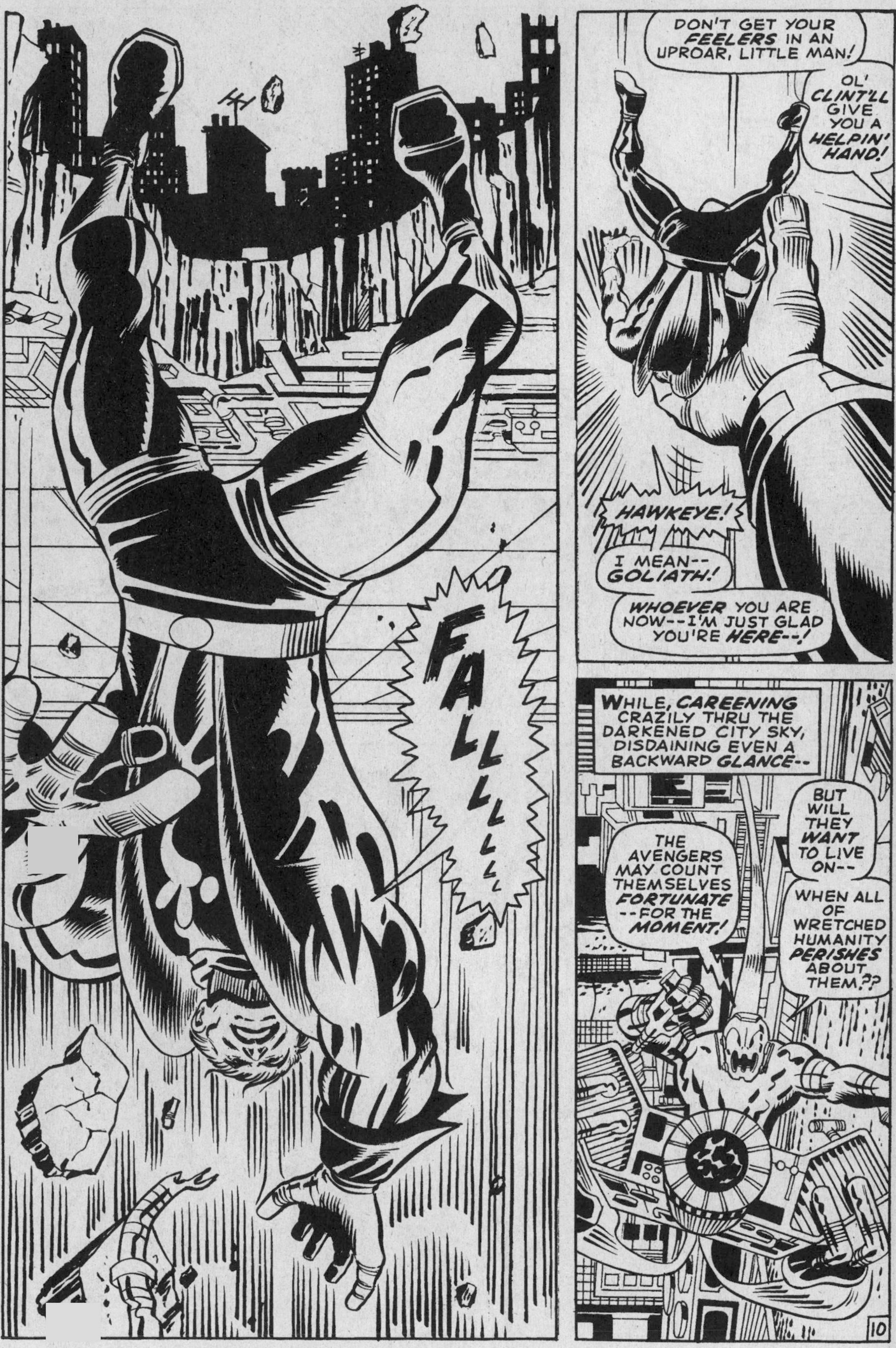
FALLLLLLL
DON'T GET YOUR FEELERS IN AN UPROAR, LITTLE MAN!
OL' CLINT'LL GIVE YOU A HELPIN' HAND!
HAWKEYE!
I MEAN-- GOLIATH!
WHOEVER YOU ARE NOW--I'M JUST GLAD YOU'RE HERE--!
WHILE, CAREENING CRAZILY THRU THE DARKENED CITY SKY, DISDAINING EVEN A BACKWARD GLANCE--
THE AVENGERS MAY COUNT THEMSELVES FORTUNATE --FOR THE MOMENT!
BUT WILL THEY WANT TO LIVE ON--
WHEN ALL OF WRETCHED HUMANITY PERISHES ABOUT THEM??
10

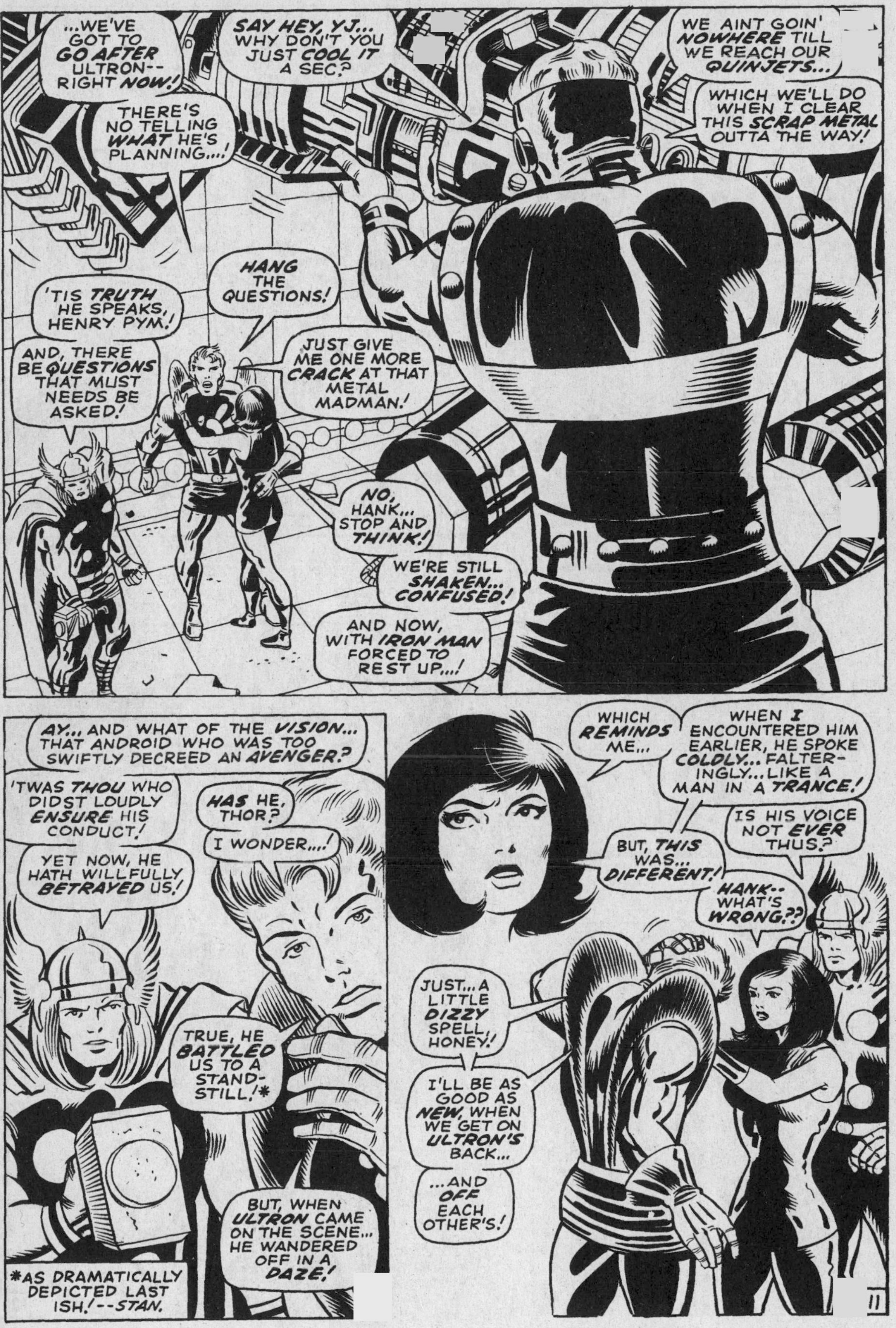
...WE'VE GOT TO GO AFTER ULTRON-- RIGHT NOW!
THERE'S NO TELLING WHAT HE'S PLANNING...!
SAY HEY, YJ... WHY DON'T YOU JUST COOL IT A SEC?
WE AINT GOIN' NOWHERE TILL WE REACH OUR QUINJETS...
WHICH WE'LL DO WHEN I CLEAR THIS SCRAP METAL OUTTA THE WAY!
'TIS TRUTH HE SPEAKS, HENRY PYM!
AND, THERE BE QUESTIONS THAT MUST NEEDS BE ASKED!
HANG THE QUESTIONS!
JUST GIVE ME ONE MORE CRACK AT THAT METAL MADMAN!
NO, HANK... STOP AND THINK!
WE'RE STILL SHAKEN... CONFUSED!
AND NOW, WITH IRON MAN FORCED TO REST UP...!
AY... AND WHAT OF THE VISION... THAT ANDROID WHO WAS TOO SWIFTLY DECREED AN AVENGER?
'TWAS THOU WHO DIDST LOUDLY ENSURE HIS CONDUCT!
YET NOW, HE HATH WILLFULLY BETRAYED US!
HAS HE, THOR?
I WONDER...!
TRUE, HE BATTLED US TO A STAND-STILL!*
BUT, WHEN ULTRON CAME ON THE SCENE... HE WANDERED OFF IN A DAZE!
*AS DRAMATICALLY DEPICTED LAST ISH!--STAN.
WHICH REMINDS ME...
WHEN I ENCOUNTERED HIM EARLIER, HE SPOKE COLDLY... FALTER-INGLY... LIKE A MAN IN A TRANCE!
BUT, THIS WAS... DIFFERENT!
IS HIS VOICE NOT EVER THUS?
HANK-- WHAT'S WRONG??
JUST... A LITTLE DIZZY SPELL, HONEY!
I'LL BE AS GOOD AS NEW, WHEN WE GET ON ULTRON'S BACK...
...AND OFF EACH OTHER'S!
11

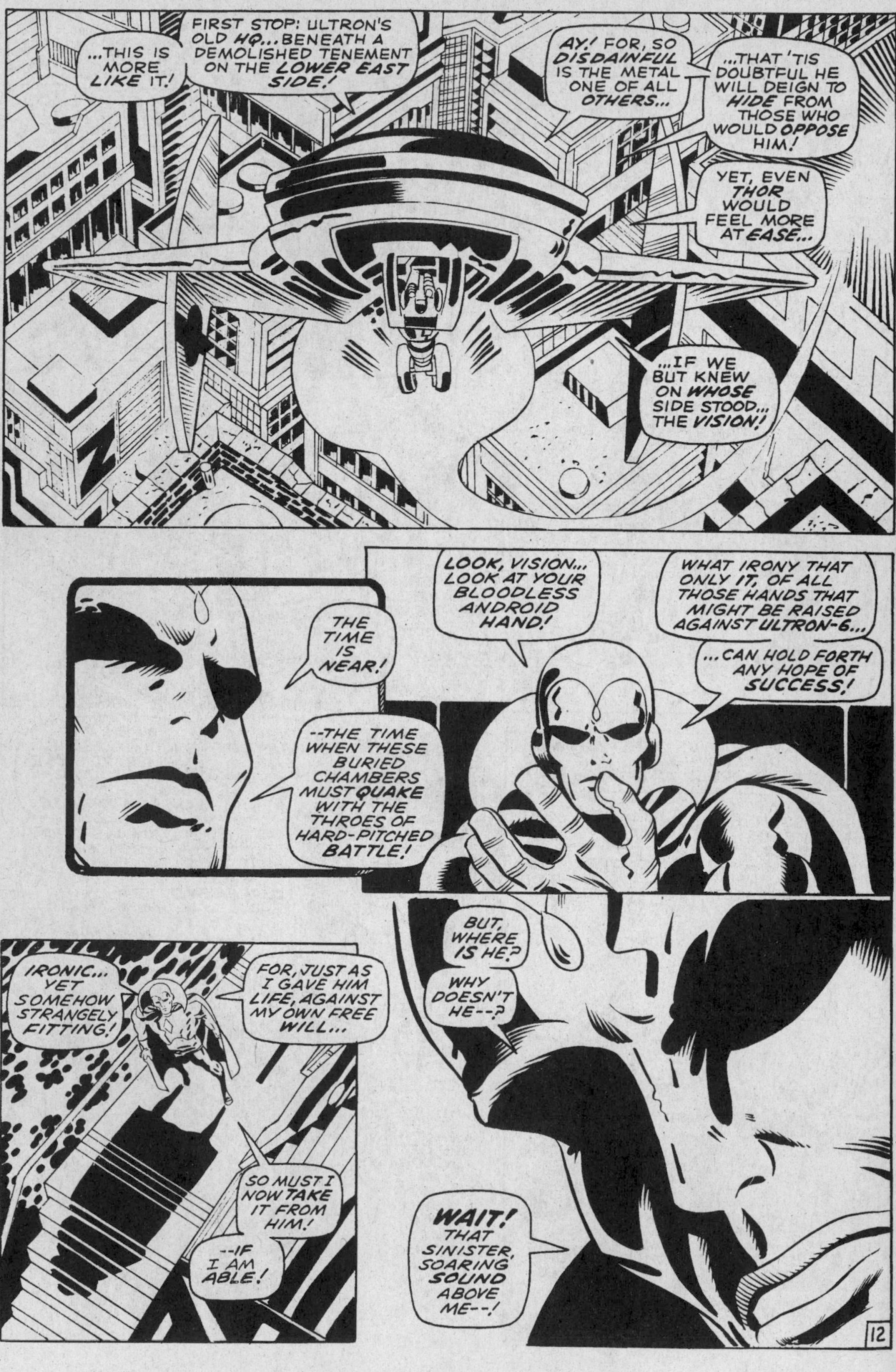
...THIS IS MORE LIKE IT!
FIRST STOP: ULTRON'S OLD HQ... BENEATH A DEMOLISHED TENEMENT ON THE LOWER EAST SIDE!
AY! FOR, SO DISDAINFUL IS THE METAL ONE OF ALL OTHERS...
...THAT 'TIS DOUBTFUL HE WILL DEIGN TO HIDE FROM THOSE WHO WOULD OPPOSE HIM!
YET, EVEN THOR WOULD FEEL MORE AT EASE...
...IF WE BUT KNEW ON WHOSE SIDE STOOD... THE VISION!
THE TIME IS NEAR!
--THE TIME WHEN THESE BURIED CHAMBERS MUST QUAKE WITH THE THROES OF HARD-PITCHED BATTLE!
LOOK, VISION... LOOK AT YOUR BLOODLESS ANDROID HAND!
WHAT IRONY THAT ONLY IT, OF ALL THOSE HANDS THAT MIGHT BE RAISED AGAINST ULTRON-6...
...CAN HOLD FORTH ANY HOPE OF SUCCESS!
IRONIC... YET SOMEHOW STRANGELY FITTING!
FOR, JUST AS I GAVE HIM LIFE, AGAINST MY OWN FREE WILL...
SO MUST I NOW TAKE IT FROM HIM!
--IF I AM ABLE!
BUT, WHERE IS HE?
WHY DOESN'T HE--?
WAIT! THAT SINISTER, SOARING SOUND ABOVE ME--!
12

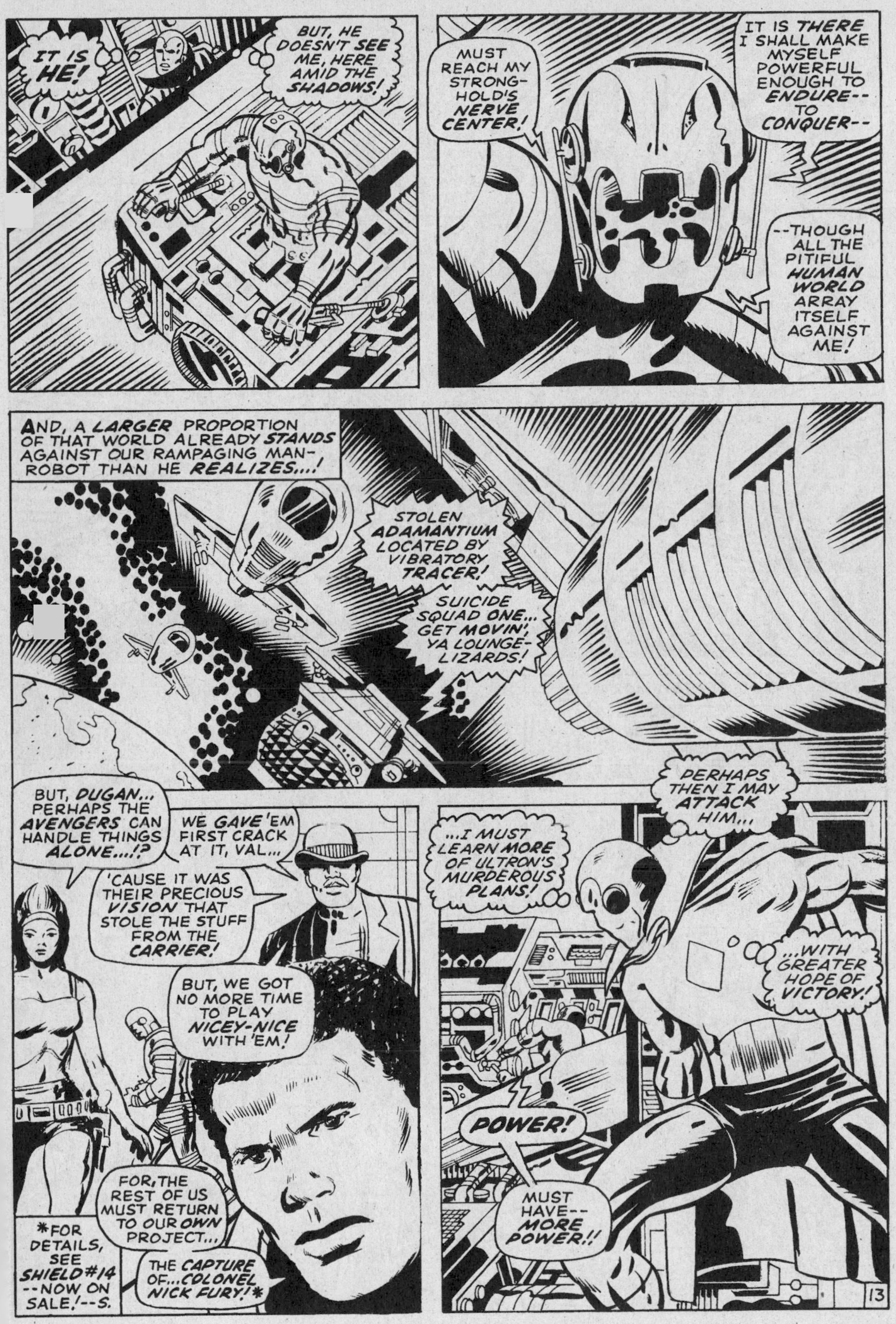

IT IS HE!
BUT, HE DOESN'T SEE ME, HERE AMID THE SHADOWS!
MUST REACH MY STRONG-HOLD'S NERVE CENTER!
IT IS THERE I SHALL MAKE MYSELF POWERFUL ENOUGH TO ENDURE-- TO CONQUER--
--THOUGH ALL THE PITIFUL HUMAN WORLD ARRAY ITSELF AGAINST ME!
AND, A LARGER PROPORTION OF THAT WORLD ALREADY STANDS AGAINST OUR RAMPAGING MAN-ROBOT THAN HE REALIZES...!
STOLEN ADAMANTIUM LOCATED BY VIBRATORY TRACER!
SUICIDE SQUAD ONE... GET MOVIN', YA LOUNGE-LIZARDS!
BUT, DUGAN... PERHAPS THE AVENGERS CAN HANDLE THINGS ALONE...!?
WE GAVE 'EM FIRST CRACK AT IT, VAL...
'CAUSE IT WAS THEIR PRECIOUS VISION THAT STOLE THE STUFF FROM THE CARRIER!
BUT, WE GOT NO MORE TIME TO PLAY NICEY-NICE WITH 'EM!
FOR, THE REST OF US MUST RETURN TO OUR OWN PROJECT...
THE CAPTURE OF... COLONEL NICK FURY!*
*FOR DETAILS, SEE SHIELD #14 --NOW ON SALE!--S.
PERHAPS THEN I MAY ATTACK HIM...
...I MUST LEARN MORE OF ULTRON'S MURDEROUS PLANS!
...WITH GREATER HOPE OF VICTORY!
POWER!
MUST HAVE-- MORE POWER!!
13

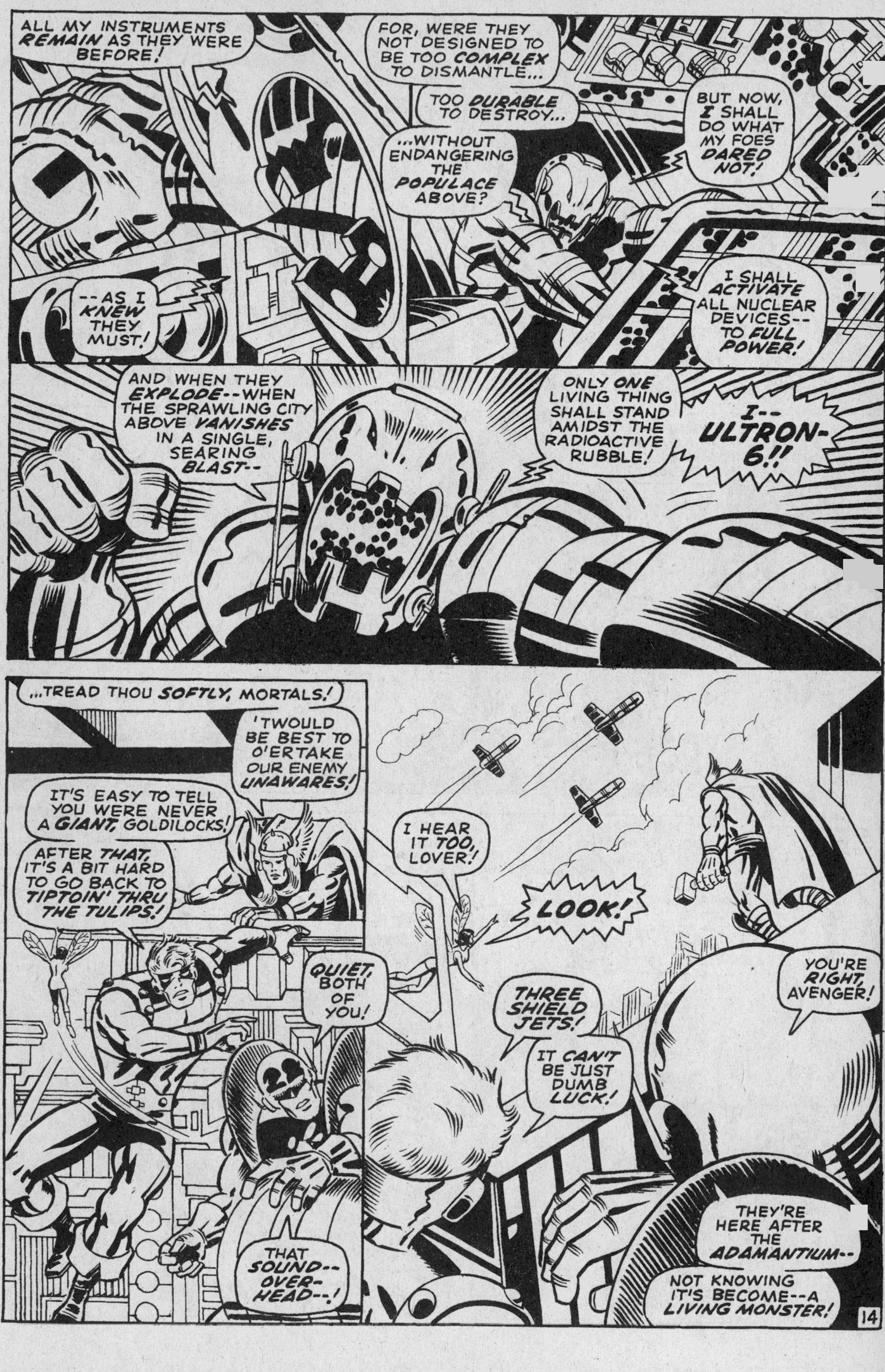
ALL MY INSTRUMENTS REMAIN AS THEY WERE BEFORE!
--AS I KNEW THEY MUST!
FOR, WERE THEY NOT DESIGNED TO BE TOO COMPLEX TO DISMANTLE...
TOO DURABLE TO DESTROY...
...WITHOUT ENDANGERING THE POPULACE ABOVE?
BUT NOW, I SHALL DO WHAT MY FOES DARED NOT!
I SHALL ACTIVATE ALL NUCLEAR DEVICES--TO FULL POWER!
AND WHEN THEY EXPLODE--WHEN THE SPRAWLING CITY ABOVE VANISHES IN A SINGLE, SEARING BLAST--
ONLY ONE LIVING THING SHALL STAND AMIDST THE RADIOACTIVE RUBBLE!
I--ULTRON-6!!
...TREAD THOU SOFTLY, MORTALS!
'TWOULD BE BEST TO O'ERTAKE OUR ENEMY UNAWARES!
IT'S EASY TO TELL YOU WERE NEVER A GIANT, GOLDILOCKS!
AFTER THAT, IT'S A BIT HARD TO GO BACK TO TIPTOIN' THRU THE TULIPS!
QUIET, BOTH OF YOU!
THAT SOUND--OVER-HEAD--!
I HEAR IT TOO, LOVER!
LOOK!
THREE SHIELD JETS!
IT CAN'T BE JUST DUMB LUCK!
YOU'RE RIGHT, AVENGER!
THEY'RE HERE AFTER THE ADAMANTIUM--
NOT KNOWING IT'S BECOME--A LIVING MONSTER!

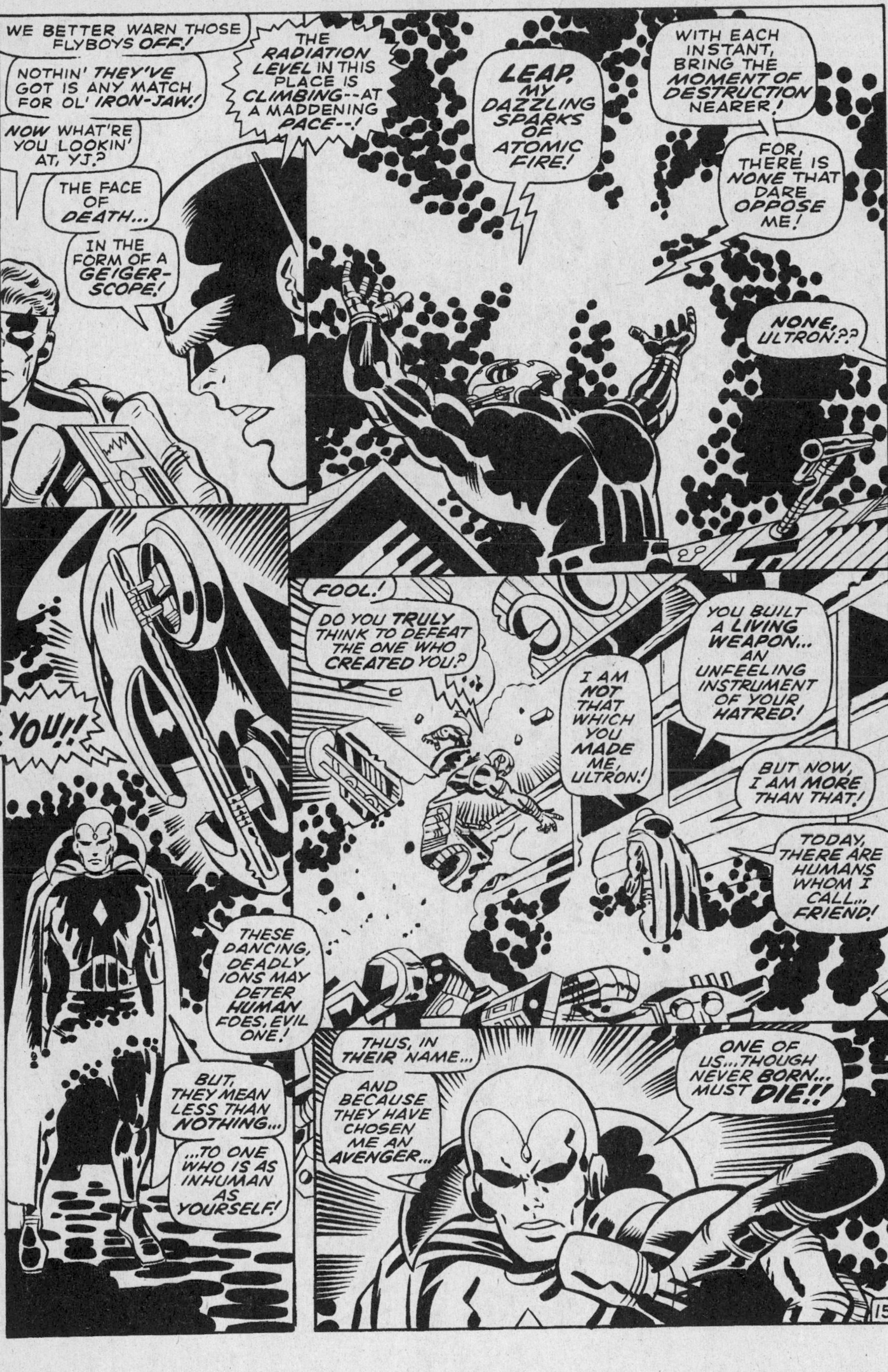

WE BETTER WARN THOSE FLYBOYS OFF!
NOTHIN' THEY'VE GOT IS ANY MATCH FOR OL' IRON-JAW!
NOW WHAT'RE YOU LOOKIN' AT, YJ.?
THE FACE OF DEATH...
IN THE FORM OF A GEIGER-SCOPE!
THE RADIATION LEVEL IN THIS PLACE IS CLIMBING--AT A MADDENING PACE--!
LEAP, MY DAZZLING SPARKS OF ATOMIC FIRE!
WITH EACH INSTANT, BRING THE MOMENT OF DESTRUCTION NEARER!
FOR, THERE IS NONE THAT DARE OPPOSE ME!
NONE, ULTRON??
YOU!!
FOOL!
DO YOU TRULY THINK TO DEFEAT THE ONE WHO CREATED YOU?
I AM NOT THAT WHICH YOU MADE ME, ULTRON!
YOU BUILT A LIVING WEAPON... AN UNFEELING INSTRUMENT OF YOUR HATRED!
BUT NOW, I AM MORE THAN THAT!
TODAY, THERE ARE HUMANS WHOM I CALL... FRIEND!
THESE DANCING, DEADLY IONS MAY DETER HUMAN FOES, EVIL ONE!
BUT, THEY MEAN LESS THAN NOTHING...
...TO ONE WHO IS AS INHUMAN AS YOURSELF!
THUS, IN THEIR NAME...
AND BECAUSE THEY HAVE CHOSEN ME AN AVENGER...
ONE OF US...THOUGH NEVER BORN... MUST DIE!!
15

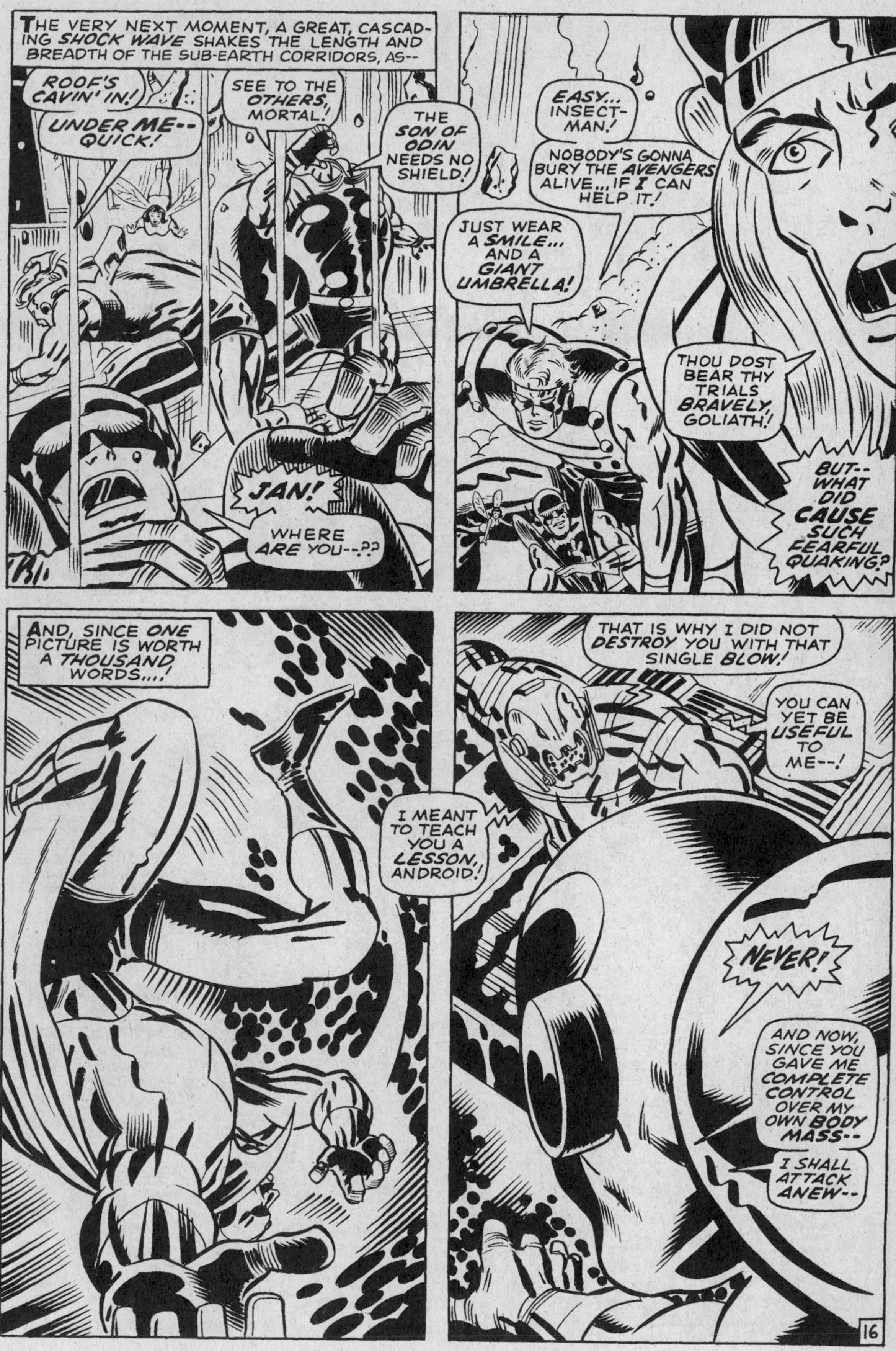
THE VERY NEXT MOMENT, A GREAT, CASCADING SHOCK WAVE SHAKES THE LENGTH AND BREADTH OF THE SUB-EARTH CORRIDORS, AS--
ROOF'S CAVIN' IN!
UNDER ME-- QUICK!
SEE TO THE OTHERS, MORTAL!
THE SON OF ODIN NEEDS NO SHIELD!
JAN!
WHERE ARE YOU--??
EASY... INSECT-MAN!
NOBODY'S GONNA BURY THE AVENGERS ALIVE... IF I CAN HELP IT!
JUST WEAR A SMILE... AND A GIANT UMBRELLA!
THOU DOST BEAR THY TRIALS BRAVELY, GOLIATH!
BUT-- WHAT DID CAUSE SUCH FEARFUL QUAKING?
AND, SINCE ONE PICTURE IS WORTH A THOUSAND WORDS....!
I MEANT TO TEACH YOU A LESSON, ANDROID!
THAT IS WHY I DID NOT DESTROY YOU WITH THAT SINGLE BLOW!
YOU CAN YET BE USEFUL TO ME--!
NEVER!
AND NOW, SINCE YOU GAVE ME COMPLETE CONTROL OVER MY OWN BODY MASS--
I SHALL ATTACK ANEW--
16

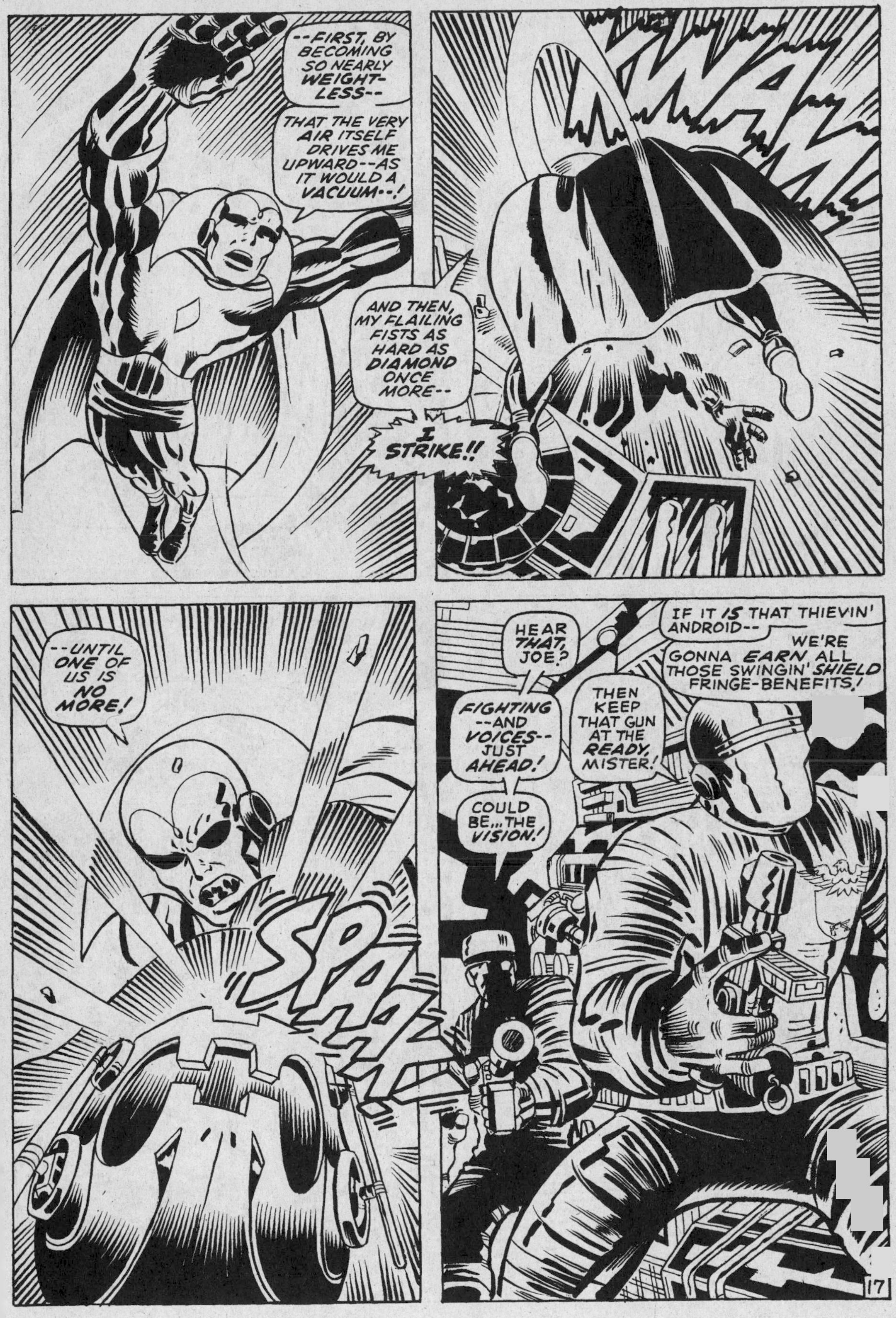
--FIRST, BY BECOMING SO NEARLY WEIGHT-LESS--
THAT THE VERY AIR ITSELF DRIVES ME UPWARD--AS IT WOULD A VACUUM--!
AND THEN, MY FLAILING FISTS AS HARD AS DIAMOND ONCE MORE--
I STRIKE!!
--UNTIL ONE OF US IS NO MORE!
SPA
HEAR THAT, JOE?
FIGHTING--AND VOICES--JUST AHEAD!
COULD BE...THE VISION!
IF IT IS THAT THIEVIN' ANDROID--
WE'RE GONNA EARN ALL THOSE SWINGIN' SHIELD FRINGE-BENEFITS!
THEN KEEP THAT GUN AT THE READY, MISTER!
17

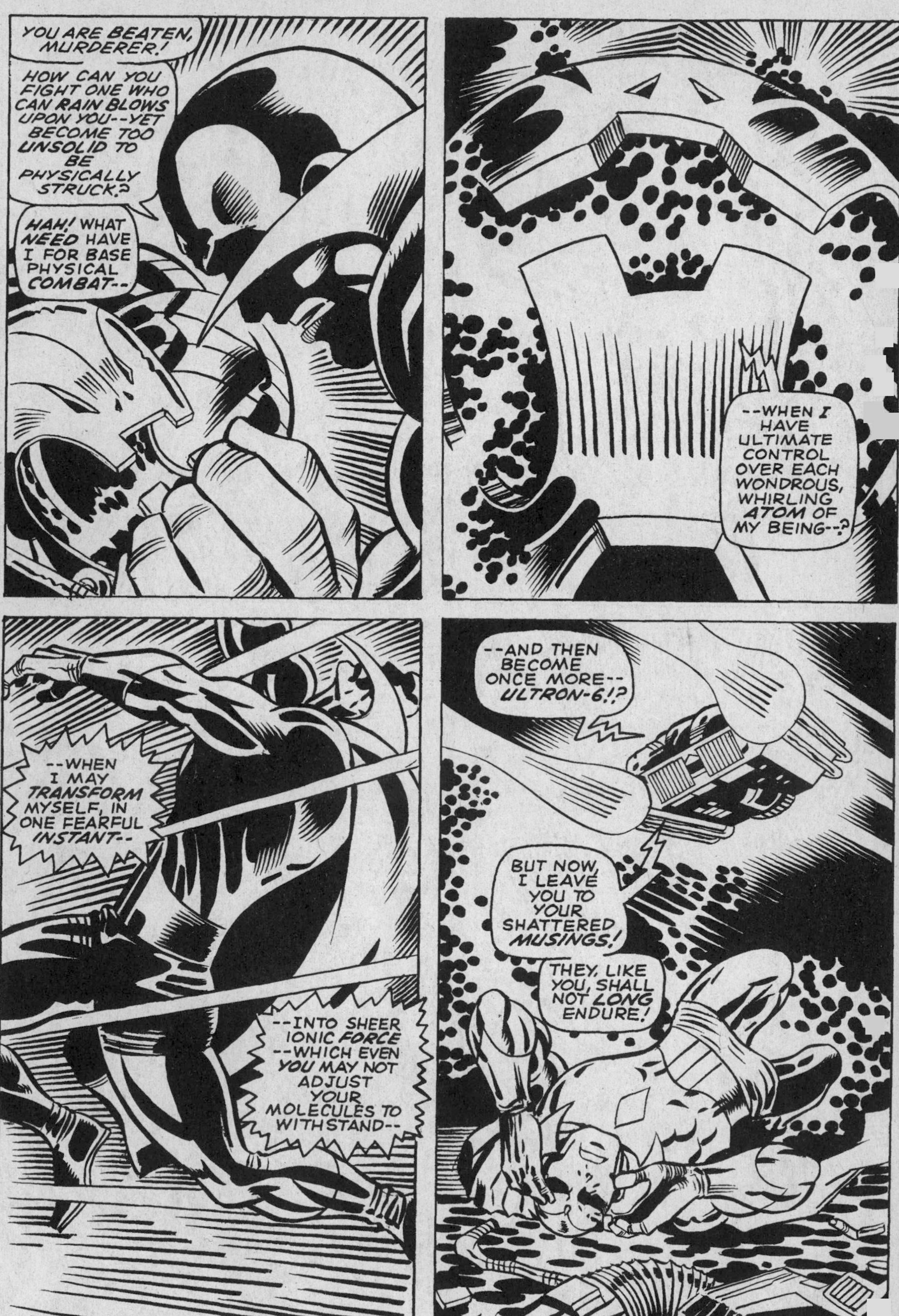
YOU ARE BEATEN, MURDERER!
HOW CAN YOU FIGHT ONE WHO CAN RAIN BLOWS UPON YOU--YET BECOME TOO UNSOLID TO BE PHYSICALLY STRUCK?
HAH! WHAT NEED HAVE I FOR BASE PHYSICAL COMBAT--
--WHEN I HAVE ULTIMATE CONTROL OVER EACH WONDROUS, WHIRLING ATOM OF MY BEING--?
--WHEN I MAY TRANSFORM MYSELF, IN ONE FEARFUL INSTANT--
--INTO SHEER IONIC FORCE --WHICH EVEN YOU MAY NOT ADJUST YOUR MOLECULES TO WITHSTAND--
--AND THEN BECOME ONCE MORE--ULTRON-6!?
BUT NOW, I LEAVE YOU TO YOUR SHATTERED MUSINGS!
THEY, LIKE YOU, SHALL NOT LONG ENDURE!
18

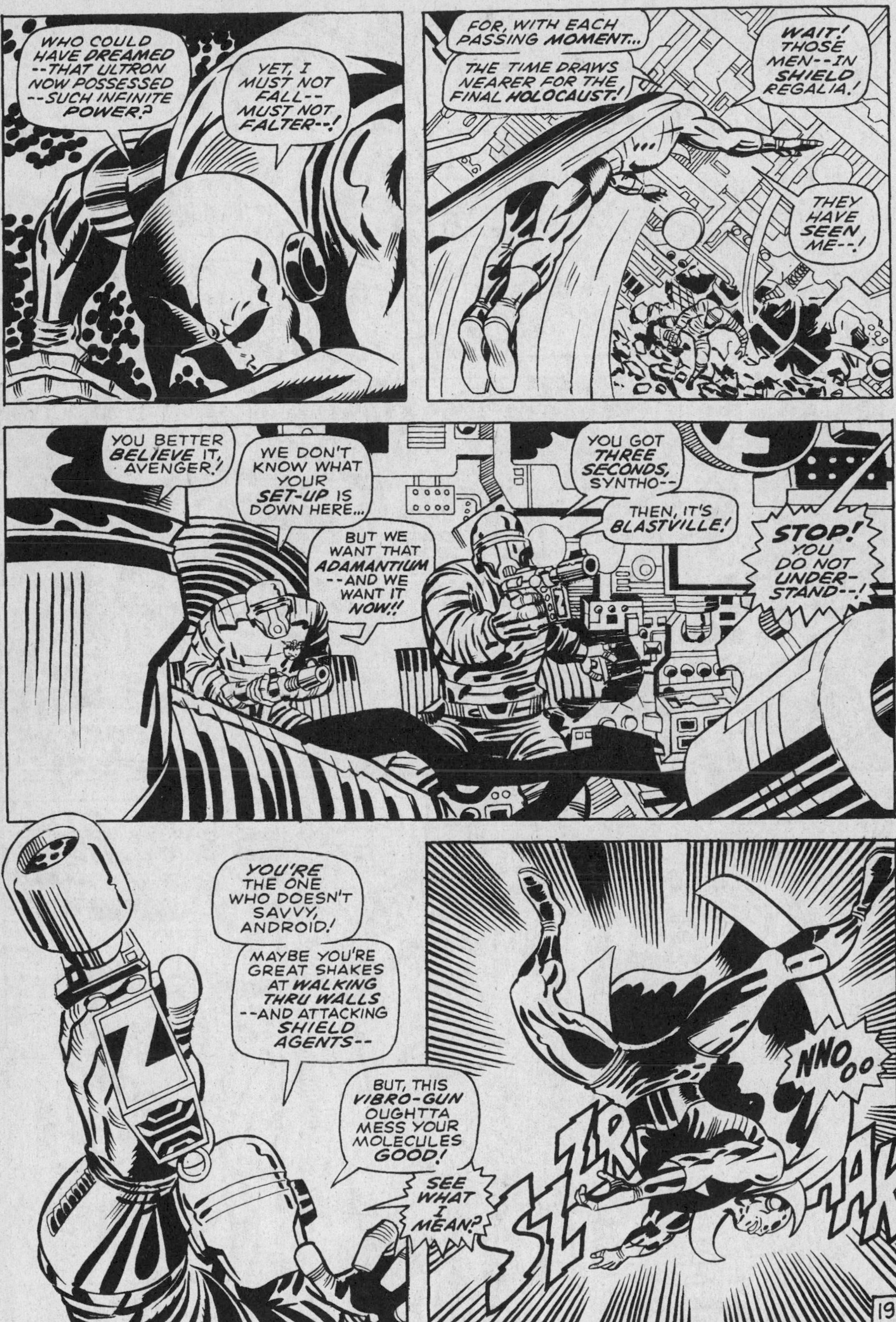
WHO COULD HAVE DREAMED --THAT ULTRON NOW POSSESSED --SUCH INFINITE POWER?
YET, I MUST NOT FALL-- MUST NOT FALTER--!
FOR, WITH EACH PASSING MOMENT...
THE TIME DRAWS NEARER FOR THE FINAL HOLOCAUST!
WAIT! THOSE MEN--IN SHIELD REGALIA!
THEY HAVE SEEN ME--!
YOU BETTER BELIEVE IT, AVENGER!
WE DON'T KNOW WHAT YOUR SET-UP IS DOWN HERE...
BUT WE WANT THAT ADAMANTIUM --AND WE WANT IT NOW!!
YOU GOT THREE SECONDS, SYNTHO--
THEN, IT'S BLASTVILLE!
STOP! YOU DO NOT UNDER-STAND--!
YOU'RE THE ONE WHO DOESN'T SAVVY, ANDROID!
MAYBE YOU'RE GREAT SHAKES AT WALKING THRU WALLS --AND ATTACKING SHIELD AGENTS--
BUT, THIS VIBRO-GUN OUGHTTA MESS YOUR MOLECULES GOOD!
SEE WHAT I MEAN?
NNOoo
ZZRAK

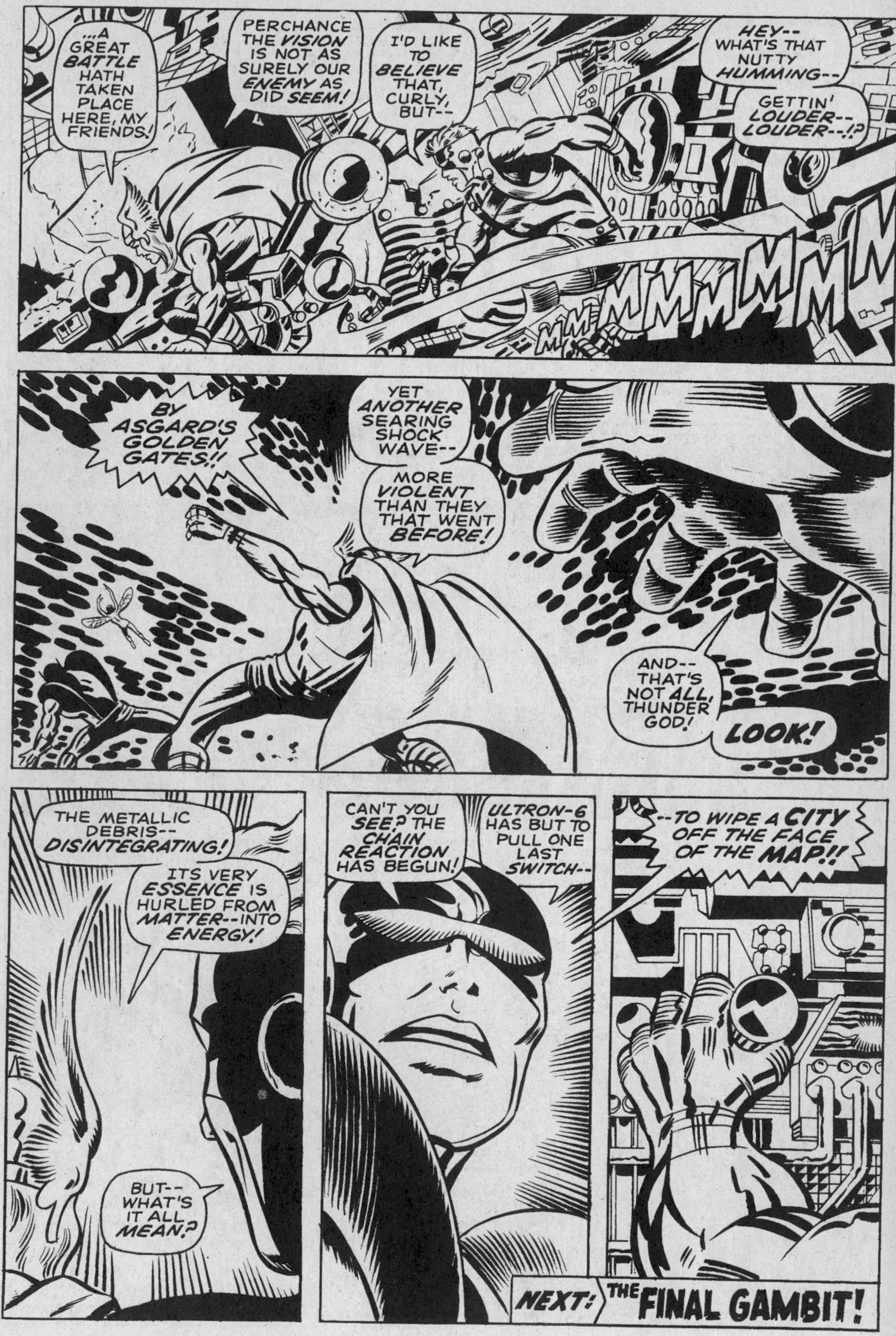

...A GREAT BATTLE HATH TAKEN PLACE HERE, MY FRIENDS!
PERCHANCE THE VISION IS NOT AS SURELY OUR ENEMY AS DID SEEM!
I'D LIKE TO BELIEVE THAT, CURLY, BUT--
HEY-- WHAT'S THAT NUTTY HUMMING--
GETTIN' LOUDER-- LOUDER--!?
MMMMMMMMMMM
BY ASGARD'S GOLDEN GATES!!
YET ANOTHER SEARING SHOCK WAVE--
MORE VIOLENT THAN THEY THAT WENT BEFORE!
AND-- THAT'S NOT ALL, THUNDER GOD!
LOOK!
THE METALLIC DEBRIS-- DISINTEGRATING!
ITS VERY ESSENCE IS HURLED FROM MATTER--INTO ENERGY!
BUT-- WHAT'S IT ALL MEAN?
CAN'T YOU SEE? THE CHAIN REACTION HAS BEGUN!
ULTRON-6 HAS BUT TO PULL ONE LAST SWITCH--
--TO WIPE A CITY OFF THE FACE OF THE MAP!!
NEXT: THE FINAL GAMBIT!

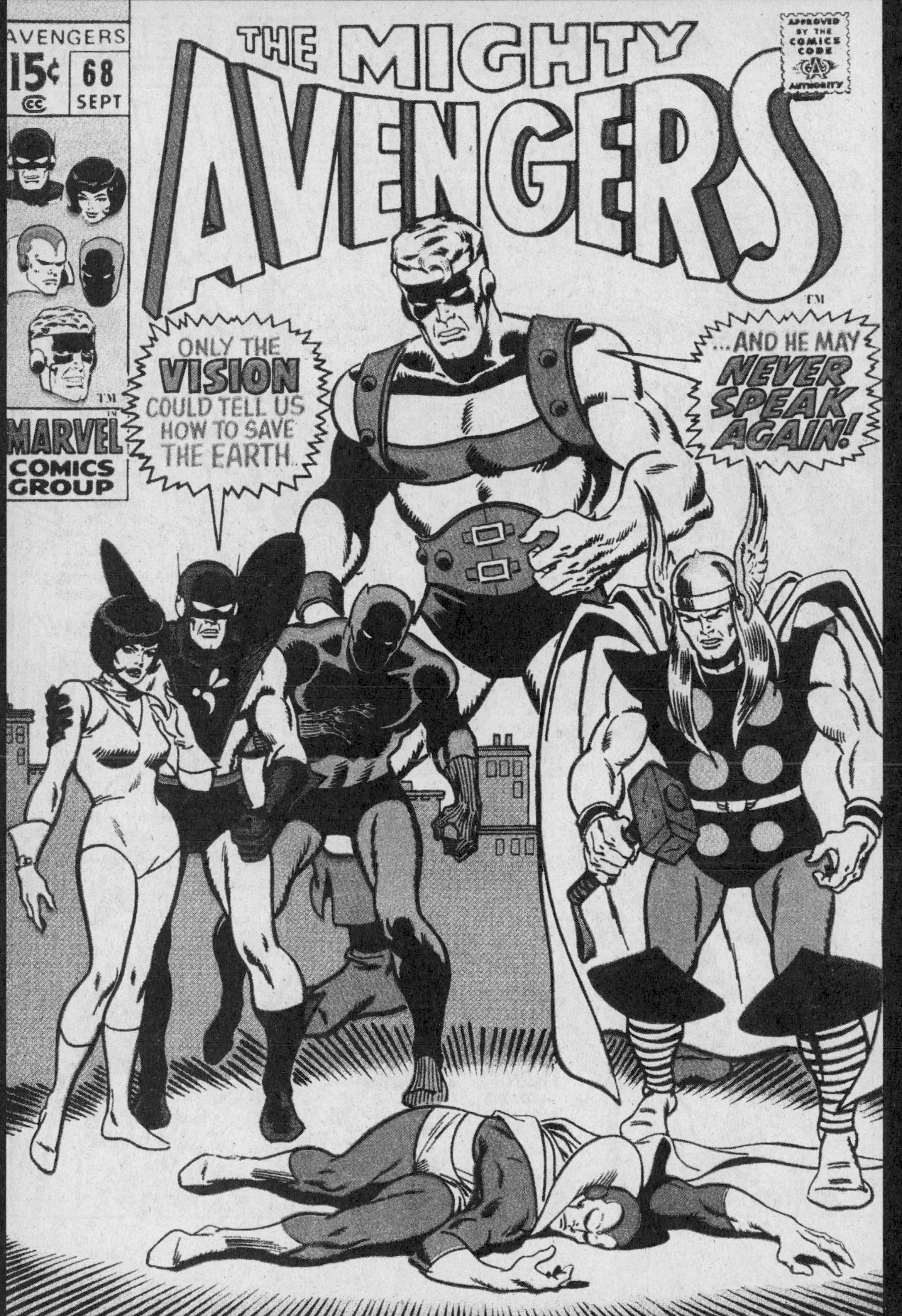
AVENGERS
15¢
68
SEPT
THE MIGHTY
AVENGERS
TM
MARVEL
COMICS
GROUP
ONLY THE VISION COULD TELL US HOW TO SAVE THE EARTH..
...AND HE MAY NEVER SPEAK AGAIN!
APPROVED BY THE COMICS CODE AUTHORITY

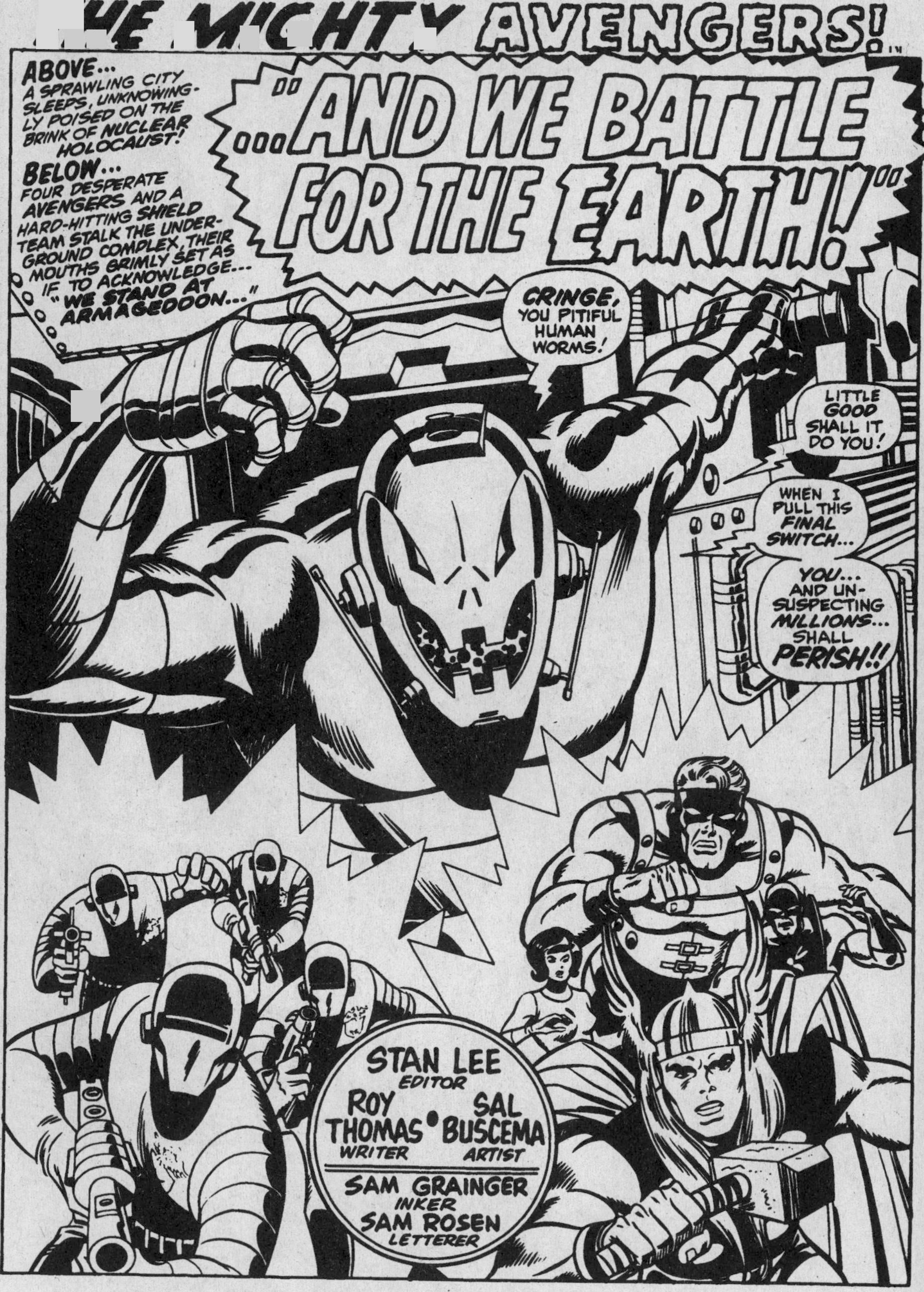
AVENGERS!
ABOVE... A SPRAWLING CITY SLEEPS, UNKNOWINGLY POISED ON THE BRINK OF NUCLEAR HOLOCAUST!
BELOW... FOUR DESPERATE AVENGERS AND A HARD-HITTING SHIELD TEAM STALK THE UNDERGROUND COMPLEX, THEIR MOUTHS GRIMLY SET AS IF TO ACKNOWLEDGE... "WE STAND AT ARMAGEDDON..."
"...AND WE BATTLE FOR THE EARTH!"
CRINGE, YOU PITIFUL HUMAN WORMS!
LITTLE GOOD SHALL IT DO YOU!
WHEN I PULL THIS FINAL SWITCH...
YOU... AND UNSUSPECTING MILLIONS... SHALL PERISH!!
STAN LEE EDITOR
ROY THOMAS WRITER
SAL BUSCEMA ARTIST
SAM GRAINGER INKER
SAM ROSEN LETTERER

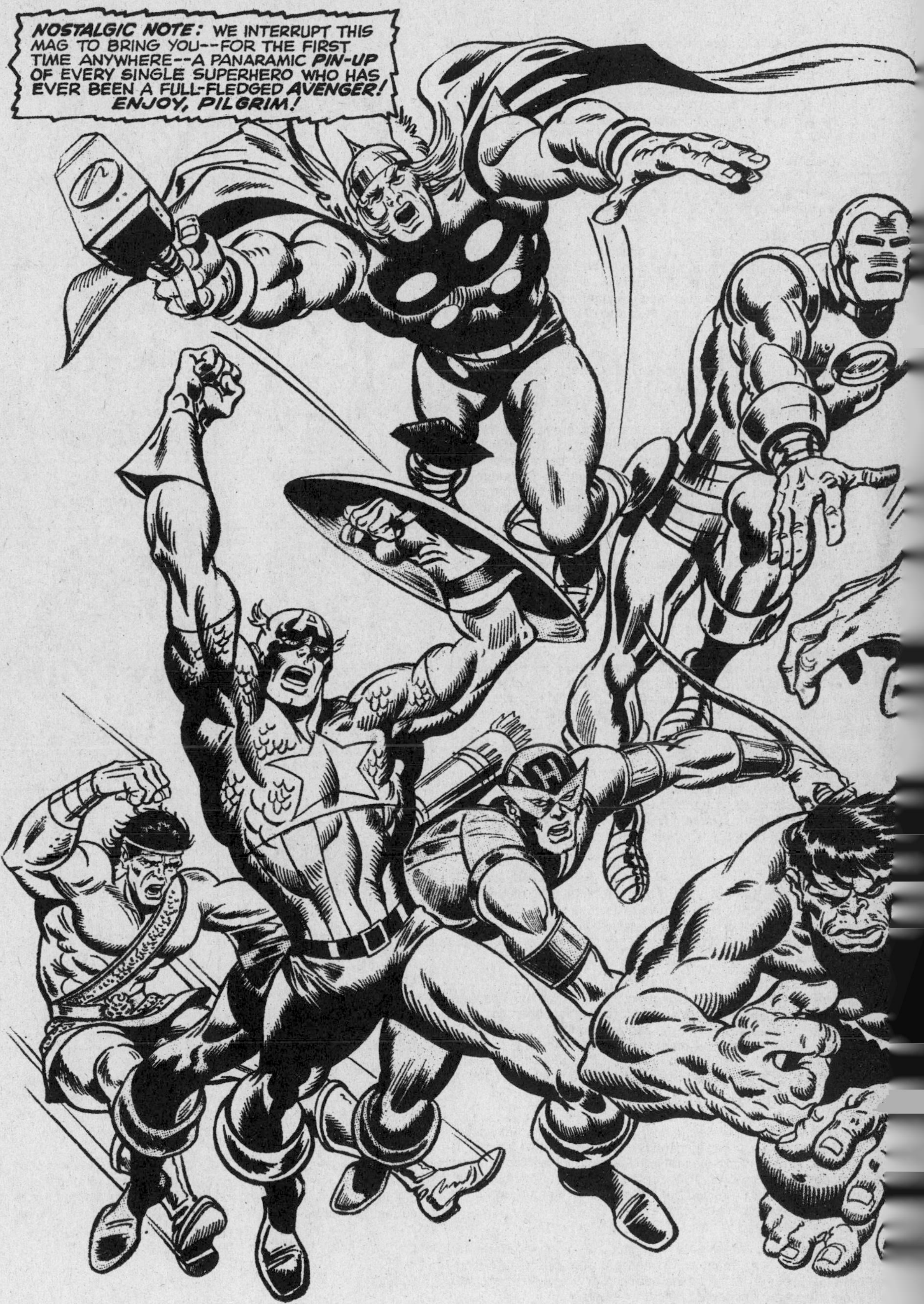
NOSTALGIC NOTE: WE INTERRUPT THIS MAG TO BRING YOU--FOR THE FIRST TIME ANYWHERE--A PANARAMIC PIN-UP OF EVERY SINGLE SUPERHERO WHO HAS EVER BEEN A FULL-FLEDGED AVENGER! ENJOY, PILGRIM!

HELLCAT

Applicant. Hellcat applied for membership in the Avengers and was granted provisional status for a number of months. Before she could be elected to membership, however, fellow provisional member Moondragon convinced Hellcat to accompany her for further training. Although she never served as an active member of the Avengers, Hellcat was a member of the now-defunct Defenders.

JOCASTA

Applicant. Jocasta was a provisional member living in Avengers Mansion since shortly after her creation as a robot. She was never granted official status. She has since been deactivated.

MS. MARVEL

Thirteenth recruit. After sharing a number of adventures with the Avengers on an unofficial basis, Ms. Marvel applied for full membership and was accepted. She served a brief stint, and resigned from the team after an unwanted pregnancy. She is now a member of the Starjammers under the name of Binary.

FALCON

Fourteenth recruit. The Falcon was drafted for Avengers membership by Henry Peter Gyrich's government edict. He served for a brief period and resigned.

WONDER MAN

Fifteenth recruit. After a long term as a provisional member, Wonder Man was elected to active membership. He served for an uninterrupted stint until, during a major membership reshuffling, he decided to leave the active roster in order to pursue a career on the West Coast. When the West Coast Avengers were organized, he was asked to rejoin. Wonder Man is currently an active member of the West Coast team.

TIGRA

Sixteenth recruit. Tigra applied for membership to the East Coast Avengers and was accepted into the active ranks. She served for a brief time and resigned for personal reasons. When the West Coast Avengers were organized, she was asked to rejoin. Tigra is currently an active member of the West Coast team.

SHE-HULK

Seventeenth recruit. She-Hulk applied for membership and was accepted into the active ranks. She served for a short term, and then requested reserve status so that she could fill a vacancy in the Fantastic Four left by the Thing. She-Hulk remains a reserve member of the East Coast Avengers.

CAPTAIN MARVEL

Eighteenth recruit. Captain Marvel was nominated to enter the Avengers' new training program by the Wasp, and accepted. After a brief period as a provisional member, she was elected to active membership. Captain Marvel is currently an active member of the East Coast Avengers.

STARFOX

Nineteenth recruit. Starfox applied for membership and was accepted into the training program. After a brief period as a provisional member, he was awarded active status. After a distinguished tour of duty, Starfox elected to leave the team for personal reasons. He is currently a reserve member of the East Coast Avengers.

MOCKINGBIRD

First recruit of the West Coast Avengers. After her husband Hawkeye was appointed chairman, Mockingbird accepted active membership in the newly organized second team. She currently resides at the Avengers Compound and is an active member of the West Coast team. Due to her SHIELD credentials, she was appointed the West Coast team's security liason with the government.

IRON MAN II

Second recruit of the West Coast Avengers. Iron Man II was invited to join the newly organized second team by the Vision, who believed him to be the original Iron Man and not his hand-picked replacement. Iron Man II accepted the offer of membership, served for a brief time, and became a reserve member when the original Iron Man became active again.

THING

Applicant to the West Coast Avengers. While on leave from the Fantastic Four, the Thing was invited to join the West Coast Avengers by Hawkeye. Although he has shared some adventures with them, he has not accepted official membership.

STARFOX
(Eros)
Joined AVENGERS #231

MOCKINGBIRD
(Barbara Morse Barton)
Joined WEST COAST
AVENGERS LS #1

IRON MAN II
(James Rhodes)
Joined WEST COAST
AVENGERS LS #1

THING
(Benjamin Grimm)
Active WEST COAST
AVENGERS #4

SUB-MARINER
(Namor McKenzie)
Joined AVENGERS #264

FIREBIRD
(Bonita Juarez)
Active WEST COAST
AVENGERS #4

RICK JONES
Honorary member
Active AVENGERS #1

HENRY PYM
Resident scientist
Active WEST COAST
AVENGERS #1

FIREBIRD

Applicant to the West Coast Avengers. A member of the loosely-organized Rangers, Firebird was invited to join the West Coast Avengers. She is currently a provisional member of the West Coast team.

SUB-MARINER

Twentieth recruit to the East Coast Avengers. A former member of the Invaders and Defenders, the Sub-Mariner was offered membership in the Avengers by Captain America and accepted. He is currently an active member of the East Coast team. ■

SCARLET WITCH
Fourth recruit, filling a vacancy in the ranks left by the departing founding members. The Scarlet Witch has taken several leaves of absence of varying duration, once after her wedding to fellow Avenger, the Vision. She and the Vision later left active duty to become reserve members, but subsequently returned to active duty. Following an official investigation of her husband's activities as Avengers chairman, she resigned her membership.

SWORDSMAN
Fifth recruit. The Swordsman served a several day stint as a member, betrayed the Avengers, and was expelled. He returned years later, having reformed, and had his membership reinstated. The Swordsman died in action.

HERCULES
Sixth recruit. Hercules served the Avengers in an unofficial capacity for a brief period before being granted official membership. He took a long leave of absence shortly thereafter, serving as an unofficial ally to the Avengers on only two occasions. He was briefly a member of the short-lived team, the Champions. He is currently an active member of the East Coast Avengers.

BLACK PANTHER
Seventh recruit, served as Captain America's replacement during his first major leave of absence. The Panther eventually returned to Wakanda, the African nation of which he is king. He has since become a reserve Avenger, serving on an irregular basis.

VISION
Eighth recruit. The Vision served as an active member of the Avengers for years before taking his first leave of absence, after his wedding to fellow member, the Scarlet Witch. The Vision and the Scarlet Witch quickly returned to active duty and continued to live at Avengers Mansion until they had saved enough to buy a house of their own. They then became reserve Avengers. The Vision later returned to active duty and assumed chairmanship of the group. At his instigation, the Avengers formed the West Coast branch. He has since stepped down as chairman and resigned from active membership.

BLACK KNIGHT
Ninth recruit. The Black Knight assisted the Avengers on several cases unofficially before being elected to membership. Rather than joining the active roster, the Black Knight applied for reserve status, and left for England where he owned an estate. He then undertook a time trip to the Tenth Century in order to fight in the Crusades, and has only recently returned. Having forfeited his British estate, he has returned to his native America and has rejoined the Avengers. He is currently an active member of the East Coast team.

BLACK WIDOW
Tenth recruit. A long-time ally of the Avengers due to her now-terminated romantic relationship with Hawkeye, the Black Widow finally accepted membership in the group for the duration of a single adventure. She then elected to stay with Daredevil in San Francisco. She was a member of the short-lived Champions, and has worked with the East Coast Avengers on several occasions since the disbanding of the Champions. Residing in New York, she is currently a reserve member of the East Coast Avengers.

MANTIS
Eleventh recruit. Mantis served as a provisional member for several months in tandem with the Swordsman, whom she helped reform. She was elected to full membership after learning she was the Celestial Madonna, but she immediately resigned from active duty to pursue her destiny in space.

BEAST
Twelfth recruit. A graduate of the X-Men, the Beast applied for Avengers membership and after a period of provisional membership was elected to active status. He served an uninterrupted stint until during a major membership reshuffling, he decided to go off active duty to pursue a life of his own. He soon joined the Defenders, however, and resigned his reserve status with the Avengers. With the demise of the Defenders, he joined the original X-Men in X-Factor.

MOONDRAGON
Applicant. Moondragon accepted a period of provisional membership after aiding the Avengers in two major adventures. When she was offered a full active membership, she declined, preferring to remain a reserve member. She later assisted the Avengers in one mission, and then encountered them twice in an adversarial role. The second time she was expelled from the Avengers for dishonorable conduct. She has since joined the Defenders and was expelled from their ranks just prior to their disbanding.

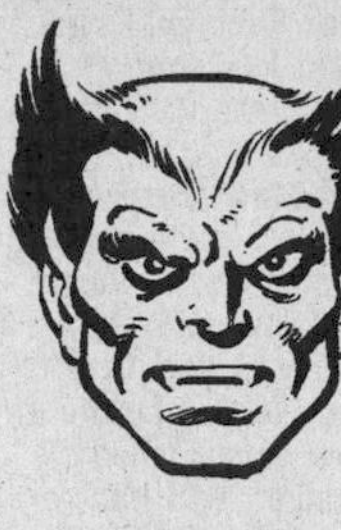

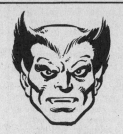

BEAST
(Henry McCoy)
Joined AVENGERS #137

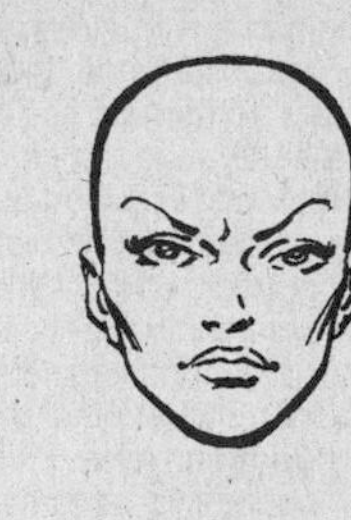

MOONDRAGON
(Heather Douglas)
Joined AVENGERS #137

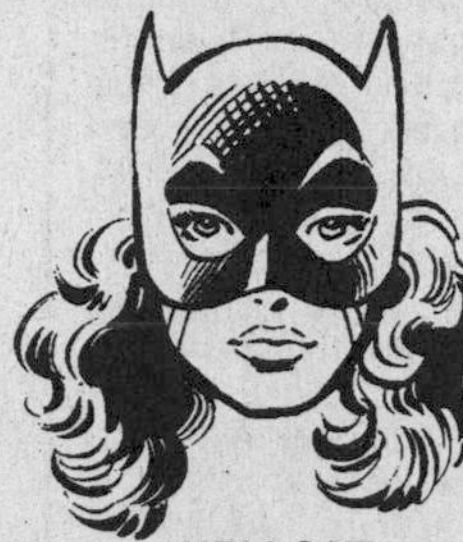

HELLCAT
(Patsy Walker)
Applied AVENGERS #144

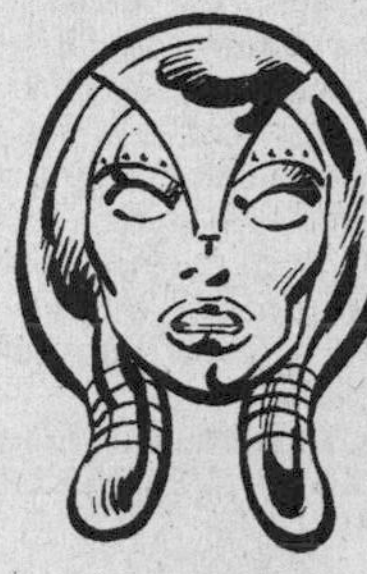

JOCASTA
(no alias used)

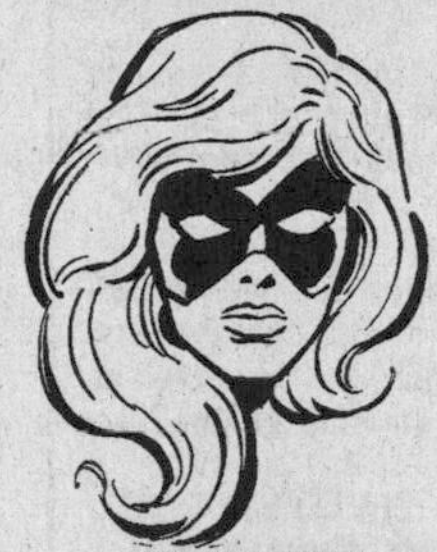

MS. MARVEL
(Carol Danvers)
Joined AVENGERS #183

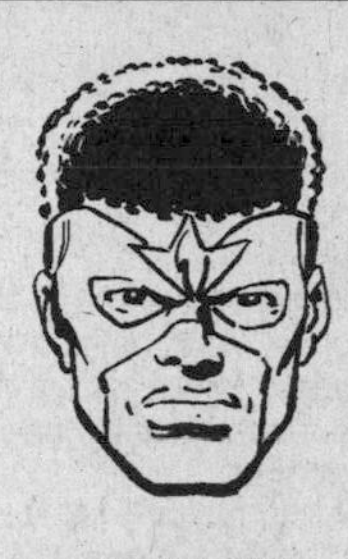

FALCON
(Sam Wilson)
Joined AVENGERS #184

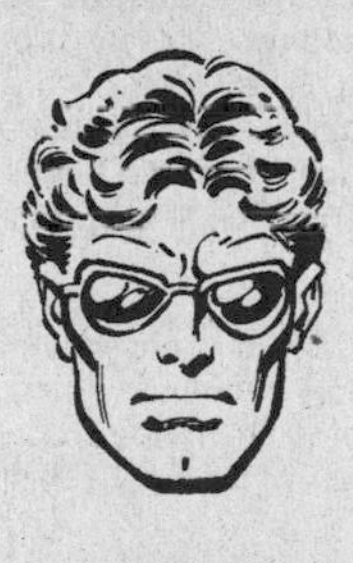

WONDER MAN
(Simon Williams)
Joined AVENGERS #194

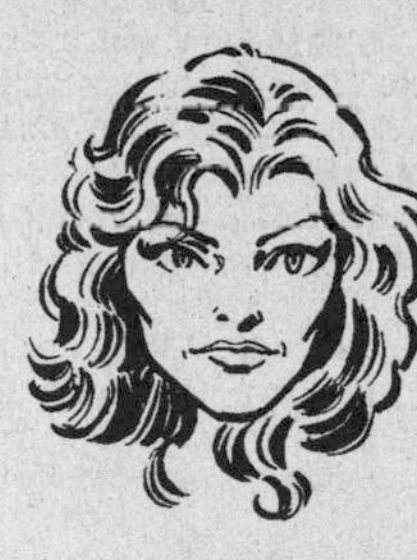

TIGRA
(Greer Nelson)
Joined AVENGERS #211

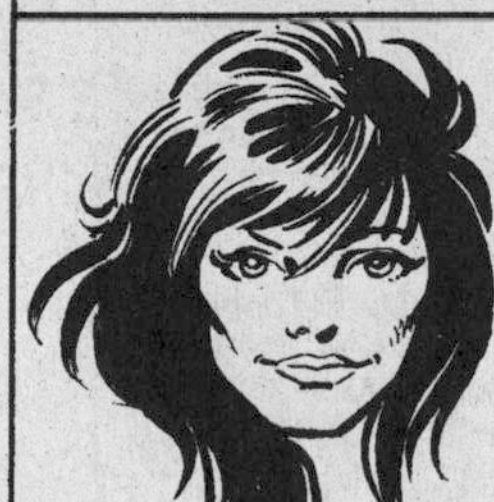

SHE-HULK
(Jennifer Walters)
Joined AVENGERS #221

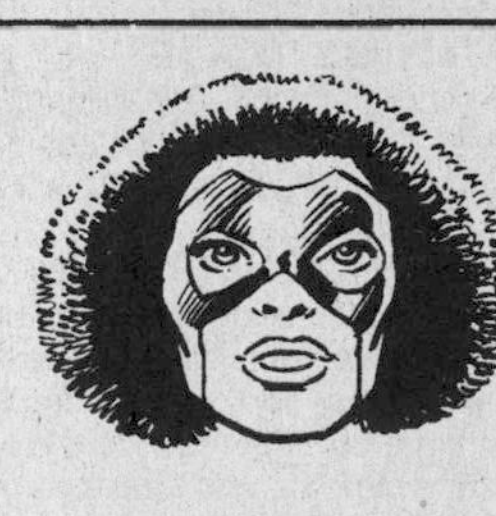

CAPTAIN MARVEL
(Monica Rambeau)
Joined AVENGERS #231

In recent months, then-current chairman the Vision petitioned the U.S. government to approve the establishment of a second team of active Avengers to be based on the West Coast. Getting official clearance, the Vision appointed Hawkeye to be the new team's chairman and sent him to Los Angeles, California, to set up a base of operations (see *Avengers Compound*). With two independently operated but fully coordinated branches of Avengers, the organization now has slots for twelve active members, six on each coast. When it was learned that the Vision planned to take benevolent control of the world government (see *Vision*), certain punitive measures were taken by the United States, despite the fact that the Vision aborted his plan before it truly endangered anyone. The government has since limited the Avengers' access to security-related information, and has revoked various special sanctions, including the privilege of launching their supersonic Quinjets from their headquarters in Manhattan. The Avengers have joined with the Fantastic Four, whose Manhattan launch privileges were also rescinded, to establish a joint airbase in the Atlantic Ocean just outside U.S. territorial limits. The operations of the West Coast Avengers have been curtailed in regard to government sanctions but not airspace rights.

The East Coast and West Coast Avengers operate autonomously of one another, with no central authority. The informal dividing line for their United States operations is the Mississippi River. The two groups routinely share all information, and occasionally join forces to meet a single threat. Together, the two teams make up Earth's largest and most powerful organization of superhuman champions.

First appearance: AVENGERS #1, (West Coast Avengers) WEST COAST AVENGERS (Limited Series) #1.

MEMBERSHIP RECORD

THOR
Founding member. Thor has taken numerous leaves of absence of varying duration. He is currently a reserve member of the East Coast team, participating in Avengers business under special circumstances.

IRON MAN
Founding member. Iron Man has taken several leaves of absence, once while being investigated on murder charges, and most recently when alcoholism incapacitated him. He served as chairman once, and is currently an active member of the West Coast Avengers.

ANT-MAN I / GIANT-MAN I / GOLIATH I / YELLOWJACKET
Founding member. Ant-Man assumed the identity of Giant-Man before his second adventure with the group. After a short leave of absence, he returned to the team under the name of Goliath. Later he changed his identity to Yellowjacket, and married his fellow member, the Wasp, in this guise. He took several leaves of absence after this, occasionally reassuming his Ant-Man identity. Following a lengthy leave, Yellowjacket returned to active status and was expelled for dishonorable conduct. He has now retired from active costumed adventuring, but serves the West Coast Avengers as resident scientist.

WASP
Founding member. Wasp has taken a few leaves of absence of varying duration, usually to accompany her partner and later husband, Yellowjacket. She has since divorced him. She is currently serving her second term as chairman of the East Coast Avengers.

HULK
Founding member. The Hulk quit the team following their second adventure. He has been an unofficial ally of the team on rare occasions since.

CAPTAIN AMERICA
First recruit of the original team. Captain America has served several lengthy stints as chairman. He has taken a few leaves of absence of short duration. He is currently an active member of the East Coast Avengers.

HAWKEYE / GOLIATH II / HAWKEYE
Second recruit, filling a vacancy in the ranks left by the departing founding members. Hawkeye has taken a few leaves of absence of varying duration. He assumed the identity of Goliath II for a short time, but resumed his Hawkeye identity thereafter. He is a founding member and chairman of the West Coast Avengers.

QUICKSILVER
Third recruit, filling a vacancy in the ranks left by the departing founding members. Quicksilver has served two major stints with the East Coast Avengers. He resigned from active membership to marry outside the group. Residing on the moon, Quicksilver is inactive in the Avengers.

SWORDSMAN
(real name classified)
Joined AVENGERS #19

GOLIATH
(formerly Giant-Man)
Active AVENGERS #28

HERCULES
(no alias used)
Joined AVENGERS #45

BLACK PANTHER
(T'Challa)
Joined AVENGERS #52

VISION
(no alias used)
Joined AVENGERS #58

YELLOWJACKET
(formerly Goliath)
Active AVENGERS #63

GOLIATH II
(formerly Hawkeye)
Active AVENGERS #63

BLACK KNIGHT
(Dane Whitman)
Joined AVENGERS #71

BLACK WIDOW
(Natasha Romanova)
Joined AVENGERS #111

MANTIS
(real name classified)
Joined AVENGERS #114

AVENGERS

The Avengers is one of Earth's foremost organizations of costumed superhuman adventurers dedicated to safeguarding the world from any threat beyond the power of conventional peacekeeping forces to handle. Founded several months after the incorporation of the Fantastic Four (see *Fantastic Four*), the Avengers became the first superhuman team to be granted official government sanctions by the National Security Council of the United States, the General Assembly of the United Nations, and later by the international intelligence agency, SHIELD. Unlike the Fantastic Four, whose ranks have been restricted to Reed Richards and his experimental rocket crew (except for an occasional substitute), membership in the Avengers has been open and in constant fluctuation. Only weeks after the Avengers' inception, one of its founding members, the Hulk, left the team, setting the precedent for future roster changes. Roughly a year into the organization's existence, all of the rest of the founding members took a leave of absence, leaving the Avengers' first recruit, Captain America, to fill the vacancies in the ranks. Eventually, all of the founding members returned for stints as active members with the exception of the Hulk.

The five founding members of the Avengers first banded together when Loki, the Asgardian god of mischief (see *Loki*), attempted to discredit the Hulk in order to draw the thunder god Thor into battle. The Hulk's teenage ally Rick Jones, believing the Hulk was innocent of the deed he was accused of, dispatched a radio call to the Fantastic Four for help. Loki intercepted the message, however, and relayed it to Thor. Inadvertantly the message was also received by Iron Man, Ant-Man, and the Wasp. The four adventurers rendevoused for the first time, tracked down the Hulk, learned that Loki was the true culprit, and apprehended him. Before they parted, Ant-Man suggested that they form a regular team. The five readily agreed, and the Wasp suggested the name "Avengers." The newly-formed team assembled a short time later at the midtown Manhattan mansion of industrialist Anthony Stark, who, unknown to them at the time, was their fellow member Iron Man. Stark soon donated the mansion to the Avengers for their exclusive use (see *Avengers Mansion*), and set up a foundation to cover all the operational expenses of the nonprofit team of adventurers. This foundation was set up under Stark's mother's name (The Maria Stark Foundation) so that his own business fortunes could not immediately affect the financial situation of the Avengers. The Stark family's trusted butler Edwin Jarvis was kept on as the principal regular domestic employee at Avengers Mansion.

Captain America became the first full-time resident of Avengers Mansion as well as the team's first recruit. When the founding members took a leave of absence, their replacements, Hawkeye, Quicksilver, and the Scarlet Witch, also made the Mansion their domicile, as did various subsequent members. Captain America became the first permanent chairman of the team, a post he held for a number of years. Chairmanship of the Avengers has been determined by election, and a number of individuals have held the positions over the years, including Iron Man, the Wasp, and the Vision. The ranks of active Avengers has varied in number from a mere three up to fifteen. In addition, certain individuals have enjoyed informal status with the group well before becoming official members. (In three cases, this informal status never culminated in official membership.)

As the official ties between the Avengers and the United States government grew to the extent that the Avengers computer system had direct access to certain U.S. governmental and military information networks, the National Security Council began to take a more active interest in the Avengers' internal affairs. In recent years, N.S.C. agent Henry Peter Gyrich was appointed to be the government's liaison with the Avengers. Gyrich instituted certain policies in the name of security which restricted active membership in the group and tightened admission requirements. Prior to this point, the Avengers screened candidates for membership themselves, and were flexible enough in their membership requirements to allow non-citizens, gods, mutants, and even synthetic humans to join. Gyrich initiated a strict screening procedure for new members and even dictated Avengers membership according to government standards of equal-opportunity employment. Happily for the Avengers, Gyrich was eventually reassigned to Project: Wideawake (see *Sentinels*), and was replaced by the more moderate Raymond Sikorsky, another N.S.C. agent. Captain America instituted a six-member ceiling on membership during his latest stint as chairman, and this ceiling has remained in effect since.

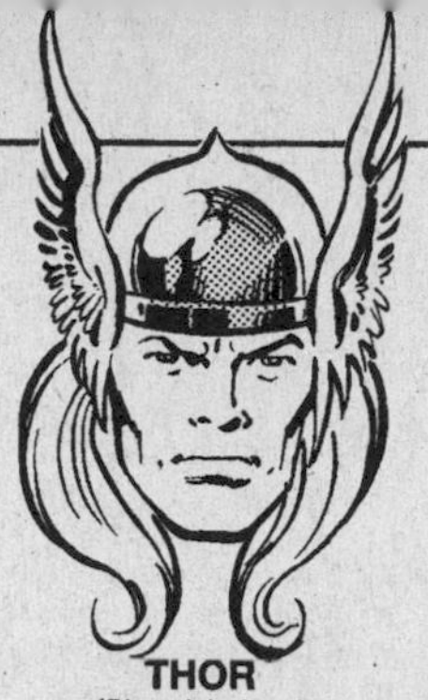

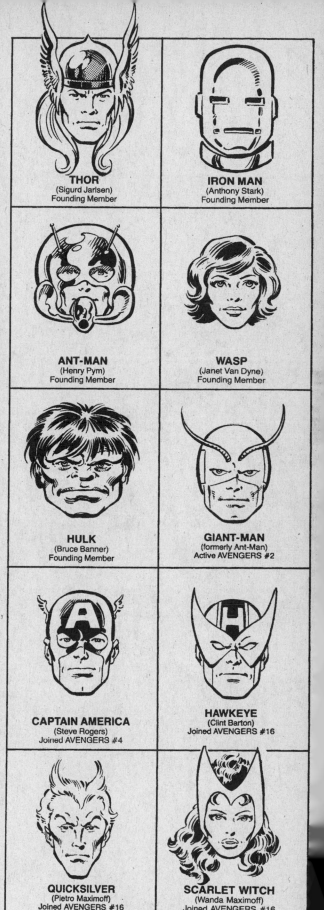

THOR
(Sigurd Jarlsen)
Founding Member

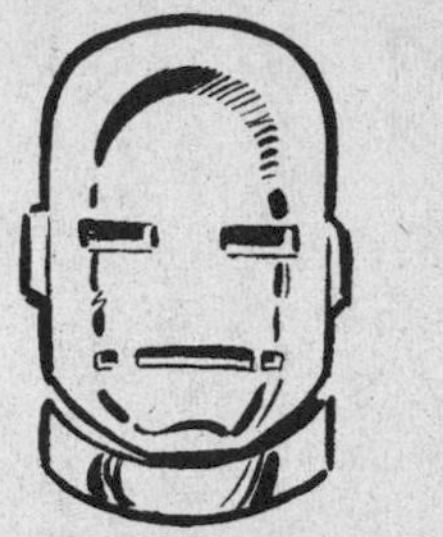

IRON MAN
(Anthony Stark)
Founding Member

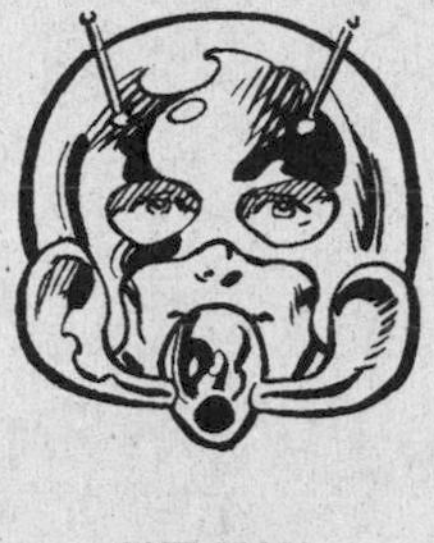

ANT-MAN
(Henry Pym)
Founding Member

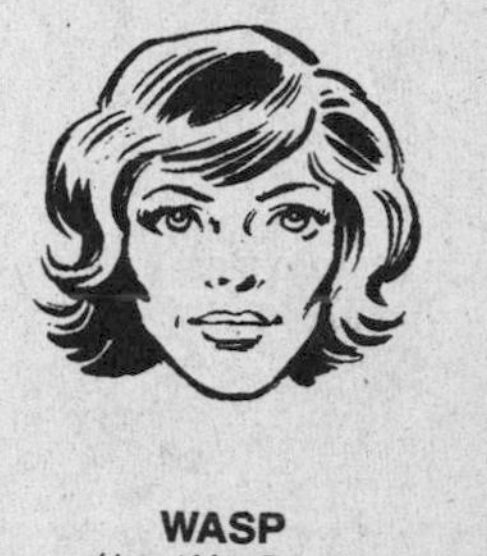

WASP
(Janet Van Dyne)
Founding Member

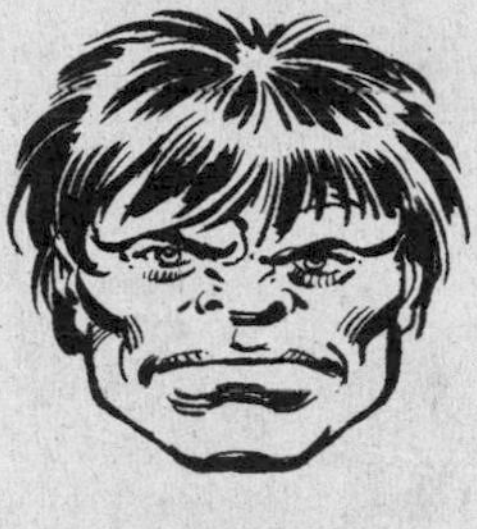

HULK
(Bruce Banner)
Founding Member

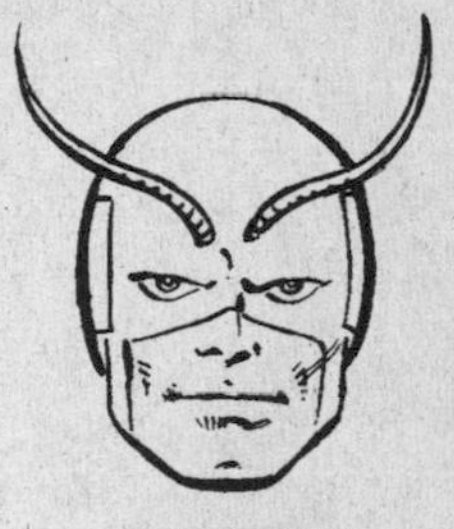

GIANT-MAN
(formerly Ant-Man)
Active AVENGERS #2

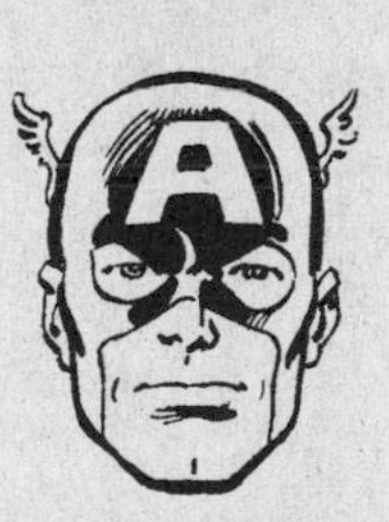

CAPTAIN AMERICA
(Steve Rogers)
Joined AVENGERS #4

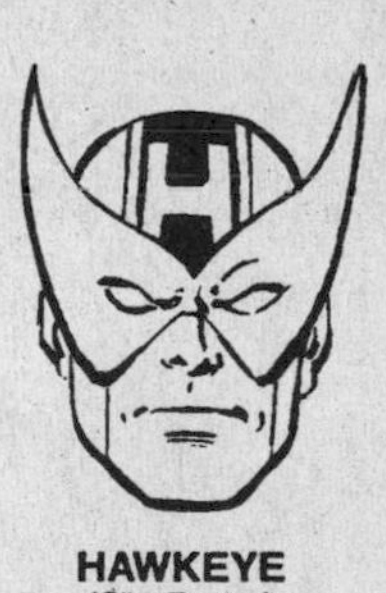

HAWKEYE
(Clint Barton)
Joined AVENGERS #16

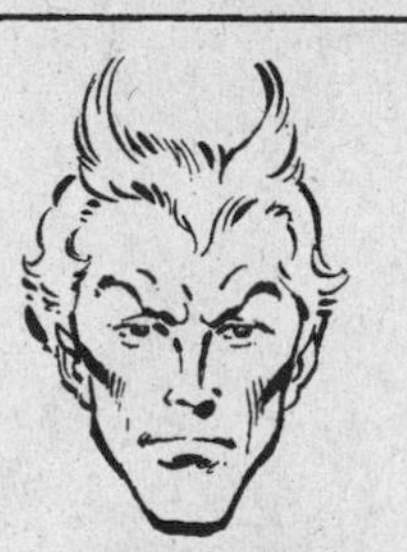

QUICKSILVER
(Pietro Maximoff)
Joined AVENGERS #16

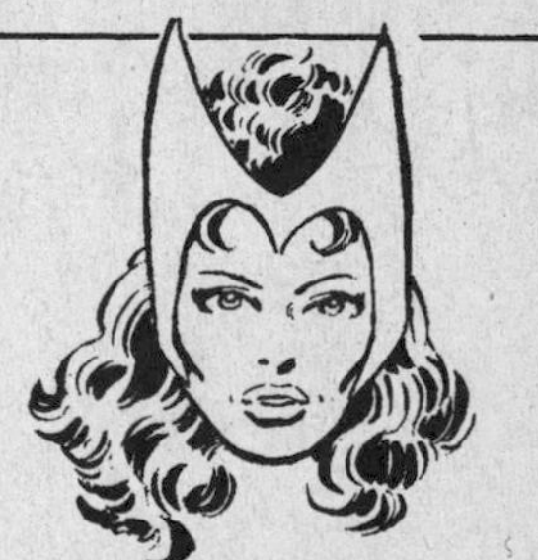

SCARLET WITCH
(Wanda Maximoff)
Joined AVENGERS #16

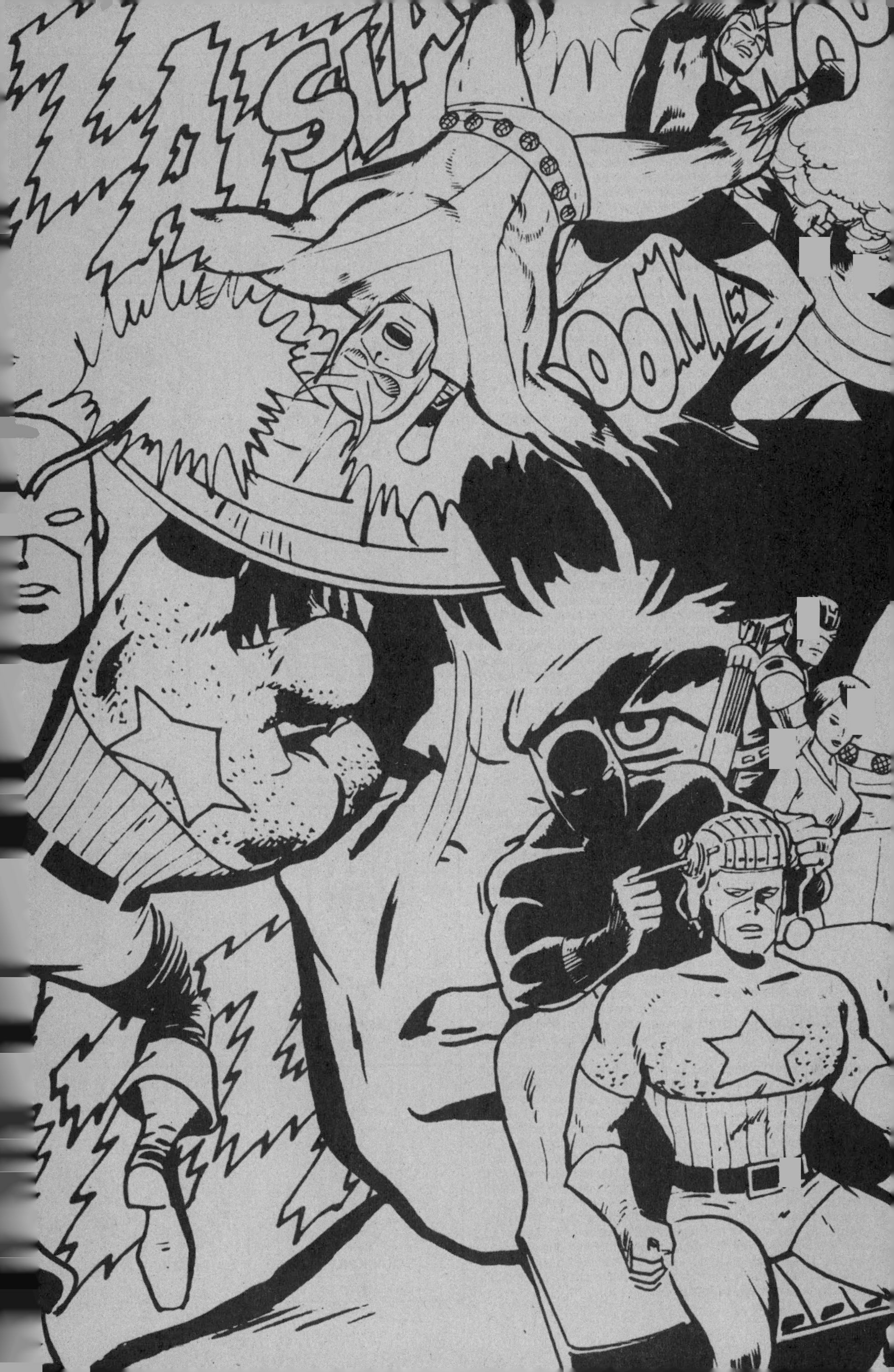

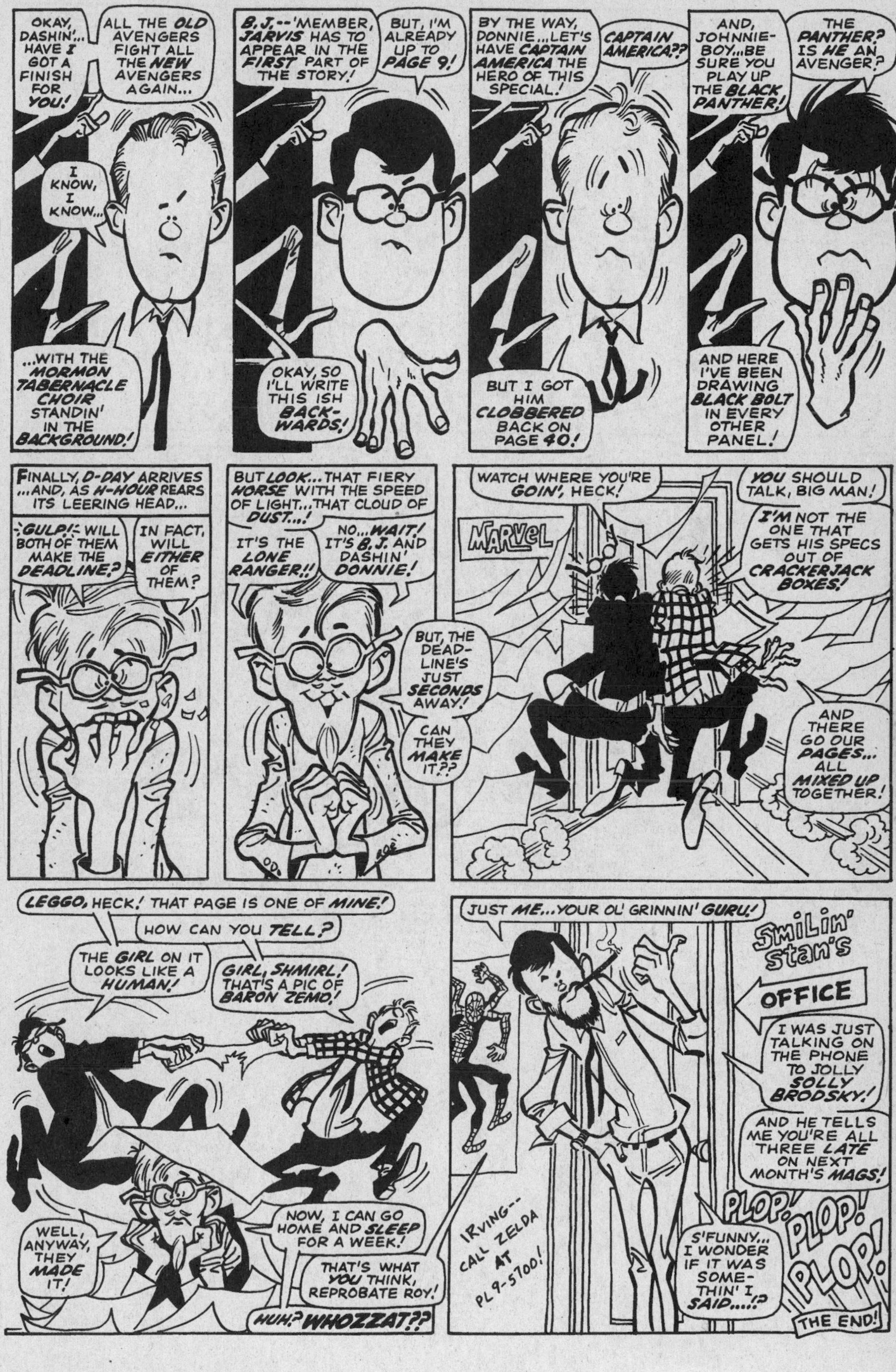
OKAY, DASHIN'... HAVE I GOT A FINISH FOR YOU!
ALL THE OLD AVENGERS FIGHT ALL THE NEW AVENGERS AGAIN...
I KNOW, I KNOW...
...WITH THE MORMON TABERNACLE CHOIR STANDIN' IN THE BACKGROUND!
B.J.--'MEMBER, JARVIS HAS TO APPEAR IN THE FIRST PART OF THE STORY!
BUT, I'M ALREADY UP TO PAGE 9!
OKAY, SO I'LL WRITE THIS ISH BACK-WARDS!
BY THE WAY, DONNIE...LET'S HAVE CAPTAIN AMERICA THE HERO OF THIS SPECIAL!
CAPTAIN AMERICA??
BUT I GOT HIM CLOBBERED BACK ON PAGE 40!
AND, JOHNNIE-BOY...BE SURE YOU PLAY UP THE BLACK PANTHER!
THE PANTHER? IS HE AN AVENGER?
AND HERE I'VE BEEN DRAWING BLACK BOLT IN EVERY OTHER PANEL!
FINALLY, D-DAY ARRIVES ...AND, AS H-HOUR REARS ITS LEERING HEAD...
-GULP!- WILL BOTH OF THEM MAKE THE DEADLINE?
IN FACT, WILL EITHER OF THEM?
BUT LOOK...THAT FIERY HORSE WITH THE SPEED OF LIGHT...THAT CLOUD OF DUST...!
IT'S THE LONE RANGER!!
NO...WAIT! IT'S B.J. AND DASHIN' DONNIE!
BUT, THE DEAD-LINE'S JUST SECONDS AWAY!
CAN THEY MAKE IT??
WATCH WHERE YOU'RE GOIN', HECK!
MARVEL
YOU SHOULD TALK, BIG MAN!
I'M NOT THE ONE THAT GETS HIS SPECS OUT OF CRACKERJACK BOXES!
AND THERE GO OUR PAGES... ALL MIXED UP TOGETHER!
LEGGO, HECK! THAT PAGE IS ONE OF MINE!
HOW CAN YOU TELL?
THE GIRL ON IT LOOKS LIKE A HUMAN!
GIRL, SHMIRL! THAT'S A PIC OF BARON ZEMO!
WELL, ANYWAY, THEY MADE IT!
NOW, I CAN GO HOME AND SLEEP FOR A WEEK!
THAT'S WHAT YOU THINK, REPROBATE ROY!
HUH? WHOZZAT??
JUST ME...YOUR OL' GRINNIN' GURU!
SMILIN' STAN'S
OFFICE
I WAS JUST TALKING ON THE PHONE TO JOLLY SOLLY BRODSKY!
AND HE TELLS ME YOU'RE ALL THREE LATE ON NEXT MONTH'S MAGS!
IRVING-- CALL ZELDA AT PL9-5700!
PLOP! PLOP! PLOP!
S'FUNNY... I WONDER IF IT WAS SOME-THIN' I SAID....!?
THE END!

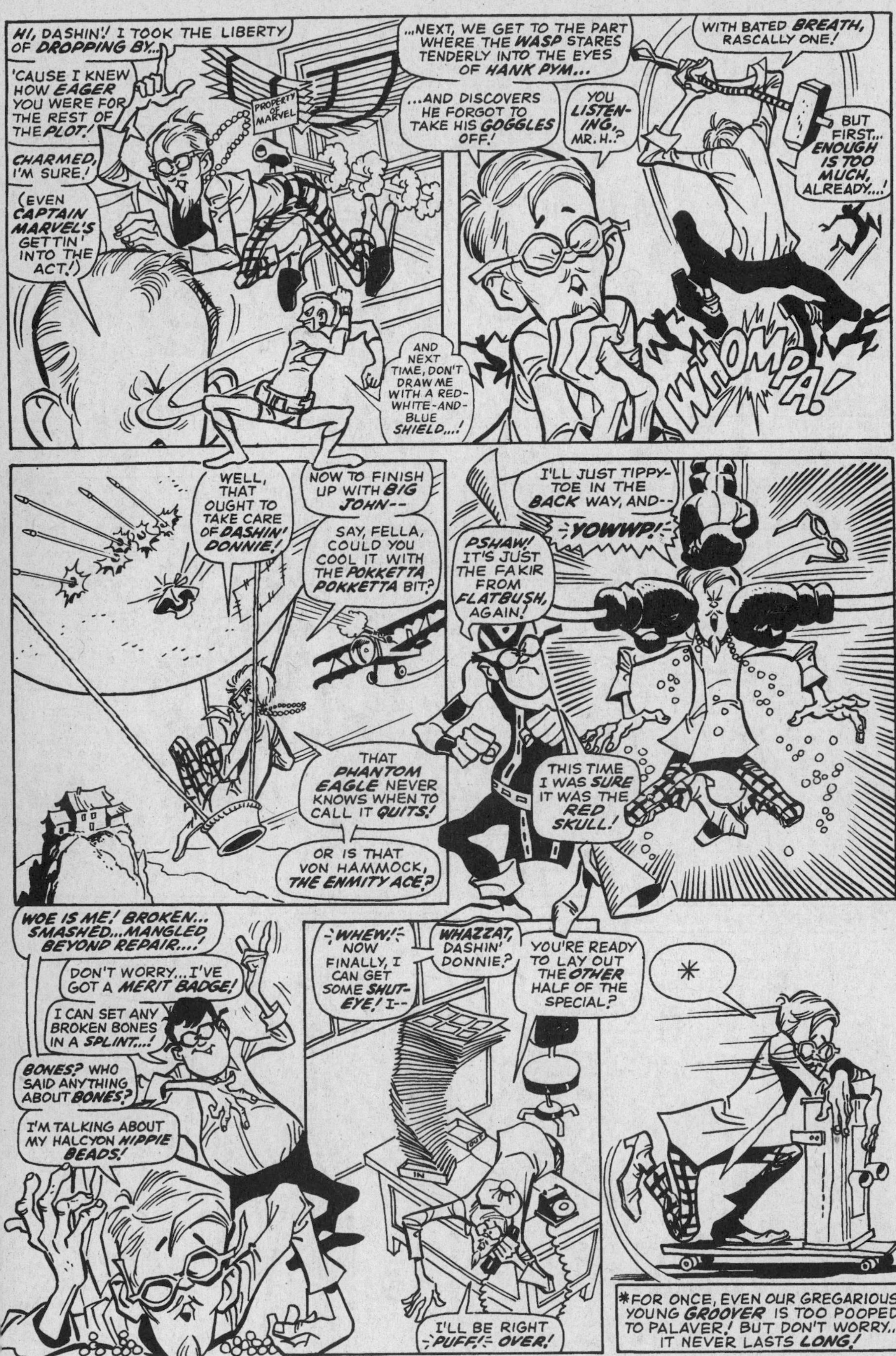
HI, DASHIN'! I TOOK THE LIBERTY OF DROPPING BY...
'CAUSE I KNEW HOW EAGER YOU WERE FOR THE REST OF THE PLOT!
PROPERTY OF MARVEL
CHARMED, I'M SURE!
(EVEN CAPTAIN MARVEL'S GETTIN' INTO THE ACT!)
AND NEXT TIME, DON'T DRAW ME WITH A RED-WHITE-AND-BLUE SHIELD...!
...NEXT, WE GET TO THE PART WHERE THE WASP STARES TENDERLY INTO THE EYES OF HANK PYM...
...AND DISCOVERS HE FORGOT TO TAKE HIS GOGGLES OFF!
YOU LISTENING, MR. H.?
WITH BATED BREATH, RASCALLY ONE!
BUT FIRST... ENOUGH IS TOO MUCH, ALREADY...!
WHOMPA!
WELL, THAT OUGHT TO TAKE CARE OF DASHIN' DONNIE!
NOW TO FINISH UP WITH BIG JOHN--
SAY, FELLA, COULD YOU COOL IT WITH THE POKKETTA POKKETTA BIT?
THAT PHANTOM EAGLE NEVER KNOWS WHEN TO CALL IT QUITS!
OR IS THAT VON HAMMOCK, THE ENMITY ACE?
I'LL JUST TIPPY-TOE IN THE BACK WAY, AND--
YOWWP!
PSHAW! IT'S JUST THE FAKIR FROM FLATBUSH, AGAIN!
THIS TIME I WAS SURE IT WAS THE RED SKULL!
WOE IS ME! BROKEN... SMASHED...MANGLED BEYOND REPAIR...!
DON'T WORRY...I'VE GOT A MERIT BADGE!
I CAN SET ANY BROKEN BONES IN A SPLINT...!
BONES? WHO SAID ANYTHING ABOUT BONES?
I'M TALKING ABOUT MY HALCYON HIPPIE BEADS!
WHEW! NOW FINALLY, I CAN GET SOME SHUT-EYE! I--
WHAZZAT, DASHIN' DONNIE?
YOU'RE READY TO LAY OUT THE OTHER HALF OF THE SPECIAL?
I'LL BE RIGHT PUFF! OVER!
IN
OUT
*
*FOR ONCE, EVEN OUR GREGARIOUS YOUNG GROOVER IS TOO POOPED TO PALAVER! BUT DON'T WORRY... IT NEVER LASTS LONG!

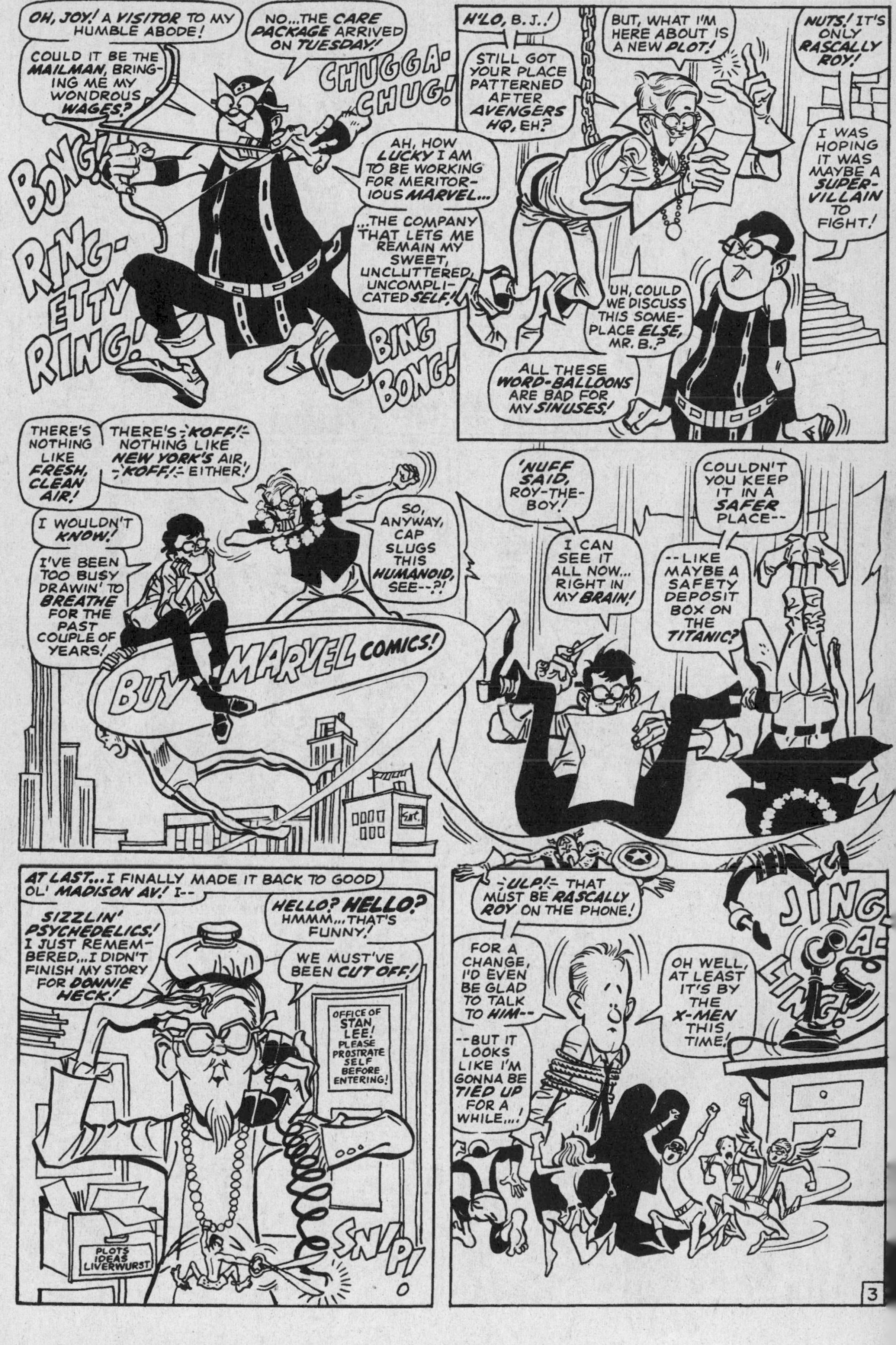
OH, JOY! A VISITOR TO MY HUMBLE ABODE!
COULD IT BE THE MAILMAN, BRINGING ME MY WONDROUS WAGES?
NO...THE CARE PACKAGE ARRIVED ON TUESDAY!
CHUGGA-CHUG!
BONG!
RING-ETTY RING!
AH, HOW LUCKY I AM TO BE WORKING FOR MERITORIOUS MARVEL...
...THE COMPANY THAT LETS ME REMAIN MY SWEET, UNCLUTTERED, UNCOMPLICATED SELF!
BING BONG!
H'LO, B.J..!
STILL GOT YOUR PLACE PATTERNED AFTER AVENGERS HQ, EH?
BUT, WHAT I'M HERE ABOUT IS A NEW PLOT!
NUTS! IT'S ONLY RASCALLY ROY!
I WAS HOPING IT WAS MAYBE A SUPER-VILLAIN TO FIGHT!
UH, COULD WE DISCUSS THIS SOMEPLACE ELSE, MR. B.?
ALL THESE WORD-BALLOONS ARE BAD FOR MY SINUSES!
THERE'S NOTHING LIKE FRESH, CLEAN AIR!
THERE'S -KOFF!- NOTHING LIKE NEW YORK'S AIR, -KOFF!- EITHER!
I WOULDN'T KNOW!
I'VE BEEN TOO BUSY DRAWIN' TO BREATHE FOR THE PAST COUPLE OF YEARS!
SO, ANYWAY, CAP SLUGS THIS HUMANOID, SEE--?!
BUY MARVEL COMICS!
'NUFF SAID, ROY-THE-BOY!
I CAN SEE IT ALL NOW... RIGHT IN MY BRAIN!
COULDN'T YOU KEEP IT IN A SAFER PLACE--
--LIKE MAYBE A SAFETY DEPOSIT BOX ON THE TITANIC?
AT LAST...I FINALLY MADE IT BACK TO GOOD OL' MADISON AV! I--
SIZZLIN' PSYCHEDELICS! I JUST REMEMBERED...I DIDN'T FINISH MY STORY FOR DONNIE HECK!
HELLO? HELLO? HMMM...THAT'S FUNNY!
WE MUST'VE BEEN CUT OFF!
OFFICE OF STAN LEE! PLEASE PROSTRATE SELF BEFORE ENTERING!
PLOTS IDEAS LIVERWURST
SNIP!
-ULP!- THAT MUST BE RASCALLY ROY ON THE PHONE!
FOR A CHANGE, I'D EVEN BE GLAD TO TALK TO HIM--
--BUT IT LOOKS LIKE I'M GONNA BE TIED UP FOR A WHILE...!
OH WELL, AT LEAST IT'S BY THE X-MEN THIS TIME!
JING-A-LING!

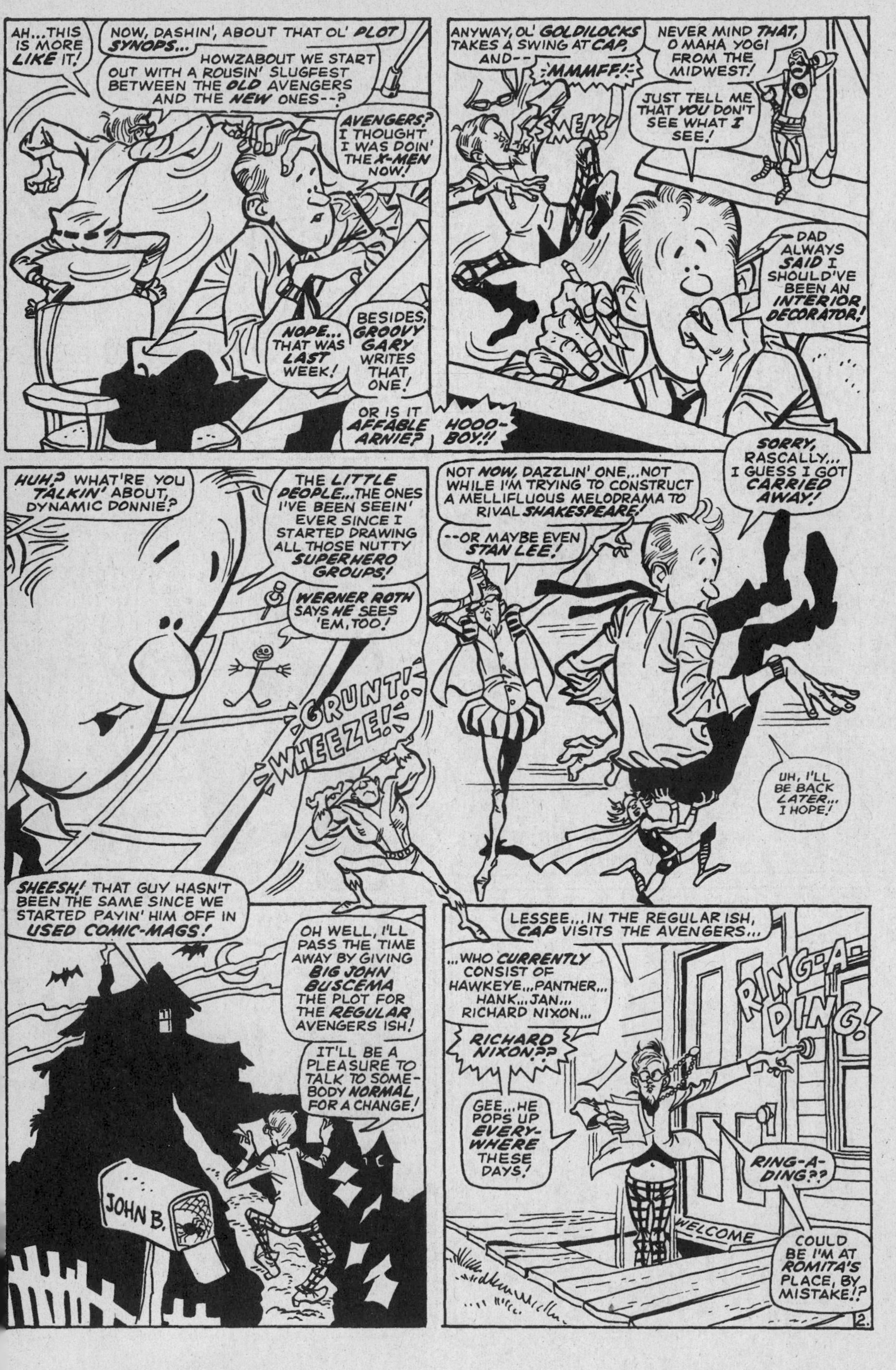
AH...THIS IS MORE LIKE IT!
NOW, DASHIN', ABOUT THAT OL' PLOT SYNOPS...
HOWZABOUT WE START OUT WITH A ROUSIN' SLUGFEST BETWEEN THE OLD AVENGERS AND THE NEW ONES--?
AVENGERS? I THOUGHT I WAS DOIN' THE X-MEN NOW!
NOPE... THAT WAS LAST WEEK!
BESIDES, GROOVY GARY WRITES THAT ONE!
OR IS IT AFFABLE ARNIE?
HOOO-BOY!!
ANYWAY, OL' GOLDILOCKS TAKES A SWING AT CAP, AND--
MMMFF!
SMEK!
NEVER MIND THAT, O MAHA YOGI FROM THE MIDWEST!
JUST TELL ME THAT YOU DON'T SEE WHAT I SEE!
DAD ALWAYS SAID I SHOULD'VE BEEN AN INTERIOR DECORATOR!
HUH? WHAT'RE YOU TALKIN' ABOUT, DYNAMIC DONNIE?
THE LITTLE PEOPLE... THE ONES I'VE BEEN SEEIN' EVER SINCE I STARTED DRAWING ALL THOSE NUTTY SUPERHERO GROUPS!
WERNER ROTH SAYS HE SEES 'EM, TOO!
GRUNT!
WHEEZE!
NOT NOW, DAZZLIN' ONE... NOT WHILE I'M TRYING TO CONSTRUCT A MELLIFLUOUS MELODRAMA TO RIVAL SHAKESPEARE!
--OR MAYBE EVEN STAN LEE!
SORRY, RASCALLY... I GUESS I GOT CARRIED AWAY!
UH, I'LL BE BACK LATER... I HOPE!
SHEESH! THAT GUY HASN'T BEEN THE SAME SINCE WE STARTED PAYIN' HIM OFF IN USED COMIC-MAGS!
OH WELL, I'LL PASS THE TIME AWAY BY GIVING BIG JOHN BUSCEMA THE PLOT FOR THE REGULAR AVENGERS ISH!
IT'LL BE A PLEASURE TO TALK TO SOMEBODY NORMAL FOR A CHANGE!
JOHN B.
LESSEE... IN THE REGULAR ISH, CAP VISITS THE AVENGERS...
...WHO CURRENTLY CONSIST OF HAWKEYE... PANTHER... HANK... JAN... RICHARD NIXON...
RICHARD NIXON??
GEE... HE POPS UP EVERYWHERE THESE DAYS!
RING-A-DING!
RING-A-DING??
WELCOME
COULD BE I'M AT ROMITA'S PLACE, BY MISTAKE!?
2.

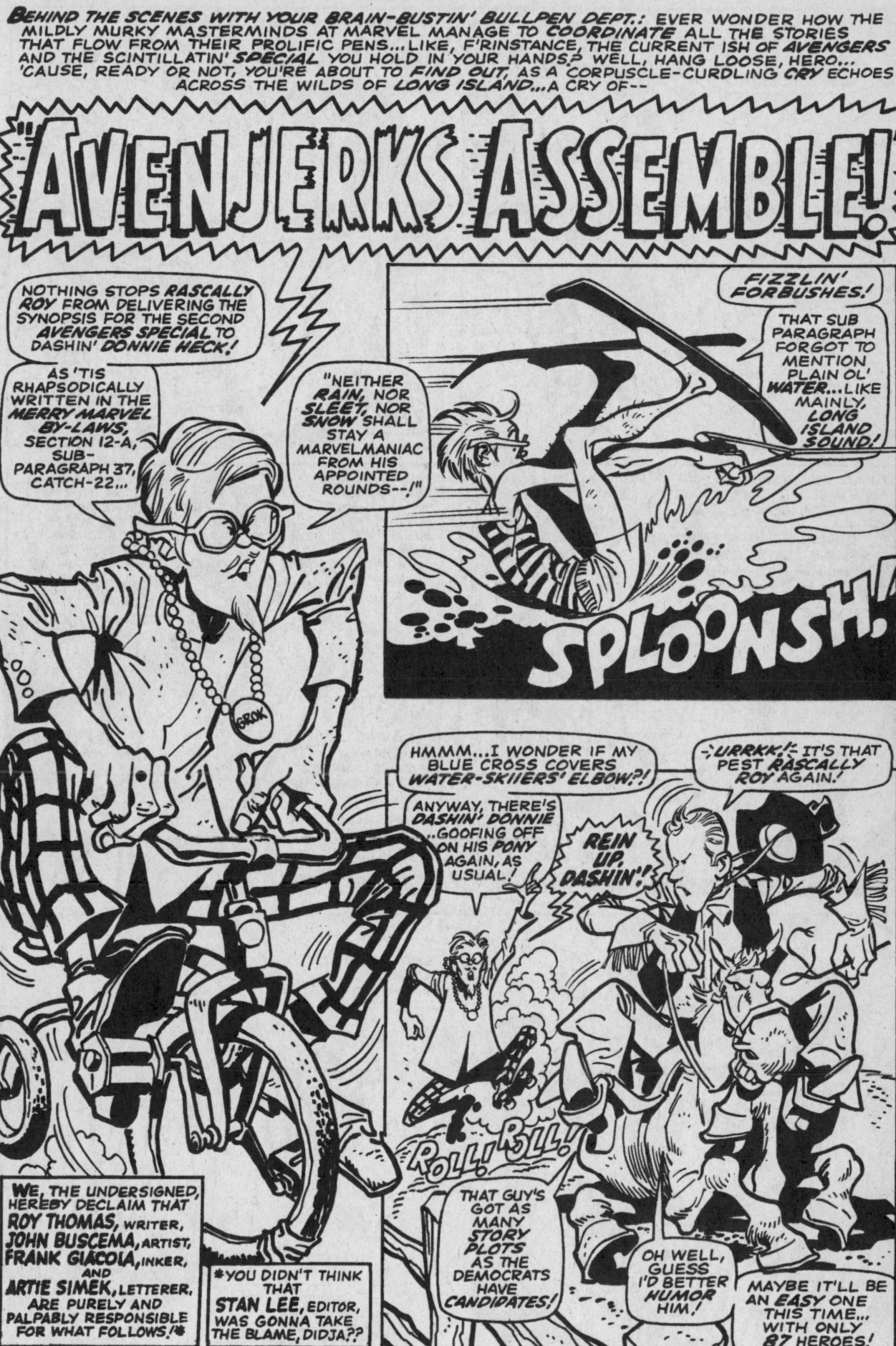
BEHIND THE SCENES WITH YOUR BRAIN-BUSTIN' BULLPEN DEPT.: EVER WONDER HOW THE MILDLY MURKY MASTERMINDS AT MARVEL MANAGE TO COORDINATE ALL THE STORIES THAT FLOW FROM THEIR PROLIFIC PENS... LIKE, F'RINSTANCE, THE CURRENT ISH OF AVENGERS AND THE SCINTILLATIN' SPECIAL YOU HOLD IN YOUR HANDS? WELL, HANG LOOSE, HERO... 'CAUSE, READY OR NOT, YOU'RE ABOUT TO FIND OUT, AS A CORPUSCLE-CURDLING CRY ECHOES ACROSS THE WILDS OF LONG ISLAND... A CRY OF--
"AVENJERKS ASSEMBLE!"
NOTHING STOPS RASCALLY ROY FROM DELIVERING THE SYNOPSIS FOR THE SECOND AVENGERS SPECIAL TO DASHIN' DONNIE HECK!
AS 'TIS RHAPSODICALLY WRITTEN IN THE MERRY MARVEL BY-LAWS, SECTION 12-A, SUB-PARAGRAPH 37, CATCH-22...
"NEITHER RAIN, NOR SLEET, NOR SNOW SHALL STAY A MARVELMANIAC FROM HIS APPOINTED ROUNDS--!"
GROK
FIZZLIN' FORBUSHES!
THAT SUB PARAGRAPH FORGOT TO MENTION PLAIN OL' WATER... LIKE MAINLY, LONG ISLAND SOUND!
SPLOONSH!
HMMM... I WONDER IF MY BLUE CROSS COVERS WATER-SKIIERS' ELBOW?!
ANYWAY, THERE'S DASHIN' DONNIE ..GOOFING OFF ON HIS PONY AGAIN, AS USUAL!
REIN UP, DASHIN'!
-URRKK!- IT'S THAT PEST RASCALLY ROY AGAIN!
ROLL! ROLL!
THAT GUY'S GOT AS MANY STORY PLOTS AS THE DEMOCRATS HAVE CANDIDATES!
OH WELL, GUESS I'D BETTER HUMOR HIM!
MAYBE IT'LL BE AN EASY ONE THIS TIME... WITH ONLY 87 HEROES!
WE, THE UNDERSIGNED, HEREBY DECLAIM THAT ROY THOMAS, WRITER, JOHN BUSCEMA, ARTIST, FRANK GIACOIA, INKER, AND ARTIE SIMEK, LETTERER, ARE PURELY AND PALPABLY RESPONSIBLE FOR WHAT FOLLOWS!*
*YOU DIDN'T THINK THAT STAN LEE, EDITOR, WAS GONNA TAKE THE BLAME, DIDJA??

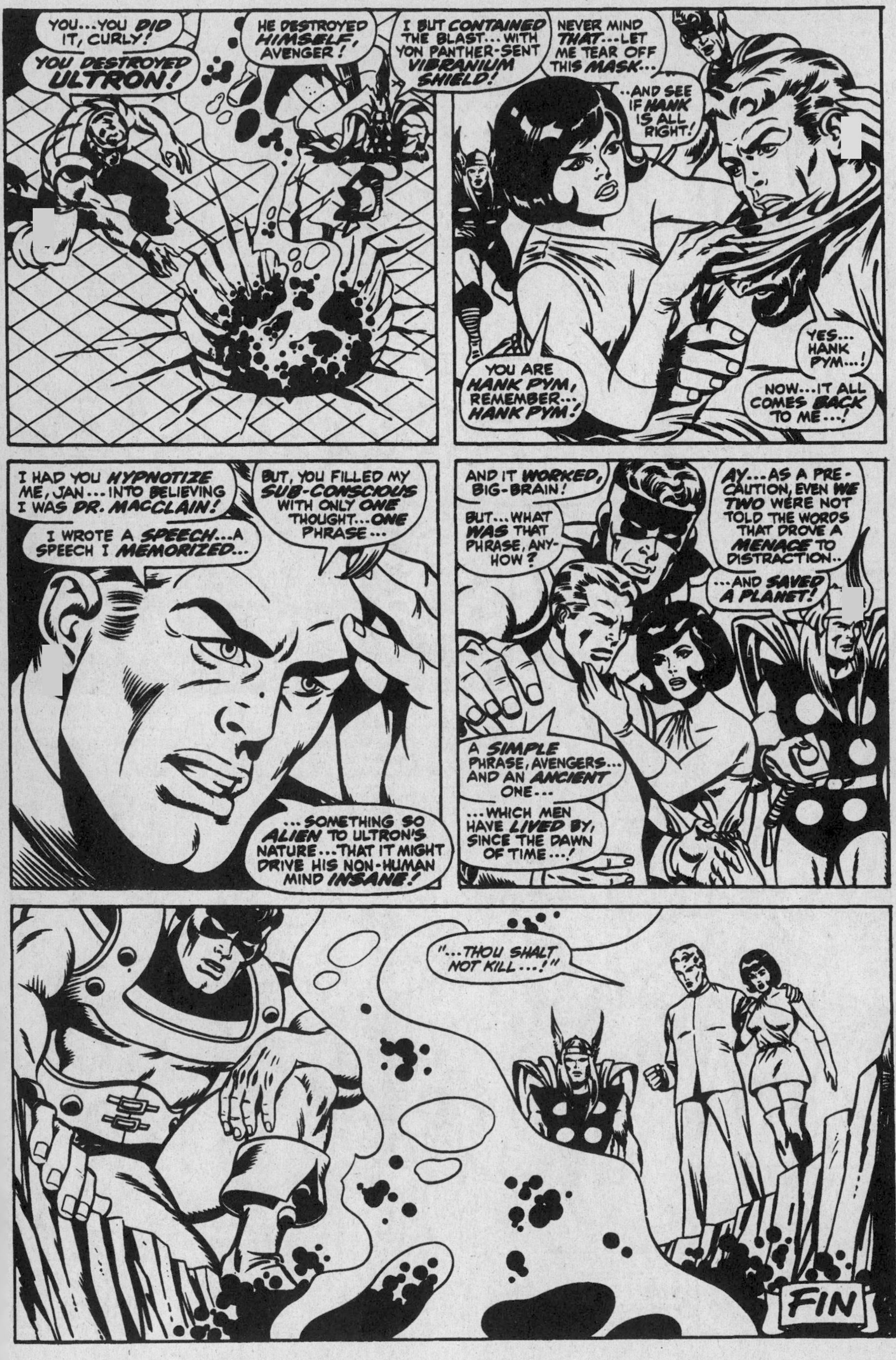
YOU...YOU DID IT, CURLY!
YOU DESTROYED ULTRON!
HE DESTROYED HIMSELF, AVENGER!
I BUT CONTAINED THE BLAST...WITH YON PANTHER-SENT VIBRANIUM SHIELD!
NEVER MIND THAT...LET ME TEAR OFF THIS MASK...
...AND SEE IF HANK IS ALL RIGHT!
YOU ARE HANK PYM, REMEMBER... HANK PYM!
YES... HANK PYM...!
NOW...IT ALL COMES BACK TO ME...!
I HAD YOU HYPNOTIZE ME, JAN...INTO BELIEVING I WAS DR. MACCLAIN!
I WROTE A SPEECH...A SPEECH I MEMORIZED...
BUT, YOU FILLED MY SUB-CONSCIOUS WITH ONLY ONE THOUGHT...ONE PHRASE...
...SOMETHING SO ALIEN TO ULTRON'S NATURE...THAT IT MIGHT DRIVE HIS NON-HUMAN MIND INSANE!
AND IT WORKED, BIG-BRAIN!
BUT...WHAT WAS THAT PHRASE, ANY-HOW?
AY...AS A PRE-CAUTION, EVEN WE TWO WERE NOT TOLD THE WORDS THAT DROVE A MENACE TO DISTRACTION...
...AND SAVED A PLANET!
A SIMPLE PHRASE, AVENGERS... AND AN ANCIENT ONE...
...WHICH MEN HAVE LIVED BY, SINCE THE DAWN OF TIME...!
"...THOU SHALT NOT KILL...!"
FIN

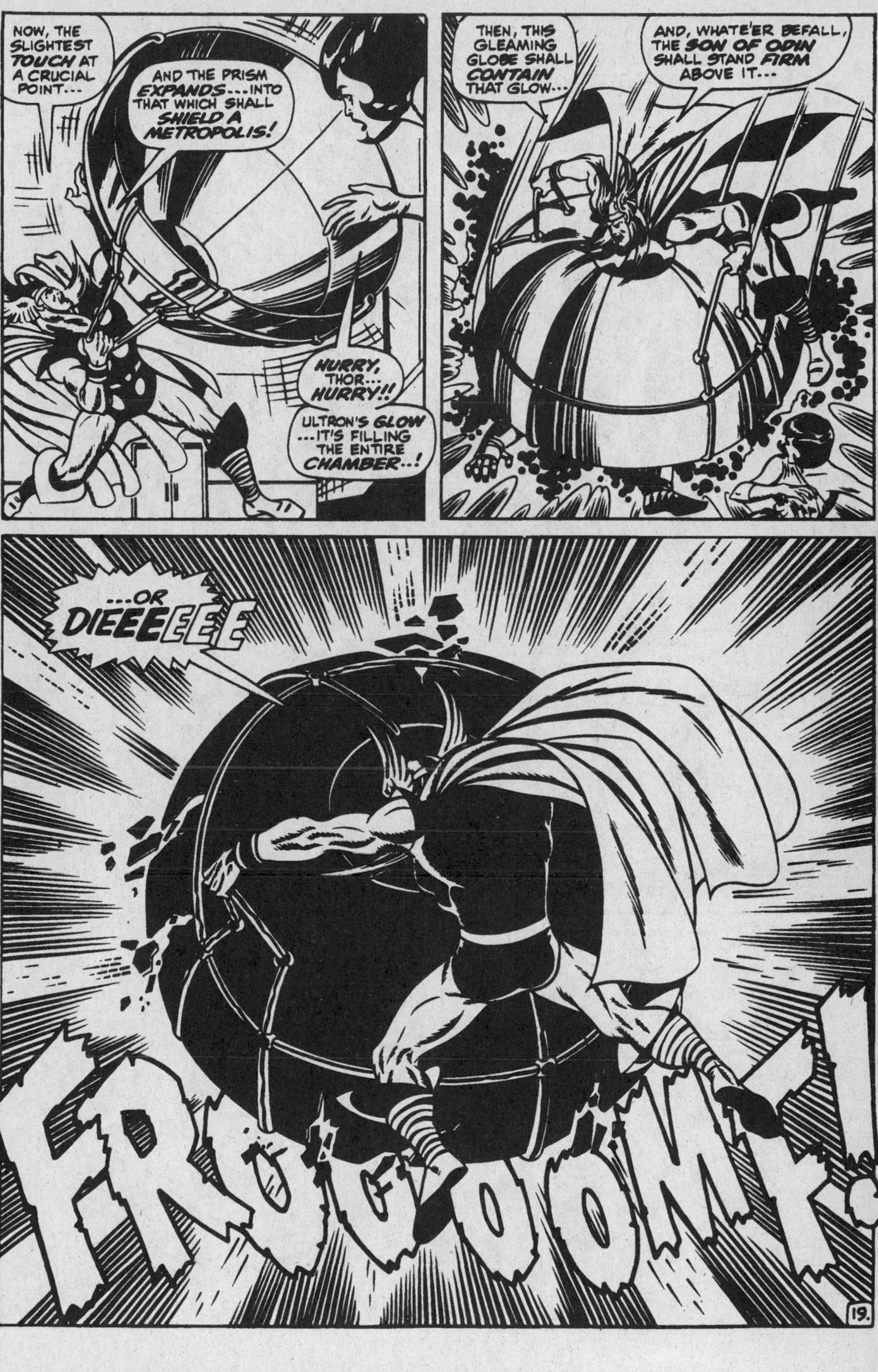
NOW, THE SLIGHTEST TOUCH AT A CRUCIAL POINT...
AND THE PRISM EXPANDS...INTO THAT WHICH SHALL SHIELD A METROPOLIS!
HURRY, THOR... HURRY!!
ULTRON'S GLOW ...IT'S FILLING THE ENTIRE CHAMBER..!
THEN, THIS GLEAMING GLOBE SHALL CONTAIN THAT GLOW...
AND, WHATE'ER BEFALL, THE SON OF ODIN SHALL STAND FIRM ABOVE IT...
...OR DIEEEEEE
FROOOOM!
19.

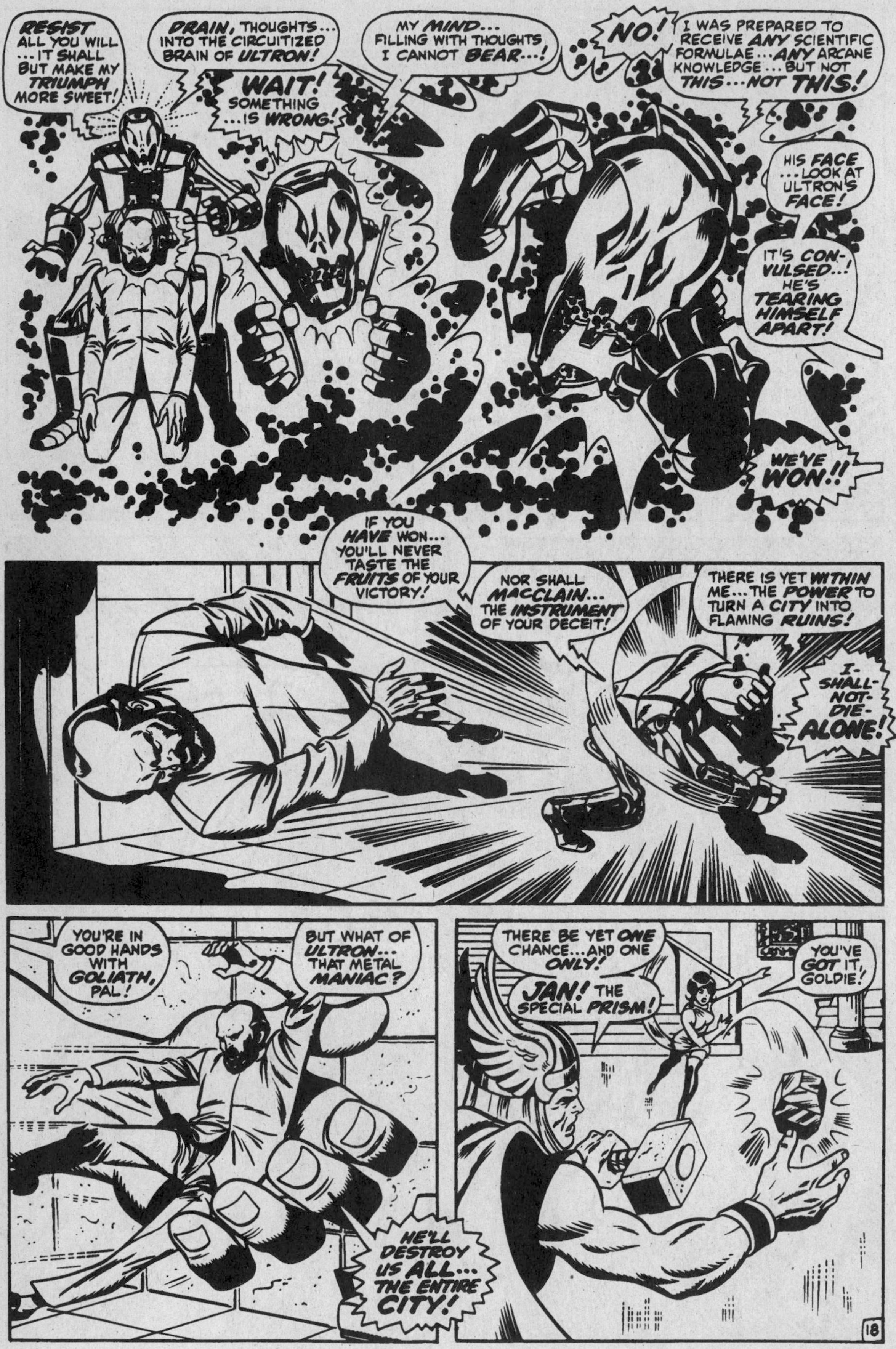

RESIST ALL YOU WILL ...IT SHALL BUT MAKE MY TRIUMPH MORE SWEET!
DRAIN, THOUGHTS... INTO THE CIRCUITIZED BRAIN OF ULTRON!
WAIT! SOMETHING ...IS WRONG!
MY MIND... FILLING WITH THOUGHTS I CANNOT BEAR...!
NO!
I WAS PREPARED TO RECEIVE ANY SCIENTIFIC FORMULAE...ANY ARCANE KNOWLEDGE... BUT NOT THIS...NOT THIS!
HIS FACE ...LOOK AT ULTRON'S FACE!
IT'S CON-VULSED...! HE'S TEARING HIMSELF APART!
WE'VE WON!!
IF YOU HAVE WON... YOU'LL NEVER TASTE THE FRUITS OF YOUR VICTORY!
NOR SHALL MACCLAIN... THE INSTRUMENT OF YOUR DECEIT!
THERE IS YET WITHIN ME... THE POWER TO TURN A CITY INTO FLAMING RUINS!
I- SHALL- NOT- DIE- ALONE!
YOU'RE IN GOOD HANDS WITH GOLIATH, PAL!
BUT WHAT OF ULTRON... THAT METAL MANIAC?
HE'LL DESTROY US ALL... THE ENTIRE CITY!
THERE BE YET ONE CHANCE...AND ONE ONLY!
JAN! THE SPECIAL PRISM!
YOU'VE GOT IT, GOLDIE!
18

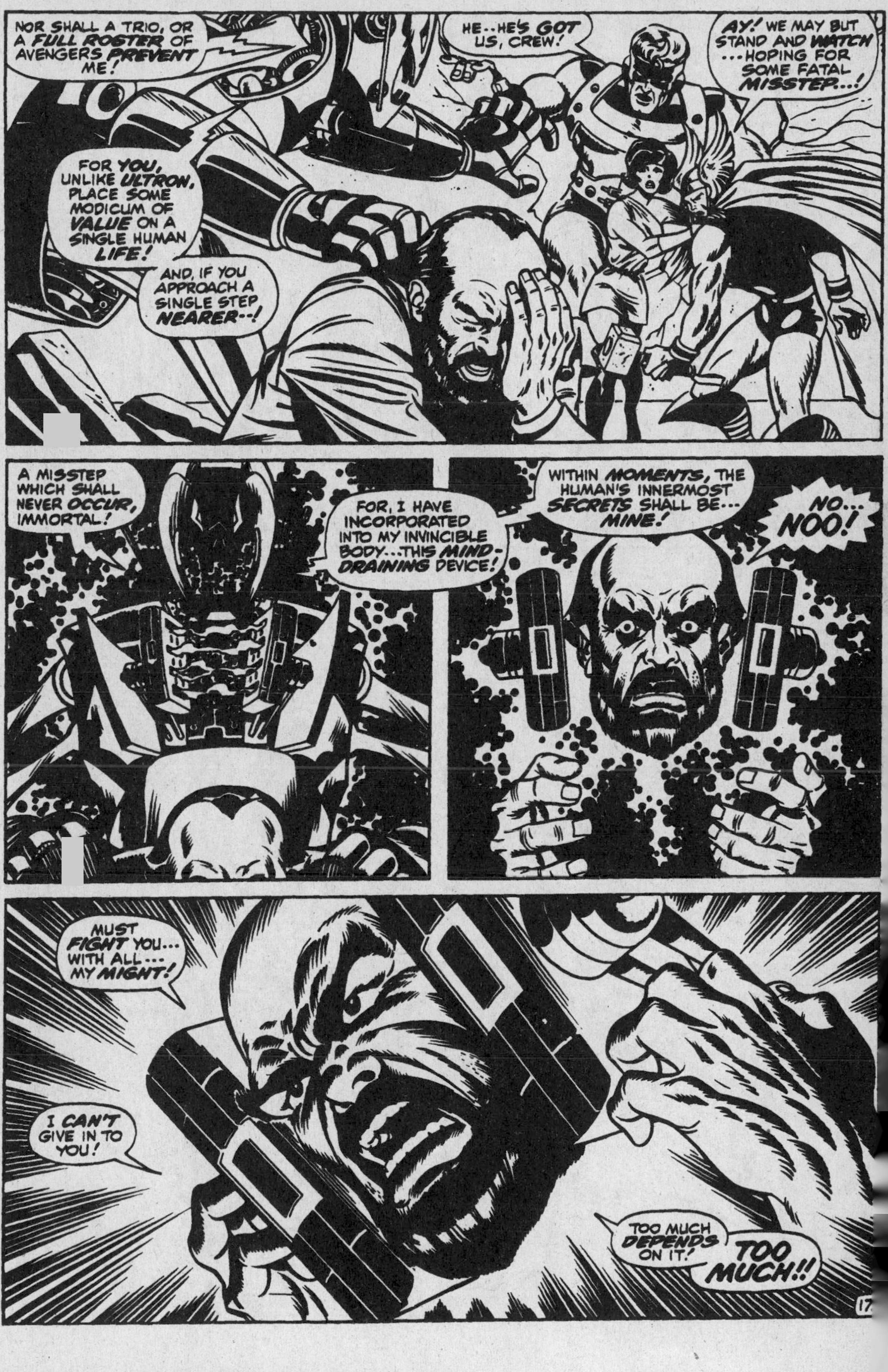
NOR SHALL A TRIO, OR A FULL ROSTER OF AVENGERS PREVENT ME!
HE..HE'S GOT US, CREW!
AY! WE MAY BUT STAND AND WATCH ...HOPING FOR SOME FATAL MISSTEP...!
FOR YOU, UNLIKE ULTRON, PLACE SOME MODICUM OF VALUE ON A SINGLE HUMAN LIFE!
AND, IF YOU APPROACH A SINGLE STEP NEARER--!
A MISSTEP WHICH SHALL NEVER OCCUR, IMMORTAL!
FOR, I HAVE INCORPORATED INTO MY INVINCIBLE BODY...THIS MIND-DRAINING DEVICE!
WITHIN MOMENTS, THE HUMAN'S INNERMOST SECRETS SHALL BE... MINE!
NO... NOO!
MUST FIGHT YOU... WITH ALL... MY MIGHT!
I CAN'T GIVE IN TO YOU!
TOO MUCH DEPENDS ON IT!
TOO MUCH!!
17

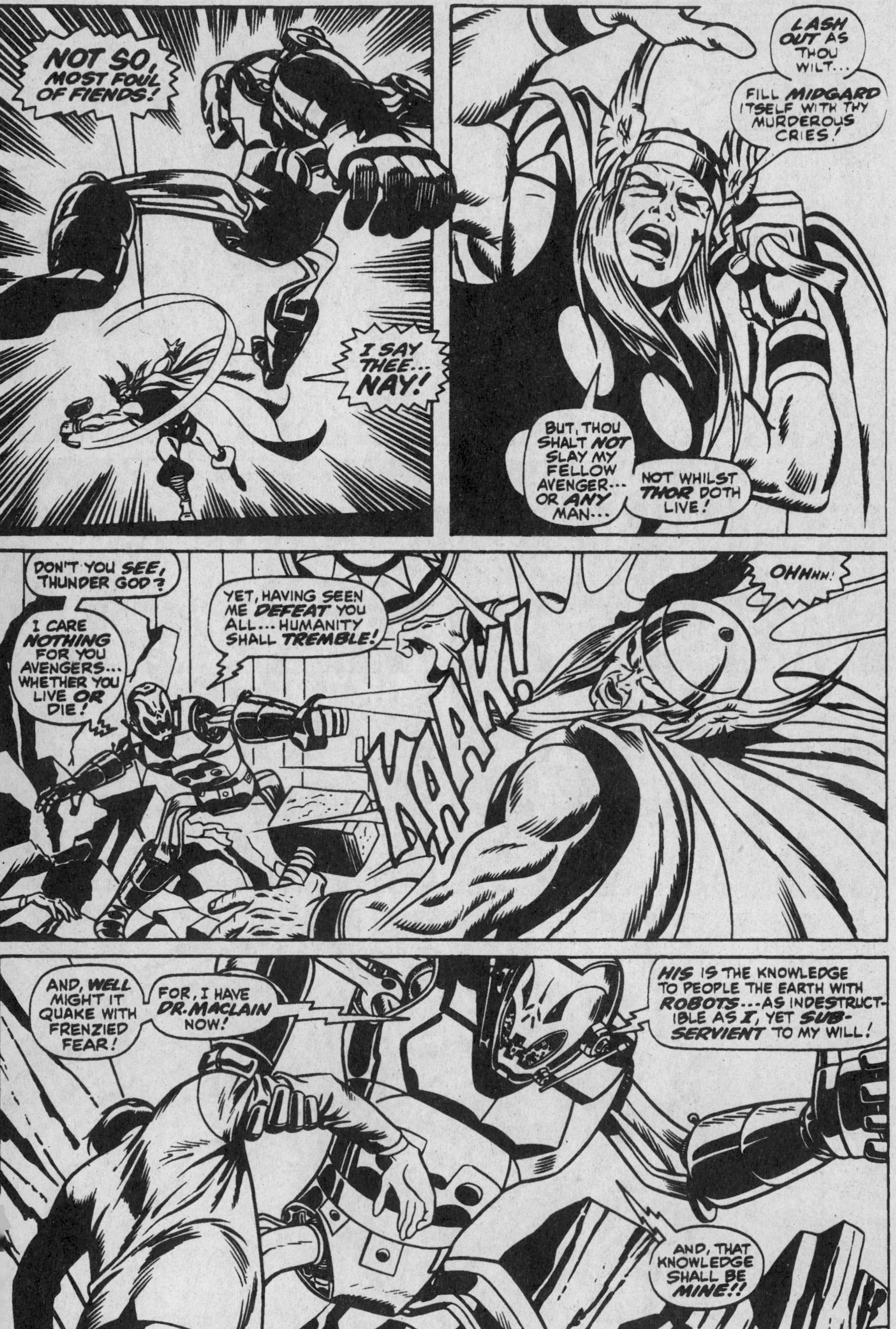

NOT SO, MOST FOUL OF FIENDS!
I SAY THEE... NAY!
LASH OUT AS THOU WILT...
FILL MIDGARD ITSELF WITH THY MURDEROUS CRIES!
BUT, THOU SHALT NOT SLAY MY FELLOW AVENGER... OR ANY MAN...
NOT WHILST THOR DOTH LIVE!
DON'T YOU SEE, THUNDER GOD?
I CARE NOTHING FOR YOU AVENGERS... WHETHER YOU LIVE OR DIE!
YET, HAVING SEEN ME DEFEAT YOU ALL... HUMANITY SHALL TREMBLE!
OHHHH!
KAAK!
AND, WELL MIGHT IT QUAKE WITH FRENZIED FEAR!
FOR, I HAVE DR. MACLAIN NOW!
HIS IS THE KNOWLEDGE TO PEOPLE THE EARTH WITH ROBOTS... AS INDESTRUCTIBLE AS I, YET SUBSERVIENT TO MY WILL!
AND, THAT KNOWLEDGE SHALL BE MINE!!

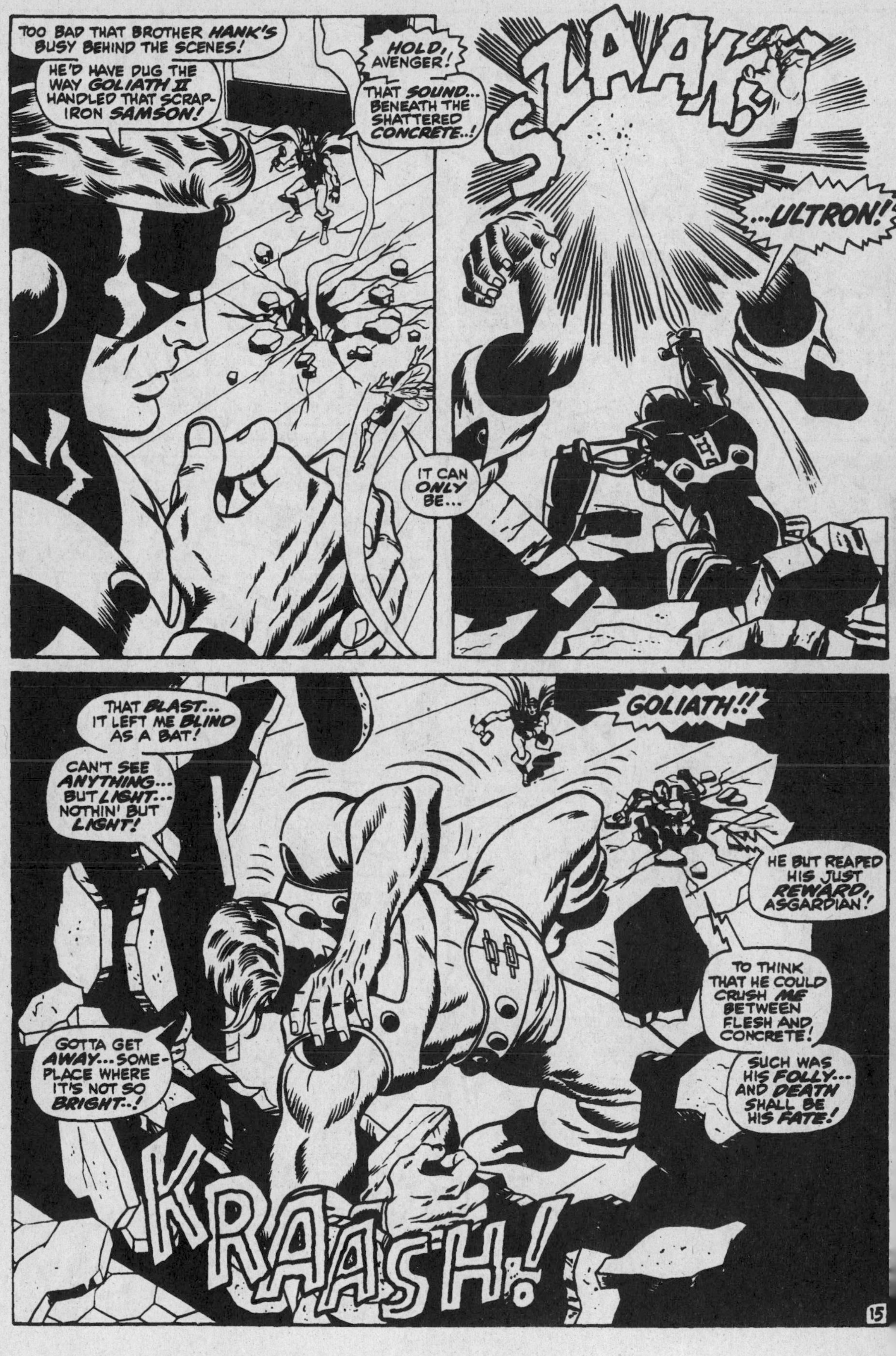

TOO BAD THAT BROTHER HANK'S BUSY BEHIND THE SCENES!
HE'D HAVE DUG THE WAY GOLIATH II HANDLED THAT SCRAP-IRON SAMSON!
HOLD, AVENGER!
THAT SOUND... BENEATH THE SHATTERED CONCRETE..!
IT CAN ONLY BE...
SZAAK!
...ULTRON!
THAT BLAST... IT LEFT ME BLIND AS A BAT!
CAN'T SEE ANYTHING... BUT LIGHT... NOTHIN' BUT LIGHT!
GOLIATH!!
HE BUT REAPED HIS JUST REWARD, ASGARDIAN!
TO THINK THAT HE COULD CRUSH ME BETWEEN FLESH AND CONCRETE!
SUCH WAS HIS FOLLY... AND DEATH SHALL BE HIS FATE!
GOTTA GET AWAY... SOME-PLACE WHERE IT'S NOT SO BRIGHT..!
KRAASH!
15

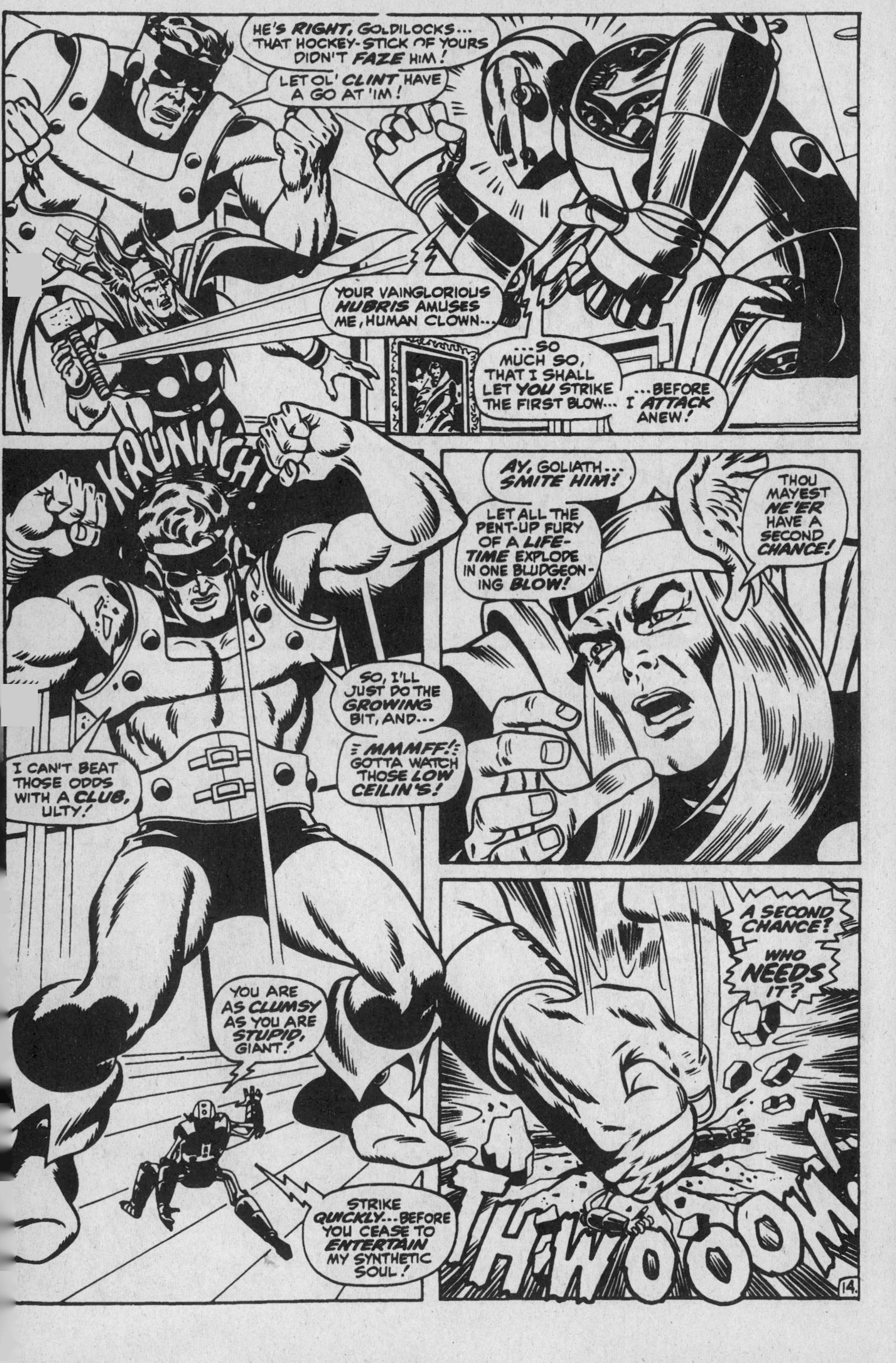
HE'S RIGHT, GOLDILOCKS... THAT HOCKEY-STICK OF YOURS DIDN'T FAZE HIM!
LET OL' CLINT HAVE A GO AT 'IM!
YOUR VAINGLORIOUS HUBRIS AMUSES ME, HUMAN CLOWN...
...SO MUCH SO, THAT I SHALL LET YOU STRIKE THE FIRST BLOW...
...BEFORE I ATTACK ANEW!
KRUNNCH!
I CAN'T BEAT THOSE ODDS WITH A CLUB, ULTY!
SO, I'LL JUST DO THE GROWING BIT, AND...
MMMFF! GOTTA WATCH THOSE LOW CEILIN'S!
YOU ARE AS CLUMSY AS YOU ARE STUPID, GIANT!
STRIKE QUICKLY...BEFORE YOU CEASE TO ENTERTAIN MY SYNTHETIC SOUL!
AY, GOLIATH... SMITE HIM!
LET ALL THE PENT-UP FURY OF A LIFE-TIME EXPLODE IN ONE BLUDGEON-ING BLOW!
THOU MAYEST NE'ER HAVE A SECOND CHANCE!
A SECOND CHANCE? WHO NEEDS IT?
HWOOOOM!
14.

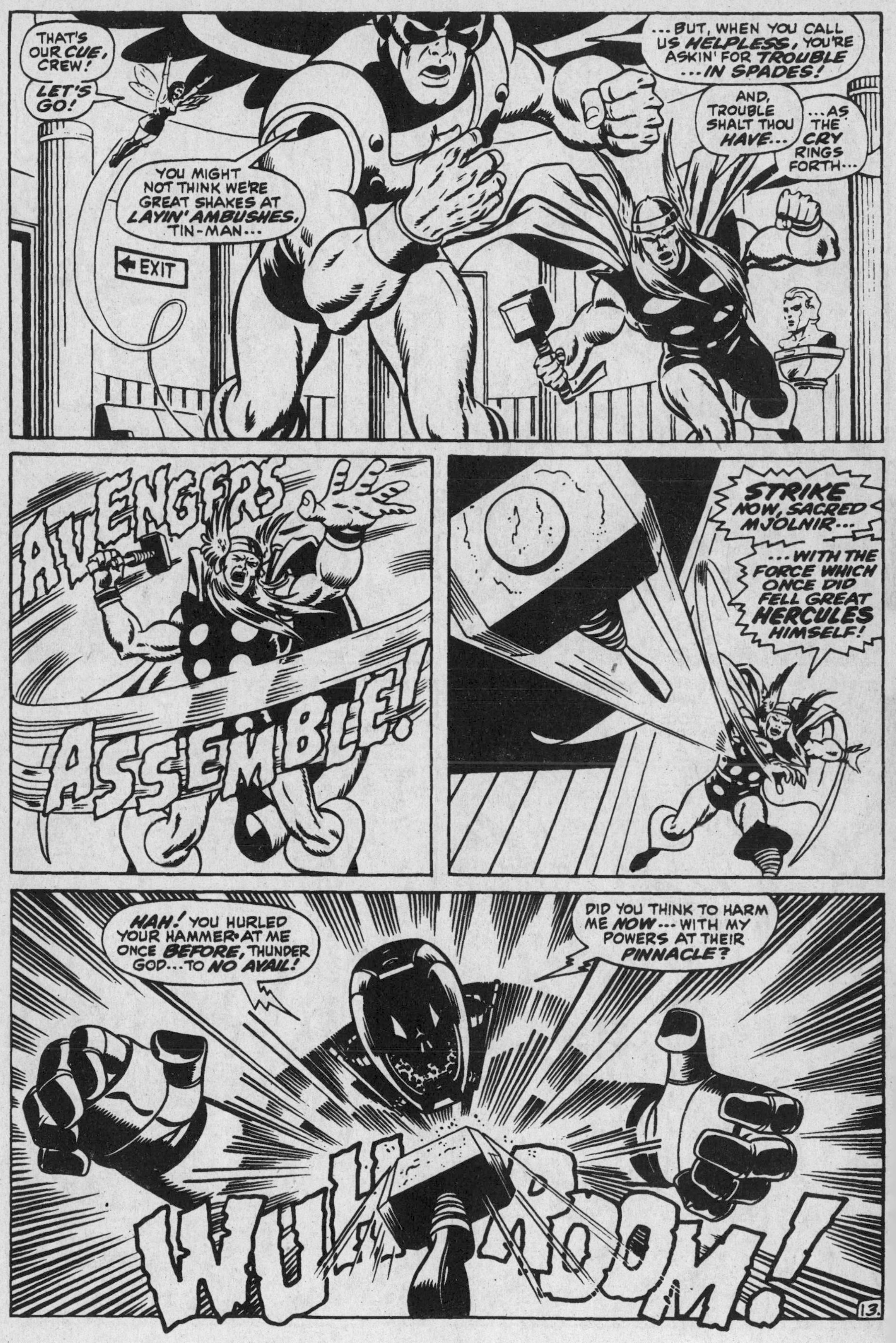
THAT'S OUR CUE, CREW!
LET'S GO!
YOU MIGHT NOT THINK WE'RE GREAT SHAKES AT LAYIN' AMBUSHES, TIN-MAN...
...BUT, WHEN YOU CALL US HELPLESS, YOU'RE ASKIN' FOR TROUBLE ...IN SPADES!
AND, TROUBLE SHALT THOU HAVE...
...AS THE CRY RINGS FORTH...
EXIT
AVENGERS ASSEMBLE!
STRIKE NOW, SACRED MJOLNIR...
...WITH THE FORCE WHICH ONCE DID FELL GREAT HERCULES HIMSELF!
HAH! YOU HURLED YOUR HAMMER AT ME ONCE BEFORE, THUNDER GOD...TO NO AVAIL!
DID YOU THINK TO HARM ME NOW...WITH MY POWERS AT THEIR PINNACLE?
WHOOOM!
13.

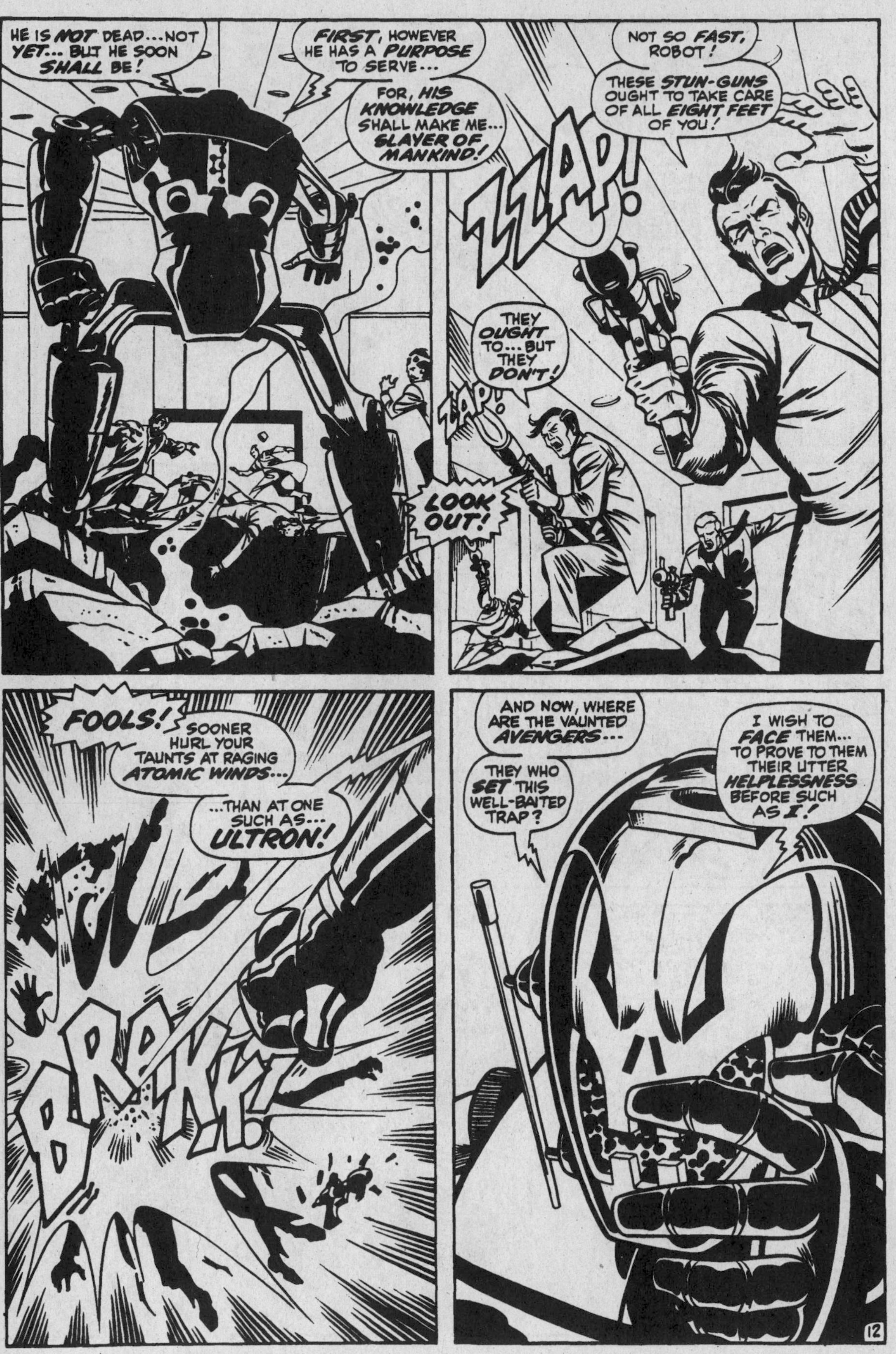

HE IS NOT DEAD...NOT YET... BUT HE SOON SHALL BE!
FIRST, HOWEVER HE HAS A PURPOSE TO SERVE...
FOR, HIS KNOWLEDGE SHALL MAKE ME... SLAYER OF MANKIND!
NOT SO FAST, ROBOT!
THESE STUN-GUNS OUGHT TO TAKE CARE OF ALL EIGHT FEET OF YOU!
ZZAP!
THEY OUGHT TO... BUT THEY DON'T!
ZAP!
LOOK OUT!
FOOLS!
SOONER HURL YOUR TAUNTS AT RAGING ATOMIC WINDS...
...THAN AT ONE SUCH AS... ULTRON!
BRAKK!
AND NOW, WHERE ARE THE VAUNTED AVENGERS...
THEY WHO SET THIS WELL-BAITED TRAP?
I WISH TO FACE THEM... TO PROVE TO THEM THEIR UTTER HELPLESSNESS BEFORE SUCH AS I!

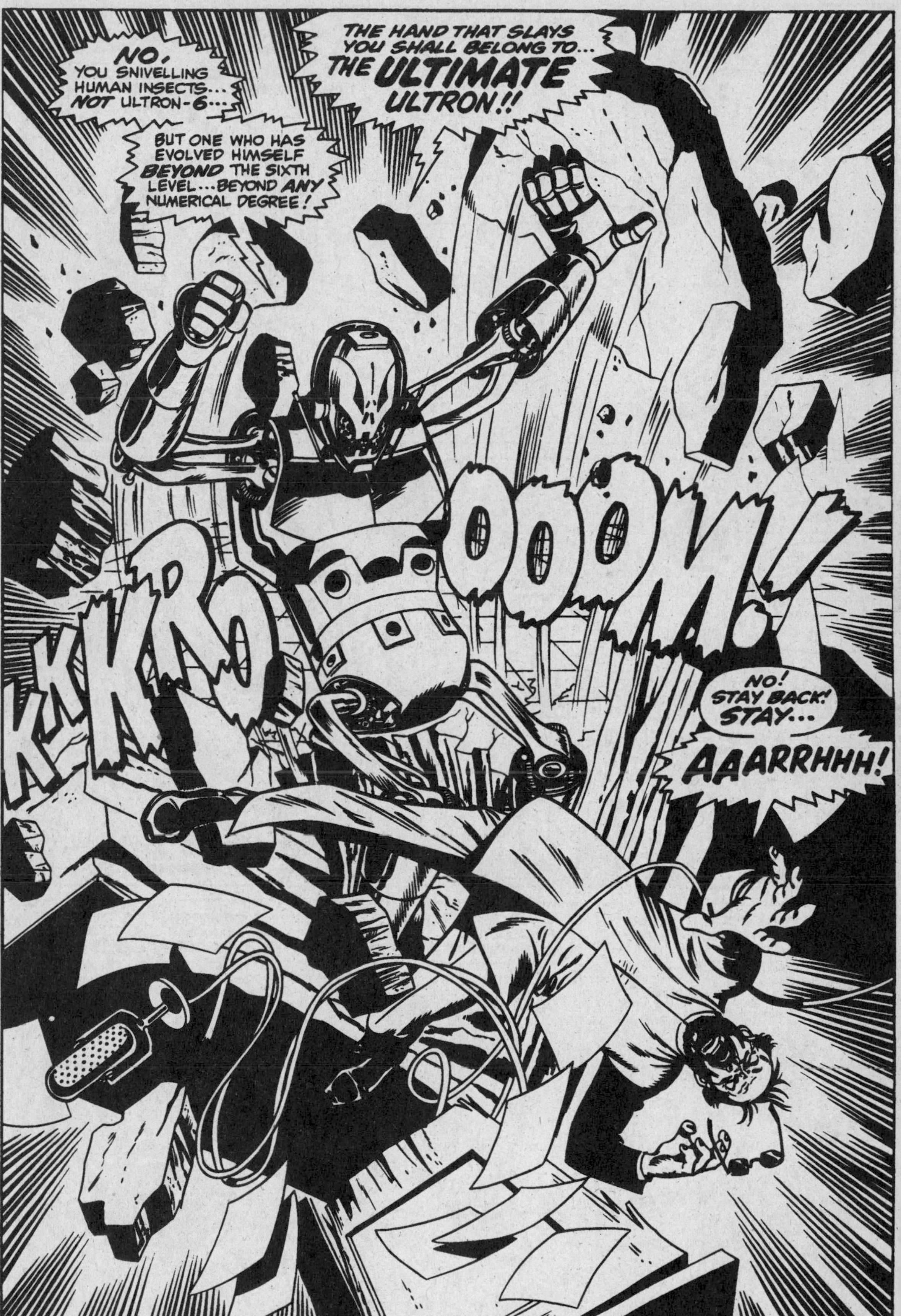
NO, YOU SNIVELLING HUMAN INSECTS... NOT ULTRON-6...
THE HAND THAT SLAYS YOU SHALL BELONG TO... THE ULTIMATE ULTRON!!
BUT ONE WHO HAS EVOLVED HIMSELF BEYOND THE SIXTH LEVEL...BEYOND ANY NUMERICAL DEGREE!
KKKROOOOM!!
NO! STAY BACK! STAY...
AAARRHHH!
11.

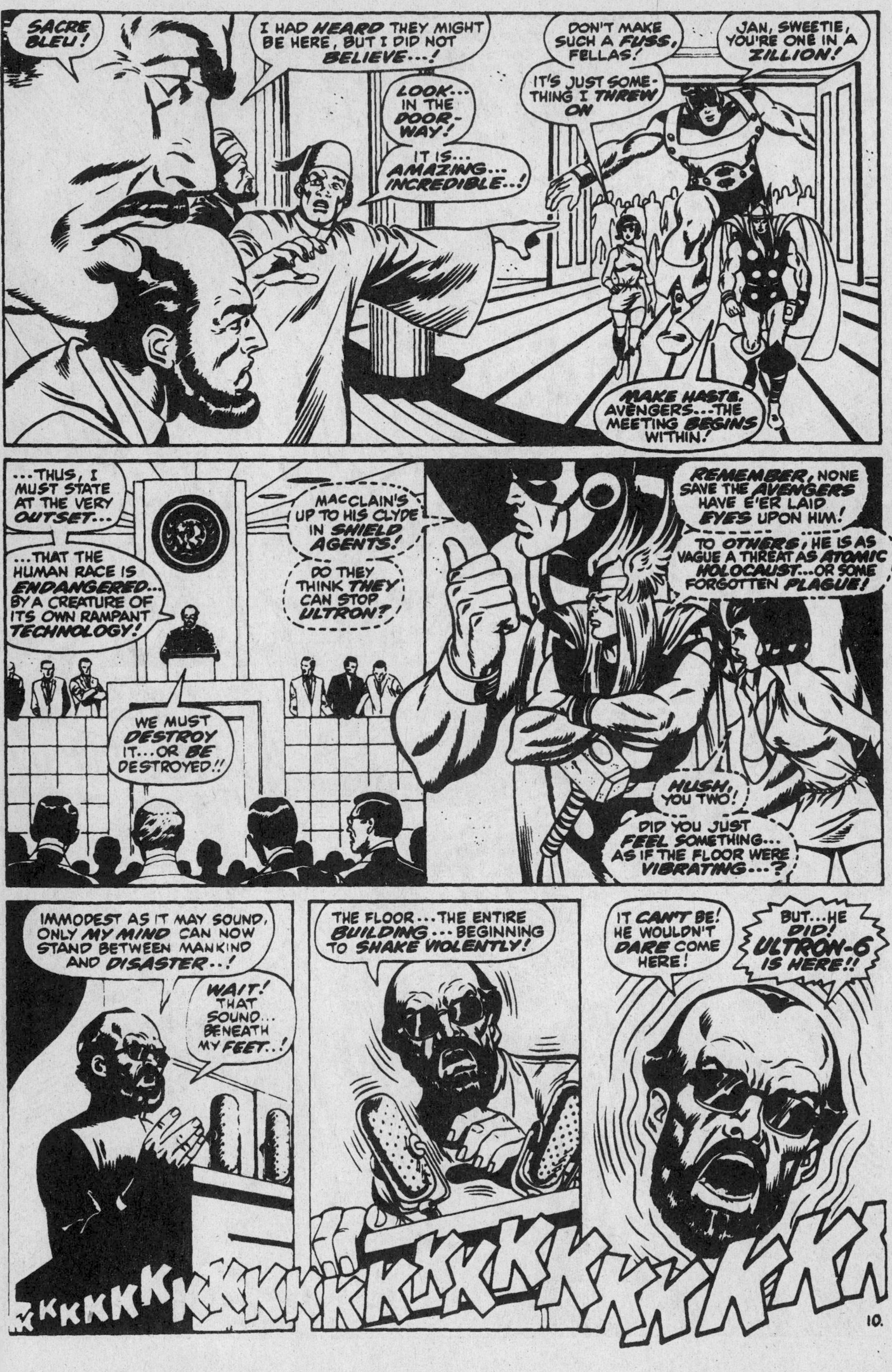
SACRE BLEU!
I HAD HEARD THEY MIGHT BE HERE, BUT I DID NOT BELIEVE...!
LOOK... IN THE DOORWAY!
IT IS... AMAZING... INCREDIBLE..!
DON'T MAKE SUCH A FUSS, FELLAS!
IT'S JUST SOMETHING I THREW ON
JAN, SWEETIE, YOU'RE ONE IN A ZILLION!
MAKE HASTE, AVENGERS... THE MEETING BEGINS WITHIN!
...THUS, I MUST STATE AT THE VERY OUTSET...
...THAT THE HUMAN RACE IS ENDANGERED... BY A CREATURE OF ITS OWN RAMPANT TECHNOLOGY!
WE MUST DESTROY IT... OR BE DESTROYED!!
MACCLAIN'S UP TO HIS CLYDE IN SHIELD AGENTS!
DO THEY THINK THEY CAN STOP ULTRON?
REMEMBER, NONE SAVE THE AVENGERS HAVE E'ER LAID EYES UPON HIM!
TO OTHERS, HE IS AS VAGUE A THREAT AS ATOMIC HOLOCAUST...OR SOME FORGOTTEN PLAGUE!
HUSH, YOU TWO!
DID YOU JUST FEEL SOMETHING... AS IF THE FLOOR WERE VIBRATING...?
IMMODEST AS IT MAY SOUND, ONLY MY MIND CAN NOW STAND BETWEEN MANKIND AND DISASTER..!
WAIT! THAT SOUND... BENEATH MY FEET..!
THE FLOOR... THE ENTIRE BUILDING... BEGINNING TO SHAKE VIOLENTLY!
IT CAN'T BE! HE WOULDN'T DARE COME HERE!
BUT... HE DID! ULTRON-6 IS HERE!!
KKKKKKKKKKKKKKKKKKKKKKKKKKKKKK

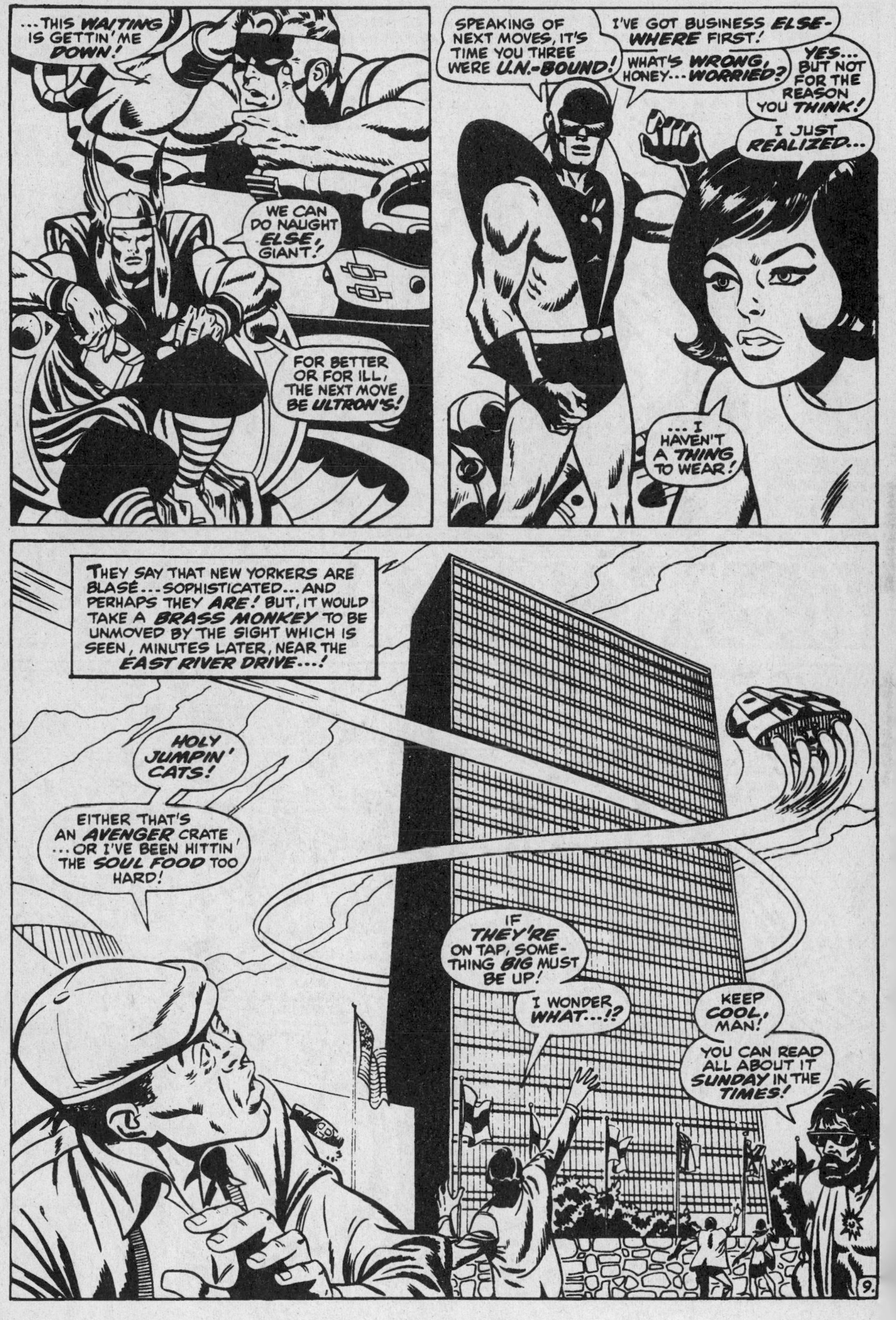

...THIS WAITING IS GETTIN' ME DOWN!
WE CAN DO NAUGHT ELSE, GIANT!
FOR BETTER OR FOR ILL, THE NEXT MOVE BE ULTRON'S!
SPEAKING OF NEXT MOVES, IT'S TIME YOU THREE WERE U.N.-BOUND!
I'VE GOT BUSINESS ELSEWHERE FIRST!
WHAT'S WRONG, HONEY... WORRIED?
YES... BUT NOT FOR THE REASON YOU THINK!
I JUST REALIZED...
...I HAVEN'T A THING TO WEAR!
THEY SAY THAT NEW YORKERS ARE BLASÉ... SOPHISTICATED... AND PERHAPS THEY ARE! BUT, IT WOULD TAKE A BRASS MONKEY TO BE UNMOVED BY THE SIGHT WHICH IS SEEN, MINUTES LATER, NEAR THE EAST RIVER DRIVE...!
HOLY JUMPIN' CATS!
EITHER THAT'S AN AVENGER CRATE ...OR I'VE BEEN HITTIN' THE SOUL FOOD TOO HARD!
IF THEY'RE ON TAP, SOMETHING BIG MUST BE UP!
I WONDER WHAT...!?
KEEP COOL, MAN!
YOU CAN READ ALL ABOUT IT SUNDAY IN THE TIMES!

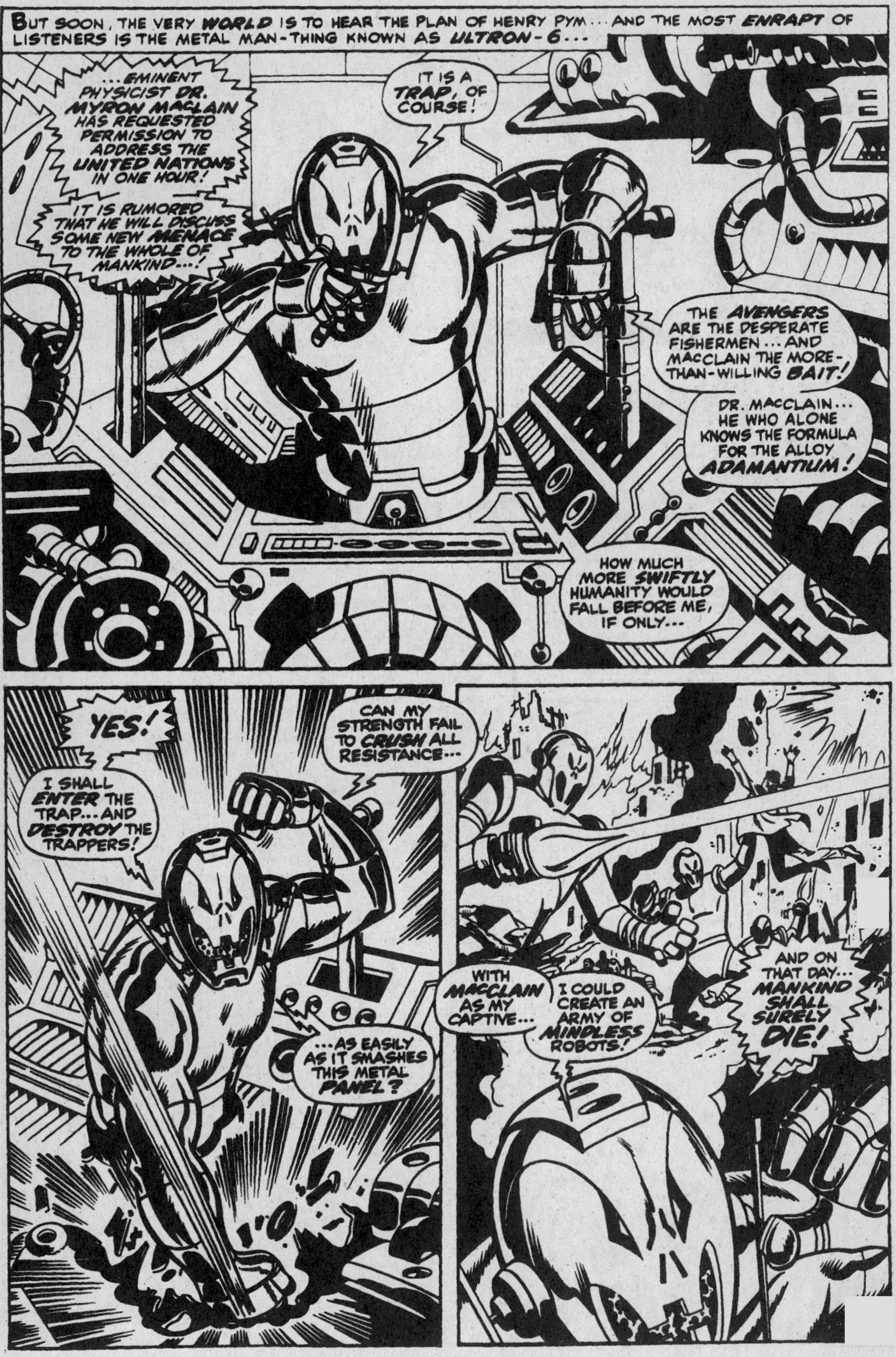
BUT SOON, THE VERY WORLD IS TO HEAR THE PLAN OF HENRY PYM... AND THE MOST ENRAPT OF LISTENERS IS THE METAL MAN-THING KNOWN AS ULTRON-6...
...EMINENT PHYSICIST DR. MYRON MACLAIN HAS REQUESTED PERMISSION TO ADDRESS THE UNITED NATIONS IN ONE HOUR!
IT IS RUMORED THAT HE WILL DISCUSS SOME NEW MENACE TO THE WHOLE OF MANKIND...!
IT IS A TRAP, OF COURSE!
THE AVENGERS ARE THE DESPERATE FISHERMEN... AND MACCLAIN THE MORE-THAN-WILLING BAIT!
DR. MACCLAIN... HE WHO ALONE KNOWS THE FORMULA FOR THE ALLOY ADAMANTIUM!
HOW MUCH MORE SWIFTLY HUMANITY WOULD FALL BEFORE ME, IF ONLY...
YES!
I SHALL ENTER THE TRAP... AND DESTROY THE TRAPPERS!
CAN MY STRENGTH FAIL TO CRUSH ALL RESISTANCE...
...AS EASILY AS IT SMASHES THIS METAL PANEL?
WITH MACCLAIN AS MY CAPTIVE...
I COULD CREATE AN ARMY OF MINDLESS ROBOTS!
AND ON THAT DAY... MANKIND SHALL SURELY DIE!

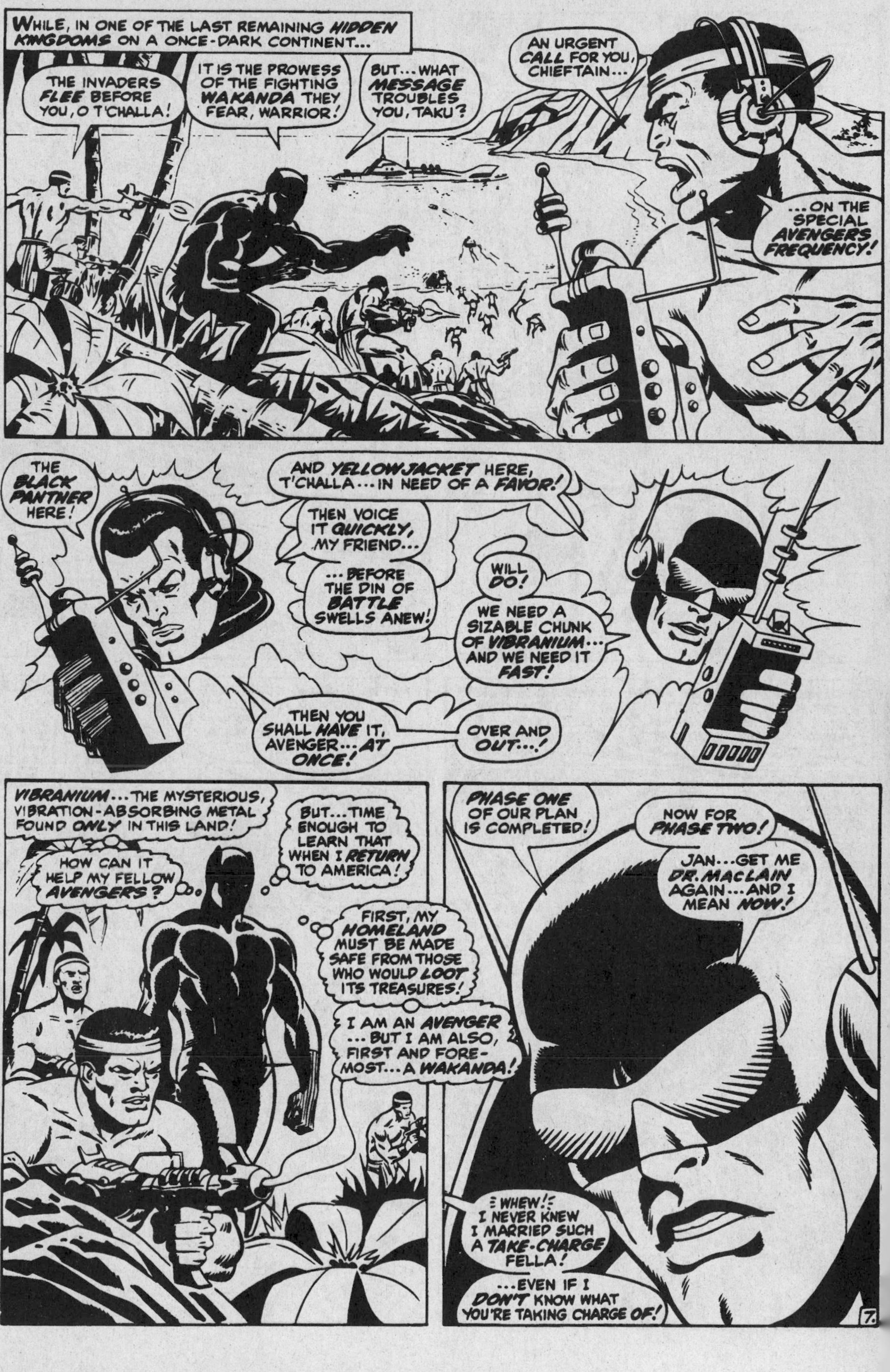

WHILE, IN ONE OF THE LAST REMAINING HIDDEN KINGDOMS ON A ONCE-DARK CONTINENT...
THE INVADERS FLEE BEFORE YOU, O T'CHALLA!
IT IS THE PROWESS OF THE FIGHTING WAKANDA THEY FEAR, WARRIOR!
BUT...WHAT MESSAGE TROUBLES YOU, TAKU?
AN URGENT CALL FOR YOU, CHIEFTAIN...
...ON THE SPECIAL AVENGERS FREQUENCY!
THE BLACK PANTHER HERE!
AND YELLOWJACKET HERE, T'CHALLA...IN NEED OF A FAVOR!
THEN VOICE IT QUICKLY, MY FRIEND...
...BEFORE THE DIN OF BATTLE SWELLS ANEW!
WILL DO!
WE NEED A SIZABLE CHUNK OF VIBRANIUM... AND WE NEED IT FAST!
THEN YOU SHALL HAVE IT, AVENGER...AT ONCE!
OVER AND OUT...!
VIBRANIUM...THE MYSTERIOUS, VIBRATION-ABSORBING METAL FOUND ONLY IN THIS LAND!
HOW CAN IT HELP MY FELLOW AVENGERS?
BUT...TIME ENOUGH TO LEARN THAT WHEN I RETURN TO AMERICA!
FIRST, MY HOMELAND MUST BE MADE SAFE FROM THOSE WHO WOULD LOOT ITS TREASURES!
I AM AN AVENGER ...BUT I AM ALSO, FIRST AND FORE-MOST...A WAKANDA!
PHASE ONE OF OUR PLAN IS COMPLETED!
NOW FOR PHASE TWO!
JAN...GET ME DR. MACLAIN AGAIN...AND I MEAN NOW!
WHEW! I NEVER KNEW I MARRIED SUCH A TAKE-CHARGE FELLA!
...EVEN IF I DON'T KNOW WHAT YOU'RE TAKING CHARGE OF!

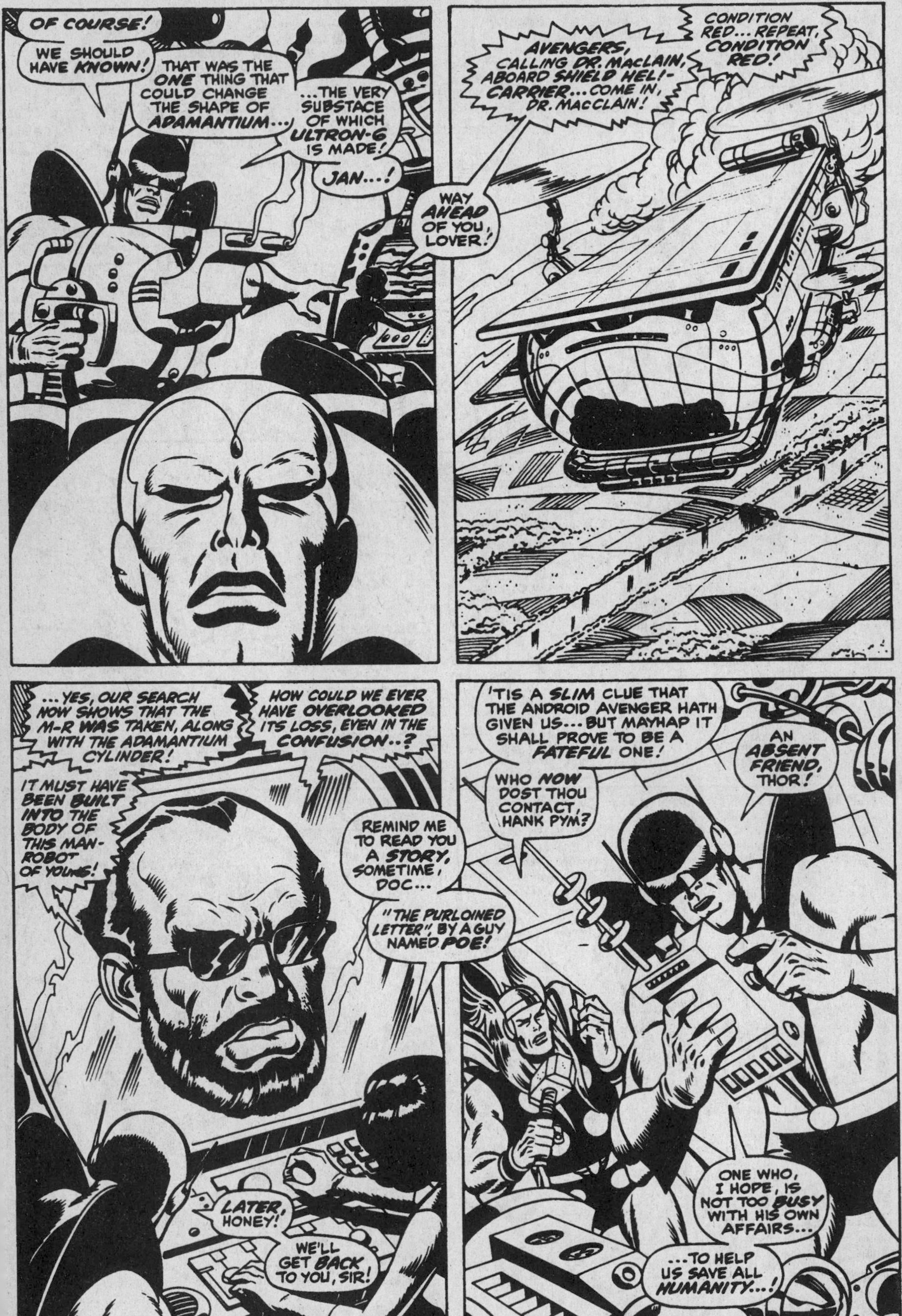
OF COURSE!
WE SHOULD HAVE KNOWN!
THAT WAS THE ONE THING THAT COULD CHANGE THE SHAPE OF ADAMANTIUM...
...THE VERY SUBSTACE OF WHICH ULTRON-6 IS MADE!
JAN...!
WAY AHEAD OF YOU, LOVER!
AVENGERS, CALLING DR. MACLAIN, ABOARD SHIELD HELI-CARRIER... COME IN, DR. MACCLAIN!
CONDITION RED... REPEAT, CONDITION RED!
...YES, OUR SEARCH NOW SHOWS THAT THE M-R WAS TAKEN, ALONG WITH THE ADAMANTIUM CYLINDER!
HOW COULD WE EVER HAVE OVERLOOKED ITS LOSS, EVEN IN THE CONFUSION..?
IT MUST HAVE BEEN BUILT INTO THE BODY OF THIS MAN-ROBOT OF YOURS!
REMIND ME TO READ YOU A STORY, SOMETIME, DOC...
"THE PURLOINED LETTER", BY A GUY NAMED POE!
LATER, HONEY!
WE'LL GET BACK TO YOU, SIR!
'TIS A SLIM CLUE THAT THE ANDROID AVENGER HATH GIVEN US... BUT MAYHAP IT SHALL PROVE TO BE A FATEFUL ONE!
WHO NOW DOST THOU CONTACT, HANK PYM?
AN ABSENT FRIEND, THOR!
ONE WHO, I HOPE, IS NOT TOO BUSY WITH HIS OWN AFFAIRS...
...TO HELP US SAVE ALL HUMANITY...!
6

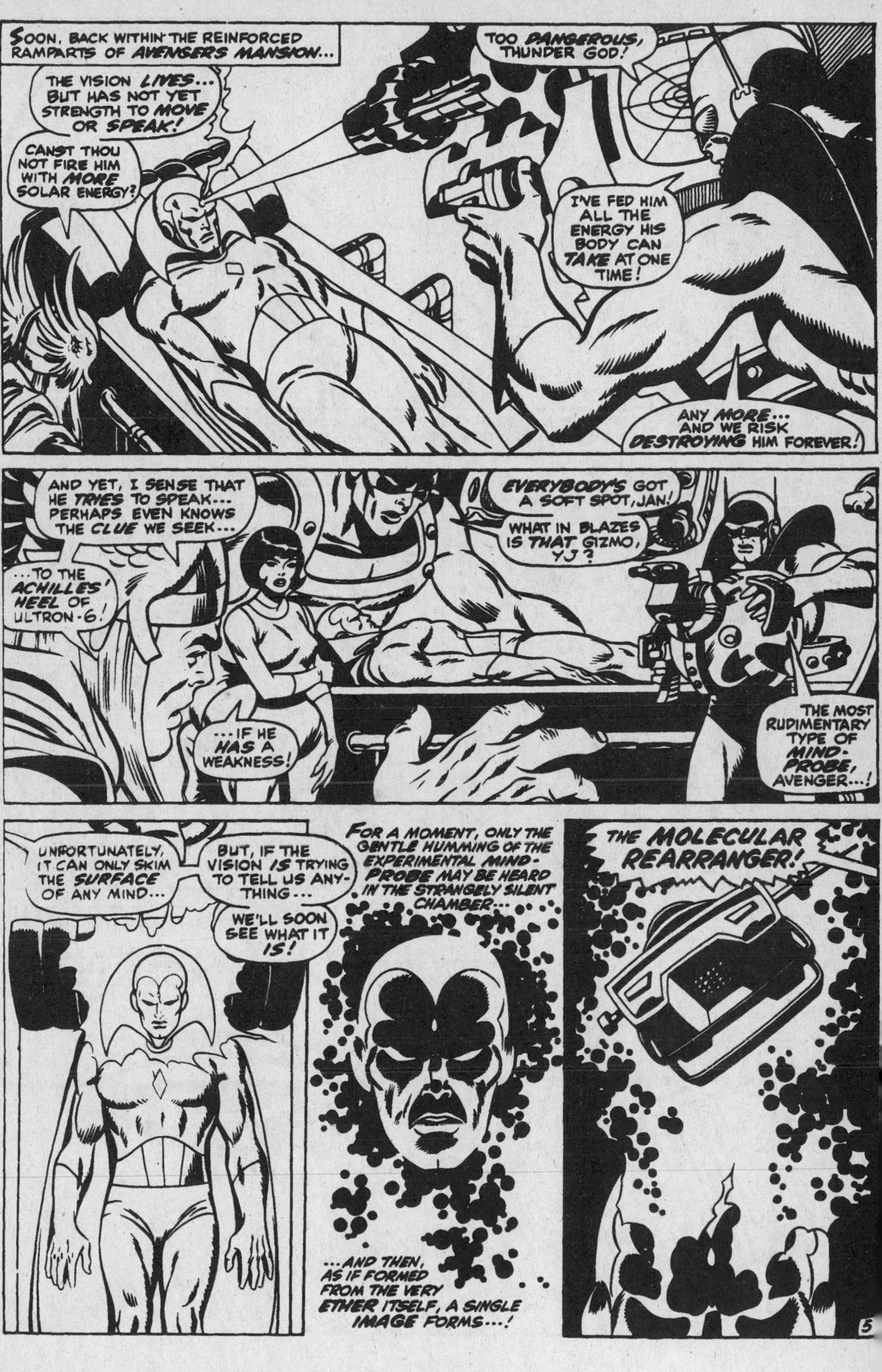
SOON, BACK WITHIN THE REINFORCED RAMPARTS OF AVENGERS MANSION...
TOO DANGEROUS, THUNDER GOD!
THE VISION LIVES... BUT HAS NOT YET STRENGTH TO MOVE OR SPEAK!
CANST THOU NOT FIRE HIM WITH MORE SOLAR ENERGY?
I'VE FED HIM ALL THE ENERGY HIS BODY CAN TAKE AT ONE TIME!
ANY MORE... AND WE RISK DESTROYING HIM FOREVER!
AND YET, I SENSE THAT HE TRIES TO SPEAK... PERHAPS EVEN KNOWS THE CLUE WE SEEK...
...TO THE ACHILLES' HEEL OF ULTRON-6!
...IF HE HAS A WEAKNESS!
EVERYBODY'S GOT A SOFT SPOT, JAN!
WHAT IN BLAZES IS THAT GIZMO, YJ?
THE MOST RUDIMENTARY TYPE OF MIND-PROBE, AVENGER...!
UNFORTUNATELY, IT CAN ONLY SKIM THE SURFACE OF ANY MIND...
BUT, IF THE VISION IS TRYING TO TELL US ANY-THING...
WE'LL SOON SEE WHAT IT IS!
FOR A MOMENT, ONLY THE GENTLE HUMMING OF THE EXPERIMENTAL MIND-PROBE MAY BE HEARD IN THE STRANGELY SILENT CHAMBER...
...AND THEN, AS IF FORMED FROM THE VERY ETHER ITSELF, A SINGLE IMAGE FORMS...!
THE MOLECULAR REARRANGER!

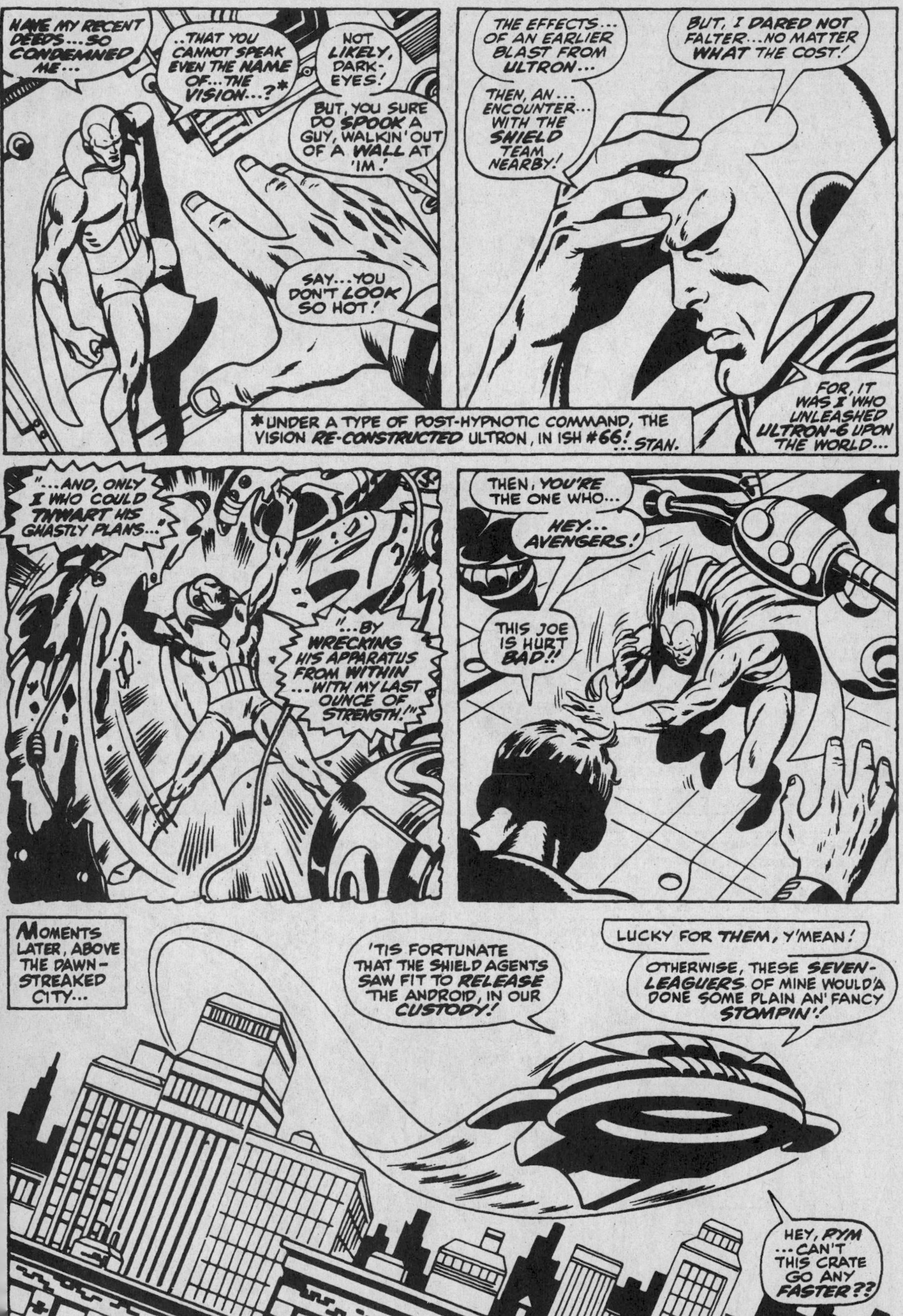
HAVE MY RECENT DEEDS... SO CONDEMNED ME...
..THAT YOU CANNOT SPEAK EVEN THE NAME OF... THE VISION...?*
NOT LIKELY, DARK-EYES!
BUT, YOU SURE DO SPOOK A GUY, WALKIN' OUT OF A WALL AT 'IM!
SAY... YOU DON'T LOOK SO HOT!
THE EFFECTS... OF AN EARLIER BLAST FROM ULTRON...
THEN, AN... ENCOUNTER... WITH THE SHIELD TEAM NEARBY!
BUT, I DARED NOT FALTER... NO MATTER WHAT THE COST!
FOR, IT WAS I WHO UNLEASHED ULTRON-6 UPON THE WORLD...
*UNDER A TYPE OF POST-HYPNOTIC COMMAND, THE VISION RE-CONSTRUCTED ULTRON, IN ISH #66! ...STAN.
"...AND, ONLY I WHO COULD THWART HIS GHASTLY PLANS..."
"...BY WRECKING HIS APPARATUS FROM WITHIN ...WITH MY LAST OUNCE OF STRENGTH!"
THEN, YOU'RE THE ONE WHO...
HEY... AVENGERS!
THIS JOE IS HURT BAD!!
MOMENTS LATER, ABOVE THE DAWN-STREAKED CITY...
'TIS FORTUNATE THAT THE SHIELD AGENTS SAW FIT TO RELEASE THE ANDROID, IN OUR CUSTODY!
LUCKY FOR THEM, Y'MEAN!
OTHERWISE, THESE SEVEN-LEAGUERS OF MINE WOULD'A DONE SOME PLAIN AN' FANCY STOMPIN'!
HEY, PYM ...CAN'T THIS CRATE GO ANY FASTER??
4

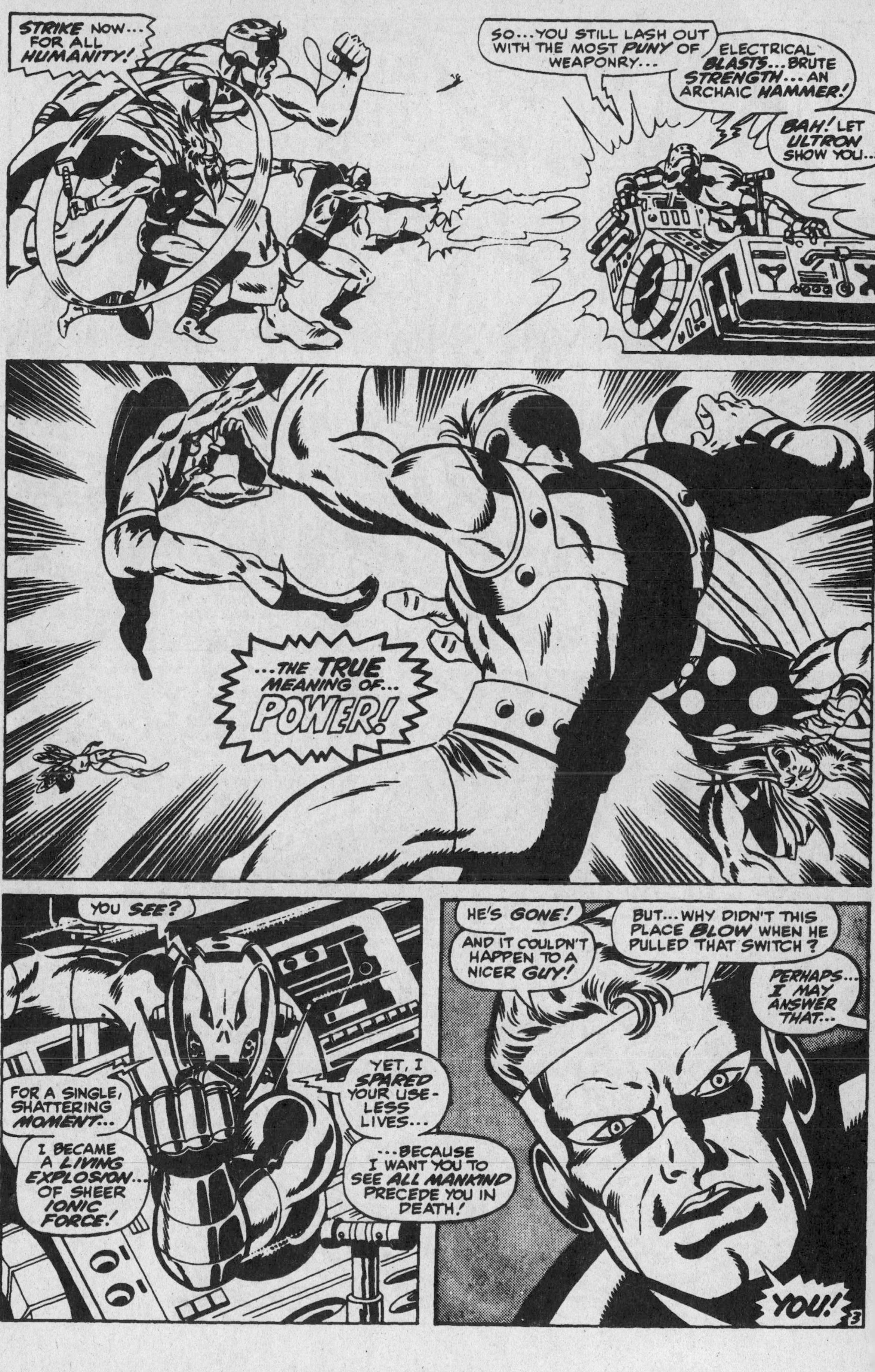

STRIKE NOW... FOR ALL HUMANITY!
SO...YOU STILL LASH OUT WITH THE MOST PUNY OF WEAPONRY...
ELECTRICAL BLASTS...BRUTE STRENGTH...AN ARCHAIC HAMMER!
BAH! LET ULTRON SHOW YOU...
...THE TRUE MEANING OF... POWER!
YOU SEE?
FOR A SINGLE, SHATTERING MOMENT...
I BECAME A LIVING EXPLOSION... OF SHEER IONIC FORCE!
YET, I SPARED YOUR USE-LESS LIVES...
...BECAUSE I WANT YOU TO SEE ALL MANKIND PRECEDE YOU IN DEATH!
HE'S GONE!
AND IT COULDN'T HAPPEN TO A NICER GUY!
BUT...WHY DIDN'T THIS PLACE BLOW WHEN HE PULLED THAT SWITCH?
PERHAPS... I MAY ANSWER THAT...
YOU!
3

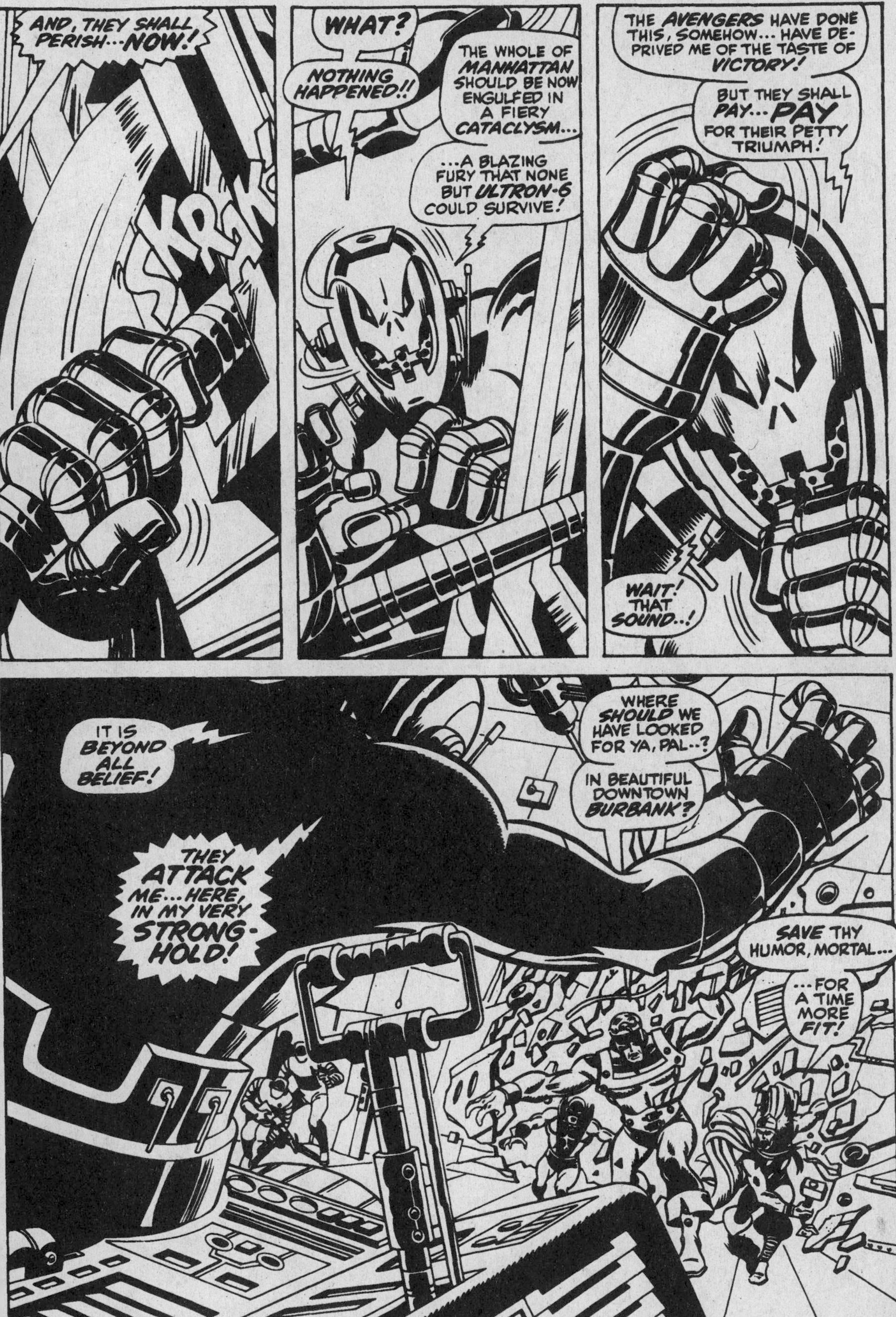
AND, THEY SHALL PERISH...NOW!
SKRAK
WHAT?
NOTHING HAPPENED!!
THE WHOLE OF MANHATTAN SHOULD BE NOW ENGULFED IN A FIERY CATACLYSM...
...A BLAZING FURY THAT NONE BUT ULTRON-6 COULD SURVIVE!
THE AVENGERS HAVE DONE THIS, SOMEHOW... HAVE DEPRIVED ME OF THE TASTE OF VICTORY!
BUT THEY SHALL PAY...PAY FOR THEIR PETTY TRIUMPH!
WAIT! THAT SOUND...!
IT IS BEYOND ALL BELIEF!
THEY ATTACK ME...HERE, IN MY VERY STRONGHOLD!
WHERE SHOULD WE HAVE LOOKED FOR YA, PAL...?
IN BEAUTIFUL DOWNTOWN BURBANK?
SAVE THY HUMOR, MORTAL...
...FOR A TIME MORE FIT!
2.

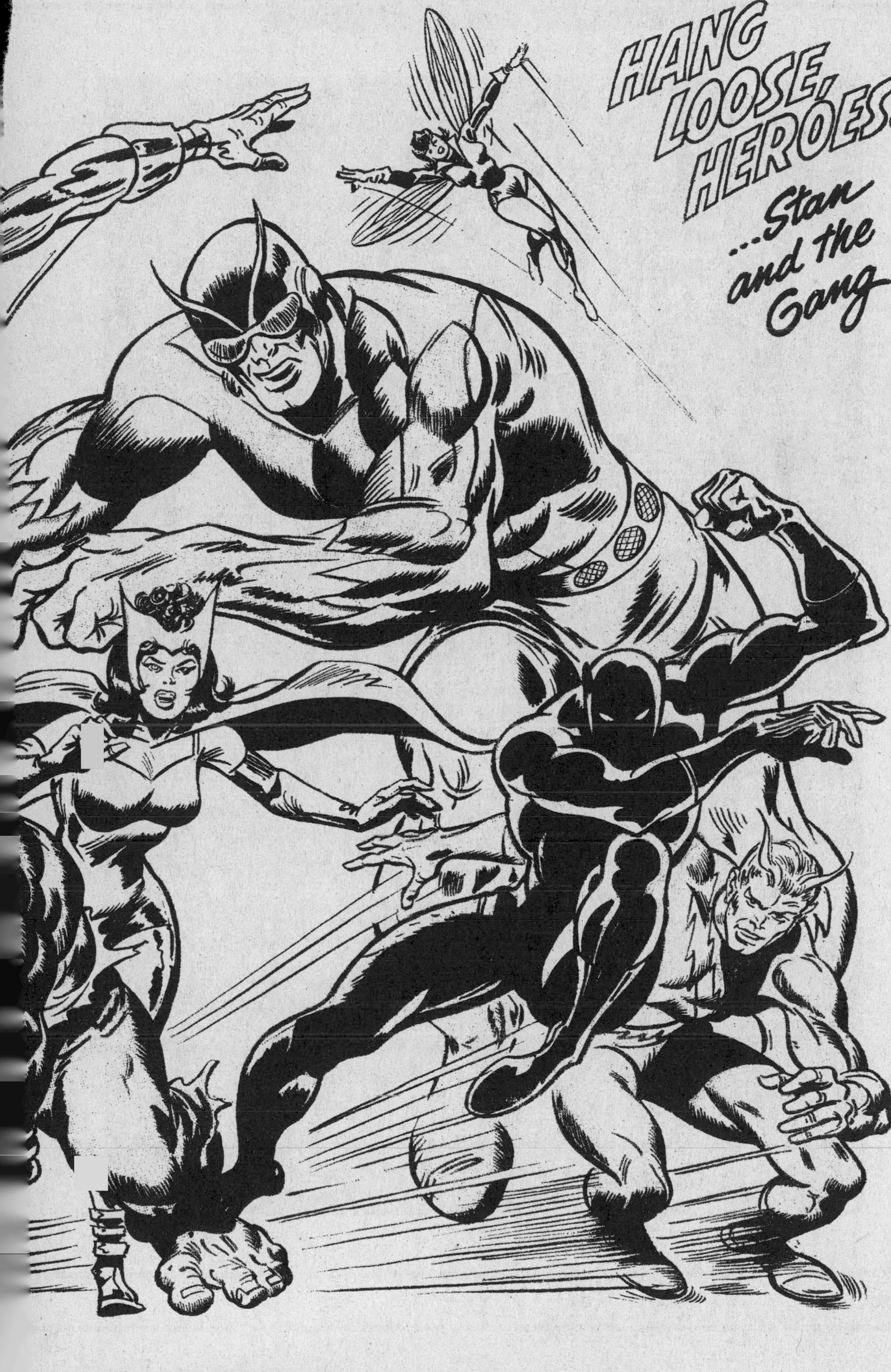
HANG LOOSE, HEROES!
...Stan and the Gang

ALSO AVAILABLE: